Anonymous

Blackie's Comprehensive History of England

Civil and military, religious, intellectual, and social: from the earliest period to the Jubilee of Victoria, queen and empress

Anonymous

Blackie's Comprehensive History of England

Civil and military, religious, intellectual, and social: from the earliest period to the jubilee of Victoria, queen and empress

ISBN/EAN: 9783337328566

Printed in Europe, USA, Canada, Australia, Japan

Cover: Foto ©ninafisch / pixelio.de

More available books at **www.hansebooks.com**

BLACKIE'S
COMPREHENSIVE HISTORY
OF
ENGLAND

CIVIL AND MILITARY,

RELIGIOUS, INTELLECTUAL, AND SOCIAL.

FROM THE EARLIEST PERIOD

TO THE JUBILEE OF VICTORIA, QUEEN AND EMPRESS.

ILLUSTRATED BY A SERIES OF FINELY ENGRAVED HISTORICAL PICTURES,

AND ABOVE 1000 ENGRAVINGS IN THE TEXT.

DIVISIONAL-VOLUME I.
FROM EARLIEST TIMES TILL THE REIGN OF EDWARD I.

BLACKIE & SON, LIMITED,
LONDON, GLASGOW, EDINBURGH, AND DUBLIN.
1895.

CONTENTS OF DIVISIONAL-VOL. I.

INTRODUCTION.

ENGLAND BEFORE THE ROMAN INVASION.—Fabulous part of British history—The first sovereign—Albion and the Danaides—Arrival of Brutus and the Trojans—Their conquest of Britain—Early kings—Bladud, Lear, Brennus, Elidure, &c.—Laws of Queen Mertia—Reigns of Hely and Lud—Cassivelaunus—The Druids—Merchandise of the Britons—Resort of Phœnician traders to the Tin Islands—Civilization of the Britons—Their funeral depositories, Druidical structures, and fortresses, pp. 1-16.

BOOK I.—BRITISH AND ROMAN PERIOD. B.C. 55-A.D. 449.

CIVIL AND MILITARY HISTORY.

Chap. I. INVASION BY JULIUS CÆSAR: B.C. 55-A.D. 43. —Early inhabitants—Motives of Julius Cæsar for invading Britain—Gallant resistance of the Britons —Their cavalry and infantry, war-chariots, and weapons, pp. 17-28.

Chap. II. INVASION UNDER CLAUDIUS TO ARRIVAL OF SAXONS: A.D. 43-449.—Resistance of Caractacus— Capture of Mona—Revolt under Boadicea—Her defeat and death—Agricola appointed governor— His victory at Mons Grampius—Graham's Dyke built—Campaign of Severus—Decay of the Roman power in Britain—Invasions of Scots and Picts— Religious controversies—Saxons invited—Hengist and Horsa, pp. 29-46.

HISTORY OF RELIGION.

Chap. III. RELIGION OF THE ANCIENT BRITONS AND INTRODUCTION OF CHRISTIANITY: B.C. 55-A.D. 449.— Cæsar's account of Druidism—Its priesthood—Their costume and modes of divination—Their doctrines —Human sacrifices—Origin of Druidism—Warfare of the Romans against it—Entrance of Christianity —The early church in Britain, pp. 46-58.

HISTORY OF SOCIETY.

Chap. IV. FROM CÆSAR'S INVASION TO THE ARRIVAL OF THE SAXONS: B.C. 55-A.D. 449.—Derivation of the names Albion and Britain—Cæsar's account of the island and its inhabitants—Their habits, dress, and modes of subsistence—Their government— Their mutual wars, pp. 59-65.

BOOK II.—PERIOD FROM THE ARRIVAL OF THE SAXONS TO THE ARRIVAL OF THE NORMANS. A.D. 449-1066.

CIVIL AND MILITARY HISTORY.

Chap. I. ARRIVAL OF THE SAXONS TO UNION OF THE HEPTARCHY: A.D. 449-825.—Origin and early history of the Saxons—Their arrival in Britain—Fabulous history of King Arthur—The Heptarchy—Office of Bretwalda—Wars of the Heptarchy—Reigns of Offa and Egbert—England becomes one kingdom, pp. 66-79.

Chap. II. INVASION OF THE DANES TO DEATH OF ALFRED: A.D. 825-901.—History and character of the Danes—Succession of Saxon kings—Alfred the Great—His struggles with the Danes—Review of his history and character, pp. 79-97.

Chap. III. ACCESSION OF EDWARD TO DEATH OF HARDICANUTE: A.D. 901-1042.— Reign of Athelstane—Victory at Brunnaburgh—Edward the Martyr—Danes invade England—Massacre by the English—Invasions by Sweyn—Martyrdom of Alphege —Canute becomes king—Harold and Hardicanute, pp. 97-116.

Chap. IV. EDWARD THE CONFESSOR TO THE NORMAN CONQUEST: A.D. 1042-1066.—Edward the Confessor —His quarrels with Earl Godwin—William, Duke of Normandy—Earl Godwin and his son Harold— Death of Edward—Harold proclaimed king—William asserts his right to the crown—Hardrada of Norway invades England—Defeated and slain at Stamford Bridge—William's invasion—His proposals to Harold—Battle of Hastings—Death of Harold, pp. 117-139.

Chap. V. SCOTTISH AND IRISH ANNALS: A.D. 300-1066.—The Picts and Scots—History of the Scottish kings to Malcolm III.—Early peoples of Ireland— Their conversion by St. Patrick—Their contests with the Danes—State of Ireland at the time of the Norman Conquest, pp. 140-148.

HISTORY OF RELIGION: A.D. 449-1066.

Chap. VI. Religion of the Saxon invaders—Missionaries sent to England by Gregory the Great— Their progress—Controversies about the tonsure and celebration of Easter—Corruptions among the clergy—St. Dunstan, pp. 148-159.

HISTORY OF SOCIETY: A.D. 449-1066.

Chap. VII. Union of the Saxon tribes in England— The ceorls and serfs—Architecture— Houses, food, and dress of the Anglo-Saxons—Social and domestic life—Superstitions—Amusements—Education, pp. 160-176.

BOOK III.—PERIOD FROM THE NORMAN CONQUEST TO THE DEATH OF KING JOHN. A.D. 1066-1216.

CIVIL AND MILITARY HISTORY.

Chap. I. WILLIAM I., SURNAMED THE CONQUEROR: A.D. 1066-1087.—Battle Abbey founded—William crowned at Westminster—Revolts suppressed with merciless severity—Resistance of Hereward—Completion of the conquest—Formation of the New Forest—Death of William—His inglorious funeral, pp. 177-208.

Chap. II. WILLIAM II., SURNAMED RUFUS: A.D. 1087-1100.—Opposition to the succession—William's contentions with his brothers—Wars with Scotland and Wales—Death of William in the New Forest —His character, pp. 209-218.

Chap. III. HENRY I., SURNAMED BEAUCLERK: A.D. 1100-1135.— Henry seizes the crown — Marries Princess Maud, a descendant of Alfred—Contests with his brother Robert—Wars on the Continent —Wreck of the "White Ship"—Death of Henry, pp. 219-232.

Chap. IV. STEPHEN: A.D. 1135-1154.—Matilda opposes Stephen—Scots invade England—Battle of the Standard—Wars between Matilda and Stephen —Matilda's son Henry invades England—His treaty with Stephen, pp. 233-248.

Chap. V. HENRY II., SURNAMED PLANTAGENET: A.D. 1154-1172.—Henry's queen Eleanor—His reforms —Wars on the Continent—Career of Thomas à Becket—His quarrels with Henry—His assassination, pp. 248-267.

Chap. VI. HENRY II.: A.D. 1064-1189.—Summary of Irish history—Conquest of Ireland commenced — Rebellion of Henry's sons — Commencement of the Crusades—Death of Henry—Story of "Fair Rosamond", pp. 268-290.

Chap. VII. RICHARD I., SURNAMED CŒUR DE LION: A.D. 1189-1199.—Massacre of the Jews—Richard departs for the Crusades—His marriage with Berengaria—His quarrels with Philip of France—Taken prisoner on his return—His ransom and return to England—War with France—Richard mortally wounded before Chaluz, pp. 291-321.

Chap. VIII. JOHN, SURNAMED SANS-TERRE, OR LACK-LAND: A.D. 1199-1216.—Unpopularity of John—Claims of his nephew Arthur to the crown—Quarrels with the Pope—John's abject submission —The barons combine against him—Magna Charta signed—His death, pp. 322-339.

Chap. IX. SCOTTISH ANNALS, &c.: A.D. 1057-1214.—Review of Scottish history—Dominions of Malcolm Canmore—He invades England—Reigns of Donald Bane, Duncan, and Edgar—Alexander I.—His contests with the church—Useful reign of David I.—Malcolm IV. and William the Lion—Alexander II. —Summary of Irish affairs, pp. 339-349.

HISTORY OF RELIGION: A.D. 1066-1216.

Chap. X.—The English church at the Conquest— Lanfranc's reforms—A uniform church-service introduced—Anselm's quarrels with William Rufus and Henry I.—Clerical celibacy—Thomas à Becket —Constitutions of Clarendon—Monastic orders in England—Hospitallers and Templars, pp. 350-363.

HISTORY OF SOCIETY: A.D. 1066-1216.

Chap. XI.—Colleges and schools of the period—Institution of chivalry—Growth of cities—Extent of London—Mercantile progress—Architecture— Modes of life among the nobles—Female dress and ornaments—Domestic life of the upper classes— Minstrels, jugglers, &c.—Sports and amusements of the common people, pp. 363-381.

BOOK IV.—PERIOD FROM THE ACCESSION OF HENRY III. TO THE END OF THE REIGN OF RICHARD II. A.D. 1216-1399.

CIVIL AND MILITARY HISTORY.

Chap. I. HENRY III., SURNAMED OF WINCHESTER: A.D. 1216-1272.—Earl of Pembroke appointed Protector—The dauphin attempts to obtain the crown, but is defeated at Lincoln—Reforms in the laws— Unpopularity of Henry—The "Mad Parliament" Civil war begins—Battle of Evesham—Death of Henry, pp. 382-400.

Chap. II. EDWARD I., SURNAMED LONGSHANKS: A.D. 1272-1290.—Edward I. proclaimed—His exploits in Syria—His expedients to raise money—Invades Wales—Llewellyn slain and Wales reduced—Affairs in Scotland—Edward's interference—Norwegians invade Scotland and are defeated at Large—Death of Alexander III.—His daughter Margaret proclaimed—She is contracted to Edward's son—Her death, pp. 401-416.

LIST OF ILLUSTRATIONS.

HISTORICAL PICTURES AND MAP.

Page

BAPTISM OF ETHELBERT KING OF KENT, by St. Augustine at Canterbury, A.D. 597.
From the fresco painting by W. Dyce, R.A., in the House of Lords,......................*Frontis.* 151

CELTIC RELICS—Personal Ornaments, &c., of Gold and Bronze.
Drawn chiefly from the objects themselves by J. L. Williams,........................*to face* 14

KING ALFRED INCITING THE ANGLO-SAXONS TO REPEL THE INVASION OF THE
DANES, A.D. 876.
From a cartoon executed by G. F. Watts, R.A., now in the Houses of Parliament,......... ,, 86

CORONATION OF HAROLD, KING OF THE ANGLO-SAXONS, A.D. 1066.
From the drawing by D. Maclise, R.A.,... ,, 130

THE FIRST PREACHING OF CHRISTIANITY IN BRITAIN.
From a drawing by C. W. Cope, R.A., now in the South Kensington Museum,............... ,, 150

ANGLO-SAXON RELICS—Personal Ornaments of Gold and Bronze.
Drawn from the objects themselves by J. L. Williams,................................. ,, 172

RICHARD CŒUR DE LION FORGIVING BERTRAND DE GURDUN, A.D. 1199.
From the picture by John Cross, now in the Houses of Parliament,...................... ,, 320

RELICS ASSOCIATED WITH THOMAS À BECKET.
Drawn from the objects themselves by J. L. Williams,................................. ,, 356

COLOURED MAP OF SAXON ENGLAND.
Drawn and engraved by Edward Weller, F.R.G.S., ... *to follow* 104

ILLUSTRATIONS IN THE TEXT.

No.		Page	No.		Page
1.	INITIAL LETTER.—Mythological,	1	24.	BRITISH FORTIFIED CAMP, in Strathmore, called White Cather-Thun,	27
2.	THE LAND'S END, Cornwall,	7	25.	BARBARIAN PRISONER, from a marble in the British Museum,	30
3.	STONE CELTS AND ARROW HEADS,	9	26.	PLAN OF BRITISH CAMP ON COXAL KNOLL,	31
4.	BRONZE CELTS, from examples in British Museum,	10	27.	HADRIAN, from a fine bronze in the British Museum,	35
5.	MOULD FOR CASTING CELTS AND RINGS, found near Wallington, Northumberland,	10	28.	REMAINS OF HADRIAN'S VALLUM, near Haltwhistle,	36
6.	CIST CONTAINING A SKELETON.—From the Archæologia,	11	29.	PLAN—THE ROMAN WALL BETWEEN THE SOLWAY AND THE TYNE,	37
7.	TRINKETS AND ARTICLES OF THE TOILET, found in barrows,	11	30.	PLAN—THE ROMAN WALL BETWEEN THE CLYDE AND FORTH,	37
8.	ARTICLES OF JEWELLERY, found in barrows,	12	31.	COURSE OF THE WALL OF SEVERUS, and Mile-castle,	38
9.	INTERIOR OF A CROMLECH ON THE PLAIN OF L'ANCRESSE, Guernsey,	12	32.	SECTION OF THE ROMAN WALL near the South Agger Port Gate,	39
10.	CELTIC FUNERAL URNS,	13	33.	SECTION OF THE WALL AND DITCH OF SEVERUS,	39
11.	MOUNT CABURN BEACON, near Lewes, Sussex,	13	34.	GOLD COIN OF CARAUSIUS,	40
12.	INCENSE VESSELS,	13	35.	REMAINS OF THE WALLS OF LONDON,	41
13.	ANCIENT QUERN, in British Museum,	14	36.	PLAN OF THE WALLS OF LONDON,	42
14.	WELSH FISHERMAN OF THE PRESENT DAY WITH CORACLE,	15	37.	MADRON HOLY WELL, Cornwall,	49
15.	REMAINS OF BRITISH BREASTPLATE OR GORGET OF GOLD, found at Mold,	15	38.	MISLETOE PLANT, AND GOLDEN HOOK with which it was cut,	49
16.	INITIAL LETTER, with Roman Ornaments,	17	39.	DRUIDS, from a bas-relief found at Autun,	50
17.	JULIUS CÆSAR, from a marble in the British Museum,	18	40.	DRUIDICAL INSIGNIA OF GOLD, found in Ireland,	50
18.	MAP.—THE STRAITS OF DOVER, with the opposite Coasts of Gaul and Britain,	19	41.	NIMBUS OF GOLD, presumed to have been worn on the head by Druids,	51
19.	DOVER CLIFFS.—From Turner's England and Wales,	20	42.	LIUTH MESSEATH, OR PLATE OF JUDGMENT, found in Ireland,	51
20.	ROMAN GALLEY, from the model in Greenwich Hospital,	22	43.	DRUID COLLAR OR GORGET OF GOLD, found in Ireland,	51
21.	STAKE, from the bed of the Thames at Coway Stakes, now in the British Museum,	23	44.	GROUND PLAN OF DRUIDICAL CIRCLE at Avebury,	52
22.	BRONZE WEAPONS, answering to the description of hooks or scythes appended to the axle of British war-chariots.—British Museum,	26	45.	GROUND PLAN OF STONEHENGE,	53
			46.	VIEW OF STONEHENGE, Salisbury Plain,	54
23.	BRITISH SWORDS, DAGGER, SPEAR HEADS, AND JAVELIN HEADS, of Bronze.—British Museum,	26	47.	GAULISH DEITIES, from Roman bas-reliefs,	54

LIST OF ILLUSTRATIONS.

No.	Page
49. GAULISH DEITIES, from Roman bas-reliefs,	54
49. MALABAR TOLMEN,	55
50. REMAINS OF TEMPLE OF MINERVA, discovered at Bath in 1755, and preserved in Bath Museum,	57
51. RESTORATION BY SMIRKE OF PORTICO OF TEMPLE OF MINERVA, at Bath,	57
52. WOAD PLANT, *Isatis tinctoria*,	60
53. TORQUES, with manner of wearing it,	62
54. INITIAL LETTER—Style of Saxon illuminations,	66
55. MAP OF THE CIMBRIC CHERSONESE AND ADJOINING MAINLAND, the original seat of the Saxon nations,	67
56. SAXON SWORDS, SPEAR HEADS, AND BOSSES OF SHIELDS,	68
57. FLAMBOROUGH HEAD,	70
58. TOWN AND HEADLAND OF WHITBY,	70
59. BRASS COIN OF OFFA, in British Museum,	78
60. DANISH CHICLE.—From a tombstone in Iona,	83
61. DANISH SWORDS AND AXE HEAD,	83
62. GOLDEN BRACELET,	86
63. MAP—SKETCH OF THE COUNTRY BETWEEN ATHELNEY AND CHIPPENHAM, to illustrate Alfred's campaign of 878,	87
64. MAP—SKETCH TO ILLUSTRATE PART OF THE SAXON AND DANISH CAMPAIGNS OF 893-897,	91
65. SAXON LANTERN,	95
66. ALFRED'S JEWEL, in Ashmolean Museum, Oxford,	96
67. CORFE CASTLE, Dorsetshire,	104
68. CROWNING-STONE OF THE SAXON KINGS, at Kingston-on-Thames,	105
69. CANUTE AND HIS QUEEN.—From an illumination in the Registry of Hyde Abbey,	110
70. DANISH SOLDIER OF THE PERIOD,	110
71. IMPRESSIONS FROM THE GREAT SEAL OF EDWARD THE CONFESSOR.—British Museum,	119
72. CASTLE OF FALAISE,	122
73. HAROLD SWEARING ON THE RELICS.—Bayeux Tapestry,	128
74. CHAPEL AND SHRINE OF EDWARD THE CONFESSOR, in Westminster Abbey,	130
75. THE CROWN OFFERED TO HAROLD, AND THE CORONATION OF HAROLD.—From the Bayeux Tapestry,	131
76. NORMAN SHIP.—Restored from the Bayeux Tapestry,	133
77. SAXON SHIP.—Restored from the Bayeux Tapestry,	134
78. MAP—SKETCH TO ILLUSTRATE THE LANDING OF THE NORMANS AND THE BATTLE OF HASTINGS,	135
79. PEVENSEY BAY,	136
80. PEVENSEY CASTLE,	136
81. THE CATHEDRAL AND ST. ORAN'S CHAPEL, Iona,	150
82. NORTH WALLS OF RICHBOROUGH CASTLE AND FOUNDATIONS OF ST. AUGUSTINE'S CHURCH,	151
83. ALTAR OF DIANA, excavated in London,	152
84. HOLY ISLAND, and REMAINS OF THE CHURCH OF LINDISFARNE,	153
85. ROCK HERMITAGE AT GUY'S CLIFF, Warwickshire,	156
86. ST. DUNSTAN, from an Anglo-Saxon MS.,	158
87. ORDERS OF THE CLERGY,	159
88. SERF OR THEOW.—From Cotton MS.,	161
89. SOUTH VIEW OF GREENSTEAD CHURCH, Essex,	162
90. WEST END OF GREENSTEAD CHURCH, Essex,	162
91. COLUMN IN MONKWEARMOUTH CHURCH,	163
92. CARVED FRAGMENTS, Monkwearmouth Church,	163
93. TOWER OF SOMPTING CHURCH, Sussex,	163
94. WINDOW in Barnack Church, Northamptonshire,	163
95. DOORWAY OF THE TOWER OF EARLS-BARTON CHURCH,	164
96. BALUSTER WINDOW, Monkwearmouth Church, Durham,	164
97. FONT IN BRIDEKIRK CHURCH, Cumberland,	164
98. SAXON HAND-BELLS,	165
99. GLASS VESSELS, found in Saxon graves,	165
100. SAXON BED.—From Cotton MS.,	166
101. SAXON BANQUET.—From Cotton MS.,	166
102. ARMED MAN.—Benedictional of St. Ethelwold,	168

No.	Page
103. SAXON KING AND EOLDERMEN Cotton MS.,	169
104. SAXON COSTUMES.—From illuminated MS., Bodleian Library,	169
105. SAXON NECKLACE AND PIN,	170
106. SAXON BUCKLES AND BROOCH,	170
107. HEADS, from the Saxon Cross of Rothbury,	170
108. NECKLACE OR BRACELET, and BEADS,	171
109. BEADS OF GLASS, AND OF COLOURED PASTE,	171
110. SAXON BOAR HUNT.—From Strutt,	174
111. CHURCH AND REMAINS OF THE MONASTERY AT JARROW,	175
112. INITIAL LETTER—Style of Norman illumination,	177
113. BATTLE ABBEY,	178
114. ROUGEMONT CASTLE, part of the old defences of Exeter,	184
115. KEEP OF RICHMOND CASTLE, Yorkshire,	189
116. WATER TOWER AND WALLS OF CHESTER,	191
117. RHUDDLAN CASTLE, Flintshire,	192
118. MAP—THE ISLE OF ELY and adjoining Fen Country, with the courses of the rivers, at the period,	194
119. NORWICH CASTLE,	198
120. MAP—THE NEW FOREST and adjacent country,	204
121. MANTES, on the Seine,	206
122. ROCHESTER CASTLE, Kent,	211
123. BAMBOROUGH CASTLE, Northumberland,	215
124. TOMB OF WILLIAM RUFUS, Winchester Cathedral,	217
125. DUKE ROBERT'S TOWER, Cardiff Castle,	225
126. GEOFFREY PLANTAGENET, from monumental tablet,	229
127. CHAPTER HOUSE AND PART OF THE CATHEDRAL OF ST. OMER,	230
128. MANS, France,	231
129. REMAINS OF READING ABBEY,	232
130. ARMOUR of the time of Stephen.—Cotton MS.,	237
131. KNIGHT, in tegulated armour, time of Stephen,	237
132. QUEEN MAUD'S CHAMBER, Arundel Castle,	240
133. TOWER OF OXFORD CASTLE,	245
134. CRYPT OF BRISTOL CASTLE,	246
135. GATE OF THE ABBEY CHURCH, St. Edmundsbury,	247
136. FAVERSHAM ABBEY, Kent,	248
137. EFFIGY OF HENRY II., from his tomb at Fontevraud,	249
138. SILVER PENNY OF HENRY II.—British Museum,	251
139. SILVER COIN OF HENRY II.—British Museum,	251
140. REMAINS OF BRIDGENORTH CASTLE,	252
141. ABBEY OF PONTIGNY, France,	260
142. MOUNT ST. MICHAEL, Normandy,	261
143. REMAINS OF ST. AUGUSTINE MONASTERY, Canterbury,	265
144. ASSASSINATION OF BECKET.—From an ancient painting,	266
145. REGINALD'S, OR THE RING TOWER, Waterford,	273
146. SITE OF CARRICK OR CARRIG CASTLE, near Wexford,	275
147. CASHEL, co. Tipperary,	276
148. ELEANOR, QUEEN OF HENRY II.—From the effigy at Fontevraud,	277
149. CRYPT OF CANTERBURY CATHEDRAL,	289
150. CASTLE OF CHINON,	288
151. ABBEY OF FONTEVRAUD,	288
152. REMAINS OF THE NUNNERY OF GODSTOW,	290
153. EFFIGY OF RICHARD I.—From his tomb at Fontevraud,	291
154. SHIPS OF THE TIME.—Cambridge, Matt. Paris,	295
155. CRYPT OF THE SANCTUARY OF ST. JANUARIUS, Naples,	296
156. MAP—THE ITALIAN COAST, from Naples southwards, with part of Sicily,	297
157. EFFIGY OF BERENGARIA, Queen of Richard I.,	301
158. MAP—THE PLAIN AND BAY OF ACRE,	303
159. ACRE, from the Beach,	304
160. RUINS OF ASCALON,	306
161. JAFFA,	309
162. CASTLE OF TIERNSTEIN, on the Danube,	311
163. CRYPT OF ST. MARY OF THE ARCHES, London,	319
164. CASTLE OF ROUEN,	320
165. COVER OF THE CASE WHICH CONTAINED THE HEART OF RICHARD I.,	321
166. EFFIGY OF KING JOHN.—From his tomb in Worcester Cathedral,	323

LIST OF ILLUSTRATIONS.

No.	Page
167. CHATEAU-GAILLARD, near the Seine,	328
168. GREAT SEAL OF JOHN, appended to Magna Charta,	331
169. DOVER CASTLE,	337
170. REMAINS OF THE CASTLE OF NEWARK-ON-TRENT,	338
171. CASTLE OF NEWCASTLE-ON-TYNE,	341
172. CONSECRATION OF BECKET AS ARCHBISHOP,	355
173. BENEDICTINE MONK,	359
174. CARTHUSIAN MONK,	359
175. KNIGHT HOSPITALLER,	362
176. KNIGHTS TEMPLARS,	362
177. SOUTH TRANSEPT AND NAVE, Peterborough Cathedral,	369
178. NORMAN CUSHION CAPITAL,	370
179. NORMAN CAPITAL, in the Chapel, Tower of London,	370
180. TRANSITION NORMAN CAPITAL, Hall of Oakham Castle,	370
181. TRANSITION NORMAN CAPITAL, Canterbury Cathedral,	370
182. NORMAN WINDOW, Steetley, Derbyshire,	370
183. NORMAN WINDOW, St. Cross, Hampshire,	370
184. NORMAN DOORWAY, Earls-Barton, Northamptonshire,	371
185. CHEVRON MOULDING,	371
186. LOZENGE MOULDING,	371
187. BILLET MOULDING,	371
188. NAIL-HEAD MOULDING,	371
189. INTERLACING ARCADE, Norwich Cathedral,	371
190. TRANSITION, INTERLACING, AND POINTED ARCADES. —West Front of Croyland Abbey,	372
191. NORMAN DWELLING.—The Jews' House, Lincoln,	372
192. NORMAN FIREPLACE, Hedingham Castle, Essex,	373
193. BIRDS'-EYE VIEW OF NORMAN CASTLE,	373

No.	Page
194. NORMAN KEEP, Hedingham Castle, Essex,	374
195. SHIELD, HELMET, SWORD, AND BANNER,	375
196. SHIELDS BEARING BADGES,	375
197. GENTLEMEN OF THE TIME OF KING JOHN,	376
198. SLEEVE OF TWELFTH CENTURY, AND FEMALE WITH LONG KNOTTED SLEEVES.—From a Psalter,	376
199. LONG TRESSES AND FEMALE COSTUME,	377
200. LADIES OF THE TIME OF KING JOHN,	377
201. JUGGLER AND MUSICIAN.—Cotton MS.,	379
202. BOB-APPLE.—MS. Royal Library,	379
203. SWORD-DANCE AND PIPER.—From Strutt,	380
204. WATER-TOURNAMENT.—MS. Royal Library,	380
205. ANCIENT QUINTAIN, at Offham, Kent,	381
206. INITIAL LETTER—Style of illuminations of the period,	382
207. EFFIGY OF HENRY III.—From his tomb in Westminster Abbey,	383
208. HERTFORD CASTLE,	384
209. SHIP OF THE TIME.—Camb. Matt. Paris,	385
210. SEA FIGHT.—Matt. Paris, Bennett Coll.,	385
211. WILLIAM MARESCHAL (the elder), Earl of Pembroke,	387
212. SIMON DE MONTFORT, Earl of Leicester,	393
213. LEWES PRIORY, as it appeared in 1773,	396
214. KENILWORTH CASTLE,	398
215. GREAT SEAL OF EDWARD I.—British Museum,	401
216. EFFIGY OF ELEANOR, Queen of Edward I.—From her tomb in Westminster Abbey,	403
217. HAWARDINE CASTLE, Flintshire,	408
218. FLINT CASTLE,	409
219. CAERNARVON CASTLE.—J. S. Prout,	410

THE

COMPREHENSIVE
HISTORY OF ENGLAND.

INTRODUCTION.

ENGLAND BEFORE THE ROMAN INVASION.

Claims of the fabulous part of British history to our attention—Its commencement—Samothes, the first sovereign of Britain, and his four successors—Albion conquers the island—Marriage of his giants with the Danaides—Arrival of Brutus and the Trojans—Their conquest of Britain—Successors of Brutus—The reigns of Ebranc, Bladud, Lear, and Cordelia—Brennus declared to have been a Briton—Laws of Queen Mertia—Romantic history of King Elidure—Reigns of Hely and Lud—They are succeeded by Cassivellaunus—Causes of the remote antiquity claimed in the fabulous history of Britain—Power of the Druids—Influence of the sovereigns—Evidences of a superior race having lived among the Britons—Merchandise of the Britons—Their tin—Resort of Phœnician traders to the Tin Islands—The secret of these islands carefully concealed—People of the Cassiterides—Remissness of the Britons in navigation—Their measure of civilization, as attested by buried remains of weapons, tools, utensils, &c.—Account of funeral depositories and their contents—Beacon stations, Druidical structures, and fortresses of the Britons—Their sailing vessels—Their ornaments.

IN commencing the history of a country, the mythic or fabulous portion of it is commonly treated by modern writers as a ravelled skein, wherein truth is so mingled with error, as to defy extrication. But in the legendary records of our land, however garbled by the allegories of early fabulists and bards, and the accidents of oral tradition, we may discover traces of the origin of the people, and the changes that operated upon their habits and character up to the period at which these become associated with authentic history. The fabulous history of Britain continued to be an article of faith during the time of the Plantagenets, and it supplied Edward I. with arguments for his aggressions upon Scotland, and the commencement of the longest and most important warfare in which England was ever engaged. It continued to be received in the Elizabethan age, and was studied as veritable historic truth by the brightest intellects which this country has produced. I' en at a still later period, also, the same pen that wrote *Paradise Lost* did not disdain to illustrate those shadowy ages in which a Trojan rule was established in England. With these reflections we are justified in glancing at those early legends upon which Milton employed his learning, and from which Shakspeare himself derived some of his happiest illustrations.

The collectors of these earliest traditions who first adventured upon a written history of England, after alluding to the people by whom England was inhabited before the Deluge—and about the records of whom they modestly profess their ignorance—are contented to begin as late as 200 years after that memorable event. It was then that Samothes or Dis, who was either the fourth or the sixth son of Japheth, planted Gaul and Britain with the Celtic race, and from him the island was originally called Samothea. This Samothes is also alleged, upon the authority of Berosus, to have taught his people the arts of government and the use of letters. After him succeeded Magus, who was not only a learned scholar, but a mighty magician; Sarron, a founder of schools and colleges; Druis, the originator of the order of Druids; and Bardus, the father of the Bards. In this way, four great stages of improvement are comprised within four short generations, and impersonated in as many names:

VOL. I. 1—2

it was, perhaps, a desperate attempt to comprise within a brief intelligible sketch whole centuries of general progress, about which no record existed beyond the fact that such changes had actually occurred. It was necessary for the earliest writers of the records of these four reigns to give them a historic aspect, and, therefore, they quote Berosus for their authority. But where is this record of Berosus? It was evidently nothing better than a historic forgery, in the absence of authentic documents; and, while it sufficed for present inquiry, it only enveloped truth in deeper darkness, and increased the difficulties of research.

Having thus peopled the island with a Celtic race, and described those institutions by which the people were distinguished, a change occurred, under which the ancient name of Samothen, that was first affixed to Britain, was to pass away, and be superseded by that of Albion. This was in consequence of an arrival of hostile strangers, who landed in Britain during the reign of Bardus, and became masters of the island. These victorious invaders, who have been described as giants, were under the command of Albion, the son of Neptune; and on winning possession of the country, they commemorated the valour and good fortune of their chief by giving his name to the island at large. But the career of Albion was brief; for Hercules, the destroyer of giants, was abroad, and the gigantic sons of Neptune were his special enemies. Bergion, King of Ireland and the Orkneys, having been assailed by this formidable wanderer, Albion, his brother, hastened to his assistance; but in an engagement that followed, the two brethren fell, with the greater part of their army. In this story, Hercules, instead of going forth alone with his club and lion's skin, is at the head of a host, and makes war in regular fashion, and with the ordinary weapons, while the provocations that have moved him are such as any ancient chief would have made the ground of a warlike enterprise. The whole narrative, indeed, is evidently nothing more than that of a hostile invasion which was made upon Britain at a very early period, while the rude chroniclers who first reduced the report to writing, invested the successful assailant with the well-known classical name of Hercules, to give additional interest to the story.

The success of this story of Hercules upon the credulous minds of the British nobles and priests of the early ages, was not lost sight of; and the next arrival of strangers into the island was allegorized in the same spirit of classical license. It was the old Greek story of Danaus and his daughters, naturalized into the annals of England. This Danaus, whom our early writers by mistake call Dioclesian, King of Syria, had fifty daughters, whom as many of his nephews sought in marriage, and that, too, at the sword's point. Compelled to submit, but still resolved that his nephews should not profit by his submission, he gave a sword to each of his daughters, with which she was to murder her husband on the wedding night. With this they all complied, except one, who saved her husband, Lynceus; and, in requital of their barbarity, this young prince caused the forty-nine faithless brides to be put on board a ship, and set adrift to the mercy of the waves. The vessel was borne by the winds to Britain, and the giants, whom the death of Albion had set free to follow their own devices, were so delighted with the arrival of these congenial spirits, that they took them in marriage, and became fathers of an offspring more gigantic and tyrannical than themselves. In this way, it may be, the arrival of a foreign female influence, and the origin of an unpopular aristocracy in Britain, were embodied under the guise of the old Greek story.

In such a fashion as this, the mythic history of England is carried onward through the earliest periods of antiquity to the era of the Trojan war. It is well known how eagerly this event was laid hold of by the Roman poets and historians, to aggrandize the origin of their countrymen, as well as that of their noblest families. But in spite of these fables, by which historic truth was so much obscured, we also know how greatly a Pelasgic, if not a Trojan ancestry belonged to the founders of Rome. The idea of such an honoured derivation was not confined exclusively to the Romans; the Britons also claimed a similar paternity, and Geoffrey of Monmouth, who was its chief recorder and advocate, continued to be copied by his successors until the beginning of the seventeenth century. It was only then that they dismissed it indignantly as a pious fraud, without inquiring as to what particles of truth it may have contained, or even what important change or era in our ancient history it may have obscurely symbolized.

The commencement of the strange story, by which a Trojan ancestry is secured for the ancient Britons, is thus told by Giovani Villani, a Florentine, in his *Universal History*, as quoted by Holinshed: "Sylvius, the son of Æneas by his wife Lavinia, fell in love with a niece of his mother, the same Lavinia; and by her he had a son, of whom she died in travail, and therefore he was called Brutus; who after, as he grew in some stature, and hunting in a forest, slew his father at unawares; and thereupon, for fear of his grandfather, Sylvius Posthumus, he fled the country, and with a retinue of such as followed him, passing through diverse seas, at length he arrived in the isle of Britain."

Such is the earlier portion of the tale, embellished with many a strange circumstance, partly of the classical, and partly of the chivalrous ages. On arriving in Albion (not yet called Britain) the roving Trojan had been directed in his choice by a dream, in which Diana had delivered to him an oracle in Greek, afterwards rendered into Latin, and finally translated by Milton into English, to the following effect:—

"Brutus, far to the west, in the ocean wide,
Beyond the realm of Gaul, a land there lies;
Begirt it lies, where giants dwelt of old;
Now void, it fits thy people; thither bend
Thy course—there shalt thou find a lasting seat,
There to thy sons another Troy shall rise;
And kings be born of thee, whose dreaded might
Shall awe the world, and conquer nations bold."

On landing, Brutus found the promised island wasted of its ancient inhabitants; none now dwelt in it except a remnant of those giants, the descendants of the Danaides, whose ferocious rule had been so sanguinary, that they are termed "devils" in the ancient legends. The strangers on commencing their exploration, had roused the Titanic brood, who sallied out from their caves and dens to give the intruders battle; but it fared with them as it had done with every other people who have exceeded the standard measure of humanity, for they were quickly put to the rout, and cut down with ease by their puny antagonists. One of the strongest of these giants, called Gogmagog, who was twelve cubits high, having been preserved alive, either as a specimen or a trophy, Corineus, a gallant champion of the Trojans, longed to wrestle a fall with him; but at the outset was encountered with such a hug, that three of his ribs were broken. Nothing daunted, however, by this unpromising embrace, he heaved the giant up by main force upon his shoulders, carried him to the next high rock, and there hurled him into the sea. That part of the cliffs of Dover from which the unfortunate Gogmagog was thus thrown, as Milton writes, "has been called ever since Langoëmagog, which is to say, the Giant's Leap." To reward him for his valour, Brutus bestowed upon Corineus the whole county of Cornwall. These events, which are stated to have taken place about the time that Eli the high-priest governed Israel, betoken the monkish origin of this part of the legend, and show how its author must have thought of the occupation of Canaan by the Israelites, and the destruction of the gigantic race of Anak. On becoming undisputed lord of the island, Brutus erected his capital city of Troia Nova, afterwards called Trinovantum, and now London; parted Britain among his three sons, and, after a reign of twenty-four years, died in peace.

After Brutus succeeded a line of kings, as long, and withal as shadowy, perhaps, as those which passed before the bewildered eye of Macbeth in the cave of Hecate. These different sovereigns, love and hate, make peace and war, build cities and subdue provinces, in the usual fashion of ancient history, until their very names as well as deeds are confounded with each other; but amidst the throng, who might otherwise have passed into utter oblivion, are some whom accident, strangely enough, has exalted into full immortality. Of these, Ebranc, the fifth King of Britain after Brutus, was the first of British sovereigns who invaded France, where he seems to have been as successful as Edward III. more than 2000 years afterwards; he also built Mount Agned, or the Castle of the Maidens, round which Edinburgh was to grow in future years. The fourth in succession to him was Bladud, who had the singular merit of discovering the medicinal virtues of the hot springs of Bath, and of founding that famous city, which was originally called Caerbad. The end of this king, which was truly dolorous, supplied, in future ages, an important chapter to Johnson's *Rasselas*. "'This Bladud,' says Holinshed, 'took such pleasure in artificial practices and magic, that he taught the art throughout all his realm. And to show his cunning in other points, upon a presumptuous pleasure which he had therein, he took upon him to fly in the air; but he fell upon the temple of Apollo, which stood in the city of Troynovant, and there was torn in pieces, after he had ruled the Britons by the space of twenty years." [Here we find a temple of Apollo in London before Rome itself was founded!]

Bladud was succeeded by his son Lear—and what a name to British memory and British feeling! It seems as if King Lear had died but yesterday; and that our own eyes had seen him, first as an arrogant sovereign, and unreasonable exacting father, and afterwards as a discrowned king, wandering helpless and unattended upon the heath, with his white locks beaten by the tempest, and streaming in the wind. The whole story of his dotage, in which his daughters duped him with a show of fulsome and flattering affection, and the manner in which they stripped him of the last relics of his royalty, and cast him loose into the world, were presented to Shakspeare in all the bald, dry circumstantial narrative of the legendary scroll—and with a touch he lighted its letters into living fire, and made it a tale that shall live for ever. According to the original story, however, the old king left the land in which he had no longer a hovel to shelter him, and betook himself to France, of which his rejected Cordelia was queen. And then it was that she enjoyed the full meaning of that simple reply for which he had disinherited her, when she said to him, after her sisters had done speaking: "Father, my love towards you is as my duty bids; what should a father seek, what can a child promise more? They who pretend beyond this, flatter." For, with the permission of her husband she raised an army, passed over to England, and replaced Lear upon the throne. This close is different from that of Shakspeare; but heart-rending as is that of the poet, it would have been the best after all, compared with the sequel as it exists in the original history. For we are there informed, that after the death of Lear, Cordelia, now a widow, succeeded to the sovereignty of England, where she ruled in peace, until two sons of her unnatural sisters, having now grown to man's estate, conceived themselves defrauded of their inheritance, and made war against her. She was defeated, deposed and imprisoned; "wherewith," we are told, "she took such grief, being a woman of a manly courage, and despairing to recover liberty, there she slew herself, when she had reigned the term of five years." The two victors, who were the veritable children of such mothers as Goneril and Regan, after having parted the island between them, soon quarrelled about their share of the spoil, and Margan, the elder, in a battle that ensued in Wales, was slain by Cunedag, his cousin, who became sole sovereign of Britain.

We now pass over an interval during which Rome was built, reigned over by its seven kings, and finally changed into a republic. We might well wonder what Britain could have to do with such remote events; but so it was; for Brennus and his formidable troops were not Gauls, as the Roman historians have erroneously reported, but true-born Britons. This Brennus, it appears, according to British chroniclers, was the younger son of Dunwallo Molmutius; and being discontented with his inheritance, which comprised the whole of England north of the Humber, he made war upon his elder brother, Belinus, to obtain the sovereignty of the whole realm. But being defeated, he afterwards joined his forces to those of his brother, overran Gaul and part of Italy, and finally approached the gates of Rome. Having thus settled the most essential part of the story, which was to convert the Gaulish invaders into Britons, the narrative falls into the track of the Roman writers, in the capture of the city and the final defeat of Brennus by Camillus. This was surely enough to console the wounded pride of the Britons for the subsequent conquest of their island by the Romans! Their countrymen had been a civilized people when their proud enemies had been mere barbarians; and had entered as masters the city gates of the world's metropolis, and compelled it to purchase their forbearance. At this point, however, Milton shows his incredulity, and professes himself unable to reconcile the different parts of the story, so that he dismisses it with this brief statement: "Thus much is more generally believed, that both this Brennus, and another famous captain, Britomarus, whom the epitomist Florus and others mention, were not Gauls but Britons; the name of the first in that tongue signifying a king, and of the other, a great Briton."

After this feat of the sacking of Rome, we have another long array of kings, of whom the early annalists had by this time begun to grow weary, for their deeds are very briefly recorded. During this course, also, if these early legends are to be believed, England must already have been overspread with those stately cities which the Romans had afterwards the credit of founding, and been governed by those wise laws which are usually referred to a Saxon origin. Thus the Mercian law, which has usually been attributed to Alfred the Great, is represented to have been actually devised and formulated by Mertia, wife of King Guithelin or Guintolin; but here Milton, who admits the fact of such an early origin of the Mercian law, while he scorns the thought of a female legislator, thus gets out of the difficulty: "In the minority of her son, she [Mertia] had the rule, and then, as may be supposed, brought forth these laws, not herself, for laws are masculine births, but by the advice of her sagest counsellors; and therein she might do virtuously, since it befell her to supply the nonage of her son: else nothing more awry from the law of God and nature, than that a woman should give laws to men." Among the kings who followed, was Elidure, whose fate as a sovereign was a rarity in royal annals; for he was thrice deposed, and as often replaced on his throne. He was also a very paragon of justice and generosity, as may be learned from the following romantic incident. His elder brother, Archigallo, who had reigned oppressively, having been displaced, and himself advanced in his room, it happened that one day, after having reigned five years, Elidure, while hunting in a forest, met his deposed brother, now an impoverished wanderer, and meanly attended, after he had vainly roamed about through the different courts of Europe in search of aid to replace him in his kingdom. The forlorn Archigallo was recognized; but Elidure, instead of sweeping such a dangerous rival from his path, as the kings of that period would have done without scruple, took him privately to the city Alclud, and hid him in his own bed-chamber. He then feigned himself to be grievously sick; and, as if unable to endure a crowd, he summoned his nobles one by one to his bedside, that he might consult with them about the affairs of his kingdom. The nobles singly repaired to him, and then the apparently dying Elidure prevailed upon them to swear allegiance to Archigallo.

Having in this way obtained the consent of the whole nobility, the dying king quickly got well again, summoned a council to meet him at York, and there so handled the matter, that Archigallo was received by the commons as he had been by the lords; after which, Elidure, with his own hands, placed the royal crown upon his brother's head, and was the first to hail him as king. Penetrated to the heart's core by such a wondrous instance of justice, generosity, and brotherly love, the now restored wanderer became one of the best of kings, and dying childless after a reign of ten years, was succeeded once more by Elidure.

We now gladly rush to the close of this array of shadows and phantoms, and hasten into the dawn which begins with the period of Cæsar's Cassivellaunus. The father of this last-mentioned king was Eli or Hely, who reigned forty years, and the most distinguished event of whose reign is thus specified by Holinshed, on the authority of the old British historians:—"Marry, this is not to be forgotten, that of the aforesaid Hely, the last of the said thirty-three kings, the Isle of Ely took the name, because that he most commonly did there inhabit, building in the same a goodly palace, and making great reparations of the sluices, ditches, and causeways about that isle, for conveyance away of the water, that else would sore have endomaged the country." Nineteen years before the arrival of the Romans, Hely was succeeded by his eldest son, Lud, who is described in high terms as a jolly feaster, warrior, legislator, and reformer of abuses, and also a great builder, repairing many of the old towns and stately edifices that had gone to decay. He also enlarged the city of Troynovant, and surrounded it with a strong wall of stone, in consequence of which it thenceforth obtained the name of Lud-town, or London. Among those architectural undertakings with which he aggrandized the capital, are particularly mentioned Lud's Gate, afterwards called Ludgate; the palace in its neighbourhood, afterwards the Bishop of London's palace; and a temple, which subsequently became St. Paul's Church. Such were but a few of his many undertakings, which are recorded by the old British historians with careful circumstantiality and most praiseworthy gravity.

On the death of Lud, whose two sons were still minors, Cassivellaunus, his brother, succeeded to the royal power. And now it is that the old British annalists, feeling themselves hampered between the *Commentaries* of Cæsar on the one hand, and the fanciful traditions of the country on the other, proceed in their course with unwonted caution. On this account they are unable precisely to determine whether Cassivellaunus was raised to the throne, or merely appointed regent. By their statement, however, his administration was so just and able that he was worthy of the esteem of the Britons, who set aside the claims of his nephews, and recognized him as their only king. Cassivellaunus acted a generous part towards these orphans, by investing the elder with the sovereignty of London and Kent, and the younger with that of Cornwall.

And here the Muse of ancient British history abruptly retires, like one detected in falsehood, and gives place to a more credible witness, after having fabled for the long course of 1058 years. And here also Milton, who had followed the narrative, frequently in doubt, and sometimes in utter disbelief, thus welcomes the approaching change:—"By this time, like one who had set out on his way by night, and travelled through a region of smooth or idle dreams, our history now arrives on the confines, where daylight and truth meet us with a clear dawn, representing to our view, though at a far distance, true colours and shapes. For albeit Cæsar, whose authority we are now first to follow, wanted not who taxed him of mis-reporting in his *Commentaries*, yea, in his *Civil Wars against Pompey*, much more may we think in the British affairs, of whose little skill in writing he did not easily hope to be contradicted; yet now, in such variety of good authors, we hardly can miss from one hand or other to be sufficiently informed as of things passed so long ago."

In the foregoing history of Britain, which we have so briefly passed over, the first thought that strikes us is the long series of kings, whose characters and deeds are as confidently sketched as if they had been men of yesterday; and the extended period of time which they necessarily occupy, stopping short only within a brief distance of the Deluge itself. But this difficulty is easily got rid of when we remember the nature of that government which prevailed among the Celtic people. Among them a king was but the chieftain of his own tribe, and not of the nation at large; and, therefore, sometimes not less than a dozen of sovereigns might have been found reigning in Britain at one and the same time. Nothing was more natural, at a later period, than to mistake these *reguli* for sole kings of the whole country, and to arrange their histories into successive periods, instead of making them contemporaneous. Such has been the case in the early annals of many other countries where this patriarchal system of government prevailed; and the great perplexity of antiquaries and historians, in such instances, has been occasioned by a long course of life and action, to which the earliest antiquity could afford no room.

By keeping, then, the fact in mind, that our island was divided into many families and septs, each of which had its own ruler, several kings may be comprised within a single generation, and a whole century condensed into a few years. In this way the mythic history of Britain before the Roman invasion can be reduced, in point of time, within a very reasonable compass, and the wonderful achievements, stripped of their poetical embellishments, may become sober realities. And keeping in mind the evidence of a mixed population set forth by these writers, corroborated, moreover, by the veritable authors who succeeded them, it is to be conceived that there existed within the compass of the island many peoples—not a community: some in a degree of civilization approaching that of the nations of antiquity; others, and by far the greater number, in a rude and barbarous state. The Druid priesthood, indeed, who were likewise the lawgivers, by their superior knowledge, as well as through the superstitious deference of their votaries, maintained a community of power in all affairs, civil and religious; but in other respects we see no evidences of that combination of classes which constitutes a nation. In most parts of the island the king, or military chief of a tribe, and his principal warriors, usurped the lion's share in the resources of his dominion; while the herd, the tiller of the soil, and the hunter, stood in much the same relation as that of an Irish kerne of the fifteenth century to his feudal superior. On parts of the coast, however, communities of a more settled and more uniform character were held together by the mutual interest of traffic, and the benefits ensuing from an intercourse with strangers from the opposite shores, as in the instance of the Trinobantine mart of London, which is described by Tacitus (A.D. 62) as a place most renowned for the concourse of merchants, and for its stores of goods. The period quoted is only nineteen years after the Romans had got possession of South Britain, and were still struggling to maintain it, and therefore not likely to have had a part in the establishment of this early seat of British commerce. Allowing for this, and taking a broad view of the fabulous relations, we may observe the growth of a population fed by the incursions of wandering and adventurous bands, who flowed on these shores in successive waves of population. Striving for a footing in the land, the conquerors or colonists still brought in an accession of strength or diversity of character, such as, by a view of subsequent annals, we observe to have been infused down to the period of the Norman conquest. Hence, it may be conceived, was derived that spirit of enterprise which has obtained for the British race such a wide geographical extension, and so potent a predominance. The original colonists, a branch of the Celtic family, to whom, as the descendants of Japheth, were given the isles of the Gentiles, were replenished by successive offshoots of the same prolific stock, carrying with them such modifications of character as had been induced by the influences of climate and situation, and the nature of their resources. Hence, whatever features of barbarism may appear in our first view of the Britons, as they are delineated by the authenticated writers of antiquity, these may be looked upon rather as proper to a condition declined from early civilization, than as the signs of a primitive state. If, for instance, they were incapable of steering their wicker, hide-covered vessels any distance beyond that of a mere coasting voyage, or, at the furthest, to the neighbouring islands, they must have then been in a worse condition than when they first effected a landing on these shores;—and if they be found dwelling in holes and caves, or in miserable huts of daub and wattle, and we contrast with such mean fabrics the colossal and symmetrical structures of Stonehenge, Avebury, and other similar monuments, whose vast relics seem the production of a race of giants and sorcerers—these must appear, in such a point of view, the vestiges of a vastly superior age, or the memorials of a race elevated far above those who surrounded them.

But respecting these considerations there is but slight footing even for speculation; for the few authentic authors of antiquity who treat of the Celtic Britons evidently do so upon very partial information. That Britain had become the seat of several tribes differing greatly in many respects, and bringing with them the characteristics of their race, is evident in the observations of authors of the period, especially those of Tacitus, who, in his *Life of Agricola*, thus writes:— "Now what manner of men the first inhabitants of Britain were, foreignly brought in, or born in the land as among a barbarous people, it is not certainly known. Their complexions are different, and thence may some conjectures be taken; for the red hair of the dwellers in Caledonia, and mighty limbs, import a German descent. The coloured countenances of the Silures,[1] and hair most commonly curled, and site against Spain, seem to induce that the old Spaniards passed the sea and possessed those places. The nearest to France likewise resemble the French, either because they retain of the race from which they descended, or that in countries abutting together the same aspects of the heavens do yield the same complexions of bodies. But, generally, it is most likely the French, being the nearest, did people the land."[2] Diodorus Siculus, whose *Bibliothecæ Historicæ* is considered to have been written

---

[1] The inhabitants of South Wales (Dehenbarth). The qualification appears here to mean naturally swart or dark, and not the artificial appearance produced by dyeing the skin, said to have been practised by the Britons. [2] Greneway's *Trans*.

shortly after the death of Julius Cæsar, places the Britons somewhat on a parallel with the Homeric warriors. After describing the position and bearings of the island—"Further," he continues, "they say that its original tribes inhabit Britain, in their usages still preserving the primitive modes of life; for in their war they use chariots, as the ancient Greek heroes are reported to have done in the Trojan war."

The people of the Cape of Cornwall are distinguished by the same author as "singularly partial to strangers; and, from their intercourse with foreign merchants, civilized in their habits." "These people," he continues, with reference to their traffic, "obtain the tin by skilfully working the soil which produces it. This, being rocky, has earthy interstices, in which working the ore, and then fusing, they reduce to metal, and when they have formed it into cubical shapes, they convey it to a certain island, lying off Britain,

THE LAND'S END, CORNWALL.—Drawn from nature and on wood, by J. Skinner Prout.

named Ictis; for at the low tides, the intervening space being laid dry, they carry thither in waggons the tin in great abundance." But previous to that era this production, so valuable before the art of tempering iron was discovered, had attracted the Phœnicians to our shores. A history of early Britain would be incomplete without a fuller notice of the subject. This trade of the Phœnicians may be considered the beginning of that British commerce which has outlived its ancient teachers, extinguished every successive rivalry, and secured a main part of the wide world's traffic, in all its numberless departments, up to the present day.

It is now generally allowed, that what the Greeks termed *chalcus*, although translated brass, was not the metal commonly known under that name. It was rather that composition of copper and tin which we denominate bronze. It was with this bronze that the Greeks and Romans composed their statues, and many of their implements and ornaments; and of this also the Carthaginians, and even the early Homeric heroes, fashioned their swords and spears, as well as their defensive armour. Tin was likewise used, as is supposed, by the Tyrians, in producing the rich purple dye, for which they were famous, and was known to the Israelites, before the Babylonish captivity, under the name *bedil*. But going still further back, we find that brass (that is, bronze) was not only an important material in the construction of Solomon's temple, but a metal precious as gold, with which the Israelites, who must have obtained it from the Egyptians, adorned their tabernacle in the wilderness. In the former instance, we learn from the Sacred Writings that the artificer employed by Solomon in the decoration of the temple was Hiram, a native of Tyre, one of the cities of the Phœnicians, the early traders in tin. Here we trace the use of bronze up to the Mosaic period, and consequently of tin also, without which bronze cannot be made. And where was this tin obtained? At such early periods it was only to be found in two countries—Spain and Britain. These were, then, the valued sources from which the nations of earliest antiquity derived a metal that ministered so largely to their wealth, their luxury, and convenience. And these countries, perhaps, were that mysterious Tarshish, lying somewhere beyond the Pillars of Hercules, from which such precious shipments returned, and whose locality our biblical commentators and able hydrographers have so long endeavoured to discover.

In such an important fact, it matters little whether the hidden treasures of Spain or of Britain had the honour of the first discovery. It is sufficient for us to know that that portion of the British territory called the Scilly Islands was known to the Carthaginians ages before the Christian era. This is pretty distinctly intimated in the account given to us by Festus Avienus of the voyage of Hamilco, an ancient Carthaginian navigator. In this voyage, we are told, Hamilco reached the islands of the Œstrymnides within less than four months after he had set sail from Carthage, and from the description of Avienus we are compelled to conclude that these Œstrymnides could be no other than our Scilly Islands. They were, he tells us, in the neighbourhood of Albion and of Ireland, and within two days' sail of the latter, which he terms the Sacred Island. He describes those islands as abounding in tin and lead, and inhabited by a bold, active, trafficking people, who, having no timber for the building of ships, make adventurous voyages in boats made of hides. These islands, also, he intimates, were not first discovered by Hamilco, but had previously been visited for traffic by the people of Tartessus and Carthage. They were afterwards explored with such industry, that their tin was at length exhausted, and nothing apparently remains of it except the traces of the ancient mines; but Cornwall was not far off as a field for fresh operations. It was probably this peninsula which afterwards obtained the name of Cassiteros (from the Greek word *cassiteron*, signifying tin), while the Scilly Isles, described as ten in number, of which only one was uninhabited, were called Cassiterides, or the Tin Islands. Under this name they are mentioned by Herodotus, the father of history, nearly 500 years before the Christian era, although their geographical position he was unable to discover.

The causes of this ignorance in so important a matter it is not difficult to explain. In their knowledge of these Tin Islands the Carthaginians possessed a treasure which they were resolved to monopolize, and hence their particular locality was carefully concealed from all the world, and especially from their formidable and enterprising rivals, the Romans, who were anxious to learn the secret. The latter, therefore, lay on the watch, and were ready to give chase, while the former studied to out-manœuvre or out-sail them. At length, as we are informed by Strabo, a ship of Carthage having set out on a voyage to the Cassiterides for tin, the captain of a Roman galley, who had been appointed to observe him, followed in close pursuit. The Carthaginian tried every expedient to elude his adversary, but being closely pressed, and finding escape impossible, he ran his vessel aground, and thus sacrificed both ship and cargo. His fidelity in thus concealing the route to the Tin Islands was so highly appreciated by his countrymen, that on returning home he was repaid, to the full value of his loss, out of the public treasury.

But cunning although the Carthaginians were, it was impossible that such a profitable route, pursued for centuries, could always remain exclusively their own. The Greek colonists of Marseilles had turned their attention to the subject; and from their superior intelligence and nautical skill, they were at length enabled to discover the whereabouts of this rich *terra incognita*. Accordingly we are told, that only a century after the time of Herodotus, Pytheas, a Marseillais navigator, was the first of his countrymen who penetrated into the British seas. This enterprise appears to have been so successfully followed, that the secret of the Cassiterides was at length laid open to the Roman colonies on the south coast of Gaul; and thus, even before the arrival of Julius Cæsar, a brisk trade in tin had been carried on between them and the people of the Scilly Islands and Cornwall. The effects of this traffic were exhibited in the superior comfort and civilization of those parts of the British coast which the strangers visited. Diodorus informs us that the Britons inhabiting the Land's End (Bolerium) were much more civilized than the rest of their countrymen, in consequence of their traffic with the foreigners. Such was also the case with the natives of the Cassiterides, although they are pictured of a somewhat strange appearance, not unlike that of figures upon some of the earlier Etruscan vases. According to Strabo, they wore comfortable dresses, and these also of cloth, while most of their inland countrymen had nothing but their own painted skins. He tells us that they wore long black cloaks, which reached to their ankles, and were girded about the waist; that they walked about with staves in their hands, and that their long beards gave them the appearance of goats. He is careful especially to mention the lead and tin mines with which these islands abounded, and their traffic with foreign traders in these metals and skins, in return for bronze articles, earthenware, and salt.

It might be asked why Rome herself, who had been so solicitous to discover these wealthy mines, was afterwards contented to purchase their treasures at second hand from her own tributaries? But the Romans were no navigators, and cared little for commerce, unless it was brought to their doors; and as for wealth in general, they regarded every country as their storehouse, which they could empty at their own good pleasure. While the sword could procure tin at any time, they would neither condescend to sail in quest of it, nor labour in digging it;

BEFORE THE ROMAN INVASION.

and hence, until they conquered Britain, they regarded its people as "*toto orbe divisos.*"

And why, it might also be asked, were the Britons themselves so remiss in improving to the full those advantages of intercourse with foreigners, which they had enjoyed for so many centuries? They had been visited successively by the most enterprising and civilized of the nations, and yet had learned comparatively so little! It may be answered that civilization had entered, but had not pervaded the land. Even the most important, and yet most obvious step in advance which the Britons might have been expected to adopt—that of constructing good barks for themselves, modelled from those of the strangers, and thus carrying on such a gainful trade on their own account—appears incomprehensible. This discrepancy, however, is to some extent met by the statement of Festus Avienus, that the islands frequented by the Phœnician mariners did not produce wood for the construction of ships. Further, the peculiar genius and circumstances of the people may be taken into account—the influence of superstition under the

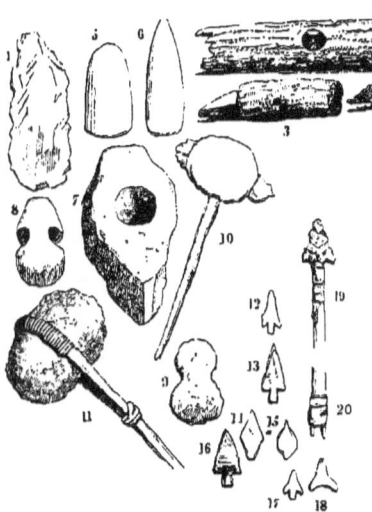

STONE CELTS AND ARROW HEADS.—Drawn by J. W. Archer, from examples in the British Museum.

rule of the Druids so similar to that of the Egyptian priesthood. The ancient Egyptians had the same commercial temptations, and the ability to build ships; but it appears from Herodotus that they abstained, from a loathing of the sea, looking upon it as the domain of the abhorred Typhon. The Britons evidently did not possess those national qualities that are need-

ful for patient and enduring sailors. It was not until the Saxon and the Dane had become settled inhabitants, that the "meteor flag of England" was to float in undisputed ascendency.

Where tradition and history are both insufficient to enlighten our inquiries into the origin and condition of our early population, we have buried beneath the soil, a history which a high state of intellectual cultivation enables the inquirer to discover; and to read in obscure caverns—the places of sepulture—a lesson on the condition of those early tribes, whose record we might otherwise have abandoned in despair.

In the endeavour to comprehend the bearing of those vestiges upon our prehistoric era, a classification has been adopted, by which the implements, weapons, &c., found in barrows and excavations, are arranged under the Stone, the Bronze, and the Iron periods. This formula, however convenient, is not founded upon such sufficient authority that it can be adopted as an arbitrary rule, and instead of periods, it is more prudent to say conditions; for, with regard to the use of the materials of bronze and stone, it is probable that the one appertained to the great, and the other to the lowly, in the same way that the rich man of the present day eats his fish with a silver fork, and the poor man with an implement of Sheffield hardware. In adverting to the stone condition of the Celtic Britons, we find a great variety of weapons and implements, along with the buried remains, as the things most valued by the departed, or adapted to his use in a future state. Among these the stone hammer appears in a variety of forms, from that of a rude stone to those in which it has been fashioned into a shapely and convenient instrument, such as is represented in the accompanying cut, No. 8. In Nos. 1, 2, 3, we see implements in their original handles of deer's horn, one a rude flake of flint, the other two chisel-shaped, and suitable for flaying the carcasses of animals, &c. No. 4 is a large flake of flint, found in a tumulus at Alfriston, in Sussex, which has been chipped into an imperfect shape. Nos. 5 and 6 are composed of a hard greenish flint, symmetrically formed and finely polished, but of a shape unsuited for handles. In No. 9 we observe a stone with a flexure in the sides, by which it could be held by a pliable handle bent round it, and tied at the junction, like No. 11, a stone hammer used by the natives of Northern Australia. In No. 7 the stone implement is perforated for the insertion of a handle, like No. 10, a stone hammer from Western Australia, in which a wooden handle is inserted, and further secured by a cement of native gum; but in No. 8

HISTORY OF ENGLAND.

the sides of the stone are scooped as well as pierced, for the purpose of binding the handle with thongs or osiers. There are likewise found a variety of javelin heads, Nos. 12, 13, 16, and arrow heads, Nos. 14, 15, 17, 18, of flint, for war or the chase, and which, in dexterous hands, may have served to knock down the deer or beaver, but are scarcely of sufficient deadliness for the capture of the urus or mountain bull, or the wolf and boar of the great British forests. Nos. 19 and 20 are the flint pile and knock of a Patagonian arrow, the former showing the manner in which the pile is bound to the shaft with vegetable fibre, probably resembling the mode of attachment employed by the ancient Britons. In the British tumuli are likewise found flint knives and daggers, and weapons of bone and horn. Of this description were the lances or harpoons which have been found alongside the relics of stranded whales, pins and bodkins of bone and wood, with a variety of ornaments, such as beads, bits of amber, &c.; the drinking cup of the departed Briton; and,

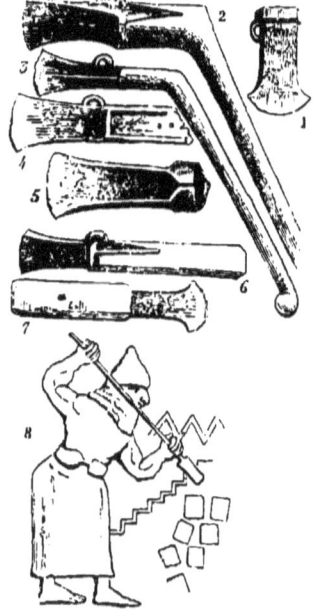

BRONZE CELTS.—Drawn by J. W. Archer, from examples in the British Museum.—1, Bronze Celt; 2, 3, 6, 7, Bronze Celts with handles speculatively adapted; 4, 5, Ditto. various; 8, Figure using Celt, from Nimroud Sculptures.

where cremation has been practised, the funeral urn, containing the ashes of the deceased, wrapped in a linen cloth, and secured by a pin of bone, wood, or bronze.

Articles of bronze found in British barrows have been subjected to analysis, and found to contain, in the instance of a spear head, one part of tin to six parts of copper; in an axe head, one

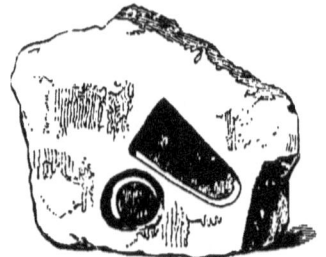

MOULD FOR CASTING CELTS AND RINGS, found near Wallington, Northumberland, now in the British Museum.

of tin to ten of copper; and in a knife, one of tin to seven and a half of copper.[1] Among these are found a variety of the hatchet-shaped instruments commonly denominated celts. In the accompanying cut is represented a selection of those instruments, some of which are speculatively adapted to handles, together with the representation of an Assyrian sapper and miner employed in reducing the wall of a beleaguered city by means of an instrument precisely similar to the British celt, No. 1, which is shaped for the longitudinal insertion of a handle. Moulds for casting these implements, as well as swords and spear heads, have been found both in Britain

CIST CONTAINING A SKELETON.—From the Archæologia.

and Ireland—in some instances together with lumps of metal and quantities of cinders—and

---

[1] Meyric's *Original Inhabitants*, and *Phil. Trans. for 1796.*

hence it is concluded that the Britons were in the practice of casting their own tools and weapons. Of the funeral depositories in which these articles are discovered, the stone cist appears to have been the earliest. This is made evident, by the series of subsequent interments in the mounds beneath which the cist is found. The last cut on p. 10 represents a cist found under such an accumulation, near Driffield, in the East Riding of Yorkshire. This rude sarcophagus was reached after the removal of the remains of superincumbent interments. It was found sunk in the ground, till the upper edges of the sides, which were formed of four slabs of sandstone, came on a level with the natural surface, and was paved with small irregular pieces of the same kind of tone. The dimensions were, on the north sides three feet nine inches, on the south four feet two inches, on the east two feet five inches, and on the west two feet eleven inches. It was two feet six inches in depth. On the floor lay a skeleton of large size, the thigh-bones measuring nineteen inches. It was placed, as is common in cist burial, with the knees drawn up, and lying on the left side, the arms bent, and the palms of the hands together; the bones of the right arm were laid in a very singular and beautiful armlet, No. 4, made of some large animal's bone, about six inches long, and the extremities (which were a little broader than the middle), neatly squared. In this were two perforations, about half an inch from each end, through which were bronze pins or rivets, with gold heads, most probably to attach it to a piece of leather, which had passed round the arm, and been fastened by a small bronze buckle, that was found underneath the bones. Immediately behind the vertebræ, as if it had fallen from the waist, was a small bronze dagger in a wooden sheath, having a handle of the same, No. 2; round the neck were three large amber beads of conical form, No. 1, having the under side flat, and which were pierced by two holes, running upwards in a slanting direction, until they met at the centre. At the lower end of the vault, between the extremity of the spine and the feet, was a highly ornamented drinking cup, No. 5, completely covered with rows of marks and indentations, each row being divided by ridges or bands. About the centre of the pavement, in front of the body, was the upper part of a hawk's head and beak, No. 3. A mass of what seemed to be linen cloth lay under the entire length of the skeleton.[1] In some instances it is observed that bodies were inclosed in wooden coffins, composed of planks riveted together with bronze, or of a length cut from the stem of a tree, and hollowed out for their reception. In the southern parts of the country the burial repositories are barrows or

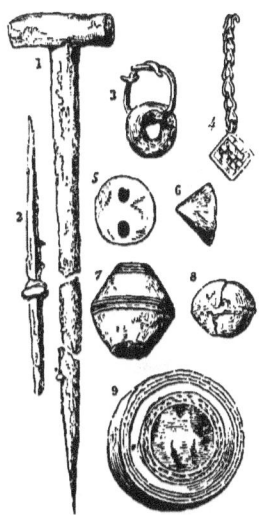

TRINKETS AND ARTICLES OF THE TOILET, found in barrows on the Wiltshire Downs.—From Hoare's Ancient Wiltshire.—Nos. 1, 2, Pins; 3, 4, Gold Ear-rings; 5, 6, Beads; 7, 8, Gold Beads; 9, Ornament of amber set in gold, to be worn suspended.

tumuli; in the north, piled-up heaps of stones, called cairns. The former are mounds of a diversity of shapes, some extending to the great length of 400 feet. On being opened some of these large tumuli were found to contain but few bones, and are supposed to have been dedicated to great chiefs; others are conical or bell-shaped, which latter, from containing trinkets and articles of female use, are taken to have been appropriated to women of high rank. A classification of the various shapes and destinations of these mounds has been attempted, but the formula is not entirely satisfactory. A cromlech on the plain of L'Ancresse, in the Island of Guernsey, is described[2] as a vault formed of vertical single stones, or shafts, in close lateral approximation, or actual contact, supporting a roof of large transverse blocks, the flatter surface of which, as of the shafts, is turned toward the interior. The area is usually of a long triangular shape, having the apex directed toward the east; the capstones lie from north to south. The eastern narrow end of the cromlech is prolonged into a contracted avenue, rarely more than three feet high. The difficulty of conveying the dead by the depressed passage into the penetralia, is explained by the fact that bones

---

[1] *Archæologia*, vol. xxxiv. [2] *Archæologia*, vol. xxxv.

only, burned or otherwise, were conveyed there. The western end is closed like the sides. This large cromlech is forty-five feet in length, by

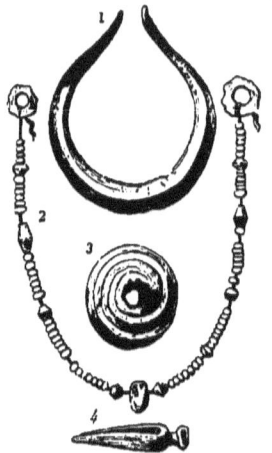

ARTICLES OF JEWELLERY,[1] found in barrows on the Wiltshire Downs.—From Hoare's Ancient Wiltshire.

fifteen feet wide, and nearly eight feet in height within the area at the western end. This space is covered by five larger and two smaller blocks of granite. The western is computed to weigh about thirty tons; it is nearly seventeen feet long, ten and a half wide, by four and a half in thickness. The second is sixteen feet long, the third again smaller, and so they gradually diminish to the seventh. The cromlech contains two layers or burial floors, on which were human bones, urns of coarse red and black clay, amulets and beads, pins, &c., the layers being separated by flat fragments of granite; the first stratum lay on a rude pavement, placed on the natural soil. The remains were disposed in the following remarkable manner:—
Unburned bones covered either end of the floor, the middle third being allotted to those which had been submitted to the action of fire. The urns in this part were of remarkably rude shape and material. The bones were heaped together confusedly, and each heap surrounded by a ring of small flat pebbles. The urns were near or within the rings. Some heaps consisted, as it were, of parents' and children's ashes mingled together, for within the same ring of pebbles were the bones of individuals of all ages. In this cromlech was an abundance of the bones of very young children. The next stratum contained only burned bones, among which were interspersed the tusks of boars. Be it remarked, that in no instance was the urn found to contain the ashes of the dead, but had, no doubt, been filled with food or liquor. Four flat discs, from six to twelve inches in diameter, and one inch in thickness, were found formed of the same ware as the urns, and doubtless they served as lids to some which had broad flat edges. As these lids are furnished with central handles, it may be inferred that the urns were visited and replenished from time to time. About 150 urns —some whole—were removed from this vault. When these repositories had become filled by successive deposits, it is found that additions were made of collateral cists, to supply room for further interments. The custom of cremation and urn burial appears, by the independent style of many vessels containing burned funeral remains, to have prevailed before the intercourse

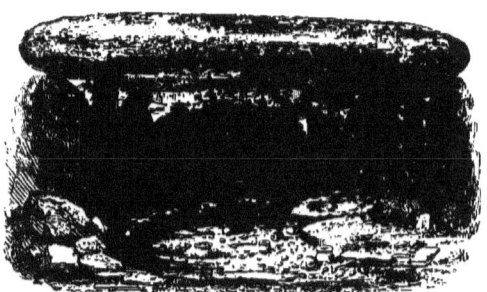

INTERIOR OF A CROMLECH ON THE PLAIN OF L'ANCRESSE, GUERNSEY.
From the Archæologia.

of the Romans with Britain. A very large and fine series of sepulchral urns, discovered by Sir Richard Colt Hoare, Bart., attest the variety of pattern used in the formation of these vessels;

---

[1] No. 1, Ornament of bronze plated with gold, to be worn suspended; 2, Necklace; 3, Glain Neidyr, or Adder-stone; 4, Tweezers.—The Glain Neidyr was found in a bell-shaped barrow—for reasons adverted to in the text, supposed to have been reserved for women of consequence. The Gemmæ Anguinæ, or Glain, were sacred to the Druid order; and the fact of this specimen having been found in a barrow of the kind conjectured to have been set apart for the interment of women, corroborates in some measure the conjecture, founded upon some ancient writers, that females were likewise initiated into the Druid rites and mysteries. These insignia are small glass amulets, commonly about as wide as our finger-rings, but much thicker, of a green colour usually, though some of them are blue, as in the present specimen, and others curiously waved, with blue, red, and white. Mr. Owen (Owen's *Dict.*) says they were worn by the different orders of Bards, each having its appropriate colour. The blue ones belonged to the presiding Bards, the white to the Druids, the green to the Ovates, and the three colours blended to the disciples.

one in particular, which was found in a tumulus near Stonehenge, is of entirely unique pattern, and from this peculiarity, as well as on account of its large size—fifteen inches in diameter at

CELTIC FUNERAL URNS.—From Sir R. Colt Hoare's Ancient Wiltshire.

the top, and twenty-two inches in height—it is distinguished as the Stonehenge Urn, and contained an interment of burned bones. It forms the largest figure in the accompanying wood-cut. The vessels on either side are a richly ornamented drinking cup, found with a skeleton (primary deposit), in a barrow at Amesbury Downs, and a small urn inverted over an interment of burnt bones. Other kinds of vessels discovered, two examples of which are here represented, are supposed to have been used as incense cups. They are about three inches in diameter, one of them is studded over with projecting knobs, which seem to have been first made in the form of glass stoppers to a bottle, and afterwards inserted into circular holes in the cup, which appear to have been previously drilled for receiving them. Between these grape-like protuberances are other perforations which remain open. This curious vessel was found in a tumulus near Heytesbury.

The dwellings of the dead have proved more permanent than those once appropriated to the living. "What they," the Britons, "call a town," Cæsar says, "is a tract of woody country, surrounded by a vallum and a ditch, for the security of themselves and cattle against the incursion of their enemies;" and Strabo corroborates this in the following words:—"The forests of the Britons are their cities; for when they have inclosed a very large circuit with felled trees, they build within it houses for themselves and hovels for their cattle. These buildings are very slight, and not designed for permanence."

It is conjectured that these notices refer only to the winter habitations of the Britons, and that the circumvallated hills called British camps were in summer the residences and sanctuaries of the Celtic rural populations. These are the *caer* of the Welsh and the Gaelic *dun*. A lengthy range of these intrenched hills appears on the downs of the Sussex coast, and interspersed with them are a series of hills which present a smaller surface at the top, and their site so chosen that where one occurs between two of the larger hills, the next in succession is situated on a spur of the downs, at an angle with the preceding one, so as to be visible clear of the chain of hills to the next eminence of a similar kind. These are surmised to have been adapted as beacons, for spreading an alarm in case of invasion, or for the rites and observances of fire worship. The Herefordshire Beacon, one of the Malvern Hills, is a conspicuous example, being surrounded by a triple rampart; and with others of a similar kind bears

INCENSE VESSELS.—From Hoare's Ancient Wiltshire.

MOUNT CABURN BEACON, near Lewes, Sussex.—Drawn from nature and on wood, by H. G. Hine.

a striking analogy to the presumed original form of the great tower of Babel, of which, perhaps, its construction was a tradition, and its purpose a similar temple of Belus, for the adoration of the sun and fire, its type and symbol. We have the authority of Cæsar for the skill of the Britons in the art of castrametation; and he instances the capital of Cassivellaunus, which he describes as "admirably defended, both by nature and art." A Celtic stronghold in Cornwall, called Chun Castle, may be cited as a remarkable specimen of this kind of fortified habitation. It is girt about by two circular walls, each separated by a space of thirty feet; the walls are of the kind of masonry called Cyclopean, being constructed of granite masses of various forms and sizes, some of which are five or six feet long, fitted together without cement so artificially as to offer an equal external surface. The outer wall was surrounded by a ditch nineteen feet wide. A portion of the wall is ten feet high, and about five feet in thickness. It is surmised by Borlase that the inner wall must have been at least fifteen feet high, in consideration of its bulk, which is full twelve feet in thickness. This stronghold has only one entrance, which is towards the south-west; and it attests great proficiency in the art of defence. This opening is six feet wide in the narrowest part, and sixteen where the walls diverge and are rounded off on either side. There are also indications of steps up to the level of the area within the castle; and the remains of a wall, which crossed the terrace from the outer wall, divided the entrance into two parts at its widest end. The inner wall of the castle comprehends an area of 175 feet north and south, by 180 feet east and west. No indication of buildings appears in the centre, but all round the inner side of the wall are the bases of circular inclosures, which appear to have been the chambers or habitable parts of the castle, similarly disposed to those in the walls of the Saxon castle at Coningsburgh in Yorkshire, and the subsequent early Norman castles. These chambers are from eighteen to twenty feet in diameter, but on the northern side there is a larger apartment measuring thirty feet by twenty-six.[1] Other vestiges of Celtic castles of a similar kind exist in Cornwall and Wales. The remains found within these inclosures throw but little light upon the habits of their ancient occupants; deer horns, heaps of bones, and the quern or hand-mill, for grinding

ANCIENT QUERN, from an example in the British Museum.

meal, only attest the pursuit of the hunter, and the produce of agriculture, by which the lords of those ancient strongholds employed the time which was not engrossed in the more stirring affairs of defence and warlike aggression.

The observation of these vestiges serves to prepare us for the contemplation of the more august remains connected with the faith of our early progenitors, among which the monuments of Stonehenge and Avebury are conspicuous. The symbolism of the sun and the serpent, it is conjectured, was betokened in their mystic order and disposition, as well as in the kindred monument of Carnac in Brittany, in which land many of the tribes of Britain found a retreat on the departure of the Romans, and the inroad of Hengist and Horsa—the Teutonic Castor and Pollux. The dolmen or quoit—the witch stone of the sacred rustic—is conceived to have been the Druid altar on which the human offering was immolated, when the Vates took their prediction from the convulsion of the limbs, and the particular direction in which the blood of the victim flowed. Whatever may have been its purpose, the dolmen abounds in Armorica, as here, and is to be found in most parts of the Old World. In the ship temples of Ireland the tradition of the ark is thought to have been symbolized. The hare stone[2] is associated with the patriarchal boundary and memorial stones, and may be relics of a tribe who reached this island at a period prior to the Celtic inroad, and among whom there shone a ray from the dawning of the light now spread over the world in the books of Moses. But while indulging in many a surmise conjured up by the evidence of those monuments, whose interpretation lies buried in the depth of ages, we are awakened by the question of by what means of transport those ancient tribes made their way to the shores of Britain.

It has been inferred, from some passages in Cæsar, that the Britons were in possession of a navy. In one of these passages he states that his enemies, the Veneti of Western Gaul, having taken into alliance other neighbouring tribes, sent for aid from Britain, which lay directly over against their coast; but while it is not stated that the aid thus sought was of shipping, no other account indicates that such was the case; and we find no remains of vessels, but those of the simplest and most rude description, to inform us of the attainments of the Britons in the naval art. The canoes that still continue to be dug up from the alluvial beds of our rivers, and the antiseptic depths of our mosses, both in England and Scotland, are of the rudest description. They are made of the entire trunk of a tree, and have been partly hollowed by fire, and partly by the operation of the stave adze, while the outside exhibits no trace of ornament, and very little even of close lopping and smoothness. Of the canoes thus discovered, the length of the smallest

---

[1] *Archæologia*, vol. xxii. p. 300.

[2] Hoar or hare stones, signifying border or boundary stones, the *maen hir* or *mennie greyr* of Wales; *men hars* in Armorica, a bound-stone.—A Letter by the late William Hamper, F.S.A., *Archæologia*, vol. xxvi.

CELTIC RELICS.

1. Gold Bracelet; found near Egerton Hall, Cheshire.
2. Bronze Fibula; found at Arras, Yorkshire.
3. Do. late Celtic; from Horæ Ferales.
4. Do. do. found at Borough, Westmoreland.
5. Bronze Horse Trapping, enamelled; found in London, now in British Museum.
6. Enamelled Ring, found at Stanwick; from Horæ Ferales.
7. Bronze Torque, found at Embsay, near Skipton, in Yorkshire; from the Archæologia.
8. Gold Torque, found in Needwood Forest; the property of the Queen.
9. Gold Ear-ring, found near Castlerea, county Roscommon; in the Royal Irish Academy.
10. Bronze Ornament, found at Brighthampton, in Oxfordshire; in the British Museum.
11. Bronze Horse Trapping, enamelled, found at Westhall, Suffolk; in the British Museum.
12. Bronze Horse Trapping, enamelled, found at Kileevan, near Analore; Kilkenny Archæological Association.
13. Bronze Horse Trapping, found on Polden Hill, Somersetshire.
14. Bronze Bracelets, late Celtic, enamelled; found near Drummond Castle, Perthshire.
15. Belt of thin brass *repoussé*, found at Standwick; from Horæ Ferales.

CELTIC RELICS.
PERSONAL ORNAMENTS &c OF GOLD AND BRONZE.

varies from seven to eleven feet, and, like those of the Indians, they have been impelled by paddles. One of the largest, now in the British Museum, measures thirty-five feet four inches in length, one foot ten inches in depth, and four feet six inches in width at the centre. Another vessel of similar character is described by Sir John Clark as having been exhumed in the Carse of Falkirk in May, 1726. It measured thirty-six feet in length, and four in extreme breadth, and was finely smoothed and polished, both inside and outside, having the usual pointed stem and square stern. It was in such vessels as these that the ruder Britons carried on their coasting and river navigation; and in these also they fished with hooks of bone, and even ventured to attack the whales that happened to get stranded on their coasts or in their estuaries. As such vessels were evidently not intended for adventurous voyages, they required little labour or ingenuity of construction, beyond the mere hollowing of a pine, to render it more buoyant upon the waters. The circumstance of locality, or the genius of a different tribe, may have produced the variety of canoes of lighter but more fragile materials.

WELSH FISHERMAN OF THE PRESENT DAY WITH CORACLE.

These were the barks of osier, covered with the skins of animals, which were of more ample stowage and lighter draught, but which also required a greater degree of skill to manage, as well as to construct them. The Britons, at the arrival of the Romans, were famed for their ingenuity in basket-work, and this they had turned to the purposes of navigation, when they substituted for the clumsy log a large floating basket. In such, we are told, they could make a six days' voyage, and maintain a close connection with Ireland. These vessels, upon a small scale, and for the purposes of fishing and river navigation, are still used in Wales under the name of *cwrwgyl*, or coracles; and are so light and portable that, on leaving the stream, the fisherman commonly carries off his boat on his back.

At the period of Cæsar's invasion a great change had taken place in the transition of the export trade of the Britons, from the western to the southern shores of the island; and an extensive intercourse with the Gauls, together with the intermixture of Germanic tribes, had greatly assimilated the manners and resources of the inhabitants of South Britain to those of the opposite coasts. Their land produced grain in abundance, and they possessed numerous flocks and herds; whereas the people of the interior, according to Cæsar, grew no grain, but lived on the milk and flesh of their cattle. The inland people, living among their forests and marshes, and in the course of intestine wars of tribe against tribe, had lapsed into a state calculated to develop only the ruder energies; and the more northern parts of the island were yet lower in the scale, procuring a sustenance from the milk of their flocks, and wild fruits, and whatsoever they could procure in hunting; but when these resources failed they eked out a sustenance by devouring roots and leaves, and in extremity they had recourse to a certain composition, by which, it is said, when they had eaten about the quantity of a bean, their spirits were so admirably supported that they no longer felt hunger or thirst.[1]

In addition to the abundance of fuel possessed by the Britons in their vast forests, they appear to have been acquainted with the use of coal, quantities of which have been found in British deposits. According to Strabo, they had in use cups, and other vessels of glass, probably imported. Many articles fashioned in gold and silver of great purity, have been found, which attest the possession and appreciation of those metals. A fine specimen in gold was discovered in a cairn at Mold in Flintshire. It is a gold breastplate or gorget, embossed with a figured pattern in various degrees of relief. It was found,

REMAINS OF BRITISH BREASTPLATE OR GORGET, found at Mold, and now in the British Museum.

with bones of the former owner, as it had been worn, with remnants of coarse cloth or serge, amber beads, and pieces of copper, upon which the gold had been probably fastened. Its extreme length is three feet seven inches, being made apparently to pass under the arms, and meet in the centre of the back, and its width in front, where it is shaped to fit the neck, eight inches.

Such are a few of the specimens of early British life that have survived the wreck of eighteen

---

[1] *Xiphilin. in Sever.*

centuries, and which a growing spirit of inquiry, and greater diligence in exploration, are continually enriching with many and valuable additions. It is by such antiquarian researches, be it remembered, however lightly they may be esteemed, that the conditions of a race who have departed are made accessible to the world. The buildings which constitute the homes of a people, and the household utensils that minister to the comforts of daily life, have passed away; the costume by which one nation is distinguished from another, and the personal ornaments by which the different ranks of the same people are indicated, have been more perishable still; even the weapons that were forged for the violence of mortal hatred, and the endurance of hereditary feuds, have become so dimmed and deformed by the rust of ages that their original uses are sometimes matter of question. But, even in the relics of a barbarous people, this utter decay seldom extends to the shrines of their devotion and the dwellings of the dead. The tomb and the temple—the sacred repose of death, and the cheering promise of immortality—excite a stronger solicitude than even that which suffices for the erection of ramparts and palaces, and are manifested in grander and more enduring memorials. And hence it is that in every country they have survived the monuments of active everyday life, and still remain, not only in all their original solemn silence, but with much of their primitive entireness. It is in these mausoleums of buried ages that we are often left to read the history of a people who have passed away; and it is in this manner that we are obliged to study the modes of life and condition of character that prevailed among the early Britons. Their own legends, as we have already seen, are of little avail to guide us; the more consistent accounts that were reduced to writing, and embodied in classical history, were the testimonies of their enemies, and therefore to be received with suspicion, and only in part. But in the circle of stones and its crumbling altars—in the barrow and its funeral urns—we learn, as from safe though very limited resources, how our earliest ancestors may have lived, and worshipped, and warred, and died, before the destroying enemy had arrived among them, or the doom of extinction been carried into effect.

BOOK I.

BRITISH AND ROMAN PERIOD.—504 YEARS.

FROM B.C. 55 TO A.D. 449.

CHAPTER I.—CIVIL AND MILITARY HISTORY.

INVASION BY JULIUS CÆSAR—B.C. 55—A.D. 43.

Early inhabitants of Britain—Motives of Julius Cæsar for invading it—Gallant resistance of the natives—Cæsar's second invasion—His successes and progress—Submission of the Britons, and its terms—Means of resistance possessed by the Britons—Their war-chariots, cavalry and infantry, weapons—Superior discipline and appointments of the Roman legions.

THE conquests of Julius Cæsar in Gaul brought him within sight of the coast of Britain; and, having established the Roman authority in the nearest countries on the Continent, which are now called France and Belgium, it was almost as natural for him to aim at the possession of our island, as for the masters of Italy to invade Sicily, or the conquerors of India the contiguous island of Ceylon. The disjunction of Britain from the rest of the world, and the stormy but narrow sea that flows between it and the main, were circumstances just sufficient to give a bold and romantic character to the enterprise, without being real barriers to a skilful and courageous general. But there were other motives to impel Cæsar. Britain, or the far greater part of it, was inhabited by a people of the same race, language, and religion as the Gauls; and during his recent and most arduous campaigns, the islanders had assisted their neighbours and kindred of the Continent, sending important aid more particularly to the Veneti, who occupied Vannes in Bretagne, and to other people of Western Gaul who lived near the sea-coast. Cæsar, indeed, says himself that in all his wars with the Gauls the enemies of the Republic had always received assistance from Britain, and that this fact made him resolve to pass over into the island. (This island, moreover, seems to have had the character of a sort of Holy Land among the Celtic nations, and to have been considered the great centre and stronghold of the Druids, the revered priesthood of an iron superstition, that bound men, and tribes, and nations together, and inflamed them far more than patriotism against the Roman conquerors. With respect to Druidism, Britain perhaps stood in the same relation to Gaul that the island of Mona or Anglesey bore to Britain; and when the Romans had established themselves in Gaul, they had the same motives for attacking our island that they had, a century later, when they had fixed themselves in Britain, for falling upon Anglesey, as the centre of the Druids and of British union, and the source of the remaining national resistance.

It is to be remembered, also, that, whatever may have been the views of personal ambition from which Cæsar principally acted, the Romans really had the best of all pleas for their wars with the Gauls, who had been their constant enemies for centuries, and originally their assailants. Their possession of Italy, indeed, could not be considered as secure until they had subdued, or at least impressed with a sufficient dread of their arms, the fierce and restless nations both of Gaul and Germany, some of whom—down almost to the age of Cæsar—had not ceased occasionally to break through the barrier of the Alps, and to carry fire and sword into the home territories of the Republic. These, and the other Northern barbarians, as they were called, had had their eye upon the cultivated fields of the Italic peninsula ever since the irruption of Bellovesus, in the time of the elder Tarquin; and the war the Gauls were now carrying on with Cæsar was only a part of the long contest, which did not terminate till the Empire was overpowered at last by its natural enemies, nearly five centuries afterwards. In the meantime, it was the turn of the Gauls to find the Roman valour, in its highest condition of discipline and efficiency, irresistible;

VOL. I.

and the Britons, as the active allies of the Gauls, could not expect to escape sharing in their chastisement.

According to a curious passage in Suetonius, it was reported that Cæsar was tempted to invade Britain by the hopes of finding pearls.[1] Such an inducement seems scarcely of sufficient importance, although we know that pearls were very highly esteemed by the ancients; and Pliny, the naturalist, tells us that Cæsar offered or dedicated a breastplate to Venus, ornamented with pearls, which he pretended to have found in Britain. But Cæsar might be tempted by other real and more valuable productions, and he could not be ignorant of the existence of the British lead and tin which the Phœnicians had imported into the Mediterranean ages before his time, and in which the Phocæan colony of Massilia or Marseilles was actually carrying on a trade. Cæsar himself, indeed, says nothing of this; but within a few miles of our coasts, and among a people with whom the

JULIUS CÆSAR.—From a marble in the British Museum.

British had constant intercourse, he must have acquired more information than appears respecting the natural fertility of the soil, and the mineral and other productions of the island. From evident reasons, indeed, the Gauls in general might not be very communicative on these subjects; but among that people Cæsar had allies and some steady friends, who must have been able and ready to satisfy all his inquiries. His subservient instrument, Comius, who will presently appear upon the scene, must have possessed much of the information required. His love of conquest and glory alone might have been sufficient incentive to Cæsar, but a recent and philosophic writer assigns other probable motives for his expeditions into Britain—such as his desire of dazzling his countrymen, and of seeming to be absorbed by objects remote from internal ambition, by expeditions against a new world, or of furnishing himself with a pretence for prolonging his provincial command, and keeping up an army devoted to him, till the time should arrive for the execution of his projects against liberty at Rome.[2]

Whatever were his motives, in the year B.C. 55, Cæsar resolved to cross the British Channel, not, as he has himself told us, to make then a conquest, for which the season was too far advanced, but in order merely to take a view of the island, learn the nature of the inhabitants, and survey the coasts, harbours, and landing-places. He says that the Gauls were ignorant of all these things; that few of them, except merchants, ever visited the island; and that the merchants themselves only knew the sea-coasts opposite to Gaul. Having called together the merchants from all parts of Gaul, he questioned them concerning the size of the island, the power and customs of its inhabitants, their mode of warfare, and the harbours they had capable of receiving large ships. He adds, that on none of these points could they give him information; but, on this public occasion, the silence of the traders probably proceeded rather from unwillingness and caution than ignorance, while it is equally probable that the conqueror received a little more information than he avows. He says, however, that for these reasons he thought it expedient, before he embarked himself, to despatch C. Volusenus, with a single galley, to obtain some knowledge of these things, commanding him, as soon as he had obtained this necessary knowledge, to return to head-quarters with all haste. He then himself marched with his whole army into the territory of the Morini, a nation or tribe of the Gauls, who inhabited the sea-coast between Calais and Boulogne—"because thence was the shortest passage into Britain." Here he collected many ships from the neighbouring ports.

Meanwhile many of the British states, having been warned of Cæsar's premeditated expedition, by the merchants that resorted to their island, sent over ambassadors to him, with an offer of hostages and submission to the Roman authority. He received these ambassadors most kindly, and exhorting them to continue in the same pacific intentions, sent them back to their own country, despatching with them Comius, a Gaul whom he had made King of the Atrebatians, a Belgic nation then settled in Artois. Cæsar's choice of this envoy was well directed. The Belgæ, at a comparatively recent period, had colonized, and they still occupied all the south-eastern coasts of Britain; and these colonists, much more civilized than the rest of the islanders, no doubt held frequent com-

---

[1] *Vit. Jul. Cæs.* c. xlvii.   [2] Sir James Mackintosh, *Hist. Eng.*

mercial and friendly intercourse with the Atrebatians in Artois, and the rest of the Belgic stock settled in other places.[1] Cæsar himself says, not only that Comius was a man in whose virtue, wisdom, and fidelity he placed great confidence, but one "whose authority in the island of Britain was very considerable." He therefore charged Comius to visit as many of the British states as he could, and persuade them to enter into an alliance with the Romans, informing them, at the same time, that Cæsar intended to visit the island in person as soon as possible.

C. Volusenus appears to have done little service with his galley. He took a view of the British coast, as far as was possible for one who had resolved not to quit his vessel or trust himself into the hands of the natives, and on the fifth day of his expedition returned to head-quarters. With such information as he had, Cæsar embarked the infantry of two legions, making about 12,000 men, on board eighty transports, and set sail from Portus Itius, or Witsand, between Calais and Boulogne. The cavalry, embarked in eighteen other transports, were detained by contrary winds at a port about eight miles off, but Cæsar left orders for them to follow as soon as the weather permitted. This force, however, as will be seen, could never make itself available; and hence, mainly, arose the reverses of the campaign.

The Straits of Dover, with the opposite Coasts of GAUL & BRITAIN.

At ten o'clock in a morning in autumn (Halley the astronomer, in a paper in the *Philosophical Transactions*, has almost demonstrated that it must have been on the 26th of August), Cæsar reached the British coast, near Dover, at about the worst possible point to effect a landing in face of an enemy; and the Britons were not disposed to be friends. The submission they had offered through their ambassadors was intended only to prevent or retard invasion; and seeing it fail of either of these effects, on the return of their ambassadors with Comius, as Cæsar's envoy, they made that prince a prisoner, loaded him with chains, prepared for their defence as well as the shortness of time would permit; and when the Romans looked from their ships to the steep white cliffs above them, they saw them covered all over by the armed Britons. Finding that this was not a convenient landing-place, Cæsar resolved to lie by till the third hour after noon, in order, he says, to wait the arrival of the rest of his fleet. Some laggard vessels appear to have come up, but the eighteen transports bearing the cavalry were nowhere seen. Cæsar, however, favoured by both wind and tide, proceeded at the appointed hour, and sailing about seven miles further along the coast, prepared to land his forces on an open, flat shore, which presents itself between Walmer Castle and Sandwich.[2] The Britons on the cliffs, perceiving his design, followed his motions, and sending their cavalry and war-chariots before, marched rapidly on with their main force, to oppose his landing anywhere. Cæsar confesses that the opposition of the natives

---

[1] "It is almost impossible, at this distance of time, to ascertain how far the Belgian settlements extended inland in Britain; though there are strong reasons for supposing that they covered a large portion of the south of England. The narrative of Cæsar would lead us to infer that the Britons with whom he came in contact were not of two distinct races. He must, therefore, as is evident from his own account, have fought against the Belgian settlers, and have had nothing to do with the more ancient Celtic population. The Belgæ were at that time, as they are at present, a busy, commercial people; and had spread, even in the time of Cæsar, as far as the Seine, towards the west of France. If this view of the extent of the Belgian settlements in Britain be correct, it removes a great deal of the difficulty which surrounds the story of the Britons having been exterminated in after ages by the Saxons. It is not likely that military invaders like the Saxons would either slay all the peasants of the country, or drive them into Wales; and it is morally certain that so poor a country as Wales would suffer from famine, both then and now, from the sudden influx of 100,000 foreigners. The Saxons would be more likely to retain the original British population as servants to till their grounds; and if that population were of Belgian or German descent, as were the Saxons themselves, their amalgamation with a kindred race would be speedy and complete. But it is, as yet, uncertain how far the Celts themselves were originally of German descent also."—Giles' *History of the Ancient Britons*, vol. i. p. 37. It is remarkable that the islands of North-Western Europe should have presented in Cæsar's time what we find in those of Eastern Asia at this day—many tribes divided generally into two different races, the one inhabiting the interior and mountainous parts, short in stature, averse to the sea, and addicted to hunting; the other ranged along the shores, tall, and addicted to navigation, commerce, and agriculture.—Ed.

[2] Horsley (*Brit. Rom.*) shows that Cæsar must have proceeded to the north of the South Foreland, in which case the landing must have been effected between Walmer Castle and Sandwich. Others, with less reason, think he sailed southward from the South Foreland, and landed on the flats of Romney Marsh.

was a bold one, and that the difficulties he had to encounter were very great, on many accounts; but superior skill and discipline, and the employment of some military engines on board the war-galleys, to which the British were unaccustomed, and which projected missiles of various kinds, at last triumphed over them, and he disembarked his two legions. We must not omit the act of the standard-bearer of the tenth legion, which has been thought deserving of particular commemoration by his general. While the Roman soldiers were hesitating to leave the ships—chiefly deterred, according to Cæsar's account, by the depth of the water—this officer, having first solemnly besought the gods that what he was about to do might prove fortunate for the legion, and then exclaiming with a loud voice, "Follow me, my fellow-soldiers, unless you will give up your eagle to the enemy!—I, at least, will do my

ing the blame of the harsh treatment his envoy had met with upon the multitude or common people, and entreating Cæsar to excuse a fault which proceeded solely from the popular ignorance. The conqueror, after reproaching them for sending of their own accord ambassadors into Gaul to sue for peace, and then making war upon him, *without any reason*, forgave them their offences, and ordered them to send in a certain number of hostages, as security for their good behaviour in future. Some of these hostages were presented immediately, and the Britons promised to deliver the rest, who lived at a distance, in the course of a few days. The native forces then seemed entirely disbanded, and the several chiefs came to Cæsar's camp to offer allegiance, and negotiate or intrigue for their own separate interests.

On the day that this peace was concluded, and not before, the unlucky transports with the Roman cavalry were enabled to quit their port on the coast of Gaul. They stood across the Channel with a gentle gale; but when they neared the British coast, and were even within view of Cæsar's camp, they were dispersed by a tempest, and were finally obliged to return to the port where they had been so long detained. That very night, Cæsar says, it happened to be full moon, when the tides always rise highest—

THE CHALK CLIFFS OF DOVER.—From Turner's England and Wales.

duty to the Republic and to our general!" leaped into the sea as he spoke, and dashed with his ensign among the enemy's ranks. The men instantly followed their heroic leader; and the soldiers in the other ships, excited by the example, also crowded forward along with them. The two armies were for some time mixed in combat; but at length the Britons withdrew in disorder from the well-contested beach. As their cavalry, however, was not yet arrived, the Romans could not pursue them, or advance into the island, and thus render the victory complete.

The native maritime tribes, thus defeated, sought the advantages of a hollow peace. They despatched ambassadors to Cæsar, offering hostages, and an entire submission. They liberated Comius, and restored him to his employer, throw-

"a fact at that time wholly unknown to the Romans"[1]—and the galleys which he had with him, and which were hauled up on the beach, were filled with the rising waters, while his heavier transports, that lay at anchor in the roadstead, were either dashed to pieces, or rendered altogether unfit for sailing. This disaster spread a general consternation through the camp; for, as every legionary knew, there were no other vessels to carry back the troops, nor any materials with the army to repair the ships that were disabled;

---

[1] The operations of the Roman troops had hitherto been almost confined to the Mediterranean, where there is little perceptible tide. Yet during their stay on the coast of Gaul, on the opposite side of the Channel, they ought to have become acquainted with these phenomena. Probably they had never attended to the irregularities of a spring-tide.

and, as it had been from the beginning Cæsar's design not to winter in Britain, but in Gaul, he was wholly unprovided with corn and provisions to feed his troops. Suetonius says, that during the nine years Cæsar held the military command in Gaul, amidst a most brilliant series of successes, he experienced only three signal disasters; and he counts the almost entire destruction of his fleet by a storm in Britain, as one of the three.

Nor were the invaded people slow in perceiving the extent of Cæsar's calamity, and devising means to profit by it. They plainly saw he was in want of cavalry, provisions, and ships; a close inspection showed that his troops were not so numerous as they had fancied, and probably familiarized them in some measure to their warlike weapons and demeanour; and they confidently hoped that, by defeating this force, or surrounding and cutting off their retreat, and starving them, they should prevent all future invasions. The chiefs in the camp having previously held secret consultations among themselves, retired, by degrees, from the Romans, and began to draw the islanders together. Cæsar says, that though he was not fully apprised of their designs, he partly guessed them, from their delay in sending in the hostages promised from a distance, and from other circumstances; and instantly took measures to provide for the worst. He set part of his army to repair his shattered fleet, using the materials of the vessels most injured to patch up the rest; and as the soldiers wrought with an indefatigability suiting the dangerous urgency of the case, he had soon a number of vessels fit for sea. He then sent to Gaul for other materials wanting, and probably for some provisions also. Another portion of his troops he employed in foraging parties, to bring into the camp what corn they could collect in the adjacent country. This supply could not have been great, for the natives had everywhere gathered in their harvest, except in one field; and there, by lying in ambush, the Britons made a bold and bloody attack, which had well-nigh proved fatal to the invaders. As one of the two legions that formed the expedition were cutting down the corn in that field, Cæsar, who was in his fortified camp, suddenly saw a great cloud of dust in that direction. He rushed to the spot with two cohorts, leaving orders for all the other soldiers of the legion to follow as soon as possible. His arrival was very opportune, for he found the legion, which had been surprised in the corn-field, and which had suffered considerable loss, now surrounded and pressed on all sides by the cavalry and war-chariots of the British, who had been concealed in the neighbouring woods. He succeeded in bringing off the engaged legion, with which he withdrew to his intrenched camp, declining a general engagement for the present. Heavy rains that followed confined the Romans for some days within their intrenchments. Meanwhile the British force of horse and foot was increased from all sides, and they gradually drew round the intrenchments. Cæsar, anticipating their attack, marshalled his legions outside of the camp, and, at the proper moment, fell upon the islanders, who, he says, not being able to sustain the shock, were soon put to flight. In this victory he attaches great importance to a body of thirty horse, the Atrebatian, had brought over from Gaul. The Romans pursued the fugitives as far as their strength would permit; they slaughtered many of them, set fire to some houses and villages, and then returned again to the protection of their camp. On the same day the Britons again sued for peace, and Cæsar, being anxious to return to Gaul as quickly as possible, " because the equinox was approaching, and his ships were leaky," granted it to them, on no harder condition than that of doubling the number of hostages they had promised after their first defeat. He did not even wait for the hostages, but a fair wind springing up, he set sail at midnight, and arrived safely in Gaul. Eventually only two of the British states sent their hostages; and this breach of treaty gave the Roman commander a ground of complaint by which to justify his second invasion.

In the spring of the following year (B.C. 54) Cæsar again embarked at the same Portus Itius for Britain. This time peculiar attention had been paid to the build and equipment of his fleet: he had 800 vessels of all classes, and these carried five legions and 2000 cavalry—an invading force in all not short of 32,000 men.[1] At the approach of this formidable armament the natives retired in dismay from the coast, and Cæsar disembarked without opposition, at "that part of the island which he had marked out the preceding summer as being the most convenient landing-place." This was probably somewhere on the same flat, between Walmer Castle and Sandwich, where he had landed the year before. Having received intelligence as to the direction in which the Britons had retired, he set out about midnight in quest of them, leaving ten cohorts, with 300 horse, behind him on the coast, to guard his camp and fleet. After a hurried night-march, he came in sight of the islanders, who were well posted on some rising grounds behind a river—probably the Stour, near Canterbury. The confederate army gallantly disputed the passage of the river with their cavalry and chariots; but being repulsed by the Roman horse, they retreated to-

[1] In this calculation an allowance of 500 is made for sickness, casualties, and deficiencies. At this period the infantry of a legion, when complete, amounted to 6100 men.

wards the woods, to a place strongly fortified both by nature and art, and which Cæsar judged had been strengthened before, on occasion of some internal native war; "for all the avenues were secured by strong barricades of felled trees laid upon one another." This stronghold is supposed to have been at or near to the spot where the city of Canterbury now stands. Strong as it was, the soldiers of the seventh legion (the force that had suffered so much the preceding campaign in the corn-field) carried it, by means of a mound of earth they cast up in front of it; and then they drove the British from the cover of the wood. The evening closed on their retreat, in which they must have suffered little loss; for Cæsar, fearful of following them through a country with which he was unacquainted, strictly forbade all pursuit, and employed his men in fortifying their camp for the night. The Roman eagles were scarcely displayed the following morning, and the trumpets had hardly sounded the advance, when a party of horse brought intelligence from the coast that nearly all the fleet had been driven on shore and wrecked during the night. Cæsar flew to the sea-shore, whither

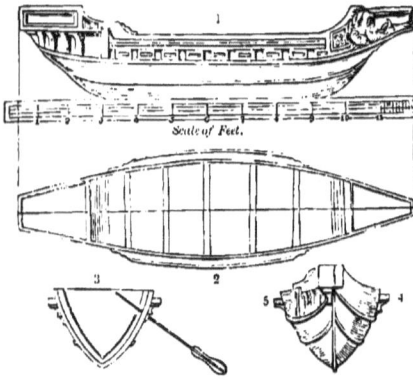

ROMAN GALLEY, from the model presented by Lord Anson to Greenwich Hospital.—1, Side Elevation; 2, Plan; 3, Midship Section; 4, Elevation of Stem; 5, Elevation of Stern.

he was followed by the legions in full retreat. The misfortune had not been exaggerated: forty of his ships were irretrievably lost, and the rest so damaged that they seemed scarcely capable of repair. With his characteristic activity, he set all the carpenters of the army to work, wrote for more artisans from Gaul, and ordered the legions stationed on that coast to build as many new ships as they could. Apprehensive alike of the storms of the ocean and of the fierce attack of the natives, Cæsar ordered that all his ships should be drawn up on dry land, and inclosed within his fortified camp. Although the ancient galleys were small and light compared to our modern men-of-war, and the transports and tenders of his fleet in all probability little more than sloops and barges, this was a laborious operation, and occupied the soldiers ten days and nights. Having thus secured his fleet, he set off in pursuit of the enemy, who had made a good use of his absence, by increasing their army, and appointing one chief to the supreme command of it. The choice of the confederated states fell upon Cassivellaunus (his Celtic name was perhaps Caswallon), whose territories were divided from the maritime states of the river Thames, at a point which was between seventy and eighty miles from Cæsar's camp on the Kentish coast. This prince had hitherto been engaged in almost constant wars with his neighbours, whose affection to him must have therefore been of recent date, and of somewhat doubtful continuance; but he had a reputation for skill and bravery, and the dread of the Romans made the Britons forget their quarrels for a time, unite themselves under his command, and intrust him with the whole conduct of the war. Cæsar found him well posted at or near to the scene of the last battle. Cassivellaunus did not wait to be attacked, but charged the Roman cavalry with his horse, supported by his chariots. Cæsar says that he constantly repelled these charges, and drove the Britons to their woods and hills; but that, after making great slaughter, venturing to continue the pursuit too far, he lost some men. It does not appear that the British retreated far; and some time after these skirmishes they gave the Romans a serious check. Sallying unexpectedly from the wood, they fell upon the soldiers, who were employed, as usual, in fortifying the camp or station for the night, and cut up the advanced guard. Cæsar sent two cohorts to their aid, but the Britons charged these in separate parties, broke through them, routed them, and then retired without loss. A military tribune was slain; and, but for the timely arrival of some fresh cohorts, the conflict would have been very disastrous. Even as it was, and though Cæsar covers the fact by a somewhat confused narrative, it should appear that a good part of his army was beaten on this occasion. He says that from this action, of which the whole Roman army were spectators, it was evident that his heavy-armed legions were not a fit match for the active and light-armed Britons, who always fought in detachments, with a body of reserve in their rear, which advanced fresh supplies when needed, and covered and protected the forces when in retreat; that even his cavalry could not engage without great danger, it being the custom of the Britons to counterfeit a retreat, until they had drawn the Roman horse a considerable way from the legions, when, suddenly leaping from their chariots, they charged them on foot, and, by this *unequal* manner of fighting, rendered it equally dangerous to pursue or retire.

The next day the Britons only showed small bodies on the hills at some distance from the Roman camp. This made Cæsar believe they were less willing to skirmish with his cavalry; but no sooner had he sent out *all his cavalry* to forage, supported by *three legions* (between horse and foot this foraging party comprised considerably more than half the forces he had with him), than the Britons fell upon them on all sides, and even charged up to the solid and impenetrable legions. The latter bold step was the cause of their ruin: the superior arms, the defensive armour, and the perfect discipline of those masses, rendered the contest too unequal; the British warriors were repulsed— thrown off like waves from a mighty rock—confusion ensued, and Cæsar's cavalry and infantry, charging together, utterly broke the confederate army. The conqueror informs us that after this defeat the auxiliary troops, which had repaired from all parts to Cassivellaunus' standard, returned severally to their own homes; and that during the rest of the campaign the enemy never again appeared against the Romans with their whole force.

These severe contests had not brought Cæsar far into the interior of the island; but now he followed up Cassivellaunus, who retired, for the defence of his own kingdom, beyond the Thames. Marching through Kent and a part of Surrey, or the beautiful country which now bear those names, the Romans reached the right bank of the Thames, at Co way Stakes, near Chertsey,[1] in Surrey, where the river was considered fordable. The passage, however, was not undisputed. Cassivellaunus had drawn up his troops in great numbers on the opposite bank; he had likewise fortified that bank with sharp stakes, and driven similar stakes into the bed of the river, yet so as

STAKE.[2]

to be concealed or covered by the water. Of these things Cæsar says he was informed by prisoners and deserters. It should appear that he overcame the obstacles raised at the ford with great ease; he sent the horse into the river before, ordering the foot to follow close behind them, which they did with such rapidity that, though nothing but their heads appeared above water, they were presently on the opposite bank, where the enemy could not stand their charge, but fled. The rest of his army having disbanded, Cassivellaunus now retained no other force than 4000 war-chariots, with which he harassed the Romans, always keeping at a distance from their main body, and retiring, when attacked, to woods and inaccessible places; whither also he caused such of the inhabitants as lay on Cæsar's line of march to withdraw with their cattle and provisions. Being perfectly acquainted with the country, and all the roads and defiles, he continued to fall upon detached parties; and the Romans were never safe, or masters of any ground, except in the space covered by their intrenched camp or their legions. On account of these frequent surprises, Cæsar would not permit his horse to forage at any distance from the legions, or to pillage and destroy the country, unless where the foot was close at hand to support them.

The fatal want of union among the petty states into which the island was frittered, and the hatred some of them entertained against their former enemy, Cassivellaunus, now began to appear, and to disconcert all that chief's measures for resistance. The Trinobantes, who dwelt in Essex and Middlesex, and who formed one of the most powerful states in those parts, sent ambassadors to Cæsar. Of this state was Mandubratius, who had fled into Gaul to Cæsar, in order to avoid the fate of his father, Imanuentius, who had held the sovereignty of the state, and whom Cassivellaunus had defeated and put to death. The ambassadors entreated Cæsar to restore their prince, who was then a guest in the Roman camp, to defend him and them against the fury of Cassivellaunus, promising, on these conditions, obedience and entire submission in the name of all the Trinobantes. Cæsar demanded forty hostages, and a supply of corn for his army. The general does not confess it, but it is very probable that, through the wise measures of Cassivellaunus, the Romans were at this time sorely distressed by want of provisions. The Trinobantes delivered both the corn and the hostages, and Cæsar restored to them their prince. Immediately upon this, other tribes, whom Cæsar designates the Cenimagni, Segontiaci, Ancalites, Bibroci, and Cassi, also sent in their submission. Some of these people informed Cæsar that he was not far from the capital of Cassivellaunus, which was situated amidst woods

---

[1] This point, like most of the other localities mentioned by Cæsar, has been the subject of dispute. We venture to fix it where we do on the authority of Camden, and Mr. Gale, a writer in the *Archæologia*, vol. i. p. 183.

[2] Stake drawn from the bed of the Thames at Coway Stakes, presumed to be one of those planted by Cassivellaunus; now in the British Museum. A number of similar stakes still remain in the bed of the river.

and marshes, and whither multitudes of the British had retired with their cattle, as to a place of safety.¹ This town is supposed to have been near to the site of St. Alban's, and on the spot where the flourishing Roman colony of Verulamium arose many years after. Though called a town and a capital, it appears from Cæsar to have been nothing but a thick wood or labyrinth, with clusters of houses or villages scattered about it; the whole being surrounded by a ditch and a rampart, the latter made of mud or felled trees, or probably of both materials mixed.

Cæsar soon appeared with his legions before the capital of Cassivellaunus; and he says, that though the place seemed very strong both by art and nature, he resolved to attack it in two several points. He was once more successful; the Britons fled to another wood, after a short stand, and the Romans took many prisoners and vast numbers of cattle. Though thus defeated in the inland districts, Cassivellaunus still hoped to redeem the fortunes of his country by a bold and well-conceived blow, to be struck on the sea-coast. While the events related were passing beyond the Thames, he despatched messengers to the four princes or kings of Cantium (Kent), to instruct them to draw all their forces together, and attack the camp and ships of the Romans by surprise. The Kentish Britons obeyed their instructions; but, according to Cæsar, the Romans, sallying from their intrenchments, made a great slaughter of their troops, took one of the princes prisoner, and returned in safety to the camp. At the news of this reverse, the brave Cassivellaunus lost heart; he sent ambassadors to sue for peace, and availed himself of the mediation of Comius, the king of the Atrebatians, with whom, at one time or other, he appears to have had friendly relations. The Roman general, as we have noticed, states that the authority or influence of Comius in the island was very considerable. It would be curious to see how he exercised it in favour of his Roman patron; but here we are left in the dark. Cæsar turned a ready ear to the overtures of Cassivellaunus, and granted him peace on such easy conditions, that some writers have been induced to believe he was heartily tired of the harassing war. For himself, he only says that he was in a hurry to return to Gaul, on account of the frequent insurrections in that country. He merely demanded hostages, appointed a yearly tribute (the amount of which is nowhere named, and which was probably never paid), and charged Cassivellaunus to respect Mandubratius and the Trinobantes. Having received the hostages, he led his troops back to the Kentish coast, and crowding them into his ships as closely and quickly as he could, he set sail by night for Gaul, fearing, he says, the equinoctial storms, which were now at hand. He tells us he had many prisoners; but he certainly did not erect a fort, or leave a single cohort behind him, to secure the ground he had gained in the island.²

Tacitus, writing 150 years later, says distinctly, that even Julius Cæsar, the first who entered Britain with an army, although he struck terror into the islanders by a successful battle, could only maintain himself on the sea-coast—that he was a discoverer rather than a conqueror.

We have dwelt more particularly on these campaigns, as we have the accomplished general's own account to guide us; and as many of his details may be applied to explain the other Roman wars which followed, when there was no Cæsar to describe in the closet his exploits in the field. The sequel, indeed, when we must follow professional historians, who were never even in Britain, is comparatively uninteresting and monotonous. We shall, therefore, set down the great results, without embarrassing the reader with unnecessary details; but at this point it will be well to pause, in order to offer a few general remarks, which will equally elucidate the past and future campaigns of the Romans in our island.

The contest which had thus taken place between the British bands and the famed Roman legions,

---

[1] "If we may implicitly trust the report of Cæsar, a British city in his time differed widely from what we understand by that term. A spot difficult of access, from the trees that filled it, surrounded with a rampart and ditch, and which offered a refuge from the sudden incursions of an enemy, could be dignified by the name of an *oppidum*, and form the metropolis of Cassivellaunus. Such, also, among the Sclavonians, were the *vici*, encircled by an *abbatis* of timber, or at most a paling, proper to repel not only an unexpected attack, but even capable of resisting for a time the onset of practised forces; such in our own time have been found the stockades of the Burmese, and the *pah* of the New Zealander; and if our skilful engineers have experienced no contemptible resistance, and the lives of many brave and disciplined men have been sacrificed in their reduction, we may admit that even the *oppida* of Cassivellaunus, or Caractac, or Galgacus, might, as fortresses, have serious claims to the attention of a Roman commander." "It is, however, scarcely possible that Cæsar and Strabo can be strictly accurate in their reports, or that there were from the first only such towns in Britain as these authors have described. It is not consonant to experience that a thickly-peopled and peaceful country should long be without cities. A commercial people always have some settled stations for the collection and interchange of commodities, and fixed establishments for the regulation of trade. Cæsar himself tells us that the buildings of the Britons were very numerous, and that they bore a resemblance to those of the Gauls, whose cities were assuredly considerable. Moreover, a race so conversant with the management of horses as to use armed chariots for artillery, are not likely to have been without an extensive system of roads, and where there are roads towns will not long be wanting. Hence when, less than eighty years after the return of the Romans to Britain, and scarcely forty after the complete subjugation of the island by Agricola, Ptolemy tells us of at least fifty-six cities in existence here, we may reasonably conclude that they were not all due to the efforts of Roman civilization."—Kemble's *Saxons in England*, vol. i. pp. 264-5.

[2] For the preceding part of our narrative, see *Cæsar de Bello Gallico*, from book iv. ch. xviii. to book v. ch. xix. (inclusive).

at a period when the discipline of those corps was most perfect, and when they were commanded by the greatest of their generals, was certainly very unequal; but less so (even without taking into account the superiority of numbers and other advantages, all on the side of the invaded) than is generally imagined and represented. A brief examination of the arts and practices of war of the two contending parties may serve to explain, in a great measure, what is past, and render more intelligible the events which are to ensue. The first striking result of such an examination is a suspicion, and, indeed, a proof, that the Britons were much farther advanced in civilization than the savage tribes to which it has been the fashion to compare them. Were this not the case, the somewhat unsuccessful employment against them of so large an army as that of Cæsar, would be disgraceful to the Roman name. Their war-chariots, which several times produced tremendous effects on the Romans, and the use of which seems at that time to have been peculiar to the Britons, would of themselves prove a high degree of mechanical skill, and an acquaintance with several arts. These cars were of various forms and sizes, some being rude, and others of curious and even elegant workmanship. Those most commonly in use, and called *esseda* or *essedæ* by the Romans, were made to contain each a charioteer for driving, and one, two, or more warriors for fighting. They were at once strong and light; the extremity of their axles and other salient points were armed with scythes and hooks, for cutting and tearing whatever fell in their way, as they were driven rapidly along. The horses attached to them were perfect in training, and so well in hand that they could be driven at speed over the roughest country, and even through the woods, which then abounded in all directions. The Romans were no less astonished at the dexterity of the charioteers than at the number of the chariots. The way in which the Britons brought the chariots into action was this: at the beginning of a battle they drove about the flanks of the enemy, throwing darts from the cars; and, according to Cæsar, the very dread of the horses, and the noise of the rapid wheels, often broke the ranks of his legions. When they had succeeded in making an impression, and had winded in among the Roman cavalry, the warriors leaped from the chariots, and fought on foot. In the meantime the drivers retired with the chariots a little from the combat, taking up such a position as to favour the retreat of the warriors in case of their being overmatched. "In this manner," says Cæsar, "they perform the part both of rapid cavalry and of steady infantry; and, by constant exercise and use, they have arrived at such expertness, that they can stop their horses when at full speed, in the most steep and difficult places, turn them which way they please, run along the carriage-pole, rest on the harness, and throw themselves back into their chariots with incredible dexterity."

For a long time the veteran legions of Rome could not look on the clouds of dust that announced the approach of these war-chariots without trepidation. The Gauls had once the same mode of fighting, and equally distressed the Romans with their war-chariots. Nearly 300 years before the invasion of Britain, when the Gauls were established in parts of Italy, and in close alliance with the Samnites, a successful charge of the Roman cavalry was repulsed, and the whole army thrown into dismay, by a mode of fighting to which they were utter strangers. "A number of the enemy," says Livy, "mounted on chariots and cars, made towards them with such a terrible noise, from the trampling of the horses and the rolling of the wheels, as affrighted the horses of the Romans, unaccustomed to such operations. By this means the victorious cavalry were dispersed, and men and horses, in their headlong flight, were thrown in heaps to the ground. The same cause produced disorder even in the ranks of the legions: through the impetuosity of the horses, and the carriages they dragged through the ranks, many of the Roman soldiers in the van were trodden or bruised to death; and the Gauls, as soon as they saw the enemy in confusion, followed up the advantage, nor allowed them breathing-time."[1] The use of war-chariots, however, seems to have fallen out of fashion among the Gauls during the long period that had intervened; for Cæsar never makes mention of them in describing his many battles with that people on the Continent.

The existence of the accessories—the hooks and scythes attached to the wheels or axles—has been questioned, as neither Cæsar, nor Tacitus, nor any early writer, with the exception of the geographer Pomponius Mela (who wrote, however, in the first century), expressly mentions them in describing the war-chariots. Weapons answering to the description have, however, been found on the field of some of the most ancient battles. Between the Roman invasion under Cæsar, and that ordered by the Emperor Claudius, the cars or chariots of the British attracted notice, and were exhibited in Italy. They were seen in the splendid pageantry with which Caligula passed over the sea from Puteoli to Baiæ, on his mole of masonry and bridge of boats. The emperor, Suetonius tells us, rode in a chariot drawn by two famous horses, and a party of his friends followed, mounted in British chariots. Probably Cæsar had carried some of the native war-cars to Rome as curiosities,

---

[1] *Tit. Liv.* lib. x. c. xxviii.

just as our navigators brought the canoes of the Indians and South Sea Islanders to England. At subsequent periods the war-chariots of the Britons were frequently alluded to by the poets as well as historians of Rome.

The ancient Britons were well provided with horses, of a small breed, but hardy, spirited, and yet docile. Their cavalry were armed with shields,

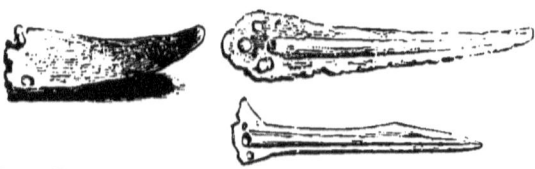

BRONZE WEAPONS, answering to the description of hooks or scythes appended to the axle of British war-chariots.—Drawn by J. W. Archer, from specimens in the British Museum.

broad-swords, and lances. They were accustomed, like the Gauls, and their own chariot-men, to dismount, at fitting seasons, and fight on foot; and their horses are said to have been so well trained, as to stand firm at the places where they were left till their masters returned to them. Another common practice among them was to mix an equal number of their swiftest foot with their cavalry, each of these foot-soldiers holding by a horse's mane, and keeping pace with him in all his motions. Some remains of this last custom were observed among the Highland clans in the last century, in the civil wars for the Pretender; and in more modern, and regular, and scientific warfare, an advantage has often been found in mounting infantry behind cavalry, and in teaching cavalry to dismount, and do the duty of foot-soldiers. A great fondness for horses, and a skill in riding them, and breaking them in for cars and chariots, were observable in all the nations of the Celtic race. The scythe-armed cars of the Britons may be assumed as one of the many links in that chain which seems to connect them with Persia and the East, where similar vehicles were in use in very remote ages.

The infantry of the Britons was the most numerous body, and, according to Tacitus, the main strength of their armies. They were very swift of foot, and expert in swimming over rivers and crossing fens and marshes, by which means they were enabled to make sudden attacks and safe retreats. They were slightly clad; throwing off in battle the whole, or at least the greater part, of whatever clothing they usually wore, according to a custom which appears to have been common to all the Celtic nations. They were not encumbered with defensive armour, carrying nothing of that sort but a small light shield; and this, added to their swiftness, gave them, in some respects, a great advantage over the heavily-armed Romans, whose foot could never keep pace with them.

This, indeed, was so much the case in the ensuing wars, that the turn of a battle was often left to depend, not on the legions, but on their barbarian auxiliaries, some of whom were as lightly equipped as the Britons themselves. In coming to their offensive arms, we reach a point where they were decidedly inferior to the Romans; and a cause, perhaps, as principal as any other, of their invariable defeat when they came to close combat. Their swords were unwieldy, awkward, and offenceless weapons, compared to the compact, manageable, cut-and-thrust swords of their enemies, which could be used in the closed *mêlée*. But an important circumstance, which throws the advantage still more on the side of the Romans, is, that while their weapons were made of well-tempered steel, the swords and dirks of the Britons were, in all probability, only made of copper, or of copper mixed with a little tin. We are told that the swords of their neighbours, the Gauls, were made of copper, and bent after the first blow, which gave the Romans a great advantage over them. In addition to their clumsy sword, the British

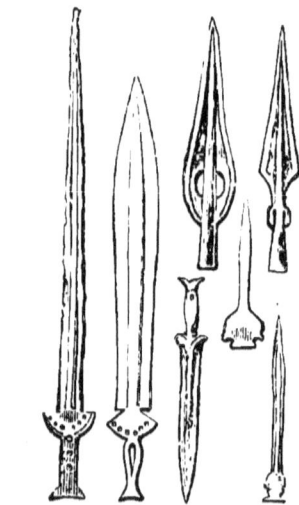

BRITISH SWORDS, DAGGER, SPEAR HEADS, and JAVELIN HEADS, of bronze.—Drawn by J. W. Archer, from examples in the British Museum.

infantry carried a short dirk and a spear. The spear was sometimes used as a missile weapon, having a leather thong fixed to it, and retained in the hand when thrown, in order that it might be recovered again: at the butt-end of this spear was sometimes a round hollow ball of copper, or mixed copper and tin, with pieces of metal inside; and, shaking this, they made a noise to frighten the horses when they engaged with cavalry.

With the exception of the Druids, all the young men among the Britons and other Celtic nations were trained to the use of arms. Frequent hostilities among themselves kept them in practice; and hunting and martial sports were among their principal occupations in their brief periods of peace. Even in tactics and strategics, the more difficult parts of war, they displayed very considerable talent and skill. They drew up their troops in regular order; and if the form of a wedge was not the very best for infantry, it has been found, by the Turks and other Eastern nations, most effective for cavalry appointed to charge. They knew the importance of keeping a body in reserve; and in several of their battles they showed skill and promptitude in outflanking the enemy, and turning him by the wings. Their infantry generally occupied the centre, being disposed in several lines, and in distinct bodies. These corps consisted of the warriors of one clan, commanded each by its own chieftain; they were commonly formed in the shape of a wedge, presenting its sharp point to the enemy; and they were so disposed that they could readily support and relieve each other. The cavalry and chariots were placed on the wings, but small flying parties of both manœuvred along the front. In the rear and on their flanks they fixed their travelling-chariots and their waggons, with their respective families in them, in order that those vehicles might serve as barriers to prevent attack in those directions, and that their courage might be inflamed by the presence of all who were most dear to them.

Some of the native princes displayed eminent abilities in the conduct of war. According to the Roman writers, Cassivellaunus, Caractacus, and Galgacus all formed combined movements and enlarged plans of operation, and contrived stratagems and surprises which would have done honour to the greatest captains of Greece and Rome. Their choice of ground for fighting upon was almost invariably judicious, and they availed themselves of their superior knowledge of the country on all occasions. In the laborious arts of fortifying, defending, or attacking camps, castles, and towns, they were, however, deficient. Their

BRITISH FORTIFIED CAMP, in Strathmore, called White Cather-Thun.—From Roy's Military Antiquities. This camp is 1480 ft. long, and 830 ft. wide.

strongest places were surrounded only by a shallow ditch and a mud wall, while some of their towns had nothing but a parapet of felled trees placed lengthwise. While the Roman camps, though made to be occupied only for a night, were strongly fortified, the British camps were merely surrounded by their cars and waggons—a mode of defence still common among the Tartar and other nomadic tribes in Asia. But as the Roman war proceeded, we frequently find them giving more attention to the defence of their night camps; and some of the more permanent positions they took up were strengthened with deep ditches and stone walls.

The armies of the ancient Britons were not divided into bodies, mixed, but distinct as a whole, consisting each of a determinate number of men, recruited from different families and in different places, and commanded by appointed officers of various ranks, like the Roman legions and our modern regiments; but all the fighting-men of each particular clan or great family formed a separate band, commanded by the chieftain or head of that family. By this system, which had other disadvantages, the command was frittered away into minute fractions. All the several clans which composed one state or kingdom were commanded in chief by the sovereign of that state; and when two or more states formed an alliance, and made war in conjunction, the king of one of these states was chosen to be generalissimo of the whole. These elections gave rise to jealousies and dissensions; and all through the system there were too many divisions of command and power, and too great a disposition in the warriors to look up only to the head of their own clan, or at furthest to the king of their own limited state.

Far different from these were the thoroughly organized and inter-dependent masses of the Roman army, where the commands were nicely defined and graduated, and the legions (each a small but perfect army in itself) acted at the voice of the consul, or its one supreme chief, like a complicated engine set in motion by its main-wheel. As long as Rome maintained her military glory the legions were composed only of free Roman citizens, no allies or subjects of conquered nations being deemed worthy of the honour of fighting in their ranks. Each legion was divided into horse and foot, the cavalry bearing what is considered, by modern scientific writers, a just proportion, and not more, to the infantry. Under the old kings a legion consisted of 3000 foot and 300 horse; under the consuls, of 4200 foot and 400 horse; but under Cæsar and the emperors it amounted to 6100 foot and 726 horse. Like our regiments, the legions were distinguished from each other by their number; being called the first, the second, the third, &c. In the early ages of the Republic they had no more than four or five legions kept on foot, but these were increased with increase of conquest and territory, and under the Empire they had as many as twenty-five or thirty legions, even in time of peace. The infantry of each legion was divided into ten cohorts. The first cohort, which had the custody of the eagle and the post of honour, was 1105 strong; the remaining nine cohorts had 555 men each.

Instead of a long, awkward sword of copper, every soldier had a short, manageable, well-tempered Spanish blade of steel, sharp at both edges as at the point; and he was always instructed to thrust rather than cut, in order to inflict the more fatal wounds, and expose his own body the less. In addition to a lighter spear, the legionary carried the formidable *pilum*, a heavy javelin, six feet long, terminating in a strong triangular point of steel, eighteen inches long. For defensive armour they wore an open helmet with a lofty crest, a breastplate or coat of mail, greaves on their legs, and a large strong shield on their left arms. This shield or buckler, altogether unlike the small, round, basket-looking thing used by the Britons, was four feet high, and two and a half broad; it was framed of a light but firm wood, covered with bull's hide, and strongly guarded with bosses or plates of iron or bronze.

The cavalry of a legion was divided into ten troops or squadrons; the first squadron, as destined to act with the strong first cohort, consisting of 132 men, while the nine remaining squadrons had only sixty-six men each. Their principal weapons were a sabre and a javelin; but at a later period they borrowed the use of the lance and iron mace or hammer from foreigners. For defensive armour they had a helmet, a coat of mail, and an oblong shield.

The legions serving abroad were generally attended by auxiliaries raised among the provinces and conquests of the Empire, who for the most part retained their national arms and loose modes of fighting, and did all the duties of light troops. Their number varied according to circumstances, being seldom much inferior to that of the legions; but in Britain, where mention of the barbarian auxiliaries constantly occurs, and where, as we have intimated, they performed services for which the legions were not calculated, they seem to have been at least as numerous as the Roman soldiers. Three legions, say the historians, were competent to the occupation of Britain; but to this force of 20,478 we must add the auxiliaries, which will swell the number to 40,956. Gauls, Belgians, Batavians, and Germans were the hordes that accompanied the legions in our island.

Such were the main features and appointments of the Roman legions in their prime, and such they continued during their conflict with the Britons, and long after all the southern parts of our island were subjugated by their might. They were afterwards sadly diminished in numbers and in consideration. They lost their discipline; the men threw off the defensive armour as too heavy for them to wear; changes were made in their weapons; and, not to notice many intermediate variations, a legion, at the final departure of the Romans from Britain, consisted only of from 2500 to 3000 indifferently armed men.

After Cæsar's departure, Britain was left undisturbed by foreign arms for nearly 100 years. But few of the events that happened, during that long interval, have been transmitted to us. We can, however, make out in that dim obscurity that the country, and more particularly those maritime parts of it occupied by the Belgæ, and facing the coast of Gaul, made considerable advances in civilization, borrowing from the Gauls, with whom they were in close communication, some of those useful and elegant arts which that people had learned from the Roman conquerors, now peaceably settled among them. Besides their journeys into Gaul, which are well proved, it is supposed that during this long interval not a few of the superior class of Britons, from time to time, crossed the Alps, and found their way to Rome, where the civilization and arts of the world then centred.

This progress, however, does not appear to have been accompanied by any improvement in the political system of the country, or by any union and amalgamation of the disjointed parts or states. Internal wars continued to be waged; and this disunion of the Britons, their constant civil dissensions, and the absence of any steady system of defence, laid them open to the Romans whenever those conquerors should think fit to revisit their fair island, and renew the struggle in earnest.

CHAPTER II.—CIVIL AND MILITARY HISTORY.

THE INVASION UNDER CLAUDIUS TO THE ARRIVAL OF THE SAXONS.—A.D. 43-449.

Roman invasion of Britain in the reign of the Emperor Claudius—Progress of the Roman generals Plautius, Vespasian, Ostorius—Brave resistance and defeat of Caractacus—Capture of Mona by Suetonius—Revolt of the Britons under Boadicea—Her defeat and death—Agricola appointed governor of Britain—His successful and wise administration—His northern campaigns and their progress—His victory at *Mons Grampius* over the Caledonians—Operations of his fleet, and its voyage round the island—Inconclusive result of his victories over the Caledonians—The Caledonians, after a long peace, attack the province of South Britain—Graham's Dyke built to repress them—Unsuccessful northern campaign of Severus—Builds a new wall of stone to protect the province—Carausius governor of Britain—Decay of the Roman power in Britain—Invasions of the Scots and Picts—Weakness of the South Britons and its causes—Their feeble resistance to the Scots and Picts—Their religious controversies—Their appeal to Rome in vain for military assistance—They invite the Saxons to their aid—Arrival of Hengist and Horsa.

IN the ninety-seventh year after Cæsar's second expedition (A.D. 43), the Emperor Claudius[1] resolved to seize the island of Britain, and Aulus Plautius, a skilful commander, landed with four complete legions, which, with the cavalry and auxiliaries, must have made above 50,000 men. The Britons, who had made no preparations, at first offered no resistance; and when they took the field under Caractacus and Togodumnus, sons of the deceased Cunobelinus, who is supposed to have been King of the Trinobantes, they were thoroughly defeated in the inland country by the Romans. Some states or tribes detaching themselves from the confederacy, then submitted; and Aulus Plautius, leaving a garrison in those parts, which included Gloucestershire and portions of the contiguous counties, followed up his victories beyond the river Severn, and made considerable progress in subduing the inhabitants. After sustaining a great defeat on the right bank of the Severn, the Britons retreated eastward to some marshes on the Thames, where, availing themselves of the nature of the ground, they made a desperate stand, and caused the Romans great loss. In these campaigns Plautius made great use of his light-armed barbarian auxiliaries (chiefly Germans), many of whom, on this particular occasion, were lost in the deep bogs and swamps. Though Togodumnus was slain, it does not appear that the natives were defeated in this battle; and Plautius, seeing their determined spirit, withdrew his army to the south of the Thames, to await the arrival of the Emperor Claudius, whose presence and fresh forces he earnestly solicited. Claudius embarked with reinforcements at Ostia at the mouth of the Tiber, landed at Massilia (Marseilles), and proceeded through Gaul to Britain. It is said that some elephants were included in the force he brought, but we hear nothing of those animals after his arrival in the island. There is some confusion as to the immediate effect of the emperor's arrival, the two brief historians[2] of the events contradicting each other; but we believe that, without fighting any battles, the pusillanimous Claudius accompanied his army on its fresh advance to the north of the Thames, was present at the taking of Camalodunum, the capital of the Trinobantes, and that then he received the proffered submission of some of the states, and returned to enjoy an easily-earned triumph at Rome, whence he had been absent altogether somewhat less than six months.

While Vespasian, his second in command, who was afterwards emperor under the same name, employed himself in subduing Vectis (the Isle of Wight), and the maritime states on the southern and eastern coasts, Aulus Plautius prosecuted a long and, in great part, an indecisive warfare with the inland Britons, who were still commanded by Caractacus. Between them both, Plautius and Vespasian thoroughly reduced no more of the island than what lies to the south of the Thames, with a narrow strip on the left bank of that river; and when Plautius was recalled to Rome, even these territories were overrun and thrown into confusion by the Britons. Ostorius Scapula, the new propraetor, on his arrival in the island (A.D. 50), found the affairs of the Romans in an all but hopeless state; their allies, attacked and plundered on all sides, were falling from them, the boldness of the unsubdued states was rapidly increasing, and the people they held in subjection were ripe for revolt. But Ostorius, who had pro-

---

[1] Pomponius Mela, who wrote in the time of Claudius, expresses a hope that the success of the Roman arms will soon make the island and its savage inhabitants better known.

[2] *Dio Cass.* (in the abridgment by Xiphilinus), lib. lx.; Suetonius in *C. Claud.* c. xvii.

bably brought reinforcements into the island, was equal to this emergency: knowing how much depends on the beginning of a campaign, he put himself at the head of the light troops, and advanced against the marauding enemy by rapid marches. The Britons, who did not expect he would open a campaign in the winter, were taken by surprise, and defeated with great loss. It should appear from Tacitus that Ostorius at once recovered all the country, as far as the Severn, that had been conquered, or rather temporarily occupied, by his predecessor Plautius; for the great historian tells us, immediately after, that he erected a line of forts on the Sabrina (Severn) and the Antona (Nene); but it is more probable that this advance was made by a series of battles rather than by one hasty blow struck in the winter by the light division of his army. Ostorius was the first to cover and protect the conquered territory by forts and lines; the line he now drew cut off from the rest of the island nearly all the southern and south-eastern parts, which included the more civilized states, who had either submitted or become willing allies, or been conquered by Plautius and Vespasian. It was by the gradual advance of lines like these that the Romans brought the whole of England south of the Tyne under subjection. Ostorius also adopted the cautious policy of disarming all such of the Britons within the line of forts as he suspected. This measure, always odious, and never to be carried into effect without shameful abuses

BARBARIAN PRISONER.[1]—From a marble in the British Museum.

of power, particularly exasperated those Britons within the line who, like the Iceni, had not been conquered, but, of their own good and free will, had become the allies of the Romans. Enemies could not treat them worse than such friends—the surrender of arms was the worst consequence that could result from defeat in a war which they

[1] This fine head, remarkable from its expression of heroic melancholy, is conjectured to represent the image of Caractacus, and is figured, accordingly, in the Dilettanti Society's publication of Antique Marbles and Bronzes, with a description by R. P. Knight.

had not yet essayed. It would also naturally occur to them, that if the Romans were permitted to coop them up within military posts, and sever them from the rest of the island, their independence, whether unarmed or armed, was completely sacrificed.

The Iceni, a brave tribe, who are supposed to have dwelt in Norfolk and Suffolk, took up arms, formed a league with their neighbours, and chose their ground for a decisive battle. They were beaten by Ostorius, after having fought obstinately to the last, and giving signal proofs of courage. After the defeat of the Iceni and their allies the Romans marched beyond their line of demarcation against a people called the Cangi; and, Tacitus says, they got within a short march of that sea that lies between Britain and Ireland. From the pursuit of this timid enemy, Ostorius was recalled by a rising of the Brigantes, who occupied Yorkshire, with parts of Lancashire and the adjoining counties. Having subdued these in their turn, and drawn a camp and fixed a colony of veterans among them, Ostorius marched rapidly against the Silures—the inhabitants of South Wales—the fiercest and most obstinate enemies the Romans ever encountered in South Britain. To their natural ferocity, say Tacitus, these people added the courage which they now derived from the presence of Caractacus. His valour, and the various turns of his fortune, had spread the fame of this heroic chief throughout the island. His knowledge of the country, and his admirable skill in the stratagems of war, were great advantages; but he could not hope, with inferior forces, to beat a well-disciplined Roman army. He therefore retired to the territory of the Ordovices, which seems to have included within it nearly all North Wales. Having drawn thither to his standard all who considered peace with the Romans as another word for slavery, he resolved to wait firmly the issue of a battle. According to the great historian, he chose his field with admirable art. It was rendered safe by steep and craggy hills. In parts where the mountains opened, and the easy acclivity afforded an ascent, he raised a rampart of massy stones. A river which offered no safe ford flowed between him and the enemy, and a part of his forces showed themselves in front of his ramparts.

As the Romans approached, the chieftains of the confederated British clans rushed along the ranks, exhorting their men, and Caractacus animated the whole. There is a lofty hill in Shropshire, near to the confluence of the rivers Colue and Teme, which is generally believed to be the scene of the hero's last action. Its ridges are furrowed by trenches, and still retain fragments of a loose stone rampart, and the hill for many centuries has been called by the people Caer-

Caradoc, or the castle or fortified place of Caradoc, supposed to be the British name of Caractacus. Ostorius was astonished at the excellent arrangement and spirit he saw, but his numbers, discipline, and superior arms, once more gained him a victory. Tacitus says that the Britons, having neither breastplates nor helmets, could not maintain the conflict—that the better Roman swords and spears made dreadful havoc—that the victory was complete. Caractacus escaped from the carnage; but his wife and daughter were taken prisoners, and his brothers surrendered soon after the battle. The hero himself did not, however, escape long, for having taken refuge with his stepmother, Cartismandua, Queen of the Brigantes, that heartless woman caused him to be put in chains, and delivered up to the Romans. From the camp of Ostorius he was carried, with his wife and all his family, to the foot of the emperor's throne. All Rome—all Italy were impatient to gaze on the indomitable Briton, who for nine years had bidden defiance to the masters of the world. His name was everywhere known, and he was everywhere received with marked respect. In the presence of Claudius his friends and family quailed and begged for mercy; he alone was superior to misfortune: his speech was manly without being insolent—his countenance still unaltered, not a symptom of fear appearing—no sorrow, no mean condescension; he was great and dignified even in ruin. This magnanimous behaviour no doubt contributed to procure him milder treatment than the Roman conquerors usually bestow on captive princes; his chains and those of his family were instantly struck off. At this crisis Tacitus leaves him, and his subsequent history is altogether unknown.

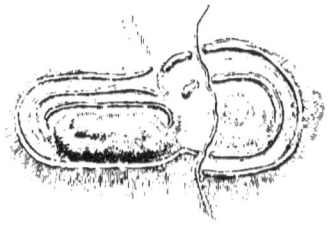

Plan of BRITISH CAMP on Coxal Knoll, Herefordshire.[1]— From Roy's Military Antiquities.

[1] Caer-Caradoc was supposed by Camden to be the scene of the final struggle between Caractacus and Ostorius; but, from various circumstances mentioned by Tacitus referring clearly to the geography of the spot, and with which the site of Coxal Knoll alone corresponds, Roy, supported by other good authorities, believes that locality to have been the true scene of the action, and Caer-Caradoc to have been merely the castle of Caractacus. Coxal Knoll is situated on the river Teme, between Knighton and Lentwardine, some miles distant from Caer-Caradoc. Here the remains of a British camp still exist, measuring 1700 ft. in length; with a breadth, where widest, of 720 ft., and, where narrowest, of 600 ft.

Their sanguinary defeat and the loss of Caractacus did not break the spirit of the Silures. They fell upon the Romans soon after, broke up their fortified camp, and prevented them from erecting a line of forts across their country. The prefect of the camp, with eight centurions and the bravest of his soldiers, was slain; and, but for the arrival of reinforcements, the whole detachment would have been sacrificed. A foraging party, and the strong detachments sent to its support, were routed; this forced Ostorius to bring his legions into action, but, even with his whole force, his success was doubtful. Continual and new harassing attacks and surprises followed, till at length Ostorius, the victor of Caractacus, sunk under the fatigue and vexation, and expired, to the joy of the Britons, who boasted that though he had not fallen in battle, it was still their war which had brought him to the grave. The country of the Silures, intersected by numerous and rapid rivers, heaped into mountains, with winding and narrow defiles, and covered with forests, became the grave of many other Romans; and it was not till the reign of Vespasian, and more than twenty years after the death of Ostorius, that it was conquered by Julius Frontinus.

For some time the Roman power in Britain was stationary, or, at most, it made very little progress under Aulus Didius and Veranius, the immediate successors of Ostorius. Indeed, under these governors, the Emperor Nero, who had succeeded his father Claudius, is said to have seriously entertained the thought of withdrawing the troops, and abandoning the island altogether —so profitless and uncertain seemed the Roman possession of Britain.

But the next governor, Paulinus Suetonius, an officer of distinguished merit (A.D. 59–61), revived the spirit of the conquerors. Being well aware that the Island of Mona, now Anglesey, was the chief seat of the Druids, the refuge-place of the defeated British warriors, and of the disaffected generally, he resolved to subdue it. In order to facilitate his approach, he ordered the construction of a number of flat-bottomed boats; in these he transported his infantry over the strait which divides the island from the main (the Menai), while the cavalry were to find their way across, partly by fording and partly by swimming. The Britons added the terrors of their superstition to the force of their arms for the defence of this sacred island. "On the opposite shore," says Tacitus, "there stood a widely diversified host: there were armed men in dense array, and women running among them, who in dismal dresses, and with dishevelled hair, like furies, carried flaming torches. Around were Druids, pouring forth curses, lifting up their hands to heaven, and striking terror, by the novelty of their appearance, into the hearts of the Roman soldiers, who, as if their limbs were paralyzed, exposed themselves motionless to the blows of the enemy. At last, aroused by the exhortations of their leader, and stimulating one another to despise a frantic band of women and priests, they make their onset, overthrow their foes, and burn them in the fires which they themselves had kindled for others. A garrison was afterwards placed there among the conquered, and the groves sacred to their cruel superstition were cut down."

But while Suetonius was engaged in securing the sacred island, events took place in his rear which went far to commit the safety of the entire empire of the Romans in Britain. His attack on the Druids and the grove of Mona could not fail to exasperate all the British tribes that clung to their ancient worship: other and recent causes of provocation were particular to certain of the states. The Romans, in the colonies they had planted in the island, indulged too freely in what are called the rights of conquest: they treated the Britons with cruelty and oppression; they drove them from their houses, and, adding insult to wrong, called them by the opprobrious name of slaves. In these acts the veterans or superiors were actively seconded by the common soldiery —a class of men who, in the words of Tacitus, are by their habits of life trained to licentiousness. The conquerors, too, had introduced priests of their own creed; and these, " with a pretended zeal for religion, devoured the substance of the land." Boadicea, widow of King Prasutagus, and now Queen of the Iceni, probably because she remonstrated against the forcible seizure of the territory her husband bequeathed her, or possibly because she attempted to resist the Romans in their plunder, was treated with the utmost barbarity: Catus, the procurator, caused her to be scourged, her daughters to be violated in her presence, and the relations of her deceased husband to be reduced to slavery. Her unheard-of wrongs, the dignity of her birth, the energy of her character, made Boadicea the proper rallying point; and immediately an extensive armed league intrusted her with the supreme command. Boadicea's own subjects were joined by the Trinobantes; and the neighbouring states, not as yet broken into a slavish submission, engaged in secret councils to stand forward in the cause of national liberty. They were all encouraged by the absence of Suetonius, and thought it no difficult enterprise to overrun a colony undefended by a single fortification. Tacitus says (and the statement is curious, considering their recent and uncertain tenure) that the Roman governors had attended to improvements of taste and elegance, but neglected the useful—that they had embellished the province, but taken no pains to put it in a state of defence. The storm first burst on the colony of Camalodunum, which was laid waste with fire and sword, a legion which marched to its relief being cut to pieces. Catus, the procurator, terrified at the fury his own enormities had mainly excited, fled, and effected his escape into Gaul. On receiving the news of these disasters, Suetonius hurried across the Menai Strait, and, marching through the heart of the country, came to London, which city, though not yet dignified with the name of a Roman colony, was a populous, trading, and prosperous place. He soon found he could not maintain that important town, and therefore determined to evacuate it. The inhabitants, who foresaw the fate of the fair town, implored him with tears to change his plan, but in vain. The signal for the march was given, the legions defiled through the gates, but all the citizens who chose to follow their eagles were taken under their protection. They had scarcely cleared out from London when the Britons entered: of all those who, from age, or weakness, or the attractions of the spot, had thought proper to remain behind, scarcely one escaped. The inhabitants of Verulamium were in like manner utterly annihilated, and, the carnage still spreading, no fewer than 70,000 Romans and their confederates fell in the course of a few days. The infuriated insurgents made no prisoners, gave no quarter, but employed the gibbet, the fire, and the cross, without distinction of age or sex.

Suetonius, having received reinforcements which made his army amount to about 10,000 men, all highly disciplined, chose an advantageous field, and waited the battle. The Britons were also reinforced, and from all quarters: Tacitus says they were an incredible multitude, but their ranks were swelled and weakened by women and children. They were the assailants, and attacked the Romans in the front of their strong position.

Previously to the first charge, Boadicea, mounted in a war-chariot, with her long yellow hair streaming to her feet, with her two injured daughters beside her, drove through the ranks, and harangued the tribes or nations, each in its turn.[1] She reminded them that she was not the first woman that had led the Britons to battle; she spoke of her own irreparable wrongs, of the wrongs of her people and all their neighbours, and said whatever was most calculated to spirit them against their proud and licentious oppressors. The Britons, however, were defeated with tremendous loss, and the wretched Boadicea put an end to her existence by taking poison. As if not to be behind the barbarity of those they emphatically

---

[1] Dio has described her costume as being a plaited tunic of various colours, a chain of gold round her waist, and a long mantle over all.—*Dio Nic. apud Xiphil.*

styled barbarians, the Romans committed an indiscriminate massacre, visiting with fire and sword not only the lands of those who had joined the revolt, but of those who were only suspected of having wavered in their allegiance to the emperor. Tacitus estimates the number of the Britons who were thus destroyed at 80,000; and in the train of war and devastation followed famine and disease. But the despondence of sickness and the pangs of hunger could not induce them to submit; and though Suetonius received important reinforcements from the Continent (according to Tacitus, by the directions of the Emperor Nero, 2000 legionary soldiers, eight auxiliary cohorts, and 1000 horse, were sent to him from Germany), and retained the command some time longer, he left the island without finishing this war; and, notwithstanding his victories over the Druids and Boadicea, his immediate successors were obliged to relapse into inactivity, or merely to stand on the defensive, without attempting the extension of their dominions.

Some fifteen or sixteen years after the departure of Suetonius, the Romans recommenced their former movements (A.D. 75–78), and Julius Frontinus at last subdued the Silures. This general was succeeded by Cnaeus Julius Agricola, who was fortunate, as far as his fame is regarded, in having for his son-in-law the great Tacitus, the partial and eloquent recorder of his deeds. Exaggeration and favour apart, however, Agricola appears to have had skill in the arts both of peace and war. He had served under Suetonius during the Boadicean conflicts, he was beloved by his army, and well acquainted with the country, and now, before he left the supreme command, he completed the conquest of South Britain, and showed the victorious eagles of Rome as far north as the Grampian Hills. One of his first operations, which proves with what tenacity the Britons held to their own, was the reconquest of Mona; for scarcely had Suetonius turned his back, when they repossessed themselves of that most holy island. Having made this successful beginning, and also chastised the Ordovices, who had cut a division of cavalry to pieces, he endeavoured, by mild measures, to endear himself to the acknowledged provincials of Rome, and to conciliate the British tribes generally by acts of kindness. "For," says Tacitus, "the Britons willingly supply our armies with recruits, pay their taxes without a murmur, and perform all the services of government with alacrity, provided they have no reason to complain of oppression. When injured their resentment is quick, sudden, and impatient; they are conquered, not spirit-broken; they may be reduced to obedience, not to slavery."

At the same time Agricola endeavoured to subdue their fierceness, and change their erratic habits, by teaching them some of the useful arts, and accustoming them to some of the luxuries of civilized life. He persuaded them to settle in towns, to build comfortable dwelling-houses, to raise halls and temples. It was a capital part of his policy to establish a system of education, and give to the sons of the leading British chiefs a tincture of polite letters. He praised the talents of the pupils, and already saw them, by the force of their natural genius, outstripping the Gauls, who were distinguished for their aptitude and abilities. Thus, by degrees, the Britons began to cultivate the beauties of the Roman language, which they had before disdained—to wear the Roman toga as a fashionable part of dress—and to indulge in the luxuries of baths, porticoes, and elegant banquets.

In the second year of his government (A.D. 79), Agricola advanced into the north-western parts of Britain, and partly by force, and more by clemency, brought several tribes to submission. These are not named by Tacitus, but they probably dwelt in the heart of the country, to the east of the Ordovices and the Silures. Wherever he gained a district he erected fortifications, composed of castles and ramparts.

In his third campaign (A.D. 80) Agricola led his army still farther north; but the line of march, and the degree of progress made in it, are not easily ascertained. The outlines presented to us by Tacitus are vague and indistinct, which may be ascribed both to the generality of that writer's language, and to the limits of his information.

It is the opinion of a late writer,[1] however, that Agricola, setting out from Mancunium, the Manchester of present times, led his army towards the north-western coasts, and not towards the north-eastern, as is commonly stated; and that, after traversing parts of Lancashire, Westmoreland, and Cumberland, he came to the *Tau*, which this writer contends was not the river Tay, but the Solway Frith. The *Tau*, he says (the Taus of Tacitus), was a British word, signifying an estuary, or any extending water; it might equally imply the Solway, the Tay, or any other estuary. Besides, it was the plan of this cautious general, it is argued, to advance by degrees, and fortify the country as he advanced; and we accordingly find him spending the remainder of this season in building a line of forts, in the most convenient situations for keeping possession of the territory he had gained. The raising of a part, if not of the whole, of that rampart drawn right across the island from the Solway near to the mouth of

---

[1] Chalmers' *Caledonia.*

the Tyne, and called Agricola's Wall, is supposed to have taken place in this year. It must be confessed, however, that the tenor of Tacitus' narrative, and some of his expressions in particular, require considerable straining before we can reconcile them with this account. In the first place, it is to be observed, that he speaks of Agricola's march to the Taus in his third summer as merely an inroad, the effects of which were to discover the country, to lay it waste, and to strike terror into the inhabitants. It appears to be clear that the occupation of it was not at that time attempted or thought of. Then, when the historian proceeds to relate the operations of the next campaign, he expressly informs us that the country which Agricola employed this fourth summer in taking possession of and fortifying, was that which he had thus in the preceding summer overrun. No words are used which can imply that he penetrated into any new country in his fourth campaign; the statement distinctly is, that he only occupied and secured what he had already surveyed and laid waste.

According to the view, however, which supposes him not till now to have ever been beyond the Solway, his fourth summer (A.D. 81) was employed in exploring and overrunning the country extending from that arm of the sea to the Friths of Clyde and Forth, and in securing, as usual, the advance he had thus made. Tacitus describes the place where the waters of the Glotta and Bodotria (the Friths of Clyde and Forth) are prevented from joining only by a narrow neck of land, and tells us that Agricola drew a chain of forts across that isthmus. These forts are supposed to have stood in the same line where Lollius Urbicus afterwards erected his more compact rampart, and not far from the modern canal which connects the two estuaries.

But in making this advance Agricola seems to have neglected the great promontory of Galloway, which lay between the Solway and the Clyde, and was then occupied by the Novantæ, and, in part, by the Selgovæ and Damnii; we mean more particularly the country now included in Wigton, Kirkcudbright, Dumfries, and Ayrshire. In his fifth campaign (A.D. 82), therefore, he thought it prudent to subdue these tribes, who, in the advance he contemplated for the next year beyond the Frith of Forth, would, from their western position, have been in his rear. He accordingly invaded "that part of Britain," says Tacitus, "which is opposite to Ireland," being the whole extent of Galloway; and to do this he is supposed to have sailed from Kilbride Loch, in Cumberland, and on the Solway, and to have landed on the estuary of Locher.[1] From the Galloway coast he saw the distant hills of Ireland, and the sight is said to have suggested the idea of a fresh invasion, to which, moreover, he was incited by an Irish chieftain, who, being expelled from his native country, had taken refuge with the Roman commander. Having, after various engagements, cleared the south-west of Scotland as far as his fortified works on the Frith of Clyde, he seems to have put the mass of his army into winter quarters along the line he had drawn from that estuary to the Frith of Forth, so as to have them ready for next year's campaign.

In his sixth year (A.D. 83) Agricola resolved to extend his conquests to the north-east, beyond the Frith of Forth. His fleet had already surveyed the coasts and harbours, and his naval officers showed him the most commodious passage—at Inchgarvey, as it is supposed—where he seems to have been met by a part of his fleet, and to have been wafted over to the advancing point in Fife, now called Northferry.[2] Other writers, however, suppose that he marched along the southern side of the Forth, to a point where the river was narrow and fordable, and crossed it somewhere near Stirling. It is possible that both courses may have been adopted by different divisions of the troops. On the north side of the Forth the troops were attended and supported by the ships, so that their march must have been along the east coast. The fleet kept so near the shore that the mariners frequently landed and encamped with the land forces; each of these bodies entertaining the other with marvellous tales of what they had seen and done in these unknown seas and regions.[3]

Having crossed the Frith of Forth, Agricola found himself, for the first time, fairly engaged with the real Caledonians—a people at the least as fierce and brave as any he had hitherto contended with. They were not taken by surprise, nor did they wait to be attacked. Descending from the upper country as Agricola advanced into Fife, strong bands of them fell upon the new Roman forts on the isthmus between the Forth and Clyde, which had been left behind without sufficient defence. Soon after they made a night attack on the ninth legion, one of the divisions of the main army, and nearly succeeded in cutting it to pieces, in spite of the strong camp in which it was intrenched. This camp was probably situated at Loch Ore, about two miles to the south of Loch Leven, where ditches and other traces of a camp are still seen. In a general battle, however, to which this nocturnal attack led, the Caledonians were beaten, and, without any other successful exploit, the Romans wintered north of the Frith of Forth, in Fife, where

---

[1] Chalmers' *Caledonia*.   [2] Chalmers' *Caledonia*.   [3] Tacit. *Vit. Agric.* c. xxv.

their fleet supplied them with provisions, and kept open their communication with the forts in the south. The Caledonians, no way dispirited, mustered all their clans for the next summer's campaign, and submitted to the supreme command of Galgacus, who ranks with Cassivellaunus and Caractacus as one of the heroes of the British wars.

At the opening of his seventh and last campaign (A.D. 84), when Agricola moved forward he found the enemy, to the number of 30,000, posted on the acclivities of *Mons Grampius*, determined to oppose his progress in a general battle. The positions of the Caledonians on this occasion, and the field of the great battle, although they have been much disputed, seem to admit of being fixed on very probable grounds. From the nature of the country, Agricola would direct his line of march by the course of the Devon, would turn to the right from Glen Devon, through the opening of the Ochil Hills, along the course of the rivulet which forms Glen-Eagles, leaving the Braes of Ogilvie on his left. He would then pass between Blackford and Auchterarder, towards the Grampians (or Gran-Pen of the British, meaning the head or chief ridge or summit), which he would see before him as he defiled from the Ochils. An easy march would then bring him to the Moor of Ardoch, at the roots of the Grampians, where there are very evident signs of ancient conflicts. The large ditch of a Roman camp can still be traced for a considerable distance; weapons, both British and Roman, have been dug up; and on the hill above Ardoch Moor are two enormous heaps of stones, called Carnwochel and Carnlee, probably the sepulchral cairns of the Caledonians who fell in the battle.[1]

The host of Galgacus fought with great obstinacy and bravery, but they were no more able to resist the disciplined legions of Rome in a pitched battle than their brethren, the southern Britons, had been. They were defeated, and pursued with great loss, and the next day nothing was seen in front of the Roman army but a silent and deserted country, and houses involved in smoke and flame. Tacitus relates that some of the fleeing natives, after tears and tender embraces, killed their wives and children, in order to save them from slavery and the Romans. In the battle the Caledonians used war-chariots, like the southern Britons, and the Roman writer mentions their broad-swords and small targets, which remained so long after the peculiar arms of the Highlanders. The victory of Agricola, however valueless in its results, was complete; and though Tacitus does not record his death on the field, he speaks no more of the brave Galgacus.

In the course of these two campaigns north of the Forth, the Romans seem to have derived an uncommon degree of assistance from their fleet, which was probably much better appointed and commanded than on any former occasion. After defeating Galgacus, Agricola sent the ships from the Frith of Tay to make a coasting voyage to the

HADRIAN, from a fine bronze found in the Thames, now in the British Museum.—Drawn by J. W. Archer.

north, which may very properly be called a voyage of discovery; for though nearly a century and a half had passed since Cæsar's invasions, the Romans were not yet quite certain that Britain was an island, but thought it might have joined the European continent either at the extreme north or north-east, or at some other, to them unknown, point. Agricola's fleet doubled the promontory of Caithness and Cape Wrath, ran down the western coast from the end of Scotland to the Land's End in Cornwall, then turning to the east, arrived safe at the Trutulensian harbour (supposed to be Sandwich), and sailing thence along the eastern coast, returned with glory to the point from which it had started, having thus, according to Tacitus, made the first certain discovery that Britain was an island.

The fears and imagination of the mariners were no doubt much excited during this periplus; and Tacitus, who probably heard the recital from his father-in-law, Agricola, and some of the officers of the fleet, was not proof against exaggeration. He tells us that the cluster of islands called the Orcades, till then wholly unknown, was added to the Roman empire (he omits all mention of the Hebrides); that Thule, which had lain concealed in gloom and eternal snows, was seen by the navigators, and that the sea in those parts was *a sluggish mass of stagnated water, hardly yielding to the stroke of the oar, and never agitated by winds and storms.*[2]

---

[1] Chalmers' *Caledonia*, book i. ch. iii.; Roy's *Military Antiquities*, plate 10; Stobie's Map of Perth.

[2] *Vit. Agric.* c. x. and xxxviii.

Agricola did not keep his army this second winter north of the friths, but withdrawing them by easy marches, put his troops in cantonments behind his works on the isthmus, if not behind those on the Solway and Tyne. Soon after this he was recalled from his command by the jealous, tyrannical Domitian. There is no evidence that Agricola left any garrison on the north of the Frith of Forth, and it appears probable that most of the forts thrown up in the passes of the Grampians, to check the incursions of the Caledonians (remains of which still exist at Cupar-Angus, Keithock, Herefaulds, Invergowrie, and other places), were either temporary encampments made on his march northwards, or were erected at a later period by the Emperor Severus, and never maintained by the Romans for any length of time. The great difficulty in these regions was not the act of advancing, but that of remaining; and the poverty of the country was, no doubt, as good a defence as the valour of its inhabitants.

It was under Agricola that the Roman dominion in Britain reached its utmost permanent extent; for a few hurried marches, made at a later period, farther into the north of Caledonia, are not to be counted as conquests or acquisitions of territory. During the long period of thirty years the island remained so tranquil that scarcely a single mention of its affairs occurs in the Roman annals; and we need scarcely remark that, as history has usually been written, the silence of historians is one of the best proofs of a nation's happiness.

But in the reign of Hadrian[1] the Romans were attacked all along their northern frontiers by the Caledonians, and the whole state of the island was so disturbed as to demand the presence of that energetic emperor (A.D. 120). The conquests of Agricola north of the Tyne and Solway were lost; his advanced line of forts between the Forth and the Clyde swept away; and Hadrian contented himself, without either resigning or reconquering all that territory, with raising a new rampart (much stronger than that drawn by Agricola) between the Solway Frith and the German Ocean. Perhaps it would have been wise in the Romans to have kept to this latter line, but in the following reign of Antoninus Pius (A.D. 138), the governor of Britain, Lollius Urbicus, advanced from it, drove the barbarians before him, and again fixed the Roman frontier at the isthmus between the Clyde and Forth, where he erected a strong rampart on the line of Agricola's forts. The prætentum, or rampart of Lollius Urbicus, consisted of a deep ditch, and an earthen wall raised on a stone foundation. There were twenty-one forts at intervals along the line, which, from one extremity to the other, measured about thirty-one miles. A military road, as a necessary appendage, ran within the rampart, affording an easy communication from station to station. The opposite points are fixed at Caerridden on the Forth, and Dunglas on the Clyde. The works appear to have been finished about A.D. 140; and, notwithstanding the perishable materials, the mound can be traced after the lapse of seventeen centuries. Among the people, whose traditions have always retained some notion of its original destination, it is called Græme's or Graham's Dyke. Inscribed stones have been discovered there, recording that the second legion, and detachments from the sixth and the twentieth legions, with some auxiliaries, were employed upon the works.[3]

REMAINS OF HADRIAN'S VALLUM,[2] near Haltwhistle.—Drawn from nature and on wood, by J. W. Archer.

It had been the boast of the Romans, even from the time of Agricola, that this fortified line was to cover and protect all the fertile territories of the south, and to drive the enemy, as it were, into another island, barren and barbarous like

[1] In a general description of the Roman empire under Trajan, the immediate predecessor of Hadrian, Appian says that the emperor possessed more than one-half of Britain, that he neglected the rest of the island as useless, and derived no profit from the part he possessed.

[2] This earthwork, originally constructed by Agricola, consisted of an earthen mound, with a ditch, on the borders of which he built, at unequal distances, a range of forts or castles. It was repaired (about A.D. 121) by Hadrian, who dug an additional and much larger ditch, and raised a higher rampart of earth, making his new works run in lines nearly parallel with the old. From these operations the association of the name of Agricola with the work merged into that of Hadrian.—*Hutton.*

[3] Roy's *Military Antiquities.*

themselves. But the northern tribes would not so understand it. In the reign of Commodus (A.D. 183) they again broke through this barrier, and swept over the country which lay between it and the wall of Hadrian, and which became the scene of several sanguinary battles with the Romans. About the same time a mutinous spirit declared itself among the legions in Britain, and symptoms were everywhere seen of that decline in discipline and military virtue which led on rapidly to the entire dissolution of the Roman empire. Shortly after, the succession to the empire was disputed with Severus by Clodius Albinus, the governor of Britain. The unequal contest was decided by a great battle in the south of France; but as the pretender Albinus had drained the island of its best troops, the northern tribes took that favourable opportunity of breaking into and desolating the settled Roman provinces. These destructive ravages continued for years, and cost the lives of thousands of the civilized British subjects of Rome.

The Emperor Severus, in his old age (A.D. 207), and though oppressed by the gout and other maladies, resolved to lead an army in person against the northern barbarians. Having made great preparations, he landed in South Britain, and almost immediately began his march to the

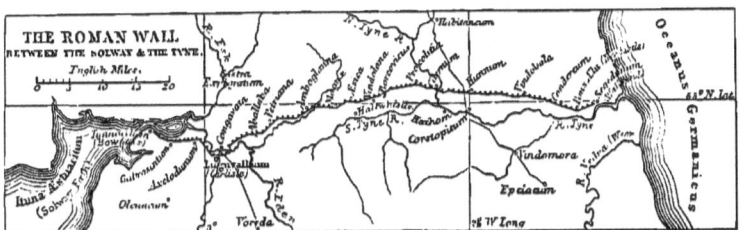

northern frontier, which was once more marked by the walls of Agricola and Hadrian, between the Solway Frith and the mouth of the Tyne. The tremendous difficulties he encountered as soon as he crossed that line, sufficiently show that the country beyond it had never been thoroughly conquered and settled by the Romans, who invariably attended to the construction of roads and bridges. Even so near to the walls as the present county of Durham, the country was an impassable wilderness. Probably there are some exaggerations in the number, and a part of the victims may have fallen under the spears and javelins of the natives, but it is stated that Severus, in his march northward, lost 50,000 men, who were worn out by the incessant labour of draining morasses, throwing raised roads or causeways across them, cutting down forests, levelling mountains, and building bridges. By these means he at length penetrated farther into the heart of Caledonia than any of his predecessors, and struck such terror into the native clans or tribes, who, however, had most prudently avoided any general action, that they supplicated for peace. He went so far to the north, that the Roman soldiers were much struck with the

length of the summer days and the shortness of the nights; but the *Aræ Finium Imperii Romani*, and the extreme point to which Severus attained in this arduous campaign, seems to have been the end of the narrow promontory that separates the Moray and Cromarty Friths, the conqueror or explorer still leaving Ross, Suther- land, and Caithness, or all the most northern parts of Scotland, untouched. The uses of this most expensive military promenade (for, with the exception of the road-making, it was nothing better) are not very obvious; no Roman army ever followed his footsteps, and he himself could not maintain the old debatable ground between the Tyne and the Forth. Indeed, after his return from the north, his first care was to erect a new frontier barrier, in the same line as those of Agricola and Hadrian, but stronger than either of them; thus acknowledging, as it were, the uncertain tenure the Romans had on the country beyond the Solway and the Tyne. For two years the Romans and their auxiliaries were employed in building a wall, which they vainly hoped would for ever check the incursions of the northern clans.

The wall of Agricola, which has been so frequently alluded to, was in reality a long bank or mound of earth, with a ditch, on the borders of which he built, at unequal distances, a range of forts or castles. This work very nearly extended from sea to sea, being about seventy-four miles long; beginning three miles and a half east of Newcastle, and ending twelve miles west of Carlisle. After existing thirty-seven years, this work, which had been much injured, was repaired (about A.D. 121) by Hadrian, who added works of his own to strengthen it. He dug an additional and much larger ditch, and raised a higher rampart of earth, making his new works run in nearly parallel lines with the old. From the date of these operations and repairs, the name of Agricola was lost; and the whole, to this day, has retained the name of Hadrian's Wall. During the ninety years that intervened between the labours of Hadrian and those of Severus, the rampart, not well calculated to withstand the frosts and rains of a cold and wet climate, had, no doubt, suffered extensively, and the barbarians had probably broken through the earthen mound in more places than one. Severus—in this surpassing his predecessors—determined to build with stone: the wall he raised was about eight feet thick, and twelve feet high to the base of the battlements. To the wall were added, at equal distances, a number of stations or towns, eighty-one castles, and 330 castelets or turrets. At the outside of the wall (to the north) was dug a ditch, about thirty-six feet wide, and from twelve to fifteen feet deep. Severus' works run nearly parallel with the other two (those of Agricola and Hadrian), lie on the north of them, and are never far distant, but may be said always to keep them in view; the greatest distance between them is less than a mile, the nearest distance about twenty yards, the medium distance forty or fifty yards. Exclusive of his wall and ditch, these stations, castles, and turrets, Severus constructed a variety of roads —yet called *Roman roads*—twenty-four feet wide, and eighteen inches high in the centre, which led from turret to turret, from one castle to another; and still larger and more distant roads from the wall, which led from one station or town to another; besides the grand military way (now our main road from Newcastle to Carlisle), which covered all the works, and no doubt was first formed by Agricola, improved by Hadrian, and, after lying neglected for 1500 years, was made complete in 1752.[2]

COURSE OF THE WALL OF SEVERUS,[1] with Mile-castle at Cawfield, near Haltwhistle.—Drawn by H. G. Hine, from his sketch on the spot in 1854.

---

[1] This fortification, says Bruce (*On the Roman Wall*), consists of three parts:—
1. A stone wall, strengthened by a ditch on its northern side.
2. An earth wall, or vallum, to the south of the stone wall.
3. Stations, castles, watch-towers, and roads for the accommodation of the soldiery who manned the barrier, and for the transmission of military stores. These lie, for the most part, between the stone wall and the earthen rampart.

The Mile-castle at Cawfield (the name of the farm-house to the north) is the most perfect mile-castle remaining of the line. The building is a parallelogram, but the corners at its lower side are rounded off. It measures inside 63 ft. east to west, and 49 ft. north to south. The stones used are of the same character as those employed in the wall. The side walls of the castle have not been tied to the great wall, but have been brought close up to it, and the junction cemented with mortar. It is provided with a gateway of 10 ft. opening, both on its northern and southern side, and formed of large slabs of rustic masonry, the walls being thicker here than in other parts. Two folding doors have closed the entrance, which, when thrown back, have fallen into recesses. Some of the pivot-holes of the doors remained tinged with oxide of iron. . . . In clearing out the interior, no traces of party walls, of a substantial character at least, were found. Some fragments of gray slate, pierced for roofing, were found among the rubbish. It is, therefore, not improbable that a shed was laid against the southern wall for the protection of the soldiers. At about the elevation which the raised floor would reach, the wall is in one place eaten away by the action of fire, and here the hearth probably stood. Plots of chives, supposed to be surviving relics of the common salad accompaniment to the black bread of the Roman soldier, planted there during their occupation, still grow near those castles.

[2] Hutton's *Hist. of the Roman Wall*.

BRITISH AND ROMAN PERIOD.

As long as the Roman power lasted, this barrier was constantly garrisoned by armed men. The stations were so near to each other, that if a fire was lighted on any one of the bulwarks, it was seen at the next, and so repeated from bulwark to bulwark, all along the line, in a very short time.

Severus had not finished his works of defence when the Caledonian tribes resumed the offensive. The iron-hearted and iron-framed old emperor marched northward with a dreadful vow of extermination; but death overtook him at Eboracum (York), in the early part of the year 211. Caracalla, his son and successor, who had been serving with him in Britain, tired of a warfare in which he could gain comparatively little, hopeless, perhaps, of ever succeeding in the so-frequently-foiled attempt of subjecting the country north of the walls, and certainly anxious to reach Rome, in order the better to dispose of his brother Geta, whom his father had named co-heir to the Empire, made a hasty peace with the Caledonians, formally ceding to them the debatable ground between the Solway and Tyne, and the Friths of Clyde and Forth, and then left the island for ever.

After the departure of Caracalla, there occurs another long blank—supposed to have been a tranquil interval—for during nearly seventy years, history scarcely devotes a single page to Britain and its affairs. The formidable stone rampart of Severus had, no doubt, its part in preserving the tranquillity of the southern division of the island, but it was not the sole cause of this happy effect. The territory ceded by Caracalla, extending eighty miles to the north of Severus' Wall, and averaging in breadth, from sea to sea, not less than seventy miles, was, in good part, a fertile country, including what are now some of the best lands in Scotland. The clans left in possession of this valuable settlement would naturally acquire some taste for the quiet habits of life—would imbibe some civilization from the Roman provincials on the south side of the wall—and then their instinctive love of property and quiet would make them restrain, with arms in their hands, the still barbarous mountaineers to the north of their own territory, whilst their own civilization, such as it might be, would make some little progress among the clans in that direction. And it certainly did happen that, even when the Roman power had long been in a state of decrepitude, no great or decisive invasions took place from the north to the south,

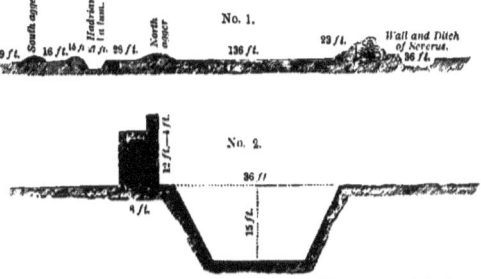

No. 1, Section of the Roman Wall near the South Agger Port Gate; No. 2, Section of the Wall and Ditch of Severus.—From Hodgson's Northumberland.

until the Scots, a new enemy, pouring in from Ireland with an overwhelming force, drove clan upon clan, and advanced beyond the wall of Severus. This latter event ought always to be taken in connection with the growing weakness of Rome, in order to account for the catastrophe which followed.

Though it has been generally overlooked, there is another, and a great cause too, which will help to account for the tranquillity enjoyed in the south, or in all Roman Britain. Caracalla imparted the freedom of Rome, and the rights and privileges of the Roman citizen, to all the provinces of the Empire; and thus the Briton, exempted from arbitrary spoliation and oppression, enjoyed his patrimony without fear or challenge.[1] Such a boon merited seventy years of a grateful life.[2]

---

[1] Palgrave's *Rise and Progress of the English Commonwealth*, chap. x.

[2] "The Roman influence in Britain must have been very great, if Pancirolus be right in his calculations. There were three great military commands—one for the interior parts of the island, another for the defence of the coast against the Saxons, and a third for guarding the frontiers against the barbarians in Britain itself; and the whole force must have amounted to 99,000 foot and 1700 horse. In order to feed these, the Roman agriculture must have been introduced; and when the Romans left Britain, there must have been great fulness of corn. But the Roman arts also must have been introduced, and were probably perpetuated. For, besides the three military commanders-in-chief, there was a *procurator gynæcii*, president of the wardrobe in Britain, in which the emperor's and soldiers' clothes were woven. Thus the Roman system, by leaving nothing to be done by the native Britons for their own defence, and stimulating, at the same time, agriculture and manufactures, must have left them, on the withdrawal of the legions, a tempting object of conquest to the Saxons, who would have found a very different reception in the island had the Romans, by forming the native Britons into a militia, trained them to the military as well as the agricultural and textile arts."—(See Giles' *History of the Ancient Britons*, vol. i. p. 299.) The great fulness of corn in Britain during the Roman period may partly be accounted for by the invaders finding, like the first European settlers in North America, a virgin soil, covered with a rich layer of vegetable mould, the exhaustion of which goes far to account for the famines and dearths of subsequent times.

When Britain reappears in the annals of history, we find her beset by fresh foes, and becoming the scene of a new enterprise, which was frequently repeated in the course of a few following years. In the reign of Diocletian and Maximian (A.D. 288), the Scandinavian and Saxon pirates began to ravage the coasts of Gaul and Britain. To repress these marauders, the emperors appointed Carausius, a Menapian, to the command of a strong fleet, the head-quarters of which was in the British Channel. The Menapians had divided into several colonies; one was settled in Belgium, one in Hibernia, one in the islands of the Rhine, one at Menevia (now St. David's) in Britain—and Carausius was by birth either a Belgian or a Briton—it is not very certain which. Wherever he was born, he appears to have been a bold and skilful naval commander. He beat the pirates of the Baltic, and enriched himself and his mariners with their plunder. It is suspected that he had himself been originally a pirate. He was soon accused of collusion with the enemy, and anticipating, from his great wealth and power, that he would throw off his allegiance, the emperors sent orders from Rome to put him to death. The wary and ambitious sailor fled, in time, with his fleet to Britain, where the legions and auxiliaries rallied round his victorious standard, and bestowed upon him the imperial diadem. The joint emperors of Rome, after seeing their attempts to reduce him repelled,

GOLD COIN OF CARAUSIUS.[1]

with disgrace to their own arms, were fain to purchase peace by conceding to him the government of Britain, of Bologne, and the adjoining coast of Gaul, together with the proud title of Emperor. Under his reign we see, for the first time, Britain figuring as a great naval power.

Carausius built ships of war, manned them in part with the intrepid Scandinavian and Saxon pirates, against whom he had fought; and, remaining absolute master of the Channel, his fleet swept the seas from the mouths of the Rhine to the Straits of Gibraltar. He struck numerous medals, with inscriptions and devices, "which show the pomp and state he assumed in his island empire." The impressive names he borrowed were, "Marcus Aurelius Valerius Carausius."[2]

He had escaped the daggers of pirates and emperors, but a surer executioner rose up in the person of a friend and confidential minister. He was murdered, in the year 297, at Eboracum (York), by Allectus, a Briton, who succeeded to his insular empire, and reigned about three years, when he was defeated and slain by an officer of Constantius Chlorus, to whom Britain fell in succession on the resignation of Diocletian and Maximian (A.D. 296). In this short war we hear of a strong body of Franks and Saxons, who formed the main strength of Allectus' army, and who attempted to plunder London after his defeat. Thus, under Carausius and Allectus, the Saxons must have become acquainted even with the interior of England. Constantius Chlorus died in the summer of A.D. 306, at Eboracum, or York. Constantine, afterwards called the Great, then began his reign at York, where he was present at his father's death. After a very doubtful campaign north of the wall of Severus, the details of which are very meagre and confused, this prince left the island, taking with him a vast number of British youths, as recruits for his army. From this time to the death of Constantine, in 337, Britain seems again to have enjoyed tranquillity.[3]

The Roman power was, however, decaying; the removal of the capital of the Empire from Rome to Constantinople had its effects on the remote provinces of Britain; and, under the immediate successors of Constantine, while the Frank and Saxon pirates ravaged the ill-defended coasts of the south, the Picts, Scots, and Attacots—all mentioned for the first time by historians in the earlier part of the fourth century—began to press upon the northern provinces, and defy Severus' deep ditches and wall of stone. As the Scots

---

[1] This coin is in the collection of C. Roach Smith, Esq. It is believed to be unique, and is considered to represent a veritable likeness of Carausius.
[2] Palgrave's *Hist. England*, ch. l.
[3] "The first half of the fourth century is chiefly remarkable, as regards Britain, on account of the harmony with which the natives and Romans, as well as other settlers, brought together in no small number by their common faith, united in the arts of peace. The cultivation of grain had been carried to such a height that Britain became the granary of the northern provinces of the Empire; and, by yearly exports, supplied other countries with food, while it enriched itself. Civic establishments were so flourishing that builders and other artificers were demanded from Britain for the restoration of the desolated provinces.—The country was crossed by highroads in various directions, many of which have served the later settlers in their marches, as well as their commercial operations. It is probable that the Romans themselves found some of those great highways already in existence, which were afterwards known by the name of Watling-street, leading from the southern shore of Kent, from Rhutupiæ and London, through St. Alban's and Stony-Stratford, to Carnarvon (*Segontium*); Ikenild or Rikenild-street, from Tynemouth, through York, Derby, and Birmingham, to St. David's; the Irmin (*Ermin*) Street, which led from the latter place to Southampton; the Foss, from Cornwall to Caithness, or, perhaps more correctly, only to Lincoln. These roads, which, if not formed, were at least greatly improved by Roman labour, prove, by their direction, a lively internal traffic, as well as a commercial connection with countries lying east and west of Britain."—Lappenberg's *History of England under the Anglo-Saxon Kings*, vol. i. p. 51.

came over from Ireland in boats, and frequently made their attacks on the coast-line, it seems not improbable that in some instances their depredations were mistaken for, or mixed up with those

REMAINS OF THE WALLS OF LONDON.1—J. W. Archer, from his original drawing.

of the Saxons. According to our insufficient guide,[2] however, it was the Picts and Scots alone that, after breaking through the wall of Severus, and killing a Roman general, and Nectaridus, the "Count of the Saxon Shore," in the reign of Julian the Apostate, were found, about three years after (A.D. 367), in the time of the Emperor Valentinian, pillaging the city of London (Augusta), and carrying off its inhabitants as slaves. Theodosius, the distinguished general, and father of the emperor of that name, repelled these invaders, and repaired the wall and the ruined forts in different parts of the south; but the northern districts were never afterwards reduced to order or tranquillity, and even for the partial and temporary advantage they obtained, the Romans were compelled to follow the host of pirates to the extremity of the British islands, "when," as it is expressed in the verses of the poet Claudian upon this achievement, "the distant Orcades were drenched with *Saxon* gore."

By watching these occurrences, with others that were equally fatal, step by step, as they happen, we shall be the better able to understand how Britain, when abandoned by the Romans legions, was in so reduced and helpless a state as to fall a prey to the barbarians. If that fact is presented to us in an isolated manner, it almost passes our comprehension; but taken in connection with great causes, and the events of the two

---

[1] The exact period when London was first walled about is not clearly ascertained. Simeon of Durham ascribes the foundation of the wall to the Emperor Constantine the Great, and it appears probable that it was either built or repaired in his time, from the discovery of coins of his mother Helena under its site. But it is probable that the effective fortification of London was completed during the reign of Valentinian I., and after the rescue of the city by Theodosius, as related in the text, when it is said he restored the defences throughout the country. The city having been ravaged and burned by Danish pirates about the year 839, it remained utterly waste for nearly half a century, when it was again rendered habitable by Alfred, King of the West Saxons, who restored its defences so effectually that about the end of the tenth century the citizens were able to assert their independence. Fitz-stephen says, concerning the walls of London as they appeared in the reign of Henry II., when he compiled his account of London:—"The wall is high and great, well towered on the north side, with due distance between the towers. On the south side also the city was walled and towered, but the fishful river of Thames, by his ebbing and flowing, has long since subverted them." The towers were fifteen in number, and their remains were still visible down to the middle of the last century. The above view represents a large fragment of London wall, which abutted on the Tower postern, still in existence, but concealed by the erection of some livery stables. Here the wall is upwards of 25 ft. high, the masonry at the base is regularly laid, and the stones are well squared. Over the first course of stones is a double layer of the large tile found in Roman masonry, of which the dimensions are as follows:—17 in. long, 11 in. broad, and nearly 1½ in. in thickness, the depth of the course, including the mortar, being 4½ in. This course, which is evidently of Roman construction, and the basement of the original wall, is succeeded by another layer of squared stones, repaired in many parts with rubble and bits of tile. The stones are here five deep, and they occupy a space of 46 in. between the first layer of tiles and another which lies upon it, and above this there are vestiges of a third course of regular masonry, greatly mingled with the material of coarse and unartificial repair. Here probably we see the work of the Saxon rebuilding of the wall, consisting of large masses of stone, roughly composed with rubble, bits of Roman tile, and flints. The upper portion of this mural monument of the ancient strength of London may, in its diversity of masonry, contain a stratification of the successive repairs it had undergone from the period of its first erection to the time when the brick made from the clay of Moorfields, with the Kentish chalk, were combined with its structure in the reign of Edward IV.

[2] *Ammianus Marcellinus*, lib. xxvii. and xxviii.

centuries that preceded the Saxon conquest, it becomes perfectly intelligible.

Following an example which had become very prevalent in different parts of the disorganised Empire, and which had been first set in Britain by Carausius, several officers, relying on the devotion of the legions and auxiliaries under their command, and supported sometimes by the affection of the people, cast off their allegiance to the emperor, and declared themselves independent sovereigns. It was the fashion of the servile historians to call these provincial emperors "tyrants," or usurpers, and to describe Britain especially as being "insula tyrannorum fertilis," an island fertile in usurpers. But, in sober truth, these provincial monarchs had as pure and legitimate a basis for their authority as any of the later emperors of Rome, in whose succession hereditary right and the will of the governed were alike disregarded, and whose election depended on the chances of war and the caprices of a barbarian soldiery; for the right of nomination to the vacant Empire, so long assumed by the Prætorian band, and which right, questionable as it was, was still certain and ascertainable—still something like a settled rule—was soon overset, and disallowed by the men of all nations in arms on the frontiers in the pay of Rome. If a pretension had been set up for purity of Roman blood, or a principle established that the sovereign should be at least a Roman born, there would have been a line of exclusion drawn against the provincial officers; but so far from this being the case, we find that the large majority of the so-called *legitimate* Roman emperors were barbarians by race and blood—natives of Illyria and other more remote provinces—while several of the most distinguished of their number sprung from the very lowest orders of society.

The most noted of the provincial emperors or pretenders that raised their standard in Britain was Maximus (A.D. 382); certainly a man of rank, and probably connected with the imperial family of Constantine the Great. If not born in Britain, he was of British descent, and had long resided in the island, where he had repelled the Picts and Scots. Brave, skilful, and exceedingly popular in Britain, Maximus might easily have retained the island, but his ambition induced him to aim at the possession of all that portion of the Western Roman empire which remained to Gratian; and this eventually not only led to his ruin, but inflicted another dreadful blow on British prosperity. He withdrew nearly all the troops; and so many of the Britons followed him to Gaul that the island was left almost defenceless, and utterly deprived of the flower of its youth and nobility. Many of these were swept off on the field of battle, many prevented by other causes from ever returning home. Gaul and Germany also gave willing recruits to the army of Maximus, who was left, by the defeat and death of Gratian, the undisputed master of Britain, Gaul, Spain, and Italy. He established the seat of his government

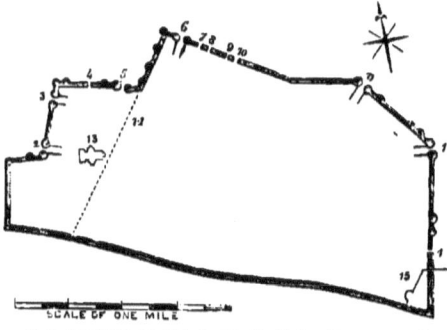

PLAN OF THE WALLS OF LONDON.[1]—The black portions represent the existing remains.

---

[1] The gates and posterns were twelve in number, namely:—1, Tower postern; 2, Ludgate; 3, Newgate; 4, Greyfriars postern; 5, Aldersgate; 6, Cripplegate postern; 7, Aldermanbury postern; 8, Basinghall postern; 9, Moorgate; 10, Moorgate postern; 11, Bishopsgate; 12, Aldgate. No. 13 shows the position of St. Paul's Cathedral, 14 the supposed line of original Roman wall, and 15 the site of the Tower. The four principal gates of the city are understood to have been Aldgate on the eastern side, Newgate on the west, Aldersgate on the north, and the gate which stood on the north end of London Bridge, on the south. Fitzstephen states that there were seven double gates in the wall of London, but fails to specify them; it is to be conjectured, however, that the others were the Tower postern, Ludgate, and Aldersgate or Cripplegate. The gates eastward of Cripplegate, on the northern side of the city, were opened in times comparatively late. The ground on which St. Paul's Cathedral (No. 13) is situated was a cemetery, in which the vestiges of British and Roman interments were found by Wren, in digging for the foundations of the present edifice; and, according to the law and practice of the Romans, the dead were forbidden to be interred within the walls of their cities, it is therefore to be presumed that the walls of London were so planned as to exclude this site. It has consequently been conjectured that the original west wall had run from Cripplegate to the Thames bank, and it is indicated accordingly on the plan, No. 14; but the evidence of a Roman causeway, discovered on the rebuilding of Newgate—which, however, stood to the east of the prison so called—goes to prove that the road presumed to have been the Prætorian way entered the city at this angle. how much further to the east cannot be determined. The further projection on the south-west, at No. 2, was carried out at the beginning of the thirteenth century, to inclose the precincts of the monastery of the Blackfriars, erected in the year 1215. It is conjectured that a Roman Palatinate tower stood upon the site of the present Tower, No. 15, and that a corresponding stronghold was situated at the opposite extremity of the wall on the west. Outside the wall was a ditch 200 ft. broad, which was completed in the fifteenth year of the reign of King John (1213).—*Vestiges of Old London.*

for some time at Treves, and is said to have declared Victor, his son by a British wife, his partner in the empire of the West—a proceeding which could scarcely fail of gratifying the host of Britons in his army. But Theodosius, called the Great, the emperor of the East, marched an overpowering army into the West, and, after being defeated in two great battles, Maximus retired to Aquileia, near the head of the Adriatic Gulf, on the confines of Italy and Illyria, where he was betrayed to the conqueror, who ordered him to be put to death in the summer of 388.

Theodosius the Great now reunited the Roman empires of the East and West. While Maximus was absent, conquering many lands, the Scots and Picts renewed their depredations in Britain. The moment of crisis is now at hand. Chrysantus, an able general, and the lieutenant of Theodosius in Britain, wholly or partially expelled the invaders. Soon after this Theodosius the Great died (A.D. 365), and again divided, by his will, the Empire which his good fortune had reunited. Britain, with Gaul, Italy, and all the countries forming the empire of the West, he bequeathed to his son, Honorius, a boy only ten years of age, whom he placed under the guardianship of the famous Stilicho, who fought long and bravely, but in vain, to prop the fallen dignity of Rome. Theodosius was scarcely cold in his grave, when Picts, Scots, and Saxons again sought what they could devour. Stilicho claimed some temporary advantages over them, but the inflated verses of his panegyrist are probably as far from the truth as Claudian is from being a poet equal to Virgil.[1]

While these events were passing in Britain (A.D. 403), the withered majesty of Rome was shrouded for ever: Africa was dismembered from her empire; Dacia, Pannonia, Thrace, and other provinces were laid desolate; and Alaric the Goth was ravaging Italy, and on his way to the Eternal City. In this extremity, some Roman troops, which had been lately sent into the island by Stilicho, were hastily recalled for the defence of Italy, and the Britons, again beset by the Picts and Scots, were left to shift for themselves.

The islanders seem to have felt the natural love of independence, but there was no unanimity, no political wisdom, and probably but little good principle among them. Seeing the necessity of a common leader to fight their battles, they permitted their soldiery to elect one Marcus emperor of Britain (A.D. 407); and, shortly after, they permitted the same soldiery to dethrone him, and put him to death. The troops then set up one Gratian, whom, in less than four months, they also deposed and murdered. Their third choice fell upon Constantine, an officer of low rank, or, according to others, a common soldier. They are said to have chosen him merely on account of his bearing the imperial and auspicious name of Constantine; but he soon showed he had other properties more valuable than a name; and had he been contented with the sovereign possession of Britain, he might possibly have foiled its invaders, and reigned with peace and some glory. But, like Maximus, he aspired to the whole empire of the West, and, like Maximus, he fell (A.D. 411), after having caused the loss of vast numbers of British youths, whom he disciplined and took with him to his wars on the Continent. At one part of his short career, Constantine made himself master of nearly the whole of Gaul, and put his son Constans, who had previously been a monk at Winchester, in possession of Spain. In the course of this Spanish campaign, it is curious to remark that in Constantine's army there were two bands of Scots or Attacotti.[2]

Soon after the fall of Constantine we find Gerontius, a powerful chief, and a Briton by birth, cultivating a close connection with the Teutonic tribes; and, at his instigation, the barbarians from beyond the Rhine, by whom we are to understand the Saxons, continued to invade the unhappy island. Such underhand villainies are always common in the downfall of nations (but can the Romanized Britons fairly be called a nation?); and we find other chiefs, worse than Gerontius, in secret league with the more barbarous Picts and Scots.

It appears that, after the death of Constantine, Honorius, during the short breathing-time allowed him by his numerous enemies, twice sent over a few troops for the recovery and protection of Britain, the sovereignty of which he still claimed; but his exigencies soon obliged him to recall them; and about the year 420, nearly five centuries after Cæsar's first invasion, and after being masters of the best part of it during nearly four centuries, the Roman emperors finally abandoned the island. The Britons had already deposed the magistrates appointed by Rome, proclaimed their independence, and taken up arms for that defence against their invaders, which the emperor could no longer give; but the final disseverance was not accompanied by reproach or apparent ill-will. On the contrary a mutual friendship subsisted for some time after between the islanders and the Romans; and the Emperor Honorius, in a letter addressed to the states or cities of Britain, seemed formally to release them from their allegiance, and to acknowledge the national independence.

For some years after the departure of the Romans, the historian has to grope his way in the

---

[1] *Claud. de Bello Gallico.*   [2] *Notitia Imperii*, sect. xxxviii.

dark; nor is it possible to determine the precise condition of the country. It appears, however, that the free municipal government of the cities was presently overthrown by a multitude of military chiefs, who were principally of British, but partly of Roman origin. It was a period to appreciate the warrior who could fight against the Scots and Picts, rather than the peaceful magistrate; and the voice of civil liberty would be rarely heard in the din of war and invasion. In a very few years all traces of a popular government disappeared, and a number of petty chiefs reigned absolutely and tyrannically, under the pompous name of kings, though the kingdoms of few of them could have been so large as a second-rate modern county of England. Instead of uniting for their general safety, at least until the invaders were repelled, these *roitelets*, or kinglings, made wars upon each other in the presence of a common danger; and, unwiser even than their far less civilized ancestors in the time of Cæsar, they never thought of forming any great defensive league until it was too late.

It is chiefly in this mad disunion that we must look for the cause of—what has created astonishment in so many writers—the miserable weakness of Britain on the breaking up of the Roman government.[1] Other causes of decline, however, had long been at work. Almost from the first establishment of the Roman power, the British troops raised as recruits were drafted off to the Continent, where they were disciplined, and whence few ever returned. It was contrary to the policy of the Romans to teach the provincials the arts of war, and establish them as troops in their own country. The soldiers of Britain were scattered from Gaul to the extremities of the Empire; the sedentary and unwarlike remained at home. All this, we think, may account for the absence of a well-disciplined force in the time of need. Moreover, during nearly a century and a half, the drain upon the population for the purposes of Roman war must have been prodigious. In 308 Constantine took with him a vast number of Britons to the Continent; this example was followed, as the enemies of the Empire increased in number and audacity, or as one pretender disputed the imperial crown with another;

and we have shown, at periods so recent as A.D. 383 and 411, how the pride and flower of the youth were sacrificed in foreign warfare. The exterminating inroads of the Scots and Picts, which began early in the fourth century, and lasted, almost without intermission, until long after the departure of the Roman legions in the fifth century, must have fearfully thinned the population in the north, where arms were most wanted. The curses that destroy mankind were many, and there were none of the blessings that tend to their increase. Gaul, and other provinces with which Britain traded, were in as bad a condition as herself, and thus an end was put to foreign commerce, while the internal trade of the country was gradually destroyed by divisions and wars, which made it unsafe for the inhabitant of one district to transport his produce into the next, although only at a few miles' distance. Under such a state of things, moreover, agriculture would be neglected, for men would not sow in the sad uncertainty whether they or the enemy should reap. Famine and pestilence ensued; and Britain, in common with the greater part of Europe, where the same causes had been in operation, was still further depopulated by these two scourges.

We can scarcely credit Gildas, or the history which bears his name, and which is supposed to have been written about the middle of the sixth century, when he or it asserts that, at the departure of the legions, the Britons were sunk in such helplessness and ignorance, that they could not repair the stone wall of Severus without the guidance and assistance of Roman workmen; but we can understand how they could not muster forces sufficient to man that rampart, and also how the Picts and Scots should render it of no avail, by turning the wall on its flanks, and landing in its rear, at such distances as best suited their convenience. To maintain an adequate garrison against a vigilant and restless enemy, along a line upwards of seventy miles in length, would demand a very large disposable force. The northern barbarians would not hesitate to launch their boats in the Solway Frith, or at the mouth of the Tyne, north of the wall, and, by sailing south, pass that rampart at one of its extremities, and land on the coast within the wall, or ascend rivers, where that defence, left far in their rear, could present no obstacle to their progress. Their rudest coracles might have performed this coasting service in fine weather; but it is not improbable that during their occasional connections with the Teutonic or Saxon pirates, who had made some progress in naval architecture, the Scots came into possession of larger and better vessels. An obvious fact is, that from the arrival of the latter people from Ireland, the rampart of Severus began signally to fail in an-

---

[1] M. Guizot, in his *Essais sur l'Histoire de France*, remarks, that the resistance of the Romanized Britons to the barbarians was, in point of fact, far more obstinate than that of any other Roman province. "It was chiefly," he says, "in the provinces that had been longest subject to Rome, and where civilization was farthest advanced, that the people thus disappeared.... The Britons, less civilized, less Roman than the other subjects of Rome, resisted the Saxons, and their resistance has a history. At the same epoch in the same situation, the Italians, the Gauls, the Spaniards have none. The Empire retired from their territories, and the barbarians occupied them, without the mass of the inhabitants having acted the smallest part, or marked their place in any way, in the events that made them the victims of so many calamities."

swering the purposes for which it was intended; though, perhaps, if, instead of taking the usual expression of their breaking through the wall, we read that they turned it at one or other of its extremities, by means of their shoals of boats, we shall generally, in regard to their earlier inroads, be nearer the truth.

But the time was now come when such stratagems, or circuitous courses, were unnecessary, and the Scots and Picts leaped the ditches and scaled the ill-defended walls at all points. The fertile provinces of the south tempted them forward, till they reached the very heart of the country, which they racked with a most barbarous hand. It was not their object to occupy the country and settle in it as conquerors (had such been their plan, the Britons would have suffered less); their expeditions were forays; they came to plunder and destroy; and the booty they carried off, season after season, was a less serious loss than the slaughter and devastation that marked their advance and retreat.

At this horrid crisis, the more southern and least exposed parts of the island appear to have been occupied by two great parties or factions, which had absorbed all the rest, but could not come to a rational understanding with each other. One of these was a Roman party, including, no doubt, thousands of Roman citizens, who had remained on the estates they had acquired, and the many native families that must have been connected with them by marriage and the various ties of civil life; the other was a British party, composed, or pretending to be composed, exclusively of Britons. As soon as such a line of distinction was drawn, dissension was inevitable. The Roman party was headed by Aurelius Ambrosius, a descendant of one of the emperors; the British rallied round the notorious Vortigern. It is not very clear whether, when it was determined a third time to implore the aid of the Romans, both these parties consented to that measure, or whether Aurelius Ambrosius did not take it upon himself, as his rival Vortigern did the calling in of the Saxons only three years after.

The abject prayer, however, entitled "The Groans of the Britons," and addressed to Ætius, thrice consul, was sent to the Continent (A.D. 441). "The barbarians," said the petitioners, "chase us into the sea; the sea throws us back upon the barbarians; and we have only the hard choice left us of perishing by the sword or by the waves." But Ætius, though as great a warrior as Stilicho, was then contending with Attila, a more terrible enemy even than Alaric, and could not afford a single cohort to the supplicants, whose last faint reliance on Rome thus fell to the ground.

Religious controversy, and the mutual hatred that inflames men when they fix the charge of heresy on one another, completed the anarchy of Britain. This is also a very common, though a very strange concomitant with the fall and last agonies of nations; and the Britons, like the Jews some centuries before, and like the Greeks at Constantinople, besieged by the Turks, ten centuries after, consumed their time in theological subtleties and disputations when the enemy was at their gates, and their last defences were falling above their heads. Had some of the disputants been animated with the same martial spirit as Germanus of Auxerre, a Gallic bishop, who was sent over by the pope to decide the controversy, their ruin might have been delayed; but his was a solitary instance. Germanus, who had been a soldier before he became a priest, sallied out with a number of Britons, and to the shouts of hallelujah (if we may believe the venerable Bede), cut up a party of Picts that were plundering the coast. But this hallelujah victory, as it was called, was far from being sufficient to stay the march of the invaders, and at length Vortigern took his memorable step, and called the Saxons to his assistance. The people of Armorica or Brittany had already set the example, and, more fortunate than their neighbours proved in the end, they had succeeded, by means of some Saxon allies, in maintaining the independence, and securing the tranquillity of their country.

It may be suspected that, even at this extremity, Vortigern applied for the aid of foreign arms, as much for the purpose of destroying the Roman party in the island as for the expulsion of its invaders; and this suspicion, though not proved, gains some strength from their past and existing disputes; from the reports of the deadly hatred and bloody contests which ensued between Aurelius Ambrosius, the head of the Roman party, and Vortigern; and from the circumstance that Aurelius, from the first landing, made head against the Saxons, while his enemy lived in peace and amity with them for some time.

But, whatever were his motives, Vortigern (A.D. 449) called the hardy freebooters of the Baltic and Northern Germany, and they came most readily at his call. Three *chiules* (keels), or long ships, were cruising in the British Channel, under the command of two brothers, distinguished warriors or pirates among the Saxons, who are called Hengist and Horsa, though it is possible those may not have been really their names, but designations merely derived from the standards they bore.[1] It appears to have

---

[1] *Hengst*, or *hengist*, signifies a stallion; and *horsa*, or *hross*, does not require any explanation. It may be remarked, however, that

been on the deck of these marauding vessels that the Saxons received the invitation which eventually led to the conquest of a great kingdom. Vortigern appointed his ready guests to dwell in the east part of the land, and gave them the Isle of Thanet for their residence, an insulated and secure tract to those who, like the Saxons, had the command of the sea; for the narrow, and, at times, almost invisible rill which now divides Thanet from the rest of Kent, was then a channel of the sea, nearly a mile in width. From this date begins the history of the Saxons in Britain.[2]

CHAPTER III.—HISTORY OF RELIGION.

RELIGION OF THE ANCIENT BRITONS AND INTRODUCTION OF CHRISTIANITY.—B.C. 55—A.D. 449.

Druidism—Cæsar's account of the Druids—Account of them by Seneca and Lucan—Druidical groves and wells—The mistletoe—Classes of the Druidical priesthood—Costume of the Druids—Their modes of divination—Their doctrines and religious observances—Their human sacrifices—Origin of Druidism—Warfare of the Romans against it—Its influence after the suppression of the Druids—Entrance of Christianity into Britain—State of the early Christian Church there.

THAT very ancient and far-extended faith known by the name of Druidism, flourished among the ancient Britons in all its vigour. It appears, indeed, that Druidism was considered by the Gauls to have originated in Britain; but those, perhaps, are nearer to the truth who give to the broad principles of the religion an Eastern origin. Much of the subject is concealed in a darkness very favourable to conjecture and speculation; but we possess very few materials whereupon to found a positive account of the system. Julius Cæsar, who was altogether only a short time in our island, but who resided six or seven years in Gaul, and made himself well acquainted with the institutions of that country, has left the fullest ancient account we possess of the Gallic Druids. He states generally that the same system existed in Britain; but as his stay was so short, and as he saw so little of our island, he was scarcely competent to judge whether Druidism prevailed in all parts of the country, and whether it did not vary in some of its rites and practices from the Gallic establishment. He, however, says that those of the Gauls who wished to obtain a perfect knowledge of the system, were wont to pass over into Britain to study it.

Cæsar's account of the Gallic Druids is this:—"They are the ministers of sacred things; they have the charge of sacrifices, both public and private; they give directions for the ordinances of religious worship (*religiones interpretantur*). A great number of young men resort to them for the purpose of instruction in their system, and they are held in the highest reverence. For it is they who determine most disputes, whether of the affairs of the state or of individuals; and if any crime has been committed, if a man has been slain, if there is a contest concerning an inheritance or the boundaries of their lands, it is the Druids who settle the matter; they fix rewards and punishments; if any one, whether in an individual or public capacity, refuses to abide by

---

in Danish, *hors* signifies not a *horse*, but a *mare*. The snow-white steed still appears as the ensign of Kent, in England, as it anciently did in the shield of the "Old Saxons" in Germany. Hence the white horse is still borne on the royal shield of Brunswick-Hanover. --Palgrave, *History of England*, ch. ii.

[2] "We have considered the general principles of Roman provincial government; and we now ask, How were these applied in the case of Britain? The answer is much more difficult to give than might be imagined. Wealthy as this country was, and capable of conducing to the power and wellbeing of its masters, it seems never to have received a generous or even fair treatment from them. The Briton was to the last, as at the first, *penitus toto divisus orbe Britannus*, and his land, always *ultima Thule*, was made, indeed, to serve the avarice or ambition of the ruler, but derived little benefit to itself from the rule. 'Levies, corn, tribute, mortgages, slaves'—under these heads was Britain entered in the vast *ledger* of the Empire. The Roman records do not tell us much of the details of government here, and we may justly say that we are more familiar with the state of an eastern or an Iberian city, than we are with that of a British one. A few technical words, perfectly significant to a people who, above all others, symbolized a long succession of facts under one legal term, are all that remain to us; and unfortunately the jurists, and statesmen, and historians, whose works we painfully consult in hopes of rescuing the minutest details of our early condition, are satisfied with the use of general terms, which were perfectly intelligible to those for whom they wrote, but teach us little. . . . Temples there were; food, porticoes, baths, and luxurious feasts; Roman manners and Roman vices; not to support them, loans, usurious mortgages, and ruin. But we seek in vain for any evidence of the Romanized Britons having been employed in any offices of trust and dignity, or permitted to share in the really valuable results of civilization; there is no one Briton recorded, of whom we can confidently assert that he held any position of dignity and power under the imperial rule; the historians, the geographers, nay, even the novelists (who so often supply incidental notices of the utmost interest), are here consulted in vain; nor in the many inscriptions which we possess relating to Britain can we point out one single 'British name.'"—Kemble's *The Saxons in England*, book ii. ch. vii.

their sentence, they forbid him to come to the sacrifices. This punishment is among them very severe; those on which this interdict is laid are accounted among the unholy and accursed; all flee from them, and shun their approach and their conversation, lest they should be injured by their very touch; they are placed out of the pale of the law, and excluded from all offices of honour.

"Over all these Druids one presides, to whom they pay the highest regard of any among them. Upon his death, if there is any of the other Druids of superior worth, he succeeds; if there are more than one who have equal claims, a successor is appointed by the votes of the Druids; and the contest is sometimes decided by force of arms. These Druids hold a meeting at a certain time of the year, in a consecrated spot in the country of the Carnutes (people in the neighbourhood of Chartres), which country is considered to be in the centre of all Gaul. Hither assemble all from every part, who have a litigation, and submit themselves to their determination and sentence. The system of Druidism is thought to have been formed in Britain, and from thence carried over into Gaul; and now those who wish to be more accurately versed in it, for the most part go thither (*i.e.*, to Britain), in order to become acquainted with it.

"The Druids do not commonly engage in war, neither do they pay taxes like the rest of the community; they enjoy an exemption from military service, and freedom from all other public burdens. Induced by these advantages, many come of their own accord to be trained up among them, and others are sent by their parents and connections. They are said in this course of instruction to learn by heart a number of verses; and some accordingly remain twenty years under tuition. Nor do the Druids think it right to commit their instructions to writing, although in most other things, in the accounts of the state and of individuals, the Greek characters are used. They appear to me to have adopted this course for two reasons; because they do not wish either that the knowledge of their system should be diffused among the people at large, or that their pupils, trusting to written characters, should become less careful about cultivating the memory; because in most cases it happens that men, from the security which written characters afford, become careless in acquiring and retaining knowledge. It is especially the object of the Druids to inculcate this—that souls do not perish, but after death pass into other bodies; and they consider that by this belief, more than anything else, men may be led to cast away the fear of death, and to become courageous. They discuss, moreover, many points concerning the heavenly bodies and their motion, the extent of the universe and the world, the nature of things, the influence and ability of the immortal gods; and they instruct the youth in these things.

"The whole nation of the Gauls is much addicted to religious observances, and, on that account, those who are attacked by any of the more serious diseases, and those who are involved in the dangers of warfare, either offer human sacrifices, or make a vow that they will offer them, and they employ the Druids to officiate at these sacrifices: for they consider that the favour of the immortal gods cannot be conciliated, unless the life of one man be offered up for that of another; they have also sacrifices of the same kind appointed on behalf of the state. Some have images of enormous size, the limbs of which they make of wicker-work, and fill with living men, and setting them on fire, the men are destroyed by the flames. They consider that the torture of those who have been taken in the commission of theft or open robbery, or in any crime, is more agreeable to the immortal gods; but when there is not a sufficient number of criminals, they scruple not to inflict this torture on the innocent.

"The chief deity whom they worship is Mercury; of him they have many images, and they consider him to be the inventor of all arts, their guide in all their journeys, and that he has the greatest influence in the pursuit of wealth and the affairs of commerce. Next to him they worship Apollo and Mars, and Jupiter and Minerva; and nearly resemble other nations in their views respecting these, as that Apollo wards off diseases, that Minerva communicates the rudiments of manufactures and manual arts, that Jupiter is the ruler of the celestials, that Mars is the god of war. To Mars, when they have determined to engage in a pitched battle, they commonly devote whatever spoil they may take in the war. After the contest, they slay all living creatures that are found among the spoil; the other things they gather into one spot. In many states, heaps raised of these things in consecrated places may be seen: nor does it often happen that any one is so unscrupulous as to conceal at home any part of the spoil, or to take it away when deposited; a very heavy punishment, with torture, is denounced against that crime.

"All the Gauls declare that they are descended from Father Dis (or Pluto), and this they say has been handed down by the Druids; for this reason, they distinguish all spaces of time, not by the number of days, but of nights: they so regulate their birthdays, and the beginning of the months and years, that the day shall come after the night."[1]

---

[1] *Cæsar de Bell. Gall.* lib. vi. 13, 14, 16, 17, 18, as translated in the *Penny Cyclopædia*.

It is to be supposed that in speaking of the divinities worshipped by the Druids, Cæsar describes the unknown by the known, or calls this divinity Mercury, and this Apollo, or Mars, or Jupiter, because the attributes of the said divinities resembled those of the gods of the Grecian and Roman mythology; and that, if we possessed a more ample knowledge of the subject, we should find that the descent, pedigree, origin, and connection of the Druidical divinities had nothing whatever to do with those of the divinities in the classical mythology.

Among the various derivations which have been given of the name of the Druids, the most probable seems to be that which brings it from *drui*, the Celtic word for an oak, corruptly written in the modern Irish *droi*, or more corruptly, *draoi*, and making in the plural *druidhe*. *Drui* is the same word with *drus*, which signifies an oak in the Greek language; and also, indeed, with the English word *tree*, which in the old form was written *triu*. We cannot name the Druids of England without thinking of our woods and national oaks. The things are inseparable in our imagination; yet it is remarkable that Cæsar nowhere has any mention of the sacred groves, and the reverence paid to the oak, which make so great a figure in the other accounts of Druidism, and which indisputably formed very important features in that religion.

"If you come," says the philosopher Seneca, "to a grove thick planted with ancient trees, which have outgrown the usual altitude, and which shut out the view of the heaven with their interwoven boughs, the vast height of the wood, and the retired secrecy of the place, and the wonder and awe inspired by so dense and unbroken a gloom in the midst of the open day, impress you with the conviction of a present deity."[1] These natural feelings of the human mind were turned to account by the Druids, even as they were in the other most primitive and simple forms of ancient superstition. Pliny informs us that the oak was the tree which they principally venerated, that they chose groves of oak for their residence, and performed no sacred rites without the leaf of the oak. The geographer Pomponius Mela describes the Druids as teaching the youths of noble families that thronged to them, in caves, or in the depths of forests. We have seen, in the preceding chapter, that when (A.D. 61) Suetonius Paulinus made himself master of the Isle of Anglesey, he cut down the Druidical groves. These groves, says Tacitus, were "hallowed with cruel superstitions; for they held it right to stain their altars with the blood of prisoners taken in war, and to seek to know the mind of the gods from the fibres of human victims."[2] The poet Lucan, in a celebrated passage on the Druids, has not forgotten their sacred groves:—

"The Druids now, while arms are heard no more,
Old mysteries and barbarous rites restore;
A tribe, who singular religion love,
And haunt the lonely coverts of the grove.
To these, and these of all mankind alone,
The gods are sure revealed, or sure unknown.
If dying mortals' dooms they sing aright,
No ghosts descend to dwell in dreadful night;
No parting souls to grisly Pluto go,
Nor seek the dreary silent shades below;
But forth they fly, immortal in their kind,
And other bodies in new worlds they find.
Thus life for ever runs its endless race,
And like a line Death but divides the space;
A stop which can but for a moment last,
A point between the future and the past.
Thrice happy they beneath their northern skies,
Who that worst fear, the fear of death, despise;
Hence they no cares for this frail being feel,
But rush undaunted on the pointed steel;
Provoke approaching fate, and bravely scorn
To spare that life which must so soon return."[3]

No Druidical grove, it is believed, now remains in any part of our island; but within little more than a century, ancient oaks were still standing around some of the circles of stones set upright in the earth, which are supposed to have been the temples of the old religion. These sacred inclosures seem, in their perfect state, to have generally consisted of a circular row or double row of great stones in the central open space (the proper *lucus* or place of light), and beyond these, of a wood surrounded by a ditch and a mound of earth. The sacred grove appears to have been usually watered by a holy fountain. The reverence for rivers or streams, springs or wells, is another of the most prevalent of ancient superstitions; and it is one which, having, along with many other Pagan customs, been adopted, or at least tolerated, by Christianity as first preached by the Roman missionaries, and being, besides, in some sort recommended to the reason by the high utility of the object of regard, has not even yet altogether passed away. The holy wells, to which some of our early monks gave the names of their saints, had, in many instances, been objects of veneration many centuries before; and the cultivation of the country, or the decay from lapse of time, which has almost everywhere swept away the antique religious grove, has for the most part spared the holy well. In the centre of the circle of upright stones is sometimes found what is still called a *cromlech*, a flat stone supported in a horizontal position upon others set perpendicularly in the earth, being apparently the altar on which the sacrifices were offered up, and on which the sacred fire was kept burning. Near to the temple frequently rises a *carnedd*, or

---

[1] M. A. Seneca, *Epist.* 14.
[2] Tacitus, *Ann.* xiv. 30.
[3] Lucan, *Pharsalia*, l. 462; Rowe's translation.

sacred mount, from which it is conjectured the priests were wont to address the people.

The most remarkable of the Druidical supersti-

MADRON HOLY WELL,[1] Cornwall.—J. S. Prout, from his drawing on the spot.

tions connected with the oak, was the reverence paid to the parasitical plant called the misletoe, when it was found growing on that tree. Pliny has given us an account of the ceremony of gathering this plant, which, like all the other

MISLETOE PLANT,[2] and Golden Hook with which it was cut.

sacred solemnities of the Druids, was performed on the sixth day of the moon, probably because the planet has usually at that age become distinctly visible. It is thought that the festival of gathering the misletoe was kept always as near to the 10th of March, which was their New-year's Day, as this rule would permit. Having told us that the

Druids believed that God loved the oak above all the other trees, and that everything growing upon that tree came from heaven, he adds that there is nothing they held more sacred than the misletoe of the oak. Whenever the plant was found on that tree, which it very rarely was, a procession was made to it on the sacred day, with great form and pomp. First, two white bulls were bound to the oak by their horns; and then a Druid clothed in white mounted the tree, and with a knife of gold cut the misletoe, which another, standing on the ground, held out his white robe to receive. The sacrifice of the victims and festive rejoicings followed. The sacredness of the misletoe is said to have been also a part of the ancient religious creed of the Persians, and not to be yet forgotten in India; and it is one of

DRUIDS, from a bas-relief found at Autun.[3]—From Montfaucon.

the Druidical superstitions, of which traces still survive among our popular customs. Virgil, a diligent student of the poetry of old religions, has been thought to intend an allusion to it by the golden branch which Æneas had to pluck to be his passport to the infernal regions. Indeed, the poet expressly likens the branch to the misletoe:—

"Quale solet silvis brumali frigore viscum
Fronde virere nova, quod non sua seminat arbos,
Et croceo fetu teretes circumdare truncos;
Talis erat species auri frondentis opacâ
Ilice; sic leni crepitabat bractea vento."
—Æn. vi. 209.

As in the woods, beneath mid-winter's snow,
Shoots from the oak the fresh-leaved misletoe,
Girding the dark stem with its saffron glow;
So sprung the bright gold from the dusky rind,
So the leaf rustled in the fanning wind.

---

[1] An ancient baptistery, one mile north of Madron church, Cornwall. It was partially destroyed by Major Ceely, one of Cromwell's officers. The altar, pierced with a hole to receive the foot of the cross or an image of the saint, is still entire.

[2] The misletoe, *Viscum album*, is a common parasite of apple-trees and others, but the sacred misletoe of the Druids, growing on an oak, is rare. The golden hook is from Hoare's *Ancient Wiltshire*.

[3] The figure crowned with a coronal of oak leaves (without which,

The entire body of the Druidical priesthood appears to have been divided into several orders or classes; but there is some uncertainty and difference of opinion as to the characters and offices of each. Strabo and Ammianus Marcellinus are the ancient authorities upon this head; and they both make the orders to have been three—the Druids, the Vates, and the Bards. It is agreed that the Bards were poets and musicians. Marcellinus says that they sung the brave deeds of illustrious men, composed in heroic verses, with sweet modulations of the lyre; and Diodorus Siculus also mentions them in nearly the same terms. The Vates, according to Strabo, were priests and physiologists; but Marcellinus seems to assign to them only the latter office, saying that they inquired into nature, and endeavoured to discover the order of her processes, and her sublimest secrets. The Druids Strabo speaks of as combining the study of physiology with that of moral science; Marcellinus describes them as persons of a loftier genius than the others, who addressed themselves to the most occult and profound inquiries, and rising in their contemplations above this human scene, declared the spirits of men to be immortal.[1] A remarkable fact mentioned by Marcellinus is that the Druids, properly so called, lived together in communities or brotherhoods. This, however, cannot have been the case with all the members of the order; for we have reason to believe that the Druids frequently reckoned among their number some of the sovereigns of the Celtic states, whose civil duties, of course, would not permit them to indulge in this monastic life. Divitiacus, the Æduan prince, who performed so remarkable a part, as related by Cæsar, in the drama of the subjugation of his country by the Roman arms,

DRUIDICAL INSIGNIA of gold, found in Ireland.—From the Archæologia.

is stated by Cicero to have been a Druid. Strabo records it to have been a notion among the Gauls that the more Druids they had among them, the more plentiful would be their harvests, and the greater their abundance of all good things; and we may therefore suppose that the numbers of the Druids were very considerable.

Toland, who, in what he calls his *Specimen of the Critical History of the Celtic Religion and Learning*, has collected many curious facts, has given us the following account of the dress of the Druids. Every Druid, he informs us, carried a wand or staff, such as magicians in all countries have done, and had what was called a Druids' egg (to which we shall advert presently) hung about his neck, inclosed in gold. All the Druids wore the hair of their heads short, and their beards long; while other people wore the hair of their heads long, and shaved all their beards, with the exception of the upper lip. "They likewise," he continues, "all wore long habits, as did the Bards and the Vaids (the Vates); but the Druids had on a white surplice whenever they religiously officiated. In Ireland they, with the graduate Bards and Vaids, had the privilege of wearing six colours in their breacans or robes (which were the striped braccæ of the Gauls, still worn by the Highlanders); whereas the king and queen might have in theirs but seven, lords and ladies five, governors of fortresses four, officers and young gentlemen of quality three, common soldiers two, and common people one." These particulars appear to have been collected from the Irish traditions or Bardic manuscripts.

The art of divination was one of the favourite pretensions of the Druidical, as it has been of most other systems of superstition. The British Druids, indeed, appear to have professed the practice of magic in this and all its other departments. Pliny observes that in his day this supernatural art was cultivated with such astonishing ceremonies in Britain, that the Persians themselves might seem to have acquired the knowledge of it from that island; and Ælian tells us that the Druids of Gaul were liberally paid by those who consulted them for their revelations of the future, and the good fortune they promised. Among their chief methods of divination was that from the entrails of victims offered in sacrifice. One of their practices was remarkable for its strange and horrid cruelty, if we may believe the account of Diodorus Siculus. In sacrificing a man they would give him the mortal blow by the stroke of a sword above the diaphragm, and then, according to rules which had descended to them from their forefathers, they would draw their predictions from inspection of the posture in which the dying wretch fell, the convulsions of his quivering limbs,

---

or some such symbol, no act of their mysteries could be performed), and bearing a sceptre, is conjectured to represent an arch-Druid. The other figure holds in his hand a crescent, equivalent to the form of the moon on the sixth day of the month, which was the period ordained for the ceremony of cutting the misletoe.

[1] Strabo, iv.; Ammian. Marcell. xv. 9; Diod. Sic. v. 31; Toland's *Hist. of the Druids*, pp. 24-29; Rowland's *Mona Antiqua*, p. 65; Borlase's *Cornwall*, p. 67; Macpherson's *Dissertations*, p. 203; Bouche's *Histoire de Provence*, i. 68; Fosbroke's *Encyclopædia of Antiquities*, ii. 662.

and the direction in which the blood flowed from his body.

There is reason to believe that the Druids, like other ancient teachers of religion and philosophy,

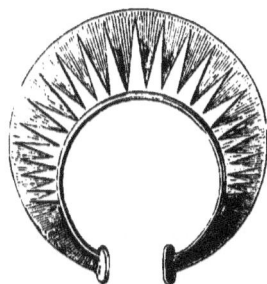

NIMBUS OF GOLD, presumed to have been worn on the head by Druids.—From Vallancey, Collect. de Reb. Hibernicis.

had an esoteric or secret doctrine, in which the members of the order were instructed, of a more refined and spiritual character than that which they preached to the multitude. Diogenes Laertius acquaints us that the substance of their system of faith and practice was comprised in three precepts, namely, to worship the gods, to do no evil, and to behave courageously. They were reported, however, he says, to teach their philosophy in enigmatic apophthegms. Mela also ex-

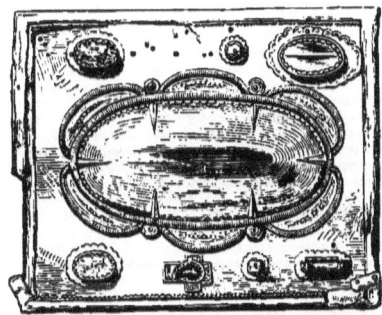

LIUTH MESSEATH,[1] or Plate of Judgment, found in Ireland. From the Archæologia.

presses himself as if he intended us to understand that the greater part of their theology was reserved for the initiated. One doctrine, he says, that of the immortality of the soul, they published,

in order that the people might be thereby animated to bravery in war; and he tells us that, in consequence of their belief in this doctrine, they were accustomed, when they buried their dead, to burn and inter along with them things useful for the living—a statement which is confirmed by the common contents of the barrows or graves of the ancient Britons. He adds a still better evidence of the strength of their faith. They were wont, it seems, to put off the settlement of accounts *and the exaction of debts* (!) till they should meet again in the shades below. It also sometimes happened, that persons not wishing to be parted from their friends who had died, would throw themselves into the funeral piles of the objects of their attachment, with the view of thus accompanying them to their new scene of life. In this belief, also, the ancient Britons, when they buried their dead, were wont to address letters to their deceased friends and relations, which they threw into the funeral pile, as if the persons to whom they were addressed would in this way receive and read them.

It has been conjectured that the fundamental principle of the Druidical esoteric doctrine was the belief in one God. For popular effect, however, this opinion, if it ever was really held, even by the initiated, appears to have been from the first wrapped up and disguised in an investment

DRUID COLLAR OR GORGET of gold,[2] found in Ireland.—From the Archæologia.

of materialism, as it was presented by them to the gross apprehension of the vulgar. The simplest, purest, and most ancient form of the public religion of the Druids seems to have been the

---

[1] The Liuth Messeath is understood to have been worn upon the girdle of the Druid, and it bears a remarkable resemblance to the breastplate worn by the Jewish high-priest. This relic is composed of pure silver; in the centre is a large crystal, and smaller stones are inserted around it.

[2] This article, called also Jodhan Morain, is supposed to have been worn on the neck of the judge when on the bench, and it was believed it would choke him if he gave unjust judgment. Some authorities say that it was called Morain from a great judge of that name, who formerly flourished in Ireland. "My surprise,"

says Governor Pownall (*Early Irish Antiquities, Archæologia*, vol. vii.), "was great when I found in Buxtorf, that Jodhan Morain was the Chaldee name for Urim and Thummim. Not satisfied with Buxtorf, I wrote to the learned Rabbi Heideck, now in London; his answer was satisfactory, and contained a dozen quotations from various Talmud commentators. In short, my friend the Rabbi will have it that none but Jews or Chaldees could have brought the name and the thing to Ireland. . . . The measurement of this relic was nearly 11 in. at the caps or circles, by much the same in depth; and the weight was exactly 20 guineas."

worship of the celestial luminaries and of fire. The sun appears to have been adored under the same name of Bel or Baal, by which he was distinguished as a divinity in the paganism of the East.[2] We have already had occasion to notice their observance of the moon in the regulation of the times of their great religious festivals. These appear to have been four in number: the first was the 10th of March, or the sixth day of the moon nearest to that, which, as already mentioned, was their New-year's Day, and that on which the ceremony of cutting the mistletoe was performed; the others were the 1st of May, Midsummer Eve, and the last day of October.

On all these occasions the chief celebration was by fire. On the eve of the festival of the 1st of May, the tradition is that all the domestic fires throughout the country were extinguished, and lighted again the next day from the sacred fire kept always burning in the temples. "The Celtic nations," observes Toland, "kindled other fires on Midsummer Eve, which are still continued by the Roman Catholics of Ireland, making them in all their grounds, and carrying flaming brands about their corn-fields. This they do likewise all over France, and in some of the Scottish isles. These Midsummer fires and sacrifices were to obtain a blessing on the fruits of the earth, now becoming ready for gathering; as those of the 1st of May, that they might prosperously grow; and those of the last of October were the thanksgiving for finishing their harvest." In Ireland, and also in the north of Scotland, the 1st of May, and in some places the 21st of June, is still called Beltein or Beltane, that is, the day of Bel Fire; and imitations of the old superstitious ceremonies were not

PLAN OF DRUIDICAL CIRCLE AT AVEBURY.1—From Hoare's Ancient Wiltshire.

top, according to Sir R. Colt Hoare, 4442 ft. The area within the mound is upwards of 28 acres. About midway upon the inner slope was a terrace, apparently meant as a stand for spectators. Within the periphery of the great circle were two other small circles, one being a double circle of upright stones, with a single stone raised near the centre, which Stukeley calls the aimbire or obelisk; this small temple consisted of forty-three stones. Another circle of forty-five stones, some of which are still standing, and of great size, stood a little north of the former, consisting also of two concentric circles, inclosing a group of three tall stones, called the cove. These composed the triple circle or temple. This work was distinguished from other similar monuments, by avenues of approach, consisting of double rows of upright stones, which branched off from the central work, each to the extent of upwards of a mile. One of these branched southward, and terminated in two elliptical ranges of upright stones. This avenue was formed by 200 upright stones, being finished at its eastern extremity with 58 stones. The width of the avenue varied from 56 ft. to 35 ft. between the stones, which were on an average 86 ft. apart from each other in their linear direction. The outer oval of the terminating temple to the south-east, on an eminence called Overton Hill, or the Hackpen, measured about 146 ft. in diameter; the inner oval was 45 ft. across. The western avenue extended about one mile and a half, and consisted of 203 stones; its extremity ended in a point with a single stone. Those avenues were formed in curved lines, and, according to Dr. Stukeley's theory, were intended to represent or typify the figure of the serpent. This vast work is surrounded by numerous tumuli, cromlechs, and ancient trackways, over which rises the lofty cone of Silbury Hill. The great earthen mound of Avebury now contains a village, with its fields and appurtenances, and its original figure is not to be made out by the present vestiges. Aubrey (A.D. 1663) makes out sixty-three stones as remaining within the intrenched inclosure in his time; these were reduced to twenty-nine, when Stukeley made his survey; and in 1812, when Sir R. Colt Hoare described it, only seventeen stones remained. Two upright stones of the western avenue remain, and about sixteen of those of the southern avenue.

[1] This plan is taken from Stukeley's survey in the year 1724. Since that time this vast monument has become nearly obliterated, through the pillage of the stones for a variety of unworthy purposes. The site of the temple is a platform, bounded on the east by undulating hills, and within a short distance of the source of the Kennet, a tributary to the Thames. "This," Stukeley remarks, "might have been regarded as the grand national cathedral, while the smaller circles in different parts of the island might be compared to the parish or village churches." Numbers of detached stones, called grey weathers, lie in the neighbouring parts, and from this source the materials of the temple appear to have been selected. The number of these masses employed in the construction of the temple amounted to 650 stones. The dimensions of these stones vary from 5 ft. to 20 ft. in elevation above the surface of the ground, and from 3 ft. to 12 ft. in bulk. One hundred vertical stones surrounded in a circle an area of about 1400 ft. in diameter, and bounding these stones, the work was completed by a deep ditch and a high bank, having two openings corresponding with the original avenues, although other two openings have subsequently been broken in the mound. The inner slope of the mound measured 80 ft., and its whole extent and circumference at the

[2] The author of *Britannia after the Romans*, however, denies that the Celtic Beli or Belinus has any connection with the Oriental Baal or Bel.

long ago still generally performed.[1] In Scotland a sort of sacrifice was offered up, and one of the persons present, upon whom the lot fell, leaped three times through the flames of the fire. In Ireland the cottagers all drove their cattle through the fire. Even in some parts of England the practice still prevails of lighting fires in parishes on Midsummer Eve.[2]

Another of the most remarkable principles of primitive Druidism appears to have been the worship of the serpent; a superstition so widely extended, as to evince its derivation from the most ancient traditions of the human race. Pliny has given us a curious account of the anguinum, or serpent's egg, which he tells us was worn as their distinguishing badge by the Druids. He had himself seen it, he says, and it was about the bigness of an apple, its shell being a cartilaginous incrustation, full of little cavities, like those on the legs of the polypus. Marvels of all kinds were told of this production. It was said to be formed, at first, by a great number of serpents twined together, whose hissing at last raised it into the air, when it was to be caught, ere it fell to the ground, in a clean white cloth, by a person mounted on a swift horse, who had immediately to ride off at full speed, the enraged serpents pursuing him until they were stopped (as witches still are supposed to be, in the popular faith) by a running water. If it were genuine it would, when enchased in gold, and thrown into a river, swim against the stream. All the virtues also of a charm were ascribed to it. In particular, the person who carried it about with him was insured against being overcome in any dispute in which he might engage, and might count upon success in his attempts at obtaining the favour and friendship of the great. It has been conjectured, on highly probable grounds, that the massive

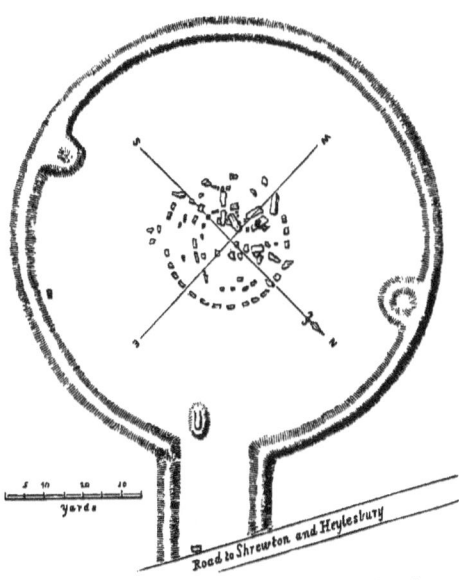

GROUND PLAN OF STONEHENGE.[3]—From Sir R. Colt Hoare's Ancient Wiltshire.

Druidical temples of Avebury, of Stonehenge, of Carnac in Brittany, and most of the others that remain both in Britain and Gaul, were dedicated to the united worship of the sun and the serpent, and that the form of their construction is throughout emblematical of this combination of the two religions.[4]

But however comparatively simple and restricted may have been the Druidical worship in its earliest stage, there is sufficient evidence that, at a later period, its gods came to be much more

---

[1] "The needfire, nydfyr, New German nothfeuer, was called, from the mode of its production, confrictione de lignis; and though probably common to the Kelts as well as Teutons, was long and well known to all the Germanic races at a certain period. All the fires in the village were to be relighted from the virgin flame produced by the rubbing together of wood; and in the Highlands of Scotland and Ireland it was usual to drive the cattle through it, by way of lustration, and as a preservative against disease."—Kemble's *Saxons in England*, vol. ii. p. 360, where a curious illustration of the subject is given, from an ancient English MS. Perthshire seems to have retained most pertinaciously the old superstitions connected with the worship of fire, probably from Benledi having been specially consecrated to it. So late as in 1826, an old farmer in that county, who had lost several cattle by an epidemic disease, was persuaded by a weird sister in his neighbourhood to try the effect of a lustration of the survivors, by making them pass through the flame of a fire kindled in the barnyard by friction.—(See the *Mirror* for June, 1826, quoted by Kemble.)

[2] See *Statistical Account of Scotland*, vol. iii. p. 105, vol. v. p. 84, and vol. xi. p. 620; Vallancey's *Essay on the Antiquity of the Irish Language*, p. 19; and Brande's *Popular Antiquities*, vol. i. p. 238, &c.

[3] The site of Stonehenge, the plain of Sarum, is on a platform of undulating downs, about six miles from Salisbury. The structure consists of two circles and two ovals, composed of huge stones, uprights and imposts. The outer or largest circle is 105 ft. in diameter, and between that and the interior smaller circle is a space of about 9 ft. Within this smaller circle, which is half the height (8 ft.) of the exterior one, was a portion of an ellipse formed by five groups of stones, which have been called *trilithons*, because formed by two vertical and one horizontal stone. Within this ellipse is another of single stones, half the height of the trilithons. The outer circle was originally composed of thirty upright stones, at nearly equal distances apart, sustaining as many stones in a horizontal position, forming a continuous impost. The inner circle consisted of about the same number of upright stones of smaller size, and without imposts. Within the inner elliptical inclosure was a block of stone 16 ft. long, 4 ft. broad, and 20 in. thick. This has been usually called the altar stone. Round the larger circle, and at the distance of 100 ft., was a vallum 52 ft. in width, and 15 ft. in height.

[4] See on this subject a curious dissertation, by the Rev. B. Deane, in the *Archæologia*, vol. xxv. (for 1834) pp. 188-229.

numerous. Cæsar, as we have already seen, mentions among those adored by the Gauls, Mercury, Apollo, Mars, Jupiter, and Minerva. It is to be regretted that the historian did not give us the Celtic names of the deities in question, rather than the Roman names, which he considered, from the

STONEHENGE, Salisbury Plain.

similarity of attributes, to be their representatives. Livy, however, tells us that the Spanish Celts called Mercury Teutates; the same word, no doubt, with the Phœnician Taaut, and the Egyptian Thoth, which are stated by various ancient writers to be the same with the Hermes of the Greeks, and the Mercury of the Latins.[1] Jupiter is thought to have been called Jow, which means *young*, from his being the youngest son of Saturn, whom both Cicero and Dionysius of Halicarnassus affirm to have been also adored by the Celtic nations. Bacchus, Ceres, Proserpine, Diana, and other gods of Greece and Rome, also appear to have all had their representatives in the Druidical worship; if, indeed, the classic theology did not borrow these divinities from the Celts. Another of the Celtic gods was Taranis, whose name signifies the god of thunder.

The earliest Druidism seems, like the kindred superstition of Germany, as described by Tacitus, to have admitted neither of covered temples nor of sculptured images of the gods. Jupiter, indeed, is said to have been represented by a lofty oak, and Mercury by a cube—the similarity of that geometrical figure on all sides typifying that perfect truth and unchangeableness which were held to belong to this supreme deity; but these

GAULISH DEITIES, from Roman bas-reliefs under the choir of Notre Dame, Paris.—From Montfaucon.

are to be considered, not as attempts to imitate the supposed bodily forms of the gods, but only as emblematic illustrations of their attributes. At a later period, however, material configurations of

GAULISH DEITIES, from Roman bas-reliefs under the choir of Notre Dame, Paris.—From Montfaucon.

the objects of worship seem to have been introduced. Gildas speaks of such images as still existing in great numbers in his time, among the unconverted Britons. They had a greater number of gods, he says, than the Egyptians themselves, there being hardly a river, lake, mountain, or wood, which had not its divinity.

As for the human sacrifices of which Cæsar speaks, his account is fully borne out by the testimonies of various other ancient authors. Strabo describes the image of wicker or straw, in which, he says, men and all descriptions of cattle and beasts were roasted together. He also relates that sometimes the victims were crucified, sometimes shot to death with arrows. The statement of Diodorus Siculus is, that criminals were kept

---

[1] Philobiblius ex Sanconiath.—*Cic. de Nat. D.* iii. 22.

under ground for five years, and then offered up as sacrifices to the gods, by being impaled, and burned in great fires along with quantities of other offerings. He adds, that they also immolated the prisoners they had taken in war, and along with them devoured, burned, or in some other manner destroyed, likewise, whatever cattle they had taken from their enemies. Plutarch tells us that the noise of songs and musical instruments was employed on these occasions to drown the cries of the sufferers.[1] Pliny is of opinion that a part of every human victim was eaten by the Druids; but what reason he had for thinking so does not appear, nor does the supposition seem to be probable in itself. Upon the subject of the practice of human sacrifice, it has been observed, that "if we rightly consider this point we shall perceive that, shocking as it is, it is yet a step towards the humanizing of savages; for the mere brute man listens only to his ferocious passions and horrid appetites, and slays and devours all the enemies he can conquer; but the priest, persuading him to select only the best and bravest as sacrifices to his protecting deity, thereby, in fact, preserves numberless lives, and puts an end to the cannibalism which has justly been looked upon as the last degradation of human nature."[2]

The origin of Druidism, and its connection with other ancient creeds of religion and philosophy, have given occasion to much curious speculation. Diogenes Laertius describes the Druids as holding the same place among the Gauls and Britons with that of the Philosophers among the Greeks, of the Magi among the Persians, of the Gymnosophists among the Indians, and of the Chaldeans among the Assyrians. He also refers to Aristotle as affirming, in one of his lost works, that philosophy had not been taught to the Gauls by the Greeks, but had originated among the former, and, from them, had passed to the latter. The introduction into the Greek philosophy of the doctrine of the Metempsychosis is commonly attributed to Pythagoras; and there are various passages in ancient authors which make mention of, or allude to some connection between that philosopher and the Druids. Abaris, the Hyperborean, is by many supposed to have been a Druid; and he, Iamblicus tells us, was taught by Pythagoras to find out all truth by the science of numbers.[3] Marcellinus, speaking of the conventual associations of the Druids, expresses himself as if he conceived that they so lived in obedience to the commands of Pythagoras; "as the authority of Pythagoras hath decreed," are his words.[4] Others affirm that the Grecian philosopher derived his philosophy from the Druids. A report is preserved, by Clement of Alexandria, that Pythagoras, in the course of his travels, studied under both the Druids and the Brahmins.[5] The probability is that both Pythagoras and the Druids drew their philosophy from the same fountain.

Several of the ablest and most laborious among the modern investigators of the subject of Druidism have found themselves compelled to adopt the theory of its Oriental origin. Pelloutier, from the numerous and strong resemblances presented by the Druidical and the old Persian religion, concludes the Celts and Persians, as Mr. O'Brien has lately done, to be the same people, and the Celtic tongue to be the ancient Persic.[6] The late Mr. Reuben Burrow, distinguished for his intimate acquaintance with the Indian astronomy and mythology, in a paper in the *Asiatic Researches*, decidedly pronounces the Druids to have been a race of emigrated Indian philosophers, and Stonehenge to be evidently one of the temples of Buddha.[7] Some of

MALABAR TOLMEN.[8]—From Higgins' Celtic Druids.

the Welsh antiquaries have, on other grounds, brought their assumed British ancestors from Ceylon, the great seat of Buddhism. This question has been examined at great length in a *Dissertation on the Origin of the Druids*, by Mr. Maurice, who, considering the Buddhists to have

---

[1] *De Superstitione.*   [2] Introd. to History, *Ency. Metrop.* p. 63.
[3] *Vita Pythag.* c. xix.   [4] *Ammian. Marcell.* xv. 9.   [5] *Strom.* i. 35.
[6] *Histoire des Celtes*, p. 19. See also Borlase's *Antiquities of Cornwall*, ch. xxii.: "Of the Great Resemblance betwixt the Druid and Persian Superstition, and the Cause of it inquired into."
[7] *Asiatic Researches*, ii. 488.
[8] The similarity of remains found in parts of India, Persia, Palestine, &c., to those of Druidical character still existing in this country, tends strongly to confirm the hypothesis of the Eastern origin of Druidism. The above representation of a tolmen in Malabar is taken by Higgins from Sir R. Colt Hoare, who has omitted to state his authority, but the author of the *Celtic Druids* quotes it, remarking that from Sir Richard's care and acumen, he is persuaded that it is given upon sufficient grounds.

been a set of the Brahmins, comes to the conclusion that "the celebrated order of the Druids, anciently established in this country, were the immediate descendants of a tribe of Brahmins situated in the high northern latitudes bordering on the vast range of Caucasus; that these, during a period of the Indian empire, when its limits were most extended in Asia, mingling with the Celto-Scythian tribes who tenanted the immense deserts of Grand Tartary, became gradually incorporated, though not confounded with that ancient nation; introduced among them the rites of the Brahmin religion, occasionally adopting those of the Scythians; and, together with them, finally emigrated to the western regions of Europe."[1]

It must be confessed that the Druidical system, as established in Gaul and Britain, has altogether very much the appearance of something not the growth of the country, but superinduced upon the native barbarism by importation from abroad. The knowledge and arts of which they appear to have been possessed, seem to point out the Druids as of foreign extraction, and as continuing to form the depositories of a civilization greatly superior to that of the general community in the midst of which they dwelt. It was quite natural, however, that Druidism, supposing it to have been originally an imported and foreign religion, should nevertheless gradually adopt some things from the idolatry of a different form which may have prevailed in Britain and Gaul previous to its introduction; just as we find Christianity itself to have become adulterated in some countries by an infusion of the heathenism with which it was brought into contact.

The Germans, Cæsar expressly tells us, had no Druids; nor is there a vestige of such an institution to be discovered in the ancient history, traditions, customs, or monuments of any Gothic people. It was probably, indeed, confined to Ireland, South Britain, and Gaul, until the measures taken to root it out from the Roman dominions compelled some of the Druids to take refuge in other countries. The Emperor Tiberius, according to Pliny and Strabo, and the Emperor Claudius, according to Suetonius, issued decrees for the total abolition of the Druidical religion, on the pretext of an abhorrence of the atrocity of the human sacrifices in which it indulged its votaries. The true motive may be suspected to have been a jealousy of the influence, among the provincials of Gaul and Britain, of a native order of priesthood so powerful as that of the Druids. Suetonius, indeed, states that the practice of the Druidical religion had been already interdicted to Roman citizens by Augustus. We have seen, in the course of the preceding narrative, how it was extirpated from its chief seat in the south of Britain by Suetonius Paulinus. Such of the Druids as survived this attack are supposed to have fled to the Isle of Man, which then became, in place of Anglesey, the head-quarters of British Druidism. It was probably after this that the Druidical religion penetrated to the northern parts of the island. The vestiges, at all events, of its establishment at some period in Scotland, are spread over many parts of that country, and it has left its impression in various still surviving popular customs and superstitions. The number and variety of the Druid remains in North Britain, according to a late learned writer, are almost endless. The principal seat of Scottish Druidism is thought to have been the parish of Kirkmichael, in the recesses of Perthshire, near the great mountainous range of the Grampians.[2]

Druidism long survived, though in obscurity and decay, the thunder of the imperial edicts. In Ireland, indeed, where the Roman arms had not penetrated, it continued to flourish down nearly to the middle of the fifth century, when it fell before the Christian enthusiasm and energy of St. Patrick. But even in Britain, the practice of the Druidical worship appears to have subsisted among the people long after the Druids, as an order of priesthood, were extinct. The annals of the sixth, seventh, and even of the eighth century, contain numerous edicts of emperors, and canons of councils, against the worship of the sun, the moon, mountains, rivers, lakes, and trees.[3] There is even a law to the same effect of the English king Canute, in the eleventh century. Nor, as we have already more than once had occasion to remark, have some of the practices of the old superstition yet altogether ceased to be remembered in our popular sports, pastimes, and anniversary usages. The ceremonies of All-Hallowmass, the bonfires of May Day and Midsummer Eve, the virtues attributed to the mistletoe, and various other customs of the villages and country parts of England, Scotland, and Ireland, still speak to us of the days of Druidism, and evince that the impression of its grim ritual has not been wholly obliterated from the popular imagination, by the lapse of nearly twenty centuries.

On the settlement of the Romans in Britain, the established religion of the province of course became the same classic superstition which these conquerors of the world still maintained in all its ancient honours and pre-eminence in their native Italy, which was diffused alike through all the customs of their private life and the whole system of their state-economy, and which they

---

[1] *Indian Antiquities*, vol. vi. part i. p. 18. [2] *Chalmers*, i. pp. 69-78. [3] Pelloutier, *Hist. des Celtes*, iii. 4.

carried with them, almost as a part of themselves, or at least as the very living spirit and sustaining power of their entire policy and civilization, into every foreign land that they colonized. In this far island, too, as in the elder homes of poetry and the arts,

"An age hath been when earth was proud
Of lustre too intense
To be sustained; and mortals bowed
The front in self-defence."

Beside the rude grandeur of Stonehenge, and surrounded by the gloom of the sacred groves, glittering temples, displaying all the grace and pomp of finished architecture, now rose to Jupiter, and Apollo, and Diana, and Venus; and the air of our northern clime

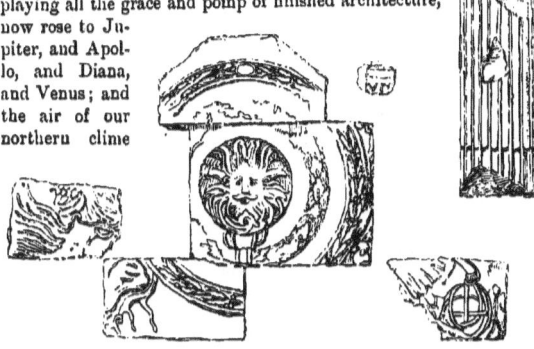

REMAINS OF TEMPLE OF MINERVA, discovered at Bath in 1755, now in Bath Museum.

was peopled with all the bright dreams and visions of the mythology of Greece. A temple of Minerva, and probably other sacred edifices, appear to have adorned the city of Bath; London is supposed to have had its temple of Diana, occupying the same natural elevation which is now crowned by the magnificent cathedral of St. Paul's; and the foundations and other remains of similar monuments of the Roman paganism have been discovered in many of our other ancient towns. But perhaps no such material memorials are so well fitted to strike the imagination, and to convey a lively impression of this long past state of things, as the passage in the *Annals* of Tacitus, in which we find a string of prodigies recounted to have happened in different parts of the province of Britain, immediately before the insurrection of Boadicea, just as the same events might have taken place in Italy, or in Rome itself. First, in the town of Camalodunum, the image of the goddess Victory, without any apparent cause, suddenly falls from its place, and turns its face round, as if giving way to the enemy. Then females, seized with a sort of prophetic fury, would be heard mournfully calling out that destruction was at hand, their cries penetrating from the streets both into the *curia* or council-chamber, and into the theatre. A representation, in the air, of the colony laid in ruins, was seen near the mouth of the Thames, while the sea assumed the colour of blood, and the receding tide seemed to leave behind it the phantoms of human carcasses. The picture is completed by the mention of the temple, in which the Roman soldiery took refuge on the rushing into the city of their infuriated assailants—of the undefended state of the place, in which the elegance of the buildings had been more attended to than their strength—of another temple which had been raised in it to Claudius the Divine—and, finally, of its crew of rapacious priests, who, under the pretence of religion, wasted every man's substance, and excited a deeper indignation in the breasts of the unhappy natives than all the other cruelties and oppressions to which they were subjected.

One result of the Roman invasion was the introduction into Britain of the Christian faith. But the obscurity which pervades the ecclesiastical records of the first century, and the unobtrusive silence with which the first steps of Christianity were made, involve this part of the religious history of Britain in much uncertainty. Some

RESTORATION BY SMIRKE OF PORTICO OF TEMPLE OF MINERVA at Bath.—From Lyson's Reliquiæ Romanæ.

investigators have attributed the work of founding Christianity in Britain to St. Peter, to James the son of Zebedee, to Simon Zelotes, and some to St. Paul himself. Others, again, have attributed it to such inferior personages as Aristobulus, who is incidentally mentioned by St. Paul, Joseph of Arimathea, and the disciples of Polycarp. Some of these accounts would imply that British Christianity is as old as the apostolic age; but all that can be regarded as well established is, that at a comparatively early period Christianity found its way into the British Islands. Before the close of the first century Christian refugees may have fled thither from the Continent to escape persecution, and Christian soldiers and civilians may have accompanied the invading armies. The destruction which had befallen the teachers of the old or Druidical religion, would facilitate the progress of Christianity, and the wars between the Romans and the natives allow it to go on unchecked. The monastic writers decorate their history of the first centuries of the British church with the legend of King Lucius, the son of Coilus, who, according to their account, was king of the whole island, was baptized, and became so earnest for the conversion of his people that he sent to Eleutherius, Bishop of Rome, for assistance in the important work. It is possible that, in this monkish legend, we see dimly shadowed forth some petty British king or chieftain, in vassalage to Rome, who, with the aid of Roman missionaries, effected the conversion of his tribe. In Tertullian's work against the Jews, written A.D. 209, he says that "even those places in Britain hitherto inaccessible to the Roman arms have been subdued by the gospel of Christ." This expression, however, may very possibly refer to Ireland, which was then accounted part of Britain.

During the Diocletian persecution, St. Alban, the first martyr of our Island, perished, with many others who names have not been recorded. Bede says this event took place in A.D. 286; but if it really happened in the great persecution under Diocletian, a date at least seventeen or eighteen years later must be assigned to it. In the year 314, Eborius, Bishop of York, Restitutus, Bishop of London, and Adelphius, Bishop of Richborough, attended the council at Arles; and as three bishops formed the full representation of a province, it appears that Britain was thus placed on an equality with the churches of Spain and Gaul. In the fourth century, according to Gildas, Arianism was very prevalent in our island; but, on the other hand, St. Jerome and St. Chrysostom, frequently allude, in their writings, to the orthodoxy of the British Church. In the fifth century the opinions of Pelagius were zealously disseminated by his countrymen, Agricola and Celestius; and, says Bede, the British ecclesiastics, in great alarm, and unable to refute them, implored assistance from the Bishops of Gaul. The latter sent two of their number, who arrived in Britain about the year 429, and completely silenced the Pelagians by their arguments. But the baffled Pelagians again raised their heads, and again, in 446, Germanus, Bishop of Auxerre, accompanied by Severus, Bishop of Treves, came to Britain, and this time not only silenced the Pelagians, but procured the banishment of their leaders from the island.

After the Christian church had been established, the same results were exhibited in Britain as in other countries; and while the Italian or Greek infused into the Christian faith the classical paganism of his fathers, the Briton leavened it with his ancestral Druidical superstitions.[1]

It should appear that the order of monks soon became numerous, though they were obliged for a long time to procure their subsistence by manual labour. Even the British bishops, partly through the poverty of the country, and, perhaps, still more through the partial conversion of the people —many of whom still remained attached either to the Roman paganism or to the Druidical worship—were, and long continued to be, very poor. When the successor of Constantine offered to maintain the bishops of the West from the imperial revenues, only those of Britain acceded to the proposal, while the rest rejected it. The number of churches and houses of religion seems to be only matter of conjecture; but it is pretty certain that, even at the time when the Romans abandoned the island, many parts of it had never heard of the Christian gospel.

---

[1] Southey, *Book of the Church*.

CHAPTER IV.—HISTORY OF SOCIETY.

CÆSAR'S INVASION TO THE ARRIVAL OF THE SAXONS.—B.C. 55—A.D. 449.

Derivation of the names Albion and Britain—Cæsar's account of the island—Britain peopled by two distinct races—Cæsar's account of the inhabitants—Personal appearance of the Britons—Their painted skins—Strange marriage institutions of the Britons—Their habitations—Their handicraft ingenuity—Their war-chariots, baskets, furniture, dress, ornaments—Their means and modes of subsistence—Their form of government—Disunion of the tribes, and their mutual wars—Their towns and fortifications—Roman civilization, and its effect on the Britons.

CÆSAR'S own account of the island and its inhabitants, as given in his *Commentaries*, shows that he spent but a brief period in his British invasion, and thus its results were indecisive. It was not a conquest, but a mere hostile landing; and the account which he has given us of the ancient Britons was perhaps little more than he might easily have learned from the Gaulish traders, whom he consulted before he commenced the expedition. Still, his brief notices are valuable, characterized as they are by his wonted sagacity and power of observation, and also by their forming the first introduction of the British people into the records of accredited history.

In a former chapter we had occasion to notice the names, first, of Samothea, and afterwards of Albion, by which the island was distinguished. We also adverted to the historical legends in which they are said to have originated. These sources, however, were unsatisfactory to our earliest antiquaries, who turned their inquiries to another source, and they have derived the name of Albion from *alb* or *albus*, signifying *white*, which is supposed to have been given to the island from the whiteness of its cliffs, as seen from the opposite coast of Gaul. That of BRITAIN, by which name the island was first known to the Romans, is still more doubtful in its origin; so that, while some of our antiquaries, at the head of whom is Camden, have derived it from *brit* or *brith* ("painted"), in allusion to the blue painted skins of the natives, others, with Carte, suppose it a corruption of a British word, *prydhain*, but of the true meaning of which they are uncertain.

From this unprofitable investigation about names, we gladly turn to the account of the island itself, as given by Julius Cæsar. "The inland part of Britain," he says in his *Commentaries*, "is inhabited by those who, according to the existing tradition, were the aborigines of the island; the sea-coast by those who, for the sake of plunder, or to make war, had crossed over from among the Belgæ, and who, in nearly every case, retain the names of their native states, from which they emigrated to this island, wherein they made war, and settled, and began to cultivate the ground." Taking this statement in connection with the whole tenor of antiquarian discovery among the earliest ages of Britain, we find that its first inhabitants were Celts, children of that large Asiatic family who emigrated during the primitive ages into Europe, and afterwards, under the names of Gauls and Cimbri, carried such terror into Italy and Greece, and secured so many fair European settlements, among which Britain was not the least important. In process of time, however, according to Cæsar's intimation, they had formidable rivals in the Belgæ, a Gothic race, located in Gaul, and renowned for their superior valour and activity, who, crossing the narrow sea, obtained possession of the south-eastern coast of Britain, and drove its Celtic population into the interior. In this way two distinct races, and one considerably superior to the other, as well as later in its arrival, are recognized as occupying the island at the commencement of the Roman invasion. Some additional information upon this important head might have thrown much light upon our primitive history, and explained those perplexing anomalies of civilization, combined with barbarism, which the ancient relics of our island present to the study of the antiquary. But Cæsar, although the most observant and intellectual of conquerors, was not the conqueror of Britain, and his hostile advance into it never appears to have exceeded eighty miles, commencing at the east coast of Kent and terminating at the capital of Cassivellaunus, supposed to have been afterwards the ancient town of Verulam, in Hertfordshire. The tribes dignified with the name of nations, with whom he successively came in contact in his hasty inroad, were the people of Cantium, the Trinobantes, the Cenimagni, the Segontiaci, the Aucalites, the Bibroci, and the Cassi—clans sufficiently numerous within so short a compass, and probably living in the old Celtic fashion, either of isolation or downright hostility; but the different localities they occupied is now a matter of mere conjecture. It is worthy of remark, also, that he has not mentioned the name of a single British town in the whole course of his expedition.

From this very limited account of the island, we pass to that which he has given of the inhabitants; and here his brevity is sufficiently characteristic of his limited knowledge of the subject. "The population," he says, "is very great, and the buildings very numerous, closely resembling those of the Gauls: the quantity of cattle is considerable. For money they use copper, or rings of iron of a certain weight. Tin is produced there in the midland districts, and iron near the seacoast; but the quantity of this is small. The copper which they use is imported. There is timber of every kind that is found in Gaul, except beech and fir. They reckon it unlawful to eat the hare, the hen, and the goose. These animals, however, they breed for amusement. The country has a more temperate climate than Gaul, the cold being less intense." After several geographical statements, which are irrelevant to our purpose, Cæsar thus continues his account of the Britons:—"Of all the natives, those who inhabit Kent (*Cantium*)—a district the whole of which is near the coast—are by far the most civilized, and do not differ greatly in their customs from the Gauls. The inland people for the most part do not sow corn, but subsist on milk and flesh, and have clothing of skins. All the Britons, however, stain themselves with woad, which makes them of a blue tinge, and gives them a more formidable appearance in battle. They also wear their hair long, and shave every part of the body except the head and the upper lip. Every ten or twelve of them have their wives in common, especially brothers with brothers, and parents with children; but if any children are born, they are accounted the children of those by whom each virgin was first espoused."

Such is the brief account of Julius Cæsar concerning that strange people, of whom his own countrymen appear to have but vaguely heard, until he landed an army in the island, and overran part of it in two campaigns. So little interest, however, did the Romans feel about Britain, or so difficult had a conquest of it been reckoned, that an interval of nearly a century followed before another invasion was attempted. The superior opportunities for information which were then acquired by his successors, not only sufficed to give a general confirmation of his statements, but also materially to enlarge their amount.

The first circumstance that arrests our attention in these notices of the ancient Britons, is their personal appearance. The physical qualifications of those rude warriors, who fought with the greatest of Roman conquerors, and who, of all his enemies, reduced him to the honours of a doubtful victory, could have been of no ordinary character. The strength and courage of these half-naked, scantily armed, mustachioed warriors, were well-attested by the stout resistance they offered to the Roman legions. Their large correspondent stature is mentioned by Strabo, who tells us he had seen some British youths at Rome half a foot taller than the Gauls, who in turn were superior in height to the Romans. This writer adds, that they were not gracefully and strongly formed in proportion to their great stature, and that they did not stand very firmly upon their legs; but it must be remembered that these juvenile specimens were perhaps longer in attaining to full maturity than persons of a smaller size and warmer climate. As for their painted skins, with which the Britons endeavoured to dismay their enemies, the idea prevailed among the Romans of Cæsar's day, that this was nothing more than a mere painting or staining with the juice of woad—something, indeed, like the war-painting of the Red Indians when they prepare for fight or festival. But instead of this mere surface-colouring, which may be washed off at pleasure, we learn from several ancient Roman writers that it was a permanent tattooing, like that of the South Sea Islanders, which, once impressed, could never be eradicated. The process, they inform us, was effected in early youth, by puncturing the skin with a sharp-pointed instrument, and squeezing out the juice of certain herbs upon the punctures, which were made to represent the forms of animals, and that these pictures, which assumed a blue colour, grew with the growth of the body, and descended with it to the grave. When the first steps of Roman civilization introduced a more abundant clothing, this rude fashion soon disappeared in South Britain, and was retained only in the still unconquered north, where it continued to form almost the only kind of dress and ornament, and whose inhabitants were therefore called *Picti* (or painted men) by their Romanized brethren of South Britain. In

Woad Plant, *Isatis tinctoria.*

this simple way we can easily account for the sudden disappearance of the Caledonians in history, which has so sorely puzzled our antiquaries: instead of being utterly exterminated, as has sometimes been supposed, they only reappear under the nickname of Picts. It is worth noticing, by the way, that in their practice of tattooing, and their adherence to the pastoral life, the ancient Britons closely resembled two classes of the most hopeful and energetic of our modern savages. These, it will at once be seen, are the inhabitants of the South Sea Islands and the Caffres of South Africa.

But what shall we say of that strange form of the marriage institution which Cæsar declares to have prevailed among the Britons? It appears so gross and revolting, and so opposed to that exclusive possession which forms the great principle of marriage, that modern writers have discarded the fact, by declaring such a state of society impossible. Polygamy, indeed, has prevailed almost since the world commenced, but in every case it has consisted of a plurality of wives, and not of husbands. Man, and not woman has always been the legislator, and he took care to frame the indulgence for his own special benefit. Besides, could such a strong, healthy, and numerous race as the ancient Britons have been the produce of such promiscuous intercourse? It is also alleged that Cæsar, whose testimony is quoted as the authority for such a revolting fact, was but a short time in the island, and saw little of the natives, except in actual conflict. He may have seen them, indeed, dwelling by whole families under one roof, from the want of more abundant accommodation, and thus have hastily come to the conclusion that they also lived in common sexual intercourse. But to this it may be answered, on the other hand, that no such mistake was made about the ancient Germans, who also lived by whole families in a single habitation. Cæsar, too, is not the only authority for the statement, for it was repeated by Dio Cassius and St. Jerome, when Britain was fully known to the world at large. Unpalatable, therefore, though it be, it descends to us with all the stubbornness of an historical fact. And that the ideas of the Britons upon the subject of marriage in general differed from those of other nations, is attested by the old Roman writer, Solinus, when he describes the government of the western islands of Caledonia, afterwards called the Hebrides. Speaking of the sovereign, he states, "This prince is not even allowed to have a wife of his own; but he has free access to the wives of all his subjects, that, having no children which he knows to be his own, he may not be prompted to encroach on the privileges of his subjects, in order to aggrandize his family." Strange, also, though these British marriages were, they scarcely exceeded in guilt or extravagance the marriage institutions which prevail among the Nairs of India. Perhaps the Asiatic origin of the Celtic race who finally settled in Britain, and the strange expedients of the earliest Eastern nations to make marital jealousy a feeling not worth entertaining, might account in some measure for these matrimonial usages of the Britons, and show that they were not wholly improbable. At all events, we may hope that, like the permission given to polygamy, they were only confined to the higher classes, and not participated by the people at large; and this, too, long before the entrance of Christianity into the island, when they utterly disappeared.

We have seen, in a former chapter, what kind of houses the Britons occupied on the arrival of Julius Cæsar. On that part of the sea-coast opposite Gaul, where intercourse with strangers had effected a higher civilization, the houses were like those of the Gauls, being poles set up in a circle, forming a sharp point at the top, with the interstices filled up with wattled work, and having neither window nor chimney; but far inferior to these were the common dwellings of the interior, which were little better than the holes of foxes. As for the ancient British towns, according to Cæsar they were nothing else than a cluster of these huts planted in the heart of a forest, guarded by a rampart of felled trees, and sometimes also by a *dun*, or fortress, composed of loose blocks of granite. As safety and the means of absolute subsistence were of more account at such a period than even domestic comfort, the principal British constructions of those days were the strongholds of princes, while those of the common people might be worn out in a year. Little better than this were the Border houses in Scotland, even so late as the fourteenth century.

In their handicraft operations these islanders showed considerable ingenuity. This was especially manifested in the construction of their *essedæ* or war-chariots, which must not only have been strong and well-poised, to encounter the rough fields over which they were driven at full speed, but also to have tasked much skill in the fabrication of the scythes with which they were armed, and the harness with which the horses were yoked. These chariots, indeed, the Britons appear to have derived from their remote Eastern ancestry, and such vehicles for the purposes of warfare occur in the earliest records of Sacred History, as well as in the poems of Homer. Even at a late period they were also occasionally used by the nations of Asia against the armies of the Roman republic, and were continued by the Britons the last of all, until they learned to imitate the military arts of their conquerors. The same ingenuity, indeed, might have constructed war-canoes equal to those of the New Zealanders, and made the Britons an adventurous maritime people; but, as we have already stated, they had that aversion for the sea which has characterized the whole Celtic race. Next to their war-chariots, the skill of the Britons was exerted in the various operations of basket-work, from the walls of a house and the sides of a coracle, down to the lightest utensil for household purposes. It was the same kind of ingenuity as that of the Caffres of South Africa, who form elegant vessels of grass, so closely plaited together as to hold milk and other liquids. The baskets of the Britons were so highly admired at Rome, that the Latin word *bascauda* is supposed to have been of British origin. From the earliest coins we also find that the houses of the Britons were furnished with stools, like the modern crickets; while the contents of the barrows attest that, even before the entrance of the Romans, they made various kinds of pottery, such as drinking cups, jars, and cinerary urns. In the article of clothing, although the Britons of the interior wore nothing but the skins of animals at the arrival of Julius Cæsar, yet it is certain that the inhabitants of the coast opposite Gaul, in consequence of their higher civilization, and intercourse with foreign traders, were better provided. Even before this period, it is evident that the checkered cloth and *braccæ* of the Gauls had found their way into the island, and been adopted by the wealthier inhabitants. With regard to personal

Torques, with manner of wearing it, from the sculptures on the monument of Vigna Amendola.

ornaments, the principal one worn by the Britons was the torques, a chain composed of flexible bars twisted into the form of a rope, and clasped behind by a hook. In its highest state of improvement, it was composed of links elaborately carved and ornamented. These were badges of distinction for kings and chieftains, and, as such, were made of silver, and sometimes even of gold; but, in the absence of these metals, they were usually of bronze or iron. The Britons, also, as well as the Gauls, wore a ring on the middle finger. The ornaments of the females were still more numerous, as is attested by the remains found in bell-shaped barrows, which appear to have been chiefly the burial-places of women. These ornaments consist of beads of granite, flint, and pebble; amber and bead necklaces; bronze pins, some of them with bone and ivory handles; and bracelets of ivory.[1] All this, however, was poor and rude enough, even at the best, and its nakedness must have been keenly felt when brought in contact with the wealth, grandeur, and taste of the Roman conquerors. It was natural, therefore, that Caractacus should have burst into the exclamation, while he was led a prisoner through the stately streets of Rome: "Alas! that those who inhabit such palaces should envy me a hut in Britain!"

The inhabitants of the island being so dependent upon their own native produce, subsisted upon the resources of agriculture, rearing of tame animals, and the chase, each pursuit being prosecuted according to the facilities of the particular district, or the advanced condition of the tribe that occupied it. In this way the inhabitants of the southern coast, and especially those of Cantium or Kent, were, like their brethren the Belgæ, addicted to agriculture; while the more inland tribes were chiefly shepherds, who were unacquainted with tillage, and lived upon the produce of their flocks and herds—or hunters, with whom the pursuit of game and wild beasts was more a necessity than an amusement. It is strange that to these three occupations fishing cannot be added, considering the plentiful supplies of food with which the rivers and coasts abounded; but Xiphilinus informs us that none of the Britons ever tasted fish. Whether this abstinence arose from a religious prejudice, or from the general Celtic aversion to the sea, it is impossible to determine. We learn from Pliny, that in agriculture the people of the south coast manured the soil, not only with the usual appliances, but with marl, a practice confined to themselves and their neighbours the Gauls alone. He informs us, also, that of this marl, one kind, which was white and chalky, was so effectual for the purpose, that ground once manured with it would retain its productive qualities for eighty years, so that no man using this to a field needed to apply it twice during his lifetime. In the pastoral life each proprietor had the boundary of his land marked by a large upright stone, within which he confined his range; but the knowledge of his occupation was so limited, that the milk of his cattle was only useful for daily subsistence; for, according to Strabo, the Britons were unacquainted with the making of cheese. In the hunter's life the sacrilege of eating hares must have often been felt as a severe game-law, even though religion had enforced the prohibition. Such, also, may have

---

[1] See illustrations in vol. i. pp. 11, 12.

been the case with the shepherd or the husbandman in his abstinence from the hen and the goose.

While such were the limited means of subsistence possessed by the inhabitants of the southern part of the island, it was still worse with those of the northern division. The tribes of the north, whom the earliest Roman historians comprised under the two classes of Mæatæ, or inhabitants of the lowlands, and Caledonians, or those of the great forest and highlands, because they resisted to the last the degradation of Roman conquest, were longest deprived of the advantages of Roman civilization. We find them, therefore, so late as the invasion of Severus, in the same condition as the southern Britons had been at the time of Cæsar's arrival—or even lower in the scale—in consequence of the greater sterility of the soil, that offered fewer temptations to the civilizing exertions of husbandry. We are informed that they had neither walls nor towns, but were a pastoral people, living in tents; and that they subsisted on milk and wild fruits, and such animals as they caught in hunting. But to a people so imperfectly armed, their chief articles of game, which must have been the deer, the wild bull, and the boar, were not always attainable; and Xiphilinus, as we have already stated, informs us that the chief resource of these northern hunters in such a strait was to swallow a certain drug, about the size of a bean, by which their spirits were exhilarated, and the cravings of hunger deadened. When milk and wild fruits failed, we are also told by the same writer, that those who dwelt in the woods had recourse to roots and leaves. Even worse modes of subsistence appear to have been adopted in cases of desperate famine; for, on the testimony of St. Jerome, they are charged with actual cannibalism. He declares that in his youth, when he was in Gaul, he saw people of the Attacotti, one of the northern tribes, devouring human flesh; and he even specifies those particular parts of the body which these man-devourers held in highest account. All this would be incredible, did we not know that the same practice even yet prevails among the islands of the South Seas, and in a part of Sumatra, where the people are at least as civilized as the rudest tribes of the Britons of the north, while they had not their plea of urgent necessity.

§ Although little has been told us by the Roman writers of the form of government which was established in Britain, yet, from the fact of the people belonging to the Celtic race, we can easily conclude that it was the same patriarchal institution to which the Celts have invariably adhered, whatever might be the country in which they obtained a settlement. Politically, the Britons did not constitute a collective nation, but a congeries of tribes, each ruled by its own independent head. On this account, if the Belgæ of the southern coast had been a united people, they might have anticipated the Saxon conquest, and obtained a complete predominance over the whole island. But, from Cæsar's account, it appears that these colonists still retained the names of the different peoples from whom they had sprung; and in all likelihood, therefore, were as much divided among themselves as were the rude tribes whom they dispossessed. Ptolemy, in his classification of the Britons, gives us not less than seventeen tribes for the south, and eighteen for the north part of the island, making thirty-five in all!—a comparatively easy conquest for Agricola, and afterwards for the successors of Hengist and Horsa. One wonders, indeed, that, from the difficulty of bringing so many independent and rival sovereigns together, they could in any case be united for a common resistance; but a common danger, which brings animals the most hostile to each other within a peaceful ring until the danger is over-past, could combine several, or even the whole of the tribes against a dangerous foreign invasion, as was evinced in the one case by the army of Caractacus, and in the other by that of Cassivellaunus. But these unions were of such uncertain continuity that, when the tide of fortune turned, the one leader was betrayed and the other deserted. Of the amount of regal authority which these kings possessed over their subjects, and the specific manner in which it was exercised, the Roman historians have not informed us; all we can learn of this subject is, that the nobles or inferior chiefs had a controlling voice in every public movement; and that the authority of the Druids, when they were pleased to interpose it, was superior even to that of the sovereigns. They were the sacred Brahmins of Britain—the race who were sprung from the highest and holiest portion of that divine body, out of which all the other classes of society proceeded—and who, therefore, by virtue of their superior descent, could claim a paramount authority over both king and soldier. Here was a check upon the otherwise unlimited and irresponsible power of a Celtic chief, which was common to Britain alone—making the conclusion obvious, that the Druids had not originally been Celts, but strangers of a higher and more civilized race, who had assumed the pre-eminence which knowledge unscrupulously exercised will always obtain over barbarism and ignorance. Of this Druidical supremacy, even in political matters, we are assured by Dio Chrysostom, who informs us that even a royal edict could not be carried into effect without the sanction of the Druids; and that the kings were nothing more than the servants and instruments of the priesthood.

Such a divided state of society as thus existed in Britain, at once suggests the idea of incessant strife and contention. Each tribe was a nation in itself; every king had a rival in his neighbour; and where none of those obstacles interposed which keep hostile kingdoms apart, the wars of the Britons among each other must have been both rancorous and incessant. A boundary line, a pasture field, even a personal or family pique, would be enough, in the first instance, to set two tribes at variance, and afterwards to involve others in the contest. That such a state of internal warfare was common among the Britons, we may learn from the immense earthen ramparts that can still be traced in the island, of which that of Wansdyke is a specimen. As they seem to have extended for several miles, they were probably thrown up for the defence of a whole tribe against their neighbours—a sort of Chinese wall on a limited scale. The same state of insecurity is indicated by the remains of broad and deep covered ways, strongly embanked on either side, which served as lines of communication from one forest-town to another. Of these, the specimens that exist in Wiltshire attest not only the vast labour with which they were constructed, but the military skill and experience that had planned them. In warfare, indeed, the Britons showed that they were no tyros, by their resistance to Cæsar and his legions. This was evidently their chief department of knowledge, even as their war-chariots were the most ingenious of their fabrications. Strange, indeed, must have been the contrast between the miserable clusters of hovels in the heart of a wood, which constituted a British town —if we are to put faith in Roman authorities,— and the array of armed warriors, and prancing steeds, and rattling chariots, that poured from it through the long, broad, covered way, to attack some rival town! And where were the Druids the while, to prevent such terrible collisions? Being men of like passions with their worshippers, perhaps they sympathized in the feud. Or perhaps they were cautious of interposing against such outbursts, from the fear that their own ascendency might be swept away in the popular storm.

Such were the Britons at the period of the Roman invasion. The sketch is not only narrow, but imperfect, owing to the very scanty information on the subject which the Roman writers have bequeathed to us. A new school of British antiquarianism has also lately risen to assert that this scantiness is not the grentest defect in their statements—that they have been partial and one-sided, as well as careless and brief, in their accounts of Britain and its inhabitants. While they saw and announced the barbarism of the people, why were they so silent about those Cyclopean erections with which the island abounded, and those relics of a higher civilization which the graves still continue to yield up? It has been thought, from these most substantial evidences of an early civilization, that the Britons were not such utter savages as they have been represented; and that they must have had science, and skill, and long-descended experience among them, as well as brute force, and the labour of countless hands. It has been alleged, also, that with the Druids for their schoolmasters, they must have learned a more comfortable style of life, and attained a higher style of intellectual culture, than have been attributed to them in Cæsar's *Commentaries*. It is unfortunate that these Druids have passed away and left no historians to record their deeds, except those who were their enemies and destroyers. If either the records of the past of our island can be more clearly deciphered, or the buried treasures of its antiquarianism more plentifully exhumed, it may be that we shall have a more favourable account of the Britons than can be found in Roman history. We may then also learn from what race and country the Druids came, at what time they arrived in Britain, what were their real qualifications and character; and whether such wattled, mud-built hovels as the Romans found at their arrival, had always stood in full neighbourhood with the stately erections of Stonehenge and Avebury.

Although the stay of Cæsar in Britain was so brief, and his two campaigns so indecisive of results, compared with his usual career of conquest, his visit was not without important consequences. It opened the island more completely to the knowledge of the world, and was attended with not only more frequent arrivals from Gaul, but even visits from Rome itself. The effect of such intercourse was that, even in the time of Augustus, the arts, the manners, and religion of Rome had obtained an entrance into the island. This we are told by Strabo, who also informs us of the increase of traffic that had already taken place in Britain; and while he mentions gold, silver, and iron, corn, dogs, cattle, and skins as its exports, the imports were ivory, bridles, gold chains, cups of amber, drinking glasses, and other similar articles. Then, too, the ring money of bronze and iron gave place to a regular coinage of the valuable metals, better fitted for foreign circulation; and of these, the mintage of Cunobelinus, usually stamped with a human effigy on the one side and an animal or emblematic device on the other, gives ample indications of the commercial improvement that had taken place during the century which followed the invasion of Julius Cæsar. But that of Claudius succeeded, when the island was conquered and occupied as well as invaded, and when not only the style of British life and character, but the whole aspect of the country, were to assume a new physiognomy.

These changes, introduced by the establishment of the Roman dominion, need only to be hastily glanced at, being of the same kind with those they impressed upon every conquered country, and the ineffaceable tokens of which are still distinctly marked over the whole map of Europe. The land of many tribes was reduced into a single province; and although native kings in some cases were allowed to retain their titles, it was only in subservience to the paramount rule of the Roman governor. Municipia or free towns were established, with the privileges of Roman citizenship; highways were constructed, that linked the scattered districts into a single country; and while Roman laws, courts of justice, temples, and academies took the place of Celtic legislation and Druidical training, the rich natural resources of the country—its lead, copper, and tin—its fertilizing marl and valuable chalk—its pearls, and even its oysters—its spirited horses, and fleet, stanch, hunting-dogs—all were brought to their full perfection, introduced into the markets of Rome and the Continent, and converted into plentiful sources of commercial wealth, as well as motives to increased British immigration. It is in this way, perhaps, that we are to account for the discrepancies between the statements of Cæsar respecting the temporary forest villages of the Britons, and the numerous towns by which they were superseded in the days of Tacitus, 130 years afterwards. The energy and rapidity of Roman civilization, especially among a rude people, generally corresponded with the previous work of conquest. It was then also that the youths of Britain awoke as to a new life, and learned to despise the rude habits of their fathers: Roman dresses and ornaments were speedily adopted in lieu of sheep-skins or Gaulish tartan; and while they attended the courts and theatres of the conquerors, they did their best to imitate—and even to ape when they could not imitate—the fashions of Rome itself, and the refinements that had newly issued from the imperial palace. Such we could easily imagine to have been the case, without turning for confirmation to the turgid and lugubrious pages of Gildas, in which he describes the change, and bewails the vices that had followed it.

It happened, unfortunately for the Britons, in this great transformation from their primitive state to the high artificial style of their conquerors, that the progress was not a gradual one. Had it been so, it would have laid a firmer hold upon the native character, and produced more vital results. We might then have had British orators, poets, and historians of these early ages, whose works would have been worth reading, as well as warriors and statesmen, whom history would have been proud to commemorate. But the change was effected so rapidly, that it seemed little else than an external show; it was a gay, superficial varnishing, rather than an internal and thorough permeation; a few years would have dimmed it, and a single storm effaced it for ever. For only three centuries this gay show continued; and what a brief period for a national history!—and when the Roman fell, the Briton could stand no longer. A woeful picture of this helplessness was presented in the inability of the Britons to defend themselves from such enemies as the Scots and Picts, and their calling in the Saxons to their aid. It was, indeed, full time that a new people should enter upon the scene—that fresh elements should be introduced for the construction of a new national character!

BOOK II.

PERIOD FROM THE ARRIVAL OF THE SAXONS TO THE ARRIVAL OF THE NORMANS.—617 YEARS.

FROM A.D. 449—1066.

CHAPTER I.—CIVIL AND MILITARY HISTORY.

THE ARRIVAL OF THE SAXONS TO THE UNION OF THE HEPTARCHY.——A.D. 449—825.

Origin of the Saxons—Their early history—Their arrival in Britain—Progress of their conquest of England—Fabulous history of King Arthur—The Heptarchy—The office of Bretwalda—Reigns of the successive Bretwaldas—Introduction of Christianity among the Anglo-Saxons—Wars of the Heptarchy--Reign of Offa—Of Egbert—England reduced into one kingdom.

SOME etymologists have derived the word Saxon from the term *Seax*, a short sword, with which the warlike natives of the shores of the Baltic, the Elbe, the Weser, and the Rhine, are supposed, but on somewhat doubtful authority, to have been generally armed. It is much more probable, however, that the Saxons are the Sakai-Suna, or descendants of the Sakai, or Sacæ, a tribe of Scythians, who are mentioned by ancient writers as making their way towards Europe from the East so early as in the age of Cyrus. Pliny tells of a branch of the Sacæ who called themselves Sacassani; and Ptolemy designates another branch by the name Saxones, which seems to be merely another form of the same word. But whatever was the etymology of the name, it was certainly, at the time of the British invasion, applied, in a very general sense, to tribes or nations who were separate, and differing in some essentials, though they had most probably all sprung from the same stock at no very distant period, and still preserved the same physical features, the same manners and customs, and nearly, though not quite, the same unaltered language which, at the distance of fourteen centuries, is the basis and staple of the idiom we speak. They were all of the pure Teutonic or Gothic race, and all their kings claimed their descent from Woden, or Odin, an ancient sovereign, magnified by veneration and superstition into a god, the traces of whose capital (real or traditional) are still shown to the traveller at Sigtuna, on the borders of the great Mälar Lake, between the old city of Upsala and Stockholm, the present capital of Sweden. Other tribes that issued both before and after the fifth century from that fruitful storehouse of nations, Scandinavia, were of the same Teutonic origin; and the Franks, the Danes, the Norwegians, the Norse or Northmen, and the most distinguished of the last-mentioned, those known throughout Europe under the name of Normans, were all of the same race, and commenced their career from the same regions, though differing subsequently, owing to the time and circumstances of their disseverance from the great northern stock, the direction in which their migrations and conquests had lain, and the character physical and moral, the habits, and the language of the people they had conquered, or among whom they had settled and been mixed.[1] It would neither be a profitable nor a very easy task to trace all these kindred streams to their primitive fountainhead, by the shores of the Caspian, in Asia, and

---

[1] "For successive generations the tribes, or even portions of tribes, may have moved from place to place, as the necessities of their circumstances demanded; names may have appeared, and vanished altogether from the scene; wars, seditions, conquests, the rise and fall of states, the solemn formation or dissolution of confederacies, may have filled the ages that intervened between the first settlement of the Teutons in Germany, and their appearance in history as dangerous to the quiet of Rome. The heroic lays may possibly preserve some shadowy traces of these events; but of all the changes in detail we know nothing: we argue only that nations, possessing in so pre-eminent a degree as the Germans the principles, the arts, and institutions of civilization, must have passed through a long apprenticeship of action and suffering, and have learned in the rough school of practice the wisdom they embodied in their lives."—Kemble's *Saxons in England*, vol. i. p. 4.

thence follow them back again to the coasts, promontories, and islands of the Baltic and the Rhine; but it is necessary to give a local habitation to the particular tribes that now began to work a total change in Britain.

Although classed under one general head, as Saxons, these tribes were three in number: 1. The Jutes. 2. The Angles. 3. The Saxons. The Jutes and the Angles dwelt in the Cimbric Chersonesus, or peninsula of Jutland (now a province of Denmark), and in parts of Schleswig and Holstein, the territory of the Angles extending as far as the modern town of Flensborg. In Holstein there is a district still called Auglen (the real Old England); and the narrowness of its limits need not interfere with our belief that this was the seat of the tribe (the Angles) that gave its name to our island. The Saxons proper, to the south of the Jutes and Angles, were far more widely spread, extending from the Weser to the delta of the Rhine, and occupying the countries now called Westphalia, Friesland, Holland, and probably a part of Belgium. Their precise limits are not fixed, but it seems their gradual encroachments on the Continent had brought them from the Baltic to the neighbourhood of the British Channel, when they embraced, as it were, our south-eastern coast. From the very close resemblance the old Frisick dialect bears to the Anglo-Saxon, a recent writer conjectures that the conquerors of Britain must have come principally from Friesland.[1] But many known fluxes and refluxes of population took place between the fifth and the twelfth centuries; the Jutes and the Angles, whose language may have been as like that of our Anglo-Saxon ancestors as the old Frisick dialect, were partially dispossessed of their territory in the peninsula of Jutland, and mixed up with newer tribes from Scandinavia, who eventually formed the Danish kingdom, and must have influenced the dialect there, as afterwards in Schleswig and Holstein. On the other hand, the occupants of the remarkable district of Friesland, where language, manners, usages—where all things seem, even in our days, to retain an ancient and primitive stamp, may, from local situation or other causes, have escaped the intermixture that befell the other Saxons. It is generally admitted that Horsa, Hengist, and their followers, were Jutes, and that the tribe or nation they first called in to partake in the pay and spoils of the Britons were their neighbours the Angles, from Holstein, and not the Saxons, from Friesland, though the latter soon joined the enterprise, and probably derived some advantage from being nearer than the others to the scene of action.

When the conquests of the Romans, in the first century of our era, brought them into contact with the Saxons, they found them as brave as the Britons, but, like the latter people, unprovided with steel blades and the proper implements of war. During the three centuries, however,

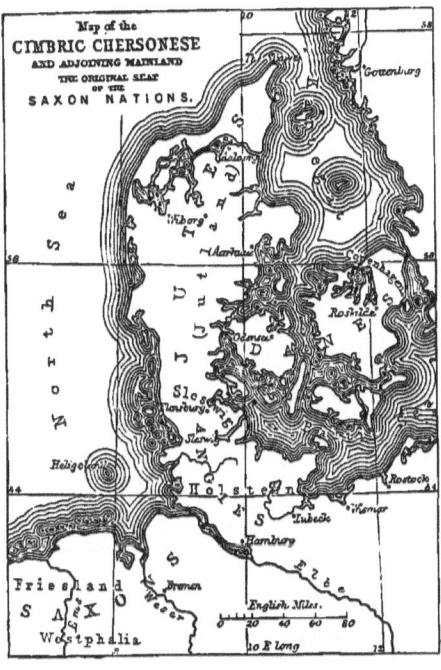

Map of the CIMBRIC CHERSONESE AND ADJOINING MAINLAND THE ORIGINAL SEAT OF THE SAXON NATIONS.

that had elapsed since then, in their wars with the Roman armies, and their friendly intercourse with the Roman colonies in Gaul and on the Rhine, they had been made fully sensible of their wants, and learned, in part, how to supply them. In their long-continued piratical excursions they had looked out for bright arms and well-wrought steel, as the most valuable article of plunder, and a constant accumulation must have left them well provided with that ruder metal, which commands gold. When they appeared in Britain, they certainly showed no want of good arms. Every warrior had his dagger, his spear, his battle-axe, and his sword, all of steel. In addition to these weapons, they had bows and arrows, and their champions frequently wielded a ponderous club, bound and spiked with iron, a sort of sledge-hammer, a copy, possibly, from the Scandinavian type of Thor's "mighty hammer." These two

---

[1] Palgrave, *Hist. Eng.*

weapons, the battle-axe and the hammer, wielded by nervous arms, were the dread of their enemies, and constantly recurring images in the songs of their bards, who represent them as cleaving helmets and brains with blows that nothing could withstand. When their depredations first attracted the notice of the Romans, they ventured from the mouth of the Baltic and the Elbe in crazy little boats; and shoals of these canoes laid the coasts of Gaul, Britain, and other parts of the Empire under contribution. Though larger, the best of these vessels could scarcely have been better than the coracles of the British; they were flat-bottomed, their keels and ribs were of light timber, but the sides and upper works consisted only of wicker, with a covering of strong hides. In the fifth century, however, their chiules,[1] or war-ships, were long, strong, lofty, and capable of containing each a considerable number of men, with provision and other stores. If they had boldly trusted themselves to the stormy waves of the Baltic, the German Ocean, the British Channel, and the Bay of Biscay, in their frail embarkations, they would laugh at the tempest in such ships as these. All their contemporaries speak of their love of the sea, and of their great familiarity with it and its dangers. "Tempests," says Sidonius, "which inspire fear in other men, fill them with joy; the storm is their protection when they are pressed by an enemy—their veil and cover when they meditate an attack." This love of a maritime life afterwards gained for some of the Northmen the title of Sea-kings. The passion was common to all the Saxons, and to the whole Teutonic race.[2]

SAXON SWORDS, SPEAR HEADS, AND BOSSES OF SHIELDS, all of iron.
From examples in the British Museum.

Thus, supposing that the Britons retained the arms of the Roman legions—and there is no reason to doubt that they did, though the Roman discipline was lost—their new enemy was as well armed as themselves; while the Saxons had over them all the advantages of a much greater command of the sea, and could constantly recruit their armies on the Continent, in the midst of their warlike brethren, bring them over in their ships, and land them at whatever point they chose.

At the period of their invasion of Britain, the Saxons were as rough and uncouth as any of the barbarian nations that overturned the Roman empire. Of civilization and the arts, they had only borrowed those parts which strengthen the arm in battle by means of steel and proper weapons, and facilitate the work of destruction. They were still pagans, professing a bloody faith, that made them hate or despise the Christian Britons. Revenge was a religious duty, and havock and slaughter a delight to their savage tempers. Their enemies and victims who drew their portraits, darkened the shades; and the Saxons had, no doubt, some of those rude virtues which are generally attached to such a condition of society.

The obscurity that comes over the history of Britain with the departure of the Romans, con-

---

[1] Hence our word *keel*.

[2] "Meagre, indeed, are the accounts which thus satisfied the most inquiring of our forefathers; yet, such as they are, they were received as the undoubted truth, and appealed to in later periods as the earliest authentic record of our race. The acuter criticism of an age less prone to believe, more skilful in the appreciation of evidence, and familiar with the fleeting forms of mythical and epical thought, sees in them only a confused mass of traditions, borrowed from the most heterogeneous sources, compacted rudely and with little ingenuity, and in which the smallest amount of historical truth is involved in a great deal of fable. Yet the truth which such traditions do nevertheless contain, yields to the alchemy of our days a golden harvest; if we cannot undoubtingly accept the details of such legends, they still point out to us at least the course we must pursue to discover the elements of fact upon which the Mythus and Epos rest, and guide us to the period and locality where these took root and flourished."—Kemble's *Saxons in England*, vol. i. p. 3.

"Possessing no written annals, and trusting to the poet the task of the historian, our forefathers have left but scanty records of their early condition. Nor did the supercilious or unsuspecting ignorance of Italy care to inquire into the mode of life and habits of the barbarians, until their strong arms threatened the civilization and the very existence of the Empire itself. Then first, dimly through the twilight in which the sun of Rome was to set for ever, loomed the Colossus of the German race, gigantic, terrible, inexplicable; and the vague attempt to define its awful features came too late to be fully successful. In Tacitus the City possessed, indeed, a thinker worthy of the exalted theme; but his sketch, though vigorous beyond expectation, is incomplete in many of its most material points; yet this is the most detailed and fullest account which we possess, and nearly the only certain source of information, till we arrive at the moment when the invading tribes in every portion of the Empire entered upon their great task of reconstructing society from its foundations."—Kemble' *Saxons in England*, vol. i. p. 5.

tinues to rest upon it for the two following centuries.¹ In the first instance, Hengist and Horsa appear to have fulfilled their part of the engagement upon which they had come over, by marching with the Jutes, their followers, against the Picts and Scots, and driving these invaders from the kingdom. Soon after this, if it occurred at all, must be placed the story of the feast given by Hengist, at his stronghold of Thong-caster, in Lincolnshire, to the British king, Vortigern, and of the bewitchment of the royal guest by the charms of Rowena, the young and beautiful daughter of his entertainer. Rowena's address, as she gracefully knelt and presented the wine-cup to the king, *Liever Kyning wass heal* (Dear king, your health), is often quoted as the origin of our still existing expressions, wassail and wassail-cup, in which, however, the word *wassail* might mean health-drinking, or pledging, although it had never been uttered by Rowena. But, as the story goes on, the action and the words of the Saxon maid finished the conquest over the heart of the king, which her beauty had begun; and, from that time, he rested not till he had obtained the consent of her father to make her his wife. The latest writer who has investigated the history of this period, sees no reason to doubt the story of Rowena, and has advanced many ingenious and plausible arguments in proof of its truth.² But, at any rate, it appears that, either from Vortigern's attachment thus secured, or from his gratitude for martial services rendered to him, or from an inability on his part to prevent it, the Jutes were allowed to fortify the Isle of Thanet, and to invite over fresh forces. The natural fertility and beauty of Britain, as well as its disorganization and weakness, must long have been familiar to the pirates on the Continent; and as soon as they got a firm footing in the land, they conceived the notion of possessing at least a part of it, not as dependent allies or vassals, but as masters. The conquest of the whole was probably an after-thought, which did not suggest itself till many generations had passed away. The sword was soon drawn between the Britons and their Saxon guests, who thereupon allied themselves with their old friends the Scots and Picts, to oppose whom they had been invited by Vortigern. That unfortunate king is said to have been deposed, and his son Vortimer elected in his stead. A partial and uncertain league was now formed between the Roman faction and the Britons; and several battles were fought by their united forces against the Saxons. In one of these engagements Vortigern is said to have commanded the Britons. Then, after a time, the two nations, according to the story commonly told, agreed to terminate their contention; and a meeting was held, at which the chief personages of both were mixed together in festive enjoyment, when suddenly, Hengist, exclaiming to his Saxons, *Nimed eure seaxas* (Unsheath your swords), they pulled forth each a short sword or knife, which he had brought with him concealed in his hose, and slew all the Britons present, Vortigern only excepted. This story, too, has been treated as a fiction by most recent writers; but the same ingenious and accomplished inquirer who has vindicated the historic existence of Rowena, has also argued ably and powerfully in favour of the truth of this other ancient tradition.³ He thinks, however, that the Britons were the conspirators on this occasion, and that the Saxons only acted in self-defence. The bloody congress is conjectured to have taken

---

[1] This obscurity rests particularly over the history and fate of the cities of Britain. Of these, Lappenberg speaks thus:—"When the Romans abandoned Britain, it contained twenty-eight cities, besides a considerable number of castella, forts, and small communities. Among the first, we know of two municipia—York and Verulam; nine colonies—Camolodunum (Maldon or Colchester), Rhutupiæ (Richborough), Londinium Augusta (London), Glevum Claudia (Gloucester), Thermæ Aquæ Solis (Bath), Isca Silurum (Carleon, in Monmouthshire), Camboricum (Chesterford, near Cambridge), Lindum (Lincoln), and Deva Colonia (Chester); also ten cities which had obtained the right of Latium—Pterotone (Inverness), Victoria (Perth), Durnomagus (Caister, in Lincolnshire), Lugubalia (Carlisle), Cattaractone (Catterick), Cambodunum (Slack, in Longwood), Coccium (Blackrode, in Lancashire?), Theodosia (Dumbarton), Corinum (Cirencester), and Sorbiodunum (Old Sarum), the last colony to the south-west in the country of the free Damnonii. Volantium (Ellenborough, in Cumberland), so rich in Roman remains, preserves an inscription, from which we learn that it had decurions, who assembled in a public building destined for the purpose. These cities, therefore, possessed a council (*decuriones, curiales, municipes*), with magistrates of their own choosing (*duumviri* and *principales*), and the right of contentious as well as of voluntary jurisdiction. To them was committed the levying of taxes in their districts; and it is known how the joint security of the civic decurions became both a burden to themselves, and brought the greatest obloquy on their order. That these abuses had also found their way into Britain, we learn from an ordinance of Constantine, for the remedying of the same in this country. Subsequently to the time of that emperor, the defensor, elected by the whole city, more especially against the oppressions of the governor, had become of consideration. The establishment of corporations at Rome, into which certain artisans and handicraftsmen were united, was extremely advantageous to them when they were removed into foreign provinces."—See *Lappenberg*, vol. I. p. 35.

[2] *Britannia after the Romans*, pp. 42, 62, &c.

[3] *Britannia after the Romans*, pp. 42, 62, &c. "It strikes the inquirer at once with suspicion, when he finds the tales supposed peculiar to his own race and to this island shared by the Germanic population of other lands; and with slight changes of locality, or trifling variations of detail, recorded as authentic parts of their history. The readiest belief in fortuitous resemblances and coincidences gives way before a number of instances, whose agreement defies all the calculations of chances. Thus, when we find Hengist and Horsa approaching the coasts of Kent in three keels, and Ælli effecting a landing in Sussex with the same number, we are reminded of the Gothic tradition which carries a migration of Ostrogoths, Visigoths, and Epidæ, also in three vessels, to the mouths of the Vistula, certainly a spot where we do not look for recurrence to a trivial calculation which so peculiarly characterizes the modes of thought of the Cymri. The murder of the British chieftains by Hengist is told *totidem verbis* by Widikund and others of the old Saxons in Thuringia."—Kemble's *Saxons in England*, vol. I. p. 18.

place at Stonehenge, on a May Day. In the end, Eric, the son of Hengist, remained in possession of all Kent, and became the founder of the Kentish, or first Saxon kingdom, in our island.

The conquerors of "Cantwara Land," or Kent, seem to have been Jutes mixed with some Angles; but now the Saxons appeared as their immediate neighbours. In the year 477, Ella, the Saxon, with his three sons, and a formidable force, landed in the ancient territory of the Regni, now Sussex, at or near to Withering, in the Isle of Selsey. The Britons were defeated with great slaughter, and driven into the forest of Andrede or An-

FLAMBOROUGH HEAD.[1]—From a sketch by G. Balmer.

dredswold.[2] According to the old writers this forest was 120 miles long, and 30 broad; prodigious dimensions, which astonish us, although informed that, even at the evacuation of the country by the Romans, a considerable portion of the island was covered with primeval woods, forests, and marshes. Continuing to receive accessions of force, Ella defeated a confederacy of the British princes, became master of nearly all Sussex, and established there the second kingdom, called that of the *South Saxons*. Taking the coast-line, the invaders now occupied from the estuary of the Thames to the river Arun; and to obtain this short and narrow slip had cost them half a century of conflict. Cerdic, with another band of Saxons, extended the line westward, a few years after, as far as the river Avon, by conquering Hampshire and the Isle of Wight; when he founded *Wessex*, or the kingdom of the *West Saxons*. The country to the west of the Hampshire Avon remained for many years longer in possession of the Britons, who now yielded no ground without hard fighting.

The next important descent was to the north of the estuary of the Thames, where Ercenwine, about 527-9, took possession of the flats of Essex, with some of the contiguous country, and formed the state of the *East Saxons*. Other tribes carried their arms in this direction as far as the Stour, when there was a short pause, which was not one of peace, for the Britons, driven from the coasts, pressed them incessantly on the land side. About the year 547, Ida, at the head of a formidable host of Angles, landed at Flamborough Head, and leaving a long lapse on the coast between him and the East Saxons, proceeded to settle between the Tees and the Tyne, a wild country, which now includes the county of Durham, but which was then abandoned to the beasts of the forest. This conquest obtained the name of the *Kingdom of Bernicia*. Other invaders, again, stepped in between the Tees and the Humber, but it cost them much time and blood before they could establish their southern frontier on the Humber. Their possessions were called the *Kingdom of Deira*. At the end of the sixth century, a general emigration seems to have taken place from Anglen, or Old England; and under chiefs that have not left so much as a doubtful name behind them, the Angles, in two great divisions, called the Southfolk and the Northfolk, rushed in between the Stowe and the Great Ouse and Wash, and gave a lasting denomination to our two counties of Suffolk and Norfolk. Their conquest was called the *Kingdom of East Anglia*. The territory thus seized by the East Angles was almost insulated from the rest of the island by a succession (on its western side) of bogs, meres, and broad lakes, connected, for the most part, by numerous streams. Where these natural defences ended, the East Angles dug a deep ditch, and cast up a lofty rampart of earth. In the middle ages this was called the "Giants' Dyke," a name which was afterwards changed into the more popular denomination of the "Devil's Dyke." The marshes upon which it leaned have been drained, but the remarkable mound is still very perfect.

---

[1] This remarkable promontory, on the Yorkshire coast, is composed of chalk cliffs, extending about six miles, and rising in many parts to an elevation of 300 ft. perpendicularly from the sea. The bases of the cliffs are worn into extensive caverns. On the extreme point of the promontory, at a height of 214 ft. above sea-level, is a lighthouse with a revolving light, visible from a distance of thirty miles. These cliffs are frequented by immense numbers of sea-fowl.

[2] The forest or wold is also called Anderida.

The other Angles advanced from beyond the Humber, and fresh tribes pouring in from the peninsula of Jutland and Holstein, the territory now forming Lincolnshire, between the Wash and the Humber, was gradually but slowly conquered from the Britons, and the only lapse or chasm filled up, that existed in the Saxon line of coast, from the Hampshire Avon to the Northumbrian Tyne. This line was extended as far north as the Frith of Forth by the Angles of Bernicia and Deira, who were united under one sceptre about the year 617, and thenceforward were called *Northumbrians*.[1] All the western coast, from the Frith of Clyde to the Land's End, in Cornwall, and the southern coast, from the Land's End to the confines of Hampshire, remained unconquered by the Saxons. Such had been the security of Cornwall, and its indifference to the fate of the rest of the island, that, while the states of the south were falling one by one under the sword of the Saxon invaders, 12,000 armed Britons left its shore to take part in a foreign war. This curious event took place about the year 470, when Gaul was overrun by the Visigoths, and Anthemius, who reigned in Italy, was unable to protect his subjects north of the Alps. He purchased or otherwise procured the services of Riothamus, an independent British king, whose dominion included, besides Cornwall, parts of Devonshire. The Britons sailed up the river Loire, and established themselves in Berry, where, acting as oppressive and insolent conquerors, rather than as friends and allies, they so conducted themselves, that the people were rejoiced when they saw them cut to pieces or dispersed by the Visigoths.[2]

The breadth of the Saxon territories or their frontiers inland, were long uncertain and wavering, now advancing, and now receding, according to the fortune of war. Under the name of *Myrcna-ric*, Latinized *Mercia*,[3] a branch of the Angles, penetrating into the heart of the island, founded a kingdom that extended over all the midland counties, from the Severn to the Humber, and that pressed on the borders of Wales. In this district, however, the population was not destroyed or expelled; the Britons lived mixed up, in about equal numbers, with the Saxons. The Mercian Angles, who at one period had spread to the south and east, until they reached the Thames, and included London in their dominion, contributed most extensively to the conquest of the island, and formed a kingdom, which was one of the last of the Heptarchy to be overthrown or absorbed. During their power, the Mercians more than once followed the bold mountaineers of Wales, who maintained a constant hostility, right through their country to the shores of St. George's Channel and the Irish Sea; but they were never able to subdue that rugged land. The other Anglo-Saxons, who seized their dominion in the ninth and tenth centuries, were not more successful than the Mercians; and although, at a later day, some of its princes paid a trifling tribute, and the country was reduced to its present limits of Wales and Monmouthshire, Cambria was never conquered by the Saxons during the 600 years of their domination.[4]

The people of Strathclyde and Cumbria, which territories extended along the western coast, from the Frith of Clyde to the Mersey and the Dee, appear to have been almost as successful as the Welsh, and by the same means. Their disposition was fierce and warlike, their hatred to the Saxons inveterate, and, above all, their country was mountainous, and abounded with lakes, marshes, moors, and forests. Part of the territory of Strathclyde, moreover, was defended by a ditch and a rampart of earth. This work, which is popularly called the Catrail or the March Dykes, can still be traced from the Peel-fell, on the Borders, between Northumberland and Roxburghshire, to Galashiels, a little to the north of Melrose and the river Tweed, and near to Abbotsford.[5] But lower down on the western coast the Saxon arms were more successful. Even there, however, the slowness of their progress denotes the sturdy resistance they met with. Nearly two centuries had elapsed since their landing at Thanet before they found their way into Dumnonia or Devonshire, which, together with Cornwall, appears to have remained in the occupation of a great undisturbed mass of British population. The king, Cadwallader, had resigned his earthly crown, and gone to Rome as a pilgrim,

---

[1] "The great extent of ground which the Angles occupied in Britain is quite sufficient to explain the statement of the old historians, that they had completely evacuated their native land, and left it uninhabited. From them, as the earliest settlers, and the most numerous, the island became known among foreign writers by the names of *Anglia* and *Anglorum Terra*; and among the Saxons themselves it was usually called *Engla-land* (England), and the language of its inhabitants *Englisc* (English). The population of the Teutonic portion of the island is still known by no other name than that of Englishmen."—*The Celt, the Roman, and the Saxon*, p. 394. As the Anglian settlements in England were afterwards so completely conquered and occupied by the Danes, that Danish superseded English names of many important towns, and as the south of England was chiefly occupied by Jutes and Saxons, it would seem that the Teutonic inhabitants of Scotland are now the purest English.—See *Palgrave*.

[2] *Jornandes*, c. xlv.; *Sidonius*, lib. iii. epist. 9.

[3] "We are generally told that *Mercia* signifies the *march* or *frontier*—a signification peculiarly improper for a central country. *Myrcna-ric*, in the Anglo-Saxon, signifies the *woodland kingdom*, which agrees very closely with *Coitani*, the Latinized name of the old British inhabitants, signifying *woodland men* or *foresters*."—Macpherson's *Annals of Commerce*, i. 237.

[4] A portion of Monmouthshire was, however, thoroughly conquered a short time before the Norman invasion, when the Saxons occupied the towns of Monmouth, Chepstow, Caerwent, and Caerleon.—Coxe, *Monmouthshire*.

[5] Gordon's *Iter Septentrionale*; Chalmers' *Caledonia*.

in search of a crown of glory; disunited and disheartened, the nobles of the land fled beyond sea to Armorica or Brittany, and, at the approach of the invaders, hardly any were left to oppose them except the peasantry. From the traditions of the country, and the signs of camps, trenches, and fields of battle spread over it, we should judge that the rustics made a vigorous defence.[1] They made a stand on the river Exe; but, being routed there, retreated to the right bank of the Tamar, abandoning all the fertile plains of Devonshire, but still hoping to maintain themselves in the hilly country of Cornwall. Defeat followed them to the Tamar and the country beyond it, upon which they, in A.D. 647, submitted to the Anglo-Saxons, who by this time may be called the English.

In this rapid and general sketch of the Saxon conquest, which, from the dates that have been given, will be perceived to have occupied altogether a space of nearly 200 years—of which above 100 were consumed even before the eastern and central parts of the island were subdued, and the last of the several new Saxon kingdoms established, a sufficient proof of the obstinate resistance of the Britons—we have omitted all details of the achievements of the British champions, not excepting even—

—— "what resounds
In fable or romance of Uther's son,"

as Milton has chosen to designate the history of the famous King Arthur. It seems impossible to arrive at any certainty with regard to the chronology or particular events of a period, the only accounts of which are so dark and confused, and so mixed up and overrun with the most palpable fictions. But as to Arthur, there appear to be the strongest reasons for suspecting that he was not a real but only a mythological personage, the chief divinity of that system of revived Druidism which appears to have arisen in the unconquered parts of the west of Britain after the departure of the Romans, the name being often used in the poetry of the bards as the hieroglyphical representative of the system. This is the most important of the subjects upon which new light has been thrown by the researches of the author of *Britannia after the Romans*, and his elaborate and masterly examination of the question of Arthur certainly seems to go very near to settle the controversy. "The *Saxon Chronicle*," he observes, upon the several probabilities of the case (the only part of his argument to which we can here advert), "does not suppress the names of islanders with whom the Saxons had to deal, but mentions those of Vortigern, Natanleod, Aidan, Brochvael, Geraint, Constantine of Scots, and Cadwallon. Its author betrays no knowledge of Arthur's existence. The venerable Beda either never heard of it, or despised it as a fable." Nor is it mentioned, he goes on to remark, either by Florence of Worcester or by Gildas. Yet, as he observes elsewhere, "the name of Arthur is so great, that if such a man ever reigned in Britain, he must have been a man as great as the circumscribed theatre of his actions could permit." And again: "The Arthurian era was one in the course of which the British frontier receded, and Hants, Somerset, and other districts passed for ever into the hands of the invader. It is not by suffering a series of severe defeats that any Saxon or other man conquers provinces; it is done by gaining successive victories. If Arthur lived and fought, he did so with a preponderance of ill success, and with the loss of battles and of provinces. But exaggeration must be built upon homogeneous truth. For a Cornish prince to be renowned through all countries, and feigned a universal conqueror, he must really have been a hero in his own land, and a signal benefactor to it. No man was ever deified in song for being vanquished and losing half a kingdom. But the god of war would retain his rank in any case. . . . The god of war would keep his station and preside over valiant acts, whether the results of war were fortunate or not. But the disasters of the British, historically and geographically certain as they are, make it also clear that they were commanded by no king fit for their bards to canonize."[2]

---

[1] Borlase; Mrs. Bray's *Letters to Southey*.
[2] *Britannia after the Romans*, pp. 70-141. For a defence of the historic reality of Arthur, see Turner's *Anglo-Saxons*, i. 268-283.
"The glory of one of the last champions of Christendom against ferocious pagans was alluring to ingenious fablers. The absence of authentic particulars set free their fancy; actions seen in so dim a twilight put on the size and shape which best pleased the poet; and the wonders of mythology, which always gradually withdraw before the advance of civilization, found a natural and last retreat in the most remote regions of Western Europe. To these circumstances, or to some of them, it may probably be ascribed that in a few centuries a Cornish or Welsh chieftain came to share the popularity of Charlemagne himself. The historical name of the great ruler of the Franks has, perhaps, borrowed a brighter lustre from the heroic legends with which it was long surrounded. In this country, on the contrary, a disposition has been shown to take revenge on the memory of Arthur for the credulity of our forefathers, by ungratefully and unreasonably calling into question his existence."—*Sir James Mackintosh*, vol. i. p. 26. "The authentic actions of Arthur have been so disfigured by the gorgeous additions of the minstrels and of Jeffrey, that many writers have denied that he ever lived; but this is an extreme as wild as the romances which occasioned it. His existence is testified by his contemporaries, whose genius has survived the ruin of twelve centuries; and the British bards are a body of men too illustrious for their personal merit and wonderful institution, to be discredited when they attest. . . . This state of moderate greatness suits the character in which the Welsh bards exhibit Arthur; they commemorate him, but it is not with that excelling glory with which he has been surrounded by subsequent traditions. . . . Yet, on perusing the British triads, we discern some traits which raise Arthur above the situation of a provincial chieftain. They give him three palaces; and the positions of these imply a sovereignty on the western part of the island, from Cornwall to Scotland."—*Sharon Turner's History of the Anglo-Saxons*, i. 228, 237.

To bring the course of the invaders and the permanent settlement of the Anglo-Saxons under one point of view, we have glanced from the middle of the fifth to the middle of the seventh century. We may now retrace our steps over part of that dark and utterly confused interval; but in doing so we shall not venture into the perplexing labyrinth presented by the more than half fabulous history of the Heptarchy, or seven separate and independent states or kingdoms of the Anglo-Saxons. Modern writers have assumed, that over these separate states there was always a lord paramount, a sort of Emperor of England, who might be, by inheritance or conquest, sometimes the king of one state and sometimes the king of another.[1] This ascendant monarch is called the Britwalda, or Bretwalda, a Saxon term, which signifies the wielder, or dominator, or ruler, of Brit (Britain).[2] According to Bede and the *Saxon Chronicle*, seven or eight of the Saxon princes in irregular succession bore this proud title; and perhaps it may be inferred from Bede's expressions that the other six kings of the island acknowledged themselves as the vassals of the Bretwaldas. We are not thoroughly convinced of any such supremacy (even nominal), and in the real operations of war and government we continually find each state acting in an independent manner, as if separate from all the rest—a proof at least that the authority of the lord paramount was very limited or very uncertain. As, however, their whole history is uninteresting, and as it is easier to trace the reigns of the more marking monarchs than to enter into seven separate dynasties, we shall follow the modern example.

ELLA, the conqueror of Sussex, and the founder, there, of the kingdom of the South Saxons—the smallest of all the new states—was the first Bretwalda, and died, little noticed by the English chroniclers, about the year 510. After a long vacancy, CEAWLIN, King of Wessex, who began to reign about 568, stepped into the dignity, which, however, was contested with him by ETHELBERT, the fourth King of Kent, who claimed it in right of his descent from Hengist, the brother of Horsa. The dispute led to hostilities; for long before the Anglo-Saxons had subdued all the Britons, they made fierce wars upon one another. The first example of this practice, which must have retarded their general progress in the subjugation of the island, was set by Ethelbert, who, after sustaining two signal defeats from his rival, and many other reverses during the twenty-two years that Ceawlin reigned, acquired the dignity of Bretwalda (A.D. 593) soon after that prince's death. Ceawlin, by the law of the sword, had taken possession of the kingdom of Sussex, and seems to have fought as often against his Saxon brethren as against the Britons.

The grand incident under the reign of this, the third Bretwalda, was the conversion of himself and court by Augustine and 40 monks, chiefly Italians, who were sent for that purpose into Britain by Pope Gregory the Great. Ethelbert's change of religion was facilitated by the circumstance of his having espoused a Christian wife shortly before. This was the young and beautiful Bertha, sister or daughter of Charibert, King of Paris, to whom, by stipulation, he granted the free exercise of her religion when she came into

---

[1] Mr. Kemble utterly rejects the idea of there ever having been any such lord paramount:—"Much less," says he, "can we admit that there was any central political authority, recognized, systematic, and regulated, by which the several kingdoms were combined into a corporate body. There is, indeed, a theory, respectable for its antiquity, and reproduced by modern ingenuity, according to which this important fact is assumed; and we are not only taught that the several kingdoms formed a confederation, at whose head, by election or otherwise, one of the princes was placed, with imperial power, but that this institution was derived by direct imitation from the custom of the Roman empire; we farther learn, that the title of this high functionary was Bretwalda, or Emperor of Britain, and that he possessed the imperial decorations of the Roman state." This learned author, who considers the Roman part of the theory, as adopted by Palgrave, very well exploded by Lappenberg—though the latter gives far too much credence to the rest—then proceeds to refute what Rapin, Sh. Turner, and others have said on the subject, and sums up his own ideas upon it as follows:—"I therefore again conclude that this so-called Bretwaldadom was a mere accidental predominance; there is no peculiar function, duty, or privilege anywhere mentioned as appertaining to it; and when Beda describes Eadwini of Northumberland proceeding with the Roman *tufa* or banner before him, as an ensign of dignity, he does so in terms which show that it was not, as Palgrave seems to imagine, an ensign of imperial authority used by all the Bretwaldas, but a peculiar and remarkable affectation of that particular prince."—*Saxons in England*, vol. ii. p. 18.

[2] The supposed universal empire held over Britain by particular Anglo-Saxon kings, in so far as it rests on the etymology of the word Bretwalda, is overthrown by Mr. Kemble, who shows—first, that that word, Bretwalda, arises from a clerical error; and, secondly, that the right word has nothing to do with Britain at all.

"Let us now inquire," says he, "to what the passage in the *Saxon Chronicle* amounts, which has put so many of our historians upon a wrong track, by supplying them with the suspicious name Bretwalda. Speaking of Ecgberht, the chronicler says: 'And the same year King Ecgberht overran the kingdom of the Mercians, and all that was south of the Humber; and he was the eighth king who was Bretwalda.' And then, after naming the seven mentioned by Beda, and totally omitting all notice of the Mercian kings, he concludes: 'The eighth was Ecgberht, King of the West Saxons.'

"Now it is somewhat remarkable, that of six manuscripts in which this passage occurs, one only reads Bretwalda; of the remaining five, four have Bryten-walda or wealda, and one Bretenanweald, which is precisely synonymous with Bryten-wealda. All the rules of orderly criticism would, therefore, compel us to look upon this as the right reading; and we are confirmed in so doing, by finding that Æthelstan, in one of his charters, calls himself also 'Bryten-wealda ealles thæses calondes'—ruler or monarch of all this island. Now, the true meaning of this word, which is compounded of *wealda*, a ruler, and the adjective *bryten*, is totally unconnected with Bret or Bretwealh, the name of the British aborigines, the resemblance to which is merely accidental; *bryten* is derived from *bréótan*, to distribute, to divide, to break into small portions, to disperse; it is a common prefix to words denoting wide or general dispersion, and, when coupled with *wealda*, means no more than an extensive, powerful king—a king whose power is widely extended."—Kemble, *Anglo-Saxons*.

the island. Ethelbert's close connection with the more enlightened nations of the Continent, and his frequent intercourse with French, Roman, and Italian churchmen, who, ignorant as they were, were infinitely more civilized than the Saxons, proved highly beneficial to England; and in the code of laws which this prince published before his death, he is supposed to have been indebted to the suggestions and science of those foreigners, although the code has far more of the spirit of the old German lawgivers than of Justinian and the Roman jurisconsults. This code was not published as from an absolute sovereign (a quality to which none of the Saxon princes ever attained), but was enacted by Ethelbert with the consent of the states of his kingdom of Kent, and formed the first written laws promulgated by any of the northern conquerors; the second being the code of the Burgundians, published a little later; and the third, that of the Longobardi or Lombards, which was promulgated in their dominions in the north of Italy, about half a century after Ethelbert's code. As King of Kent, Ethelbert's reign was a very long and happy one; as Bretwalda he exercised considerable authority or influence over all the Saxon princes south of the Humber. He died in 616, and was succeeded, as King of Kent, but not as Bretwalda, by his son Eadbald. The Anglo-Saxons at this period were very volatile and fickle in their faith, or very imperfectly converted to the Christian religion. Passionately enamoured of the youth and beauty of his step-mother, Ethelbert's widow, Eadbald took her to his bed; and as the Christians reprobated such incestuous marriages, he broke with them altogether, and returned to his priests of the old Teutonic idolatry. The whole Kentish people turned with him, forsook the missionaries and the churches, expelled the Christian bishop, and again set up the rude altars of the Scandinavian idols. Such a relapse as this was not uncommon among the recently converted heathen of other countries; but the sequel is curious, and makes our Saxon ancestors appear like a flock of sheep following the bell-wether. Laurentius, the successor of Augustine in the archbishopric of Canterbury, prevailed on Eadbald to put away his step-mother, and return to his fold; and no sooner had the king done so than all his subjects returned with him, without murmur or disputation.

We have said that Eadbald did not succeed to the dignity of Bretwalda. It appears, however, he made a claim to it, and that the other princes refused their concurrence and obedience. The dignity of Bretwalda would seem, from this and other instances, not to have been obtained by regular and free election, but to have been conceded to him who showed himself ablest to maintain his claim to it by the sword. The three first Bretwaldas, Ella, Ceawlin, and Ethelbert, were Saxons or Jutes; but now the dignity passed to the more powerful Angles, in the person of REDWALD, about the year 617. Redwald was King of East Anglia, and by profession a Christian, having been converted some years before by the Bretwalda Ethelbert. But his wife and people were attached to the old idolatry; and, yielding to their importunities, he reopened the temples, taking care, however, to place a Christian altar by the side of the statue of Woden,[1] in doing which he no doubt hoped to conciliate both parties. During his reign the Scots, who had renewed hostilities in the north, were beaten by the now united and extended Saxon kingdom of Northumbria. At a later period Redwald himself was hostilely engaged with the Northumbrian king Edilfrid, who is said to have destroyed more Britons than all the other Saxon kings. The armies of the Saxon kings met on the banks of the river Idel, in Nottinghamshire, where victory, after a sanguinary engagement, rested on the crest of the Bretwalda. Edilfrid was slain.

EDWIN, the fifth Bretwalda, succeeded (about 621) both to the dignity of Redwald and the kingdom of Edilfrid; and so successful was he in his wars and his politics, that he raised Northumbria to a superiority over all the Saxon kingdoms, thus transferring the ascendency from the south to the north of the island. After wavering some time between the old national faith of the Saxons and Christianity, Edwin was converted by the preaching of Paulinus, a Roman missionary, and the influence of his fair wife Edilberga, who was daughter of Ethelbert, the Bretwalda and King of Kent, and a Christian before she married Edwin. The happiest effects are asserted to have followed the conversion of the hitherto ferocious Northumbrians. Edwin added the Isles of Man and Anglesey to his Northumbrian dominions; and was so powerful, that all the Saxon kings acknowledged his authority, and paid him a kind of tribute. According to some accounts, he also maintained a supremacy over the Scots and Picts. In writing to him, in the year 625, the pope styles Edwin "Rex Anglorum"—King of the Angles, or English. In his person the dignity of Bretwalda had a significant and clear meaning; but he did not hold it very long. About the year 633, Penda, the Saxon Prince of Mercia, rebelled against his authority; and, forming an alliance with Ceadwalla, or Cadwallader, the King of North Wales, he fought a great battle at Hatfield, or Heathfield, near the river Trent, in which Edwin was defeated and slain (A.D. 634). The alliance of one party of the Saxons with the Welsh, to fight

[1] Bede.

against another party of Saxons, is remarkable; but the case was often repeated. The confederate armies between them committed a horrible slaughter, sparing neither old men nor children, women nor monks. Cadwallader and the Welsh remained in the territory of the Northumbrians at York, but Penda marched into Norfolk, against the East Angles. This people had embraced the Christian faith some seven years before, at the earnest representations of the Bretwalda Edwin; and Sigebert, their old king, had lately renounced his crown to his cousin Egeric, and retired into a monastery. But at the approach of Penda and his pagan host the old soldier left his holy retirement, and directed the manœuvres of his army, with a white rod or wand, his religious scruples not permitting him to resume the sword and battle-axe. Penda was as successful here as he had been against the Christians of Northumbria, and both Sigebert and Egeric fell in battle. At this time a struggle for supremacy seems to have existed between the converted and unconverted Saxons; and Penda, as head of the latter, evidently aimed at possessing the full dignity of Bretwalda, as it had been exercised by Edwin of Northumbria. But the latter prince had laid a broad and sure basis, which enabled the Northumbrians to retain the advantage in their own country, and transmit the dignity to two members of his family.

In the year 634, OSWALD, the nephew of Edwin, raised his banner in Northumbria, where Cadwallader, after many successes, seemed to despise precaution. He and his Welsh were surprised near Hexham, and totally defeated by inferior numbers. On the part of the Anglo-Saxons the battle began with kneeling and prayers; it ended, on the part of the Welsh, in the death of Cadwallader, and in the annihilation of his army, which appears to have assumed the title of "the invincible."[1] Oswald being equally recognized by the two Northumbrian states of Bernicia and Deira, then regained all that his uncle Edwin had lost, and soon after most of the Saxons acknowledged him as Bretwalda. He attributed his success to the God he worshipped; and, to show his gratitude, he invited many monks to complete the conversion of the people of Northumbria. The donation of Lindisfarne, or Holy Island, and the splendid monastery that rose there, testified to his munificence. Churches and monasteries sprung up in other parts of the north, and undoubtedly forwarded civilization, to a certain point, more than any other measures of establishments. Oswald, who repaired to the court of Cynegils, the king of that country, to demand his daughter in marriage, took an active part in the conversion of Wessex; and when Cynegils made a donation of land to Birinus, the Roman missionary and bishop, he confirmed it in his quality of Bretwalda.

As Bretwalda, Oswald exercised an authority over the Saxon nations and provinces fully equal to that of his uncle Edwin; and he is said, beside, although the fact is disputed, to have compelled the Pictish and Scottish kings to acknowledge themselves his vassals. Oswald was slain in battle (A.D. 642), like his uncle Edwin, and by the same enemy, the fierce and still unconverted Penda, King of Mercia, who was as desirous as ever of establishing his own supremacy. But the Northumbrians once more rallied round the family of the beloved Edwin, and on the retreat of the heathens from the well-defended rock of Bamborough, they enabled Oswald's brother, named Oswy, or Oswio, whose wife was the daughter of the great Edwin, to ascend the throne of his father-in-law. His succession, however, was not undisputed, nor did his murder of one of his competitors preserve the integrity of the Northumbrian kingdom. About the year 651 it was redivided into its two ancient independent states; and whilst Oswy retained to himself Bernicia, the more northern half, Odelwald reigned in Deira, or the southern part. The disseverance was a fatal blow, from which Northumbria never recovered.

Oswy had soon to contend with the old enemy of his house, the slayer of his two predecessors. Penda, still anxious to obtain the dignity of Bretwalda, which, as on other occasions, seems to have been in abeyance for some years, after driving the Christian King of Wessex from his throne (A.D. 652), advanced once more, and this time with fire and sword, into Northumberland. Burning every house or hut he found in his way, this savage marched as far as Bamborough. Trembling at his recollections of the past, and his present danger, Oswy entreated for peace, which he at length obtained by means of rich presents, hostages, and an arrangement of intermarriage. His second son was sent as a hostage to Penda's court. Alchfrid, his eldest son, espoused one of Penda's daughters, and shortly after Penda's son, Penda or Weda, married one of Oswy's daughters, the fair and Christian Alchfreda, who carried four priests in her train, and became instrumental in converting the people of Mercia.

But as long as Penda was alive in the land,

---

[1] "In Cædwalla expired the last renowned hero of old British race; in fourteen pitched battles and sixty encounters he had revived and confirmed the military fame of his country, and acquired dominion over a considerable part of Lloegria (Lloegyr). No wonder, then, if his life and death, though claiming a far higher degree of credibility than Arthur's, were soon surrounded by the glittering imagery of tradition, and that we are now unable to ascertain the truth, either in the apotheosis of his adoring countrymen, or in the vindictive narrative of the Anglo-Saxons."
—*Lappenberg*, vol. i. p. 158.

there could be no lasting peace. Having desolated East Anglia (A.D. 654), he advanced once more against the Northumbrians, his army being swelled by the forces of thirty vassal kings or chieftains, Welsh or Cumbrians, as well as Saxons. This time gifts and offers were of no avail. Oswy was obliged to fight; and the hardest fought battle that had been seen for many years, took place between him and Penda not far from York. Here, at last, this scourge of Britain or England (for the first name is now scarcely appropriate) perished by that violent death he had caused so many princes, and thirty of his chief captains were slain with him. Another account is, that of the thirty vassal kings or chiefs who followed him to the field, only one escaped, and that this one was the King of Gwynedh, a state in North Wales, which seems to have comprised Cardiganshire, part of Merionethshire, and all Carnarvonshire. Twelve abbeys, with broad lands attached, showed the gratitude of Oswy for his unexpected victory; and, according to a custom which was now obtaining among all the northern conquerors, he dedicated an infant daughter to the service of God, and took her to the Lady of Hilda, who shortly after removed with her nuns from Hartlepool to the vale of Whitby, where there soon arose one of the most famed and splen-

THE TOWN AND HEADLAND OF WHITBY.[1]

did monasteries of the middle ages. But all the proceedings of the victor were not of so pious or tranquil a nature. After Penda's death, Oswy rapidly overran the country of his old enemies the Mercians, on whom he inflicted a cruel vengeance. He attached all their territory north of the Trent to his Northumbrian kingdom; and Penda, his son-in-law, being treacherously murdered soon after (it is said by his own wife, who was Oswy's daughter), he seized the southern part of Mercia also. It was probably at this high tide of his fortune (A.D. 655) that Oswy assumed the rank of Bretwalda. The usual broad assertion is made, that the Picts and Scots, and the other natives of Britain, acknowledged his supremacy. There was soon, however, another Bretwalda; the first instance, we believe, of two such suns shining in our hemisphere.

In 656 the eoldermen or nobles of Mercia rose up in arms, expelled the Northumbrians, and gave the crown to WULFERE, another of Penda's sons, whom they had carefully concealed from the eager search of Oswy. This Wulfere not only retained possession of Mercia, but extended his dominions by conquests in Wessex and the neighbouring countries; after which he became king of all the "australian regions," or Bretwalda in all those parts of the island that lie south of the Humber. About the same time, Oswy was further weakened by the ambition of his eldest son, Alchfrid, who demanded and obtained a part of Northumbria in independent sovereignty. The sickness called the yellow, or the yellers plague, afflicted Oswy and his enemies alike; for it began in the south, gradually extended to the north, and at length raged over the whole island, with

[1] Whitby is understood to have risen from the neighbourhood of an abbey, founded by Oswy, King of Northumberland, in 667. Both abbey and town were utterly destroyed by the Danes, and lay in ruins till after the Norman conquest, when the abbey was rebuilt, and a considerable fishing town was established. The ruins of Whitby Abbey overlook the sea at an elevation of 240 ft. The fine central tower fell in 1830; the existing vestiges consist of the choir, the north transept, which is nearly entire, and part of the west front. The town of Whitby is situated on both sides of the mouth of the river Esk. It has a good harbour, protected by piers.

the exception of the mountains of Caledonia. Among the earliest victims of this pestilence were kings, archbishops, bishops, monks, and nuns. As the plague now makes its appearance annually in some of the countries of the East, so did this yellow sickness break out in our island for twenty years. King Oswy, who is generally considered the last of the Bretwaldas, though others continue the title to Ethelbald, King of Mercia, died in 670, during the progress of this fearful disease, but not of it.

Although we here lose the convenient point of concentration afforded by the reigns of the Bretwaldas, it is at a point where the seven kingdoms of the Heptarchy had merged into three; for the weak states of Kent, Sussex, Essex, and East Anglia, were now reduced to a condition of vassalage by one or the other of their powerful neighbours; and the great game for supreme dominion remained in the hands of Northumbria, Mercia, and Wessex. We are also relieved from any necessity of detail. The preceding narrative will convey a sufficient notion of the wars the Anglo-Saxon states waged with one another; and as we approach the junction of the three great streams of Northumbria, Mercia, and Wessex, which were made to flow in one channel under Egbert, we shall notice only the important circumstances that led to that event.

Oswy was succeeded in the greater part of his Northumbrian dominions by his son EGFRID, who was scarcely seated on that now tottering throne, when the Picts seated between the Tyne and the Forth broke into insurrection. With a strong body of cavalry, Egfrid defeated them in a bloody battle, and again reduced them to a doubtful obedience. Some eight years after, ambitious of obtaining all the power his father had once held, Egfrid invaded Mercia. A drawn battle was fought (A.D. 679) by the rival Saxons, on the banks of the Trent, and peace was then restored by means of a holy servant of the church; but it was beyond the bishop's power to restore the lives of the brave who had fallen, and whose loss sadly weakened both Mercia and Northumbria. In 685 Egfrid was slain in a war with Brude, the Pictish king; and the Scots and some of the northern Welsh joined the Picts, and carried their arms into England. In the exposed parts of Northumbria the Anglo-Saxons were put to the sword or reduced to slavery, and that kingdom became the scene of wretchedness and anarchy. In the course of a century fourteen kings ascended the throne, in a manner as irregular as their descent from it was rapid and tragical. Six were murdered by their kinsmen or other competitors, five were expelled by their subjects, two became monks, and one only died with the crown on his head.

Although exposed, like all the Anglo-Saxon states, to sanguinary revolutions in its government, Mercia, the old rival of Northumbria, for a considerable period seemed to rise on the decline of the latter, and to bid fair to be the victor of the three great states. After many hardly contested battles, the kings of Wessex were reduced to serve as vassals, and by the year 737, ETHELBALD, the Mercian king, ruled with a paramount authority over all the country south of the Humber, with the exception only of Wales. But five years after, the vassal state asserted its independence, and in a great battle at Burford, in Oxfordshire, victory declared for the Golden Dragon, the standard of Wessex. Between the years 757 and 794 the superiority of Mercia was successfully reasserted by king Offa, who, after subduing parts of Sussex and Kent, invaded Oxfordshire, and took all that part of the kingdom of Wessex that lay on the left of the Thames. Then turning his arms against the Welsh, he drove the kings of Powis from Pengwern (now Shrewsbury) beyond the river Wye, and planted strong Saxon colonies between that river and the Severn. To secure these conquests, and protect his subjects from the inroads and forays of the Welsh, he resorted to means that bear quite a Roman character. He caused a ditch and rampart to be drawn all along the frontier of Wales (a line measuring 100 miles), beginning at Basingwerke, in Flintshire, not far from the mouth of the Dee, and ending on the Severn, near Bristol. There are extensive remains of the work, which the Welsh still call "Clawdh Offa," or Offa's Dyke. But the work was scarcely finished when the Welsh filled up part of the ditch, broke through the rampart, and slew many of Offa's soldiers while they were pleasantly engaged in celebrating Christmas. Offa the Terrible, as he was called, took a terrible vengeance. He met the mountaineers at Rhuddlan, and encountered them in a battle there, in which the King of North Wales, and the pride of the Welsh youth and nobility, were cut to pieces. The prisoners he took were condemned to the harshest condition of slavery. Master of the south, it is said that he now compelled the Northumbrians beyond the Humber to pay him tribute; but the year is not mentioned, and the fact is not very clear. Ten years of victory and conquest, say his monkish eulogists, neither elated him nor swelled him with pride; "yet," adds one of them, "he was not negligent of his regal state; for that, in regard of his great prerogative, and not of any pride, he first instituted and commanded that, even in times of peace, himself and his successors in the crown should, as they passed through any city, have *trumpeters going and sounding before them*, to show that the presence of the king should breed both fear and honour in all who either see or hear him."[1] William of Malmesbury declares he is at a loss to determine whether the merits or crimes of this prince preponderated; but as Offa was a most munificent benefactor to the church, the monks in general (the only historians of these times) did not partake of this scruple, and praised him to excess. As a sovereign, however, Offa had indisputable and high merits, and the country made some progress under his reign and by his example. He had some taste for the elegancies of life and the fine arts; he built a palace at "Tamworth Town," which was the wonder of the age; and his medals and coins are of much better

BRASS COIN OF OFFA.—British Museum.

taste and workmanship than those of any other Saxon monarch.[2] He maintained an epistolary correspondence with Charlemagne; and it is highly interesting, and a consoling proof of progression, to see the trade of the nation and the commercial intercourse between England and France made a subject of discussion in these royal letters. When, towards the close of his reign, his body being racked with disease and his soul with a late remorse, he gave himself up to monkish devotion and superstitious observances, there was still a certain taste as well as grandeur in his expiatory donations, and a remarkable happiness of choice (though this is said to have been directed by the accidental discovery of a few bones) in his site for the abbey of St. Alban's, the most magnificent of all the ecclesiastical edifices he erected.[3] According to some of the old writers, his last warlike exploit was the defeat of a body of Danish invaders; and it is generally allowed that, during the latter part of his reign, a few ships' crews, the precursors of those hordes that desolated England soon after, effected a landing on our coast, and did some mischief. On the death of Offa, after a long reign, in the year 795, the great power of Mercia, which his craft, valour, and fortune had built up, and which his energies alone had supported, began rapidly to decline; and as Northumbria continued in a hopeless condition, Wessex, long the least of the three great rival states, soon had the field to herself.

[1] *The Ligger Book of St. Alban's*, as quoted in Speed's *Chronicles*.
[2] Palgrave, *Hist*.
[3] The present venerable Abbey church of St. Alban's, which stands on the site of that erected by Offa, was built, three centuries later, by William Rufus. A considerable portion of the materials employed are Roman bricks or tiles, taken from the ruins of the ancient city of Verulamium, which stood in the neighbourhood, between St. Alban's and Gorhambury Park.

At the time of Offa's death the throne of Wessex was occupied by Brihtric, or Beortric, whose right was considered very questionable even in those days, when the rule of succession was very far from being settled. Egbert, the son of Alchmund, had a better title, but fewer partisans; and, after a short and unsuccessful struggle for the crown, he fled for his life, and took refuge in the court of Offa, the Mercian. His triumphant rival, Beortric, then despatched ambassadors into Mercia, charged with the double duty of demanding the hand of Eadburgha, one of Offa's daughters, and the head of Egbert. Offa readily gave his daughter (he could hardly have given a greater curse), but he refused the second request. He, however, withdrew his protection from his royal guest, who fled a second time for his life. Egbert repaired to the court or camp of the Emperor Charlemagne, who received him hospitably, and employed him in his armies. During a residence of fourteen or fifteen years on the Continent, living chiefly among the French, who were then much more polished than the Saxons, Egbert acquired many accomplishments; and, whether as a soldier or statesman, he could not have found a better instructor than Charlemagne. Eadburgha, the daughter of Offa, and wife of Beortric, was a woman of a most depraved character—incontinent, wanton, perfidious, and cruel. When men thwarted her love, or otherwise gave her offence, she armed the uxorious king against them; and when he would not be moved to cruelty, she became the executioner of her own vengeance. She had prepared a cup of poison for a young nobleman who was her husband's favourite; by some inadvertence this was so disposed that the king drank of it as well as the intended victim, and died a horrid death (A.D. 800). According to another version of the story, she had filled the bowl expressly for the king, and many of his household and warriors were poisoned by it. The crime was discovered, and the queen degraded and expelled; the thanes and men of Wessex decreeing, at the same time, that for the future no kings' wives should be called queens, nor suffered to sit by their husbands' sides upon the throne. She also took refuge with Charlemagne, who assigned her a residence in a convent or abbey. But in process of time she began to conduct herself so viciously, that she was turned out of this place of shelter. Some years after her expulsion, a woman of foreign mien and faded beauty was seen begging alms in the streets of Pavin, in Italy; it was Eadburgha, the widow of the King of the West Saxons—the daughter of Offa, monarch of all England south of the Humber. It is believed she ended her days at Pavia.

As soon as Egbert learned the death of Beortric, he returned from France to Wessex, when the thanes and the people received him with open arms. The first years of his reign were employed in establishing his authority over the inhabitants of Devonshire and Cornwall; but he had then to meet the hostility of the jealous Mercians, who invaded Wessex with all their forces. Egbert met them at Elyndome, or Ellandum, near Wilton, in Wiltshire, with an army very inferior in numbers, but in superior fighting condition; being, to use the expression of one of our old quaint chroniclers, "lean, meagre, pale, and long-breathed," whereas the Mercians were "fat, corpulent, and short-winded." He gained a complete victory, and was soon after enabled to attach Mercia and all its dependencies to his kingdom. He established sub-reguli, or under-kings, in Kent and East Anglia; and not satisfied with the dominion of the island south of the Humber, he crossed that river, and penetrated into the heart of Northumbria. He invaded that once powerful state when anarchy was at its height. Incapable of resistance, the Northumbrians made an offer of entire submission (A.D. 825); and Eanred, their king, became the vassal and tributary of the great monarch of Wessex. It appears, however, that Egbert granted much milder terms of dependence to the Northumbrians than to any of the rest. Thus, in the first quarter of the ninth century, and 376 years after the first landing of Hengist and Horsa, was effected what some historians call the reduction of all the kingdoms under one sovereign.

CHAPTER II.—CIVIL AND MILITARY HISTORY.

INVASION OF THE DANES TO THE DEATH OF ALFRED.——A.D. 825—901.

England invaded by the Danes—Reign of Ethelwulf—His wars with the Danes—His pilgrimage to Rome—Reigns of Ethelbald and Ethelbert—Their wars with the Danish invaders—History of the Danes—Their character at the period of their invasion of England—Their modes of invasion and warfare—Ethelbert succeeded by Alfred the Great—Alfred's early conflicts with the Danes—His attempts to create an English navy—His defeat and flight to Athelney—His victory over the Danes at Ethandune—His treaty with Guthrun, and assignment of the Danelagh to the enemy—Intercourse of Alfred with Asser, his biographer—Hasting invades England—Various conflicts of the three years' warfare between Alfred and Hasting—Hasting compelled to leave England—Alfred's navy—Review of Alfred's history and character—His education, studies, and acquirements—His proceedings as a sovereign and legislator—His death and character.

ALTHOUGH Egbert had now attained to paramount authority, he did not assume the title of King of England. He contented himself with the style of King of Wessex, and with the dignity and authority of Bretwalda. This authority was sometimes questioned or despised in more than one part of the kingdom; but, counting from the river Tweed to the shores of the British Channel and the extremity of Cornwall, there were none who could make head against him; and during the last ten years of his reign he possessed, or absolutely controlled, more territory, not only than any Saxon sovereign that preceded him, but than any that followed him. Even Wales, if not conquered, was at one time coerced and kept in a dependent state.

But no sooner had England made some approaches towards a union and consolidation, and the blessings of a regular government, than the Danes or Northmen appeared in force, and began to throw everything into confusion and horror. In the year 832, when Egbert was in the plenitude of his power, a number of these ferocious pirates landed in the Isle of Sheppey, and having plundered it, escaped to their ships without loss or hindrance. The very next year the marauders landed from thirty-five ships, and were encountered by the brave and active Egbert at Charmouth, in Dorsetshire. The English were astonished at the ferocity and desperate valour of these new foes, who, though they lost great numbers, maintained their position for a while, and then made good their retreat to their ships. Indeed, some accounts state that Egbert's army was defeated in the engagement; that two chief captains and two bishops were slain; and that Egbert himself only escaped by the covert of night. In cruising along the English coasts, where they frequently landed in small bodies at defenceless places, the robbers of the North formed an acquaintance with the inhabitants of Cornwall, which ended in an ill-assorted alliance. The rugged promontory which stretches out to the Land's End had never been invaded by the Saxon conquerors of the island until the comparatively recent period of 647, and even then, as we have shown, the native population there was not much disturbed. As recently as 809, Egbert had invaded their territory, where he found them in such force and spirit that he lost many of his troops before he could reduce them to a nominal obedience. They must even now have been numerous and warlike, for on the stipulated landing in their territory of their Danish allies, in 834, they joined them in great force, and marched with them into Devonshire, where they found many old Britons equally willing to rise against the Saxons who had settled among them. But Egbert was again on the alert. He met them with his well-appointed army at Hengsdown-hill, and defeated them with enormous slaughter.

This was the last martial exploit of Egbert, who died in 836, after a long reign. The kingdom he had in a manner built up out of many pieces, began to fall asunder almost before his coffin was deposited in the church of Winchester. He was succeeded by his eldest surviving son, ETHELWULF, one of the first operations of whose government was to give the kingdom of Kent, with its dependencies, Sussex and Essex, in separate sovereignty to his son Athelstane.[1] He retained Wessex; but Mercia, which Egbert had subdued, again started into independence; and thus, when union was becoming more and more necessary, to face an enemy as terrible to the Saxons as the Saxons had been to the Britons, the spirit of disunion, jealousy, and discord assumed a fatal ascendency.

The Scandinavian pirates soon found there was no longer an Egbert in the land. They ravaged all the southern coasts of the kingdoms of Wessex and Kent; they audaciously sailed up the Thames and the Medway; and stormed and pillaged London, Rochester, and Canterbury. The idea of the need of a common co-operation at last suggested itself, and a sort of congress, composed of the bishops and thanes of Wessex and Mercia, was held at Kingsbury, in Oxfordshire (A.D. 851). Some energetic, and for the most part successful measures followed these deliberations. Barhulf, King of Mercia, was defeated and slain; but Ethelwulf and his son Ethelbald, at the head of their men of Wessex, gained a complete victory over the Danes at Okeley, in Surrey, and achieved such a slaughter as those marauders had never before suffered in any of the several countries they had invaded. Soon after Athelstane, the King of Kent, with Alchere, the eolderman, defeated the pirates, and took nine of their ships at Sandwich. The west of England also contributed a victory; for Ceorl, with the men of Devon, defeated the Danes at Wenbury. These severe checks, together with the disordered state of France, which favoured their incursions in that direction, where they soon laid Paris in ashes, seem to have induced the marauders to suspend for a while their great attacks on England; but such was the mischief they had done, and the apprehensions they still inspired, that the Wednesday of each week was appointed as a day of public prayer to implore the Divine assistance against the Danes. During the confusion their attacks caused in England, the Welsh many times descended from their mountains, and fell upon the Saxons. Ethelwulf is said to have taken vengeance for this, by marching through their country as far as the Isle of Anglesey, and compelling the Welsh to acknowledge his authority; but precisely the same stories are vaguely related (as this is) of several Saxon kings, who certainly never preserved any conquest or authority there for any length of time.

Ever since their conversion, the Saxons of superior condition had been singularly enamoured of journeys or pilgrimages to Rome; and besides the prelates who went upon business, many princes and kings, crowned, or uncrowned and dethroned, had told their orisons before the altar of St. Peter. Ethelwulf, whose devotion was fervent, though his sense of some moral duties was languid, now felt the general desire, and, as the island was tranquil, he passed over to the Continent (A.D. 853), and crossing the Alps and the Apennines, arrived at Rome, where he was honourably received, and where he tarried nearly one year. On his return, forgetting that he was an old man, he became enamoured of Judith, the fair and youthful daughter of Charles the Bald, King of the Franks, and espoused that princess with great solemnity in the cathedral of Rheims, where he placed her by his side, and caused her to be crowned as queen. Athelstane, his eldest son, was dead, but Ethelwulf had still three sons of man's estate—Ethelbald, Ethelbert, and Ethelred, besides Alfred, then a boy, who was destined to see his brothers ascend and descend the throne in rapid succession, and to become himself "the Great." From the usual thirst for power, it is probable that, before this French marriage, Ethelbald, who was already intrusted with the government of part of his father's kingdom, was anxious to possess himself of the whole; but the marriage and the circumstances attending it gave plausible grounds of complaint, and Prince Ethelbald, Adelstane, Bishop of Sherborn, Eanwulf, Earl of Somerset, and the other thanes and men of Wessex that joined in a plot to dethrone the absent king, set forth in their manifesto that he had given the name and authority of Queen to his French wife, had seated her by his side on the throne, and *"openly eaten with her at the table;"* all which

---

[1] Ethelwulf had been sub-regulus of Kent under his father, but then he was in reality subordinate to Egbert, who maintained full authority. It is not quite clear whether Athelstane was the eldest son or the brother of Ethelwulf.

was against the constitution and laws of Wessex, which had for ever abolished the queenly dignity, in consequence of the crimes of Eadburgha. It is probable, also, that the favour shown to the boy Alfred had some share in Ethelbald's resentment. Ethelwulf had carried his favourite son with him to Rome, where the pope anointed him as king with holy oil, and with his own hands. It is more than likely that Alfred had always been destined by his father to fill a minor throne in the kingdom, but this act, and the wonderful estimation in which the oil of consecration was held in those days, especially when administered by the pontiff of the Christian world, may have induced his brothers to suspect that the Benjamin of the family was to be preferred to them all. A recent historian—an indefatigable searcher into the old chronicles and records of the kingdom—is of opinion that, though the fact is not mentioned in express terms in our ancient historians, Osburgha, his first wife, and the mother of his children, was not dead at the time, but merely put away by Ethelwulf to make room for Judith.[1] In spite of their devotion and zeal for the church, such proceedings were not uncommon among kings in the middle ages; but if Ethelwulf so acted, the undutifulness of his eldest son, who had a mother's wrongs to avenge, would appear the more excusable. Whatever were their motives and grievances, a formidable faction, in arms, opposed Ethelwulf when he returned to the island with his young bride. Yet the old king had many friends; his party gained strength after his arrival among them, and it was thought he might have expelled Ethelbald and his adherents. But the old man shrunk from the accumulated horrors of a civil war waged between father and son, and consented to a compromise, which, on his part, was attended with great sacrifices. Retaining to himself the eastern part of the kingdom of Wessex, he resigned all the western, which was considered the richer and better portion, to Ethelbald. Ethelwulf did not long survive this partition, dying in 857, in the twenty-first year of his reign.

ETHELBALD then not only succeeded to the whole of his father's kingdom, but to his young widow also; for, according to the chroniclers, howsoever unwilling he had been that this fair queen should sit in state by his father's side, yet, contrary to all laws both of God and man, he placed her by his own, and by nuptial rites brought her to his sinful and incestuous bed. A tolerably well-grounded supposition that Judith was only twelve years old when Ethelwulf married her, and that their marriage had never been consummated, may diminish our horror; but such a union could in no sense be tolerated by the Romish Church, which, by means of its bishops in England, at last gained Ethelbald's reluctant consent to a divorce. According to other old authorities, the marriage was only dissolved by his death, and priests and people generally attributed the shortness of his reign, which did not last two years, to the sinful marriage, which had drawn down God's vengeance. As she is connected by her posterity with many succeeding ages of our history, we must devote a few words to the rest of the checkered career of Judith. Either on her divorce, or at the death of Ethelbald, she retired to France, and lived some time in a convent at Senlis, a few miles to the north of Paris. From this convent she either eloped with or was forcibly carried off by Baldwin, the grand forester of Ardennes. Her father, Charles the Bald, made his bishops excommunicate Baldwin for having ravished a widow; but the pope took a milder view of the case, and by his mediation the marriage of the still youthful Judith with her third husband was solemnized in a regular manner, and the earldom of Flanders was bestowed on Baldwin. Judith then lived in great state and magnificence; her son, the second Earl of Flanders, espoused Elfrida, the youngest daughter of our Alfred the Great, from whom, through five lineal descents, proceeded Maud, or Matilda, the wife of William the Conqueror, from whom again descended all the subsequent kings of England.

Ethelbald was succeeded in the kingdom of Wessex by his brother ETHELBERT, who had a short reign, troubled beyond measure by the Danes, who now made inroads in almost every part of the island. He had the mortification to see them burn Winchester, his capital, and permanently establish themselves in the Isle of Thanet, which they made their nucleus, and the key of their conquests, just as the Saxons had done more than four centuries before. This king died in the year 866 or 867, and was succeeded by his brother ETHELRED, who, in the course of one year, had to fight nine pitched and murderous battles against the Danes. Whilst he was thus busied in resisting the invaders in the south and west parts of the island, the kings and chiefs of Mercia and Northumbria wholly withdrew from their covenanted subjection or alliance, and, only thinking of themselves, they gave no timely aid to one another or to the common cause. Thus left to their own resources, the men of Wessex maintained a doubtful struggle, at times losing, and at others gaining battles. According to the old writers, the destruction of the Danes was immense; and during the five or six years of Ethelred's reign there were killed in the field nine yarls or earls, one king, "besides others of the

---

[1] According to some of the chroniclers, the Queen Osburgha was alive twenty-seven years after Ethelwulf's marriage with Judith, and in 878 repaired to Athelney, in Somersetshire, the retreat of her son Alfred.

meaner sort without number." But this loss was constantly supplied by fresh forces from the North, who brought as eager an appetite for plunder as their precursors, and whose vengeance became the more inflamed as the number of deaths of their brethren was increased. In most of these conflicts Alfred, who was already far more fitted to command, fought along with Ethelred, the last of his brothers; and at Aston or Ashenden, in Berkshire, while the king was engaged at his prayers, and would not move with his division of the Saxon army till mass was over, Alfred sustained the brunt of the whole Danish force, and mainly contributed to a splendid victory. The victory of Aston was followed by the defeats of Basing and Mereton; and, soon after, Ethelred died (871), at Whittingham, of wounds received in battle, upon which the crown fell to ALFRED, the only surviving and the best of all the sons of Ethelwulf. But, under existing circumstances, the crown was a jewel of no price, and for many years the hero had to fight for territory and for life against the formidable Danes.

The piratical hordes called Danes or Norsemen by the English, Normans by our neighbours the French, and Normanni by the Italians, were not merely natives of Denmark, properly so called, but belonged also to Norway, Sweden, and other countries spread round the Baltic Sea. They were offshoots of the great Scandinavian branch of the Teutons, who, under different names, conquered and recomposed most of the states of Europe on the downfall of the Roman empire. Such of the Scandinavian tribes as did not move to the South and the West to establish themselves permanently in fertile provinces, but remained in the barren and bleak regions of the North, devoted themselves to piracy as a profitable and honourable profession. The Saxons, then scattered along the south of the Baltic, did this in the fourth and fifth centuries, and now, in the ninth century, they were becoming the victims of their old system, carried into practice by their kindred, the Danes, Swedes, Norwegians, and others. All these people were of the same race as the Saxons, being an after-torrent from the same Scandinavian fountain-head; and though time, and a change of country and religion on the part of the Anglo-Saxons, had made some difference between them, the common resemblance in physical appearance, language, and other essentials, was still strong. It is indeed remarkable that the three different conquests of England, made in the course of six centuries, were all the work of one race of men, bearing different names at different epochs; for the Normans of the eleventh century were called Danes in the ninth, and were of the same stock as the Danes and Saxons they subdued in England. A settlement of 200 years in France, and an intermixture with the people of that country, had wonderfully modified the Scandinavian character, but still the followers of William the Conqueror had a much greater affinity with the Danes and Anglo-Saxons than is generally imagined.

Hume and other historians are of opinion that the remorseless cruelties practised by Charlemagne from the year 772 to 803, upon the pagan Saxons settled on the Rhine and in Germany, were the cause of the fearful reaction and the confirmed idolatry of that people.[1] There can be little doubt that this was partly the case; and it is a well-established fact, that the Northmen or Normans made the imbecile posterity of Charlemagne pay dearly for their father's cruelty. Retreating from the arms, the priests, and the compulsory baptisms of this conqueror, many of these Saxons fixed their homes in the peninsula of Jutland, which had been nearly evacuated three centuries before by the Jutes and Angles, who went to conquer England. A mixed population, of which the Jutes formed the larger portion, had, however, grown up in the interval on that peninsula, and, as they were unconverted, they were inclined to give a friendly reception to brethren suffering in the cause of Woden. The next step was obvious; and in the reprisals made on the French coasts, which were ravaged long before those of England were touched, the men of Jutland were probably joined by many of their neighbours from the mouth of the Baltic, the islands of Seeland, Funen, and the islets of the Kattegat. All these might probably be called Danes; but there are reasons for believing that the invaders of our island, under Alfred and his predecessors, were chiefly Norwegians, and not Danes; and that the real Danish invasions, which ended in final conquest, were not commenced until nearly a century later. Our old chroniclers, who applied one general name to all, call Rollo " the Ganger," one of the most formidable of our invaders, a Dane, and yet it is well ascertained that he was a Norwegian nobleman. It is difficult, however, and not very important, to distinguish between two nations speaking the same language, and having the same manners and pursuits. All the maritime Scandinavian tribes, from Jutland to the head of the Baltic—from Copenhagen nearly to the North Cape—were pirates alike; and the fleet that sailed from the coasts of Norway would often be mixed with ships from Jutland and Denmark, and *vice versâ*. Moreover, on certain great occasions, when their highest

---

[1] Charlemagne massacred the Saxons by thousands, even after they had laid down their arms. The alternative he offered was death or a Christian baptism. Those who renounced their old gods, or pretended to do so, he sent in colonies into the interior of France. Some were even hurried into Italy.

numerical force was required, the "Sea-kings," the leaders of these hordes, were known to make very extensive leagues.

In their origin, the piratical associations of the Northmen partook somewhat of the nature of our privateering companies in war-time, but still more closely resembled the associations of the corsairs of the Barbary coast, who, crossing the Mediterranean, as the Danes and Norwegians did the German Ocean and the British Channel, for many ages plundered every Christian ship and country they could approach. The governments at home, such as they were, licensed the depre-

DANISH CHIULE,[1] from tombstone in Iona.

dations, and partook of the spoils, having, as it seems, a regularly fixed portion allotted them after every successful expedition. Like the Saxons we have described, the Danes, Norwegians, and all the Scandinavians, were familiar with the sea and its dangers, and expert mariners. Every family had its boat or its ship, and the younger sons of the noblest of the land had no other fortune than their swords and their chiules (keels). With these they fought their way to fame and fortune, or perished by the tempest or battle, which were both considered most honourable deaths. All the males were practised in the use of arms from their infancy, and the art of war was cultivated with more success than by any nation in Europe. The astonishing progress of the Danes (as they were called) in England, of the Normans in France, and later in Italy and Sicily, not only prove their physical vigour, their valour, and perseverance, but their military skill and address. Their religion and literature (for they had a literature at least as early as the eighth century) were subservient to the ruling passions for war and plunder; or, more properly speaking, they were both cast in the mould of those passions, and stamped with the deep impress of the national character. The blood of their enemies in war, and a rude hospitality, with a barbarous excess in drinking, were held to be the incense most acceptable to the god Woden, who himself had perhaps been nothing more than a mighty slayer and drinker. War and feasting were the constant themes of their scalds or bards; and what they called their history, which is mixed with fable to such a degree that the fragments remaining of it are seldom intelligible, recorded little else than piracy and bloodshed. Like their brethren the Saxons, they were not at one time very bigoted, or very intolerant to other modes of faith; but when they came to England, they were embittered by recent persecution, and they treated the Saxons as renegadoes, who had forsaken the faith of their common ancestors to embrace that of their deadly enemies. This feeling was shown in their

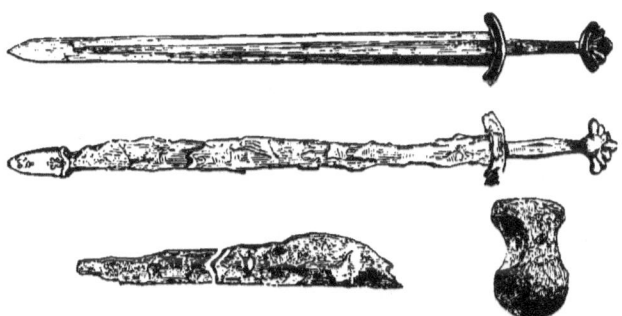

DANISH SWORDS AND AXE HEAD.—From specimens in the British Museum.

merciless attacks on priests, churches, monasteries, and convents.

With good steel arms the Danes were abundantly provided. Their weapons seem to have been much the same as those used by the Saxons at their invasion of the island, but the Scandinavian mace and battle-axe were still more conspicuous, particularly a double-bladed axe. "To shoot well with the bow" was also an indispensable qualification to a Danish warrior; and as the Saxons had totally neglected archery, it should seem the English were indebted to the

---

[1] This illustration, taken from the tombstone in Iona of Lachlan M'Kinnon, a descendant of a race of Norwegian kings in the Isle of Man, can only be regarded as an exaggerated type of the Scandinavian chiule. It presents, however, this difference from the Roman galleys, characteristic of the vessels of the Northmen generally, of being sharp at both ends, and being propelled by a sail rigged upon a mast, placed nearly equidistant between the stem and the stern of the vessel. Instead, however, of a rudder inserted on the quarter at either end of the vessel, this example has it placed as we use it in modern times. The coal-boats on the Tyne, called keels, are formed like the Danish chiule.

conquest, and intermixture with them of the Danes, for the high fame they afterwards enjoyed as bowmen. They had great skill in choosing and fortifying the positions they took up. Wherever a camp was established, a ditch was dug, and a rampart raised with extraordinary rapidity; and all the skill and bravery of the Saxons were generally baffled by these intrenchments. Their ships were large, and capable of containing many men; but in most of their expeditions they were attended by vessels drawing little water, that could easily run up the creeks and rivers of our island. Many of our rivers, however, must have been deeper in those times, for we constantly hear of their ascending such as would not now float the smallest embarkation. They frequently drew their vessels on shore, and having formed an intrenchment around them (as Cæsar had done with his invading fleet), they left part of their force to guard them, and then scattered themselves over the country to plunder and destroy. On many occasions they dragged their vessels overland from one river to another, or from one arm of the sea to another inlet.[1]

If they met a superior force, they fled to their ships, and disappeared; for there was no dishonour in retreat, when they carried off the pillage they had made. They then suddenly appeared on some other distant or unprepared coast, and repeated the same manœuvres; thus, at length, as their numbers increased more and more, keeping every part of England in a constant state of alarm, and preventing the people of one country from marching to the assistance of those of another, lest in their absence their own district should be invaded, and their own families and property fall the victims of the marauders. The father and brothers of Alfred had established a sort of local district militia; but the same causes of self-interest and alarm continued, and it was seldom that a sufficient force could be concentrated on one point, in time to prevent the depredations of the pirates. On some occasions, however, these armed burghers and peasants, throwing themselves between the Danes and their ships, recovered their booty, and inflicted a fearful vengeance; quarter was rarely given to the defeated invaders. For a considerable time the Danes carefully avoided coming to any general engagement; for, like the Picts and Scots of old, there object was merely to make forays, and not conquests and settlements. Their success, with the weakness and divisions of England, gradually enlarged their views. They brought no horses with them; but as cavalry was necessary to scour the country, and an important component of an armed force, they seized and mounted all the horses they could catch; and as their operations extended inland, their first care was to provide themselves with those animals, for the procuring of which they would promise neutrality or an exemption from plunder, to the people or districts that furnished them. Thus, on one occasion, the men of East Anglia mounted the faithless robbers, who rushed upon the men of Mercia, vowing they would not injure the horse-lenders. But no promises or vows were regarded—no treaty was kept sacred by the Danes, who had always the ready excuse (when they thought fit to make one) that the peace or truce was broken by other bands, over whom those who made the treaty had no control. Thus, when the men of Kent resorted to the fatal expedient of offering money for their forbearance, the Danes concluded a treaty, took the gold, and, breaking from their permanent head-quarters in the Isle of Thanet, ravaged the whole of their country shortly after. The old writers continually call them "truce-breakers;" and the Danes well deserved the name.

We need not follow the gradual development of this sanguinary story, nor trace, step by step, how the Danes established themselves in the island. It will be enough to show their possessions and power on the accession of Alfred to the degraded throne. They held the Isle of Thanet, which gave them the command of the river Thames and the coasts of Kent and Essex; they

---

[1] "The northern fleets and vessels, however dispersed in action, were always in communication with each other; so that the several hosts and bands might assist in their mutual exigencies, or best profit by their mutual good fortunes. In the British Islands, as well as on the Continent, their operations were uniform. Fleet after fleet, squadron after squadron, vessel after vessel, they sought to crush the country between river and river, or between river and sea, a battue encircling the prey.

"The *littoral* has sustained many alterations; cliff and beach, length and level, height and depth have changed and interchanged. Estimated according to a general average, we may assert that, bordering on the North Sea and the Channel, and as far as the Scheldt, the land has lost and the sea has gained. The bays on the coasts of France and England were generally much deeper than they are at present, and the rivers more abundant in water, whether flowing in the stream, spreading on the sheeted broad, or stagnating in the marsh. It is very important to notice these facts: such physical mutations, rarely recollected by historians, have been almost universally neglected in historical geography, a branch of science yet imperfectly pursued. We have, for example, never seen a single map of Roman Britain whose delineator has not joined the Isle of Thanet to the Kentish land. On the Gaulish coasts, the tides, particularly in the Seine, rose much higher up than at present; and many of the existing peninsulas, which cause the river's sinuous course, increasing the landscape's beauty, were then not *præqu'-isles*, but completely eyots and islands. The French academicians, who have investigated these questions with the most conscientious diligence, leave us in no doubt whether the Isle d'Oisselle, so important and celebrated military post during the northern invasions, has not been obliterated by alluvion.

"The facilities thus afforded for penetrating into the country encouraged the Northmen's desperate pertinacity; the seas, the blue billows, the *bolgen blau* of the Danish ballads were their home. Beaten off from the Belgic or Neustrian coast, they would ply the oar and hoist the black sail for Essex or Kent, East Anglia or Northumbria."—Palgrave, *Hist. Normandy and England*, vol. i. p. 320.

had thoroughly overrun or conquered all Northumbria, from the Tweed to the Humber; they had planted strong colonies at York, which city, destroyed during the wars, they rebuilt. South of the Humber, with the exception of the Isle of Thanet, their iron grasp on the soil was less sure, but they had desolated Nottinghamshire, Lincolnshire, Cambridgeshire, Norfolk, and Suffolk; and, with numbers constantly increasing, they ranged through the whole length of the island, on this side of the Tweed, with the exception only of the western counties of England, and had established fortified camps between the Severn and the Thames. The Anglo-Saxon standard had been gradually retreating towards the southwestern corner of our island, which includes Somersetshire, Devonshire, and Cornwall, and which was now about to become the scene of Alfred's most romantic adventures. For a while, the English expected the arrival of their foes during the spring and summer months, and their departure at the close of autumn; but now a Danish army had wintered seven years in the land, and there was no longer a hope of the blessing of their ever departing from it.

But Alfred, the saviour of his people, did not despair, even when worse times came: he calmly abode the storm over which his valour, but still more his prudence, skill, and wisdom finally triumphed. Though only twenty-three years of age, he had been already tried in many battles. He had scarcely been a month on the throne, when his army, very inferior in force to that of the Danes, was forced into a general engagement at Wilton. After fighting desperately through a great part of the day, the heathens fled; but seeing the fewness of those who pursued, they set themselves to battle again, and got the field. Alfred was absent at the time, and it is probable his army was guilty of some imprudence; but the Danes suffered so seriously in the battle of Wilton, that they were fain to conclude a peace with him, and evacuate his kingdom of Wessex, which they hardly touched again for three years. The invading army withdrew in the direction of London, in which city they passed the winter. In the following spring, having been joined in London by fresh hosts, both from Northumbria and from their own country, they marched into Lyndesey, or Lincolnshire, robbing and burning the towns and villages as they went, and reducing the people, whose lives they spared, to a complete state of slavery. From Lincolnshire they marched to Derbyshire, and wintered there at the town of Repton.

The next year (A.D. 875) one army, under Halfden, or Halfdane, was employed in settling Northumbria, and in waging war with that probably mixed population that still dwelt in Cumberland, Westmoreland, and Galloway, or what was called the kingdom of Strathclyde. They now came into hostile collision with the Scots, who were forced to retreat beyond the Friths of Clyde and Forth. Halfdane then divided the mass of the Northumbrian territory among his followers, who, settling among the Anglo-Saxons there, and intermarrying with them, became, in the course of a few generations, so mixed as to form almost one people. It is not easy, from the vagueness of the old writers, to fix limits; but this fusion was probably felt strongest along our northeastern coast, between the Tees and the Tweed, where some Danish peculiarities are still detected among the people. While Halfdane was pursuing these measures in the north, a still stronger army, commanded by three kings, marched upon Cambridge, which they fortified and made their winter-quarters. By this time the Anglo-Saxon kingdoms of Northumbria, Mercia, and East Anglia, were entirely obliterated, and the contest lay between the Danes and Alfred's men of Wessex.

At the opening of the year 876, the host that had wintered in Cambridge took to their ships, and, resolving to carry the war they had renewed into the heart of Wessex, they landed on the coast of Dorsetshire, surprised the castle of Wareham, and scoured the neighbouring country. But in the interval of the truce, Alfred's mind had conceived an idea which may be looked upon as an embryo of the naval glory of England. After their establishment in our island, the Saxons, who, at their first coming, were as nautical a people as the Danes, imprudently neglected sea affairs; but in his present straits Alfred saw the advantages to be derived from the employment of ships along the coast, where they might either prevent the landing of an enemy, or cut off their supplies and reinforcements, which generally came by sea, and as frequently from the Continent as elsewhere. The first flotilla he launched was small, and almost contemptible; but in its very first encounter with the enemy it proved victorious, attacking a Danish squadron of seven ships, one of which was taken, the rest put to flight. This happened immediately after the surprise of Wareham; and when, in a few days, the Danes agreed to treat for peace, and evacuate the territory of Wessex, the consequences of the victory were magnified in the eyes of the people. In concluding this peace, after the Danish chief or kings had sworn by their golden bracelets—a most solemn form of oath with them—Alfred, who was not above all the superstitions of his age, insisted that they should swear upon the relics of some Christian saints.[1] The Danes swore by both, and the very next night fell upon Alfred as he was

---

[1] *Asser*, 28

riding with a small force, and suspecting no mischief, towards the town of Winchester. The king had a narrow escape; the horsemen who attended

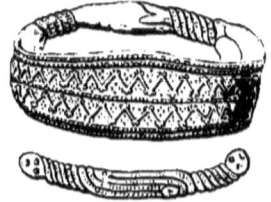

GOLDEN BRACELET.[1]—From Vallancey, Col. Reb. Heb.

him were nearly all dismounted and slain; and seizing their horses, the Danes galloped off in the direction of Exeter, whither, as they were no doubt informed, another body of their brethren were proceeding, having come round by sea, and landed at the mouth of the Exe. Their plan now was to take Alfred in the rear of his stronghold in the west of England, and to rouse again the people of Cornwall against the Saxons. A formidable Danish fleet sailed from the mouth of the Thames to reinforce the troops united in Devonshire; but Alfred's infant navy, strengthened by some new vessels, stood ready to intercept it. A storm which arose caused the wreck of half the Danish ships on the Hampshire coast; and when the others arrived, tardily and in a shattered condition, they were met by the Saxon fleet that blockaded the Exe, and entirely destroyed, after a gallant action. Before this, his second sea-victory, Alfred had come up with his land forces and invested Exeter, and King Guthrun, the Dane who held that town, on learning the destruction of his fleet, capitulated, gave hostages and oaths, and marched with his Northmen from Exeter and the kingdom of Wessex, into Mercia.

Alfred had now felt the value of the fleet he had created, and which, weak as it was, maintained his cause on the sea during the retreat to which he was now about to be condemned. The crews of these ships, however, must have been oddly constituted; for, not finding English mariners enough, he engaged a number of Friesland pirates, or rovers, to serve him. These men did their duty gallantly and faithfully. It is curious to reflect that they came from the same country which, ages before, had sent forth many of the Angles to the conquest of Britain; and they may have felt, even at that distance of time, a strong sympathy with the Anglo-Saxon adherents of Alfred. The reader has already weighed the value of a Danish treaty of peace. Guthrun had no sooner retreated from Exeter than he began to prepare for another war, and this he did with great art, and by employing all his means and influence, for he had learned to appreciate the qualities of his enemy, and he was himself the most skilful, steady, and persevering of all the invaders. He fixed his head-quarters at no greater distance from Alfred than the city of Gloucester, around which he had broad and fertile lands to distribute among his warriors. His fortunate raven attracted the birds of rapine from every quarter; and when everything was ready for a fresh incursion into the west, he craftily proceeded in a new and unexpected manner. A winter campaign had hitherto been unknown among the Danes, but on the first day of January, 878, his choicest warriors received a secret order to meet him on horseback at an appointed place. Alfred was at Chippenham, a strong residence of the Wessex kings. It was the feast of the Epiphany, or Twelfth Night, and the Saxons were probably celebrating the festival when they heard that Guthrun and his Danes were at the gates. Surprised thus by the celerity of an overwhelming force, they could offer but an ineffectual resistance. Many were slain; the foe burst into Chippenham, and Alfred, escaping with a little band, retired, with an anxious mind, to the woods and the fastnesses of the moors. As the story is generally told, the king could not make head against the Danes, but other accounts state that he immediately fought several battles in rapid succession. We are inclined to the latter belief, which renders the broken spirits and despair of the men of Wessex more intelligible; but all are agreed in the facts that, not long after the Danes stole into Chippenham, they rode over the kingdom of Wessex, where no army was left to oppose them; that numbers of the population fled to the Isle of Wight and the opposite shores of the Continent, while those who remained tilled the soil for their hard taskmasters, the Danes, whom they tried to conciliate with presents and an abject submission. The brave men of Somerset alone retained some spirit, and continued, in the main, true to their king; but even in their country, where he finally sought a refuge, he was obliged to hide in fens and coverts, for fear of being betrayed to his powerful foe, Guthrun. Near the confluence of the rivers Thone and Parret there is a tract of country still called Athelney, or the Prince's Island. The waters of the little rivers now flow by corn-fields, pasture-land, a farm-house, and a cottage; but in the time of Alfred the whole tract was covered by a dense wood, the secluded haunt of deer, wild boars, wild goats, and other beasts of the forest. It has now long ceased to be an island; but in those days, where not washed by the two rivers,

[1] This bracelet, presumed to be of the period spoken of, was found in Ireland; weight, 17 oz. 6 grs.

KING ALFRED INCITING THE ANGLO-SAXONS.

When King Alfred came to the throne in 871 A.D. he found his kingdom of Wessex beset by the conquering Danes. Everywhere along the eastern seaboard of England they had raided, until Northumbria, Mercia, and East Anglia had passed into their hands. To arrest this persistent invasion the young king determined to fight the Norsemen upon the sea before they could effect a landing. He instructed his Saxon followers, therefore, to prepare a few vessels, and with these he attacked and defeated the Danes at various times. His fleet increased in numbers and strength; and the incident chosen by the artist is from the year 876 A.D., when Alfred incited his seamen to push boldly out from Exmouth to meet the Danes. This they did, and after some tough fighting the Danish flotilla was destroyed.

KING ALFRED INCITING THE ANGLO-SAXONS

it was insulated by bogs and inundations, which could only be passed in a boat. In this secure lurking-place the king abode some time, making himself a small hold or fortress there. For sustenance he and his few followers depended upon hunting and fishing, and the spoil they could make by sudden and secret forays among the Danes. From an ambiguous expression of some of the old writers, we might believe he sometimes plundered his own subjects; and this is not altogether improbable, if we consider his pressing wants, and the necessity under which he lay of concealing who he was. This secret seems to have been most scrupulously kept by his few adherents, and to have been maintained on his own part with infinite patience and forbearance. A well-known story, endeared to us all by our earliest recollections, is told by his contemporary and bosom friend, the monk Asser; it is repeated by all the writers who lived near the time, and may safely be considered as authentic as it is interesting. In one of his excursions he took refuge in the humble cabin of a swineherd, where he stayed some time. On a certain day it happened that the wife of the swain prepared to bake her *loudas*, or loaves of bread. The king, sitting at the time near the hearth, was making ready his bow and arrows, when the shrew beheld her loaves burning. She ran hastily, and removed them, scolding the king for his shameful negligence, and exclaiming, "You man! you will not turn the bread you see burning, but you will be glad enough to eat it." "This unlucky woman," adds Asser, "little thought she was talking to the King Alfred."

From his all but inaccessible retreat in Athelney, the king maintained a correspondence with some of his faithful adherents. By degrees a few bold warriors gathered round him in that islet, which they more strongly fortified, as a point upon which to retreat in case of reverse; and between the Easter and Whitsuntide following his flight, Alfred saw hopes of his emerging from obscurity. The men of Somersetshire, Wiltshire, Dorsetshire, and Hampshire began to flock in; and, with a resolute force, Alfred was soon enabled to extend his operations against the Danes. In the interval, an important event in Devonshire had favoured his cause. Hubba, a Danish king or chief of great renown, in attempting to land there, was slain, with 800 or 900 of his followers, and their magical banner, a raven, which had been embroidered in one noontide by the hands of the three daughters of the great Lodbroke, fell into the hands of the Saxons. Soon after receiving the welcome news at Atheluey, the king determined to convert his skirmishes and loose partisan warfare into more decisive operations. Previously to this, however, he was anxious to know the precise force and condition of the army which Guthrun kept together; and, to obtain this information, he put himself in great jeopardy, trusting to his own resources and address. He assumed the habit of a wandering minstrel, or gleeman, and with his instruments of music in his hands, gained a ready entrance in the camp, and the tents and pavilions of the Danes. As he amused these idle warriors with songs and interludes, he espied all their sloth and negligence, heard much of their councils and plans, and was soon enabled to return to his friends at Athelney with a full and satisfactory account of the state and habits of that army. Then secret messengers were sent to all quarters, requesting the trusty men of Wessex to meet in arms at Egbert's Stone, on the east of Selwood Forest.[1] The summons was obeyed, though most knew not the king had sent it; and when Alfred appeared at the place of rendezvous he was received with enthusiastic joy, the men of Hampshire, and Dorset, and Wilts, rejoicing as if he had been risen from death to life. In the general battle of Ethandune which ensued (seven weeks after Easter), the Danes were taken by surprise, and thoroughly beaten. Alfred's concealment, counting from his flight from Chippenham, did not last above five months.

It is reasonably supposed that the present Yatton, about five miles from Chippenham, is the representative of Ethandune, or Assandune; but that the battle was fought a little lower on the Avon, at a place called "Slaughterford,"

Sketch of the Country BETWEEN ATHELNEY & CHIPPENHAM, to illustrate ALFRED'S CAMPAIGN OF 878. *English Miles.*

where, according to a tradition of the country people, the Danes suffered a great slaughter. Guthrun retreated with the mournful residue of his army to a fortified position. Alfred followed him thither, cut off all his communications, and

---

1 *Asser*, 33. The wood extended from Frome to Burham, and was probably much larger at one time.

established a close blockade. In fourteen days, famine obliged the Danes to accept the conditions offered by the Saxons. These conditions were liberal; for, though victorious, Alfred could not hope to drive the Danes by one, nay, nor by twenty battles, out of England. They were too numerous, and had secured themselves in too considerable a part of the island. The first points insisted upon in the treaty were, that Guthrun should evacuate all Wessex, and submit to be baptized.[1] Without a conversion to Christianity, Alfred thought it impossible to rely on the promises or oaths of the Danes; he saw that a change of religion would, more than anything else, detach them from their savage Scandinavian brethren across the seas; and as he was a devout man, with priests and monks for his counsellors, religion, no doubt, was as precious to him as policy, and he was moved with an ardent hope of propagating and extending the Christian faith. Upon Guthrun's ready acceptance of these two conditions, an extensive cession of territory was made to him and the Danes; and here the great mind of Alfred probably contemplated the gradual fusion of two people—the Saxons and the Danes—who differed in but few essentials; and foresaw that the pursuits of agriculture and industry, growing up among them, after a tranquil settlement, would win the rovers of the North from their old plundering, piratical habits. As soon as this took place, they would guard the coasts they formerly desolated. If it had even been in Alfred's power to expel them all (which it never was), he could have had no security against their prompt return and incessant attacks. There was territory enough, fertile, though neglected, to give away, without straitening the Saxons. In the most happy time of the Roman occupation, a great part of Britain was but thinly inhabited; and the famines, the pestilences, the almost incessant wars which had followed since then, had depopulated whole counties, and left immense tracts of land without hands to till them, or mouths to eat the produce they promised the agriculturist.[2]

Alfred thus drew the line of demarcation between him and the Danes:—" Let the bounds of our dominion stretch to the river Thames, and from thence to the water of Lea, even unto the head of the same water; and thence straight unto Bedford; and finally, going along by the river Ouse, let them end at Watling-street." Beyond these lines, all the east side of the island, as far as the Humber, was surrendered to the Danes; and as they had established themselves in Northumbria, that territory was soon united, and the whole eastern country from the Tweed to the Thames, where it washes a part of Essex, took the name of the *Danelagh*, or "Dane-law," which it retained for many ages, even down to the time of the Norman conquest. The cession was large; but it should be remembered that Alfred, at the opening of his reign, was driven into the western corner of England, and that he now gained tranquil possession of five, or perhaps ten times more territory than he then possessed.[3] In many respects, these his moderate measures answered the end he proposed. Soon after the conclusion of the treaty, Guthrun, relying on the good faith of the Saxons, went with only thirty of his chiefs to Aulre, near Athelney. His old but gallant and generous enemy, Alfred, answered for him at the baptismal font, and the Dane was christened under the Saxon name of Athelstan. The next week the ceremony was completed with great solemnity at the royal town of Wedmor, and after spending twelve days as the guest of Alfred, Guthrun departed (A.D. 878), loaded with presents, which the monk Asser says were *magnificent*. Whatever were his inward convictions, or the efficacy and sincerity of his conversion, the Danish prince was certainly captivated by the merits of his victor, and ever after continued the faithful friend and ally (if not vassal) of Alfred. The subjects under his rule in the Danelagh, or "Dane-law," assumed habits of industry and tranquillity, and gradually adopted the manners and customs of more civilized life. By mutual agreement, the laws of the Danes were assimilated to those of the Saxons; but the former long retained many of their old Scandinavian usages. All sales, whether of *men*, horses, or oxen, were declared illegal, unless the purchaser produced the voucher of the seller. This was to

---

[1] "We meet with nothing which can be construed into an indication of Alfred's having made this determination (to embrace Christianity) one of the conditions of peace. The first idea of such a thing, although it might not have been sincere, but merely suggested by the straits to which he was reduced, appears to have arisen in the soul of the heathen. He himself ruled over Christian subjects, who showed more courage for their religion than they did in war; and already, too, were the first signs of that so frequently recurring phenomenon apparent, namely, that the Christian religion generally triumphs, in the course of time, over the weapons of its oppressors."—Pauli, *Life of Alfred the Great*, p. 181.

[2] "The magnanimity of the plan was as great as its wisdom. Had Alfred suffered fear or revenge to have been his counsellors, he would never have sheathed the exterminating sword till every Northman or every Saxon had perished. Common minds and vehement feelings would have chosen this alternative. But Alfred had the wisdom to discern and the virtue to believe, that the existence of his enemies was not incompatible with his own honour and his people's safety. He felt that the addition of Mercia was an increase of power, which placed him above any perilous assault, and he was contented to be secure."—Sh. Turner, *Hist. of Anglo-Saxons*, vol. ii, p. 200.

[3] Mercia fell completely into the power of Alfred after the defeat of Guthrun. He abolished the regal honours of that state, and intrusted the military command of it to Ethelred, who was afterwards married to one of his daughters. Ethelred seems to have been merely styled the "Folklerman of Mercia."

put a stop on both sides to the lifting of cattle, and the carrying off of the peasantry as slaves. Both kings engaged to promote the Christian religion, and to punish apostasy. We are not well informed as to the progress the faith made among his subjects on Guthrun's conversion; but it was probably rapid, though imperfect, and accompanied with a lingering affection for the divinities of the Scandinavian mythology.

It was about this time, or very soon after Alfred's breaking up from his retreat at Athelney, and gaining the victory of Ethandune, that, moved by the love of humane letters which distinguished him all his life, he invited Asser, esteemed the most learned man then in the island, to his court or camp, in order that he might profit by his instructive conversation. The monk of St. David's, who was not a Saxon, but descended from a Welsh family, obeyed the summons, and, according to his own account, he was introduced to the king at Dene, in Wiltshire, by the thanes who had been sent to fetch him. A familiar intercourse followed a most courteous reception, and then the king invited the monk to live constantly about his person. The vows of Asser, and his attachment to his monastery, where he had been nurtured and instructed, interfered with this arrangement; but after some delays, it was agreed he should pass half his time in his monastery, and the rest of the year at court. Returning, at length, to Alfred, he found him at a place called Leonaford. He remained eight months constantly with him, conversing and reading with him all such books as the king possessed. On the Christmas Eve following, Alfred, in token of his high regard, gave the monk an abbey in Wiltshire, supposed to be at Amesbury, and another abbey at Banwell, in Somersetshire, together with a rich silk pall, and as much incense as a strong man could carry on his shoulders, assuring him, at the same time, that he considered these as small things for a man of so much merit, and that hereafter he should have greater. Asser was subsequently promoted to the bishopric of Sherburn, and thenceforward remained constantly with the king, enjoying his entire confidence and affection, and sharing in all his joys and sorrows. This rare friendship between a sovereign and subject continued unbroken till death; and when the grave closed over the great Alfred, the honourable testimony was read in his will, that Asser was a person in whom he had full confidence. To this singular connection Alfred and his subjects were, no doubt, indebted for some improvements in the royal mind, which wrought good alike for the king and for the people; and *we*, at the distance of nearly 1000 years, owe to it an endearing record of that monarch's personal character and habits.

But some time had yet to pass ere Alfred could give himself up to quiet enjoyments, to law-making, and the intellectual improvement of his people. Though Guthrun kept his contract, hosts of marauding Danes, who were not bound by it, continued to cross over from the Continent, and invest the shores and rivers of our island. In 879, the very year after Guthrun's treaty and baptism, a great army of pagans came from beyond the sea, and wintered at Fullanham, or Fulham, hard by the river Thames. From Fulham, this host proceeded to Ghent, in the Low Countries. At this period the Northmen alternated their attacks on England, and their attacks on Holland, Belgium, and East France, in a curious manner, the expedition beginning on one side of the British Channel and German Ocean, frequently ending on the other side. The rule of their conduct, however, seems to have been this—to persevere only against the weakest enemy. Thus, when they found France strong, they tried England; and when they found the force of England consolidated under Alfred, they turned off in the direction of France, or the neighbouring shores of the Continent. It is a melancholy fact, that England then benefited by the calamities of her neighbours. In the year 886, while the armies of the Northmen were fully employed in besieging or blockading the city of Paris, Alfred took that favourable opportunity to rebuild and fortify the city of London. Amongst other cities, we are told, it had been destroyed by fire, and the people killed; but he made it habitable again, and committed it to the care and custody of his son-in-law, Ethelred, Earl or Eolderman of the Mercians, to whom, before, he had given his daughter Ethelfleda. Each of the six years immediately preceding the rebuilding of London, he was engaged in hostilities; but he was generally fortunate by sea as well as by land, for he had increased his navy, and the care due to that truly national service. In the year 882 his fleet, still officered by Frieslanders, took four, and, three years after (in one fight), sixteen of the enemy's ships. In the latter year (885) he gained a decisive victory over a Danish host that had ascended the Medway, and were besieging Rochester, having built them a strong castle before the gates of that city. By suddenly falling on them, he took their tower with little loss, seized all the horses they had brought with them from France, recovered the greater part of their captives, and drove them to their ships, with which they returned to France in the utmost distress.

Alfred was now allowed some breathing time, which he wisely employed in strengthening his kingdom, and bettering the condition of his people. Instead, however, of tracing these things strictly in their chronological order, it will add to the perspicuity of the narrative, if we follow at once the warlike events of his reign to their close.

The siege of Paris, to which we have alluded, and which began in 886, employed the Danes or Northmen two whole years. Shortly after the heathens burst into the country now called Flanders, which was then a dependency of the Frankish or French kings, and were employed there for some time in a difficult and extensive warfare. A horrid famine ensued in those parts of the Continent, and made the hungry wolves look elsewhere for sustenance and prey. England had now revived, by a happy repose of seven years; her corn-fields had borne their plentiful crops; her pastures, no longer swept by the tempests of war, were well-sprinkled with flocks and herds; and those good fatted beeves, which were always dear to the capacious stomachs of the Northmen, made the island a very land of promise to the imagination of the famished. It is true that of late years they had found those treasures were well defended, and that nothing was to be got under Alfred's present government without hard blows, and a desperate contest, at least doubtful in its issue. But hunger impelled them forward; they were a larger body than had ever made the attack at once; they were united under the command of a chief equal or superior in fame and military talent to any that had preceded him; and therefore the Danes, in the year 893, once more turned the prows of their vessels toward England. It was indeed a formidable fleet. As the men of Kent gazed seaward from their cliffs and downs, they saw the horizon darkened by it; as the winds and waves wafted it forward, they counted 250 several ships; and every ship was full of warriors and horses brought from Flanders and France, for the immediate mounting of them as a rapid, predatory cavalry. The invaders landed near Romney Marsh, at the eastern termination of the great wood or weald of Anderida (already mentioned in connection with an invasion of the Saxons), and at the mouth of a river, now dry, called Limine. They towed their ships four miles up the river towards the weald, and there mastered a fortress the peasants of the country were raising in the fens. They then proceeded to Apuldre, or Appledore, at which point they made a strongly fortified camp, whence they ravaged the adjacent country for many miles. Nearly simultaneously with these movements, the famed Haesten or Hasting, the skilful commander-in-chief of the entire expedition, entered the Thames with another division of eighty ships, landed at and took Milton, near Sittingbourne, and there threw up prodigiously strong intrenchments. Their past reverses had made them extremely cautious; and for nearly a whole year, the Danes in either camp did little else than fortify their positions, and scour the country in foraging parties. Other piratical squadrons, however, kept hovering round our coasts, to distract attention and create alarm at many points at one and the same time. The honourable and trustworthy Guthrun had now been dead three years; and to complete the most critical position of Alfred, the Danes settled in the Danelagh, even from the Tweed to the Thames, violated their oaths, took up arms against him, and joined their marauding brethren under Hasting. It was in this campaign, or rather this succession of campaigns, which lasted altogether three years, that the military genius of the Anglo-Saxon monarch shone with its greatest lustre, and was brought into full play by the ability, the wonderful and eccentric rapidity, and the great resources of his opponent Hasting. To follow their operations the reader must place the map of England before him, for they ran over half of the island, and shifted the scene of war with almost as much rapidity as that with which the decorations of a theatre are changed.

The first great difficulty Alfred had to encounter was in collecting and bringing up sufficient forces to one point, and then keeping them in adequate number in the field; for the Saxon "fyrd," or *levée en masse*, were only bound by law to serve for a certain time (probably forty days), and it was indispensible to provide for the safety of the towns, almost everywhere threatened, and to leave men sufficient for the cultivation of the country. Alfred overcame this difficulty by dividing his army, or militia, into two bodies; of these he called one to the field, while the men composing the other were left at home. After a reasonable length of service those in the field returned to their homes, and those left at home took their places in the field. The spectacle of this large and permanent army, to which they had been wholly unaccustomed, struck Hasting and his confederates with astonishment and dismay. Nor did the position the English king took up with it give them much ground for comfort. Advancing into Kent, he threw himself between Hasting and the other division of the Danes: a forest on one side, and swamps and deep waters on the other, protected his flanks, and he made the front and rear of his position so strong that the Danes dared not look at them. He thus kept asunder the two armies of the Northmen, watching the motions of both, being always ready to attack either, should it quit its intrenchments; and so active were the patrols and troops he threw out in small bodies, and so good the spirit of the villagers and townfolk, cheered by the presence and wise dispositions of the sovereign, that in a short time not a single foraging party could issue from the Danish camp without almost certain destruction. Worn out in body and spirit, the Northmen resolved to break up from their camps, and, to deceive the king as to their intentions, they sent submissive messages and hostages, and promised to leave the kingdom. Hasting took to his shipping, and actually made sail, as if to leave the well-defended island; but while the eyes of the Saxons were fixed on his departure, the other division, in Alfred's rear, rushed suddenly from their intrenchments into the interior of the country, in order to seek a ford across the Thames, by which they hoped to be enabled to get into Essex, where the rebel Danes that had been ruled by Guthrun would give them a friendly reception, and where they knew they should meet Hasting and his division, who, instead of putting to sea, merely crossed the Thames, and took up a strong position at Benfleet, on the Essex coast. Alfred had not ships to pursue those who moved by water; but those who marched by land he followed up closely, and brought them to action on the right bank of the Thames, near Farnham, in Surrey. The Danes were thoroughly defeated. Those who escaped the sword and drowning marched along the left bank of the Thames, through Middlesex, into Essex; but being hotly pursued by Alfred, they were driven right through Essex, and across the river Coln, when they found a strong place of refuge in the Isle of Mersey. Here, however, they were closely blockaded, and soon obliged to sue for peace, promising hostages, as usual, and an immediate departure from England. Alfred would have had this enemy in his hand through sheer starvation, but the genius of Hasting, and the defection of the Northmen of the Danelagh, called him to a distant part of the island. Two fleets, one of 100 sail, the second of forty, and both in good part manned by the Danes who had been so long, and for the last fifteen years so

peacefully settled in England, set sail to attack in two points, and made a formidable diversion. The first of these, which had probably been equipped in Norfolk[1] and Suffolk, doubled the North Foreland, ran down the southern coast as far as Devonshire, and laid siege to Exeter: the smaller fleet, which had been fitted out in Northumbria, and probably sailed from the mouth of the Tyne, took the passage round Scotland, ran down all the western coast, from Cape Wrath to the Bristol Channel, and, ascending that arm of the sea, beleaguered a fortified town to the north of the Severn. Though Alfred had established friendly relations with the people of the west of England, who seem on many occasions to have served him with as much ardour as his Saxon subjects, he still felt that Devonshire was a vulnerable part. Leaving, therefore, a portion of his

---

[1] That Norfolk was now peopled by the Normans, under the name of Danes, may be inferred from its having the same reputation for producing litigants and lawyers that Normandy has in France, although Camden, oddly enough, attributes this to the *goodness of the soil*, which he admits to be very various. "The soil," says he, "is different, according to the several quarters; in some places it is fat, luscious, and moist; in others poor, lean, and sandy; and in others, clayey and chalky. But (to follow the directions of Varro) the goodness of the soil may be gathered from hence, that the inhabitants are of a bright, clear complexion; not to mention their sharpness of wit, and singular sagacity in the study of our common law, so that it is at present, and always has been reputed, the most fruitful nursery of lawyers. But even among the common people you may meet with many who, as one expresses it, if no quarrel offers, are able to pick one out of the quirks and niceties of the law." "And," adds Bishop Gibson, "for the preventing of the great and frequent contentions that might ensue thereupon, and the inconveniences of too many attorneys, a special statute was made, as long since as the time of King Henry VI., to restrain the number of attorneys in Norfolk, Suffolk, and Norwich." Thus Norfolk and Normandy add their testimony to the force of the expression of a man's "being too far *north* to be cheated."

army on the confines of Essex, he mounted all the rest on horses, and flew to Exeter. Victory followed him to the west; he obliged the Danes to raise the siege of Exeter; he beat them back to their ships with great loss, and soon after the minor expedition was driven from the Severn. The blockade of the Danes in the Isle of Mersey does not appear to have been well conducted during his absence, and yet that interval was not devoid of great successes: for, in the meantime, Ethelred, Eolderman of the Mercians, and Alfred's son-in-law, with the citizens of London and others, went down to the fortified post at Benfleet, in Essex, laid siege to it, broke into it, and despoiled it of great quantities of gold, silver, horses, and garments; taking away captive also the wife of Hasting and his two sons, who were brought to London, and presented to the king on his return. Some of his followers urged him to put these captives to death—others to detain them in prison as a check upon Hasting; but Alfred, with a generosity which was never properly appreciated by the savage Dane, caused them immediately to be restored to his enemy, and sent many presents of value with them. By this time the untiring Hasting had thrown up another formidable intrenchment at South Showbury, in Essex, when he was soon joined by numbers from Norfolk and Suffolk, from Northumbria, from all parts of the Danelagh, and by fresh adventurers from beyond sea. Thus reinforced, he sailed boldly up the Thames, and thence spread the mass of his forces into the heart of the kingdom, while the rest returned with their vessels and the spoil they had so far made to the intrenched camp at South Showbury. From the Thames, Hasting marched to the Severn, and fortified himself at Buttington. But here he was surrounded by the Saxons and the men of North Wales, who now cordially acted with them; and in brief time Alfred, with Ethelred and two other eoldermen, cut off all his supplies, and blockaded him in his camp. After some weeks, when the Danes had eaten up nearly all their horses, and famine was staring them in the face, Hasting rushed from his intrenchments. Avoiding the Welsh forces, he concentrated his attack upon the Saxons, who formed the blockade on the east of his position. The conflict was terrific; several hundreds (some of the chroniclers say *thousands*) of the Danes were slain in their attempt to break through Alfred's lines; many were thrown into the Severn and drowned; but the rest, headed by Hasting, effected their escape, and, marching across the island, reached their intrenchment and their ships on the Essex coast. Alfred lost many of his nobles, and must have been otherwise much crippled, for he did not molest Hasting, who could have had hardly any horse in any part of his retreat. Most of the Saxons who fought at Buttington were raw levies, and hastily got together. When Hasting next showed front it was in the neighbourhood of North Wales, between the rivers Dee and Mersey. During the winter that followed his disasters on the Severn, he had been again reinforced by the men of the Danelagh, and at early spring he set forth with his usual rapidity, and marched through the midland counties. Alfred was not far behind him, but could not overtake him until he had seized Chester, which was then almost uninhabited, and secured himself there. This town had been very strongly fortified by the Romans, and many of the works of those conquerors still remaining,[1] no doubt gave strength to Hasting's position, which was deemed too formidable for attack. But the Saxon troops pressed him on the land side, and a squadron of Alfred's ships, which had put to sea, ascended the Mersey and the river Wirall, and prevented his receiving succour in that direction. Dreading that Chester might become a second Buttington, the Danes burst away into North Wales. After ravaging part of that country, they would have gone off in the direction of the Severn and the Avon, but they were met and turned by a formidable royal army, upon which they retraced their steps, and finally marched off to the north-east. They traversed Northumbria, Lincolnshire, Norfolk, Suffolk—nearly the whole length of the Danelagh—where they were among friends and allies, and by that circuitous route at length regained their fortified post at South Showbury, in Essex, where they wintered and recruited their strength as usual.

Early next spring the persevering Hasting sailed to the mouth of the Lea, ascended that river with his ships, and at or near Ware,[2] about twenty miles above London, erected a new fortress on the Lea. On the approach of summer, the burgesses of London, with many of their neighbours, attacked the stronghold on the Lea, but were repulsed with great loss. As London was now more closely pressed than ever, Alfred found it necessary to encamp his army round about the city until the citizens got in their harvest. He then pushed a strong reconnoissance to the Lea, which (far deeper and broader than now) was covered by their ships, and afterwards surveyed, at great personal risk, the new fortified camp of the Danes. His active ingenious mind forthwith conceived a plan, which he confidently hoped would end in their inevitable destruction. Bringing up his army, he raised two fortresses,

---

[1] Some noble arched gateways, built by the Romans, were standing almost entire until a recent period, when they were laid low by a barbarous decree of the Chester corporation.

[2] Some topographers contend that this fortified camp was not at Ware, but at Hertford.

one on either side of the Lea, somewhat below the Danish station, and then he dug three deep channels from the Lea to the Thames, in order to lower the level of the tributary stream. So much water was thus drawn off, that "where a ship," says an old writer, "might sail in time afore passed, then a little boat might scarcely row;"—and the whole fleet of Hasting was left aground, and rendered useless. But yet again did that remarkable chieftain break through the toils spread for him, to renew the war in a distant part of the island. Abandoning the ships where they were, and putting, as they had been accustomed to do, their wives, their children, and their booty under the protection of their friends in the Danelagh, the followers of Hasting broke from their intrenchments by night, and hardly rested till they had traversed the whole of that wide tract of country which separates the Lea from the Severn. Marching for some distance along the left bank of the Severn, they took post close on the river at Quatbridge, which is supposed to be Quatford, near Bridgenorth, in Shropshire. When Alfred came up with them there, he found them already strongly fortified.

On our first introducing the Northmen, we mentioned their skill in choosing and strengthening military positions; and the course of our narrative will have made their skill and speed in these matters evident, especially in the campaigns they performed under Hasting, who had many of the qualities that constitute a great general. Alfred was compelled to respect the intrenchments at Quatbridge, and to leave the Danes there undisturbed during the winter. In the meantime the citizens of London seized Hasting's fleet, grounded in the Lea. Some ships they burned and destroyed, but others they were enabled to get afloat and conduct to London, where they were received with exceeding great joy.

For full three years this Scandinavian Hannibal had maintained a war in the country of the enemy; but now, watched on every side, worn out by constant losses, and probably in good part forsaken as an unlucky leader, both by his brethren settled in the Danelagh and by those on the Continent, his spirit began to break, and he prepared to take a reluctant and indignant farewell of England. In the following spring of 897, by which time dissensions had broken out among the leaders, the Danes tumultuously abandoned their camp at Quatbridge, and utterly disbanded their army soon after, fleeing in small and separate parties, in various directions. Some sought shelter among their brethren of the Danelagh, either in Northumbria, or Norfolk and Suffolk; some built vessels, and sailed for the Scheldt and the mouth of the Rhine; while others, adhering to Hasting in his evil fortune, waited until he was ready to pass into France. A small fleet, bearing his drooping raven, was hastily equipped on our eastern coast, and the humbled chieftain, according to Asser, crossed the Channel "*sine lucro et sine honore*," without profit or honour. It appears that he ascended the Seine, and soon after obtained a settlement on the banks of that river (probably in Normandy) from the weak King of the French.

A few desultory attacks made by sea, and by the men of the Danelagh, almost immediately after Hasting's departure, only tended to show the naval superiority Alfred was attaining, and to improve the Anglo-Saxons in maritime tactics. A squadron of Northumbrian pirates cruised off the southern coasts, with their old objects in view. It was met and defeated on several occasions by the improved ships of the king. Alfred, who had some mechanical skill himself, had caused vessels to be built, far exceeding those of his enemies in length of keel, height of board, swiftness, and steadiness; some of these carried sixty oars or sweepers, to be used, as in the Roman galleys, when the wind failed; and others carried even more than sixty. They differed in the form of the hull, and probably in their rigging, from the other vessels used in the North Sea. Hitherto the Danish and Friesland builds seem to have been considered as the best models; but these ships, which were found peculiarly well adapted to the service for which he intended them, were constructed after a plan of Alfred's own invention. At the end of his reign they considerably exceeded the number of 100 sail; they were divided into squadrons, and stationed at different ports round the island, while some of them were kept constantly cruising between England and the main. Although he abandoned their system of ship-building, Alfred retained many Frieslanders in his service, for they were more expert seamen than his subjects, who still required instruction. After an obstinate engagement near the Isle of Wight, two Danish ships, which had been much injured in the fight, were cast ashore and taken. When the crews were carried to the king at Winchester, he ordered them all to be hanged. This severity, so much at variance with Alfred's usual humanity, has caused some regret and confusion to historians. One writer says that the Danes do not seem to have violated *the law of nations*, as such law was then understood, and that, therefore, Alfred's execution of them was inexcusable. Another writer is of opinion that Alfred always, and properly, drew a distinction between pirates and warriors. This line would be most difficult to draw, when all were robbers and pirates alike; but the real rule of Alfred's conduct seems to have been this—to distinguish between such Danes as attacked him from abroad, and such Danes as attacked him from the Danelagh at home. On the services and gratitude of the former he had no claim, but the men of Northumbria, Norfolk, and Sussex had, through their chiefs and princes, sworn allegiance to him, had received benefits from him, and stood bound to the protection of his states, which they were ravaging. From the situation they occupied they could constantly trouble his tranquillity, and in regard to them he may have been led to consider, after the experience he had had of their bad faith, that measures of extreme severity were allowable and indispensable. The two ships captured at the Isle of Wight came from Northumbria, and the twenty ships taken during the three remaining years of his life, and of which the crews were slain or hanged on the gallows, came from the same country, and the other English lands included in the Danelagh.

The excursions of Hasting were accompanied with other calamities, "so that," to use the words of the chronicler Fabian, "this land, for three years, was vexed with three manner of sorrows —with war of the Danes, pestilence of men, and murrain of beasts." The horrors of famine, to escape which the Danes had come to England, are not alluded to, but the pestilence, which is mentioned by all the chroniclers, carried off vast numbers. It seems to have continued some time after Hasting's departure, and then, on its cessation, Alfred enjoyed as much comfort as his rapidly declining health would permit.

Before we descend to the far inferior reigns of his successors, we select from his biographers a few personal details, and cull a few of those flowers which adorned the great Alfred's reign, and which give it a beauty and an interest we look for in vain elsewhere during those barbarous ages.

Historians have generally attached great consequences to his travels on the Continent through France and Italy; and, mere child as he was, it is not improbable that Alfred's mind received impressions in those countries that were afterwards of benefit to himself and his kingdom. On the first of these journeys to Rome, Alfred was only in his fifth year, but on the second, when he was accompanied by his father, and anointed by the pope, he was eight years old. On this last occasion he stayed nearly a year at Rome, and returning thence through France, he resided some time at Paris. The Eternal City, though despoiled by the barbarians, and not yet enriched with the works of modern art, must have retained much of its ancient splendour; the Coliseum, and many other edifices that remain, are known to have been much more perfect in the days of Alfred than they are now; the proud Capitol was comparatively entire, and in various parts of the city, where we now trace little but foundations of walls and scattered fragments, there then stood lofty and elegant buildings. Alfred, who at home had lived in wooden houses, and been accustomed to see mud huts with thatched roofs, could hardly fail of being struck with the superior splendour of Rome. The papal court, though as yet modest and unassuming, was regulated with some taste and great order, while the other court at which he resided (the French) was more splendid than any in Europe, with the exception of Constantinople.

But whatever effect these scenes may have had in enlarging the mind of Alfred, it should appear he had not yet learned to read—an accomplishment, by the way, not then very common, even among princes and nobles of a more advanced age. He, however, delighted in listening to the Anglo-Saxon ballads and songs, which were constantly recited by the minstrels and gleemen attached to his father's court. From frequent vocal repetition, to which he listened day and night,[1] he learned them by heart; and the taste he thus acquired for poetry lasted him, through many cares and sorrows, to the last day of his life. The story told by Asser is well known. One day his mother, Osburgha, was sitting, surrounded by her children, with a book of Saxon poetry in her hands. The precious MS. was gilded or illuminated, and the contents were probably new, and much to the taste of the boys. "I will give it," said she, "to him among you who shall first learn to read it." Alfred, the youngest of them all, ran to a teacher, and studying earnestly, soon learned to read Anglo-Saxon, and won the book. But, with the exception of popular poetry, Anglo-Saxon was the key to only a small portion of the literature or knowledge of the times; and as his curiosity and intellect increased, it became necessary for him to learn Latin. At a subsequent period of his life Alfred possessed a knowledge of that learned language, which was altogether extraordinary for a prince of the ninth century. It is not very clear when he obtained this degree of knowledge, but after teaching himself by translating, he was probably greatly improved in his mature manhood, when the monk Asser, Johannes Erigena, Grimbald, and other learned men, settled at his court. Alfred was accustomed to say that he regretted the neglected education of his youth, the entire want of proper teachers, and also the difficulties that then barred his progress to intellectual acquirements, much more than all the hardships, and sorrows, and crosses that befell him afterwards. As one of his great impediments had been the Latin language, which, even with our improved system of tuition, and with all our facilities and advantages, is not mastered without long and difficult study, he earnestly recom-

[1] *Asser*, 16.

mended from the throne, in a circular letter addressed to the bishops, that thenceforward "all good and useful books be translated into the language which we all understand, so that all the youths of England, but more especially those who are of gentle kind, and in easy circumstances, may be grounded in letters, for they cannot profit in any pursuit until they are well able to read English." Alfred's own literary works were chiefly translations from the Latin into Anglo-Saxon, the spoken language of his people. It excites surprise how he could find time for these laudable occupations; but he was steady and persevering, regular in his habits, when not kept in the field by the Danes, and a great economist of his time. Eight hours of each day he gave to sleep, to his meals, and exercise; eight were absorbed by the affairs of government; and eight were devoted to study and devotion. Clocks, clepsydras, and the other ingenious instruments for measuring time were then unknown in England. Alfred was, no doubt, acquainted with the sun-dial, which was in common use in Italy and parts of France; but this index is of no use in the hours of the night, and would frequently be equally unserviceable during our foggy sunless days. He, therefore, marked his time by the constant burning of wax torches or candles, which were made precisely of the same weight and size, and notched in the stem at regular distances. These candles were twelve inches long; six of them, or seventy-two inches of wax, were consumed in twenty-four hours, or 1440 minutes; and thus, supposing the notches at intervals of an inch, one inch would mark the lapse of twenty minutes.

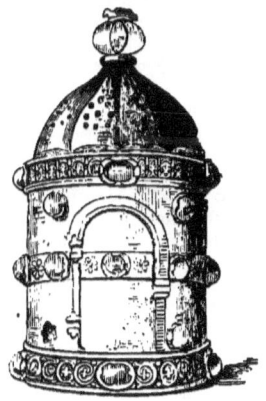

SAXON LANTERN.—From Strutt's Chronicle of England

It appears that these time-candles were placed under the special charge of his mass-priests or chaplains. But it was soon discovered that sometimes the wind, rushing in through the windows and doors, *and the numerous chinks in the walls of the palace*, consumed the wax in a rapid and irregular manner. Hence Asser makes the great Alfred the inventor of horn lanterns! He says the king went skilfully and wisely to work; and having found out that white horn could be rendered transparent like glass, he, with that material, and with pieces of wood, admirably (*mirabiliter*) made a case for his candle, which kept it from wasting and flaring.

In his youth Alfred was passionately fond of field sports, and was famed as being "excellent cunning in all hunting;" but after his retreat at Athelney he indulged this taste with becoming moderation; and during the latter years of his reign he seems to have ridden merely upon business, or for the sake of his health. He then considered every moment of value, as he could devote it to lofty and improving purposes.

We have already mentioned the care and ingenuity he employed in creating a navy. Sea affairs, geography, and the discovery of unknown countries, or rather the descriptions of countries then little known, obtained by means of bold navigators, occupied much of his time, and formed one of his favourite subjects for writing. He endeavoured, by liberality and kindness, to attract to England all such foreigners as could give good information on these subjects, or were otherwise qualified to illuminate the national ignorance. From Audher, or Ohthere, who had coasted the continent of Europe from the Baltic to the North Cape, he obtained much information; from Wulfstan, who appears to have been one of his subjects, and who undertook a voyage round the Baltic, he gathered many particulars concerning the diverse countries situated on that sea; and from other voyagers and travellers whom he sent out expressly himself, he obtained a description of Bulgaria, Sclavonia, Bohemia, and Germany. All this information he committed to writing in the plain mother tongue, and with the noble design of imparting it to his people. Having learned that there were colonies of Christian Syrians settled on the coasts of Malabar and Coromandel, he sent out Swithelm, Bishop of Sherburn, to India—a tremendous journey in those days. The stout-hearted ecclesiastic, however, making what is now called the overland journey, went and returned in safety, bringing back with him presents of gems and Indian spices. Hereby was Alfred's fame increased, and the name and existence of England probably heard of for the first time in that remote country, of which, nine centuries after, she was to become the almost absolute mistress.[1]

[1] For further details relating to the commerce of this and subsequent periods, we refer the reader to *History of British Commerce from the Earliest Times*, by Geo. L. Craik, M.A.

While his active mind, which anticipated the national spirit of much later times, was thus engaged in drawing knowledge from the distant corners of the earth, he did not neglect home affairs. He taught the people how to build better houses; he laboured to increase their comforts; he established schools; he founded or rebuilt many towns; and having learned the importance of fortifications during his wars with the Danes, he fortified them all as well as he could. He caused a survey to be made of the coast and navigable rivers, and ordered castles to be erected at those places which were most accessible to the landing of the enemy. Fifty strong towers and castles rose in different parts of the country, but the number would have been threefold had Alfred not been thwarted by the indolence, ignorance, and carelessness of his nobles and people. He revised the laws of the Anglo-Saxons, being aided and sanctioned therein by his witenagemot or parliament; and he established so excellent a system of police, that towards the end of his reign it was generally asserted that one might have hung golden bracelets and jewels on the public highways and cross-roads, and no man would have dared to touch them, for fear of the law.

ALFRED'S JEWEL.[1]—Ashmolean Museum, Oxford.

Towards arbitrary, unjust, or corrupt administrators of the law, he was inexorable; and, if we can give credit to an old writer,[2] he ordered the execution of no fewer than forty-four judges and magistrates of this stamp in the course of one year. Those who were ignorant or careless he reprimanded and suspended, commanding them to qualify themselves for the proper discharge of their office before they ventured to grasp its honours and emoluments. He heard all appeals with the utmost patience, and, in cases of importance, revised all the law proceedings with the utmost industry. His manifold labours in the court, the camp, the field, the hall of justice, the study, must have been prodigious; and our admiration of this wonderful man is increased by the well-established fact, that all these exertions were made in spite of the depressing influences of physical pain and constant bad health. In his early years he was severely afflicted by the disease called the *ficus*. This left him; but, at the age of twenty or twenty-one, it was replaced by another and still more tormenting malady, the inward seat and unknown mysterious nature of which battled all the medical skill of his "leeches." The accesses of excruciating pain were frequent—at times almost uninterminent; and then if, by day or by night, a single hour of ease was mercifully granted him, that short interval was imbittered by the dread of the sure returning anguish.[3] This malady never left him till the day of his death, which it must have hastened. He expired in the month of October, six nights before All-Hallows-mass Day, in the year 901, when he was only in the fifty-third year of his age, and was buried at Winchester, in a monastery he had founded.

In describing his brilliant and incontestable deeds, and in tracing the character of the great Alfred, we, in common with nearly all the writers who have preceded us in the task, have drawn a general eulogy, and a character nearly approaching to ideal perfection. But were there no spots in all this brilliancy and purity? As Alfred was a mortal man, there were, no doubt, many; but to discover them, we must ransack his private life, and his vaguely reported conduct when a mere stripling king; and the discovery, after all, confers no honour of sagacity, and does not justify the exultation with which a recent writer announces to the world that Alfred had not only faults, but crimes to bemoan. It is passed into a truism that he will seldom be in the wrong who deducts alike from the amount of virtue and vice in the characters recorded in history; but this deduction will be made according to men's tempers; and while some largely reduce the amount of virtue, they seem to leave the vice untouched—their incredulity extending rather to what elevates and ennobles human nature, than to the things which degrade and debase it. The directly contrary course, or that of reducing the crime, and leaving the virtue, if not the more correct (which we will not decide), is certainly

---

[1] This highly interesting relic, an ornament of gold, seemingly intended to be hung round the neck, was found near Athelney, in Somersetshire, the very place of Alfred's retreat and deliverance from the Danes. The jewel contains an effigy, conjectured to be that of St. Cuthbert, enamelled on gold, surrounded by the following inscription, which identifies it with the bost of the Saxon kings —AELFRED ME HEAT GEWRCAN (Alfred bad me wrought). On the other side is represented a flower. The jewel measures about 3 in. long, and the workmanship of the whole is good. Malmesbury relates that St. Cuthbert appeared to Alfred in a vision at Athelney, and predicted his future triumph over the infidel Danes.

[2] Andrew Horne, author of *Miroir des Justices*, who wrote, in Norman French, under Edward I. or Edward II.

[3] *Asser*.

the more generous and improving. Every people above the condition of barbarity have their heroes and their national objects of veneration, and are probably improved by the high standard of excellence they present, and by the very reverence they pay to them. We may venerate the memory of our Alfred with as little danger of paying an unmerited homage as any of them. On this subject the late Sir James Mackintosh, whose historical sagacity was equal to his good feeling, says, " The Norman historians, who seem to have had his diaries and note-books in their hands, chose Alfred as the glory of the land which had become their own. There is no subject on which unanimous tradition is so nearly sufficient evidence as on the eminence of one man over others of the same condition. His bright image may long be held up before the national mind. This tradition, however paradoxical the assertion may appear, is, in the case of Alfred, rather supported than weakened by the fictions which have sprung from it. Although it be an infirmity of every nation to ascribe their institutions to the contrivance of a man, rather than to the slow action of time and circumstances, yet the selection of Alfred by the English people, as the founder of all that was dear to them, is surely the strongest proof of the deep impression, left on the minds of all, of his transcendent wisdom and virtue."[1]

CHAPTER III.—CIVIL AND MILITARY HISTORY.

FROM THE ACCESSION OF EDWARD TO THE DEATH OF HARDICANUTE.—A.D. 901–1042.

Reign of Edward—Account of his sister, Ethelfleda—Reign of Athelstane—His victory at Brunnaburgh—Reigns of Edmund the Atheling, Edred, and Edwy—Contest of Edwy with Dunstan—Tragical fate of Elgiva, the wife of Edwy—Reign of Edgar—His prosperity—His marriage with Elfrida—Reign of Edward the Martyr—His assassination at Corfe Castle—He is succeeded by Ethelred—Reign of Ethelred, surnamed the Unready—The Danes invade England—Their forbearance purchased with money—Massacre of the Danes in England—Invasion of England by Sweyn, King of Denmark—His invasion repeated—Ethelred's unwise proceedings—Invasion of Thurkill's host—Martyrdom of Alphege by the Danes—Sweyn once more invades England, and is proclaimed king—Ethelred's return to England, and death—Succeeded by Edmund Ironside—Canute becomes King of England—Marries the widow of Ethelred—His prosperous reign—His pilgrimage to Rome—His rebuke of the flattery of his courtiers—He is succeeded by his son Harold—Treacherous murder of Edward the son of Ethelred—Harold succeeded by Hardicanute—Death of Hardicanute at a banquet.

DWARD. A.D. 901. Alfred, with all his wisdom and power, had not been enabled to settle the succession to the throne on a sure and lasting basis. On his death it was disputed between his son Edward and his nephew Ethelwald, the son of Ethelbald, one of Alfred's elder brothers. Each party armed; but as Ethelwald found himself the weaker, he declined a combat at Wimburn, and fled into the Danelagh, where the Danes hailed him as their king. Many of the Saxons who lived in that country mixed with the Danes, preferred war to the restraints of such a government as Alfred had established; and an internal war was renewed, which did infinite mischief, and prepared the way for other horrors. Ethelwald was slain in a terrible battle fought in the

---

[1] *Hist. Eng.* ch. xi. "The qualities of his mind were those of a statesman and a hero, but elevated, and, at the same time, softened, by his ardent longing for higher and more imperishable things than those on which all the splendour and power of this world generally rest. The most unshakable courage was most certainly the first component of his being; he showed it, while still a youth, in the tumult of the battle of Ascesdunc. There was one period when his courage seemed about to desert him. This was when the young king imagined that he saw his country for ever in the hands of the foe, and his people doomed to never-ending despair; but from the ordeal of Athelney he came out proved and victorious, and a large number of brave men rivalled each other in imitating his example.

"We have already had occasion, several times, in the course of this work, to notice another peculiarity of Alfred's mind that was attended with no less gratifying results; he possessed a decided turn for invention, which enabled him not only to extricate himself from personal difficulties, but to suggest new and original ideas in the execution of all sorts of artistic productions and handiwork. The pillars on which the church at Athelney was built, the long ships he constructed, the manner in which he turned a river from its natural course, and his clock of tapers, afford us as convincing evidence of his powers of thought as the battles which he gained. . . . .

"Elevated by his piety above all his subjects and contemporaries, no one could he farther than he was from becoming a weak bigot, willingly bending beneath the yoke of an arrogant priesthood; and, while immersed in the fulfilment of his religious duties, forgetting the prosperity of worldly affairs, as well as that of his subjects. He was well aware what the country had suffered from the too yielding disposition of his father to the will of the higher ecclesiastics. It is impossible to draw a parallel between Alfred and his descendant Edward the Confessor. The latter lost his kingdom, and was made a saint; the former kept it by the aid of his sword and a firm reliance on the Almighty. The Church of Rome, it is true, did not thank him for this; but he lived, through his works, in the hearts of his people, who celebrated his praises in their songs."—Pauli's *Life of Alfred the Great*.

year 905, upon which the Danes concluded a peace upon equal terms; for Edward was not yet powerful enough to treat them as a master. The sons of the princes and yarls, and in many instances the individuals themselves, who had been tranquil and submissive under Alfred, soon aimed, not merely at making the Danelagh an independent kingdom, but at conquering the rest of the island. Edward was not deficient in valour or military skill. In the year 911 he gained a most signal victory over the Danes, who had advanced to the Severn; but the whole spirit of Alfred seemed more particularly to survive in his daughter Ethelfleda, sister of Edward, and wife of Ethelred, the Eolderman of Mercia, who has been so often mentioned, and whose death, in 912, left the whole care of that kingdom to his widow. Her brother Edward took possession of London and Oxford, but she claimed and then defended the rest of Mercia, with the bravery and ability of an experienced warrior. Following her father's example, she fortified all her towns, and constructed ramparts and intrenched camps in the proper places; allowing them no rest, she drove the Danes out of Derby and Leicester, and compelled many tribes of them to acknowledge her authority. In the assault of Derby, four of her bravest commanders fell, but she boldly urged the combat until the place was taken. As some of the Welsh had become troublesome, she conducted an expedition, with remarkable spirit and rapidity, against Breccannere or Brecknock, and took the wife of the Welsh king prisoner. In seeing these, her warlike operations, says an old writer, one would have believed she had changed her sex. The Lady Ethelfleda, as she is called by the chroniclers, died in 920, when Edward succeeded to her authority in Mercia, and prosecuted her plan of securing the country by fortified works. He was active and successful: he took most of the Danish towns between the Thames and the Humber, and forced the rest of the Danelagh that lay north of the Humber to acknowledge his supremacy. The Welsh, the Scots, the inhabitants of Strathclyde and Cumbria (who still figure as a separate people), and the men of Galloway, are said to have done him homage, and to have accepted him as their "father, lord, and protector."

ATHELSTANE. A.D. 925. Edward's dominion far exceeded in extent that of his father Alfred; but his son Athelstane, who succeeded him in 925, established a more brilliant throne, and made a still nearer approach to the sovereignty of all England. By war and policy he reduced nearly all Wales to an inoffensive tranquillity, if not to vassalage. A tribute was certainly paid during a part of the reign, and, together with gold and silver, and beeves, the Welsh were bound to send their best hounds and hawks to the court of Athelstane. He next turned his arms against the old tribes of Cornwall, who were still turbulent, and impatient of the Saxon yoke. He drove them from Devonshire, where they had again made encroachments, and reduced them to obedience and good order beyond the Tamar.

In 937 he was assailed by a more powerful confederacy than had ever been formed against a Saxon king. Olave or Anlaf, a Danish prince, who had already been settled in Northumbria, but who had lately taken Dublin, and made considerable conquests in Ireland, sailed up the Humber with 630 ships; his friend and ally, Constantine, King of the Scots, the people of Strathclyde and Cumbria, and the northern Welsh were all up in arms, and ready to join him. Yet this coalition, formidable as it was, was utterly destroyed on the bloody field of Brunnaburgh,[1] where Athelstane gained one of the most splendid of victories, and where five Danish *kings* and seven earls fell. Anlaf escaped, with a wretched fragment of his forces, to Ireland; Constantine, bemoaning the loss of his fair-haired son, who had also perished at Brunnaburgh, fled to the hilly country north of the friths. After this great victory, none seem to have dared again to raise arms against Athelstane in any part of the island.

It appears to have been from this time that Athelstane laid aside the modest and limited title of his predecessors, and assumed that of "King of the Anglo-Saxons," or "King of the English," a title which had been given to several of them in the letters of the Roman popes and bishops, but had never till now been used by the sovereigns themselves. His father, and his grandfather Alfred, had simply styled themselves Kings of Wessex, or of the West Saxons.

Under Athelstane the English court was polished to a considerable degree, and became the chosen residence or asylum of several foreign princes. Harold, the King of Norway, intrusted his son Haco to the care and tuition of the enlightened Athelstane; and his son, by the aid of England, afterwards succeeded to the Norwegian throne, on which he distinguished himself as a legislator. Louis d'Outremer, the French king, took refuge in London before he secured his throne; and even the Celtic princes of Armorica or Brittany, when expelled their states by the Northmen or Normans, fled to the court of Athelstane in preference to all others. He bestowed his sisters in marriage on the first sovereigns of those times, and, altogether, he enjoyed a degree of respect, and exercised an influence on the general politics of Europe, that were not surpassed by any living sovereign.[2] A horrid suspicion of guilt

---

[1] Supposed by some to be Bourn, in the south of Lincolnshire; by others, Brugh, in the north of the same county.

[2] Among the costly presents sent to Athelstane by foreign

—the crime of murdering his own brother Edwin—has been cast upon him; but this is scarcely proved by any contemporary evidence, and his conduct as a sovereign seems almost irreproachable. He revised the laws, promulgated some new and good ones, made a provision for the poor and helpless, and encouraged the study of letters by earnest recommendations and by his own example. Like his grandfather Alfred, he was exceedingly fond of the Bible, and promoted the translation of it into the spoken language of the people. The life of this king was, in the words of William of Malmesbury, "in time little—in deeds great." Had it been prolonged, he might possibly have consolidated his power, and averted those tempests from the north which soon again desolated England. He died A.D. 940, being only in his forty-seventh year, and was buried in the abbey of Malmesbury.

EDMUND the Atheling, his brother, who was not quite eighteen years old, succeeded to the throne. In him the family virtue of courage knew no blemish or decrease; and he showed a determined taste for elegance and improvement, which obtained for him the name of "the Magnificent;" but his reign was troubled from the beginning, and he was cut off in his prime by the hand of an assassin. He had scarcely ascended the throne when the Danes of Northumbria recalled from Ireland Anlaf, the old opponent of Athelstane at Brunnaburgh. The Danish prince came in force, and the result of a war was, that Edmund was obliged to resign to him, in separate sovereignty, the whole of the island north of Watling-street. But Anlaf did not enjoy these advantages many months; and when he died Edmund repossessed himself of all the territory he had ceded. During his troubles the people of Cumbria, who had submitted to Athelstane, broke out in rebellion. He marched against them in 946, expelled their king, Dunmail, and gave the country as a fief to Malcolm of Scotland, whom he at the same time bound to defend the north of the island against Danish and other invaders. The two sons of Dunmail, whom he took prisoners, he barbarously deprived of their eyes. Such abominable operations, together with the amputating of limbs, cutting off of tongues and noses of captive princes, had become common on the Continent, but hitherto had very rarely disgraced the Anglo-Saxons. Edmund did not long survive the perpetration of this atrocity. On the festival of St. Augustine, in the same year, as he was carousing with his nobles and officers, his eye fell upon a banished robber, named Leof, who had dared to mingle with the company. The royal cup-bearer, or *dapifer*, ordered him to withdraw. The robber refused. Incensed at his insolence, and heated by wine, Edmund started from his seat, and seizing him by his long hair, tried to throw him to the ground. Leof had a dagger hid under his cloak, and in the scuffle he stabbed the king in a vital part. The desperate villain was cut to pieces by Edmund's servants, but not before he had slain and hurt divers of them. The body of the king was interred in Glastonbury Abbey, where Dunstan, who was soon to occupy a wider scene, was then abbot.

EDRED (946), who succeeded his brother Edmund, was another son of Edward the Elder, and grandson of Alfred. He was not twenty-three years old, but a loathsome disease had brought on a premature old age. He was afflicted with a constant cough, he lost his teeth and hair, and he was so weak in his lower extremities that he was nick-named "Edredus debilis pedibus" (Edred weak in the feet). According to some authorities his mind was as feeble as his body, and the vigour that marked his reign sprung from the energy of Dunstan, the abbot of Glastonbury, who now began to figure as a statesman, and of Torketul, another churchman, who was chancellor of the kingdom. Other writers, however, affirm that Edred's weak and puny body did not affect his mind, which was resolute and vigorous, and such as became a grandson of Alfred. Though, in common with the other states of the north, the Danes of Northumbria had sworn fealty to Edred at Tadwine's Cliff, they rose soon after his accession, and being joined by Eric, and other princes and pirates from Denmark, Norway, Ireland, the Orkneys, and the Hebrides (where the sea-kings had established themselves), they once more tried the fortune of war with the Saxons. The operations of Edred's armies, though disgraced by cruelty and the devastation of the land, were marked with exceeding vigour and activity, and, after two or three most obstinate and sanguinary battles, they were crowned with success. The Danes in England, humbled and apparently crushed, were condemned to pay a heavy pecuniary fine; Northumbria was incorporated with the rest of the kingdom much more completely than it had hitherto been; the royal title was abolished, and the administration put into the hands of an earl appointed by the king. Even the victorious Athelstane had left the title of king, or sub-king, to the Danish rulers of Northumbria, and it is assumed that the constant rebellions of those rulers were principally excited by their anxious wish to throw off the allegiance due to the English crown. We believe, however, there was a powerful excitement from without. The sea-kings still roamed the ocean in search of plunder or settlements; many princes or chiefs in Denmark and Norway claimed kindred with

---

sovereigns, was one from the King of Norway, "of a goodly ship of fine workmanship, with gilt stern and purple sails, furnished round about the deck within with a row of gilt pavises (or shields)."

those who had made conquests and obtained kingdoms in England, and whenever an opportunity offered they pretended to those possessions by an indefeasible, hereditary right. Such a right might not be recognized by the Anglo-Saxons, but it would pass unquestioned among the Scandinavian rovers, who would profit by its being enforced. The names of a whole series of these Danish pretenders may probably be found in the mythical historians—in the more than half fabulous Edda and Sagas of the north—but we are not aware that the discovery of them would cast any very important light on our annals.

Edred died soon after the reduction of Northumbria, and, leaving no children, was succeeded by the son of his brother and predecessor on the throne.

EDWY was a boy of fifteen when he began his troublous reign (A.D. 955). One of the first acts of his government seems to have been the appointment of his brother Edgar (whom the monks soon played off against him) to be sub-regulus or vassal-king of a part of England,[1] most probably of the old kingdom of Mercia, where he was to acknowledge Edwy's supremacy. As the Northumbrians remained in subjection, and as the Danes generally seem to have ceased from troubling the land, he might have enjoyed a tranquil reign but for some irregularities of his own, and his quarrels with a body more powerful then than warriors and sea-kings, and who fought with a weapon more deadly than the sword.

We now reach an interesting part of our history, which, after passing current for many ages, has been fiercely disputed by some recent writers, whose main course of argument is weakened by the glaring fact, that in shifting all the blame from Dunstan to Edwy, they had party or sectarian purposes to serve. For ourselves, who are perfectly impartial between the king and the monk, we think the old narrative has been disturbed without rendering any service to historical truth, and that this is proved to be the case, almost to a demonstration, by a learned and acute writer who has sifted the whole question.[2] Like nearly every other part of the Saxon history, the story of Edwy and Elgiva is certainly involved in some difficulties or obscurities. Avoiding discussion and disputation, we will briefly state the facts as they seem to us best established.

Edwy, who was gay, handsome, thoughtless, and very young, became enamoured of Elgiva, a young lady of rank, and married her, although she was related to him in a degree within which the canonical laws forbade such union. She was probably his first or second cousin; and we need not go nearer, as such marriages are still illegal in Catholic countries, without the express dispensation of the pope. Her mother, Ethelgiva, lived with her at the court of Edwy, and seems to have been a person of good repute, for, under the honourable designation of the "king's wife's mother," she attested an agreement between St. Ethelwold and the Bishop of Wells, to which three other bishops were subscribing witnesses. We are entitled to assume, that had there been anything more than a slight infringement of church-law in the marriage of Elgiva, or had she and her mother been the depraved characters some writers have represented them, such personages as saints, and bishops, and most orthodox churchmen would not be found frequenting the court, where both the ladies lived in pre-eminence and honour. Dunstan and his party, however, must surely have had other provocations than the irregularity of the marriage, or the thoughtlessness of Edwy in quitting their company, when they proceeded to the insolent extremities we are now to relate. On the day of the king's coronation the chief nobles and clergy were bidden to a feast, where they sat long carousing, deep in their cups, which they were too much accustomed to do.[3] The stomach of the youthful king may have been incapable of such potations—his taste may have been revolted by such coarse excesses—he was still passionately enamoured of his beautiful bride; and, stealing from the banqueting-hall, he withdrew with her and her mother to an inner apartment of the palace. His absence was remarked by Odo, the Archbishop of Canterbury, a Dane by birth,[4] a harsh, ambitious man, who may be more than suspected of having played false with Edwy's father, King Edmund, when engaged in the Northumbrian troubles, and obliged to renounce half the island to Aulaf. Odo was probably exasperated himself, and perceiving that the company were displeased at the king's leaving them, he ordered some persons to go and bring him back to partake of the general conviviality. The individuals addressed seem to have declined the office, from motives of respect and decency; but Dunstan, the friend of Odo, feeling no such scruples, rushed to the inner apartment, dragged the young king from the side of his wife, and thrust him back into the banqueting-hall by main force. Such an outrage—such a humiliation in the face of his assembled

---

[1] "This fact, which is of some importance, is proved, like many other points of a similar description, not by historians, but by a charter. The document, however, does not designate the locality of the dominions assigned to Edgar."—Palgrave, *Hist. Eng.* ch. xii. We follow this learned investigator in supposing it was Mercia.

[2] See article on Lingard's *Antiquities of the Anglo-Saxon Church*, in *Edinburgh Review*, vol. xxv. pp. 346-354; and article on Lingard's *History of England*, in the same work, vol. xliii. pp. 1-31. Both these reviews are acknowledged to be by the late John Allen, Esq., in his *Letter to Francis Jeffrey, Esq., in reply to Dr. Lingard's Vindication*, 8vo. Lond. 1827.

[3] "Quibus Angli nimis sunt assueti."—*Wallingford.*

[4] He was the son of one of the chieftains who had invaded England.

subjects—must have passed Edwy's endurance. Nor was this all the wrong. While in the chamber Dunstan addressed the queen and her mother in the most brutal language, and threatened the latter with infamy and the gallows. The king had a ready rod wherewith to scourge the monk. Dunstan, among other offices, filled that of treasurer to Edred, the preceding sovereign, and Edwy, it is said, had all along suspected him of having been guilty of peculation in his charge. If Edwy had ever whispered these suspicions—and from his youth, imprudence, and hastiness of temper, he had probably done so often—this alone would account for Dunstan's ire. However this may be, the fiery abbot of Glastonbury, who returned from the festival to his abbey, was now questioned touching the moneys; his property was sequestered; his court places were taken from him; the monks who professed celibacy were driven out, and his monastery was given to the secular clergy, who still insisted on having wives like other men; and finally a sentence of banishment was hurled at Dunstan. He fled for the monastery of St. Peter's, in Ghent, but was scarcely three miles from the shore, on his way to Flanders, when messengers reached it, despatched by Edwy or his mother-in-law, and who, it is said, had orders to put out his eyes if they caught him in this country.

Before this extreme rupture Edwy had probably meddled with the then stormy politics of the church, or betrayed an inclination to favour the secular clergy in opposition to the monks; and this again would, and of itself, suffice to account for Dunstan's outrageous behaviour at the coronation feast. After Dunstan's flight the king certainly made himself the protector of the "married clerks;" for, expelling those who professed celibacy, he put the others in possession, not only of Glastonbury and Malmesbury, but of several other abbeys, which he thus made (to speak the language of Dunstan's adherents and successors) "styes for canons." In so doing, Edwy, fatally for himself, espoused the weaker party, and still further exasperated Odo, the Archbishop of Canterbury, who entertained the same views in state matters and church discipline as his friend Dunstan.

Shortly after the departure of Dunstan, a general rising of the people, instigated by Odo, took place in Northumbria (the reader will bear in mind that the archbishop was a Dane), and a corresponding movement following, under the same influence or holy sanction, in Mercia, it was determined to set one brother in hostile array against the other; and, in brief time, Edgar was declared independent sovereign of the whole of the island north of the Thames! Dunstan then returned in triumph from his brief exile, which had scarcely lasted a year.

But while these events were in progress, and before they were completed, the young soul of Edwy was racked by an anguish more acute than any that could be caused by the loss of territory and empire. Some knights and armed retainers of the implacable archbishop tore his beautiful wife Elgiva from one of his residences, branded her in the face with a red-hot iron, to destroy her beauty, and then hurried her to the coast, whence she was transported to Ireland, probably as a slave. Her melancholy fate, her high birth, gracefulness, and youth (for she seems to have been now not more than sixteen or seventeen years old), probably gained her friends among a kind-hearted people. She was cured of the cruel wounds inflicted; her scars were obliterated; and, as radiant in beauty as ever, she was allowed (and no doubt assisted) to return to England. It is not clear whether Elgiva had actually joined her husband or was fleeing to his embraces, when she was seized near Gloucester; but all the early accounts agree in stating that she was there barbarously mangled and hamstrung, and that she expired a few days after in great torture. The generally received statement is, that the perpetrators of this atrocious deed were armed retainers of the Archbishop Odo: others, however, are of opinion that the young queen fell into the hands of the Mercians, who were in insurrection against her husband, and that in neither case was the execution ordered either by Odo or Dunstan. However this may be, the deed was undeniably done by the adherents of those churchmen (for the Mercians were armed in their quarrel), and praised as an act of inflexible virtue by their encomiasts. The palliation set up by a recent historian—who cannot deny the fact of the hamstringing—that such a mode of punishment, "though cruel, was not unusual in that age," leaves the question of justice and law untouched, and seems to us to be conceived in the spirit of an inquisitor of the worst ages. Edwy did not long survive his wife: he died in the following year (958), when he could not have been more than eighteen or nineteen years old. His death is generally attributed to grief and a broken heart, but it is just as probable that he was assassinated by his enemies.[1] From the comeliness of his person, he was generally called Edwy the Fair.

EDGAR (958-9), his brother, who had been put forward against him in his lifetime, now succeeded to all his dignities. As a boy of fifteen, he could exercise little authority: he was long a passive instrument in the hands of Dunstan and

---

[1] An old MS. in the Cottonian Library says explicitly, "In pago Glocestrensi interfectus fuit." Another old MS., quoted by Mr. Sharon Turner, says, "Misera morte exspiravit;" but this would apply as well (or better) to death by grief as to death by the dagger.

his party, who used their power in establishing their cause, in enforcing the celibacy of the clergy, and in driving out, by main force, from all abbeys, monasteries, cathedrals, churches, and chantries, all such married clergymen as would not separate from their wives. At the same time, it cannot be denied that Dunstan and the monks ruled the kingdom with vigour and success, and consolidated the detached states into more compact integrity and union than had ever been known before. Several causes favoured this process. Among others, Edgar, who had been brought up among the Danes of East Anglia and Northumbria, was endeared to that people, who, in consequence, allowed him to weaken their states, by dividing them into several separate earldoms or governments, and to make other innovations, which they would have resented with arms in their hands under any of his predecessors. His fleet was also wisely increased to the number of 360 sail; and these ships were so well disposed, and powerful squadrons kept so constantly in motion, that the sea-kings were held in check on their own element, and prevented from landing and troubling the country. At the same time, tutored by the indefatigable Dunstan, who soon was made, or rather who soon made himself, Archbishop of Canterbury, the king accustomed himself to visit in person every part of his dominions annually. In the land progresses he was attended by the primate, or by energetic ministers of Dunstan's appointing; and as he went from Wessex to Mercia, from Mercia to Northumbria, courts of justice were held in the different counties, audiences and feasts were given, appeals were heard, and Edgar cultivated the acquaintance of all the nobles and principal men of the kingdom. The neighbouring princes—his vassals or allies—of Wales, Cumbria, and Scotland, were awed into respect or obedience, and on several occasions seem to have bowed before his throne. When he held his court at Chester, and had one day a wish to visit the monastery of St. John's, on the river Dee, eight crowned kings (so goes the story) plied the oars of his barge, while he guided the helm. These sovereign-bargemen are said to have been Kenneth, King of Scotland; Malcolm, his son, King of Cumbria; Macens the Dane, King of Anglesey, the Isle of Man, and the Hebrides; the Scottish Kings of Galloway and "Westmere;" and the three Welsh Kings of Dynwall, Siferth, and Edwall.[1]

Edgar certainly bore prouder and more sounding titles than any of his predecessors. He was styled Basileus or Emperor of Albion, King of the English, and of all the nations and islands around.[2] He obtained the more honourable epithet of the Peaceable or Pacific; for, luckily, during his whole reign, his kingdom was not troubled by a single war.[3] He commuted a tribute he received from a part or the whole of Wales, into 300 wolves' heads annually, in order to extirpate those ravenous animals; and, according to William of Malmesbury, this tribute ceased in the fourth year, for want of wolves to kill. The currency had been so diminished in weight by the fradulent practice of clipping, that the actual value was far inferior to the nominal. He therefore reformed the coinage, and had new coins issued all over the kingdom. Though Edgar was now in mature manhood, there is pretty good evidence to show that these measures, with others, generally of a beneficial nature, were suggested and carried into effect by Dunstan, who, most indubitably, had his full share in the next operations, which are mentioned with especial laud and triumph by the monkish writers. He made married priests so scarce or so timid, that their faces were nowhere to be seen; and he founded or restored no fewer than fifty monasteries, which were all subjected to the rigid rules of the Benedictine order. It is curious that the monks, who had a debt of gratitude to pay, and who, in their summary of his whole character, indeed, uphold Edgar as a godly, virtuous prince, should have recorded actions which prove him to have been one of the most viciously profligate of

---

[1] "Hence, his fame being noised abroad, foreigners—Saxons, Flemings, and even Danes—frequently sailed hither, and were on terms of intimacy with Edgar, though their arrival was highly prejudicial to the natives; for from the Saxons they learned an untamable ferocity of mind; from the Flemings, an unmanly delicacy of body; and from the Danes, drunkenness; though they were before free from such propensities, and disposed to observe their own customs with native simplicity, rather than admire those of others."—*William of Malmesb.* book ii. ch. viii. Yet, in spite of these corrupting influences, the monk of Malmesbury adds: "At this time the light of holy men was so resplendent in England, that you would believe the very stars from heaven smiled upon it. Among these was Dunstan," . . . who, without preaching total abstinence as a remedy for the growing vice of drunkenness, "ordered gold or silver pegs to be fastened in the pots; that whilst every man knew his just measure, shame should compel each neither to take more himself, nor to oblige others to drink more than their proportional share."—See Giles' ed. p. 148.

[2] "Nothing," says Mr. Turner, "can more strongly display Edgar's vanity than the pompous and boasting titles which he assumes in his charters. They sometimes run to the length of fifteen or eighteen lines. How different from Alfred's 'Ego occidentalium Saxonum Rex!'"—Sharon Turner's *History of the Anglo-Saxons.*

[3] "Edgar the Pacific, as he was called, gave a greater extent and majesty to the Anglo-Saxon dominion than any Bretwalda had hitherto obtained. Peace, it was believed, was prophesied to him by Dunstan, and peace certainly prevailed. A combat with the Britons, faintly indicated, is the only sign of war which can be traced in the annals of his reign. Yet such obedience was rendered to Edgar as no sovereign of Britain had ever claimed before. Circumnavigating the island with a fleet whose numbers are said to have amounted to 5000 vessels, he led his mighty force to the city of Chester, where the vassals of the Anglo-Saxon crown had assembled, pursuant to his behest."—Palgrave's *History of the Anglo-Saxons.*

the Saxon kings. The court of this promoter of celibacy and chastity swarmed at all times with concubines, some of whom were obtained in the most violent or flagitious manner. To pass over less authentic cases, in an early part of his reign, during the life of his first wife, he carried off from the monastery of Wilton a beautiful young lady of noble birth, named Wulfreda, who was either a professed nun, or receiving her education under the sacred covering of the veil. It has been said that Dunstan here interfered with a courage which absolves him from the charge of reserving his reproofs for those who stood, like the unfortunate Edwy, in the position of enemies. But what was the amount of his interference in this extreme case, where the sanctity of the cloister itself was violated? He condemned the king to lay aside an empty, inconvenient bauble—not to wear his crown on his head for seven years—and to a penance of fasting, which was probably in good part performed by deputy. This was not the measure of punishment that was meted out to Edwy; and, for all that we can learn to the contrary, Edgar was allowed to retain Wulfreda as his mistress! On another occasion, when the guest of one of his nobles at Andover, he ordered that the fair and honourable daughter of his host should be sent to his bed. The young lady's mother artfully substituted a handsome slave or servant; and this menial was added to his harem, or taken to court, where, according to William of Malmesbury, she enjoyed his exceeding great favour, until he became enamoured of Elfrida, his second *lawful* wife. Romantic as are its incidents, the story of his marriage with the execrable Elfrida rests on about as good authority as we can find for any of the events of the time. The fame of this young lady's beauty reached the ears of Edgar, ever hungry of such reports. To ascertain whether her charms were not exaggerated, the royal voluptuary despatched Athelwold, his favourite courtier, to the distant castle of her father, Ordgar, Earl of Devonshire. Athelwold became himself enamoured of the beauty, wedded her, and then represented her to the king as being rich, indeed, but not otherwise commendable. Edgar suspected or was told the real truth. He insisted on paying her a visit. The unlucky husband was allowed to precede him, that he might put his house in order; but he failed in his real object, which was to obtain his wife's forgiveness for having stepped between her and a throne, and to induce her to disguise or conceal the brilliancy of her charms by homely attire and rustic demeanour. The visit was made: the king was captivated, as she intended he should be. Soon after Athelwold was found murdered in a wood, and Edgar married his widow. This union, begun in crime, led to the foul murder of Edgar's eldest son: and under the imbecile Ethelred, the only son he had by Elfrida, the glory of the house of Alfred was eclipsed for ever. He himself did not survive the marriage more than six or seven years, when he died, at the early age of thirty-two, and was buried in the abbey of Glastonbury, which he had made magnificent by vast outlays of money and donations of land.[1]

EDWARD, commonly called the Martyr, who succeeded (A.D. 975), was Edgar's son by his first marriage. Like all the kings since Athelstane, he was a mere boy at his accession, being not more than fourteen or fifteen years old. His rights were disputed, in favour of her own son, Ethelred, who was only six years old, by the ambitious and remorseless Elfrida, who boldly maintained that Edward, though the elder brother, and named king in his father's will, was excluded by the illegitimacy of his birth. The legitimacy of several of the Saxon princes who had worn the crown was more than doubtful; but in the case of Edward the challenge seems to have been unfounded. The cause of Edward and his half-brother was decided on far different grounds. As soon as Edgar was dead the church war was renewed, and Dunstan, after a long and unopposed triumph, was compelled once more to descend to the arena with his old opponents, the "married clerks," or secular clergy, who again showed themselves in force in many parts of the kingdom, and claimed the abbeys and churches of which they had been dispossessed. The nobles and the governors of provinces chose different sides. Alfere, the powerful Eolderman of Mercia, declared for the secular clergy, and drove the monks from every part of his extensive dominions. Alwyn, of East Anglia, on the contrary, stood by Dunstan and the monks, and chased the seculars. Elfrida, no doubt because Dunstan and his friends had got possession of Edward, gave the weight of her son Ethelred's name and herself to the party of Alfere and the seculars, which soon proved again to be the weaker of the two factions. Had it been the stronger, Ethelred would have been crowned; as it turned out, Dunstan was enabled to place Edward upon the

---

[1] ' Edgar's reign has been celebrated as the most glorious of all the Anglo-Saxon kings. No other sovereign, indeed, converted his prosperity into such personal pomp, and no other sovereign was more degraded in his posterity. With his short life—for he died at thirty-two—the gaudy pageantry ceased, and all the vast dominion in which he had so ostentatiously exulted vanished from his children's grasp. His eldest son perished by the scheme of his beloved Elfrida; his youngest reigned only to show that one weak reign is sufficient to ruin even a brave and great people. Edgar made kings his watermen; the son of his love five times bought his kingdom from Danish rovers, was the fool of traitors, and surrendered his throne to a foreign invader. Of Edgar's grandsons, one perished violently soon after his accession. The other was the last of his race who ruled the Anglo-Saxon nation."—Sharon Turner's *History of the Anglo-Saxons*, vol. iii. p. 186.

throne. But the animosities of two religious parties were not to be reconciled by the decisions of national or church councils, by disputations, or even by miracles; nor was the ambition of the perfidious Elfrida to be cured by a single reverse. She continued her intrigues with the secular party; she united herself more closely than ever with Alfere, the Eolderman of Mercia; and soon saw herself at the head of a powerful confederacy of nobles, who were resolved her son should reign, and Dunstan deprived of that immense power he had so long held. But not even this resolution would prepare us for the horrible catastrophe that followed. About three years after his accession, as Edward was hunting one day in Dorsetshire, he quitted his company and attendants to visit his half-brother, Ethelred, who was living with his mother, hard by, in Corfe Castle. Elfrida came forth with her son to meet him at the outer gate: she bade him welcome with a smiling face, and invited him to dismount; but

CORFE CASTLE, Dorsetshire.[1]—From Turner's Southern Coast.

the young king, with thanks, declined, fearing he should be missed by his company, and craved only a cup of wine, which he might drink in his saddle to her and his brother, and so be gone. The wine was brought, and as Edward was carrying the cup to his lips, one of Elfrida's attendants stabbed him in the back. The wounded king put spurs

[1] The foundation of this castle is considered to date from the tenth century. Its great strength, and its situation on a high hill, caused it to be regarded formerly as a fortress of peculiar importance, and it was used as a resting-place by the West Saxon princes. It was the occasional residence of King John, and here he deposited his regalia for security. Here Edward II., when he fell into the hands of his enemies, was for a time imprisoned; it was stoutly defended in the war of the Parliament, but taken by treachery in 1645-6, when it was dismantled. The castle is separated from the town to which it gives its name by a ditch, now dry, crossed by a bridge of four very narrow, high arches.

to his horse, but soon fainting from loss of blood, he fell out of the saddle, and was dragged by one foot in the stirrup through woods and rugged ways until he was dead. His but too negligent companions in the chase traced him by his blood, and at last found his disfigured corpse, which they burned, and then buried the ashes of it at Wareham, without any pomp or regal ceremonies. "No worse deed than this," says the *Saxon Chronicle*, "had been committed among the people of the Angles since they first came to the land of Britain."

It is believed that Alfere, the Eolderman of Mercia, with other nobles opposed to Dunstan and the monks, was engaged with the queen-dowager in a plot to assassinate Edward, but that Elfrida, impatiently seizing an unlooked-for opportunity, took the bloody execution instantly and wholly upon herself. The boy ETHELRED, who was not ten years old, had no part in the guilt which gave him a crown, though that crown certainly sat upon him like a curse. It is related of him that he dearly loved his half-brother Edward, and wept his death, for which his virago mother, seizing a large torch, beat him with it until he was almost dead himself. Such, however, was the popular odium that fell both on son and mother, that an attempt was made to exclude him from the throne, by substituting Edgitha, Edgar's natural daughter by the lady he had stolen from the nunnery of Wilton. This Edgitha was herself at the time a professed nun in the same monastery from which her mother had been torn; and it is said that nothing but her timidity and the dread inspired by her brother Edward's murder, and her firm refusal to exchange the tranquillity of the cell for the dangers of the throne, prevented Dunstan from causing her to be proclaimed Queen of all England. There was no other prince of the blood-royal—no other pretender to set up; so the prelates and thanes, with no small repugnance, were compelled to bestow the crown on the son of the murderess; and Dunstan, as primate, at the festival of Easter (A.D. 979) put it on his weak head in the old chapel of Kingston, at this time the usual crowning place of the Saxon monarchs. The vehement monk, who was now soured by age, and exasperated at the temporary triumph of his enemies, is said to have pronounced a malediction on Ethelred, even in the act of crowning him, and to have given public vent to a prophecy of woe and misery, which some think was well calculated to ensure its own fulfilment; for Dunstan already enjoyed among the nation the reputation of being both a seer and a saint, and the words he dropped could hardly fail of being treasured in the memory of the people, and of depressing their spirits at the approach of danger. Ethelred, moreover, began his reign with an unlucky nickname, which it is believed was given him by Dunstan—he was called "the Unready." His personal and moral qualities were not calculated to overcome a bad prestige, and the unpopular circumstances attending his succession: in him the people lost their warm affection for the blood of Alfred, and by degrees many of them contemplated with indifference, if not with pleasure, the transfer of the crown to a prince of Danish race. This latter feeling more than half explains the events of his reign. During the first part of the minority, the infamous Elfrida enjoyed great authority, but as the king advanced in years her influence declined, and, followed by the execrations of nobles and people (even by those of her own party), she at last retired to expiate her sins, according to the fashion of the times, in building and endowing monasteries.

Although the Northmen settled in the Danelagh had so frequently troubled the peace of the kingdom, and had probably at no period renounced the hope of gaining an ascendency over the Saxons of the island, and placing a king of their own race on the throne of England, the Danes beyond sea had certainly made no formidable attacks since the time of Athelstane, and of late years had scarcely been heard of. This suspension of hostility on their part is not to be attributed solely to the wisdom and valour of the intermediate Saxon kings. There were great political causes connected with the histories of

CROWNING-STONE OF THE SAXON KINGS.1—J. W. Archer, from his drawing on the spot.

Norway and Denmark, and France and Normandy; and circumstances which, by giving the Danes employment and settlement in other countries, kept them away from England. But now, when unfortunately there was neither wisdom nor valour in the king and council, nor spirit in the people, these extraneous circumstances had changed, and instead of checking, they threw the men of the North on our shores.

Sweyn, a son of the King of Denmark, had quarrelled with his father, and been banished from his home. Young, brave, and enterprising, he soon collected a host of mariners and adventurers round his standard, with whom he resolved to obtain wealth, if not a home in our island. His first operations were on a small scale, intended merely to try the state of defence of the island, and were probably not conducted by himself.

In the third year of Ethelred's reign (A.D. 981) the Danish raven was seen floating in Southampton Water, and that city was plundered, and its inhabitants carried into slavery. In the course of a few months Chester and London partook of the fate of Southampton, and attacks were multiplied on different points—in the north, in the south, and in the west—as far as the extremity of Cornwall. These operations were continued for some years, during which Ethelred seems to have been much occupied by quarrels with his bishops and nobles. Alfere, the Mercian, who had conspired with Elfrida against Edward the Martyr, was dead, and his extensive earldom had fallen to his son Alfric, a notorious name in these annals. In consequence of a conspiracy, real or alleged, this Alfric was banished. The weak king was soon obliged to recall him, but the revengeful nobleman never forgot the past. In the year 991 a more formidable host of the sea-kings ravaged all that part of East Anglia that lay between Ipswich and Maldon, and won a great battle, in which Earl Brithnoth, a Dane by descent, but a Christian, and a friend to the established government, was slain. Ethelred then, for the first time, had recourse to the fatal expedient of purchasing their forbearance with money. *Ten thousand* pounds of silver were paid down, and the sea-kings departed for a while, carrying with them the head of Earl Brithnoth as a trophy. In the course of the following year

---

[1] This stone was invested with a traditionary sanctity somewhat similar to that in the coronation chair at Westminster Abbey. It formerly stood in the ancient chapel of St. Mary, at Kingston-on-Thames, which fell down about fifty years ago. It has been recently set up upon a new pedestal in the High Street of that town.

"The Anglo-Saxon kings were crowned at Winchester until that city was burned by the Danes, in the reign of Ethelbert, when the court was removed to Kingston. Edward (called the Elder) was the first Anglo-Saxon king crowned at Kingston."—Brayley's *Surrey*.

the witenagemot adopted a wiser plan of defence. A formidable fleet was collected at London, and well manned and supplied with arms. But this wise measure was defeated by Alfric the Mercian, who, in his hatred to the king, had opened a correspondence with the Danes, and being intrusted with a principal command in the fleet, he went over to them on the eve of a battle, with many of his ships. The traitor of course escaped, and Ethelred wreaked his savage vengeance on Elfgar, the son of Alfric, whose eyes he put out. In 993 a Danish host landed in the north, and took Bamborough Castle by storm. Three chiefs, of Danish origin, who had been appointed to command the natives, threw down the standard of Ethelred, and ranged themselves under the Danish raven. All through Northumbria, and the rest of the Danelagh, the Danish settlers gradually either joined their still pagan brethren from the Baltic, or offered them no resistance. In the meantime, the fortunes of Sweyn the exile had undergone a change. By the murder of his father he had ascended the throne of Denmark, and, formidable himself, he had gained a powerful ally in Olave, King of Norway, a prince of the true Scandinavian race, a son of an old pirate, who, in former times, had often pillaged the coast of England. In 994 the two North kings ravaged all the southern provinces of our island, doing "unspeakable harm," and meeting nowhere with a valid resistance. It was again agreed to treat, and buy them off with money. Their pretensions of course rose, and this time *sixteen thousand* pounds of silver were exacted and paid. By a clause in the treaty, Olave and some chiefs were bound to embrace the Christian religion. Sweyn had been baptized already more than once, and had relapsed to idolatry. One of the chiefs boasted that he had been washed *twenty times* in the water of baptism, by which we are to understand that the marauder had submitted to what he considered an idle ceremony, whenever it suited his convenience. Olave, the Norwegian king, however, stood at the font with a better spirit; his conversion was sincere; and an oath he there took, never again to molest the English, was honourably kept. During the four following years the Danes continued their desultory invasions; and when (in 998) Ethelred had got ready a strong fleet and army to oppose them, some of his own officers gave the plunderers timely warning, and they retreated unhurt. On their next returning in force (A.D. 1001), Ethelred seems to have had neither fleet nor army in a condition to meet them; for, after two conflicts by land, they were allowed to ravage the whole kingdom from the Isle of Wight to the Bristol Channel, and then they were stayed, not by steel, but by gold. Their price of course still rose; this time *twenty-four thousand* pounds were paid to purchase their departure. These large sums were raised by direct taxation upon land; and the "Dane-geld," as it was called, was an oppressive and humiliating burden, that became permanent. Nor was this all. The treaties of peace or truce generally allowed bands of the marauders to winter in the island, at Southampton or some other town; and during their stay the English people, whom they had plundered and beggared, were obliged to feed them. Their appetites had not decreased since the days of Guthrun and Hasting.

As if the Danes were not enemies enough, Ethelred had engaged in hostilities with Richard II., Duke of Normandy, and had even, at one time, prepared an armament to invade his dominions. The quarrel was made up by the mediation of the pope; and then the English king, who was a widower, thought of strengthening his hands by marrying Emma, the Duke of Normandy's sister. The alliance, which laid the first grounds for the pretext of Norman claims on England, afterwards pressed by William the Conqueror, was readily accepted by the Duke Richard, and in the spring of 1002 Emma, "the Flower of Normandy," as she was styled, arrived at the court of Ethelred, where she was received with great pomp.

The long rejoicings for this marriage were scarcely over when a memorable atrocity covered the land with amazement, blood, and horror. This was the sudden massacre of the Danes, perpetrated by the people with whom they were living intermixed as fellow-subjects. It is universally asserted that the plot was laid beforehand, the fatal order given by the king himself; and there is little in Ethelred's general conduct and character to awaken a doubt in his favour. At the same time, be it observed, the people must have been as guilty, as secret, as treacherous, as cruel as the king, and must have entered fully into the spirit which dictated the bloody order of which they were to be the executioners. Such being the case, we think they were fully equal to the conception of the plot themselves, and that, from the loose, unguarded manner in which the Danes lived scattered among them, such a mode of disposing of them would naturally suggest itself to a very imperfectly civilized people, maddened by the harsh treatment and insults of their invaders. In the simultaneous massacre of the French invaders all over Sicily, in 1282, the same mystery was observed; but it is still a matter of doubt whether the "Sicilian Vespers" were ordered by John of Procida, or sprung spontaneously from the people. These two cases, which belong alike to the class of the terrible acts of vengeance that signalize a nation's despair, are nearly parallel in their circumstances; and in

England, as afterwards in Sicily, it was the insults offered by the invaders to their women that extinguished the last sentiments of humanity in the hearts of the people. The outrages of the Danish *pagans* were extreme. According to the old chroniclers, they made the English yeomanry among whom they were settled perform the most menial offices for them; they held their houses as their own, and, eating and drinking of the best, scantly left the real proprietor his fill of the worst; the peasantry were so sorely oppressed that, out of fear and dread, they called them, *in every house where they had rule*, "Lord Danes." Their wives and daughters were everywhere a prey to their lust, and when the English made resistance or remonstrance, they were killed, or beaten and laughed at. All this description seems to point at soldiers and adventurers, and men recently settled in the land, and not to the converted married Danes, who had been living a long time in different parts of the country (as well as in the Danelagh, where they were too numerous to be touched), who had contracted quiet, orderly habits, and successfully cultivated the friendship of the English. It was resolved, however, to destroy them all at one blow; the good with the bad, the innocent infant at the breast with the hardened ruffian, the neighbour of years with the intruder of yesterday. As the story is told, Ethelred sent secretly to all his good burghs, cities, and towns, charging the rulers thereof to rise, all on a fixed day and hour, and, by falling suddenly on the Danes, exterminate them from the land by sword and fire. By whatever means this simultaneous movement was arranged, it certainly took place. On Nov. 13, 1002 (the holy festival of St. Brice), the Danes, dispersed through a great part of England, were attacked by surprise, and massacred, without distinction of quality, age, or sex, by their hosts and neighbours. Gunhilda, the sister of Sweyn, King of Denmark, who had embraced Christianity, and married an English earl of Danish descent, after being made to witness the murder of her husband and child, was barbarously murdered herself.

This tale of horror was soon wafted across the ocean, where Sweyn prepared for a deadly revenge. He assembled a fleet more numerous than any that had hitherto invaded England. The Danish warriors considered the cause a national and sacred one; and in the assembled host there was not a slave, or an emancipated slave, or a single old man, but every combatant was a freeman, the son of a freeman, and in the prime of life.[1]

These choice warriors embarked in lofty ships, every one of which bore the ensign or standard of its separate commander. Some carried at their prow such figures as lions, bulls, dolphins, dragons, or armed men, all made of metal, and gaily gilded; others carried on their topmast-head the figures of large birds, as eagles and ravens, that stretched out their wings and turned with the wind; the sides of the ships were painted with different bright colours, and, larboard and starboard, from stem to stern, shields of burnished steel were suspended in even lines, and glittered in the sun. Gold, silver, and embroidered banners were profusely displayed, and the whole wealth of the pirates of the Baltic was made to contribute to this barbaric pomp. The ship that bore the royal standard of Sweyn was moulded in the form of an enormous serpent, the sharp head of which formed the prow, while the lengthening tail coiled over the poop. It was called "The Great Dragon." The first place where the avengers landed was near Exeter, and that important city was presently surrendered to them, through the treachery of Ethelred's governor, a Norman nobleman, and one of the train of favourites and dependents that had followed Queen Emma. After plundering and dismantling Exeter, the Danes marched through the country into Wiltshire, committing every excess that a thirst for vengeance and rapine could suggest. In all the towns and villages through which they passed, after gaily eating the repasts the Saxons were forced to prepare for them, they slew their hosts, and, departing, set fire to their houses.[2] At last an Anglo-Saxon army was brought up to oppose their destructive progress; but this force was commanded by another traitor—by Alfric the Mercian—who had already betrayed Ethelred, and whose son, in consequence, had been barbarously blinded by the king. We are not informed by what means he had been restored to favour and employment after such extreme measures, but Alfric now took the opportunity offered him for further revenge on the king. He pretended to be seized with a sudden illness, called off his men when they were about to join battle, and permitted Sweyn to retire with his army and his immense booty through Salisbury to the sea-coast. In the following year Norwich was taken, plundered, and burned, and the same fate befell nearly every town in Norfolk, Suffolk, Cambridgeshire, Huntingdonshire, and Lincolnshire. The Danes then (A.D. 1004) returned to the Baltic, retreating from a famine which their devastations had caused in England.

By marrying the Norman princess Emma, Ethelred had hoped to secure the assistance of her brother, Duke Richard, against the Danes; but it was soon found that the only Normans who crossed the Channel were a set of intriguing, am-

---

[1] *Sax. Chron.*   [2] Hen. Hunting. *Hist.*

bitious courtiers, hungry for English places and honours; and by his inconstancy and neglect of his wife, Ethelred so irritated that princess that she made bitter complaints to her brother, and caused a fresh quarrel between England and Normandy. Duke Richard seized all the native English who chanced to be in his dominions, and after shamefully killing some, threw the rest into prison. According to Walsingham, and some of the old Norman writers, Ethelred then actually sent a force to invade Normandy, and this force, after effecting a landing near Coutances, was thoroughly defeated. We are inclined to believe that the expedition was less important than the Norman chronicles represent it, but it shows the impolicy of the Saxon king, and had, no doubt, some effect in weakening an already weak and dispirited nation.

In 1006 Sweyn, whose vengeance and rapacity were not yet satisfied, returned, and carried fire and sword over a great part of the kingdom; and when it was resolved in the great council to buy him off with gold, £36,000 was the sum demanded. The frequent raising of these large sums utterly exhausted the people, whose doors were almost constantly beset either by the king's tax-gatherers or the Danish marauders. Those few who had, as yet, the good fortune of escaping the pillage of the Danes, could not now escape the exactions of Ethelred, and, under one form or another, they were sure of being plundered of all they possessed. By an insolent and cruel mockery, the royal tax-gatherers were accustomed to demand an additional sum from those who had paid money to the Danes directly, in order to save their persons and their houses from destruction, affecting to consider such transactions with the enemy as illegal.

In 1008 the people were oppressed with a new burden; but had this been properly apportioned, had the country been less exhausted, and had the measure for which the money was to be applied been carried vigorously and honestly into effect, it seems as if it ought to have saved England from the Danes. Every 310 hides of land were charged with the building and equipping of one ship for the defence of the kingdom; and in addition to this, every nine hides of land were bound to provide one man, armed with a helmet and iron breastplate. It is calculated that, if all the land which still nominally belonged to Ethelred had supplied its proper contingent, more than 800 ships and about 35,000 armed men would have been provided. The force actually raised is not stated, but, in spite of the exhaustion of the country, it appears to have been large; some of the old writers stating, particularly as to the marine, that there never were so many ships got together in England before. This fleet, however, was soon rendered valueless by dissensions and treachery at home. Ethelred, who had always a favourite of some kind, was now governed by Edric, a man of low birth, but eloquent, clever, and ambitious. He obtained in marriage one of the king's daughters, and about the same time one of the highest offices in the state. His family shared, as usual, in his promotion. Brihtric, the brother of this powerful favourite, conspired against Earl Wulfnoth. Wulfnoth fled, and carried twenty of the new ships with him, with which he plundered all the southern coast of England, even as if he had been a Danish pirate. Eighty other ships were placed under the command of Brihtric, who pursued the man he had sought to ruin. A storm arose; these eighty vessels were wrecked on the coast, where Wulfnoth succeeded in burning them all; and then the rest of the king's fleet appear to have dispersed in anarchy and confusion. This story, like so many others of the period, is imperfectly told; but the annalists agree in stating that the new navy was dissipated or lost; and that thus perished the last hope of England.

As soon as the intelligence of this disaster reached the mouth of the Baltic, a large army of Danes, called, from their leader, "Thurkill's host," set sail for England, where, during the three following years, they committed incalculable mischief, and by the end of that period had made themselves masters of a large part of the kingdom. They now and then sold short and uncertain truces to the Saxons, but they never evinced an intention of leaving the island, as Sweyn had left it on former occasions, when well loaded with gold. As Ethelred's difficulties increased, he was surrounded more and more by the basest treachery, and he seems, at last, not to have had a single officer on whom he could depend. During this lamentable period of baseness and cowardice, a noble instance of courage and firmness occurred in the person of a churchman.[1] Alphege, Archbishop of Canterbury, defended that city for twenty days, and when a traitor opened its gates to the Danes, and he was made prisoner and

---

[1] "In the earlier years of Ethelred, the struggle commenced between the two races of the inhabitants of England. The superiority of the Saxons in art and wealth was, for a time, compensated by the inexhaustible aid which their opponents drew from Scandinavia, now almost united under one king paramount. The Saxon people continued faithful, though dispirited. But the defection and treachery of several of the provincial chiefs, especially of Elfric, Earl of Mercia, seem to indicate a growing familiarity between men of rank in both nations, and a disposition to regard the war as the contest of two national parties for the mastery. Thrice did Ethelred purchase a momentary respite from their ravages by large bribes, which served to ensure their return. In the midst of these ignominious submissions, the Archbishop of Canterbury, a prisoner in the Danish camp, acted with a magnanimity more signal than that which patriotic fiction ascribed to Regulus."—*Sir James Mackintosh.*

loaded with chains, he refused to purchase liberty and life with gold, which he knew must be wrung from the people. Tired out by his resistance, they thought to overcome it by lowering the rate of his ransom; and they proposed to take a small sum from him, if he would engage to advise the king to pay them a further amount as a largess. "I do not possess so much money as you demand from me," replied the Saxon archbishop, "and I will not ask or take money from anybody, nor will I advise my king against the honour of my country." He continued immovable in this resolution, even refusing the means of ransom voluntarily offered by his brother, saying it would be treason in him to enrich, in any degree, the enemies of England. The Danes, more covetous of money than desirous of his blood, frequently renewed their demands. "You press me in vain," said Alphege; "I am not the man to provide Christian flesh for pagan teeth, by robbing my poor countrymen to enrich their enemies." The Danes at length lost patience, and one day, when they were assembled at a drunken banquet, they caused him to be dragged into their presence. "Gold, bishop! give us gold! gold!" was their cry, as they gathered about him in menacing attitudes. Still unmoved, he looked round that circle of fierce men, who presently broke up in rage and disorder, and running to a heap of bones, horns, and jaw-bones, the remains of their gross feast, they threw these things at him, until he fell to the ground half dead. A Danish pirate, whom he had previously converted, or, at least, baptized with his own hands, then took his battle-axe, and put an end to the agony and life of Archbishop Alphege.[1]

This heroic example had no effect upon King Ethelred, who continued to pay gold as before. After receiving £48,000 (for still their demands rose), and the formal cession of several counties, Thurkill took the oaths of peace, and became, with many of his chiefs and a large detachment of his host, the ally and soldier of the weak Saxon monarch. It is probable that Earl Thurkill entered the service of Ethelred for the purpose of betraying him, and acted all along in concert with Sweyn; but the Danish king affected to consider the compact as treason to himself, and, with a show of jealousy towards Thurkill, prepared a fresh expedition, which he gave out was equally directed against Ethelred and his vassal Thurkill. The fact at all events was, that Sweyn, who had so often swept the land from east to west, from north to south, had now resolved to attempt the permanent conquest of our island. He sailed up the Humber with a numerous and splendid fleet, and landed as near as he could to the city of York. As the Danes advanced into the country they stuck their lances into the soil, or threw them into the current of the rivers, in sign of their entire domination over England. They marched escorted by fire and sword, their ordinary satellites.[2] Nearly all the inhabitants of the Danelagh joined them at once: the men of Northumbria, Lindesey, and the "Five Burghs" welcomed the banner of Sweyn, and finally all the "host" north of Watling-street took up arms in his favour.[3] Even the provinces in the centre of England, where the Danish settlers or troops were far less numerous, prepared themselves for a quiet surrender. Leaving his fleet to the care of his son Canute, Sweyn conducted the main body of his army to the south, exacting horses and provisions as he marched rapidly along. Oxford, Winchester, and other important towns threw open their gates at his approach; but he was obliged to retire from before the walls of London, and the determined valour of its citizens, among whom the king had taken refuge. Sweyn then turned to the west, where he was received with open arms. The eoldermen of Devonshire, and nearly every other thane in that part of the kingdom, repaired to his head-quarters at Bath, and did homage to him as their lawful or chosen sovereign. Seeing the whole kingdom falling from him, Ethelred abandoned London, which soon followed the general example, and submitted to the Danes. This unready king then fled to the Isle of Wight, whence he secretly sent his children with Emma, his Norman wife, to the court of her brother at Rouen. He was for some short time doubtful where he should lay his own head; for, after the hostilities and insults which had passed between them, he reasonably doubted the good-will of his brother-in-law. The Duke of Normandy, however, not only received Emma and her children with great kindness, but offered a safe and honourable asylum to Ethelred, which that luckless prince was fain to accept as his only resource.

SWEYN was now (about the middle of Jan., 1013) acknowledged as "full King of England;" but the power which had been obtained with so much labour, and at the expense of so much bloodshed and wretchedness, remained to the conqueror a very short time. He died suddenly at Gainsborough; and, only six weeks after the time when he had been allowed to depart for Normandy, "abandoned, deserted, and betrayed" by all, Ethelred was invited by the Saxon nobles and prelates to return and take possession of his kingdom, which was pledged to his defence and support—*provided only that he would govern them better than he had done before.* Ethelred, before

---

[1] Vita Alphegi, in *Anglia Sacra*; Ingulf; *Chron. Sax.*; Eadmer; Brompton.
[2] *Scriptores Rer. Danic.*, quoted in Thierry's *Histoire de la Conquête*; Brompton. [3] *Chron. Sax.*

venturing himself, sent over his son Edward, with solemn promises and assurances. Pledges were exchanged for the faithful performance of the new compact between king and people.[1] A sentence of perpetual outlawry was pronounced against every king of Danish name and race; and before the end of Lent, Ethelred was restored to those dominions which he had already misgoverned thirty-five years. In the meantime the Danish army in England had proclaimed Canute, the son of Sweyn, as king of the whole land; and in the northern provinces they and their adherents were in a condition to maintain the election they had made. Indeed, north of Watling-street the Danes were all-powerful; and Canute, though beset by some difficulties, was not of a character to relinquish his hold of the kingdom without a hard struggle. A sanguinary warfare was renewed, and murdering and bribing, betraying and betrayed, Ethelred was fast losing ground, when he died of disease, about three years after his return from Normandy.[2]

The law of succession continued as loose as ever; and in seasons of extreme difficulty like the present, when so much depended on the personal character and valour of the sovereign, it was altogether neglected or despised. Setting aside Ethelred's legitimate children, the Saxons chose for their king a natural son, EDMUND, surnamed *Ironside*, who had already given many proofs of courage in the field and wisdom in the council. By general consent, indeed, Edmund was a hero; but the country was too much worn out and divided, and the treasons that had torn his father's court and camp were too prevalent in his own, to permit of his restoring Saxon independence throughout the kingdom. After twice relieving London, when besieged by Canute and all his host, and fighting five pitched battles with unvarying valour, but with various success, Ironside proposed that he and his rival should decide their claims in a single combat, saying "it was pity so many lives should be lost and perilled for their ambition."[3] Canute declined the duel, saying that he, as a man of slender make, would stand no chance with the stalwart Edmund; and he added, that it would be wiser and better for them both to divide England between them, even as their forefathers had done in other times. This proposal is said to have been received with enthusiastic joy by both armies; and however the negotiation may have been conducted, and whatever was the precise line of demarcation settled between them, it was certainly agreed that Canute should reign over the north, and Edmund Ironside over the south, with a nominal superiority over the Dane's portion. The brave Edmund did not survive the treaty more than two months. His death, which took place on the feast of St. Andrew, was sudden and mysterious. As Canute profited so much by it as to become sole monarch of England immediately after, it is generally believed he planned his assassination; but judging from the old chroniclers who lived at or near the time, it is not clear who were the contrivers and actual perpetrators of the deed, or whether he was killed at all. There is even a doubt as to the place of his death, whether it was London or Oxford.

CANUTE. A.D. 1017. Although the death of Edmund removed all obstacles, and the south lay prostrate before the Danes, Canute began with a show of law and moderation. A great council of the bishops, "duces," and "optimates"

CANUTE AND HIS QUEEN.—From an illumination in the Registry of Hyde Abbey.

was convened at London; and before them Canute appealed to those Saxons who had been witnesses to the convention and treaty of partition between himself and Edmund, and called upon them to state the terms upon which the compact was concluded. Intimidated by force, or won by promises, and the hopes of conciliating the favour

---

[1] "This remarkable transaction laid the foundations for the greatest alterations in the principles of the constitution. With the full acknowledgment of hereditary right, the nation stipulated that the king should not abuse his power. They imposed terms upon Ethelred—they vindicated their national liberty, at the same time that they respected the sanctity of the crown; and in the concessions made by Ethelred we may discern the germ of Magna Charta, and of all the subsequent compacts between the king and people of England."—Palgrave, *Hist of the Anglo-Saxons*, p. 303.

[2] "His death put an end to a reign in which all the elements of Anglo-Saxon society seemed to have fallen into the most complete and the most frightful dissolution."—Bonnechose, *Le quatre Conquêtes de l'Angleterre*, t. ii. p. 23. [3] *Malmesb.*

of the powerful survivor, who seemed certain to be king, with or without their consent, they all loudly testified that Edmund had never intended to reserve any right of succession to his brothers, the sons of Ethelred, who were absent in Normandy, and that it was his (Edmund's) express wish that Canute should be the guardian of his own children during their infancy. The most imperfect and faint semblance of a right being thus established, the Saxon chiefs took an oath of fidelity to Canute, as King of all England; and Canute, in return, swore to be just and benevolent, and clasped their hands with his naked hand, in sign of sincerity. A full amnesty was promised; but the promise had scarcely passed the royal lips ere Canute began to proscribe those whom he had promised to love. The principal of the Saxon chiefs who had formerly opposed him, and the relations of Edmund and Ethelred, were banished or put to death. "He who brings me the head of one of my enemies," said the ferocious Dane, "shall be dearer to me than a brother." The witenagemot or parliament, which had so recently passed the same sentence against the Danish princes, now excluded all the descendants of Ethelred from the throne. They declared Edwy, a grown-up brother of Ironside, an outlaw, and when he was pursued and murdered by Canute, they tacitly acknowledged the justice of that execution.

Edmund and Edward, the two infant sons of the deceased king, Edmund Ironside, were seized, and a feeling of shame, mingled perhaps with some fear of the popular odium, preventing him from murdering them in England, Canute sent them over sea to his ally and vassal, the King of Sweden, whom he requested to dispose of them in such a manner as should remove his uneasiness on their account. He meant that they should be murdered; but the Swedish king, moved by the innocence of the little children, instead of executing the horrid commission sent them to the distant court of the King of Hungary, where they were affectionately and honourably entertained, beyond the reach of Canute. Of these two orphans, Edmund died without issue, but Edward married a daughter of the German emperor, by whom he became father to Edgar Atheling, Christina, and Margaret. Edgar will be frequently mentioned in our subsequent pages; Margaret became the wife of Malcolm, King of Scotland, and through her the rights of the line of Alfred and Cerdic were transmitted to Malcolm's progeny, after the Norman conquest of England. There were still two princes whose claims to the crown might some day disquiet Canute, but they were out of his reach, in Normandy. These were Edward and Alfred, the sons of King Ethelred by Emma. Their uncle Richard, the Norman duke, at first sent an embassy to the Dane, demanding, on their behalf, the restitution of the kingdom; but though his power was great, he adopted no measures likely to induce Canute to a surrender or partition of the territories he was actually possessed of; and very soon after, he entered into close and friendly negotiations with that enemy of his nephews, and even offered him *their* own mother and *his* sister in marriage. According to some historians, the first overtures to this unnatural marriage, which was followed by most unnatural consequences, proceeded from Canute. However this may be, the Dane wooed the widowed "Flower of Normandy;" and the heartless Emma, forgetful of the children she had borne, and only anxious to become again the wife of a king, readily gave her hand to the man who had caused the ruin and hastened the death of her husband Ethelred. In this extraordinary transaction an old chronicler is at a loss to decide whether the greater share of dishonour falls to Queen Emma or to her brother, Duke Richard.[1] Having soon become the mother of another son, by Canute, this Norman woman neglected and despised her first-born; and those two princes, being detained at a distance from England, became by degrees strangers to their own country, forgot its language and its manners, and grew up Normans instead of Saxons. The Danish dynasty of Canute was not destined to take root; but the circumstance just alluded to most essentially contributed to place a long line of Norman princes upon the throne of England.

Canute was not one that loved blood for the sake of bloodshedding. When he had disposed of all those who gave him fear or umbrage, he stayed his hand, and was praised, like so many other conquerors, for his merciful forbearance. The Danish warriors insulted, robbed, and sorely oppressed the Saxons, and he himself wrung from them more "geld" than they had ever paid before; but by degrees Canute assumed a mild tone towards his new subjects, and partially succeeded in gaining their good-will. They followed him willingly to his foreign wars, of which there was no lack, for, besides that of England, Canute now held, or pretended to the crowns of Denmark, Sweden, and Norway. In these distant wars the Saxons, who had not been able to defend themselves, fought most bravely under their own conqueror, for the enslaving of other nations. But this is a case of very common occurrence, both in ancient and modern history. Canute's last military expedition (A.D. 1017-9) was against the Cumbrians and Scots. Duncan, the regulus or under-king of Cumbria, refused homage and

---

[1] *Malmesb.*

allegiance to the Dane, on the ground that he was an usurper; and Malcolm, King of Scotland, equally maintained that the English throne belonged of right to the legitimate heir of King Ethelred. Had the powerful Duke of Normandy seconded these demonstrations in favour of his nephews, Canute's crown might have been put in jeopardy; but the Cumbrians and Scots were left to themselves, and compelled to submit, in the face of a most formidable army which the Dane had collected.

These constant successes, and the enjoyment of peace which followed them, together with the sobering influence of increasing years, though he was yet in the prime of manhood, softened the conqueror's heart; and though he continued to rule despotically, the latter part of his reign was marked with no acts of cruelty, and was probably, on the whole, a happier time than the English had known since the days of Alfred and Athelstane.[1] He was cheerful and accessible to all his subjects, without distinction of race or nation. He took pleasure in old songs and ballads, of which both Danes and Saxons were passionately fond; he most liberally patronized the scalds, minstrels, and glee-men, the poets and musicians of the time, and occasionally wrote verses himself, which were orally circulated among the common people, and taken up and sung by them. He could scarcely have hit upon a surer road to popularity. A ballad of his composition continued long after to be a special favourite with the English peasantry. All of it is lost except the first verse, which has been preserved in the *Historia Eliensis*, or History of Ely. The interesting royal fragment is simply this:—

> Merie sungen the muneches binnen Ely,
> Tha Cnut Ching reu there by.
> Roweth, cnihtes, naer the land,
> And here we thes muneches soeng.

That is:—

> Merrily sung the monks within Ely,
> When Cnute king rowed there by.
> Row, my knights, row near the land,
> And hear we these monks' song.

The verses are said to have been suggested to him one day as he was rowing on the river Nene, near Ely minster, by hearing the sweet and solemn music of the monastic choir floating over the waters.[2] In his days of quiet the devotion of the times had also its full influence on the character of Canute. This son of an apostate Christian showed himself a zealous believer, a friend to the monks, a visitor and collector of relics, a founder of churches and monasteries. His soul was assailed with remorse for the blood he had shed and the other crimes he had committed; and, in the year 1030, he determined to make a pilgrimage to Rome. He started on his journey to the Holy City with a wallet on his back and a pilgrim's staff in his hand. He visited all the most celebrated churches on the road between the Low Countries and Rome, leaving at every one of them some proof of his liberality. According to a foreign chronicler, all the people on his way had reason to exclaim—"The blessing of God be upon the King of the English!" But no one tells us how dearly this munificence cost the English people. Returning from Rome, where he resided a considerable time, in company with other kings (there seems to have been a sort of royal and ecclesiastical congress held), he purchased, in the city of Pavia, the arm of St. Augustine, "the Great Doctor." This precious relic, for which he paid 100 talents of gold and 100 talents of silver, he afterwards presented to the church of Coventry—an act of liberality by which, no doubt, he gained many friends and many prayers.

On recrossing the Alps, Canute did not make his way direct to England, but went to his other kingdom of Denmark, where, it appears, he had still difficulties to settle, and where he remained some months. He, however, despatched the abbot of Tavistock to England with a long letter of explanation, command, and advice, addressed "to Egelnoth the metropolitan, to Archbishop Alfric, to all bishops and chiefs, and to all the nation of the English, both nobles and commoners greeting." This curious letter, which appears to have been carefully preserved, and which is given entire by writers who lived near the time, begins with explaining the motives of his pilgrimage, and the nature of the sacred omnipotence of the Church of Rome. It then continues:—

"And be it known to you that, at the solemn festival of Easter, there was held a great assemblage of illustrious persons; to wit,—the Pope John, the Emperor Conrad, and the chiefs of all the nations from Mount Garganus to the neighbouring sea. They all received me with distinc-

---

[1] "The character of the Scandinavian nations was in some measure changed from what it had been during their first invasions. They had embraced the Christian faith; they were consolidated into great kingdoms; they had lost some of that predatory and ferocious spirit which a religion invented, it seems, for pirates, had stimulated. Those, too, who had long been settled in England, became gradually more assimilated to the natives, whose laws and language were not radically different from their own. Hence the accession of a Danish line of kings produced neither any evil nor any sensible change of polity. But the English still outnumbered their conquerors, and eagerly returned, when an opportunity arrived, to the ancient stock. Edward the Confessor, notwithstanding his Norman favourites, was endeared by the mildness of his character to the English nation; and subsequent miseries gave a kind of posthumous credit to a reign not eminent either for good fortune or wise government."—Hallam's *Constitutional History of England*, vol. ii. p. 379.

[2] The meaning of the old English "merry," and "merrily," it is to be remembered, was different from that which we now attach to the words. A "merry" song was merely a sweet or touching melody, and might be plaintive as well as gay, the former being the case here.

tion, and honoured me with rich presents, giving me vases of gold and vessels of silver, and stuffs and garments of great price. I discoursed with the Lord Pope, the Lord Emperor, and the other princes, on the grievances of my people, English as well as Danes. I endeavoured to obtain for my people justice and security in their journeys to Rome; and, above all, that they might not henceforth be delayed on the road by the shutting up of the mountain passes, the erecting of barriers, and the exaction of heavy tolls. My demands were granted both by the emperor and King Rudolf, who are masters of most of the passes; and it was enacted that all my men, as well merchants as pilgrims, should go to Rome and return in full security, without being detained at the barriers, or forced to pay unlawful tolls. I also complained to the Lord Pope that such enormous sums had been extorted up to this day from my archbishops, when, according to custom, they went to the apostolic see to obtain the pallium; and a decree was forthwith made that this grievance likewise should cease. Wherefore I return sincere thanks to God that I have successfully done all that I intended to do, and have fully satisfied all my wishes. And now, therefore, be it known to you all, that I have dedicated my life to God, to govern my kingdoms with justice, and to observe the right in all things. If, in the time that is passed, and in the violence and carelessness of youth, I have violated justice, it is my intention, by the help of God, to make full compensation. Therefore I beg and command those unto whom I have intrusted the government, as they wish to preserve my good-will, and save their own souls, to do no injustice either to rich or poor. Let those who are noble, and those who are not, equally obtain their rights, according to the laws, from which no deviation shall be allowed, either from fear of me, or through favour to the powerful, or for the purpose of supplying my treasury. *I want no money raised by injustice.*" The last clause of this remarkable and characteristic epistle had reference to the clergy. "I entreat and order you all, the bishops, sheriffs, and officers of my kingdom of England, by the faith which you owe to God and to me, so to take measures that before my return among you all our debts to the church be paid up; to wit, the plough alms, the tithes on cattle of the present year, the Peter-pence due by each house in all towns and villages, the tithes of fruit in the middle August, and the kirk-shot at the feast of St. Martin to the parish church. And if, at my return, these dues are not wholly discharged, I will punish the delinquents according to the rigour of the laws, and without any grace. So fare ye well."[1]

It does not clearly appear whether the old writers refer the following often-repeated incident to a period preceding or one subsequent to this Roman pilgrimage. When at the height of his power, and when all things seemed to bend to his lordly will (so goes the story), Canute, disgusted one day with the extravagant flatteries of his courtiers, determined to read them a practical lesson. He caused his throne to be placed on the verge of the sands on the sea-shore, as the tide was rolling in with its resistless might, and, seating himself, he addressed the ocean, and said— "Ocean! the land on which I sit is mine, and thou art a part of my dominion—therefore rise not— obey my commands, nor presume to wet the edge of my robe." He sat for some time, as if expecting obedience, but the sea rolled on in its immutable course; succeeding waves broke nearer and nearer to his feet, till at length the skirts of his garments and his legs were bathed by the waters. Then, turning to his courtiers and captains, Canute said, "Confess ye now how frivolous and vain is the might of an earthly king compared to that great Power who rules the elements, and can say unto the ocean, 'Thus far shalt thou go, and no farther.'" The chroniclers conclude the apologue by adding that he immediately took off his crown, and depositing it in the cathedral of Winchester, never wore it again.

This great Danish sovereign died in A.D. 1035, at Shaftesbury, about three years after his return from Rome, and was buried at Winchester. The churches and abbeys he erected have long since disappeared, or their fragments have been imbedded in later edifices erected on their sites; but the great public work called the *King's Delf*, a causeway connecting Peterborough and Ramsey, and carried through the marshes by Canute's command, is still serviceable.[2]

On his demise there was the usual difficulty and contention respecting the succession. Canute left but one legitimate son, Hardicanute, whom he had by Ethelred's widow, the Lady Emma of Normandy. He had two illegitimate

---

[1] *Malmesb.; Florent. Wigorn.* The substance of the letter is also found in *Torfœi Hist. Norveg.*, and in *Ditmari. Script. Rer. Danicar.*

[2] "The northerns have transmitted to us the portrait of Canute. He was large in stature, and very powerful; he was fair, and distinguished for his beauty; his nose was thin, eminent, and aquiline; his hair was profuse; his eyes bright and fierce.

"He was chosen king by general assent; for who could resist his power? His measures to secure his crown were sanguinary and tyrannical; but the whole of Canute's character breathes an air of barbaric grandeur. He was formed by nature to tower over his contemporaries; but his country and his education intermixed his greatness with a ferocity that compels us to tremble even while we admire. In one respect he was fortunate—his mind and his manners refined as his age matured. The first part of his reign was cruel and despotic. His latter days shone with a glory more unclouded."—Sharon Turner's *History of the Anglo-Saxons,* vol. iii.

sons, Sweyn and Harold. In royal families bastardy was none, or a very slight objection in those days; but according to the contemporary writers it was the prevalent belief, or popular scandal, that these two young men were not the children of Canute, even illegitimately, but were imposed upon him as such by his acknowledged concubine Alfgiva, daughter of the Eolderman of Southampton, who, according to this gossip, knew full well that Sweyn was the son of a priest by another woman, and Harold the offspring of a cobbler and his wife. Whoever were their fathers and mothers, it is certain that Canute intended that his dominions should be divided among the three young men, and this without any apparent prejudice in favour of legitimacy; for Harold, and not Hardicanute (the lawful son), was to have England, which was esteemed by far the best portion. Denmark was to fall to Hardicanute, and Norway to Sweyn. Both these princes were in the north of Europe, and apparently in possession of power there, when Canute died. The powerful Earl Godwin, and the Saxons of the south generally, wished rather to choose for King of England either one of the sons of Ethelred, who were still in Normandy, or Hardicanute, the son of Emma, who was at least connected with the old Saxon line. But Earl Leofric of Mercia, with the thanes north of the Thames, and all the Danes, supported the claims of the illegitimate Harold; and when the influential city of London took this side, the cause of Hardicanute seemed almost hopeless. But still all the men of the south and the great Earl Godwin adhered to the latter, and a civil war was imminent (to escape the horrors of which many families had already fled to the morasses and forests), when it was wisely determined to effect a compromise by means of the witenagemot. This assembly met at Oxford, and there decided that Harold should have all the provinces north of the Thames, with London for his capital, while all the country south of that river should remain to his real or fictitious half-brother, Hardicanute.

Hardicanute, showing no anxiety for his dominions in England, lingered in Denmark, where the habits of the Scandinavian chiefs, and their hard drinking, were to his taste; but his mother, Emma, and Earl Godwin, governed in the south on his behalf, and held a court at Winchester. Harold, however, who saw his superiority over his absent half-brother, took his measures for attaching the provinces of the south to his dominions, and two fruitless invasions from Normandy only tended to increase his power and facilitate that aggrandizement.

Soon after the news of Canute's death reached Normandy, Edward, the eldest of the surviving sons of Ethelred by Emma, and who eventually became King of England under the title of Edward the Confessor, made sail for England with a few ships, and landed at Southampton, in the intention of claiming the crown. He threw himself in the midst of his mother's retainers, and was within a few miles of her residence at Winchester. But Emma had no affection for her children by Ethelred; she was at the moment making every exertion to secure the English throne for her son by Canute, and, instead of aiding Edward, she set the whole country in hostile array against him. He escaped with some difficulty, from a formidable force, and fled back to Normandy, determined, it is said, never again to touch the soil of his fathers.

The second invasion from Normandy was attended with more tragical results, and part of the history of it is enveloped in an impenetrable mystery.

An affectionate letter,[1] purporting to be written by the queen-mother, Emma, was conveyed to her sons Edward and Alfred, reproaching them with their apathy, and urging that one of them at least should return to England, and assert his right against the tyrant Harold. This letter is pronounced a forgery by the old writer who preserves it; but those who are disposed to take the darkest view of Emma's character, may object that this writer was a paid encomiast of that queen (and paid by her living self), and therefore not likely to confess her guilty of being a participator in her own son's murder, even if such were the fact. The same authority, indeed, even praises her for her ill-assorted, shameful marriage with Canute, which undeniably alienated her from her children by the former union. For ourselves, although she did not escape the strong suspicion of her contemporaries, any more than Earl Godwin, who was then in close alliance with her, we rather incline to the belief that the letter was forged by the order of Harold, though, again there is a possibility that it may have been actually the production of the queen, who may have meant no harm to her son, and that the harm he suffered may have fallen upon him through Godwin, on that chief's seeing how he came attended. However this may be, Alfred, the younger of the two brothers, accepted the invitation. The instructions of Emma's letter were to come without any armament;[2] but he raised a considerable force (*milites non parvi numeri*)[3] in Normandy and Boulogne. When he appeared off Sandwich there was a far superior force there, which rendered his landing hopeless. He therefore bore round the North Foreland, and disembarked "opposite

[1] *Encom. Emm.*
[2] *Rogo unus vestrum ad me velociter et privaté veniat.—Encom. Emm.*
[3] *Guill. Gemeticensis.*

to Canterbury," probably about Herne Bay, between the Triculvers and the Isle of Sheppey. Having advanced some distance up the country without any opposition, he was met by Earl Godwin, who is said to have sworn faith to him, and to have undertaken to conduct him to his mother Emma. Avoiding London, where the party of Harold was predominant, they marched to Guildford, where Godwin billeted the strangers, in small parties of tens and scores, in different houses of the town. There was plenty of meat and drink prepared in every lodging, and Earl Godwin, taking his leave for the night, promised his dutiful attendance on Alfred for the following morning. Tired with the day's journey, and filled with meat and wine, the separated company went to bed suspecting no wrong; but in the dead of night, when disarmed and buried in sleep, they were suddenly set upon by King Harold's forces, who seized and bound them all with chains and gyves. On the following morning they were ranged in a line before the executioners. There are said to have been 600 victims, and, with the exception of every tenth man, they were all barbarously tortured and massacred. Prince Alfred was reserved for a still more cruel fate. He was hurried away to London, where, it should seem, Harold personally insulted his misfortunes; and from London he was sent to the Isle of Ely, in the heart of the country of the Danes. He made the sad journey mounted on a wretched horse, naked, and with his feet tied beneath the animal's belly. At Ely he was arraigned before a mock court of Danish miscreants as a disturber of the country's peace, and was condemned to lose his eyes. His eyes were instantly torn out by main force, and he died a few days after, in exquisite anguish. Some believe that Earl Godwin was guilty of betraying, or at least deserting the prince after he had landed in England, without having premeditated treachery in inviting him over; and they say his change of sentiment took place the instant he saw that Alfred, instead of coming alone to throw himself on the affections of the Saxon people, had surrounded himself with a host of ambitious foreigners, all eager to share in the wealth and honours of the land. Henry of Huntingdon, a writer of the twelfth century, supports this not irrational view of the case, and says that Godwin told his Saxon followers that Alfred came escorted by too many Normans, that he had promised these Normans rich possessions in England, and that it would be an act of imprudence in them (the Saxons) to permit this race of foreigners, known through the world for their audacity and cunning, to gain a footing in England. Shortly after the murder of Alfred, Emma was either sent out of England by Harold, or retired a voluntary exile. It is to be remarked that she did not fix her residence in Normandy, where her son Edward, brother of Alfred, was living, but went to the court of Baldwin, Earl of Flanders.

HAROLD had now little difficulty in getting himself proclaimed "full king" over all the island. The election, indeed, was not sanctioned by legislative authority; but this authority, always fluctuating and uncertain, was at present almost worthless. A more important opposition was that offered by the church, in whose ranks the Saxons were far more numerous than the Danes, or priests of Danish descent; and in all these contentions the two hostile races must be considered, and not merely the quarrels or ambition of the rival princes. The question at issue was, whether the Danes or the Saxons should have the upper hand. Ethelnoth, the Archbishop of Canterbury, who was a Saxon, refused to perform the ceremonies of the coronation. Taking the crown and sceptre, which it appears had been intrusted to his charge by Canute, he laid them on the altar, and said, "Harold! I will neither give them to thee, nor prevent thee from taking the ensigns of royalty; but I will not bless thee, nor shall any bishop consecrate thee on the throne." It is said that on this, like a modern conqueror, the Dane put the crown on his head with his own hands. According to some accounts, he subsequently won over the archbishop, and was solemnly crowned. His chief amusement was hunting; and, from the fleetness with which he could follow the game on foot, he acquired the name of "Harold Harefoot." Little more is known about him, except that he died after a short reign of four years, in A.D. 1040, and was buried at Westminster.

HARDICANUTE, his half-brother, was at Bruges, and on the point of invading England, when Harold died. After long delays in Denmark he listened to the urgent calls of his exiled mother, the still stirring and ambitious Emma; and, leaving a greater force ready at the mouth of the Baltic, he sailed to Flanders with nine ships to consult his parent. He had been but a short time at Bruges when a deputation of English and Danish thanes arrived there to invite him to ascend the most brilliant of his father's thrones in peace. The two great factions in England had come to this agreement, but, according to the chroniclers, they were soon made to repent of it by the exactions and rapacity of Hardicanute. Relying more on the Danes, among whom he had lived so long, than on the English, and being averse to part with the companions of his revels and drinking-bouts, he brought with him a great number of Danish chiefs and courtiers, and retained an expensive Danish army and navy. This obliged him to have frequent recourse to "Danegelds," the arbitrary levying of which by his "huscarles," or household troops, who were all Danes, caused frequent insurrections or commotions. The people of Worcester resisted the huscarles with arms in their hands, and slew Feader and Turstane, two of the king's collectors. In revenge for this contempt that city was burned to the ground, a great part of the surrounding country laid desolate, and the goods of the citizens put to the spoil "by such power of lords and men-of-war as the king sent against them." It should appear that not even the church was exempted from these oppressive levies of Danegeld, for a monkish writer complains that the clergy were forced to sell the very chalices from the altar in order to pay their assessments.

DANISH SOLDIER of the period. From Strutt.

On his first arriving in England, Hardicanute showed his horror of Prince Alfred's murder, and his revenge for the injury done by Harold to himself and his relatives, in a truly barbarous manner. By his order the body of Harold was dug up from the grave, its head was struck off, and then both body and head were thrown into the Thames. To increase the dramatic interest of the story, some of the old writers, who maintain that the great earl had murdered Alfred to serve Harold, say that Godwin was obliged to assist at the disinterment and decapitation of the corpse, the mutilated remains of which were soon after drawn out of the river by some Danish fishermen, who secretly interred them in the churchyard of St. Clement Danes, "without Temple Bar at London." Earl Godwin, indeed, a very short time after, was formally accused of Alfred's murder, but he cleared himself in law by his own oath, and the oaths of many of his peers, and a rich and splendid present is generally supposed to have set the question at rest between him and Hardicanute, though it failed to quit him in popular opinion. This present was a ship of the first class, covered with gilded metal, and bearing a figure-head in solid gold; the crew, which formed an intrinsic part of the gift, were fourscore picked warriors, and each warrior was furnished with dress and appointments of the most costly description; a gilded helmet was on his head, a triple hauberk on his body, a sword with a hilt of gold hung by his side, a Danish battle-axe, damasked with silver, was on his shoulder, a gold-studded shield on his left arm, and in his right hand a gilded *ategar*.[1]

During the remainder of Hardicanute's short reign, Earl Godwin and Emma, the queen-mother, who were again in friendly alliance, divided nearly all the authority of government between them, leaving the king to the tranquil enjoyment of the things he most prized in life—his banquets, which were spread four times a-day, and his carousals at night. From many incidental passages in the old writers we should conclude that the Saxons themselves were sufficiently addicted to drinking and the pleasures of the table, and required no instructors in those particulars; yet it is pretty generally stated that hard drinking became fashionable under the Danes, and more than one chronicler laments that Englishmen learned from the example of Hardicanute "their excessive gormandizing and unmeasurable filling of their bellies with meats and drinks."

This king's death was in keeping with the tenor of his life. When he had reigned two years all but ten days, he took part, with his usual zest, in the marriage feast of one of his Danish thanes, which was held at Lambeth, or, more probably, at Clapham.[2] At a late hour of the night, as he stood up to pledge that jovial company, he suddenly fell down speechless, with the wine-cup in his hand: he was removed to an inner chamber, but he spoke no more; and thus the last Danish king in England died drunk. He was buried in the church of Winchester, near his father Canute.

---

[1] The same scythe-shaped weapon as the Moorish "assagai," the Turkish "yataghan," &c. It was a common weapon with the Danes, and is still so in the East.

[2] The name of the bride's father, in whose house the feast is supposed to have been held, was Osgod Clapa; and *Clapaham*, the *hame* or *home* of Clapa, is taken as the etymology of our suburban village.—Palgrave, *Hist.* ch. xiii.

CHAPTER IV.—CIVIL AND MILITARY HISTORY.

EDWARD THE CONFESSOR TO THE NORMAN CONQUEST.—A.D. 1042—1066.

Hardicanute succeeded by Edward the Confessor—Edward's behaviour to his wife and mother—His favour towards the Normans—Visit of Eustace, Count of Boulogne, and its consequences—Quarrels between the Confessor and Earl Godwin—William, Duke of Normandy, visits England—His gracious reception by Edward the Confessor—Earl Godwin drives the Normans out of England—Popular character and achievements of his son, Harold—Death of Edward the Atheling in London—Harold's journey to Normandy—He falls into the hands of William, Duke of Normandy—Promises and oaths exacted of him by William—Unpopular proceedings of Tostig, the brother of Harold—Last illness of Edward the Confessor—Question of the succession to the throne—Harold proclaimed king—William of Normandy asserts his right to the throne of England—His preparations to maintain it—Hardrada, King of Norway, invades England—Is defeated and slain at Stamford Bridge—Hostile arrival of William, Duke of Normandy—His proposals to Harold—Battle of Hastings—Defeat and death of Harold.

EDWARD THE CONFESSOR. Hardicanute was scarcely in his grave, when his half-brother Edward, who was many years his senior, ascended the throne (A.D. 1042) with no opposition, except such as he found from his own fears and scruples, which, had he been left to himself, would probably have induced him to prefer a monastery, or some other quiet retirement in Normandy. During his very brief reign Hardicanute had recalled the exile to England, had received him with honour and affection, granted him a handsome allowance, and even proposed, it is said, to associate him in his government. Edward was, therefore, at hand, and in a favourable position at the moment of crisis; nor, according to the *modern* laws of hereditary succession, could any one have established so good a right; for his half-nephew Edward, who was still far away in Hungary, was only illegitimately descended from the royal line of Cerdic and Alfred, his father, Edmund Ironside, though older than Edward, being a natural son of their common father Ethelred. But, in truth, rules of succession had little to do with the settlement of the crown, which was affected by a variety of other and more potent agencies. The connection between the Danish and English crowns was evidently breaking off; there was a prospect that the two parties in England would soon be left to decide their contest without any intervention from Denmark; for some time the Saxon party had been gaining ground, and, before Hardicanute's death, formidable associations had been made, and more than one successful battle fought against the Danes. On their side the Danes, having no descendant of the great Canute around whom to rally, became less vehement for the expulsion of the Saxon line, while many of them settled in the south of the island were won over by the reputed virtue and sanctity of Edward. If we may judge by the uncertain light of some of the chronicles many leading Danes quitted England on Hardicanute's decease; and it seems quite certain that when the nobles and prelates of the Saxons (were there not Danes among these?) assembled in London, with the resolution of electing Edward, they encountered no opposition from any Danish faction. But the great Earl Godwin, the still suspected murderer of the new king's brother, Alfred, had by far the greatest share in Edward's elevation. This veteran politician, of an age considered barbarous, and of a race (the Saxon) generally noted rather for stupidity and dulness than for acuteness and adroitness, trimmed his sails according to the winds that predominated, with a degree of skill and remorselessness which would stand a comparison with the manœuvres of the most celebrated political intriguers of the most modern and civilized times. In all the struggles that had taken place since the death of Canute he had changed sides with astonishing facility and rapidity—going back more than once to the party he had deserted, then changing again, and always causing the faction he embraced to triumph just so long as he had adhered to it, and no longer. Changes, ruinous to others, only brought him an accession of strength. At the death of Hardicanute he was Earl of all Wessex and Kent, and by his alliances and intrigues he controlled nearly the whole of the southern and more Saxon part of England. His abilities were proved by the station he had attained, for he had begun life as a cow-herd. He was a fluent speaker; but his eloquence, no doubt, owed much of its faculty of conveying conviction, to the power or material means he had always at hand to enforce his arguments. When he rose in the assembly of thanes and bishops, and gave it as his opinion that

Edward the Atheling, the only surviving son of Ethelred, should be their king, there were but very few dissentient voices; and the earl carefully marked the weak minority, who seem all to have been Saxons, and drove them into exile shortly after. It is pretty generally stated that his relation, William, Duke of Normandy (afterwards the Conqueror), materially aided Edward by his influence, having firmly announced to the Saxons, that if they failed in their duty to the sons of Emma they should feel the weight of his vengeance; but we more than doubt the authenticity of this fact, from the simple circumstances of Duke William's being only fifteen years old at the time, and his states being in most lamentable confusion and anarchy, pressed from without by the French king, and troubled within by factious nobles, who all wished to take advantage of his youth and inexperience.

The case, perhaps, is not very rare, but it must always be a painful and perplexing one. Edward hated the man who was serving him; and while Godwin was placing him on the throne he could not detach his eyes from the bloody grave to which, in his conviction, the earl had sent his brother Alfred. Godwin was perfectly well aware of these feelings, and, like a practised politician, before he stirred in Edward's cause, and when the fate of that prince, even to his life or death, was in his hands, he made such stipulations as were best calculated to secure him against their effects. He obtained an extension of territories, honours, and commands for himself and his sons; a solemn assurance that the past was forgiven; and, as a pledge for future affection and family union, he made Edward consent to marry his daughter. The fair Editha, the daughter of the fortunate earl, became Queen of England; but the heart was not to be controlled, and Edward was never a husband to her. Yet, from contemporary accounts, Editha was deserving of love, and possessed of such a union of good qualities as ought to have removed the deep-rooted antipathies of the king to herself and her race. Her person was beautiful; her manners graceful; her disposition cheerful, meek, pious, and generous, without a taint of her father's or brother's pride and arrogance. Her mental accomplishments far surpassed the standard of that age; she was fond of reading, and had read many books.

If Edward neglected, and afterwards persecuted his wife, he behaved in a still harsher and more summary manner to his mother Emma, who, though she has few claims on our sympathy, was, in spite of all her faults, entitled to some consideration from him. But he could not forgive past injuries; he could not forget that, while she lavished her affections and ill-gotten treasures on her children by Canute, she had left him and his brother to languish in poverty in Normandy, where they were forced to eat the bitter bread of other people; and he seems never to have relieved her from the horrid suspicion of having had part in Alfred's murder. These feelings were probably exasperated by her refusing to advance him money at a moment of need, just before or at the date of his coronation. Shortly after his coronation he held a council at Gloucester, whence, accompanied by Earls Godwin, Leofric, and Siward, he hurried to Winchester, where Emma had again established a sort of court, seized her treasures, and all the cattle, the corn, and the forage on the lands which she possessed as a dower, and behaved otherwise to her with great harshness. Some say she was committed to close custody in the abbey of Wearwell; but according to the more generally received account, she was permitted to retain her lands, and to reside at large at Winchester, where, it appears, she died in 1052, the tenth year of Edward's reign.

In the second year of Edward's reign (A.D. 1043) a faint demonstration to re-establish the Scandinavian supremacy in England was made by Magnus, King of Norway and Denmark; but the Saxons assembled a great fleet at Sandwich; the Danes in the land remained quiet; and, his last hopes expiring, Magnus was soon induced to declare that he thought it "right and most convenient" that he should let Edward enjoy his crown, and content himself with the kingdoms which God had given him. But though undisturbed by foreign invasions, or the internal wars of a competitor for the crown, Edward was little more than a king in name. This abject condition arose in part, but certainly not wholly, from his easy, pacific disposition; for he not unfrequently showed himself capable of energy, and firm and sudden decisions; and, although superstitious and monk-ridden, he was, when roused, neither deficient in talent nor in moral courage. A wider and deeper spring that sapped the royal authority, was the enormous power of which Godwin and other earls had possessed themselves before his accession; and this power, be it remembered, he himself was obliged to augment before he could put his foot on the lowest step of the throne. When he had kept his promises with the "great earl"—and he could not possibly evade them—what with the territories and commands of Godwin, and of his six sons, Harold, Sweyn, Wulnot, Tostig, Gurth, and Leofwin, the whole of the south of England, from Lincolnshire to the end of Devonshire, was in the hands of one family. Nor had Edward's authority a better basis elsewhere, for the whole of the north was unequally divided between Leofric and the greater Earl Siward, whose dominions extended from the Humber to the Scottish border. These earls possessed all that was valuable in sovereignty within the territories they held. They appointed their own judges, received fines, and levied what troops they chose. The chief security of the king lay in the clashing interests and jealousies of these mighty vassals. As the king endeared himself to his people by reducing taxation and removing the odious Danegeld altogether, by reviving the old Saxon laws, and administering them with justice and promptitude—as he gained their reverence by his mild virtues, and still more by his ascetic devotion, which eventually caused his canonization, he might have been enabled to curb the family of Godwin and the rest, and raise his depressed throne by means of the popular will and affection; but unfortunately there were circumstances interwoven which neutralized Edward's advantages, and gave the favourable colour of nationality and patriotism to the cause of Godwin, whenever he chose to quarrel with the king. It was perfectly natural—and it would have been as excusable as natural, if the imprudence of a king ever admitted of an excuse—that Edward should have an affection for the Normans, among whom the best years of his life had been passed, and who gave him food and shelter when abandoned by all the rest of the world. He was only thirteen years old when he was first sent into Normandy; he was somewhat past forty when he ascended the English throne, so that for twenty-seven years, commencing with a period when the young mind is not formed, but ductile, and most susceptible of impressions, he had been accustomed to foreign manners and habits, and to convey all his thoughts and feelings through the medium of a foreign language. He was accused of a predilection for the French or "Romance," which by this time had superseded their Scandinavian dialect, and become the vernacular language of the Normans; but it is more than probable he had forgotten his Saxon. Relying on Edward's gratitude and friendship, several Normans came over with him when he was invited to England by Hardicanute; this number was augmented after his accession to the throne; and as the king provided for them all, or gave them constant entertainment at his court, fresh adventurers continued to cross the Channel. It should appear it was chiefly in the church that Edward provided for his foreign favourites. Robert, a Norman, and, like most of his race, a personal enemy to Earl Godwin, was promoted to be Archbishop of Canterbury and Primate of all England; Ulf and William, two other Normans, were made Bishops of Dorchester and London; and crosiers and abbots' staffs were liberally distributed to the king's exotic chaplains and houseclerks, who are said to have closed all the avenues of access to his person and favour against the English-born. Those Saxon nobles who yet hoped to prosper at court learned to speak French, and imitated the dress, fashions, and manner of living of the Normans. Edward adopted, in all documents and charters, the handwriting of the Normans, which he thought handsomer than that of the English; he introduced the use of the "great seal," which he appended to his parchments, in addition to the simple mark of the cross, which had been used by the Anglo-Saxon kings; and as his chancellor, secretaries of state, and legal advisers were all foreigners, and, no doubt, like the natives of France of all ages, singularly neglectful of the tongue of the people among whom they were settled, the English lawyers were obliged to study French, and to employ a foreign language in their deeds and papers. Even in those rude ages fashion had her influence and her votaries. The study of the French language, to the neglect of the Saxon, became very general; and the rich, the young, and the gay of both sexes were not satisfied unless their tunics, their *chaussés*, their streamers, and mufflers were cut after the latest Norman pattern. Not one of these things was trifling in its influence—united, their effect must have been most important; and it seems to us that historians in general have not sufficiently borne them in mind, as a prelude to the great drama of the Norman conquest.

IMPRESSIONS FROM THE GREAT SEAL OF EDWARD THE CONFESSOR.[1] British Museum.

All this, however, was distasteful to the great body of the Saxon people, and highly irritating to Earl Godwin, who is said to have exacted an express and solemn promise from the king not to inundate the land with Normans, ere he consented to raise him to the throne. The earl could scarcely take up a more popular ground; and he made his more private wrongs—the king's treatment of his daughter, and disinclination to the society of himself and his sons—all close and revolve round this centre. Even personally the sympathy of the people went with him. "Is it astonishing," they said, "that the author and supporter of Edward's reign should be wroth to see *new* men, of a foreign nation, preferred to himself?"[2]

---

[1] This seal measures 3 in. in diameter.　　[2] *Malmesb.*

In 1044 a crime, committed by a member of his family, somewhat clouded Godwin's popularity. Sweyn, the earl's second son, and a married man, violated an abbess, and was exiled by the king—for this, of all others, was the crime Edward was least likely to overlook. After keeping the seas for some time as a pirate, Sweyn returned to England, on the promise of a royal pardon. Some delay occurred in passing this act of grace; and it is said that Beorn, his cousin, and even Harold, the brother of Sweyn, pleaded strongly against him at court. The fury of the outlaw knew no bounds; but, pretending to be reconciled with his cousin Beorn, he won his confidence, got possession of his person, and then caused him to be murdered. In spite of this accumulated guilt Edward was fain to grant a pardon to the son of the powerful earl; and Sweyn, though he had rendered himself odious, and injured the popularity of his family, was restored to his government.

But in 1051 an event occurred which exasperated the whole nation against the Normans, and gave Godwin the opportunity of recovering all his reputation and influence with the Saxon people. Among the many foreigners that came over to visit the king was Eustace, Count of Boulogne, who had married the Lady Goda, a daughter of Ethelred, and sister to Edward. This Eustace was a prince of considerable power, and more pretension. He governed hereditarily, under the supremacy of the French crown, the city of Boulogne and the contiguous territory on the shores of the Channel; and as a sign of his dignity as chief of a maritime country, when he armed for war he attached two long aigrettes, made of whalebone, to his helmet. This loving brother-in-law, with rather a numerous retinue of warriors and men-at-arms, was hospitably entertained at the court of Edward, where he saw Frenchmen, and Normans, and everything that was French and foreign, so completely in the ascendant, that he was led to despise the Saxons as a people already conquered. On his return homewards Eustace slept one night at Canterbury. The next morning he continued his route for Dover, and when he was within a mile of that town he ordered a halt, left his travelling palfrey, and mounted his war-horse, which a page led in his right hand. He also put on his coat of mail; all his people did the same; and in this warlike harness they entered Dover. The foreigners marched insolently through the town, choosing the best houses in which to pass the night, and taking free quarters on the citizens without asking permission, which was contrary to the laws and customs of the Saxons. One of the townsmen boldly repelled from his threshold a retainer who pretended to take up his quarters in his house. The stranger drew his sword, and wounded the Englishman; the Englishman armed in haste, and he, or one of his house, slew the Frenchman. At this intelligence Count Eustace and all his troop mounted on horseback, and, surrounding the house of the Englishman, some of them forced their way in, and murdered him on his own hearth-stone. This done, they galloped through the streets with their naked swords in their hands, striking men and women, and crushing several children under their horses' hoofs. This outrage roused the spirit of the burghers, who armed themselves with such weapons as they had, and met the mailed warriors in a mass. After a fierce conflict, in which nineteen of the foreigners were slain and many more wounded, Eustace, with the rest, being unable to reach the port and embark, retreated out of Dover, and then galloped with loose rein towards Gloucester, to lay his complaints before the king. Edward, who was, as usual, surrounded by his Norman favourites, gave his pence to Eustace and his companions; and believing, on the simple assertion of his brother-in-law, that the inhabitants of Dover were in the wrong, and had begun the affray, he sent immediately to Earl Godwin, in whose government the city lay. "Set out forthwith," said the king's order;[1] "go and chastise with a military execution those who attack my relations with the sword, and trouble the peace of the country." "It ill becomes you," replied Godwin, "to condemn, without a hearing, the men whom it is your duty to protect."[2] The circumstances of the fight at Dover were now known all over the country; the assault evidently had begun by a Frenchman's daring to violate the sanctity of an Englishman's house, and, right or wrong, the Saxon people would naturally espouse the cause of their countrymen. Instead, therefore, of chastising the burghers, the earl sided with them. Before proceeding to extremities, Godwin proposed that, instead of exercising that indiscriminate vengeance on all the inhabitants which was implied by a military execution, the magistrates of Dover should be cited in a legal manner to appear before the king and the royal judges, to give an account of their conduct. It should seem that, transported by the indignation of his brother-in-law, the Earl Eustace, and confounded by the clamours of his Norman favourites, Edward would not listen to this just and reasonable proposition, but summoned Godwin to appear before his *foreign* court at Gloucester; and on his hesitating to put himself in so much jeopardy, threatened him and his family with banishment and confiscation. Then the great earl armed; and though some of the chroniclers assert it was only to redress the popular grievances, and to make an appeal to the English against the

---

[1] *Chron. Sax.*   [2] *Malmesb.*

courtiers from beyond sea, and that nothing was farther from his thoughts than to offer insult or violence to the king of his own creation, we are far from being convinced of the entire purity of his motives, or the moderation of his objects.

Godwin, who ruled the country south of the Thames, from one end to the other, gathered his forces together, and was joined by a large body of the people, who voluntarily took up arms. Harold, the eldest of his sons, collected many men all along the eastern coast between the Thames and the Wash; and Sweyn, his second son, whose guilt was forgotten in the popular excitement, arrayed his soldiers, and formed a patriotic association among the Saxons who dwelt on the banks of the Severn and along the frontiers of Wales. These three columns soon concentrated near Gloucester, then the royal residence; and, with means adequate to enforce his wish, Godwin demanded that the Count Eustace, his companions, and many other Normans and Frenchmen, should be given up to the justice of the nation. Edward, knowing he was wholly at the mercy of his irritated father-in-law, was still firm. To gain time he opened a negotiation; and so much was he still esteemed by the people, that Godwin was obliged to save appearances, and to grant him that delay which, for a while, wholly overcast the earl's fortunes. Edward had secured the good-will of Godwin's great rivals—Siward, Earl of Northumbria, and Leofric, Earl of Mercia: to these chiefs he now applied for protection, summoning to his aid at the same time Ranulf or Ralph, a Norman knight, whom he had made Earl of Worcestershire. When these forces united and marched to the king's rescue, they were equal or superior in number to those of Godwin, who had thus lost his moment. The people, however, had improved in wisdom; and on the two armies coming in front of each other, it was presently seen, by their respective leaders, that old animosities had in a great measure died away —that the Anglo-Danes from the north were by no means anxious to engage their brethren of the south for the cause of Normans, and men equally alien to them both—and that the Saxons of the south were averse to shedding the blood of the Anglo-Danes of the north. The whispers of individual ambition—the mutterings of mutual revenge—the aspirations of the great were mute, for once, at the loud and universal voice of the people. An armistice was concluded between the king and Godwin, and it was agreed to refer all differences to an assembly of the legislature, to be held at London in the following autumn. Hostages and oaths were exchanged—both king and earl swearing "God's peace and full friendship" for one another. Edward employed the interval between the armistice and the meeting of the witenagemot in publishing a ban for the levying of a royal army all over the kingdom, in engaging troops, both foreign and domestic, and in strengthening himself by all the means he could command. In the same time the forces of Harold, which consisted in chief part of burghers and yeomen, who had armed under the first excitement of a popular quarrel, and who had neither pay nor quarters in the field, dwindled rapidly away. According to the *Saxon Chronicle* the king's army, which was cantoned within and about London, soon became the most numerous that had been seen in this reign. The chief, and many of the subordinate commands in it, were given to Norman favourites, who thirsted for the blood of Earl Godwin. At the appointed time the earl and his sons were summoned to appear before the witenagemot, without any military escort whatsoever, and that, too, in the midst of a most formidable army and of deadly enemies, who would not have spared their persons, even if the king and the legislative assembly had been that way inclined. Godwin, who before now had frequently both suffered and practised treachery, refused to attend the assembly unless proper securities were given that he and his sons should go thither and depart thence in safety. This reasonable demand was repeated, and twice refused; and then Edward and the great council pronounced a sentence of banishment, decreeing that the earl and all his family should quit the land for ever within five days. There was no appeal; and Godwin and his sons, who, it appears, had marched to Southwark, on finding that even the small force they had brought with them was thinned by hourly desertion, fled by night for their lives. The sudden fall of this great family confounded and stupefied the popular mind. "Wonderful would it have been thought," says the *Saxon Chronicle*, "if any one had said before that matters would come to such a pass." Before the expiration of the five days' grace a troop of horsemen was sent to pursue and seize the earl and his family; but these soldiers were wholly or chiefly Saxons, and either could not or would not overtake them. Godwin, with his wife and his three sons, Sweyn, Tostig, and Gurth, and a ship well stored with money and treasures, embarked on the east coast, and sailed to Flanders, where he was well received by Earl Baldwin; Harold and his brother Leofwin fled westward, and, embarking at Bristol, crossed the sea to Ireland. Their property, their broad lands, and houses, with everything upon them and within them, were confiscated; their governments and honours distributed, in part among foreigners; and scarcely a trace was left in the country of the warlike earl or his bold sons. But a fair daughter of that house remained; Editha was still Queen of England,

and on *her* Edward determined to pour out the last vial of his wrath, and complete his vengeance on the obnoxious race that had given him the throne. He seized her dower, he took from her her jewels and her money, "even to the uttermost farthing," and allowing her only the attendance of one maiden, he closely confined his virgin wife in the monastery of Wearwell, of which one of his sisters was lady abbess; and in this cheerless captivity she, in the language of one of the old chroniclers, "in tears and prayers expected the day of her release and comfort."

Delivered from the awe and timidity he had always felt in Earl Godwin's presence, the king now put no restraint on his affection for the Normans, who flocked over in greater shoals than ever to make their fortunes in England. A few months after Godwin's exile he expressed his anxious desire to have William, Duke of Normandy, for his guest; and that ambitious and most crafty prince, who already began to entertain projects on England, readily accepted the invitation, and came over with a numerous retinue, in the fixed purpose of turning the visit to the best account, by personally informing himself of the strength and condition of the country, and by influencing the councils of the king, who had no children to succeed him, and was said to be labouring under a vow of perpetual chastity, even as if he had been a cloistered monk.

William was the natural son of Robert, Duke of Normandy, the younger brother of Duke Richard III., and the son of Duke Richard II., who was brother to Queen Emma, the mother of King Edward and of the murdered Alfred, by Ethelred, as also of the preceding kings, Harold and Hardicanute, by her second husband, Canute the Great. On the mother's side William's descent was sufficiently obscure. One day, as the Duke Robert was returning from the chase, he met a fair girl, who, with companions of her own age, was washing clothes in a brook. Struck by her surpassing beauty, he sent one of his discreetest knights to make proposals to her family. Such a mode of proceeding is startling enough in our days, but in that age of barbarism and the license of power, the wonder is he did not seize the lowly maiden by force, without treaty or negotiation. The father of the maiden, who was a currier or tanner of the town of Falaise, at first received the proposals of Robert's love-ambassador with indignation; but, on second thoughts, he went to consult one of his brothers, a hermit in a neighbouring forest, and a man enjoying a great religious reputation; and this religious man gave it as his opinion that one ought, in all things, to conform to the will of the powerful man. The name of the maid of Falaise was Arlete, Harlotta, or Herleva, for she is indiscriminately called by these different appellations, which all seem to come from the old Norman or Danish compound, *Her-leve,* "the much-loved." And the duke continued to love her dearly; and he brought up the boy William, he had by her, with as much care and honour as if he had been the son of a lawful

THE CASTLE OF FALAISE.[1]—From Cotman's Antiquities of Normandy.

spouse. Although—or perhaps it will be more correct to say *because*—their conversion was of a comparatively recent date, no people in Europe surpassed the Normans in their devotion, or their passion, for distant pilgrimages. When William was only seven years old, his father, Duke Robert, resolved to go to Jerusalem as a pilgrim, to obtain the remission of his sins. As he had governed his states wisely, his people heard of his intention with alarm and regret, but his worldly advantage could not be put in the balance against his spiritual welfare. The Norman chiefs, still anxious to retain him among them, represented that it would be a bad thing for them to be left without a head. The native chroniclers put the following naive reply into the mouth of Duke Robert—"By my faith, Sirs, I will not leave you without a seigneur. I have a little bastard, who will grow big, if it pleases God! Choose him from this moment, and, before you all, I will put

---

[1] The keep of the castle was built in the year 1000, or prior to that date. The lofty circular tower was added in the year 1430, by the English general Talbot, then governor of the town, and to the present day it bears his name. A room in the keep is still shown, in which, according to tradition, William the Conqueror was born. —Dawson Turner, in Cotman's *Normandy.*

him in possession of this duchy as my successor." The Normans did what the Duke Robert proposed, "because," says the chronicle, "it suited them so to do." According to the feudal practice they, one by one, placed their hands within his hands, and swore fidelity to the child. Robert had a presentiment that he should not return; and he never did; he died about a year after (A.D. 1034), on his road home. He had scarcely donned his pilgrim's weeds and departed from Normandy, when several of the chiefs, and above all the relations of the old duke, protested against the election of William, alleging that a bastard was not worthy of commanding the children of the Scandinavians. A civil war ensued, in which the party of William was decidedly victorious. As the boy advanced in years he showed an indomitable spirit, and a wonderful aptitude in learning those knightly and warlike exercises which then constituted the principal part of education. This endeared him to his partisans; and the important day on which he first put on armour, and mounted his battle-steed without the aid of stirrup, was held as a festal day in Normandy. Occasions were not wanting for the practice of war and battles, but were, on the contrary, frequently presented both by his own turbulent subjects and his ambitious neighbours. From his tender youth upwards William was habituated to warfare and bloodshed, and to the exercise of policy and craft, by which he often succeeded when force and arms failed. His contemporaries tell us that he was passionately fond of fine horses, and caused them to be brought to him from Gascony, Auvergne, and Spain, preferring above all those steeds which bore proper names, by which their genealogy was distinguished. His disposition was revengeful and pitiless in the extreme. At an after period of life, when he had imposed respect or dread upon the world, he scorned the distinctions between legitimate and illegitimate birth, and more than once bravingly put "We, William the Bastard," to his charters and declarations;[1] but at the commencement of his career he was exceedingly susceptible and sore on this point, and often took sanguinary vengeance on those who scoffed at the stain of his birth.

The fame of William's doings had long preceded him to this island, where they created very different emotions, according to men's dispositions and interests. But when he arrived himself in England, with a numerous and splendid train, it is said that the Duke of Normandy might have doubted, from the evidence of his senses, whether he had quitted his own country. Normans commanded the Saxon fleet he met at Dover, Normans garrisoned the castle and a fortress on a hill at Canterbury; and as he advanced on the journey, Norman knights, bishops, abbots, and burgesses met him at every relay to bid him welcome. At the court of Edward, in the midst of Norman clerks, priests, and nobles, who looked up to him as their "natural lord," he was more a king than the king himself; and every day he spent in England must have conveyed additional conviction of the extent of Norman influence, and of the weakness and disorganization of the country.

It is recorded by the old writers that King Edward gave a most affectionate welcome to his good cousin Duke William, that he lived lovingly with him while he was here, and that at his departure he gave him a most royal gift of arms, horses, hounds, and hawks.[2] But what passed in the private and confidential intercourse of the two princes these writers knew not, and attempted not to divine; and the only evident fact is that, after William's visit, the Normans in England carried their assumption of superiority still higher than before.

But preparations were in progress for the interrupting of this domination. Ever since his flight into Flanders, Godwin had been actively engaged in devising means for his triumphant return, and in corresponding with and keeping up the spirits of the Saxon party at home. In the following summer (A.D. 1052), the great earl having well employed the money and treasure he took with him, got together a number of ships, and, eluding the vigilance of the royal fleet, which was commanded by two Normans, his personal and deadly enemies, he fell upon our southern coast, where many Saxons gave him a hearty welcome. He had previously won over the Saxon garrison and the mariners of Hastings, and now sent secret emissaries all over the country, at whose representations hosts of people took up arms, binding themselves by oath to the cause of the exiled chief, and "promising, all *with one voice*," says Roger of Hoveden, "to live or die with Godwin." Sailing along the Sussex coast to the Isle of Wight, he was met there by his sons Harold and Leofwin, who had brought over a considerable force in men and ships from Ireland. From the Isle of Wight the Saxon chiefs sailed to Sandwich, where they landed part of their forces without opposition, and then, with the rest, boldly doubled the North Foreland, and sailed up the Thames towards London. As they advanced, the popularity of their cause was manifestly displayed; the Saxon and Anglo-Danish troops of the king, and all the royal ships they met, went over to them; the burghers and peasants hastened to supply them with provisions,

---

[1] In one of his English charters, preserved in Hickes, he styles himself, with less truth, "Rex Hereditarius."

[2] Maistre Wace, *Roman du Rou*.

and to join the cry against the Normans. In this easy and triumphant manner did the exiles reach the suburb of Southwark, where they anchored, and landed without being obliged to draw a sword or bend a single bow. Their presence threw everything into confusion; and the court party soon saw that the citizens of London were as well affected to Godwin as the rest of the people had shown themselves. The earl sent a respectful message to the king, requesting for himself and family the revision of the irregular sentence of exile, the restoration of their former territories, honours, and employments, promising, on these conditions, a dutiful and entire submission. Though he must have known the critical state of his affairs, Edward was firm or obstinate, and sternly refused the conditions. Godwin despatched other messengers, but they returned with an equally positive refusal, and then the old earl had the greatest difficulty in restraining his irritated partisans. But the game was in his hand, and his moderation and aversion to the spilling of kindred blood greatly strengthened his party. On the opposite side of the river a royal fleet of fifty sail was moored, and a considerable army was drawn up on the bank, but it was soon found there was no relying either on the mariners or the soldiers, who, for the most part, if not won over to the cause of Godwin, were averse to civil war. Still, while most of his party were trembling around him, and not a few seeking safety in flight or concealment, the king remained inflexible, and, to all appearance, devoid of fear. The boldest of his Norman favourites, who foresaw that peace between the Saxons would be their ruin, ventured to press him to give the signal for attack; but the now openly expressed sentiments of the royal troops, and the arguments of the priest Stigand and many of the Saxon nobles, finally induced Edward to yield, and give his reluctant consent to the opening of negotiations with his detested father-in-law. At the first report of this prospect of a speedy reconciliation there was a hurried gathering together of property or spoils, and a shoeing and saddling of horses for flight. No Norman or Frenchman of any consequence thought his life safe. Robert, the Archbishop of Canterbury, and William, Bishop of London, having armed their retainers, took horse, and fought their way, sword in hand, through the city, where many English were killed or wounded. They escaped through the eastern gate of London, and galloped with headlong speed to Ness, in Essex. So great was the danger or the panic of these two prelates, that they threw themselves into an ill-conditioned, small, open fishing-boat, and thus, with great suffering and at imminent hazard, crossed the Channel to France. The rest of the foreign favourites fled in all directions, some taking refuge in the castles or fortresses commanded by their countrymen, and others making for the shores of the British Channel, where they lay concealed until favourable opportunities offered for passing over to the Continent.

In the meantime the witenagemot was summoned, and when Godwin, in plenitude of might, appeared before it, after having visited the humbled king, the "earls" and "all the best men of the land" agreed in the proposition that the Normans were guilty of the late dissensions, and Godwin and his sons innocent of the crimes of which they had been accused. With the exception of four or five obscure men, a sentence of outlawry was hurled against all the Normans and French; and, after he had given hostages to Edward, Godwin and his sons, with the exception only of Sweyn, received full restitution; and, as a completion of his triumph, his daughter Editha was removed from her monastic prison to court, and restored to all her honours as queen. The hostages granted were Wulnot, the youngest son, and Haco, a grandson of Godwin. Edward had no sooner got them into his hands than, for safer custody, he sent them over to his cousin, William of Normandy, and from this circumstance there arose a curious episode, or under-act, in the treacherous and sanguinary drama. The exclusion of Sweyn from pardon and a nominal restoration to the king's friendship, did not arise from the active part he had taken in the Norman quarrel, but was based in his old crimes, and more particularly the treacherous murder of his cousin Beorn. It seems that his family acquiesced in the justice of his sentence of banishment, and that Sweyn himself, now humble and penitent, submitted without a struggle. He threw aside his costly mantle and his chains of gold, his armour, his sword, and all that marked the noble and the warrior; he assumed the lowly garb of a pilgrim, and, setting out from Flanders, walked barefoot to Jerusalem—that great pool of moral purification, which, according to the notion of the times, could wash out the stains of all guilt. He reached the Holy City in safety, he wept and prayed at all the holiest places there; but, returning through Asia Minor, he died in the province of Lycia.

Godwin did not long survive the re-establishment of Saxon supremacy, and his complete victory over the king. According to Henry of Huntingdon, and other chroniclers, a very short time after their feigned reconciliation, as Godwin sat at table with the king at Windsor, Edward again reproached the earl with his brother Alfred's murder. "O, king!" Godwin is made to say, "whence comes it that, at the least remembrance of your brother, you show me a bad countenance? If I have contributed, even indirectly, to his cruel fate, may the God of heaven cause this morsel of bread to choke me!" He put the bread to his mouth, and, of course, according to this story, was choked, and died instantly. But it appears, from better authority, that Godwin's death was by no means so sudden and dramatic; that though he fell speechless from the king's table on Easter Monday (most probably from apoplexy), he was taken up and carried into an inner chamber by his two sons, Tostig and Gurth, and did not die till the following Thursday. Harold, the eldest, the handsomest, the most accomplished, and in every respect the best of all the sons of Godwin, succeeded to his father's territories and command, and to even more than Godwin's authority in the nation; for, while the people equally considered him as the great champion of the Saxon cause, he was far less obnoxious than his father to the king; and whereas his father's iron frame was sinking under the weight of years, he was in the prime and vigour of life. The spirit of Edward, moreover, was subdued by misfortune, the fast-coming infirmities of age, and a still increasing devotion, that taught him all worldly dominion was a bauble not worth contending for. He was also conciliated by the permission to retain some of his foreign bishops, abbots, and clerks, and to recall a few other favourites from Normandy.

The extent of Harold's power was soon made manifest. On succeeding to Godwin's earldom he had vacated his own command of East Anglia, which was bestowed by the court on Algar, the son of Earl Leofric, the hereditary enemy of the house of Godwin, who had held it during Harold's disgrace and exile. As soon as he felt confident of his strength, Harold caused Algar to be expelled his government and banished the land, upon an accusation of treason; and, however unjust the sentence may have been, it appears to have been passed with the sanction and concurrence of the witenagemot. Algar, who had married a Welsh princess, the daughter of King Griffith, fled into Wales, whence, relying on the power and influence possessed by his father, the Earl Leofric, and by his other family connections and allies, he shortly after issued with a considerable force, and fell upon the county and city of Hereford, in which latter place he did much harm, burning the minster and slaying seven canons, besides a multitude of laymen. Rulph or Radulf, the Earl of Hereford, who was a Norman, and nephew of the king's, made him a feeble resistance; and it is said he destroyed the efficiency of the Saxon troops by making them fight the Welsh on *horseback*, "against the custom of their country." Harold soon hastened to the scene of action, and advancing from Gloucester with a well-appointed army, defeated Algar, and followed him in his retreat through the mountain defiles, and across the moors and morasses of Wales. Algar, however, still showed himself so powerful that Harold was obliged to treat with him. By these negotiations he was restored to his former possessions and honours; and when, very shortly after, his father Leofric died, Algar was allowed to take possession of his vast earldoms. The king seems to have wished that Algar should have been a counterpoise to Harold, as Leofric had once been to Godwin; but, both in council and camp, Harold carried everything before him, and his jealousy being again excited, he again drove Algar into banishment. Algar, indeed, was no mean rival. Both in boldness of character and in the nature of his adventures he bore some resemblance to Harold. This time he fled into Ireland, whence he soon returned with a small fleet and an army, chiefly raised among the Northmen who had settled on the Irish coasts, and who thence made repeated attacks upon England. With this force, and the assistance of the Welsh under his father-in-law, King Griffith, he recovered his earldoms by force of arms, and held them in defiance of the decrees of the king, who, whatever where his secret wishes, was obliged openly to denounce these proceedings as illegal and treasonable. After enjoying this triumph little more than a year, Algar died (A.D. 1059), and left two sons, Morcar and Edwin, who divided between them part of his territories and commands.

While these events were in progress, other circumstances had occurred in the north of England which materially augmented the power of Harold. Siward, the great Earl of Northumbria, another of Godwin's most formidable rivals, had died, after an expedition into Scotland, and as his elder son Osberne had been slain, and his younger son Waltheof was too young to succeed to his father's government, the extensive northern earldom was given to Tostig, the brother of Harold. Siward, as will be presently related more at length, had proceeded to Scotland to assist in seating his relation, Prince Malcolm, the son of the late King Duncan, upon the throne of that country, which had been usurped by Duncan's murderer, Macbeth. It was in this enterprise, and before it was crowned with final success, that, as has just been mentioned, Osberne, the pride of his father's heart, was slain. He appears to have fallen in the first battle fought with Malcolm (A.D. 1054), near the hill of Dunsinnane.

Siward, who was a Dane, either by birth or near descent, was much beloved by the Northumbrians, who were themselves chiefly of Danish extraction. They called him *Sigward-Digr*, or Siward the Strong; and many years after his death they showed, with pride, a rock of solid granite which they pretended he had split in two with a single blow of his battle-axe. To his irregular successor, Tostig, the brother of Harold, they showed a strong dislike from the first, and this aversion was subsequently increased by acts of tyranny on the part of the new earl. In another direction the popularity of Harold was increased by a most successful campaign against the Welsh, who had inflamed the hatred of the Saxon people by their recent forays and cruel murders. Their great leader, King Griffith, had been weakened and exposed by the death of his son-in-law and Alfred's rival, the Earl Algar, in 1059; and after some minor operations, in one of which Rees, the brother of Griffith, was taken prisoner and put to death, by the order of King Edward, as a robber and murderer, Harold was commissioned, in 1063, to carry extreme measures into effect against the ever-turbulent Welsh. The great earl displayed his usual ability, bravery, and activity; and by skilfully combined movements, in which his brother Tostig and the Northumbrians acted in concert with him—by employing the fleet along the coast, by accoutring his troops with light helmets, targets, and breastpieces made of leather (instead of their usual heavy armour), in order that they might be the better able to follow the fleet-footed Welsh—he gained a succession of victories, and finally reduced the mountaineers to such despair that they decapitated their king, Griffith, and sent his bleeding head to Harold as a peace-offering and token of submission. The two half-brothers of Griffith swore fealty and gave hostages to King Edward and Harold. They also engaged to pay the ancient tribute; and a law was passed, that every Welshman found in arms to the east of Offa's Dyke should lose his right hand. From this memorable expedition, the good effects of which were felt in England, through the tranquillity of the Welsh, for many years after, Harold returned in a sort of a Roman triumph to the mild and peaceable Edward, to whom he presented the ghastly head of Griffith, together with the rostrum or beak of that king's chief war-ship.

The king's devotion still kept increasing with his years, and now, forgetful of his bodily infirmities, which in all probability would have caused his death on the road, and indifferent to the temporal good of his people, he expressed his intention of going in pilgrimage to Rome, asserting that he was bound thereto by a solemn vow. The Witan objected that, as he had no children, his absence and death would expose the nation to the danger of a disputed succession; and then the king, for the first time, turned his thoughts to his nephew and namesake, Edward, the son of his half-brother, Edmund Ironside. The long

neglect of this prince of the old race of Cerdic and Alfred, which, counting from the time of King Edward's accession, had extended over a period of more than twenty years, shows but slight affection for that Saxon family; and, as the king had never expected any children of his own to succeed him, it seems to confirm the statement of those old writers who say he had all along intended to bequeath his crown to his cousin, William of Normandy. But at this moment Norman interest and influence, though not dried up, were at a low ebb; be his wishes what they might, Edward durst not propose the succession of William, and being pressed by the Witan, and his own eager desire of travelling to Rome, he sent an embassy to the German emperor, Henry III., whose relative the young prince had married, requesting he might be restored to the wishes of the English nation. Edward the Atheling, or Edward the Outlaw, as he is more commonly called, obeyed the summons with alacrity, and soon arrived in London, with his wife Agatha and his three young children—Edgar, Margaret, and Christina. The race of their old kings was still dear to them; Edmund Ironside was a national hero, inferior only to the great Alfred; his gallantry, his bravery, his victories over the Danes, were sung in popular songs, and still formed the subject of daily conversation among the Saxon people, who therefore received his son and grandchildren with the most hearty welcome and enthusiastic joy. But though King Edward had invited over his nephew with the professed intention of proclaiming him his heir to the crown, that prince was never admitted into his presence. This circumstance could not fail of creating great disgust; but this and all other sentiments in the popular mind were speedily absorbed by the deep and universal grief and despondence caused by Prince Edward's death, who expired in London shortly after his arrival in that city, and was buried in the cathedral of St. Paul's. This sudden catastrophe, and the voluntary or constrained coyness of the king towards his nephew, awakened horrible suspicions of foul play. The more generally received opinion seems to have been that the prince was kept at a distance by the machinations and contrivances of the jealous Harold, and that that earl caused him to be poisoned, in order to remove what he considered the greatest obstacle to his own future plans. In justice, however, the memory of Harold ought not to be loaded with a crime which, possibly, after all, was never committed; for the prince might very well have died a natural death, although his demise tallied with the views and interests of Harold. There is no proof, nor shadow of proof, that Harold circumvented and then destroyed the prince. It is merely presumed that, because the earl gained most by his death, he caused him to be killed. But William of Normandy gained as much as Harold by the removal of the prince, and was, at the very least, as capable of extreme and treacherous measures. During his visit in England, the king may have promised the duke that he would never receive his nephew Edward; and while this circumstance would of itself account for the king's shyness, the coming of the prince would excite the jealousy and alarm of William, who had emissaries in the land, and friends and partisans about the court. Supposing, therefore, Prince Edward to have been murdered (and there is no proof that he was), the crime was as likely to have been committed by the orders of the duke as by those of the earl.

The demise of Edward the Outlaw certainly cut off the national hope of a continuance of the old Saxon dynasty; for though he left a son, called Edgar the Atheling, that prince was very young, feeble in body, and in intellect not far removed from idiotcy. The latter circumstance forbade all exertion in his favour; but had he been the most promising of youths, it is very doubtful whether a minor would not have been crushed by one or other of two such bold and skilful competitors as William and Harold. As matters stood, the king, whose journey to Rome could be no more talked of, turned his eyes to Normandy, while many of the Saxons began to look up to Harold, the brother of the queen, as the best and most national successor to the throne.

That Harold went to Normandy at this time is certain, but it is said that his sole object in going was to obtain the release of his brother Wulnot and his nephew Haco, the two hostages for the Godwin family, whom Edward had committed to the custody of Duke William, but whom he was now willing to restore. Another opinion is, that Harold's going at all was wholly accidental. According to this version, being one day at his manor of Bosenham, or Bosham, on the Sussex coast, he went into a fishing-boat for recreation, with but few attendants, and those not very expert mariners; and scarcely was he launched into the deep, when a violent storm suddenly arose, and drove the ill-managed boat upon the opposite coast of France; but whether he went by accident or design, or whatever were the motives of the voyage, the following facts seem to be pretty generally admitted.

Harold was wrecked or stranded near the mouth of the river Somme, in the territory of Guy, Count of Ponthieu, who, according to a barbarous practice, not uncommon, and held as good law in the middle ages, seized the wreck as his right, and made the passengers his prisoners until they should pay a heavy ransom for their release. From the castle of Belram, now Beaurain, near Montreuil, where the earl and his retinue were shut up, after they had been despoiled of the best part of their baggage, Harold made his condition known to Duke William, and entreated his good offices. The duke could not be blind to the advantages that might be derived from this accident, and he instantly and earnestly demanded that Harold should be released, and sent to his court. Careful of his money, William at first employed threats, without talking of ransom. The Count of Ponthien, who knew the rank of his captive, was deaf to these menaces, and only yielded on the offer of a large sum of money from the duke, and a fine estate on the river d'Eaune. Harold then went to Rouen; and the Bastard of Normandy had the gratification of having in his court, and in his power, and bound to him by this recent obligation, the son of the great enemy of the Normans, one of the chiefs of the league that had banished from England the foreign courtiers—the friends and relations of William—those on whom his hopes rested —the intriguers in his favour for the royalty of that kingdom. Although received with much magnificence, and treated with great respect and even a semblance of affection, Harold soon perceived he was in a more dangerous prison at Rouen than he had been in the castle of Belram. His aspirations to the English crown could be no secret to himself, and his inward conscience would make him believe they were well known to William, who could not be ignorant of his past life and present power in the island. If he was indeed uninformed as yet as to William's intentions, that happy ignorance was soon removed, and the whole peril of his present situation placed full before him by the duke, who said to him one day, as they were riding side by side—"When Edward and I lived together, like brothers, under the same roof, he promised me that, if ever he became King of England, he would make me his successor. Harold! I would, right well, that you helped me in the fulfilment of this promise; and be assured that if I obtain the kingdom by your aid, whatever you choose to ask shall be granted on the instant." The liberty and life of the earl were in the hands of the proposer, and so Harold promised to do what he could. William was not to be satisfied with vague promises. "Since you consent to serve me," he continued, "you must engage to fortify Dover Castle, to dig a well of good water there, and to give it up to my men-at-arms; you must also give me your sister, that I may marry her to one of my chiefs; and you yourself must marry my daughter Adele. Moreover, I wish you at your departure to leave me, in pledge of your promises, one of the hostages whose liberty you now reclaim; he will stay under my guard, and I will restore him to you in England when I arrive there as king." Harold felt that to refuse or object would be not only to expose himself, but his brother and nephew also, to ruin; and the champion of the Saxon cause, hiding his heart's abhorrence, pledged himself verbally to deliver the principal fortress of his country to the Normans, and to fulfil all the other engagements, which were as much forced upon him as though William had held the knife to his defenceless throat. But the ambitious, crafty, and suspicious Norman was not yet satisfied.

In the town of Avranches, or, according to other authorities, in the town of Bayeux, William summoned a grand council of the barons and headmen of Normandy, to be witnesses to the oaths he should exact from the English earl. The sanctity of an oath was so frequently disregarded in these devout ages, that men had begun to consider it not enough to swear by the majesty of heaven and the hopes of eternal salvation; and had invented sundry plans, such as swearing upon the host or consecrated wafer, and upon the relics of saints and martyrs, which, in their dull conception, were things far more awful and binding. But William determined to gain this additional guarantee by a trick. On the eve of the day fixed for the assembly, he caused all the bones and relics of saints preserved in all the churches and monasteries in the country, to be collected and deposited in a large tub, which was placed in the council-chamber, and covered and concealed under a cloth of gold. At the appointed meeting, when William was seated on his chair of state, with a rich sword in his hand, a golden diadem on his head, and all his Norman chieftains round about him, the missal was brought in, and being opened at the evangelists, was laid upon the cloth of gold which covered the tub, and gave it the appearance of a rich table or altar. Then Duke William rose and said, "Earl Harold, I require you, before this noble assembly, to confirm by oath the promises you have made me— to wit, to assist me in obtaining the kingdom of England after King Edward's death, to marry my daughter Adele, and to send me your sister, that I may give her in marriage to one of mine." Harold, who, it is said, was thus publicly taken

HAROLD SWEARING ON THE RELICS.[1]—From the Bayeux Tapestry.

by surprise, durst not retract; he stepped forward with a troubled and confused air, laid his hand upon the book, and swore. As soon as the oath was taken, at a signal from the duke the missal was removed, the cloth of gold was taken off, and the large tub was discovered, filled to the very brim with dead men's bones and dried-up bodies of saints, over which the son of Godwin had sworn without knowing it. According to the Norman chroniclers, Harold shuddered at the sight.[2]

Having, in his apprehension, thus made surety

---

[1] The Bayeux Tapestry is a long piece of embroidery, worked with coloured worsted thread, on a tissue of linen, about 233 ft. (71 mètres) long and 20 in. (52 centimètres) broad. It was discovered in the town-hall of Bayeux, in Normandy, whence its name. Tradition assigns the work to Matilda, queen of William the Conqueror, and her maids of honour. It is certainly a product of the eleventh century, though still in the freshest condition, and was probably sewed by some high-born châtelaine of the time, and her ladies. It is a pictorial representation of the conquest of England by the Normans, in seventy-two distinct compartments, every leading incident immediately preceding, during, and following which, is depicted in the most expressive manner, accompanied by all the accessories of architecture, fixed and floating, costume, armour, &c. Every compartment has a superscription in Latin, indicating its subject. The pantomime of the actors in the successive scenes is singularly eloquent; and the apparent movement of the figures—allowance made for the imperfect art of the time— is really spirited. This fine relic of the olden time—really an historical document of the utmost value—has had several locations, but is at present reposited in the hôtel-de-ville of Bayeux, where it is kept coiled round a roller, from which it is unwound for inspection.

[2] Mém. de l'Acad. des Inscriptions; Roman du Rover; Eadmer; Gulielmus Pictaviensis, or William of Poitou. William of Poitou received the particulars from persons who were present at this extraordinary scene.

Among the chief objects of attraction to the Anglo-Saxons, both at home and in their pilgrimages, were relics. In finding this superstition so extremely prevalent among them, we are almost led to the supposition that it did not originate in the (R.) Catholic

doubly sure, William loaded Harold with presents, and permitted him to depart. Liberty was restored to young Haco, who returned to England with his uncle; but the politic duke retained the other hostage, Wulnot, as a further security for the faith of his brother the earl.

Harold had scarcely set foot in England when he was called to the field by circumstances which, for the present, gave him an opportunity of showing his justice and impartiality, or his wise policy, but which soon afterwards tended to complicate the difficulties of his situation. His brother Tostig, who had been intrusted with the government of Northumbria on good Siward's death, behaved with so much rapacity, tyranny, and cruelty as to provoke a general rising against his authority and person. The insurgents—the hardiest and most warlike men of the land—marched upon York, where their obnoxious governor resided. Tostig fled; his treasury and armoury were pillaged, and 200 of his bodyguard were massacred on the banks of the Ouse. The Northumbrians then, despising the weak authority of the king, determined to choose an earl for themselves; and their choice fell on Morcar, one of the sons of Earl Algar, the old enemy of Harold and his family. Morcar, whose power and influence were extensive in Lincoln, Nottingham, and Derbyshire, readily accepted the authority offered him, and gathering together an armed host, and securing the services of a body of Welsh auxiliaries, he not only took possession of the great northern earldom, but advanced to Northampton, with an evident intention of extending his power towards the south of England; but here he was met by the active and intrepid Harold, who had never yet returned vanquished from a field of battle. Before drawing the sword against his own countrymen, the son of Godwin proposed a conference. This was accepted by the Northumbrians, who at the meeting exposed the wrongs they had suffered from Tostig, and the motives of their insurrection. Harold endeavoured to palliate the faults of his brother, and promised in his name better conduct for the future, if they would receive him back as their earl lawfully appointed by the king. But the Northumbrians unanimously protested against any reconciliation with the chief who had tyrannized over them. "We were born freemen," said they, "and were brought up in freedom; a proud chief is to us unbearable—for we have learned from our ancestors to live free, or die."

The crimes of Tostig were proved, and Harold, giving up his brother's cause as lost, agreed to the demands of the Northumbrians, that the appointment of Morcar as earl should be confirmed. A truce being concluded, he hastened to obtain the consent of the king, which was little more than a matter of form, and granted immediately. The Northumbrians then withdrew with their new earl, Morcar, from Northampton; but during Harold's short absence at court to complete the treaty of pacification, and at their departure, they plundered and burned the neighbouring towns and villages, and carried off some hundreds of the inhabitants, whom they kept for the sake of ransom. As for the expelled Tostig, he fled to Bruges, the court of Baldwin, Earl of Flanders, whose daughter he had married, and, burning with rage and revenge, and considering himself betrayed or unjustly abandoned by his brother Harold, he opened a correspondence, and sought friendship and support, with William of Normandy.

The childless and now childish Edward was dying. Harold arrived in London on the last day of November; the king grew worse and worse; and in the first days of January it was evident that the hand of death was upon him. The veil of mystery and doubt again thickens round the royal deathbed. The writers who go upon the authority of those who were in the interest of the Norman, positively affirm that Edward repeated the clauses of his will, and named William his successor; and that when Harold and his kinsmen forced their way into his chamber to obtain a different decision, he said to them with his dying voice, "Ye know right well, my lords, that I have bequeathed my kingdom to the Duke of Normandy; and are there not those *here* who have plighted oaths to secure William's succession?" On the other side it is maintained with equal confidence, that he named Harold his successor, and told the chiefs and churchmen that no one was so worthy of the crown as the great son of Godwin.

The Norman duke, whose *best* right (if *good* or *right* can be in it) was the sword of conquest, always insisted on the intentions and last will of Edward. But although the will of a popular king was occasionally allowed much weight in the decision, it was not imperative or binding to the Saxon people without the consent and concurrence of the witenagemot—the parliament or great council of the nation—to which source of right the Norman, very naturally, never thought of applying. The English crown was in great measure an elective crown. This fact is suffi-

---

faith, but was rather, if not entirely produced, at least greatly promoted by the belief of the Germanic nations, who solemnly buried the bones of the dead in barrows, threw up vast mounds over them, raised monuments of rude workmanship, and thought to conquer in battle with the aid of the corpses of their dead chieftains. The judicial superstition, brought to Britain by the Saxons, that the lifeless body of a murdered person would begin to bleed on the approach of the murderer, also supposes the presence of supernatural powers in the corpse.—*Lappenberg.*

ciently proved by the irregularity in the succession, which is not reconcilable with any laws of heirship and primogeniture, for we frequently see the brother of a deceased king preferred to all the sons of that king, or a younger son put over the head of the eldest. As the royal race ended in Edward, or only survived in an imbecile boy, it became imperative to look elsewhere for a successor, and upon whom could the eyes of the nation so naturally fall as upon the experienced, skilful, and brave Harold, the defender of the Saxon cause, and the near relation by marriage of their last king? Harold, therefore, derived his authority from what ought always to be considered its most legitimate source, and which was actually acknowledged to be so in the age and country in which he lived. William, a foreigner of an obnoxious race, rested his claim on Edward's dying declaration, and on a will that the king had no faculty to make or enforce without the consent and ratification of the states of the kingdom; and, strange to say, this will, which was held by some to give a plausible, or even a just title (which it did not), *was never produced*, whence people concluded it had never existed. The chroniclers agree in stating that Edward was visited by frightful visions—that he repeated the most menacing passages of the Bible, which came to his memory involuntarily, and in a confused manner—and that the day before his death he pronounced a fearful prophecy of woe and judgment to the Saxon people. At these words there was "dole and sorrow enough;" but Stigand, the Archbishop of Canterbury, could not refrain from laughing at the general alarm, and said the old man was only dreaming and raving, as sick old men are wont to do.

CHAPEL AND SHRINE OF EDWARD THE CONFESSOR.[1]

During these his last days, however, the anxious mind of the king was in good part absorbed by the care for his own sepulture, and his earnest wish that Westminster Abbey, which he had rebuilt from the foundation, should be completed and consecrated before he departed this life. The works, to which he had devoted a tenth part of his revenue, were pressed—they were finished; but on the festival of the Innocents, the day fixed for the consecration, he could not leave his chamber; and the grand ceremony was performed in presence of Queen Editha, who represented her dying husband, and of a great concourse of nobles and priests, who had been bidden in unusual numbers to the Christmas festival, that they might partake in this solemn celebration. He expired on the 5th of January, 1066; and on the very next day, the festival of the Epiphany, all that remained of the last Saxon king of the race of Cerdic and Alfred was interred, with great pomp and solemnity, within the walls of the sacred edifice he had just lived time enough to complete. He was in his sixty-fifth or sixty-sixth year, and had reigned over England nearly twenty-four years.

The body of laws he compiled, and which were so fondly remembered in after times, when the Saxons were ground to the dust by Norman tyranny, were selected from the codes or collections of his predecessors, Ethelbert, Ina, and Alfred, few or none of them originating in himself, although the gratitude of the nation long continued to attribute them all to him. In his personal character pious, humane, and temperate, but infirm and easily persuaded, his whole life showed that he was better fitted to be a monk than a king.

HAROLD was proclaimed king in a vast assembly of the chiefs and nobles, and of the citizens of London, almost as soon as the body of Edward was deposited in the tomb, and the same evening witnessed his solemn coronation, only a few hours intervening between the two ceremonies. The common account is that Stigand, the Archbishop of Canterbury, who in right of his office should have crowned the king, having quarrelled with the court of Rome, and then lying under a sen-

---

[1] The chapel in Westminster Abbey, and the shrine which contains the ashes of the Confessor, were erected by direction of Henry III., the latter being the work of the Italian artist Cavallini. The coffin containing the king's remains is suspended by iron rods firmly inserted in the stone-work, at about half the depth of the shrine.

THE CORONATION OF KING HAROLD.

At the death of Edward the Confessor in 1066 there were rival claimants for the English throne. The favourite of the English nobles was Harold, who held an earldom among the West Saxons. Nature had equipped this youth for kingship, for to her generous gift of a handsome figure she had added sagacity, military skill, and personal courage. His rival was Duke William of Normandy, whose claim to the throne was repudiated by the whole nation. It was natural, therefore, that when the king died the chiefs and nobles should lose no time in appointing his successor. They met, accordingly, in Westminster Abbey, two hours after the burial of Edward, and hailed the new king, who was crowned by the Archbishop of York.

CORONATION OF HAROLD KING OF THE ANGLO-SAXONS, A.D. 1066.

FROM THE DRAWING BY F. HAYTER, R.A.
BY PERMISSION OF THE ART UNION OF LONDON

tence of suspension, the ecclesiastic next in dignity, Aldred, Archbishop of York, officiated in his stead; other authorities affirm that Harold put the crown on his head with his own hands; but both William of Poitiers, a contemporary writer, and Ordericus Vitalis, who lived in the next century, assert that the act was performed by Stigand. This account seems to be confirmed by the representation of the ceremony on the Bayeux Tapestry, where Harold appears seated on the throne, with Stigand standing on his left. In this moment of excitement the strong mind of the Saxon, though not destitute of superstition, may have risen superior to the terrors of the dead men's bones, and the oaths that had been extorted from him most foully and by force in Normandy; but the circumstances, no doubt, made an unfavourable impression on the minds of most of such of his countrymen as were acquainted with them. Still all the southern counties of England hailed his accession with joy; nor was he wanting to himself in exertions to increase his well-established popularity. "He studied by all means which way to win the people's favour, and omitted no occasion

THE CROWN OFFERED TO HAROLD, AND THE CORONATION OF HAROLD.—From the Bayeux Tapestry.

whereby he might show any token of bounteous liberality, gentleness, and courteous behaviour towards them. The grievous customs, also, and taxes which his predecessors had raised, he either abolished or diminished; the ordinary wages of his servants and men-of-war he increased, and further showed himself very well bent to all virtue and goodness."[1] A writer who lived near the time adds that from the moment of his accession he showed himself pious, humble, and affable, and that he spared himself no fatigue, either by land or by sea, for the defence of his country.[2]

The court was effectually cleared of the unpopular foreign favourites, but their property was respected; they were left in the enjoyment of their civil rights, and not a few retained their employments. Some of these Normans were the first to announce the death of Edward and the coronation of Harold to Duke William. At the moment when he received this great news he was in his hunting-grounds near Rouen, holding a bow in his hand, with some new arrows that he was trying. On a sudden he was observed to be very pensive; and giving his bow to one of his people he threw himself into a skiff, crossed the river Seine, and then hurried on to his palace of Rouen, without saying a word to any one. He stopped in the great hall, and strode up and down that apartment, now sitting down, now rising, changing his seat and his posture, as if unable to find rest in any. None of his attendants durst approach, he looked so fierce and agitated.[3] Recovering from his reverie, William agreed that ambassadors should be immediately sent to England. When these envoys appeared before Harold, they said, "William, Duke of the Normans, reminds thee of the oath thou hast sworn him with thy mouth, and with thy hand on good and holy relics." "It is true," replied the Saxon king, "that I made an oath to William, but I made it under the influence of force; I promised what did not belong to me, and engaged to do what I never could do; for my royalty does not belong to me, nor can I dispose of it without the consent of my country. In the like manner I cannot, without the consent of my country, espouse a foreign wife. As for my sister, whom the duke claims, in order that he may marry her to one of his chiefs, she has been dead some time—will he that I send him her corpse?" A second embassy terminated in mutual reproaches; and then William, swearing that in the course of the year he would come to exact all that was due to him, and pursue the perjured

---

[1] *Holinshed.* *Roger of Hoveden.* [3] Thierry, *Hist. de la Conquête de l'Angleterre; Chron. de Norm.*

Harold even unto the places where he believed his footing the most sure and firm, pressed those preparations for war which he had begun almost as soon as he learned the course events had taken in England.

On the Continent the opinion of most men was in favour of William, and Harold was regarded in the light of a sacrilegious oath-breaker, with whom no terms were to be kept. The habitual love of war, and the hopes of obtaining copious plunder and rich settlements in England, were not without their effect. In the cabinet council which the duke assembled there was not one dissentient voice; all the great Norman lords were of opinion that the island ought to be invaded; and knowing the magnitude of the enterprise, they engaged to serve him with their body and goods, even to the selling or mortgaging their inheritance. Some subscribed for ships, others to furnish men-at-arms, others engaged to march in person; the priests gave their gold and silver, the merchants their stuffs, and the farmers their corn and provender. A clerk stood near the duke, with a large book open before him; and as the vassals made their promises, he wrote them all down in his register. The ambitious William looked far beyond the confines of Normandy for soldiers of fortune to assist him in his enterprise. He had his ban of war published in all the neighbouring countries; he offered good pay to every tall, robust man who would serve him with the lance, the sword, or the cross-bow. A multitude flocked to him from all parts—from far and near—from the north and the south. They came from Maine and Anjou; from Poitou and Bretagne; from the country of the French king and from Flanders; from Aquitaine and from Burgundy; from Piedmont beyond the Alps and from the banks of the Rhine. Adventurers by profession, the idle, the dissipated, the profligate, the *enfans perdus* of Europe hurried at the summons.[1] Of these some were knights and chiefs in war, others simple foot-soldiers; some demanded regular pay in money, others merely their passage across the Channel, and all the booty they might make. Some demanded territory in England— a domain, a castle, a town; while others, again, simply wished to secure some rich Saxon lady in marriage. All the wild wishes, all the pretensions of human avarice were wakened into activity. "William," says the *Norman Chronicle*, "repulsed no one; but promised and pleased all as much as he could." He even sold beforehand a bishopric in England to a certain Remi of Fescamp (afterwards canonized as St. Remigius), for a ship and twenty men-at-arms.

When the pope's bull arrived, justifying the expedition, and with it the consecrated banner that was to float over it, the matrons of Normandy sent their sons to enroll themselves for the health of their souls; and the national eagerness for war was increased twofold. Three churchmen—the celebrated Lanfranc, Robert of Jumièges (Archbishop of Canterbury, who had been expelled by Earl Godwin and his sons), and a deacon of Lisieux—had been sent on an embassy to Rome, where they urged the cause of William with entire success, and obtained from Alexander III. a holy license to invade England, on the condition, however, that the Norman duke, when he had conquered our island, should hold it as a fief of the church. This measure was not carried through the consistory without opposition. The man who combated most warmly in its favour was the fiery Hildebrand, then archdeacon of the Church of Rome, and afterwards the celebrated Pope Gregory VII. The most valid reasons William or his ambassadors could present to the pope were—the will of King Edward the Confessor (which was never produced), the perjury and sacrilege of Harold, the forcible expulsion from England of the Norman prelates, and the old massacre of the Danes on St. Brice's Day by King Ethelred. But if there was any want of plausibility in the argumentative statement of his case, William, as already intimated, was most liberal and convincing in his promises to the pope.

A pontifical diploma, signed with the cross, and sealed, according to the Roman usage, with a seal in lead, of a round form,[2] was sent to the Norman duke; and, in order to give him still more confidence and security in his invasion, a consecrated banner, and a ring of great price, containing one of the hairs of St. Peter, were added to the bull. William repaired in person to St. Germain, in order to solicit the aid of Philip I., King of the French. This sovereign, though tempted by flattering promises, thought fit to refuse any direct assistance; but he permitted (what he probably could not prevent) that many hundreds of his subjects should join the expedition. William's father-in-law, Baldwin of Flanders, gave some assistance in men, ships, and stores; and the other continental princes pretty generally encouraged William, in the politic hope that a formidable neighbour might be kept at a distance for the rest of his life if the expedition succeeded, or so weakened as to be no longer formidable if it failed. But there was one state, whose history in old times had been singularly mixed and interwoven with that of Britain, which might have proved an impediment. Armorica, now called Bretagne or Brittany, had become a

---

[1] Thierry, *Chron. de Normandie.*

[2] Called in Latin *bullæ;* hence the common name, "bull," for the pope's letters, &c.

sort of fief to Normandy; but Conan, the reigning chief or Duke of the Bretons, sent a message to William, requiring that, since he was going to be King of England, he should deliver up his Norman duchy to the legitimate descendants of Rollo the Ganger,[1] from whom the Breton said he issued by the female line. Conan did not long survive this indiscreet demand; and his sudden death by poison was generally, and above all in Brittany, imputed to William the Bastard. Eudes or Eudo, the successor of Conan, raised no pretensions; but voluntarily yielding to the influence of William, sent him two of his sons (which he was not bound to do) to serve him in his wars against the English. These two young Bretons, named Brian and Allan,[2] came to the rendezvous, accompanied by a troop of men of their own country, who gave them the title of Mac Tierns (the sons of the chief), while the Normans styled them Counts. Other rich Bretons—as Robert de Vitry, Bertrand De Dinan, and Raoul de Gael—flocked to William's standard, to offer their services as volunteers or as soldiers of fortune.

From early spring all through the summer months the most active preparations had been carried on in all the seaports of Normandy. Workmen of all classes were employed in building and equipping ships; smiths and armourers forged lances, and made coats of mail; and porters passed incessantly to and fro, carrying the arms from the workshops to the ships. These notes of preparation soon sounded across the Channel, and gave warning of the coming invasion. The first storm of war that burst upon England did not, however, proceed from Normandy, but from Harold's own unnatural brother. It will be remembered how his brother, Tostig, expelled from Northumbria, fled with treacherous intentions to the court of the Earl of Flanders, and opened communications with the Duke of Normandy. Soon after Harold's coronation Tostig repaired in person to Rouen, where he boasted to William that he had more credit and real power in England than his brother, and promised him the sure possession of that country if he would only unite with him for its conquest. William was no doubt too well informed to credit this assertion; but he saw the advantage which might be derived from this fraternal hate; and gave Tostig a few ships, with which that miscreant ravaged the Isle of Wight and the country about Sandwich. Retreating before the naval force of his brother, Tostig then went to the coast of Lincolnshire, where he did great harm. He next sailed up the Humber, but was presently driven thence by the advance of Morcar, Earl of Northumbria, and his brother Edwin, which two powerful chiefs were now living in friendship with Harold, who had espoused their sister, Algitha, and made her Queen of England. From the Humber, Tostig fled with only twelve small vessels to the north of Scotland, whence, forgetful of his alliance with the Norman duke, he sailed to the Baltic, to invite Sweyn, the king of Denmark, to the conquest of our island. Sweyn wisely declined the dangerous invitation; and then, caring little what rival he raised to his brother, he went to Norway, and pressed Harold Hardrada, the king of that country, to invade England. Hardrada could not resist the temptation; and early in autumn he set sail with a formidable fleet, consisting of 200 war-ships, and 300 store-ships and vessels of smaller size. Having touched at the Orkneys, where he left his queen, and procured a large reinforcement of pirates and adventurers, Hardrada made for England, and sailed up the Tyne, taking and plundering several towns. He then continued his course southwards, and being joined

NORMAN SHIP.—Restored from the Bayeux Tapestry, by C. Jal, Archæologie Navale.

by Tostig sailed up the Humber and the Ouse. The Norwegian king and the Saxon traitor landed their united forces at Riccall or Richale, not far from the city of York. Notwithstanding his former infamous conduct, Tostig had still some friends and retainers in that country; those now rallied round his standard, and many others were won over or reduced to an unpatriotic neutrality by the imposing display of force on the part of the invaders. The Earls Morcar and Edwin, true to Harold and their trust, marched boldly out from York; but they were defeated after a des-

---

[1] The founder of the duchy of Normandy.
[2] This Allan is supposed by some to have been the original stock of the royal house of Stuart.

perate conflict, and compelled to flee. The citizens of York then opened their gates to the Norwegian conqueror, who made himself the more formidable to Harold by the wisdom and moderation of his conduct.

SAXON SHIP—HAROLD'S SHIP.—Restored form the Bayeux Tapestry, by H. G. Hine.

Through all the summer months the last of the Saxon monarchs had been busily engaged watching the southern coast, where he expected William to land; but now, giving up for the moment every thought of the Normans, he united nearly all his forces, and marched most rapidly to the north, to face his brother and the King of Norway. This march was so skilfully managed that the invaders had no notion of the advance; and they were taken by surprise when Harold burst upon them like a thunderbolt, in the neighbourhood of York, a very few days after their landing. Hardrada drew up his forces as best he could, at Stamford Bridge; as he rode round them his horse stumbled, and he fell to the ground; but he presently sprang up unhurt, and, in order to stop a contrary augury, exclaimed that this was a good omen. Harold saw what had happened, and inquired who that Norwegian chief was in the sky-blue mantle and with the splendid helmet. He was told that it was the King of Norway; upon which he added, "He is a large and strong person, but I augur that fortune has forsaken him." Before joining battle Harold detached twenty mail-clad horsemen to parley with that wing of the enemy where the standard of Tostig was seen; and one of these warriors asked if Earl Tostig was there. Tostig answered for himself, and said, "You know he is here." The horsemen then, in the name of his brother King Harold, offered him peace and the whole of Northumbria, or, if that were too little, the third part of the realm of England. "And what territory would Harold give in compensation to my ally Hardrada, King of Norway?" The horsemen replied, "Seven feet of English ground for a grave; or a little more, seeing that Hardrada is taller than most men." "Ride back, ride back," cried Tostig, "and bid King Harold make ready for the fight. When the Northmen tell the story of this day, they shall never say that Earl Tostig forsook King Hardrada, the son of Sigurd. He and I have one mind and one resolve, and that is, either to die in battle or to possess all England." Soon after, the action commenced; it was long, fierce, and bloody, but the victory was decisive, and in favour of Harold. Hardrada fell, with nearly every one of his chiefs, and the greater part of the Norwegians perished. Tostig, the cause of the war, was slain soon after Hardrada. Even the Norwegian fleet fell into the hands of the conqueror, who had the generosity to permit Olave, the son of Hardrada, to depart, with all the survivors, in twenty-four ships, after that prince had sworn that he would for ever maintain faith and friendship to England.

Only three days after this signal victory the Normans landed in the south. Harold received this news as he was sitting joyfully at table in the good city of York; but, taking his measures with his usual rapidity, he instantly began his march towards London. Upon his way his forces, which had suffered tremendously in the battle against the Norwegians, were weakened by discontents and desertion; and not a few men were left behind by the speed of his march, from the effects of their wounds and from sheer fatigue. In number, spirit, discipline, appointment, and in all other essentials, the enemies he had now to encounter were most formidable. They have well been called "the most remarkable and formidable armament which the western nations had seen, since some degree of regularity and order had been introduced into their civil and military arrangements."[1]

By the middle of August the whole of William's fleet, with the land troops on board, had assembled at the mouth of the Dive, a small river which falls into the sea between the Seine and the Orne. The total number of vessels amounted to about 3000, of which 600 or 700 were of a superior order. During a whole month the winds were contrary, and kept the Norman fleet in that port. Then a breeze sprang up from the south, and carried the ships

---

[1] Sir J. Mackintosh, *Hist. Eng.*

as far as St. Valery, near Dieppe; but there the weather changed; a storm set in, and they were obliged to cast anchor and wait for several days. During this delay some of the ships were wrecked, and their crews drowned on the coast. In consequence of all this, not a few of the discouraged adventurers broke their engagements, and withdrew from the army; and the rest were inclined to believe that Providence had declared against the war. To check these feelings, which might have proved fatal to his projects, William caused the bodies of the shipwrecked to be privately buried as soon as they were found, and increased the rations both of food and strong drink. But this inactivity still brought back the same sad and discouraging ideas. "He is mad!" murmured the soldiers, "that man is very mad who seeks to take possession of another's country! God is offended at such designs, and this he shows now by refusing us a fair wind." The duke then had recourse to something more potent than bread and wine. He caused the body of St. Valery, the patron of that place, where a town had grown up around his cell, to be taken from his shrine, and carried in procession through the camp, the knights, soldiers, camp-followers, and sailors all devoutly kneeling as it passed, and praying for the saint's intercession. In the course of the ensuing night the weather changed, and the wind blew fair from the Norman to the English coast. The troops repaired to their several ships, and at an early hour the next morning the whole fleet set sail. William led the van, in a vessel which had been presented to him for the occasion by his wife Matilda, and which was distinguished by its splendid decorations in the day, and in the darkness of night by a brilliant light at its masthead. The vanes of the ship were gilded; its sails were of different bright colours; the three lions, the arms of Normandy, were painted in several places; and its sculptured figure-head was a child with a drawn bow, the arrow ready to fly against the hostile land. The consecrated banner, sent from Rome by the pope, floated at the main-top mast, and the invader had put a cross upon his flag, in testimony of the holiness of his undertaking. This ship sailed faster than all the rest, and, in his impatience, William neglected to order the taking in of sail to lessen its speed. In the course of the night he left the whole fleet far astern. Early in the morning he ordered a sailor to the mast-head, to see if the other ships were coming up. "I can see nothing but the sea and sky," said the mariner; and then they lay-to. To keep the crew in good heart, William ordered them a sumptuous breakfast, with wines strongly spiced. The sailor was again sent aloft, and this time he said he could make out four vessels in the distance; but mounting a third time shortly after, he shouted, "Now I see a forest of masts and sails!" A few hours after this the united Norman fleet came to anchor on the Sussex coast, without meeting with any resistance; for Harold's ships, which so long had cruised on that coast, had been called elsewhere, or had returned into port through want of pay and provisions.[1] It was on the 28th of September, 1066, that the Normans landed unopposed at a place called Bulverhithe, between Pevensey and Hastings. The archers landed first; they wore short dresses, and their hair was shaved off; then the horsemen landed, wearing iron casques and tunics and *chaussés* (or defences for the thighs) of mail, being armed with long and strong lances, and straight, double-edged swords. After them descended the workmen of

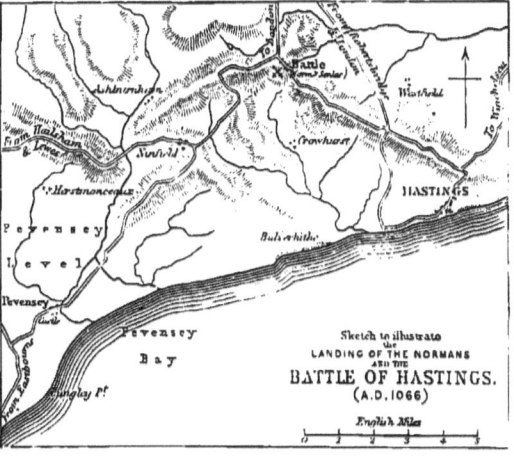

Sketch to illustrate the
LANDING OF THE NORMANS
AND THE
BATTLE OF HASTINGS.
(A.D. 1066)

the army, pioneers, carpenters, and smiths, who carried on shore, piece by piece, three wooden castles, which had been cut and prepared beforehand in Normandy. The duke was the last man to land; and as his foot touched the sand, he made a false step, and fell upon his face. A murmur instantly succeeded this trifling mishap, and the soldiery cried out, "God keep us! but here is a bad sign!" In those days the Conqueror's presence of mind never forsook him, and, leaping gayly to his feet, and showing them his hand full of English earth or sand, he ex-

---

[1] Thierry, *Hist. de la Conquête;* Southey's *Naval Hist. of Eng.;* *Chron. de Normand.;* *Gul. Pictav.*

claimed, "What now? What astonishes you? I have taken seisin of this land with my hands, and, by the splendour of God! as far as it extends it is mine—it is yours!"

From the landing-place the army marched to Hastings, near to which town he traced a fortified camp, and set up two of the wooden castles or towers that he had brought with him from

PEVENSEY BAY.—From a drawing by J. M. W. Turner, R.A.

Normandy, and there placed his provisions. Detached corps of Normans then overran all the neighbouring country, pillaging and burning the houses. The English fled from their abodes, concealed their goods and their cattle, and repaired in crowds to the sacred protection of their inland

ment. It should appear that he was presently welcomed into England by several foreigners, the remnant of the old Norman court party which had been so predominant in the days of the late king. One Robert, a Norman thane, who was settled in the neighbourhood of Hastings, is particularly mentioned as giving him advice immediately after his landing. It is probable that the disembarking the army, horse and foot, and the landing of the provisions and military stores, would occupy two or three days; but sixteen days elapsed between their arrival and the battle, and in all that time William made no advance into the country, but lingered within a few miles of the coast where he had landed.

PEVENSEY CASTLE.[1]—H. G. Hine, from his drawing on the spot.

On reaching London, where he appears to have been well received by the people, Harold manned 700 vessels, and sent

churches. William personally surveyed all the neighbouring country, and occupied the old Roman castle of Pevensey with a strong detach-

them round to hinder William's escape; for he made no doubt of vanquishing the Normans, even as he had so recently vanquished the Norwegians. Reinforcements of troops came in from all quarters except from the north; and another of his Norman spies and advisers, who was residing in the capital, informed the duke there were grounds for apprehending that in a few days the Saxon army would be swelled to 100,000 men. But Harold was irritated by the ravages committed in the country by the invaders; he was impatient to meet them; and, hoping to profit a second time by a sudden

---

[1] The remains of Roman masonry visible in Pevensey Castle indicate an origin prior to the times both of Saxons and Normans. The outer walls, the most ancient part of the building, inclose an area of 7 ac., and stand from 20 ft. to 25 ft. high. The moat on the south is wide and deep. Works of more modern character stand within the walls, consisting of a fortification of pentagonal form, with five circular towers. It is entered from the outer court by a drawbridge on the west side, between two towers. The principal barbican or watch-tower is towards the north-east corner. The walls are 9 ft. thick; the towers are two and three stories high.

and unexpected attack, he marched off for the Sussex coast by night, only six days after his arrival in London, and with forces inferior in numbers to those of William. The camp of William was well guarded, and to prevent all surprise he had thrown out advanced posts to a considerable distance. These posts, composed of good cavalry, fell back as the Saxons approached, and told William that Harold was rushing on with the speed and fury of a madman. On his side Harold despatched some spies, who spoke the French language, to ascertain the position and state of preparation of the Normans. Both these the returning spies reported to be formidable, and they added with astonishment that there were more priests in William's camp than there were soldiers in the English army. These men had mistaken for priests all the Norman soldiers that had short hair and shaven upper lips; for it was then the fashion of the English to let both their hair and their moustaches grow long. Harold smiled at their mistake, and said, "Those whom you have found in such great numbers are not priests, but brave men of war, who will soon show us what they are worth." He then halted his army at *Senlac*, since called Battle, and changing his plan, surrounded his camp with ditches and palisades, and waited the attack of his rival in that well-chosen position. One whole day was passed in fruitless negotiations, the nature of which is differently reported by the old chroniclers. According to William of Poitiers, who was chaplain to the Conqueror, and had the best means of information, and the writer or writers of the *Chronicle of Normandy*, a monk named Hugh Maigrot was despatched to demand from Harold, in the name of William, that he would do one of three things—resign his crown in favour of the Norman; submit to the arbitration of the pope; or decide the quarrel by single combat. Harold sent a refusal to each of these proposals, upon which William charged the monk with this last message:—"Go, and tell Harold, that if he will keep his old bargain with me, I will leave him all the country beyond the river Humber, and will give his brother Gurth all the lands of his father, Earl Godwin; but if he obstinately refuse what I offer him, thou wilt tell him, before all his people, that he is perjured, and a liar; that he and all those who shall support him are excommunicated by the pope, and that I carry a bull to that effect." The *Norman Chronicle* says that the monk Hugh pronounced his message in a solemn tone, and at the word "excommunication" the English chiefs gazed upon one another in great dismay; but that, nevertheless, they all resolved to fight to the last, well knowing that the Norman had promised their lands to his nobles, his captains, and his knights, who had already done homage for them.

The Normans quitted Hastings, and occupied an eminence opposite to the English, plainly showing that they intended to give battle on the morrow. Several reasons had been pressed upon Harold by his followers, and were now repeated, why he should decline the combat, or absent himself from its perilous chances. It was urged that the desperate situation of the Duke of Normandy forced him to bring matters to a speedy decision, and put his whole fortune on the issue of a battle, for his provisions were already exhausted, and his supplies from beyond sea would be rendered precarious, both by the storms of the coming winter and the operations of the English fleet, which had already blockaded all the ships William kept with him in the ports of Pevensey and Hastings; but that he, the King of England, in his own country, and well provided with provisions, might bide his own time, and harass with skirmishes a decreasing enemy, who would be exposed to all the discomforts of an inclement season and deep miry roads; that if a general action were now avoided, the whole mass of the English people, made sensible of the danger that threatened their property, their honour, and their liberties, would reinforce his army from all quarters, and by degrees render it invincible. As he turned a deaf ear to all these arguments, his brother Gurth, who was greatly attached to him, and a man of bravery and good counsel, endeavoured to persuade him not to be present at the action, but to set out for London and bring up the levies, while his best friends should sustain the attack of the Normans. "O! Harold," said the young man, "thou canst not deny that, either by force or free-will, thou hast made Duke William an oath upon the body of saints; why then adventure thyself in the dangers of the combat with a perjury against thee? To us, who have sworn nothing, this war is proper and just, for we defend our country. Leave us, then, alone to fight this battle—thou wilt succour us if we are forced to retreat, and if we die thou wilt avenge us." To this touching appeal Harold answered, that his duty forbade him to keep at a distance whilst others risked their lives; and, determined to fight, and full of confidence in the justice of his cause, he waited the morrow with his usual courage. The night was cold and clear; it was spent very differently by the hostile armies; the English feasted and rejoiced, singing with a great noise their old national songs, and emptying their horn-cups, which were well filled with beer and wine: the Normans having looked to their arms and to their horses, listened to their priests and monks, who prayed and sang litanies; and that over, the soldiers confessed themselves, and took the sacrament by thousands at a time.

The day of trial—Saturday, the 14th of October—was come. As day dawned, Odo, the Bishop of Bayeux, a half-brother of Duke William, celebrated mass, and gave his benediction to the troops, being armed the while in a coat of mail, which he wore under his episcopal rochet; and when the mass and the blessing were over, he mounted a war-horse, which the old chroniclers, with their interesting minuteness of detail, tell us was large and white, took a lance in his hand, and marshalled his brigade of cavalry. The whole army was divided into three columns of attack; the third column, composed of native Normans, and including many great lords and the choicest of the knights, being headed by the duke in person. William rode a fine Spanish horse, which a rich Norman had brought him on his return from a pilgrimage to the shrine of St. Iago of Galicia: he wore suspended round his neck some of those revered relics upon which Harold had sworn, and the standard blessed by the pope was carried at his side, by one Tonstain, surnamed "the White," or "the Fair,"[1] who accepted the honourable but dangerous office, after two Norman barons had declined it. Just before giving the word to advance, he briefly addressed his collected host—"Make up your minds to fight valiantly, and slay your enemies. A greaty booty is before us; for if we conquer we shall all be rich; what I gain you will gain; if I take this land, you will have it in lots among you. Know ye, however, that I am not come hither solely to take what is my due, but also to avenge our whole nation, for the felonies, perjuries, and treachery of these English. They massacred our kinsmen the Danes—men, women, and children—on the night of St. Brice; they murdered the knights and good men who acccompanied Prince Alfred from Normandy, and made my cousin Alfred expire in torture. Before you is the son of that Earl Godwin who was charged with these murders. Let us forward, and punish him, with God to our aid!"

A gigantic Norman, called Taillefer, who united the different qualities of champion, minstrel, and juggler, spurred his horse to the front of the van, and sung with a loud voice the popular ballads which immortalized the valour of Charlemagne, and Roland, and all that flower of chivalry that fought in the great fight of Roncesvalles. As he sang he performed feats with his sword, throwing it into the air with great force with one hand, and catching it again with the other. The Normans repeated the burden of his song, or cried *Dieu aide! Dieu aide!* This accomplished bravo craved permission to strike the first blow: he ran one Englishman through the body, and felled a second to the ground; but in attacking a third cavalier he was himself mortally wounded. The English, who, in reply to the *Dieu aide!* or "God is our help!" of the Normans, shouted "Christ's rood!—the holy rood!" remained in their position on the ridge of a hill fortified by trenches and palisades; and within these defences they were marshalled after the fashion of the Danes, shield against shield, presenting an impenetrable front to the enemy. According to old privilege the men of Kent were in the first line, and the burgesses of London had the honour of being the body-guard, and were drawn up close round the royal standard. At the foot of this banner stood Harold, with his two brothers, Gurth and Leofwin, and a body of the bravest thanes of England. The Normans attacked along the line with their bowmen and cross-bowmen, who produced no impression; and when their cavalry charged, the English, in a compact body, received the assailants with battle-axes, with which they broke the lances and cut the coats of mail on which the Normans relied. The Normans, despairing of forcing the English palisades and ranks, retired in some disorder to the division where William commanded in person. The duke then threw forward all his archers, and supported them by a charge of cavalry, who shouted, as they couched their lances, "*Notre Dame! Notre Dame! Dieu aide! Dieu aide!*" Some of this cavalry broke through the English line, but presently they were all driven back to a deep trench, artfully covered over with brushes and grass, where horses and riders fell in *pêle-mêle*, and perished in great numbers. According to some accounts more Normans fell here than in any other part of the field. For a moment there was a general panic; a cry spread that the duke was killed, and at this report a flight commenced. William threw himself before the fugitives, and stopped their passage, threatening them, and striking them with his lance; then, uncovering his face and head, he cried, "Here I am! look at me! I am still alive, and I will conquer by God's help." In another part of the field the rout was stopped by the fierce Bishop of Bayeux, and the attacks on the English line were renewed and multiplied. From nine in the morning till three in the afternoon the successes were nearly balanced, or, if anything, seemed rather to preponderate on the English side. William had expected the greatest advantage from the charges of his numerous and brilliant cavalry; but the English foot stood firm (a thing which infantry seldom did in those days under such circumstances), and they were so well

---
[1] The readers of *Marmion* will remember the brave bearing of "stainless Tunstall's banner white," long after in the fight of Flodden.

defended by their closed shields, that the arrows of the Normans had little effect upon them. The duke then ordered his bowmen to alter the direction of their shafts, and instead of shooting point-blank, to direct their arrows upward, so that the points should come down like hail from above upon the heads of the enemy. The manœuvre took effect, and many of the English were wounded, most of them in the face; but still they stood firm, and the Normans, almost disheartened, had recourse to a stratagem. William ordered 1000 horse to advance, and then turn and flee; at the view of this pretended rout the English lost their coolness, and leaving their positions, a part of the line gave pursuit, with their battle-axes slung round their necks. At a certain distance a fresh corps of Normans joined the 1000 horse, who drew rein and faced about; and then the English, surprised in their disorder, were assailed on every side by lances and swords. Here many hundreds of the English fell; for, encompassed by horse and foot, they could not retreat, and they would not surrender. The latter word, indeed, is never once used in any of the old accounts of the battle of Hastings. The Norman writers speak with admiration of the valour of several of Harold's thanes, who fought single-handed against a host of foes, as though each of them thought to save his country by his individual exertions. They have not preserved his name, but they make particular mention of one English thane, armed with a battle-axe, who spread dismay among the invaders. The battle-axe appears to have been the arm chiefly used by the English. This ponderous weapon had its advantages and its disadvantages; wielded by nervous men, it broke in pieces the coats of mail, and cleft the steel casques of the Normans, as no swords could have done; but from its weight and size it required both hands to wield it, and was awkward and difficult to manage in close combat.

The feint flight, which had succeeded so well, was repeated by the Normans in another part of the field, and, owing to the impetuosity of the English, with equal success. But still the main body maintained its position behind its stakes and palisades on the ridge of the hill; and such was their unshaken courage, that the Normans were obliged to try the same stratagem a third time—and a third time the brave but imprudent victims fell into the snare. Then the Norman horse and foot burst into the long-defended inclosure, and broke the English line in several points. But even now the English closed again round Harold, who, throughout the day, had shown the greatest activity and bravery. At this juncture he was struck by an arrow, shot at random, which entered his left eye and penetrated into his brain. The English then gave way, but they retreated no further than their standard, which they still sought to defend. The Normans hemmed them in, making the most desperate efforts to seize the banner. Robert Fitz-Ernest had almost grasped it, when a battle-axe laid him low for ever. Twenty Norman knights then undertook the task, and this attempt succeeded, after ten of their number had perished. The standard of England was then lowered, and the consecrated banner sent from Rome raised in its stead, in sign of victory. Gurth and Leofwin, the brave brothers of Harold, died at that last rallying point. The combat had lasted nine hours, for it was now six o'clock in the evening, and the sun was setting. After a desperate attempt at rallying made by the men of Kent and the East Angles, which cost the lives of many of the victors, the English troops, broken and dispirited by the loss of their leader, dispersed through the woods which lay in the rear of their position; the enemy followed them by the light of the moon; but, as they were ignorant of the country, which was in some places intersected by ditches, and as the English turned and made a stand wherever they could, they suffered severely in this pursuit, and soon gave it up. In every clause of their narrative the Norman writers express their admiration of the valour of the foe; and most of them confess that the great superiority of his forces alone enabled William to obtain the victory. During the sanguinary conflict the fortunate duke had three horses killed under him, and at one moment he was nearly laid prostrate by a blow struck upon his helmet by an English cavalier. The proud band of lords and knights that followed him from the Continent was fearfully thinned, as was well proved on the morrow, when the muster-roll he had prepared before leaving the port of St. Valery was called over. He lost one-fourth of his army, and he did not gain by the battle of Hastings a fourth part of the kingdom of England; for many an after-field was fought, and his wars for the conquest of the west, the north, and the east, were protracted for seven long years. The conquest effected by the Normans was a slow, and not a sudden one.[1] "Thus," to use the energetic language of an old writer,[2] "was tried, by the great assize of God's judgment in battle, the right of power between the English and Norman nations; a battle the most memorable of all others; and howsoever miserably lost, yet most nobly fought on the part of England."[3]

---

[1] Sir J. Mackintosh, *History of England*.
[2] Samuel Daniel.
[3] It has not been sufficiently noticed by historians, that the same mistaken views of Christian perfection which, by withdrawing the most moral part of the population into convents and solitudes, weakened the social system of the Roman empire in the fourth and fifth centuries, and thus insured its overthrow by the barbarians of the North, weakened Anglo-Saxon society in the

CHAPTER V.—SCOTTISH AND IRISH ANNALS.

A.D. 300–1066.

Different occupants of Britain—The Picts—The Scots—They are united into one nation—History of the Scottish kings to Malcolm III.—Annals of Ireland—Its early populations—Conversion of the Irish to Christianity by St. Patrick—Their contests with the Danes—State of Ireland at the period of the Norman Conquest of England.

DURING the course of the preceding narrative, we have seen the Saxons frequently engaged in wars, and occasionally also connected by alliances, with various other nations dwelling around them in the same island. The largest as well as the fairest portion of Britain was conquered and occupied, during the period we have been reviewing, by these Germanic invaders; but much of it still remained in the possession of the races of other lineage, by whom it had been earlier colonized, or was seized upon by invaders like themselves, but from a different quarter. All the east and south, from the Channel to the Tweed, was Saxon; in the west, along the whole extent of the Saxon dominion, were the alien and generally hostile tribes of Cornwall and Wales; on the north-west were the independent sovereignties of Cumbria and Strathclyde (if these were really two distinct kingdoms); and to the east and north of these was the powerful and extensive kingdom of the Picts, originally, it should seem, embracing the whole of the rest of modern Scotland. Behind the Picts, however, in the north-west, a colony of Scots from Ireland, not long after the arrival of the Saxons in the south, founded another new power of foreign origin, destined in like manner, in course of time, to bear down before it the elder thrones of its own part of the island.

The doubtful and confused annals of the several Cornish and Welsh principalities of those times offer nothing to detain the historian. Cornwall appears to have usually formed one kingdom, South Wales another, and North Wales a third. But the subjects of these several states, and also those of Cumbria and Strathclyde, farther to the north, may be regarded as having been in the main one people. It seems not improbable that they may have been a mixture of the old Celtic Britons who fled before the Saxons, or were the original inhabitants of this strip of

eleventh century, and thus insured the triumph of the Normans. Dissipation in one part of the people, and asceticism in another, tended to the same result. Christianity became either quite unknown, or did not bear on the ordinary relations of civil and domestic life. Retreating from the world it should have purified, it left it to perish from it own corruptions. William of Malmesbury gives a graphic picture of both excesses. The whole passage is instructive:—"This was a fatal day to England—a melancholy havock of our dear country, through its change of masters. For it had long since adopted the manners of the Angles, which bad been very various according to the times; for in the first years of their arrival they were barbarians in their look and manners, warlike in their usages, heathen in their rites; but after embracing the faith of Christ, by degrees and in process of time, from the peace they enjoyed, regarding arms only in a secondary light, they gave their whole attention to religion. I say nothing of the poor, the meanness of whose fortune often restrains them from overstepping the bounds of justice. I omit men of ecclesiastical rank, whom sometimes respect to their profession, and sometimes the fear of shame, suffer not to stray from the truth. I speak of princes, who, from the greatness of their power, might have full liberty to indulge in pleasure; some of whom in their own country, and others at Rome, changing their habit (that is, becoming monks) obtained a heavenly kingdom and a saintly intercourse. Many during their whole lives in outward appearance only embraced the present world, in order that they might exhaust their treasures on the poor, or divide them among monasteries. What shall I say of the multitudes of bishops, hermits, and abbots? Does not the whole island blaze with such numerous relics of its natives, that you can scarcely pass a village of any consequence but you hear the name of some new saint, besides the numbers of whom all notices have perished, from the want of records?"

Anglo-Saxon England had evidently become much like the Roman provinces in the days of Sulpicius Severus. Social, domestic, and military life had not received those purifying and invigorating Christian influences that make a people disposed to peace, yet irresistible against foreign attack. On the contrary, monkish superstition and asceticism, by leading the conscientious and pious away from the world they should have purified and preserved, left vice and ignorance, profligacy and moral cowardice, to usurp their place. We need not wonder, therefore, at what follows, from the same author:—

"Nevertheless, in process of time, the desire after literature and religion had decayed, for several years before the arrival of the Normans. The clergy, contented with a very slight degree of learning, could scarcely stammer out the words of the sacraments; and a person who understood grammar was an object of wonder and astonishment. The monks mocked the rule of their order by fine vestments and the use of every kind of food. The nobility, given up to luxury and wantonness, went not to church in the morning, after the manner of Christians, but merely, in a careless manner, heard matins and masses from a hurrying priest in their chambers, amid the blandishments of their wives. The commonalty, left unprotected, became a prey to the most powerful, who amassed fortunes by either seizing on their property, or by selling their persons into foreign countries: although it be an innate quality of this people to be more inclined to revelling than to the accumulation of wealth. There was one custom repugnant to human nature which they adopted, namely, to sell their female servants, when pregnant by them, and after they had satisfied their lusts, either to public prostitution, or to foreign slavery. Drinking in parties was an universal practice, in which occupation they passed entire nights as well as days. They consumed their whole substance in mean and despicable houses, unlike the Normans and French, who, in noble and splendid houses, lived with frugality."—*William of Malmesbury,* book iii.

country, and of Cimbrians, originally from the north of Germany and Denmark, the proper progenitors of the present Welsh. At what date these Cimbrians first found their way from the east coast of Scotland, where they seem to have earliest settled, to the west coast of England, and there mixed with and established a dominion over the native British occupants, no chronicles have told us. But some ancient relation between the Welsh and the Picts seems to be indicated by the strong evidence of language; and the close connection that subsisted between Wales and the Scottish kingdom of Strathclyde, down to the extinction of the latter, is established by abundance of historic testimony. If, in the mixture of the two races, the ascendency remained with the Celtic Britons anywhere, it was most probably in Cornwall. Everywhere else both the government and the language appear to have become chiefly Cimbrian, the national denomination of the Welsh in their vernacular tongue to this day. One of the northern Welsh kingdoms was actually called the kingdom of Cumbria, whence our modern county of Cumberland; and if the kingdom of Strathclyde was a different state from this (which is doubtful), we know at least that in that district of Scotland also, the native land and residence of Merlin and Aneurin, and many other personages famous in Cumbrian song and story, the language, and government, and all things else were Welsh.[1]

At what time the various tribes of the north, often spoken of under the general appellation of the Caledonians, although that name was properly applicable only to the occupants of the woody and mountainous regions of the west and northwest, came to be united in the single monarchy of the Picts, it is impossible to ascertain. The Picts are first mentioned about the beginning of the fourth century, at which time the name appears to have been understood to comprehend all the northern tribes. Antiquaries are generally agreed that a kingdom, under the name of the kingdom of the Picts—which, in pretension at least, extended over the whole of what is now called Scotland, with the exception of the district of Strathclyde in the south-west—had been established some considerable time before the evacuation of South Britain by the Romans in the middle of the fifth century. Records, the authenticity of which does not admit of any reasonable doubt, make the Pictish sovereign, when this event took place, to have been Durst, the son of Erp, for whom his warlike achievements against the provincialized Britains of the south, and the length of his reign, have obtained from the Irish annalists the poetic title of King of a Hundred Years and a Hundred Battles. The Picts came into collision with the Saxons of Northumberland not long after the establishment of the two kingdoms of Deira and Bernicia, the princes of the latter of which appear to have claimed, as within their boundaries, the whole of the territory along the east coast, as far as to the Frith of Forth. For

---

[1] This is not the place to discuss the genealogy of the Picts; but if we adopt the theory of their Germanic origin, the enigma of the passing away of the Romano-British population, if not made quite plain, will appear less difficult than before.

"The supposition is not destitute of support. The migratory tendencies of the Gothic tribes have always been conspicuous. From the earliest periods of our history, the inhabitants of Jutland and its neighbouring provinces were in the habit of making descents on the coasts of Britain. After the departure of the Romans, their attempts were probably more bold and frequent; but they did not then for the first time commence. The Norfolk and Suffolk coast was, from its position, peculiarly exposed to these incursions; and as early as the close of the third century, was placed under the command of a military count, called *Comes litoris Saxonici*. This district was called the Saxon shore, as Sir Francis Palgrave observes, not merely because it was open to the incursion of the Saxons, but, most probably, because they had succeeded in fixing themselves in some portions of it. The weak hold which the Romans, at all times, had of Scotland, would render it an easier prey than England to the Franks and Saxons. Tacitus informs us that the ruddy hair and lusty limbs of the Caledonians indicate a Germanic extraction. Richard of Cirencester tells us, that a little before the coming of Severus, the Picts landed in Scotland; from which we are entitled to infer, that the Picts were not the original inhabitants of North Britain; and probably the statement is substantially correct, inasmuch as large reinforcements landed in Scotland at this period, as previously observed. The Scots—the other branch of the people classed under the general term Caledonians—are confessedly of Irish origin. When St. Columba, whose mother-tongue was the Irish Gaelic, preached to the Picts, he used an interpreter. Fordun, the father of Scottish history, tells us: 'The manners of the Scots are various as to their languages; for they use two tongues—the Scottish and the Teutonic. The last is spoken by those on the sea-coasts and in the low countries, while the Scottish is the speech of the mountaineers and the remote islanders.' The proper Scots Camden describes as those commonly called Highlandmen; 'for the rest,' he adds, 'more civilized, and inhabiting the eastern part, though comprehended under the name of Scots, are the farthest in the world from being Scots, but are of the same German origin with us English.' Dr. Jamieson, whose researches in physiology are well known, is decidedly of opinion that the Picts and Saxons had a common origin. Upon what other theory, he argues, can the prevalence of the Saxon tongue in the lowlands of Scotland be accounted for? William the Conqueror could not change the language of South Britain. Was it likely that a few Saxon fugitives at the Scottish court could supplant that of their benefactor?

"The theory of the Germanic origin of the Picts removes another difficulty. How is the disappearance of the Celtic tongue from England to be accounted for? The Saxons, on seizing the soil, would not exterminate the inhabitants, but retain them as bondsmen. Had the majority of the original occupants of England been the original Britons or Romanized Celts, we should have found in our daily speech, and in the names of our towns and villages, a large intermixture of Gaelic and Latin; but such is not the case. Grant that the Picts were a branch of the great Gothic family, and that successive waves of them had, long before the time of Cerdic, poured from the Lowlands of Scotland over the plains of England, and the almost entire extermination of the ancient Britons is easily accounted for.

"If the theory here advocated cannot be sustained, it must at least be allowed that the population of North Britain was largely leavened with individuals of the Saxon race. These strangers would, doubtless, obtain that supremacy over the natives which the Franks did in Gaul; so that, even upon this limited view of the question, the influence of the Germanic race in fixing the destinies of Britain at this critical period, is apparent."—*The Roman Wall*, by the Rev. John C. Bruce, M.A.

some time, accordingly, all this district formed a sort of debateable land, alternately subject to the Northumbrian Saxons and to the Picts. The Saxons are believed to have begun to settle in the territory as early as the middle of the fifth century, and probably from this date the population continued to be mainly Saxon; but after the great battle of Dunnechtan (supposed to be Dunnichen in Angus), fought in 685 between the Pictish king Bridei, the son of Beli, and the Northumbrian Egfrid, it became permanently a part of the Pictish dominions. This is the tract of country which, in a later age, came to be called by the name of Lodonia or Laodonia, still surviving in the Lothians, the modern designation of the greater part of it.

In the earliest times of the Pictish monarchy, its capital appears to have stood near the present town of Inverness. It was here that King Bridei or Brude, son of Merlothon, was visited, soon after the middle of the sixth century, by St. Columba. Afterwards, on the extension of their power towards the south, the kings of the Picts transferred their residence to Forteviot in Perthshire, and here they seem to have fixed themselves so long as the monarchy subsisted. The history of the state, so far as it has been preserved, is made up of little else than a long succession of hostilities, sometimes with the Saxons, sometimes with the neighbouring kingdom of Strathclyde, sometimes with the Scots from Ireland, who from the commencement of the sixth century continued to encroach upon the territories of the Picts, and the pressure from whom perhaps had some share in inducing the latter eventually to remove the chief seat of their sovereignty from its ancient position in the heart of the true Caledonia. The meagre narrative is also varied by some domestic wars, principally arising out of the competition of various claimants for the crown, to which there seem to have been no definitely settled rule of succession. In the end of the eighth and the beginning of the ninth century, the Picts found a new enemy in the northern pirates or sea-kings, the same maranders who in the same age ravaged the neighbouring coasts of England and France, and indeed it may be said generally of all the north-west of Europe. The dissolution of the ancient Pictish royalty, however, and the extinction of the name of the Picts as that of an independent people, were now at hand.

The earliest colony of Irish, or Scots, as they were called, is said to have settled on the west coast of North Britain about the middle of the third century. They were led by Carbry Rinda, prince or sub-regulus of a district called Dalriada in Ulster; and they were long known by the name of the Dalriadians, from this their native seat. The Dalriadians, however, do not appear to have set up any pretences to an independent sovereignty in the country of their adoption until after the beginning of the sixth century, when their numbers were greatly augmented by an immigration of their Irish kindred, under the conduct of Lorn, Fergus, and Angus, the three sons of Erek, the then prince of Dalriada. This new colonization seems to have amounted to an actual invasion of North Britain, and the design of its leaders probably was from the first to wrest the country or a part of it from its actual possessors. Very soon after this we find the Picts and Scots meeting each other in arms. A still more decided proof of the growing strength of the latter nation is, in course of time, afforded by a matrimonial alliance between the King of the Dalriadians and the Pictish royal house. This connection took place in the reign of Achaius, who is reckoned the twenty-seventh of the Scottish kings from Fergus, in whose line and in that of the descendants of his elder brother, Lorn, the sovereign power had been all along preserved. Achaius married Urgusia, the sister of the Pictish kings Constantine and Ungus, who reigned in succession from A.D. 791 to 830. The issue of this marriage, and the successor of Achaius, was Alpin, and his son and successor was Kenneth II., who mounted the throne of his ancestors in the year 836. Three years after, the Pictish king Uven, the son and successor of Ungus, fell in battle with the Danes. Kenneth, as the near relation of its deceased occupier, immediately claimed the vacant throne: a contest of arms between the two nations appears to have ensued; but at last, in A.D. 843, Kenneth, having subdued all opposition, was acknowledged king, both of the Scots and the Picts. There is no reason to suppose, as is asserted by some of the Scottish chroniclers who wrote in a comparatively recent age, that the Pictish people were upon this event either destroyed or driven from their country; it is probable enough that the chiefs of the faction that had resisted the claim of Kenneth, and also perhaps many of their followers, may have fled from the vengeance of the conqueror, and taken refuge in the Orkney Islands and elsewhere; but the great body of the inhabitants, no doubt, remained the subjects of the new king. It appears that Kenneth and his immediate successors styled themselves, not Kings of Scotland and of Pictavia or Pictland, but Kings of the Scots and the Picts; and the Picts are spoken of as a distinct people for a century after they thus ceased to form an independent state.[1]

---

[1] The account here given is that which is now generally received; but it is proper to notice that the whole story of the conquest of the Picts by Kenneth, and also Kenneth's extraction from the old royal line of the Irish Scots, have been called in question and

SAXON PERIOD.

Meanwhile the kingdom of Strathclyde, the capital of which was Alcluyd, the modern Dumbarton, still subsisted, and withheld a large portion of the present Scotland from the sway of the Dalriadian prince. There is some appearance of Kenneth Mac Alpin having attempted to possess himself of that additional throne by the same combination of policy and force by which he had acquired the dominion of the Picts. After long fighting, he concluded a peace with Cu or Caw, the King of Strathclyde, and gave him his daughter in marriage. No opportunity, however, was found of turning this arrangement to account in the manner which its projector probably contemplated; and the kingdom of Strathclyde, though distressed and weakened, both by the pressure of its powerful neighbour, and the frequent predatory and devastating attacks of the Danes from beyond seas, continued to maintain a nominal independence till the native government was finally subverted, and the country incorporated with the rest of the Scottish dominions, by the defeat of its last king, Dunwallon, by Kenneth III., King of the Scots (the great-great-grandson of Kenneth Mac Alpin), at the battle of Vacornar, in A.D. 973. Even before this event, however, North Britain had begun to be known, after its Irish conquerors, by the name of Scotland. It is so called for the first time in the *Saxon Chronicle* under the year 934.

Meanwhile the united Scottish kingdom, founded by Kenneth Mac Alpin, continued to consolidate and strengthen itself under the sway of his descendants. Kenneth himself, in the remaining part of his reign, had to make good his position by his sword, sometimes in defensive, sometimes in aggressive contests, both with the Danes, the Saxons, and his neighbours of Strathclyde; but he died at last in bed, at his capital of Forteviot, A.D. 859. He was succeeded by his brother, Donald III., who reigned till A.D. 863. Constantine II., the son of Kenneth, followed, and, during a reign of eighteen years, was engaged in almost uninterrupted warfare with the Danes, who harassed him both from Ireland and from the Continent, and penetrated into the heart of the kingdom by all its maritime inlets. It is asserted by the old historians, that these invaders were first called in by the fugitive or subjugated Picts, a fact which may be taken as some confirmation of the common Northern origin of both.

The enemy, therefore, with whom Constantine had to contend, had friends and supporters in the heart of his dominions; and while he endeavoured to repel the foreigners with one hand, he must have had to keep down his own subjects with the other. Nor were the Picts altogether defrauded of their revenge on the son of their conqueror. They and their allies the Danes appear to have wrested from the Scottish king not only the Orkney and Western Islands, but also the extensive districts of Caithness, Sutherland, and part of Ross-shire, on the continent of Scotland; and these acquisitions continued to be governed for many ages by Norwegian princes entirely independent of the Scottish crown. The traditionary account, repeated by the later historians, of the termination of Constantine's disastrous reign is, that he was killed in a battle with the Danes, or put to death by them immediately after the battle, near Crail, in Fife. A cave in which he was massacred is still shown, and called the Devil's Cave. The older writers, however, place his death in A.D. 882, a year after the great battle in Fife.

Constantine's immediate successor was his brother Hugh; but he was dethroned the same year by Grig, the chieftain of the district now forming the shires of Aberdeen and Banff, who, associating with himself on the throne Eocha or Eth, son of the King of Strathclyde, by a daughter of Kenneth Mac Alpin, is said to have reigned for about twelve years, with a more extensive authority than had been enjoyed by any of his predecessors. The monkish chroniclers, indeed, who designate him by the pompous title of Gregory the Great, absurdly make him not only to have held his own with a strong hand, but to have actually reduced to subjection all the neighbouring states, including both the English and the Irish. He appears to have been a favourer of the church, upon which he probably leaned for support in the deficiency of his hereditary title. However, he and his partner in the sovereignty were at length dethroned by a popular insurrection, A.D. 893; on which their place was supplied by Donald IV., the son of Constantine II. A succession of combats with the Danes, again—one of the most memorable of which was fought at Collin, near Scone, for the possession of the famous Stone of Destiny, which Kenneth Mac Alpin had transferred thither from the original British nestling-place of his antique race in Argyleshire—form almost the only recorded events of his reign. The Northern invaders were beaten at Collin; but a few years after, in 904, Donald fell in fight near Forteviot, against another band of them from Ireland. He was succeeded by Constantine III., the son of his uncle Hugh. This was the Scottish king who, as related in a

---

denied by Pinkerton, in his *Inquiry into the History of Scotland preceding the reign of Malcolm III.*, a work of much learning and acuteness, and also of great value for the quantity of materials collected in it from previously unexplored sources, but disfigured by many precipitate assertions, and a pervading spirit of prejudice and paradox. In our abstract we have principally adhered to the dates and order of events as settled by the latest investigator of this part of our national history, Chalmers, in his *Caledonia*, vol. i. pp. 374-428.

preceding page, made an inroad, in 937, into the dominions of the Saxon Athelstane, in conjunction with Olave or Anlaf, the Danish chief of Northumberland, when their united forces were routed in the bloody day of Brunnaburgh, and Constantine with difficulty escaped from the slaughter, in which his eldest son fell. A few years after this humiliating defeat, in A.D. 944, he exchanged his crown for a cowl, and he passed the last eight or nine years of his life as abbot of the Culdees of St. Andrews. Meanwhile the throne was ascended by Malcolm I., son of Donald IV. The most important event of this reign was the cession, by the Saxon king, Edmund, of the district of Cumbria, which he had recently conquered from its last king, Dunmail, to Malcolm, to be held by him on condition of his arming when called upon, in the defence either of that or of any other part of the English territory. Cumberland remained an appanage of the Scottish crown from this time till 1072, when it was recovered by William the Conqueror.

Malcolm I. came to a violent death at the hands of some of his own subjects in 953, and left his sceptre to Indulf, the son of his predecessor, Constantine III. The reign of Indulf was grievously troubled by repeated attacks of the Northmen; and he at last lost his life in what the old writers call the battle of the Bauds, fought in 961, near the Bay of Cullen, in Banffshire, where several barrows on a moor still preserve the memory of the defeat of the foreigners. Duff, the son of Malcolm I., now became king, according to what appears to have been the legal order of succession at this time, when each king for many generations was almost uniformly succeeded, not by his own son, but by the son of his predecessor. But the effects of the natural disposition of the sovereign in possession to retain the succession exclusively in his own line now began to show themselves; and the right of Duff was disputed from the first by Indulf's son, Culen, whose partisans, although defeated in the fair fight of Duncrub, in Perthshire, are asserted to have afterwards opened the way to the throne for their leader by the assassination of his rival. This event took place at Forres, in 965. But Culen did not long retain his guiltily acquired power. Disregarding all the duties of his place, he abandoned himself to riot and licentiousness, and soon followed up the murder of Duff by an act of atrocious violence, committed on another near relation, the daughter of the King of Strathclyde. The nation of the injured lady took arms against her violator; and Culen fell in a battle fought with them at a place situated to the south of the Forth, in A.D. 970.

The crown now fell to Kenneth III., another son of Malcolm I., and the brother of Duff. The reign of Kenneth III. is one of the most important in the early history of Scotland. He was a prince of remarkable ability, and of a daring and unscrupulous character; he occupied the throne for a sufficient length of time to enable him to lay a deep foundation for his schemes of policy, if not to carry them into complete effect; and he came at a crisis when the old order of things was naturally breaking up, and the most favourable opportunity was offered to a bold and enterprising genius like his of establishing, or at least originating a new system. It was one of those conjunctions of circumstances, and of an individual mind fitted to take advantage of them, by which most of the great movements in national affairs have been produced. His first effort was to follow up the war with the declining state of Strathclyde, until he wound it up, as has been intimated above, with the complete subjugation of that rival kingdom, and its incorporation with his hereditary dominions. With the exception, therefore, of the nominal independence, but real vassalage in everything except in name, of the Welsh, the whole of Britain was now divided into the two sovereignties of England and Scotland. The Saxon power of Wessex had swallowed up and absorbed everything else in the south, and in the north every other royalty had in like manner fallen before that of the Celtic princes of Dalriada. Peace and intimate alliance, also, had now taken the place of the old enmity between the two monarchies; and an opening must have been made for the passage to Scotland of some rays from the superior civilization of her neighbour, which would naturally be favourable to imitation in the arrangements of the government, as well as in other matters. It was in this position of affairs that Kenneth proceeded to take measures for getting rid of what we have seen was the most remarkable peculiarity of the Scottish regal constitution, the participation of two distinct lines in the right of succession to the throne, a rule or custom to which, notwithstanding some advantages, there would seem to exist an all-sufficient objection in its very tendency to excite to such attempts as that which Kenneth now made. Kenneth's mode of proceeding was characteristically energetic and direct. To put an end in the most effectual manner to the pretensions of Malcolm, the son of his brother Duff, he had that prince put to death, although he had been already recognized as Tani016, or next heir to the throne, and had as such been invested, according to custom, with the lordship of Cumberland. We shall see, however, that this deed of blood was after all perpetrated to no purpose. Another of Kenneth's acts of severity, and perhaps also of cruelty and vengeance, recoiled upon him to his own destruction. After the suppression of a commotion in the Mearns, he had thought it necessary to signalize the triumph of the royal authority by taking the life of the only son of the chief of the district, either because the young man had been one of the leaders of the vanquished faction, or perhaps because his father had not shown sufficient energy in meeting and putting down their designs. By some means or other, however, Kenneth was some time after induced to trust himself in the hands of Fenella, the mother of his victim, by visiting her in her castle, near Fettercairn. Here he was murdered, either by her orders, or not improbably by her own hands, for it is related that she fled the instant the deed was done, although she was soon taken, and suffered the same bloody death she had avenged and inflicted. The reign of Kenneth was thus terminated, A.D. 944.

The throne left vacant by the death of Kenneth appears to have been contested from the first by three competitors. Of these a son of Culen, under the name of Constantine IV., is regarded as having been first crowned; but within a year he fell fighting against one of his rivals, a son of King Duff, and younger brother of the murdered Prince Malcolm, who immediately assumed the sovereignty as Kenneth IV. The Scottish chroniclers call him Kenneth the Grim. There was still, however, another claimant to the succession to Kenneth III.; this was Malcolm, the son of that king, whom his father had designed to be his heir, and invested as such with the principality of Cumberland, after the violent removal of his cousin, the other Malcolm. The two competitors met at last, in A.D. 1003, at Monivaird, when a battle took place, in which Kenneth the Grim lost both the day and his life.

The vigorous line of Kenneth III. was now again seated on the throne, in the person of Malcolm II. The earlier part of Malcolm's reign appears to have been consumed in a long succession of fierce contests with the Danes, in the course of which these persevering invaders are said to have been defeated in the several battles of Mortlach in Moray, in the parish church of which place the skulls of the slaughtered foreigners were, not many years ago, to be seen built into the wall; of Aberlemno, where barrows and sculptured stones are held still to preserve the memory and to point out the scene of the conflict; of Panbride, where the Danish commander, Camus, was slain; and of Cruden, near Forres, where a remarkable obelisk, covered with engraved figures, is supposed, but probably erroneously, to have been erected in commemoration of the Scottish victory. It was in 1020 also, in the reign of this king, that a formal cession was obtained from Eadulf, the Danish Earl of Northumberland, of the portion of modern Scotland south of the Forth, then called Lodonia, the possession of which had for a long time been disputed between the Scots and the Saxons, although in the meantime such numbers of the latter had settled in it, that its population appears already to have become in the greater part Saxon, and the country itself was often called Saxonia or Saxony. Malcolm II., the ability of whose administration was long held in respectful remembrance, died in 1033.

This king, unfortunately for the peaceful success of his father's scheme of changing the old rule of succession, left no son; but, imitating his father's remorseless policy, he had done his utmost to make a similarity even in that respect between himself and the rival branch of the royal stock, by having, a short time before his decease, had the only existing male descendant of Kenneth the Grim, a son of his son Boidhe, put in the most effectual manner out of the way. In these circumstances no opposition appears to have been made in the first instance to the accession of Duncan, the grandson of Malcolm II., by his daughter Bethoc or Beatrice, who was married to Crinan, abbot of Dunkeld, in those days a personage of great eminence in the state. Boidhe, however, besides the son who was murdered, had left a daughter, Gruoch; and this lady had other wrongs to avenge besides those of the line from which she was sprung. Her first husband, Gilcomcain, marmor or chief of Moray, having been defeated in an attempt to support the cause of his wife's family by arms against King Malcolm, had been burned in his castle, along with fifty of his friends, when she herself had to flee for her life, with her infant son Lulach. She sought shelter in the remoter district of Ross, of which the famous Macbeth appears to have then been the hereditary lord, maintaining probably within his bounds an all but nominal independence of the royal authority. This part of Scotland, it may be remembered, had been torn, scarcely a century before, from Constantine II. by the Danes, and Macbeth himself may possibly have been of Danish lineage. Be this as it may, to him the Lady Gruoch now gave her hand. She is the Lady Macbeth made familiar to us all by the wonderful drama of Shakspeare. It would appear that, for some time after the accession of Duncan, Macbeth and his wife had feigned an acquiescence in his title, and had probably even won the confidence of the good and unsuspecting king (the pure-breathed Duncan, as he is designated in Celtic song), by their services or professions. The end of their plot, however, was, that Duncan was barbarously assassinated in 1039, not, as Shakspeare has it, in Macbeth's castle at Inverness, but at a place called

Bothgouanau, near Elgin.[1] Macbeth immediately mounted the throne, and the accounts of the oldest chroniclers gave reason to believe that he filled it both ably and to the general satisfaction of the people. The partisans of the race of Kenneth III., however, resisted the new king from the first; for Duncan had left two sons, the elder of whom, Malcolm, fled on his father's assassination to Cumberland, and the younger, Donald, to the Western Isles. One revolt in favour of Malcolm's restoration was headed by his grandfather, the abbot of Dunkeld; but this and several other similar attempts failed. At length, in 1054, Macduff, marmor or chief (improperly called by later writers thane) of Fife, his patriotism inflamed, it is said, by some personal injuries, called to arms his numerous retainers; and Siward, the Danish Earl of Northumberland, whose sister Duncan had married, having joined him at the head of a formidable force, the two advanced together upon Macbeth. Their first encounter appears to have taken place, as tradition and Shakspeare agree in representing, in the neighbourhood of Dunsinnane Hill, in Angus, on the summit of which Macbeth probably had a stronghold.[2] Defeated here, the usurper retreated to the fastnesses of the north, where he appears to have protracted the war for about two years longer. His last place of refuge is supposed to have been a fortress in a solitary valley in the parish of Lunfanan, in Aberdeenshire. In this neighbourhood he was attacked by the forces under the command of Macduff and Malcolm, on the 5th of December, 1056, and fell in the fight, struck down, it is said, by the hand of Macduff. His followers, however, did not even yet everywhere throw down their arms. They immediately set up as king, Lulach, the son of Lady Macbeth, who indeed, as descended from Duff, the elder son of Malcolm I., in the same degree in which his rival was descended from Malcolm's younger son, Kenneth III., might be affirmed to have had the better right to the throne of the two. Lulach, however, a fugitive all the while that he was a king, did not long bear the empty title that thus mocked his fortunes. His forces and those of Malcolm met on the 3d of April, 1067, at Eassie, in Angus; and that day ended his life, and also broke for ever the power of his faction. In a few days after this (on the 25th of April, the festival of St. Mark) Malcolm III. was crowned at Scone. But the history of his reign belongs to the next period.

It will be convenient, also, before we close the present chapter, to turn for a few moments to the course of events in Ireland, which, although not politically connected with England in the period under review, had already acquired a remarkable celebrity, and begun to maintain a considerable intercourse both with Britain and with continental Europe. We find the country at the commencement of our era subjected to the rule of the Scots, a foreign people, who had wrested the supreme dominion of it from the Tuath de Danaus, in the same manner as the latter had displaced their predecessors the Firbolgs. The fables of the bards made mention of three still earlier races by whom the island was successively colonized. But all that can be gathered from the chaos of wild inventions which forms this first part of the Irish story is, that probably before the arrival of the Firbolgs the country had been peopled by that Celtic race to which the great body of its population still continues to belong. These primitive Celtic colonists, whose blood, whose speech, whose manners and customs remain—in spite of all subsequent foreign infusions—dominant throughout the island to this day, would seem to be the Partholans of the legendary account. The Fomorians, again, who came from Africa, were perhaps the Phœnicians or Carthaginians. The Nemedians, the Tuath de Danans, the Firbolgs, and the Scots or Milesians, are affirmed to have all been of the same race, which was different from that of the Partholans; a statement which is most easily explained by supposing that all these subsequent bodies of colonists or invaders were of the Gothic or Teutonic stock, and came, as indeed the bardic narrative makes them to have done, from the north of continental Europe. It seems, at all events, to be most probable that the Scots were a Gothic people; Scythæ, Scoti, Gothi, Getæ, indeed, appear to be only different forms of the same word.[3] The Scots are supposed, by the ablest inquirers, not to have made their appearance in Ireland very long before the commencement of our era, if their colonization be not, indeed, a still more recent event; for we believe no trace of their occupation is to be discovered before the second or third century. From the fourth century down to the eleventh, that is, during the whole of the period with which we are at present engaged, Ireland was known by the name of Scotia or Scotland, and the Irish generally by that of the Scoti or Scots; nor till the close of the tenth century were these names ever

---

[1] "The word Bothgouanan means in Gaelic, the Smith's Dwelling. It is probable that the assassins lay in ambush, and murdered him at a smith's house in the neighbourhood of Elgin."—Hailes' *Annals*, i. 1 (edit. of 1819).

[2] The foundations of an ancient stone building are still to be found buried in the soil on the top of the hill. Dunsinnane is about eight miles north-east from Perth; the hill is of very regular shape, and although more than 1000 ft. above the level of the sea, it has been supposed to be in great part artificial.—See Chalmers' *Caledonia*, vol. i.

[3] See this matter very ably treated in Pinkerton's *Dissertation on the Origin and Progress of the Scythians or Goths*, part I. chap. 1.

otherwise applied.¹ If the Scots of North Britain were spoken of, they were so designated as being considered to be a colony of Irish.

The bardic account, however, carries back the arrival of the Scotic colony, under the conduct of Heber and Heremon, the sons of Milesius, to a much more ancient date; and the modern inquirers who have endeavoured to settle the chronology of that version of the story, have assigned the event, in the most moderate of their calculations, to the fifth or sixth century before the birth of Christ. Others place it nearly 1000 years earlier. It is related that the two brothers at first divided the island between them, Heber the elder taking to himself Leinster and Munster, and Heremon getting Ulster and Connaught; but, in imitation of Romulus and Remus (if we ought not rather to suppose the Irish to have been the prototype of the classic incident), they afterwards quarrelled, and Heber having been slain, Heremon became sole sovereign. From him is deduced a regular succession of monarchs of all Ireland down to Kimbaoth, who is reckoned the fifty-seventh in the list, and is said to have reigned about 200 years before our era. Besides the supreme monarch, it is admitted that there were always four subordinate kings, reigning each over his province; and the history is made up in great part of the wars of these reguli, not only with one another, but frequently also with their common sovereign lord. Tacitus relates that one of the reguli of Ireland, who had been driven from his country by some domestic revolution, came over to Britain, to Agricola, who kept him with him under the semblance of friendship, in the hope of some time or other having an opportunity of making use of him. It was the opinion of Agricola that Ireland might have been conquered and kept in subjection by a single legion and a few auxiliaries. Tacitus observes, however, that its ports and harbours were better known than those of Britain, through the merchants that resorted to them, and the extent of their foreign commerce.²

We need not further pursue the obscure, and in great part fabulous annals of the country before the introduction of Christianity. It is probable that some knowledge of the Christian religion had penetrated to Ireland before the mission of St. Patrick; but it was by the labours of that celebrated personage that the general conversion of the people was effected, in the early part of the fifth century. The first Christian King of Ireland was Leogaire or Laogaire Mac Neil, whose reign is stated to have extended from A.D. 428 to A.D. 463. The twenty-ninth king, counting from him, was Donald III., who reigned from A.D. 743 to A.D. 763. It was in his time (A.D. 748) that the Danes or Northmen made their first descent upon Ireland. In 815, in the reign of Aodhus V., these invaders obtained a fixed settlement in Armagh; and thirty years afterwards, their leader, Turgesius or Turges, a Norwegian, was proclaimed King of all Ireland. At length a general massacre of the foreigners led to the restoration of the line of the native princes. But new bands speedily arrived from the north to avenge their countrymen, and in a few years all the chief ports and towns throughout the south and along the east coast were again in their hands. The struggle between the two races for the dominion of the country continued, with little intermission and with various fortune, for more than a century and a half, although the Danes, too, had embraced Christianity about the year 948. The closing period of the long contest is illustrated by the heroic deeds of the renowned Brien Boroihme or Boru, the "Brien the Brave" of song, who was first King of Munster, and afterwards King of all Ireland. He occupied the national throne from 1003 to 1014, in which latter year he fell, sword in hand, at the age of eighty-eight, in the great battle of Clontarf, in which, however, the Danish power received a discomfiture from which it never recovered. Brien, however, though his merits and talents had raised him to the supreme power, not being of the ancient royal house, is looked upon as little better than an usurper by the Irish historians; and the true king of this date is reckoned to have been Maelsechlan Mac Domhnaill, more manageably written Melachlan or Malachi, whom Brien deposed. Malachi, too, was a great warrior; the same patriotic poet who, in our own day and in our Saxon tongue, has celebrated "the glories of Brien the Brave," has also sung—

"Let Erin remember the days of old,
Ere her faithless sons betrayed her;
When Malachi wore the collar of gold
Which he won from her proud invader;"

and on the death of Brien, Malachi was restored to the throne, which he occupied till 1022. He is reckoned the forty-second Christian King of Ireland.³ The interruption of the regular succession, however, by the elevation of Brien, now brought upon the country the new calamity of a contest among several competitors for the throne; and the death of Malachi was followed by a season of great confusion and national misery. The game was eventually reduced to a trial of strength between Donchad, the son of Brien, and Donchad's nephew, Turlogh; and in 1064 Turlogh

---

¹ See this completely established, and all the authorities collected, in Pinkerton's *Inquiry*, part v. ch. iv.
² Tacit. *Vit. Agric.* xxiv.
³ In these dates we have followed the authority of the *Catalogus Chronologicus Regum Christianorum Hiberniæ*, in O'Connor's *Rerum Hibernicarum Scriptores Veteres*, vol i. pp. lxxv. &c.

succeeded in overpowering his uncle, who, bidding farewell to arms and to ambition, retired across the sea, and ended his days as a monk at Rome. Turlogh, reckoned an usurper by the native annalists, but acknowledged to have ruled the country ably and well, occupied the Irish throne at the epoch of the Norman conquest of England.

CHAPTER VI.—HISTORY OF RELIGION.

A.D. 449-1066.

Religion of the Saxon invaders of England—Its deities—Its doctrines of a future state—Its sanguinary rites—State of Christianity in North and South Britain at the Saxon Invasion—Missionaries sent to England by Gregory the Great—Progress of the missionaries among the kingdoms of the Heptarchy—Conversion of Northumbria—Controversies about the form of the tonsure and period for the celebration of Easter—Corruptions among the clergy through wealthy donations—Multiplication of monasteries and nunneries—Havoc wrought among them by the Danish invaders—Life of St. Dunstan—His miracles and adventures—He becomes Primate of England—His strange expedients to reform the church—Its condition after his death till the Norman conquest.

HEN Hengist and Horsa and their followers arrived in Britain, they certainly found Christianity professed by a large part of the island; but the religion of the South Britons had become mixed with many corruptions of doctrine. The Saxons one and all were pagans, but of a paganism which differed essentially from the old Druidism. Woden or Odin was the head of their mythology. The source from whence their religion issued, the period of its first promulgation, and the agents by whom it was planted in the several countries where it flourished, are historical difficulties which yet remain to be settled. Long before the fourth century of the Christian era it prevailed throughout Scandinavia, and in other countries besides those which we now call Sweden, Norway, and Denmark.[1] It was a grim and terrible theology. Woden or Odin was "the terrible and severe god; the father of slaughter; the god that carries desolation and fire; the active and roaring deity; he who gives victory, and who names those that are to be slain." The worship of such a divinity kept up the ferocity and warlike habits of these iron men of the North. Under him figured Frea, his wife, as the goddess of love, pleasure, and sensuality; the god Thor, who controlled the tempests; Balder, who was the god of light; Kiord, the god of the waters; Tyr, the god of champions; Brage, the god of orators and poets; and Heimdal, the janitor of heaven, and the guardian of the rainbow. Eleven gods and as many goddesses, all the children of Odin and Frea, assisted their parents, and were objects of worship. But in addition to all these there were very many inferior divinities. There were three Fates, by whom the career of men was predestined; and every individual was supposed, besides, to have a Fate attending him, by whom his life was controlled and his death determined. There were also the Valkeries, a species of inferior goddesses, who acted as celestial attendants, and who were also employed by Odin to determine victory, and select the warriors that were to perish in battle. There were genii and spirits, who mingled in every mortal event. Infernal agents there were in abundance; and Lok, the personification of the evil principle, was the head of them all. Lok is described as beautiful in form, but depraved in mind; the calumniator of the gods, the grand contriver of deceit and fraud, the reproach of gods and men, whom the deities, in consequence of his malignity, had been constrained to shut up in a cavern. The goddess Hela, the wolf Fenris, the great dragon, and giants of measureless size and strength, contended the dark array.

On the subject of a future state, this religion of the North was particularly explicit; and a heaven was formed, congenial to a people whose chief employment and greatest pleasure was war. Those who had led a life of heroism, or perished bravely in battle, ascended to Valhalla. In that blessed region the day was spent in war and furious conflict; but at evening-tide the battle ceased, all wounds were suddenly healed, and the contending warriors sat down to the banquet, and feasted on the exhaustless flesh of the boar Serimner, and drank huge draughts of mead from the skulls of their enemies. Such was the para-

---

[1] Mallet, *Northern Antiquities.*

dise, the hope of which wakened to rapture the imagination of the Saxon and the Dane. There was a hell for the wicked; but by the word wicked was merely understood the cowardly and the slothful. This hell was called Niflheim. Here Hela dwelt, and exercised her terrible supremacy. Her palace was Anguish, her table Famine, her waiters were Expectation and Delay, the threshold of her door was Precipice, her bed was Leanness, and her looks struck terror into every beholder.

But nothing of all this was to be strictly eternal. After the revolution of countless ages, the malignant powers so long restrained are to burst forth again; the gods are to perish, and even Odin himself expire; while a conflagration bursts forth, in which Valhalla, their heaven, and the world, and Niflheim or hell, with all their divine and human inhabitants, are consumed, and pass away. But from this second chaos a new world is to emerge, fresh and full of beauty and grandeur, with a heaven more glorious than Valhalla, and a hell more fearful than Niflheim; while over all a God appears pre-eminent and alone, possessed of incomparably greater might and nobler attributes than Odin. Then, too, the human race are finally to be tried, and higher virtues than bravery, and heavier guilt than cowardice and sloth, are to form the standard of good and evil. The righteous shall then be received into Gimle, and the wicked shall be sent to the unutterable punishments of Nastrande; and this heaven and this hell shall continue through all eternity under the reign of Him who is eternal.

But among the fierce worshippers of Odin we can discover no practical results of this better faith that lay immediately beneath the surface of their own system. They thought more of the temporal, but immediate, than of the eternal—more of Valhalla than of Gimle. Their tempest-breathing god, and his paradise of battles, and drinking and feasting, though these were finally to be consumed and to pass away, were more attractive than the excellences of a more spiritual Deity, and the eternity of a purer heaven.

The Scandinavian temples, in which Odin was represented by a gigantic image, armed and crowned, and brandishing a naked sword, were rude and colossal; and rugged were the rites performed therein. Animals were offered up as sacrifices, and their blood was sprinkled upon the worshippers. The rough altar was frequently drenched with the blood of human victims. Crowds of captives and slaves were immolated for the welfare of the people at large; and princes often sacrificed their own children to avert a mortal sickness or to secure an important victory.[1] Believing that the exclusion from Valhalla, which a natural death entailed, could be avoided by the sacrifice of a substitute, every warrior who could procure a captive to put to death with this object had a motive peculiarly powerful for so horrid a practice.

Mixed with all this ferocity, the Scandinavian tribes had a more delicate and romantic feeling about women than any other ancient people. As females among them were regarded with a veneration elsewhere unknown, and were supposed to be chosen receptacles of Divine inspiration, they were therefore considered as being well fitted to preside over the worship of the gods. The daughters of Scandinavian princes officiated as priestesses of the national faith, were consulted as the oracles of heaven, and were frequently dreaded as the ministers of its vengeance; while other women who cultivated the favour of the malignant divinities were held to be witches. Of the authority of the priests little is known. Among the Saxons, they were not permitted to mount a horse or handle a warlike weapon.[2] Tacitus represents them in Germany as being invested with magisterial authority. He says that they settled controversies, attended the armies in their expeditions, and not only awarded punishments, but inflicted them with their own hands, the fierce warriors submitting to their stripes as to inflictions from the hand of Heaven.

The grim Scandinavian faith was, however, subject to great modifications, according to the situation and circumstances of the several tribes who professed it. It was of a more sanguinary complexion among the reckless followers of the sea-kings than among those who dwelt on shore. Perhaps the Saxon invaders of Britain might be classed with those among whom the religion assumed its least revolting shape; while the Danes, who afterwards followed in their track, exhibited the worship of Odin in its fiercest and most pernicious aspect. With the latter the primitive superstition was amplified by the principles and tales of the Scalds, who clothed it in their songs with horrors, of which its first founders had probably no conception. Although both Saxons and Danes worshipped the same gods, and believed alike in Valhalla, yet the Saxons, even while they continued heathens, became peaceful cultivators of the soil which their swords had won; while the Danes did not subside into the same social condition until they had abandoned their original creed and embraced Christianity.

On the first coming of the Saxons into Britain there was visible, not only in Wales but in other parts of the island, a strange intermixture of

---

[1] Mallet, *Northern Antiquities*; Dithmar, *Chronicles of Merselung*; Wormius in *Monument. Dan. Saxo Grammatic.*
[2] *Bede.*

Christianity and Druidism; and it is thought that throughout the protracted struggle which ensued for the dominion of the country, it was in the spirit and in the ritual of this Neo-Druidism, and not of Christianity, that the national feeling was chiefly appealed to, and the resistance to the invaders sustained and directed.

About a quarter of a century before the Saxons began their conquest, Ninian is said to have converted the Picts that lived southward of the Grampian Hills. Nearly at the same time that illustrious missionary, St. Patrick, had appeared in Ireland, and, after sweeping away much of the old heathenism, had established Christianity as the national religion. About the year 550, Kentigern, or St. Mungo, is supposed to have founded the see of Glasgow. But the most distinguished of the missionaries to Caledonia was St. Columba, venerated as the patron saint of Scotland until that honour was conferred upon St. Andrew. Columba was born at Garten, a village now included in the county of Donegal, in Ireland. He was illustrious by his birth, being connected with the royal families of the Irish and of the Scots. He landed in Scotland with twelve companions in the year 563, and undertook the task of converting the heathen Picts that occupied the country north of the Grampians. He soon converted and baptized the Pictish king, whose subjects immediately followed the royal example. Columba then settled in Iona, where he founded his celebrated monastery, and established a system of religious discipline which became the model of many other monastic institutions. The small and barren Island of Iona soon became illustrious in the labours and triumphs of the Christian church; and the Culdees, or priests, animated with the zeal of their founder, not only devoted their efforts to enlighten their own country, but became adventurous missionaries to remote and dangerous fields. Of the care with which they were trained to be the guardians of learning and instructors of the people, some idea may be formed from the fact that eighteen years of study were frequently required of them before they were ordained.[2]

In the south of Britain in the first fury of the Saxon invasion, if Christianity was not completely overthrown, the Christian church and every trace of it were destroyed. Without a clergy, or any apparatus for the administration of the ordinances of religion, it is not easy to conceive that such of the native Britons as were Christians would very long retain their knowledge and profession of the truth. But meanwhile the Saxon conquerors themselves, becoming settled and peaceful, gradually acquired habits and a disposition favourable for their conversion to a religion of love and peace. When things were in this state a simple incident led to great results. Gregory, afterwards pope, and surnamed the Great, passing one day through the streets of Rome, was arrested at the market-place by the sight of young slaves from Britain who were publicly exposed for sale. Struck with the brightness of their complexions, their fair long hair, and the remarkable beauty of their forms, he eagerly inquired to what country they belonged; and being told that they were Angles, he said, "They would not be Angles, but angels, if they were but Christians." Gregory resolved, at every hazard, to carry the gospel to their shores, and he actually set off upon the dangerous pilgrimage; but the pope was prevailed upon to command his return. When, some years after, Gregory succeeded to the popedom, he appointed Augustine, prior of the convent of St. Andrew's at Rome, with forty monks, to proceed on a mission to England. There were many delays and misgivings upon the road, Augustine and his companions being alarmed by the reports they heard of the Anglo-Saxon ferocity; but Pope Gregory passionately urged them on, and procured them all the assistance he could in France; and in the year 597 they landed in the Isle of Thanet, and forthwith announced the object of their coming to Ethel-

THE CATHEDRAL AND ST. ORAN'S CHAPEL, IONA. Mull in the distance.

---
[1] The remains of religious establishments on this little island of the Hebrides, though popularly attributed to Columba, are of a much more recent date than the time of that venerated saint, whose structures were of very slight materials. The principal ruins are those of the cathedral church of St. Mary, of a nunnery, five chapels, and a building called the Bishop's House. Numerous kings of Scotland, Ireland, and Norway were buried in the island.

[2] Adomnani. *Vit. Sti. Columbæ.*

THE FIRST PREACHING OF CHRISTIANITY IN BRITAIN.

When Pope Gregory the Great was but a monk in the convent of St. Andrews, behind the Coliseum, he saw three fair-haired boys set up for sale in the market-place at Rome. He asked whence these bright-faced boys came and what was their religion, and on learning that they belonged to a Pagan race that dwelt in Britain, he determined to journey to this far region that he might preach the gospel. He was prevented from fulfilling this desire, however, by an arresting augury; but when he afterwards became Pope he selected Augustine, the prior of his old convent, and forty monks, to undertake the enterprize. *Ebbes Fleet, in the Isle of Thanet, was the place at which the prior and his companions landed, and there, for the first time in Britain, they preached Christ and Him crucified.*

THE FIRST PREACHING OF CHRISTIANITY IN BRITAIN.

bert, the King of Kent, who also held the rank of Bretwalda, while his authority extended to the right bank of the Humber.¹ His queen, Bertha, was a Christian princess,² and having stipulated at her marriage for the liberty of professing her own religion, she had some French priests in her household, and a bishop named Liudhard, by whom the rites of the Christian faith were performed in a little church outside the walls of Canterbury.³ The conversion of the king was easily brought about, and the opposition of the pagan priesthood was but feeble and momentary. When Ethelbert had been baptized, 10,000 of his people soon followed his example. The joy of Pope Gregory was so great that he conferred the primacy of the whole island upon Canterbury, the capital of Kent, and sent the pall to Augustine, who had already been consecrated Archbishop of Canterbury by the prelate of Arles.

From the facility with which he had established his faith in Kent, Augustine hoped for a similar conversion in the whole island; but, although Pope Gregory sent him additional aid, the work proved long and difficult, and was not completed until many years after Augustine had been laid in his grave, in the churchyard of the monastery in Canterbury which goes by his name. Among the mountains of Wales, where the Saxon conquerors could not penetrate, there existed many Christians, and a regular clergy; but when Augustine applied for the assistance of the Welsh ecclesiastics, and demanded their submission to the universal supremacy of the Bishop of Rome, he found that the Welsh clergy would not co-operate with him. They disagreed on very many points, and notably as to the proper period for the celebration of Easter, a question which divided many churches, and which was once disputed with a most fierce and uncompromising spirit. Yet, without the aid of the Welsh ecclesiastics, the progress of the Christian faith was rapid. In the year 604 Sebert, King of Essex,

NORTH WALLS OF RICHBOROUGH CASTLE, AND FOUNDATIONS OF ST. AUGUSTINE'S CHURCH.⁴—From a drawing on the spot, by J. W. Archer.

and nephew to Ethelbert, the converted King of Kent, and Bretwalda, received the rite of baptism. As usual, great numbers of the people forthwith followed the example of their king; and a Christian church was erected in London, Sebert's capital, upon the rising ground which had formerly been the site of the Roman temple of Diana. This London church was dedicated to St. Paul, and each successive building upon the same site has retained the name. Nearly at the same time Redwald, the King of East Anglia, was converted.⁵ In the same year (604) Augustine died, after having seen the gospel firmly established in Kent and Essex. He had consecrated Justus Bishop of Rochester, and Miletus Bishop of the East Saxons, and appointed his faithful follower Lau-

---

¹ Bede. ² See vol. i. p. 73. ³ Bede.
⁴ Richborough Castle, near Sandwich, is the Ritupæ or Ad Portum Rituptis of the Romans. It exhibits one of the most noble vestiges of the Romans in Britain. The walls have formed a parallelogram, but the east wall has disappeared. It stands upon a slight eminence, at the base of which flows the Stour. The walls are constructed in blocks of chalk and stone, and faced with square blocks of grit stone. The northern wall, which is perfect, measures 560 ft. in length; it contains seven courses, each course 4 ft. thick, banded at intervals with layers of large tiles. Rising 6 ft., the thickness of the walls is 11 ft. 3 in., above which they measure 10 ft. 8 in. The greatest existing altitude of the walls is 23 ft., but the summit is everywhere broken. Leland, in his *Itinerary*, says: "Within the castle is a little parish church of St. Augustine, and an hermitage. I had antiquities of the hermit, the which is an industrious man." In the centre of the area of the walls there is a platform in the shape of a cross, corresponding with the sacellum of Roman fortifications, where the Roman standards and eagles were deposited, but which appears in this instance to have been adopted for the site of a church—that mentioned by Leland.
⁵ See vol. i. p. 74.

rentius to be his successor in the see of Canterbury.

The faith so lately planted among the Anglo-Saxons soon sustained a violent shock. Sebert, the King of Essex, died; and his three sons endeavoured to re-establish the ancient idolatry. Melitus was banished, and compelled to flee from London to Rochester, to seek for shelter with his friend Justus. But even in Kent the faith was shaken, chiefly through the passion of Eadbald, the son and successor of Ethelbert, for his father's youthful widow.[2] Melitus and Justus fled to France, and the primate Laurentius was preparing to follow them, in the conviction that the cause of Christianity was for the present lost in England; but Eadbald relented, and became converted anew.

ALTAR OF DIANA.[1]—Drawn from the original by J. W. Archer.

After many sufferings and most perilous adventures, Edwin became King of Northumbria, and introduced Christianity into that very powerful and warlike kingdom. Before he was actually baptized Edwin called an assembly of his nobles, that they might discuss the claims of the new faith and the old. Coifi, the pagan high-priest, declared that the gods whom they had hitherto worshipped were utterly useless. No man, he said, had served them with greater zeal than himself, and yet many men had prospered in the world far more than he had done; therefore was he quite ready to give at least a trial to the new religion. One of the nobles followed in a wiser and purer spirit. Comparing the present life of man, whose beginning and end is in darkness, to a swallow entering a banqueting-hall to find refuge from the storm without, flitting for a moment through the warm and cheerful apartment, and then passing out again into the gloom, he proposed that if Christianity should be found to lighten this obscurity, and explain whence we came and whether we departed, it should immediately be adopted. Upon this Coifi, the pagan high-priest, moved that Paulinus the missionary should be called in to explain the Christian doctrine. Paulinus came in immediately, and made use of such cogent arguments, that the impatient Coifi declared there was no longer room for hesitation; proposed that the old Saxon idols should be immediately overturned; and, as he had been the chief of their worshippers, he now offered to be the first to desecrate them. He threw aside his priestly garments; called for arms, which the Saxon priests were forbidden to wield, and for a horse, which they were not permitted to mount, and thus accoutred he galloped forth before the amazed multitude. Advancing to a temple in the neighbourhood where the chief idol stood, he hurled his lance within the sacred inclosure, and by that act the temple was profaned. No lightning descended, no earthquake shook the ground; and the multitude, encouraged by the impunity of the daring apostate, proceeded to second his efforts. Forthwith the temple and its inclosures were levelled with the ground. This event happened at a village still called Godmundham, which means the home or hamlet of the inclosure of the god. The conversion of the king was instantly followed by that of his subjects, and Paulinus, who was afterwards consecrated Archbishop of York, is said to have baptized 12,000 converts in one day in the river Swale. This Christian king, Edwin, attained to the dignity of Bretwalda, and maintained the faith which he had adopted; but in the year 634, while in the vigour of his days, he was slain in battle against the terrible pagan king, Penda. Upon this sad event there followed such a general apostasy of the people in Northumbria, that Bishop Paulinus was obliged to abandon his see, and retire into Kent. The triumph of the heathen was, however, checked in the north by the accession of King Oswald, who had spent his youth in Iona, to which northern sanctuary he had repaired for shelter; and having been taught Christianity among that primitive community, he naturally sent thither for spiritual instructors to his people, as soon as he was established upon the throne. Corman, the first monk that was sent from Iona, quickly returned, disheartened by the difficulties of his office, and by the barbarous disposition and gross intellect of the Northumbrians; but Aidan, another monk of

---

[1] The altar is 21 in. high, 11 in. broad at the base, and 7½ in. thick. It was found May 5, 1831, at a depth of 15 ft., in a stratum of clay, when excavating the foundation for the Goldsmiths' Hall, in which it is now deposited. Under the site of Goldsmiths' Hall, and under that of the General Post-office adjoining, were found vaults and foundations, evidently of Roman masonry. It is probable these were vestiges of the temple of Diana, which were sought for in vain on the site of St. Paul's Cathedral, at the distance of little more than a stone's throw.

[2] See vol. i. p. 73.

the order, volunteered to supply Cornian's place. In the year 635 Aidan founded a monastery upon the bleak island of Lindisfarne; and there his religious community flourished for more than two centuries, until it fell beneath the fury of the Danes. Aided by King Oswald, Aidan was very successful

HOLY ISLAND, coast of Northumberland, and REMAINS OF THE CHURCH OF LINDISFARNE.[1]
From Turner's England and Wales.

in reclaiming the apostate Northumbrians, and in converting other Saxon states. Having prevailed upon the King of Wessex and his daughter to be baptized, a Christian church was established in that portion of the Heptarchy, according to the primitive and simple form of that of Iona.

The introduction of the gospel into the powerful kingdom of Mercia was the next great event. Peada, the son of the terrible Penda, in whom the Christianity of England had found its deadliest enemy, solicited the hand of the fair daughter of the converted King of Northumbria. The princess refused to marry an unbelieving husband, and the prince in consequence abjured his idols, and was baptized; and on his return to Mercia he took with him four good missionaries, who were very successful in converting the people. Towards the close of this century the kingdom of Sussex was converted; and thus, in less than ninety years from the first arrival of Augustine, Christianity was established over the whole of England.

When Christianity thus became the religion of Saxon Britain, its rude inhabitants were prepared for the further blessings of learning and civilization, and these were now introduced in the train of Theodore, Archbishop of Canterbury, who was consecrated to the primacy by Pope Vitalian, in 668. Like St. Paul, he was a native of Tarsus in Cilicia, and eminent for his extensive learning. Though already sixty-six years old, yet such was the energy of his character, that a life of usefulness was still expected from him; and these hopes were not disappointed, for he governed the English Church for twenty-two years. He brought with him a valuable library of Latin and Greek authors, among which were the works of Homer, and established schools of learning, to which the clergy and laity repaired. The consequence was, according to Bede, that soon after this many English priests were as conversant with the Latin and Greek languages as with their native tongue.[2]

Scarcely, however, was the national faith thus settled, when controversies arose in the bosom of the infant church on certain points of ceremonial practice, the triviality of which, of course, did not prevent them from being agitated with as much heat and obstinacy as if they had involved the most essential principles of morality or religion. One of the subjects of dispute was the same difference as to the mode of computing Easter that had already prevented the union of the English and Welsh Churches; it now, in like manner, threatened to divide the two kingdoms of Mercia and Northumberland, which, as already related, had been converted by Scottish missionaries, from

---

[1] In Holy Island was first established the nucleus of the opulent see of Durham, by Aidan, a monk of the monastery of Iona. The church was at first built of split oak, and covered with reeds. It was rebuilt by Eadbert, successor to St. Cuthbert, who caused the body of Cuthbert to be removed and placed in a magnificent tomb near the high altar. Here the venerated remains rested till about the middle of the ninth century, when the coast was overrun by the barbarous Danes, and the affrighted monks of Lindisfarne escaped with the remains of their beloved apostle, and commenced the series of peregrinations which ended in their establishment at Dunholm (Durham). Few traces of the monastic buildings exist, except those of the church, which is of Anglo-Norman architecture.

[2] *Bede*, iv. 2.

the other states of the Heptarchy, that had received their instructors from Rome and France. To this was added the difference between the Romish and Scottish Churches, upon the form of the ecclesiastical tonsure. While the priests of the former wore the hair round the temples, in imitation of a crown of thorns, they were horror-struck at the latter, who, according to the custom of the Eastern Church, shaved it from their foreheads into the form of a crescent, for which they were reproached with bearing the emblem of Simon Magus.[1] A council had been summoned with the view of accommodating these dissensions, by Oswy, King of Northumberland, in the year 664; but the only result of this attempt was to increase the animosity of the two factions, the clergy of the Scottish persuasion, in fact, retiring from the assembly in disgust.[2] Their departure was occasioned by the intemperate zeal and arrogance of Wilfrith, afterwards Archbishop of York, whose great aim was to reduce the English Church to a state of uniformity, by the suppression of the Culdees.[3] At a council called at Hertford, in the year 673, the bishops generally consented to the canons which Theodore had brought with him from Rome, by which a complete agreement in faith and worship was established.[4]

In the meantime, Theodore was enabled to proceed with his division of the larger dioceses. That of Mercia, in particular, which had till now embraced the whole of the state so called, was divided by king Ethelred, at his instigation, into the four dioceses of Lichfield, Worcester, Hereford, and Chester. Many other reforms were also prosecuted by the energetic primate. He encouraged the wealthy to build parish churches, by conferring upon them and their heirs the right of patronage. The sacred edifices, till now for the most part of timber, began to give place to larger and more durable structures of stone; the beautiful chanting, hitherto confined to the cathedrals, was introduced into the churches generally; and the priests, who had been accustomed in the discharge of their office to wander from place to place, had fixed stations assigned to them. They and the churches had as yet been maintained solely by the voluntary contributions of the people; but, because this was a precarious resource when the excitement of novelty had ceased, Theodore provided for the regular support of religion, by prevailing upon the kings of the different states to impose a special tax upon their subjects for that purpose, under the name of kirk-scot.[5] By these and similar measures, all England, long before the several kingdoms were united under one sovereign, was reduced to a state of religious uniformity, and composed a single spiritual empire. After living to witness many of the benefits of his important labours, this illustrious primate died in 690, after a well-spent and active life of nearly ninety years.

The age of the Christian church in England that immediately succeeded its establishment, was distinguished by the decline of true religion, and the rapid increase both of worldly-mindedness among the clergy, and of fanaticism and superstition among the people. From the humble condition of a dependence upon the alms of the faithful, the church now found itself in the possession of revenues which enabled its bishops to vie in pomp and luxury with the chief nobility, and even conferred no small consideration upon many of its inferior ministers. It is generally held that tithes were first imposed upon the Mercians in the latter part of the eighth century, by their king, Offa, and that the tax was extended over all England by King Ethelwulf, in 855. But the

---

[1] Theodore, who, when he was called to the primacy, wore the Eastern tonsure, was obliged to wait four months, that his hair might grow so as to be shaven according to the orthodox fashion.—*Bede*, iv. 1.

[2] For the lengthened discussion at this council, see *Bede*, iii. 25.

[3] "Wilfrith, by his own power, accomplished what Augustine, animated by the spirit of Gregory the Great, had begun. The Anglo-Saxon states were converted not only to Christianity, but to Catholicism. For secular learning they were chiefly indebted to the Scots and Britons—for their accession to the European system of faith, to these two men; for, however successful Augustine may appear in his first spiritual acquisitions for the Church of Rome, the course of Anglo-Saxon history, nevertheless, shows that, although the Roman ecclesiastical system was acknowledged, the influence of Rome was exceedingly weak, and that the Anglo-Saxons, even after they were no longer anti-Catholic, continued always anti-Papistical. As Wilfrith's history itself proves indeed how little even this zealous partisan of the popes could effect, it is the more desirable to take a view of the internal relations of religion in England.

"We notice, in the first place, in every kingdom a bishop, who, travelling about with his coadjutors, propagated both doctrine and discipline. This kind of church regimen was well calculated to succeed that of the pagan priesthood. The bishops, when chosen by the clergy, always required the confirmation of the prince; but, in most instances, they were nominated by him. In later times, it is observable that the royal chaplains always obtained the episcopal dignities. Over these bishops, he who resided at Canterbury, the capital of the Bretwalda Ethelbert, was set as archbishop, in like manner as the Bishop of Rome had originally assumed the supremacy over the Roman provinces. The archbishopric of York, established by Gregory the Great, which might act as a check to a primacy of the Kentish archbishop, dangerous to the Papal authority, ceased to exist after the flight of Paulinus, and was not re-established till a century afterwards, when Egbert, the brother of King Eadbert, after many representations to the Papal chair, received the pall. A third archiepiscopal see was established for the country between the Thames and the Humber, by the powerful Offa of Mercia, who held the dignity necessary for the honour of his kingdom, with the consent of Pope Hadrian, to whom this augmentation of his slight influence over the Anglo-Saxon clergy might have been welcome. The old state of things was, however, shortly after restored.—Almost contemporaneously with the bishoprics, some monasteries were founded by the bounty of the kings and their relatives, which served as residences to numerous monks. Many of these cloisters in the north of England were destroyed by the Danes, the very sites of which are not known with certainty."—*Lappenberg*, vol. i. p. 189.

[4] *Bede*, iv. 5.

[5] Bede, *Epistol. ad Egbert.*

SAXON PERIOD.

subject of this assumed donation of Ethelwulf to the church is involved in great obscurity.[1] All that is certain is, that in after ages the clergy were uniformly wont to refer to his charter as the foundation of their claim. The tithes of all England, however, at this early period, if such a general tax then existed, would not have been sufficient of themselves to weigh down the church by too great a burden of wealth. A great portion of the soil was still composed of waste or forest land; and the tithes appear to have been charged with the repair of churches, the expenses of worship, and the relief of the poor, as well as with the maintenance of the clergy. It was from the lavish benevolence of individuals that the church principally derived its large revenues. Kings, under the influence of piety or remorse, were eager to pour their wealth into the ecclesiastical treasury, to bribe the favour of Heaven, or avert its indignation; and wealthy thanes were in like manner wont to expiate their sins, as they were taught they might do, by founding a church or endowing a monastery. Among other consequences of these more ample resources, we find that the walls of the churches became covered with foreign paintings and tapestry; that the altars and sacred vessels were formed of the precious metals, and sparkled with gems; while the vestments of the priests were of the most splendid description. Other much more lamentable effects followed. Indolence and sensuality took the place of religion and learning among all orders of the clergy. The monasteries in particular, founded at first as abodes of piety and letters, and refuges for the desolate and the penitent, soon became the haunts of idleness and superstition. Many of the nunneries were mere receptacles of profligacy, in which the roving debauchee was sure of a welcome.[2] In the year 747 the Council of Cloveshoe found it necessary to order that the monasteries should not be turned into places of amusement for harpers and buffoons; and that laymen should not be admitted within their walls too freely, lest they might be scandalized at the offences they should discover there.[3] Most of the monasteries in England, too, were double houses,[4] in which resided communities of men and women; and the natural consequences often followed this perilous juxtaposition of the sexes, living in the midst of plenty and idleness. These establishments also continued to multiply with a rapidity that was portentous, not only from the tendency of the idle and depraved to embrace such a life of indulgence, but from the doctrine current at the end of the seventh century, that the assumption of the monastic habit absolved from all previous sin. Bede, who saw and lamented this growing evil, raised a warning voice, but in vain, against it; and expressed his fears that, from the increase of the monks, soldiers would at last be wanting to repel the invasion of an enemy.[5] Many nobles, desirous of an uninterrupted life of sensuality, pretended to devote their wealth to the service of Heaven, and obtained the royal sanction for founding a religious house; but in their new character of abbots, they gathered round them a brotherhood of dissolute monks, with whom they lived in the commission of every vice; while their wives, following the example, established nunneries upon a similar principle, and filled them with the most depraved of their sex.[6] To these evils was added the bitterness of religious contention. Men thus pampered could scarcely be expected to live in a state of mutual harmony; and fierce dissensions were constantly raging between the monks, or regulars, as they called themselves, and the seculars or unmonastic clergy, about their respective duties, privileges, and honours.

It was natural enough that the grossest superstition should accompany and intermingle with all this profligacy. So many Saxon kings accordingly abandoned their crowns, and retired into monasteries, that the practice became a proverbial distinction of their race;[7] while other persons of rank, nauseated with indulgence, or horror-struck with religious dread, often also forsook the world, of which they were weary, and took refuge in cells or hermitages. The penances by which they endeavoured either to expiate their crimes or attain to the honours of saintship, emblazoned though they are in chronicles, and canonized in calendars, can only excite contempt or disgust, whether they ascend to the extravagance of St. Gurthlake, who endeavoured to fast forty days, after the fashion of Elias,[8] or sink to the low standard of those noble ladies who thought that heaven was to be won by the spiritual purity of unwashed linen. In addition to the feeling of remorse by which such expiations were inspired, a profligate state of society will multiply religious observances, as a cheap substitute for the practice of holiness and virtue; and men will readily fast, and make journeys, and give alms, in preference to the greater sacrifice of amendment of life. We need not, therefore, wonder to find Saxon pilgrims thronging to the Continent and to Rome, who do not seem to have considered a little contraband traffic, when opportunity offered, as detracting from the merits of their religious tour; while ladies of rank, who undertook the same

---

[1] See Turner's *Anglo-Saxons*, i. 479-481.
[2] Bede; *De Remedio Peccatorum*; Wilkin's *Concilia*, i. 88, 99.
[3] Wilkins' *Concilia*, i. 97.
[4] Lingard's *Antiquities of the Anglo-Saxon Church*, p. 120.
[5] Bede, *Epist. ad Egbert*.
[6] Alcuin, *Epistolæ*; Lingard's *Antiquities of the Anglo-Saxon Church*, p. 133.
[7] *Hunting*, p. 337.
[8] *Flores Sanctorum*, in *Vit. Gurth.* p. 34.

journey, frequently parted with whatever virtue they possessed by the way.[1]

While such was the state of the English Church,

ROCK HERMITAGE AT GUY'S CLIFF, Warwickshire.—From a sketch on the spot, by J. W. Archer.

the invasions of the Danes commenced at the end of the eighth century, and were continued in a succession of inundations, each more terrible than the preceding. These spoilers of the North, devoted to their ancient idolatry, naturally abhorred the Christianity of the Saxons, corrupted though it was, as a religion of humanity and order; and as the treasures of the land, at the first alarm, were deposited in the sacred edifices, which were fondly believed to be safe from the intrusion even of the most daring, the tempest of the Danish warfare was chiefly directed against the churches and monasteries. Those miracles lately so plentiful, and so powerful to deceive, were impotent now to break or turn back the sword of the invader. The priest was massacred at the altar; the monk perished in his cell; the nuns were violated; and the course of the Northmen might be traced by the ashes of sacred edifices that had been pillaged and consumed. The effects of these devastations upon both religion and learning may be read in the mournful complaint of Alfred. At his accession, he tells us, in the interesting preface to his translation of Pope Gregory's tract on the *Duties of Pastors*, that he could find very few priests north of the Humber who were able to translate the Latin service into the vulgar tongue; and south of the Thames, not one.[3]

After the land had begun to recover from the immediate effects of this visitation, and the church had resumed its wonted position, the celebrated Dunstan appeared. He was born in Wessex, about the year 925. Although he was of noble birth, and remotely related to the royal family, as well as connected with the church through two uncles, one of whom was primate and the other Bishop of Winchester, these signal advantages were not deemed enough for the future aspirant to clerical supremacy, without the corroboration of a miracle. His career was, therefore, indicated

---

[1] Spelman's *Concilia*, i. p. 237.

[2] Dugdale, describing Guy's Cliff, says: "This being a great cliff on the western bank of the Avon, was made choice of by that pious man, St. *Dubritius* (who in the Britons' time had his episcopal seat at Warwick) for a place of devotion, where he built an oratory, dedicated to St. *Mary Magdalen* (Camden says St. Margaret), into which, long after, in the Saxon days, did a devout heremite repair, who, finding the natural rock so proper for his cell, and the pleasant grove wherewith it is backed yielding entertainment fit for solitude, seated himself here. Which advantages invited also the famous Guy (sometime Earl of Warwick), after his notable achievements, having weaned himself from the deceitful pleasures of this world, to retire hither, where, receiving ghostly comfort from that heremite, he abode till his death." There are several cells in the cliff. That shown in the cut is at the base of the rock, and is popularly distinguished as Guy's Cell. However doubtful that personage and his localities may be, the cell itself bears a token of early occupation, in an inscription cut in the wall in Saxon characters, but not legible.

[3] "To the distance from Rome, and their slender dependence on the Papal chair, the people of England are apparently indebted for the advantage of having retained their mother tongue as the language of the church, which was never entirely banished by the priests from their most sacred services. Their careless, sensual course of life, and perhaps the prejudice which prevented them from learning even so much Latin as was requisite to enable them to repeat the Paternoster and Creed in that language, have proved more conducive to the highest interests of the country than the dark subtilty of the learned Romanized monk, pondering over authorities. Even the mass itself was not read entirely in the Latin tongue. The wedding form, was, no doubt, in Anglo-Saxon; and its hearty, sound, and simple sterling substance, are preserved in the English ritual to the present day. The numerous versions and paraphrases of the Old and New Testaments made those books known to the laity, and more familiar to the clergy. That these were in general circulation in Bede's time, may perhaps be inferred from his omission of all mention of them, though the learned and celebrated Anglo-Saxon poet, Aldhelm, had already translated the Psalms; and Egbert, Bishop of Lindisfarne, the four gospels. Bede is also said to have translated both the Old and the New Testament into his mother tongue, an assertion which, like a similar one regarding King Alfred, must be limited to the Gospel of St. John, and, in the case of Alfred, to some fragments of the Psalms. An abridged version of the Pentateuch, and of some other books of the Old Testament, by Elfric, in the end of the tenth century, is still extant. The vast collection of Anglo-Saxon homilies, still preserved in manuscript, at once enlarged and ennobled the language and the feelings of Christianity; and the ear, which continued deaf to the mother tongue, was, in the Anglo-Saxon Church, yet more sensibly addressed, and in a way to agitate or gently move the heart. Large organs are described and spoken of as donations to the church in the beginning of the eighth century. The mention of this instrument at Malmesbury, affords ground for the conjecture that it might have been introduced by the musical Welsh. Church music was first brought into Kent by the Roman clergy, and from thence into the northern parts, where it underwent improvement. This was an object of such interest, that the arrival of a Roman singing-master is mentioned by contemporary authors as a matter of almost equal importance with a new victory gained by the Catholic faith over the Pagans or Scots."—Lappenberg, *History of England*, vol. i. p. 202.

by a miracle in a church, even before he was born. His youth also was a series of miracles. His early studies having been pursued with an intensity that exhausted his feeble constitution, a fever ensued; but an angel visited his couch by night, and suddenly restored him to health. By another miracle he was taught how he must enlarge the church in Glastonbury, &c. Dunstan, however, accomplished himself in all the learning and in most of the arts that might give him an influence in society. He was an excellent composer in music; he played skilfully upon various instruments; was a painter, a worker in design, and a caligrapher; a jeweller, and a blacksmith. After he had taken the clerical habit, he was introduced by his uncle, Aldhelm, the primate, to King Athelstane, who seems to have been delighted with his music. At this time of his life he was accustomed to sing and play some of the heathen songs of the ancient Saxons, and for this he was accused by his enemies as a profane person. Incurring the envy of Athelstane's courtiers, and losing the favour of the king, who was made to suspect him of sorcery, Dunstan was driven from the court, was kicked, and cudgelled, and thrown into a bog, and there left to perish. He escaped, however, from this peril, and sought refuge with his uncle, the Bishop of Winchester. His whole life was now altered. Contiguous to the church of Glastonbury he erected a very small cell, more like a sepulchre than a human habitation; and this was at once his bed-chamber, his oratory, and his workshop; and it was here that he had that most celebrated combat with the devil which all have heard of. His character for sanctity now began to wax illustrious. A noble dame, who had renounced the world, and who occupied a cell near his own, died in the odour of sanctity, and left him all her property. He distributed the personal property among the poor, and bestowed the lands upon the church at Glastonbury, endowing that establishment at the same time with the whole of his own patrimony, which had lately fallen to him. His ambition, though inordinate, was of too lofty a character to stoop to lucrative considerations. Edmund having now succeeded to the throne, Dunstan was recalled to court; but his ambition and the dread of his talents again united the courtiers against him, and he was once more dismissed through their intrigues. An opportune miracle, however, induced the king to make him abbot of Glastonbury, and to increase greatly the privileges of that famous monastery. Edred, the successor of Edmund, showed him equal favour, and would have made him Bishop of Crediton; but Dunstan, who seems to have contemplated a much higher preferment, declined the offer. The very next day (having always miracles at his hand) he declared that St. Peter, St. Paul, and St. Andrew had visited him in the night, and that the last, having severely chastised him with a rod for rejecting their apostolic society, commanded him never to refuse such an offer again, *or even the primacy*, should it be offered him; assuring him withal that he should one day travel to Rome.

It is probable that Dunstan's ultimate aim was to effect what he deemed a reformation of the church, and that, according to the morality of the times, he justified to himself the means to which he resorted by the importance of the object he had in view. A fierce champion for the fancied holiness of celibacy, he determined to reduce the clergy under the monastic yoke, and to carry out the celibate rule of Pope Gregory II.; and as during the late troubles many both of the secular and the regular priests had married, he insisted that those who had so acted should put away both their wives and families. Those clergymen also who dwelt with their respective bishops were required to become the inmates of a monastery. In these views Dunstan was happy in having for his coadjutor Archbishop Odo. This personage, born of Danish parents, and distinguished in the early part of his life as a warrior, retained ever after the firmness and ferocity of his first calling. We have already related the part he acted along with Dunstan in the tragedy of the unhappy Elgiva.[1] When Dunstan, shortly after this, was obliged to flee from England, on being accused of embezzlement in the administration of the royal revenues, it is related that while the king's officers were employed at the abbey of Glastonbury in taking an inventory of his effects, his old adversary, the devil, made the sacred building resound with obstreperous rejoicings. But it is added that Dunstan checked the devil's triumph by the prophetic intimation of a speedy return.[2] In effect the death of Edwy immediately brought about the recall of Dunstan, and the restoration of his influence; and he was appointed Bishop of Worcester by King Edgar in 957. Three years after he obtained the primacy, being promoted to the archbishopric of Canterbury upon the death of his friend Odo. According to custom he repaired to Rome, to receive the pall at the hands of the pope, thus fulfilling the predictions of his vision.

Dunstan was now possessed of unlimited ecclesiastical authority;[1] and he was seconded by the zealous efforts of Oswald and Ethelwald, the former of whom he promoted to the see of Worcester, and the latter to the see of Winchester, and both of whom were afterwards canonized as well as himself. The superstitious King Edgar, and afterwards the youthful King Edward, were completely under his control. With none to check

---

[1] See vol. i. p. 101.   [2] *Anglia Sacra.*

him, he proceeded with merciless zeal in his projects of reformation, and alternately adopted force and stratagem. The clergy were imperiously required to dismiss their wives and children, and conform to the law of celibacy or resign their charges; and when they embraced the latter alternative they were represented as monsters of wickedness. The secular canons were driven out of the cathedrals and monasteries, and their places were filled with monks. Miracles were not spared for converting the obstinate recusants, and, besides the wonderful legends that were propagated in praise of St. Benedict and his severe institution, Archbishop Dunstan vouchsafed to them a sign for their conviction. A synod being held at Winchester in the year 977, at which the canons hoped that the sentence against them would be reversed, all at once a voice issued from a crucifix in the wall, exclaiming, "Do it not! do it not! You have judged well, and you would do ill to change it." This miracle or ventriloquism, however, so far from convincing the canons, only produced confusion, and broke up the meeting. A second meeting was held, with no better success. A third was appointed at Calne, and there a prodigy was to be exhibited of a more tremendous and decisive character. The opponents of Dunstan had chosen for their advocate Beornelm, a Scottish bishop, who is described as a person of subtle understanding and infinite loquacity. Dunstan, perplexed by the arguments of the logical and loquacious Scot, proceeded to his final demonstration. "I am now growing old," he exclaimed, "and you endeavour to overcome me. I am more disposed to silence than to contention. Yet I confess I am unwilling that you should vanquish me; and to Christ himself, as judge, I commit the cause of his church!" Scarcely had he said the words, when part of the scaffolding and flooring suddenly gave way, and fell with a mighty crash, with his adversaries, of whom some were crushed to death, and many grievously injured; while the part of the edifice which Dun-

ST. DUNSTAN.
From an Anglo-Saxon MS.

stan and his adherents occupied remained safe and unmoved—sound as a rock. It is no violation of charity to suspect from this incident that the archbishop was skilled in the profession of the carpenter and builder as well as in that of the blacksmith.

Dunstan lived for ten years after this sanguinary trick, and spent them in prosecuting his favourite schemes of ecclesiastical reform. His last moments are irradiated in the legend of his life by a whole galaxy of miracles. He died in the reign of Ethelred, A.D. 988.

The history of the Anglo-Saxon Church, from the death of Dunstan to the Norman conquest, presents little to interest the general reader. The cause for which Dunstan and his coadjutors had laboured, with the celibacy of the clergy, remained completely in the ascendant. Monasteries continued to be founded or endowed in every part of the kingdom; and such were the multitudes who devoted themselves to the cloister, that the foreboding of the venerable Bede was at length accomplished—the monks were so numerous that there were not left soldiers enough to defend the country, and above a third of the property of the land was in possession of the church, and exempted from taxes and military service.

With the remnant of the superstitions of the ancient Britons were blended many of the superstitions and customs which the Saxons and Danes brought with them from Northern Germany and Scandinavia, and of which traces are still to be found in sundry usages and in many parts of England and Scotland. An increase of superstition of a certain kind was one of the consequences of the invasion of the Danes. In a canon of the reign of King Edgar the clergy are enjoined to be diligent in withdrawing the people from the worship of trees, stones, and fountains, and from other evil practices; and the laws of King Canute prohibit the worship of heathen gods, of the sun, moon, fire, rivers, fountains, rocks, or trees, the practice of witchcraft, or the commission of murder by magic, or other infernal devices.[2]

---

[1] "The Christian clergy occupied an influential station among the Anglo-Saxons, which, considering the numerous calamities that had befallen them, as well as their disputes with the Scots, is the more remarkable. In explanation of this striking phenomenon among barbaric hordes, may be adduced the account given by Tacitus of the vast influence in secular affairs possessed by the pagan German priesthood, in whom exclusively resided the power of life and death. Such a primitive influence tended, no doubt, greatly to facilitate the domination of the Roman Papal Church, and a part of their jurisdiction—the ordeals or so-called judgments of God—may have had their origin in the legal usages of the heathen priests. Religion became a national concern, and priests enacted a principal part in the Anglo-Saxon witenagemot. The rank of an archbishop was equal to that of an atheling, of a bishop to that of an ealderman. The bishop presided with the eolderman in the county court (scir-gemot), the jurisdiction of which was frequently coextensive with the diocese."—Lappenberg, ii. 322.

[2] "No Germanic people preserved so many memorials of paganism as the Anglo-Saxons. Their days of the week have to the present time retained their heathen names; even that of Woden (Wednesday) is still unconsciously so called in both worlds, and by more tongues than when he was the chief object of religious veneration. In the north of England and the Germanic parts of Scotland, the Yule feast (geohol, geol) has never been supplanted by the name of Christmas. That these denominations throughout ages were not a senseless echo of superannuated customs, is evident

In the canons of Elfric, who was Archbishop of Canterbury from 995 to 1005, we learn that there were seven orders of clergy in the church, whose names and offices were the following:—(1) the ostiary, who took charge of the church doors, and rang the bell; (2) the lector or reader of Scripture to the congregation; (3) the exorcist, who drove out devils by sacred adjurations or invo-

ORDERS OF THE CLERGY.—1, An acolyte, from an early Salisbury missal; 2, Sub-deacon in a tunicle, 3, Deacon in his dalmatic, 4, Anglo-Saxon priest wearing a stole, from a MS. in public library, Rouen.

cations; (4) the acolyte, who held the tapers at the reading of the gospels and the celebration of mass; (5) the sub-deacon, who produced the holy vessels, and attended the deacon at the altar; (6) the deacon, who ministered to the mass-priest, laid the oblation on the altar, read the gospel, baptized children, and gave the eucharist to the people; (7) the mass-priest or presbyter, who preached, baptized, and consecrated the eucharist. Of the same order with the last of these, but higher in honour, was the bishop.[1]

from the Anglo-Saxon laws of later times, which strictly forbid the worship of heathen gods, of the sun, the moon, fire, rivers, water-wells, stones, or forest-trees. It is, however, probable, that some of this heathenism may have been awakened by contact with the pagan Northmen. A part of the old theology lost its pernicious power; when reduced to history it became subservient to the purposes of epic poetry, as instances of which may be cited the genealogies of the Anglo-Saxon kings and the poem of Beowulph. Of many superstitions, which long retained their ground, relative to the power of magic, to amulets, magical medicaments, as well as to the innocent belief—so intimately connected with poetry—in elves and swarms of benevolent, or at least harmless unearthly, though sublunary spirits, it is often difficult to point out the historic elements from which they have sprung; as precisely in the northern parts of England, where they were longest preserved, the intermixture of the Britons with the Germans was the most intimate."—*Lappenberg.*

[1] "A preceding bishop, probably his immediate predecessor, Elfric, in the year 1006, had directed, in one of the canons published at a council in which he presided, that every parish priest should be obliged, on Sundays and on other holidays, to explain the Lord's Prayer or the Creed, and the gospel for the day, before the people, in the English tongue. While historians enlarge on the quarrels between the Papacy and the civil power, and descant, with tedious prolixity, on the superstitions which were in vogue during the dark ages, they are too apt to pass over in a cursory manner such facts as this. Let the reader reflect on the preciousness of the doctrines which the Lord's Prayer, the Creed, and some of the plainest and most practical passages of the New Testament either exhibit or imply, and he will be convinced that, if the canon of Elfric had been obeyed with any tolerable degree of spirit and exactness in a number of parishes in England, the ignorance and darkness could not have been so complete or so universal as we are generally taught to believe. . . . That elementary knowledge which is the object of the canon is ever more salutary in its influence than the most ingenious subtleties of literary refinement in religion."—Milner, *Hist. of the Church of Christ,* cent. 11, ch. iv.

CHAPTER VII.—HISTORY OF SOCIETY.

FROM THE ARRIVAL OF THE SAXONS TO THE ARRIVAL OF THE NORMANS.—A.D. 449—1066.

Union of the Saxon tribes in England into one people—Classes into which they were divided—Condition of the ceorls and serfs—Different kinds of servitude—Ecclesiastical architecture—Houses—Furniture—Food—Cookery—Anglo-Saxon banquets—Drinking practices—Dress of the Anglo-Saxons—Ornaments—Female costume and ornaments—Social and domestic life of the Anglo-Saxons—Female occupations—Superstitions of the people—Their course of life from the beginning to the close—Amusements of the Anglo-Saxons—State of education—Learned Englishmen.

HEN the Saxons, Jutes, and Angles had obtained possession of England, and when the Heptarchy had been resolved into a monarchy, it was in the ordinary course of things that these distinctions of races should cease, and the whole become one people. This was the more natural, as they were previously assimilated in character, language, customs, and institutions, as well as by the fact of a common origin. Accordingly they soon came to be spoken of, first under the name of Angles, and afterwards under the compound term of Anglo-Saxons. An equally natural, but still more important change, was that which converted them from restless pirates into peaceful industrious agriculturists. In obtaining not the mere plunder of the English coast, but the permanent possession of England itself, they had got all and more than they had hoped for; and, therefore, nothing further remained for them but to sheathe their swords, and sit down to the full enjoyment of their conquest. In this way the three Germanic tribes became a single nation; and from these causes, also, they acquired that distinctive nationality which was best suited to their common character. The country was divided into shires and hundreds, and into cities, burghs, and townships;[1] while the people, in like manner, were parted into their respective classes, whether of rich or poor, whether of bond or free.[2] But it is to these divisions of

---

[1] The police of the Anglo-Saxons was established and secured by the principle of mutual guarantee. This system began with the *mægburh*, or family-bond, including whole communities, related by blood and occupying the same localities. These seem to have given their names to their respective possessions in the lands they had conquered. Mr. Kemble gives two lists of patronymical names, which he believes to be those of ancient marks—the first derived from the *Codex Diplomaticus* and other authorities; the second inferred from actual local names in England. The total number of the latter is 627; but as several are found repeated in various counties, the grand total is 1329. Thus, the Æbingas are supposed to have given their name to Abinger, Abinghall, and Abington; the Aldingas, to Allingbourn, Aldingham, and Aldington; the Buslingas, to Buslingthorpe; the Fenldingas, to Faldingworth; the Ferdingas, to Firdlingbridge; the Gildingas, to Gildingwells; the Hemingas, to Hemingbrough and Hemingby, &c.; while many of these names stand alone, without any addition of *ton, ham, thorpe, worth*, &c. Mr. Kemble supposes that, as of 190 of these last, 140 occur in counties on the eastern and southern coasts, and twenty-two more in counties easily accessible through great navigable streams, they were possibly the original seats of the marks bearing those names; and that the settlements distinguished by the addition of *ham, wic*, &c., to these original names, were filial settlements, or, as it were, colonies from them.

"In looking over a good county map," says Mr. K., "we are surprised to see the systematic succession of places ending in *den, holt, wood, hurst, fald*, and other words, which invariably denote forests and out-lying pastures in the woods. *These are all in the mark*; and within them we may trace, with equal certainty, the *hams, tuns, worths*, and *stedes*, which imply settled habitations."

Thus, while the British and Celtic races seem to have named places almost invariably from some natural peculiarity of the ground, the Anglo-Saxons, it appears, named them from the families or relationships that settled on them. And each of these small communities had its police maintained originally by the *mægburh*, or family-bond, according to which all were held responsible for the offence committed by one; and an offence done to one, it became the right and duty of all to avenge.

But this, though a natural, could not be a lasting system. A time inevitably comes when the members of a *sibsceaft*, or cognation, gradually disperse, and neighbours cease to be kinsmen. This naturally led to a new system of guarantee, founded simply on number and neighbourhood. The free inhabitants of the mark came thus to be classed in tens and hundreds—technically tithings and hundreds—each forming a corporation, probably comprising a corresponding number of members respectively, together with a tithing-man for each tithing, and a hundred-man for each hundred; thus making 111 men in each territorial hundred.

It must not be supposed that these 111 heads of houses were, with their children and domestic servants, the sole inhabitants of the hundred; a large allowance must be made for slaves. Neither did the territorial hundred contain always neither more nor fewer heads of houses than those with which it commenced. A distinction seems, indeed, to have been for some time observed between the numerical and the territorial division—the numerical being called the *hynden*, which consisted of ten tithings, and the territorial being called the *hundred*, although originally they were identical. The tendency of land divisions being to remain stationary for ages, while their population varies incessantly, two very distinct things seem to have grown up together in England - a constantly increasing number of the *gylds*, or corporations, yet a nearly or entirely stationary tale of territorial tithings and hundreds. There seems to have been elbow-room within the marks, to admit a considerable elasticity of the population, without disturbing their ancient boundaries, but merely by extending and improving cultivation within those boundaries. Assuming that our present hundreds nearly represent the original in number and extent, we might conclude that, if in the year 400 Kent was first divided, Thanet then contained only 100 heads of houses, or *hydes*, upon 3000 acres of cultivated land; while, in the time of Bede, three centuries later, it comprised 600 families, upon 18,000 cultivated acres.

[2] "The population of the country consisted of two elements—the chiefs and their followers, who had obtained possession and lordship of the lands; and the agriculturists and labourers, who

the people that we confine our attention at present, and to the development and progress of their character in intellectual, social, and domestic life.

The Anglo-Saxon society, after it had assumed a settled and regularly organized form, may be divided into six classes. These were—1, the king and his family; 2, the ethelborn, or nobly-born, who were men of the highest birth; 3, men high in office or possessed of large property; 4, a freeman; 5, a freed man; 6, a serf.[1] In simplifying these nice distinctions, however, the people, properly so called, were divided into two great classes—the *eorls* and the *ceorls*. The former comprised the ethelborn, eoldermen, or men of princely descent; the *twelfhaendmen*, or men of twelve hands, and the *sixhaendmen*, or men of six hands; that is, the nobility of inferior rank. As for the ceorls (or churls), who were also called villains (or inhabitants of a villa), they were the free-born and the liberated, who dwelt in the township, village, or farm, under the rule of their feudal superior, and were the agriculturists and handicraftsmen of the country, and traders and small landholders of every description under the rank of priest and noble. These constituted the middle classes, out of which the commons of England were ultimately formed. An idea of the inferior place which the ceorls occupied, although they constituted the bulk of the community, may be obtained from the following scale, established in the courts of law. The word of a king or bishop was of itself conclusive, and required no additional corroboration. The compurgatory oath of a priest was equivalent to that of 120 ceorls, and the oath of a deacon to that of sixty. But when we descend from these sacred privileges of the church in the matter of legal testimony and oath-taking, to the lay nobles, it is gratifying to find that the eorl was equivalent to not more than six ceorls. This was a liberal allowance, according to the standard of the age; but still it was hard enough that five good men and true might be outfaced in a court by the testimony of only one six-handed man. The ceorls, also, although they were not the absolute property of a master, were yet so strictly bound to the soil that they could not remove from the estate on which they were born; and when this was sold, they were transferred with it to the new purchaser, like the cattle that grazed, or even the trees that grew upon it.[2] This was nothing more or less than the condition in which these ceorls, villani, or bondmen had been placed in the forests of Germany, which Tacitus thus describes: "The rest of their slaves have not, like ours, particular employments in the family allotted them. Each is the master of a habitation and household of his own. The lord requires from him a certain quantity of grain, cattle, or cloth, as from a tenant; and so far only the subjection of the slave extends." Mild though this form of servitude might be in a rude state of society, the Roman historian characterizes it under the name of slavery; and there are few of the present day who will not agree with him. To be mere part and parcel of the soil, though it were that of Eden itself, and to be bound to it beyond the power or liberty of removal, is bondage indeed. It is evident that a long period had to intervene, and many a step of transition to be effected, before these land-enthralled churls could become the happy, bold-hearted, and free-born, free-moving commons of merry England.

A worse condition still than this was that of the serfs or slaves, in the proper acceptation of the term. These men, who constituted a large portion of the Anglo-Saxon population, were not only bondmen of the soil, but of the proprietor also, and, as such, were bound to serve him at home or a-field without wages, except the clothing and sustenance which he was pleased to give them. It was not merely that they were bought and sold with the land, like

SERF OR THEOW.—Cotton MS. Cleopatra C. 8.

---

were in the position of serfs and bondmen, and comprised chiefly the old Romano-British population, which, under the Anglo-Saxons, was probably quite as well off as under the Romans. The Saxons thus held the country, while the Roman cities continued to hold the towns as tributaries of the Saxon kings, within whose bounds they stood. The country thus exhibited Teutonic rudeness, while the towns were the representatives of Roman civilization; and though the intercourse between the two, and the gradual infusion of Saxon blood into the towns, laid the foundation of modern society, there was a feeling of hostility and rivalry between town and country which has hardly yet disappeared. Between the aristocratic feeling of the Saxon landholders, and the republican principles that existed in the towns, arose, under the balancing influence of the crown, the modern political constitution."—See *The Celt, the Roman, and the Saxon*, p. 435. In illustrating the only effects by which his view was demonstrated,

the same author adds, at p. 440:—"It may be cited as a proof of the correctness of this view of the mode in which the Roman corporations influenced the shock of invasion, and *thus became a chief instrument in the civilization of subsequent ages*, that even the Danes, in their predatory excursions, often entered into similar compositions with the Saxon towns, as with Canterbury, in 1009. It may be added, that there is no greater evidence of the independence and strength of the towns under the Saxons than the circumstance, that while the king and his earls, with the forces of the counties, were not able to make a successful stand against the Danish invaders, it frequently happened that a town singly drove a powerful army from its gates, and the townsmen sometimes issued forth, and defeated the enemy in a pitched battle."

[1] Sharon Turner's *History of the Anglo-Saxons*.
[2] Ibid.; Palgrave's *English Commonwealth*.

cattle or other property—for this was also the destiny of the churls, who considered themselves as freemen notwithstanding—but they were bequeathed by will on the death of their masters, and not only they, but their posterity to the remotest generations, in the fashion of a modern entail. While the ceorl also was protected by the laws in such liberty as he possessed, the slave might be confined, whipped, or branded without appeal, and was frequently yoked to the car or plough; and in this way, we read of "teams of men" in the inventories of the day, to distinguish them from horses and oxen.[1] Such was the condition of the slaves, or *theows*, as they were denominated among the Anglo-Saxons. But in this also there were several ameliorating circumstances. Thus the practice of manumission, which was recommended as a Christian duty, was frequent, especially at the hour of death, and by the wills of testators. A serf might also buy out his freedom by a little extra industry, for which he had many opportunities. But the greatest blow at slavery was struck by the institutions of Alfred, which decreed that when a Christian man was purchased as a slave, he should only serve for six years, but on the seventh be set at liberty. In this way it was decided that, in the ordinary course of nature, and without any other interference, slavery should gradually die out in England. As to the kinds of people upon whom this unfortunate lot of slavery had fallen, it is perhaps not very difficult to ascertain them. As the Saxons had been accustomed to the institution in their own country, they would scarcely scruple to continue it in their new home, and retain in serfage the classes whom they had been wont to hold in thraldom in Germany. But besides their own hereditary bondmen, who were of the same race with themselves, there were the vanquished Britons, over whom they probably exercised that right of the stronger which every country has used in turn, and whom they converted not only into ceorls, but in many cases into theows. Finally, there were but too many Saxons who either had forfeited their liberty by their crimes, or been fain to sell it in consequence of their poverty, out of whom the ranks of servitude were constantly supplied. A slave-market, indeed, was not unknown in England; and in the frequent famines that occurred, chiefly from the Danish invasions, parents sold their own children to save them from a death of hunger. In this way each noble household was abundantly supplied with such kind of service, as is evident from the single example of Alcuin, the Saxon abbot, who had 10,000 slaves to his own share.[2] But besides these numerous serfs, the princes and eorls had retinues, composed of men of a higher grade. These were *huscarles* (house ceorls), who waited upon their master's person at home, or upon a journey; and *cnihts*, or knights. As this last word bulked so largely during the Norman ascendency, it is necessary to mention, that among the Anglo-Saxons it only signified a boy, afterwards a servant who was not a slave, and finally a military attendant. In this last capacity the cnihts were distinguished for their fidelity and devotedness, as was manifested by an instance that occurred during the period of the Heptarchy. When Cynewulf, King of Mercia, was about to be assassinated, his military attendants were offered immunity if they ceased to resist; but they scorned the bribe, and died to a man in the hopeless defence of their master. When Cyneheard, his murderer, a few hours after, was attacked by a greatly superior force, who sought to revenge their sovereign's death, his cnihts, who might have escaped, rallied in his

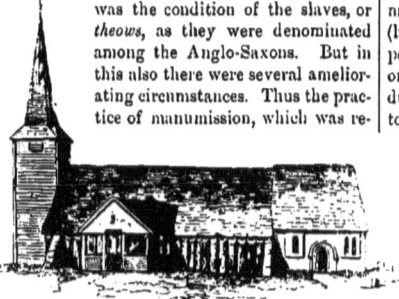

SOUTH VIEW OF GREENSTEAD CHURCH, Essex.—Drawn 1748.

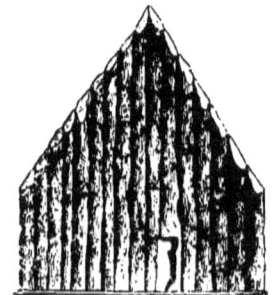

WEST END OF GREENSTEAD CHURCH, Essex.

defence, and fell one by one before he could be reached.

Before turning our attention to the social and domestic life of the Anglo-Saxons, and the homes

---

[1] Sharon Turner's *History of the Anglo-Saxons*.

[2] *Strutt.*—It is to the various works of this indefatigable antiquarian that we are mainly indebted for our knowledge of the condition, costume, and manners of the Anglo-Saxons. This intimation will make it the less necessary to refer to his name as our authority in the following pages.

they inhabited, it is necessary to give a few particulars regarding the condition of their ecclesiastical and public architecture. When Christianity was established in the seventh century in England, the first churches that were erected partook of the rude simplicity of the period, being constructed only of timber and roofed with thatch, as in the instances of Lindesfarne and York, while nothing but the altar was of stone. Of this primitive kind of edifice, the church at Greenstead is believed to be an existing specimen. According to ancient legends, this simple structure was erected to serve as a shrine for the body of St. Edmund, A.D. 1010. The nave is entirely composed of the trunks of large oaks, split and roughly hewed on both sides; they are set upright, and close to each other, being let into a sill at the bottom and a plate at the top, where they are fastened with wooden pins. This was the whole of the original fabric, which still remains entire, although much decayed by time. It is twenty-nine feet nine inches long, fourteen feet wide, and five feet six inches high on the side which supported the primitive roof. The addition at the east end is of Anglo-Norman architecture, and forms a further evidence of the antiquity of this timber edifice.

In the seventh century churches in England began to be built of stone; and of this early ecclesiastical masonry specimens are still to be found in the remains of the monasteries erected by Benedict Biscop, at Wearmouth, A.D. 674, and at Jarrow, A.D. 684. Those in the former place consist of a banded cylindrical column that has belonged to a small window, and of very rude design, but which corresponds precisely with some columns

COLUMN IN MONKWEARMOUTH CHURCH.

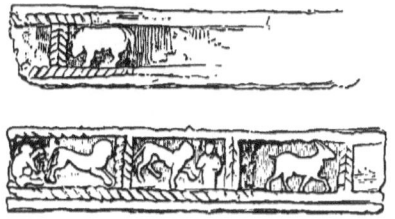

CARVED FRAGMENT, Monkwearmouth Church.

delineated in Anglo-Saxon illuminations; and another fragment, supposed to have belonged to the same edifice, being part of a string course, on which are rude carvings of animals, &c. The architectural zeal of Biscop was manifested not only by the sacred edifices he erected, but his diligence in bringing foreign artisans into England; but amidst the growing improvement it is evident that the architectural styles both of the Saxons and the Normans were only imitations of the Romanesque style of Italy, and that the chief difference lay in the degree of ability in imitating a debased original.

The towers of Earls-Barton Church in Northamptonshire, and of Sompting Church in Sussex — as structures admitted to belong to the Anglo-Saxon period—present a remarkable feature in the peculiar mode of their construction, being built rather in the manner of timbered edifices than of those raised in masoury. "Beyond the face of the walls long thin stones project, placed vertically at nearly equal distances, which continue from one horizontal course or story to another, and in the spaces between are semicircular and diagonal pieces, which give it a great similarity to wood quartering. The quoins are of the description of masonry which is always identified with the Anglo-Saxon style, and called long and short work, from their being arranged with stones of equal size, placed alternately in a vertical and horizontal position upon each other, thus bearing resemblance to debased rustic work. The walls of the tower of St. Peter's Church, Barton-upon-Humber, are built in a similar manner to those just described, of rubble stone and grout, interspersed with a sort of framework of projecting freestone in compartments, and incasing the doors and windows; the openings of the windows in the upper story are covered by two stones, inclining together, without any cur-

TOWER OF SOMPTING CHURCH, Sussex.

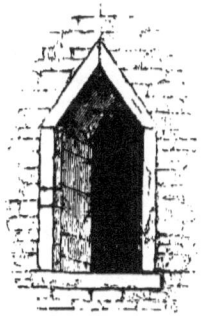

WINDOW, Barnack Church, Northamptonshire.

vature."[1] This peculiarity in the Anglo-Saxon bell towers is not recognized in the Norman architecture, nor in any other, except in some of the numerous tombs of Asia Minor; and it may be presumed to have originated in the transition from the practice of executing edifices composed

DOORWAY OF THE TOWER OF EARLS-BARTON CHURCH.

of timber, to that of working in stone. The heads of windows and doors in Anglo-Saxon architecture are triangular or semicircular; the former shape seems to have been copied from the debased Roman form which is to be seen on sarcophagi in the catacombs of Rome. "The extreme of the triangle rests upon a plain abacus, the impost in some cases projecting from the wall."[2] The semicircular arch is the most frequent, the earliest of which were constructed of large tiles, probably borrowed from the debris of Roman edifices. These tiles were placed on end, and the spaces between, which are nearly equal in width, filled in

BALUSTER WINDOW, Monkwearmouth Church, Durham.

with rubble-work; the jambs or imposts of the arches were generally of stone, as well as the walls, in which were sometimes laid courses of tile, either in horizontal layers, or in the diagonal manner called herring-bone, being evidently an imitation of the Romano-British structures. A massive but rude imitation of the Roman models before them seems to have characterized the works of the Saxon architects. Their mouldings were few and simple, consisting of a square-faced projection, with a chamfer or splay on the upper or lower edge. Another feature in the Anglo-Saxon bell towers is to be re-

marked in the rude columns which divide the openings of the windows, and form a kind of balustrade, frequently represented in Anglo-Saxon manuscripts. These appear in the tower of Earls-Barton, Jarrow, Monkwearmouth, and other churches. Of the genius of Anglo-Saxon sculpture we have a few examples, chiefly consisting of crosses and fonts, in which the human figure and animals are sometimes rudely carved,

FONT IN BRIDEKIRK CHURCH, Cumberland.

but the adornments of interlaced knot-work and foliage display some ingenuity of design and execution, as in the font of Bridekirk, Cumberland, on which is a Saxon inscription, evidently part of the original design.

Of the domestic architecture of the Anglo-Saxons, all we can learn is only to be gathered from a few scattered hints, which show that the houses of our Saxon ancestors were piles constructed without art, or mere imitations of the Roman edifices which existed among them. Such is the testimony of William of Malmesbury,[3] who contrasts the low and mean dwellings of the people with those stately edifices which the Normans afterwards introduced. That such was the condition even of the palaces of kings at the introduction of Christianity, is apparent from the speech of the venerable thegn to Edwin, King of Northumbria, when the question of adopting the new faith was discussed. He compared the state of man to the entrance and departure of a swallow; and from the whole picture we see nothing better than the king and his nobles seated round a fire in the midst of the apartment, from which the smoke was allowed to escape as it best might, while the whole building was so open that, even in the winter storm, a bird could enter and depart at pleasure. When Alfred had settled the Danelagh, and commenced a life of study in earnest, we also find that he was obliged to invent a lantern to guard his candles from being blown out by the winds that swept through his apartment. As often happens, however, all this squalor and discomfort was contrasted

---

[3] This historian, who wrote after the Norman Conquest, abounds with incidental notices of the manners and customs of the Anglo-Saxons prior to that event.

[1] Talbot Bury, *Rudimentary Architecture.* [2] Ibid.

with the occasional richness of the furniture; and the walls within, notwithstanding their apertures, and the dust with which they were begrimed, were hung with rich tapestry. These hangings are frequently mentioned in the inventories of the day; and in the houses of the wealthy and noble they were generally of silk, sometimes adorned with rich needle-work of gold, representing birds and other animals. One of these, mentioned by Iugulphus,[1] which was made in the ninth century, represented the destruction of Troy; and another, wrought by Edelfleda, for the church of Ely, was embroidered with the actions of her husband Brithnod, Duke of Northumberland, in needle-work of gold. The chairs, benches, and stools were sometimes covered with the same kind of tapestry, and the wood-work ornamented with carved likenesses of the heads and legs of animals. The tables also were rich, being sometimes described as made of silver, and even of gold,[2] while the same costly materials were abundantly used in the manufacture of drinking-cups, and the furniture of a banquet. In these consisted the chief wealth of their owners, and they were at any time convertible into money. Besides the above articles, a silver mirror is mentioned in Dugdale's *Monasticon* as an accompaniment of the toilet, and silver candelabra and cressets occur in the notices of the period. To these may be added the indispensable conveni-

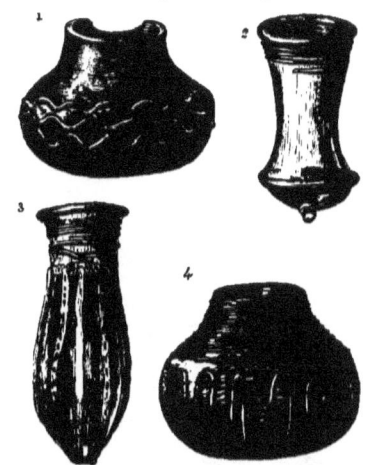

GLASS VESSELS, found in Saxon graves.[3]—1 and 4, found at Cuddison, Oxon; 2 and 3, from a cemetery in East Kent.—Akerman's Pagan Saxondom.

authority informs us that Benedict Biscop, who erected a monastery at Wearmouth, A.D. 674, introduced workers in glass into England, who not only glazed the windows of his edifices, but also made glass for lamps and other uses, and gave instruction in those manufactures to the English.[4] When the hour of rest arrived, the tables of the hall were removed, and beds laid in their places, where those who had feasted during the day betook themselves to repose, each man with his weapons above his head. This, however, was during the earlier stage of the Saxon occupation of England; for afterwards, as appears by an illuminated MS., bedsteads, with a roof shaped like that of a house, and hung with curtains, were introduced; and in the Anglo-Saxon poem of *Judith*, we read also of one being surrounded with the luxury of a "golden fly-net." As for the beds themselves, they were sacks stuffed with soft materials, furnished with pillows of straw, and the usual complement of blankets and sheets. These accounts, as will at once be seen, only apply to the houses of the noble and wealthy; what kind of habitations were used by the lower classes, and how they were furnished, the chroniclers of the period have not informed us.

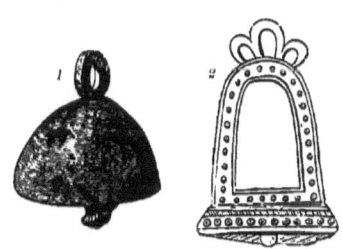

SAXON HAND-BELLS.—1, found at Little Wilbraham. Neville's Saxon Obsequies.—2, from Strutt.

ence of a hand-bell, with which the lord or lady summoned the attendants. As for cups and vessels of glass, these were rarely used in England before the period of the Norman conquest; and Bede mentions that the people were "ignorant and helpless in the art of glass-making." The same

[1] Secretary of William the Conqueror. This writer is also a valuable authority upon the condition of the Anglo-Saxons.
[2] Probably they were only overlaid or ornamented with these precious metals. In the same manner, Turgot informs us that Malcolm Canmore, King of Scotland, was served at table in vessels of gold and silver, and then adds, that at least they were over-gilt.
[3] These vessels are of a fine material. No. 2 is of extremely delicate fabric, and of a rich brown tint. It is so exceedingly light, as scarcely to be felt in the hand. No. 3 is of very transparent light green glass; it holds exactly a pint. Drinking-glasses distinguished by the same peculiarities have been found in the Frank cemeteries of France and Germany. The form of those glasses, not being adapted to set down until emptied, is conjectured to have originated the name of tumbler, given to modern drinking-glasses.
[4] Local tradition accounts for several outlandish names, such as Tyzack, Henzell, &c., still flourishing among the Tyne glass-works, by stating that Biscop's artificers planted themselves on the Tyne, and established the first English glass-works in that quarter, which continued to be carried on by their descendants for several centuries afterwards.

This mention of the Anglo-Saxon houses suggests the subject of indoor and domestic life; and here the department of cookery claims our first attention. But on this we must confess that our knowledge is extremely limited. The people,

SAXON BED.—Cotton MS. Claud. B. IV.

it is well known, were vigorous feeders; but before the arrival of the more refined Normans, it is probable that quantity rather than quality was the chief mark of their solicitude. The principal animal food used among them was pork; and the landholders kept such large herds of swine, that the swineherd was an important functionary among the rural offices of a farm establishment. This was the more natural, as swine could be easily maintained in the woods, which were of common access before the Norman game-laws were introduced; and fattened upon the fruit of the beech and oak, that required no cultivation. Mutton was not so abundantly used, as the Saxons appear to have valued the sheep more for its wool than its flesh; but beef, venison, and fowls were common articles of sustenance. In striking contrast to the Britons, however, the Anglo-Saxons were partial to a fish diet, and next to pork, eels appear to have been their principal articles of food. These were carefully fattened in eel-ponds and inclosures, and were so abundant that they were sometimes paid by the thousand as rent. Besides eating every kind of fish used in the present day, we learn that the Saxons also ate the porpoise. The processes of cooking food among them were broiling, baking, and roasting, but chiefly boiling; and a drawing in one of the Saxon MSS. represents a caldron resting on a trivet, with the fire beneath, while the cook stands beside it with an iron flesh-fork, for the purpose of removing the meat when it is ready. In boiling meat they also seasoned it with various herbs, among which

colewort appears to have held the chief place. Bread was not so plentiful among the Saxons as animal food, and was therefore more sparingly used, and wheaten bread was a luxury confined to the tables of the rich.

From various pictures in the MSS. of this period, a pretty distinct idea can be formed of an Anglo-Saxon banquet. The table was commonly covered with a table-cloth, and abundantly provided with knives and spoons, but no forks; dishes of various shapes and sizes, loaves of bread, and services of soup and fish; and cups or drinking-horns, which were still more numerous than the dishes. Sometimes the table-cloth was so large as to cover the knees of the guests, and serve the purposes of a napkin. The roast meats were generally presented by servants on the spits to the company, and each man cut from the offered joint, with his knife, the portion he required. One picture in the Cotton MS. represents the servants kneeling in the performance of this duty. It is pleasing to remark, also, that at these tables the women were seated on equal terms with the men, instead of being kept apart, or obliged to wait upon the other sex, as was generally the case in a rude state of society. In pledging each other with the cup at table, a

SAXON BANQUET.—Cotton MS. Tib. C. 7.

curious practice prevailed—by no means unnecessary in the revels of such a pugnacious people—which was also common at a comparatively late period in the Highlands of Scotland. This was, for the person pledged to hold up his knife or sword, in token that he would protect the drinker from assault or assassination while he was thus off his guard. This custom, we are informed by William of Malmesbury, originated in the treacherous murder of Edward the Martyr, who was stabbed in the back while drinking a cup of wine which his stepmother Elfrida had offered him. When the meats were removed, and the guests were warmed with wassail, it was the custom, as we are informed by Bede, to bring in a harp, which was sent round the company, and each man was expected to play and sing in turn for the amusement of the rest. Thus it was even in Athens in the days of Themistocles and Pericles. But in spite of the charms of music and poetry, these Saxon feastings were so gross, and the drinking was so excessive, as frequently to be followed with fatal consequences: in this way Hardicanute, after a life of gluttony, died of an over-abundant dinner; and Edmund I. was assassinated at table, because his nobles and attendants were too drunk to defend him. This style of living, especially among the great, was at last so exaggerated, that at court four abundant meals were served up daily—a profusion which an historian of the twelfth century, regretfully contrasts with the single daily dinner introduced by the Normans, as if the spirit of hospitality and social intercourse had been banished by the change.

As the Anglo-Saxons were still more notorious for their drinking than eating propensities, an account of their principal beverages demands full notice. And first in the list must be mentioned ale, which had been their favourite liquor before they left the shores of Germany. This we are informed by Tacitus, who describes the chief drink of the German tribes as a distillation from barley "corrupted into a likeness of wine." Besides ale they used mead, which probably they had learned to make from the Britons, as this constituted for centuries afterwards the national beverage of the Welsh. The Saxons also knew the art of making cider, which they may have acquired after their settlement in England. Pigment and morat were in use among them, but probably more sparingly than the other liquors, on account of their superior richness and costliness, the former being a composition of wine, honey, and various spices, and the latter of honey diluted with the juice of mulberries. As wine was not a native produce, and imported at great expense, its use in England before the Conquest was limited to the higher classes. Of the immense spilth of these liquors at the great festivals, or even common revelries of the Anglo-Saxons, and the vociferous mirth and desperate excesses which they occasioned, the continued history of the people makes frequent mention; and the following extract, from a translation of the Saxon poem of *Judith*, was no doubt a faithful picture of the noble and even royal banquets of the author's own day:—

"Then was Holofernes
Enchanted with the wine of men:
In the hall of the guests
He laughed and shouted,
He roared and dinned,
That the children of men might hear afar,
How the sturdy one
Stormed and clamoured,
Animated and elated with wine;
He admonished amply
Those sitting on the bench
That they should bear it well.
So was the wicked one all day,
The lord and his men,
Drunk with wine;
The stern dispenser of wealth;
Till that they swimming lay
Over drunk,
All his nobility
As they were death slain,
Their property poured about.
So commanded the lord of men
To fill to those sitting at the feast,
Till the dark night
Approached the children of men."

This national vice of inebriety, however it might be indulged uncensured among the worshippers of Thor and Woden, was too flagrant for the toleration of a Christian priesthood, and the statutes of the church were both frequent and severe against the prevailing tendency. That no one, also, might be ignorant of the mark at which he should stop short, the following specification of the crime was given in one of the canons: "This is drunkenness, when the state of the mind is changed, the tongue stammers, the eyes are disturbed, the head is giddy, the belly is swelled and pain follows." But as such definitions are only found useful to those who do not need them, a more tangible corrective was devised by Edgar the Peaceable, at the suggestion, it is said, of St. Dunstan. As it was discovered that one great source of the excess arose from the practice of handing round a large vessel at the table, while each guest vied with the others in the amplitude of his draught, these vessels were ordered by royal statute to be made with knobs or pins of brass placed at regular distances, while each drinker was only to go from one mark to another. But it was easy to elude such a formal restriction; and the phrase "He is in a merry pin," came to designate a person who had transgressed the graduated scale of temperance, or, in common parlance, "got more than enough." It is probable, also, that the penances imposed by the church on such transgressors were frequently commuted or overlooked, as the Anglo-Saxon clergy were too much addicted to the same excesses. This we learn from the decrees of different councils, in which the incentives to intemperance were strictly prohibited—gambling, dancing, and singing in the monasteries, "even to the very middle of the night;" while every priest was forbid to have harpers or any music, or to permit jokes or plays to be performed in his presence; and every monastery was debarred from being a haunt of practisers of the sportive arts; that is—as the decree particularly indicates them—poets, harpers, musicians, and buffoons.

It is difficult to ascertain the national costume of the Saxons at the period of their arrival in England, and until the time of their conversion to Christianity. But that it largely partook of barbarism is testified by the fact that they sometimes tattooed their bodies, like the primitive Britons; and although this practice was condemned in the year 785, it was not wholly rooted out of England till after the Norman conquest. The church, also, that set itself against this practice of skin-engraving, as a relic of the former heathenism, was equally zealous against their earlier clothing, from the same cause, and endeavoured to have it wholly set aside. This is evident from the rebuke addressed to the people, who still adhered in whole or in part to the costume of their ancestors, by the council of Cealhythe, A.D. 787. "You put on," it said, "your garments in the manner of pagans, whom your fathers expelled from the world; an astonishing thing that you imitate those whose life you always hated." At this time, as we learn from Paulus Diaconus, the dress of the Christianized Anglo-Saxons was similar to that of the Lombards, of whom he says, "Their garments were loose and flowing, and chiefly made of linen, adorned with broad borders, woven or embroidered with various colours." Fortunately we are enabled, from the many illuminated MSS. of the eight and ninth centuries, to specify the particular parts of this briefly described costume, and ascertain with distinctness how our ancestors were dressed in the days of Alfred, Canute, and William the Conqueror.

First of all, then, we should mention the shirt, which was made of linen, and was in general use among the Anglo-Saxons so early as the eighth century. Over this was a tunic of linen or woollen, which was worn by all classes, from the sovereign to the peasant. This garment—of fine or coarse texture according to the means of the wearer—descending no lower than the knee, appears to have formed the outer covering of the common people when employed in their usual avocations, and was probably the origin of the English smock-frock. It was open at the neck, and occasionally at the sides also, while the sleeves, which descended to the wrists, were either close and tight, or puckered into small folds. If ornamented, it was generally with needle-work of different colours, round the border and collar. This garment was usually girded round the waist with a sash or belt. Last in the article of a working man's costume was the shoe, which appears to have been in common use, even among those who otherwise went bare-legged. These shoes, not only in material and colour, but also in form, resembled those of the present day, having an opening at the top to receive the foot, which opening was fastened by two *thwangs* or thongs. The usual covering for the head was a cap or cowl, shaped like a Phrygian bonnet. Thus attired, we can form a distinct idea of the appearance of the English peasantry of this period, while travelling on the highway or engaged in the labours of the field. To these we can add other articles of dress belonging to the better classes, but which were also probably used by the common people upon particular occasions. The first of these was a short cloak or mantle, thrown over the tunic, and fastened either across the breast or shoulder with a buckle. Next came a pair of drawers, which begin to make their appearance in the pictures of the ninth century. These were either of linen or woollen, and at first were so short that they were fastened above the knee; but in process of time they were elongated into trousers, or rather pantaloons, where drawers and stockings composed one piece of attire. In addition to this, the stocking was frequently bandaged from ankle to knee with strips of cloth or leather; and as the colour and arrangement of such strips gave ample scope to the love of finery and display, we can imagine that not a few Malvolios of the period were "cross-gartered most villainously." Sometimes, instead of this cross-gartering, a half-stocking or sock was worn over the drawers, supposed to have been made

ARMED MAN.—Benedictional of St. Ethelwold.

of woollen, and ornamented with fringes. In this progress of addition, and perhaps of improvement in the common national costume, we shall do well to take into account, first, the settlement of the Danes in England, who were distinguished, even beyond the Saxons, for their love of finery and display; and afterwards, the introduction of Norman fashions into the court of Edward the Confessor. These causes, it is probable, tended

SAXON KING AND EOLDERMAN.—Cotton MS. Claud. B. IV.

to make the dress of the people not only more complete, but also more elegant.

We now ascend to the costume of the rich and the noble, which mainly consisted of certain additional garments that were used on public or state occasions. The first of these was a long tunic that descended below the knee; the second a kind of surcoat, that had short wide sleeves, and an aperture at the top to admit the head. These, which were frequently made of silk, after the eighth century had introduced the use of that luxury into the court of England, were also ornamented with rich embroideries of gold and silver, and silk thread of various colours, and lined with the fur of the beaver, sable, or fox. Such are the chief distinctions in costume of princes and nobles in the illuminated MSS. of the times. Except when the regal crown appears no distinctive head-dress occurs, beyond the Phrygian shaped bonnet, which was worn by all classes, but in the case of the higher ranks improved, as may be supposed, in texture, colour, and ornament. Indeed, in all these delineations we find nothing in the form of a hat, an article which was worn among the Britons, in shape similar to that of a modern carman or coal-heaver, as may be seen in the coins of Cunobelinus. But the Saxons were independent of this head-covering, in consequence of the long hair they wore, and of which they were not a little proud. This was parted on either side from the middle of the head, and flowed, waving or in ringlets, to the shoulders; and such was either the time they consumed in dressing this ornament of nature, so prized by all the Teutonic tribes, or the superstitious veneration attached to it, that the English clergy inveighed against it with a vehemence equal to that of Prynne himself, when he so terribly denounced the "unloveliness of love-locks." But the long fair hair of our ancestors remained unshorn, and even unshaken, amidst the clerical tempest. The beard, however, was more mutable in its character; and the first change it underwent was by the shaving of the upper and lower lip, so that it became a continuation of the whiskers, terminating below the chin in two forked points. Afterwards the beard was shaven away, and the moustaches left entire—the former being resigned wholly to the clergy—and hence the ridiculous error of the English spies whom Harold sent to the camp of William the Conqueror, when they mistook the Norman soldiers for priests, because they wore short hair and shaved the upper lip.

In the articles of rich ornament the Anglo-Saxons were not behind the other nations of the period; but it speaks little for their gallantry that the men in this particular seem to have appropriated the costliest share to themselves. These were chiefly bracelets, brooches, and buckles made of gold, silver, and ivory; chains, armlets, and crosses, made of gold and silver, and set with jewels; sword-belts, mounted with the same

SAXON COSTUMES.—From an illuminated MS. of 10th century. Bodleian Library.

rich accompaniments; and fillets or coronets, by whose lustre an additional brightness was imparted to their long flowing hair. As might have been expected among a people essentially warlike, the hilts and sheaths of their weapons were not neglected amidst the general adornment. The ring was an indispensable ornament, and as it was worn on the finger of the right hand next to the little one, this was called the

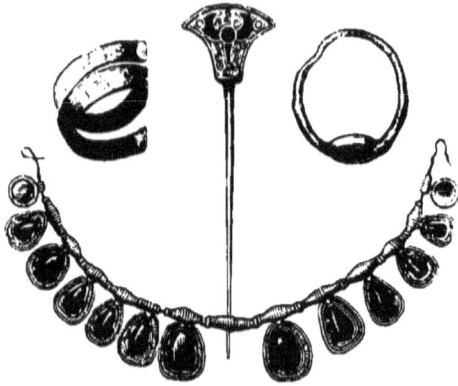

NECKLACE AND PIN,[1] from a tumulus at Callige Lowe, Derbyshire; RINGS, from Little Wilbraham.

"gold finger." This distinct badge of the wearer's rank could at all times be recognized, as gloves,

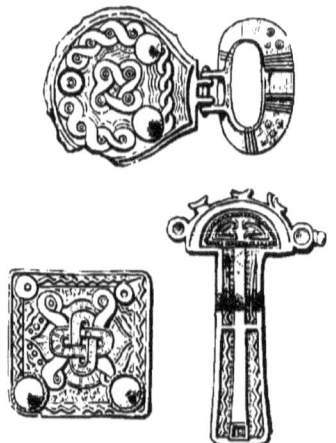

BUCKLES AND BROOCH, half the actual size.[2]—Proceedings of the British Archæol. Assoc.

which were a Norman innovation, were not worn by the Anglo-Saxons until the twelfth century.

In advancing to the more difficult subject of female costume, it may be premised that the dress of the Anglo-Saxon ladies was not only splendid and graceful, but in strict accordance with the most rigid modesty. The outer garment (*gunna* or gown) was a long tunic, the skirts of which nearly reached the ground, while the sleeves, that were loose and wide, reached only to the elbows. It was of various colours, but generally white, probably being made of linen, and was bound at the waist with a girdle. As this garment was a fair ground work, upon which the wearer's taste and skill in embroidery could be exhibited to best advantage, we find it in the illuminated MSS. frequently adorned with needle-work of variegated stripes, or small sprigs, diverging gracefully from a centre. Over this, ladies of rank appear to have worn a cloak or mantle, probably for visiting or travelling. Under the gown was worn a more succinct tunic, perhaps the original kirtle, the sleeves of which descended to the wrist. The head-dress was a kerchief or veil of linen or silk, which, being fastened near the top of the forehead, or wrapped round the head and neck, enveloped the shoulders,

MODE OF WEARING THE HAIR, from the Saxon Cross of Rothbury, Northumberland.[3]

and fell on either side as low as the knees. Shoes, of which the colour is always black, form part

---

[1] The necklace is composed of gold drops, set with garnets, and is probably of late Roman workmanship. The jewelled hair-pin was found in the grave of a woman, at Wingham, Kent. The rings are of gold; one of them has been formed to encircle the finger in a series of elastic hoops.—Akerman's *Pagan Saxondom.*

[2] The buckles were discovered, together with spear heads and an iron sword, at Bellevue, in the parish of Lympne, Kent; the second of them has been gilt. The brooch was found near the turnpike road at Folkestone Hill, between Folkestone and Dover. The body is of bronze, gilt; the central band has been ornamented with slices of garnet, one of which remains at the bottom in a silver rim; the upper part has also been set with stones, or some kind of glass.

[3] The top of this cross, which is greatly fractured, shows fragments of the crucified figure of our Saviour. The group of heads is from one side of the base, and is supposed to represent the spectators who assembled to witness the crucifixion. This illustration is given to show the manner of the Anglo-Saxon women in wearing the hair rolled back, or parted and confined by a fillet, with an ornament over the forehead, like that shown on some Roman coins.

of a lady's dress in the Anglo-Saxon delineations; and although, from the length of her gown skirts, we are unable to perceive any token of stockings or socks, yet we may presume that such a useful article of dress, which was worn by the men, was common to the women also. Although the veil or headrail, which we have already described, must have concealed the greater part of the head, yet we learn from Aldhelm that the Anglo-Saxon ladies, at the close of the eighth century, were at least as careful of their hair as the other sex; and he describes them as wearing it artificially dressed, and delicately curled with irons. From the same authority we are informed of another practice by which the ladies endeavoured to heighten their beauty, that was scarcely so commendable—it was the painting of their cheeks with the red colour of stibium. This practice, however, has prevailed not only in every stage of human existence, but at some time or other among every race of mankind, from the naked savage girl, who plasters her face with chalk or ochre, to the fashionable court belle, who delicately tints her cheek with more than the bloom of youth. In the enumeration of female ornaments we find that they chiefly consisted of golden half-circles or fillets for the head, ear-rings, necklaces, beads, jewelled neck-crosses, rings, girdles adorned with gold or precious

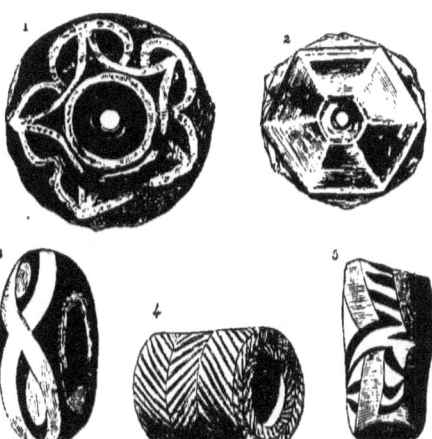

BEADS OF GLASS, AND OF COLOURED PASTE, found at Little Wilbraham. 1, 2, half-size; 3, 4, 5, full size.—Neville's Saxon Obsequies.

stones, a bulla, and a golden fly beautifully set with gems.

Having thus endeavoured to describe the broad outlines of an English home and its inmates, before they were modified or altered by the Norman conquest, we proceed to add a few minute particulars, by which the picture will become more complete. While the master and mistress were thus attired in full costume, the servants of the household are represented as waiting upon them bareheaded and barefooted. Within doors, the master generally wore his bonnet; but on leaving the house his covering was laid aside, and he went forth bareheaded. A practice which he had perhaps derived from his warlike ancestors, made him always carry his weapons with him wherever he went; but even when England was most settled there was too little cause to discontinue the habit. Thus equipped, with sword or spear, or both weapons together, he repaired to the social meeting or the market-place, ready equally to kiss his friend or chastise his enemy, as the case might require. Besides the possession of good dress and ornaments, and the full pleasures of the table, the Anglo-Saxon loved the enjoyment of a warm bath; but to plunge into cold water was so utterly revolting to his feelings, that he only endured it at the command of the priest, and for the remission of his sins. In this way he sauntered, ate, and chatted during the

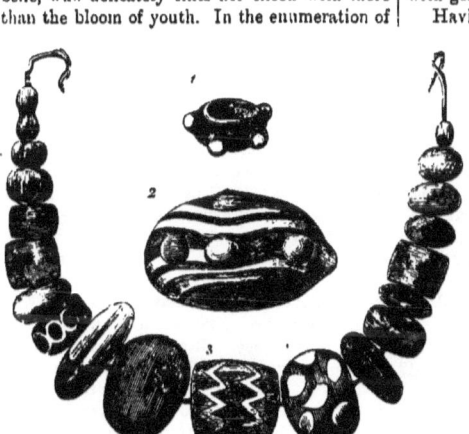

NECKLACE OR BRACELET,[1] from a grave near Stamford; and BEADS, found at Syston Park, Lincolnshire.—British Museum.

[1] The necklace is composed of glass beads of various colours, sizes, and degrees of opacity. Deep blue is the predominant tint, and this is relieved by a light green specimen, and by others nearly resembling, both in colour and substance, "Sainian ware." The beads Nos. 1 and 2 are remarkable for their construction. No. 1 is of a pale brown, the knobs yellow, with a red band at the base. No. 2 was found in the Anglo-Saxon cemetery at Fairford in Gloucestershire. It is banded with stripes of red, yellow, and green. The knobs are alternately red and yellow.

day, until the afternoon's banquet arrived, with its subsequent revelry, that was often kept up till midnight. It was through this luxurious disposition and love of enjoyment, that the church endeavoured to coerce him into full submission; and in the following extract from the laws of Edgar, we perceive how completely the penance was fitted for the man, however the man might be for the penance:—"He must lay aside his weapons, and travel barefoot a long way; nor be sheltered of a night. He must fast, and watch, and pray, both day and night, and willingly weary himself, and be so careless of his dress, that the iron should not come to his hair or nails. He must not enter a warm bath, nor a soft bed; nor eat flesh, nor anything by which he can be intoxicated; nor may he go inside of a church, but seek some holy place, and confess his guilt and pray for intercession. He must kiss no man, but be always grieving for his sins." In this way was the Saxon sinner assailed at every possible point of enjoyment: the whole world was tabooed against his entrance; and he lived "a man forbid," until the church was pleased to absolve him. Whether he contrived, in any of these cases, "to boil the pease," so that he might walk through his penance more lightly, we are not informed; but it may be suspected that such was the fact, from the dexterous plan which he adopted in what was to him the most odious of all penances —the penance of fasting. In this case he hired a whole regiment of penitents to fast with him on bread, green herbs, and cold water; and as each man's share was of full account in the sum total, himself and 800 auxiliaries could thus get through a hungry seven years' penance in three days and a few odd hours. When such was the permission of the church, even in sins of greatest enormity, the peccadilloes of smaller account were liquidated in a way which the clergy must have found very profitable to their own private revenues. Thus, a man might redeem one day's fasting by the fine of a penny, or a whole year of such penance by the payment of thirty shillings, or the manumission of a slave worth that sum.

While the occupations of the men—such at least as were exempted from the necessity of toil —were of such an unintellectual and unprofitable character, those of the ladies appear to have been of a more industrious description. An idea of the multitude of their domestic occupations may be formed from the thronged households over which they presided, where almost every trade and craft was comprised; and the huge daily flesh-feasts and carousals of their lords, for which they had to make due preparation. But besides these, there was the complicated needle-work of robes and hangings, that were so indispensable to every family above the rank of servitude, and the embroidery of clerical vestments, drapery for the church walls, and coverings for the altars, by which the ladies of the day manifested their religious zeal. No lady, however high in rank, was too proud for such occupations; and the hall of the palace, as well as the kitchen of the grange, was animated with the boom of the spinning-wheel and the click of the loom. We are informed incidentally in this way, by William of Malmesbury, that the four princesses, daughters of Edward the Elder, and sisters of Athelstane, were distinguished for their superior skill in spinning, weaving, and embroidery; and that Queen Editha, the wife of Edward the Confessor, was a complete mistress of the needle, and embroidered with her own hands the rich state robes of her husband.[1] Of this lady a touching delineation is given in the following simple statement of Ingulphus:—"I have often seen her, while I was yet a boy, when my father was at the king's palace; and as I came from school, when I have met her, she would examine me in my learning; and from grammar, she would proceed to logic (which she also understood), concluding with me in the most subtle argument; then causing one of her attendant maids to present me with three or four pieces of money, I was dismissed, being sent to the larder, where I was sure to get some eatables." Although many ladies in England might be as skilful, industrious, and hospitable as Editha, perhaps few were equally capable of conducting a logical argument. It is gratifying to find, that, while female industry was thus encouraged in England, female chastity was duly prized and carefully protected. This is evident from the severe laws enacted against those men who were guilty of outrage upon the female sex, not even excepting the female slaves, and where the punishment was proportioned to the rank of her against whom the offence was committed. The law was still more merciless against her who had willingly yielded to the crime.[2] Even the approaches also to immodesty and unchastity in households where servants of both sexes were numerous, were strictly guarded, as may be learned from the following notice of Bede: "In the courts of princes there are certain men and women moving continually in more splendid vestments, and retain-

---

[1] Hence the term "spinster," by which every unmarried woman still continues to be designated in England, upon a certain important occasion. Daughters were also termed children of the "spindle side," in the enumeration of a family.

[2] The adulteress was driven from place to place by crowds of her own sex, and mangled with their knives until she expired, or hanged herself to escape further torture. Her body was then burned, and her seducer put to death upon the spot. Such is the testimony of St. Boniface or Winfrith, in the early part of the eighth century. This, however, seems to have been a popular *emeute*, or Lynch-law process, rather than the result of the usual form of legislation.

ANGLO-SAXON RELICS.

1. Enamelled Ring of King Ethelwulf; in British Museum.
2. Brooch set with garnets and enamelled, found at Sarre, in Kent; in British Museum.
3, 3, 3. Pins, enriched with engraving, found in river Witham; in British Museum.
4. Bronze Cross, enamelled, with gold mount, found near Gravesend; in British Museum.
5. Gold Cross; found in Kent.
6. Bronze Buckle, part gilt; found at Gilton, in Kent.
7. Bronze Fibula; found at Badby, in Northamptonshire.
8. Pendant of gold and enamel; in the Fausset Collection.
9. Enamelled Pendant; in the C. R. Smith Collection.
10. Gold Ring; found at Bosington, Hants.
11. Necklace, found at Sarre, in Kent; in British Museum.
12. Bronze Brooch, inlaid with pearls and garnets; found near Canterbury.
13. Gold and Enamelled Brooch; found in Kent.

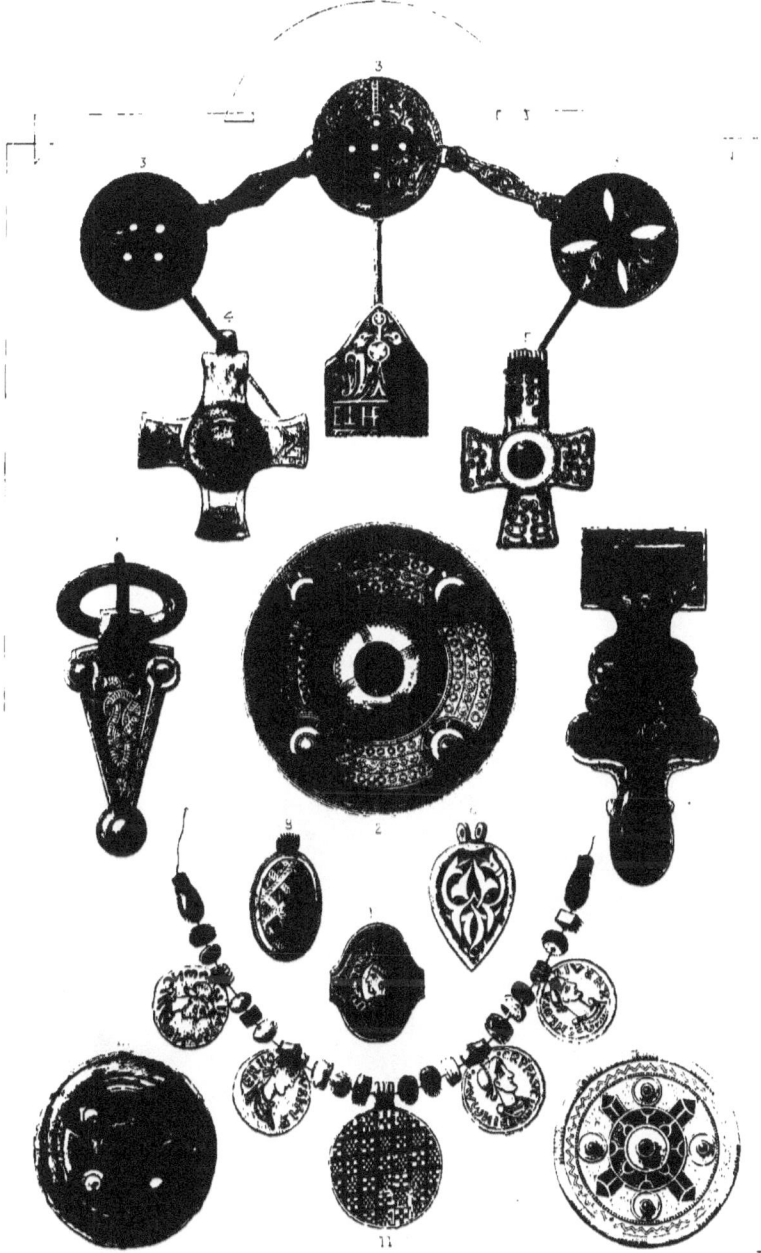

ing a great familiarity with their lord and lady. There it is studiously provided that none of the women there who are in an enslaved state should remain with any stain of unchastity; but if by chance she should turn to the eyes of men with an immodest aspect, she is immediately chided with severity. There some are deputed to the interior, some to the exterior offices, all of whom carefully observe the duties committed to them, that they may claim nothing but what is so intrusted."

The other domestic usages of the Anglo-Saxons may be briefly dismissed. As each day is fraught with its own doubts and difficulties, and as the people in general were not particularly addicted to the toil of profound thinking, they were wont, like other nations of a similar character, to solve the question by lot. In this case a white sheet was thrown upon the ground, and slips from a fruit-bearing tree, marked on either side, were cast down at random upon it. The number of lucky or unlucky marks lying uppermost decided the matter at once, and saved all further speculation. Was it from this compendious way of solving a doubt that their descendants acquired such a wondrous aptitude for betting? But in matters of greater importance, where a heavy wrong had been inflicted, or grievous crime committed, while the culprit could not be directly convicted, the same chance-medley system was adopted, under a more solemn form. The accused was bound hand and foot and cast into deep water, where, if he floated on the surface without stir or motion, he was held innocent, but if he struggled or sunk he was accounted guilty. This was the trial reserved exclusively for witches and wizards at a later period. Another form of the water ordeal was for the accused to plunge his naked arm into boiling water, from which if he could withdraw it unscalded, he was absolved from suspicion. These forms of trial, which originally must have been the right of every noble householder to exercise among his own serfage, were reckoned a direct appeal to heaven, and as such their superintendence was claimed by the clergy, at first, it may be, from motives of pure humanity, but which afterwards degenerated in a selfish spirit of rule and aggrandizement. In the same way they became the umpires of the ordeal by fire, the most solemn form of trial in Saxon legislation when sufficient proof of guilt was wanting. By this process the accused was obliged to walk blindfold and barefooted over nine red-hot ploughshares, placed at equal distances, or to carry a bar or red-hot mass of iron to a certain distance unhurt. But in this case the culprit was previously put under the charge of the clergy, who also heated the irons; and when his probation was over, his hands or feet were muffled up for three days, at the end of which he was to exhibit them in open court. Who does not at once see his numerous chances of escape, especially if he was rich and liberal? At all events, it is certain that several persons thus tried passed the ordeal unhurt—and it is equally certain that the same feat can be achieved by an ordinary juggler.

On the birth of a child, after the conversion of the people to Christianity, the first great subject of thought was the administration of baptism and the imposition of a name. The sacred rite was performed by immersion; and as for the name, it was not a patronymic, but one expressive of some peculiar quality or circumstance, and generally a compound word. Thus, Egbert means the bright eye; Æthelwulf, the noble wolf; Ealdwulf, the old wolf; Eadward, the prosperous guardian; Æthelgifa, the noble gift. To these was frequently added a surname, expressive either of locality, occupation, or family, when the Christian name itself would not have been a sufficient designation. The period spent by the boy between infancy and manhood was called cnihthade (knighthood); but, as we have seen, this was a term indicative of servitude, rather than liberty and distinction. The paternal authority, however, was limited. Thus, if a boy of fifteen years old had an inclination to become a monk, he might pursue his purpose, notwithstanding his father's inclination to the contrary. After the age of fifteen, also, a father might not give his daughter in marriage against her will. What is commonly called the school-boy period of life, and remembered in after stages as the darkest or brightest of our existence, had scarcely a place in England during the Anglo-Saxon ascendancy, as it was confined only to the higher ranks, and, even in their case, only for a brief season. It was not wonderful, therefore, if so many of their kings and nobles were unable to read, or to sign their own names. When scholarship was required, the chief teachers were the ecclesiastics; and flogging appears to have been their principal incentive in accelerating the progress of their pupils. At the age of fourteen, the stripling, now a young man, threw aside his previous occupations and commenced the study of arms, which was reckoned the proper profession of the high-born. How the rest of his life was usually spent we have already seen. When this was closed, and the only office that remained was to return dust to dust, the last duties were performed by the survivors with that reverential care and affection which is common to every people, however diversified may be the mode. In that of the Anglo-Saxons we have abundant information, as it forms the frequent subject of their pictorial illustrations. From these we perceive that the body, after being washed in pure water, was wrapped in a shirt, and clothed according to the rank of the wearer; and if he had held a high office, it was often adorned with his robes of state, and the rich insignia he had worn when living. All this was finally enveloped in a winding-sheet, while the face was carefully left uncovered, that the friends of the deceased might view it to the last. When the period for burial had arrived, a *sudarium* or napkin was spread upon the face, the extremities of the winding-sheet were drawn over it, and the body consigned to the coffin, which at first was made of wood, but afterwards of stone, often richly carved, as is found on opening the graves of illustrious personages. The funeral procession, the chant of monks with which it was accompanied, the prayers over the closing grave, and the plentiful dole of bread and meat that was usually administered at the gate of the house of mourning, may be left to the imagination of the reader. One funeral custom, however, we must not omit, as it originated during the Anglo-Saxon period. This was the ringing of the passing bell when the person's death occurred, that all who were within hearing might pray for the repose of his soul.

Of the sedentary sports and pastimes used by the Anglo-Saxons before the Norman conquest we can say little, as scarcely any notice occurs of them among the writers of the day. We may presume, however, that they were, for the most part, such as were followed at a later period, which we must, therefore, reserve for a subsequent era of this history. With the stirring and active out-door amusements we are better acquainted, and can speak of them with greater

SAXON BOAR HUNT.—From Strutt.

certainty. We learn, from Asser's *Life of Alfred*, that the young noblemen of the day, after having acquired what was reckoned a sufficient knowledge of the Latin language, betook themselves to "the arts adapted to manly strength, such as hunting;" and we know that this last sport has been reckoned essential in every age in the training of young gentlemen for a military life. The animals chiefly hunted in England were the wolf, until it was finally extirpated—wild boars and deer, the hare, and sometimes the goat. These were either run down with horse and hound, amidst the joyous cheer of the horn, or driven into nets. As each proprietor was at full liberty to hunt the game upon his own ground, the extinction of this right by the Norman game-laws was considered by the Anglo-Saxons as one of the most oppressive results of the Conquest. Hawking was also a favourite sport among them, and was in such high account with the great Alfred, that, amidst his many important cares, he instructed his falconers in the proper training of hawks, and wrote a book on the subject. The falcons of England, however, were judged so inferior, that the best were brought from abroad, and purchased at high prices. After hawking came fowling, the sport of those who were not rich enough to keep falcons, but where variety made amends for the want of splendour and bustle. In this case the birds of game were sometimes allured with decoys, sometimes trapped with snares and gins, and sometimes caught with bird-lime; but to bring them down upon the wing, the bow and arrow were used, as also the sling and stone. Two pictures occur in the Cotton MS. of fowling practised with these simple weapons, which were probably used also by the poorer classes in hunting. As horse-racing may be termed an English passion, it would have been strange if at least the germ of it had not been indicated among the earlier amusements of our Saxon ancestors. But that it was in usual practice among them, although in its simplest form, we can conclude from a passage in Bede, where he mentions incidentally, and as a thing of course, that when himself and his school-fellows were riding together, they tried the mettle and speed of their horses in a race as soon as they entered upon the open plain.

We have already spoken of the state of education in England at this period, and the unprofitable results with which it was followed. Was

SAXON PERIOD.

this, then, to be attributed to any inherent deficiency in the Anglo-Saxon intellect, or disinclination to the pursuit of knowledge from the toil and difficulty with which it was attended? We scarcely think that any will venture to answer in the affirmative. The cause, perhaps, is to be found in the unsettled state of the people from the landing of Hengist and Horsa to that of William the Conqueror. Learning being a plant of slow growth, requires a long and peaceful interval; but the protracted struggle of the Saxons before their occupation of England was secured, then the wars of the Heptarchy, and, finally, the Danish invasions, allowed no such interval to occur. Still, however, their opportunities, such as they were, do not appear to have been wholly neglected; and, in common with the scholars of every country, English students of all ranks repaired to Ireland, at that period abounding in learned and liberal scholastic institutions, where they were received with hospitable welcome, and gratuitously supplied with food, books, and instruction. Of this we are informed by Bede; while the high intellectual rank of the Irish schools, and the eagerness with which they were sought by our countrymen, is thus reluctantly attested by Aldhelm:—"Why should Ireland, whither troops of students are

CHURCH AND REMAINS OF THE MONASTERY AT JARROW.[1] - From Surtee's Durham.

daily transported, boast of such unspeakable excellence, as if, in the rich soil of England, Greek and Roman masters were not to be had to unlock the treasures of Divine knowledge? Though Ireland, rich and blooming in scholars, is adorned, like the poles of the world, with innumerable bright stars, it is Britain that has her radiant sun, her sovereign-pontiff Theodore." This "radiant sun," who, as we have seen, was the Primate of England during the latter part of the seventh century, fully deserved the commendations bestowed on him, by the zeal with which he laboured to introduce learning into the country in the train of Christianity, and the successors whom his instructions had prepared or his example stimulated.

Of these learned Englishmen, Aldhelm himself was one. A cotemporary of Theodore, and originally the pupil of one of those monks whom the archbishop had brought with him from Italy, his scholarship was matured and perfected by one of those Irish preceptors against whom he afterwards declaimed with such patriotic jealousy. Although he was eminent, and deservedly so, among the writers of the day, yet his subjects were of a contracted and temporary character, that afforded little scope for the development of genius, as they consisted chiefly of laudations of virginity, both in prose and verse, and the right method of computing the period of Easter; while his writings, which were in Latin, were turgid, pedantic, and artificial. Eddius, surnamed Stephanus, who wrote a *Life of Bishop Wilfred* in Latin, and was the first who instructed the churches of Northumbria in the science of sacred music, was another literary English character of note. A third distinguished luminary among

[1] "— Almost at the very mouth of the Tyne," says Camden, "is to be seen Girwy, now Jarrow, the native soil of the Venerable Bede, where also in ancient times flourished a little monastery. The foundation whereof, and the time of the foundation, this inscription showeth, which is yet extant in the church wall:"—

DEICATIO BASILICÆ
S PAVLI VIII KL MAII
ANNO XVI. ECFRIDI REG
CEOLFRIDI ABB. FIVS DEMO.
ECCLES DEO AVCTORE
CONDITORIS ANNO IIII.

Bede died and was buried in this monastery, but his remains were afterwards removed to Durham, and laid in the same coffin or chest with those of St. Cuthbert. Some remains of the original edifice may be observed in the church. Bede's Well, near the church, is still venerated; the bottom of it is covered with pins, from the custom observed by visitors of dropping a pin into the water. His chair is preserved in the church.

the learned men of the eighth century was Winfrith, better known as St. Boniface, a native of Devonshire, who finally became Archbishop of Mentz, and suffered martyrdom from the pagans of East Friesland, and whose letters, illustrative of the period in which he lived, have been published in the *Magna Bibliotheca Patrum*. One unlucky proof which he afforded of his orthodoxy and religious zeal, was to denounce the Irishman Virgilius, Bishop of Saltzburgh, as a heretic, for asserting the existence of the antipodes! But far more illustrious than any of these was Venerable Bede, whose name and writings are still as fresh in the present as ever they were in past ages. He was born at Jarrow, in the county of Durham, somewhere about the years 672 and 677, and died in 735. His chief work was the *Ecclesiastical History of England*, and it is from this well-known production, devoted though it be to the affairs of the church, that the best portion of our information on the civil affairs of the country is derived. As the greater part of his life was spent in a cloister, while his whole time was devoted to writing, he produced, besides his voluminous history, many other works, chiefly on theology and educational subjects, and a Martyrology. He was also the author of a volume on the metrical art, and another of hymns and epigrams. These works were written in Latin; but his last literary labour, upon which he was engaged when he died, was a translation of St. John's Gospel into his native tongue. The literary exertions of Alfred the Great, by which he sought to become the teacher as well as the liberator and lawgiver of his country, are too well known to require particular notice here. His various productions, both original and translated, which he executed in the midst of difficulties such as few sovereigns have been able to surmount, were as remarkable, and perhaps as beneficial, as his victories. It will be seen, however, that at the best the history of Anglo-Saxon literature forms a very scanty record. The genius of England, like its political constitution, required the labour of generations and the lapse of ages to bring it into full form and maturity.

BOOK III.

PERIOD FROM THE NORMAN CONQUEST TO THE DEATH OF KING JOHN.—150 YEARS.

FROM A.D. 1066—1216.

CONTEMPORARY PRINCES.

England.
1066 WILLIAM I.
1087 WILLIAM II.
1100 HENRY I.
1135 STEPHEN.
1154 HENRY II.
1189 RICHARD I.
1199 JOHN.

Scotland.
1057 MALCOLM III.
1093 DONALD BANE.
1094 DUNCAN.
1095 DONALD BANE (restored).
1098 EDGAR.
1107 ALEXANDER I.
1124 DAVID I.

1153 MALCOLM IV.
1165 WILLIAM.
1214 ALEXANDER II.

Ireland.
1064 TURLOGH.
1086 INTERREGNUM.
1094 MURTACH O'BRIEN in the South,
... DONALD MACLACHLAN O'NEIL in the North.
1119 DONALD MACLACHLAN O'NEIL.
1121 INTERREGNUM.
1136 TURLOGH O'CONNOR the Great.
1156 MURTACH MACLACHLAN O'NEIL.
1166 RODERIC O'CONNOR.

France.
1060 PHILIP I.
1109 LOUIS VI.
1137 LOUIS VII.
1180 PHILIP II.

Germany.
1056 HENRY IV.
1107 HENRY V.
1125 LOTHAIRE.
1139 CONRAD III.
1152 FREDERICK I.
1191 HENRY VI.
1209 OTTO IV.

Popes.
1061 ALEXANDER II.
1073 GREGORY VII.

1086 VICTOR III.
1088 URBAN II.
1099 PASCAL II.
1118 GELASIUS II.
1119 CALIXTUS II.
1124 HONORIUS II.
1130 INNOCENT II.
1143 CELESTINE II.
1144 LUCIUS II.
1145 EUGENIUS III.
1153 ANASTASIUS IV.
1154 ADRIAN IV.
1159 ALEXANDER III.
1181 LUCIUS III.
1185 URBAN III.
1187 GREGORY VIII.
1188 CLEMENT III.
1191 CELESTINE III.
1198 INNOCENT III.

CHAPTER I.—CIVIL AND MILITARY HISTORY.

WILLIAM I., SURNAMED THE CONQUEROR.—ACCESSION, A.D. 1066—DEATH, A.D. 1087.

Battle Abbey founded—William's advance to London—Feeble resistance of the English—William crowned at Westminster—Riot at his coronation—He revisits Normandy—Revolt in England during his absence—His merciless proceedings to complete the conquest at his return—Anarchy and sufferings thereby occasioned—William's military operations in the north of England—Desertion among his nobles—Revolt in Northumberland—William suppresses it—Confiscations and oppressions which follow—Resistance of Hereward, Lord of Brunn, in Lincolnshire—Hereward's Camp of Refuge at Ely—His successes over the Normans—He is obliged to capitulate—Completion of the conquest—William departs to the Continent—Revolt of his nobles during his absence—They are defeated—Execution of Waltheof, Earl of Northumberland—Rebellion of William's family against him—Demand of Robert, his eldest son, for a separate government—He makes war upon his father—Combat between William and his son under the walls of Gerberoy—The Northumbrians again in rebellion—They kill their Norman governor and his garrison—Their suppression by Odo, brother of William—Odo intrigues for the popedom—He is arrested and imprisoned by William—Tyrannical formation of the New Forest—William's inordinate love of hunting—He repairs with an army to France—His death occasioned by an accident—Ingratitude of his sons and courtiers—Inglorious funeral of William the Conqueror.

THE first feelings of the Normans after the battle of Hastings seem to have been sensations of triumph and joy, amounting almost to a delirium. They are represented by a contemporary[1] as making their horses to prance and bound over the thickly strewed bodies of the Anglo-Saxons; after which they proceeded to rifle them, and despoil them of their clothes. By William's orders the space was cleared round the pope's standard, which he had set up; and there his tent was pitched, and he feasted with his followers amongst the dead. The critical circumstances in which he had so recently been placed, and the difficulties which still lay before him, disposed the mind of the Conqueror to serious thoughts. Not less, perhaps, in gratitude for the past than in the hope that such a work would procure him heavenly favour for the future, he solemnly vowed that he would erect a splendid abbey on the scene of this his first victory; and

[1] William of Poitiers. This writer asserts that although Harold's mother offered its weight in gold for the dead body of her son, the stern victor was deaf to her request, professing indignation at the proposal that he should enjoy the rites of sepulture for whose

VOL. I.   23—24

when, in process of time, this vow was accomplished, the high altar of the abbey church stood on the very spot where the standard of Harold had been planted and thrown down. The exterior walls embraced the whole of the hill, the centre of their position, which the bravest of the English had covered with their bodies, and all the surrounding country, where the scenes of the combat had passed, became the property of the holy house, which was called, in the Norman or French language, *l'Abbaye de la Bataille*, and was dedicated to St. Martin, the patron of the soldiers of Gaul. Monks, invited from the great convent of Marmontier, near Tours, took up their residence in the new edifice. They were well endowed with the property of the English who had died in the battle, and prayed alike for the repose of the souls of those victims, and for the prosperity and long life of the Normans who had killed them.[2] In the archives of the house was deposited a long roll, on which were inscribed the names of the nobles and gentlemen of mark who came with the Conqueror and survived the battle of Hastings.[3]

BATTLE ABBEY.[1]—From a drawing in the King's Library, British Museum.

The most sanguine of the Normans, in common with the most despondent among the English, expected that, immediately after the battle of Hastings, the Conqueror would march straight to London, and make himself master of that capital. But the first move was a retrograde one; nor did William establish himself in the capital until more than two months had passed. While the army of Harold kept the field at Senlac or Battle, several new ships with reinforcements came over from Normandy to join William. Mistaking the proper place for landing, the commanders of these vessels put in to Romney, where they were at once assaulted and beaten by the people of the coast. William learned this unpleasant news the day after his victory, and to save the other recruits whom he still expected from a similar disaster, he resolved before proceeding farther to make himself master of all the south-eastern coast. He turned back, therefore, from Battle to Hastings, at which latter place he stayed some days, awaiting his transports from beyond sea, and hoping, it is said, that his presence would induce the population of those parts to make voluntary submission. At length, seeing that no one came to ask for peace, William resumed his march with the remnant of his army and the fresh troops which had arrived in the interval from Normandy. He kept close to the sea-coast, marching from south to north, and spreading devastation on his passage. He took a savage vengeance at Romney for the reverse his

---

excessive cupidity so many men lay unburied. Harold, it is added, was buried on the beach. Most of the English historians, however, say that the body was given to his mother without ransom, and interred by her in Waltham Abbey, which had been founded by Harold before he was king. The Cottonian MS., Julius D. 6, which appears to have been written in Waltham Abbey about a century after the event, relates that two monks, who were allowed by William to search for the body, were unable to distinguish it among the heaps of slain, until they sent for Harold's mistress, Edītha, "the Swan-necked," whose eye of affection was not to be eluded or deceived. The improbable story told by Giraldus Cambrensis (and in more detail in the Harleian MS. 3776) about Harold, after receiving his wound, having escaped from the battle, and living for some years as an anchorite in a cell near St. John's Church, in Chester, though a pretty enough romance, is palpably undeserving of notice in an historical point of view.

[1] The building of Battle Abbey was commenced by the Conqueror in A.D. 1067, the year following that on which the battle of Hastings was fought. In the reign of Edward III. the abbey was fortified by permission of the king. The circuit of the ruins is computed at about a mile. Gilpin considers that the prevailing style indicates the rebuilding of the greater part of the edifice in the time of the later Henries. The remains consists of three sides of a quadrangle, the fourth having been removed. The grand entrance was a large square building, embattled, with an octagon tower at each corner. The abbey church is supplanted by the edifice of Sir Thomas Webster. The refectory lies in utter ruin, and the crypts have been converted into a stable. Many fine minor vestiges exist in different parts of the ruin.

[2] Thierry, *Histoire de la Conquête*.

[3] The original roll of Battle Abbey is lost; but some copies have been preserved, from which the document has been repeatedly printed. It is believed, however, that these pretended transcripts are far from faithful, and that, besides other corruptions, many names have been inserted in later times by the monks of the abbey, to gratify families or individuals that wish to make it appear they were sprung from followers of the Conqueror. To date from the Conquest, as is well known, is still the ambition of noble English families.

troops had sustained there, by massacring the inhabitants and burning their houses. From Romney he advanced to Dover, the strongest place on the coast—"the lock and key of all England," as Holinshed calls it. With little or no opposition he burst into the town, which his troops set fire to; and the strong castle, which the son of Godwin had put into an excellent state of defence, was so speedily surrendered to him, that a suspicion of treachery rests on the Saxon commander. The capture of this fortress was most opportune and important, for a dreadful dysentery had broken out in the Norman army, and a safe receptacle for the sick had become indispensable. Dover Castle also commanded the best landing-place for troops from the Continent, and William was not yet so sure of his game as not to look anxiously for a place of retreat on the coast, in case of meeting with reverses in the interior. He spent eight or nine days in strengthening the castle, and repairing some of the damage done to the town by his lawless soldiery. Meanwhile, in order to conciliate the inhabitants, he made them some compensation for the losses and injuries they had sustained; and in the same interval he received more recruits from Normandy.

When the Conqueror at last moved from Dover, he ceased to creep cautiously round the coast, but, penetrating into Kent, marched direct to London. A confused story is told by some of our early historians about a popular resistance, organized by Archbishop Stigand and the abbot Egelnoth, in which the men of Kent, advancing like the army of Macduff and Siward against Macbeth, under the cover of cut-down trees and boughs, disputed the passage of the Normans, and with arms in their hands exacted from them terms most favourable to themselves and the part of England they occupied. But the plain truth seems to be that, overawed by the recent catastrophe of Hastings, and the presence of a compact and numerous army, the inhabitants of Kent made no resistance, and meeting William with offers of submission, placed hostages in his hands, and so obtained mild treatment.

During these calamities the Saxon Witan had assembled in London, to deliberate and provide for the future; but evidently, as far as the lay portion of the meeting was concerned, with no intention of submitting to the Conqueror. The first care that occupied their thoughts was to elect a successor to the throne. Either of Harold's brave brothers, at such a crisis, when valour and military skill were the qualities most wanted, might probably have commanded a majority of suffrages; but they had both fought their last fight; and, owing to their youth, their inexperience, their want of popularity, or to some other circumstance, the two sons of Harold seem never to have been thought of. Many voices would have supported Morcar or Edwin, the powerful brothers-in-law of Harold, who had already an almost sovereign authority in Northumbria and Mercia; but the citizens of London, and the men of the south of England generally, preferred young Edgar Atheling, the grandson of Edmund Ironside, who had been previously set aside on account of his little worth: and when Stigand the primate, and Aldred the Archbishop of York, threw their weight into this scale, it outweighed the others, and Edgar was proclaimed king. It should seem, however, that even at this stage, many of the bishops and dignified clergymen, who were even then Frenchmen or Normans, raised their voice in favour of William, or let fall hints that were all meant to favour his pretensions. The pope's bull and banner could not be without their effect, and, motives of interest and policy apart, some of these ecclesiastics may have conscientiously believed they were performing their duty in promoting the cause of the elect of Rome. Others there were who were notoriously bought over, either by money paid beforehand, or by promises of future largesse.

The party that ultimately prevailed in the Witan did not carry their point until much precious time had been consumed; nor could the blood of Cerdic, Alfred, and Edmund make the king of their choice that rallying point which conflicting factions required, or a hero capable of facing a victorious invader, advancing at the head of a more powerful army than England could hope to raise for some time. In fact, Edgar was a mere cipher—a boy incapable of government as of war—with nothing popular about him except his descent. The primate Stigand took his place at the council board, and the military command was given to Earls Edwin and Morcar. A very few acts of legal authority had been performed in the name of Edgar, when William of Normandy appeared before the southern suburb of London. If the Normans had expected to take the capital by a *coup-de-main*, and, at once, they were disappointed; the Londoners were very warlike; and the population of the city, great even in those days, was much increased by the presence of the thanes and chiefs of all the neighbouring counties, who had come in to attend the Witan, and had brought their servants and followers with them. After making a successful charge, with 500 of his best horse, against some citizens who were gathered on that side of the river, William set fire to Southwark, and marched away from London, with the determination of ravaging the country around it, destroying the property of the thanes who had assembled at the Witan, and, by interrupting all communication, induce the well-defended capital to surrender.

Detachments of his army were soon spread over a wide tract; and in burning towns and villages, in the massacre of men armed and men unarmed, and in the violation of helpless females, the people of Surrey, Sussex, Hampshire, and Berkshire were made to feel the full signification of a Norman conquest. William crossed the Thames at Wallingford, near to which place he established an intrenched camp, where a division of his army was left, in order to cut off any succours that might be sent towards London from the west. This done, he proceeded across Buckinghamshire into Herefordshire, "slaying the people," till he came to Berkhampstead, where he took up a position, in order to interrupt all communication with London from the north. The capital, indeed, at this time seems to have been girded round by the enemy, and afflicted by the prospect of absolute famine. Nor were there wanting other causes of discouragement. The Earls Edwin and Morcar showed little zeal in the command of a weak, and, as yet, unorganized army, and soon withdrew towards the Humber, taking with them all the soldiers of Northumbria and Mercia, who constituted the best part of King Edgar's forces, but who looked to the earls much more than to the king. These two sons of Alfgar probably hoped to be able to maintain themselves in independence in the north, where, in reality, they at a later period renewed, and greatly prolonged the contest with the Normans. Their departure had a baneful effect in London; and while the spirit of the citizens waxed fainter and fainter, the partisans and intriguers for William, encouraged at every move by the prevalent faction among the clergy, raised their hopes and extended their exertions.

After some time, however, Earls Morcar and Edwin appear to have returned to the capital. On many an intermediate step the chroniclers are provokingly silent: but at last it was determined that a submissive deputation should be sent from London to Berkhampstead; and King Edgar himself, the primate Stigand, Aldred, Archbishop of York, Wolfstan, Bishop of Worcester, with other prelates and lay chiefs, among whom the Saxon chronicler expressly names the two Earls of Northumbria and Mercia, and many of the principal citizens, repaired to William, who received them with an outward show of moderation and kindness. It is related that when the man whom he most hated, as the friend of Harold and the energetic enemy of the Normans — that when Stigand came into his presence, he saluted him with the endearing epithets of father and bishop. The puppet-king Edgar made a verbal renunciation of the throne, and the rest swore allegiance to the Conqueror — the bishops swearing for the whole body of the clergy, the chiefs for the nobility, and the citizens for the good city of London.[1] During a part of this singular audience, William pretended to have doubts and misgivings as to the propriety of his ascending the vacant throne; but these hypocritical expressions were drowned in the loud acclamations of his Norman barons, who felt that the crown of England was on the point of their swords. Having taken oaths of fidelity and peace, the Saxon deputies left hostages with the Norman, who, on his side, promised to be mild and merciful to all men. On the following morning the foreigners began their march towards London, plundering, murdering, and burning, just as before.[2] They took their way through St. Alban's. Even now William did not enter London in person, but, sending on part of his army to build a fortress for his reception, he encamped with the rest at some distance from the city. This fortress, which was built on the site, and probably included part of a Roman castle, grew gradually in after times into the Tower of London. Some accounts state that William's vanguard was hostilely engaged by the citizens, but according to others they met with no resistance, and were permitted to raise their fortifications without any serious molestation.

As soon as the Normans had finished his stronghold, William took possession of it, and then they fixed his coronation for a few days after. The Conqueror is said to have objected to the performance of this ceremony while so large a part of the island was independent of his authority; and he certainly hoped, by delaying it, to obtain a more formal consent from the English nation, or something like a Saxon election, which would be a better title in the eyes of the people than the right of conquest. Little, however, was gained by delay; and the coronation, which, for the sake of greater solemnity, took place on Christmas Day, was accompanied by accidents and circumstances highly irritating to the people. It is stated, on one side, that William invited the primate Stigand to perform the rites, and that Stigand refused to crown a man "covered with the blood of men, and the invader of others' rights."[3] Although there might have been some policy in making this great champion of the Saxon cause hallow the Conqueror, it does not appear probable that William would ask this service of one who was lying under the severe displeasure of Rome; and it is said, on the other side, that he refused to be consecrated by Stigand, and con-

---

[1] "Bugon tha for ncode," says the *Saxon Chronicle*, "tha macst waes to learm gedon; and thaet waes micel unread thaet man acror awa ne dyde tha hit god betan nolde for urum synnum." (They submitted them for need, when the most harm was done. It was very ill-advised that they did not so before, seeing that God would not better things for our sins.—Ingram's *Translation*.)

[2] *Roger Hoveden; Chron. Sax.*   [3] *William of Newbury.*

ferred that honour on Aldred, Archbishop of York, whom some of the chroniclers describe as a wise and prudent man, who understood the expediency of accommodating himself to circumstances. The new abbey of Westminster, the last work of Edward the Confessor, was chosen as the place for the coronation of our first Norman king. The suburbs, the streets of London, and all the approaches to the abbey were lined with double rows of soldiers, horse and foot. The Conqueror rode through the ranks, and entered the abbey church, attended by 260 of his warlike chiefs, by many priests and monks, and a considerable number of English, who had been gained over to act a part in the pageantry. At the opening of the ceremony one of William's prelates, Geoffrey, the Bishop of Coutances, asked the Normans, in the French language, if they were of opinion that their chief should take the title of King of England? and then the Archbishop of York asked the English if they would have William the Norman for their king? The reply on either side was given by acclamation in the affirmative, and the shouts and cheers thus raised were so loud that they startled the foreign cavalry stationed round the abbey. The troops took the confused noise for a cry of alarm raised by their friends, and, as they had received orders to be on the alert, and ready to act in case of any seditious movement, they rushed to the English houses nearest the abbey, and set fire to them all. A few, thinking to succour their betrayed duke and the nobles they served, ran to the church, where, at sight of their naked swords, and the smoke and flames that were rising, the tumult soon became as great as that without its walls. The Normans fancied the whole population of London and its neighbourhood had risen against them; the English imagined that they had been duped by a vain show, and drawn together, unarmed and defenceless, that they might be massacred. Both parties ran out of the abbey, and the ceremony was interrupted, though William, left almost alone in the church, or with none but the Archbishop Aldred and some terrified priests of both nations near him at the altar, decidedly refused to postpone the celebration. The service was therefore completed amidst these bad auguries, but in the utmost hurry and confusion, and the Conqueror took the usual coronation oath of the Anglo-Saxon kings, making, as an addition of his own, the solemn promise that he would treat the English people as well as the best of their kings had done.[1] Meanwhile the commotion without continued, and it is not mentioned at what hour of the day or night the conflagration ended. The English, who had been at the abbey, ran to extinguish the fire—the Normans, it is said, to plunder, and otherwise profit by the disorder; but it appears that some of the latter exerted themselves to stop the progress of the flames, and to put an end to a riot peculiarly unpalatable to their master, whose anxious wish was certainly, at that time, to conciliate the two nations.

Soon after his coronation, William withdrew from London to Barking, where he established a court, which gradually attracted many of the nobles of the south of England. Edric, surnamed the Forester, Coxo, a warrior of high repute, and others are named; and, as William extended his authority, even the thanes and the great earls from the north, where the force of his arms was not yet felt, repaired to do him homage. In return William granted them the confirmation of their estates and honours, which he had not at present the power to seize or invade. It appears that the Conqueror's first seizures and confiscations, after the crown lands, were the domains of Harold, and his brothers Gurth and Leofwin, and the lands and property of such of the English chiefs as were either very weak, or unpopular, or indifferent to the nation.

Edgar Atheling was an inmate of the new court, and William, knowing he was cherished by many of the English on account of his descent, pretended to treat him with great respect, and left him the earldom of Oxford, which Harold had conferred on him when he ascended the throne in his stead. From Barking the new king made a progress through the territory, that was rather militarily occupied than securely conquered, displaying as he went as much royal pomp, and treating the English with as much courtesy and consideration, as he could. The extent of this territory cannot be exactly determined, but it appears the Conqueror had not yet advanced, in the north-east beyond the confines of Norfolk, nor in the south-west beyond Dorsetshire. Both on the eastern and western coast, and in the midland counties, the invasion was gradual and slow, and, as yet, the city of Oxford had certainly not fallen.

All William's measures at this time were mild and conciliating; he respected the old Anglo-Saxon laws; he established good courts of justice, encouraged agriculture and commerce, and (at least nominally) enlarged the privileges of London and some other towns. At the same time, however, the country he held was bristled with castles and towers; and additional fortresses erected in and around the capital, showed his distrust of what was termed, in the language of the Normans, an over-numerous and too proud population. Next to London, the city of Winchester, which had been a favourite residence of the

---

[1] *Guil. Pictav.; Orderic. Vital.; Chron. Sax.*

Anglo-Saxon kings, excited most suspicion; "for," says William of Poitiers, the Conqueror's chaplain, "it is a noble and powerful city, inhabited by a race of men rich, fearless, and perfidious." A castle was therefore erected at Winchester, and a strong Norman garrison put into it. Such operations could not be otherwise than distasteful to the English, who were further irritated by seeing proud foreign lords fixed among them, and married to the widows and heiresses of their old lords, who had fallen at Hastings. The rapacious followers of William were hard to satisfy; and, to secure their attachment, he was frequently obliged to go beyond those bounds of moderation he was inclined to set for himself. A most numerous troop of priests and monks had come over from the Continent, and their avidity was scarcely inferior to that of the barons and knights. Nearly every one of them wanted a church, a rich abbey, or some higher promotion. To pass over other wrongs and provocations inseparable from foreign conquest, the people presently saw the coming on of that sad state of things which they soon after suffered, "when England became the habitation of new strangers, in such wise, that there was neither governor, bishop, nor abbot remaining therein of the English nation."[1] It was, however, to these foreign churchmen that our country was chiefly indebted for whatever intellectual improvement or civilization was imported at the Conquest.

In the month of March, 1067, the English in the north and west being yet untouched, and their countrymen in the south beginning to harbour violent feelings—while the Normans were anxious to provoke an insurrection, and prosecute the war in the land where so many broad acres remained to reward the victors—William resolved to pass over into Normandy. Had he determined to vex and rouse the English, he could scarcely have left a more fitting instrument than his half-brother, Odo, to whom he confided the royal power during his absence, associating with him as councillors of state, William Fitz-Osborn, Hugo of Grantmesnil, Hugo de Montfort, Walter Gifford, and William de Garenne. On the other hand, as if to make an English revolt hopeless should it be attempted, he carried in his train Stigand, the Archbishop of Canterbury, the abbot Egelnoth, Edgar Atheling, Edwin, Earl of Mercia, Morcar, Earl of Northumbria, Waltheof, Earl of Northampton and Huntingdon, and many others of high nobility. The place chosen for his embarkation was Pevensey, near Hastings; and when he had made a liberal distribution of money and presents to a part of his army which had followed him to the beach, he set sail with a fair wind for Normandy, just six months after his landing in England. According to every account, he was received with enthusiastic joy by his continental subjects, who were filled with wonderment at his success, and the quantity of gold and silver and other precious effects he brought back with him. A part of this wealth, the fruit of blood and plunder, was sent to the pope, with the banner of Harold, which had been taken at the battle of Hastings, and another portion was distributed among the abbeys, monasteries, and churches of Normandy; "neither monks nor priests remaining without a guerdon." William gave them coined gold, and gold in bars, golden vases, and, above all, richly embroidered stuffs, which on high feast-days they hung up in their churches, where they excited the admiration of all travellers and strangers. The whole of the account given by William's chaplain tends to raise our idea of the wealth of England. "That land," says the Poitevin, "abounds more than Normandy in the precious metals. If in fertility it may be termed the granary of Ceres, in riches it should be called the treasury of Arabia. The English women excel in the use of the needle, and in embroidering in gold; the men in every species of elegant workmanship. Moreover, the best artists of Germany live amongst them; and merchants, who repair to distant countries, import the most valuable articles of foreign manufacture, unknown in Normandy." The same contemporary informs us that at the feast of Easter, which William held with unusual splendour, a relation of the King of France, named Raoul, came with a numerous retinue to the Conqueror's court, where he and his Frenchmen, not less than the Normans, considered with a curiosity, mingled with surprise, the chased vases of gold and silver brought from England; and, above all, the drinking-cups of the Saxons, made of large buffalo-horns, and ornamented at either extremity with precious metal. The French prince and his companions were also much struck with the beauty of countenance and the long flowing hair of the young Englishmen whom William had brought over with him as guests or hostages.

While all thus went on merrily in Normandy, events of a very different nature were taking place on the other side of the Channel. The rule of Odo and the barons left in England pressed harshly on the people, whose complaints and cries for justice they despised. Without punishment or check, their men-at-arms were permitted to insult and plunder, not merely the peasants and burgesses, but people of the best condition, and the cup of misery and degradation was filled up, as usual in such cases, by violence offered to the women. The English spirit was not yet so depressed, and, in fact, never sank so low as to tole-

---

[1] Holinshed.

rate such wrongs. Several popular risings took place in various parts of the subjugated territory, and many a Norman, caught beyond the walls of his castle or garrison-town, was cut to pieces. These partial insurrections were followed by concerted and extensively combined movements. A grand conspiracy was formed, and the Conqueror's throne was made to totter before it was nine months old. The men of Kent, who had been the first to submit, were the first to attempt to throw off the yoke. A singular circumstance attended their effort. Eustace, Count of Boulogne, the same who had caused such a stir at Dover in the time of Edward the Confessor, was then in open quarrel with William the Norman, who kept one of his sons in prison. This Eustace was famed far and wide for his military skill; and his relationship to the sainted King Edward, whose sister he had married, made the English consider him now in the light of a natural ally. Forgetting, therefore, their old grievances, the people of Kent sent a message to Count Eustace, promising to put Dover into his hands if he would make a descent on the coast, and help them to wage war on their Norman oppressors. Eustace accepted the invitation, and crossing the Channel with a small but chosen band, he landed, under favour of a dark night, at a short distance from Dover, where he was presently joined by a host of Kentish men in arms. A contemporary says, that had they waited but two days, these insurgents would have been joined by the whole population of those parts; but they imprudently made an attack on the strong castle of Dover, were repulsed with loss, and then thrown into a panic, by the false report that Bishop Odo was approaching them with all his forces. Count Eustace fled, and got safely on board ship, but most of his men-at-arms were slain or taken prisoners by the Norman garrison, or broke their necks by falling over the cliffs on which Dover Castle stands. The men of Kent with a few exceptions found their way home in safety, by taking by-paths and roads with which the Normans were unacquainted.

In the west the Normans were much less fortunate. Edric the Forester, who had visited the Conqueror at Barking, and done homage to him, was the lord of extensive possessions that lay on the Severn and the confines of Wales. This powerful chief was at first desirous of living in peace, but being provoked at the depredations committed by some Norman captains who had garrisoned the city of Hereford, he took up arms, and forming an alliance with two Welsh princes, he was enabled to shut the foreigners close up within the walls of the town, and to range undisputed master of all the western part of Herefordshire.

At this favourable moment the two sons of King Harold appeared in the west; but though they were nearly a year older than at the time they were passed over unnoticed by the Witan assembled at London, they soon showed that neither of them had the qualities requisite for the saviour of the Anglo-Saxon nation. Their proceedings would be altogether inexplicable if we did not reflect that they were allied with, and probably controlled by, a host of pirates. These two young men sailed over from Ireland with a considerable force, embarked in sixty ships. They ascended the Bristol Channel and the river Avon, and landing near Bristol plundered that fertile country. Whatever were their pretexts and claims, they acted as common enemies, and were met as such by the English people, who repulsed them when they attempted to take the city of Bristol, and soon after defeated them upon the coast of Somersetshire, whither they had repaired with their ships and plunder. The invaders, who suffered severely, took to their ships, and returned immediately to Ireland. In Shropshire, Nottinghamshire, and other parts of the kingdom, both where they had felt the Norman oppression, and where, as yet, they only apprehended it, bodies of English rose in arms, and urged their neighbours to join them. The indignation of the people was general, and encouraged by the Conqueror's absence, efforts were made, and others contemplated, for throwing off the yoke. Rumours spread that a simultaneous massacre, like that perpetrated on the Danes, was intended; and it was equally natural that the English should make use of such threats in their moments of rage, and that the Normans, conscious of oppression, and well versed in the history of St. Brice's Day, should believe them and tremble at them. Letter after letter and message after message were sent into Normandy; but the Conqueror, either because he was insensible to the alarm, or thought sufficient provocation had not been given, lingered there for more than eight months. When at last he departed, it was in hurry and agitation. He embarked at Dieppe on the 6th of December, and sailed for England by night. On arriving, he placed new governors, whom he had brought from Normandy, in his castles and strongholds in Sussex and Kent. On reaching London he was made fully sensible of the prevailing discontent; but with his usual crafty prudence he applied himself to soothe the storm for awhile, deeming that the time had not yet arrived for his openly declaring that the fickle, faithless English were to be exterminated or treated as slaves, and all their possessions and honours given to the Normans. He celebrated the festival of Christmas with unusual pomp, and invited many Saxon chiefs to London to partake in the celebration. He received these guests with smiles and caresses.

giving the kiss of welcome to every comer.[1] If they asked for anything, he granted it; if they announced or advised anything, he listened with respectful attention; and it should seem that they were nearly all the dupes of these royal artifices. He then propitiated the citizens of London by a proclamation, which was written in the Saxon language, and read in all the churches of the capital. "Be it known unto you," said this document, "what is my will. I will that all of you enjoy your national laws in the days of King Edward; that every son shall inherit from his father, after the days of his father; and that none of my people do you wrong." William's first public act after all these promises was to impose a heavy tax, which was made more and more burdensome as his power increased.

The war of 1068, or what may be called the Conqueror's second campaign in England, opened in the fertile province of Devonshire, where the people, supported by their hardy neighbours of Cornwall, and animated by the presence of the mother and some other relations of King Harold, refused to acknowledge his government, and had prepared to resist the advance of his lieutenants. Some of the thanes to whom the command of the insurrection had been intrusted, proved cowards or traitors; the Normans advanced, burning and destroying and breathing vengeance; but the men of Exeter, who had had a principal share in organizing the patriotic resistance, were resolute in the defence of their city. Githa or Editha, Harold's mother, had fled there after the battle of Hastings, and carried with her considerable riches. When the Conqueror came within four miles of Exeter, he summoned the citizens to submit and take the oath of fealty. They replied, "We will not swear fealty to this man, who pretends to be our king, nor will we receive his garrison within our walls; but if he will receive as tribute the dues we were accustomed to pay to our kings, we will consent to pay them to him." To this somewhat novel proposal William said, "I would have subjects, and it is not my custom to take them on such conditions."[2] Some of the magistrates and wealthiest of the citizens then went to William, and, imploring his mercy, proffered the submission of the city, and gave hostages; but the mass of the population either did not sanction this proceeding, or repented of it; and when William rode up at the head of his cavalry, he found the gates barred and the walls manned with combatants, who bade him defiance. The Normans, in sight of the men on the ramparts, then tore out the eyes of one of the hostages they had just received; but this savage act did not daunt the people, who were well prepared for

ROUGEMONT CASTLE, part of the old defences of Exeter.[3]—From a view in the King's Library, British Museum.

defence, having raised new turrets and battlements on the walls, and brought in a number of armed seamen both native and foreigners, that happened to be in their port. The siege continued for eighteen days, and cost William a great number of men; and when the city surrendered at last, if we are to believe the *Saxon Chronicle*, it was because their chiefs had again betrayed them. The brave men of Exeter, however, obtained much more favourable terms than were then usual; for, though they were forced to take the oath and admit a Norman garrison, their lives, property, and privileges were secured to them, and successful precautions were taken by the Conqueror to prevent any outrage or plunder. Having ordered a strong castle to be built in the captured town, William returned eastward to Winchester, where he was joined by his wife Matilda, who had not hitherto been in England. At the ensuing festival of Whitsuntide she was publicly crowned by Aldred, the Archbishop of York. On the surrender of Exeter, the aged Githa, with several ladies of rank,

---

[1] Dulciter ad oscula invitabat.—*Orderic*. [2] Ibid.

[3] Bishop Grandison, on the authority of an old chronicle, states that King Athelstane founded a castle here, which was destroyed by the Danes in 1003. It was rebuilt by William the Conqueror. After the surrender of Exeter to General Fairfax, it was dismantled, and all its towers and battlements destroyed. There are now few remains of the building. The lofty gateway represented in the wood-cut is one of the most ancient vestiges. The name Rougemont is considered to have been derived from the red colour of the soil on which the castle stands.—Lyson's *Magna Britannia*.

escaped to Bath, and finding no safety there, they fled to the small islands at the mouth of the Severn, where they lay concealed until they found an opportunity of passing over to Flanders.

Harold's sons, Godwin and Edmund, with a younger brother named Magnus, again came over from Ireland; and with a fleet hovered off the coast of Devonshire and Cornwall, landing occasionally, and inviting the people to join them against the Normans. Nothing could be more absurdly concerted than these movements. Having rashly ventured too far into the country, they were suddenly attacked by a Norman force from Exeter, and defeated with great slaughter. Their means were now exhausted, and, wearied by their ill success, their Irish allies declined giving any further assistance to these exiles. The sons of Harold next appeared as suppliants at the court of Sweyn, King of Denmark.

During the spring and early summer of this same year (1068), William established his authority in Devonshire, Somersetshire, and Gloucestershire, and besides taking Exeter, made himself master of Oxford and other fortified cities which he had left in his rear when he advanced into the west. Wherever his dominion was imposed, the mass of land was given to his lords and knights, and fortresses and castles were erected and garrisoned by Normans and other foreigners, who continued to cross the Channel in search of employment, wealth, and honours. Meanwhile, the accounts of the sufferings of the conquered people, as given by the native chroniclers, are thus condensed in a striking passage of Holinshed:—"He took away from divers of the nobility, and others of the better sort, all their livings, and gave the same to his Normans. Moreover, he raised great taxes and subsidies through the realm; nor anything regarded the English nobility; so that they who before thought themselves to be made for ever by bringing a stranger into the realm, did now see themselves trodden under foot, to be despised, and to be mocked on all sides, insomuch that many of them were constrained (as it were, for a further testimony of servitude and bondage) to shave their beards, to round their hair, and to frame themselves, as well in apparel as in service and diet, at their tables, after the Norman manners, very strange and far differing from the ancient customs and old usages of their country. Others, utterly refusing to sustain such an intolerable yoke of thraldom as was daily laid upon them by the Normans, chose rather to leave all, both goods and lands, and, after the manner of outlaws, got them to the woods with their wives, children, and servants, meaning from thenceforth to live upon the spoil of the country adjoining, and to take whatsoever came next to hand. Whereupon it came to pass within a while that no man might travel in safety from his own house or town to his next neighbours." The bands of outlaws thus formed of impoverished, desperate men, were not suppressed for several successive reigns; and while the Normans considered and treated them as banditti, the English people long regarded them in the light of unfortunate patriots.

Men of higher rank and more extended views were soon among the fugitives from the pale of the Conqueror. When in his conciliating mood, William had promised Edwin, Earl of Mercia, one of his daughters in marriage, and flattered by the prospect of such a prize, this powerful brother-in-law of Harold had rendered important services to the Norman cause; but now, when he asked his reward, the Conqueror not only refused the fair bride, but insulted the suitor. Upon this, Edwin, with his brother Morcar, absconded from the Norman court, and went to the north of England, there to join their incensed countrymen, and make one general effort for the recovery of their ancient liberties. No foreign soldier had as yet passed the Humber; and it was behind that river that Edwin and Morcar fixed the great camp of independence, the most southern bulwark of which was the fortified city of York. Among the men of Yorkshire and Northumbria they found some thousands of hardy warriors, who swore they would not sleep under the roof of a house till the day of victory, and they were joined by some allies from the mountains of Wales and other parts. The ever active Conqueror, however, came upon them before they were prepared. His march, considering the many obstacles he had to overcome, was wonderfully rapid. Advancing from Oxford, he took Warwick and Leicester, the latter of which places he almost entirely destroyed. Then crossing the Trent, which he had not seen till now, he fell upon Derby and Nottingham. From Nottingham he marched upon Lincoln, which he forced to capitulate and deliver hostages, and thence pressing forward, might and main, he came to the river Ouse, near the point where it falls into the Humber. Here he found Edwin and Morcar drawn out to oppose him. The battle which immediately ensued was fierce in the extreme; but, as at Hastings, their superiority in number, arms, and discipline, gave the Normans the victory. Many of the English perished; the rest retreated to York, within the walls of which they hoped to find refuge; but the conquerors following them closely, broke through the walls and entered the city, destroying everything with fire and sword, and massacring all they found, from the boy to the old man. The wreck of the patriotic army fled to the Humber, and descended that estuary in boats; they then turned to the north, and landed in the country of the Scotch, or in the territory near the Borders, which became the places of refuge of all the brave men of the north, who did not yet despair of liberty.[1]

The victors, who were not prepared to advance farther, built a strong citadel at York, which became their advanced post and bulwark towards the north. A chosen garrison of 500 knights and men-at-arms, with a host of squires and servants-at-arms, was left at this dangerous post. So perilous, indeed, was it considered, from the well-known martial and obstinate character of the men that dwelt beyond its walls, that the Normans laboured day and night to strengthen their position, forcing the poor inhabitants of York who had escaped the massacre to dig deep ditches and build strong walls for them. Fearing to be besieged in their turn, they also collected all the stores and provisions they could.

In spite of his successes in the north, and his firm establishment in the midland counties, where he built castles and gave away earldoms, the Conqueror's throne was still threatened, and the country still agitated from one end to the other. The English chiefs, who had hitherto adhered to his cause, fell off, at first one by one, and then in troops together, following up their defection with concerted plans of operation against him. To these was added a fugitive of still higher rank, of whose custody the Conqueror was very negligent. At the instance of Marleswine, Cospatric, and some other noblemen, Edgar Atheling fled by sea into Scotland, taking his mother, Agatha, the widow of Edmund, son of Edmund Ironsides, and his two sisters, Margaret and Christina, with him. These royal fugitives were received with great honour and kindness, and conducted to his castle of Dunfermline by the Scottish monarch, Malcolm Canmore. Edgar's sister Margaret was young and handsome; "and in process of time, the said King Malcolm cast such love unto the said Margaret, that he took her to wife."[2] Some of the English nobles had preceded Edgar to Scotland; many followed him; and these emigrants, and others that arrived from the same quarter on various subsequent occasions, became

[1] "A more general proof of the ruinous oppression of William the Conqueror may be deduced from the comparative condition of the English towns in the reign of Edward the Confessor, and at the compilation of *Doomsday*. At the former epoch there were, in York, 607 inhabited houses—at the latter, 967; at the former there were, in Oxford, 721—at the latter, 243; of 172 houses in Dorchester, 100 were destroyed; of 243 in Derby, 103; of 487 in Chester, 205. Some other towns had suffered less, but scarcely any one fails to exhibit marks of a decayed population. As to the relative numbers of the peasantry and value of lands at these two periods, it would not be easy to assert anything without a laborious examination of *Doomsday Book*."—Hallam, *State of Europe during the Middle Ages*, vol. ii, p. 426.
[2] *Grafton*.

the founders of a principal part of the Scottish nobility.

It is probable that William did not mourn much for the departure of the English thanes; but presently he was vexed and embarrassed by the departure of some of his Norman chiefs who had followed him from the Continent. These warriors, wearied by the constant surprises and attacks of the English, and seeing no term to that desultory and destructive warfare, longed for the quiet of their own homes. Some considered themselves enriched enough by the plunder they had made; others thought that estates in England were not worth the trouble and danger with which they were to be obtained and secured; others, again, wanted to join their wives, who were constantly pressing them to return; for it appears that few or none of them had as yet thought it safe to bring their families to England. William tried to reanimate their zeal by offers more bountiful than ever, and by promising lands, money, and honours in abundance the moment the conquest of England should be completed. In spite, however, of all these manœuvres, Hugh de Grantmesnil, Earl of Norfolk, his brother-in-law, Humphrey Tilleuil, the warden of Hastings Castle, and a great number of others, retired from the service, and recrossed the Channel. The king punished this desertion by immediately confiscating all the possessions they had obtained in our island. Foreseeing, however, that he was about to be surrounded by great difficulties and dangers, he sent his own wife Matilda back to Normandy, that she might be in a place of safety. At the same time he invited fresh adventurers and soldiers of fortune from nearly every country in Europe; and, allured by his brilliant offers, bands flocked to him from the banks of the Rhine, the Seine, the Loire, the Garonne, and the Tagus—from the Alps, and the Italian peninsula beyond the Alps.

A.D. 1069. The strong garrison which the Conqueror had left at York could scarcely adventure a mile in advance of that post without being attacked by the natives, who lay constantly in ambush in all the woods and glens. The governor, William Malet, was soon fain to declare that he would not answer for the security of York itself unless prompt succour was sent him. On receiving this alarming news, William marched in person, and arrived before York just as the citizens, in league with all the country people of the neighbourhood, were besieging the Norman fortress. Having raised this siege by a sudden attack, he laid the foundations of a second castle in York, and, leaving a double garrison, returned southward. Soon after his departure the English made a second attempt to drive the enemy from their fortress, but they were repulsed with loss; and the second castle and other works were finished without further interruption. Thinking themselves now secure in this advanced post, the Normans resumed the offensive, and made a desperate attempt to extend their frontier as far north as Durham. The advance was made by a certain Robert de Comine, to whom William had promised a vast territory yet to be conquered.

This Robert set out from York with much pomp and circumstance, having assumed, by anticipation, the title of Earl of Northumberland. His army was not large, consisting only of 1200 lances; but his confidence was boundless. He crossed the Tees, and was within sight of the walls of Durham, which the Normans called "the stronghold of the rebels of the north," when Egelwin, the English bishop of that place, came forth to meet him, and informed him that the natives had vowed to destroy him, or be destroyed, and warned him not to expose himself with so small a force. Comine treated the warning with contempt, and marched on. The Normans entered Durham, massacring a few defenceless men. The soldiers quartered themselves in the houses of the citizens, plundering or wasting their substance; and the chief himself took possession of the bishop's palace. But when night fell, the people lighted signal-fires on the hills, that were seen as far as the Tees to the south, and as far northward as the river Tyne; and, at the summons, the inhabitants gathered in great numbers, and hurried to Durham. At the point of day they rushed into the city, and attacked the Normans on all sides. Many were killed before they could well rouse themselves from the deep sleep induced by the fatigue of the preceding day's march, and the revelry and debauch of the night. The rest attempted to rally in the bishop's house, where their leader had established his quarters. They defended this post for a short time, discharging their arrows and other missiles on the heads of their assailants, but the English ended the combat by setting fire to the house, which was burned to the ground, with Robert de Comine and all the Normans in it. The chroniclers relate, that of all the men engaged in the expedition only two escaped.

When the Northumbrians struck the blow at Durham, they were expecting powerful allies, who soon arrived. As we have so often had occasion to repeat, these men, with the inhabitants of most of the Danelagh, were exceedingly fierce and warlike, and chiefly of Danish blood. Many of the old men had followed the victorious banner of the great Canute into England, or had served under his sons, Kings Harold Harefoot and Hardicanute; and the sons of these old warriors were now in the vigour of mature manhood. They had always maintained an intercourse with Denmark, and as soon as they saw themselves threatened by the Normans, they applied to that country for assistance. The court of the Danish king was soon crowded by supplicants from the Danelagh, from Norwich and Lincoln, to York, Durham, and Newcastle. There were also envoys from other parts of the kingdom, where the Saxon blood predominated, and the sons of King Harold added their efforts to urge the Danish monarch to the invasion of England. At the same time the men of Northumberland had opened a correspondence with Malcolm Canmore and his guest Edgar Atheling, and allied themselves with the English refugees in Scotland and on the Border. Even supposing that the sons of Harold made no pretensions to the crown, there must have been some jealousy and confusion in this confederacy; for while one party to it held the weak Edgar as legitimate sovereign, another maintained that by right of succession the King of Denmark was King of England. It seems well established that the Danish monarch, Sweyn Estridsen, held the latter opinion; and the ill success of the confederacy may probably be attributed to the disunion inevitably arising from such clashing interests and pretensions. As soon as the battle of Hastings was known, and before any invitations were sent over, Sweyn had contemplated a descent on England. To avert this danger, William had recourse to Adelbert, the Archbishop of Bremen, who, won by persuasion and presents of large sums of money, undertook the negotiation, and endeavoured to make the Danish king renounce his project.

Two years passed without anything more being heard of the Danish invasion; but when in this, the third year after the battle of Hastings, the solicitations of the English emigrants were more urgent than ever, and the men of the north, his natural allies, were up in arms, the powerful Dane despatched a fleet of 240 sail, with orders to act in conjunction with the King of Scotland and the Northumbrians. The army embarked in this fleet was composed of almost as many heterogeneous materials as the mercenary force of William; besides Danes and Holsteiners, there were Frisians, Saxons, Poles, and adventurers from other countries, tempted by the hope of plunder.[1] The Danish king gave the supreme command of the fleet to his brother Osborn. After alarming the Normans in the south-east, at Dover, Sandwich, and Ipswich, the Danes went northward to the Humber, and sailed up that estuary to the Ouse, where they landed about the middle of August. It appears that Osborn was not able to prevent his motley army from plundering and wasting the country. As

---

[1] Southey, *Naval Hist.*

soon, however, as the Anglo-Danes, the men of Yorkshire and Northumberland, were advised of the arrival of the armament, they flocked to join it from all parts of the country; and Edgar Atheling, with Marleswine, Cospatric, Waltheof the son of Siward, the great enemy of Macbeth, Archil, the five sons of Carl, and many other English nobles, arrived from the frontiers of Scotland, bearing the consoling assurance that, in addition to the force they brought with them, Malcolm Canmore was advancing with a Scottish army to support the insurgents. York was close at hand, and they determined to commence operations by the attack of the Norman fortifications in that city. The Normans had rendered the walls of the town so strong that they defended them seven days; on the eighth day of the siege they set fire to the houses that stood near their citadels, in order that their assailants might not use the materials to fill up the ditches of the castles, and then they shut themselves up within those lines. A strong wind arose—the flames spread in all directions; the minster, or cathedral church, with its famous library, and great part of the city, was consumed; and even within their castles the Normans saw themselves threatened with a horrid death by the fire they had kindled. Preferring death by the sword and battle-axe to being burned alive, they made a sally, and were slain, almost to a man, by an enemy far superior in number, and inflamed with the fiercest hatred. They had suffered no such loss since the fight of Hastings; 3000 Normans and mercenaries of different races fell; and only William Malet, the governor of York, with his wife and children, and a few other men of rank, were saved and carried on board the Danish fleet, where they were kept for ransom. Such parts of the city of York as escaped the conflagration were occupied by or for Edgar Atheling. A rapid advance to the south, after the capture of York, with no enemy in their rear, might have insured the confederates a signal and perhaps a decisive success; but the King of Scotland did not appear with his promised army, and at the approach of winter the Danes retired to their ships in the Humber, or took up quarters between the Ouse and the Trent. William was thus allowed time to collect his forces and bring over fresh troops from the Continent.

The Conqueror was hunting in the forest of Dean when he received the first news of the catastrophe of York; and then and there he swore, by the splendour of the Almighty, that he would utterly exterminate the Northumbrian people, nor ever lay down his lance when he had once taken it up, until he had done the deed. He forthwith opened secret negotiations with Osbeorn, and finally succeeded, by means of gold and other presents, in inducing him to agree to withdraw his Danish fleet and army, and to give no more assistance to the Northumbrians. With the earliest spring William took the field, riding at the head of the finest and most numerous cavalry that had ever been seen in England, and causing his infautry to follow by forced marches. As he thus advanced the English rose nearly everywhere in his rear, recommencing a war on many different points at once. An inferior commander would have been confused by this multiplicity of attacks, and inevitably ruined; but William did not suffer his attention to be distracted, and steadily pursued his course to the north, where he knew the great blow must be struck.

The defenders of York learned nearly at the same moment that the ruthless Conqueror was approaching their walls, and that their faithless allies, the Danes, had abandoned them, and were sailing away for the south, where, according to the compact they had made, they were to be permitted to victual, and to plunder the English. Abandoned as they were, and ill provided with defences—for in their rage they had utterly destroyed the two castles—they made an obstinate resistance; nor was York taken until many hundreds of English and Normans lay dead together. Edgar Atheling, escaping with his life, and little else, fled for a second time to the court of the Scottish king. Elated by his victory, William spent but a short time in York, and then continued his march northward. His rage had not moderated with time, and he thought it wise and good policy to carry into effect the fearful vow he had made in the forest of Dean. His troops required no excitement from him; the destruction of their comrades at Durham and York in the preceding year, and the loss they had just sustained themselves at the latter city, rankled in their savage minds, and they threw themselves on the territory of Northumbria in a frenzy of vengeance, wasting the cultivated fields, burning towns and villages, and massacring indiscriminately flocks, herds, and men. To accomplish this havoc over a great width of country, they marched in separate columns. An English army, commanded by Cospatric, and very inferior in numbers, retreated before the Normans into Scotland. Egelwin, the Bishop of Durham—the same who had given the fruitless warning to Robert de Comine—assembled the inhabitants of that city, and, like a good shepherd, proposed to conduct his flock to a place of safety, out of the reach of what an old rhyming chronicler calls "Normans, Burgolouns,[1] thieves, and felons." Leaving their homes to become the prey of the enemy, but

---

[1] Burgundians.

carrying with them the body or bones of St. Cuthbert, these wretched people followed their bishop across the Tyne to Lindisfarne or Holy Island, near the mouth of the Tweed; and the Normans a second time entered Durham, but in such force as to leave them no grounds for apprehending a repetition of the tragedy that had terminated their first visit. Having fortified Durham, the invaders pushed forward to the Tyne, continuing their work of devastation, and feeling their thirst for blood unslaked. A havoc more complete and diabolical was never perpetrated. The Norman and French chroniclers and historians join the English in narrating and deploring the catastrophe which, even in those times of violence and blood, seems to have overpowered men's minds with a wild horror and wonderment. William of Malmesbury, who wrote in the reign of Stephen, about eighty years after, says, "From York to Durham not an inhabited village remained. Fire, slaughter, and desolation made a vast wilderness there, which continues to this day." From Durham north to Hexham, from the Wear to the Tyne, the remorseless Conqueror continued the same infernal process. Orderic Vitalis denounces the "*feralis occisio*," the dismal slaughter; and says that more than 100,000 victims perished. The fields in culture were burned, and the cattle and the corn in the barns carried off by the conquerors, who made a famine where they could not maintain themselves by the sword. After eating the flesh of dead horses which the Normans left behind them, the people of Yorkshire and Northumberland, driven to the last extremity, are said to have made many a loathsome repast on human flesh.[1] Pestilence followed in the wake of famine; and as a completion to this picture of horror, we are informed that some of the English, to escape death by hunger, sold themselves, with their wives and children, as slaves to the Norman soldiery, who were well provided with corn and provisions, purchased on the Continent with gold and goods robbed from the English.

On his return from Hexham to York, by an imperfectly known and indirect route across the Fells, William was well nigh perishing. The snow was still deep in those parts, and the rivers, torrents, ravines, and mountains continually presented obstacles to which the Normans had been little accustomed in the level counties of England. The army fell into confusion, the king lost the track, and passed a whole night without knowing where he was, or what direction his troops had taken. He did not reach York without a serious loss, for he left behind him most of his horses, which were said to have perished in the snow; his men also suffered the severest privations.

Confiscation now became almost general. All property in land, whether belonging to patriotic chiefs, or to men who had taken no active part in the conflict, began to pass into the possession of the Normans and other foreigners. Nor was movable property safer or more respected. William's commissioners, who in many places performed their work sword in hand, did not always draw a distinction between the plate and jewels left in deposit and the treasures that belonged to the monasteries themselves, but carried off the church ornaments and the vessels of silver or gold that were attached to the service of the altar. They also removed or destroyed all deeds and documents, charters of immunities, and evidences of property. The newly-conquered territory in the north was distributed in immense lots. William de Garenne had twenty-eight villages; William de Percy more than eighty manors. In *Doomsday Book*, which was drawn up fifteen

KEEP OF RICHMOND CASTLE,[2] Yorkshire.—Whitaker's *History of Richmondshire.*

years after the Norman occupation of them, most of these domains are described as lying fallow or waste. Vast tracts of country to the north of the city of York fell to the lot of Allan the Bre-

---

[1] *Florent. Wigorn.*

[2] Richmond Castle is understood to have been founded by Alan Rufus, son of Hoel, Count of Bretagne, a kinsman of William the Conqueror, by whom he was created Earl of Richmond. It is situated on a precipitous rock, which rises upwards of 100 ft. above the river Swale. The successors to the founder in the earldom of Richmond added to the exterior defences, but the Norman keep, about 100 ft. high, with walls 11 ft. thick, remains unchanged, and almost entire.

ton, who erected a castle and other works of defence on a steep hill, nearly surrounded on all sides by the river Swale. Like most of the chiefs of the conquering army, he gave a French name to the place—he called it *Richemont* or Richmount, now Richmond. Dreux Bruère, the chief of a band of Flemish auxiliaries, had the eastern part of Yorkshire between the rivers and the sea. The territory of this Fleming was afterwards conferred on Eudes of Champaign, who married a half-sister of the Conqueror. When Eudes' wife was delivered of a son, he represented to the king that his lands were not at all fertile, producing only oats, and prayed he would make him a grant of an estate proper to bear wheat, that he might have wherewith to make wheaten bread for his infant, the king's nephew. King William presented him with some lands to his heart's wish, in Lincolnshire. Gamel, who came from Meaux, with a troop of his own townsmen, established himself in lands adjoining the Yorkshire possessions of Eudes of Champaign; and Basin, Sivard, Fraucon, and Richard D'Estoutevilleare mentioned as landholders and neighbours of Gamel of Meaux. The vast domain of Pontefract was the share of Gilbert de Lacy, who soon afterwards extended the Norman conquest in Lancashire and Cheshire, and obtained three estates still more extensive.[1] Every baron erected his castle; and in every populous town there was a strong fortress, where the Normans confined the principal natives as hostages, and into which they could retire in case of an insurrection. William did not advance farther than Hexham; but some of his captains continued the progress both to the north and to the west, though their tenure of the land was scarcely secured until some years later, when the mountainous country of Westmoreland and Cumberland, and the adjacent part of Northumberland, were reduced by various chiefs. The first Earl of Cumberland was a certain Renouf Meschines, who divided the domains and handsome women of the country among his followers, thus following out the feudal system fully established by William. Simon, the son of Thorn, the English proprietor of two rich manors, had three daughters; one of these Meschines gave to Humphrey, his man-at-arms; the second he gave to Raoul, nicknamed *Tortes-mains* (crooked hands); and the third he reserved for his squire, William of St. Paul. In the north of Northumberland, Ives de Vescy took possession of the town of Alnwick, along with the granddaughter and all the inheritance of a Saxon who had died in battle. Robert de Bruce obtained, by conquest, several manors, and the dues of Hartlepool, the seaport of Durham. Robert D'Omfreville had the forest of Riddesdale, which belonged to Mildred the Saxon, the son of Akman. On his receiving investiture of this domain, D'Omfreville swore that he would clear the land of wolves and the enemies of the Conqueror. The nominal government of Northumberland was, however, intrusted to a native who had recently borne arms against William. This was Cospatric, who came in with Waltheof, the brave son of Siward, with Morcar and Edwin, the brothers-in-law of King Harold, and submitted to William for the second time, being probably induced thereto by liberal promises from the Conqueror, who then considered them as the main prop of the English cause, wanting whom Edgar Atheling would at once fall into insignificance. The reward of Cospatric we have mentioned; Waltheof was made Earl of Huntingdon and Northampton, and received the hand of Judith, one of King William's nieces; and Morcar and Edwin were restored to their paternal estates. In reality, however, these four men were little better than prisoners, and three of them perished miserably in a very short time.[2]

The insurrections which broke out in William's rear, during his march to York, were partially suppressed by his lieutenants, who suffered some

---

[1] Thierry, *Histoire de la Conquête*.
[2] "A peculiar aspect is given to the English annals by the Norman conquest. In tracing the progress of the other great nations of modern Europe, from their first establishment on the ruins of the Roman empire to their full development as states and kingdoms, we pursue our inquiries, amidst the changes and revolutions of dynasties, with difficulty and hesitation; yet we do not meet with any catastrophe occasioning so sudden and jarring an interruption as that great event, which, considered as an historical incident, has no parallel in character. Even in Spain, where so many kingdoms were rendered aliens to Christendom, the lineal succession of the nation seems to be more unbroken than in England. We arrive at the period when the whole Gothic monarchy is sheltered in the caverns of Covadonga, yet it still survives; Pelayo and his descendants are the lawful successors of Hermeneric and Athanagild; Castile and Leon are gradually repeopled by those who, proud of the name of Goths, issue forth from the mountain fastnesses, in which they have preserved the laws which their ancestors adopted and the language which they assumed. Not so in England, where the Norman conquest forms a dark, determined boundary-line—where the accession of William becomes an era upon which we are accustomed to found chronologies and calculations—a term of beginning and of ending. Hence it has become extremely difficult to disconnect the train of ideas suggested by the Conquest, from the views which we take of Anglo-Saxon history and of the growth and progress of the law; and we should be always on our guard lest we should be misled by the impressions which we unconsciously receive.

"Whatever colour of right may be given to the title by which William claimed the crown—by whatever efforts he may have attempted to acquire the character of a lawful sovereign, and not of an invader—still his triumph appeared to place the English people in the lowest state of degradation. Even after the lapse of centuries, the Conquest could not be considered with impartiality; for when England was contending against those sovereigns who laboured to subvert her civil and religious liberties, the arguments founded upon the occupation of the kingdom by the Normans were still mooted by the zealous advocates who fanned the flames of mutual hostility, and who prosecuted their discussions, not as points of abstract inquiry, or as the themes of historical research, but as subjects of vital and practical importance. *Doomsday* was the authentic record of the entire and unqualified subjection of the

reverses, and perpetrated great cruelties. The garrison of Exeter, besieged by the people of Cornwall, was relieved by Fitz-Osborne; Montacute repulsed the insurgents of Devonshire and Somersetshire; and Edric the Forester, who took the town of Shrewsbury, with the help of the men of Chester and some Welsh, was foiled in his attempt to reduce the castle. The whole of the north-west was, however, in a very insecure state; and the haste with which William marched thither on his return to York from Hexham, seems to denote some greater peril on the side of the Normans than is expressed by any of the annalists. The weather was still inclement, and his troops were fatigued by their recent exertions, their rapid marches and counter-marches in Northumberland; yet he led them, amidst storms of sleet and hail, across the mountains which divide our island lengthwise, and which have been called, not inappropriately, the Appenines of England. The roads he took, as being those which led direct to Chester, were scarcely passable for cavalry, and his troops were annoyed and disheartened by actual difficulties and prospective hardships and dangers. The auxiliaries, particularly the men of Anjou and Brittany, began to murmur aloud; and not a few of the Normans, complaining of the hard service to which their chief was exposing them, talked of returning beyond sea. William silenced their murmurs with his wonted art; and on the rough way over the wealds he partook in the fatigues

WATER TOWER AND WALLS OF CHESTER.[1]—J. Skinner Prout, from his sketch on the spot.

of the common soldiers, marching on foot with them, and faring as they fared. Chester, which still retained the outer features of a Roman city, and where the Conqueror gazed on Roman walls and gates then comparatively entire, had not yet been invaded by the Normans. No defence, however, was attempted there; and, after entering in triumph, William proceeded to lay the foundations of a new and strong castle, while detachments of his army reduced the surrounding country. During the Conqueror's stay Edric the Forester submitted, and was received into favour. From Chester William marched to Salisbury, where he distributed rewards among the mercenaries, a part of whom he disbanded; and from Salisbury he repaired to his strong citadel or palace at Winchester, which city became a favourite abode with him, as it had been with his Saxon predecessors. To retain the newly-conquered province in the north-west, he had left a strong body of troops behind him, under the command of a Fleming, named Gherband, who became the first

---

English race in the eyes of the inculcators of indefeasible hereditary right, who sought to prove that all the boasted franchises of England had proceeded from the mere motion and bounty of the sovereign, and were therefore revocable at the will and pleasure of him who had made the grants. In reasoning against these opinions, the earnest antagonists of prerogative and arbitrary power sought to strengthen the rights of the people by the assertion of their antiquity; they discovered the English parliament, with all its powers and members, in the obscure witenagemot of the Saxon age, and endeavoured to prove that the safeguards of liberty survived, though Harold had fallen on the field."—Palgrave, *The Rise and Progress of the English Commonwealth*, vol. i. p. 51.

[1] Chester is conjectured to have had its origin in one of the fortresses constructed by Ostorius Scapula, for the security of the Roman army after the discomfiture of Caractacus. It is certain that Chester was a walled city before 908, and there is no reason to doubt that the walls were originally built by the Romans. It had four principal gates, besides posterns—these were the North-gate, East-gate, Bridge-gate, and Water-gate; and on the walls there were formerly several towers. The Water Tower projects towards the river Dee, and large iron rings are attached to it, for the purpose of fastening vessels, which, before the harbour was choked with sands, came up to the walls.—Lyson's *Magna Britannia*.

Count or Earl of Chester. This Gherbaud was soon wearied by the constant fatigues and dangers of his post; for the English rose whenever they found an opportunity, and the mountaineers from North Wales harassed them incessantly, so that he was glad to resign his command, fiefs, and honours, and return to his own country. The Conqueror then granted the earldom of Chester to Hugh D'Avranches, a more warlike and much fiercer commander, who earned, even in that age, the surname of "the Wolf." Not satisfied with defensive operations, the new earl immediately crossed the Dee, invaded North Wales, made himself master of a part of Flintshire, and built a castle at Rhuddlan, thus taking an important step

RHUDDLAN CASTLE, Flintshire.[1] —Gorse's Antiquities.

towards the subjugation of the Welsh, a project the Normans never abandoned until it was completed, two centuries later, by Edward I. Hugh the Wolf and his ferocious followers, roused to even more than their usual ferocity by the obstinate and fierce resistance they encountered, shed the blood of the Welsh like water, and burned and wasted their houses and lands. The fearful tragedy of Northumberland and Yorkshire was repeated on a smaller scale in this corner of the island, and famine and pestilence stalked along the banks of the Clwyd, the Dee, and the Mersey, as they had done by the rivers of the north-eastern coast.

The disturbances on the eastern coast, which had been overlooked, now grew to such importance as to demand attention. Hereward, "England's darling," as he was called by his admiring countrymen, was Lord of Brunn or Bourn, in Lincolnshire, and one of the most resolute chiefs the Normans ever had to encounter. Having expelled the foreigners who had taken possession of his patrimony, he assisted his neighbours in doing the like, and then established a fortified camp in the Isle of Ely, where he raised the banner of independence, and bade defiance to the Conqueror. His power or influence soon extended along the eastern sea-line, over the fen country of Lincolnshire, Huntingdon, and Cambridge; and English refugees of all classes—thanes dispossessed of their lands, bishops deprived of their mitres, abbots driven from their monasteries to make room for foreigners—repaired from time to time to his "camp of refuge." The jealous fears of the king increased the danger they were intended to lessen. Though Edwin and Morcar remained perfectly quiet, and showed every disposition to keep their oaths of allegiance, he dreaded them, on account of their great popularity with their countrymen, and he finally resolved to seize their persons. The two earls received timely notice of this intention, and secreted themselves. When he thought the vigilance of the Normans was lulled, Edwin endeavoured to escape to the Scottish border; but he was betrayed by three of his attendants, and fell on the road, gallantly fighting against his Norman pursuers, who cut off his head, and sent it as an acceptable present to the Conqueror.[2] Morcar effected his escape to the morasses of Cambridgeshire, and joined Hereward, whose camp was further crowded about this time by many of the English chiefs of the north, who had been driven homeless into Scotland. Among the ecclesiastics of Northumbria who took this course was Egelwin, the Bishop of Durham. Even Stigand, the Primate of all England, but now degraded by king and pope, and replaced by Lanfranc, an Italian, is mentioned among the refugees of Ely.[3]

---

[1] This castle stands on the eastern side of the river Clwyd, within about two miles of its influx into the sea. It was built, according to Camden, by Llewellin ap Sitshilt, Prince of Wales, and is reported to have been a principal palace of the Welsh princes; but was burned, A.D. 1063, in an excursion made by Harold, afterwards King of England, in retaliation for the depredations committed by the Welsh on the English borders. It was strengthened by Edward I. in 1275. It belongs to the crown.

[2] *Orderic. Vital.*; *H. Hunt.*

[3] M. Thierry's view of the Norman conquest is, that it was the result of a conspiracy between Rome and William of Normandy.

WILLIAM THE CONQUEROR.

William at length moved with a formidable army. The difficulties of this war on the eastern coast was different from, but not inferior to what the Normans had encountered in the west and the north. There were no mountains and defiles, but the country was in good part a swamp, on which no cavalry could tread; it was cut in all directions by rivers, and streams, and broad meres; and the few roads that led through this dangerous labyrinth were little known to the foreigners. The country, too, where the banner of independence floated was a sort of holy land to the English; the abbeys of Ely, Peterborough, Thorney, and Croyland, the most ancient, the most revered of their establishments, stood within it; and the monks, however professionally timid or peaceful, were disposed to resistance—for they well knew that the coming of the Normans would be the signal for driving them from their monasteries.

During two or three years the Conquest was checked in this direction. The Normans, surprised among the bogs and the tall rushes that covered them, suffered many severe losses. The sagacious eye of William at last saw that the proper way of proceeding would be by a blockade that should prevent provisions and succour from reaching the Isle of Ely. He accordingly stationed all the ships he could collect in the Wash, with orders to watch every inlet from the sea to the fens; and he so stationed his army as to block up every road that led into the fens by land. When he resumed more active operations, he undertook a work of great note and difficulty.

---

which had been maturing for years, and which had for its grand object the humiliation of the Anglo-Saxon Church and people, by subjecting the one to the absolute empire of the pope, and the other to the civil and military despotism of the Norman bastard. This view he supports by special proofs; but the strongest is, doubtless, to be found in the Normans in general, and William in particular, being so largely endowed with those qualities which Rome required, and which she knew so well how to enlist in her service. Rome's quarrel with Anglo-Saxon England, for want of absolute submission to her will, bore a striking analogy to her quarrel with the inhabitants of Dauphiné, Provence, and Languedoc, not long after, for the same deadly offence. In both cases the revenge taken by her wounded pride was fierce, bloody, relentless; and in both her grand agents were the feudal chiefs of the north of France, whom she employed also in enslaving Ireland to her will.

The following facts, from that author's *History of the Norman Conquest*, are in this view particularly memorable:—

"From the period of England's deliverance from the Danish domination, King Canute's law for raising the yearly impost of Peter's pence, had shared the fate of all the other laws decreed by the foreign government. The public administration compelled no one to observe it, and Rome now received from England only the offerings and free gifts of individual devotion. Thus the ancient regard of the Romish Church for the English nation rapidly declined. Conversations to their and their king's prejudice were held in enigmatical language, in the halls of St. John of Lateran."

Rome, accustomed to sell all things herself, accused the Anglo-Saxon bishops of simony. Eldred, as Archbishop of York, went to Rome for the pallium, and obtained it only on an Anglo-Saxon chief, who had accompanied him, threatening that, if refused, he would obtain a law prohibiting the sending of money to Rome. Hence deep resentment was felt even in granting the pallium.

"The Norman, Robert de Jumièges, expelled by the Anglo-Saxon patriots from the see of Canterbury, immediately went to Rome, and denounced Stigand, the native churchman whom the national desire had put in his place, and returned to Normandy with papal letters, declaring him to be lawful archbishop. . . . The journey from Canterbury to Rome was in those days a painful one; Stigand was in no haste to go and justify himself before the fortunate rival of Benedict X.; and the old leaven of hatred against the English people fermented more strongly than ever."

Finally, Lanfranc, a monk of Lombard origin, famous for his knowledge of the civil law, after having incurred William's displeasure by blaming his marriage with Matilda as a kinswoman within the forbidden degrees, found it convenient to seek a reconciliation with so powerful a prince by pleading the cause of that very marriage with the pope, and obtaining a formal dispensation for it. Thus "he became the soul of his (William's) councils, and his plenipotentiary at the court of Rome. The respective pretensions of the Romish clergy and the Duke of Normandy, with regard to England, and the possibility of realizing them, and of meeting with joint success therein, were, it would appear, from that time the subject of serious negotiations. An armed invasion was, perhaps, not yet thought of; but William's relationship to Edward seemed one great cause for hope, and, at the same time, an incontestible title in the eyes of the Roman priests, who favoured throughout Europe the maxims of hereditary royalty, in opposition to the practice of election."

"The Duke of Normandy preferred an accusation of sacrilege against his enemy before the pontifical court; he demanded that England should be laid under interdict by the church, and declared to be the property of him who should first take possession, with the reservation of the pope's approval. . . . But Harold was in vain cited to defend himself before the tribunal of Rome. He refused to acknowledge himself amenable to that court; he deputed no ambassador thither, being too haughty to submit the independence of his crown to any foreign dictation, and, at the same time, possessed of too much good sense to confide in the impartiality of judges appealed to by his enemy."

Add to this, that Norman knights had been of great service to the Roman see already in Italy. In short, Hildebrand, whose constant object it was to transform the religious supremacy of Rome into an universal sovereignty over all Christian states, began to consider the Normans as destined to fight all its battles, and to do homage to it for its conquests.

Such, says Thierry, were the very singular relations which accidental events had recently established, when the complaints and the appeal of the Duke of Normandy were laid before the court of Rome. Fraught with his long-cherished hope, Archdeacon Hildebrand thought the propitious hour had arrived for attempting, with regard to the kingdom of England, those designs which had been so happily carried into effect in Italy. His most strenuous efforts were directed to substitute, instead of ecclesiastical pleadings relative to the lukewarmness of the English people, the simony of its prelates and the perjury of its king, a formal treaty with the Norman *for the conquest of the island at common cost and for mutual profit*. Although the real design was thus converted to a purely political purpose, the cause of William against Harold was examined in the conclave, without other motive appearing than to sift the question of hereditary right, or to uphold the sanctity of an oath as inviolable, and the veneration for relics as obligatory. These pleas, to many of the judges, seemed not enough to justify the church in sanctioning hostile aggression against a Christian nation, or a military invasion of its territory. When Hildebrand insisted, loud murmurs arose, the more conscientious prelates declaring that it would be infamous to authorize so murderous a course; but he was not to be moved, and his sentiments prevailed at last.

"According to the terms of the Papal sentence, pronounced by the pope himself, William, Duke of Normandy, had leave to enter England, *to bring it back to its obedience to the Holy See*, and to re-establish for ever the tax of St. Peter's pence. Harold and all his adherents were excommunicated by a Papal bull, transmitted to William by the hands of his envoy; and to it was added the gift of a banner from the apostolical church, and a ring, containing one of St. Peter's hairs, enchased beneath a diamond of some price."

In order to approach the fortified camp in the midst of marshes, and an expanse of water in some places shallow, in others deep, he began to build a wooden causeway, two miles long, with bridges over the beds of the rivers. Hereward frequently interrupted these operations, and in a manner so murderous, sudden, and mysterious, that the affrighted workmen and soldiers became firmly convinced that he was leagued with the devil, and aided by some necromancer. William, who had brought over with him from Normandy a conjuror and soothsayer as an essential part of his army of invasion, was readily induced to employ a sorceress on the side of the Normans, in order to neutralize or defeat the spells of the English.[2] This sorceress was placed, with much ceremony, on the top of a wooden tower at the head of the works; but Hereward, the "cunning captain," watching his opportunity, set fire to the dry reeds and rushes; the flames were rapidly spread by the wind, and tower and sorceress, workmen and soldiers, were consumed.

When the Isle of Ely had been blockaded three months, provisions became scarce there. Those whose profession and vowed duties included frequent fasting were the first to become impatient under privation. The monks of Ely sent to the enemy's camp, offering to show a safe passage across the fens, if the king would only promise to leave them in undisturbed possession of their houses and lands. The king agreed to the condition, and two of his barons pledged their faith for the execution of the treaty. Under proper guides the Normans then found their way into the Isle of Ely, and took possession of the strong monastery which formed part of Hereward's line of defence. They killed 1000 Englishmen, that either occupied an advanced position, or had made a sortie; and then, closing round the "camp of refuge," they finally obliged the rest to lay down their arms. Some of these brave men were liberated on paying heavy fines or ransoms; some were put to death; some deprived of their sight; some maimed and rendered unfit for war, by having a right hand or a foot cut off; some were condemned to perpetual imprisonment. Hereward, the soul of the confederacy, would not submit; but making an effort which appeared desperate to all, he rushed from the beleaguered camp, and escaped by throwing himself into the marshes, where the Normans would not venture to follow him. Passing from fen to fen, he

ISLE OF ELY
AND THE
ADJOINING FEN COUNTRY.

---

[1] This map is intended to exhibit, as nearly as existing authorities render possible, the extent of the fens, with the courses of the rivers, and the direction of the adjacent sea-coast, prior to the works undertaken for their drainage. The following maps, compared with various historical notices, have served to supply the materials for its construction:—"A General Plott and Description of the Funnes and Surrounded Grounds," &c. By H. Hondius (Amstelodami, 1680?). "A Mapp of the Great Levell of the Fenns." By Sir Jonas Moore. Sixteen sheets. (London, 1684.) The roads that are indicated are mostly (if not all) of ancient date—chiefly of Roman, or else of early British construction.

[2] Croyland, it appears, had a particularly ill name in this respect; and evil spirits, that did not respect the monks, might well be supposed to have no mercy on the Normans. Camden's description of the place, however, even as it existed in his day, shows how admirably it was adapted for defence; while the abundance of water-fowl must have made starving it out almost impossible. He begins with its demonology:—

"If, out of the same author (Ingulphus), I should describe the devils of Crowland (with their blubber lips, fiery mouths, scaly faces, beetle heads, sharp teeth, long chins, hoarse throats, black skins, hump shoulders, big bellies, burning loins, bandy legs, tailed

gained the low, swampy lands in Lincolnshire, near his own estate, where he was joined by some friends, and renewed a partisan or guerilla warfare, which lasted four or five years, and cost the Normans many lives, but which could not, under existing circumstances, produce any great political result. At last, seeing the hopelessness of the struggle, he listened to terms from William, who was anxious to pacify an enemy his armies could never reach, and who probably admired, as a soldier, his wonderful courage and address. Hereward made his peace, took the oath of allegiance, and was permitted by the Conqueror to preserve and enjoy the estates of his ancestors. The exploits of the last hero of Anglo-Saxon independence formed a favourite theme of tradition and poetry; and long after his death the inhabitants of the Isle of Ely showed with pride the ruins of a wooden tower, which they called the castle of Hereward.

After the destruction of the camp of refuge in Ely, the Norman forces, naval as well as military, proceeded to the north, to disperse some bands which had again raised the standard of independence, and invoked the presence of Edgar Atheling, who was enjoying the tranquillity and obscurity for which he was fitted in Scotland. After some bloody skirmishes, the confederates were driven beyond the Tweed; and then William crossed that river, to seize the English emigrants and punish Malcolm Canmore. A Scottish army, which had been so anxiously expected by the English insurgents at York two years before, when its weight in the scale might have proved fatal to the Normans, had tardily marched, at a moment when the Northumbrians and people of Yorkshire were almost exterminated, and when it could do little more than excite the few remaining inhabitants to a hopeless rising, and burn the houses of such as refused to join in it. The want of provisions in a land laid waste soon made the Scots recross the Border. To avenge this mere predatory inroad, however, William now advanced from the Tweed to the Frith of Forth, as if he intended to subdue the whole of the "land of the mountain and flood," taking with him the entire mass of his splendid cavalry, and nearly every Norman foot-soldier he could prudently detach from garrison duty in England. The emigrants escaped his pursuit, nor would Malcolm deliver them up; but, intimidated by the advance of an army infinitely more numerous and better armed than his own, the Scottish king, says the *Saxon Chronicle*, "came and agreed with King William, and delivered hostages, and was his man; and the king went home with all his force."

On his return from Scotland, during his stay at Durham, the king summoned Cospatric to appear before him, and, on the idle ground of old grievances, which had been pardoned when that nobleman surrendered with Edwin and Morcar, he deprived him of the earldom of Northumberland, for which, it appears, he had paid a large sum of money. Cospatric, fearing worse consequences, abandoning whatever else he had in England, fled to Malcolm Canmore, who gave him a castle and lands. The earldom of Northumberland was conferred on Waltheof, an Englishman like himself, but now the nephew of the Conqueror, by marriage with his niece Judith.

The Normans had now been seven years in the land, engaged in almost constant hostilities; and at length England, with the exception of Wales, might fairly be said to be conquered. In most abridgments and epitomes of history, the events we have related, in not unnecessary detail, are so faintly indicated, and huddled together in so narrow a space, as to leave an impression that the resistance of our ancestors after the battle of Hastings was trifling and brief—that the sanguinary drama of the Conquest was almost wholly included in one act. Nothing can be more incorrect than this impression, or more unfair to that hardy race of men, who were the fountain-source of at least nine-tenths of the blood that flows in the large and generous veins of the English nation.

Not long after his return from Scotland, circumstances imperatively called for the presence of William in his continental dominions. His talents as a statesman and warrior are indisputable, yet few men have owed more to good for-

---

buttocks, &c.), which haunted these places, and very much annoyed Guthlacus and the monks, you would laugh at the history, and much more at my madness in relating it. But since the situation and nature of the place is strange, and different from all others in England, and since the monastery was particularly famous in former times, I shall give you the description of it somewhat more at large.

"This Crowland (anno 1607) lies in fens so inclosed and incompassed with deep bogs and pools, that there is no access to it but on the north and east sides, and there, too, only by narrow causeways. This monastery and Venice (if we may compare small things with great) have the same sort of situation; it consists of three streets, separated from each other by water-courses planted with willows, and raised on piles driven into the bottom of the pool, having communication by a triangular bridge of curious workmanship, under which the inhabitants say there was a very deep pit, that was dug to receive the concourse of waters there. Beyond the bridge, where, as one words it, 'a bog is become firm ground' (in solum mutatur humus), formerly stood that famous monastery, though of a small compass, about which, unless on the side where the town stands, the ground is so rotten and boggy, that a pole may be thrust down 30 ft. deep; and there is nothing round about but reeds, and, next the church, a grove of alders. However, the town is pretty well inhabited; but the cattle are kept at some distance from it, so that, when the owners milk them, they go in boats which will hold but two, called skerries. Their greatest gain is from the fish and wild-ducks that they catch, which are so many, that in August they can drive into a single net 3000 ducks at once; and they call these pools their corn-fields, there being no corn growing within five miles of the place. For this liberty of catching fish and wild ducks, they formerly paid yearly to the abbot, as they do now to the king, £3000 sterling."

time. Their wrongs and provocations were the same then as now, and policy would have suggested to the people of Maine to exert themselves a year or two before, when William, engaged in difficult wars in England, would have been embarrassed by their insurrection on the Continent. But they made their great effort just as England was reduced to the quietude of despair, and when William could proceed against them unencumbered by any other war. Herbert, the last count or national chief, bequeathed the county of Maine, bordering on Normandy, to Duke William, who, to the displeasure of the people, but without any important opposition, took possession of it several years before he invaded England. Instigated by Fulk, Count of Anjou, and vexed by a tyrannical administration, the people of Maine now rose against William, expelled the magistrates he had placed over them, and drove out from their towns the officers and garrisons of the Norman race. Deeming it imprudent to remove his Norman forces from this island, he collected a considerable army among the English population, and carrying them over to Normandy he joined them to some troops levied there, and putting himself at their head, marched into the unfortunate province of Maine. The national valour, which so often opposed him, was now exerted with a blind fury in his favour. The English beat the men of Maine, burned their towns and villages, and did as much mischief as the Normans (among whom was a strong contingent from Maine) had perpetrated in England.

While these things were passing on the Continent, Edgar Atheling received an advantageous offer of services and co-operation from Philip, King of France, who at last, and too late, roused himself from the strange sloth and indifference with which he had seen the progress made by his overgrown vassal, the Duke of Normandy. The events in Maine, the dread inspired in all the neighbouring country, even to the walls of Paris, and William's exhibition of force, were probably the immediate causes that dispelled Philip's long sleep. He invited Edgar to come to France and be present at his council, promising him a strong fortress, situated on the Channel, at a point equally convenient for making descents upon England or incursions or forays into Normandy. Closing with the proposals, Edgar got ready a few ships and a small band of soldiers—being aided therein by his sister, the Queen of Scotland, and some of the Scottish nobility—and made sail for France. His usual bad luck attended him; he had scarcely gained the open sea when a storm arose, and drove his ships ashore on the coast of Northumberland, where some of his followers were drowned, and others taken prisoners by the Normans. He and a few of his friends of superior rank escaped and got into Scotland, where they arrived in miserable plight, with nothing but the clothes on their backs, some walking on foot, some mounted on sorry beasts. After this misfortune, his brother-in-law, King Malcolm, advised him to seek a reconciliation with William, and Edgar accordingly sent a messenger to the Conqueror, who at once invited him to Normandy, where he promised proper and honourable treatment. Instead of sailing direct from Scotland, the Atheling, whose feelings were as obtuse as his intellect, took his way through England, the desolated kingdom of his ancestors, feasting at the castles of the Norman invaders as he went along. William received him with a show of kindness, and allotted him an apartment in the palace of Rouen, with a pound of silver a-day for his maintenance; and there the descendant of the great Alfred passed eleven years of his life, occupying himself with dogs and horses.

The king, who had gone to the Continent to quell one insurrection, was recalled to England by another of a much more threatening nature, planned, not by the English, but by the Norman barons, their conquerors and despoilers. William Fitz-Osborn, the prime favourite and counsellor of the Conqueror, had died a violent death in Flanders, and had been succeeded in his English domains, and the earldom of Hereford, by his son, Roger Fitz-Osborn. This young nobleman negotiated a marriage with Raoul or Ralph de Gaël, a Breton by birth, and Earl of Norfolk in England by the right of the sword. For some reason not explained, this alliance was displeasing to the king, who sent from Normandy to prohibit it. The parties were enraged at this prohibition, which they also determined not to obey; and on the day which had been previously fixed for the ceremony, Emma, the affianced, was conducted to Norwich, where a wedding-feast was celebrated, that was fatal to all who were present at it.[1] Among the guests who had been invited, rather for the after-act than to do honour to the bride and bridegroom, were Waltheof, the husband of Judith, sundry barons and bishops of the Norman race, some Saxons who were friends to the Normans, and even some chieftains from the mountains of Wales, with whom their neighbour, the Earl of Hereford, the brother of the bride, had thought proper to cultivate amicable relations. A sumptuous feast was followed by copious libations; and when the heads of the guests were heated by wine, the Earls of Hereford and Norwich, who were already committed by carrying the forbidden marriage into effect, and who knew the implacable temper of William, opened their plans with a wild and energetic

---

[1] *Chron. Sax.*

eloquence. They inveighed against the arbitrary conduct of the king, his harsh and arrogant behaviour to his noblest barons, and his apparent intention of reducing the Normans to the same condition of misery and servitude as the English, whose wrongs and misfortunes they affected to compassionate. Hereford complained of his conduct with regard to the marriage, saying it was an insult offered to the memory of his father, Fitz-Osborn, the man to whom the Bastard incontestably owed his crown. By degrees the excited assembly broke forth in one general curse against the Conqueror. The old reproach of his birth was revived over and over again. "He is a bastard, a man of base extraction," cried the Normans; "it is in vain he calls himself a king; it is easy to see he was never made to be one, and that God hath him not in his grace." "He poisoned our Conan, that brave Count of Brittany," said the Bretons. "He has invaded our noble kingdom, and massacred the legitimate heirs to it, or driven them into exile," cried the English. "He is ungrateful to the brave men who have shed their blood for him, and raised him to a higher pitch of greatness than any of his predecessors ever knew," said the foreign captains; "and what has he given to us conquerors covered with wounds? Nothing but lands naturally sterile or devastated by the war; and then, as soon as he sees we have improved those estates, he takes them from us, or diminishes their extent." The guests cried out tumultuously that all this was true—that William the Bastard was in odium with all men—that his death would gladden the hearts of men.[1]

The great object of the Norman conspirators was to gain over Earl Waltheof, whose warlike qualities and great popularity with the English were well known to them; and, when they proceeded to divulge the particulars of their plan, the Earls of Hereford and Norwich allured him with the promise of a third of England, which was to be partitioned into the old Saxon kingdoms of Wessex, Mercia, and Northumberland. With the fumes of wine in his head, and a general ardour and enthusiasm around him, Waltheof, it is said, gave his approval to the conspiracy; but, according to one version of the story, the next morning, "when he had consulted with his pillow, and awaked his wits to perceive the danger whereunto he was drawn, he determined not to move in it," and took measures to prevent its breaking out. A more generally received account, however, is, that Waltheof, seeing from the first the madness of the scheme, and the little probability it offered of benefiting the English people, refused to engage in it, and only took an oath of secrecy. The whole project, indeed, was insane; the discontented barons had scarcely a chance of succeeding against the established authority and the genius of William; and their success, had it been possible, would have proved a curse to the country; a step fatally retrograde; a going back toward the time of the Saxon Heptarchy, when England was fractured into a number of petty hostile states. It is quite certain that Waltheof never took up arms, nor did any overt act of treason, but in his uneasiness of mind, and his confidence in so dear a connection, he disclosed to his wife Judith all that had been done in Norwich Castle; and this confidence is generally believed to have been the main cause of his ruin. Roger Fitz-Osborn and Ralph de Gaël, the real heads of the confederacy, were hurried into action before their scheme was ripe, for their secret was betrayed by some one. The first of these earls, who had returned to his government, and collected his followers and a considerable number of Welsh, was checked in his attempt to cross the Severn at Worcester, nor could he find a passage at any other point, as Ours, the Viscount of Worcester, and Wulfstan the bishop, occupied the left bank of that river with a great force of Norman cavalry. Egelwin, the abbot of Evesham, who, like Wulfstan, was an Englishman, induced the population of Gloucester to rise and co-operate with the king's officers; and Walter de Lacy, a great baron in those parts, soon brought up a mixed host of English and Normans, that rendered the Earl of Hereford's project of crossing the Severn, to co-operate with his brother-in-law in the heart of England, altogether hopeless. Lanfranc, the Italian Archbishop of Canterbury, who acted as viceroy during William's absence, proceeding with the greatest decision, also sent troops from London and Winchester to oppose Fitz-Osborn, at whose head he hurled, at the same time, the terrible sentence of excommunication. In writing to the king in Normandy, the primate said, "It would be with pleasure, and as envoy of God, that we could welcome you among us; but," added the energetic old priest, "do not hurry yourself to cross the sea, for it would be putting us to shame to come and aid us in destroying such traitors and thieves." The Earl of Hereford fell back from the Severn, and his brother-in-law, the Earl of Norfolk, left to himself, and unable to procure in time assistance, for which he had applied to the Danes, was suddenly attacked by a royal army of very superior force, led on by Odo, the Bishop of Bayeux, Geoffrey, Bishop of Coutances, and Richard de Bienfait and William de Warenne, the two justiciaries of the kingdom, who obtained a complete victory, and cut off the right foot of every prisoner they made. The earl retreated to

---

[1] Wm. Malm.; Matt. Paris.; Orderic.

Norwich, garrisoned his castle with the most trusty of his followers, and, leaving his bride to defend it, passed over to Brittany, in hopes of obtaining succour from his countrymen. The daughter of William Fitz-Osborn defended Norwich Castle with great bravery; and when at the end of three months she capitulated, she obtained mild terms for her garrison, which was almost entirely composed of Bretons. They did not suffer in life or limb, but were shipped off to the Continent within the term of forty days. The Bretons generally had rendered themselves unpopular at William's court. With the true character of their race, they were irascible, turbulent, factious, and much more devoted to the head of their clan than to the king. When they were embarked, Lanfranc wrote to his master, "Glory be to God, your kingdom is at last purged of the filth of these Bretons." The king invaded Brittany, in the hope of exterminating the fugitive Earl of Norwich in his native castle, and reducing that province to entire subjection; but, after

NORWICH CASTLE, as in 1735.[1]—From Buck.

laying an unsuccessful siege to the town of Dol, he was obliged to retire before an army of Bretons, who were supported by the French king.[2] William then crossed the Channel to suppress the insurrection in England; but by the time he arrived there was little left for him to do except to punish the principal offenders. The Earl of Hereford had been followed, defeated, and taken prisoner, and many of his adherents, Welsh, English, and Normans, hanged on high gibbets, or blinded, or mutilated. At a royal court De Gaël was outlawed, and his brother-in-law, Fitz-Osborn, condemned to perpetual imprisonment and the forfeiture of his property. Scarcely one of the guests at the ill-augured marriage of Emma Fitz-Osborn escaped with life, and even the inhabitants of the town of Norwich felt the weight of royal vengeance. The last and most conspicuous victim was Waltheof, who had been guilty, at most, of a misprision of treason. His secret had been betrayed by his wife Judith, who is said, moreover, to have accused him of inviting over the Danish fleet, which now made its appearance on the coast of Norfolk. The motive that made this heartless woman seek the death of her brave and generous husband, was a passion she had conceived for a Norman nobleman, whom she hoped to marry if she could but be made a widow. Others, however, although acting under different impulses, were quite as urgent as the Conqueror's niece for the execution of the English earl. These were Norman barons, who had cast the eyes of affection on his honours and estates—"his great possessions being his greatest enemies." The judges were divided in opinion as to the proper sentence that ought to be passed upon the earl, some of them maintaining that, as a revolted *English* subject, Waltheof should be put to death; others, that as an officer of the king, and according to *Norman* law, he ought only to suffer the minor punishment of perpetual imprisonment.

---

[1] The site of Norwich Castle was probably occupied by one belonging to the East Anglian kings. It had three nearly circular concentric lines of defence, each consisting of a wall and ditch, inclosing a court. Besides these, there was the keep, the only part now standing, and which has been covered by a modern casing of granite. The whole comprehended an area of 23 acres. The inner ditch and the bridge over it still remain. The bridge is 150 ft. long, and has one arch of 40 ft. span, supposed to be the largest and most perfect arch remaining of what has been popularly but erroneously termed Saxon architecture. The wall of the innermost ballium has long been destroyed, but there are the remains of two round towers, part of the original gateway at the inner end of the bridge. The central keep is a substantial quadrangular building, of 110 ft. from east to west, including a small tower, through which was the principal entrance. From north to south it is 93 ft.; its height to the battlements is upwards of 69 ft.

[2] Daru, *Hist. de la Bretagne*.

These differences of opinion lasted nearly a whole year, during which the earl was confined in the royal citadel of Winchester. At length his wife and other enemies prevailed, the sentence of death was pronounced, and confirmed by the king, who is said to have long wished for the opportunity of putting him out of his way. The unfortunate son of that great and good Earl Siward, whom Shakspeare has immortalized, was executed on a hill a short distance from the town of Winchester, at a very early hour in the morning, and in great haste, lest the citizens should become aware of his fate, and attempt a rescue.[1] His body was thrown into a hole dug at a cross-road, and covered with earth in a hurry; but the king was induced to permit its removal thence, and the English monks of Croyland, to whom the deceased earl had been a benefactor, took it up and carried it to their abbey, where they gave it a more honourable sepulture. The patriotic superstition of the nation soon converted the dead warrior into a saint, and the universal grief of the English people found some consolation in giving a ready credence to the miracles said to be performed at his tomb. The Anglo-Saxon hagiology seems to have abounded, beyond that of most other nations, in unfortunate patriots and heroes who had fallen in battle against the invaders of the country. And what became of the widow of the brave son of Siward—of the "infamous Judith," as she is called by nearly all the chroniclers? So far from permitting her to marry the man of whom she was enamoured, her uncle William, who was most despotic in these matters, and claimed as part of his prerogative the right of disposing of female wards, insisted on her giving her hand to one Simon, a Frenchman of Senlis, a very brave soldier, but lame and deformed; and when the perverse widow rejected the match with insulting language, he drove her from his presence, deprived her of all Waltheof's estates, and gave them to Simon, without the incumbrance of such a wife. Cast from the king's favour, and reduced to poverty, she became almost as unpopular with the Normans as she was with the English; and the wretched woman, hated by all, or justly contemned, passed the rest of her life in wandering in different corners of England, seeking to hide her shame in remote and secluded places.

The Normans had been gradually encroaching on the Welsh territory, both on the side of the Dee and on the side of the Severn, and now William in person led a formidable army into Wales, where he is said to have struck such terror, that the native princes performed feudal homage to him at St. David's, and delivered many hostages

[1] Orderic gives some curious particulars respecting the execution.

and Norman and English prisoners, with which he returned as a "victorious conqueror." In the north of England he made no further progress, and had considerable difficulty in retaining the land he had occupied. The Scots again crossed the Tweed and the Tyne, and much harassed the Norman barons. At the approach of a superior army they retired; but William's officers did not follow them, and the only result of the expedition, on the king's side, was the founding of the city of Newcastle-upon-Tyne. The impression made upon Scotland by the Conqueror when he had marched in person, must have been of the slightest kind, and his circumstances never permitted him to return.

A.D. 1077-9. He was now wounded by the sharp tooth of filial disobedience, and obliged to be frequently, and for long intervals, on the Continent, where a fierce and unnatural war was waged between father and son. When William first received the submission of the province of Maine, he had promised the inhabitants to make his eldest son, Robert, their prince; and before departing for the conquest of England he stipulated that, in case of succeeding in his enterprise, he would resign the duchy of Normandy to the same son. So confident was he of success, that he permitted the Norman chiefs, who consented to and legalized the appointment, to swear fealty and render homage to young Robert as their future sovereign. But all this was done to allay the jealousy of the King of France and his other neighbours, uneasy at the prospect of his vastly extending power; and when he was firmly seated in his conquest, and had strengthened his hands, William openly showed his determination of keeping and ruling both his insular kingdom and his continental duchy. Grown up to man's estate, Robert claimed what he considered his right. "My son, I wot not to throw off my clothes till I go to bed," was the homely but decisive answer of his father. Robert was brave to rashness, ambitious, impatient of command; and a young prince in his circumstances was never yet without adherents and counsellors, to urge him to those extreme measures on which they found their own hopes of fortune and advancement. He was suspected of fanning the flames of discontent in Brittany as well as in Maine, and to have had an understanding with the King of France, when that monarch frustrated William's attempt to seize the fugitive Breton, Raoul de Gaël, and forced the King of England to raise the siege of Dol. Some circumstances, which added to the number of the unnatural elements already engaged, made Robert declare himself more openly. In person he was less favoured by nature than his two younger brothers, William and Henry, who seemed to engross all their father's favour, and who probably made an improper use of the nickname of *Courte-heuse*,[1] which was given to Robert on account of the shortness of his legs. One day, when the king and his court were staying in the little town of L'Aigle, William and Henry went to the house of a certain Roger Chaussiègue, which had been allotted to their brother Robert for his lodging, and installed themselves, without his leave, in the upper gallery or balcony. After playing for a time at dice, "as was the fashion with military men,"[2] they began to make a great noise and uproar, and then they finished their boyish pranks by emptying a pitcher of water on the heads of Robert and his comrades, who were passing in the court below. Robert, naturally passionate, probably required no additional incentive; but it is stated that one of his companions, Alberic de Grantmesnil, a son of Hugh de Grantmesnil, whom King William had formerly deprived of his estates in England, instigated the prince to resent the action of his brothers as a public affront, which could not be borne in honour. Robert drew his sword and ran up stairs, vowing that he would wipe out the insult with blood. A great tumult followed, and the king, who rushed to the spot, had much difficulty in quelling it. That very night Robert fled with his companions to Rouen, fully determined to raise the standard of revolt. He failed in his first attempt, which was to take the castle of Rouen; and soon after some of his warmest partisans were surprised and made prisoners by the king's officers. The prince escaped across the frontiers of Normandy into the district of Le Perche, where Hugh, nephew of Albert le Ribaud, welcomed him, and sheltered him in his castles of Sorel and Reynalard. By the mediation of his mother, who seems to have been fondly attached to him, Robert was reconciled to his father; but the reconciliation did not last long, for the prince was as impatient for authority as ever; and the young counsellors who surrounded him found it unseemly, and altogether abominable, that he should be left so poor, through the avarice of his father, as not to have a shilling to give his faithful friends who followed his fortunes.[3] Thus excited, Robert went to his father, and again demanded possession of Normandy; but the king again refused him, exhorting him, at the same time, to change his associates for serious old men, like the royal counsellor and prime minister, Archbishop Lanfranc. "Sire," said Robert bluntly, "I came here to claim my right, and not to listen to sermons; I heard plenty of them, and tedious ones, too, when I was learning my grammar;" and then he added that he insisted on a positive answer to his demand of the duchy. The king wrathfully replied that he would never give up Normandy, his native land, nor share with another any part of England, which he had won with his own toil and peril. "Well, then," said Robert, "I will go and bear arms among strangers, and perhaps I shall obtain from them what is refused to me by my father."[4] He set out accordingly, and wandered through Flanders, Lorraine, Gascony, and other lands, visiting dukes, counts, and rich burgesses, relating his grievances and asking assistance; but all the money he got on these eleemosynary circuits he dissipated among minstrels and jugglers, parasites and prostitutes, and was thus obliged to go again a-begging, or borrow money at an enormous interest. Queen Matilda, whose maternal tenderness was not estranged by the follies and vices of her son, contrived to remit him several sums when he was in great distress. William discovered this, and sternly forbade it for the future. But her heart still yearning for the prodigal, the queen made further remittances, and her secret was again betrayed. The king then reproached her, in bitter terms, for distributing among his enemies the treasures he gave her to guard for himself, and ordered the arrest of Samson, her messenger, who had carried the money, and whose eyes he vowed to tear out as a proper punishment. Samson, who was a Breton, took to flight, and became a monk, "for the salvation both of body and soul."[5]

After leading a vagabond life for some time, Robert repaired to the French court, and King Philip, still finding in him the instrument he wanted, openly espoused his cause, and established him in the castle of Gerberoy, on the very confines of Normandy, where he supported himself by plundering the neighbouring country, and whence he corresponded with the disaffected in the duchy. Knights and troops of adventurers on horseback flocked to share the plunder and the pay he now had to offer them: in the number were as many Norman as French subjects, and not a few men of King William's own household. Burning with rage, the king crossed the Channel with a formidable English army, and came in person to direct the siege of the strong castle of Gerberoy, where he lost many men in fruitless operations, and from sorties made by the garrison. With all his faults, Robert had many good and generous qualities, which singularly endeared him to his friends when living, and which, along with his cruel misfortunes, caused him to be mourned when dead. Ambition, passion, and evil counsel had lulled and stupefied, but had not extirpated his natural feelings. One day, in a sally from his

---

[1] Literally "short-hose," or "short-boot."—*Brevis Ocrea.*—*Orderic. Vital.*
[2] "Ibique super solarium (sicut militibus mos est) tesseris ludere cœperunt."—*Orderic. Vital.* [3] Ibid.
[4] Orderic.
[5] Pro salvatione corporis et animæ.—*Orderic. Vital.*

castle, he chanced to engage in single combat with a stalwart warrior clad in mail, and concealed, like himself, with the visor of his helm. Both were valiant and well skilled in the use of their weapons; but, after a fierce combat, Robert wounded and unhorsed his antagonist. In the voice of the fallen warrior, who shouted for assistance, the prince, who was about to follow up his advantage with a death-stroke, recognized his father, and, instantly dismounting, fell on his knees, craved forgiveness with tears, and, helping him to his saddle, saw him safely out of the *mêlée*, which now thickened. The men who were coming up to the king's assistance, and bringing a second horse for him to mount, were nearly all killed. William rode away to his camp on Robert's horse, smarting with his wound, and still cursing his son, who had so seasonably mounted him.[1] He relinquished the siege of Gerberoy in despair, and went to Rouen, where, as soon as his temper permitted, his wife and bishops, with many of the Norman nobles, laboured to reconcile him again to Robert. For a long time the iron-hearted king was deaf to their entreaties, or only irritated by them. "Why," cried he, "do you solicit me in favour of a traitor who has seduced my men—my very pupils in war, whom I fed with my own bread, and invested with the knightly arms they wear?"[2] At last he yielded, and Robert, having again knelt and wept before him, received his father's pardon, and accompanied him to England. But even now the reconciliation on the part of the unforgiving king was a mere matter of policy, and Robert, finding no symptoms of returning affection, and fearing for his life or liberty, soon fled for the third time, and never saw his father's face again. His departure was followed by another paternal malediction, which was never revoked.

A.D. 1080. Walcher of Lorraine, installed in the bishopric of Durham and his strong castle "on the highest hill," united to his episcopal functions the political and military government of Northumberland. The earl-bishop boasted that he was equally skilful in repressing rebellion with the edge of the sword, and reforming the morals of the English by eloquent discourse. But the Lorrainer was a harsh taskmaster to the English, laying heavy labours and taxes upon them, and permitting the officers under him and his men-at-arms to plunder, insult, and kill them with impunity.[3] Liulf, an Englishman of noble birth, and endeared to the whole province, ventured, on being robbed by some of Walcher's satellites, to lay his complaint before the bishop. Shortly after making this accusation, Liulf was murdered by night in his manorhouse, near the city of Durham, and it was well proved that one Gilbert, and others in the bishop's service, were the perpetrators of the foul deed. "Hereupon," says an old writer, "the malice of the people was kindled against him, and when it was known that he had received the murderers into his house, and favoured them as before, they stomached the matter highly." Secret meetings were held at the dead of night, and the Northumbrians, who had lost none of their old spirit, and were absolutely driven to madness, because, among other causes of endearment, Liulf had married the widow of Earl Siward, the mother of the unfortunate Earl Waltheof, resolved to take a sanguinary vengeance. Both parties met by agreement at Gateshead;[4] the bishop, who protested his innocence of the homicide, in the pomp of power, surrounded by his retainers; the Northumbrians in humble guise, as if to petition their lord for justice, though every man among them carried a sharp weapon hid under his garment. The bishop, alarmed at the number of English that continued to flock to the place of rendezvous, retired with all his retinue into the church. The people then signified in plain terms that, unless he came forth and showed himself, they would fire the place where he stood. As he did not move, the threat was executed. Then, seeing the smoke and flames arising, he caused Gilbert and his accomplices to be thrust out of the church. The people fell with savage joy on the murderers of Liulf, and cut them to pieces. Half-suffocated by the heat and smoke, the bishop himself wrapped the skirts of his gown over his face, and came to the threshold of the door. There seems to have been a moment of hesitation; but a voice was heard among the crowd, saying, "Good rede, short rede! slay ye the bishop!" and the bishop was slain accordingly.[5] The foreigners had nothing left but the alternative of being burned alive or perishing by the sword. The bishop's chaplain seemed to give a preference to the former death, for he lingered long in the burning church; but in the end he was compelled, by the raging fire, to come out, and was also slain and hacked to pieces—"as he had well deserved," adds an old historian, "being the main promoter of all the mischief that had been done in the country."[6] Of all who had accompanied the bishop to the tragical meeting at Gateshead, only two were left alive, and these were menials of English birth. Above 100 men, Normans and Flemings, perished with Walcher.[7]

A.D. 1082. William intrusted to one bishop the office of avenging another. His

---

[1] *Chron. Sax.; Florent. Wigorn.* The story is told somewhat differently in the *Chron. Lambardi.*
[2] *Tirones meos, quos alui et armis militaribus decoravi, abduxit.—Orderic. Vital.* [3] *Matt. Paris.; Anglia Sacra.*
[4] The name means "goat's head;" "ad caput capræ."—*Florent Wigorn.* [5] *Matt. Paris.* [6] *Holinshed.*
[7] *Saxon Chronicle.*

half-brother, Odo, the fierce bishop of Bayeux, marched to Durham with a numerous army. He found no force on foot to resist him, but he treated the whole country as an insurgent province, and making no distinction of persons, and employing no judicial forms, he beheaded or mutilated all the men he could find in their houses. Some persons of property bought their lives by surrendering everything they possessed. By this exterminating expedition Odo obtained the reputation of being one of the greatest "dominators of the English;" but it seems to have been the last he commanded, and disgraced with cruelty, during the reign of William. This churchman, besides being bishop of Bayeux in Normandy, was Earl of Kent in England, and held many high offices in this island, where he had accumulated enormous wealth, chiefly by extortion, or a base selling of justice. For some years a splendid dream of ambition, which he thought he could realize by means of money, increased his rapacity. There were many instances in those ages of kings becoming monks, but not one of a Catholic priest becoming a king. Profane crowns being out of his reach, Odo aspired to a sacred one—to the tiara—that triple crown of Rome, which gradually obtained, in another shape, a homage more widely extended than that paid to the Cæsars. His dream was cherished by the predictions of some Italian astrologers, who, living in his service, and being well paid, assured him that he would be the successor of Gregory VII., the reigning pope. Odo opened a correspondence with the Eternal City by means of English and Norman pilgrims who were constantly flocking thither, bought a palace at Rome, and sent rich presents to the senators. His project was not altogether so visionary as it has been considered by most writers, and we can hardly understand why his half-brother, William, should have checked it, unless indeed his interference proceeded from his desire of getting possession of the bishop's wealth. Ten years before the Conqueror invaded England, Robert Guiscard, one of twelve heroic Norman brothers, had acquired the sovereignty of the greater part of those beautiful countries that are now included within the kingdom of Naples. The Norman lance was dreaded in all the rest of Italy, and with a Norman pope established at Rome, the supremacy of that people might have been extended from one end of the peninsula to the other. The Bishop of Bayeux had some reason for counting on the sympathy of his powerful countrymen in the south, the close neighbours of Rome; and the influence of gold had been felt before now in the college of cardinals and the elections of popes. It is quite certain that a considerable number of the Norman chiefs entered into Odo's views; and when he made up his mind to set out for Italy in person, a brilliant escort was formed for him. "Hugh the Wolf," the famous Earl of Chester, who had a long account of sin to settle—if he considered the butchering of English and Welsh as crimes—was anxious to go to Rome, and joined the bishop, with some considerable barons, his friends, and much money.

The king was in Normandy when he heard of this expedition, and being resolute in his determination of stopping it, he instantly set sail for England. He surprised the aspirant to the popedom at the Isle of Wight, seized his treasures, and summoned him before a council of Norman barons hastily assembled at that island. Here the king accused his half-brother of "untruth and sinister dealings"—of having abused his power, both as viceroy and judge, and as an earl of the realm—of having maltreated the English beyond measure, to the great danger of the common cause—of having robbed the churches of the land—and finally, of having seduced and attempted to carry out of England, and beyond the Alps, the warriors of the king, who needed their services for the safe-keeping of the kingdom. Having exposed his grievances, William asked the council what such a brother deserved at his hands? No one durst answer. "Arrest him, then!" cried the king, "and see that he be well looked to!" If they had been backward in pronouncing an opinion, they were still more averse to lay hands on a bishop; not one of the council moved, though it was the king that ordered them. William then advanced himself, and seized the prelate by his robe. "I am a clerk—a priest," cried Odo; "I am a minister of the Lord: the pope alone has the right of judging me!" But his brother, without losing his hold, replied, "I do not arrest you as Bishop of Bayeux, but as Earl of Kent."[1] Odo was carried forthwith to Normandy, and, instead of crossing the Alps and the Apennines, was shut up in a castle.

Soon after imprisoning his brother, William lost his wife, Matilda, whom he tenderly loved; and after her death it was observed or fancied he became more suspicious, more jealous of the authority of his old companions in arms, and more avaricious than ever. The coming on of old age is, however, enough in itself to account for such a change in such a man. After a lapse of ten years the Danes were again heard of, and their threats of invading England kept William in a state of anxiety for nearly two whole years, and were the cause of his laying fresh burdens upon his English subjects. He revived the odious Danegeld; and because many lands and manors which had been charged with it in the time of

---

[1] *Chron. Sax.*; *Florent.*; *Malmesb.*; *Orderic*

the Anglo-Saxon kings had been specially exempted from this tax when he granted them in fief to his nobles, he made up the deficiency by raising it upon the other lands, to the rate of six shillings a-hide. The money he thus obtained, with part of the treasures he had amassed, was employed in hiring and bringing over foreign anxiliaries; for though he could rely on an English army when fighting against Frenchmen, or the people of Normandy, Maine, and Brittany, he could not trust them at home; and he well knew that many of them on the eastern and north-eastern shores would join the Danish invaders heart and hand, instead of opposing them. He therefore collected, as he had done before, men of all nations; and these came across the Channel in such numbers that, according to the chroniclers, people began to wonder how the land could feed so many hungry bellies. These hordes of foreigners sorely oppressed the natives, for William quartered them throughout the country, to be paid as well as supported.

To complete the miseries inflicted upon England at this time, William ordered all the land lying near the sea-coast to be laid waste, so that if the Danes should land, they would find no ready supply of food or forage.[1]

The Conqueror had often felt the want of a naval force, and knowing that to encourage commerce was the best means of fostering a navy, he repeatedly invited foreigners to frequent his ports, promising that they and their property should be perfectly secure. But he did not live to possess a navy of his own.

Another domestic calamity afflicted the latter years of the Conqueror—for he saw a violent jealousy growing up between his favourite sons, William and Henry. Robert, his eldest son, continued an exile or fugitive; and Richard, his second son in order of birth (but whom some make illegitimate), had been gored to death by a stag,[2] some years before, as he was hunting in the New Forest; and he was noted by the old English annalists as being the first of several of the Conqueror's progeny that perished in that place—" the justice of God punishing in him his father's dispeopling of that country."

Perhaps no single act of the Conqueror inflicted more misery within the limits of its operation, and certainly none has been more bitterly stigmatized, than his seizure and wasting of the lands in Hampshire, to make himself a hunting-ground. Like most of the great men of the time, who had few other amusements, William was passionately fond of the chase. The Anglo-Saxon kings had the same taste, and left many royal parks and forests in all parts of England wherein he might have gratified a reasonable passion; but he was not satisfied with the possession of these, and resolved to have a vast hunting-ground "for his insatiate and superfluous pleasure" in the close neighbourhood of the royal city, Winchester, his favourite place of residence. In an early part of his reign he therefore seized all the south-western part of Hampshire, measuring thirty miles from Salisbury to the sea, and in circumference not much less than ninety miles. This wide district, before called Ytene or Ytchtene (a name yet partially preserved), was to some extent uninhabited, and fit for the purposes of the chase, abounding in sylvan spots and coverts; but it included, at the same time, many fertile and cultivated manors, which he caused to be totally absorbed in the surrounding wilderness, and many towns or villages, with no fewer than thirty-six mother or parish churches, all which he demolished, and drove away the people, making them no compensation. According to the indisputable authority of *Doomsday Book*, in which we have an account of the state of this territory both before and after its "afforestation," the damage done to private property must have been immense. In an extent of nearly ninety miles in circumference, *one hundred and eight* places, manors, villages, or hamlets, suffered in a greater or less degree.[3] Some melancholy traces of these ancient abodes of the Anglo-Saxons are still to be found in the recesses of the New Forest, and have been described by a gentleman[4] who passed much of his life in and near those woods, and who was the successor in office to Sir Walter Tyrrel, as bow-bearer to the king. In many spots, though no ruins are visible above ground, either the line of erections can be traced by the elevation of the soil, or fragments of building materials have been discovered on turning up the surface. The traditional names of places still used by the foresters, such as "Church-place," "Church-moor," "Thompson's Castle," seem to mark the now solitary spots as the sites of ancient buildings where the English people worshipped their God, and dwelt in peace, before they were swept away by the Conqueror; and the same elegant writer we have last referred to suggests that the termination of *ham* and *ton*, yet annexed to some woodlands, may be

---

[1] *Saxon Chronicle*.
[2] Other accounts say he was killed by a "pestilent blast" which crossed him while hunting; but, we believe, all fix the scene of his death in the New Forest.
[3] Warner, *Topographical Remarks on the South-Western Parts of Hampshire*.

[4] The late William Stewart Rose, Esq. The office of bow-bearer for the New Forest is now, of course, a sinecure, and it is almost purely honorary, the salary being 40s. in the year, and one buck in the season. In his oath of office the bow-bearer swears "to be of good behaviour towards his majesty's wild beasts."

taken as evidence of the former existence of hamlets and towns in the Forest.¹

We have entered into these slight details because some foreign writers, at the head of whom

THE NEW FOREST AND ADJACENT COUNTRY.
English Miles

1. Ashley Walk.
2. Ashurst Walk.
3. Holderwood Walk.
4. Bramblehill Walk.
5. Broomy Walk.
6. Durley Walk.
7. Castle Malwood Walk.
8. Denny Lodge Walk.
9. Eyeworth Walk.
10. Holmsley Walk.
11. Irons Hill Walk.
12. Lady Cross Walk.
13. Rinefield Walk.
14. Whitley Ridge Walk.
15. Wilverley Walk.
16. Beaulieu Manor.
17. Minestead Manor.

is Voltaire, have professed a disbelief of the early history of the New Forest, and because some native writers, including even Dr. Warton, who was "naturally disposed to cling to the traditions of antiquity," fancying there were no existing ruins or traces of such desolation, have doubted whether William destroyed villages, castles, and churches, though that demolition is recorded by chroniclers who wrote a very short time after the event, and is proved beyond the reach of a doubt by *Doomsday Book*. If any other proof were necessary, it ought to be found in the universal tradition of the people in all ages, that on account of the unusual crimes and cruelties committed

there by William, God made the New Forest the death-scene of three princes of his own blood. The seizure of a waste or wholly uninhabited district would have been nothing extraordinary: it was the sufferings of the people who were driven from their villages—the wrongs done the clergy, whose churches were destroyed—that made the deep and ineffaceable impression.

At the same time that the Conqueror thus enlarged the field of his own pleasures at the expense of his subjects, he enacted new laws, by which he prohibited hunting in any of his forests, and rendered the penalties more severe than ever had been inflicted for such offences. At this period the killing of a man might be atoned for by payment of a moderate fine or composition; but not so, by the New Forest laws, the slaying of one of the king's beasts of chase. "He ordained," says the *Saxon Chronicle*, "that whosoever should kill a stag or a deer should have his eyes torn out; wild boars were protected in the same manner as deer, and he even made statutes equally

¹ See notes to *The Red King*, a spirited poem, by William Stewart Rose, Esq., the royal bow-bearer, in which the manners and costume of the period are carefully preserved. Mr. Rose justly observes, "that this cannot be considered as one of those 'historical doubts,' the solution of which involves nothing beyond the mere disentanglement of an intricate knot. It may be considered as making one of a series of acts of tyranny, unvarnished with any plea which might palliate or disguise its enormity; and, as such, forming a curious feature in the history of manners."

severe to preserve the hares. This savage king loved wild beasts as if he had been *their father.* These forest laws, which were executed with rigour against the English, caused great misery; for many of them depended on the chase as a chief means of subsistence. By including in his royal domain all the great forests of England, and insisting on his right to grant or refuse permission to hunt in them, William gave sore offence to many of his Norman nobles, who were as much addicted to the sport as himself, but who were prohibited from keeping sporting dogs, even on their own estates, unless they subjected the poor animals to a mutilation of the fore-paws, that rendered them unfit for hunting. From their first establishment, and through their different gradations of "forest-laws" and "game-laws," these jealous regulations have constantly been one of the most copious sources of dissension, litigation, violence, and bloodshed.[1]

Towards the end of the year 1086 William summoned all the chiefs of the army of the Conquest, the sons of those chiefs, and every one to whom he had given a fief, to meet him at Salisbury. All the barons and all the abbots came attended with men-at-arms and part of their vassals, the whole assemblage, it is said, amounting to 60,000 men. The chiefs, both lay and churchmen, took again the oath of allegiance and homage to the king; but the assertion that they rendered the same to Prince William, as his successor, seems to be without good foundation. Shortly after receiving these new pledges, William, accompanied by his two sons, passed over to the Continent, taking with him "a mighty mass of money fitted for some great attempt," and being followed by the numberless curses of the English people. The enterprise he had on hand was a war with France, for the possession of the city of Mantes with the territory situated between the Epte and the Oise, which was then called the country of Vexin. William at first entered into negotiations for this territory, which he claimed as his right; but Philip, the French king, after amusing his rival for a while with quibbles and sophisms, marched troops into the country, and secretly authorized some of his barons to make incursions on the frontiers of Normandy. During the negotiations William fell sick, and kept his bed. As he advanced in years he grew excessively fat; and, spite of his violent exercise, his indulgence in the pleasures of the table had given him considerable rotundity of person. On the score of many grudges his hatred of the French king was intense; and Philip now drove him to frenzy by saying, as a good joke among his courtiers, that his cousin William was a long while lying-in, but that no doubt there would be a fine churching when he was delivered. On hearing this coarse and insipid jest, the conqueror of England swore by the most terrible of his oaths—by the splendour and birth of Christ—that he would be churched in Notre Dame, the cathedral of Paris, and present so many wax torches that all France should be set in a blaze.[2]

It was not until the end of July (1087) that he was in a state to mount his war-horse, though it is asserted by a cotemporary that he was convalescent before then, and expressly waited that season to make his vengeance the more dreadful to the country. The corn was almost ready for the sickle, the grapes hung in rich ripening clusters on the vines, when William marched his cavalry through the corn-fields, and made his soldiery tear up the vines by the roots, and cut down the pleasant trees. His destructive host was soon before Mantes, which either was taken by surprise and treachery, or offered but a feeble resistance. At his orders the troops fired the unfortunate town, sparing neither church nor monastery, but doing their best to reduce the whole to a heap of ashes. As the Conqueror rode up to view the ruin he had made, his horse put his fore-feet on some embers or hot cinders, which caused him to swerve or plunge so violently that the heavy rider was thrown on the high pummel of the saddle, and grievously bruised. The king dismounted in great pain, and never more put foot in stirrup.[3] He was carried

---

[1] These laws, however, did not much affect the main fabric of the national jurisprudence, as to which Sir F. Palgrave remarks as follows:—"Notwithstanding the violence and desolation attendant upon the Conquest, William the Norman governed with as much equity and justice as was compatible with the forcible assumption of the regal power; and the main fabric of the Anglo-Saxon jurisprudence remained unchanged, although some alterations had been effected in the executive details. If William ever contemplated the introduction of the Norman jurisprudence as the law of the whole people of England, that plan had been defeated, and probably by the opposition of the Normans themselves, united to the unwillingness of the natives. Had the Conqueror succeeded, the royal prerogatives would have gained a great accession; for it was the English laws which protected the Norman barons, whose franchises were established by pleading the usages which had prevailed under Edward the Confessor. So great, indeed, was the traditionary veneration inspired by the hallowed name of the last legitimate Anglo-Saxon king, that the Normans themselves were willing to claim him as the author of the wise customs of their native country. And we may be also inclined to believe that notwithstanding the very strong terms in which the chroniclers describe the despotism of the Conqueror—'all things,' it is said, 'Divine and human, obeyed his beck and nod'—his supremacy over the church was the principal oppression of which they complained. But the employment of foreign functionaries was followed by new forms of proceeding, not accompanied, perhaps, by any decided intention of innovating, and dictated merely by the pressure of circumstances, which, nevertheless, had afterwards the effect of displacing much of the old jurisprudence as it existed before the invasion, or of causing it to assume another guise."—Palgrave's *Rise and Progress of the English Commonwealth*, part i. p. 240.

[2] *Chron. de Normand.; Brompton.* It was the custom for women, at their churching, to carry lighted tapers in their hands.

[3] *Orderic.; Anglia Sacra.*

slowly in a litter to Rouen, and again laid in his bed. The bruise had produced a rupture; and being in a bad habit of body, and somewhat advanced in years, it was soon evident to all, and even to himself, that the consequence would be fatal. Being disturbed by the noise and bustle of Rouen, and no doubt desirous of dying in a holy place, he had himself carried to the monastery of St. Gervas, outside of the city walls. There he lingered for six weeks, surrounded by doctors who could do him no good, and by priests and monks, who, at least, did not neglect the opportunity of doing much good for themselves. Becoming sensible of the approach of death, his heart softened for the first time; and though he preserved his kingly decorum, and conversed calmly on the wonderful events of his life, he is said to have felt the vanity of all human gran-

MANTES.¹—Drawn by H. G. Hine, from his sketch on the spot.

deur, and a keen remorse for the crimes and cruelties he had committed. He sent money to Mantes to rebuild the churches he had burned, and he ordered large sums to be paid to the churches and monasteries in England. It was represented to him that one of the best means of obtaining mercy from God was to show mercy to man; and at length he consented to the instant release of his state-prisoners, some of whom had pined in dungeons for more than twenty years. Of those that were English among these captives the most conspicuous were—Earl Morcar, Beorn, and Ulnoth or Wulnot, the brother of Harold; of the Normans—Roger Fitz-Osborn, formerly Earl of Hereford, and Odo, Bishop of Bayeux, his own half-brother. The pardon which was wrung from him with most difficulty was that of Odo, whom, at first, he excepted in his act of grace, saying he was a firebrand that would ruin both England and Normandy if set at large.

His two younger sons, William and Henry, were assiduous round the death-bed of the king, waiting impatiently for the declaration of his last will. A day or two before his death the Conqueror assembled some of his chief prelates and barons in his sick chamber, and declared in their presence that he bequeathed the duchy of Normandy, with Maine and its other dependencies, to his eldest son, Robert, whom, it is alleged, he could not put aside in the order of succession, as the Normans were mindful of the oaths they had taken, with his father's consent, to that unfortunate prince, and were much attached to him. "As to the crown of England," said the dying monarch, "I bequeath it to no one, as I did not receive it, like the duchy of Normandy, in inheritance from my father, but acquired it by conquest and the shedding of blood with mine own good sword. The succession to that kingdom I therefore leave to the decision of God, only desiring most fervently that my son William, who has ever been dutiful to me in all things, may obtain it, and prosper in it." "And what do you give unto me, O my father?" impatiently cried Prince Henry, who had not been mentioned in this distribution. "Five thousand pounds' weight of silver out of my treasury," was his answer. "But what can I do with five thousand pounds of silver if I have neither lands nor a home?" "Be

¹ Mantes is situated on the left bank of the Seine. Two fine stone bridges communicate, by an intervening island, with the small town of Limay, on the opposite bank of the river. The town is well built, and the streets are adorned with four public fountains. The church is a fine Gothic edifice, with two lofty towers, and there is another more ancient tower, which belonged to the old church of St. Maclou. In the infancy of the French monarchy Mantes was one of its bulwarks towards Normandy.

patient," replied the king, "and have trust in the Lord; suffer thy elder brothers to precede thee—thy time will come after theirs."[1] Henry went straight and drew the silver, which he weighed with great care, and then furnished himself with a strong coffer, well protected with locks and iron bindings, to keep his treasure in. William left the king's bedside at the same time, and, without waiting to see the breath out of the old man's body, hastened over to England to look after his crown.

About sunrise on the 9th of September the Conqueror was for a moment roused from a stupor into which he had fallen, by the sound of bells; he eagerly inquired what the noise meant, and was answered that they were tolling the hour of prime in the church of St. Mary. He lifted his hands to heaven, and saying, "I recommend my soul to my Lady Mary, the holy mother of God," instantly expired. The events which followed his dissolution not only give a striking picture of the then unsettled state of society, but also of the character and affections of the men that waited on princes and conquerors. William's last faint sigh was the signal for a general flight and scramble. The knights, priests, and doctors who had passed the night near him, put on their spurs as soon as they saw him dead, mounted their horses, and galloped off to their several homes, to look after their property and their own interests. The king's servants, and some vassals of minor rank, left behind, then proceeded to rifle the apartment of the arms, silver vessels, linen, the royal dresses, and everything it contained, and then were to horse, and away like the rest. From prime to tierce,[2] or for about three hours, the corpse of the mighty Conqueror, abandoned by all, lay in a state of almost perfect nakedness on the bare boards. The citizens of Rouen were thrown into as much consternation as could have been excited by a conquering enemy at their gates; they either ran about the streets, asking news and advice from every one they chanced to meet, or busied themselves in concealing their movables and valuables. At last the clergy and the monks thought of the decent duties owing to the mortal remains of their sovereign; and, forming a procession, they went with a crucifix, burning tapers and incense, to pray over the dishonoured body for the peace of its soul. The Archbishop of Rouen ordained that the king should be interred at Caen, in the church of St. Stephen's, which he had built and royally endowed. But even now it should seem there were none to do it honour; for the minute relater of these dismal transactions, who was living at the time, says that his sons, his brothers, his relations were all absent, and that of all his officers, not one was found to take charge of the obsequies, and that it was a poor knight who lived in the neighbourhood who charged himself with the trouble and expense of the funeral, "out of his natural good nature and love of God." The body was carried by water, by the Seine and the sea, to Caen, where it was received by the abbot and monks of St. Stephen's; other churchmen and the inhabitants of the city joining these, a considerable procession was formed; but as they went along after the coffin, a fire suddenly broke out in the town; laymen and clerks ran to extinguish it, and the brothers of St. Stephen's were left alone to conduct the corpse to the church. Even the last burial service did not pass undisturbed. The neighbouring bishops and abbots assembled for this ceremony. The mass had been performed; the Bishop of Evreux had pronounced the panegyric, and the body was about to be lowered into the grave prepared for it in the church, between the altar and the choir, when a man, suddenly rising in the crowd, exclaimed with a loud voice, "Bishop, the man whom you have praised was a robber; the very ground on which we are standing is mine, and is the site where my father's house stood. He took it from me by violence to build this church on it. I reclaim it as my right; and in the name of God I forbid you to bury him here, or cover him with my glebe." The man who spoke thus boldly was Asseline Fitz-Arthur, who had often asked a just compensation from the king in his lifetime. Many of the persons present confirmed the truth of his statement; and, after some parley, the bishops paid him sixty shillings for the grave alone, engaging, at the same time, to procure him the full value of the rest of his land. The body, dressed in royal robes, but without a coffin, was then lowered into the tomb; the rest of the ceremony was hurried over, and the assembly dispersed.[3]

The personal character of William is inscribed so distinctly in the particulars of his eventful history, that any further detail of it is unnecessary. As a brave soldier, he was distinguished at a period when mere personal bravery was of the highest account; as a sagacious leader, he was so far superior to any of his cotemporaries, that for his equal in English history we must pass onward to the days of Crecy and Azincourt. Even these qualities, however, would not have

---

[1] Orderic.
[2] The chroniclers, who were all monks or priests, always count by these and the other canonical hours, as *sexts*, *nones*, *vespers*, &c. The church service called *prime* or *prima*, and which immediately succeeded *matins*, began about six A.M., and lasted to *tierce* or *tortia*, which commenced about nine A.M.

[3] Orderic.; Wace, Roman. de Rou.; Chron. de Normand. Orderic gives further details respecting the lowering of the body into the grave, but they are too revolting to be translated for general readers of the nineteenth century.

sufficed to win for him the proud title of the "Conqueror," had he not excelled in political craft and cunning as much as in military skill.

Dynasties have been changed and provinces won by war, but William's attempt against England was the last great and permanent conquest of a whole nation achieved in Europe. The companions of his conquest became one people with those they subdued; his power was transmitted to his posterity; and after all the changes and revolutions that have happened in the course of seven centuries and a half, the blood of our reigning family is still kindred to his.[1]

---

[1] Of William the Conqueror, M. Bonnechose says:—"His insatiable ambition was served by an invincible perseverance; he had from his infancy to face innumerable difficulties; everything was at first against him—his illegitimate birth, his tender age, the ambition of relatives disputing his paternal inheritance; he grew up amid the severest trials; he inured his soul, in suppressing rebellion, to the employment of the most violent measures, and he learned, in regaining his own patrimony, how to appropriate that of others.

"With what sagacity did he foresee remote contingencies! with what consummate skill did he so arrange everything as to ensure success! When his rival is in his hands, he caresses instead of threatening him, in order to obtain from him an oath which would make him his subject if he kept it, and would disgrace him if he broke it; afterwards, when Harold occupied the throne that William claimed, the latter still temporizes, and when at the point of employing violence, studies to maintain a show of justice. With what prudence does he secure that aid from Rome which his rival disdains! how he avails himself of the passions that he needs to serve his purposes! One after another, he addresses himself to men's cupidity, to their fears, to their superstition, to their prejudices, and turns all to account. At last the moment for action comes, and that same man, whom we have seen so temporizing, so measured, and as cunning as a fox, at once becomes a lion; to him we may apply the words of Bossuet: 'The promptitude of his action affords no time for counteraction, and in the thickest of the fight at Hastings he displays a courage which would have been rash, had not the extremity of the peril been such as to render the excess of courage indispensable.'

"After gaining the battle, he trusts nothing to chance, and before risking himself in the interior, he subdues and fortifies the whole of the coast; next he establishes himself as strongly to the north of the capital as to the south, and after encompassing the city on all sides, just as he seems to have only to march in order to effect its reduction, he restrains himself. His language is not that of a conqueror or a master. William caresses the leading men among his enemies, he solicits their suffrages, he allures to him the descendant of the old Saxon kings, he gives the titles of father and bishop to the very priest who, at his own pressing request, has been declared at Rome to be an intruder and a rebel; he lays no violent hands on the crown of Cerdic, he contrives to have it offered to him; he accepts it, and swears he will govern England as the best of her kings. . . . When threatened with a formidable insurrection, we have seen how he conjured the storm, by promising to inquire into the old laws of the country, and to cause them to be observed; but the national law, as interpreted by a conqueror, is the law of the strongest. We shall see with what unheard-of ability, with what a despot's tact, William contrives to extract from ancient institutions whatever could consolidate his power, and how, in evoking from their tombs all the kings whose memory had retained popularity, from Arthur to Edward, he made all speak so as to favour his views. At last, when he found his authority fully established—when he had all England within his powerful grasp, and had made all resistance hopeless—he seizes his vast prey, he tears it to pieces as it suits his humour, and of all those portions, still reeking with the blood of a whole people, he appropriates the largest to himself. He possessed countless domains; heaps of gold were yearly poured into his treasury; immense forests grew by his command, on what were once the sites of thriving towns; and herds of game, for his gratification, found a haunt in tracts of land laid waste for the purpose, and from which man was expelled. . . . Taught by long practical acquaintance with men and affairs, he thoroughly knew human nature and despised it; nevertheless, he believed also in the existence of virtue; and when he anywhere discovered it, his confidence became as boundless as his esteem; extraordinary merit, even in his enemies, never found him indifferent or insensible, and his admiration disarmed his wrath. If he often employed criminal means to raise and strengthen himself, he also exhibited, in several acts of his life, a serious regard and sincere zeal for religion and justice; his wisdom, in fine, consolidated what violence had established."—*Les Quatre Conquêtes de l'Angleterre*, livre iv. ch. iii.

Thierry, on the subject of the conquest, has the following remarks:—"If, in collecting in his own mind all the facts detailed in the foregoing narration, the reader wishes to form a just idea of England upon its conquest by William of Normandy, he must figure to himself not a mere change of political rule—not the triumph of one of two competitors—but the intrusion of a nation into the bosom of another people, which it came to destroy, and the scattered fragments of which it retained as an integral portion of the new system of society, in the *status* merely of personal property, or, to use the stronger language of records and deeds, of a 'clothing to the soil.' He must not picture to himself, on the one hand, William, the king and despot; on the other, simply his subjects, high and low, rich and poor, all inhabiting England, and, consequently, all English; he must bear in mind that there were two distinct nations, the old Anglo-Saxon race and the Norman invaders, dwelling intermingled on the same soil; or rather he might contemplate two countries—the one possessed by the Normans, wealthy and exonerated from capitation and public burdens—the other, the Anglo-Saxons, enslaved and oppressed with a land-tax; the former full of spacious mansions, of walled and moated castles; the latter scattered over with thatched cabins and ancient walls, in a state of dilapidation; this peopled with the happy and the idle, with soldiers and courtiers, with knights and nobles; that with men in misery and condemned to labour, with peasants and artisans; on the one he beholds luxury and insolence—on the other, poverty and envy; not the envy of the poor at the sight of the opulence of men born to opulence, but that malignant envy, although justice be on its side, which the despoiled cannot but entertain in looking upon the spoilers. Lastly, to complete the picture, these two lands are in some sort interwoven with each other; they meet at every point; and yet they are more distinct, more completely separated, than if the ocean rolled between them. Each has its own tongue, and speaks a tongue that is strange to the other. French is the court language—used in all the palaces, castles, and mansions, in the abbeys and monasteries, in all places where wealth and power offer their attractions; while the ancient language of the country is heard only at the firesides of the poor and the serfs. For a long time these two idioms were propagated without intermixture—the one being the mask of noble, the other of ignoble birth, as is expressed with bitterness in the verses of a poet of the olden time, who complains that England in his day exhibited the spectacle of a land that had repudiated its mother tongue."—*History of the Norman Conquest*, conclusion of book vi.

CHAPTER II.—CIVIL AND MILITARY HISTORY.

WILLIAM II., SURNAMED RUFUS.——A.D. 1087—1100.

Accession of William II., surnamed Rufus—Opposition made to his succession—Claim of his elder brother, Robert, to the crown—Odo, who assists him, is banished—Flambard, the rapacious minister of Rufus—Contentions between Rufus and his brothers—War between England and Scotland—War between England and Wales—Conspiracy in Northumberland against Rufus defeated—Departure of Robert of Normandy to the Crusade—Rufus invades Maine—His death in the New Forest—His character.

ILLIAM RUFUS, or William the Red, who left his father at the point of death, was informed of his decease as he was on the point of embarking at Wissant, near Calais. The news only made him the more anxious to reach England, that he might, by the actual seizure of the succession, set at defiance the pretensions of any other claimant to the crown. Arriving in England, he secured the important fortresses of Dover, Pevensey, and Hastings, concealing his father's death, and pretending to be the bearer of orders from him. He then hastened to Winchester, where, with a proper conviction of the efficacy of money, he claimed his father's treasures, which were deposited in the castle there. William de Pont-de-l'Arche, the royal treasurer, readily delivered him the keys, and Rufus took possession of £60,000 in pure silver, with much gold and many precious stones. His next step was to repair to Lanfranc, the primate, in whose hands the destinies of the kingdom may almost be said to have at that moment been. Bloet, a confidential messenger, had already delivered a letter from the deceased king, commending the cause and guidance of his son William to the archbishop, already disposed by motives both of affection and self-interest in favour of William, who had been his pupil, and for whom he had performed the sacred ceremonies on his initiation into knighthood. It is stated, however, that Lanfranc refused to declare himself in favour of Rufus till that prince promised, upon oath, to govern according to law and right, and to ask and follow the advice of the primate in all matters of importance. It appears that Lanfranc then proceeded with as much activity as Rufus could desire. He first hastily summoned a council of the prelates and barons, to give the semblance of a free election. The former he knew he could influence, and of the latter many were absent in Normandy. Some preferred William's claim and character upon principle, and others were silenced by his presence and promises. Though a strong feeling of opposition existed, none was shown at this meeting; and Lanfranc crowned his pupil at Westminster, on Sunday, the 26th of September, 1087, the seventeenth day after the Conqueror's death.

William's first act of royal authority speaks little in his favour either as a man or a son—it was the imprisonment of the unfortunate Englishmen whom his father had liberated on his death-bed. Earls Morcar and Wulnot, who had followed him to England in the hope of obtaining some part of the estates of their fathers, were arrested at Winchester, and confined in the castle. The Norman state prisoners, however, who had been released at the same time by the Conqueror, re-obtained possession of their estates and honours. He then gave a quantity of gold and silver, a part of the treasure found at Winchester, to "Otho, the Goldsmith," with orders to work it into ornaments for the tomb of that father whom he had abandoned on his death-bed.

When Robert Courthose heard of his father's death, he was living, an impoverished exile, at Abbeville, or, according to other accounts, in Germany. He, however, soon appeared in Normandy, and was joyfully received at Rouen, its capital, and recognized as their duke by the prelates, barons, and chief men. Henry, the youngest brother of the three, put himself and his five thousand pounds of silver in a place of safety, waiting events, and ready to seize every chance of gaining either the royal crown or the ducal coronet.

It was not perhaps easy for the Conqueror to make any better arrangement, but it was in the highest degree unlikely, under the division he had made of England and Normandy, that peace should be preserved between the brothers. Even if the unscrupulous Rufus had been less active, and the personal qualities of Robert altogether different from what they were, causes independent of the two princes threatened to lead to inevitable hostilities. The great barons, the followers of the Conqueror, were almost all possessed of estates and fiefs in both countries: they

VOL. I.   27—28

were naturally uneasy at the separation of the two territories, and foresaw that it would be impossible for them to preserve their allegiance to two masters, and that they must very soon resign or lose either their ancient patrimonies in Normandy, or their new acquisitions in England. A war between the two brothers would at any time embarrass them as long as they held territory under both. The time, also, was not yet come to reconcile them to the thought of their native Normandy as a separate and foreign land. In short, every inducement of interest and of local attachment made them wish to see the two countries united under one sovereign; and their only great difference of opinion on this head was, as to which of the two brothers should be that sovereign; some of them adhering to William, while others insisted that, both by right of birth, and the honourableness, generosity, and popularity of his character, Robert was the proper prince to have both realms. A decision of the question was inevitable; and the first step was taken, not in Normandy, to expel Robert, but in England, to dethrone William. Had he been left to himself, the elder brother, from his love of ease and pleasure, would in all probability have remained satisfied with his duchy, but he was beset on all sides by men who were constantly repeating how unjust and disgraceful to him it was to see a younger brother possess a kingdom while he had only a duchy; by Norman nobles that went daily over to him complaining of the present state of affairs in England; and by his uncle Odo, the bishop, who moved with all his ancient energy and fierceness in the matter, not so much out of any preference of one brother to the other, as out of his hatred of the primate Lanfranc, whom he considered as the chief cause of the disgrace, the imprisonment, and all the misfortunes that had befallen him in the latter years of the Conqueror.

Robert promised to come over with an army in all haste, and Odo engaged to do the rest. At the Easter festival the Red King kept his court at Winchester. Odo was there with his friends, and took that opportunity of arranging his plans. From the festival he departed to raise the standard of Robert in his old earldom of Kent, while Hugh de Grantmesnil, Roger Bigod, Robert de Mowbray, Roger de Montgomery, William, Bishop of Durham, and Geoffrey of Coutances, repaired to do the like in their several fiefs and governments. A dangerous rising thus took place simultaneously in many parts of England; but the insurgents lost time, and alienated the hearts of the English inhabitants by paltry acts of depredation, while the army from Normandy, with which Robert had promised to come over, and which Odo was instructed to look out and provide for upon the south coast of England, was slow in making its appearance. The Courtehose, a slave to his habitual indolence and indecision, was, as usual, in great straits for money; but those who acted for him had raised a considerable force in Normandy, and but for the adoption by the new king of a novel measure, and a confidence timely placed in the natives, England would have been again desolated by a foreign army. Rufus, on learning the preparations that were making for this armament, permitted his English subjects to fit out cruisers; and these adventurers, who seem to have been the first that may be called "privateers," rendered him very important service; for the Normans, calculating that there was no royal navy to oppose them, and that when they landed they would be received by their friends and confederates, the followers of Odo and his party, began to cross the Channel in small companies, each at their own convenience, without concert or any regard to mutual support in case of being attacked on their passage; and so many of them were intercepted and destroyed by the English cruisers, that the attempt at invasion was abandoned.[1] But Rufus was also greatly indebted to another measure which he adopted at this important crisis. Before the success of the privateering experiment could be fully ascertained, seeing so many of the Normans arrayed against him, he had recourse to the native English; he armed them to fight in their own country against his own countrymen and relatives; and it was by this confidence in them that he preserved his crown, and probably his life. He called a meeting of the long-despised chiefs of the Anglo-Saxon blood, who had survived the slow and wasting conquest of his father; he promised that he would rule them with the best laws they had ever known; that he would give them the right of hunting in the forests, as their forefathers had enjoyed it; and that he would relieve them from many of the taillages and odious tributes his father had imposed.[2] "Contested titles and a disputed succession," as Sir James Mackintosh has remarked, "obliged Rufus and his immediate successors to make concessions to the Anglo-Saxons, who so much surpassed the conquering nation in numbers; and these immediate sources of terrible evils to England became the causes of its final deliverance."[3] Flattered by his confidence, the thanes and franklins who had been summoned to attend him, zealously promoted the levy; and when Rufus proclaimed his ban of war in the old Saxon form—"Let ever man who is not a man of nothing,[4] whether he live in burgh or out of burgh,

---

[1] Southey, *Naval Hist.*; *Dr. Campbell*.
[2] *Chron. Sax.*; *Waverley Annals.*   [3] *Hist. England.*
[4] In Anglo-Saxon, a "nidering," or "unnithing," one of the

leave his house and come"—there came 30,000 stout Englishmen to the place appointed for the muster.

Kent, with the Sussex coast, was the most vulnerable part of the island, and Odo, the king's uncle, the most dangerous of his enemies; Rufus, therefore, marched against the bishop, who had strongly fortified Rochester Castle, and then thrown himself into Pevensey, there to await the arrival of the tardy and never-coming Robert. After a siege of seven weeks, the bishop was obliged to surrender this stronghold, and his nephew granted him life and liberty, on his taking an oath that he would put Rochester Castle

ROCHESTER CASTLE. Kent.[1]—J. Skinner Prout, from a photograph.

into his hands, and then leave the kingdom for ever. Relying on his solemn vow, Rufus sent the prelate, with an inconsiderable escort of Norman horse, from Pevensey to Rochester. The strong castle of Rochester, Odo had intrusted to the care of Eustace, Earl of Boulogne. When, now reciting the set form of words, he demanded of the earl the surrender of the castle, Eustace, pretending great wrath, arrested both the bishop and his guards, as traitors to King Robert. The scene was well acted, and Odo, trusting to be screened from the accusation of perjury, remained in the fortress. His loving nephew soon embraced him with a close environment, drawing round him a great force of English infantry and foreign cavalry. But the castle was strong and well garrisoned, for 500 Norman knights, without counting the meaner sort, fought on the battlements; and after a long siege the place was not taken by assault, but forced to surrender either by pestilential disease or famine, or probably by both. The English would have granted no terms of capitulation; but the Norman portion of William's army, who had countrymen, and many of them friends and relations, in the castle, entertained very different sentiments, and at their earnest instance the Red King allowed the besieged to march out with their arms and horses and freely depart the land. The unconscionable Bishop of Bayeux would have included in the capitulation a proviso that the king's army should not cause their band to play in sign of victory and triumph as the garrison marched out, but this condition was refused, the king saying in great anger he would not make such a concession for 1000 marks of gold. The partisans of Robert then came forth with banners lowered, the king's music playing the while. As Odo appeared, there was a louder crash; the trumpets screamed, and the English shouted as he passed, "O! for a halter to hang this perjured, murderous bishop!" It was with these and still worse imprecations that the priest who had blessed the Norman army at the battle of Hastings, departed from England never more to enter it.[2]

Having disposed of Odo, Rufus found no very great difficulty in dealing with the other conspirators, who began to feel that Robert was *not* the man to re-unite the two countries, or give them security for their estates and honours in both. Roger Montgomery, the powerful Earl of Shrewsbury, was detached from the confederacy by a peaceful negotiation; others were won over by

---

strongest terms of contempt. The expressions of the Saxon chronicler are, "Baed thaet aelc man the waere unnithing scaolde cuman to him—Frenclisce and Englisce—of porte and of upplande."

[1] Rochester Castle was erected by William the Conqueror on what is believed to have been the site of an earlier fortress. The west wall of the castle overhangs the Medway, just above the ancient bridge erected in the reign of Richard II. The walls inclosed a quadrangular area nearly 300 ft. square. The keep stands in the south-eastern angle of this area, and is about 70 ft. square, and rises about 104 ft. from the base, having a tower at each angle rising 12 ft. above the rest of the building. On the north side is another tower, about two-thirds the height of the keep, which guarded the entrance. The walls of this castle are of Kentish ragstone, with quoins of Caen stone. The building, with the exception of a circular tower at the south-eastern angle, which was rebuilt after King John had besieged and taken the castle, is of pure Norman construction. It was dismantled in the reign of James I., and the roof and floors are entirely gone.

[2] *Thierry; Chron. Sax.; Orderic. Vital.*

blandishments; the Bishop of Durham was defeated by a division of William's army, and the Bishop of Worcester's English tenants, adhering to William, killed a host of the insurgents. The remaining chiefs of the confederacy either submitted on proclamation or escaped into Normandy. A few of them received a pardon, but the greater part were attainted, and Rufus bestowed their English estates on such of the barons as had done him best service.

In the course of the following year (1089), Lanfranc, who was in many respects a great and a good man, departed this life. A change was immediately observed in the king, who showed himself more debauched, tyrannical, and rapacious than he had been when checked by the primate's virtues and abilities. He appointed no successor to the head office in the church, but seized the rich revenues of the archbishopric of Canterbury, and spent them in his unholy revelries. Lanfranc had been, in fact, chief minister, as well as primate of the kingdom. As minister, he was succeeded by a Norman clergyman of low birth and dissolute habits, but gifted with an aspiring spirit, great readiness of wit, engaging manners, and an unhesitating devotion to the king in all things. He had first attracted attention in the English court of the Conqueror as a skilful spy and public informer. His name was Ralph, to which, in his capacity of minister, and through his violent measures, he soon obtained the significant addition of *le Flambard*, or "the destructive torch." His nominal offices in the court of the Red King were, royal chaplain, treasurer, and justiciary; his real duties, to raise as much money as he could for his master's extravagant pleasures, and to flatter and share his vices. He was ingeniously rapacious, and seems almost to have exhausted the art of extortion. Under this priest the harsh forest laws were made a source of pecuniary profit; new offences were invented for the multiplication of fines; another survey of the kingdom was begun, in order to raise the revenues of the crown from those estates which had been underrated in the record of *Doomsday*;[1] and all the bishoprics and abbeys that fell vacant by death were left so by the king, who drew their revenues and applied them to his own use. These latter proceedings could hardly fail to offend the monastic chroniclers, and the character of the Red King has in consequence come down to us darkened with perhaps rather more than its real depravity. There is, however, no reasonable ground for doubting that he was a licentious, violent, and rapacious king, nor (as has been well observed) is there either wisdom or liberality of sentiment in excusing his rapacity because it comprehended the clergy, who, after all, were the best friends of the people in those violent times.[2]

A.D. 1090. The barons who had given the preference to Robert having failed in their attempts to deprive William of England, the friends of William now determined to drive Robert out of Normandy, which country had fallen into a state of complete anarchy. The turbulent barons expelled Robert's troops from nearly all the fortresses, and then made war with one another on their own private account. Many would have preferred this state of things, which left them wholly independent of the sovereign authority; but those of the great lords who chiefly resided in England, were greatly embarrassed by it, and resolved it should cease. By treachery and bribery possession was obtained of Aumale, or Albemarle, St. Vallery, and other Norman fortresses, which were forthwith strongly garrisoned for Rufus. Robert was roused from his lethargy, but his coffers were empty, and the improvident grants of estates he had already made left him scarcely anything to promise for future service; he therefore applied for aid to his friend and feudal superior the French king, who marched an army to the confines of Normandy, as if to give assistance, but marched it back again on receiving a large amount of gold from the English king. At the same time the unlucky Robert nearly lost his capital by a conspiracy, Conau, a wealthy and powerful burgess, having engaged to deliver up Rouen to Reginald de Warenne for King Rufus. In these difficulties Robert claimed the assistance of the cautious and crafty Henry. Some very singular transactions had already taken place between these two brothers. While Robert was making his preparations to invade England, Henry advanced him £3000, in return for which slender supply he had been put in possession of the Cotentin country, which comprehended nearly a third part of the Norman duchy. Dissensions followed this unequal bargain, and Robert, on some other suspicious, either threw Henry into prison for a short time, or attempted to arrest him. Now, however, the youngest brother listened to the call of the eldest, and joined him at Rouen, where he chiefly contributed to put down the conspi-

---

[1] The measurements in *Doomsday* appear to have been made with a reference to the quality as well as the quantity of the land in each case, whereas Flambard is said to have caused the hides to be measured exactly by the line, or without regard to anything but their superficial extent. Sir Francis Palgrave believes that a fragment of Flambard's *Doomsday* is preserved in an ancient lieger or register book of the monastery of Evesham, now in the Cottonian Library, in MS. Vespasian, B. xxiv. It relates to the county of Gloucester, and must have been compiled between 1096 and 1112. See an account of this curious and hitherto unnoticed relic, with extracts, in Sir Francis' *Rise and Progress of the English Commonwealth*, ii. 449, &c.

[2] Mackintosh, *Hist. of Eng.* i. 119; *Sugeri Vit. Ludovic. Grossi*; *Ingulph.*; *Malmesb.*; *Orderic*.

racy, to repulse King William's adherent, Reginald de Warenne, and to take Conan, the great burgess, prisoner. The forgiving nature of Robert was averse to capital punishment, and he condemned Conan to a perpetual imprisonment; but Henry, some short time after, took the captive to the top of a high tower on pretence of showing him the beauty of the surrounding scenery, and while the eye of the unhappy man rested on the pleasant landscape, he suddenly seized him by the waist and flung him over the battlements. Conan was dashed to pieces by the fall, and the prince coolly observed to those who saw the catastrophe that it was not fitting that a traitor should escape condign punishment.[1]

A.D. 1091. In the following January William Rufus appeared in Normandy, at the head of an army chiefly English. The affairs of the king and duke would have now come to extremity, but Robert again called in the French king, by whose mediation a treaty of peace was concluded at Caen. Rufus, however, gained almost as much by this treaty as a successful war could have given him. He retained possession of all the fortresses he had acquired in Normandy, together with the territories of Eu, Aumale, Fescamp, and other places; and secured, in addition, the formal renunciation on the part of Robert of all claims and pretensions to the English throne. On his side, William engaged to indemnify his brother for what he resigned in Normandy by an equivalent in territorial property in England, and to restore the estates to all the barons who had been attainted in Robert's cause. It was also stipulated between the two parties that the king, if he outlived the duke, should have Normandy; and the duke, if he outlived the king, should have England; the kingdom and duchy thus in either case to be united as under the Conqueror; and twelve of the most powerful barons on each side swore that they would do their best to see the whole of the treaty faithfully executed.

The family of the Conqueror were not a family of love. No sooner were the bonds of fraternal concord gathered up between Robert and William than they were loosened between them and their younger brother Henry. The united forces of the duke and king proceeded to take possession of his castles; and Henry was obliged to retire to a fortress on Mount St. Michael, a lofty rock on the coast of Normandy, insulated at high water by the sea. In this almost impregnable position he was besieged by Robert and William. In the end Prince Henry was obliged to capitulate. He obtained with difficulty permission to retire into Brittany; he was despoiled of all he possessed, and wandered about for two years with no better attendance than grim poverty, one knight, three squires, and a chaplain. But in this, the lowest stage of his fortunes, he impressed men with a notion of his political abilities; and he was invited by the inhabitants of Damfront to take upon himself the government of that city.

Duke Robert accompanied the king to England, to take possession of those territories which were promised by the treaty. During his stay Rufus was engaged in a war with Malcolm Canmore, who, while William was absent in Normandy, had invaded England, and "overrun a great deal of it," says the *Saxon Chronicle*, "until the good men that governed this land sent an army against him and repulsed him." On his return William collected a great force, both naval and military, to avenge this insult; but his ships were all destroyed before they reached the Scottish coast. The English and Scottish armies met, however, in Lothian, in England, according to the *Saxon Chronicle*—at the river called Scotte Uatra (perhaps Scotswater) says Ordericus Vitalis—and were ready to engage, when a peace was brought about by the mediation of Duke Robert on one side, and his old friend Edgar Atheling on the other. "King Malcolm," says the *Saxon Chronicle*, "came to our king, and became his man, promising all such obedience as he formerly rendered to his father, and that he confirmed with an oath. And the King William promised him in land and in all things whatever he formerly had under his father." By the same treaty Edgar Atheling was permitted to return to England, where he received some paltry court appointment.

Returning from Scotland, Rufus was much struck with the favourable position of Carlisle; and, expelling the lord of the district, he laid the foundation of a castle, and soon after sent a strong English colony from the southern counties to settle in the town and its neighbourhood. Carlisle, with the whole of Cumberland, had long been an appanage of the elder son of the Scottish kings; and this act of Rufus was speedily followed by a renewal of the quarrel between him and Malcolm Canmore. To accommodate these differences Malcolm was invited to Gloucester, where William was keeping his court; but before undertaking this journey the Scottish king demanded and obtained hostages for his security—a privilege not granted to the ordinary vassals of the English crown.[2] On arriving at Gloucester, however, Malcolm was required by Rufus to do him right, that is, to make him amends for the injuries with which he was charged in his court there, or, in other words, to submit to the opinion and decision of the Anglo-Norman barons. Malcolm rejected the proposal, and said that the Kings of

---

[1] *Orderic.; Malmesb.*

[2] Allan's *Vindication of the Ancient Independence of Scotland; Fœdera.; Chron. Sax.*

Scotland had never been accustomed to do right to the Kings of England except on the frontiers of the two kingdoms, and by the judgment of the barons of both.[1] He then hurried northward, and having raised an army, burst into Northumberland, where he soon afterwards fell into an ambush, and was slain, together with Edward, his eldest son. Broken-hearted by this calamity, his amiable queen, Margaret, died only four days after.

Duke Robert had returned to the Continent in disgust at having pressed his claims for the promised indemnity in England without any success. He afterwards despatched messenger after messenger from the Continent, but still William would give up none of his domains. At last, in 1094, Robert had recourse to a measure deemed very efficacious in the court of chivalry. He sent two heralds who, having found their way into the presence of the Red King, denounced him before his chief vassals as a false and perjured knight, with whom his brother, the duke, would no longer hold friendship. To defend his honour, the king followed the two heralds to Normandy, where, hoping at least for the majority of voices, he agreed to submit the matter in dispute to the arbitration of the twenty-four barons who had sworn to do their best to enforce the faithful observance of the treaty of Caen. The barons, however, decided in favour of Robert; and then William appealed to the sword. The campaign went so much in favour of the Red King that Robert was again obliged to apply for assistance to the King of France; and Philip once more marched with an army into Normandy. Rufus then sustained some serious losses; and trusting no longer to the appeal of the sword, he resolved to buy off the French king. He sent his commission into England for the immediate levying of 20,000 men. By the time appointed these men came together about Hastings, and were ready to embark, "when suddenly there came his lieutenant with a counter-order, and signified to them, that the king, minding to favour them, and spare them for that journey, would require that every of them should give him ten shillings towards the charges of the war, and thereupon depart home with a sufficient safe conduct; which the most part were better content to do than to commit themselves to the fortune of the sea and bloody success of the wars in Normandy."[2] The king's lieutenant and representative in this cunning device was Ralph Flambard. Some considerable sum was raised, and King Philip accepted it, and withdrew from the field, leaving Robert, as he had done before, to shift for himself. Rufus would then in all probability have made himself master of Normandy, had he not been recalled to England by important events.

A.D. 1094-5. The Welsh, "after their accustomed manner, began to invade the English marches, taking booty of cattle, and destroying, killing, and spoiling many of the king's subjects." Laying siege to the castle of Montgomery, which had been erected on a recently occupied part of Wales, they took it by assault, and slew all whom they found within it. Before William could reach the scene of action all the Welsh were in arms, and had overrun Cheshire, Shropshire, and Herefordshire, besides reducing the Isle of Anglesey. To chastise them, he determined to follow them, as Harold had done before,[3] for he saw that the Welsh "would not join battle with him in the plain, but kept themselves still aloof within the woods and marches, and aloft upon the mountains: albeit, oftentimes when they saw advantage they would come forth, and, taking the Normans and the English unawares, kill many and wound no small numbers."[4] Stimulated, however, by the example of Harold, who had penetrated into the inmost recesses in Wales, the Red King still pursued them by hill and dale: but by the time he reached the mountains of Snowdon, he found that his loss was tremendous, and "not without some note of dishonour," began a retreat which was much more rapid than his advance. The next summer he entered the mountains with a still more numerous army, and was again forced to retire with loss and shame. He seems to have forgot that the invasions of Harold were made with light-armed troops, and he found that his heavy Norman cavalry was ill suited for such a warfare. He turned from Wales in despair, but ordered the immediate erection of a chain of forts and castles along the frontier.

Before he was free from the troubles of this Welsh war his throne was threatened by a formidable conspiracy in the north of England. The exclusive right claimed by Rufus over all the forests continued to irritate the Norman barons, and other causes of discontent were not wanting. At the head of the disaffected was Robert Mowbray, Earl of Northumberland, a most powerful chief, possessing 280 English manors, whose long-continued absence from court created suspicion. The king published a decree that every baron who did not present himself at court on the approaching festival of Whitsuntide should be outlawed. The festival came and passed without any tidings of the Earl of Northumberland, who feared he should be cast into prison if he went to the south. The king marched

---

[1] *Flor. Wigorn., Sim. Dun.*
[2] *Holinshed.* The old authorities are Matthew Paris and Simeon Dunelmensis.
[3] See vol. i. p. 125.   [4] *Holinshed.*

WILLIAM RUFUS.

with an army into Northumberland, and after taking several of his less important fortresses, shut up the earl within the walls of Bamborough Castle. Finding he could neither besiege nor blockade this impregnable place, he built another castle close to it, in which leaving a strong garrison, he returned to the south. The new castle, which was hastily constructed of wood, was called "Malvoisin" (the bad neighbour), and such it proved to Earl Mowbray. Being decoyed from his safe retreat by a feigned offer of placing the town of Newcastle-upon-Tyne in his hands, he was attacked by a large party of Normans from Malvoisin, who lay in wait for him. The earl, with thirty horsemen, fled to the monastery of St. Oswin at Tynemouth. The sanctuary was not respected; but Mowbray and his few followers defended it with desperate valour for six days, at the end of which the earl, sorely wounded, was made prisoner. But Bamborough Castle was even more valuable than the person of this noble captive, and the Red King, who had laid the snare into which the earl had fallen, had also arranged the plan upon which the captors now acted. They carried Mowbray to a spot in front of his castle, and invited his countess, the fair Matilda, to whom he had been married only a few months, to a parley. When the countess came to the outer walls, she saw her husband in the hands of his bitter enemies, who told her they would put out his eyes before her face unless she instantly delivered up the castle. It was scarcely for woman to hesitate in such an alternative: Matilda threw open the gates. Within the walls the king's men found more than they expected, for Earl Mowbray's lieutenant betrayed to them the whole secret of the conspiracy, the object of which was to place upon the throne of England, Stephen, Count of Aumale, nephew of the Conqueror, and brother to the infamous Judith. The extensive conspiracy included, among others, William, Count of Eu, a relation of the king's, William of Alderic, the king's god-father, Hugh, Earl of Shrewsbury, Odo, Earl of Holderness, and Walter de Lacey. The fates of these men were various: Earl Mowbray was condemned to perpetual imprison-

BAMBOROUGH CASTLE, Northumberland.¹—J. Skinner Prout, from a photograph.

ment, and died in a dungeon of Windsor Castle, about thirty years after; the Count of Eu rested his justification on the issue of a duel, which he fought with his accuser in the presence of the king and court; but being vanquished in the combat, he was convicted, according to the prevailing law, and condemned to have his eyes torn out, and to be otherwise mutilated.[2] William of Alderic, who was much esteemed and lamented, was hanged; the Earl of Shrewsbury bought his pardon for an immense sum of money; the Earl of Holderness was deprived of all he possessed and imprisoned; the rest escaped to the Continent, leaving their estates in England to be confiscated.

At a moment when the Red King had successfully disposed of all his enemies in England, and was in a condition to renew the war in Normandy, his thoughtless brother resigned that duchy to him for a sum of money. The Christians of the West, no longer content to appear at Jerusalem as despised and ill-treated pilgrims with beads and crosses in their hands, resolved to repair thither with swords and lances, and conquer the whole of Palestine and Syria from the infidels. The preaching of Peter the Hermit, the decisions of the council of Clermont, and the bulls of Pope Urban II., had kindled a warlike flame throughout Europe. Duke Robert had early enlisted in the crusade, engaging to take with him a numerous and well-armed body of knights and vassals; but wanting money, "no news to his coffers," he applied to his brother the Red King, who readily entered into a bargain which was concluded on terms most advantageous to himself. For the sum of £10,000, the duke resigned the government of Normandy to his brother. This act is generally considered by historians not as a sale, but as a mortgage, which

A.D. 1096.

---

¹ The castle is considered to retain masonry of the sixth century, when it was founded, according to the Saxon Chronicle, by Ida, King of Northumberland. It is founded on a platform of lofty basaltic cliffs, and is only accessible on the south-east side.

² Cæcatus et extesticulatus est.—Malmesb.

was to expire in five years. But it is almost idle to talk of conditions in such a strange transaction, which could have left Robert but a slight chance of ever recovering his dominion from his unscrupulous brother, had Rufus lived. When the bargain was struck, Rufus was almost as penniless as Robert. According to an old historian, to make up this sum with despatch, "he did not only oppress and fleece his poor subjects, but rather with importunate exactions, did, as it were, flea off their skins. All this was grievous and intolerable, as well to the spirituality as temporality; so that divers bishops and abbots, who had already made away with some of their chalices and church jewels to pay the king, made now plain answer that they were not able to help him with any more; unto whom, on the other side, as the report went, the king said again, 'Have you not, I beseech you, coffins of gold and silver full of dead men's bones?'"[1] meaning the shrines wherein the relics of saints were inclosed.

Soon after receiving his £10,000, Robert departed for Palestine, flattering himself with a splendid futurity; and then William, indulging in the less fantastic prospect of near and solid advantages, sailed to the Continent to take immediate possession of Normandy. He had long held many of the fortresses, his partisans among the nobility were numerous, and he was received by the Normans without opposition. But it was far otherwise with the people of Maine, who burst into a universal insurrection, and by rallying round Helie, Lord of La Flèche, a young and gallant adventurer, who had some claim to the country himself, gave Rufus much trouble, and obliged him to carry over an army from England more than once. About three years after Robert's departure, the brave Helie was surprised in a wood with only seven knights in company, and made prisoner by one of the English king's officers. Rufus marched into Maine, soon after, at the head of a large force of cavalry; but the French king and the Count of Anjou interfering, he was induced to negotiate, and Helie obtained his liberty by delivering up the town of Mans. In the following year (1100), as the Red King was hunting in the New Forest, a messenger arrived with intelligence that Helie had surprised the town of Mans, and was besieging the Norman garrison in the castle, being aided therein by the inhabitants. William instantly turned his horse's head, and set off for the nearest sea-port. The nobles who were hunting with him reminded him that it was necessary to call out troops, and wait for them. "Not so," replied Rufus, "I shall see who will follow me; and, if I understand the temper of the youth of this kingdom, I shall have people enough." Without stopping or turning he reached the port, and embarked in the first vessel he found. It was blowing a gale of wind, and the sailor entreated him to have patience till the storm should abate. "Weigh anchor, hoist sail, and begone," cried Rufus; "did you ever hear of a king that was drowned?"[2] Obeying his orders, the sailors put to sea, and safely landed their royal passenger at Barfleur. The news of his landing sufficed to raise the siege of the castle of Mans; and Helie, thinking he must have come in force, dismissed his troops and took to flight. The Red King then barbarously ravaged the lands of his enemies; but being wounded while laying siege to an insignificant castle, he returned suddenly to England.

William's lavish expenditure continued on the increase; but by his exactions and irregular way of dealing with church property, he still found means for gratifying his extravagance, and enjoyed abroad the reputation of being a rich, as well as a powerful king. But the dread creditor was now at hand, whom even kings cannot escape. Popular superstition had long darkened the shades and solitudes of the New Forest, and peopled its glades with horrid spectres. The fiend himself, it was said and believed, had appeared there to the Normans, announcing the punishment he had in reserve for the Red King and his wicked counsellors. The accidents that happened in that Chase, which had been so barbarously obtained, gave strength to the vulgar belief. In the month of May, Richard, an illegitimate son of Duke Robert, was killed while hunting in the forest by an arrow, reported to have been shot at random. This was the second time the Conqueror's blood had been poured out there, and men said it would not be the last time. On the 1st of August following, William lay at Malwood-keep, a hunting-seat in the forest,[3] with a goodly train of knights. A reconciliation had taken place between the two brothers, and the astucious Henry, who had been some time in England, was of the gay party. The circumstances of the

---

[1] *Holinshed; Speed.* The old authorities are *Eadmer, Orderic, Matt. Paris,* and *Wm. Malmesb.*   [2] *Wm. Malmesb.*

[3] "The Red King lies in Malwood-keep,
To drive the deer o'er lawn and steep,
He's bound him with the morn.
His steeds are swift, his hounds are good;
The like in covert or high-wood,
Were never cheer'd with horn."
— *W. Stewart Rose.*

"Malwood Castle or Keep, seated upon an eminence, embosomed in wood, at a small distance from the village of Minestead, in the New Forest, was the residence of this prince, when he met with the accident which terminated his life. No remains of it exist, but the circumference of a building is to be traced; and it yet gives its name to the walk in which it was situated."—Notes to the *Red King*. This spirited and beautiful poem, illustrative of the age and its events, is published in the same volume with *Partenopex de Blois*.

WILLIAM RUFUS.

story, as told by the monkish chroniclers, are sufficiently remarkable. At the dead of night the king was heard invoking the blessed Virgin, a thing strange in him; and then he called aloud for lights in his chamber. His attendants ran at his call, and found him disturbed by a frightful vision, to prevent the return of which he ordered them to pass the rest of the night by his bedside, and divert him by pleasant talk. As he was dressing in the morning an artisan brought him six new arrows: he examined them, praised the workmanship, and keeping four for himself, gave the other two to Sir Walter Tyrrel, otherwise called, from his estates in France, Sir Walter de Poix, saying, as he presented them— "Good weapons are due to the sportsman that knows how to make a good use of them."[1] The tables were spread with an abundant collation, and the Red King ate more meat and drank even more wine than he was wont to do. His spirits rose to their highest pitch; his companions still passed the wine cup, whilst the grooms and huntsmen prepared their horses and hounds for the chase; and all was boisterously gay in Malwood-keep, when a messenger arrived from Serlon, the Norman abbot of St. Peter's, at Gloucester, to inform the king that one of his monks had dreamed a dream foreboding a sudden and awful death to him. "The man is a right monk," cried Rufus, " and to have a piece of money he dreameth such things. Give him, therefore, an hundred pence, and bid him dream of better fortune to our person." Then turning to Tyrrel, he said—" Do they think I am one of those fools that give up their pleasure or their business because an old woman happens to dream or sneeze? To horse, Walter de Poix!"

The king, with his brother Henry, William de Breteuil, and many other lords and knights, rode into the forest, where the company dispersed here and there, after the manner used in hunting; but Sir Walter, his especial favourite in these sports, remained constantly near the king, and their dogs hunted together. As the sun was sinking low in the west, a hart came bounding by, between Rufus and his comrade, who stood concealed in the thickets. The king drew his bow, but the string broke, and the arrow took no effect. Startled by the sound, the hart paused in his speed and looked on all sides, as if doubtful which way to turn. The king, keeping his attention on the quarry, raised his bridle-hand above his eyes, that he might see clear by shading them from the glare of the sun, which now shone almost horizontally through the glades of the forest; and at the same time, being unprovided with a second bow, he shouted, "Shoot, Walter! —shoot, in the devil's name!"[2] Tyrrel drew his bow—the arrow departed—was glanced aside in its flight by an intervening tree, and struck William in the left breast, which was left exposed by his raised arm. The fork-head pierced his heart, and, with one groan, and no word or prayer uttered, the Red King fell, and expired. Sir Walter Tyrrel ran to his master's side, but finding him dead, he remounted his horse, and without informing any one of the catastrophe, galloped to the sea coast, embarked for Normandy, whence he fled for sanctuary into the dominions of the French king, and soon after departed for the Holy Land. According to an old chronicler, the spot where Rufus fell had been the site of an Anglo-Saxon church, which his father, the Conqueror, had pulled down and destroyed for the enlarging of his chase.[3] Late in the evening, the royal corpse was found alone, where it fell, by a poor charcoal-burner,[4] who put it, still bleeding, into his cart, and drove towards Winchester. At the earliest report of his death, his brother Henry flew to seize the royal treasury; and the knights and favourites who had been hunting in the forest dispersed, in several directions, to look after their interest, not one of them caring to render the last sad honours to their master. The next day the body, still in the charcoal-burner's cart, and defiled with blood and dirt, was carried to St. Swithin's, the cathedral church of Winchester. There, however, it was

Tomb of William Rufus, Winchester Cathedral.—Gough's Sepulchral Monuments.

treated with proper respect, and buried in the centre of the cathedral choir, many persons looking on, but few grieving. A proof of the bad opinion that the people entertained of the deceased monarch is, that they interpreted the fall of a certain tower in the cathedral, which happened the following year, and covered his tomb with its ruins, into a sign of the displeasure of Heaven that he had received Christian burial.[5]

---

[1] Orderic. Vital.
[2] "Trahe, trahe arcum ex parte diaboli."—*Hen. Knyghton.*
[3] Walter Hemyngforde, quoted in Grafton's *Chronicle.*
[4] "This man's name was Purkess. He is the ancestor of a very numerous tribe. Of his lineal descendants it is reported that, living on the same spot, they have constantly been proprietors of a horse and cart, but never attained to the possession of a team."—W S. Rose, notes to the *Red King.*
[5] Dr. Milner, *Hist. Winchest.*

The second king of the Norman line reigned thirteen years, all but a few weeks, and was full of health and vigour, and only forty years of age, when he died. That he was shot by an arrow in the New Forest—that his body was abandoned and then hastily interred—are facts perfectly well authenticated; but some doubts may be entertained as to the precise circumstances attending his death, notwithstanding their being minutely related by writers who were living at the time, or who flourished in the course of the following century. Sir Walter Tyrrel afterwards swore, in France, that he did not shoot the arrow; but he was probably anxious to relieve himself from the odium of killing a king, even by accident. It is quite possible, indeed, that the event did not arise from chance, and that Tyrrel had no part in it. The remorseless ambition of Henry might have had recourse to murder, or the avenging shaft might have been sped by the desperate hand of some Englishman, tempted by a favourable opportunity and the traditions of the place. But the most charitable construction is, that the party were intoxicated with the wine they had drunk at Malwood-keep, and that in the confusion consequent on drunkenness, the king was hit by a random arrow.

The Red King was never married; and his example is said to have induced all his young courtiers to prefer the licentious liberty of a single life. In describing his libertinism, the least heinous charge of the monkish historians is, that he respected not the virtue of other men's wives, and was "a most especial follower of lemans." For the honour of human nature we hope the picture is overcharged; but there are proofs enough to convince us that but little order or decorum reigned in the court of Rufus. Indeed, all writers agree in their accounts of the dissolute manners of his household and adherents. His rapacity is equally unquestionable; but this charge may be partially explained, if it cannot be excused, by his taste and magnificence. He did not spend all his money in his wars, his foreign schemes, his pleasures and debaucheries; but devoted large sums to the building of royal palaces, and to several works of great public utility.[1]

[1] William of Malmesbury, who was born in the reign of William Rufus, gives this graphic description of him:—"Greatness of soul was pre-eminent in the king, which, in process of time, he obscured by excessive severity—vices, indeed, in place of virtues, so insensibly crept into his bosom that he could not distinguish them. . . . At last, however, in his latter years, the desire after good grew cold, and the crop of evil increased to ripeness; his liberality became prodigality—his magnanimity, pride—his austerity, cruelty. . . . He was, when abroad, and in public assemblies, of supercilious look, darting his threatening eye on the bystander; and with assumed severity and ferocious voice, assailing such as conversed with him. From apprehension of poverty and of the treachery of others, as may be conjectured, he was too much given to lucre and to cruelty. At home and at table, with his intimate companions, he gave loose to levity and to mirth. He was a most facetious railer at anything he had himself done amiss, in order that he might thus do away obloquy, and make it matter of jest. . . . Military men came to him out of every province on this side of the mountains, whom he rewarded most profusely. In consequence, when he had no longer aught to bestow, poor and exhausted, he turned his thoughts to rapines. The rapacity of his disposition was seconded by Ralph, the inciter of his covetousness, a clergyman of the lowest origin, but raised to eminence by his wit and subtility. If, at any time, a royal edict issued that England should pay a certain tribute, it was doubled by this plunderer of the rich—this exterminator of the poor —this confiscator of other men's inheritance. He was an invincible pleader, as unrestrained in his words as in his actions; and equally furious against the meek or the turbulent. . . . At this person's suggestion, the sacred honours of the church, as the pastors died out, were exposed to sale. . . . Those things appeared the more disgraceful, because in his father's time, after the decease of a bishop or abbot, all rents were reserved entire, to be given up to the succeeding pastor; and persons, truly meritorious on account of their religion, were elected. But in the lapse of a very few years, everything was changed. . . . Men of the meanest condition, or guilty of whatever crime, were listened to, if they could suggest anything likely to be advantageous to the king; the halter was loosened from the robber's neck, if he could promise any emolument to the sovereign. All military discipline being relaxed, the courtiers preyed upon the property of the country people, and consumed their substance, taking the very meat from the mouths of these wretched creatures. Then was there flowing hair and extravagant dress; and then was invented the fashion of shoes with curved points; then the model for young men was to rival women in delicacy of person—to mince their gait, to walk with loose gesture, and half naked. Enervated and effeminate, they unwillingly remained what nature had made them—the assailers of others' chastity, prodigal of their own. Troops of pathics and droves of harlots followed the court; so that it was said, with justice, by a wise man, 'That England would be fortunate if Henry could reign;' led to such an opinion, because he abhorred obscenity from his youth." Such was the improved morality introduced by the Normans!

CHAPTER III.—CIVIL AND MILITARY HISTORY.

HENRY I., SURNAMED BEAUCLERK.——A.D. 1100–1135.

Henry, surnamed Beauclerk, seizes the crown—His endeavours to conciliate his English subjects—He marries the Princess Maud, the descendant of Alfred—The marriage opposed, from the report that Maud had taken the veil—Flambard's imprisonment and escape—Return of Robert of Normandy from the Crusade—He demands the crown of England—His claim defeated and relinquished—Rebellion of the Earl of Shrewsbury suppressed—Henry Beauclerk invades the territory of his brother Robert—He defeats Robert, and takes him prisoner—Miserable end of Robert—Henry Beauclerk takes possession of Normandy—Marriage of his daughter Matilda to the Emperor of Germany—Henry's successful wars and negotiations on the Continent—His only son, William, drowned while returning to England—His new plans to settle the succession of the crown—Procures Matilda, his daughter, to be acknowledged his successor—His proceedings to insure her succession—Death of Henry Beauclerk—His character.

ENRY was not unopposed in the first step he took to secure the crown. While he was imperiously demanding the keys of the royal treasury, and the officers, in whose charge they were placed, were hesitating whether they should deliver them or not, William de Breteuil, the royal treasurer, who had also been of the fatal hunting party, arrived with breathless speed from the forest, and opposed his demand. "You and I," said he to Henry, "ought to remember the faith we have pledged to your brother, Duke Robert; he has received our oath of homage, and, absent or present, he has a right to this money." Henry attempted to shake the fidelity of the treasurer with arguments, but William de Breteuil resolutely maintained that Robert was the lawful sovereign of England, to whom, and to no one else, the money in Winchester Castle belonged.[1] The altercation grew violent, and Henry, who felt he had no time to lose, drew his sword, and threatened immediate death to any that should oppose him. He was supported by some powerful barons who happened to be on the spot, or who had followed him from the forest. De Breteuil was left almost single in his honourable opposition, the domestics of the late king taking part against him; and Henry seized the money and crown-jewels before his eyes. Part of the money seems to have been distributed among the barons and churchmen at Winchester. He immediately gave the bishopric of Winchester to Henry Gifford, a most influential adherent, and then proceeded with all speed to London, where he made a skilful use of his treasures, and was proclaimed by an assembly of noblemen and prelates, no one challenging his title, but all acknowledging his consummate abilities and fitness for government. On Sunday, the 5th of August, only three days after the death of Rufus, standing before the altar in Westminster Abbey, he promised God and all the people to annul all the unrighteous acts that took place in his brother's time; and after this declaration, Maurice, the Bishop of London, consecrated him king.[2] Anselm, the Archbishop of Canterbury, who, according to ancient rule, should have performed the ceremony of the coronation, had been driven out of the kingdom some three years before; and the archbishopric of York had been left vacant for some time. A popular recommendation was, that Henry was an Englishman, born in the country,[3] and after the Conquest; and some of his partisans set up this circumstance as being, in itself, a sufficient title to the crown. But he himself, in a charter of liberties issued on the following day, and diligently promulgated throughout the land, represented himself as being crowned "by the mercy of God, and by the common consent of the barons of the kingdom."

The claims of Duke Robert were not forgotten; but Henry, who "had aforehand trained the people to his humour and vein, in bringing them to think well of him," had also caused to be reported, as a certain fact, that Robert was already created King of Jerusalem by the Crusaders, and would never leave the Holy Land for an ordinary kingdom. Although the law of succession remained almost as loose as under the Saxon dynasty, and the crown of England was still, in form at least, an elective one, Henry, who, moreover, was bound by oaths to his elder brother Robert, seems himself to have been conscious of a want of validity or security in his title, and to have endeavoured to strengthen his throne by reforms of abuses, and by large concessions to the

---

[1] *Malmesb.*

[2] *Sax. Chron.*
[3] Henry was born at Selby, in Yorkshire, A.D. 1070, in the fourth year of his father's reign as King of England.

nation. The charter of liberties passed by Henry on his accession forms an important feature in our progressive law and government. He restored all the rights of the church, promised to require only moderate and just reliefs from his vassals, to exercise his powers in wardships and marriages with equity and mildness, to redress all the grievances of the former reign, and to restore the laws of King Edward the Confessor, subject only to the amendments made in them by his father.

Still farther to conciliate his Anglo-Saxon subjects, Henry, who, on all necessary occasions, boasted of his English birth, determined to espouse an English wife. This marriage is a most important historical event, being a step made towards that intermixture and fusion of the two races which destroyed, at a much earlier period than is generally imagined, the odious distinction between Saxons and Normans. It is also exceedingly interesting in some of its details, and particularly those which have been transmitted by the pen of Eadmer,[1] who was living at the time, and who, as an Englishman himself, entertained a lively sympathy for the fortunes of the young princess. The lady of Henry's choice was, to use the words of the *Saxon Chronicle*, "Maud, daughter of Malcolm, King of Scots, and of Margaret, the good queen, the relation of King Edward, and of the right kingly kin of England." This descendant of the great Alfred had been sent from Scotland at a very early age, and committed to the care of her aunt Christina, Edgar Atheling's second sister, who was abbess of Wilton, or, as others say, of Rumsey, in Hampshire. As she grew up, several of the Norman captains aspired to the honour of her hand. She was asked in marriage by Alan, the Lord of Richmond: but Alan died before he could receive any answer from the king. William de Garenne, Earl of Surrey, was the next suitor, but the marriage was not allowed by Rufus. A cotemporary writer[2] says, he knows not why the marriage with the Earl of Surrey did not take place; but the policy of forbidding a union between a powerful vassal and a princess of the ancient royal line is evident; and the Red King, like his father, held it as part of his prerogative to give or refuse the hands of his fair subjects. When proposals were made on the part of King Henry, the fair Saxon, not being dazzled with the prospect of sharing with a Norman the throne on which her ancestors had sat for centuries, showed a decided aversion to the match. But she was assailed by arguments difficult to resist. "O! most noble and fair among women," said her Saxon advisers, "if thou wilt, thou canst restore the ancient honour of England, and be a pledge of reconciliation and friendship; but if thou art obstinate in thy refusal, the enmity between the two races will be everlasting, and the shedding of human blood know no end."[3] When her slow consent was obtained, another impediment was raised by a strong Norman party, who neither liked to see an Englishwoman raised to be their queen, nor the power of their king confirmed by means which would endear him to the native race, and render him more and more independent of the Normans. They asserted that Maud, who had been brought up from her infancy in a convent, was a nun, and that she had been seen wearing a veil, which made her for ever the spouse of Christ. Such an obstacle would have been insurmountable; and as there were some seeming grounds for the report, the celebration of the marriage was postponed, to the great joy of those who were opposed to it.[4]

Anselm, the Archbishop of Canterbury, who had returned from Italy at the pressing invitation of the new king, was a zealous promoter of the marriage—for his soul was kind and benevolent, and he was interested in favour of the English people; but when he heard the reports, he declared that nothing could induce him to unite a nun to a carnal husband. The archbishop, however, determined to question the maiden herself; and Matilda, or Maud, in reply, denied she had ever taken the vows, or even worn the veil of her free will; and she offered to give full proof of this before all the prelates of England. "I must confess," she said, "that I have sometimes appeared veiled; but listen to the cause: in my first youth, when I was living under her care, my aunt, to save me, as she said, from the lust of the Normans, who attacked all females, was accustomed to throw a piece of black stuff over my head; and when I refused to cover myself with it, she treated me very roughly. In her presence I wore that covering, but as soon as she was out of sight, I threw it on the ground, and trampled it under my feet in childish anger." To solve this great difficulty, Anselm called a council of bishops, abbots, and monks. Witnesses summoned before this council confirmed the truth of Matilda's words. Two archdeacons, who had been sent to the convent where the young lady was brought up, deposed that public report, and the testimony of the nuns, agreed with her declaration. The decision, given unanimously, was, "We, the bishops, &c., are of opinion that the young lady is free, and can dispose of herself; and we have a precedent in a

---

[1] This historian was the scholar and inmate of Archbishop Anselm, who celebrated the marriage, and afterwards crowned the young queen.

[2] *Ordericus.* This chronicler says she had formerly gone by the more Saxon name of Edith.

[3] *Matt. Paris.*   [4] *Eadmer.*

judgment, rendered, in a similar cause, by the venerable Lanfranc, when the Saxon women, who had taken refuge in the convent out of fear of the soldiers of the great William, reclaimed and obtained their liberty." On Sunday, the 11th of November, the marriage was celebrated, and the queen was crowned with great pomp and solemnity. But so wisely cautious was the prelate, and so anxious to dissipate all suspicions and false reports, that, before pronouncing the nuptial benediction, he mounted on a bench in front of the church door, and showed to the assembled people the debate and decision of the ecclesiastical council. The Normans, who had opposed the union, now vented their spite in bitter railleries. Henry dissembled his rage till a convenient moment, and, in public, laughed heartily at the insolent jests. Matilda, who had given her consent to the marriage with reluctance, and who found a most unfaithful husband, proved a "right loving and obedient wife." She was beautiful in person, and distinguished by a love of learning and great charity to the poor. Her elevation to the throne filled the hearts of the English with a momentary joy.

Another proceeding which greatly increased the new king's popularity with the English, and with all who entertained respect for virtue and decency, was his expulsion of his brother's minions. If half of the detestable vices attributed by the churchmen, their contemporaries, to these favourites, were really prevalent among them, they must have been a curse and an abomination to the land.

It was scarcely possible that Ralph Flambard, the obnoxious minister of the late king, should escape in this general purgation. The Bishop of Durham—for such was the ecclesiastical promotion Ralph had attained under Rufus—was thrown into the Tower, where he lived most luxuriously, and captivated the affections of his keepers by his conviviality, generosity, and wit. In the February following Henry's coronation, a good rope was conveyed to the bishop, hid in the bottom of a huge wine flagon. His guards drank of the wine until their senses forsook them; and then Ralph, under favour of the night, and by means of the rope, descended from his prison window and escaped. Some friends in attendance put him on board ship, and the active bishop made sail for Normandy, to see what fortune would offer him as the servant of Robert Courtehose.

When Henry caused the report to be circulated, that Robert had obtained the crown of Jerusalem, and thought not of returning to England, he knew right well that another than he had been elected sovereign in the Holy Land, and that his brother was actually in Europe, and on his way back to Normandy, in which country he arrived within a month or six weeks after the death of Rufus. The improvident duke had greatly distinguished himself in the conquest of Palestine, and the taking of Jerusalem, performing prodigies of valour, which were only surpassed, in later times, by Richard Cœur de Lion. Though valued for the good qualities he possessed, the Crusaders never thought seriously of electing so imprudent a prince to the difficult post of securing and governing the conquests they had made; nor does Robert appear ever to have fixed his eye on the throne of Jerusalem, which, by universal consent, fell to Godfrey of Bouillon, a man "born for command," and as wise and prudent as a statesman as he was gallant and fearless as a knight.[1] Soon after the capture of Jerusalem, which happened on the 15th of July, 1099, somewhat more than a year before the death of the English king in the New Forest, Duke Robert left the Holy Land covered with holy laurels, and crossed the Mediterranean to Brundusium, the nearest port of Italy, intending to travel homeward, by land, through that beautiful and luxurious country. The Norman lance, as we have already mentioned, had won the fairest portion of Southern Italy some years before the conquest of England; and as Duke Robert advanced into the land, he was everywhere met by Norman barons, and nobles of Norman descent. At every feudal castle the duke was hailed and welcomed as a countryman, a friend, a hero, a Crusader returning with victory, whom it was honourable to honour; and so much was their hospitality to the taste of the thoughtless prince that he lingered long and well pleased on his way. Of all these noble hosts was none more noble or more powerful than William, Count of Conversano; he was the son of Geoffrey, who was nephew of Robert Guiscard, the founder of the Norman dynasty in Naples; his vast possessions lay along the shores of the Adriatic, from Otranto to Bari, and extended far inland in the direction of Lucania and the other sea. He was, in short, the most powerful lord in Lower Apulia. His castle, which stood on an eminence surrounded by olive groves, at a short distance from the Adriatic, had many attractions for the pleasure-loving and susceptible son of the Conqueror. There were minstrels and jongleurs; there were fine horses and hounds, and hawks, in almost

---

[1] "Veramente è costui nato all' impero,
Sì del regnar, del commandar sa l'arti;
E non minor che duce e cavaliero;
Ma del doppio valor tutte ha le parti."
—*Tasso, Gerusalemme.*

"Well seems he born to be with honour crown'd,
So well the lore he knows of regiment;
Peerless in fight, in counsel grave and sound—
The double gift of glory excellent."—*Fairfax.*

royal abundance; and the vast plains of Apulia, with the forests and mountains that encompass them, offered a variety of the finest sport. But there was an attraction, even greater than all these, in the person of a beautiful maiden, the young Sibylla, the daughter of his host, the Count of Conversano. Robert became enamoured, and such a suitor was not likely to be rejected. Robert received the hand of Sibylla, who is painted as being as good as she was fair, together with a large sum of money as her dowry. Happy in the present, careless of the future, and little thinking that a man so young as his brother, the Red King, would die, he lingered several months in Apulia, and finally travelled thence without any eagerness or speed; and at the critical moment when the British throne fell vacant, his friends hardly knew when they might expect him. On his arrival, however, in Normandy, he appears to have been received with great joy by the people, and to have obtained peaceful possession of the whole of the country with the exception of the fortresses surrendered to Rufus, and which were now held for Henry. He made no secret of his intention of prosecuting his claim on England; but here again he lost time and threw away his last remaining chance. He was proud of showing his beautiful bride to the Normans, and, with his usual imprudence, he spent her fortune in feasting and pageantry. Ralph Flambard was the first to wake him from his splendid but evanescent dream, and at the earnest suggestion of the fugitive bishop-minister he prepared for immediate war, knowing it was vain to plead to Henry his priority of birth, his treaty with Rufus, or the oaths which Henry himself had taken to him.

When this ban of war was proclaimed, Robert's Norman vassals showed the utmost readiness to fight under a prince who had won laurels in the Holy Land; and the Norman barons expressed the same discontent at the separation of the duchy and kingdom which had appeared on the accession of William Rufus. If the nobles had been unanimous in their preference to Robert as sovereign of the country, on either side the Channel where they had domains, the dispute about the English throne must have been settled in his favour; but they were divided, and many preferred Henry (as they had formerly done Rufus) to Robert. The friends of the latter, however, were neither few nor powerless: several of high rank crossed the Channel from England, to urge him to recover the title which belonged to him in virtue of the agreement formerly concluded between him and the Red King; and Robert de Belesme, Earl of Shrewsbury and Arundel, William de la Warrenne, Earl of Surrey, Arnulf de Montgomery, Walter Gifford, Robert de Ponte-fract, Robert de Mallet, Yvo de Grantmesnil, and many others of the principal nobility, promised, on his landing, to join him with all their forces. Henry began to tremble on the throne he had so recently acquired. His fears of the Normans threw him more than ever on the support of the English people, whom he now called his friends, his faithful vassals, his countrymen—the best and bravest of men—though his brother, he insidiously added, treated them with scorn, and called them cowards and gluttons.[1] At the same time he paid diligent court to Archbishop Anselm, who, by the sanctity of his character and his undeniable virtues and abilities, exercised a great influence in the nation.

The effect of all this was, that the bishops, the common soldiers, and the native English, with a curious exception, stood firmly on the side of Henry, who could also count, among the Norman nobility, Robert de Melleut, his chief minister, the Earl of Warwick, Roger Bigod, Richard de Redvers, and Robert Fitz-Hamon, all powerful barons, as his unchangeable adherents. The exception against him, on the part of the native English, was among the sailors, who, affected by Robert's fame, and partly won over by the fugitive Bishop of Durham, deserted with the greater part of a fleet, which had been hastily equipped to intercept the duke on his passage, or oppose his landing. Robert sailed from Normandy in these very ships, and while Henry was expecting him at Pevensey, on the Sussex coast, he reached Portsmouth, and there landed. Before the two armies could meet, some of the less violent of the Normans from both parties had interviews, and agreed pretty well on the necessity of putting an end to a quarrel among countrymen and friends. When the hostile forces fronted each other, there was a wavering among his Normans; but the English continued faithful to Henry, and Anselm threatened the invaders with excommunication. To the surprise of most men, the duke's great expedition ended in a hurried peace and a seemingly affectionate reconciliation; after which the credulous Robert returned to the Continent, renouncing all claim to England, and having obtained a yearly payment of 3000 marks, and the cession to him of all the castles which Henry possessed in Normandy. It was also stipulated that the adherents of each should be fully pardoned, and restored to all their possessions, whether in Normandy or in England; and that neither Robert nor Henry should thenceforward encourage, receive, or protect the enemies of the other. There was another clause added, which, even without counting how much older he was than Henry, was not worth, to

---

[1] *Matt. Paris.*

Robert, the piece of parchment it was written upon; it imported that, if either of the brothers died without legitimate issue, the survivor should be heir to his dominions.

Robert was scarcely returned to Normandy when Henry began to take measures against the barons, his partisans, whom he had promised to pardon. He appointed spies to watch them in their castles, and, artfully sowing dissensions among them, and provoking them to breaches of the law, he easily obtained, from the habitual violence of these unpopular chiefs, a plausible pretence for his prosecutions. He summoned Robert de Belesme, Earl of Shrewsbury, to answer to an indictment containing forty-five serious charges.[1] De Belesme appeared, and, according to custom, demanded that he might go freely to consult with his friends and arrange his defence; but he was no sooner out of the court than he mounted his horse and galloped off to one of his strong castles. The king summoned him to appear within a given time, under pain of outlawry. The earl responded to the summons by calling his vassals around him, and preparing for open war. This was meeting the wishes of the king, who took the field with an army, consisting in good part of English infantry, well disposed to do his will, and delighted at the prospect of punishing one of their many oppressors. He was detained several weeks by the siege of the castle of Arundel, the garrison of which finally capitulated, and then, in part, escaped to join their Earl de Belesme, who, in the meantime, had strongly fortified Bridgenorth, near the Welsh frontiers, and strengthened himself in the citadel of Shrewsbury. During the siege of Bridgenorth the Normans in the king's service showed that they were averse to proceeding to extremities against one of the noblest of their countrymen, and some of the earls and barons endeavoured to put an end to the war by effecting a reconcilement between Robert de Belesme and the sovereign. They demanded a conference, and an assembly was held in a plain near the royal camp. A body of English infantry, posted on a hill close by, who knew what was in agitation among the Norman chiefs, cried out, "Do not trust in them, King Henry; they want to lay a snare for you. We are here; we will assist you and make the assault. Grant no peace to the traitor until you have him in your hands, alive or dead!"[2] The attempt at reconciliation failed; the siege was pressed, and Bridgenorth fell. The country between Bridgenorth and Shrewsbury, where the earl made his last stand, was covered with thick wood, and infested by his scouts and archers. The English infantry cleared the wood of the enemy, and cut a road for the king to the very walls of Shrewsbury, where De Belesme, reduced to despair, soon capitulated. He lost all his vast estates in England, but was permitted to retire into Normandy, on taking an oath he would never return to the kingdom without Henry's permission. His ruin involved that of his two brothers, Arnulf, Earl of Montgomery, and Roger, Earl of Lancaster; and the prosecution and condemnation of all the barons who had been favourable to Robert followed. One by one, nearly all the great nobles, the sons of the men who had achieved the conquest of England, were driven out of the land as traitors and outlaws, and their estates and honours were given to "new men."[3]

So scrupulous was Duke Robert in observing the treaty, that, on the first notice of De Belesme's rebellion, he ravaged the Norman estates of that nobleman; considering himself, in spite of former ties of friendship, as bound so to do by the clause which stipulated that neither brother should encourage the enemies of the other. He was soon, however, made sensible that the real crime of all the outlaws, in Henry's eyes, was the preference they had given to him; and following one of those generous impulses to which his romantic nature was prone, he came suddenly over to England and put himself completely in the power of Henry, to intercede in favour of the unfortunate barons. The crafty king received him with smiles and brotherly embraces, and then placed spies over him to watch all his motions. Robert, who had demanded no hostages, soon found he was a prisoner, and was glad to purchase his liberty by renouncing his annuity of 3000 marks. He then returned to Normandy, and, in self-defence, renewed his friendship with the barons exiled from England. Henry now pretended that Robert was the aggressor, and declared the peace between them to be for ever at an end. The simple truth was, that he had resolved to

---

[1] "Robert de Belesme, Earl of Shrewsbury, son of the great Montgomery, deserves some notice. He was the most powerful subject in England, haughty, rapacious, and deceitful. In these vices he might have many equals; in cruelty he rose pre-eminent among the savages of the age. He preferred the death to the ransom of his captives; it was his delight to feast his eyes with the contortions of the victims, men and women, whom he had ordered to be impaled; he is even said to have torn out the eyes of his godson with his own hands, because the father of the boy had committed some trivial offence, and had escaped from his vengeance. Against this monster, not from motives of humanity, but from policy, Henry had conceived the most violent hatred. He was cited before the king's court; the conduct of his officers in Normandy, as well as in England—his words, no less than his actions, were severely scrutinized; and a long list of five-and-forty offences was objected to him by his accusers. The earl, according to custom, obtained permission to retire, that he might consult his friends; but instantly mounted his horse, fled to his earldom, summoned his retainers, and boldly bade defiance to the power of his prosecutor. Henry cheerfully accepted the challenge."—*Lingard*. Compelled in the end to surrender, this monster of cruelty had his life spared, on condition of his quitting the kingdom.

[2] *Ordericus Vitalis*.

[3] Thierry, *Histoire de la Conquête*.

unite the duchy to his kingdom. Normandy, indeed, was in a deplorable state, and Robert, it must be said, had given, and continued to give, manifold proofs of his inability to manage a factious and intriguing nobility, or to govern any state, as states were then constituted. He was indeed "too trusting and merciful for his age."[1] He had, however, relapsed into his old irregularities after losing the beautiful Sibylla, who died in 1102, leaving an infant son, the only issue of their brief marriage. His court was again thronged with vagabond jongleurs, loose women, and rapacious favourites, who plundered him of his very attire—at least this sovereign prince is represented as lying in bed, at times, from want of proper clothes to put on when he should rise. A much more serious evil for the country was, that his pettiest barons were suffered to wage war on each other, and inflict all kinds of wrong on the people. When Henry first raised the mask, he declared himself the protector of Normandy against the bad government of his brother. He called on Robert to cede the duchy for a sum of money, or an annual pension. "You have the title of chief," said he, "but in reality you are no longer a chief, seeing that the vassals who ought to obey you set you at nought."[2] The duke indignantly rejected the proposal, on which the king crossed the seas with an army, and, "by large distributions of money carried out of England," won many new partisans, and got possession of many of the fortresses of Normandy. The duke, on the other hand, had now nothing to give to any one, yet still some brave men rallied around him, out of affection to his person, or in dread and hatred of his brother; and Henry found it impossible to complete his ruin in this campaign.

In the following year (1106) the king reappeared in Normandy with a more formidable army, and with still more money, to raise which he had cruelly distressed his English subjects. About the end of July he laid siege to Tenchebray, an important place, the garrison of which, incorruptible by his gold, made a faithful and gallant resistance. Robert, when informed that his friends were hard pressed, promised to march to their relief, ensue what might; and on the appointed day, most true to his word, as was usual with him in such matters, he appeared before the walls of Tenchebray, where Henry had concentrated his whole army. As a soldier, Robert was far superior to his brother, but his forces were numerically inferior, and there was treachery in his camp. As brave, however, as when he fought the Paynim and mounted the breach in the Holy City, he fell upon the king's army, threw the English infantry into disorder, and had nearly won the victory, when De Belesme most basely fled with a strong division of his forces, and left him to inevitable defeat. After a last and most brilliant display of his valour as a soldier, the duke was taken prisoner, with 400 of his knights. "This battle," observes old John Speed, "was fought, and Normandy won, upon Saturday, being the vigil of St. Michael, even the same day, forty years, that William the Bastard set foot on England's shore for his conquest; God so disposing it (saith Malmesbury) that Normandy should be subjected to England that very day wherein England was subdued to Normandy."

The fate of the captives made at Tenchebray, or taken after that battle, or who voluntarily surrendered, was various; some received a free pardon, some were allowed to be ransomed, and a few were condemned to perpetual imprisonment. The ex-Earl of Shrewsbury, De Belesme, was gratified with a new grant of most of his estates in Normandy; and the ex-bishop-minister, Ralph Flambard, who had been moving in all these contentions, obtained the restoration of his English see by delivering up the town and castle of Lisieux to King Henry. A remarkable incident in the victory of Tenchebray is, that the royal Saxon, Edgar Atheling, was among the prisoners. Duke Robert had on many occasions treated him with great kindness and liberality. According to some accounts Edgar had followed Robert to the Holy Land;[3] but this is, at the least, doubtful; and the *Saxon Chronicle* represents him as having joined the duke only a short time before the battle of Tenchebray, where he charged with the Norman chivalry. This was his last public appearance. He was sent over to England, where, to show the Norman king's contempt of him, he was allowed to go at large. At the intercession of his niece, the Queen Maud, Henry granted him a trifling pension; and this survivor of so many changes and sanguinary revolutions passed the rest of his life in an obscure but tranquil solitude in the country. So perfect was the oblivion into which he fell, that not one of the chroniclers mentions the place of his residence, or records where or how he died. The fate of his friend Duke Robert, who had much less apathy, was infinitely more galling from the beginning, and his captivity was soon accompanied with other atrocities. He was committed a prisoner for life to one of his brother's castles. At first his keepers, appointing a proper guard, allowed him to take

---

[1] William of Malmesbury says, "He forgot and forgave too much."
[2] *Ordericus Vitalis.*

[3] In 1086, the last year of the Conqueror's reign, Edgar Atheling obtained permission to conduct 200 knights to Apulia, and thence to Palestine; but we are not informed what progress he made in this journey, and Duke Robert did not set out for the Holy Land until 1096, or ten years after.

air and exercise in the neighbouring woods and fields. One day he seized a horse, and, breaking from his guard, did his best to escape; but he was presently pursued, and taken in a morass, wherein his horse had stuck fast. Upon hearing of this attempt the king not only prescribed "a greater restraint and harder durance," but commanded that his sight should be destroyed, in order to render him incapable of such enterprises, and unapt to all royal or martial duties for the future. This detestable order was executed by a method which had become horribly common in Italy[1] during these ages, and which was not unknown in other countries on the Continent. A basin of copper or iron, made red-hot, was held close over the victim's eyes till the organs of sight were seared and destroyed. The wretched prince lived twenty-eight years after this, and died in Cardiff Castle in 1135, a few months before his brother Henry. He was nearly eighty years old, and had survived all the chiefs of name who rescued Jerusalem from the Saracens.

In getting possession of Robert's person Henry became master of Normandy. Rouen, the capital, submitted, and Falaise surrended after a short resistance. At the latter place William, the only son of Sibylla and Duke Robert, fell into his hands. When the child, who was then only five years old, was brought into the presence of his uncle, he sobbed and cried for mercy. It could not escape the king's far-reaching calculations that this boy's legitimate claims might cause him future trouble; but Henry, as if making a violent effort to rid himself of evil thoughts, suddenly commanded that he should be removed from him, and given in custody to Helie de St. Saen, a Norman noble, on whom (though he had married an illegitimate daughter of Duke Robert) he thought he could rely. He soon, however, repented of this arrangement, and sent a force to surprise the castle of St. Saen, and secure the person of young William. Helie fled with his pupil, and they were both honourably received at all the neighbouring courts, where the beauty, the innocence, the early misfortunes, and claims of the boy, gained him many protectors. The most powerful of these friends were Louis VI. of France, commonly called Le Gros, and Fulk, Earl of Anjou. As William Fitz-Robert, as he was called, grew up, and gave good

promise of being a valiant prince, they espoused his cause more decidedly, Louis engaging to grant him the investiture of Normandy, and Fulk to give him his daughter Sibylla in marriage, as soon as he should be of proper age. Before that period arrived, circumstances occurred (A.D. 1113) that hurried them into hostilities, and the Earl of Flanders having been induced to sanction, if not to join their league, Henry was attacked all along the frontiers of Normandy. He lost towns and castles, and was alarmed at the same time by a report, true or false, that some friends of Duke Robert had formed a plot against his life. When the war had lasted two years, Henry put an end to it by a skilful treaty, in which he regained whatever he had lost in Normandy, and in which the interests of William Fitz-Robert were overlooked. These advantages were obtained by giving the estates and honours of the

DUKE ROBERT'S TOWER, Cardiff Castle.[2]—J. Skinner Prout, from his sketch on the spot.

faithful Helie de St. Saen to his quondam ally, Fulk, Earl of Anjou, and by stipulating a marriage between his only son, Prince William of

---

[1] The punishment was usually applied to captive princes, fallen ministers, and personages of the highest rank and political influence. The Italians had even a verb to express it—*Abbacinare*, from *bacino*, a basin. "L'abbacinare è il medesimo che l'accecare; e perchè si faceva con un bacino rovente, che avvicinato agli occhi tenuti aperti per *forza*, concentrandosi il calore struggeva quo' panicelli, e risecccava l'umidità, che, come un' uva è intorno alla pupilla, e la ricopriva di una cotal nuvola, che gli toglieva la vista, si aveva preso questo nome d'abbacinare."

Such is the formal explanation of the horrid verb in the *Dictionary Del'n Crusca*.

[2] This castle, situated on the river Taff, which washes its walls, was built, A.D. 1110, by Robert Fitz-Hamon, one of the most renowned of William the Conqueror's captains, who, in 1091, conquered Glamorganshire. The tower represented in the engraving is that in which tradition says Robert, Duke of Normandy, was confined for upwards of twenty-six years. According to Ordo Vitalis and William of Malmesbury, Henry made his imprisonment as easy as possible, furnishing him with an elegant table, and buffoons to divert him, "pleasures which, for some years, he had preferred to all the duties of sovereign power."—*Lord Lyttleton.*—Grose's *Antiquities*.

England, and Matilda, another daughter of that earl. The previous contract between Fitz-Robert and Sibylla was broken off, and the Earl of Anjou agreed to give no more aid or countenance to that young prince.

These arrangements were not made without great sacrifices of money on the part of the English people; and some years before they were concluded, the nation was made to bear another burden.[1] By the feudal customs the king was entitled to levy a tax for the marrying of his eldest daughter; and (A.D. 1110) Henry affianced the Princess Matilda, a child only eight years old, to Henry V., Emperor of Germany. The high nominal rank of the party, and the general poverty of the German emperors in those days, would alike call for a large dowry; and Henry V. drove a hard bargain with his brother (and to-be-father-in-law) of England. The marriage portion seems to have been principally raised by a tax laid upon land. The stipulated sum was at length placed in the hands of the emperor's ambassadors, who conducted the young lady into Germany.

About this time Henry checked some incursions of the Welsh, the only wars waged in the interior of England during his reign. He despaired, however, of reducing them, and was fain to content himself with building a few castles, a little in advance of those erected by the Conqueror and the Red King. He also collected a number of Flemings, who had been driven into England by the misfortunes of their own country, and gave them the town of Haverfordwest, with the district of Ross, in Pembrokeshire. They were a brave and industrious people, skilled in manufacturing woollen cloths; and, increasing in wealth and numbers, they maintained themselves in their advanced post, in spite of the long efforts of the Welsh to drive them from it. But a subject which occupied the mind of the English king much more than the conquest of Wales, was the securing the succession of all his dominions to his only legitimate son William, to whom he confidently and proudly looked, as to one who was to perpetuate his lineage and power. Having already made all the barons and prelates of Normandy swear fealty and do homage to the boy, he exacted the same oaths in England, at a great council of all the bishops, earls, and barons of the kingdom; and being still pursued by the dread of the growing popularity, on the Continent, of his nephew Fitz-Robert, he artfully laboured to get him into his power, making use, among other means, of the most enticing promises—such as the immediate possession of three great earldoms in England. But that young prince would never trust the jailer of his father.

A.D. 1118. At a moment when the most formidable confederacy that ever threatened him was forming on the Continent, Henry lost his excellent consort, Maud the Good; and in about a month after he suffered a loss, which he probably felt much more, in the death of the Earl of Mellent, the ablest instrument of his ambition, the most skilful of all his ministers, who had so managed his foreign politics as to obtain the reputation of being the greatest statesman in Europe.

Henry's want of good faith had hurried on the storm which now burst upon him. He had secretly assisted his nephew Theobald,[2] Earl of Blois, in a revolt against his feudal superior and liege lord, the French king—he had broken off the match agreed upon between his son William and the Earl of Anjou's daughter, Matilda—and he had belied many of the promises made to the Norman barons in his hour of need. The league that was formed against him, therefore, included many of his own disaffected Norman subjects, Louis of France, Fulk of Anjou, and Baldwin, Earl of Flanders—the last-mentioned having fewer interested motives, and a purer affection for the gallant son of Duke Robert, than any of the others. The beginning of the war was altogether unfavourable to the allies, and King

---

[1] While public exactions were thus pressing on people of all ranks, the churchmen found ingenious methods of raising money for building purposes. As an illustration of this, we may take the following passage from the pages of Camden. Speaking of the monastery of Crowland, or Croyland, he says:—

"It is not necessary to write the private history of this monastery, for it is extant in Ingulphus, which is now printed; yet I am willing to make a short report of that which Petrus Blesensis, vice-chancellor to King Henry II., has related at large concerning the first building of this monastery, in the year 1112, to the end that from one single precedent we may learn by what means and by what assistances so many stately religious houses were built in all parts of this kingdom. Joffrid, the abbot, obtained of the archbishops of England, 'to every one that helped forward so religious a work, an indulgence of the third part of the penance enjoined for the sins he had committed.' With this he sent our monks everywhere to make collections, and having enough, he appointed St. Perpetua's and Felicity's day to be that on which he would lay the foundation, that the work, from those fortunate names, might be auspiciously begun.

"At this time the nobles and prelates, with the common people, met there in great numbers. Prayers being said and anthems sung, the abbot himself laid the first corner-stone on the east side; after him, every nobleman, according to his degree, laid his stone, and upon it some laid money, and others writings, by which they offered lands, advowsons of churches, tenths of their sheep, and other tithes of their several churches, certain measures of wheat, or a certain number of workmen or masons. On the other side, the common people, no less generous, offered, with great devotion, some of them money, and some one day's work every month till it should be finished; some to build whole pillars, and others pedestals, and others certain parts of the walls. The abbot afterwards made a speech, commending their great zeal and bounty in contributing to so pious a work; and by way of requital, he made every one of them a member of that monastery, and gave them a right to partake in all the spiritual blessings of that church. At last, having entertained them with a plentiful feast, he dismissed them in great joy."

[2] Elder brother of Stephen, who seized the English crown on Henry's death.

Louis at one time was forced to beg a suspension of hostilities. Then fortune veered, and King Henry lost ground; but after a succession of reverses, his better star prevailed, and he was made happy by the death of Baldwin, Earl of Flanders, the soul of the confederacy, who died of a wound received at the siege of Eu. Being thus relieved from one of his formidable enemies, he proceeded to detach another by means as prevalent as sword, or lance, or arrow-shot. He sent a large sum of money to the venal Earl of Anjou, and agreed that the marriage between his son and the earl's daughter should be solemnized forthwith. Fulk took the bribe, and abandoning his allies, went to prepare for the wedding. At the same time, Henry gained over most of the disaffected Norman barons; and, after two more years of a war of petty sieges, and of skirmishes scarcely deserving the name of battles, the French king saw himself deserted by all his allies.

An end was put to the war, now only maintained on one side by Louis, through the praiseworthy mediation of the pope,[1] who, however, laboured in vain to procure a mitigation of the severity exercised on Duke Robert, and a proper settlement for his son William. By this treaty of peace, Henry was to preserve undisturbed possession of Normandy; and his pride was saved by Louis consenting to receive the homage due to him for the duchy from the son instead of the father. This son, who was in his eighteenth year, had received the oaths of the Norman nobles, as also the hand of his bride, a child only twelve years old, whose father, Fulk of Anjou, had given her a considerable dower. King Henry now resolved to return triumphantly to England. The place of embarkation was Barfleur, where Rufus had landed after his stormy passage and impious daring of the elements.[2] The double retinue of the king and prince-royal was most numerous; and some delay was caused by the providing of accommodation and means of transport for so many noble personages, among whom were counted, we scarcely know how many, illegitimate children and mistresses of the king. On the 25th of November (A.D. 1120), however, all was ready, and the sails were joyously bent, as for a short and pleasant voyage. Thomas Fitz-Stephen, a mariner of some repute, presented himself to the king, and tendering a golden mark, said—"Stephen, son of Evrard, my father, served yours all his life by sea, and he it was who steered the ship in which your father sailed for the conquest of England. Sire king, I beg you to grant me the same office in fief: I have a vessel called the *Blanche-Nef*, well equipped and manned with fifty skilful mariners." The king replied that he had already chosen a vessel for himself, but that, in order to accede to the prayer of Fitz-Stephen, he would confide to his care the prince, with his companions and attendants. Henry then embarked, and setting sail in the afternoon with a favourable and gentle wind from the south, reached the English coast in safety on the following morning. The prince was accompanied in the *Blanche-Nef*, or "White Ship," by his half-brother Richard; his half-sister the Lady Marie,[3] Countess of Perche; Richard, Earl of Chester, with his wife, who was the king's niece; her brother, the prince's governor, with a host of gay young nobles, both of Normandy and of England, 140 in number, eighteen being ladies of the first rank—all these and their retinues amounting, with the crew, to about 300 persons. On such occasions it was usual to regale the mariners with a little wine, but the prince, and the young men with him, imprudently ordered three whole casks of wine to be distributed among the men, who "drank out their wits and reason." The captain had a sailor's pride in the speed of his craft and the qualities of his crew, and, though hours passed away, he promised to overtake every ship that had sailed before him. The prince certainly did not press his departure, for he spent some hours on deck in feasting and dancing with his company. A few prudent persons quitted the disorderly vessel, and went on shore. Night had set in before the *Blanche-Nef* started from her moorings, but it was a bright moonlight, and the wind, though it had freshened somewhat, was still fair and gentle. Fitz-Stephen, proud of his charge, held the helm; every sail was set, and still to increase the speed, the fifty sturdy mariners, encouraged by their boyish passengers, plied the oar with all their vigour. As they proceeded coastwise they got engaged among some rocks at a spot called Ras de Catte (now Ras de Catteville), and the White Ship struck on one of these with such violence on her larboard side, that several planks were started, and she instantly began to fill. A cry of alarm and horror was raised at once by 300 voices, and was heard on board some of the king's ships that had gained the high sea, but nobody there suspected the cause. Fitz-Stephen lowered a boat, and putting the prince with some of his companions in it, advised them to row for the shore, and save themselves. This would not have been difficult, for the sea

---

[1] Calixtus II. He was related by marriage to King Henry, and personally visited that sovereign, who, among other signal falsehoods, assured him that his brother Robert was not a prisoner, but entertained in a sumptuous manner in one of the royal castles, where he enjoyed as much liberty and amusement as he desired.
[2] See vol. i. p. 216. Most of the old historians are of opinion that the drowning of the nephew was a judgment provoked by the presumption of the uncle.

[3] By some writers this lady is called Maud, and by others Adele or Adela. The name of her mother is not mentioned. Richard was the son of an English mistress, who is called "the widow of Anskill, a nobleman that lived near the monastery of Abingdon."

was smooth, and the coast at no great distance; but his sister, Marie, had been left behind in the ship, and her shrieks touched the heart of the prince—the best or most generous deed of whose life seems to have been his last. He ordered the boat to be put back to take her in; but such numbers leaped into it at the same time as the lady, that it was upset or swamped, and all in it perished. The ship also went down with all on board. Only two men escaped by rising and clinging to the main-yard, which floated, and was probably detached from the wreck: one of these was a butcher of Rouen, named Berold, the other a young man of higher condition, named Godfrey, the son of Gilbert de l'Aigle. Fitz-Stephen, the unfortunate captain, seeing the heads of two men clinging to the yard, swam to them. "And the king's son," said he, "what has happened to him?" "He is gone! neither he, nor his brother, nor his sister, nor any person of his company, has appeared above water." "Woe to me!" cried Fitz-Stephen; and then plunged to the bottom. The night was cold, and the young nobleman, the more delicate of the two survivors, became exhausted; and after holding on for some hours let go the yard, and, recommending his poor companion to God's mercy, sunk to the bottom of the sea. The butcher of Rouen, the poorest of all those who had embarked in the White Ship, wrapped in his sheep-skin coat,[1] held on till morning, when he was seen from the shore, and saved by some fishermen; and from him, being the sole survivor, the circumstances of the fearful event were learned. The tidings reached England in the course of the following day, but no one would venture on communicating them to the king. For three days the courtiers concealed the fact, and at last they sent in a little boy, who, weeping bitterly with "no counterfeit passion," fell at his feet, and told him that the White Ship was lost, and that all on board had perished. The hard heart of Henry was not proof to this shock—he sunk to the ground in a swoon; and though he survived it many years, and indulged again in his habitual ambition, he was never afterwards seen to smile.[2] By the people at large, the death of the young prince was regarded with satisfaction; for independently of his hateful vices, by which he had utterly forfeited their sympathy, he had been often heard to threaten that he would yoke the English natives to the plough, and treat them like beasts of burden, when he became king.

As Henry was now deprived of his only legitimate son, he was cast upon new plans for the securing of his various states in his family. At the same time, the same event seemed to brighten the prospects of his nephew, William of Normandy, whose friends certainly increased soon after the demise of the heir apparent. A circumstance connected with the marriage of the drowned prince hastened and gave a colour of just resentment to one declaration in favour of Fitz-Robert. His former friend Fulk, Earl of Anjou, demanded back from Henry his daughter Matilda, together with the dower he had given to Prince William. King Henry willingly gave up the young lady,[3] but refused to part with the money; and upon this, Fulk, who was an adept in these matters, renewed his matrimonial negotiations with the son of Duke Robert, and finally affianced to him his younger daughter Sibylla, putting him, meanwhile, in possession of the earldom of Mons. Louis of France continued to favour the young prince, and some of the most powerful of the Norman barons entered into a conspiracy in his favour against his unkind uncle, Henry. But no art—no precaution—could conceal these manoeuvres from the English king, who had spies everywhere, and who fell like a thunderbolt among the Norman lords before they were prepared. It cost him, however, more than a year to subdue this revolt; but then he made the Norman leaders of it prisoners, and induced the Earl of Anjou once more to abandon the cause of his intended son-in-law.

Some time before effecting this peace, Henry, in the vain hope of offspring, which he thought must destroy the expectations of his nephew, espoused Adelais, or Alice, daughter of Geoffrey, Duke of Louvain, and niece to the reigning pope, Calixtus II. This new queen was young, and very beautiful, but the marriage was not productive of any issue; and after three or four years had passed, the king formed the bold design of settling the crown of England and the ducal coronet of Normandy on his daughter Matilda, who had become a widow in 1124, by the death of her husband, the Emperor Henry V.

On the solemn day of Christmas (A.D. 1126) there was a general assembly in Windsor Castle, of the bishops, abbots, barons, and all the great tenants of the crown, who, for the most part acting against their inward conviction, *unanimously* declared the ex-empress Matilda to be the next heir to the throne, in the case (now not problematical) of her father's dying without legitimate male issue. They then swore to maintain her succession—the clergy swearing first, in the order of their rank, and after them the laity, among whom there seems to have been more than one dispute touching precedence.[4] The most

---

[1] Qui pauperior erat omnibus, robore amictus ex arietinis pellibus. . . . . *Orderic.*
[2] *Orderic.; Malmesb.; Hen. Hunt.; R. Hoveden.; W. Gemet.*
[3] Ten years after, Matilda became a nun in the celebrated convent of Fontevraud.
[4] David, King of Scotland, in his quality of English earl, or holder of lands in England, swore first *of all* to support Matilda, who was his own niece.

remarkable of these disputes, as being an index to hidden aspirations, was that for priority between Stephen, Earl of Boulogne, and Robert, Earl of Gloucester. Stephen was the king's nephew, by the daughter of the Conqueror, Henry's sister, Adela: Robert, on the other side, was the king's own son, but was of illegitimate birth; and the delicate point to be decided was, whether precedence was due to legitimacy of birth or to nearness of blood; or, in other words, which of the two—the lawfully begotten nephew of a king, or the unlawfully begotten son of a king—was the greater personage. The shade of the great Conqueror might have been vexed at such a discussion; but though the reigning family derived its claim from a bastard, the question was decided by the assembly in favour of the nephew, Stephen, who accordingly swore first. The question had not arisen out of the small spirit of courtly form and etiquette; the disputants had higher objects. They contemplated perjury in the very preliminary of their oaths. Feeling, in common with every baron present at that wholesale swearing, that the succession of Matilda was insecure, they both looked forward to the crown; and on that account each was anxious to be declared the first prince of the blood.

The same year that brought Matilda to England, saw Fulk, the Earl of Anjou, depart for the Holy Land, it being his destiny to become a very indifferent king of Jerusalem. He renounced the government of the province of Anjou to his son, Geoffrey, surnamed *Plantagenet*, on account of a custom he had of wearing a sprig of flowering broom[1] in his cap like a feather. Henry had many times felt the hostile power of the earls of Anjou, and various political considerations induced him to conclude a marriage between his daughter Matilda and this Geoffrey, the son of Fulk. The ex-empress, though partly against her liking, consented to the match, which was negotiated and concluded with great secrecy. The barons of England and Normandy pretended that the king had no right thus to dispose of their future sovereign without previously consulting them; they were generally dissatisfied with the proceeding, and some of them openly declared that it released them from the obligations of the oath they had taken to Matilda; but Henry disregarded their murmurs, and congratulated himself on his policy, which united the interests of the house of Anjou with those of his own. The marriage was celebrated at Rouen, in the octaves of the feast of Whitsuntide, 1127, and the festival was prolonged during three weeks. Henry somewhat despotically ordered, by proclamation, everybody to be merry, and all who refused, to be deemed as offenders, and guilty of disloyalty.

GEOFFREY PLANTAGENET.[2]
From his monumental tablet.

But, rejoice as he might, Henry felt that the succession of his daughter could never be secure, if his nephew, William Fitz-Robert, survived him; and he applied himself with all his craft to effect the ruin of that young man, who, at the moment, occupied a position that made him truly formidable. At the late peace, the French king had not abandoned his interests, like Fulk, the Earl of Anjou; on the contrary, Louis invited him again to his court, and soon after, in lieu of Sibylla of Anjou, gave him the hand of his queen's sister, and with her, as a portion, the countries of Pontoise, Chaumont, and the Vexin, on the borders of Normandy. Soon after this advantageous settlement, Charles the Good, Earl of Flanders, successor to Baldwin, the steady friend of the son of Duke Robert, was murdered in a church at the very foot of the altar. The king of France entered Flanders, as liege lord, and with the consent of the people, to punish the sacrilegious murderers; and having done this, he, in virtue of his feudal suzerainty, conferred the earldom upon young William of Normandy, who had accompanied him in the expedition, and who, had such claims been allowed, had a good hereditary right to it as the representative of his grand-

---

[1] In old French the name of the plant is *genest* (now *genêt*), from the Latin *genista*.

[2] The beautiful enamelled tablet from which this representation is derived was formerly in the church of St. Julien, and is now preserved in the museum at Mans. The earl appears at full length under an arch decorated with semicircular ornaments, and supported on either side by a pillar with a capital of foliage. He wears a steel cap in form like the Phrygian, enamelled with a leopard of gold. In his right hand is a sword, his left supports a shield, which is adorned with golden leopards on a blue field, similar to the cap. This shield is of the long kite shape, and reaches from the shoulders to the feet; it bears a striking resemblance to those represented on the Bayeux Tapestry, save that the upper part is not curved, though the angles are rounded. He wears an under tunic of light blue, ornamented with borders of gold, an upper one of green; his mantle is of light blue, and is lined with vair; above the mantle and over the right shoulder is his belt. The whole groundwork of the tablet is curiously filled up with small trefoils, scroll, and other ornaments. Over the head of the figure is this inscription:—

ENSE TVO, PRINCEPS, PREDONVM TVRBA FVGATVR,
ECCLE' IIS Q' QVIES PACE VIGENTE DATVR.

The heraldic bearings on this tablet—by some thought to be griffins (though they are in all probability leopards or lions)—have excited much attention from being perhaps the earliest specimen extant of armorial bearings. The style in which the tablet is executed leaves little doubt but that this memorial of Geoffrey Plantagenet was made about the time when he died.

mother, Matilda, who was daughter of Earl Baldwin of the old legitimate line. The Flemish people offered no opposition to their new earl; and King Louis, with his army, departed, in the gratifying conviction that he had secured a stable dominion to his gallant young brother-in-law, and placed him in a situation the most favourable for the conquest of Normandy, or at least for the curbing of that ambition in the English king, which continued to give uneasiness to Louis.

CHAPTER HOUSE AND PART OF THE CATHEDRAL, ST. OMER.[1]
Weale's Architectural Papers.

This uneasiness could not fail of being increased by the union between the Norman line and the house of Anjou, which took place at this very time.

But the French army had scarcely left the country, when the Flemish people broke out into revolt against their new earl, and asked and received assistance from King Henry. A respectable party, however, adhered to William, who had many qualities to insure respect and love. In the field he had a manifest advantage over the ill-directed insurgents, who then invited Thiedrik or Thierry, Landgrave of Alsace, to put himself at their head. Thierry gladly accepted their invitation. He advanced a claim to the succession on the ground of his descent from some old chief of the country; and Henry, who found in him the instrument he wanted, sent him money, and engaged to support him with all his might. The treacherous surrender of Lisle, Ghent, and other important places in Flanders, immediately followed; but William, who had the courage and military skill of his unfortunate father, without any of his indolence, completely defeated his antagonist, Thierry, under the walls of Alost. Most unfortunately, however, in the moment of victory, he received a pike wound in the hand, and this

[1] This fine cathedral is of the style of transition from the round to the pointed style of the twelfth century.

being neglected, or improperly treated by ignorant surgeons, brought on a mortification. He was conveyed to the monastery of St. Omer, where he died on the 27th July, 1128, in his twenty-sixth year. In his last moments he wrote to his unnatural uncle, to implore mercy for the Norman barons who had followed his fortunes. Henry, in the joy of his heart, granted the request of his deceased nephew, who left no children to prolong the king's inquietude, or serve as a rallying point to the disaffected nobles. We are not informed whether the tidings of William's brief greatness were conveyed into the dungeon of Cardiff Castle, to solace the heart of his suffering father, or whether the news of his early death, which so soon followed it, was in mercy concealed from the blind old man.

To work out his purposes, Henry had hesitated at no treachery, no bloodshed, no crime, and yet he fondly hoped to end his days in tranquillity. The winding up of his story is little more than a succession of petty family jars and discords—the very bathos of ambition and worldly grandeur. His daughter, Matilda, presuming on the imperial rank she had held, and being naturally of a proud, imperious temper, soon quarrelled with her husband: a separation took place; Matilda returned to England, and her father was occupied during many months with these family disputes, and in negotiating a peace between man and wife. At length a reconciliation was patched up, and Matilda returned to her husband. The oath-breaker, her father, thought he could never exact oaths enough from others; and before his daughter left England, he made the prelates and barons again swear fealty to her. Henry, who in spite of these precautions, well knew the chances to which Matilda would be exposed, ardently longed for a grandson, whom he hoped to see grow up; but for six years he was kept uneasy and unhappy by the unfruitfulness of the marriage. In March, 1133, however, Matilda was delivered, at Mans, of her first child, Henry, styled Fitz-Empress, who was afterwards Henry II. of England. At the birth of this grandson the king again convoked the barons of England and Normandy, and made them recognize as his successors the children of his daughter, after him and *after her*. The nobles, being accustomed to the taking of oaths which they meant to break, swore fealty afresh, not only to Matilda, but to her infant son, and the rest of her progeny as yet unborn. The ex-empress gave birth to two more princes, Geoffrey and William, in the course of the two following years; but even a growing family failed to endear her husband to her: she quarrelled with him on all possible occasions; and as her father took her part, she kept his mind almost constantly occupied with their dissensions. Under these circumstances, it was not natural that Geoffrey Plantagenet should prove a loving and dutiful son-in-law. He demanded immediate possession of Normandy, which he said Henry had promised him; and when the king refused, he broke out into threats and insults. Matilda, it is said, exerted her malignant and ingenious spirit in widening the breach between her own husband and father. The four last years of Henry's reign, which were spent wholly abroad, were troubled with these domestic broils. At length an incursion of the Welsh demanded his presence in England; and he was preparing for that journey, when death despatched him on a longer one. His health and spirits had been for some time visibly on the decline. On the 25th of November, "to drive his grief away, he went abroad to hunt." Having pursued his sport during the day, in the woods of Lions-la-Forêt, in Normandy,[1] he returned home in the evening, "somewhat amended," and being hungry, "would needs eat of a lamprey, though his physician ever counselled him to the contrary." The lamprey or lampreys he ate brought on an indigestion; and the indigestion a fever. On the third day, despairing of his recovery, he sent for the Archbishop of Rouen, who administered the sacrament and extreme unction; and on the seventh day of his illness, which was Sunday, December 1, A.D. 1135, he expired at the midnight hour. He was in his sixty-seventh year, and had reigned thirty-five years and four months, wanting four days. By his will he left to his daughter, Matilda, and her heirs for ever, all his territories on either side the sea; and he desired that when his lawful debts were discharged, and the liveries and wages of his retainers paid, the residue of his effects should be distributed among the poor. They kept the

MANS.[2]—From a modern French print.

royal bowels in Normandy, and deposited them in the church of St. Mary at Rouen, which his mother had founded; but the body was conveyed to England, and interred in Reading Abbey, which Henry had built himself.

The best circumstances attending his long reign were, the peace he maintained in England, and a partial respect to the laws which his vigorous government imposed on his haughty and ferocious barons.[3] Considering the times, extraordinary care had been taken of his education. His natural abilities were excellent; and so great was his progress in the philosophy and literature of the age, that his contemporaries honoured him

---

[1] Lions-la-Forêt, now a town, is at a short distance from Rouen, and is approached through the remains of a forest, to which it owes its surname. To this forest, once of great extent, the Norman princes eagerly resorted for the diversion of the chase. So early as 929, William I., Duke of Normandy, built a hunting-box there, which afterwards became a castle important from its strength. This forest was the scene in which, as congenial ground, were laid many of the adventures recorded in the old chronicles and romances.—*Tour in Normandy,* by H. Gally Knight.

[2] The view includes the cathedral and part of the fortifications of the town. The cathedral is built upon the foundations of an ancient temple.

The most ancient part of the edifice is the nave, which is by different authorities ascribed to the ninth and the eleventh centuries. The choir and transepts are of the fifteenth century. The choir is remarkably bold in style, and has a lofty roof; it contains a quantity of fine stained glass. A tower at the end of one of the transepts rises upwards of 200 ft. from the ground. The cathedral is surrounded by thirteen small chapels. The town contains several other churches, and an abbey of St. Vincent, now occupied as a seminary for priests. Mans contains several vestiges of Roman edifices, among which are those of an amphitheatre.

[3] "During the tyrannical reign of Rufus, the arbitrary will of the monarch constituted the only code by which the subject was ruled; but the charter of Henry I 'restored the law of Edward;' or, in other words, re-established or intended to re-establish the Anglo-Saxon jurisprudence as it existed before the invasion. To what extent the alterations, consequent upon the change of property amongst the higher orders, had modified the older institutions, we cannot entirely ascertain; and some of the doctrines introduced by the Conqueror were silently preparing the way for future revolutions. But, in theory, the customs of the ancient national monarchs still prevailed, and the administration of the law, though severe, was neither discreditable to the government nor ungrateful to a people, then advancing in good order and civilization."—Palgrave's *Rise and Progress of the English Commonwealth,* part i. p. 240.

with the name of Beauclerk, or the fine scholar. He was proud of his learning, and in the habit of saying that he considered an unlearned king as nothing better than a crowned ass. He was very fond of men of letters, and of wild beasts; and, to enjoy both, he often fixed his residence between them; or, in the words of one of the chroniclers, "He took chief pleasure to reside in his new palace, which himself built at Oxford, both for the delight he had in learned men— himself being very learned—and for the vicinity of his new park at Woodstock, which he had fraught with all kinds of strange beasts, wherein he much delighted, as lions, leopards, lynxes, camels, porcupines, and the like."[1] His love of letters, however, did not interfere with his revenge. In the last war in which he was personally engaged on the Continent, Luke de Barré, a knightly poet, who had fought against him, was made prisoner, and barbarously sentenced to lose his eyes. Charles the Good, Earl of Flanders, who was present, remonstrated against the punishment, urging, among other things, that it was not the custom to inflict bodily punishment on men of the rank of knights, who had done battle in the service of their immediate superior. Henry replied, "This is not the first time that Luke de Barré has borne arms against me: but he has been guilty of still worse things; for he has satirized me in his poems, and made me a laughing-stock to mine enemies. From his example, let other verse-makers learn what they have to expect when they offend the King of England." The cruel sentence was wholly or partly executed, and the poet, in a paroxysm of agony, burst from the savage hands of the executioners, and dashed out his brains against the wall.[3] Early in life he chose his chaplain by the rapidity with which he got through a mass, saying, that no man could be so fit a mass-priest for soldiers as one who did his work with such despatch. While making war in Normandy, Henry chanced to enter this priest's church, as it lay on his road, near Caen. "And when the royal youth," says William of Newbury, "said, 'Follow me!' he adhered as closely to him as Peter did to his heavenly Lord, uttering a similar command; for Peter, leaving his vessel, followed the King of kings—he, leaving his church, followed the prince, and, being appointed chaplain to him and his troops, became a blind leader of the blind." In some worldly respects, at least, the censure was too severe. The speedy chaplain, who will reappear under the reign of Stephen, was Roger, afterwards the famous Bishop of Sarum, and treasurer and favourite minister to Henry, who invariably made such elections from among the most able and quick-sighted of men.[4]

REMAINS OF READING ABBEY.[2]—Grose's Antiquities.

---

[1] *Rossus.*, quoted in Speed's *Chronicle*.
[2] Reading Abbey was built by Henry I., who was buried within its walls. It was subsequently converted into a royal palace, but it has long since fallen into total ruin.
[3] *Ordericus Vitalis.*
[4] During Henry's frequent and long absences from England, Roger seems almost without exception to have been lord-lieutenant, or regent of the kingdom.

CHAPTER IV.—CIVIL AND MILITARY HISTORY.

STEPHEN.—A.D. 1135—1154.

Opposition made to the succession of Matilda—Stephen is crowned in her stead—His unwise concessions to the barons—The Earl of Gloucester intrigues against him in favour of Matilda—The Scots invade England—Battle of the Standard, and defeat of the Scots—The Bishop of Sarum's rebellion against Stephen—Its suppression—Matilda lands in England and claims the crown—Wars between her and Stephen—Stephen taken prisoner—Matilda driven from London by the adherents of Stephen—She is defeated, and Stephen restored—Troubles of the land from the contest—Matilda's singular escape from Oxford—She retires to Normandy—Quarrels of Stephen with his prelates and barons—Prince Henry, son of Matilda, asserts his right to the crown—He invades England—Treaty by which Stephen retains the crown for life, with Henry for his successor—Death of Stephen.

SCARCELY was Henry Beauclerk dead when events proved how fruitless were all his pains and precautions to secure the succession to his daughter, and how utterly valueless were *unanimous* oaths which were rather the offspring of fear than of inward conviction and good-will. Passing over the always questionable obligation of oaths of this nature, there were several capital obstacles to bar the avenues of the throne to Matilda. The first among these was her sex. Since the time of the ancient Britons, England had never obeyed a female sovereign; and the Saxons for a long time had even a marked aversion to the name and dignity of queen when applied only to the reigning king's wife.[1] In the same manner, the Normans had never known a female reign, the notion of which was most repugnant to the whole course of their habits and feelings. To hold their fiefs "under the distaff" (as it was called) was considered humiliating to a nobility whose business was war, and whose king, according to the feudal system, was little else than the first of many warriors—a chief expected to be in the saddle, and at the head of his chivalry whenever occasion demanded. We accordingly find that a loud and general cry was raised by the Anglo-Norman and Norman barons, that it would be most disgraceful for so many noble knights to obey the orders of a woman. In certain stages of society, and in all the earliest, the Salic law, or that portion of it excluding females from the throne, to which we have limited its name and meaning, is a natural law. These all but insurmountable objections would not hold good against her son Henry; but that prince was an infant not yet four years old, and regencies under a long minority were as incompatible with the spirit and condition of the times, as a female reign. Queens governing in their own right and by themselves, and faithfully guarded minorities, are both the product of an age much more civilized and settled than the twelfth century, and the approach to them was slow and gradual. It was something, however, to have confined the right of succession to the legitimately born; for if the case had occurred a little earlier in England, the grown-up and experienced natural son of the king, standing in the position of Robert, Earl of Gloucester, might possibly have been elected without scruple, as had happened to Edmund Ironside, Athelstane, and others of the Saxon line.

No one was better acquainted with the spirit of the times, and the obstacles raised against Matilda and Earl Robert, than the ambitious Stephen, nephew of the late king, who had taken many measures beforehand, who was encouraged by the irregularity of the succession ever since the Conquest, and who would no doubt give the widest interpretation to whatever of elective character was held to belong to the English crown. Henry had been unusually bountiful to this nephew. He married him to Maud, daughter and heir of Eustace, Count of Boulogne, who brought him, in addition to the feudal sovereignty of Boulogne, immense estates in England, which had been conferred by the Conqueror on the family of the count. By this marriage Stephen also acquired another close connection with the royal family of England, and a new hold upon the sympathies of the English, as his wife Maud was of the old Saxon stock, being the only child of Mary of Scotland, sister to David, the reigning king, as also to the good Queen Maud, the first wife of Henry, and mother of the Empress Matilda. Still further to aggrandize this favourite nephew, Henry conferred upon him the great estate forfeited by Robert Mallet in England, and that forfeited by the Earl of Mortaigne in Normandy. He also brought over Stephen's younger brother, Henry, who, being a church-

---

[1] See vol. I. Saxon Period.

man, was created abbot of Glastonbury and Bishop of Winchester. Stephen had resided much in England, and had rendered himself exceedingly popular both to the Normans and the people of Saxon race. The barons and knights admired him for his undoubted bravery and activity—the people for his generosity, the beauty of his person, and his affable, familiar manners. The king might not know it, but he was the popular favourite in the already important and fast-rising city of London before Henry's death. When that event happened, he was nearer England than Matilda, whose rights he had long determined to dispute. Taking advantage of his situation, he crossed the Channel immediately, and though the gates of Dover and Canterbury were shut against him, he was received in London with enthusiastic joy, the populace saluting him as king without waiting for the formalities of the election and consecration. The first step to the English throne in those days, as we have seen in the cases of Rufus and Henry, was to get possession of the royal treasury at Winchester. Stephen's own brother was Bishop of Winchester, and by his assistance he got the keys into his hands. The treasure consisted of £100,000 in money, besides plate and jewels of great value. His episcopal brother was otherwise of the greatest use, being mainly instrumental in winning over Roger, Bishop of Sarum, then chief justiciary and regent of the kingdom, and William Corboil, Archbishop of Canterbury. Bishop Roger, he who had been the speedy mass-priest of King Henry, was easily gained through his constant craving after money; but the primate was not assailable on that side, being a very conscientious though weak man; it was therefore thought necessary to practise a deception upon him, and Hugh Bigod, steward of the late household, made oath before him and other lords of the land, that the king on his death-bed had adopted and chosen his nephew, Stephen, to be his heir and successor, *because* his daughter the empress had grievously offended him by her recent conduct. This was a most disgraceful measure; and those men were more honest, and in every sense occupied better ground, who maintained that the great kingdom of England was not a heritable property, or a thing to be willed away by a dying king, without the consent and against the customs of the people. After hearing Bigod's oath, the archbishop seems to have floated quietly with the current, without offering either resistance or remonstrance. But there were other oaths to be considered, for the whole body of the clergy and nobility had repeatedly sworn fealty to Matilda. We have already shown how the oaths were considered by the mass; and now the all-prevalent Roger, Bishop of Sarum,

openly declared that those vows of allegiance were null and void, because, without the consent of the lords of the land, the empress was married out of the realm; whereas they took their oath to receive her as their queen upon the express condition that she should never be so married without their concurrence.[1] Some scruples may have remained, but no opposition was offered to his election, and on the 26th of December, being St. Stephen's Day, Stephen was hallowed and crowned at Westminster by the primate, William Corboil. Immediately after his coronation, he went to Reading, to attend the burial of the body of his uncle, King Henry, and from Reading Abbey he proceeded to Oxford, where he summoned a great council of the prelates, abbots, and lay-barons of the kingdom, that he might receive their oaths of allegiance, and consult with them on the affairs of the state. When the assembly met, he allowed the clergy to annex a condition, which, as they were sure to assume the right of interpretation, rendered their oaths less binding even than usual. They swore to obey him as their king so long as he should preserve their church liberties, and the vigour of discipline, and no longer. This large concession, however, had the effect of conciliating the bishops and abbots, and the confirmation of the pope soon followed. The letter of Innocent II., which ratified Stephen's title, was brief and clear.[2]

Stephen weakened his right instead of strengthening it, by introducing a variety of titles into his charter, which, in imitation of his predecessor Henry, he issued at this time; but particular stress seems to have been laid on his election as king, "with the consent of the clergy and people," and on the confirmation granted him by the pope. In this same charter he promised to redress all grievances, and grant to the people all the good laws and good customs of Edward the Confessor. Whatever were his natural inclinations (and we are inclined to believe they were not bad or ungenerous), the circumstances in which he was placed, and the villainous instruments with which he had to work, from the beginning to the end of his troubled reign, put it wholly out of his power to keep the promises he had made, and the condition of the English people became infinitely worse under him than it had been under Henry, or even under Rufus. A concession which he made to the lay barons contributed largely to the frightful anarchy which ensued. To secure their affections and to strengthen himself, as he thought, against the empress, he granted them all permission to

---

[1] Matt. Paris.; Gesta Steph.
[2] Scrip. Rer. Franc. The letter of the pope has been preserved by Richard of Hexham. It may be possible, though it appears scarcely probable, that the pope knew nothing of the oaths previously taken to Matilda and her children.

fortify their castles and build new ones; and these, almost without an exception, became dens of thieves and cut-throats. At the same time he made large promises to the venal and rapacious nobles, to engage them the more in support of his title to the crown, and gave them strong assurances that they should enjoy more *privileges* and offices under him than they had possessed in the reigns of his Norman predecessors. The keeping of these engagements with the barons would of itself render nugatory his promises to the English people; and the non-performance of them was sure to bring down on Stephen's head the vengeance of a warlike body of men, who were almost everything in the nation, and far too much, when united, for any royal authority, however legitimately founded. At first, and probably on account of the large sum of money he had in hand to meet demands, all went on in great peace and harmony; and the court which the new king held in London during the festival of Easter, in the first year of his reign, was more splendid, and better attended in every respect, than any that had yet been seen in England.[1]

Nor were the prelates and barons in Normandy more averse to the succession of Stephen than their brethren in England. The old reasons for desiring a continuance of their union with our island were still in force with many of them; and there was an hereditary animosity between the nobles and people of Normandy and those of Anjou, so that when Geoffrey Plantagenet, Earl of Anjou, marched into the duchy to assert the rights of his wife Matilda, he and his Angevins met with a determined opposition, and he was, soon after, glad to conclude a peace or truce for two years with Stephen, on condition of receiving during that time an annual pension of 5000 marks. When Stephen appeared on the Continent he met with nothing to indicate that he was considered as an unlawful usurper: the Normans swore allegiance, and the French king (Louis VII.), with whom he had an interview, formed an alliance by contracting his young sister Constance with Eustace, Stephen's son, and, as suzerain, granted the investiture of Normandy to Eustace, who was then a mere child.

During the first year of Stephen's reign England was disturbed only by the revolt of the Earl of Exeter, who was discontented with his share in the new king's liberalities; and by a Scottish incursion made into the northern counties in support of Matilda by her uncle King David,[2] who, however, was bought off for the present, by the grant of the lordship of Huntingdon and the castle of Carlisle, with a few other concessions.

Robert, Earl of Gloucester, the late king's natural son, who had so vehemently disputed the question of precedence with Stephen, merged his own pretensions to the crown in those of his half-sister Matilda, whose cause he resolved to promote in England conjointly with his own immediate advantages. Pretending to be reconciled to his rule, he came over from the Continent (A.D. 1137) and took the oaths of fealty and homage to Stephen, by the performance of which ceremony he obtained instant possession of his vast estates in England; and the first use he made of the advantages the oaths procured him, was to intrigue with the nobles in favour of his half-sister. The happy calm in which England lay did not last long after the Earl of Gloucester's arrival. Several of the barons, alleging their services had not met with due reward, began to seize, by force of arms, different parts of the royal demesne, which they said Stephen had promised them in fief. Hugh Bigod, who had sworn that King Henry had appointed Stephen his successor, and who probably put a high price on his perjury, was foremost among the disaffected, and seized Norwich Castle. Other royal castles were besieged and taken, or were treacherously surrendered. They were nearly all soon retaken by the king, but the spirit of revolt was rife among the nobles, and the sedition, suppressed on one spot, burst forth on others. Stephen, however, was lenient and merciful beyond all precedent to the vanquished.

The Earl of Gloucester, having settled with his friends the plan of a most extensive insurrection, and induced the Scottish king to promise another invasion of England, withdrew beyond sea, and sent a letter of defiance to Stephen, in which he formally renounced his homage. Other great barons—all pleading that Stephen had not given them enough, nor extended their privileges as he had promised—fell from his side, and withdrew to their castles, which by his permission they had already strongly fortified. He was abandoned, like Shakspeare's Macbeth, but his soul was as high as that usurper's. "The traitors!" he cried, "they themselves made me a king, and now they fall from me; but by God's birth, they shall never call me a deposed king!"[3] At this crisis of his fortunes, he displayed extraordinary activity and valour; but having no other politic means of any efficacy with such men, who were all grasping for estates, honours, and employments, he trenched on the domains of the crown, and had again recourse to his old system of promising more than he could possibly perform. The history of those

---

[1] *Henry Hunting.*
[2] The Scottish king was equally uncle to Stephen's wife, but he probably remembered the oaths he had taken to the mother of Henry.

[3] *William of Malmesbury.*

petty sieges of baronial castles, wherein Stephen was almost invariably successful, is singularly uninteresting; but the campaign against the Scots has some remarkable features. While he was engaged with the revolted barons in the south, King David, true to his promise, but badly supported by the Earl of Gloucester and Matilda, who did not arrive in England to put themselves at the head of their party till a year later, gathered his forces together from every part of his dominions—from the Lowlands, the Highlands, and the Isles—from the great promontory of Galloway, the Cheviot Hills, and from that nursing-place of hardy, lawless men, the Border-land between the two kingdoms—and crossing the Tweed (March, 1138), advanced boldly into Northumberland, riding with Prince Henry, his son and heir, at the head of as numerous, as mixed, and, in the main, as wild a host as ever trode this ground. These "Scottish ants," as an old writer calls them,[1] overran the whole of the country that lies between the Tweed and the Tees. "As for the King of Scots himself," says the anonymous author of *Gesta Stephani*, "he was a prince of a mild and merciful disposition; but the Scots were a barbarous and impure nation, and their king, leading hordes of them from the remotest parts of that land, was unable to restrain their wickedness." The Normans of the time purposely exaggerated the barbarous excesses — committed chiefly by the Gallowegians, the Highlanders, and the men of the Isles—in order to make the English fight more desperately on their side; for had they relied solely on their chivalry, and the men-at-arms and mercenaries in the service of their northern barons, their case would have been hopeless. At the same time they conciliated the English people of the north by a strong appeal to the local superstitions—they invoked the names of the saints of Saxon race whom they had been wont to treat with little respect; and the popular banners of St. Cuthbert of Durham (or, according to some, of St. Peter of York), St. John of Beverley, and St. Wilfrid of Ripon, which had long lain dust-covered in the churches, were reproduced in the army, as the pledges and means of victory. So rapid was the advance of King David, that Stephen had not time to reach the scene of hostilities; and the defence of the north was, in a great measure, left to Toustain or Thurstan, Archbishop of York, an infirm, decrepid old man, but whose warlike energies, address, and cunning were not affected by age and disease. It was mainly he who organized the army of defence which was got together in a hurry. He eloquently exhorted the men to fight to the last, for God and their country, telling them victory was certain, and paradise the meed of all who should fall in battle against the Scots; he made them swear never to desert each other; he gave them his blessing and the remission of their sins; he sent forth all his clergy, bishops, and chaplains, and the curates, who led their parishioners, "the bravest men of Yorkshire;" and though sickness prevented him from putting on his own coat of mail, he sent Raoul or Ranulf, the Bishop of Durham, to represent him on the field of battle. Each lay baron of the north headed his own vassals; but a more extensive command of divisions was intrusted by the archbishop to William Piperel or Peverel, and Walter Espec, of Nottinghamshire, and Gilbert de Lacy and his brother Walter, of Yorkshire. As the Scots were already upon the Tees, the Anglo-Norman army drew up between that river and the Humber, choosing their own battle-field at Elfer-tun, now Northallerton, about equidistant from York and Durham. Here they erected a remarkable standard, from which the battle has taken its name. A car upon four wheels, which will remind the reader of Italian history of the *carroccio* of the people of Lombardy,[2] was drawn to the centre of the position; the mast of a vessel was strongly fastened in the car; at the top of the mast a large crucifix was displayed, having in its centre a silver box containing the consecrated wafer, or sacrament; and, lower down, the mast was decorated with the banners of the three English saints. Around this sacred standard many of the English yeomanry and peasants from the plains, wolds, and woodlands of Yorkshire, Nottingham, and Lincolnshire, gathered of their own accord. These men were all armed with large bows and arrows two cubits long; they had the fame of being excellent archers, and the Normans gladly assigned them posts in the foremost and most exposed ranks of the army.

The Scots, whose standard was a simple lance, with a sprig of the "blooming heather" wreathed round it, crossed the Tees in several divisions. Prince Henry commanded the first corps, which consisted of men from the Lowlands of Scotland, armed with cuirasses and long pikes; of archers from Teviotdale, and Liddesdale, and all the

---

[1] Matthew Paris.
[2] The carroccio, or great standard car, is said to have been invented or first used by Eribert, Archbishop of Milan, in the year 1035. It was a car upon four wheels, painted red, and so heavy that it was drawn by four pair of oxen. In the centre of the car was fixed a mast, which supported a golden ball, an image of our Saviour, and the banner of the republic. In front of the mast were placed a few of the most valiant warriors; in the rear of it a band of warlike music. Feelings of religion, of military glory, of local attachment, of patriotism, were all associated with the carroccio, the idea of which is supposed to have been derived from the Jewish ark of the covenant. It was from the platform of the car that the priest administered the offices of religion to the army. No disgrace was so intolerable among the free citizens of Lombardy as that entailed by the suffering an enemy to take the carroccio.

valleys of the rivers that empty their waters into the Tweed or the Solway Frith; of troopers from the mountains of Cumberland and Westmoreland, mounted on small but strong and active horses; and of the fierce men of Galloway, who wore no defensive armour, and carried long thin pikes as

ARMOUR of the time of Stephen. Cotton MS. Nero C. 4.

their chief, if not sole weapon of war. A bodyguard of knights and men-at-arms under the command of Eustace Fitz-John, a nobleman of Norman descent, rode round the prince. The Highland clans and men of the Isles came next, carrying a small round shield made of light wood covered with leather, as their only defensive armour, and the claymore or broad-sword as their only weapon: some of the island tribes, however, wielded the old Danish battle-axe instead of the claymore. After these marched the king with a strong body of knights, who were all either

KNIGHT, in tegulated armour.—Seal of Richard, constable of Chester in the time of Stephen.

of English or Norman extraction; and a mixed corps of men from the Moray Firth, and various other parts of the land, brought up the rear. With the exception of the knights and men-at-arms, who were clad in complete mail, and armed uniformly, the host of the Scottish king presented a disordered variety of weapons and dresses. The half-naked clans were, however, as forward to fight as the warriors clad in steel. The rapid advance of the Scottish forces was covered and concealed by a dense fog; and they would have taken the Anglo-Norman army by surprise, had it not been for Robert de Bruce and Bernard de Baliol, two barons of Norman descent, who held lands both in Scotland and England, and who were anxious for the conclusion of an immediate peace. Having in vain argued with David, and hearing themselves called traitors by William, the king's nephew, they renounced the Scottish part of their allegiance, bade defiance to the king, and putting spurs to their horses, galloped off to the camp at Northallerton, which they reached in good time to tell that the Scots were coming. At the sight and sound of their headlong and tumultuous approach, the Bishop of Durham read the prayer of absolution from the standard-car, the Normans and the English kneeling on the ground the while, and rising to their feet and shouting "Amen," when it was finished. The representative of the energetic old Thurstain then delivered a speech for the further encouragement of the army: it was long, and seems to have been interrupted by the onslaught of the Scots.

The Scots came on with the simple war-cry of "Alban! Alban!"[1] which was shouted at once by all the Celtic tribes. The desperate charge of the men of Galloway drove in the English infantry, and broke for a moment the Norman centre. "They burst the enemy's ranks," says old Brompton, "as if they had been but spiders' webs." Almost immediately after, both flanks of the Anglo-Normans were assailed by the mountaineers and the men of Teviotdale and Liddesdale; but these charges were not supported in time, and the Norman horse formed an impenetrable mass round the standard-car, and repulsed the Scots in a fierce charge they made to penetrate there. During this fruitless effort of the enemy, the English bowmen rallied, and took up good positions on the two wings of the Anglo-Norman army; and when the Scots renewed their attack on the centre, they harassed them with a double flank flight of arrows, while the Norman knights and men-at-arms received them in front on the points of their couched lances. The long thin pikes of the men of Galloway were shivered against the armour of the Normans, or broken by their heavy swords and battle-axes. The Highland clans still shouting "Alban! Alban!" wielded their claymores, and fighting hand to hand, tried to cut their way through the mass of iron-cased chivalry. For full two hours did the

---

[1] *Matt. Paris.*

Scots maintain the fight in front of the Norman host; and at one moment the gallant Prince Henry had nearly penetrated to the elevated standard; but, at last, with broken spears and swords, they ceased to attack—paused, retreated, and then fled in confusion. The king, however, retained near his person, and in good order, his guards and some other troops, which covered the retreat, and gave several bloody checks to the Anglo-Normans who pursued. Three days after he rallied within the walls of Carlisle, and employed himself in collecting his scattered troops, and organizing a new army. He is said to have lost 12,000 men at Northallerton. The Normans were not in a situation to pursue their advantages to any extent; and the Scots soon re-assumed the offensive, by laying siege to Wark Castle, which they reduced by famine. The famous battle of the Standard, which was fought on the 22d of August, A.D. 1138, was, however, the great event of the Scottish war, which was concluded in the following year by a treaty of peace, brought about by the intercessions and prayers of Alberic, Bishop of Ostia, the pope's legate in England, and Stephen's wife, Maud, who had an interview with her uncle, King David, at Durham. Though the Scots were left in possession of Cumberland and Westmoreland, and Prince Henry invested with the earldom of Northumberland, the issue of the war dispirited the malcontents all over England, and might have given some stability to Stephen's throne, had he not, in an evil moment, roused the powerful hostility of the church.

Roger, Bishop of Sarum, though no longer treasurer and justiciary, as in the former and at the beginning of the present reign, still possessed great influence in the nation, among laity as well as clergy—an influence not wholly arising out of his great wealth and political abilities, but in part owing to the noble use he made of his money, to his taste and munificence, and the superior learning of his family and adherents. Among other works of the same kind he rebuilt the cathedral at Sarum, which had been injured by fire, and the storms to which its elevated position exposed it, and he beautified it so greatly that it yielded to none in England at that time; and some respect is still due to the memory of a man who greatly raised the architectural taste of this country, and whose genius affected the age in which he lived. "He erected splendid mansions on all his estates," says William of Malmesbury, "with unrivalled magnificence, in merely maintaining which his successors will toil in vain. His cathedral he dignified to the utmost with matchless adornments, and buildings in which no expense was spared. It was wonderful to behold in this man what abundant authority attended, and flowed, as it were, to his hand. He was sensible of his power, and somewhat more harshly than beseemed such a character, abused the favour of Heaven. Was there anything adjacent to his possessions which he desired, he would obtain it either by treaty or purchase; and if that failed, by force." But other powerful barons, both ecclesiastical and lay, equalled his rapacity without having any of his taste and elevation of spirit; for he was in all things a most magnificent person, and one who extended his patronage to men of learning as well as to architects and other artists. He obtained the sees of Lincoln and Ely for his two nephews, Alexander and Nigel, who were men of noted learning and industry, and were said at the time to merit their promotion by virtue of the education which he had given them. Alexander, the Bishop of Lincoln, who, though called his nephew, is significantly said to have been something nearer and dearer, had the same taste for raising splendid buildings; he nearly rebuilt the cathedral of Lincoln, and built the castle of Newark: but Nigel, on the contrary, is said to have wasted his wealth on hawks and hounds. Bishop Roger, next to his own brother, the Bishop of Winchester, had contributed more than any churchman to his elevation, and Stephen's consequent liberality for a long time knew no stint. It should appear, however, that his gifts were not the free offerings of gratitude, and that he treated the bishop as one does a sponge which is permitted to fill before it is squeezed. He is reported to have said more than once to his familiar companions—"By God's birth, I would give him half England if he asked for it: till the time be ripe he shall tire of asking before I tire of giving." Roger was one of the castle-builders of that turbulent period, being, as he thought, licensed therein, by the permission granted by Stephen at his coronation: all his stately mansions were, in fact, strongly fortified places, well garrisoned, and provided with warlike stores. Besides Newark Castle, Alexander had built other houses, which were also fortified; and, when abroad, uncle and nephews were accustomed to make a great display of military force. The pomp and power of this family had long excited the envy of Stephen's favourites, who had no great difficulty in persuading their master that Bishop Roger was on the point of betraying him, and espousing the interests of Matilda. Stephen was threatened by an invasion from without, and no longer knew how to distinguish his friends from his foes within: his want of money to pay the foreign mercenary troops he had engaged, and to satisfy his selfish nobles, now drove him into irregular courses, and he probably considered that the bishop's time was *ripe*. The king was holding his court at Oxford: the town was crowded with prelates and barons, with their numerous and disorderly attendants; a quarrel, either accidental or preconcerted, arose between the bishop's retainers and those of the Earl of Brittany concerning quarters, and swords being drawn on both sides, many men were wounded and one knight was killed.[1] Stephen took advantage of the circumstance and ordered the arrest of the bishop and his nephews. Roger was seized in the king's own hall, and Alexander, the Bishop of Lincoln, at his lodging in the town; but Nigel, the Bishop of Ely, who had taken up his quarters in a house outside the town, escaped, and threw himself into Devizes, the strongest of all his uncle's castles. The two captives were confined in separate dungeons. The first charge laid against them was a flagrant violation of the king's peace within the precincts of his court; and for this they were assured that Stephen would accept of no atonement less than the unconditional surrender to him of all their castles. They at first refused to part with their houses, and offered "a reasonable compensation" in money; but, moved by the dreadful threats of their enemies and the entreaties of their friends, they at length surrendered the castles which Roger had built at Malmesbury and Sherborne, and that which he had enlarged and strengthened at Sarum. Newark Castle, the work of the Bishop of Lincoln, seems also to have been given up. But the castle of Devizes, the most important of them all, remained; and relying on its strength, the warlike Bishop of Ely was prepared to bid defiance to the king. To overcome this opposition, Stephen ordered Roger and the Bishop of Lincoln to be kept without food till the castle should be given up. In case of a less direct appeal, the defenders of Devizes might have been obstinate or incredulous of the fact that Stephen was starving two bishops; but Roger himself, already pale and emaciated, was made to state his own hard fate, in front of his own castle, to his own nephew, whom he implored to surrender, as the king had sworn to keep his purpose of famishing him and the Bishop of Lincoln to death unless he submitted. Stephen, though far less cruel by nature than most of his contemporaries, was yet thought to be a man to keep his word in such a case as the present; this was felt by the Bishop of Ely, who, overcoming his own haughty spirit out of affection to his uncle, surrendered to save the lives of the captives after they had been three whole days in a fearful fast.[2]

At these violent proceedings the whole body of the dignified clergy, including even his own brother Henry, the Bishop of Winchester, who was now armed with the high powers of Papal legate for all England, turned against Stephen, accusing him of sacrilege in laying violent hands on prelates. The legate Henry summoned his brother, the king, to appear before a synod of bishops assembled at Winchester. Stephen would not attend in person, but sent Alberic de Vere as his counsel to plead for him. Alberic exaggerated the circumstances of the riot at Oxford, and laid all the blame of that blood-shedding upon Roger and his nephews, whom, moreover, he charged with a treasonable correspondence with the empress. The legate answered that the three bishops, uncle and nephews, were ready to abide their trial before a *proper* tribunal, but demanded, as of right, that their houses and property should be previously restored to them. Alberic said that they had voluntarily surrendered their castles and treasures as an atonement for their offences; and it was insisted, moreover, on the same side, that the king had a right to take possession of all *fortified* places in his dominions whenever he considered, as circumstances now obliged him to do, that his throne was in danger. On the second day of the debate the Archbishop of Rouen, the only prelate that still adhered to the king, took a more apostolic and simple view of the case, and boldly affirmed that the three bishops were bound by their vows to live humbly and quietly according to the canons of the church, which prohibited them from all kinds of military pursuits whatsoever—that they could not claim the restitution of castles and places of war, which it was most unlawful for them, as churchmen, to build or to hold—and that, consequently, they had merited the greatest part of the punishment they had suffered. The points of canonical law thus laid down were undeniable; but the bishops there assembled were not accustomed to their practice, and every one of them *might* have said that, without making his house a castle, there was no living in it in these lawless times. As their temper was stern and uncompromising, Alberic de Vere appealed to the pope in the name of the king and dissolved the council, the knights with him drawing their swords to enforce his orders if necessary.[3] The effects of this confirmed rupture were soon made visible. But Bishop Roger did not live to see the humiliation of Stephen; he was heart-broken; and when, in the following month of December, as the horrors of a civil war were commencing, he died at an advanced age, his fate was ascribed, not to the fever and ague, from which, in Malmesbury's words, he escaped by the kindness of death, but to grief and indignation

---

[1] It appears that Bishop Roger set out on his journey to Oxford with reluctance. "For," says William of Malmesbury, "I heard him speaking to the following purpose: 'By my Lady St Mary, I know not wherefore, but my heart revolts at this journey: this I am sure of, that I shall be of much the same service at court as a fool in battle!'"

[2] *Malmesb.; Orderic.; Gesta Steph.*

[3] *Malmsb.* William of Malmesbury was present at this council.

for the injuries he had suffered. The plate and money which had been saved from the king's rapacity he devoted to the completion of his church at Sarum, and he laid them upon the high altar, in the hope that Stephen might be restrained, by fear of sacrilege, from seizing them. But these were not times for delicate scruples, and they were carried off even before the old man's death. Their value was estimated at 40,000 marks. Bishop Roger was the Cardinal Wolsey of the twelfth century, and his fate, not less tragic than the cardinal's, made a deep impression on the minds of his contemporaries. His nephew, or

QUEEN MAUD'S CHAMBER, Arundel Castle.¹—From a sketch on the spot by J. W. Archer.

son, Alexander, Bishop of Lincoln, and his nephew Nigel, Bishop of Ely, having the advantage of a younger age, did not resign themselves to despair, but, intent on taking vengeance, they openly joined Matilda, and were soon up in arms against Stephen.

The synod of bishops held at Winchester was dissolved on the first day of September (A.D. 1139), and towards the end of the same month, Matilda landed in England with her half-brother, Robert, Earl of Gloucester, and 140 knights. Some Normans who went out to meet her, on finding that she came with so insignificant a force, and brought no money, returned to the other side; and Stephen, by a rapid movement, presently surprised her in Arundel Castle, where Alice or Adelais,

the queen-widow of Henry I., gave her shelter. Stephen had both these dames in his power, but refining on the chivalrous notions which were becoming more and more in vogue, and to which he was inclined by nature more perhaps than suited good policy, he left Queen Alice undisturbed in her castle, and gave Matilda permission to go free and join her half-brother, Robert, who, immediately after their landing, had repaired by by-roads, and with only twelve followers, to the west country, where at the very moment of these generous concessions, he was collecting his friends to make war upon Stephen. The king's brother, the Bishop of Winchester, escorted Matilda to Bristol, and delivered her safely to Earl Robert. It was quickly seen that those who had declined joining Matilda on her first landing had taken a narrow view of the resources of her party, for most of the chiefs in the north and the west renounced their allegiance to Stephen, and took fresh oaths to the empress. There was a moment of wavering, during which many of the barons in other parts of the kingdom weighed the chances of success, or tried both parties, to ascertain which would grant the more ample recompense to their venal swords. While this state of indecision lasted, men knew not who were to be their friends, or who their foes, in the coming struggle; "the neighbour could put no faith in his nearest neighbour, nor the friend in his friend, nor the brother in his own brother;"² but at last the more active chiefs chose their sides, the game was made up, and the horrors of civil war, which were to decide it, were let loose upon the land. Still, however, many of the barons kept aloof, and, strongly garrisoning their own castles, took the favourable opportunity of despoiling, torturing, and murdering their weak neighbours. The whole war was conducted in a frightful manner; but the greatest of the atrocities seem to have been committed by these separationists, who cared neither for Stephen nor Matilda, and who rarely or never took the field for either party. They waged war upon one another, and besieged castles, and racked farms, and seized the

---

¹ Arundel Castle is referred to as early as the time of King Alfred, who bequeathed it to his nephew Aldhelm. William the Conqueror gave it to his kinsman, Roger de Montgomery, created Earl of Arundel and Shrewsbury. It afterwards passed into the hands of the Albini, and from them to the Fitz-Alans. The ancient keep and several towers and gates still remain. Arundel Castle confers by tenure the peerage and earldom of Arundel, without any creation, patent, or investiture, this being the only instance of the kind now existing in this country. A tower next the keep is called Queen Maud's Tower; and an upper chamber is said by tradition to have been her chamber, when Alice or Adelais, the widow queen of Henry I., gave her shelter at Arundel in the course of her contest with Stephen.

² Gervase of Canterbury.

unprotected traveller, on their own account, and for their own private spite or advantage.

At first the fortune of the greater war inclined in favour of Stephen; for though he failed to take Bristol, the head-quarters of Matilda and Earl Robert, he gained many advantages over their adherents in the west, and he defeated a formidable insurrection in the east, headed by Nigel, the Bishop of Ely, who built a stone rampart among the bogs and fens of his diocese, on the very spot, it is said, where the brave Hereward, the last champion of Saxon independence, had raised his fortress against the Conqueror. To reach the warlike and inveterate nephew of old Bishop Roger, Stephen had recourse to the same skilful measures which had been employed by the Conqueror at the same difficult place. Defeated at Ely, Nigel fled to Gloucester, whither Matilda had transferred her standard; and while Stephen was still on the eastern coast, the flames of war were rekindled in all the west. The Norman prelates had no scruples in taking an active part in these military operations; and the garrisons of their castles are said to have been as cruel to the defenceless rural population, as eager after plunder, and altogether as lawless, as the retainers of the lay barons. The bishops themselves were seen, as at the time of the Conquest, mounted on war-horses, clad in armour, directing the siege or the attack, and drawing lots with the rest for the booty.[1]

The cause of Stephen was never injured by any want of personal courage and rapidity of movement. From the east he returned to the west, and from the west marched again to the country of fens, on learning that Alexander, the Bishop of Lincoln, had got together the scattered forces of the Bishop of Ely in those parts, and, in alliance with the Earls of Lincoln and Chester, was making himself very formidable. The castle of Lincoln was in the hands of his enemies; but the town's-people were for Stephen, and assisted him in laying siege to the fortress. On the 2d of February, A.D. 1141, as Stephen was prosecuting this siege, the Earl of Gloucester, who had got together an army 10,000 strong, swam across the Trent, and appeared in front of Lincoln. Stephen, however, was prepared to receive him: he had drawn out his forces in the best position, and, dismounting from his war-horse, he put himself at the head of his infantry. But his army was unequal in number, and contained many traitors; the whole of his cavalry deserted to the enemy, or fled at the first onset; and after he had fought most gallantly, and broken both his sword and battle-axe, Stephen was taken prisoner by the Earl of Gloucester. Matilda was incapable of imitating his generosity; but her partizans lauded her mercy, because she only loaded him with chains, and threw him into a dungeon in Bristol Castle. The empress does not appear to have encountered much difficulty in persuading the Bishop of Winchester wholly to abandon his unfortunate brother, and acknowledge her title. The price paid to the bishop was the promise, sealed by an oath, that he should have the chief direction of her affairs, and the disposal of all vacant bishoprics and abbacies. The scene of the bargain was on the downs, near Winchester, and the day on which it was concluded (the 2d of March) was dark and tempestuous. The next day, accompanied by a great body of the clergy, the brother of Stephen conducted the empress in a sort of triumph to the cathedral of Winchester, within which he blessed all who should be obedient to her, and denounced a curse against all who refused to submit to her authority. As legate of the pope, this man's decision had the force of law with most of the clergy; and several bishops, and even Theobald, the new Archbishop of Canterbury, followed his example.[2] At Winchester, Matilda took possession of the royal castle, the crown, with other regalia, and such treasure as Stephen had not exhausted. On the 7th of April, she, or the legate acting for her, convened an assembly of churchmen to ratify her accession. The members of this synod were divided into three classes—the bishops, the abbots, and the archdeacons. The legate conferred with each class separately and in private, and his arguments prevailed with them all. On the following day they sat together, and the deliberations were public. William of Malmesbury, who tells us he was present, and heard the opening speech with great attention, professes to give the very words of the legate. The brother of Stephen began by contrasting the turbulent times they had just witnessed, with the tranquillity and happiness enjoyed under the wise reign of Henry I.; he glanced lightly over the repeated vows made to Matilda, and said the absence of that lady, and the confusion into which the country was thrown, had compelled the prelates and lords to crown Stephen;—that he blushed to bear testimony against his own brother, but that Stephen had violated all his engagements, particularly those made to the church;—that hence God had pronounced judgment against him, and placed them again under the necessity of providing for the tranquillity of the kingdom by appointing some one to fill the throne. "And now," said the legate, in conclusion, "in order that the kingdom may not be without a ruler, we, the clergy of England, *to whom it chiefly belongs to elect kings*

---

[1] *Gesta Stephani.* This military spirit of the ecclesiastics had been greatly increased by the Crusades.

[2] *Malmesb.; Gesta Steph.; Gervase.*

and ordain them, having yesterday deliberated on this great cause in private, and invoked, as is fitting, the direction of the Holy Spirit, did, and do, elect Matilda, the daughter of the pacific, rich, glorious, good, and incomparable King Henry, to be *sovereign lady* of England and Normandy." Many persons present listened in silence — but silence, as usual, was interpreted into consent; and the rest of the assembly hailed the conclusion of the speech with loud and repeated acclamations. The deliberations of the synod, and the proclamation of Matilda, were hurried over before the deputation from the city of London could reach Winchester; but such was the respect they imposed, that it was deemed expedient to hold an adjourned session on the following morning. When the decision of the council was announced to them, the deputies said they did not come to debate, but to petition for the liberty of their king; that they had no powers to agree to the election of this new sovereign; and that the whole community of London, with all the barons lately admitted into it, earnestly desired of the legate, the archbishop, and all the clergy, the immediate liberation of Stephen. When they ended, Christian, the chaplain of Stephen's queen, rose to address the meeting. The legate endeavoured to impose silence on this new advocate; but, in defiance of his voice and authority, the chaplain read a letter from his royal mistress, in which she called upon the clergy, by the oaths of allegiance they had taken to him, to rescue her husband from the imprisonment in which he was kept by base and treacherous vassals. But Stephen's brother was not much moved by these measures; he repeated to the Londoners the arguments he had used the day before; the deputies departed with a promise, in which there was probably little sincerity, to recommend his view of the case to their fellow-citizens; and the legate broke up the council with a sentence of excommunication on several persons who still adhered to his brother, not forgetting a certain William Martel, who had recently made free on the roads with a part of his (the legate's) baggage.

If popular opinion can be counted for anything in those days—and if the city of London, together with Lincoln and other large towns, may be taken as indexes of the popular will—we might be led to conclude that Stephen was still the sovereign of the people's choice, or, at least, that they preferred him to his competitor. The feelings of the citizens of London were indeed so decided, that it was not until some time had passed, and the Earl of Gloucester had soothed them with promises and flattering prospects, that Matilda ventured among them. She entered the city a few days before Midsummer, and made preparations for her immediate coronation at Westminster. But Matilda herself, who pretended to an indefeasible, sacred, hereditary right, would perform none of the promises made by her half-elect brother; on the contrary, she imposed a heavy tallage or tax on the Londoners, as a punishment for their attachment to the usurper; and arrogantly rejected a petition they presented to her, praying that the laws of Edward the Confessor might be restored, and the changes and usages introduced by the Normans abolished. Indeed, whatever slight restraint she had formerly put on her haughty, vindictive temper, was now entirely removed; and in a surprisingly short space of time she contrived not only to irritate her old opponents to the very utmost, but also to convert many of her best friends into bitter enemies. When the legate desired that Prince Eustace, his nephew, and Stephen's eldest son, should be put in possession of the earldom of Boulogne and the other patrimonial rights of his father, she gave him a direct and insulting refusal. [In dethroning his brother, this prelate, who was, perhaps, the most extraordinary actor in the drama, had not bargained for the impoverishment of all his family, and an insult was what he never could brook.] When Stephen's wife, who was her own cousin, and a kind-hearted, amiable woman, appeared before her, seconded by many of the nobility, to petition for the enlargement of her husband, she showed the malignancy and littleness of her soul by personal and most unwomanly upbraidings.

The acts of this tragedy, in which there was no small mixture of farce, passed almost as rapidly as those of a drama on the stage; and before the coronation clothes could be got ready, and the bishops assembled, Matilda was driven from London without having time to take with her so much as a change of raiment. One fine summer's day, "nigh on to the feast of St. John the Baptist," and about noon-tide, the dinner hour of the court in those times, a body of horse bearing the banner of Queen Maud (the wife of Stephen) appeared on the southern side of the river opposite the city; on a sudden all the church-bells of London sounded the alarm, and the people ran to arms. From every house there went forth one man at least with whatever weapon he could lay his hand upon. They gathered in the streets, says a contemporary, like bees rushing from their hives.[1] Matilda saved herself from being made prisoner by rushing from table, mounting a horse, and galloping off. She had scarcely cleared the western suburb when some of the populace burst into her apartment, and pillaged or destroyed whatever they found in it. Such was her leave-taking of London, which she never saw again.

[1] *Gesta Stephani.*

Some few of her friends accompanied her to Oxford, but others left her on the route, and fled singly by cross country roads and unfrequented paths towards their respective castles.¹

Matilda had not been long at Oxford when she conceived suspicions touching the fidelity of the Bishop of Winchester, whom she had offended beyond redress, and who had taken his measures accordingly, absenting himself from court, and manning the castles which he had built within his diocese—as at Waltham, Farnham, and other places. He had also an interview with his sister-in-law, Maud, at the town of Guildford, where he probably arranged the plans in favour of his brother Stephen, which were soon carried into execution. Matilda sent him a rude order to appear before her forthwith. The cunning churchman told her messenger that he was "getting himself ready for her;" which was true enough. She then attempted to seize him at Winchester; but, having well fortified his episcopal residence, and set up his brother's standard on its roof, he rode out by one gate of the town as she entered at the other, and then proceeded to place himself at the head of his armed vassals and the friends who had engaged to join him. Matilda was admitted into the royal castle of Winchester, whither she immediately summoned the Earls of Gloucester, Hereford, and Chester, and her uncle David, King of Scots, who had been for some time in England vainly endeavouring to make her follow mild and wise counsel. While these personages were with her, she laid siege to the episcopal palace, which was in every essential a castle, and a strong one. The legate's garrison made a sortie, and set fire to all the neighbouring houses of the town that might have weakened their position, and then, being confident of succour, waited the event. The bishop did not make them wait long. Being reinforced by Queen Maud and the Londoners, who, to the number of a thousand citizens, took the field for Stephen, clad in coats of mail, and wearing steel casques, like noble men of war,² he turned rapidly back upon Winchester, and actually besieged the besiegers there. By the 1st of August he had invested the royal castle of Winchester, where, besides the empress-queen, there were shut up the King of Scotland, the Earls of Gloucester, Hereford, and Chester, and many other of the noblest of her partizans. When the siege had lasted six weeks, all the provisions in the castle were exhausted, and a desperate attempt at flight was resolved upon. By tacit consent the belligerents of those times were accustomed to suspend their operations on the great festivals of the church. The 14th of September was a Sunday, and the festival of the Holy Rood or Cross. At a very early hour of the morning of that day, Matilda mounted a swift horse, and, accompanied by a strong and well-mounted escort, crept as secretly and quietly as was possible out of the castle: her half-brother, the Earl of Gloucester, followed at a short distance with a number of knights, who had engaged to keep between her and her pursuers, and risk their own liberty for the sake of securing the queen's. These movements were so well timed and executed, that they broke through the beleaguerers, and got upon the Devizes road, before the legate's adherents, who were thinking of their mass and prayers, could mount and follow them. Once in the saddle, however, they made hot pursuit, and at Stourbridge, the Earl of Gloucester and his gallant knights were overtaken. To give Matilda, who was only a short distance in advance, time to escape, they formed in order of battle and offered an obstinate resistance. In the end they were nearly all made prisoners; but their self-devotion had the desired effect, for the queen, still pressing on her steed, reached the castle of Devizes in safety. That fortress, the work of Bishop Roger, was, we know, very strong; but it is said that, not finding herself in security even there, Matilda almost immediately resumed her journey, and, the better to avoid danger, feigned herself to be dead, and being placed on a bier like a corpse, caused herself to be drawn in a hearse from Devizes to Gloucester. Of all who formed her strong rear-guard on her flight from Winchester, the Earl of Hereford alone reached Gloucester castle, and he arrived in a wretched state, being almost naked.³ The other barons and knights who escaped from the field of Stourbridge threw away their arms, disguised themselves like peasants, and made for their own homes. Some of them, betrayed by their foreign accent, were seized by the English peasantry, who bound them with cords, and drove the proud Normans before them with whips, to deliver them up to their enemies.⁴ The King of the Scots, Matilda's uncle, got safe back to his own kingdom; but her half-brother, the Earl of Gloucester, who was by far the most important prisoner that could be taken, was conveyed to Stephen's queen, who secured him in Rochester Castle.⁵

Both parties were now, as it were, without a head, for Matilda was nothing in the field in the absence of her half-brother. A negotiation was therefore set on foot, and, on the 1st of November, it was finally agreed that the Earl of Glou-

---

¹ *Malmesb.; Gesta Steph.; Brompt.; Flor. Wig.* ² *Gesta Steph.* ³ *Contin. Wig.* ⁴ At different times the Archbishop of Canterbury and several of the Norman bishops and abbots were stripped by the English peasants—"*equis et vestibus ab istis captis, ab illis horrende abstractis.*"—*Gesta Steph.* ⁵ *Malmesb.; Gesta Steph.; Brompt.*

cester should be exchanged for King Stephen. The interval had been filled up by unspeakable misery to the people; but, as far as the principals were concerned, the two parties now stood as they did previously to the battle of Lincoln. The clergy, and particularly the legate who had alternately sided with each, found themselves in an embarrassing position; but the brother of Stephen had an almost unprecedented strength of face. He summoned a great ecclesiastical council, which met at Westminster on the 7th of December, and he there produced a letter from the pope, ordering him to do all in his power to effect the liberation of his brother. This letter was held as a sufficient justification of all the measures he had recently adopted. Stephen then addressed the assembly, briefly and moderately complaining of the wrongs and hardships he had sustained from his vassals, unto whom he had never denied justice when they asked for it; and adding, that if it would please the nobles of the realm to aid him with men and money, he trusted so to work as to relieve them from the fear of a shameful submission to the yoke of a woman; a thing which at first they seemed much to mislike, and which now, to their great grief, they had by experience found to be intolerable. At last the legate himself rose to speak, and, as he had with a very few exceptions the same audience as in the synod assembled at Winchester only nine months before, when he pronounced the dethronement of his own brother, and hurled the thunders of excommunication against his friends and adherents, his speech must have produced a singular effect. He pleaded that it was through force, and not out of conviction or good-will, that he had supported the cause of Matilda, who subsequently had broken all her engagements with him, and even made attempts against his liberty and life. He was thus, he maintained, freed from his oaths to the *Countess of Anjou*, for he no longer deigned to style her by a higher title. The judgment of Heaven, he said, was visible in the punishment of her perfidy, and God himself now restored the rightful King Stephen to his throne. Though there were some jealousies already existing between him and the Archbishop of Canterbury, the council went with the legate, and no objection was started save by a solitary voice, which boldly asserted, in the name of Matilda, that the legate himself had caused all the calamities which had happened—that he had invited her into England—that he had planned the expedition in which Stephen was taken—and that it was by his advice that the empress had loaded his brother with chains. The imperturbable legate heard these open accusations without any apparent emotion either of shame or anger; and with the greatest composure proceeded to excommunicate all those who remained attached to the party he had just quitted. The curse and interdict were extended to all who should build new castles, or invade the rights and privileges of the church, and (a most idle provision!) to all who should wrong the poor and defenceless.[1]

No compromise between the contending parties was as yet thought of; the smouldering ashes of civil war were raked together, and England was tortured as if with a slow fire; for the flames were not brought to a head in any one place, and no decisive action was fought, but a succession of skirmishes and forays, petty sieges, and the burning of defenceless towns and villages kept people on the rack in nearly every part of the land at once. "All England," says a contemporary, "wore a face of woe and desolation. Multitudes abandoned their beloved country to wander in a foreign land: others, forsaking their own houses, built wretched huts in the church-yards, hoping that the sacredness of the place would afford them some protection."[2] This last miserable hope was generally vain, for the belligerents no more respected the houses of God than they did the abodes of humble men. They seized and fortified the best of the churches; and the belfry towers, from which the sweet sounds of the church-bells were wont to proceed, were converted into fortresses, and furnished with engines of war;[3] they dug fosses in the very cemeteries, so that the bodies of the dead were brought again to light, and the miserable remains of mortality trampled upon and scattered all about. At an early period of the contest both parties had engaged foreign mercenaries; and, in the absence of regular pay and provision, and of all discipline, bands of Brabanters and Flemings prowled through the land, satisfying all their appetites in the most brutal manner. So general was the discouragement of the suffering people, that whenever only two or three horsemen were seen approaching a village or open burgh, all the inhabitants fled to conceal themselves. So extreme were their sufferings that their complaints amounted to impiety, for, seeing all these crimes and atrocities going on without check or visible judgment, men said openly that Christ and his saints had fallen asleep.[4]

A.D. 1142. During Stephen's captivity, Matilda's husband, Geoffroy of Anjou, reduced nearly the whole of Normandy, and

---

[1] *Gervase; Malmesb.* The honest and judicious monk of Malmesbury says, "I cannot relate the transactions of this council with that exact veracity with which I did the former, *as I was not present at it.*" He tells us that the legate "commanded, therefore, on the part of God and the pope, that they should strenuously assist the king, *anointed by the will of the nation and with the approbation of the Holy See;* and that such as disturbed the peace in favour of the *Countess of Anjou* should be excommunicated, with the exception of herself, *who was sovereign of the Angevins.*" [2] *Gesta Steph.* [3] *Ibid.* [4] *Chron. Sax.*

prevailed upon the majority of the resident nobles to acknowledge Prince Henry (his son by Matilda) as their legitimate duke. The king's party thus lost all hope of aid and assistance from beyond sea; but, as they were masters of the coasts of the island, they were able to prevent the arrival of any considerable reinforcement to their adversaries. Matilda pressed her husband to come to her assistance with all the forces he could raise; but Geoffrey declined the invitation on the ground that he had not yet made himself sure of Normandy; but he offered to send over Prince Henry. Even on this point he showed no great readiness, and several months were lost ere he would intrust his son to the care of the Earl of Gloucester, whom Matilda had sent into Normandy.

Meanwhile Stephen, who had recovered from a long and dangerous illness, marched in person to Oxford, where the empress had fixed her court, and invested that city, with a firm resolution of never moving thence until he had got his troublesome rival into his hands. At his first approach, the garrison came out to meet him: these enemies he put to flight, and pursued them so hotly, that he entered the city pell-mell with them. Matilda

TOWER OF OXFORD CASTLE.[1] —J. S. Prout, from his sketch on the spot.

then retired into the castle, and the victor's troops set fire to the town. Stephen invested the cita-

del, and persevered in the operations of the siege or blockade in a winter of extraordinary severity; and so intent was he on his purpose that he would not permit his attention to be distracted even when informed that the Earl of Gloucester and Prince Henry had landed in England. The castle was strong, but when the siege had lasted some three months, Matilda again found herself in danger of starvation, to escape which she had recourse to another of her furtive flights. On the 20th of December, a little after midnight, she dressed herself in white, and, accompanied by three knights in the same attire, stole out of the castle by a postern gate. The ground being covered with deep snow, the party passed unobserved, and the Thames being frozen over, afforded them a safe and direct passage. Matilda pursued her course on foot as far as the town of Abingdon, where, finding horses, the party mounted, and she rode on to Wallingford, at or near to which place she was soon after joined by the Earl of Gloucester and her young son, who were now at the head of a considerable force. The day after Matilda's flight Oxford Castle surrendered to the king; but the king himself was defeated by the Earl of Gloucester at Wilton, in the following month of July, and, with his brother the legate, narrowly escaped being made prisoner.

After the affair of Wilton no military operation deserving of notice occurred for three years, during which Stephen's party prevailed in all the east; Matilda's maintained their ground in the west; and the young prince was shut up for safety in the strong castle of Bristol, where, at his leisure moments, his uncle, the Earl of Gloucester, who enjoyed, like his father, Henry Beauclerk, the reputation of being a learned person, attended to his education. The presence of the boy in England was of no use whatever to his mother's or his own cause, and about the feast of Whitsuntide, 1147, he returned to his father Geoffrey in Normandy. Gloucester died of a fever in the month of October; and thus, deprived of son and brother, and depressed also by the loss of the Earl of Hereford, and other staunch partizans, who fell the victims of disease, the masculine resolution of Matilda gave way, and, after a struggle

---

[1] Oxford Castle was situated at the west end of the city; its site is now occupied by the county jail. A castle was founded here in 1071 by Robert D'Oilli, at the command of William the Conqueror, and finished in 1073. By digging deep trenches he caused the river to surround it like a moat; and, according to Agas's map, it appears to have been a fortress of extraordinary strength and extent. At its entrance from the city, which was on the south-east side, was a large bridge, which led by a long and broad entry to the chief gate of the castle. On one side of the castle was a barbican or watch-tower; and within the walls were a church and convent dedicated to St. George, founded by Robert D'Oilli. The towers at the west end were pulled down when the castle was made a garrison by the Parliament, during the great Civil War; and the whole fortification, with the exception of the tower represented in the cut, was demolished in 1652.

of eight years, she quitted England and retired to Normandy. After her departure, Stephen endeavoured to get possession of all the baronial castles, and to reduce the nobles to a proper degree of subordination; but the measures he adopted were, in some instances, characterized by craft, if not treachery; and his too openly avowed purpose of curbing the power and license of the nobility was as unpalatable to his own adherents as to the friends of Matilda. At the same time he involved himself in a fresh quarrel with the church, and that, too, at a moment when his brother, the legate, and Bishop of Winchester, had lost his great authority through the death of the pope, who patronized him, and the election of another pope, who took away his legatine office, and espoused the quarrel of his now declared enemy, Theobald, Archbishop of Canterbury.

For attending the council of Rheims, against the express orders of the king, the archbishop was exiled. Caring little for his sentence, Theobald went (A.D. 1148) and put himself under the protection of Bigod, Earl of Norfolk, who was of the Angevin faction, and then published a sentence of interdict against Stephen's party, and all that part of the kingdom that acknowledged the rule of the *usurper*. Instantly, in one half of the kingdom, all the churches were closed, and the priests and monks either withdrew, or refused to perform any of the offices of religion. This was a state of things which men could not bear, and Stephen was compelled to seek a reconciliation with the archbishop. About two years after this reconciliation, a general council of the high clergy was held at London; and Stephen, who in the interval had endeavoured to win the hearts of the bishops and abbots with donations to the church, and promises of much greater things when the kingdom should be settled, required them to recognize and anoint his eldest son, Eustace, as his successor. This the Archbishop of Canterbury resolutely and most unceremoniously refused to do. He had consulted, he said, his spiritual master, and the pope had told him that Stephen was an usurper, and therefore could not, like a legitimate sovereign, transmit his crown to his posterity. It was quite natural, and perhaps excusable, that Stephen, on thus hearing his rights called in question by a man who had sworn allegiance to him, should be overcome by a momentary rage (and it was not more in effect), and ordered his guards to arrest the bishops and seize their temporalities. But putting aside the question of right, and however much they may have failed in the respect due to one who was their king at the time, the prelates, in acting as they did, indubitably took a most prudent and wise view of the case, and adopted a system which was calculated to narrow the limits of civil war.

CRYPT OF BRISTOL CASTLE.[1]—J. S. Prout, from his sketch on the spot.

As long as the contest lay between Stephen on the one side and a woman and a boy on the other, it was likely to be, on the whole, favourable to the former. But time had worked its changes; Prince Henry was no longer a boy, but a handsome, gallant young man, capable of performing all the duties of a knight and soldier, and gifted with precocious abilities and political acumen. He had also become, by inheritance and marriage, one of the most powerful princes on the Continent. When Henry Plantagenet left Bristol Castle he was about fourteen years of age. In A.D. 1149, having attained the military age of sixteen, he recrossed the seas and landed in Scotland, in order to receive the honour of knighthood at the hands of his mother's uncle, King David. The ceremony was performed with great pomp in "merry Carlisle," where the Scottish king then kept his court: crowds of nobles from most parts of England, as well as from Scotland and Normandy, were present, and had the oppor-

---

[1] The only surviving vestige of Bristol Castle is the crypt. The castle is not specified in *Doomsday Book*, and the period of its origin is unknown; but it is surmised to have been built, together with the second wall round the town, by Godfrey, Bishop of Exeter, one of the followers of the Conqueror. The first historical notice of it occurs on the death of William I., when it was fortified and held by Godfrey on behalf of Robert, the Conqueror's oldest son.

tunity of remarking Henry's many eminent qualities; and as that prince had only been returned to the Continent some twelve months when Stephen assembled the council for the anointing of his son, the impressions made by the fortunate Plantagenet were still fresh, and his character was naturally contrasted with that of Prince Eustace, who was about his own age, but who does not appear to have had one of his high endowments. Shortly after his return from Carlisle, Henry was put in full possession of the government of Normandy; by the decease of his father Geoffrey, who died in the course of the same year (1150), he succeeded to the earldom of Anjou; and in 1152, together with the hand of Eleanor, the divorced queen of Louis VII. of France, he acquired her rights over the earldom of Poictou and the vast duchy of Guienne or Aquitaine, which had descended to her from her father. The Plantagenet party in England recovered their spirits at the prospect of this sudden aggrandizement, and thinking no more of the mother, they determined to call in the son to reign in his own right. The Earl of Chester passed over to Normandy, to express what he called the unanimous will of the nation; but the King of France formed an alliance with King Stephen, Theobald, Earl of Blois, and Geoffrey of Anjou, Henry's younger brother, and marched a French army to the confines of Normandy. This attempt occasioned some delay; but as soon as Henry obtained a truce on the Continent, he sailed for England with a small fleet. The army he brought over with him did not exceed 140 knights and 3000 foot, but it was well appointed and disciplined; and as soon as he landed in England most of the old friends of his family flocked to join his standard. It was unexpectedly found, however, that Stephen was still strong in the affections and devotion of a large party. The armies of the competitors came in sight of each other at Wallingford—that of Stephen, who had marched from London, occupying the left bank of the Thames, and that of Henry, who had advanced from Marlborough, the right. They lay facing each other during two whole days, and were hourly expecting a sanguinary engagement; but the pause had given time for salutary reflection, and the Earl of Arundel had the boldness to say that it was an unreasonable thing to prolong the calamities of a whole nation on account of the ambition of two princes. Many lords of both parties, who were of the same opinion, or wearied at length with a struggle which had already lasted fifteen years, laboured to persuade both princes to come to an amicable arrangement. The two chiefs consented; and in a short conversation which they carried on with one another across a narrow part of the Thames, Stephen and Henry agreed to a truce, during which each expressed his readiness to negotiate a lasting peace. On this, Prince Eustace, who was probably well aware that the first article of the treaty would seal his exclusion from the throne, burst away from his father in a paroxysm of rage, and went into the east to get up a war on his own account. The rash young man took forcible possession of the abbey of St. Edmundsbury, and laid waste or plundered the country round about, not excepting even the lands of the abbot. His licentious

GATE OF THE ABBEY CHURCH, St. Edmundsbury.¹—From a view by Mackenzie.

career was very brief, for, as he was sitting down to a riotous banquet, he was suddenly seized with a frenzy, of which he soon died.²

The principal obstacle to concession from Stephen was thus removed, for though he had another legitimate son, Prince William, he was but a boy, and was docile and unambitious. The principal negotiators, who with great ability and address reconciled the conflicting interests of the two factions, were Theobald, the Archbishop of Canter-

¹ This fine structure was the portal opposite to the west entrance to the monastery church. It is a quadrangular building, 80 ft. high. Near the base on the western face are two bass-reliefs, one representing mankind after the fall by the figures of Adam and Eve entwined with a serpent, and the other, typical of the deliverance of mankind, represents God the Father surrounded by cherubim. Within the arch are various grotesque figures.
² Writers of a later period introduced some confusion in this matter by accounting for his death in different ways. Some of them said Eustace was drowned.

bury, and Henry, Bishop of Winchester, Stephen's brother, who played so many parts in this long and chequered drama. On the 7th of November, 1153, a great council of the kingdom was held at Winchester, where a peace was finally adjusted on the following conditions:—Stephen, who was to retain undisturbed possession of the crown during his life, *adopted* Henry as his son, appointed him his successor, and *gave* the kingdom, after his own death, to Henry and his heirs for ever. In return Henry did present homage, and swore fealty to Stephen. Henry received the homage of the king's surviving son William, and in return gave that young prince all the estates and honours, whether in England or on the Continent, which his father Stephen had enjoyed before he ascended the throne; and Henry promised, as a testimonial of his own affection, the honour of Pevensey, together with some manors in Kent. There then followed a mighty interchange and duplication of oaths among the earls, barons, bishops, and abbots of both factions, all swearing present allegiance to Stephen, and future fealty to Henry.[2]

After signing the treaty, Stephen and Henry visited together the cities of Winchester, London, and Oxford, in which places solemn processions were made, and both princes were received with acclamations by the people. At the end of Lent they parted with expressions of mutual friendship.

Henry returned to the Continent, and on the following 25th of October (1154) Stephen died at Dover, in the fiftieth year of his age. He was buried by the side of his wife, Maud, who died three years before him, at the monastery of Faversham, in the pleasant county of Kent, which she had loved so much while living.

FAVERSHAM ABBEY.[1] From an old view in the British Museum.

CHAPTER V.—CIVIL AND MILITARY HISTORY.—A.D. 1154—1172.

HENRY II., SURNAMED PLANTAGENET.—ACCESSION, A.D. 1154—DEATH, A.D. 1189.

Succession of Henry II., surnamed Plantagenet—History of his queen, Eleanor—Henry's reforms at the beginning of his reign—His resumption of crown lands, and suppression of the barons—He invades Maine and Anjou—His successful war in Wales—His acquisitions on the Continent—His war with the French king—Exploits of Thomas à Becket in the war—Previous career of Becket—He becomes Archbishop of Canterbury—His altered behaviour on becoming primate—Commencement of his quarrels with Henry—Struggles of Becket for the privileges of the clergy—He is worsted by the king—Becket's strange visit to the court at Northampton—He retreats to France—Henry's vindictive proceedings against him—Henry's unsuccessful campaign in Wales—His successes on the Continent—He is excommunicated by Becket—Attempts of the French king to reconcile Henry and Becket—Becket returns to England—His triumphant reception by the people—Henry's rage at the tidings—Assassination of Thomas à Becket—Henry's attempts to free himself from suspicion.

HEN Henry Plantagenet received the news of Stephen's death, he was engaged in the siege of a castle on the frontiers of Normandy. Relying on the situation of affairs in England, and the disposition of men's minds in his favour, he prosecuted the siege to a successful close, and reduced some turbulent continental vassals to obedience, before he went to the coast to embark

---

[1] This abbey was built and endowed by Stephen; and himself, his queen Maud, and his eldest son Eustace of Boulogne, were buried within its walls. At the dissolution this abbey was held by monks of the Benedictine order. After the suppression the remains of Stephen were thrown into the river, for the value of the leaden coffin in which they were contained.

[2] Rymer's *Fœdera*.

HENRY II.

for his new kingdom. He was detained some time at Barfleur by storms and contrary winds; and it was not till six weeks after the death of Stephen that he landed in England, where he was received with enthusiastic joy. He brought with him a splendid retinue, and Eleanor, his wife, whose inheritance had made him so powerful on the Continent. This marriage proved, that if the young Henry had the gallantry of his age and all the knightly accomplishments then in vogue, he was not less distinguished by a cool calculating head, and the faculty of sacrificing romantic or delicate feelings for political advantages. The lady he espoused was many years older than himself, and the repudiated wife of another.

Eleanor, familiarly called in her own country Aanor, was daughter and heiress of William IX.,[1] Earl of Poictou and Duke of Aquitaine; that is to say, of the sovereign chief of all the western coast of France, from the mouth of the Loire to the foot of the Pyrenees. She was married in 1137 to Louis VII., King of France, who was not less enchanted with her beauty than with the fine provinces she brought him. When the union had lasted some years, and the queen had given birth to two daughters, the princesses Marie and Alix, Louis resolved to make a pilgrimage to the Holy Land, and to take along with him his wife, whose uncle, Raymond, was Duke of Antioch. The general morality of the royal and noble crusaders and pilgrims is represented in no very favourable light by contemporary writers; and it is easily understood how camps and marches, and a close and constant association with soldiers, should not be favourable to female virtue. Suspicion soon fell upon Eleanor, who, according to her least unfavourable judges, was guilty of great coquetry and freedom of manners; and her conduct in the gay and dissolute court of Antioch at last awakened the indignation of her devout husband. She was very generally accused of an intrigue with a young and handsome Turk, named Saladin.[2] In 1152,

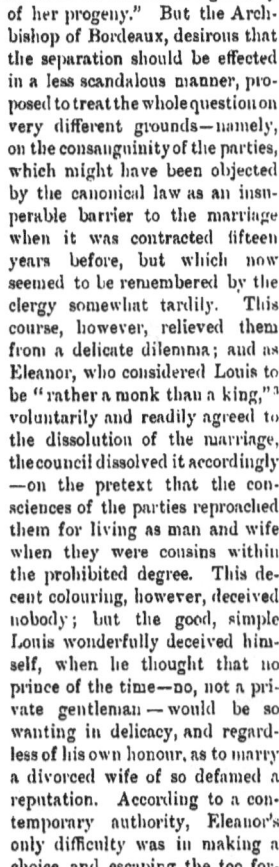

HENRY II., from his tomb at Fontevraud.—Stothard's Monumental Effigies.

about a year after their return from the Holy Land, Louis summoned a council of prelates for the purpose of divorcing him from a woman who had publicly dishonoured him. The Bishop of Langres, pleading for the king, gravely announced that his royal master "no longer placed faith in his wife, and could never be sure of the legitimacy of her progeny." But the Archbishop of Bordeaux, desirous that the separation should be effected in a less scandalous manner, proposed to treat the whole question on very different grounds—namely, on the consanguinity of the parties, which might have been objected by the canonical law as an insuperable barrier to the marriage when it was contracted fifteen years before, but which now seemed to be remembered by the clergy somewhat tardily. This course, however, relieved them from a delicate dilemma; and as Eleanor, who considered Louis to be "rather a monk than a king,"[3] voluntarily and readily agreed to the dissolution of the marriage, the council dissolved it accordingly —on the pretext that the consciences of the parties reproached them for living as man and wife when they were cousins within the prohibited degree. This decent colouring, however, deceived nobody; but the good, simple Louis wonderfully deceived himself, when he thought that no prince of the time—no, not a private gentleman—would be so wanting in delicacy, and regardless of his own honour, as to marry a divorced wife of so defamed a reputation. According to a contemporary authority, Eleanor's only difficulty was in making a choice, and escaping the too forcible addresses of some of her suitors. Henry soon presented himself, and, "with more policy than delicacy," wooed and won and married her too, within six weeks of her divorce.[4] King Louis's conduct was directly the opposite of Henry's, for he had been more delicate than politic; and, however honourable to hint individually, his delicacy was a great misfortune to France, for it dissevered states which had been

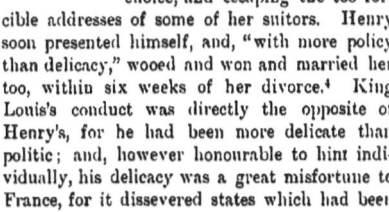

[1] This Duke William was a troubadour of high renown, and the most ancient of that class of poets whose works have been preserved.
[2] Some old writers confound this Saladin with the Great Saladin, the heroic opponent of Eleanor's son, Richard; but this is a great mistake, involving an anachronism.
[3] Mézerai, *Hist. de France*.
[4] *Script. Rer. Franc.*

united by the marriage—retarded that fusion and integration which alone could render the French kingdom respectable, and threw the finest territories of France into the hands of his most dangerous enemies. If he could have freed himself of his wife, without resigning her states, the good would have been unmixed; but this was impossible. His discarded wife, who seems to have been dear to her people, in spite of her irregularities, encountered little or no difficulty in inducing them to admit the garrisons of her new husband, the young and popular Henry. When it was too late, Louis saw the great error in policy he had committed, and made what efforts he could to prevent the by him most unexpected marriage. He prohibited Henry, as his vassal for Normandy and Anjou, to contract any such union without the consent and authority of his suzerain lord, the King of France; but Henry, who was soon by far the more powerful of the two, cared little for the prohibition, and Louis, in the end, was obliged to content himself with receiving the empty oaths of allegiance which the fortunate Plantagenet tendered for Guienne and Poictou, in addition to those he had already pledged for Anjou and Normandy. The old French historians cannot relate these transactions without losing their temper.[1]

The sacrifice was indeed immense. The French kingdom almost ceased to figure as a maritime state on the Atlantic; and when Eleanor's possessions were added to those Henry already possessed on the Continent, that prince occupied the whole coast line from Dieppe to Bayonne, with the exception only of the great promontory of Brittany, where a race of semi-independent princes were established that had sometimes supported the interests of the French kings, and at others allied themselves with the Anglo-Norman sovereigns. Henry, in fact, was master of one-fifth of the territories now included in the kingdom of France; and, deducting other separate and independent sovereignties, Louis, driven back from the Atlantic, and cooped up between the Loire, the Saône, and the Meuse, did not possess half so much land as his rival, even leaving out of the account the kingdom of England, to which he succeeded about two years after his marriage.

Eleanor was soon as jealous of Henry as Louis had been of her. The Plantagenet had not married with a view to domestic happiness, but he was probably far from expecting the wretchedness to which the union would condemn his latter days. At their first arrival in England, however, everything wore a bright aspect. The queen rode by the king's side into the royal city of Winchester, where they both received the homage of the nobility; and when, on the 19th of December, Henry took his coronation oaths, and was crowned at Westminster by Theobald, Archbishop of Canterbury, Eleanor was crowned with him, amidst the acclamations of the people. Not a shadow of opposition was offered; the English, still enamoured of their old dynasty or traditions, dwelt with complacency on the Saxon blood, which, from his mother's side, flowed in the veins of the youthful, the handsome, and brave Henry; and all classes seemed to overlook the past history of the queen in her grandeur and magnificence, and present attachment to their king. The court pageantries were splendid, and accompanied by the spontaneous rejoicings of the citizens. Henry did not permit his attention to be long occupied by these pleasures, but proceeded to business almost as soon as the crown was on his head. He assembled a great council, appointed the crown officers, issued a decree, promising his subjects all the rights and liberties they had enjoyed under his grandfather, Henry I.; and he made his barons and bishops swear fealty to his infant children, his wife Eleanor having already made him the happy father of two sons.[2]

Henry then turned his attention to the correcting of those abuses which had rendered the reign of Stephen a long agony to himself and a curse to the nation. His reforms were not completed for several years, and many events of a foreign nature intervened during their progress; but it will render the narrative clearer to condense our account of these transactions in one general statement.[3]

Henry appointed the Earl of Leicester grand justiciary of the kingdom, and, feeling that the office had hitherto been insufficiently supported by the crown, he attached to it more ample powers, and provided the means of enforcing its decisions. As happened in all seasons of trouble

---

[1] *Je qui nous couta bon.—Brantome.* Mézerai and Larrey (*Heritière de Guienne*) agree in attributing Louis's error to the want of the wise counsels of Suger. Larrey and Douchet (*Annales d'Aquitaine*), with some other writers, natives of Aquitaine or Poictou, maintained that Eleanor was unjustly calumniated; but the weight of contemporary evidence is on the other side.

[2] William and Henry. William died in his childhood.

[3] "Under the turbulent and miserable usurpation of Stephen, neither government nor law existed in England. The country was entirely given up to violence; every powerful man built his castle, which became a den of robbers; the towns and the open country, the clergy and the peasantry—all suffered equally from spoil and rapine; pestilence and famine swept away the people, and the labours of agriculture were abandoned in despair; to till the ground was to plough the sea; the earth bore no corn, for the land was all wasted by these deeds. 'Such things,' continue the monks of Peterborough, 'did we suffer for nineteen years for our sins,' until the accession of 'Henry Fitz-Empress,' considered by the English as representing the ancient national dynasty. They traced his descent to Alfred and to Cerdic; but the son of Geoffrey Plantagenet was a stranger by birth and education; and the Anglo-Saxon jurisprudence was finally subverted by the restorer of the Anglo-Saxon line."—Palgrave, *Rise and Progress of the English Commonwealth*, part I. p. 240.

and distress in those ages, the coin had been alloyed and tampered with under Stephen; and

SILVER PENNY, Henry II.—Weighs 22 grs.

now Henry issued an entirely new coinage of standard weight and purity. The foreign merce-

SILVER COIN, Henry II.

naries and companies of adventure that came over to England during the long civil war between Stephen and Matilda had done incalculable mischief. Many of these adventurers had got possession of the castles and estates of the Anglo-Norman nobles who adhered to Matilda, and had been created earls and barons by Stephen; but, treating all these as acts of usurpation, Henry determined to drive every one of them from the land, and their expulsion seems to have afforded almost as much joy to the Saxon population as to the Normans, who raised a shout of triumph on the occasion. "We saw them," says a contemporary, "we saw these Brabançons and Flemings cross the sea, to return from the camp to the plough-tail, and become again serfs, after having been lords."[1] Up to this point the operations were easy, and the king, unopposed by the conflicting interest of any important party in the state, or by claims on his own gratitude, was carried forward on the high tide of popular opinion; but in what still remained to do were great and obvious difficulties, and feelings of a private nature, which might have overcome a less determined and politic prince, for, in the impartial execution of his measures he had to despoil those who fought his mother's battles and supported his own cause

when he was a helpless infant. The generous romantic virtues natural to youth might have been fatal to him; but Henry's heart in some respects seems never to have been young, and his head was cool and calculating. In a treaty made at Winchester, shortly after his pacification with Stephen, it was stipulated that the king (Stephen) should resume all such royal castles and lands as had been alienated to the lay nobles or usurped by them. Among the resumable gifts were many made by Matilda. Stephen, poor as he was, had neglected this resumption, or made no progress in it during the few months that he survived the treaty. But Henry was determined not to be a pauper king, or to tolerate that widely-stretched aristocratic power which at once ground the people and bade fair to reduce royalty to an empty shadow. In the absence of other fixed revenues, the sovereigns of that time depended almost entirely on the produce of the crown lands; and Stephen had allowed so much of these to slip from him, that there remained not sufficient for a decent maintenance of royal dignity. Besides the numerous castles which had been built by the turbulent nobles, royal fortresses and even royal cities had been granted away; and these could hardly be permitted to remain in the hands of the feudal lords without endangering the peace of the kingdom.[2] Law was brought in to the aid of policy, and it was now established as a legal axiom, that the ancient demesne of the crown was of so sacred and inalienable a nature, that no length of time, tenure, and enjoyment could give a right of prescription to any other possessors, against the claim of succeeding princes, who might (it was laid down) at any time resume possession of what had formerly been alienated.[3]

Foreseeing, however, that this step would create much discontent, Henry was cautious not to act without a high sanction; and he therefore summoned a great council of the nobles, who, after hearing the urgency of his necessities, concurred pretty generally in the justice of his immediately resuming all that had been held by his grandfather Henry I., with the exception of the alienations or grants to Stephen's son and the church. As soon as he was armed with this sanction the

---

[1] R. de Diceto.
[2] "The judicial entries on the fly-leaves of the Exeter manuscript, written before and after the Conquest, show us that the municipal forms and conditions of that city underwent no change upon the transfer of the English crown to a Norman line of sovereigns; and such was probably the case in all other cities and towns then in existence. But although their privileges and constitution were in principle untouched, in practice they were frequently trespassed upon. A new race of feudal lords had entered upon the land, who were ignorant of the customs of the people over whom they had intruded themselves, and who had little respect for any customs which stood as obstacles in the gratification of their views of aggrandizement. This must have led to continual riots and disturbances in the old Saxon towns, and to infringements of their privileges where they had little power to obtain permanent redress. After undergoing all these vexations during a few years, they saw the advantages, or, we may perhaps better say, the necessity, of purchasing from the king written charters confirming their old rights, which became an effective protection in courts of law. Thus originated municipal charters, which are rather to be considered as a proof of the antiquity, than of the novelty of the privileges they grant. They were given most abundantly under Henry II. and his sons, when it became the policy of the English monarchs to seek the support of the independent burghers against a turbulent feudal aristocracy."—Wright, *The Celt, the Roman, and the Saxon*, p. 449.
[3] Lord Lyttelton's *Henry II*. Contemporary details are found in *Gervase of Canterbury*, *Wm. of Newbury*, and *Roger of Hoveden*.

young king put himself at the head of a formidable army, knowing right well that there were many who would not consider themselves bound by the voices of the assembly of nobles, and who would only cede their castles and lands by force. In some instances the castles, on being closely beleaguered, surrendered without bloodshed; in others, they were taken by storm, or reduced by famine. In nearly all cases they were levelled to the ground, and about 1100 of these "dens of thieves" were blotted out from the fair land they defaced. At the siege of the castle of Bridgenorth, in Shropshire, which Hugh de Mortimer

REMAINS OF BRIDGENORTH CASTLE.[1]—From an old view.

held out against the king, Henry's life was preserved by the affection and self-devotion of one of his followers, his faithful vassal Hubert de St. Clair, who stepped forward and received in his own bosom an arrow aimed at the king. After many toils, and not a few checks, Henry completed his purpose; he drove the Earl of Nottingham and some other dangerous nobles out of the kingdom; he levelled with the ground the six strong castles of Stephen's brother, the famous Bishop of Winchester, who, placing no confidence in the new king whom he had helped to make, fled with his treasures to Clugny; he reduced the Earl of Albemarle, who had long reigned like an independent sovereign in Yorkshire, to the proper state of vassalage and allegiance; and he finally obliged Malcolm, King of Scots, to resign the three northern counties of Northumberland, Cumberland, and Westmoreland, for the *bond fide* possession of the earldom of Huntingdon, which the Scottish princes claimed as descendants of Earl Waltheof. Henry was not less eager to recover everything than wisely anxious to avoid the appearance of acting from motives of party revenge; and by his equal and impartial proceeding, he left the adherents of Stephen no more reason to complain than his mother's or his own partizans. Among the latter were several who lost their all by these resumptions; but, steady to his purpose, the king would make no exceptions, not even in favour of those who had succoured his mother in the hour of need, and made the greatest sacrifices for his family. He evaded the most earnest applications by a courtesy of demeanour, and a prodigality of promises for the future, which seldom lay heavy on his conscience.

Before these measures were completed Henry's active mind was occupied by the affairs of the Continent, for his younger brother Geoffrey, advancing a title to Anjou and Maine, had invaded those provinces. A short time after his marriage, which made him Duke of Aquitaine and Earl of Poictou, Henry became Earl of Anjou by the death of his father, but under the express condition, it is said, of resigning that earldom to his younger brother if he ever should become King of England. That young prince was now encouraged by the French court, which was still smarting under the injuries received from Henry's marriage; and he seems to have had strong party in his favour in the provinces of Maine and Anjou.

The King of England crossed the seas in 1156, and again did homage to Louis VII., for Normandy, Aquitaine, Poictou, Auvergne, the Limousin, Anjou, Touraine, and a long train of dependent territories; and by this and other means, the nature of which is not explained, he induced the French king to abandon the cause of his younger brother. He then threw himself into the disputed territory, at the head of an army consisting almost entirely of native English, who soon reduced Chinon, Mirabeau, and the other castles which held for his brother. The people returned to their allegiance to Henry, and Geoffrey was soon obliged to resign all his claims for a pension of 1000 English and 2000 Angevin pounds. Having triumphed over every opposition, as much by policy as by force of arms, Henry made a magnificent progress through Aquitaine and the other dominions he had obtained by his marriage, and received the fealty of his chief vassals in a great council held in the city of Bordeaux. Wherever he appeared he commanded respect, and no sovereign of the time in Europe could equal the power and splendour of this young king.

On his return to England in 1157, he engaged in hostilities with the Welsh. Feeling over-confident in the number and quality of his army, he

---

[1] The remaining fragment of Bridgenorth Castle has, from excavations at its base, inclined so far from the perpendicular, as to have obtained the title of the Leaning Tower. It is situated at the south side of the town.

crossed Flintshire, and threw himself among the mountains. The Welsh let him penetrate as far as the difficult country about Coleshill Forest, when, issuing from their concealment, and pouring down in torrents from the uplands, they attacked Henry in a narrow defile where his troops could not form. The slaughter was prodigious. Eustace Fitz-John and Robert de Courcy, men of great honour and reputation, together with several other nobles, were dismounted and cut to pieces; the king himself was in the greatest danger, and a rumour was raised that he had fallen. Henry, Earl of Essex, the hereditary standard-bearer, threw down the royal standard and fled. The panic was now universal; but the king rushed among the fugitives, showed them he was unhurt, rallied them, and finally fought his way through the mountain-pass. The serious loss he suffered made him cautious, and instead of following Owen Gwynned, who artfully tried to draw him into the defiles of Snowdon, he changed his route, and gaining the open sea-coast, marched along the shore, closely attended by a fleet. He cut down some forests, or opened roads through them, and built several castles in advantageous situations. There was no second battle of any note, and, after a few months, the Welsh were glad to purchase peace by resigning such portions of their native territory as they had retaken from Stephen, and giving hostages and doing feudal homage for what they retained. Six years after the battle of Coleshill, the Earl of Essex was publicly accused of cowardice and treason by Robert de Montfort. The standard-bearer appealed to the trial of arms, and was vanquished in the lists by his accuser. By the law of the times, death should have followed, but the king, qualifying the rigour of the judgment, granted him his life, appointing him to be a shorn monk in Reading Abbey, and taking the earl's possessions into his hands as forfeited to the crown.[1]

Geoffrey did not live long to exact payment of his annuities from his brother. Soon after concluding the treaty with Henry, which left him without any territory, the citizens of Nantes, in Lower Brittany, spontaneously offered him the government of their city, just as the people of Domfront had done by Henry Beauclerk, when under similar depressed circumstances. But Geoffrey died in 1158, and the citizens of Nantes, returning to their old connection with the rest of the country, were governed by Conan, who was Earl of Richmond in England, as well as the hereditary Count or Duke of Brittany. To the surprise of everybody, King Henry claimed the free city of Nantes as hereditary property, devolved to him by his brother's death. It was in vain the citizens represented that they had not, by choosing Geoffrey to be their governor, resigned their independence, or converted themselves into a property to be hereditary in his family. Henry wanted to fill up the only great gap in his continental territories, and, careless of right or appearances, he resolved to seize Nantes, hoping, that if once he gained a firm footing there he should soon extend his dominion over the rest of Brittany. He affected to treat the men of Nantes as rebels, and Conan as an usurper of his rights; he confiscated his earldom of Richmond, in Yorkshire, and crossing the Channel with a formidable army, spread such terror that the people submitted, and, renouncing Conan, received his garrison within the walls of Nantes.[2] He then quietly took possession of the whole of the country between the Loire and the Vilaine, relying on his art and address for quieting the alarms these encroachments could not fail to create in the French court. He dispatched Thomas à Becket, then the most skilful and accommodating of all his ministers, to Paris, the volatile inhabitants of which capital were dazzled and delighted by the ambassador's magnificence. Henry soon followed in person, and, between them, these two adroit negotiators completely won over the obtuse French king. The price paid for his neutrality was, Henry's affiancing his eldest son to Margaret, an infant daughter Louis had had by his wife, Constance of Castile, who had succeeded Eleanor. Henry then prosecuted his views on the rest of Brittany, and concluded with Conan, whom he had driven from Nantes, a compact which threatened the independence of the whole country. He affianced his then youngest son Geoffrey to Constantia, an infant daughter of Conan, the latter engaging to bequeath to his daughter all his rights in Brittany at his death, and Henry engaging to support him in his present power during his life.[3]

If this treaty was kept secret for a time from King Louis, Henry's ambition hurried him into other schemes, which interrupted their good understanding before it had lasted a year. Not satisfied with the tranquil enjoyment of the states he had procured by his marriage, he advanced fresh claims, in right of his wife, to territories which neither she nor her father had ever enjoyed, and, by obtaining the great earldom of Toulouse, he hoped to spread his power across the whole of the broad isthmus that joins France to Spain, and to range along the French coast on the Mediterranean, as he already did along the whole Atlantic sea-board. William, Duke of Aquitaine, grandfather of Queen Eleanor, Henry's wife, and a contemporary of the Conqueror, married Philippa,

---

[1] *Dicelo.*
[2] *Newbrig.; Script. Rer. Franc.*
[3] *Chron. Norm.; Newbrig.; Daru, Hist. de la Bretagne.*

the only child of William, the fourth Earl of Toulouse. As a female succession was contrary to the laws or usages of the country, the Earl William, Philippa's father, conveyed the principality, by a contract of sale, to his brother, Raymond de St. Gilles, who succeeded at his death, and transmitted it to his posterity in the male line, who had held it many years, not without cavil on the part of the house of Aquitaine, but without any successful challenge of their title. Eleanor conveyed her rights, such as they were, and which she was determined not to leave dormant, to Louis VII., by her first marriage; and during their union the French king sent forth an army for the conquest and occupation of Toulouse. But the expedition ended in a treaty, and Raymond de St. Gilles, the grandson of the first earl of that name, was confirmed in possession of the country, and released from all claims to it, whether on the part of the French king or his wife Eleanor, by marrying Constance, the sister of Louis. Henry now urged, that by her subsequent divorce from Louis, Eleanor was restored to her original rights; and after some curious correspondence, he demanded the instant surrender of the earldom of Toulouse upon the same grounds as Louis had done before him. The Earl Raymond raised his banner of war, and applied for aid to his brother-in-law of France. "The common council of the city and suburbs," for such was the title borne by the municipal government of Toulouse,[1] seconded Raymond's negotiations with the French court, and raised their banner as a free and incorporated community. On this occasion Louis broke through the fine meshes of Henry and Becket's diplomacy, and roused himself to a formidable exertion. Perceiving that the struggle would be serious, and that success could only be obtained by the keeping on foot a large army very different in its constitution and terms of service from his feudal forces, Henry resolved, by the advice of Becket, to commute the personal services of his vassals for an aid in money,[2] with which he trusted to procure troops that would serve like modern soldiers for their daily pay, obey his orders directly without the often troublesome intermission of feudal lords, and have no objection either to the distance of the scene of hostilities, or the length of time they were detained from their homes. The term of forty days, to which the services of the vassals were limited, would have been in good part consumed in the march alone from England and the north of France to Toulouse. He began by levying a sum of money, in lieu of their presence and services, upon his vassals in Normandy, and other provinces remote from the seat of action; the commutation was agreeable to most of them; and when it was proposed in England, it was still more acceptable, on account of the greater distance, and the laudable anxiety of many of the nobles to take care of their estates, which had suffered so much during the intestine wars of the preceding reign. The *scutage*, as it is called, was levied at the rate of three pounds in England, and of forty Angevin shillings in the continental dominions, for every knight's fee. There were 60,000 knights' fees in England alone, which would produce £180,000. But, whatever was the sum, it sufficed Henry for the raising of a strong mercenary force, consisting chiefly of bodies of the famous infantry of the Low Countries. With these marched Malcolm, King of Scotland, who courted the close alliance of Henry; Raymond, King of Arragon (to whose infant daughter Henry had affianced his infant son Richard); one of the Welsh princes, and many English and foreign barons who voluntarily engaged to follow the king to Toulouse. Thomas à Becket, now chancellor of England, and the inseparable companion of his royal master, attended in this war, and none went in more warlike guise. He marched at the head of 700 knights and men-at-arms, whom he had raised at his own expense; and, when they reached the scene of action, he distinguished himself by his activity and gallantry, not permitting the circumstance of his being in holy orders to prevent him from charging with the chivalry, or mounting the deadly breach. After taking the town of Cahors, Henry marched upon the city of Toulouse. But the French king, crossing Berry, which belonged to him in good part, and the Limousin, which granted him a free passage, threw himself with reinforcements into the threatened city, where he was received with extreme joy by Earl Raymond and the citizens.[3] The force which Louis brought with him was small, and the energetic Becket advised Henry to make an immediate assault, in which the churchman judged he could hardly fail of reducing the town and taking prisoner the French king, whose captivity might be turned to incalculable advantage. But Henry was cool and cautious even in the midst of his greatest successes: he did not wish to drive the French nation to extremities— he was so woven up in the complicated feudal system, and so dependent himself on the faithful observance of its nice gradations, that he wished to avoid outraging the great principles on which it rested; and being himself vassal to Louis, and, in his quality of Earl of Anjou, hereditary seneschal of France, he declared he could not show

---

[1] Commune concilium urbis Tholosæ et suburbii.—*Script. Rer. Franc.*

[2] This seems to have been the first introduction of a practice which tended gradually to the overthrow of the feudal system.

[3] *Script. Rer. Franc.*

such disrespect to his superior lord as to besiege him. While he hesitated, a French army marched to the relief of their king. Henry then transferred the war to another part of the earldom, and soon after, leaving the supreme command to Becket, returned with part of his army to Normandy. The clerical chancellor continued to appear as if in his proper element: he fortified Cahors, took three castles, which had been deemed impregnable, and tilted with a French knight, whose horse he carried away as the proof of his victory. But Henry could not do without his favourite; and a French force having made a diversion on the side of Normandy, Becket also returned thither, leaving only a few insignificant garrisons on the banks of the Garonne and pleasant hills of Languedoc. The political condition, however, of that favoured region—the sunny land of the troubadours—declined from that hour. The habit of imploring the protection of one king against another became a cause of dependence; and with the epoch when the King of England, as Duke of Aquitaine and Earl of Poictou, obtained an influence over the affairs of the south of France, commenced the decline and misery of a most interesting population. Thenceforward, placed between two great powers, the rivals of each other, and both equally ambitious and encroaching, they sought the protection, now of the one, and now of the other, according to circumstances; and were alternately supported and abandoned, betrayed and sold by both.

In the brief war which ensued on the frontiers of Normandy, after the expedition to Toulouse, Becket maintained 1200 knights, with no fewer than 4000 attendants and foot soldiers; and when the King of France was induced to treat, the eloquent and versatile churchman was charged with the negotiations on the part of his friend and master. A truce was concluded at the end of the year, and a few months after, when the rival kings had an interview, the truce was converted into a formal peace (A.D. 1160), Henry's eldest son doing homage to Louis for the duchy of Normandy, and Henry being permitted to retain the few places he had conquered in the earldom of Toulouse. This precious peace did not last quite one month. Constance, the French queen, died without leaving any male issue; and Louis, anxious for an heir, as his daughters could not succeed, in about a fortnight after her decease, married Adelais, niece of the late English king, Stephen, and sister of the three Earls of Blois, Champagne, and Sanserre. This union with the old enemies of his family greatly troubled Henry, who, foreseeing a disposition in the French court to break off the alliance with him, which might give his progeny a hold upon France, secretly secured a dispensation from the pope, and solemnized the contract of marriage between his son Henry, who was seven years old, and the daughter of Louis, the Princess Margaret, who had been placed in his power at the conclusion of the original treaty, and who had attained the matronly age of *three* years. Becket, the prime mover in all things, brought the royal infant to London, where this strange ceremony was performed.

Another war ensued, but of too insignificant a character to demand our notice, and it was soon concluded through the mediation of the pope.

At this time, as at several other periods in the middle ages, there were two popes, each calling the other anti-pope and anti-Christ. Victor IV. was established at Rome under the patronage of the Emperor Frederick Barbarossa; and Alexander III. was a fugitive and an exile north of the Alps, where both Louis and Henry bowed to his spiritual authority, and rivalled each other in their offers of an asylum and succour, and in their reverential demeanour. When the two kings met him in person at Courcy-sur-Loire, they both dismounted, and holding each of them one of the bridle-reins of his mule, walked on foot by his side, and conducted him to the castle.[1]

A short period of tranquillity, both in England and Henry's continental dominions, followed this reconciliation; and when it was disturbed, the storm proceeded from a most unexpected quarter —from Thomas à Becket, the king's bosom friend.

Becket was born at London, in or about the year 1117. His father was a citizen and trader, of the Saxon race—circumstances which seemed to exclude the son from the career of ambition. The boy, however, was gifted with an extraordinary intelligence, a handsome person, and most engaging manners; and his father gave him all the advantages of education that were within his reach. He studied successively at Merton Abbey, London, Oxford, and Paris, in which last city he applied to civil law, and acquired as perfect a mastery, and as pure a pronunciation of the French language, as any the best educated of the Norman nobles and officers. While yet a young man, he was employed as an under-clerk in the office of the sheriff of London, where he attracted the attention of Theobald, Archbishop of Canterbury, who sent him to complete his study of the civil law at the then famous school of Bologna. After profiting by the lessons of the learned Gratian, Becket recrossed the Alps, and staid some time at Auxerre, in Burgundy, to attend the lectures of another celebrated law professor. On his return to London, he took deacon's orders,[2] and his powerful patron the archbishop gave him some valuable church preferment, which neither necessitated a residence, nor the performance of any

[1] *Newbrig.; Chron. Norm.*
[2] He never took the major orders till he became archbishop.

church duties; and he soon afterwards sent him, as the best qualified person he knew, to conduct some important negotiations at the court of Rome. The young diplomatist (for he was then only thirty-two years old) acquitted himself with great ability and complete success, obtaining from the pope a prohibition that defeated the design of crowning Prince Eustace, the son of Stephen—an important service, which secured the favour of the Empress Matilda and the house of Plantagenet. On Henry's accession, Archbishop Theobald had all the authority of prime minister, and, being old and infirm, he delegated the most of it to the active Becket, who was made chancellor of the kingdom two years after, being the first Englishman since the Conquest that had reached any eminent office. As if to empty the lap of royal bounty, Henry at the same time appointed him preceptor of the heir to the crown, and gave him the wardenship of the Tower of London, the castle of Berkhampstead, and the honour of Eye, with 340 knights' fees. His revenue, flowing in from many sources, was immense; and no man ever spent more freely or magnificently. His house was a palace, both in dimensions and appointments. It was stocked with vessels of gold and silver, and constantly frequented by numberless guests of all goodly ranks, from barons and earls to knights and pages, and simple retainers—of which he had several hundreds, who acknowledged themselves his immediate vassals. His tables were spread with the choicest viands; the best of wines were poured out with an unsparing hand; the richest dresses allotted to his pages and serving men.[1] The chancellor's out-door appearance was still more splendid, and on great public occasions was carried to an extremity of pomp and magnificence. When he went on his embassy to Paris he was attended by 200 knights, besides many barons and nobles, and a complete host of domestics, all richly armed and attired, the chancellor himself having four-and-twenty changes of apparel. As he travelled through France, his train of waggons and sumpter-horses, his hounds and hawks, his huntsmen and falconers, seemed to announce the presence of a more than king. Whenever he entered a town, the ambassadorial procession was led by 250 boys singing national songs; then followed his hounds, led in couples; and these were succeeded by eight waggons, each with five large horses, and five drivers in new frocks. Every waggon was covered with skins, and guarded by two men and a fierce mastiff. Two of the waggons were loaded with ale, to be distributed to the people; one carried the vessels and furniture of his chapel; another of his bedchamber; a fifth was loaded with his kitchen apparatus; a sixth carried his abundant plate and wardrobe; and the other two were devoted to the use of his household servants. After the waggons came twelve sumpter-horses, *a monkey riding on each, with a groom behind on his knees.* Then came the esquires, carrying the shields, and leading the war-horses of their respective knights; then other esquires (youths of gentle birth), falconers, officers of the household, knights, and priests; and last of all appeared the great chancellor himself, with his familiar friends. As Becket passed in this guise, the French were heard to exclaim, "What manner of man must the King of England be, when his chancellor travels in such state!"[2] Henry encouraged all this pomp and magnificence, and seems to have taken a lively enjoyment in the spectacle, though he sometimes twitted the chancellor on the finery of his attire. All such offices of government as were not performed by the ready and indefatigable king himself were left to Becket, who had no competitor in authority. Secret enemies he had in abundance, but never even a momentary rival in the royal favour. The minister and king lived together like brothers; and according to a contemporary,[3] who knew more of Henry than any other that has written concerning him, it was notorious to all men that they were *cor unum et animam unam* (of one heart and one mind in all things). With his chancellor Henry gave free scope to a facetious, frolicsome humour, which was natural to him, though no prince could assume more dignity and sternness when necessary. The chancellor was an admirable horseman, and expert in hunting and hawking, and all the sports of the field. These accomplishments, and a never-failing wit and vivacity, made him the constant companion of the king's leisure hours, and the sharer (it is hinted) in less innocent pleasures; for Henry was a very inconstant husband, and had much of the Norman licentiousness. At the same time, Becket was an able minister, and his administration was not only advantageous to the interests of his master, but, on the whole, extremely beneficial to the nation. Most of the useful measures which distinguished the early part of the king's reign have been attributed to his advice, his discriminating genius, and good intentions. Such were the restoration of internal tranquillity, the curbing of the baronial power, the better appointment of judges, the reform in the currency, and the encouragement given to trade. He certainly could not be accused of entertaining a low notion of the royal prerogative, or of any luke-warmness in exacting the rights of the king. He humbled the lay aristocracy whenever he could, and more than once attacked

---

[1] *Fitz-Stephen.* This amusing biographer was Becket's secretary.
[2] *Fitz-Stephen.*
[3] Petrus Blesensis, or Peter of Blois. See his *Letters.*

the extravagant privileges, immunities, and exemptions claimed by the aristocracy of the church. He insisted that the bishops and abbots should pay the scutage for the war of Toulouse like the lay vassals of the crown, and this drew upon him the violent invectives of many of the hierarchy, Gilbert Foliot, the Bishop of Hereford, among others, accusing him of plunging the sword into the bosom of mother church, and threatening him with excommunication. All this tended to convince Henry that Becket was the proper person to nominate to the primacy, as one who had already given proofs of a spirit greatly averse to ecclesiastical encroachments, and that promised to be of the greatest service to him in a project which, in common with other European sovereigns, he had much at heart—namely, to check the growing power of Rome, and curtail the privileges of the priesthood. Although his conduct had not been very priest-like, he was popular; the king's favour and intentions were well known, and accordingly, in 1161, when his old patron, Theobald, Archbishop of Canterbury, died, the public voice designated Becket as the man who must inevitably succeed him; and after a vacancy of about thirteen months, during which Henry drew the revenues, he was appointed Primate of all England.

From that moment Becket was an altered man: the soldier, statesman, hunter, courtier, man of the world, and man of pleasure, became a rigid and ascetic monk, renouncing even the innocent enjoyments of life, together with the service of his more friend than master, and resolving to perish by a slow martyrdom rather than suffer the king to invade the smallest privilege of the church. Although he then retained, and afterwards showed a somewhat inconsistent anxiety to keep certain other worldly honours and places of trust, he resigned the chancellorship in spite of the wishes of the king—he discarded all his former companions and magnificent retinue—he threw off his splendid attire—he discharged his choice cooks and his cup-bearers, to surround himself with monks and beggars (whose feet he daily washed), to clothe himself in sackcloth, to eat the coarsest food, and drink water rendered bitter by the mixture of unsavoury herbs. The rest of his penitence, his prayers, his works of charity in hospitals and pest-houses, soon caused his name to be revered as that of a saint, and his person to be followed by the prayers and acclamations of the people. With the views the king was known to entertain in church matters, the collision was inevitable; yet it certainly was the archbishop who began the contest, and it is most unfair to attempt to conceal or slur over this fact. In 1163, about a year after his elevation, Becket raised a loud complaint on the

usurpations by the king and laity of the rights and property of the church. He claimed houses and lands which, if they ever had been included in the endowments of the see of Canterbury, had been for generations in the possession of lay families. It is curious to see castles and places of war figuring in his list. From the king himself he demanded the important castle of Rochester. From the Earl of Clare—whose family had possessed them in fief ever since the Conquest—he demanded the strong castle and the barony of Tunbridge; and from other barons, possessions of a like nature. But to complete the indignation of Henry, who had laid it down as an indispensable and unchangeable rule of government, that no vassal who held *in capite* of the crown should be excommunicated without his previous knowledge and consent, he hurled the thunders of the church at the head of William de Eynsford, a military tenant of the crown, for forcibly ejecting a priest collated to the rectory of that manor by the archbishop; and for pretending, as lord of the manor, to a right over that living. When Henry ordered him to revoke the sentence, Becket told him that it was not for the king to inform him whom he should absolve and whom excommunicate—a right and faculty appertaining solely to the church. The king then resorted from remonstrances to threats of vengeance; and Becket, bending for awhile before the storm, absolved the knight, but reluctantly, and with a bad grace.[1] In the course of the following year the king matured his project for subjecting the clergy to the authority of the civil courts for murder, felony, and other civil crimes; and to this reform, in a council held at Westminster, he formally demanded the assent of the archbishop and the other prelates. The leniency of the ecclesiastical courts to offenders in holy orders, seemed almost to give an immunity to crime; and a recent case, in which a clergyman had been but slightly punished for the most atrocious of offences, called aloud for a change of court and practice, and lent unanswerable arguments to the ministers and advocates of the king. The bishops, however, with one voice, rejected the proposed innovations; upon which Henry asked them if they would merely promise to observe the ancient customs of the realm. Becket and his brethren, with the exception only of Hilary, Bishop of Chichester, answered that they would observe them, "saving their order." On this the king immediately deprived the archbishop of the manor of Eye, and the castle of Berkhampstead. Finding, however, that the bishops fell from his side, and being on one hand menaced by the king and lay nobles, and on the

[1] *Gervase of Canterbury; Diceto; Fitz-Steph. Epist. St. Thom.; Hist. Quad.*

other, it is said, advised to submit by the pope himself, Becket shortly afterwards, at a great council held at Clarendon,[1] in Wiltshire (25th January, 1164), consented to sign a series of enactments embodying the several points insisted upon by the king, and hence called the "Constitutions of Clarendon;" but he refused to put his seal to them, and immediately after withdrew from the court, and even from the service of the altar, to subject himself to the harshest penance for having acted contrary to his inward conviction. Subsequently the pope rejected the "Constitutions of Clarendon," with the exception only of six articles of minor importance; and the archbishop was then encouraged to persist by the only superior he acknowledged in this world.[2]

The king being now determined to keep no measures, assembled a great council in the town of Northampton, and summoned the archbishop to appear before it. He was charged, in the first place, with a breach of allegiance and acts of contempt against the king. He offered a plea in excuse, but Henry swore, "by God's eyes,"[3] that he would have justice in its full extent, and the court condemned Becket to forfeit all his goods and chattels; but this forfeiture was immediately commuted for a fine of £500. The next day the king required him to refund £300 which he had received as warden of Eye and Berkhampstead, and £500 which he (the king) had given him before the walls of Toulouse; and, on the third day, he was required to render an account of all his receipts from vacant abbeys and bishoprics during his chancellorship, the balance due thereon to the crown being set down at the enormous sum of 44,000 marks. Becket now perceived that the king was bent on his utter ruin. For a moment he was overpowered; but, recovering his firmness and self-possession, which never forsook him for long intervals, he said he was not bound to plead on that count, seeing that, at his consecration as archbishop, he had been publicly released by the king from all such claims. He demanded a conference with the bishops; but these dignitaries had already declared for the court, and the majority of them now advised him to resign the primacy as the only step which could restore peace to the church and nation. His health gave way under these troubles, and he was confined to a sick bed for the two following days. His indomitable mind, however, yielded none of its firmness and (we must add) its pride. He considered the bishops as cowards and time-servers; and resolved to retain that post from which, having once been placed in it, it was held, by all law and custom, he could never be deposed by the temporal power. On the morning of the decisive day (October 18, 1164), he celebrated the mass of St. Stephen, the first martyr, the office of which begins with these words:—"Sederunt principes et adversum me loquebantur" (Princes also did sit and speak against me, Ps. cxix. 23). After the mass, he set out for the court, arrayed as he was in his pontifical robes. He went on horseback, bearing the archiepiscopal cross in his right hand, and holding the reins in his left. When he dismounted at the palace, one of his suffragans would have borne the cross before him in the usual manner, but he would not let it go out of his hands, saying, "It is most reason I should bear the cross myself; under the defence thereof I may remain in safety; and, beholding this ensign, I need not doubt under what prince I serve." "But," said the Archbishop of York, an old rival and enemy of Becket, "it is defying the king, our lord, to come in this fashion to his court; but the king has a sword, the point of which is sharper than that of thy pastoral staff." As the primate entered, the king rose from his seat, and withdrew to an inner apartment, whither the barons and bishops soon followed him, leaving Becket alone in the vast hall, or attended only by a few of his clerks or the inferior clergy, the whole body of which, unlike the dignitaries of the church, inclined to his person and cause. These poor clerks trembled and were sore dismayed; but not so Becket, who seated himself on a bench, and still holding his cross erect, calmly awaited the event. He was not made to wait long: the Bishop of Exeter, terrified at the excessive exasperation of the so-

---

[1] "The assembly at Clarendon seems to have been the most considerable of those which met under the name of the Great or the Common Council of the Realm since the Norman invasion. They were not yet called by the name of a parliament. But whatever difficulty may exist concerning the qualifications of their constituent members, there is no reason to doubt that the fulness of legislative authority was exercised by the king only when he was present in such assemblies, and acted with their advice and consent."—*Mackintosh*.

[2] Dr. Lingard admits, in speaking of the articles of Clarendon, that "sentences of excommunication had been greatly multiplied and abused during the middle ages." He admits that "they were the principal weapons with which the clergy sought to protect themselves and their property from the cruelty and rapacity of the banditti in the service of the barons. They were feared by the most powerful and unprincipled; because, at the same time that they excluded the culprit from the offices of religion, they also cut him off from the intercourse of society." These remarks involve two singular admissions; first, that the Romanist clergy had failed to make society Christian enough to secure the safety of them and their property; second, that over this really heathen society, they exercised, in the name of Christ, a tremendous power of coercion. Both confirm Lappenberg's remark, that the Romish hierarchy had fallen heirs to their predecessors—the heathen priesthood. Their influence was immense; but when we analyze it, we find it not the proper influence of Christian pastors over really converted flocks, but of a pagan priesthood over unconverted "banditti."

[3] This was Henry's usual oath when much excited. The oaths of all these kings would make a curious collection of blasphemy. The chroniclers have been careful to preserve them, and, according to their records, nearly every king had his distinctive oath.

vereign, came forth from the inner apartment, and throwing himself on his knees, implored the primate to have pity on himself and his brethren the bishops, for the king had vowed to slay the first of them that should attempt to excuse his conduct. "Thou fearest," replied Becket; "flee then! thou canst not understand the things that are of God!" Soon afterwards, the rest of the bishops appeared in a body, and Hilary of Chichester, speaking in the name of all, said, "Thou wast our primate, but now we disavow thee, because, after having promised faith to the king, our common lord, and sworn to maintain his royal customs, thou hast endeavoured to destroy them, and hast broken thine oath. We proclaim thee, then, a traitor, and tell thee we will no longer obey a perjured archbishop, but place ourselves and our cause under the protection of our lord the pope, and summon thee to answer us before him." "I hear," said Becket; and he deigned no further reply.

According to Roger of Hoveden, the archbishop was accused in the council chamber of the impossible crime of magic; and the barons pronounced a sentence of imprisonment against him. The door of that chamber soon opened, and Robert, Earl of Leicester, followed by the barons, stepped forth into the hall to read the sentence, beginning in the usual old Norman-French form —"Oyez-ci." The archbishop rose, and, interrupting him, said, "Son and earl, hear *me* first. Thou knowest with how much faith I served the king—with how much reluctance, and only to please him, I accepted my present charge, and in what manner I was declared free from all secular claims whatsoever. Touching the things which happened before my consecration, I ought not to answer, nor will I answer. You, moreover, are all my children in God; and neither law nor reason permits you to sit in judgment upon your father. I forbid you therefore to judge me; I decline your tribunal, and refer my quarrel to the decision of the pope. To him I appeal: and now, under the holy protection of the Catholic church and the apostolic see, I depart in peace." After this counter-appeal to the power which his adversaries had been the first to invoke, Becket slowly strode through the crowd towards the door of the hall. When near the threshold, the spirit of the soldier, which was not yet extinguished by the aspirations of the saint, blazed forth in a withering look and a few hasty but impassioned words. Some of the courtiers and attendants of the king threw at him straw or rushes, which they gathered from the floor, and called him traitor and false perjurer. Turning round and drawing himself up to his full height, he cried, "If my holy calling did not forbid it, I would make my answer with my sword to those cowards who call me traitor!"[1] He then mounted his horse amidst the acclamations of the lower clergy and common people, and rode in a sort of triumph to his lodgings, the populace shouting, "Blessed be God, who hath delivered his servant from the hands of his enemies!" The strength of Becket's party was in the popular body; and it has been supposed, with some reason, that his English birth and Saxon descent contributed no less than his sudden sanctity, to endear him to the people, who had never since the Conquest seen one of their race elevated to such dignities.[2] Abandoned by the great, both lay and clerical, who had hitherto been proud to wait upon him, his house was empty; and in a spirit of imitation which some will deem presumptuous, he determined to fill it with the paupers of the town, and the lowly wayfarers from the road-side. "Suffer," said he, "all the poor people to come into the place, that we may make merry together in the Lord." "And having thus spoken, the people had free entrance, so that all the hall and all the chambers of the house being furnished with tables and stools, they were conveniently placed, and served with meat and drink to the full,"[3] the archbishop supping with them, and doing the honours of the feast. In the course of the evening he sent to the king to ask leave to retire beyond sea, and he was told that he should receive an answer on the following morning. The modern historians who take the most unfavourable view of the king's conduct in these particulars, intimate, more or less broadly, that a design was on foot for preventing the archbishop from ever seeing that morrow; but the circumstances of time and place, and the character of Henry, are opposed to the belief that secret assassination was contemplated; nor does any contemporary writer give reasonable grounds for entertaining such a belief, or, indeed, say more than that the archbishop's friends were sorely frightened, and thought such a tragical termination of the quarrel a probable event. Becket, however, took his departure as if he himself feared violence. He stole out of the town of Northampton at the dead of night, disguised as a simple monk, and calling himself Brother Dearman; and being followed only by two clerks and a domestic servant, he hastened towards the coast, hiding by day and pursuing his journey by night. The season was far advanced, and the stormy winds of November swept the waters of the Channel when he reached the coast; but Becket embarked in a small boat, and after many

---

[1] *Fitz-Steph.; Gervase; Grym.; Diceto*. Diceto, we know, was at this meeting; and what gives singular interest to the accounts of it is, that it is probable the other three chroniclers, who were all closely connected with Becket, were also present.
[2] *M. Thierry.*
[3] *Holinshed.*

perils and fatigues, landed at Gravelines, in Flanders, on the fifteenth day after his departure from Northampton.

From the seaport of Gravelines he and his companions walked on foot, and in very bad condition, to the monastery of St. Bertin, at St. Omer, where he waited a short time the success of his applications to the King of France, and the pope, Alexander III., who had fixed his residence for a time in the city of Sens. Their answers were most favourable; for, fortunately for Becket, the jealousy and disunion between the Kings of France and England, disposed Louis to protect the obnoxious exile, in order to vex or weaken Henry; and the pope, turning a deaf ear to a magnificent embassy despatched to him by the English sovereign, determined to support the cause of the primate as that of truth, of justice, and the church. The splendid abbey of Pontigny, in Burgundy, was assigned to him as an honourable and secure asylum; and the pope reinvested him with his archiepiscopal dignity, which he had surrendered into his hands.

As soon as Henry was informed of these particulars, he issued writs to the sheriffs of England, commanding them to seize all rents and possessions of the primate within their jurisdictions, and to detain all bearers of appeals to the pope till the king's pleasure should be made known to them. He also commanded the justices of the kingdom to detain, in like manner, all bearers of papers, whether from the pope or Becket, that purported to pronounce excommunication or interdict on the realm—all persons, whether lay or ecclesiastic, who should adhere to such sentence of interdict—and all clerks attempting to leave the kingdom without a passport from the king. The primate's name was struck out of the liturgy, and the revenues of every clergyman who had either followed him into France, or had sent him aid and money, were seized by the crown. If Henry's vengeance had stopped here it might have been excused, if not justified; but irritated to madness by the tone of defiance his enemy assumed in a foreign country, he proceeded

ABBEY OF PONTIGNY.[1]—Chaillou Desbarres, L'Abbaye de Pontigny.

to further vindictive and most disgraceful measures, issuing one common sentence of banishment against all who were connected with Becket, either by the ties of relationship or those of friendship. The list of proscription contained four hundred names, for the wives and children of Becket's friends were included; and it is said that they were all bound by an oath to show themselves in their miserable exile to the cause of their ruin, that his heart might be wrung by the sight of the misery he had brought down upon the heads of all those who were most dear to him. It is added that his cell at Pontigny was accordingly beset by these exiles, but that he finally succeeded in relieving their immediate wants by interesting the King of France, the Queen of Sicily, and the pope, in their favour.[2]

---

[1] This abbey was suppressed in 1790. The church has been preserved, and, after the cathedrals of Sens and of Auxerre, and the church of Vezelay, is the finest and largest religious edifice in the department of Yonne. The length of its interior is 354 ft., breadth, 77 ft.; height of centre of transept, 69 ft.

[2] "Odo of Kent was one of the intimate friends of Thomas Becket and of John of Salisbury, and is mentioned with expressions of great esteem by the latter writer. He appears first in history in 1172, as prior of Canterbury, when he distinguished himself by a protracted resistance to the attempts of the crown to usurp the right of electing the archbishop. In 1175 he was made abbot of Battle; and in the time of Leland a handsome marble tomb marked the place of his burial in the abbey church."—Wright's Biog. Brit. Liter. ii. 224. From the specimen given in Latin of the kind of preaching with which this Odo, John of Abbeville, and Roger of Salisbury enlightened such of their hearers as understood Latin, one cannot form any high estimate of the improvement introduced by the Norman clergy into the pulpits of England, or consider that much was lost by those plain Anglo-Saxons who could not understand them. Anything more silly than the story introduced to illustrate how the devils are to spit on the faces of popes in hell, can hardly be imagined.

In 1165, the year after Becket's flight, Henry sustained no small disgrace from the result of a campaign, in which he personally commanded, against the Welsh. That hardy people had risen once more in arms in 1163, but had been defeated by an Anglo-Norman army, which subsequently plundered and wasted with fire the county of Carmarthen. Somewhat more than a year later a nephew of Rees-ap-Gryffiths, Prince or King of South Wales, was found dead in his bed, and the uncle, asserting he had been assassinated by the secret emissaries of a neighbouring Norman baron, collected the mountaineers of the south, and began a fierce and successful warfare, in which he was presently joined by his old allies, Gwynned, the Prince of North Wales, and Owen Cyvelioch, the leader of the clans of Powisland. One Norman castle fell after another, and, when hostilities had continued for some time, the Welsh pushed their incursions forward into the level country. The king, turning at length his attention from the church quarrel, which had absorbed it, drew together an army "as well of Englishmen as strangers," and hastened to the Welsh marches. At his approach the mountaineers withdrew "to their starting-holes"—their woods and strait passages. Henry, without regard to difficulties and dangers, followed them, and a general action was fought on the banks of the Cieroc. The Welsh were defeated, and fled to their uplands. Henry, still following them, penetrated as far as the lofty Berwin, at the foot of which he encamped. A sudden storm of rain set in, and continued until all the streams and torrents were fearfully swollen, and the valley was deluged. Meanwhile the natives gathered on the ridges of the mountain of Berwin; but it appears to have been more from the war of the elements than of man that the king's army retreated in great disorder and with some loss. Henry had hitherto showed himself remarkably free from the cruelty of his age, but his mind was now embittered, and in a hasty moment he resolved to take a barbarous vengeance on the persons of the hostages whom the Welsh princes had placed in his hands, seven years before, as pledges of their tranquillity and allegiance. The eyes of the males were picked out of their heads, and the noses and ears of the females were cut off. The old chroniclers hardly increase our horror when they tell us that the victims belonged to the noblest families of Wales.[1]

This reverse in England was soon followed by successes on the Continent. A formidable insurrection broke out in Brittany against Henry's subservient ally Conan, who applied to him for succour, according to the terms of the treaty of alliance subsisting between them. The troops of the king entered by the frontier of Normandy, under pretext of defending the legitimate Earl of the Bretons against his revolted subjects. Henry soon made himself master of Dol, and several other towns, which he kept and garrisoned with his own soldiers. Conan had shown himself utterly incapable of managing the fierce Breton nobles, by whose excesses and cruelties the poor people were ground to the dust. Henry's power and abilities were well known to the suffering Bretons, and a considerable party, including the priests of the country, rallied round him, and hailed him as a deliverer.[2] Submitting in part

MOUNT ST. MICHAEL, Normandy.[3]—Cotman's Antiquities of Normandy.

to the force of circumstances and the wishes of Henry, and in part, perhaps, following his own indolent inclinations, Conan resigned the remnant of his authority into the hands of his protector, who governed the state in the name of his son Geoffrey, and Conan's heiress Constantia, the espousals of these two children being prematurely solemnized. In the month of December, 1166, Henry kept his court in the famed old castle on Mount St. Michael, whence his eye could range over the long and extending land of Brittany; and there he was visited by William the Lion, who had recently ascended the Scottish throne on the death of his brother, Malcolm IV.

[1] *Gervase; Newbria.; Girald. Camb. Itin.; Diceto.*

[2] *Script. Rev. Franc.;* Daru, *Hist. de la Bretagne.*
[3] This singular rock is situated in the province of Normandy and the modern department of Manche in France, seven miles south-west from Avranches. It is about 400 ft. high, including the building; above five miles in circumference; and lies three miles from the coast, on sandy flats that are covered each tide, and thus isolate it from the mainland. It was once strongly

While still abroad, he ordered a tax to be levied on all his subjects, whether English or foreign, for the support of the war in the Holy Land, which was taking a turn more and more unfavourable to the Christians; but at that very time his peace was broken by his own war with the church and the unremitting hostility of Becket. In the month of May the banished archbishop went from Pontigny to Vezeley, near Auxerre, and, encouraged by the pope, he repaired to the church on the great festival of the Ascension, and mounting the pulpit there, "with book, bell, and candle," solemnly cursed and pronounced the sentence of excommunication against the defenders of the Constitutions of Clarendon, the detainers of the sequestrated property of the church of Canterbury, and those who imprisoned or persecuted either laymen or clergy on his account. This done, he more particularly excommunicated by name Richard de Lucy, Joycelin Baliol, and four other of Henry's courtiers and prime favourites.[1] The king was at Chinon, in Anjou, when he was startled by this new sign of life given by his adversary. Though in general a great master of his feelings, Henry was subject to excesses of ungovernable fury, and on this occasion he seems fairly to have taken leave of his senses. He cried out that they wanted to kill him, body and soul—that he was wretched in being surrounded by cowards and traitors, not one of whom thought of delivering him from the insupportable vexations caused him by a single man. He took off his cap and dashed it to the ground, undid his girdle, threw his clothes about the room, tore off the silk coverlet from his bed and rolled upon it, and gnawed the straw and rushes —for it appears that this mighty and splendid monarch had no better bed.[2] His resentment did not pass away with this paroxysm; and after writing to the pope and the King of France, he threatened that, if Becket should return and continue to be sheltered at the abbey of Pontigny, which belonged to the Cistercians, he would seize all the estates appertaining to that order within his numerous dominions. The threat was an alarming one to the monks, and we find Becket removing out of Burgundy to the town of Sens, where a new asylum was appointed him by Louis. A paltry war was begun and ended by a truce, all within a few months: it was followed the next year by another war, equally short and still more inglorious for the French king; for although he had excited fresh disturbances in Brittany and Maine, and leagued himself with some of Henry's revolted barons of Poictou and Aquitaine, he gained no advantage whatever for himself, was the cause of ruin to most of his allies, and was compelled to conclude a peace at the beginning of the year 1169. Nothing but an empty pride could have been gratified by a series of feudal oaths; but the designations given to his sons on this occasion, by the English king, contributed to fatal consequences which happened four years later. Prince Henry of England, his eldest son, did homage to his father-in-law, the King of France, for Anjou and Maine, as he had formerly done for Normandy; Prince Richard, his second son, did homage for Aquitaine; and Geoffrey, his third son, for Brittany: and it was afterwards assumed that these ceremonies constituted the boys sovereigns and absolute masters of the several dominions named. At the same time the two kings agreed upon a marriage between Prince Richard of England, and Alice, another daughter of the King of France, the previous treaty of matrimony with the King of Arragon being set aside. Sixteen months before these events Henry lost his mother, the Empress Matilda, who died at Rouen, and was buried in the celebrated abbey of Bec, which she had enriched with the donations of her piety and penitence.

About this time Henry was prevailed upon by the pope, the King of France, and by some of his own friends, to assent to the return of Becket and his party. The Kings of France and England met at Montmirail, and Becket was admitted to a conference. Henry insisted on qualifying his agreement to the proposed terms of accommodation by the addition of the words, "saving the honour of his kingdom," a salvo which Becket met by another on his part, saying that he was willing to be reconciled to the king, and obey him in all things, "saving the honour of God and the church." Upon this, Henry, turning to the King of France, said, "Do you know what would happen if I were to admit this reservation? That man would interpret everything displeasing to himself as being contrary to the honour of God, and would so invade all my rights: but to show that I do not withstand God's honour, I will here offer him a concession—what the greatest and

---

fortified, but is now used as a state prison. Duke Rollo of Normandy is said to have endowed the monastery which crowns St. Michael's Mount on the fourth day after his baptism into the Christian faith. Richard I. of England greatly enlarged the church, and added spacious buildings for a body of monks of the Benedictine order. The base of the mount is surrounded with high thick walls, flanked with semicircular machicolated towers and bastions. Toward the west end its sides present only steep, black, bare, pointed rocks. The portions lying in an opposite direction incline in a comparatively easy slope, and are covered with houses that follow in successive lines, leaving but a scanty space for some small gardens, in which the vine, the fig-tree, and the almond flourish in great luxuriance. The walls of the castellated abbey impend, and jut out in bold, decided masses; and the whole is crowned by the florid choir of the abbey church.

[1] *Epist. S. Thomæ; Rog. Hove.; Gervase.*
[2] *Script. Rer. Franc.* Henry seems to have acted in this manner on more than one occasion.

holiest of his predecessors did unto the least of mine, that let him do unto me, and I am contented therewith." All present exclaimed that this was enough—that the king had humbled himself enough. But Becket still insisted on his salvo; upon which the King of France said he seemed to wish to be "greater than the saints, and better than St. Peter;" and the nobles present murmured at his unbending pride, and said he no longer merited an asylum in France. The two kings mounted their horses and rode away without saluting Becket, who retired much cast down. No one any longer offered him food and lodging in the name of Louis, and on his journey back to Sens he was reduced to live on the charity of the common people.[1]

In another conference the obnoxious clauses on either side were omitted. The business now seemed in fair train; but when Becket asked from the king the kiss of peace,[2] which was the usual termination to such quarrels, Henry's irritated feelings prevented him from granting it, and he excused himself by saying it was only a solemn oath taken formerly, in a moment of passion, never to kiss Becket, that hindered him from giving this sign of perfect reconciliation. The primate was resolute to waive no privilege and no ceremony, and this conference was also broken off in anger. Another quarrel between the two kings, and an impotent raising of banners on the part of Louis, which threatened at first to retard the reconciliation between Henry and his primate, were in fact the causes of hastening that event; for hostilities dwindled into a truce, the truce led to another conference between the sovereigns, and the conference to another peace, at which Henry, who was apprehensive that the pope would finally consent to Becket's ardent wishes, and permit him to excommunicate his king by name, and pronounce an interdict against the whole kingdom, slowly and reluctantly pledged his word to be reconciled forthwith to the dangerous exile. On the 22d of July, 1170, a solemn congress was held in a spacious and most pleasant meadow,[3] between Freteval and La Ferté-Bernard, on the borders of Touraine. The king was there before the archbishop; and as soon as Becket appeared, riding leisurely towards the tent, he spurred his horse to meet him, and saluted him, cap in hand. They then rode apart into the field, and discoursed together for some time in the same familiar manner as in by-gone times. Then returning to his attendants, Henry said that he found the archbishop in the best possible disposition, and that it would be sinful in him to nourish rancour any longer.

The primate came up, accompanied by the Archbishop of Sens and other priests, and the forms of reconciliation were completed; always, however, excepting the kiss of peace, which, according to some, Henry promised he would give in England, where they would soon meet.[4] The king, however, condescended to hold Becket's stirrup when he mounted. By their agreement, Becket was to love, honour, and serve the king in as far as an archbishop could "render in the Lord service to his sovereign;" and Henry was to restore immediately all the lands and livings, and privileges of the church of Canterbury, and to furnish Becket with funds to discharge his debts, and make the journey into England. These terms were certainly not all kept: the lands were not released for four months; and, after many vexatious delays, Becket was obliged to borrow money for his journey. While tarrying on the French coast, he was several times warned that danger awaited him on the opposite shore. This was not improbable, as many resolute men had been suddenly driven from the church lands on which they had fattened for years, and as he was known to carry about his person letters of excommunication from the pope against the Archbishop of York, and the Bishops of London and Salisbury, whom he held to be his chief enemies, and who were men likely to adopt strong measures to prevent his promulgating the terrible sentence. He was even assured that Ranulf de Broc, a knight of a family who all hated him to the death, and who had himself boasted that he would not let the archbishop live to eat a single loaf of bread in England, was lying with a body of soldiers between Canterbury and Dover, in order to intercept him. But nothing could move Becket, who said seven years of absence were long enough both for the shepherd and his flock, and that he would not stop though he were sure to be cut to pieces as soon as he landed on the opposite coast. The only use he made of the warnings he received, was to confide the letters of excommunication to a skilful and devoted messenger, who, preceding him some short time, stole into England without being suspected, and actually delivered them publicly to the three bishops, who were as much startled as if a thunderbolt had fallen at their feet. This last measure seems to have had as much to do with Becket's death as any anger of the king's. As he was on the point of embarking, a vessel arrived from England. The sailors were asked what were the feelings of the good English people

---

[1] *Vita S. Thomæ; Script. Rer. Franc.; Gervase; Epist. S. Thomæ.*
[2] See a curious discourse on kisses of peace in Ducange, Gloss. in voc. *Osculum Pacis.*
[3] *In prato amænissimo. Script. Rer. Franc.*

[4] *Fitz-Stephen; Epist. S. Thomæ.*

towards their archbishop. They replied, that the people would hail his return with transports of joy. This was a good omen, and he no doubt relied much more on the popular favour than on the protection of John of Oxford, one of the royal chaplains, and some others whom Henry had sent to accompany him. He sailed from France in the same gloomy month of the year in which he had begun his exile, and, avoiding Dover, landed at Sandwich on the 1st of December. At the news of his arrival, the mariners, the peasants, and the working people generally, and the English burgesses flocked to meet him; but none of the rich and powerful welcomed him; and the first persons of rank he saw presented themselves in a menacing attitude. These latter were a sheriff of Kent, Reginald de Warenne, Ranulf de Broc (who had ridden across the country from Dover), and some relatives and allies of the three excommunicated bishops, who carried swords under their tunics, and drew them when they approached the primate. John of Oxford conjured them to be quiet, lest they should make their king pass for a traitor; but it is probable that the determined countenance of the English multitude made more impression on them than his peaceful words. They retired to their castles, and spread a report among their feudal compeers that Becket was liberating the serfs of the country, who were marching in his train, drunk with joy and hopes of vengeance. At Canterbury, the primate was received with acclamations; but still it was only the poor and lowly that welcomed him. A few days after he set out for Woodstock, to visit the king's eldest son, Prince Henry, who had formerly been his pupil. Becket counted much on his influence over the young prince, but the party opposed to him succeeded in preventing his having an opportunity to exert that influence. A royal messenger met him on his journey, and ordered him, in the name of the prince, not to enter any of the royal towns or castles, but to return and remain within his own diocese. The primate obeyed, and returning, spent some days at Harrow-on-the-Hill, which belonged to the church of Canterbury a considerable time before the Norman conquest. During his stay at Harrow, Becket kept great hospitality; but this virtue was probably exercised in regard to persons of a condition resembling those whom he had bidden to his memorable feast at Northampton, and the only ecclesiastic of rank mentioned as doing him honour, was the abbot of the neighbouring monastery of St. Alban's. Two of his own clergy, Nigellus de Sackville, who was called "the usurping rector of Harrow," and Robert de Broc, the vicar, a relation of his determined foe, Ranulf de Broc, treated him with great disrespect, and when he was departing, maimed the horse which carried his provisions—an offence which was not forgotten by one who presumed to hurl the thunderbolts of damnation. Becket returned to Canterbury, escorted by a host of poor people, armed with rustic targets and rusty lances. On Christmas Day he ascended the pulpit in the great cathedral church, and delivered an eloquent sermon on the words, "Venio ad vos mori inter vos" (I come to die among you). He told his congregation that one of their archbishops had been a martyr, and that they would probably soon see another; "but," he added, "before I depart hence I will avenge some of the wrongs my church has suffered during the last seven years;" and he forthwith excommunicated Ranulf and Robert de Broc, and Nigellus, the rector of Harrow.[1] This was Becket's last public act. As soon as his messenger from the French coast had delivered his letters, the three bishops excommunicated by them hastened to Prince Henry, to complain of his insatiate thirst of revenge, and to accuse him of a fixed plan of violating all the royal privileges and the customs of the land; and almost immediately after they crossed over to the Continent, to demand redress from the king. "We implore it," said the bishops, "both for the sake of royalty and the clergy—for your own repose as well as ours. There is a man who sets England on fire; he marches with troops of horse and armed foot, prowling round the fortresses, and trying to get himself received within them."[2] The exaggeration was not needed; Henry was seized with one of his most violent fits of fury. "How!" cried he, "a fellow that hath eaten my bread—a beggar that first came to my court on a lame horse—dares insult his king and the royal family, and tread upon the whole kingdom; and not one of the cowards I nourish at my table—not one will deliver me from this turbulent priest!"[3] There were four knights present, who had probably injuries of their own to avenge, and who took this outburst of temper as a sufficient death-warrant; and, without communicating their sudden determination to the king (or, at least, there is no evidence that they did), hurried over to England. Their names were Reginald Fitz-Urse, William Tracy, Hugh de Morville, and Richard Brito; and they are described by a contemporary as being barons, and servants of the king's bed-chamber. Their intention was not suspected, nor was their absence noticed; and while they were riding with loose rein towards the coast, the king was closeted with his council of barons, who, after some discussion, which seems to have occupied more than one day, ap-

---
[1] *Fitz-Steph.; Vita S. Thomæ; Gervase; Rog. Hov.; Matt. Paris.*
[2] *Script. Rer. Franc.* [3] *Vita Quadripart.*

pointed three commissioners to go and seize, according to the forms of law, the person of Thomas à Becket, on the charge of high treason. But the conspirators, who had bound themselves together by an oath, left the commissioners nothing to do. Three days after Christmas Day they arrived secretly at Saltwood, in the neighbourhood of Canterbury, where the De Broc family had a house; and here, under the cover of night, they arranged their plans. On the 29th of December, having collected a number of adherents to quell the resistance of Becket's attendants and the citizens, in case any should be offered, they proceeded to the monastery of St. Augustine's, at Canterbury, the abbot of which, like nearly all the superior churchmen, was of the king's party. From St. Augustine's they went to the archbishop's palace, and entering his apartment abruptly, about two hours after noon, seated themselves on the floor without saluting him, or offering any sign of respect. There was a dead pause—the knights not knowing how to begin, and neither of them liking to speak first. At length Becket asked what they wanted; but still they sat gazing at him with haggard eyes. There were twelve men of the party, besides the four knights. Reginald Fitz-Urse, feigning a commission from the king, at last spoke. "We come," said he, "that you may absolve the bishops whom you have excommunicated, re-establish the bishops whom you have suspended, and answer for your offences against the king." Becket replied with boldness and with great warmth, not sparing taunts and invectives. He said that he had published the Papal letters of excommunication with the king's consent; that he could not absolve the Archbishop of York, whose heinous case was reserved for the pope alone; but that he would remove the censures from the two other bishops, if they would swear to submit to the decisions of Rome. "But of whom then," demanded Reginald, "do you hold your archbishopric—of the king, or of the pope?" "I owe the spiritual rights to God and the pope, and the temporal rights to the king." "How! is it not the king that hath given you all?" Becket's decided negative was received with murmurs, and the knights furiously twisted their long gloves. Three out of the four cavaliers had followed

REMAINS OF THE ST. AUGUSTINE MONASTERY, Canterbury.[1]—Britton's Canterbury.

Becket in the days of his prosperity and vainglory, and vowed themselves his liege men. He reminded them of this, and observed, it was not for such as they to threaten him in his own house; adding also, that if he were threatened by all the swords in England, he would not yield. "We will do more than threaten," replied the knights, and then departed. When they were gone, his attendants loudly expressed their alarm, and blamed him for the rough and provoking tone by which he had inflamed, instead of pacifying his enemies; but the prelate silenced the latter part of their discourse by telling them he had no need of their advice, and knew what he ought to do. The barons with their accomplices, who seem to have wished, if they could, to avoid bloodshed, finding that threats were ineffectual, put on their coats of mail, and taking each a sword in his hand, returned to the palace; but finding that the gate had been shut and barred by the terrified servants, Fitz-Urse tried to break it open, and the sounds of his ponderous axe rang through the building. The gate might have offered some considerable resistance, but Robert de Broc showed

---

[1] St. Augustine, having converted King Ethelbert from paganism to the Christian faith, obtained of him both permission and lands for the erection of a monastery, which was also to be the future burial-place of the Kings of Kent and Archbishops of Canterbury. For this purpose Ethelbert granted him his palace, which stood on the east side of the city of Canterbury, and just without the walls. Here St. Augustine founded his monastery, A.D. 605. It was first dedicated to the apostles Peter and Paul, but Archbishop Dunstan (A.D. 987) added St. Augustine, by which name it has been since commonly called. In 1011 the house was plundered by the Danes; in 1168 the church was almost destroyed by fire; and in 1271 the monastery was nearly ruined by floods, occasioned by a prodigious storm. In the year 1612 the back part of the building adjoining the great gate was repaired with brick. At this place it is said Charles I. consummated his marriage with the Princess Henrietta of France (anno 1625), at which time it was the mansion of the Lord Wotton of Bacton-Malherbe.—Grose's Antiquities.

them the way in at a window. The people about Becket had in vain urged him to take refuge in the church; but at this moment the voices of the monks, singing vespers in the choir, striking his ear, he said he would go, as his duty called him thither; and, making his cross-bearer precede him with the crucifix elevated, he traversed the cloister with slow and measured steps, and entered the church. His servants would have closed and fastened the doors, but he forbade them, saying that the house of God was not to be barricaded like a castle. He had passed through the north transept, and was ascending the steps which led to the choir, when Reginald Fitz-Urse appeared at the other end of the church, waving his sword,

ASSASSINATION OF BECKET.¹—From an ancient painting on a board hung at the head of the tomb of Henry IV. in Canterbury Cathedral.

and shouted, "Follow me, loyal servants of the king!" The other conspirators followed him closely, armed like himself from head to foot, and brandishing their swords. The shades of evening had fallen, and in the obscurity of the vast church, which was only broken here and there by a lamp glimmering before a shrine, Becket might easily have hid himself in the dark and intricate crypts under ground, or beneath the roof of the old church. Each of these courses was suggested by his attendants, but he rejected them both, and turned boldly to meet the intruders, followed or preceded by his cross-bearer, the faithful Edward Gryme, the only one who did not flee. A voice shouted, "Where is the traitor?" Becket answered not; but when Reginald Fitz-Urse said, "Where is the archbishop?" he replied, "Here am I, an archbishop, but no traitor, ready to suffer in my Saviour's name." Tracy pulled him by the sleeve, saying, "Come hither, thou art a prisoner." He pulled back his arm in so violent a manner, that he made Tracy stagger forward. They advised him to flee or to go with them; and, on a candid consideration, it seems to us that the conspirators, after all, are entitled to a doubt as to whether they really intended a murder, or were not rather hurried into it by his obstinacy and provoking language. Addressing Fitz-Urse, he said, "I have done thee many pleasures; why comest thou with armed men into my church?" They told him that he must instantly absolve the bishops. "Never, until they have offered satisfaction," was his answer; and he applied a foul vituperative term to Fitz-Urse. "Then die!" exclaimed Fitz-Urse, striking at his head. The faithful Gryme interposed his arm to save his master; the arm was broken, or nearly cut off, and the stroke descended on the primate's head, and slightly wounded him. Then another voice cried, "Flee, or thou diest;" but still Becket moved not, but with the blood running down his face, he clasped his hands, and bowing his head, exclaimed, "To God, to St. Mary, to the holy patrons of this church, and to St. Denis, I commend my soul and the church's cause." A second stroke brought him to the ground, close to the foot of St. Bennet's altar; a third, given with such force that the sword was broken against the stone pavement, cleft his skull, and his brains were scattered all about. One of the conspirators put his foot on his neck, and cried, "Thus perishes a traitor!"² The conspirators then withdrew, without encountering any hinderance or molestation; but when the fearful news spread through Canterbury and the neighbouring country, the excitement was prodigious; and the then inevitable inference was drawn that Becket was a martyr, and miracles would be wrought at his tomb. For some time, however, the superior orders rejected this faith, and made

---

¹ The piece represents the sufferer on his knees after the first stroke he received from Tracy, who is represented by the figure with the shield and the uplifted sword tinged with blood. The knight who is plunging his sword into the prelate's brains appears to be Fitz-Urse, by the bears depicted on his surcoat. The other, distinguished by the muzzled boars' or bears' heads, with the horizontal sword, must be Morville, as the lower figure, by the position of his sword and apparent inactivity, certainly is Brito, the last actor in this bloody tragedy. Edward Gryme, with terror strongly marked in his countenance, appears behind the altar with the episcopal cross in his hand, which history mentions to have been carried before our prelate as he entered the church, and his cap besprinkled with blood lies on the middle step of the altar.—Milner's *Account of the murder of Thomas à Becket*.

² *Gervase; Fitz-Steph.; Gryme* (who was present, and suffered on the occasion); *Newbrig*.

efforts to suppress the veneration of the common people. An edict was published, prohibiting all men from preaching in the churches or reporting in the public places that Becket was a martyr. His old foe, the Archbishop of York, ascended the pulpit to announce his death as an infliction of Divine vengeance, saying that he had perished in his guilt and pride like Pharaoh.[1] Other ecclesiastics preached that the body of the traitor ought not to be allowed to rest in consecrated ground, but ought to be thrown into a ditch, or hung on a gibbet. An attempt was even made to seize the body, but the monks, who received timely warning, concealed it, and hastily buried it in the subterranean vaults of the cathedral. But it was soon found that the public voice, echoed, for its own purposes, by the court of France, was too loud to be drowned in this manner. Louis, whom Henry had so often humbled, wrote to the pope, imploring him to draw the sword of St. Peter against that horrible persecutor of God, who surpassed Nero in cruelty, Julian in apostasy, and Judas in treachery. He chose to believe, and the French bishops believed with him, that Henry had ordered the murder.

On receiving the intelligence of Becket's assassination, Henry expressed the greatest grief and horror, shut himself up in his room, and refused to receive either food or consolation for three days; and if he took care to have a touching detail of his distressed feelings transmitted to the pope, in which he declared his innocence in the strongest terms, and entreated that censure might be suspended till the facts of the case were examined, such a measure is not to be taken, in itself, as indicating the insincerity of his grief and horror. He must have felt that his own hasty exclamations had led to the deed, and that all the penalties of a deliberate crime would be exacted at his hand.

When Henry's envoys first appeared at Rome —for the pope (Alexander) was no longer a dependent exile—they were coldly received, and everything seemed to threaten that an interdict would be laid upon the kingdom, and the king excommunicated by name. In the end, however, Alexander rested satisfied with an excommunication, in general terms, of the murderers and the abettors of the crime. It is said that Henry's gold was not idle on this occasion; but the employment of it is rather a proof of the notorious rapacity of the cardinals, than of his having a bad cause to plead. In the month of May, 1172, in a council held at Avranches, at which two legates of the pope attended, Henry swore, on the holy gospels and sacred relics—a great concourse of the clergy and people being present—that he had neither ordered nor desired the murder of the archbishop. This oath was not demanded from him, but taken of his own free will. As, however, he could not deny that the assassins might have been moved to the deed by his wrathful words, he consented to maintain 200 knights during a year, for the defence of the Holy Land; and to serve himself, if the pope should require it, for three years against the infidels, either the Saracens in Palestine or the Moors in Spain, as the church should appoint. At the same time, he engaged to restore all the lands and possessions belonging to the friends of the late archbishop; to permit appeals to be made to the pope in good faith, and without fraud, reserving to himself, however, the right of obliging such appellants as he suspected of evil intentions to give security that they would attempt nothing abroad to the detriment of him or his kingdom. To these conditions he made an addition too vague to have any practical effect—that he would relinquish such customs against the church as had been introduced in his time. The legates then fully absolved the king; and thus terminated this quarrel, less to Henry's disadvantage than might have been expected.[2]

In the short interval of this negotiation he had added a kingdom to his dominions. The year that followed the death of Becket was made memorable by the conquest of Ireland.

---

[1] *Epist. Joan. Sarisb.*

[2] *Hoveden; Epist. S. Thomæ.; Epist. Joan. Sarisb.; Gervase.*

CHAPTER VI.—CIVIL AND MILITARY HISTORY.—A.D. 1064—1189.

HENRY II., SURNAMED PLANTAGENET.—ACCESSION, A.D. 1154—DEATH, A.D. 1189.

Summary of Irish history to the time of Henry II.—Slight connection between England and Ireland—Adrian IV. grants Ireland to Henry II. by a Papal bull—The King of Leinster driven from his throne—He applies to Henry for aid—Obtains assistance from the Earl of Pembroke—The conquest of Ireland commenced by the English—They take Wexford—Their successes—Pembroke arrives in Ireland—Takes Waterford by storm—The Irish everywhere defeated—Henry arrives to secure Ireland to the English crown—The Irish chiefs tender their submission—The whole country except Ulster conquered—Dissensions in the family of Henry II.—Prince Henry, his eldest son, commences a rebellion—His brothers join him—They are aided by the King of France and other foreign princes—The Scots invade England—Henry II., in his distress, does penance at the tomb of Becket—The King of Scots taken prisoner—Henry subdues his sons and their allies—Wisdom and promptitude of Henry's proceedings—His sons again rebel—Conflicts on the Continent—Prince Henry dies—Bertrand de Born, the head of the confederacy, taken prisoner—Death of Geoffrey, Henry's second son—Richard, the third son, compelled to submit—Commencement of the Crusades—Preparations in France and England—Fresh rebellion of Richard, son of Henry II.—Its cause—He is countenanced by Philip of France—Henry II. obliged to submit to humbling conditions—He dies broken-hearted at Chinon—Richard's conduct at his father's funeral—Character of Henry II.—His family—The story of "Fair Rosamond."

N the preceding Book, the sketch of Irish history was brought down to the reign of Turlogh, the commencement of which is assigned to the year 1064. Turlogh, however, like his uncle Donchad, whom he had succeeded, and Donchad's father, the great O'Brien, is scarcely acknowledged by the old annalists as having been a legitimate king, not being of the blood of the O'Niells of Ulster, in which line, say the rather inventive Irish historians, the supreme sceptre had been transmitted, with scarcely any interruption, till its seizure by Brien, from the time of O'Niell or Nial of the Nine Hostages, who flourished in the beginning of the fifth century. The long acquiescence of the other provincial regal houses in the superiority thus assumed by that of Ulster was broken by the usurpation of the Munster O'Briens, and we shall find that ere long both the O'Connors of Connaught and the MacMurroghs of Leinster made their appearance on the scene, as competitors for the prize of chief dominion, along with the other two families. The whole history of the country from this date is merely the history of these contests for the crown, of which contests we confine ourselves to the following summary.

Turlogh, who kept his court in the palace of his ancestors, the Kings of Munster, at Kinkora, in Clare, died there in July, 1086. His second son, Murtach or Murkertach, acquired the sole possession of the throne of Munster by the death of one of his two brothers, and the banishment of the other; but his attempt to retain the supreme monarchy in his family was resisted by the other provincial kings, who united in supporting, against his claims, those of Domnal MacLochlin, or Donald MacLachlan, the head of the ancient royal house of O'Niell. At last, after much fighting, it was arranged, at a solemn convention held in 1094, that the island should be divided between the two competitors—the southern half, called Leath Mogh, or Mogh's Half, remaining subject to Murtach, and the northern, called Leath Cuinn, or Conn's Half, being resigned to the dominion of MacLochlin. This was a well-known ancient division, which, in former times, even when the nominal sovereignty of the whole country was conceded to the Kings of Ulster, had often left those of Munster in possession not only of the actual independence, but of a share of the supremacy over both Connaught and Leinster; for the line of partition was drawn right across the island from the neighbourhood of the town of Galway to Dublin, and consequently cut through each of these provinces. With this real equality in extent of dominion and authority between the two houses, one circumstance chiefly had for a long period held in check the rising fortunes of that of Munster, the law or custom, namely, of the succession to the crown in that province, which was divided into two principalities, Desmond or South Munster, and Thomond or North Munster, the reigning families of which, by an arrangement somewhat similar to that which has been described as anciently subsisting in the Scottish monarchy,[1] enjoyed the supreme sovereignty alternately. The two lines of princes derived this right of equal participation from the will of their common ancestor Olill Ollum; those

---

[1] See vol. I. p. 144.

of Desmond, which comprehended the present counties of Kerry, Cork, and Waterford, being descended from that king's eldest son Eogan, whence the people of that principality were called Eoganacths or Eugenians; while the princes of Thomond, which consisted of Clare, Limerick, and the greater part of Tipperary, were sprung from his second son Cormac Cas, whence their subjects took the name of Dalgnis or Dalcassians. But Brien Boru, himself of the Dalcassian family, had begun his course of inroad upon the ancient institutions of his country by setting at defiance the rights of his Eugenian kindred, and had possessed himself, by usurpation, of the provincial throne of Munster, before he seized upon the supreme power. The Munster kings had ever since continued to be of his race.

The compact between MacLochlin and Murtach did not put an end to their contention. Several more battles were fought between them, till at length, in 1103, Murtach sustained a defeat at Cobha, in Tyrone, which so greatly weakened his power as to prevent him from ever after giving his adversary any serious annoyance. They continued to reign, however—MacLochlin at Aileach or Alichia, in Donegal, Murtach at Cashel—till the death of the latter, in 1119, after he had spent the last three or four years of his life in a monastery, the management of affairs having been meanwhile left in the hands of his brother Dermot. From the date of the death of Murtach, MacLochlin is regarded as having been sole monarch; but he also died in 1121.

Fifteen years of confusion followed, during which a contest between various competitors for the supreme authority spread war and devastation over every part of the country. At last, in 1136, Turlogh or Tordelvac O'Connor, King of Connaught, was acknowledged monarch of all Ireland; the ancient sceptre of the O'Niells thus passing a second time into a new house. O'Connor, however, had to maintain himself on the throne he had thus acquired by a great deal of hard fighting with his neighbours and rivals. Connor O'Brien, the King of Munster, who had vigorously opposed his elevation, and his successor Turlogh O'Brien, did not cease to dispute his power, till the overthrow of the latter at the great battle of Moinmor, fought in 1151, placed Munster for the moment completely under the tread of the victor. O'Brien was driven from his kingdom, and the territory was again divided into two principalities, over which O'Connor set two princes of the Eugenian house, that had some time before joined him in his contest with the Dalcassians. A few years after, however, the expelled king was restored by the interference of Murtogh O'Lochlin, or Murtach MacLachlan, O'Niell, the King of Ulster, and the legitimate heir of the ancient monarchs of Ireland, who now also took arms to recover for himself the throne of his ancestors. With this new rival, O'Connor, for whom his martial reign has procured from the annalists the title of The Great, continued at war during the remainder of his life; and at his death, in 1156, O'Lochlin was acknowledged supreme king. Some opposition was made to his accession by Roderick O'Connor, the son of the late king, and his successor to the provincial throne of Connaught; but he also, at last, as well as the Princes of Munster and Leinster, acquiesced in the restoration of the old sovereign house, and submitted to O'Niell.

The rule of Murtogh O'Lochlin was distinguished by vigour and ability; but its close was unfortunate. He was killed along with many of his nobility, in 1166, in a battle with some insurgent chiefs of his own province of Ulster; to whom he had given abundant cause for taking up arms against him, if it be true that, after having been professedly reconciled to one of them, with whom he had had a quarrel, and sealing the compact by the acceptance of hostages, he had suddenly seized the unfortunate chief, together with three of his friends, and caused his eyes to be put out, and them to be put to death. On his decease the sovereignty of Ireland devolved upon his rival, Roderick O'Connor, of Connaught, the son of its former possessor, O'Connor the Great.

Up to this time almost the only connection between England and Ireland was that of the commerce carried on between some of the opposite ports; scarcely any political intercourse had ever taken place between the two countries. Her church, indeed, attached Ireland to the rest of Christendom; and some correspondence is still preserved, that passed between her kings and prelates and the English archbishops Lanfranc and Anselm, relating chiefly to certain points in which the latter conceived the ecclesiastical discipline of the neighbouring island to stand in need of reformation. The bishops also of the Danish towns in Ireland appear to have been usually consecrated by the Archbishop of Canterbury. But almost the single well-authenticated instance of any interference by the one nation in the civil affairs of the other since the Norman conquest, was in the rebellion of Robert de Belesme, in the beginning of the reign of Henry I., when that nobleman's brother, Arnulph de Montgomery, is said by some of the Welsh chroniclers to have passed over to Ireland, and to have there obtained from King Murtach O'Brien, both supplies for the war and the hand of his daughter for himself. It is said, indeed, that both the Conqueror and Henry I. had meditated the subjugation of Ireland; and Malmesbury affirms that the latter English king had Murtach and his successors so entirely at his devotion, that they wrote nothing but adulation of him, nor did anything but what he ordered.

It would appear that a project of conquest had been entertained by Henry II., from the very commencement of his reign. The same year in which he came to the throne, witnessed the elevation to the popedom of the only Englishman that ever wore the triple crown—Nicholas Breakspear, who assumed the name of Adrian IV. Very soon after his coronation, Henry sent an embassy to Rome, at the head of which was the learned John of Salisbury, ostensibly to congratulate Adrian on his accession, but really to solicit the new pope for his sanction to the scheme of the conquest of Ireland. Adrian granted a bull, in the terms or to the effect desired, and before the end of the same year, the matter was submitted by Henry to a great council of his barons; but the undertaking was opposed by many of those present, and especially by his mother, the empress; and in consequence it was for the time given up.

Henry's attention was not recalled to the subject till many years after. The course of the story now carries us back again to Ireland, and to another of the provincial kings of that country of whom we have yet said nothing—Dermond MacMurrogh, or Dermot MacMurchad, King of Lagenia or Leinster. This prince had early signalized himself by his sanguinary ferocity, even on a stage where all the actors were men of blood. So far back as the year 1140, in order to break the power of his nobility, he had seventeen of the chief of them seized at once, all of whom that he did not put to death he deprived of their eyes. His most noted exploit, however, was of a different character. Dervorgilla, a lady of great beauty, was the wife of Tiernan O'Ruarc, the Lord of Breffny, a district in Leinster, and the old enemy of MacMurrogh. The sworn foe of her husband, however, was the object of Dervorgilla's guilty passion; and, at her own suggestion, it is said, when her husband was absent on a military expedition, the King of Leinster came and carried her off. This happened in the year 1153, when the supreme sovereignty was in the possession of Turlogh O'Connor. To him O'Ruarc applied for the means of avenging his wrong, and received from him such effective assistance as to be enabled to recover both his wife and the property she had carried off with her. But from this time MacMurrogh and O'Ruarc kept up a spiteful contest, with alternating fortunes, for many years. So long as Turlogh lived, O'Ruarc had a steady ally in the common sovereign, and the King of Leinster was effectually kept in check by their united power. The succeeding reign of O'Lochlin, on the other hand, was, for the whole of the ten years that it lasted, a period of triumphant revenge to MacMurrogh. But the recovery of the supremacy, on O'Lochlin's death, by the house of O'Connor, at last put an end to the long and bitter strife. A general combination was now formed against the King of Leinster; King Roderick, the Lord of Breffny, and his father-in-law, the Prince of Meath, united their forces for the avowed purpose of driving him from his kingdom; they were joined by many of his own subjects, both Irish and Danish, to whom his tyranny had rendered him odious; and O'Ruarc put himself at the head of the whole. MacMurrogh made some effort to defend himself; but finding himself deserted by all, he sought safety in flight, and left his kingdom for the present to the disposal of his conquerors. They set another prince of his own family on the vacant throne. Meanwhile the deposed and fugitive king had embarked for England, to seek the aid of King Henry, in return for which he was ready to acknowledge himself the vassal of the English monarch. On landing at Bristol, some time in the summer of 1167, he found that Henry was on the Continent, and thither he immediately proceeded. Henry, when he came to him in Aquitaine, was "busied," says Giraldus, "in great and weighty affairs, yet most courteously he received him and liberally rewarded him. And the king, having at large and orderly heard the causes of his exile, and of his repair unto him, he took his oath of allegiance and swore him to be his true vassal and subject, and thereupon granted and gave him letters-patent in manner and form as followeth: 'Henry, King of England, Duke of Normandy and Aquitaine, and Earl of Anjou, unto all his subjects, Englishmen, Normans, Scots, and all other nations and people being his subjects, sendeth greeting. Whensoever these our letters shall come unto you, know ye that we have received Dermond, Prince of Leinster, into our protection, grace, and favour; wherefore, whosoever within our jurisdiction will aid and help him, our trusty subject, for the recovery of his land, let him be assured of our favour and license in that behalf.'"[1]

It would scarcely appear, from the tenor of these merely permissive letters, that Henry looked forward to any result so important as the conquest of Ireland; the other "great and weighty affairs" had long withdrawn his thoughts from that project; and embarrassed both by his war with the French king, and his more serious contest with

[1] *Giraldus Cambrensis* (Gerald the Welshman). This writer's real name was Gerald Barry. He was nearly related to some of the chief personages who figure in the story of the conquest of Ireland, and he was living in Ireland at the time

Becket at home, he was at present as little as ever in a condition to resume the serious consideration of it. MacMurrogh, however, returned to England, well satisfied with what he had got. "And by his daily journeying," proceeds Giraldus, "he came at length unto the noble town of Bristow (Bristol), where, because ships and boats did daily repair, and come from out of Ireland, he, very desirous to hear of the state of his people and country, did, for a time, sojourn and make his abode; and whilst he was there, he would oftentimes cause the king's letters to be openly read, and did then offer great entertainment and promised liberal wages to all such as would help or serve him; but it served not." At length, however, he chanced to meet Richard de Clare, Earl of Pembroke, surnamed Strongbow, with whom he soon came to an agreement. Strongbow, on the promise of the hand of Dermond's eldest daughter, Eva, and the succession to the throne of Leinster, engaged to come over to Ireland, with a sufficient military force to effect the deposed king's restoration, in the following spring. A short time after this, Dermond, having gone to the town of St. David's, there made another engagement with two young noblemen, Maurice Fitz-Gerald and Robert Fitz-Stephen, both sons of the Lady Nesta, a daughter of one of the Welsh princes, who, after having been mistress to Henry I., married Gerald, governor of Pembroke Castle, and Lord of Carew, and finally became mistress to Stephen de Marisco or Maurice, constable of the castle of Cardigan: Fitz-Gerald was her son by her marriage, and Fitz-Stephen by her last-mentioned connection. To these two half-brothers, in consideration of their coming over to him with a certain force at the same time with Strongbow, Dermond engaged to grant the town of Wexford, with two cantreds (or hundreds) of land adjoining, in fee for ever. These arrangements being completed, "Dermond," continues the historian, "being weary of his exiled life and distressed estate, and therefore the more desirous to draw homewards for the recovery of his own, and for which he had so long travelled and sought abroad, he first went to the church of St. David's to make his orisons and prayers, and then, the weather being fair and wind good, he adventured the seas about the middle of August, and having a merry passage, he shortly landed in his ungrateful country; and, with a very impatient mind, hazarded himself among and through the middle of his enemies; and, coming safely to Ferns, he was very honourably received of the clergy there, who after their ability did refresh and succour him. But he for a time dissembling his princely estate, continued as a private man all that winter following among them." It would appear, however, that he was rash enough to show himself in arms in the beginning of the year 1169, before any of his promised English succours had arrived; and that the result of this premature attempt was, that he was again easily beaten by King Roderick and O'Ruarc.

His allies in England meanwhile did not forget him. Robert Fitz-Stephen was the first to set out about the beginning of May, accompanied with thirty gentlemen of his own kindred, sixty men in coats of mail, and 300 picked archers; they shipped themselves in three small vessels, and sailing right across from St. David's Head, landed at a creek now called the Bann, about twelve miles to the south of the city of Wexford. Along with them also came the paternal uncle of Strongbow, Hervey de Montemarisco or Mountmaurice. On the day following, two more vessels arrived at the same place, bearing Maurice of Prendergast, "a lusty and a hardy man, born about Milford, in West Wales," with ten more gentlemen and sixty archers. MacMurrogh was not long in hearing of their arrival, on which he instantly sent 500 men to join them, under his illegitimate son Donald, and "very shortly after, he himself also followed with great joy and gladness."[1]

It was now determined to march upon the town of Wexford. "When they of the town," proceeds the narrative, "heard thereof, they being a fierce and unruly people, but yet much trusting to their wonted fortune, came forth about 2000 of them, and were determined to wage and give battle." On beholding the imposing armour and array of the English, however, they drew back, and, setting the suburbs on fire, took refuge within the walls of the town. For that day all the efforts of the assailants to effect an entrance were vain. The next morning, after the solemn celebration of mass, they made ready to renew the assault upon the town; but the besieged, seeing this, lost heart, and saved them further trouble by offering to surrender. Four of the chief inhabitants were given up to MacMurrogh as pledges for the fidelity of their fellow-citizens; and he, on his part, immediately performed his promise to his English friends, by making over to Fitz-Stephen and Fitz-Gerald the town that had thus fallen into his hands, with the territories thereunto adjoining and appertaining. To Hervey of Mountmaurice he also gave two cantreds, lying along the sea-side between Wexford and Waterford.

This first exploit was followed up by an incursion into the district of Ossory, the prince of which had well earned the enmity of MacMurrogh by having some years before seized his eldest son, and put out his eyes. The Ossorians at first boldly stood their ground, and as long as they

---

[1] *Giraldus Cambrensis.*

kept to their bogs and woods, the invading force, though now increased by an accession from the town of Wexford to about 3000 men, made little impression upon them; but at last they were imprudent enough to allow themselves to be drawn into the open country, when Robert Fitz-Stephen fell upon them with a body of horse, and threw down the ill-armed and unprotected multitude, or scattered them in all directions; those that were thrown to the ground the foot-soldiers straight despatched, cutting off their heads with their battle-axes. Three hundred bleeding heads were laid at the feet of MacMurrogh, "who, turning every of them, one by one, to know them, did then for joy hold up both his hands, and with a loud voice thanked God most highly. Among these there was the head of one whom especially and above all the rest he mortally hated; and he, taking up that by the hair and ears, with his teeth most horribly and cruelly bit away his nose and lips!" So nearly did an Irish king of the twelfth century resemble a modern savage chief of New Zealand. After this disaster, the people of Ossory made no further resistance; they suffered their invaders to march across the whole breadth of their country, murdering, spoiling, burning, and laying waste wherever they passed.

All this had taken place before anything was heard of MacMurrogh's old enemies, King Roderick and O'Ruarc, whom surprise and alarm seem to have deprived at first of the power of action. But news was now brought that the monarch was levying an army, and that the princes and nobility of the land were, at his call, about to meet in a great council at the ancient royal seat of Tara, in Meath. On receiving this intelligence, MacMurrogh and his English friends, withdrawing from Ossory, took up a position of great natural strength in the midst of the hills and bogs in the neighbourhood of Ferns. Their small force was speedily surrounded by the numerous army of King Roderick, and it would seem that, if they could not have been attacked in their stronghold, they might have been starved into a surrender, at no great expense of patience. But, notwithstanding the inferiority of their numbers, Roderick appears to have been a good deal more afraid of them than they were of him: disunion had broken out in the council, which, after assembling at Tara, had adjourned to Dublin; and the Irish king had probably reason to fear that, if he could not bring the affair to a speedy termination, he would soon be left in no condition to keep the field at all.

In this feeling he attempted, by presents and promises, to seduce Fitz-Stephen; failing in that, he next tried to persuade MacMurrogh to come over and make common cause with his countrymen against the foreigners; at last, when there was reason to apprehend that the enemy, encouraged by these manifestations of timidity, were about to come out and attack him, he actually sent messengers to sue for peace; on which, after some negotiation, it was agreed that MacMurrogh should be reinstated in his kingdom.

It does not appear what terms MacMurrogh professed to make in his treaty for his English allies. It is affirmed, that it was agreed between him and Roderick, that he should send them all home as soon as he had restored his kingdom to order, and in the meantime should procure no more of them to come over. But other forces were already on their way from England, and those in Ireland looked to remain there. This was soon proved by the arrival at Wexford of two more ships, bringing over Maurice Fitz-Gerald, with an additional force of ten gentlemen, thirty horsemen, and about 100 archers and foot soldiers. On receiving this accession of strength, MacMurrogh immediately cast his recent engagements and oaths to the winds. His first movement with his new auxiliaries was against the city of Dublin, which had not fully returned to its submission: he soon compelled the citizens to sue for peace, to swear fealty to him, and to give hostages. He then sent a party of his English friends to assist his son-in-law, the Prince of Limerick, whose territory had been attacked by King Roderick. The royal forces were speedily defeated.

From this time MacMurrogh and the English adventurers seem to have raised their hopes to nothing short of the conquest of the whole country. By their advice, he despatched messengers to England to urge the Earl of Pembroke to come over with his force immediately. All Leinster, he said, was completely reduced, and there could be no doubt that the earl's presence, with the force he had engaged to bring with him, would soon add the other provinces to that conquest. Strongbow deemed it prudent, before he took any decided step, to inform King Henry of the proposal, and obtain the royal sanction to comply with it. Henry, with his usual deep policy, would only answer his request evasively; but the earl ventured to understand him in a favourable sense, and returned home with his mind made up for the venture. As soon as the winter was over, he sent to Ireland, as the first portion of his force, ten gentlemen and seventy archers, under the command of his relations, Raymond Fitz-William, surnamed, from his corpulency, Le Gros, or the Gross, afterwards altered into the Anglo Irish name of Grace. He and his company landed at a rock about four miles east from the city of Waterford, then called Dundonolf, afterwards the site of the castle of Dundorogh, in the beginning of May, 1170. They had scarcely time to cast a trench and to build themselves a temporary fort of turf and twigs, when they were attacked by a body of 3000 of the people of Waterford; but this mob were scattered with frightful slaughter. Five hundred of them were cut down in the pursuit; and then, as Giraldus asserts, the "victors, being weary with killing, cast a great number of those whom they had taken prisoners headlong from the rocks into the seas, and so drowned them."

The Earl of Pembroke did not set sail till the beginning of September. He then embarked at Milford Haven, with a force of 200 gentlemen, and 1000 inferior fighting men, and on the vigil of St. Bartholomew, landed in the neighbourhood of the city of Waterford, which still remained unreduced. On the following day, Raymond le Gros came with great joy to welcome him, attended by forty of his company. "And on the morrow, upon St. Bartholomew's Day, being Tuesday, they displayed their banners, and in good array they marched to the walls of the city, being fully bent and determined to give the assault." The citizens, however, defended themselves with great spirit; and the assailants were twice driven back from the walls. But Raymond, who, by the consent of all, had been appointed to the command, now "having espied a little house of timber, standing half upon posts without the walls, called his men together, and encouraged them to give a new assault at that place; and having hewed down the posts whereupon the house stood, the same fell down, together with a piece of the town wall; and then, a way being thus opened, they entered into the city, and killed the people in the streets without pity or mercy, leaving them lying in great heaps; and thus, with bloody hands, they obtained a bloody victory." MacMurrogh arrived along with Fitz-Gerald and Fitz-Stephen while the work of plunder and carnage was still proceeding; and it was in the midst of the desolation which followed the sacking of the miserable city, that, in fulfilment of his compact with Strongbow, the marriage ceremony was solemnized between his daughter Eva and that nobleman.

Immediately after this they again spread their banners, and set out on their march for Dublin. The inhabitants of that city, who were mostly of Danish race, had taken the precaution of stationing troops at different points along the common road from Waterford; but MacMurrogh led his followers by another way among the mountains, and, to the consternation of the citizens, made his appearance before the walls ere they were aware that he had left Waterford. A negotiation was attempted, but, while it was still going on, Raymond and his friend, Miles or Milo de Cogan, "more willing to purchase honour in the wars than gain it in peace, with a company of lusty young gentlemen, suddenly ran to the walls, and, giving the assault, brake in, entered the city, and obtained the victory, making no small slaughter of their enemies." Leaving Dublin in charge of Milo de Cogan, Strongbow next proceeded, on the instigation of MacMurrogh, to invade the district of Meath, anciently considered the fifth province of Ireland, and set apart as the peculiar territory of the supreme sovereign, but which King Roderick had lately made over to his friend O'Ruarc. The Anglo-Norman chief, although he seems to have met with no resistance from the inhabitants, now laid it waste from one end to the other. While all this was going on, the only effort in behalf of his crown or his country that Roderick is recorded to have made, was the sending a rhetorical message to MacMurrogh, commanding him to return to his allegiance and dismiss his foreign allies, if he did not wish that the life of his son, whom he had left in pledge, should be sacrificed. To this threat MacMurrogh at once replied that he never would desist from his enterprise until he had not only subdued all Connaught, but won to himself the monarchy of all Ireland. Infu-

REGINALD'S OR THE KING TOWER, Waterford.¹—From the Picturesque Annual.

¹ The Irish name of this tower is Dundery, or the King's Fort. Its history is briefly recorded in the following inscription placed over the doorway:—"In the year 1003, this Tower was erected by Reginald the Dane—in 1171, was held as a fortress by Strongbow, Earl of Pembroke—in 1463, by statute 3d of Edward IV., a mint was established here—in 1819, it was re-edified in its original form, and appropriated to the police establishment by the corporate body of the city of Waterford."

riated by this defiance, the other savage instantly gave orders to cut off MacMurrogh's son's head.

But now the adventurers were struck on a sudden with no little perplexity by the arrival of a proclamation from King Henry, prohibiting the passing of any more ships from any port in England to Ireland, and commanding all his subjects now in the latter country to return from thence before Easter, on pain of forfeiting all their lands and being for ever banished from the realm. A consultation being held in this emergency, it was resolved that Raymond le Gros should be despatched to the king, who was in Aquitaine, with letters from Strongbow reminding Henry that he had taken up the cause of Dermond MacMurrogh (as he conceived) with the royal permission; and acknowledging for himself and his companions, that whatever they had acquired in Ireland, either by gift or otherwise, they considered not their own, but as held for him their liege lord, and as being at his absolute disposal. The immediate effect of the proclamation was to deal a heavy blow at their cause, by the discouragement it spread among their adherents, and by cutting off the supplies both of men and victuals they had counted upon receiving from England.

Things were in this state when a new enemy suddenly appeared—a body of Danes and Norwegians brought to attack the city of Dublin by its former Danish ruler, who had made his escape when it was lately taken, and had been actively employed ever since in preparing and fitting out this armament. They came in sixty ships, and as soon as they had landed proceeded to the assault. "They were all mighty men of war," says the description of them in Giraldus, "and well appointed after the Danish manner." The attack was made upon the east gate of the city, and Milo de Cogan soon found that the small force under his command could make no effective resistance. But the good fortune that had all along waited upon him and his associates was still true to them. His brother, seeing how he was pressed, led out a few men by the south gate, and attacking the assailants from behind, spread such confusion through their ranks, that after a short effort to recover themselves, they gave way to their panic and took to flight. Great numbers of them were slain, and their leader himself, being taken prisoner, so exasperated the Anglo-Norman commander when he was brought into his presence, that Milo de Cogan ordered his head to be struck off on the spot.

It would appear to have been not long after this that Dermond MacMurrogh died, on which it is said that Strongbow took the title and assumed the authority of King of Leinster in right of his wife. Raymond le Gros had now also returned from Aquitaine; he had delivered the letter with which he was charged, but Henry had sent no answer, and had not even admitted him to his presence. Meanwhile, on the side of the Irish, there was one individual, Laurence, Archbishop of Dublin, who saw that the moment was favourable for yet another effort to save the country. Chiefly by his exertions, a great confederacy was formed of all the native princes, together with those of Man and the other surrounding islands, and a force was assembled around Dublin, with King Roderick as its commander-in-chief, of the amount, it is affirmed, of 30,000 men. Strongbow and Raymond, and Maurice Fitz-Gerald had all thrown themselves into the city, but their united forces did not make twice as many hundreds as the enemy numbered thousands. For the space of two months, however, the investing force appears to have sat still in patient expectation. Their hope was, that want of victuals would compel the garrison to surrender; and at length a message came from Strongbow, and a negotiation was opened; but before any arrangement was concluded, an extraordinary turn of fortune suddenly changed the whole position of affairs. While the besieged were anxiously deliberating on what it would be best for them to do, Donald Kavenagh, a son of the late King MacMurrogh, contrived to make his way into the city, and informed them that their friend, Fitz-Stephen, was besieged by the people of Wexford in his castle of Carrig, near that place, and that, if not relieved within a few days, he would assuredly, with his wife and children, and the few men who were with him, fall into the hands of the enemy. Fitz-Gerald proposed, and Raymond seconded the gallant counsel, that, rather than seek to preserve their lives with the loss of all besides, they should make a bold attempt to cut their way to their distressed comrades, and, at the worst, die like soldiers and knights. The animating appeal nerved every heart. With all speed each man got ready and buckled on his armour, and the little band was soon set in array in three divisions. All things being thus arranged, about the hour of nine in the morning, they suddenly rushed forth from one of the gates, and threw themselves upon the vast throng of the enemy, whom their sudden onset so bewildered and confounded, that, while many were killed or thrown to the ground, the bold assailants scarcely encountered any resistance, and in a short time the scattered host was flying before them in all directions. King Roderick himself escaped with difficulty, and almost undressed, for he had been regaling himself with the luxury of a bath. Great store of victuals, armour, and other spoils was found in the deserted camp, with which the victors returned at night to the city, and there set everything in order, and left a garrison well provided with all necessaries, before setting out the next morning to the relief of their friends at Wexford.

SITE OF CARRICK OR CARRIG CASTLE, near Wexford.[1]—From Hall's Ireland.

The earl and his company marched on unopposed till they came to a narrow pass in the midst of bogs, in a district called the Odrone or Idrone. Here they found the way blocked up by a numerous force, but after a sharp action, in which the Irish leader fell, they succeeded in overcoming this hinderance, and were enabled to pursue their journey. They had nearly reached Wexford when intelligence was received that Fitz-Stephen and his companions were in the hands of the enemy. After standing out for several days against the repeated attacks of 3000 men, he and those with him, consisting of only five gentlemen and a few archers, had been induced to deliver up the fort, on receiving an assurance, solemnly confirmed by the oaths of the Bishops of Kildare and Wexford, and others of the clergy, that Dublin had fallen, and that the earl, with all the rest of their friends there, were killed. They promised Fitz-Stephen that, if he would surrender, they would conduct him to a place of safety, and secure him and his men from the vengeance of King Roderick. But as soon as they had got possession of their persons, "some," according to Giraldus, "they killed, some they beat, some they wounded, and some they cast into prison." Fitz-Stephen himself they carried away with them to an island called Beg-Eri, or Little Erin, lying not far from Wexford, having fled thither, after setting that town on fire, when they heard that Strongbow had got out of Dublin, and was on his march to their district. They now sent to inform the earl that, if he continued his approach, they would cut off the heads of Fitz-Stephen and his companions. Deterred by this threat, Strongbow deemed it best to turn aside from Wexford, and to take his way to Waterford.

Meanwhile, it had been determined to make another application to Henry; and Hervey of Mountmaurice had been despatched to England for that purpose. On reaching Waterford, Strongbow found Hervey there, just returned, with the king's commands that the earl should repair to him without delay. He and Hervey accordingly took ship. As soon as they landed, they proceeded to where Henry was, at Newnham, in Gloucestershire. He had returned from the Continent about two months before, and had ever since been actively employed in collecting and equipping an army and fleet, and making other preparations for passing over into Ireland. When Strongbow presented himself, he at first refused to see him; but after a short time he consented to receive his offers of entire submission. It was agreed that the earl should surrender to the king, in full possession, the city of Dublin, and all other towns and forts which he held along the coast of Ireland; on which condition he should be allowed to retain the rest of his acquisitions under subjection to the English crown. This arrangement being concluded, the king, attended by Strongbow and other lords, embarked at Milford. His force consisted of 500 knights or gentlemen, and about 4000 common soldiers. He landed at a place now called the Crook, near Waterford, on the 18th of October, 1171.

In the short interval that had elapsed since the departure of Strongbow, another attack had been made upon Dublin by Tiernan O'Ruarc; but the forces of the Irish prince were dispersed with great slaughter in a sudden sally by Milo de Cogan. This proved the last effort, for the present, of Irish independence. When the English king made his appearance in the country, he found its conquest already achieved, and nothing remaining for him to do except to receive the eagerly-offered submission of its various princes

---

[1] "A little further on and we arrive at a most interesting relic of ancient days—the site of Carrick Castle, the first castle that was built by the Anglo-Normans in Ireland—not the small antique tower which, situated on the pinnacle of a rock, forms one of the most strikingly picturesque objects in the kingdom, and which has long usurped the name and 'honours' of the fortress of Fitz-Stephen. The true castle of the first Anglo-Norman 'adventurer and conqueror'—was on the opposite side of the river, a stately pile that crowned the summit of a rugged hill, barely enough of which now remains to mark the space it occupied—for the plough has passed over nearly the whole of it."—Hall's Ireland.

and chieftains. The first that presented themselves were the citizens of Wexford, who had so treacherously obtained possession of the person of Fitz-Stephen; and they endeavoured to make a merit of this discreditable exploit—bringing their prisoner along with them as a rebellious subject, whom they had seized while engaged in making war without the consent of his sovereign. Before Henry removed from Waterford, the King of Cork, or Desmond, came to him of his own accord, and took his oath of fealty. From Waterford he proceeded with his army to Lismore, and thence to Cashel, near to which city, on the banks of the Suir, he received the homage of the other chief Munster prince, the King of Thomond or Limerick. The Prince of Ossory, and the other inferior chiefs of Munster, hastened to follow the example of their betters; and Henry, after receiving their submission, and leaving garrisons both in Cork and Limerick, returned through Tipperary to Waterford. Soon after, leaving Robert Fitz-Bernard in command there, he set out for Dublin. Wherever he stopped on his march, the neighbouring princes and chiefs repaired to him, and acknowledged themselves his vassals. Among them was Tiernan O'Ruare. "But Roderick, the monarch," it is added, "came no nearer than to the side of the river Shannon, which divideth Connaught from Meath, and there Hugh de Lacy and William Fitz-Aldelm, by the king's commandment, met him, who, desiring peace, submitted himself, swore allegiance, became tributary, and did put in (as all others did) hostages and pledges for the keeping of the same. Thus was all Ireland, saving Ulster, brought in subjection." After this Henry kept his Christmas in Dublin, the feast being held in a temporary erection, constructed, after the Irish fashion, of wicker work, while the Irish princes, his guests, were astonished at the sumptuousness of the entertainment.

Henry remained in Ireland for some months longer, and during his stay called together a council of the clergy at Cashel, at which a number of constitutions or decrees were passed for the regulation of the church, and the reform of the ecclesiastical discipline, in regard to certain points where its laxity had long afforded matter of complaint and reproach. He is also said by Matthew Paris to have held a lay council at Lismore, at which provision was made for the extension to Ireland of the English laws. Henry employed all his arts of policy to attach Raymond le Gros, and the other principal English adventurers settled in Ireland, to his interest, that he might thereby the more weaken the Earl of Pembroke and strengthen himself. At last, about the middle of Lent, ships arrived both from England and Aquitaine, and brought such tidings as determined the king to lose no time in again taking his way across the sea. So, having appointed Hugh de Lacy to be governor of Dublin, and, as such, his chief representative in his realm of Ireland, he set sail from Wexford at sunrise on Easter Monday, the 17th of April, 1172, and about noon of the same day landed at Porthnnan, in Wales.

CASHEL.[1] Drawn by J. S. Prout, from his sketch on the spot.

[1] On the rock of Cashel, which rises boldly from a fertile plain, formerly was situated the residence of the Kings of Munster. Here, in 1608, we are informed by Sir James Ware (Ware's works), that he has seen the stone on which those reguli were inaugurated, and where they are said to have received their subordinate toparchs. The town, now much decayed, is chiefly planted round the southern and eastern sides of a mass of limestone. A remarkable stone-roofed chapel, and a round tower adjoining, are ascribed to Cormac, son of Cullenan, King of Munster and Bishop of Cashel about the beginning of the tenth century, whose ancestor, Angus, was a disciple of the famous Patric at the period of the introduction of Christianity into Ireland; but the chapel is considered, upon better authority, to have been founded by Cormac MacCarthy, King of Munster and Bishop of Cashel, in the eleventh century. Both the chapel and the round tower were evidently erected prior to the foundation of the cathedral, which was built by Donald O'Brien, King of Limerick, immediately before the arrival of the English, towards the latter part of the twelfth century. The cathedral is cruciform, the choir and southern transept embracing Cormac's chapel on two sides. The abbey of the rock of Cashel, of which some remains still exist, was founded by David MacCarwell about 1260. A wall, intended for defence, surrounds the platform on which the ruins stand. Some of the bastions belonging to this wall were standing at the beginning of the present century.

It is probable that Henry's very imperfect occupation of Ireland did not greatly increase his resources, but it added to his reputation both in England and on the Continent. The envy that accompanied his successes, and the old jealousy of his power, might have failed to do him any serious injury, or touch any sensitive part, but for the dissensions existing in his own family. At this period the king had four sons living—Henry, Richard, Geoffrey, and John—of the respective ages of eighteen, sixteen, fifteen, and five years. He had been an indulgent father, and had made a splendid, and what he considered a judicial provision, for them all. His eldest son was to succeed, not only to England, but to Normandy, Anjou, Maine, and Touraine; Richard was invested with the states of his mother, Aquitaine and Poictou; Geoffrey was to have Brittany, in right of his wife, the daughter of Conan; and Ireland was destined to be the appanage of John.

At the coronation of Prince Henry by the Archbishop of York, which had already occasioned much trouble, his consort, the daughter of the French king, was not allowed to be crowned with him; and this omission being resented by Louis, led to fresh quarrels. The king at last consented that the ceremony should be repeated; and Margaret was then crowned as well as her husband. Soon after this, the young couple visited the French court, where Louis stimulated the impatient ambition of his youthful son-in-law, and incited him to an unnatural rebellion against his own father. It had been the practice in France, ever since the establishment of the Capetian dynasty, to crown the eldest son during the father's lifetime, without giving him any present share of the territories or government; but young Henry was persuaded by Louis, that by being crowned, he obtained a right of immediate participation; and, as soon as he returned, he expressed his desire that the king, his father, would resign to him either England or Normandy. Henry rejected this strange demand, telling the youth to have patience till his death, when he would have estates and power enough. His son expressed astonishment at the refusal, used very undutiful language, and never more exchanged words of real love or sincere peace with his parent. The vindictive Eleanor gave encouragement to her son, and fomented his horrible hatred; and the "elder king,"[1] as Henry was now called, was punished for the infidelities which had long since alienated the affections of his wife. Being at Limoges, Raymond, the Earl of Toulouse, who had quarrelled with the King of France and renounced his allegiance, went suddenly to Henry, and warned him to have an eye on his wife and son, and make sure of the castles of Poictou and Aquitaine. Without showing his suspicions to young Henry, who was with him, the king contrived to provision his fortresses, and assure himself of the fidelity of the commanders. On their return from Aquitaine, he and his son stopped to sleep at the town of Chinon; and during the night the son fled. The father pursued, but could not overtake the fugitive, who reached Argenton, and thence passed by night into the territories of the French king.

A.D. 1173 (March). A few days after the flight of Henry, his brothers Richard and Geoffrey also fled to the French court, and Queen Eleanor herself, who had urged them to the step, absconded from her husband. Though not for any love that he bore her, the king was anxious to recover his wife; and at his orders the Norman bishops threatened her with the censures of the church, unless she returned and brought her sons with her. She was seized as she was trying to find her way to the French court (where she must have met her former husband), dressed in man's clothes. Henry, the husband of her old age, was not so soft and meek towards her as Louis, the consort of her youthful years. He committed

ELEANOR, QUEEN OF HENRY II.[2]
From the effigy at Fontevraud.

---

[1] Rex senior.
[2] It was commonly understood that the royal effigies at Fontevraud were destroyed during the French revolution. The depositary of our early kings was found by Stothard, in the course of his researches, in a state of ruin; but proceeding further, he found the whole of the effigies in a cellar of one of the buildings adjoining the abbey. When the fury of the Revolution had subsided, they were removed from the ruined church to a building called the Tour d'Evraud, where they remained for eighteen years; but this being converted into a prison, they were again removed to the place where they were discovered by Stothard. The effigies are four in number:—Henry II., his queen Eleanor de Guienne, Richard I., and Isabel d'Angoulême, the queen of John. They have all been painted and gilt three or four times; and from the style of the last painting, it is probable that it was executed when the effigies were removed from their original situation in the choir.—Stothard's *Monumental Effigies of Great Britain*.

her to the custody of one of his most trustworthy chatelains; and with the exception of a few weeks, when her presence was necessary for a political object, she was kept in confinement for sixteen years,[1] and not liberated till after his death. Before matters came to extremities, Henry despatched two bishops to the French court to demand, in the name of paternal authority, that his fugitive sons should be delivered up to him. Louis received these ambassadors in a public manner, having at his right hand young Henry, who wore his crown as King of England; and when they recapitulated, as usual, the titles and style of their employer, they were told that there was no other King of England than the one beside him. In fact, young Henry was recognized as sole King of England in a general assembly of the barons and bishops of the kingdom of France. King Louis swore first, and his lords swore after him, to aid and assist the son with all their might to expel his father from his kingdom; and then young Henry swore first, and his brothers swore after him, in the order of their seniority, that they would never conclude peace or truce with their father without the consent and concurrence of the barons of France.[2] A great seal, like that of England, was manufactured, in order that young Henry might affix it to his treaties and charters. By the feast of Easter the plans of the rebellious boy and his confederates were matured. The scheme was bold and extensive; the confederates were numerous, including, besides the King of France, whose reward was not committed to a written treaty, William, King of Scotland, who was to receive all that his predecessors had possessed in Northumberland and Cumberland, in payment of his services, and Philip, Earl of Flanders, who was to have a grant of the earldom of Kent, with the castles of Dover and Rochester, for his share in the parricidal war.

Like the great Conqueror under similar circumstances, Henry saw himself deserted even by his favourite courtiers, and by many of the men whom he had taught the art of war, and invested with the honours of chivalry with his own hands. According to a contemporary, it was a painful and desolating sight for him to see those whom he had honoured with his confidence, and intrusted with the care of his chamber, his person, his very life, deserting him, one by one, to join his enemies; for nearly every night some of them stole away, and those who had attended him in the evening did not appear at his call in the morning.[3] But Henry's strength of character and consummate abilities were quite equal to the difficulties of his situation, and in the midst of his greatest trouble he maintained a cheerful countenance, and pursued his usual amusements, hunting and hawking, even more than his wont, and was more gay and affable than ever towards the companions that remained with him.[4] His courtiers and knights might flee, but Henry had a strong party, and wise ministers and commanders, selected by his sagacity, in most of his states, and in England more than all; he had also money in abundance; and these circumstances gave him confidence, without relaxing his precaution and exertions. Twenty thousand Brabançons, who sold their services to the best bidder, flocked to the standard of the richest monarch of the west of Europe. Not relying wholly on arms, he sent messengers to all the neighbouring princes who had sons, to interest them in his favour; and, as his case might be their own, should encouragement and success attend filial disobedience, their sympathy was tolerably complete. In addressing the pope, he worked upon other feelings; and here his present object hurried him into expressions of submission and vassalage, which contributed no doubt to form the grounds of future and dangerous pretensions. He declared that the kingdom of England belonged to the jurisdiction of the pope, and that he, as king thereof, was bound to him by all the obligations imposed by the feudal law; and he implored the pontiff to defend with his spiritual arms the *patrimony of St. Peter.* The rebellious son applied to the court of Rome as well as his father; and it may be stated generally, that if the popes meddled largely with the secular affairs of princes, it was not without their being tempted and invited so to do. The letter of the "junior king," as the young Henry was called, was a composition of singular impudence and falsehood. He attributed his quarrel with his father to the interest he took in the cause of Becket, and his desire of avenging his death. "The villains," he said, "who murdered within the walls of the temple my foster-father, the glorious martyr of Christ, St. Thomas of Canterbury, remain safe and sound; they still strike their roots in the earth, and no act of royal vengeance has followed so atrocious and unheard-of a crime. I could not suffer this criminal neglect, and such was the first and strongest cause of the present discord; the blood of the martyr cried to me; I could not render it the vengeance and honours that were due to him, but at least I showed my reverence in visiting the tomb of the holy martyr in the view and to the astonishment of the whole kingdom. My father was wrathful against me therefore, but I fear not offending my father when the cause of Christ is concerned."[5] The youthful hypocrite made most

---

[1] *Hoved.; R. Dicto; Neub.; Script. Rer. Franc.*
[2] *Gervase.*   [3] *Ibid.*
[4] *Hoved.; Matt. Par.; Gerv. Dorob.*
[5] *Script. Rer. Franc.*

liberal offers to the church; but the pope rejected his application, and even confirmed the sentence of excommunication pronounced by the bishops of Normandy against the king's revolted subjects. At the same time a legate was despatched across the Alps with the laudable object of putting an end to the unnatural quarrel by exhortation and friendly mediation; but before he arrived, the sword was drawn which it was difficult to sheathe; for national antipathies, and popular interests and passions were engaged, that would not follow the uncertain movements of paternal indulgence, on one side, or filial repentance on the other. In the month of June, the war began on several points at once. Philip, Earl of Flanders, entered Normandy, and gained considerable advantages; but his brother and heir being killed at a siege, he thought he saw the hand of God in the event, and he soon left the country, most bitterly repenting having engaged in such an impious war. The King of France, with his loving son-in-law, Prince Henry of England, were not more successful than the Earl of Flanders, and were first checked and then put to rapid flight by a division of the Brabançons. Prince Geoffrey, who had been joined by the Earl of Chester, was equally unfortunate in Brittany, and the cause of the confederates was covered with defeat and shame. King Louis, according to his old custom, soon grew weary of the war, and desired an interview with Henry, who condescended to grant it. This conference of peace was held on an open plain, between Gisors and Trie, under a venerable elm of "most grateful aspect," the branches of which descended to the earth,[1] the centre of the primitive scene where the French kings and the Norman dukes had been accustomed for some generations to hold their parleys for truce or peace.

Instead of leading to peace, the present conference embittered the war, and ended in a disgraceful exhibition of violence. The Earl of Leicester, who attended with the princes, insulted Henry to his face, and, drawing his sword, would have killed or wounded his king had he not been forcibly prevented. Hostilities commenced forthwith; but when Louis was a principal in a war against Henry, it was seldom prosecuted with any vigour, and the rest of that year was spent on the Continent in insignificant operations. In England, however, some important events took place; for Richard de Lucy repulsed the Scots, who had begun to make incursions, burned their town of Berwick, ravaged the Lothians, and, on his return from this victorious expedition, defeated and took prisoner the great Earl of Leicester, who had recrossed the Channel, and, in alliance with Bigod, Earl of Norfolk, was

[1] Ulmus erat visu gratissima, ramis ad terram redeuntibus.— *Script. Rer. Franc.*

attempting to light the flames of civil war in the heart of England. It is honourable alike to Henry and his government and the people, that the insurgents never had a chance of success in England.

A.D. 1174. The allies now showed more re solution than during the preceding year, and acted upon a plan which was well calculated to embarrass Henry. Louis, with the junior King of England, attacked the frontiers of Normandy. Geoffrey tried his fortune again in Brittany. Prince Richard, who began his celebrated warlike career by fighting against his own father, headed a formidable insurrection in Poictou and Aquitaine. Relying on the Norman barons for the defence of Normandy and Brittany, Henry marched against his son Richard, and soon took the town of Saintes and the fortress of Taillebourg, drove the insurgents from several other castles, and partially restored order to the country. Returning then towards Anjou, he devastated the frontier of Poictou, and was preparing to reduce the castles there, when the Bishop of Winchester arrived with news which rendered the king's presence indispensable on the other side of the sea. The Scots, as had been preconcerted, were again pouring into the northern counties, and had already taken several towns. Roger de Mowbray had raised the standard of revolt in Yorkshire; Earl Ferrers, joined by David, Earl of Huntingdon, brother to the Scottish king, had done the same in the central counties. In the east, Hugh Bigod, with 700 knights, had taken the castle of Norwich; and at the same time a formidable fleet, prepared by his eldest son and the Earl of Flanders, was ready on the opposite coast to attempt a descent on England, where endeavours were again making to alienate the affections of the people by the old story of the king being guilty of Becket's murder. The bishop had scarcely finished his dismal news ere the king, with his court, was on horseback for the coast, and, embarking in the midst of a storm, he sailed for England, taking with him, as prisoners, his own wife Eleanor, and his eldest son's wife Margaret, who had not been able to follow her husband to the court of her father. Although he had still maintained an outward appearance of tranquillity, his heart was aching at the rebellion of his children and the treachery of his friends. Sorrow disposes the mind to devotional feelings, and Henry's high powers of intellect did not exempt him from the superstition of the times. Some sincerity may possibly have mingled in the feelings and motives that dictated the extraordinary course he now pursued, though, seeing the political expediency of resorting to a striking measure to remove all doubts from the people, and bring *their* devotional feelings to his side, we would not venture to affirm that this sincerity was very great, or was the sole motive of his conduct. All attempts to depress the fame of Becket had failed—the pope had recently inscribed his name in the list of saints and martyrs—the miracles said to be wrought over his festering body were now recognized by bishops and priests, and reported with amplifications which grew in proportion to their distance from the spot, by the credulous multitude. The English had not had a native saint for a long time, and they determined to make the most of him. It was on the 8th of July that Henry landed at Southampton. He had scarcely set foot on shore, when, without waiting to refresh himself after the fatigues and discomforts of a rough sea voyage, he mounted his horse and took the nearest road to Canterbury, performing his pilgrimage in a manner far from being so agreeable as those jocund expeditions described by Chaucer a century and a half later. He took no refreshment save bread and water, and rode on his way by night. As the day dawned he came in sight of the towers of Canterbury Cathedral, still at the distance of some miles, and instantly dismounting from his horse, he threw off his royal dress, undid his sandals, and walked the rest of his way barefoot like the veriest penitent. The roads were rough, and as the king passed through the gateway of Canterbury, his subjects were touched and edified by the sight of his blood, which fell at every step he took from his wounded feet. When he arrived at the cathedral, he descended at once into the crypt, and while the bells tolled slowly, he threw himself with sobs and tears upon the grave of Becket, and there remained with his face pressed to the cold earth in the presence of many people; an attitude more affecting and convincing perhaps than the discourse of the bishop overhead. Gilbert Foliot, formerly Bishop of Hereford, now of London, and the same who, three years and a half before, had proposed to throw the body of Becket into a ditch, or hang it on a gibbet, but who now, with the rest, acknowledged him to be a blessed and glorious martyr, ascended the pulpit and addressed the multitude. "Be it known to you, as many as are here present, that Henry, King of England, invoking, for his soul's salvation, God and the holy martyrs, solemnly protests before you all that he never ordered, or knowingly caused, or even desired the death of the saint; but, as possibly the murderers took advantage of some words imprudently pronounced, he has come to do penance before the bishops here assembled, and has consented to submit his naked flesh to the rods of discipline." The bishop conjured the people to believe the assertions of their king; and, as he ceased speaking, Henry arose like a spectre, and walked through the church and cloisters to the chapter-house, where, again prostrating himself, and throwing off the upper part of his dress, he confessed to the minor offence, and was scourged by all the ecclesiastics present, who amounted to eighty persons. The bishops and abbots, who were few, handled the knotted cords first, and then followed the monks, every one inflicting from three to five lashes, and saying, as he gave them, "Even as Christ was scourged for the sins of men, so be thou scourged for thine own sin." The blows, no doubt, were dealt with a light hand, but the whole show was startling, and such as had never before been heard of. Nor was the penance of the king yet over. He returned to the subterranean vault, and again prostrating himself by Becket's tomb, he spent the rest of the day and the following night in prayers and tears, taking no nourishment, and never quitting the spot; "but as he came so he remained, without carpet or any such thing beneath him."[1] At early dawn, after the service of matins, he ascended from the vault and made the tour of the upper church, praying before all the altars and relics there. When the sun rose he heard mass, and then, having drunk some holy water blessed by the martyr himself,

CRYPT OF CANTERBURY CATHEDRAL, looking north-west.

---

[1] *Gerv. Dorob.*

and having filled a small bottle with the precious fluid, he mounted his horse and rode to London with a light and joyous heart. A burning fever, however, followed all this fatigue and penance, and confined him for several days to his chamber.[1] On the fifth night of his malady, a messenger arrived from the north, and announced himself to the suffering monarch as the servant of Ranulf de Glanville, a name memorable in the history of our laws and constitution, and a most dear friend of Henry. "Is Glanville in health?" said the king. "My lord is well," replied the servant, "and your enemy, the King of Scots, is his prisoner." Starting upright, Henry cried, "Repeat those words." The man repeated them, and delivered his master's letters, which fully informed the overjoyed king of the fact. On the morning of the 12th of July, Glanville had surprised William the Lion as he was tilting in a meadow near Alnwick Castle, with only sixty Scottish lords near him, and had made the whole party captives. By a remarkable coincidence, this signal advantage was gained on the very day (it was said by some on the very hour) on which Henry achieved his reconciliation with the martyr at Canterbury.[2]

Indisposition, and the languor it leaves, soon departed, and Henry was again on horseback, and at the head of a numerous and enthusiastic army; for the people of England flocked to his standard, and filled the land with an indignant cry against the leaders and abettors of an unnatural revolt. The insurgents did not wait the coming of the king, but dispersed in all directions, their chiefs purchasing their pardon by the surrender of their castles. According to a French chronicler, so many were taken that it was difficult to find prisons for them all.[3] The Scots, disheartened by the capture of their sovereign, retreated beyond the border, and peace being restored at home, the active Henry was enabled, within three weeks, to carry the army which had been raised to subdue the revolt in England, across the seas to Normandy.

When the Earl of Flanders, who was now the soul of the confederacy, had made ready to invade England, he counted on the absence of the king, whose prompt return disconcerted that measure. Changing his plan, therefore, he repaired to Normandy, and joining his forces with those of King Louis and Henry's eldest son, laid siege to Rouen, the capital. But he was scarcely there when the King of England was after him, and surprised all his stores and provisions. In a few days the allied army was not only obliged to raise the siege, but also to retreat out of Normandy. Humbled by the rapidity, the genius, and good fortune of the English monarch, the confederates, following the advice of Louis, the very king of conferences, requested an armistice and a meeting for the arrangement of a general peace. Of his rebellious children, Henry and Geoffrey offered to submit to these arrangements; but young Richard, who had begun to taste the joys of war, and the "raptures of the fight," which were to be his greatest pleasures till the hour of his death —and who was supported by the restless nobility of Aquitaine, and was led by the counsels of the indefatigable lord who held Hauteforte,[4] the famous Bertrand de Born—refused to be included, and persisted in open war against his father. But the rash boy lost castle after castle, and, at the end of six weeks, was fain to throw himself at the feet of his forgiving parent, and accompany him to the congress or conference.

The conditions of the peace were made easy by the mildness and moderation of Henry. He received from the French king and the Flemish earl all the territories they had overrun since the commencement of the war, and he restored to those princes whatever he had conquered or occupied himself. With *one* important exception, he also set at liberty all his prisoners, to the number of 969 knights. To his eldest son he assigned, for present enjoyment, two castles in Normandy, and a yearly allowance of £15,000 Angevin money; to Richard, two castles in Poictou, with half the revenue of that earldom; to Geoffrey, two castles in Brittany, with half the rents of the estates that had belonged to his father-in-law elect (for the marriage was not yet consummated) Earl Conan, with a promise of the remainder. With these conditions the impatient youths professed themselves satisfied, and they engaged henceforth to love, honour, and obey their father. Richard and Geoffrey did homage, and took the oaths of fealty; but Henry, the eldest son, was exempted from these ceremonies. The exception made in liberating the prisoners, was in the important person of the Scottish king, who had been carried over to the Continent, and thrown into the strong castle of Falaise, where he was kept until the following month of December, when he obtained his enlargement by kneeling to Henry, and acknowledging himself, in the set forms of vassalage, his "liege man against all men." By the degrading treaty of Falaise, the independence of Scotland was nominally sacrificed; and from the signing of it in December, 1174, to the accession of Richard I., in December,

---

[1] *Gervase; Hen. Hunt.; Girald.; Diceto; Hoved.; Neub.* Previous to this pilgrimage to Canterbury, Henry had done penance for Becket's murder in the cathedral of Avranches in Normandy. The church is now a ruin, but according to tradition, a flat stone, with a cup engraved upon it, still marks the spot of kingly humiliation.—Stothard's *Tour in Normandy.*
[2] *Neub.; Hoved.; Gervase.* [3] *Script. Rer. Franc.* [4] "Colui che già tenne Altaforte."—Dante's *Inferno.*

1189, when a formal release from all obligations was granted for the sum of 10,000 marks, she may be said to have figured as a dependent province of England.[1]

A.D. 1175. Henry now enjoyed about eight years of profound peace; but, as active in civil affairs as in those of war, he devoted this time, and all his energies, to the reform of the internal administration of his dominions. His reputation for wisdom, judicial ability, and power, now stood so high in Europe, that Alfonso, King of Castile, and his uncle, Sancho, King of Navarre, who had been disputing for some years about the boundaries of their respective territories, turning from the uncertain arbitrament of the sword, referred their difference to the decision of the "just and impartial" English monarch, binding themselves in the most solemn manner to submit to his award, be it what it might. And in the month of March, 1177, Henry, holding his court at Westminster, attended by the bishops, earls, barons, and justices, both of England and Normandy, heard and discussed the arguments proposed on the part of King Alfonso by the Bishop of Palencia, and on the part of King Sancho by the Bishop of Pampeluna; and, after taking the opinion of the best and most learned of the court, pronounced a wise and conciliating award, with which both ambassadors expressed their entire satisfaction.[2]

We have some curious evidence of Henry's personal activity, as evinced by his rapid change of residence, just at this period of peace and tranquillity, in a letter addressed to him, in the most familiar terms, by his confidential friend, Peter of Blois. Peter, who was not a timid, loitering wayfarer, or a luxurious, ease-loving churchman, but a bold and experienced traveller himself, seeing that, in the discharge of his duty, he had fought his way more than once across the then pathless Alps, in the heart of winter, braving the snow hurricane and the tremendous avalanches, seems to have been lost in amazement at the incessant and untiring progresses of the king. He had just returned from a royal mission to King Louis, the results of which he was anxious to report. He tells Henry that he has been hunting after him up and down England, but in vain!—that when Solomon set down four things as being too hard for him to discover, he ought to have added a fifth—and that was, the path of the King of England! Poor Peter goes on to say, that he really knoweth not whither he is going —that he has been laid up with the dysentery at Newport, from fatigue in travelling after his majesty, and has sent scouts and messengers on all sides to look for him. He proceeds to express an earnest wish that Henry would let him know where he is to be found, as he really has important affairs to treat of, and the ambassadors of the Kings of Spain have arrived with a great retinue, in order to refer the old quarrel of their masters to his majesty.

The moment was now approaching when those energies, as yet undiminished by age or the premature decay which they probably caused in the end, were again to be called into full exercise; for foreign jealousies and intrigues, the name and history of his captive wife Eleanor, and the unpopularity of the Anglo-Norman rule in the provinces of the South, contributed, with their own impatience, turbulence, and presumption, to drive his children once more into rebellion.

A.D. 1183. Richard, who was the darling of his imprisoned mother, and who, on account of the more general unpopularity of his father in Aquitaine and Poictou, was stronger than his brothers, was the first to renew the family war. When called upon by his father to do homage to his elder brother, Henry, for the duchy of Aquitaine, which he was to inherit, he arrogantly refused. Upon this, young Henry, or the junior king, allied himself with Prince Geoffrey, and marched with an army of Bretons and Brabançons into Aquitaine, where Richard had published his ban of war. The king flew to put an end to these disgraceful hostilities, and having induced his two sons to come into his presence, he reconciled them with one another. But the reconciliation was rather apparent than real, and Prince Geoffrey had the horrible frankness to declare, shortly after, that they could never possibly live in peace with one another, unless they were united in a common war against their own father. The recorded gallantries, and the worse whispered offences of Eleanor, did not alienate the affections of the people of Poictou and Aquitaine, among whom she had been born and brought up. In their eyes she was still their chieftainess — the princess of their old native stock; and Henry had no right over them except what he could claim *through* her, and by his affectionate treatment of her. Now, he had kept her for years a prisoner, and in their estimation it was loyal and right to work for her deliverance, and punish her cruel husband by whatever means they could command, even to the arming of Eleanor's sons against their sire. In the fervid heads and hearts of these men of the South such feelings became absolute passions; and the graces as well as the ardour of their popular poetry were engaged in the service of their captive princess. The troubadours, with Bertrand de Born at their head, never tired of this theme; and even the local chroniclers raised their monkish Latin into a sort of poetical prose,

---
[1] Allen's *Vindication of the Ancient Independence of Scotland.*
[2] Rymer; *Rog. Hoved.*

whenever they touched on the woes and wrongs of Eleanor—for in Poictou and Aquitaine the manifold provocations she had given her husband were all unknown or forgotten.

With the exception of Richard, whose fiery nature now and then, for transitory intervals, gave access to the tenderer feelings, the ambitious young men seem to have cared little about their mother; but they could raise no such good excuse for being in arms against one parent as that of their anxiety to procure better treatment for the other; and Henry, and Geoffrey, and Richard, at times in unison, and at times separately, continued to take the name of Eleanor as their *cri de guerre* in the South. These family wars were more frequent, of longer duration, and of far greater importance than would be imagined from the accounts given of them in our popular English histories.

The reconciliation which took place in 1182-4 was speedily interrupted; for Bertrand de Born, nearly indifferent as to which prince he acted with, but who, of the three, rather preferred Henry, on seeing that Richard was inclined to keep his oaths to his father, renewed his intrigues with the eldest son, and got ready a formidable party in Aquitaine, who pressed Prince Henry to throw himself among them. Henry consequently revolted again, and his brother Geoffrey soon followed his example. The French sovereign openly announced himself as the ally of the junior king and the nobles of Aquitaine. As Richard continued steady for a while, the King of England joined his forces with his, and they marched together to lay siege to Limoges, which had opened its gates to Henry and Geoffrey. In little more than a month, however, the younger Henry deserted his partizans of Aquitaine, and submitted to his father, who forgave him as he had forgiven him before, and once more accepted his oath of fealty. Geoffrey did not on this occasion follow his eldest brother's example; and the men of Aquitaine and Poictou, now regarding *him* as their chief, confirmed him in his resistance, apprehending that the King of England would not extend the remarkable clemency he had shown to his children, to men who were strangers to his blood, and who had incensed him by repeated revolt. Prince Henry kept up a private correspondence with Bertrand de Born and others of the insurgents, and this enabled him to arrange a meeting for the purpose of conciliation. The King of England rode to Limoges, which was still in the hands of the insurgents, to keep his appointment with his son Geoffrey and the Aquitaine barons: to his surprise he found the gates of the town closed against him, although he had taken only a few knights with him, and when he applied for admittance, he was answered by a flight of arrows and cross-bow bolts from the ramparts, one of which pierced his cuirass, while another of them wounded a knight at his side. This treacherous-looking occurrence was explained away as being a mere mistake on the part of the soldiery, and it was subsequently agreed that the king should have free entrance into the town. He met his son Geoffrey in the midst of the market-place of Limoges, and began the conference for peace; but here again he was saluted by a flight of arrows from the battlements. One of these arrows wounded the horse he rode. He ordered an attendant to pick up the arrow, and presenting it to Geoffrey with sobs and tears, he said—"O, son! what hath thy unhappy father done to deserve that thou shouldest make him a mark for thine arrows?"[1]

This foul attempt at assassination is laid by some writers to the charge of Geoffrey himself; but it is quite as probable that the bows were drawn without any order from the prince, by some of the fiery spirits of Aquitaine, labouring under the conviction that their interests were about to be sacrificed in the accommodation between father and son. Prince Henry, who accompanied his father, expressed horror at the attempt, and disgust at the obstinacy of the men of Aquitaine; and he declared he would never more have alliance, or peace, or truce with them.[2] Not many days after, he once more deserted and betrayed his sire, and went to join the insurgents, who then held their head-quarters at Dorat, in Poictou. The bishops of Normandy, by command of the pope, fulminated their excommunications; but as Prince Henry had been excommunicated before this, it was probably not the thunders of the church, but other considerations, that induced him to abandon the insurgents at Dorat as suddenly as he had abandoned his father, and to return once more to the feet of the king, who, with unexampled clemency or weakness, once more pardoned him, and not only permitted him to go at large, but to meddle again with political affairs. Having persuaded his father to adopt measures which cost him the lives of some of his most faithful followers, this manifold traitor, or veriest wheel-about that ever lived, again deserted his banner, and prepared, with his brother Geoffrey and the insurgent barons of the South, to give him battle. A short time after this revolt, which was destined to be his last, and before his preparations for aiming at his father's life or throne, or both, were completed, a messenger announced to the king that his eldest son had fallen dangerously sick at Chateau-Marcel, near Limoges, and desired most earnestly that his father would for-

---

[1] *Script. Rer. Franc.* [2] *Hoved.*

give him and visit him. The king would have gone forthwith, but his friends implored him not to hazard his life again among men who had proved themselves capable of so much treachery and cruelty; and they represented that the accounts he had received might be all a feigned story, got up by the insurgents of Aquitaine and Poictou, for the worst of purposes. Taking, then, a ring from his finger, he gave it to the Archbishop of Bordeaux, and begged that prelate to convey it with all speed to his repentant son, as a token of his forgiveness and paternal affection. He cherished the hope that the youth and robust constitution of the invalid would triumph over the disease; but soon there came a second messenger, to announce that his son was no more.

Prince Henry died at Chateau-Marcel, on the 11th of June, 1183, in the twenty-seventh year of his age.[1] In his last agony he expressed the deepest contrition; he pressed to his lips his father's ring, which had mercifully been delivered to him; he publicly confessed his undutifulness to his indulgent parent, and his other sins, and ordered the priests to drag him by a rope out of his bed, and lay him on a bed of ashes, that he might die in an extremity of penance.[2]

The heart of the king was divided between grief at the death of his first-born and rage against the insurgents, whom he held to have been not only the cause of his son's decease, but the impediment which had prevented him from seeing and embracing him in his last moments. The feeling of revenge, however, allying itself with the sense of his immediate interests, soon obtained entire mastery, and he proceeded with all his old activity against the barons of Aquitaine and Poictou. The very day after his son's funeral he took Limoges by assault; then castle after castle was stormed and utterly destroyed; and at last Bertrand de Born—the soul of the conspiracy, the seducer of his children—fell into his hands. Never had enemy been more persevering, insidious, and dangerous—never had vassal so outraged his liege lord, or in such a variety of ways; for Bertrand, like Luke de Barré, was a poet as well as knight, and had cruelly satirized Henry in productions which were popular wherever the *langue d' Oc*[3] was understood. All men said he must surely die, and Henry said so himself. The troubadour was brought into his presence, to hear his sentence; the king taunted him with a boast he had been accustomed to make—namely, that he had so much wit in reserve as never to have occasion to use one-half of it, and told him he was now in a plight in which the whole of his wit would not serve him. The troubadour acknowledged he had made the boast, and that not without truth and reason. "And I," said the king—"I think thou hast lost thy wits." "Yes, sire," replied Bertrand, mournfully; "I lost them that day the valiant young king died!—then, indeed, I lost my wits, my senses, and all wisdom." At this allusion to his son, the king burst into tears, and nearly swooned. When he came to himself his vengeance had departed from him. "Sir Bertrand," said he, "Sir Bertrand, thou mightest well lose thy wits because of my son, for he loved thee more than any other man upon earth; and I, for love of him, give thee thy life, thy property, thy castle."[4] The details of this singular scene may have been slightly over-coloured by the warm poetical imagination of the South, but that Henry pardoned his inveterate enemy is an historical fact.

If Bertrand de Born was a villain, he was a most accomplished one; he appears to have excelled all his contemporaries in insinuation, elegance, and address—in versatility of talent, and abundance of resource.[5] Attempts have been made by M. Thierry to set off his patriotism against his treachery; and it has been hinted, that while labouring to free his native country from the yoke of the English king, he was justifiable in making use of whatever means he could. It is perhaps difficult to fix precise limits to what may be done in such a cause; but though we may affect to admire the conduct of the elder Brutus, who slew his own son for the liberties of Rome, we doubt whether the sympathies of our nature will not always be against the man who armed the sons of another against their father's life. Such appears to have been the sentiment of the time; and Dante, who wrote about 120 years after the event, and who merely took up the popular legend, placed Bertrand de Born in one of the worst circles of hell.[6]

Prince Geoffrey sought his father's pardon soon after the death of his brother Henry, and abandoned the insurgents of Aquitaine, who then saw themselves opposed to a united family (for Richard was as yet true to his last oaths) whose unnatural divisions had hitherto proved their main strength

---

[1] *Rog. Hoved.* [2] *Ibid.; also Diceto.*
[3] The dialect spoken in the south of France, where, instead of *oui* (yes) they said *oc;* hence the name of the part of this district, still called Languedoc. The rest of France was called *Langue-d'oui*, or *Langue-d'oyl.*

[4] *Poésies des Troubadours, Collection de Raynouard; Millot, Hist. Littéraire des Troubadours.*
[5] We learn from Dante, who seems to have been forcibly impressed with his strange character, that besides poems on other subjects, Sir Bertrand "treated of war, which no *Italian* poet had yet done."—(Arma vero nullum Italum adhuc poemate invenio.—*De Vulg. Eloq.* Bertrand left a son of the same name, who was also a poet, and who satirized King John.
[6] *Inferno*, canto xxviii. The passage is terrific, and one of the most characteristic in the whole poem.

and encouragement. The confederacy, no longer formidable, was partly broken up by the victorious arms of the king, and partly dissolved of itself. A momentary reconciliation took place between Henry and Eleanor, who was released for a short time to be present at a solemn meeting, wherein "peace and final concord" was established between the king and his sons, confirmed by "writing and by sacrament."¹ In this transaction Prince John was included, who had hitherto been too young to wield the sword against his father. The family concord lasted only a few months, when Geoffrey demanded the earldom of Anjou; and on receiving his father's refusal, withdrew to the French court, to prepare for another war. But soon after (in August, 1186), his turbulent career was cut short at a tournament, where he was dismounted and trampled to death under the feet of the horses. Louis VII., the soft and incompetent rival of Henry, had now been dead several years, and his son, Philip II., a young and active prince, sat on the throne of France. He buried Geoffrey with great pomp, and then invited to his court his brother Richard, the Lion-hearted, who was to hate him with a deadly hatred in after years, but who now accepted his invitation, and lived with him on the most affectionate terms, "eating at the same table and out of the same dish by day, and sleeping in the same bed by night."² King Henry well knew that this friendship betokened mischief to him, and he sent repeated messages to recal Richard, who always replied that he was coming, without hastening his departure. At last he moved, but it was only to surprise and seize a treasure of his father's, deposited at Chinon, and then to raise the banner of revolt once more in Aquitaine. But this time his standard failed to attract a dispirited people, and he was fain to accept his father's pardon. Henry, who had seen so many oaths disregarded, made him swear fealty, upon this occasion, on a copy of the Holy Evangelists, in the presence of a great assembly of churchmen and laymen.

A.D. 1188. The misfortunes of the Christians in the Holy Land were the means of producing a brief peace between Henry and Philip, who had been waging an insignificant war with each other, and preparing for more decisive hostilities. Jerusalem had fallen again before the Mahometan crescent, in the September of the preceding year; the reigning pontiff was said to have died of grief at the news; and the new pope called upon all Christian princes to rescue the tomb of Christ and the wood of the true cross, which latter, it was said, had been carried away by the victorious Saladin. No one responded to the appeal more promptly and enthusiastically than Henry, who at once declared himself willing to proceed with an army to Asia. A well-settled peace with France was, however, an indispensable preliminary; and Philip being also pressed by the pope to take the cross, an interview for the settlement of all differences was easily arranged. The two kings met in the month of January, at the usual place between Trie and Gisors, near to the old elm-tree. William, the eloquent and enthusiastic Archbishop of Tyre, attended the meeting, with many bishops and priests, of whom some had witnessed the reverses of the Christians in Palestine. Henry and Philip swore to be "brothers in arms for the cause of God;" and in sign of their voluntary engagement, each took the cross from the hands of the Archbishop of Tyre, and attached it to his dress, swearing never to quit it or neglect the duties of a soldier of Christ, "either upon land or sea, in town or in the field," until his victorious return to his home. Many of the great vassals of both monarchs followed their masters' example, and took the same oaths.³

The crosses given to the King of France and his people were red; those distributed to the King of England and his people were white. Richard, who was to connect his name inseparably with the subject of the Crusades, had neither waited for his father's example nor permission, but had taken the cross some time before.⁴ The old elm-tree witnessed another *solemn* peace, which was about as lasting as its predecessors; and Henry returned to England, evidently with a sincere desire of keeping it on his part, and making ready for the Holy War. In the month of February he called together a great council of the kingdom at Gidington, in Northamptonshire, to provide the means of such a costly expedition. The barons, both lay and ecclesiastic, readily enacted that a tenth of all rents for one year, and a tenth of all the moveable property in the land, with the exception of the books of the clergy, and the arms and horses of the knights, should be levied to meet the expenses. The lords of manors who engaged to accompany the king in person were permitted to receive the assessments of their own vassals and tenants; but those of all others were to be paid into the royal exchequer. It appears that no more than £70,000 was raised in this manner. To make up the deficiency, Henry had

---

¹ Scripto et sacramento.—*Rog. Hoved.*
² Singulis diebus in una mensa ad unum catinum manducatant et in noctibus non separabat eos lectus.—*Rog. Hoved.*
³ *Rog. Hoved.; Script. Rer. Franc.*
⁴ Nor was this the first time the king talked of going to the Holy Land. Several years before, the Patriarch of Jerusalem offered him that kingdom, with the keys of the city and of the holy sepulchre. Henry, who was not then carried away by the popular enthusiasm, referred the matter to an assembly of his bishops and barons, who, *most wisely*, determined that "for the good of his own soul," he would do much better by remaining at home and taking care of his own subjects.

recourse to extortion and violent measures against the Jews, whom he had hitherto treated with leniency; and from that oppressed fragment of an unhappy people he procured £60,000, or almost as much money as he got from all the rest of his kingdom put together. Another council of bishops, abbots, and lay barons, held at Mans, regulated the tax for Henry's continental dominions.

But the money wrung from Jew and Gentile was never spent against the Turk. "The malice of the ancient enemy of mankind," says the honest chronicler, "was not asleep;"[1] and he goes on to deplore how that infernal malice turned the oaths of Christian princes into a mockery, and relit the flames of war among Christian people on the continent of Europe. The fiery Richard appears to have been the first cause of this new commotion, in which the French king soon took a part. Another conference was agreed upon, and the two kings again met under the peaceful shadow of the elm; they could not, however, agree as to terms of accommodation; and Philip, venting his spite on the tree, swore by all the saints of France, that no more parleys should be held there, and cut it down.[2] Had causes of dissension been wanting, the ingenuity of the King of France, and the jealous impatience of Richard, would have raised imaginary wrongs; but unfortunately for the fame of Henry, there *was* a real existing cause, and one singularly calculated to excite and combine those two princes against him. Richard, when a child, had been affianced, as already mentioned, to the infant Aliz, or Adelais, of France. Henry had obtained possession of the person of the royal infant, and of part of her dowry, and had kept both. By the time the parties were of proper age for the completion of the marriage, Richard was at open war with his father; but it is curious to remark, that at none of the numerous peaces and reconciliations was there any deep anxiety shown, either by her affianced spouse Richard, or her father King Louis, or her brother Philip, about the fate of the fair Adelais, who remained some time *ostensibly* as a hostage, but, of late years, in a very ambiguous situation, at the court of Henry. A report, true or false, had got abroad that the king was enamoured of her person; and when he made an unsuccessful application to the Church of Rome for a divorce from Richard's mother, Eleanor, it was believed that he had taken the step in order to espouse Richard's affianced bride. Of late, however, King Philip, feeling that the reputation of his sister was committed, had repeatedly urged that Adelais should be given to Richard, and the marriage completed; and the Church of Rome had even threatened Henry with its severest censures in case of his resisting this demand. An air of mystery involves the whole story and every part of it: how Henry evaded the demand we know not, but of this we are perfectly well informed, that he had detained the lady—that no consequences had ensued therefrom on the part of the pope—and that Philip had even made peace more than once, and had vowed eternal friendship to him while he was thus detaining her. If Richard credited the worst part of the current reports (as he afterwards averred he did), he was not likely to feel anything but the strongest aversion to the marriage. Affection for his affianced bride was, however, a very colourable pretext; and as he was now haunted by a more real and serious uneasiness—namely, by the belief that his father destined the English crown for his youngest son John—he set this plea forward in justification of his rebellion, and co-operated heart and hand with the French king. In the month of November in this same year (A.D. 1188) another conference was held, not, however, between Trie and Gisors, but near to Bonsmoulins in Normandy. Philip proposed that Adelais should be given up to Richard, and that Henry should declare that prince heir, not only to his kingdom of England, but also to all his continental dominions, and cause his vassals immediately to swear fealty to Richard. Henry, who could not forget the miseries he had suffered in consequence of elevating his eldest son in this manner, resolutely refused the latter proposition. A violent altercation ensued, and ended in a manner which sufficiently proved that Richard was thinking little of the first proposition or of his bride. Turning from his father, he furiously exclaimed, "This forces me to believe that which I before deemed impossible" (that is, the report concerning his younger brother John). He then ungirded his sword, and kneeling at the feet of King Philip, and placing his hands between his, said, "To you, sire, I commit the protection of myself and my hereditary rights, and to you I do homage for all my father's dominions on this side the sea." Philip ostentatiously accepted his homage, and made him a present grant of some towns and castles he had captured from his father. Henry, violently agitated, rushed from the scene, and, mounting his horse, rode away to Saumur, to prepare for the further prosecution of the interminable war.[3] But his iron frame now felt the inroads of disease and grief; his activity and decision *at last* forsook him, and, relying on exertions making in his favour by the pope's legate, he remained supine while Philip and Richard took several of his towns and se-

---

[1] *Rog. Hoved.*   [2] Ibid.; *Script. Rer. Franc.*   [3] *Hoved.*; *Diceto*; *Script. Rer. Franc.*

duced many of his knights. Even at this extremity the good people of Normandy were faithful to him, and, wishing to secure that duchy for his favourite son, of whose love and faith he had never doubted, he was careful to procure an oath from the seneschal of Normandy, that he would deliver the fortresses of that province to John in case of his death. The church was on this occasion zealously engaged on the side of Henry; Richard and the French king were menaced with excommunication, and though elated by unusual success, Philip was obliged to consent to another conference. The meeting took place in the month of June in the following year (A.D. 1189), at La Ferté-Bernard; and Richard, John of Anagni, cardinal and legate, the Archbishops of Canterbury, Rouen, Rheims, and Bourges, were present. Philip proposed the same conditions as at the conference of Bonsmoulins seven months before; Henry, who had been hurt in every feeling by Richard, in the interval, rejected them, and proposed that Adelais should be united to his dutiful son John—an overture that tends to shake the credibility of the existing scandal even more than does the circumstance of Henry's advanced age. Should Philip agree to this arrangement, he declared his readiness to name Prince John heir to his continental dominions—a distribution which he seems to have long contemplated. But Philip would not enter into the new plan, or abandon Richard, who was present, and who joined the French king in violent abuse of his father. John of Anagni, the cardinal-legate, then threatened to put the kingdom of France under an interdict; but these menaces depended much for their effect on circumstances and the character of the princes to whom they were addressed. Philip had boldness enough to despise them: he even accused the legate of partial and venal motives; telling him it was easy to perceive he had already scented the pounds sterling of the English king.[1] Richard, who was never exemplary for command of temper, went still further: he drew his sword against the cardinal, and would have cut him down but for the timely interposition of some more moderate members of the party.

Henry again rode away from the conference, and this time with a desponding heart. The people of Aquitaine, Poictou, and Brittany were induced to rise in mass against their now falling master; and, under the command of Richard, they fell upon him on the west and south, while the French king attacked him in Anjou, on the north. He had, on former occasions, made head against almost equally formidable confederacies; but the strength of frame, the eagle-glance, and the buoyancy of spirits which had then carried him through a victor, were now crippled and dimmed by sickness and sorrow. His barons continued their open desertions or secret treachery; and at last he was induced to solicit peace, with the offer of resigning himself to whatever terms Philip and Richard should propose.[2] The two monarchs met on a plain between Tours and Azay-sur-Cher. It appears that Richard did not attend to witness the humiliation of his father, but expected the issue of the negotiations at a short distance. While the kings were conversing together in the open field and on horseback, a loud peal of thunder was heard, though the sky appeared cloudless, and the lightning fell between them, but without hurting them. They separated in great alarm, but after a brief space met again. Then a second peal of thunder, more awful than the first, rolled over their heads. The state of Henry's health rendered him more nervous than his young and then triumphant rival; he dropped the reins, and, reeling in his saddle, would have fallen from his horse had not his attendants supported him.[3] He recovered his self-possession, but he was too ill to renew the conference, and the humiliating conditions of peace, reduced to writing, were sent to his quarters for his signature. It was stipulated that Henry should pay an indemnity of 20,000 marks to Philip, renounce all his rights of sovereignty over the town of Berry, and submit in all things to his decisions;[4] that he should permit all his vassals, both English and continental, to do homage to Richard; that all such barons as had espoused Richard's party should be considered the liege men and vassals of the son, unless they voluntarily chose to return to the father; that he should deliver Adelais to one out of five persons named by Richard, who, at the return of Philip and Richard from the crusade, on which they proposed to depart immediately (there was no longer any talk of Henry's going), would restore her in all honour, either to her brother or her affianced; and, finally, that he should give the kiss of peace to Richard, and banish from his heart all sentiments of anger and animosity against him.[5] The envoys of the French king read the treaty, article by article, to Henry as he lay suffering on his bed. When they came to the article which regarded the vassals who had deserted him to join Richard, he asked for a list of their names. The list was given him, and the very first name upon it which struck his eye was that of his darling son John, of whose

[1] Jam sterlingos regis Angliæ olfecerat.—*Rog. Hoved.*; *Matt. Par.*
[2] *Roger Hoved.; Script. Rer. Franc.* [3] *Rog. Hoved.*
[4] "Ex toto se posuit in voluntate regis Franciæ," says Roger of Hoveden. Except in one clause the name of England seems hardly to have been mentioned; and this *submission* was evidently limited to the continental dominions, over which (at least in theory) the authority of the French crown was always extensive.
[5] *Rog. Hoved.; Script. Rer. Franc.*

base treachery he had hitherto been kept happily ignorant. The broken-hearted king started up from his bed and gazed wildly around. "Is it true," he cried, "that John, the child of my heart behind me!" Some priests exhorted the disordered raving man to retract these curses, but he would not. He was sensible, however, to the affection and unwearying attentions of his na-

CASTLE OF CHINON.—Touchard Lafosse, La Loire Historique, Pittoresque, &c.

tural son, Geoffrey, who had been faithful to him through life, and who received his last sigh. As soon as the breath was out of his body, all the ministers, priests, bishops, and barons, that had waited so long, took a hurried departure, and his personal attendants followed their example, but not before they had stripped his dead body, and seized everything of any value in the apartment where he died.

—he whom I have cherished more than all the rest, and for love of whom I have drawn down on mine own head all these troubles, hath verily betrayed me!" They told him it was even so. "Now, then," he exclaimed, falling back on his bed, and turning his face to the wall, "let everything go as it will—I have no longer care for myself or for the world!"[1]

The disrespect and utter abandonment which had followed the demise of the great Conqueror 102 years before, were repeated towards the corpse of his great-grandson. It was not without delay and difficulty that people were found to wrap the body in a winding-sheet, and a hearse and horses to convey it to the abbey of Fontevraud.[3] While it was on its way to receive the last rites of se-

Shortly after, he caused himself to be transported to the pleasant town of Chinon;[2] but those favourite scenes made no impression on his profound melancholy and hopelessness of heart, and in a few days he laid himself down to die. In his last moments, as his intellects wandered, he was heard uttering unconnected exclamations. "O shame!" he cried, "a conquered king! I, a conquered king! . . . . Cursed be the day on which I was born, and cursed of God the children I leave

ABBEY OF FONTEVRAUD.[4]—Mrs. Stothard's Normandy.

pulture, Richard, who had learned the news of his father's death, met the procession and accom-

---

[1] Script. Rer. Franc. "Iterum se lecto reddens, et faciem suam ad parietem vertens," &c.
[2] Chinon, beautifully situated on the river Loire, was the French Windsor of our Norman kings; and Fontevraud, at the distance of about seven miles, their favourite place of burial.
[3] Script. Rer. Franc.; Girald; Ang. Sac.; Rog. Hoved.
[4] Fontevraud, or Fontrevauld (anciently Fons Ebraldi), a town of France, in the department of the Maine and Loire. The abbey, to which it owes its origin, was most richly endowed, and was the head of an order in which the men of the establish-

ment were subservient to the women. It was founded in 1099, by Robert d'Arbrissel, a celebrated preacher in Brittany, charged by Pope Urban II. to preach in favour of the second crusade. His popularity induced so many of all classes to follow him, that he resolved to choose a spot where he might establish them in regular order. The wild forest of Fontevraud, watered by a pure fountain that issued from a rock, was selected as a suitable retreat, and a lady named Arambourge gave them the valley in which the great church was afterwards erected.—Mrs. Stothard's Tour in France.

panied it to the church. Here, as the dead king lay stretched on the bier, his face was uncovered, that his son might look upon it for the last time. Marked as it was with the awful expression of a long agony, he gazed on it in silence and shuddered. He then knelt and prayed before the altar, but only for "a modicum of time, or about as long as it takes to say the Lord's Prayer;" and when the funeral was over he quitted the church, and entered it not again until that hour when, cut off in the full strength and pride of manhood, he was carried thither a corpse to be laid at the feet of his father.[1] It was a popular superstition which both Normans and Anglo-Saxons had derived from their common ancestors, the Scandinavians, that the body of the dead would bleed in presence of its murderer; and more than one chronicler of the time avers that this miracle was seen at the church of Fontevraud, where (say they), from the moment that Richard entered until that in which he departed, the king never ceased to bleed at both nostrils.[2] On the day of Henry's death (July 6, 1189), he was in the fifty-seventh year of his age, and he had reigned over England thirty-four years, seven lunar months, and five days, counting from the day of his coronation.[3] This long reign had been highly beneficial to the country. With a few brief exceptions, peace had been maintained in the interior, and there is good evidence to show that the condition of the people generally had been elevated and improved. The king's personal character has been differently represented, some dwelling only on its bright qualities, and others laying all their emphasis on his vices, which, in truth, were neither few in number nor moderate in their nature, although, for the most part, common attributes to the princes of those ages, few of whom had his redeeming virtues and splendid abilities. To say, with Hume, that his character, in private as well as in public life, was almost without a blemish, is a manifest defying of the testimony and authority of contemporary history; but yet, when every fair deduction is made, he will remain indisputably an illustrious prince, and a man possessed of many endearing qualities.

Besides his five legitimate sons, of whom three preceded him to the grave, Henry had three daughters by his wife Eleanor. Matilda, the eldest, was married to Henry, Duke of Saxony, Bavaria, Westphalia, &c.; and from her is descended the present royal family of Great Britain: Eleanor, the second daughter, was married to Alfonso the Good, King of Castile; and Joan, the youngest, was united to William II., King of Sicily, a prince of the Norman line of Guiscard. Two of his natural children have obtained the general notice of history on account of the celebrity of their mother, and of their own eminent qualities. The first, who was born while Stephen was yet on the throne of England, was William, surnamed "Longsword," who married the heiress of the Earl of Salisbury, and succeeded to the high titles and immense estates of that baron; the second was the still better known Geoffrey, who was born about the time when Henry became king, and who was made Bishop of Lincoln at a very early age. He had much of Henry's spirit and ability, and, if an indifferent prelate, he was a bold and successful warrior in his *nonage*, when (during the first insurrection promoted by his father's legitimate sons) he gained in the north some signal advantages for the king, to whom he and his brother, William Longsword, were ever faithful and affectionate. Geoffrey was subsequently made chancellor, when, like Becket in the same capacity, he constantly accompanied the king. In his dying moments, Henry expressed a hope or a wish that he might be made Archbishop of York, a promotion which, as we shall find, he afterwards obtained.

---

[1] *Script. Rer. Franc.*
[2] *Benedict. Abbas; Script. Rer. Franc.; Hoved.*: Speed, *Chron.*
[3] *Diceto; Hoved.;* Sir Harris Nicolas' *Chronology of History.*
[4] "If we seek the character of the founder of the Common Law in the pages of the justiciar (Glanville), we shall view him as greater and more powerful than any king who had hitherto borne sway in England. Just, discreet, and merciful—a lover of peace, but whose humanity did not degenerate into indolence or supineness—mighty, but who never allowed his strength to tempt him into tyranny. By the force of his right hand he crushed the violence of the proud and intractable, while he extended his sceptre to the indigent and lowly. None of the judges of his court could dare to deviate, however slightly, from the path of righteousness, nor to utter a sentence contrary to the dictates of truth. In his supreme tribunal, the power of the adversary oppressed not the poor man; neither could favour or credit drive the lowly from the seat of judgment. Such are the sentences which preface the earliest treatise on the Law. But, in the portrait which we receive from the ecclesiastic, every virtue disappears: unchaste, greedy, avaricious, capricious, and cruel, he abolished all the old and rightful laws of the country, by the new ordinances termed 'assizes,' which he promulgated every year. Severe beyond example, his jurisprudence was subversive both of natural justice and of the laudable customs of the realm. Attacking, with an even hand, the honour, the privileges, and the property of the aristocracy, and the franchises of the clergy; no individual was so exalted as to be above the reach of his arbitrary power; no one so insignificant as to be sheltered by obscurity from his searching tyranny. This strange discrepancy between the minister and the monk may be attributed in part to the difference of their respective stations. The persecutor of Becket could find little favour from the churchman; and the charge preferred against him that 'he kept the guilty priest in fetters, making no distinction between the clerk and the churl,' may not be considered as a proof of the impartiality of the complainant; but the fiscal extortions of Henry, together with the abuses resulting from the sale of right and justice, have been faithfully recorded. In opposition to the praises of his equity, so loudly bestowed by Glanville, we can quote the declaration of the suitor, who counts the bribes which he paid to the monarch; and the testimony afforded by the justiciar is rendered suspicious by his known perversion of the law to answer his own sinister designs."—Palgrave, *Rise and Progress of the English Commonwealth.*

The history of their mother, the "Fair Rosamond," has been enveloped in romantic traditions which have scarcely any foundation in truth, but which have taken so firm a hold on the popular mind, and have been identified with so much poetry, that it is neither an easy nor a pleasant task to dissipate the fanciful illusion, and unpeople the "bower" in the sylvan shades of Woodstock. Rosamond de Clifford was the daughter of a baron of Herefordshire, the beautiful site of whose antique castle, in the valley of the Wye, is pointed out to the traveller between the town of the Welsh Hay and the city of Hereford, at a point where the most romantic of rivers, after foaming through its rocky, narrow bed in Wales, sweeps freely and tranquilly through an open English valley of surpassing loveliness. Henry became enamoured of her in his youth, before he was king, and the connection continued for many years; but long before his death, and even long before his quarrel with his wife and legitimate sons (with which, it appears, she had nothing to do), Rosamond retired, to lead a religious and penitent life, into the "little nunnery" of Godestow, in the "rich meadows of Eveulod near unto Oxford." As Henry still preserved gentle and generous feelings towards the object of his youthful passion, he made many donations to the "little nunnery," on her account; and when she died (some time, at least, before the first rebellion) the nuns, in gratitude to one who had been both directly and indirectly their benefactress, buried her in their choir, hung a silken pall over her tomb, and kept tapers constantly burning around it. These few lines, we believe, comprise all that is really known of the Fair Rosamond. The legend, so familiar to the childhood of all of us, was of later and gradual growth, not being the product of one imagination. The chronicler Brompton, who wrote in the time of Edward III., or more than a century and a half after the event, gave the first description we possess of the secret bower of Rosamond. He says, that in order that she might not be "easily taken unawares by the queen," Henry constructed, near "Wodestock," a bower for this "most sightly maiden," of wonderful contrivance, and not unlike the Dædalean labyrinth; but he speaks only of a device against surprise, and intimates, in clear terms, that Rosamond died a natural death. The clue of silk, and the poison-bowl forced on her fair and gentle rival by the jealous and revengeful Eleanor, were additions of a still more modern date.

The adventures of the amiable frail one's unoffending bones are better authenticated. A rigid bishop caused them to be cast out of the church, and interred in the common cemetery, observing to the nuns, that the tomb of a harlot was no fit object for a choir of virgins to contemplate, and that religion made no distinction between the mistress of a king and the mistress of any other man. But gratitude rebelled against this salutary doctrine, and the virgin sisterhood of Godestow gathered up the remains, perfumed the dry bones, laid them again in their church, under a fair, large gravestone, and set up a cross hard by, with an inscription, imploring requiem or rest for Rosamond.

REMAINS OF THE NUNNERY OF GODESTOW.[1]—From an old view in the British Museum.

---

[1] It appears that John de St. John has the best claim to be considered the founder of the monastery of Godestow. In the latter end of the reign of King Henry I., he gave some ground here to a religious matron called Editha, or Edira, who built thereon an abbey for Benedictine nuns, which was consecrated at the latter end of December, 1138, to the honour of the Virgin Mary and St. John Baptist.—*Monasticon.* The remains of Godestow consist of ranges of wall on the north, south, and east sides of an extensive area, and a small building at one of the angles.

CHAPTER VII.—CIVIL AND MILITARY HISTORY.

RICHARD I., SURNAMED CŒUR DE LION.——ACCESSION, A.D. 1189—DEATH, A.D. 1199.

Richard I. succeeds to the crown—Massacre of the Jews at his coronation—His expedients to raise money for the crusade—Appoints a regency and departs on the expedition—His adventures during the voyage—His quarrels and aggressions in Sicily—His misunderstandings with his ally, Philip of France—Richard's marriage to Berengaria—He is driven by a storm to Cyprus—His war with the sovereign of the island—His landing at Acre—Acre taken from the Saracens—Disagreements between Richard and Philip—Philip returns to France—Massacre of the Saracen hostages at Acre—March of the crusaders towards Jerusalem—They are compelled to winter at Ascalon—Quarrels among the crusaders and failure of the crusade—Richard's victory over the Saracens at Jaffa—He embarks for England—His dangerous land journey—He is taken prisoner by the Duke of Austria—The Emperor of Germany claims and imprisons him—Troubles in England during King Richard's absence—Jewish massacres—Quarrels between the chiefs of the regency—Quarrels between Prince John and the chancellor, Longchamp—Longchamp defeated, and obliged to leave England—John assumes the government—He aims at the crown in his brother's absence—The emperor compelled to liberate Richard on ransom—Richard's return to England—His treacherous welcome from Prince John—Longbeard's rebellion in London—He is executed—War between England and France—The Bishop of Beauvais captured—Defeat of the French at the river Epte—Richard besieges Chaluz—He is mortally wounded—His behaviour in his last moments.

AS soon as his father was buried, Richard laid hands on Stephen of Tours, the seneschal of Anjou and treasurer to Henry II. This unfortunate officer was loaded with chains, and thrown into a dungeon, from which he was not released until he delivered up, not only the funds of the late king, but his own money also, to the last penny he possessed. Letters were sent over to England for the immediate enlargement of the queen-dowager; and, on quitting her prison, Eleanor was invested for a short time with the office of regent, and especially charged to have an eye on the monies in England. Her misfortunes seem for awhile to have had a beneficial effect on her imperious character, for during her brief authority she relieved the people by many works of mercy; releasing those who were arbitrarily detained in prison, pardoning offences against the crown, moderating the severity of the forest laws, and reversing several attainders. She also distributed bountiful alms to the poor, that they might pray for the soul of the husband whom she, more than any one, had contrived to send with sorrow to the grave. She hastened to Winchester, where the royal treasure was deposited, and having made sure of that city, summoned thither the barons and prelates of the realm, that they might recognize and receive their

EFFIGY OF RICHARD I.—From the tomb at Fontevraud.

new sovereign. The state of affairs, however, detained Richard on the Continent for nearly two months. At last he crossed the Channel, accompanied by his brother John, and landed at Portsmouth, whence he repaired to Winchester. Henry had left in his treasury there a large sum in gold and silver, besides plate, jewels, and precious stones. All these Richard caused to be weighed and examined in his presence, and carefully inventoried. His soul was occupied by an enterprise that was likely to absorb all the money he could possibly procure; and, to find means for a most lavish expenditure, he resorted to the cares and expedients that more properly characterize avarice. It was this enterprise, however, that gave him the benefit of an undisputed succession to all his father's dominions; for John, expecting to be left in full authority by the immediate departure of his brother for Palestine, and hoping that he would never return alive from the perils of the Holy War, submitted to what he considered would be a very brief arrangement, and made no effort to dispute Richard's right. But for these circumstances it is very clear, from the character of the crafty and ambitious John, that the old story of a disputed succession would have been repeated. As it was, it was wiser for him to wait awhile for the chance of getting peaceful possession of the whole, than to risk life or failure for a part. The confidence reposed in him may excite some surprise, and the more, perhaps, because one of Richard's first acts as a sovereign, was to discard and persecute all those who had plotted against his father, not excepting even his own most familiar friends, who had plotted for his own advantage; thus reading a good lesson to those who embark their fortunes in the family quarrels of princes. On the 3d of September, the coronation festival was held at Westminster with unusual magnificence; the abbots, and bishops, and most of the lay barons attending on the occasion. The unction over, and the king being royally arrayed, he was led up to the altar, where the archbishop adjured him, in the name of Almighty God, not to assume the royal dignity unless he fully proposed to keep the oaths he had sworn. Richard repeated his solemn promises, and with his own hands taking the ponderous crown from off the altar, "in signification that he held it only from God," he delivered it to the archbishop, who instantly put it on his head, and so completed all the ceremonies of coronation.[1] "Which act," says old Speed, "with a cold-bloodedness less excusable than his superstition, "was accidentally hanselled and auspicated by the blood of many Jews (though utterly against the king's will), who, in a tumult raised by the multitude, were furiously murdered, which, though it was afterwards punished by the laws, might seem a presage, that this lion-hearted king should be a special destroyer of the enemies of our Saviour." The modern historian cannot permit these atrocities to pass off so easily. We have mentioned the Jews under the preceding reign; and our cursory allusion to them has shown that they were already in possession of great wealth in England, where they were persecuted by the government, though most useful, and indeed essential to it; and hated by the whole nation, though nearly all the comforts, and, without exception, all the ornaments and luxuries of civilized life, brought from foreign markets, were introduced by their commercial enterprise. Their wealth seems to have had as much to do in rendering them odious as the religious faith to which they heroically adhered; and the advance they had made in the rate of interest on their loans to men who were about departing on the dangerous expeditions to the Holy Land—though the necessary consequence of the great and sudden demand for money, and of the augmented risk incurred by the lenders—had recently the effect of exasperating many of the noble but needy crusaders, and had increased that rancour against them which was always a prevalent feeling among the superstitious and ignorant populace—if the populace deserve these distinguishing epithets when ignorance and superstition were so prevalent among all classes. At the accession of Philip to the throne of France, all the Jews had been banished that kingdom, their property confiscated, the obligations of their numerous debtors annulled; and though Henry II. had declined taking this iniquitous course, it was expected by many that Richard, on coming to the throne of England, would follow the example of his friend Philip. The Jews probably expected something of the sort; they assembled in London from all parts of the kingdom, "meaning to honour the coronation with their presence, and to present to the king some honourable gift, whereby they might declare themselves glad for his advancement, and procure his friendship towards themselves, for the confirming of their privileges and liberties, according to the grants and charters made to them by the former king."[2] On the day before the coronation, Richard being "of a zealous mind to Christ's religion, abhorring their nation, and doubting some sorcery by them to be practised, issued a proclamation forbidding Jews *and women* to be present at Westminster, either within the church when he should receive the crown, or within the hall whilst he was at dinner.[3] A few, however, persevering in a custom sanctioned by remote antiquity among all Oriental people, ventured, on this day of general grace and joy, to lay their offerings at the king's feet. Their humble suit was heard—their rich presents were accepted, "gladly enough;" but a Christian raised an outcry, and struck a Jew that was trying to enter the gate with the rest of the crowd. The courtiers and king's servants, catching the contagion of the quarrel, then fell on the wealthy Jews who had obtained admittance, and drove them out of the hall. A report spread among the multitude gathered outside the palace that the king had commanded the destruction of the unbelievers, and therefore, following up an example already set them by their superiors, the people cruelly beat the Jews and drove them with "staves, bats, and stones, to their houses and lodgings." This violence being left unchecked, and the rumour of the king's intention still spreading, fresh crowds of fanatic rioters collected, and after barbarously murdering every Jew they found in the streets, they assaulted the houses they occupied and in which they had barricaded themselves. As many of these houses were strongly built they set fire to them, and burned men, women, and children, with

---

[1] Hoveden and Diceto, who were both present. At the coronation feast, which immediately followed, the citizens of London were the king's butlers, and the citizens of Winchester served up the meats.

[2] *Holinshed.* [3] Ibid.

everything they contained. In some cases they forced their way into the apartments, and hurled their victims, not excepting even the aged, the sick, and bed-ridden, out of the windows into fires which they had kindled below. The king, alarmed at length by the riot, sent Ranulf de Glanville, the lord-justiciary, and other officers, to appease it; but the authority of these high functionaries was despised, their own lives were threatened, and in the end they were obliged to flee back to Westminster Hall, where the banquet still continued. When night set in, the "rude sort" were lighted in their horrid work of plunder and murder by the flames that rose from the Jewish houses, and that, at one time, threatened a general conflagration of the town. The magazines and shops of the Jews were plundered; the defenceless wretches who attempted to escape from their burning dwellings "were received upon the points of spears, bills, swords, and gleaves of their adversaries, that watched for them very diligently." These atrocities continued from about the hour of noon on one day till two o'clock in the afternoon of the next, when the infuriated populace seem to have ceased plundering and butchering out of sheer weariness. One or two days after, Richard hanged three men, not because they had robbed and murdered the Jews, but because (at least so it was declared in the public sentence) they had burned the houses of Christians, some of which were indeed unintentionally consumed by the spreading of the flames. He then issued a proclamation, in which, after stating that he took the Jews under his own immediate protection, he commanded that no man should personally harm them, or rob them of their goods and chattels; and these were the only judicial measures that followed the terrific outrage.[1] All that the new king could think of at this moment, was how he should go to Palestine with a splendid army, and leave the care of his kingdom and of all his subjects to others. To raise money he had recourse to expedients similar to those which ruined Stephen and the nation under him. He alienated the demesne lands, publicly selling, by a sort of auction, royal castles, fortresses, and towns; and, together with estates that were his own, not a few that were the property of other men. When some friends ventured to remonstrate, he swore he would sell London itself if he could only find a purchaser for it.[2] Thus most of those royal lands, which his father with so much prudence and address had recovered out of powerful private hands and re-annexed to the crown, were again detached from it. In the same way places of trust and honour —the highest offices in the kingdom—were publicly sold to the highest bidder. "Richard's presence chamber," says a recent writer, "was a market overt, in which all that the king could bestow—all that could be derived from the bounty of the crown or imparted by the royal prerogative—was disposed of to the best chapman. Hugh Pudsey, the Bishop of Durham, purchased the earldom of Northumberland, together with the lordship of Sadburgh. For the chief justiciarship he paid, at the same time, the sum of 1000 marks. In the bargain was included a dispensation to the bishop, or at least such dispensation as the king could grant, from his vow or promise of joining in the crusade."[3] The new king also hastily filled all the vacant bishoprics and abbacies, exacting a heavy fee from each prelate and abbot he appointed. In consideration of 20,000 marks received from the Scottish king, he granted to him a release from all the obligations which had been extorted from him and from his subjects during his captivity, and gave back to him all the charters and documents of his servitude, with this

---

[1] *Hoved.; Dicdo; Newb.; Hemingford.* "This impunity, however, encouraged the enemies of the Israelites; and the crusaders, in their way to the coast, were careful to imitate their brethren in the capital. The excesses at Lynn, Norwich, Stamford, Edmundsbury, and Lincoln, seem to have been caused by the impulse of the moment; those at York were the result of an organized conspiracy. Before sunset a body of men entered the city, and in the darkness of the night they attacked the house of Bennet, a wealthy Jew who had perished in the riot in London. His wife and children were massacred, his property was pillaged, and the building was burned. The house marked for destruction the following night belonged to Jocen, another Jew, equally wealthy, but who had escaped from the murder of his brethren in the metropolis. He had, however, the wisdom to retire into the castle with his treasures and family, and was imitated by most of the Jews in York and the neighbourhood. Unfortunately, one morning the governor left the castle; at his return, the fugitives, who amounted to 500 men, independently of the women and children, mistrusting his intentions, refused him admission. In conjunction with the sheriff, he called the people to his assistance; the fortress was besieged night and day; a considerable ransom was offered and rejected; and the Jews, in their despair, formed the horrible resolution of disappointing, with their own hands, the malice of their enemies. They buried their gold and silver, threw into the flames everything that was combustible, cut the throats of their wives and children, and consummated the tragedy by stabbing each other. The few who had not the courage to join in this bloody deed told the tale from the walls to the assailants, and, to save their lives, implored permission to receive baptism. The condition was accepted; and the moment the gates were thrown open they were massacred. The conquerors then marched to the cathedral, extorted from the officers the bonds which the Jews had deposited with them for greater security, and making a bonfire, burned them in the middle of the nave. These outrages brought the chancellor to York; but the principal offenders fled into Scotland, and he contented himself with deposing the sheriff and governor, and taking the recognizances of the city to appear and answer in the king's court. In narrating so many horrors, it is a consolation to find them uniformly reprobated by the historians of the time. If the ringleaders endeavoured to inflame the passions of the populace by religious considerations, it was merely as a cloak to their real design of sharing among themselves the spoils of their victims, and of extinguishing their debts by destroying the securities, together with the persons of their creditors."—Lingard's *History of England.*
[2] *William of Newbury.*
[3] Introduction to *Rotuli Curiæ Regis* (published by the Record Commission), by Sir Francis Palgrave.

proviso, that he should nevertheless duly and fully perform all the services which his brother Malcolm had performed, or ought of right to have performed, to Richard's predecessors.[1] For the sum of 3000 marks he granted his peace to his half-brother, Geoffrey, who had been elected Archbishop of York, according to the wish expressed by his father Henry on his death-bed; and other sums of money were obtained by means much less justifiable.

It was now necessary to nominate a regency. At this step Prince John saw his hopes disappointed; but he remained perfectly quiet, being anxious, no doubt, that nothing should occur to prevent or delay his formidable brother's departure. A great council was held at the monastery of Pipwell, in Northamptonshire. Here the king formally announced the appointment of Hugh Pudsey, the Bishop of Durham, to be Rector Regni and Procurator Regni; but he included with him, in the commission of justiciarship, William de Mandeville, Earl of Albemarle. This great earl, however, quitted England soon after, leaving the bishop in full possession of the high office; but he did not retain it long, for his authority was first of all weakened and subdivided by Richard before he began his journey, and finally during the king's absence; but while he was yet in Normandy, it was wrenched from him altogether by the much abler hands of Longchamp, Bishop of Ely and chancellor of England. To satisfy his brother John, besides the earldom of Moreton or Moretaine, in Normandy, Richard gave him the earldoms of Cornwall, Dorset, Somerset, Gloucester, Nottingham, Derby, and Lancaster, in England, forming together not less than a third part of the whole kingdom. To gratify his mother, he added to the estates she already possessed all the lands that had been enjoyed by Matilda, the Saxon wife of Henry I., or by Alice, the French widow of the same monarch. She was also to be consulted in sundry matters of government; and at a subsequent period, during Richard's confinement in Germany, Eleanor exercised considerable authority with the consent of the king, though whatever power in the state his brother John acquired was usurped and against his will.

Richard had proceeded with a most arbitrary haste; but Philip of France, being ready before him, and doubting he might delay, sent messengers to remind him that the time of departure for the Holy Land was unchangeably fixed at the coming festival of Easter. At the arrival of these messengers, Richard, with a vast number of the earls, barons, and knights who had taken the cross with him, swore he would be ready by the time appointed, and Philip's envoys took a like oath on behalf of themselves. The form of these oaths was somewhat unusual, the Frenchmen swearing by the soul of the King of France, the Englishmen by the soul of the King of England. By this time Richard had got all the money he could on this side of the Channel; and towards the end of the year, and a little more than three months after his coronation, he crossed over to his continental dominions to see what money he could raise and extort there.

A.D. 1190. In the month of February following, Richard held a great council in Normandy, which was attended by the queen-dowager, by his brother John, and by various bishops, who are stated to have crossed the Channel by the king's command. At this meeting there was an abundant pledging of oaths, which were but indifferently kept in the sequel. Soon after the two kings made a compact of alliance and fraternity of arms, swearing that each would defend the life and honour of the other—that neither would desert the other in his danger—that the King of France would cherish and protect the rights of the King of England, even as he would protect his own city of Paris; and that the King of England would do the like by his majesty of France, even as he would protect his own city—of *Rouen!*[2]

Owing to the death of Philip's young queen, their departure was postponed from the feast of Easter till Midsummer. At last they met in the plains of Vezelai, each accompanied by a gallant and a numerous army; for their forces, when united, are said to have amounted to 100,000 men. They marched in company from Vezelai to Lyons, and the people, though much distressed by the passage of such a host, comforted themselves with the thought that the Paynim could never withstand them, and that the city of the Lord, with the whole of Palestine, would be recovered by their swords and lances. At Lyons the two kings separated, with the mutual understanding that they should meet again in the port of Messina, in Sicily. Philip, with his forces, took the nearest road to Genoa; for he had no fleet of his own, and that flourishing commercial republic had agreed with him for the furnishing of transports and some ships of war. From the time of his expedition to Ireland, Henry II. had paid great attention to maritime affairs, and an English *royal* navy had gradually grown up. We do not possess much information on this interesting subject, but we learn from the chroniclers that he had some vessels which would be considered, even now, of a large size, and that one of the "chiefest and newest," was capable of

---

[1] Allen, *Vindic. Anc. Ind. Scot.*; *Fædera*; *Benedict. Abb.*   [2] *Roger of Hoveden.*

carrying 400 persons. Some time before his death, he began to build vessels expressly for the voyage to Palestine; and when his son succeeded, he found these preparations so far advanced, that he was soon able to launch or equip fifty galleys of three banks of oars, and many other armed galleys inferior in size to them, but superior to those generally in use at the period. He had also selected transports from the shipping of all his ports; and perhaps there is not much danger in assuming that, in size and strength of ships, this was the most formidable naval armament that had as yet appeared in modern Europe.[1] Having thus a fleet of his own, Richard was not dependent, like Philip, on arrangements with the maritime Italians, and, instead of crossing the Alps, he kept his course by the beautiful valley of the Rhone towards Marseilles—a free trading city, belonging neither to the English nor the French king,[2] where he had ordered that his ships should meet him, to convey him and his army thence across the Mediterranean to Sicily, and then to Palestine.

When Richard reached the coast, he found his fleet had not arrived. After passing eight impatient days at Marseilles, he hired twenty galleys and ten great busses or barks there, and proceeded coastwise with some of his forces to Genoa, where he again met the French king. His English ships, for which he left orders at Marseilles to follow him to Sicily, had met with some strange adventures, even before reaching the Straits of Gibraltar and entering the Mediterranean. In his absence discipline was at a low ebb among the forces embarked, in spite of the severe, and, in some respects, singular scale of punishment he had drawn up for the preservation of order. Two prelates, Gerard, Archbishop of Aix, and Bernard, Bishop of Bayeux, and three knights, Robert de Saville, Richard de Camville, and William de Fortz, were intrusted with the command of the fleet, with the title of "constables." The ships sailed from Dartmouth with a gallant display of banners and painted shields; but in crossing the Bay of Biscay, they encountered a storm which scattered them in all directions. One of them which belonged to London suffered more than the rest, and was well-nigh foundering; but, according to the superstitious chroniclers, there were 100 pious men on board, who cried aloud to St. Thomas of Canterbury; and Becket not only came himself, with crozier and pall, but also brought with him Edmund, the Saxon king, saint, and martyr, and St. Nicholas, the protector of distressed seamen, and told the crew that God and our Lady had instructed him

SHIPS OF THE TIME.[3]—Cambridge, Matt. Paris.

and his beatified companions to watch King Richard's fleet, and see it safe. Many of the ships put into the Tagus and anchored at Lisbon, where the crews behaved in a very tumultuous manner; and the Portuguese, glad to be rid of such visitors, promised to aid and succour all future pilgrims bound for the Holy War that might put into their ports.[4] The crusaders then sailed from Lisbon. At the mouth of the Tagus they were joined by thirty-three vessels; and, with a fleet now amounting to 106 sail, they steered for the Straits of Gibraltar. Passing those straits, and hugging the coast of Spain and Southern France, they reached, in less than four weeks from the time they had quitted Lisbon, the prosperous city of Marseilles, where they found their impatient king was gone. According to his orders, the fleet took on board the mass of the army which he had left behind at that port, and made sail again with all expedition for Messina, which city it reached several days before either the French or English king.[5]

---

[1] Southey, Nav. Hist.
[2] Marseilles was not even nominally under Philip, but acknowledged the suzerainty of the King of Arragon. The same appears to have been the case with all the French ports on the Mediterranean, from the Pyrenees to the Maritime Alps.
[3] In this quaint but characteristic illumination we see a vessel fitted with a stage or tower raised on scaffolding at the poop, on which are men discharging arrows and missiles from the bow, and from slings. A figure at the prow fights with a flail. The castle or vessel—for which it is seems uncertain—is defended by men throwing stones and shooting with the bow and cross-bow. This illumination is strikingly illustrative of the various modes of assault and defence of the period.
[4] Southey, Nav. Hist.
[5] The English fleet sailed from Marseilles on the 30th of August, and entered the port of Messina on the 14th of Sep-

Richard, in the meanwhile, had had several adventures of his own. After coasting the Riviera of Genoa and a part of Tuscany, he entered the river Arno, and visited the splendid city of Pisa. Continuing his voyage along the coast from the mouth of the Arno, he came to the desolate spot where the Tiber pours his brown waters into the sea. His galley required some repairs, and he brought her to anchor in the famous river where the galleys of the Cæsars had once lain. He was there within a few miles of Rome; but though a liberal curiosity and devotion would alike have suggested a pilgrimage to the Eternal City, he did

CRYPT OF THE SANCTUARY OF ST JANUARIUS, Naples.—From Bellermann, die ältesten christlichen Begräbniss-stätten.

not go thither. The cardinal Bishop of Ostia, a town close to the mouth of the Tiber, went to welcome him to the patrimony of St. Peter; but, availing himself of the opportunity, he pressed the irascible Richard for the payment of certain fees due to the see of Rome. Instead of money, Richard gave this prince of the church abuse, reproaching the Papal court with simony, rapacity, and gross corruption; and for this reason, it is said, he refused to visit Rome.[1] When his galley was repaired, he made his way to Naples, where he again landed, and whence he determined to continue his journey to the Straits of Messina by land—his active body and restless mind being, no doubt, alike wearied with the close confinement of ship-board, and the slow progress made during the dead calms of summer in the Mediterranean. While at Naples, he visited the sanctuary of St. Januarius, the protector of that city, and told his orisons in a crypt, where the bodies of the dead stood up in niches, dry and shrivelled, but arrayed in their usual dresses, and otherwise looking as if they were still alive. The beauties of Naples or some other inducements made him loiter several days in that city; but he then mounted his horse, and, taking the picturesque pass of the Apennines which leads by Nocera, the Benedictine abbey of La Cava, and Vietri, he went to Salerno, then celebrated for its school of medicine, the foundation of which had been laid by the Arabs as early as the eighth century, and which had been carried to its height of fame (by Orientals, or by persons who had travelled and studied in the East) under the reign and by the liberal patronage of Robert Guiscard, the Norman conqueror of the south of Italy. But the city of Salerno, which the lances of the Normans had won from the Saracen invaders, and which the bold Guiscard had made for a time his capital, was redundant with Norman glory, and crowded with objects to interest Richard. The Normans had built the cathedral in the plain, and rebuilt the noble castle on the hill. Princes, descended like himself from the first Duke Rollo, slept in sculptured tombs in the great church; and goodly epitaphs, with many a Leonine (or rhyming Latin) verse—that favourite measure of the Normans—recorded their praise. Every castle that met his eye on the flanks and crests of the neighbouring mountains was occupied by the descendant of some Norman knight; for the time, though approaching, was not yet come, when the dynasty of Swabia made a fresh distribution, and introduced a new race of Northern lords into the most glowing regions of the South. Salerno, too, then one of the most civilized, as always one of the most beautifully situated towns of Italy, had other schools besides that of medicine, though it was held not unworthy of a king, and a fitting accomplishment in a true knight, to know something of the healing art. Moral and natural philosophy, such as they were, geometry, astronomy, dialectics, rhetoric, and poetry were all cultivated; and Richard himself was a professed poet, being one of the troubadours.[2] After staying at this interesting spot several days, during which the galleys he had hired at Marseilles came round to him from Naples, he

---

tember, without having lost a single vessel in the Mediterranean. The French fleet from Genoa arrived on the 16th, having lost several ships.

[1] Baronius speaks at some length, and with great emphasis, of this singular interview on the Tiber.—Annal. Eccles.

[2] He was born a poet—if not in the sense of Horace, at least genealogically—for his mother, Eleanor, as well as his maternal grandfather, were troubadours, and the rank was made hereditary in some families. He merited it by his compositions.

mounted his horse, and left Salerno on the 13th of September. He rode across the Pæstan plain, and through the luxuriant district of Cilento, into Calabria, his galleys following along shore, from which his own path was seldom very distant.

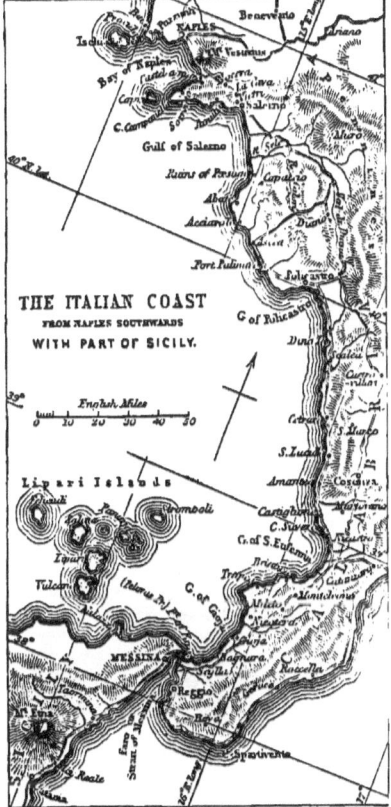

THE ITALIAN COAST
FROM NAPLES SOUTHWARDS
WITH PART OF SICILY.

Roads there were none; and as it was the commencement of the rainy season, he must have encountered great difficulties in crossing the mountain-streams, for he did not reach Mileto till the 21st. From that town he spurred on with only one knight to accompany him. At last he reached the shore of the narrow strait, commonly called the Faro, which separates Calabria from Sicily, and passed the night in a tent hard by the famed rocks and caverns of Scylla. The next morning (September 23), being either advised by signal, or by some one of the Marseilles galleys, the mass of his fleet crossed over from the island to receive him. He embarked, and scorning, or being ignorant of the Homeric dangers of Scylla and Charybdis, was presently wafted over to the noble harbour of Messina, which he entered with so much splendour and majesty, and such a clangour of horns and trumpets, and other warlike instruments, that he astonished and alarmed the Sicilians, and the French also, who had reached that port with a shattered fleet a week before him. The first feelings of the allies and confederates in the Holy War towards each other were not of an amicable nature; and Philip, foreseeing, it is said, that dissensions would be inevitable if the two armies passed much time together in inactivity, got ready his fleet as soon as he could, and set sail for the East. But contrary winds and storms drove him back to Messina; and it was then resolved, for the misfortune of the country, that the two kings should winter there together, and find supplies for their armies as best they could.

The kingdom of Sicily, which then comprised Calabria and Apulia, and all those parts of Lower Italy now included in the Neapolitan realm, was in a distracted state. A few years before, under the reign of William I., or of his heroic father, Ruggiero, when the kingdom was united, and their powerful fleets of galleys gave the law in both seas (the Tyrrhenian and the Adriatic), the Sicilians might have been able to defend themselves against the insolent crusaders, numerous as they were; but Richard, who had a private account to settle with their king, well knew their present weakness, and determined to take advantage of it. The King of Sicily, who had scarcely been ten months on the throne, and who reigned by a disputed title, was Tancred, a prince of the Norman line, of great valour and ability. Richard's sister, Joan, who had been wedded when a mere child, had borne her husband no children; and, after nine years' marriage with her, King William II., commonly called "The Good," became uneasy about the succession, and resorted to curious measures in order to keep it in the legitimate line. The only legitimate member of the family living was an aunt about the same age as himself—a posthumous child of his grandfather, the great Ruggiero. The Princess Constance had been brought up from her infancy in religious retirement, and was living in a convent —some writers say she had taken the veil and the vows of a nun long before—when her nephew, the king, fixed his eyes upon her for his successor. Notwithstanding her acknowledged legitimacy, William the Good knew it would be worse than useless to propose a single woman to his warlike barons as their queen; for in their eyes a female sovereignty, notwithstanding their chivalrous devotedness to the fair sex, was an absolute absurdity. William therefore looked abroad for a powerful husband that might assert her rights; or, considering the age of the parties, he might reasonably have hoped to live to see a son of his aunt's grow up before he died. He, therefore, negotiated a marriage with Henry, the son and heir of the Emperor Frederick Barbarossa. Considering the country and climate, and the juvenile age at which royal ladies were then given in marriage, Constance was rather in advanced life, for she was thirty-two years old! The dower and the hope of succession, were, however, brilliant and tempting; and Henry espoused her with great pomp and magnificence, in 1186, in the city of Milan. In the month of November, 1189—little more than three years after this marriage, and between nine and ten months before the arrival of the crusaders at Messina—William the Good died at Palermo, in the thirty-sixth year of his age, leaving his childless widow, Joan, the sister of Richard, who was only in her twenty-fourth year, to the care of his successor. This successor was declared by his will to be his aunt Constance, to whom, and to her husband Henry, some time before his decease, he had, according to the practice of the age, made the barons of the kingdom, on both sides the Faro, take an anticipatory oath of allegiance, at the town of Troja, in Apulia. But he was no sooner dead than his will and the oaths he had exacted were alike disregarded. The prejudice against a female succession was as strong as ever; and it was not prejudice, but laudable policy, in the people of the South to be adverse to the rule of the German emperors, who were already formidable in the north of Italy, which they had deluged with blood, and who threatened the independence of the whole peninsula. By the insular portions of the kingdom, or in Sicily proper, the notion of being governed by Henry, a foreign prince, was held in abhorrence. Constance and Henry were both far away at the time, and, encouraged by these feelings and circumstances, several of the great barons, more or less closely connected with the royal family, advanced claims to the crown. It was difficult, and in part impossible, to reconcile these pretensions; but at length the mass of the people and a large majority of the nobles agreed to elect Tancred, Count of Lecce, cousin to the deceased king, William the Good, but reputed of illegitimate birth, though avowedly born of a lady of the noblest rank. In Sicily, as in England, the church had made great advances in the establishment of the rights of legitimacy; but these rights were, as yet, far from being imperative or sacred in the eyes of the people, who, in all circumstances, would have preferred a bastard to a woman, and whose choice on the present occasion fell on a prince of ripe manhood and mature experience, who had many qualities to recommend him, besides that of his descent from the great Ruggiero, the founder of the dynasty. Tancred was, therefore, hailed king by public acclamation,[1] and solemnly crowned at Palermo, in the beginning of the year 1190. His election by the nobles and people, or his right, was acknowledged by the court of Rome, just as that of Stephen had been in England, and the reigning pope (Clement III.) sent him the usual bulls of investiture and the benediction. Though acceptable and dear to the people, Tancred's throne was immediately disturbed by his disappointed competitors, and by Archbishop Walter, and some of the Apulian barons, who declared for Constance, and armed in her cause. In the island of Sicily this insurrection was defeated by the unanimity of the people; and passing over to the continent in person, Tancred presently reduced most of the Apulian barons to his obedience. But the civil war had weakened him; plots and conspiracies were forming against him; and Henry of Swabia, now emperor, by the death of his father, Barbarossa, was on his march to the south with a powerful army, to claim the throne for Constance, when Richard, received as a guest, commenced his course of aggressions.[2]

The question of Tancred's legitimacy was not, in itself, likely to claim much of the Lion-heart's attention; his quarrel had a more private ground. When the late king, William the Good, married his sister Joan, in the first impulse of love and generosity, he gave her a magnificent dower—the cities of Monte Sant' Angelo and Vesti; the towns and tenements of Ischitella, Peschici, Vico, Caprino, Castel Pagano, and others, with their several castles; Lesina and Varano, with their lakes and the forests adjoining; two stately monasteries, with their pastures, woods, and vineyards—in short, in one extensive and solid mass, the whole of the beautiful country comprised in the great promontory of Monte Gargano, between the provinces of Apulia and the Abruzzi, was allotted to the fair daughter of our Henry II. Tancred, on his accession, had withheld this splendid dower, and had even, it was said, deprived the young queen-dowager of her personal liberty.[3] Richard's first demand was for the enlargement of his sister; and, whether she had been a prisoner or not, it is quite certain that Tancred sent her immediately to her brother, from Palermo to Messina, escorted by the royal galleys. The impetuous King of England then demanded her dower, which, under circumstances, it would not have been easy for Tancred to put her in possession of, as the territories lay in the

---

[1] Giannone says, "Tancredi adunque non altro titolo più plausibile poteva allegar per sè, se non la volontà de' Popoli." This great writer, no doubt, thought the "will of the people" one of the best of rights, but he durst not say so, *when and where* he wrote.

[2] *Angelo di Costanza; Giannone; Fazello; Muratori.*

[3] This fact is not admitted by the oldest Sicilian historians.

very heart of the great fiefs of the continental barons, who were again in revolt. Without waiting the result of peaceful negotiations, into which Tancred readily entered, Richard, embarking part of his army, crossed the Straits of Messina, and took possession, by force of arms, of the town and castle of Bagnara, on the opposite coast of Calabria. Leaving his sister Joan with a good garrison in this castle, he returned to Messina to commit another act of aggression. There was a monastery on the sea-shore (a little beyond the port of Messina) that covered one of the flanks of his army, which was encamped outside the town. The place was capable of being strongly fortified, and was otherwise well suited to his purpose; so he drove the monks out of it, and, garrisoning it for himself, converted it into a place of arms and military storehouse. Whether the poor Sicilians loved these monks[1] or not, the honour of their wives and daughters was dear to them, and they were probably as jealous as at the time of the "Vespers," a century later; and when Richard's disorderly soldiers of the cross, the very day after this seizure of the monastery, "strolled licentiously through the city, with much lasciviousness,"[2] the town's-people set upon them in the streets, killed several of them, and then closed the gates of the town. On this, the whole camp armed, and English, Normans, Angevins, Poictevins, with the rest that followed Richard's standard, rushed to the walls, and would have scaled them then, had not their king ridden among them, and commanded them to desist, beating them the while with his truncheon as hard as he could.[3] He then went to the quarters of the King of France, whither the magistrates of the town soon repaired. After mutual complaints, promises of redress were made on both sides, and the king drew off his men to their tents and ships. On the following morning a solemn meeting was held, with a view of providing for future tranquillity and concord among all parties; for Richard's men and the followers of the French king regarded each other with evil eyes, and had already shed some blood in brawls. The prelates and chief barons of the two nations, and the principal men of Messina, went with Philip to the quarters of Richard. While they were deliberating, a troop of incensed Sicilians gathered on the hills above the English camp, with the intention, it is said, of attacking the king. A Norman knight was wounded by these people, and so great an uproar arose, that Richard rushed from the conference, and called all his men to arms. The English and Normans rushed up the hill-side; but the French did not move, and Philip at one moment seemed inclined to take part with the Sicilians. Richard drove the multitude from the hill and followed them at sword-point to the city. Some of the English entered pell-mell with the fugitives, but the gates were then closed, and the citizens prepared to defend their walls. Five knights and twenty men-at-arms were killed before the walls, but Richard, having brought up nearly the whole of his force, took the town by storm, and planted his banner on its loftiest tower, as if it had been his own town, or one taken in regular warfare. At this exhibition Philip was greatly incensed; but an open rupture between the two sworn brothers in arms was avoided for the present, by Richard's consenting to lower his banner, and commit the city to the keeping of the Knights Hospitallers and Templars, till his demands upon Tancred should be satisfied.

Two of Tancred's nobles and prime favourites —his admiral and another—commanded at Messina at the time of Richard's arrival. Seeing that resistance was vain, and feeling that their dignity was committed by remaining in a town where a foreign prince gave the law, they both retired with their families and moveable property; upon which, Richard seized their houses, galleys, and whatever else they had not been able to carry off with them. He made a complete castle of the monastery on the sea-side, digging a broad and deep ditch round it, and he built a new fort on the hills above the town.[4] These, and other proceedings, excited the envy and disgust of Philip; but they probably hastened the conclusion of a treaty with Tancred, who, in the difficulties under which he was labouring, could hardly contend with so fierce and powerful a disputant. Richard demanded for his sister all the territories before-mentioned, together with a golden chair, a golden table, twelve feet long, and a foot and a half broad, two golden trestles for supporting the same, twenty-four silver cups, and as many silver dishes—to all which, it appears, she as queen was, by the custom of that kingdom, entitled. After all this, he demanded for himself, as representative and heir of his father, a tent of silk, large enough to accommodate 200 knights sitting at meals, 60,000 measures of wheat, and 60,000 of barley, with 100 armed galleys equipped and provisioned for two years. In the end, Richard either proposed or agreed to a compensation in money. Twenty thousand golden oncie[5] were paid in satisfaction of all Joan's demands, and 20,000 more were paid to

---

[1] From some accounts it appears that the monastery was occupied by Greek monks. If that were the case, they were not likely to be very dear to the Messinese.
[2] *Fazello; Ist. de Sic.* [3] *Howd.; Vinesauf.*
[4] This castle, called Mattagriffone, after having been enlarged and repaired at different periods, still frowns over Messina.
[5] An *oneia* is a Sicilian gold coin; the present value is about ten shillings English.

Richard himself, but not in satisfaction for his claim, which he waived (caring little, probably, on what ground he obtained the money, so long as he got it), but on a treaty of marriage which he concluded.[1] He affianced his young nephew Arthur, who was his heir presumptive,[2] to an infant daughter of Tancred, and engaged, in case the marriage should be prevented by the death of either of the parties, that he or his heirs would repay to Tancred or his heirs the 20,000 oncie then received by him, as the dower of the infant. But the treaty went further than this; for Richard guaranteed to Tancred the possession of Apulia, which was partly in revolt, and of the important city of Capua, which had never submitted to the new king. He, indeed, contracted with him what we now call an alliance offensive and defensive—a league he had cause to regret when his evil fortune threw him into the power of Tancred's competitor, the Emperor Henry. The treaty was sent to Rome, to be placed in the hands of the pope, who was invited, both by Richard and by Tancred, to enforce its observance, should any want of faith be shown by either of the contracting parties in the sequel. The money obtained was lavished by Richard in a manner which appeared thoughtless and wild; but his liberality had the effect of increasing his popularity with the crusading host. Such a multitude of men collected on one point had greatly raised the price of provisions; and Richard's treasure, and his table too, were open to the crossed knights of all countries, who complained of the expensiveness of their sojourn at Messina. On the feast of Christmas he gave a splendid banquet, to which he invited every man of the rank of a knight or gentleman, in both armies; and when the dinner was over, he made a present in money to each, the amount being more or less, according to the rank of the parties. A little army of troubadours and minstrels, who had followed him from Aquitaine and the rest of the south of France, constantly sang his praises. Part of the winter months were spent in repairing the ships, and in preparing catapults, manginalls, and other warlike engines, wherewith to batter the walls of the infidel towns in Syria and Palestine, the timber for which was cut on the mountains of Sicily and in the extensive forests of Calabria. But still time hung heavily on the hands of the impatient Richard. In a period of inactivity he was seized with a fit of devotion and penitence. He called all the prelates together that were then with his host at Messina, into the chapel of Reginald de Moiac, in whose house he then resided; and there, in presence of them all, falling down upon his knees, he confessed his sins and the profligate life which he had hitherto led, humbly received the penance enjoined him by the bishops; "and so," adds an old historian, who did not sufficiently bear in mind the deeds of his after life, "he became a new man, fearing God, and delighting to live after his laws."[3]

A short time after these exercises, Richard mounted his horse, and rode to the flanks of the towering and smoking Mount Etna, which had recently been in active eruption. At the city of Catania he was met, by appointment—and it appears for the first time—by Tancred. The two kings embraced, and, walking in splendid procession to the cathedral church (another work of the Normans), prayed, kneeling side by side, before the shrine of St. Agatha. They lived in great cordiality, and each seemed to entertain a high respect for the valour and character of the other. Like the heroes of Homer, they exchanged presents, Tancred giving Richard a ring, and Richard giving Tancred a sword, reputed to be the enchanted blade, Excalebar, or Caliburn, of the British King Arthur. But his Sicilian majesty also gave, as a contribution to the Holy War, four large ships and fifteen galleys. On his return to Messina, he accompanied his guest for many miles, even as far as the town of Taormina; and before they parted there, it is said, he gave to Richard a letter, wherein the French king declared his majesty of England to be a traitor, who meant to break the peace and treaty he had concluded with the King of Sicily, and offered to assist Tancred to drive him and his English out of the island. Cœur de Lion, after a furious explosion, expressed a doubt whether Philip, his liege and sworn comrade in that pilgrimage, could be guilty of so much baseness. Tancred declared that the letter had really been delivered to him, as from the King of France, by the Duke of Burgundy; and he vowed that, if the duke should deny having so delivered it, he would made good his charge upon him, in the lists, by one of his barons.[4] When he arrived at the camp, Richard met Philip with a clouded brow,

---

[1] The Sicilian historians mention only one payment of 20,000 oncie, and this they put down to the account of the dota, or dower of Tancred's daughter.

[2] In the treaty, Richard styled him his "most dear nephew and heir," mentioning, however, the condition of his dying without children—"*Si forte sine prole nos obire contingeret.*"—Recueil des Historiens de France; Daru, *Hist. de la Bretagne.* The unfortunate Arthur was little more than two years old at the time of this contract. [3] *Holinshed.*

[4] There are several versions of this mysterious story; we have chosen that which appears most natural. If there was any deceit about the letter, it was practised by Tancred. It is said that before Richard's arrival the Sicilian prince had offered one of his daughters to Philip for his infant son, and that the French king had rejected the alliance. But, again, it is said, that, a few hours after Richard had left him at Taormina, Tancred met Philip at the same town, and passed the night with him in a friendly manner. The native historians are provokingly silent on nearly all the transactions of the crusaders in Sicily.

and a day or two after, in the course of one of their many altercations, he produced the letter, and asked the French king if he knew it. Philip pronounced it to be a vile forgery, and, changing defence into attack, accused Richard of seeking a pretext for breaking off his marriage with the French princess. All the clamour Richard had raised for his affianced bride, in the last months of his father's reign, was merely for political purposes : as soon as Henry died he dropped all mention of the Lady Aliz; and at this very moment, as Philip no doubt well knew, he had contracted a very different alliance, and was every day expecting another wife. "I see what it is," said Philip; "you seek a quarrel with me, in order not to marry my sister, whom by oath you are bound to marry; but of this be sure, that if you abandon her and take another, I will be all my life the mortal enemy of you and yours." Richard replied that he could not and never would marry the princess, as it was of public notoriety that his own father, Henry, had had a child by her; and, according to a minute relater of these curious passages, he produced many witnesses to prove to Philip the dishonour and shame of his own sister. True or false, this exposure was a cruel and degrading blow, not likely ever to be forgotten or forgiven.[1] For the present, however, Philip bartered his sister's honour for a pension, agreeing to release Richard from his previous matrimonial contract, and permit him to marry whatsoever wife he chose, for 2000 marks a-year, to be paid for the term of five years. Besides promising this money, Richard engaged to restore the Princess Aliz, together with the fortresses received as her marriage portion, as soon as he should return from the Holy Land.—[Eventually the lady was not restored till some years after that event, when she espoused the Count of Ponthieu.]—This precious arrangement, and the settlement of other differences, were confirmed on both sides by fresh oaths. Philip then got ready for sea, and after receiving some vessels and stores bountifully given him by Richard, he set sail on the 30th of March, 1191, for Acre. Richard, with a few of his most splendid galleys, accompanied him down the Straits of Messina, and returning the same evening to Reggio, on the Calabrian coast, took on board his new bride, who had been for some time in the neighbourhood, waiting only for the departure of the French king. This lady was Berengaria, the beautiful daughter of the King of Navarre. Richard had seen her in her own country a year or two before his father's death, and was passionately enamoured of her at the moment when, to annoy Henry, he was raising such a clamour for the Princess Aliz. His passion was disinterested; for he gained no territories by the union, and seems to have stipulated for no political advantages when he despatched his mother Eleanor to ask the hand of Berengaria. It is said that the fair maiden partook of his generous passion, and that, without being deterred by the many dangers and privations to which she exposed herself, she joyfully consented to travel with her mother-in-law from the Pyrenees to the Alps and Apennines, and thence to follow her husband beyond sea to the land of Paynim. Leaving Navarre with a suitable escort of barons, knights, and priests, the young Beren-

EFFIGY OF BERENGARIA, Queen of Richard I.[2]

---

[1] According to an old French writer the insult was "a nail stuck in and driven through the heart of Philip."—De Serres, *Inventaire Général de l'Hist. de France*. Roger of Hoveden gives the fullest account of this quarrel. See also *Dicrto*.

[2] The architectural parts of Queen Berengaria's tomb, from which the effigy is derived, were discovered in the ruined church of the abbey of L'Espau, near Mans, which had been converted into a barn. The effigy itself was concealed beneath a considerable quantity of wheat. Beside the effigy were lying the bones of the queen. Three men, who had assisted in the work of destruction, stated that the monument with the figure upon it stood in the centre of the aisle at the east end of the church; that there was no coffin found within it, but a small square box containing bones, pieces of linen, some stuff embroidered with gold, and a slate on which was an inscription. The slate alluded to in this statement was found in the possession of a canon of the church of St. Julien, at Mans. Upon it was engraved the inscription following:—"Mausoleum Istud Serenissime Berengariæ Anglorum Reginæ hujus Cenobii Fundatricis Inclitæ restauratum et in augustiorem locum hunc translatum fuit in eoq. recondita sunt ossa haec quae reperta fuerunt in antiquo tumulo die 27 Maii Anno Domini 1672." The effigy represents the queen with her hair unconfined, but partly concealed by the coverchief, over which is placed an elegant crown. Her mantle is fastened by a narrow band crossing her breast; a large permail or brooch richly set with stones confines her tunic at the neck. To an ornamented girdle which encircles her waist, is attached a small almoniere or purse to contain alms. The queen holds in her hands a book, singular from the circumstance of having embossed on the cover a second representation of herself as lying on a bier, with waxen torches burning in candlesticks by her side.—Stothard's *Monumental Effigies of Great Britain*. The tomb and effigy are supposed to belong to the commencement of the thirteenth century.

garia and Eleanor, whose activity was not destroyed by age, travelled by land to Naples, and from that gay city on through the passes of Monteforte and Bovino, and across the vast Apulian plain, to the ancient city of Brindisi, there to wait until the French king should be out of the way. As the expedition of Richard was so nearly ready for sea when the royal travellers arrived, it was not thought proper to delay its sailing, and, as the penitential season of Lent was not quite over, the marriage was not celebrated at Messina; and the queen-mother, having placed the bride under the matronly care of her own daughter Joan, the dowager queen of Sicily, embarked for England four days after.

The day after Eleanor's departure the whole fleet set sail for Acre. As a rapid current carried it through the Straits of Messina, it presented an imposing appearance, that called forth the involuntary admiration of the people of either shore—the Sicilians saying that so gallant an armament had never before been seen there, and never would be seen again. The size and beauty of the ships excited this admiration not less than their number. The flag of England floated over fifty-three galleys, thirteen dromones, "mighty great ships with triple sails,"[1] one hundred carikes or busses, and many smaller craft. Thirty busses from England had arrived just before, bringing out fresh stores and men. The mariners of England, however, were not then what centuries of struggle and experience have made them; and when a great tempest arose, soon after leaving the Sicilian sea, the whole navy was "sore tossed and turmoiled," and scattered in all directions, not a few of the ships being foundered or cast on shore.[2] After a narrow escape himself on the coast of Candia or Crete, Richard got safely into Rhodes; but the ship which bore his sister and his bride was not with him, and he passed several days in distressing anxiety as to their fate. At Rhodes he fell sick, and was detained there several days. Incapable of taking the sea himself, he despatched some of his swiftest vessels to look after the ladies and collect the scattered fleet. This storm blew more mischief to the petty tyrant of Cyprus than to any one else. One of the English scouts returned to Rhodes with the information that two of his ships had been cast ashore on the island of Cyprus, and that the people of the country had barbarously plundered the wrecks, and cast the mariners and crusaders into prison. Vowing vengeance, Richard embarked, and, departing immediately with all of the fleet that had joined him at Rhodes, made way, with press of oars and sails, for the devoted island. Off Limisso, or Limasol, then the principal seaport town of Cyprus, he found the galley of his bride and sister. The sovereign of the island was one Isaac, a prince of the imperial race of the Comneni, who pompously styled himself "Emperor of Cyprus." When harshly called upon for satisfaction, he put himself in a posture of defence, throwing out some armed galleys to the mouth of the harbour of Limasol, and drawing up his troops along shore. These troops were ill calculated to contend with the steel-clad warriors of Richard; for, with the exception of a body-guard which was splendidly armed and appointed, they had no defensive armour, but were half naked, and the mass of them had no better weapons than clubs and stones. Richard boarded and took the galleys, dispersed the troops, and made himself master of the city with little difficulty. The inhabitants fled, but had not time to carry off their property, which the crusaders made prize of. They found an abundance of provisions of all kinds; and when Queen Joan and Berengaria landed at Limasol, they were welcomed with a feast. Having rallied to make another impotent attempt at resistance, the Cypriots were surprised the next morning, and "killed like beasts," their "emperor" saving his life by fleeing "bare in serke and breke."[1] Isaac, who had now learned to his cost the might and fury of the enemy he had provoked, sent to sue for a conference of peace. Richard, gaily mounted on a Spanish charger, and splendidly attired in silk and gold, met the humbled Greek in a plain near Limasol. The terms he imposed were sufficiently hard. That very night the Greek fled to make another vain effort at resistance; but Richard had no great right to complain of this, seeing that he treated Isaac not as a reconciled enemy and ally, but as a prisoner of war, having actually placed guards over him, whose brute force the Greek defeated by a very excusable exercise of cunning. Despatching part of his army by land into the interior of the country, Richard embarked with the rest, and, sailing round the island, took all the maritime towns, and cut off Isaac's flight by sea, for he seized every ship, and even every boat, though of the smallest dimensions. Isaac fought another battle; but the contest was in every way unequal. Nicosia, the capital, surrendered, and Isaac's beautiful daughter fell into the hands of Richard, who gave her as a companion to Berengaria. Isaac, who doated on

---

[1] By this is meant that they were three-masted.
[2] It is said, however, by one who was on board the fleet, that the sailors did everything that it was possible for human skill to do; but old Vinesauf was a landsman, and not a good judge, and people then allowed very narrow limits to the extent of human skill in many things.

[1] *Robert of Brunne*. From *Vinesauf* and *Hoveden* it appears that Isaac, betrayed by the Cypriots, was surprised before he was out of bed, and fled without armour or clothes.

his child, lost all heart in losing her, and quitting a strong castle or fortified monastery in which he had taken refuge, he again sought the presence of the conqueror, and threw himself at his feet, imploring only for the restoration of his child, and for the preservation of his own life and limbs. The conqueror would not restore his fair captive, and he sent her father away to be confined in a strong castle at Tripoli, in Syria. The unfortunate captive was loaded with chains; but it is said that, in consideration of his rank, Richard ordered that his fetters should be forged of silver instead of rude iron.[1] If the Cypriots had been discontented with their old master, they had little reason to be satisfied with their new one. Richard's first act of government was to tax them to the amount of half of their moveable property, after which he gave them an empty confirmation of the rights and privileges which they had enjoyed in former times under the Emperors of Constantinople. The amount of provisions and stores of all kinds which he carried off was so considerable, that it enabled the crusaders to carry on their operations with much greater vigour and success than they could otherwise have done. Having conquered, and in a manner settled the island, he returned to Limasol, and at length celebrated his marriage with the Lady Berengaria, who was anointed and crowned by the Bishop of Evreux. All these important operations did not occupy more than a month, and granting the present government of the island to Richard de Camville, one of the constables of the fleet, and Robert de Turnham,[2] Richard embarked with his fleet for Acre. Sailing between Cyprus and the Syrian coast, he fell in with a dromon, or ship of the largest size, which was carrying troops and stores to the great Saladin. He attacked her with his usual impetuosity, threatening to crucify all his sailors if they suffered her to escape. She was taken after a gallant action, in which the superior height of her board, and an abundant use of the Greek fire, to which Richard's followers were as yet unaccustomed, gave her for some time a decided advantage. There were on board seven emirs, or Saracens of the highest rank, and 650—some say 1500—picked men. Thirty-five individuals only were saved, the rest were either massacred or drowned, the great ship sinking before the crusaders could remove much of her cargo.[3]

On the 8th of June an astounding clangour of trumpets and drums, and every instrument of war in the Christian camp, hailed the arrival of Richard and his host in the roadstead of Acre.

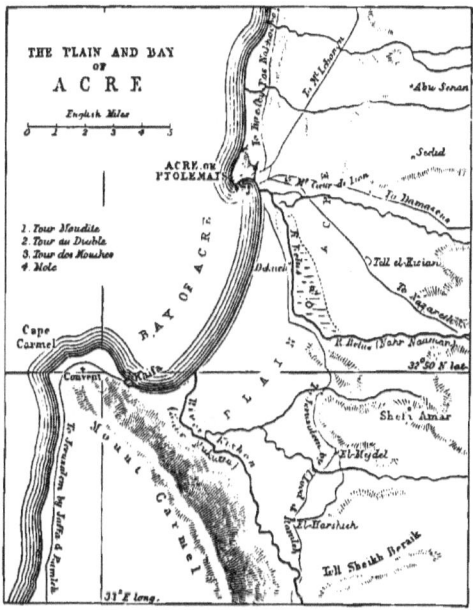

The welcome was sincere, for their aid was indispensable. The French king had arrived some time before, but had done nothing, and the affairs of the crusaders were in a deplorable condition; for, after prosecuting the siege of Acre the best part of two years, they were not only still outside the walls, but actually pressed and hemmed in, and almost besieged themselves, by Saladin, who occupied Mount Carmel and all the neighbouring heights with an immense army. The loss of human life was fearful. The sword and the plague had swept away six archbishops, twelve bishops, forty earls, and 500 barons, whose names are recorded in history, and 150,000 of "the meaner sort," who went to their graves without any such record.[4] This heavy draft upon population had been supplied by fresh and continuous arrivals from all parts of Christendom, for, like a modern conqueror, Europe then believed that the fate of Syria and the East lay

---

[1] Isaac died a prisoner four years after.
[2] Several of the Italian historians say he sold the government of Cyprus to the order of the Templars; but this does not appear very probable.
[3] Vinesauf; Hoveden; Bohadin, the Arab historian.
[4] We have taken the very lowest estimate. Vinesauf calculates that 300,000 Christians perished during the siege. Bohadin and other Arabic writers, carry the number to 500,000 or 600,000.

within the narrow circuit of Acre. The operations of the crusaders, which had languished for some weeks, were vigorously renewed on Richard's arrival; but the Kings of France and England quarrelled again almost as soon as they met; the besiegers became again inactive, and then threw away some thousands of lives from mere pique and jealousy of each other. The French and the English soldiery took a full share in the animosities of their respective leaders; and of the other bodies of crusaders, some sided with Philip, and some with Richard. The Genoese and Templars espoused the quarrel of France; the Pisans and Hospitallers stood for England; and, on the whole, it appears that Richard's more brilliant valour, and superior command of money and other means, rendered the English faction the stronger of the two. The French tried to take the town by an assault without any assistance from the English, and then the English, wishing to have all the honour to themselves, repeated the like experiment without the French, and with the like ill success. These two fatal attempts showed the necessity of co-operation, and another brief reconciliation was effected between the rivals.

Richard's personal exertions[1] attracted universal admiration in the camp, and gave rise to fresh

Acre, from the Beach.—Chesney's Euphrates Expedition.

jealousies in the breast of Philip. At length, being disappointed of aid from Cairo, and seeing that Saladin could no longer penetrate the Christian lines to throw in provisions, the brave Mussulman garrison offered to capitulate. After some negotiation, during which Philip and Richard once more disagreed, it was finally stipulated that the city should be surrendered to the crusaders, and that the Saracens, as a ransom for their lives (for their property, even to their arms, was forfeited), should restore the wood of the holy cross, set at liberty 1500 Christian captives, and pay 200,000 pieces of gold. Some thousands of Saracens were detained as hostages in the fortress for the performance of these conditions. Immediately afterwards—it was on the 12th of June, 1191—the crusaders entered Acre, and Saladin, evacuating all his positions, retired a short distance into the interior. The banners of the two kings were raised with equal honour on the ramparts; but it appears that Richard took the best house in the place for the accommodation of himself and family, leaving Philip to take up his lodgings with the Templars. Scarcely, however, had they entered this terrible town, ere the French king expressed his determination to return to Europe. The cause he alleged for his departure was the bad state of his health;[2] but this probably was not the true one—it certainly was not the only cause. Though Jerusalem was in the hands of the Mussulmans, there was a disputed succession to the throne among the Christians. Guy of Lusignan had worn the crown in right of his wife, a descendant of the great Godfrey of Bouillon, the first Christian King of Jerusalem; but Sybilla was dead, and Conrad, Marquis of Montferrat and Prince of Tyre, who had married her sister, contended that the sole right of Guy of Lusignan was extinct by the demise of his wife, and that the crown devolved to himself as the husband of the legitimate heiress. The dispute was referred to the English and French monarchs, and it was not likely that they, who, from the commencement of the crusade, had never agreed in anything, should act with concord in this important matter. As soon as Philip reached Acre, without waiting for the opinion of Richard, he declared in favour of the claims of Conrad, who seems to have been much better qualified for a throne that was to be won and maintained by the sword than his

---

[1] He worked like a common soldier at the heavy battering engines. When sick, he caused himself to be carried to the intrenchments on a silk pallet or mattress.
[2] Philip had been sick. Some of the French chroniclers accuse Richard of having given him poison!

miserable competitor Lusignan. Richard, however, swayed by other motives, or possibly merely out of pique, had declared against Conrad, and when Lusignan visited him as a suppliant in Cyprus, he had acknowledged him as King of Jerusalem, and, with his usual liberality, had given him a sum of money, his majesty being penniless and almost in want of bread. This subject had given rise to many disputes during the siege, and they were renewed with increased violence when the capture of Acre gave the French and English kings more leisure. In the end, Philip was obliged to yield so far to his fiery and determined rival as to allow that Lusignan should be King of Jerusalem during his life.

The King of France was otherwise irritated by the absolute will and constant domineering of his rival, who was as superior to him as an adventurous warrior, as he was superior to Richard in policy and political forethought. One of our old rhyming chroniclers no doubt hit part of the truth when he said—

"So that King Philip was annoyed there at the thing,
That there was not of him a word, but all of Richard the king."[1]

But, after all, we should be doing a manifest injustice to Philip's consummate king-craft, were we not to suppose that one of his strongest motives for quitting an unprofitable crusade, was to take advantage of Richard's absence in order to raise and consolidate the French kingdom—an end perfectly natural, and perhaps laudable in itself, however dishonourable the means that were employed to effect it. Dazzled as he was by dreams of chivalry and glory, Richard himself was yet not so blind as to overlook the danger that threatened him in the West; and, after his efforts to persuade Philip to remain had all failed, he exacted from him an oath not to make war upon any part of the territories of the English king, nor attack any of his vassals or allies, until at least forty days after the return of Richard from Palestine. Besides taking this oath, Philip agreed to leave at Acre 10,000 of his followers, to be immediately commanded by the Duke of Burgundy, who, however, was bound to recognize the superior authority of the English monarch. In the popular eye, Philip appeared as a deserter, and the mob of all nations that witnessed his departure from Acre hissed him and cursed him.[2] His absence, however, saved him from direct participation in an atrocious deed. Forty days was the term fixed for the fulfilment of the articles of capitulation. Receiving neither the Christian captives, nor the cross, nor the money, Richard made several applications to Saladin, who was unable or unwilling to fulfil the conditions, though he sent to offer Richard some costly presents for himself. A rumour—apparently false—was spread through the Christian camp and the town of Acre, that Saladin had massacred his Christian captives, and the soldiers demanded instant vengeance, making a fearful riot, and killing several of their officers who attempted to pacify them. On the following day the term of forty days expired. At an appointed hour a signal was given, and all the Saracen hostages were led out beyond the barriers of the French and English camps, and butchered by the exulting and rejoicing crusaders. Richard presided over the slaughter at one camp—the Duke of Burgundy at the other. Between 2000 and 3000 prisoners[3] were thus destroyed, and only a few emirs and Mohametans of rank were saved from the carnage, in the hope of obtaining valuable ransoms from their families. Some centuries had to elapse ere this deed excited any horror or disgust in Christendom. At the time, and indeed long after, it was considered as a praiseworthy smiting of the infidels—as a sacrifice acceptable to Heaven.

Having restored the battered works of Acre, Richard prepared to march upon Jerusalem. The generality of the crusaders by no means shared his impatience, "for the wine (says old Vinesauf) was of the very best quality, and the city abounded with most beautiful girls"—the gravest knights had made a Capua of Acre. At length, however, Richard tore them from these enjoyments, and, leaving behind him his sister and wife, and the fair Cypriot, and strictly prohibiting women from following the camp, he began his march on the 22d of August. Thirty thousand men, of all countries, obeyed his orders, marching in five divisions: the Templars led the van; the knights of St. John brought up the rear. Every night, when the army halted, the heralds of the several camps cried aloud three times, "Save the holy sepulchre!" and every soldier bent his knee, and said "Amen!" Saladin, who had been reinforced from all parts, infested their march every day, and encamped near them every night, with an army greatly superior in numbers. On the 7th of September, Richard brought him to a general action near Azotus, the Ashdod of the Bible, on the sea-shore, and about nine miles from Ascalon; and after a display of valour which was never surpassed, and of more cool conduct and generalship than might have been expected, he gained a complete victory. Mourning the loss of 7000 men and thirty-two

[3] We have again taken the very lowest number. Bohadin, the Arab, says that 3000 were destroyed by Richard alone, and that the Duke of Burgundy sacrificed a like number. Hoveden says that 5000 were slain by the king and the duke.

---

[1] *Robert of Gloucester.*   [2] *Vinesauf; Roger of Hoveden.*

emirs, Saladin, the victor of many a field, retreated in great disorder, finding time, however, to lay waste the country, and dismantle the towns he could not garrison or defend; and Richard advanced without further opposition to Jaffa, the Joppa of Scripture, of which he took possession. As the country in advance of that position was still clear of enemies, the Lion-heart would have followed up his advantages, but many of the crusaders, less hardy than himself, were worn out by the heat of the climate, and the rapid marches on which he had already led them; and the French barons urged the necessity of restoring the fortifications of Jaffa before they advanced. No sooner had Richard consented to this arrangement, than the crusaders, instead of prosecuting the work with vigour, abandoned themselves to a luxurious ease; and Richard himself gave many of his days to the sports of the field, disregarding the evident fact that Saladin was again making head, and that hordes of Saracens were scouring the country in detached parties. Several skirmishes ensued. On such onslaughts, say the chroniclers, Richard's cry was still "St. George! St. George!" Many romantic feats and adventures are related of this flower of chivalry—this pearl of crusading princes. His battle-axe seems to have been the weapon most familiar to his stalwart arm. He had caused it to be forged by the best smiths in England before he departed for the East, and twenty pounds of steel were wrought into the head of it, that he might "break therewith the Saracens' bones."[1] Nothing, it was said, could resist this mighty axe, and wherever it fell, horseman and horse went to the ground. When the fortifications of Jaffa were restored, the Lion-heart was duped into a further loss of time, by a negotiation artfully proposed by Saladin, and skilfully conducted by his brother Saphadin, who came and went between the two armies, and spite of his turban, ingratiated himself with Richard. At last, the crusaders set forth from Jaffa; but it was now the month of November, and incessant rains, nearly equal to those in tropical countries, wetted them to the skin, rusted their arms, spoiled their provisions, and rendered the roads almost impassable. Crossing the plain of Sharon, where "the rose of Sharon and the lily of the valley" no longer bloomed, they pitched their tents at Ramula,[2] only fifteen miles in advance of Jaffa; but the wind tore them up and rent them. They then sought quarters at Bethany, where they were within twelve miles of the Holy City; but their condition became daily worse—famine, disease, and desertion thinned their ranks, and Richard was compelled, sore against his will, to turn his back on Jerusalem. He retreated rapidly to Ascalon, followed closely by the loose light cavalry of the Kourds and Turks, who, though they could make no impression on the main body, or even penetrate the rear-guard, where the gallant knights of St. John wielded sword and lance, yet did much mischief by cutting off stragglers, and caused great distress by keeping the whole force constantly on the alert by night as well as by day. Ascalon, so celebrated in the ancient history of the Jews, was still a city of great importance, being the connecting link between the Mahometans in Jerusalem and the Mahometans in Egypt. Saladin had dismantled its fortifications, which Richard now determined to restore in all haste. To set a good example, he worked, as he had already done at Acre, upon the walls and battlements, like a common mason, and he expected every prince and noble would do the same; for the common

RUINS OF ASCALON.[3]—From Forbin, Voyage en Orient.

---

[1] Weber, *Metrical Romances*.
[2] Ramula, Ramla, or Ramah, is the Arimathea of Scripture. A little beyond it begin the almost impracticable mountain defiles of Judea, which extend to Jerusalem.
[3] The town stood on an extensive semicircular hill, abrupt towards the sea, but declining very gradually landward. Its walls, with their towers and battlements, still remain; and among the ruins, mingled with vestiges of more ancient date, are a great Gothic church, a palace, and a chapel dedicated to the Virgin. Forty columns of rose granite, still standing, are supposed to be the remains of a temple dedicated to the "heavenly Venus," mentioned by Herodotus as having been plundered by the Scythians, B.C. 630. There are also the remains of a Roman amphitheatre. The site is entirely abandoned to jackals and other wild creatures. The Arabs call it "Djaurah," and believe it to be the abode of evil spirits.

crusaders required a stimulus, and the Saracens seemed to be gathering for an assault or siege. All the men of rank, with the exception of the proud Duke of Austria, thought it no dishonour to do as the King of England did. There was an old quarrel between these two princes. During the siege of Acre, the Duke of Austria took one of the towers, and planted his banner upon it; Richard, enraged at this step, which appears to have been, at least, out of order, tore down the banner, and cast it into the ditch. Such an affront could never be forgotten. And now, when urged by Richard to work on the fortifications of Ascalon, the duke replied that he would not, seeing that he was the son neither of a mason nor of a carpenter. Upon this, it is reported that Richard struck him or kicked him, and turned him and his vassals out of the town, with threatening and most insulting language. Notwithstanding the duke's refusal, the greatest personages there, including bishops and abbots, as well as lay lords, worked as masons and carpenters, and the repairs were soon completed. Richard then turned his attention to the other towns which Saladin had dismantled, or which had not been previously fortified; and in the course of the winter, and the following spring, he made the whole coast from Ascalon to Acre a chain of well-fortified posts; and below Acre he rebuilt the walls of Gaza. Before these works were completed, however, his forces were considerably diminished; his lavish generosity had hitherto kept the French and other soldiers, not his subjects, together; but now his treasures were nearly exhausted. Hence arose a wonderful cooling of zeal—a disposition even to criticise his military skill, and a pretty general defection on the part of all except his English and Norman subjects. Acre, a pleasanter place than Ascalon, was again crowded with jealous and mercenary chieftains, and became a very hot-bed of corruption and political intrigue. The Genoese and Pisans fought openly in the streets of the town, hiding their old animosities under the pretence of combating for the rights of the lawful King of Jerusalem; for Richard's treaty in favour of Guy had not settled that question. The Genoese had declared for Conrad of Montferrat—the Pisans for Guy of Lusignan; and when Conrad himself, disregarding the treaty and the power of the English king, joined his troops with those of the Genoese, a sort of civil war seemed imminent among all the Christians in Palestine. On this, Richard moved from Ascalon to Acre, effected a reconciliation between the Genoese and Pisans, and forced Conrad to retire. He attempted to conciliate that nobleman, who had given him many other causes of complaint; but Montferrat insultingly rejected all overtures, and withdrew to his strong town of Tyre, where he opened a correspondence with the common enemy, Saladin, and where he was soon joined by 600 French knights and soldiers, whom he had seduced from Richard's garrison at Ascalon. Saladin, who was, in all respects, a rival worthy of Richard, gaining fresh heart from the dissensions of the Christians, once more condensed his forces, in the hope of striking a decisive blow. About this time the Lion-heart, in some distress of mind, wrote to the abbot of Clairvaux,[1] who had great interest in several of the European courts, earnestly entreating him to rouse the princes and people of Christendom to arms, in order that he might have a force sufficient for the occasion, and that Jerusalem, the inheritance of the Lord, might be rescued, and made secure for the future. This letter apparently was scarcely despatched when he received others from his mother Eleanor, informing him that his own throne in England was beset by the greatest of dangers. At this crisis he opened a negotiation for peace, declaring to Saladin that he wanted nothing more than the possession of Jerusalem, and the wood of the true cross. To this Saladin is reported to have replied, that Jerusalem was as dear to the Mussulmans as to the Christians,[2] and that his conscience and the law of the Prophet would not permit him to connive at idolatry or the worshipping of a piece of wood.

Another proposal which Richard is said to have made was still more unlikely to be complied with: it was, that the kingdom of Jerusalem should be peacefully occupied by the contending powers under a government partly Christian and partly Mahometan; and that this strange rule should be ratified by the marriage of Joan, Richard's sister, to Saphadin, the brother of Saladin. If such a proposal was ever made, we can easily believe how keenly it was opposed both by Christian and Mussulman, and how speedily it was silenced. Centuries, indeed, were yet to elapse before such friendly co-operation could be established between the followers of these opposite creeds, and hence the general scepticism with which the narrative of this treaty between Richard and Saladin has been regarded. It is pleasing, however, to find that amidst the atrocities of the crusade, and the wholesale massacres of captives on both sides, the contending parties evinced a chivalrous courtesy towards each other during the intervals of truce, which modern wars have seldom surpassed. The soldiers of both armies were wont at these seasons to mingle in

---

[1] The successor of St. Bernard, who had done more than any other single individual, after Peter the Hermit, to promote the Crusades.

[2] The Arabs still call Jerusalem "El Gootz," or "The Blessed City."

friendly intercourse and military sports; and when the Lion-heart himself was stretched on a bed of sickness, his noble rival sent him presents of the rich fruits of Syria, and the more valuable luxury of snow from the distant mountains in the interior. It is also stated that Saladin had sought and obtained the honour of Christian knighthood, and that his nephew, the son of Saphadin, had received the accolade, in like manner, from the sword of Richard himself.

In order to reconcile parties, and facilitate his own return to Europe, Richard now abandoned the cause of Guy of Lusignan, whom he liberally recompensed by the gift of the island of Cyprus, and consented that Conrad of Montferrat, who was supported by the French, the German, and the Genoese factions, should be crowned King of Jerusalem. But Conrad was murdered in the streets of Tyre, while preparing for his coronation, by two of the assassins, the fanatic subjects of the Old Man of the Mountain. The murderers were seized and put to the torture. Hoveden and Vinesauf both say that the wretches declared that they had murdered Conrad by the order of their master, in revenge for injuries done to his people, and insults offered to himself by Conrad, whose imprudent quarrel with the Old Man of the Mountain was notorious. Bohadin, the Arab historian, indeed, affirms that the men said they were employed by the King of England; but another Arabic writer, of equal weight, says that the murderers would make no confession whatever, but that, triumphing amidst their agonies, they rejoiced that they had been destined by Heaven to suffer in so just and glorious a cause; and this account agrees better with the character of the wonderful association to which they belonged, and is more probable than any other. So little, indeed, did Conrad himself join in these first suspicions, that, with his dying breath, he recommended his widow to Richard's protection. But the French king, the German emperor, the Austrian duke, and other sovereigns, were burning with spite and revenge against him; and Philip, more especially, who was contemplating an attack on Richard's dominions, in order to cover his infamy, filled all the West with exclamations against his rival's perfidy. In the meanwhile the French within the town, declaring that Richard had employed the murderers, rose in arms, and demanded from the widow of Conrad that she would resign Tyre to them: this she refused to do, and the people, siding with the countess, took up arms against the French. In the midst of the tumult Count Henry of Champagne, King Richard's own nephew, made his appearance, and, at the invitation of the people, took possession of Tyre, and the other territories in Palestine which had been held by Conrad. Soon after, by marrying Conrad's widow, young Henry of Champagne received her claim to the imaginary crown, and the crusaders, with the Christians in the country, generally acknowledged him as King of Jerusalem.

Richard had attempted to conceal his many causes of uneasiness; and when the army showed that they were aware that his presence was most earnestly prayed for in his own dominions, he issued a proclamation stating his fixed resolution of remaining in Palestine another year. By his promises and exertions he again restored something like unanimity of purpose, and at the end of May the crusaders once more set out on their march towards Jerusalem, under his command. Early in June he encamped in the valley of Hebron, where he received some messengers from England bringing fresh accounts of plots within, and armed confederacies without his dominions. We follow the most consistent, though not the most generally received account, in saying that, on this intelligence, and at the prospect of the increasing power of the Saracens, and of the increasing weakness and destitution of the Christian forces, to whose wants he could no longer administer, Richard now came to a stand, and turned his heart to the West. A council, assembled at his suggestion, declared that, under present circumstances, it would be better to march and besiege Cairo, whence Saladin drew his main supplies, than to attack Jerusalem. This decision was perhaps a wise one, but it came too late. Richard, however, pretended that he would follow it, upon which the Duke of Burgundy wrote a song reflecting, in severe terms, on his vacillation. Richard did not reply by despatching two emissaries of the Old Man of the Mountain, or by adopting any other unfair measure; he revenged himself with the same instrument with which the offence had been given, and wrote a satire on the vices and foibles of the Duke of Burgundy. It could not be expected, however, that the Lion-heart should renounce his great enterprise without feelings of deep mortification. It is related of him that, when a friend led him to the summit of a mountain which commanded a full view of Jerusalem, he raised his shield before his eyes, declaring that he was not worthy to look upon the Holy City which he had not been able to redeem. If the expedition to Egypt had ever been seriously contemplated, it was presently seen that it was impracticable; for as soon as a counter-march from the Hebron was spoken of, all discipline abandoned the camp, and, after some conflicts among themselves, the mass of the French and Germans deserted the standard altogether. Richard then fell back upon Acre. Taking advantage of the circumstance, the vigilant Saladin descended from the mountains of Judea and took the town of Jaffa all but the citadel. At the first breath of this intelligence, Richard ordered such troops as he had been able to keep together to march by land, while he, with only seven vessels, should hasten by sea to the relief of Jaffa. On arriving in the road he found the beach covered with a host of the enemy; but, turning a deaf ear to the advice and fears of his companions, and shouting, "Cursed for ever be he that followeth me not!" he leaped into the water. The knights in the ships were too high-minded to abandon their king, and this small body dispersed the Saracens and retook the town. On the following day, between night and morning, Saladin came up with the main body of his army, and Richard, who had been joined by the troops that had marched by land, went out to meet him in the open country behind Jaffa. The Lion-heart made up for his immense inferiority in point of number by careful and judicious arrangement; and the victory of Jaffa, which was most decisive, is generally esteemed as the greatest of his many exploits. Overpowered by a generous admiration, Saphadin, seeing him dismounted, sent him, during the action, two magnificent horses, and on one of these Richard pursued his successes till night-fall. Every champion that met him that day was killed or dismounted; and the ordinary troops, whenever he headed a charge against them, are said to have turned and fled at the very sight of him. It was by deeds like these that Richard left a traditionary fame behind him, that grew and brightened with the passing years, and that his name became a word of fear in the mouth of the Mussulman natives.

JAFFA.¹—From Forbin, Voyage en Orient.

¹ Jaffa, or Joppa, is built upon a conical eminence overhanging the sea. The town is girt on the land side by a wall, with towers at unequal distances. Its harbour is so choked with sand that small boats only can enter. The roadstead is dangerous, the anchorage being near a ledge of rocks. Jaffa is the common landing-place of the pilgrims who resort to Jerusalem, of which place it may be considered the port.

As the battle of Jaffa was the most brilliant so also was it the last fought by the Lion-heart in the Holy Land. His health and the health of his glorious adversary were both declining; and a mutual respect facilitated the terms of a treaty which was concluded shortly after. A truce was agreed upon for three years, three months, three weeks, three days, and three hours; Ascalon was to be dismantled, after Richard had been reimbursed the money it had cost him; but Jaffa and Tyre, with all the castles and all the country on the coast between them, were to be left to the peaceful enjoyment of the Christians. The pilgrims of the West were to have full liberty of repairing to Jerusalem at all seasons, without being subjected to those tolls, taxes, and persecutions which had originally provoked the Crusades. All parties immediately prepared to avail themselves of the treaty, and since they could not enter Jerusalem as conquerors, to visit it as licensed pilgrims. A violent fever, brought on by his tremendous exertions in the field of Jaffa, is said to have been the cause why Richard himself did not visit Jerusalem; but it is at least probable that his reluctance to enter merely on sufferance that town which he had so vehemently hoped to conquer, had some share in this omission.

In the month of October, 1192, on the feast-day of St. Dionysius, Richard finally set sail from Acre with his queen, his sister Joan, the Cypriot princess, and the surviving bishops, earls, and knights of England, Normandy, Anjou, and Aquitaine. The next morning he took a last view of the mountains of Lebanon and the hills above the Syrian shore. With outstretched arms he exclaimed, "Most holy land, I commend thee to God's keeping. May he give me life and health to return and rescue thee from the infidel." A storm arose and scattered the fleet—it was the usual season for tempestuous weather in the Mediterranean; but people attributed the storm to the wrath of Heaven at the Christians sailing away and leaving the tomb and the cross of Christ unredeemed. Some of the vessels were wrecked on the hostile shores of Egypt and Barbary, where the crews were made slaves; others reached friendly ports, and, in time, returned to England. The galley in which Richard's wife and the other ladies were embarked reached Sicily in safety. It is not very clear why Richard sailed in another vessel, or why he did not take his way homeward through the friendly land of Navarre; but we are told that when within three days' sail of the city of Marseilles, fearing the malice of his numerous enemies, he suddenly changed his course for the Adriatic, resolving, it should seem, to pursue his way homeward from the head of that sea through Styria and Germany. He reached the island of Corfu about the middle of November, and there he hired three small galleys to carry him and his suite, which consisted of Baldwin of Bethune, a priest, Anselm, the chaplain, and a few Knights Templars — in all twenty individuals. After escaping capture by the Greeks, who were among his numerous enemies, he landed at Zara, on the coast of Dalmatia, where his liberal expenditure attracted attention, and defeated the object of his disguise. He had put on the humble weeds of a pilgrim, hoping that this dress, with his beard and hair, which he suffered to grow long, would enable him to cross the Continent without being discovered. A storm drove him on the coast of Istria, between Venice and Aquileia. From this point he and his companions, crossing the Friuli mountains, proceeded inland to Goritz, a principal town of Carinthia. He could hardly have taken a worse course; for Maynard, the governor of this town, was a near relation to Conrad of Montferrat. Richard sent a page to Maynard to ask for a passport for Baldwin of Bethune and Hugh the merchant, who were pilgrims returning from Jerusalem. To forward his request, the young man presented a very valuable ring as a proof of his master the merchant's good-will towards the governor. Maynard, much struck with the beauty and value of the ruby, exclaimed, "This is the present of a prince, not of a merchant; your master's name is not Hugh, but King Richard: tell him, from me, that he may come and go in peace." The king was alarmed at this discovery, and, having purchased some horses, he fled by night. Baldwin of Bethune and seven others who remained behind, were arrested by Maynard, and the news was spread far and wide that the King of England was advancing into Germany in a helpless state. The fugitives rode on without accident or molestation till they reached Freisach, in the territory of Salzburg, where Richard was recognized by a Norman knight in the service of Frederick of Beteson, another near connection of Conrad. The Norman's sense of duty to his native prince overcame the love of money—for a large reward had been offered for the detection and apprehension of the disguised king—and instead of seizing him, he warned him of his danger, and presented him with a swift horse. Richard escaped with one knight and a boy who spoke the language of the country, but all the rest of his companions who had been able to keep up with him thus far were taken and thrown into prison. After tra-velling three days and three nights without entering a house, and almost without nourishment of any kind, he was compelled by hunger and sickness to enter Erperg, a village close to Vienna. His ignorance of the country was probably the cause of his lighting on a spot which, of all others, he ought most carefully to have avoided. Though sensible of his danger, Richard was too weak to renew his flight. He sent the boy to the marketplace of Vienna to purchase provisions and a few comforts which he greatly needed. With his usual thoughtlessness in these matters, he had given the boy a quantity of money, and dressed him in costly clothes. These things excited attention, but the messenger eluded inquiry by saying that his master was a very rich merchant, and would presently make his appearance in Vienna. The boy was again sent into the town to make purchases, and for some days escaped further notice; but one day that he went as usual, the citizens saw in his girdle a pair of such gloves as were not worn save by kings and princes. The poor lad was instantly seized and scourged, and on being threatened with torture and the cutting out of his tongue, he confessed the truth, and revealed the retreat of the king. A band of Austrian soldiers surrounded the house where Richard was, forgetting his pains and anxieties in a deep sleep. Surprised and overpowered as he was, Richard drew his sword, and refused to surrender to any but their chief. That chief soon made his appearance in the person of his deadliest enemy, Leopold, Duke of Austria, who had arrived from the Holy Land some time before him. "You are fortunate," said Leopold, with a triumphant smile, as he received the sword which had often made him quail; "and you ought to consider us rather as deliverers than as enemies: for, by the Lord, if you had fallen into the hands of the Marquis Conrad's friends, who are hunting for you everywhere, you had been but a dead man though you had had a thousand lives." The duke then committed the king to the castle of Tiernsteign, which belonged to one of his barons called Hadmar of Cunring.[1]

When the Emperor Henry, the degenerate son of the great Frederic Barbarossa, was informed of this arrest, he claimed the prisoner, saying, "A duke must not presume to imprison a king— that belongs to an emperor." Henry, the sixth of the name in the list of emperors, and whom old historians designate as a "beggar of a prince, ferocious and avaricious,"[2] hated Richard almost

---

[1] There are several versions of Richard's adventures from the time he left Acre to his captivity in the hands of the emperor, but they do not differ very essentially, and are about equally romantic. We have adopted what appears to us the simplest and most consistent story, the chief authorities being Hoveden, Brompton, R. Coggeshall, William of Newbury, and Matthew Paris. [2] Legendre, *Hist. de France*.

as much as Leopold of Austria did. This arose chiefly out of the English king's close alliance with Tancred of Sicily, whom the emperor held as the usurper of his or his wife Constance's rights. In the summer of 1191, the year in which Richard sailed from Messina for Acre, Henry, accompanied by his Sicilian wife, advanced with a powerful German army into the south of Italy, and laid siege to the city of Naples, which made a faithful and gallant stand for Tancred. During the heats of summer a *malaria* fever carried off a vast number of his men, and some nobles of high rank; and, as soon as Henry fell sick himself, he raised the siege of Naples, and made a disgraceful retreat. Tancred then established himself on the disputed throne more firmly than ever, nor had the emperor been able to retrieve his honour in the South. He was, however, at the moment of Richard's capture, engaged in preparations for that object, and he was overjoyed at an event which would save him from the dangerous hostility of so great a warrior and so powerful a prince; for the English king, it will be remembered, had entered into an alliance, offensive and defensive, with the occupant of the Sicilian throne, and Henry and his advisers had little doubt that, if he reached England in time, Richard would perform his part of the treaty, and prevent the success of the emperor.[2] The Duke of Austria would not resign his prisoner without a reservation of his own claims, and a payment, or at least a promise, of a large sum of money from Henry. The disgraceful sale and transfer took place at the feast of Easter, 1193, after which, it appears that even in Germany, Richard was entirely lost sight of, and men knew not where he was confined for some time.

In following the romantic adventures of one who was rather a knight-errant than a king, and whose history is more that of a crusade than a reign,' we have strayed far and long from England. And what were the home events during the interval? Our information is scanty, but enough is on record to show that they were of a gloomy nature.

The tragedy of the Jews, enacted at Richard's coronation, was speedily repeated in several of the other principal towns of the kingdom, beginning at Lynn, in Norfolk, in the month of February, 1190, while Richard was in Normandy. All these horrors, indeed, were committed before he sailed for Palestine; but though so near home he was unable or unwilling to check them in their progress, or inflict a proper punishment on the offenders. Within a month the populace rose and robbed and slaughtered the Jews at Norwich, Stamford, St. Edmundsbury, and Lincoln. The great massacre of York was not a mere popular tumult; it was conducted in a systematic manner, and assuredly had for one of its objects the destruction of the bonds that were evidence of, and security for the great debts owing by the nobles to the York Jews. In this horrid affair 500 Jews, besides women and children, had recourse to mutual slaughter that they might escape the more terrible alternative of falling into the hands of their enemies.

The next important events during Richard's absence arose out of the struggle for power between Hugh Pudsey, the Bishop of Durham, and Longchamp, the Bishop of Ely. The reader has been already informed how Pudsey purchased the post of chief justiciary for 1000 marks. Richard, before he departed from England, unfairly nominated a new regency and appointed other justiciaries, by which measures Pudsey's bought authority was wofully reduced. These additional justiciaries were Hugh Bardolf, William Briwere, and Longchamp, the last-named being the royal favourite, in whose hands Richard openly showed his intention of placing the whole power of the government. Besides his justiciaryship, Long-

---

[1] Tiernsteign, or Dürrenstein, is a small town situated on the left bank of the Danube, forty-one miles west by north from Vienna. The castle, perched upon a craggy sterile rock, overlooks the town, and behind, at a higher elevation, rises the Wunderberg, covered with a dark wood of fir. In the town are the fine ruins of a monastery of the Augustine order.

[2] Tancred died at the end of 1193, during Richard's imprisonment. He died a king, and transmitted the crown to his young son, William, who, however, could not keep it on his head. The Emperor Henry, in 1195, enriched with Richard's ransom, invaded his dominions, and became master of them after much treachery and bloodshed. The cruelties committed by the jailer of Cœur de Lion were most atrocious; his advent in Sicily and Naples was made memorable by an apparently interminable process of burning, hanging, blinding, and mutilating.

[3] *Sir James Mackintosh.*

champ held the chancellorship, for which he had paid 3000 marks. He was, moreover, intrusted with the custody of the Tower of London. He was a man of great worldly wisdom, activity, and talent for business; his ambition was immense, and must soon have made itself felt; but the first accusation his opponents seem to have brought against him was his lowness of birth. His grandfather, they said, had been nothing but a serf in the diocese of Beauvais. Richard, however, who did not judge of him by the condition of his grandfather, issued letters-patent, addressed to all his lieges, commanding them to obey Longchamp in all things, even as they would obey the king himself. He also wrote to the pope, to obtain for him the legation of England and Ireland; and when Longchamp was appointed legate—which he was immediately—his power in spiritual matters completed his authority.

Poor Pudsey would not, without a struggle, sink into the obscurity for which he seems to have been best fitted. Complaints against Longchamp's excessive power had been sent after Richard, and he arrived in great triumph in London with letters from the king, importing that he should be restored to some part, or to the whole of his former authority. Although Longchamp was absent from London, his rival received an immediate check there from the barons of the exchequer, who refused to admit him on the bench. Thus rejected, Pudsey posted after Longchamp, who was in the north, and surrounded by an armed force devoted to his interest. When the brother bishops met, he of Ely was all courtesy and compliance. He said he was quite willing to obey the king's commands; and then he invited his lordship of Durham to visit him that day se'nnight in the royal castle of Tickhill. Pudsey, with "singular simplicity," accepted the invitation; and as soon as he was within the castle walls Longchamp laid hands on him, exclaiming, "As sure as my lord the king liveth, thou shalt not depart hence until thou hast surrendered all the castles which thou holdest. This is not bishop arresting bishop, but chancellor arresting chancellor." Nor was Pudsey released from this duresse until he surrendered the castle of Windsor, and the custody of the forest, together with the shrievalty of the county, as well as the earldom of Northumberland and the lordship of Sadburgh—everything, in short, which he had purchased from the king. Longchamp's power was now without check or control. He had the whole powers of civil and military, and, we may add, ecclesiastical government; and he is represented as tyrannizing equally over clergy and laity. "Had he continued in office," said his enemies, "the kingdom would have been wholly exhausted; not a girdle would have remained to the man, nor a bracelet to the woman, nor a ring to the knight, nor a gem to the Jew." Another writer says he was more than a king to the laity, and more than a pope to the clergy. Abroad and at home he made a display of as much or more power and parade than had been exhibited by any Norman king. A numerous guard always surrounded his house; wherever he went he was attended by 1000 horse; and when he passed the night at an abbey, or any house on the road, his immense and greedy retinue consumed the produce of three whole years—a poetical exaggeration, implying that they ate and drank, and probably wasted a great deal. He was a munificent patron of minstrels, troubadours, and jongleurs; he enticed many of them over from France, and these sang his praises in the public places, saying there was not such a man in the world.[1] It is evident that Longchamp was vain of his authority; but there is nothing to indicate that he was not most loyal to the king, and anxious for the preservation of peace in the kingdom. The worst shades in his portrait were put in by men who were notoriously disloyal to Richard, and careless of deluging the country with blood, so long as they fancied that they were forwarding their own views; and it was the bishop's decided opposition to these men that first called forth the accusations against him. Peter of Blois, whose testimony carries no small weight, speaks most highly of Longchamp, and styles him a man famed for wisdom and unbounded generosity, as also for his amiable, benevolent, and gentle temper. In those turbulent times, and with such crafty, remorseless opponents as Prince John and his advisers, it was almost impossible that he should preserve peace; but while the ambitious and the great envied him, it is probable that the humbler and quieter classes in the land saw him with pleasure get that power into his hands which alone could give him a chance of averting the storm. He was the first to see that John was endeavouring to secure the succession to the throne, and he steadily opposed those pretensions. After many violent dissensions, John wrote to his brother to tell him that the chief justiciary was ruining king and kingdom, and several barons of his faction put their signatures or crosses to this letter. Richard, whose confidence in Longchamp was scarcely to be shaken, sent, however, from Messina, two letters-patent, in which he ordered that, *if* the accusations against him were true, then Walter, Archbishop of Rouen, was to assume the regency, or chief justiciaryship, with William Mareschal and Geoffrey Fitz-Peter as his colleagues; if false, the three were, nevertheless, to be associated with

---

[1] Sir Francis Palgrave, *Introduct. Rot. Cur. Reg.*; *Matt. Par.*; *Hoved.*; *Neub.*; *Gervase.*

him in the government. Although these letters are preserved in the contemporary chronicle of Ralph de Diceto, their authenticity has been questioned; and it appears quite certain that if they were really written, Richard repented of his doubts, and that, immediately before he set sail from Messina, he addressed letters to his subjects in nearly the same terms as those written about a year before from France, requiring them all to obey Longchamp, whom he again mentions with the greatest affection and honour. It is also equally certain, that though the Archbishop of Rouen came into England from Sicily, he never showed any royal order until a year later, when Longchamp was overwhelmed by his enemies.

As soon as John knew for a certainty that his brother had departed from Sicily, beyond which the real perils of the crusade were supposed to begin, he assumed the state and bearing of an heir-apparent about to enter upon his inheritance. He knew that Richard had named his nephew Arthur for his heir, but that circumstance irritated without discouraging him; he felt that a child would be no formidable rival if he could only dispose of Longchamp, who was bent on doing his master's will in all things, and who, by Richard's orders, had opened a treaty with the King of Scotland, to support Arthur's claims in case of necessity. The decisive conflict, which had been postponed as long as Richard was in Europe, began as soon as his loving brother thought he was fairly in Asia. Gerard de Camville, a factious baron and a partizan of John, claimed the custody of Lincoln Castle, and kept that place in defiance of the regent's authority. Raising an army, Longchamp marched to Lincoln; but, while he was besieging the castle, John put himself at the head of a still more numerous army and attacked the royal castles of Nottingham and Tickhill, and took them both after a siege of two days. This done, he sent a threatening message to the regent. Longchamp was taken by surprise; he gave up the siege at Lincoln, and Gerard de Camville did homage for his castle to John.[1] The regent then convened the chiefs of the king's army and the barons most attached to Richard, and warned them that John was seeking the government: but he was not properly supported, and being compelled to yield, a truce, most disadvantageous to Longchamp, was concluded between the contending parties. He was forced to agree that a certain number of the royal castles, the possession of which had hitherto constituted his greatest strength, should be placed in the custody of various bishops and barons, who were sworn to keep the fortresses in the king's fealty until he should return from Palestine; but should he die during his pilgrimage, then they were to deliver them to John. At the same time another concession, of almost equal importance, was extorted from Longchamp; the settlement in favour of Arthur was formally set aside, and, the regent himself directing the act, the earls and primates of the kingdom took the oath of fealty to John, acknowledging him, should Richard die without issue, as heir to the throne.[2] For a short time John was satisfied with the progress he had made, and left to the chancellor-regent his places and honours; but the tranquillity thus insured was disturbed by circumstances artfully arranged.

Geoffrey, Archbishop of York, the son of Henry II. by "Fair Rosamond," had been compelled to swear that he would live out of England. He was now preparing to return to obtain possession of his church. The whole board of justiciaries joined their chief in prohibiting his landing; and Longchamp, fairly acting in the exercise of his authority, commanded the sheriffs to arrest Geoffrey, should he disregard the injunction. At the instigation of his half-brother John, Geoffrey defied the regent, and landed at Dover, where, however, he was presently obliged to take refuge in a church. When the requisition was made by the sheriff or the constable of Dover, he replied that he would never submit to that "traitor, the Bishop of Ely." It was required of him that he should swear fealty anew or depart the kingdom. For three days he refused to answer, and his asylum was respected the while; but on the fourth morning the officers broke into the church where the archbishop had just concluded mass, seized him at the foot of the altar, and, after literally dragging him through the streets, lodged him in Dover Castle. At the news of this transaction, which excited considerable indignation among the people, John and his party were overjoyed. They had got Longchamp fast in the snare they had laid for him; and now they produced what they called Richard's authority for displacing him altogether, and substituting the Archbishop of Rouen. In vain did the regent plead that he had not directed the more violent and offensive part of the proceedings against Geoffrey—that the authorities of Dover had thought fit to understand much more from his warrant than he ever intended. It was equally in vain that, at the solicitation of the Bishop of London, who gave security for his good behaviour, Longchamp released Geoffrey within a very few days, and allowed him to go to London. John, acting with the Archbishop of Rouen, who assumed all

---

[1] John seems to have assumed a royal authority in the domains which Richard had too liberally given him. From the importance of these possessions the chroniclers call John the "Tetrarch."

[2] B. Abbas; Hoved.; Ricardus Divisiensis; Diceto.

the right of a chief justiciary, peremptorily summoned him to make amends to the Archbishop of York, and to answer for the whole of his public conduct before the king's council. The semblance of an affection which was as sudden as it was tender, sprang up between John, who had hitherto hated him, and his illegitimate brother. On the one side all the prelates and barons in the kingdom were invited or ordered by John to assemble—on the other they were all forbidden by Longchamp (who declared that John's object was to disinherit his sovereign) from holding any such meeting. The meeting, however, was held at Loddon Bridge on the Thames, between Reading and Windsor; and Longchamp himself, who was in Windsor Castle, was ordered to attend—an order he did not care to obey. There John and Geoffrey embraced each other weeping; and John, who was a good actor, fell on his knees before the bishops and barons, and implored them to avenge his dear brother's wrongs. Soon after this meeting Longchamp marched from Windsor Castle to the capital, being informed by Richard Bisset that John intended to seize the city of London. The regent required the citizens to close their gates against the prince; but Geoffrey, the Archbishop of York, who was beforehand with him, had spread disaffection, and John was close behind him with a considerable army. Under these circumstances the Londoners replied to the regent's summons by declaring that they would not obey a traitor and disturber of the public peace. Sorely disappointed, Longchamp took refuge in the Tower of London; and John was joyfully received on taking a solemn oath that he would be faithful to his brother Richard, and would maintain and enlarge the franchises of the city.

On the following day, the 9th of October, 1191, it was decreed by what was called the unanimous voice of the bishops, earls, barons, and citizens of London, that the chief justiciar should be deposed, and that John should be proclaimed "the chief governor of the whole kingdom." On receiving this news Longchamp fainted and fell on the floor. At an early hour the next morning John assembled his troops in the East Smithfield, which was then a great, open, green plain. A part of his forces, united with a London mob, had already closely blockaded the Tower both by land and water. The deposed regent came out of the fortress to receive the propositions of his opponents, which were rather liberal, in order, probably, to induce him to ratify John's title. They offered him his bishopric of Ely, and the custody of three of the royal castles. But he was not to be won, and his conduct on this occasion was honourable and dignified; he refused to commit any of the king's rights, or to surrender any of the powers intrusted to him by his master. "But," said he, "you are stronger than I: and, chancellor and justiciary as I am, I yield to force." So saying, he delivered up the keys of the Tower to John.

It is rather surprising that, after these proceedings, Longchamp should have been left at large, and allowed to escape from the kingdom. It appears, however, that he was obliged to put on an unseemly disguise. Some fishermen's wives saw the tall figure of a woman sitting on the sea-shore near Dover, with a web of cloth under one arm, and a mercer's yard-measure in the right hand; upon a nearer inspection, the women discovered under the "green hood," the "black face and new-shorn beard of a man."[1] It was the Bishop of Ely, the regent, the chancellor, on his way to Normandy! John appointed the Archbishop of Rouen grand justiciary and chancellor in his place, and sequestrated the revenues of his bishopric to answer for public monies which he was accused of having dissipated or purloined. Longchamp offered to account for every farthing which had come into his hands. He maintained in the face of the world that his beloved master had never ordered his removal, which had been effected by force, in order that John might with the more ease usurp the crown. The pope, to whom he wrote from Normandy, took this view of the case, and warmly espoused Longchamp's quarrel, denouncing excommunication against all those who had seized his authority. This time the anathema had little or no effect, for not a bishop in England would obey the commands of pope or legate. The displaced minister wrote to his master, who assured him that he had not withdrawn his confidence from him; and it should appear (we venture no positive assertion where all is mystery and confusion) that Richard made representations to his mother in his behalf, for in the following year Longchamp was in friendly correspondence with Eleanor, and soon after, through her means, with John himself, who had probably not found all he expected in the new chief justiciary, the Archbishop of Rouen—a man acknowledged by all parties as a prudent and upright minister, one who conducted himself mildly and conscientiously, refusing all bribes, and deciding equitably and according to law. Prince John, on the contrary, was only to be gained by money, and when

---

[1] "Viderunt faciem hominis nigram et noviter rasam."—Hoved. We have omitted the indelicate and improbable parts of the story of Longchamp's escape which were written by Hugh, Bishop of Coventry, the bitter enemy of the chancellor. Peter of Blois took Hugh to account for this satire, which was evidently intended to put Longchamp in a more ridiculous and degrading light than Archbishop Geoffrey had been in at the same place—Dover.

Longchamp made him a large offer for repurchasing his places, he invited the exile back to England, promising to reinstate him. Eleanor, it is said, had been already propitiated by *gifts* and *promises;* and she certainly joined John in setting up Longchamp, and endeavouring to persuade the Archbishop of Rouen and the other prelates and nobles to reinstate the legate. John, who, in fact, had displaced Longchamp under a colour of acting in obedience to his brother's orders, now unblushingly urged that it would much displease the king to know how Longchamp had been removed from the government without his command. It is quite evident that this fickle, selfish prince only wanted to make money.

A council being assembled at London during these negotiations, a messenger suddenly presented himself, and announced the arrival of his master, Longchamp, "legate and chancellor," at Dover. Alarmed at this intelligence, the new ministers sent for John, who soon appeared and told them that Longchamp defied them all, provided he could obtain his (John's) protection, for which he offered £700, to be paid within a week; and he concluded this significant speech by saying that he was in great want of money, and that "a word to the wise is enough." Such a monition could not be misunderstood, and, anxious to prevent the return of their great rival, the ministers agreed to buy John off by lending him £500 from the king's treasury. John then withdrew his proposition; Eleanor did the same, and a harsh and threatening letter was addressed to Longchamp in the name of the queen, the clergy, and the people, insisting upon his immediate departure from England.[1] The fallen minister withdrew again to Normandy, there to await the return of his master.

Such was the state of the government in England. On the Continent, the French king, who was in close correspondence with John, and who disregarded all his solemn oaths, was preparing most dishonourably to take advantage of Richard's absence. Almost as soon as he returned to France, Philip had demanded the cession of Gisors and the other places in the Vexin constituting the dower of that princess, together with the person of Aliz, whom (strange to say) he offered in marriage to John, who (stranger still) listened to the proposition with a willing ear. The governor of Normandy replied that he had no orders from his master; and all of them knew that, by the treaty of Messina, these restitutions were not to be made until the return of Richard. Philip then threatened to invade Normandy; but, when his army was partly assembled, some of the French nobles refused to accompany him, alleging the oaths they had taken to protect his states, and in no way make war on Richard till he should be returned from the crusade. As the pope, too, expressed his abhorrence of the project of invasion, and threatened him with the thunders of the church, Philip was obliged to renounce his disgraceful enterprise, and to satisfy himself with hatching mischief to his rival by intrigues still more disgraceful.

John offered no objection whatever to the marriage with Aliz, and Philip engaged to put him in possession of all that his heart had so long coveted.[2] These intrigues were in full activity when the news of Richard's departure from the Holy Land arrived in England. The people were daily expecting his arrival, when vague and contradictory, and then very inauspicious intelligence began to circulate. Some returned crusaders asserted that he must have fallen into the hands of the Moors, others that he must have perished at sea, and others again affirmed that they had seen the ship in which he had embarked safe in the Italian port of Brindisi. We are sorry at being again forced to reject a touching and beautiful legend, but, leaving Blondel in the congenial hands of the poets, we fear that in historical soberness we must attribute the discovery of Richard's imprisonment to the copy of a letter from his jailer, the Emperor Henry, to King Philip. The emperor told the king that the enemy of the empire—the disturber of France—was loaded with chains, and safely lodged in one of his castles of the Tyrol, where trusty guards watched over him, day and night, with drawn swords. This discovery shocked and disgusted all Europe. Longchamp, who was still on the Continent, was one of the first to learn it, and the first to adopt measures for his master's deliverance. Prince John openly rejoiced at the intelligence; but Richard's English subjects voluntarily renewed their oaths of allegiance. The Archbishop of Rouen, and the bishops and barons, met at Oxford, and immediately sent two deputies—the abbots of Broxley and Pont-Robert—into Germany to give the king advice and consolation. Beyond the Alps, as everywhere else, where the cause of the Crusades was cherished, and Richard known as the greatest champion of the cross, a most violent indignation was excited. The pope at once excommunicated Leopold, the Austrian duke, and threatened the emperor with the same sentence. Seeing that he could not work his ends with English means, John hastened over to Paris, where he surrendered the greater part of Normandy to the French king, and did Philip homage for the rest of his brother's con-

---

[1] Palgrave, *Rot. Cur. Reg.*   [2] *Script. Rer. Franc.; Hoved.; Newb.*

tinental dominions. He then engaged some troops of foreign mercenaries, and returned home, having agreed with his ally, that Philip should fall upon Normandy with a powerful army, while he (John) overran England.

John took the castles of Windsor and Wallingford, and, marching on London, reported that his brother was dead in prison, and demanded the crown as lawful heir. For a moment the steadiness of the grand justiciary, the Archbishop of Rouen, was doubtful; but the prelates and barons raised Richard's standard, defeated John's mercenaries, and compelled him to retreat. He, however, obtained an armistice, during which he extended the threads of his intrigues. Philip was still less fortunate in Normandy; for, after advancing to Rouen, he was beaten by the indignant and enthusiastic people commanded by Richard's old comrade, the brave Earl of Leicester, who had got safely from Palestine.

In the meantime, though irritated by the indignities he suffered, and occasionally depressed by the notion that his subjects would abandon him—a captive as he was in the hands of his ungenerous enemies—Richard's sanguine and jovial spirit saved him from any long fits of despair or despondence. He whiled away the weary hours by singing or composing troubadour verses, and when tired of this resource, he caroused with his keepers, who seem to have been about equally pleased with his music, his facetiousness, and his powers of drinking. Borne down by the weight of European opinion, and the authority of the church, the emperor was at length obliged to relax his hold; and Longchamp, who was now with Richard, seems to have been instrumental in inducing him to produce his captive before the diet at Hagenau. Richard was on his way to that place, when the two abbots despatched from England first met him. He received them in a gay and courteous manner. The full accounts they gave him of his brother's treachery made him look grave; but it was only for a moment, and he said, laughing, "My brother John, however, will never gain a kingdom by his valour." On his arrival at Hagenau, Richard was received with a show of courtesy; but his first interview with the emperor was discouraging. Henry revealed all his avarice and unjustifiable pretensions, and made many demands, with which his captive would not comply, saying he would rather die where he was than so drain his kingdom and degrade his crown. On the following day, Richard appeared before the diet of the empire; and Henry, who had no right over him, except what he gained by treachery and force, and from the exploded theory of the imperial supremacy over all the kings of the West, accused him of many crimes and misdemeanours, the chief of which were:—1. His alliance with Tancred, the usurper of Sicily. 2. His treatment of Isaac, the Christian sovereign of Cyprus. 3. His insults offered to the Duke of Austria, and through him to the whole German nation. 4. His impeding the crusade by his quarrels with the French king. 5. His having employed assassins to murder Conrad of Montferrat. 6. The most impudent charge of all—his having concluded a base truce with Saladin, and left Jerusalem in his hands.

Richard, after asserting that his royal dignity exempted him from answering before any jurisdiction except that of Heaven, yet condescended, for the sake of his reputation, to justify his conduct before that august assembly, which was composed of all the ecclesiastical and secular princes of Germany. His speech is not given by any original writer; but it is stated by Hoveden and other contemporaries, that his reply to all the charges was manly, clear, and convincing—that his eloquence filled the members of the diet with admiration, and left no suspicion of guilt in their minds.[1] Matthew Paris says that the emperor was convinced of Plantagenet's innocence, and that he treated him thenceforth with humanity. He still, however, exacted a heavy ransom, though it is difficult to understand by what right, or under what decent pretext, he could detain Richard, or put him to ransom, if his innocence was acknowledged. But there was no right in the transaction—no decency in the actors in it; it began in revenge, and was to end in money, and as much money as could be possibly obtained, without a care or a thought about guilt or innocence. After fixing one price, the emperor raised it to another, and the bargain was protracted for five tedious months, during which, though his fetters were removed, Richard was still kept in prison. This was, no doubt, the most anxious and most painful part of his captivity. He sent Longchamp as his chancellor, to the council of regency, to press the raising of the ransom. The captivity of the king, or superior lord, was a case especially provided for by the feudal tenures on which the vassals of the crown and others held their estates; and a tax of twenty shillings was, therefore, imposed on every knight's fee. The clergy and laity were besides called upon for a fourth part of their yearly incomes. While the money was slowly raising, the emperor still kept increasing his demands.

---

[1] Richard produced two letters from the Old Man of the Mountain, or the Prince of the Assassins, who, in them, gloried in having ordered the murder of the Marquis of Montferrat, because the marquis had robbed and murdered one of his subjects. These letters are generally set down as spurious; but they may have been written, and, as Sir James Mackintosh remarks, the unskilful hands of the chroniclers may have disfigured them, without encroaching on their substantial truth. But, true or false, such evidence was scarcely wanted.

At last, on the 22d of September, 1193, the terms were fixed. It was agreed that Richard should pay 100,000 marks of pure silver of Cologne standard to the imperial court; that he should also pay 50,000 marks to the Emperor and the Duke of Austria conjointly, giving sixty hostages to the emperor for 30,000 marks, and other hostages to the Duke of Austria for 20,000 marks; on condition, however, that these 50,000 marks should be remitted altogether if Richard performed certain private promises. Several clauses of this treaty were either secret or added afterwards. It was also agreed that Richard should restore Isaac of Cyprus to his liberty, though not to his dominions, and deliver Isaac's beautiful daughter to the care of the Duke of Austria, and send his own niece, Eleanor of Brittany, the sister of young Arthur, to be married to the Duke of Austria's son. Henry, on his side, agreed to aid Richard against all his enemies; and, that he might have the air of giving something for so much money, invested him with the feudal sovereignty of the kingdom of Arles, or Provence—an obsolete right which the emperors long claimed without being able to enforce it. According to Hoveden, one of the very best of contemporary authorities, Richard, in an assembly of the German princes and English envoys, by delivering the cap from his head, resigned his crown into the hands of Henry, who restored it to him again, to be held as a fief of the empire, with the obligation attached to it, of paying a yearly tribute of £5000. But is there not some error in the transmission of this statement, or was not the fanciful crown of Arles here intended? Such a debasing tender may, however, have been made by Richard to cajole the German, and defeat the active intrigues of his brother John and King Philip. These precious confederates offered to pay the emperor a much larger sum than that fixed for the ransom, if he would detain Richard in captivity. Henry was greatly tempted by the bait; but the better feelings of the German princes, who had attended the diet, compelled him to keep his bargain. More difficulties than might have been expected were encountered in obtaining the money for the ransom; and what was procured seems to have been raised almost wholly in England, the continental dominions contributing little or nothing. In our island, the plate of all churches or monasteries was taken; the Cistercian monks, who had no plate, gave up their wool; and England, in the words of an old annalist, "from sea to sea was reduced to the utmost distress." Seventy thousand marks were sent over to Germany, and in the month of February, 1194, Richard was at length freed.[1] He landed at Sandwich, on the 13th of March, after an absence of more than four years—about fourteen months of which he had passed in the prisons of the duke and emperor. Though they had been sorely fleeced, the English people received him with an enthusiastic and honest joy. There was wealth enough left to give him a magnificent reception in London; and one of the German barons who accompanied him is said to have exclaimed, "O king, if our emperor had suspected this, you would not have been let off so lightly."[2]

After spending only three days at London, Richard headed such troops as were ready, and marched against Nottingham Castle, belonging to John, which surrendered at discretion. As for John himself, being timely advised by his ally, Philip—who wrote to him as soon as he learned Richard's deliverance, "Take care of yourself—the devil is broken loose"—he had put himself in safety at a distance. On the 30th of March, Richard held a great council at Nottingham, at which it was determined, among other things, that if John did not appear within forty days, all his estates in England should be forfeited, and that the ceremony of the king's coronation should be repeated, in order that every unfavourable impression which his captivity had made might be thereby effaced.[3] Accordingly he was recrowned with great pomp (not at Westminster, but at Winchester) on the feast of Easter. All his attention was again turned to the raising of money; and he proceeded with as little scruple or delicacy as he had done four years before when filling his purse for the Holy War.

A.D. 1194. Even from a nature much less fiery and vindictive than Richard's, the forgiveness of such injuries as had been inflicted by the French king could scarcely be expected. Philip, moreover, who during his confinement had sent him back his homage, was now actually in arms within, or upon the frontiers of his continental states. Richard prepared for war, and his people of England were as eager for it as himself. About the middle of May, he landed at Barfleur, in Normandy, bent on revenge. He was met at his landing by his craven-hearted brother John, who threw himself at his feet, and implored forgiveness. At the intercession of his mother Eleanor, Richard forgave him, and received him into favour. This is a noble trait, and a wonderful one, considering the amount of provocation and the barbarous usages of the times. "I forgive him," said Richard, "and hope I shall as easily forget his injuries as he will forget my pardon."[4] The

[1] *Hoved.; Brompt.; Diceto; Newb.; Matt. Par.; Rymer, Fœd.; Michaud, Hist. des Croisades; Mills, Hist. Crusades; Raumer, House of Hohenstaufen.* [2] *Brompt.; Hemingford.*
[3] It appears that Richard was opposed to this re-coronation, but submitted to it in deference to the opinion of the council. [4] *Brompt.*

demoniac character of John was placed in a not less forcible light. Before quitting Philip's party, he invited to dinner all the officers of the garrison which that king had placed in Evreux, and massacred them all during the entertainment. His hands were wet with this blood when he waited upon Richard; but with all his vices, we think too well of the Lion-heart to believe that such a deed facilitated his pardon. Although begun with fury, this campaign was carried on rather languidly and on a confined scale; in part owing to the impoverished state of Richard's exchequer, and in part to the disaffection prevalent in most of his dominions on the Continent. He, however, defeated Philip in several engagements, took several towns, and in one encounter got possession of his adversary's military chest, together with the cartulary, the records, and the archives of the crown. The campaign terminated, on the 23d of July, in a truce for one year.

A.D. 1195. Hubert Walter, who had been lately advanced from the bishopric of Salisbury to the archbishopric of Canterbury, was appointed guardian of England and grand justiciary. He had shown his bravery and attachment to Richard in the wars of Palestine, and now he displayed admirable talent and conduct as a peaceful minister. He deserved better times and a more prudent master. He had been educated under the great Ranulf de Glanville, and was versed in the science of the English laws. Under his administration the justices made their regular circuits; a general tranquillity was restored; and men, gradually recovering from the late oppressions and vexations, began to be re-animated with the spirit of order and industry. The absence of the king might have been felt as a real benefit to the nation, but for his constant demands for money to carry on his wars abroad, and complete the payment of his ransom, which demands frequently obliged the minister to act contrary to the conviction of his better judgment. Hubert, however, seems to have raised more money with less actual violence and injustice than any of his predecessors. Longchamp was employed in some important embassies, and continued to hold the office of chancellor till his death, which happened about a year before that of his master.

Towards the end of the preceding year death had delivered Richard from a part of his anxieties. Fearing that the brutal Leopold would take the lives of the hostages placed in his hands, the English king fulfilled one of his agreements, by sending the Princess of Cyprus and his niece, "the Maid of Brittany," into Germany. Before the ladies reached Vienna they received news of the duke's death. As he was tilting on St. Stephen's Day, his horse fell upon him, and crushed his foot; a mortification ensued; and, when his physicians told him he must die, he was seized with dread and remorse; and, to obviate some of the effects of the excommunication under which he still lay, he ordered that the English hostages should be set free, and that the money he had extorted should be returned to Richard.[1] When war broke out again in France—which it did before the term of the truce had expired—it was carried on in a desultory manner, and a strange treaty of peace was proposed, by which Richard was to give "the Maid of Brittany," who had returned to him on learning the Duke of Austria's death, in marriage to the son of the French king. Peace was, however, concluded at the end of the year without this marriage.

Great discontents had long prevailed in London, on account of the unequal assessment of the taxes: the poor, it was alleged, were made to pay out of all proportion with the rich. The people found an advocate and champion in William Fitz-Osbert, commonly called "Longbeard"—a man of great activity and energy, "somewhat learned and very eloquent," who, in his first proceedings seems to have been perfectly in the right. He went over to the Continent to lay his complaints before the king; and as he admitted that the war which called for so much money was perfectly just, and even necessary; and as he contended for nothing more than that the rich should not throw all the burden of the supplies upon the poor, Richard received him without anger, and promised that the matter should be properly examined. It appears, however, that nothing was done. Longbeard then (A.D. 1196) had recourse to secret political associations—an expedient always dangerous, but particularly so with an unenlightened people. Fifty-two thousand persons are said to have sworn implicit obedience to the orders of their "advocate," the "saviour of the poor," whose somewhat obscure and mystical harangues[2] delivered every day at St. Paul's Cross, filled the wealthier citizens with alarm.

It is pretty clear that Fitz-Osbert now became a dangerous demagogue, but the particular accusation brought against him is curious—he was charged with inflaming the poor and middling people with *the love of liberty and happiness.* He was cited to appear before a great council of prelates and nobles; he went, but escorted by so many of the inferior classes, who proclaimed him "the *king* of the poor," that it was not con-

---
[1] It does not appear what part, or whether any of the money was restored. It is asserted that Richard's ransom was spent in beautifying and fortifying Vienna.
[2] It appears that Fitz-Osbert, or Longbeard, took a text from Scripture, and gave to his political discourses the form and character of sermons. He wore his beard that he might look like a true Saxon.

sidered safe to proceed against him. The agents of government then endeavoured to gain over a part of the mob, and succeeded by a cunning alternation of promises and threats. The Archbishop of Canterbury and the other justiciaries met the poorest citizens on several occasions, and at last induced them to give up many of their children as hostages for their peaceable behaviour. Longbeard, however, was still so formidable that they durst not arrest him openly. One Geoffrey, and another wealthy citizen whose name is not recorded, undertook to seize him by surprise: they watched all his motions for several days, being always followed by a body of armed men ready to act at their signal. At length they caught him as he was walking quietly along with only nine adherents. They approached him as if they had no business with him, but when sufficiently near they laid hands on him, and the armed men, who were concealed close at hand, ran up to secure him. Longbeard drew his knife, stabbed Geoffrey to the heart, and then with his comrades fought his way to the church of St. Mary of Arches. He barricaded the church tower, and there made a desperate resistance. On the fourth day fire was set to the tower, and the besieged were driven forth by the flames. They were all taken and bound, and, while they were binding Longbeard, the son of that Geoffrey whom he had slain plunged his long knife into his bowels. He fell, but was not so fortunate as to die there. Wounded and bleeding as he was, they tied him to the tail of a horse, and so dragged him to the Tower, where he was presented to the archbishop-regent, who presently sentenced him to the gallows. From the Tower they dragged him at the horse's tail to "the Elms" in West Smithfield, and there hanged him on a high gibbet, and his nine companions along with him.

The mob, who had done nothing to rescue him while living, honoured him as a saint and martyr when dead. They stole away the gibbet on which he was hanged, and distributed it in precious morsels for relics; they preserved the very dust on which he had trod; and by degrees not only the people in the neighbourhood of London, but the peasantry from distant parts of the kingdom, made pilgrimages to Smithfield, believing that miracles were wrought on the spot where the "king of the poor" had breathed his last. The archbishop sent troops to disperse these rustic enthusiasts; but driven away by day, they reassembled in the darkness of night; and it was not until a permanent guard was established on the spot, and many men and women had been scourged and thrown into prison, that the pilgrimages were stopped, and the popular ferment abated.[1] Not many months after these events England was afflicted with a dreadful scarcity, and the famine was accompanied or followed by the plague, a frequent visitor, but which, on this

CRYPT OF ST. MARY OF THE ARCHES, London.[2]—J. W. Archer, from his drawing on the spot.

particular occasion, committed unusual havoc. The monasteries alone were exempted.

A.D. 1197. A war, contemptible in its results, but savagely cruel, again broke out between Richard and Philip, and ended when their barons were tired of it, or when they, the kings, had no more money to purchase the services of Brabanters and other mercenaries. Even had the vengeance of Richard been less implacable, and the ambition of Philip to establish his supremacy in France, at the cost of the Plantagenets, a less fixed and ruling passion, there were other causes which would have sufficed for the disturbance of peace. In Brittany the rule or paramount authority of the English king

---

[1] Newb.; Hoved.; Matt. Par.
[2] Stow says, "This church, in the reign of William the Conqueror, being the first in this city builded on arches of stone, was therefore called New Mary Church of St. Mary de Arcubus, or Le Bow, as Stratford Bridge, being the first builded (by Matilda the queene, wife to Henry I.) with arches of stone, was called Stratford le Bow.

The Court of the Arches is kept in this church, and takes its name of the place." The building of the Arches which survives appears only to have become a crypt from the accumulation of the soil. The roof is vaulted and supported by massive piers and pillars, similar to those in the chapel of St. John in the White Tower of London, except that the capitals are without ornament.

was most unpopular, and the same was the case in Aquitaine, where Bertrand de Born, who had so often intrigued with Richard against his father Henry, was now intriguing with the French king against Richard.

The most memorable incident of this campaign was the capture of the Bishop of Beauvais, a near connection to the French king, and one of the most bitter of Richard's enemies. He was taken, fighting in complete armour, by Marchadee, the leader of the Brabanters in Richard's service. The king ordered him to be loaded with irons, and cast into a dungeon in Rouen Castle. Two thy son's coat or no." Though, as usual, sorely in want of money, Richard refused 10,000 marks which were offered as a ransom, and the Bishop of Beauvais occupied his dungeon and wore his chains till Richard went to the grave.[1]

In the month of September of this same year, disease, misfortune, remorse, and a premature decay, did the English king justice on another of his foes. The Emperor Henry died at Messina, after suffering an extremity of humiliation at the hands of his Sicilian wife; and in his dying moments he confessed his shameful injustice to Richard, and ordered that the money he had extorted as his ransom should be restored. Though a bishop was charged with a message to Richard, and though the clause was solemnly inserted in the emperor's will, the money was never repaid.

CASTLE OF ROUEN, built by Philip Augustus.—After a miniature in the townhall, Rouen.

As the war in France again waxed languid, and the powerful vassals of both potentates showed again that they were actuated by other motives and interests than those of their masters', the two kings again spoke of peace, and meeting at Andely, on the Seine, finally "concluded upon an abstinence of war, to endure from the feast of St. Hilary for one whole year."

of his chaplains waited on Richard to implore for milder treatment. "You yourselves shall judge whether I am not justified," said Richard. "This man has done me many wrongs. Much I could forget, but not this. When in the hands of the emperor, and when, in consideration of my royal character, they were beginning to treat me more gently and with some marks of respect, your master arrived, and I soon experienced the effect of his visit: over-night he spoke with the emperor, and the next morning a chain was put upon me such as a horse could hardly bear. What he now merits at my hands declare yourselves, and be just." The chaplains were silent, and withdrew. The bishop then addressed the pope, imploring him to intercede. Celestine rated him severely on his flagrant departure from the canons of the church; and told him that though he might ask mercy as a friend, he could not interfere in such a case as pope. Soon after this the pontiff wrote to Richard, imploring him to pity "his son," the bishop. Richard replied to the pope by sending him the Bishop of Beauvais' coat of mail, which was besmeared with blood, and had the following scroll attached to it—an apposite quotation from the Old Testament— "This have we found; know now whether it be

A. D. 1198. When the truce expired, hostilities were again renewed, and with greater ferocity than ever. Near Gisors, Richard gained another victory, and Philip in his flight was nearly drowned in the river Epte, a bridge he had to cross breaking down under the weight of the fugitives. In his triumphant bulletin, Richard said, "This day I have made the King of France drink deep of the waters of the Epte!" As for himself, he had unhorsed three knights at a single charge, and made them prisoners. It was *Cœur de Lion's* last fight. A truce was concluded, and early in the following year, through the mediation of Peter of Capua, the pope's legate, it was prolonged and solemnly declared to be binding for five years. A fresh ground of quarrel arose almost immediately after, but the differences were made up, and, marching from Normandy, Richard repaired to Aquitaine, to look after his intriguing and ever-turbulent vassals in that quarter.

A strange ballad had for some time been current in Normandy. Its burden purported, that in the Limousin the arrow was making by which

---
[1] *Hoved.; Brompt.; Matt. Par.; Newb*

RICHARD CŒUR DE LION FORGIVING BERTRAND DE GURDUN.

After many a fierce conflict with Saladin and his Saracens it befell that Richard of the Lion Heart died among his own people. And this was the manner of his death. Richard was besieging the castle of a refractory vassal, and approached the walls to see where a breach might best be made. His presence was observed from the ramparts by a youth named Bertrand de Gurdun, who discharged an arrow, which struck and mortally wounded the monarch. When the castle was captured Bertrand was taken bound before his dying king, who said: "Wretch, what have I done that thou shouldst seek my life?" "You slew my father and my two brothers," was the ready answer. "Then, I forgive thee, youth," cried Richard; "loose his chains and give him a hundred shillings."

RICHARD CŒUR DE LION FORGIVING BERTRAND DE GURDUN.

the tyrant would die. The learned writer[1] who has collected all the discrepancies and contradictious respecting the circumstances by which Richard's death was attended, will not venture to decide whether these shadows cast before the event arose out of the wishes of the people, or indicated any organized conspiracy. We are inclined to believe ourselves that there was no conspiracy beyond the old settled hatred and vindictive spirit of his vassals of the South. Those fiery men, it will be remembered, had attempted the life of his father Henry more than once by shooting arrows at him. There are many contradictions which throw doubt upon parts of the commonly received story of the death of Richard, but all accounts agree in stating that the heroic Lion-heart fell before an obscure castle, and in consequence of a wound received either from an arrow or a quarrel. The usual narrative, which has almost a prescriptive right to insertion, is to this effect:—Arriving from Normandy in the south, Richard learned that Vidomar, Viscount of Limoges, his vassal, had found a treasure in his domains. This, as superior lord, he demanded; and when the viscount offered only half of it, and refused to give more, Richard besieged him in his castle of Chaluz. The want of provisions reduced the garrison to the greatest straits, and they offered to surrender at the king's mercy, their lives only being spared. Richard refused the terms, telling them he would take the place by storm, and hang every man of them upon the battlements. The garrison of the castle were driven to despair. The king, with Marchadee, the leader of his mercenaries, then surveyed the walls to see where the assault should be made, when a youth, by name Bertrand de Gurdun, having recognized him from the ramparts, praying God to speed it well, discharged an arrow, and hit the king in the left shoulder. Soon after the castle was taken by assault, and all the men in it were butchered, with the exception of Bertrand. The wound was not in itself dangerous, but it was made mortal by the unskilfulness of the surgeon in extracting the arrow-head, which had been broken off in the shoulder. Feeling his end approach, Richard summoned Bertrand de Gurdun into his presence. "Wretch!" he exclaimed, "what have I done unto thee that thou shouldest seek my life?" The chained youth replied firmly—"My father and my two brothers hast thou slain with thine own hand, and myself thou wouldest hang! Let me die now, in cruel torture, if thou wilt; I am content if thou diest, and the world be freed of an oppressor!" "Youth, I forgive thee!" cried Richard: "loose his chains, and give him a hundred shillings!" But Marchadee[2] would not let him go, and after the king's death he flayed him alive, and hanged him. Richard expired in anguish and contrition, on Tuesday, the 6th of April, 1199, a date in which all the contemporary writers of best note seem to be agreed. He had reigned nearly ten years, not one of which was passed in England, but which had all been wasted in incessant wars, or in preparations for war. He was only forty-two years old, and he left no children to succeed him. By his will he directed that his heart should be car-

COVER OF CASE WHICH CONTAINED THE HEART OF RICHARD I.[3]
From the Archæologia.

ried to his faithful city of Rouen for interment in the cathedral; that his bowels, "as his ignoble parts," should be left among the rebellious Poictevins; and that his body should be buried at the feet of his father at Fontevraud.[4]

---

[1] Sir Francis Palgrave, *Introduct. Rot. Cur. Reg.*

[2] Here there is a varying account. The MS. chronicle of Winchester says that Marchadee surrendered the prisoner to Richard's sister Joan, and that *she* plucked out his eyes, and caused him to suffer other horrible mutilations and tortures, under which he expired.

[3] After the discovery of the lost effigy of Richard I. beneath the pavement of the choir of Rouen Cathedral, a further search was made beneath the spot where it had lain, with the hope of discovering the heart of Richard. The interesting relic was at length found concealed in a closed cavity which had been formed on purpose in the adjoining lateral wall, built at the time the sanctuary had been raised, between the piers by which it is surrounded, and inclosing the newly elevated area. On July 31, 1838, was this remarkable relic brought to light. The heart was found inclosed within two boxes of lead; the external one measuring 17 in. by 11 in., and about 6 in. in height; within this was a second interior case, lined with a thin leaf of silver that time had in great part decayed, inscribed within, in rudely graven characters, as seen in the accompanying wood-cut. The heart itself was described as being withered to the semblance of a faded leaf.—*Archæologia*, vol. xxix.

[4] "Richard I. was a gay, wild, thoughtless, unscrupulous young Englishman, with fair hair, blue eyes, and a tall, handsome, muscular person, differing in no respect from hundreds of his countrymen who every autumn excite the contempt of the graver inhabitants of the more frequented towns of the Continent by their wayward and boyish pranks, whilst at the same time they enlist the good-will of the whole community by their generosity and courage, and not unfrequently by the elegance of

CHAPTER VIII.—CIVIL AND MILITARY HISTORY.

JOHN, SURNAMED SANS-TERRE, OR LACKLAND.[1]——ACCESSION, A.D. 1199—DEATH, A.D. 1216.

John obtains the crown—His unpopularity—War between England and France—The claims of Arthur to the crown of England supported against his uncle John—John's progress through Aquitaine—Defeat and suspicious death of Arthur—John suspected of the murder—His forfeiture of all his continental possessions proclaimed—John's cowardly proceedings—He quarrels with the pope—The nation laid under an interdict—Its effects—John's tyranny continued—The pope proclaims his deposition—John's abject submission—Terms on which he is absolved—Great naval victory of the English at Damme—The English barons refuse to follow John—Victory of the French king at Bouvines—The barons combine against John—They present their claims and are refused—Magna Charta finally signed by the king—He tries to elude it, and makes war upon the barons—John's useless invasion of Scotland—The English crown offered to the Dauphin of France—The Dauphin lands with an army in England—John's ineffectual resistance—His disastrous loss at the Wash—His death at Newark.

PRINCE JOHN was in Normandy when his brother died. As soon as he received the intelligence, he sent to retain the foreign mercenaries who had been in Richard's pay, promising them large gifts and increased salaries. Despatching Hubert Walter, the Archbishop of Canterbury, and William Mareschal, into England, to overawe the barons there, he himself hastened to Chinon to seize his brother's treasure, which was deposited in that castle. Chinon, with several other castles in the neighbourhood, voluntarily received him; but, in the meanwhile, the barons of Touraine, Maine, Anjou, and Brittany proclaimed his nephew, the young Arthur, as their lawful sovereign. John proceeded to chastise the citizens of Mans for the support they afforded his nephew; then, returning to Normandy, he was received at Rouen without opposition, and on Sunday, the 25th of April, he was there inaugurated, being girt with the sword of the duchy, and having the golden coronal put upon his head. News, whether good or bad, travelled but slowly in those days. A vague report of Richard's death was spread in England, but nothing certain was known, and the friends of John seem purposely to have concealed the fact for many days. When the Archbishop of Canterbury and his companion arrived, they required all the lieges in the cities and burghs throughout the kingdom, and all the earls, barons, and freeholders, to be in the fealty, and keep the peace, of John, Duke of Normandy, son of King Henry, son of the Empress Matilda.[2] But John had never been popular in the nation, and the more powerful classes seemed disposed to resist his accession. Bishops, earls, and barons—most of those who had castles—filled them with armed men and stocked them with provisions. The poorer classes committed great devastations, for in those times a king's death was the signal for the general disorganization of society. The primate and his associate acted with great alacrity and vigour, seeing that nothing less would save the country from a frightful anarchy. They convened a great council at Northampton, and there, by secret gifts and open promises of justice and good government on the part of John, they induced the assembled prelates and barons to swear fealty and faithful service to the "Duke of Normandy," as the pretender was carefully called, until his coronation at Westminster.

John did not arrive until the 25th of May, when he landed at Shoreham. On the 27th he repaired to the church of St. Peter, at Westminster, to claim the crown. He well knew that many preferred the right of his nephew, the son of an elder brother, who had repeatedly been declared

---

their appearance and manners. In regarding him as such, and nothing more, Dr. Pauli has, in our opinion, taken the correct view of his character; and when Sir James Mackintosh said he was more a knight-errant than a king, he did him too much honour. He had his own share unquestionably of the superstitious reverence with which holy things and places were viewed in his day, but beyond this we see no more reason to think that he was actuated by Christian principle, or any other principle, in fighting against Saladin, than to suppose that the ultimate triumph of truth over error has been the motive which, during the last few months, has carried forth so many of the young gentlemen of whom we have spoken, to fight against the czar. Like them he loved travelling and fighting, and hated working and thinking; and in this simple fact we find a sufficient explanation of all the actions of his life and reign."—*North British Review*, No. xlii.

[1] A nickname, according to Brompton, given him by his father, who, in a will which he made at Domfront, in 1170, left John no lands, but only recommended him to be provided for by his eldest brother.

[2] *Roger of Hoveden; Matthew Paris; Sir Francis Palgrave; Rot. Cur. Reg.*

his heir by the late king, and now John professed to be in possession of a will, drawn up in his last hours, by which Richard revoked former wills, and appointed him his successor. But this testament, whether true or false, seems to have carried no weight with it, and to have been altogether disregarded on this solemn occasion. The fact that the crown was not considered heritable property was stated in the broadest terms, and never was the elective character of the monarchy so forcibly put by such high authority. The Archbishop Hubert, having announced to the audience that the Duke of Normandy had been elected king at Northampton, laid it down as a known principle that no one could be entitled by any previous circumstances to succeed to the crown unless he were chosen to be king by the body of the nation—"ab universitate regni electus." According to Matthew Paris, John assented without starting the question, either of his inherent right by birth or of his right by will; and when he had taken the usual oaths to protect the church and govern justly, all persons hailed him with "Long live the king!"[2]

John was at this time thirty-two years old—a manly age—which gave him many advantages over kings commencing their reigns in youth. He was robust, healthy, and, like most of his race, handsome; but his evil passions distorted his countenance, and gave him a treacherous and cruel expression. He was already hated by the people, and his reign opened inauspiciously. Many of the nobles in England immediately showed disaffection. The King of Scotland, William the Lion, who had quarrelled with him on account of the provinces of Northumberland and Cumberland, threatened him with invasion; and on the Continent, with the exception of those in Normandy, all the great vassals were up in arms for his nephew, and in close alliance with the French king, who had renewed the war, and was promising himself every success, well knowing the difference between the warlike Richard and the cowardly John, as also the weakness that must arise out of a disputed succession, for the election at London and the inauguration at Rouen had no legal effect in those provinces which had declared for Arthur.[3] Leaving William de Stuteville to keep in check the Scots, John crossed over to Normandy, where the Earl of Flanders, and other great lords who had confederated with Richard, brought in their forces.

KING JOHN.[1]—From his effigy in Worcester Cathedral.

---

[1] John, in his last moments, committed his soul to God and his body to St Wulstan; his body, royally attired, was conveyed to Worcester; over his head was placed a monk's cowl, as a sort of cover for all his sins and a passport to heaven. He was interred between St. Oswald and St. Wulstan, whose graves are in the chapel of the Virgin, at the eastern extremity of the cathedral. Thence, in all probability, they underwent translation to their present situation before the high altar in the choir. The effigy of John, carved in gray marble, which forms the superstructure of his present tomb, was originally the lid of the stone coffin which contained his remains, and in its first position must have been placed on a level with the floor of the building within which he was interred. His head is adorned with a crown of state, and is supported by the figures of two bishops, one on either side, and each holding a censer, undoubtedly intended for St. Oswald and St. Wulstan. He is represented as wearing a dalmatic of crimson lined with green, the neck and cuffs edged with a gold and jewelled border; his tunic is yellow or cloth of gold; he is girt with a belt; on his hands are jewelled gloves, and his right hand supports a sceptre, while his left grasps a sword. He wears red hose, golden spurs; his feet have on them black shoes, and rest upon a lion. The greater part of these details will be recognized as emblems of royalty.—Stothard's *Nonumental Effigies of Great Britain*.

[2] The succession of John has certainly passed in modern times for an usurpation. I do not find that it was considered as such by his own contemporaries on this side of the Channel. The question of inheritance between an uncle and the son of his deceased elder brother was yet unsettled, as we learn from Glanvil, even in private succession. In the case of sovereignties, which were sometimes contended to require different rules from ordinary patrimonies, it was, and continued long to be, the most uncertain point in public law. John's pretensions to the crown might therefore be such as the English were justified in admitting, especially as his reversionary title seems to have been acknowledged in the reign of his brother Richard. If, indeed, we may place reliance on Matthew Paris, Archbishop Hubert, on this occasion, declared in the most explicit terms that the crown was elective, giving even to the blood royal no other preference than their merit might challenge. Carte rejects this as a fiction of the historian; and it is certainly a strain far beyond the constitution, which, both before and after the Conquest, had invariably limited the throne to one royal stock, though not strictly to its nearest branch. In a charter of the first year of his reign, John calls himself king 'by hereditary right, and through the consent and favour of the church and people.'"—Hallam's *State of Europe during the Middle Ages*.

[3] Daru, *Hist. de la Bretagne*; Matt. Par.; Hoved.

Philip demanded and obtained a truce for six weeks, at the end of which term he met John to propose a definitive peace. His demands led to an instant renewal of war; for he not only required the surrender by the English king of all his French possessions (Normandy excepted) to Arthur, but the cession also of a considerable part of Normandy itself to the French crown.

The only being engaged in this game of ambition that can at all interest the feelings was the innocent Arthur, who was too young and helpless to play his own part in it. The greatest of our poets has thrown all the intensity, both of pathos and horror, around the last days of this prince; but all the days of his brief life were marked with touching vicissitudes. Like William of Normandy, the hapless son of Duke Robert, Arthur was the child of sorrow from his cradle upwards. His misfortunes, indeed, began before he came into the world; his father Geoffrey was killed in a tournament eight months prior to his birth, and Brittany, to which he had an hereditary right through his mother, was divided into factions, fierce, yet changeable, destructive of present prosperity and unproductive of future good; for the national independence, their main object, was an empty dream in the neighbourhood of such monarchs as the Plantagenets of England and the Capetians of France. The people of Brittany, however, hailed the birth of the posthumous child of Geoffrey with transports of patriotic joy. In spite of his grandfather Henry, who wished to give the child his own name, they insisted on giving him the name of Arthur. That mysterious hero was as dear to the people of Brittany as to their kindred of our own island: tradition painted him as the companion-in-arms of their "King Hoel the Great;" and though he had been dead some centuries, they still expected his coming as the restorer of their old independence. Merlin had predicted this, and Merlin was still revered as a prophet in Brittany as well as in Wales. Popular credulity thus attached ideas of national glory to the cherished name of Arthur; and, as the child was handsome and promising, the Bretons looked forward to the day when he should rule them without the control of French or English.[1] His mother Constance, a vain and weak woman, could spare little time from her amours and intrigues to devote to her son, and, at the moment when his uncle John threatened him with destruction, she was occupied by her passion for a third husband, whom she had recently married, her second husband being still living. During the lifetime of Richard she had bandied her son between that sovereign and the French king, as circumstances and her caprice varied; and now, when awakened to a sense of his danger, the only course she could pursue was to carry him to Paris, and place him under the protection of the astute and selfish Philip, to whom she offered the direct vassalage, not only of Brittany, which Arthur was to inherit through her, but also of Normandy, Anjou, Aquitaine, and the other states he claimed as heir to his father. The troops of John, composed almost entirely of mercenaries, fell with savage fury upon Brittany, burning and destroying the houses and fields, and selling the inhabitants as slaves. Philip assisted William Desroches, the commander of the small Breton army, and took several castles on the frontiers of Brittany and France from the English. But as soon as he gained these fortresses he destroyed them, in order, evidently, to leave the road open to himself when he should throw off the mask and invade the country on his own account. Desroches, incensed at these proceedings, withdrew Arthur and his mother from the French court, and they would both have sought his peace, and delivered themselves up to John, had they not been scared away by the report that he intended the murder of his nephew. After this, young Arthur returned to Philip, who knighted him, notwithstanding his tender age, and promised to give him his daughter Mary in marriage. But Philip only intended to make a tool of the unfortunate boy; and when some troublesome disputes, in which he was engaged with the pope, induced him to treat with John, he sacrificed all his interests without any remorse. By the treaty of peace which was concluded between the two kings in the spring of 1200, John was to remain in possession of *all* the states his brother Richard had occupied; and thus Arthur was completely disinherited, with the connivance and participation of the French king; for it is said that, by a secret article of the treaty, Philip was to inherit his continental dominions if John died without children. Circumstances, and the unruly passions of John, soon nullified the whole of this treaty.

In the summer of this same year, John made a progress into Aquitaine, to receive the homage of the barons. He delighted the lively people of the south with his magnificence and parade; he captivated some of the volatile and factious nobles with a display of a familiar and festive humour; but these feelings were only momentary; for neither with the people nor their chiefs could he keep up the favourable impression he had made. Though a skilful actor, his capability was confined to a single scene or two; it could never extend itself over a whole act; his passions, which seem to have partaken of insanity, were sure to baffle his hypocrisy in anything like a lengthened intercourse. He had

---

[1] Daru, *Hist. de la Bretagne.*

thus shown his true character, and disgusted many of the nobles of Poictou and Aquitaine, when his lawless passion for the young wife of one of them completed their irritation and disgust. Isabella, the daughter of the Count of Angoulême, was one of the most celebrated beauties of her time; she had been recently married to the Count of la Marche, a powerful noble; and John had been married ten years to Avisa, a daughter of the Earl of Gloucester, a fair and virtuous woman, who had brought him an immense dower. In spite of these obstacles, John got possession of the person of Isabella, and married her at Angoulême, the Archbishop of Bordeaux performing the ceremony. In the autumn, he brought his new wife to England, and caused her to be crowned at Westminster. He himself was re-crowned at the same time, the Archbishop of Canterbury officiating. He then gave himself up to idleness and luxurious enjoyment. But in the following spring he was disturbed by the vengeance of the Count of la Marche, whom he had robbed of his wife. That nobleman, with his brother, the Earl of Eu, and several other barons, took up arms in Poictou and Aquitaine. When summoned to attend their liege lord, many of the English vassals refused, declaring that it was too insignificant and dishonourable a warfare for them to embark in. They afterwards said that they would sail with him if he would restore their rights and liberties. For the present, John so far triumphed over their opposition as to make the refractory barons give him hostages, and pay scutage in lieu of their personal attendance. Their resistance was not yet organized; but as John's insolence, rapacity, and lawless lust had provoked lay and clergy, and as he had engaged in a personal quarrel with one of the most powerful of the monastic orders, a regular and an extensive opposition was in due process of formation. John, accompanied by Isabella, went through Normandy to Paris, where he was courteously entertained by Philip, a much greater master in deceit, who was, at the very moment, in league with the Count of la Marche, in Aquitaine, and preparing a fresh insurrection against his guest in Brittany. From Paris John marched without his wife into Aquitaine, but not to fight; and, after a paltry parade through the safe part of the country, he marched back again to his pleasures, leaving the insurgents in greater power and confidence than ever.

A.D. 1202. The moment had now arrived for the decision of the question at issue—whether the Plantagenets or the Capetians should be lords of France. The superiority of the former race had been established by the wisdom of Henry II., and pretty well maintained by the valour of Richard; but under the unwise and pusillanimous John it had no longer a chance. Having settled his disputes with the pope, and freed himself from other troubles, Philip now broke the peace, by openly succouring the insurgents in Aquitaine, and by reviving and again espousing the claims of young Arthur. The poor orphan (his mother had died the preceding year) was living under the protection of the French king, because, says a chronicler, he was in constant fear of treachery on the part of John. "You know your rights," said Philip to the youth; "and would you not be a king?" "That truly would I," replied Arthur. "Here, then," said Philip, "are 200 knights; march with them, and take possession of the provinces which are yours, while I make an inroad on Normandy." In the treaty drawn up between these most unequal allies, Arthur was made to agree that the French king should keep all that he pleased of the territories in Normandy which he had taken, or might henceforth take, with God's aid; and he agreed to do homage for the rest of the continental dominions.[1] Arthur then raised his banner of war; the Bretons sent him 500 knights and 4000 foot soldiers; the barons of Touraine and Poictou 110 men-at-arms; and this, with the insignificant contingent supplied by Philip, was all the force at his disposal. The young orphan —for, even now, Arthur was only in his fifteenth year—was of course devoid of all military experience, and dependent on the guidance of others. Some of his friends—or they may have been his concealed enemies—advised him, as his first trial in arms, to march against the town of Mirebeau, about six miles from Poitiers, because his grandmother Eleanor, who had always been the bitter enemy of his mother, was residing there; and because (it was reasoned) if he got possession of her person, he would be enabled to bring his uncle to terms. He marched, and took the town, but not his grandmother. The veteran Amazon, though surprised, had time to throw herself into a strong tower, which served as a citadel. Arthur and his small army established themselves in the town, and laid siege to the tower where the "Ate"—the stirrer "to blood and strife"—stoutly defended herself. John, with an activity of which he was not deemed capable, marched to her rescue; and his troops were before Mirebeau, and had invested that town, ere his nephew was aware of his departure from Normandy. On the night between the 31st of July and the 1st of August the savage John, by means of treachery, got possession of the town. Arthur was taken in his bed, as were also most of the nobles who had followed him on that dismal expedition.

---

[1] *Daru; Guil. Armoric.; Matt. Par.*

The Count of la Marche, Isabella's husband, on whom he had inflicted the most insupportable of wrongs, and whom John considered as his bitterest enemy, the Viscounts of Limoges, Lusignan, and Thouars, were among the distinguished captives, who amounted in all to 200 noble knights. The captor revelled in base vengeance; he caused them to be loaded with irons, tied in open carts, drawn by bullocks, and afterwards to be thrown into dungeons in Normandy and England. Of those whose confinement fell in our island, twenty-two noblemen are said to have been starved to death in Corfe Castle.[1] Young Arthur was carried to Falaise, and from Falaise he was removed to the castle of Rouen, where all positive traces of him are lost. Such damnable deeds are not done in the light of day, or in the presence of witnesses, and some obscurity and mystery must always rest upon their horrors. The version of Shakspeare has made an impression which no time and no scepticism will ever efface; and, after all, it is probably not far from being the true one. Of the contemporary writers who mention the disappearance of Arthur, Matthew Paris is the one who expresses himself in the most measured terms; yet his words convey a fearful meaning. He says John went to his nephew at Falaise, and besought him with gentleness to trust his uncle. Arthur replied indignantly, "Give me mine inheritance—restore to me my kingdom of England." Much provoked, John immediately sent him to Rouen, with orders that he should be more closely guarded. "Not long after," proceeds Matthew Paris, "he suddenly disappeared; I trust not in the way that malignant rumour alleges." It was suspected by all that John murdered his nephew with his own hand, and he became the object of the blackest hatred. The monks of Margan tell us, in their brief yearly notes, "that John being at Rouen in the week before Easter, 1203, after he had finished his dinner, instigated by drunkenness and malignant fiends, literally imbrued his hands in the blood of his defenceless nephew, and caused his body to be thrown into the Seine, with heavy stones attached to his feet; that the body was notwithstanding cast on shore, and buried at the abbey of Bec secretly, for fear of the tyrant."

According to the popular traditions of the Bretons, John, pretending to be reconciled with his nephew, took Arthur from his dungeon in the castle of Rouen, and proceeded with him towards Cherbourg, travelling on horseback, and keeping near the coast. Late one evening, when the king and his nephew had outridden the rest of the party, John stopped on a high cliff which overhung the sea; after looking down the precipice he drew his sword, and, riding suddenly at the young prince, ran him through the body. Arthur fell to the ground and begged for mercy, but the murderer dragged him to the brink of the precipice, and hurled him, yet breathing, into the waves below.[2]

But Ralph, the abbot of Coggeshall, who tells the pitiable tale most minutely, is probably the most correct of all. His account is as follows:—Some of the king's councillors, representing how many slaughters and seditions the Bretons were committing for their lord Arthur, and maintaining that they would never be quiet so long as that prince lived in a sound state, suggested that he should deprive the noble youth of his eyes, and so render him incapable of government. Some wretches were sent to his prison at Falaise to execute this detestable deed; they found Arthur loaded with chains, and were so moved with his tears and prayers that they staid their bloody hands. The compassion of his guards, and the probity of Hubert de Burgh—the kind Hubert of Shakspeare—saved him for this time. Hubert, who was warden of the castle, took upon him to suspend the cruelties till the king should be further consulted. This merciful appeal only produced his removal from Falaise to Rouen. On the 3d of April, in the year of mercy 1203, the helpless orphan was startled from his sleep, and invited to descend to the foot of the tower, which was washed by the peaceful waters of the Seine. At the portal he found a boat, and in it his uncle, attended by Peter de Maulac, his esquire. The lonely spot, the dark hour, and the darker countenance of his uncle, told the youth his hour was come. Making a vain and last appeal, he threw himself on his knees and begged that his life at least might be spared. But John gave the sign, and Arthur was murdered. Some say that Peter de Maulac shrunk from the deed, and that John seized his nephew by the hair, stabbed him with his own hand, and threw his body into the river. Hemingford and Knyghton, who wrote near the time, say that the squire was the executioner, and this statement is confirmed by the circumstance which they mention, and which is otherwise established, of John having bestowed on De Maulac the heiress of the barony of Mulgref in marriage, as the reward of his iniquity. In the essential parts of the crime nearly all writers agree.

The rumour of the murder, which was certainly spread in the month of April of this year, excited a universal cry of horror and indignation. The Bretons, among whom the young prince had been born and brought up, were the loudest of all:

---

[1] Rigord. *Gest. Phil. Aug.*; Matt. Par.; Guil. Armoric.

[2] Argentré, *Hist. de Bretagne*; Dumoulin, *Hist. de Normandie*.

their rage amounted to an absolute frenzy; and even when cooler moments came, they unanimously swore to revenge their prince's death. The Maid of Brittany—the fair and unfortunate Eleanor, Arthur's eldest sister—was in John's hands, and closely confined in a monastery or prison at Bristol, where she consumed forty years of her life; but the enthusiastic people rallied round Alice, an infant half-sister of the prince, and appointed her father, Guy de Thouars, the last husband of their duchess Constance, their regent and general of their confederacy. At a meeting of the estates of the province, held at Vannes, it was determined that Guy, with a deputation, should forthwith carry their complaints before the French king, "their suzerain lord," and demand justice.[1] He listened to their petition, and summoned John to a trial before his peers, as a vassal of the French crown. The process was in the regular order of feudal justice. But the accused monarch did not appear, on which, with the concurrence of the barons, this sentence was pronounced on him:—"That John, Duke of Normandy, unmindful of his oath to Philip, his lord, had murdered his elder brother's son, a homager to the crown of France, within the seignory of that realm; whereon he is judged a traitor; and, as an enemy to the crown of France, to forfeit all his dominions which he held by homage; and that re-entry be made by force of arms."

Philip, who had been obliged to retreat from Normandy after the capture of Prince Arthur and the barons at Mirebeau in the preceding year, was now on the frontier of Poictou, where a general insurrection took place, and most of the nobles joined him against the murderer John. They surrendered to Philip most of the strong places, and then marched with him to Normandy. Here the enraged Bretons were before him, having invaded and occupied all the territory near their own frontiers; they took the strong castle of Mount St. Michael by assault, made themselves masters of Avranches, and then advancing, burned all the towns between that city and Caen. These movements facilitated the progress of the French king, who, being joined by John's subjects of Anjou and Maine, advanced by Andely, Evreux, Domfront, and Lisieux, all of which places he took, and then effected his junction with the army of the Bretons at Caen. While tower and town thus fell before the invaders, John was passing his time in a voluptuous indolence at Rouen, surrounded by women and effeminate courtiers. He wished to remain ignorant of the loss of his towns, the miseries of his people, his own shame; and, when obliged to listen to some dismal news, he was accustomed to say, in the fulness of his infatuation, "Let them go on; let these French and this rabble of Bretons go on; I will recover in a single day all that they are taking from me with so much pains." At last his enemies appeared at Radepont, in the neighbourhood of Rouen, and then (in the month of December) he fled over to England to demand succour.[2]

We are not sufficiently acquainted with the history of the noble families of the time, and the transmission or division of their estates; but it appears that the Norman barons of England had no longer that property at stake in Normandy which on all former occasions had made them resolute to prevent the separation of the two countries. There were, no doubt, other causes for their apathy; but, in spite of John's demerits, we cannot but believe that they would have made great exertions if they had been in the same position as formerly, when the same barons held great estates in Normandy as well as in England. Now they would make no strenuous effort; and we find John complaining on this occasion, as a little later, when his other continental provinces were occupied by the French king, that his English nobles had forsaken him.

A.D. 1204. Unable to meet Philip with the sword, John attempted to stop his progress with the spiritual weapons of Rome: he applied to the pope, imploring him to interfere. Innocent despatched two legates to plead in the recreant's favour; but, in the high tide of his success, the French king, made the bolder by the universal odium John had fallen into, turned a deaf ear to their representations and menaces, and the legates departed without producing any apparent effect.

When John fled, nothing remained to him save Rouen, Verneuil, and Chateau-Gaillard. The last was a strong castle, the pride of the late king, who took extraordinary pains in its construction, and it was held for John by a brave warrior who was true to his trust. In Rouen, the people, animated by an hereditary hatred of the French, determined to defend themselves; but when, pressed by a vigorous siege, they applied for aid to their sovereign, the King of England, John had no aid to give It was in vain he punished his lukewarm barons of England by fines and forfeitures—it was in vain that he collected a considerable army at Portsmouth—the nobles resolutely told him that they would not follow his standard out of England. Thus abandoned to themselves, and suffering from famine, the citizens of Rouen surrendered to the French king. Verneuil was taken about the same time, and

---

[1] *Daru.*   [2] *Matt. Parr.; Annal. de Margan.*

Chateau-Gaillard fell after nobly sustaining a siege of seven months. Thus, John had no longer an inch of ground in Normandy, which duchy, after a separation of 292 years, was finally re-annexed to the French kingdom. Within this year Brittany, Anjou, Maine, Touraine, and Poictou, equally acknowledged the authority of Philip, and John had nothing left in those wide

CHATEAU-GAILLARD.¹—From Cotman's Normandy.

provinces except a few castles. Aquitaine, or Guienne, retained its connection with the English crown, but there the authority of the king was limited and uncertain.

A.D. 1206. Philip soon found that it was much easier to incite the people against the detested John, than to keep them obedient to himself. The men of Brittany, who indulged in their old dream of national independence, were soon disgusted by seeing their country treated as a mere province of France; and discontents also broke out in Anjou and Poictou. John contrived to land an English army at Rochelle, and even to take the strong castle of Montauban; then marching to the Loire, he took and burned Angers, committing many cruelties. He then reposed on his laurels, and gave himself up to feasting and debauchery. When again roused, he descended the Loire, and laid siege to Nantes. This siege he raised, to offer battle to Philip. As the battle was about to commence, he proposed a negotiation, and while the proposal was under discussion, he ran away to England, loaded with new infamy. Philip, who had nothing more to do, as it was not convenient for him to attack Guienne, and an invasion of England was as yet a thing not to be contemplated, listened to another legate from the pope, who induced him to consent to a truce with John for two years.

A.D. 1207. The next step of the recreant John was to quarrel with the pope, and provoke to the utmost—and by deeds which gave an odious colouring to his cause, even where he was wholly or partially in the right—the enduring enmity of that power which had shaken the throne of his great and wise father. The dispute arose out of the conflicting claims of the crown and the church in the appointment of bishops. While John insisted that his favourite minister, John de Gray, Bishop of Norwich, should be elevated to the see of Canterbury, the pope *canonically* appointed Stephen Langton; and the monks of Canterbury would receive no other archbishop. Never was time, never was place so ill chosen for an attack on the church; but John, blinded by passion, despatched two knights with an armed band to drive the monks of Canterbury from the land. The ministers of his vengeance entered with drawn swords into the cloisters which had alike witnessed the slaughter of Becket and the subsequent humilia-

---

¹ Chateau-Gaillard was founded about the year 1196, shortly after the treaty of Louviers had been concluded between Philip Augustus and Richard Cœur de Lion. The Norman duke, considering how frequently inroads had been made into his territories by the way of Andelys, resolved to strengthen himself by means of a formidable barrier in that quarter. With this view he built a fortress upon an island in the Seine, opposite the village of Lesser Andelys; and at the same time erected upon the brow of the rock that overhung the river a castle of the greatest possible strength. The circular keep is of extraordinary strength, and in its construction differs wholly from any of our English donjon-towers. It may be described as a cylinder placed upon a truncated cone. The massive perpendicular buttresses, which are ranged round the upper wall, whence they project considerably, lose themselves at their bases in the cone from which they arise. The building, therefore, appears to be divided into two stories. The wall of the second story is upwards of 12 ft. in thickness. The base of the conical portion is perhaps twice as thick. It seldom happens that the military buildings of the middle ages have such a *talus* or slope on the exterior face, agreeing with the principle of modern fortification; and it is difficult to guess why the architect of Chateau-Gaillard thought fit to vary from the established model of his age.—Cotman's *Antiquities of Normandy*.

tion of his sovereign. "In the king's name," exclaimed the knights, "we command you, as traitors, to quit the realm; begone in a moment, or we will set fire to these walls, and burn you with your convent." All the monks who were not bedridden departed forthwith, and going into Flanders, were there received and hospitably entertained in different religious houses. John seized their effects; but as no one would labour upon them for the king, the lands of the archbishopric and of the convent of Canterbury lay without culture.[1] When Innocent in a gentle but most decided tone asked for redress, John braved his authority; and thus an open struggle began between one of the ablest priests that ever wore the tiara, and the meanest and basest king that ever disgraced the English throne. While John amused himself with terrible but impotent threats against the monks, the pope wrote to the already disaffected English barons, ordering them to do all they could with the arms of the flesh to save their king and kingdom from perdition; and he called upon the prelates and abbots of the kingdom to fight with their spiritual weapons for Langton and the liberties of the church. He then sent orders to the Bishops of London, Ely, and Worcester to wait upon the king in his name, and, if they found him still refractory, to threaten him with the interdict. John at last received these prelates; when they came to the threat he grew pale with rage, and his lips quivered and frothed. "By God's teeth," he cried, "if you, or any of your body, dare to lay my states under interdict, I will send you and all your clergy to Rome, and confiscate your property. As for the Roman shavelings, if I find any in my dominions, I will tear out their eyes and cut off their noses, and so send them to the pope, that the nations may witness their infamy." The bishops trembled and withdrew; but these were not times when personal fear stopped the triumphant march of Rome. A few weeks after (on Monday, the 23d of March, 1208, in Passion week), they pronounced the sentence of interdict against all John's dominions, and then fled for safety to the Continent. To secure himself at this moment of danger, the king obliged as many of his nobles as he could, to place their children in his hands as securities for their allegiance; a measure which created fresh disgust.

In the meantime the nation was plunged in mourning by the interdict. The churches were instantly closed, and the priests ceased their functions, refusing to administer any of their usual sacred rites, except baptism to infants, and the sacrament to the dying. The dead were buried, without prayers, in unconsecrated ground

---

[1] *Matt. Par.; Annal. de Marg.*

—the relics of the saints were taken from their places and laid upon ashes in the silent church—their statues and pictures were covered with veils of black cloth—the chime of church bells no longer floated on the air; and everything was so arranged under an interdict as to give a most lugubrious aspect to the whole country upon which it had fallen. When this had lasted a year, the pope followed up the sentence of interdict by a bull of excommunication against John. Although by narrowly watching the ports, he prevented the entrance of the Roman envoy and the official publication of the latter bull, the king was seriously alarmed, for he knew that excommunication would be followed by a sentence of dethronement, and that Philip was making ready to invade England with a banner that would be blessed by the pope. He also saw that the disaffection of his barons was still increasing; and that there was no part of Christian Europe to which he could apply for succour or alliance. At this critical moment, if we are to believe a curious story picturesquely told by Matthew Paris, he applied for aid to the Mahometans of Spain and was refused, the great Emir al Nassir, to whom the embassy was sent, resolving to have nothing to do with such a tyrant as the English king.

A.D. 1210. John employed the spring of this year in raising money by the most arbitrary means: all classes suffered, but none like the unfortunate Jews, who were seized, imprisoned, and tortured all over the kingdom. A great sum is said to have been collected, and with this he levied an army, pretending that he would go and drive Philip out of Normandy. When all was ready, he sailed for Ireland, where the English nobles had for some time defied his authority. On the 6th of June he landed on the Irish coast, and proceeded to Dublin, where more than twenty of the native chieftains repaired to do him homage and offer tribute. He then marched into the province of Connaught, reduced the castles of some of the revolted English nobles, and drove Hugh de Lacy, Earl of Ulster, and his brother Walter de Lacy, Earl of Meath, out of the island. He divided such parts of the island as were subjected to England into counties, established English laws, and appointed sheriffs and other officers. He also ordered, for the convenience of traffic, that the same moneys should be equally current in both countries; and then, intrusting the government of Ireland to his favourite the Bishop of Norwich, whom he had not been able to make Archbishop of Canterbury, he returned from this safe and easy expedition to England, after an absence of twelve weeks. In the following year he determined to show his prowess in Wales. Money was again wanted: he summoned all the abbots and lady-abbesses—all the heads of monastic houses, whether male or female, to meet him in London; he urged his wants in a manner which was not to be resisted, and, having got what he could from these servants and handmaidens of Christ, he again racked the unbelieving Jews, putting them to torture and throwing them into dungeons, where they were kept until they paid enormous fines to the king. It was on this occasion that he is said to have extorted 10,000 marks from a wealthy Jew, by casting him into prison, and causing a tooth to be torn daily from his jaws until the money was paid. With the sums obtained John raised a mighty army, and penetrated into Wales, as far as the foot of Snowdon. He was not a man to do more than his great and warlike predecessors, and he marched back again immediately, having, however, forced the Welsh to pay him a tribute in cattle and horses, and to give him twenty-eight hostages, youths of the best families. Whenever John had a glimpse of success, he increased his arbitrary proceedings against his English subjects. On a former occasion he gave new rigour to the barbarous forest laws, and now he levied scutage-money in an unjust manner. In the following year the Welsh again were up in arms to assert their independence. John savagely hanged the twenty-eight hostages, and was preparing for a fresh invasion when he was terrified by a report that many of his own barons were conspiring against him. He shut himself up in the castle of Nottingham for fifteen days, seeing no one but the personal attendants on whom he most relied. He then marched to Chester, still collecting troops, and vowing to exterminate the Welsh; but from Chester he turned suddenly back to London, where he kept strong bodies of foreign mercenaries constantly about him, and seldom showed himself to his people. His enemies increased every day, and the crowd of English exiles were incessantly urging the pope to take vengeance on their king.

A.D. 1213. At last Innocent hurled his deadliest thunder-bolt at the head of John; he pronounced his deposition, absolved his vassals from their oaths of allegiance, and called upon all Christian princes and barons to take part in the meritorious act of dethroning an impious tyrant. He then sent Stephen Langton, the exiled Archbishop of Canterbury, with other English and some Italian prelates, to the French court, there to convoke a solemn meeting, and declare to the king and the whole nation that the pope authorized an immediate invasion of England. The worldly temptation was so great that Philip probably required none other, but the pope promised him *the remission of his sins* if he executed this pious purpose and drove John from his throne. About the middle of March Philip collected a great army in Normandy, and prepared a fleet of 1700 vessels, of all sizes, at Boulogne and the other ports on the Channel. John, being well informed of these preparations, took for once a bold step: he summoned every man capable of bearing arms to be ready to march to the coasts of Kent and Sussex, and he collected every vessel in his dominions capable of carrying six or more horses. When the ships were ready, he anticipated Philip's attack: the English mariners crossed the Channel, took a French squadron at the mouth of the Seine, destroyed the ships in the harbour of Fecamp, and burned Dieppe to the ground. They swept the whole coast of Normandy, and returned in triumph, the main division of the French fleet at Boulogne not hazarding an attack. On Barham Downs 60,000 landsmen stood as yet firm around the standard of John; but he dreaded these his own brave subjects, and he was always spiritless and unmanly. It was quickly seen, after all his vain boasting, and his threats against the Church of Rome, that he would lower himself to the dirt before that incensed enemy—that he would do anything rather than fight. The pope's legate, Pandulph, well knew his dastardly character, and now skilfully took advantage of it. Two knights of the Temple (travelled men and crafty diplomatists) landed at Dover and proceeded to the English camp. "We come," said they, with great respect, "from Pandulph, the subdeacon and servant of our lord the pope: for your advantage, and for that of the realm of England, he asks to see you in private." "Let him come forthwith," said John. Pandulph came, and drew so formidable a picture of the French army of invasion, and represented the general and just disaffection of the great barons of England in such forcible, and, on the whole, true colours, that the paltry despot's heart died away within him. What added to his fears, was the prediction of a certain Peter, called "the Hermit," that before the feast of the Ascension should be passed (it was distant only three days) King John would be unkinged. As he trembled before the astute churchman, Pandulph bade him repent, and remember that the pontiff was a merciful master, who would require nothing which was not absolutely necessary either to the honour of the church or to the security of the king himself. After a little wavering John gave way, and subscribed an instrument which, in itself, was not *very* objectionable, and which had been offered him some time before, when, by accepting it, he might have avoided his present excessive debasement. It was agreed, on the 13th of May, that John should obey the pope in all things for which he had been excommunicated—that he should receive into favour the exiled bishops and others, particularly Stephen Langton and the prior and monks of Canterbury—that he should make full satisfaction to the clergy and laity for the damages they had suffered at his hands, or otherwise, on account of the interdict, and that he should pay down, in part of restitution, the sum of £8000. John further agreed not to prosecute any person for any matter relating to the late disagreement; and, on his part, Pandulph promised that, on the performance of those conditions, the sentences of interdict should be recalled, and that the bishops and other proscribed churchmen, on their return, should swear to be true and faithful to the king. John set his seal to the instrument, and four of

GREAT SEAL OF JOHN, appended to Magna Charta, in British Museum.

his greatest barons, William, Earl of Salisbury, Reginald, Earl of Boulogne, and the Earls of Warenne and Ferrers, swore, "on the soul of the king," that he would keep this compact inviolate. The dastardly spirit of John, the over-reaching policy and ambition of the pope, and the address of the envoy Pandulph, can alone account for the consummation of ignominy which followed. On the 14th of May, the following day, John was closeted with the Italian in secret consultation, and when seen for a moment abroad, his countenance was sadly dejected. Though depraved in morals, and notoriously irreligious, he was a prey to superstition, and he was now thinking more of the prediction of a hare-brained recluse than of his kingdom, for he fancied that Peter the Hermit's prophecy betokened he must die.

On the 15th of May, at an early hour of the morning, John repaired to the church of the Templars at Dover, and there, surrounded by bishops, barons, and knights, took on his knees, before Pandulph, an oath of fealty to the pope—the same oath which vassals took to their lords

At the same time he put into the envoy's hands a charter, testifying that he, the King of England and Lord of Ireland, in atonement for his offences against God and the church, not compelled by the interdict or by any fear of force, but of his own free will, and with the general consent of his barons, surrendered to our lord the pope Innocent, and Innocent's successors for ever, the kingdom of England and the lordship of Ireland, which were henceforth to be held as fiefs of the Holy See, John and his successors paying for them an annual tribute of 700 marks of silver for England, and 300 marks for Ireland. He then offered some money as an earnest of his subjection, but Pandulph trampled it under his feet—an act which called forth an angry remonstrance from the Bishop or Archbishop of Dublin. The next day was the fatal term, the feast of the Ascension, during which John watched the progress of the sun with an anxious eye: it set and he died not—it rose on the morrow, and he was still alive: instantly, in punishment for the vile terror he had suffered, he ordered Peter and his son to be dragged at the tails of horses, and hanged on gibbets. The people contended that Peter, after all, was no false prophet, and that John, by laying his crown at the feet of a foreign priest, had verified the prediction.[1]

Five or six days after these transactions, Pandulph went over to France, and, to the astonishment and great wrath of Philip, announced to him that he must no longer molest a penitent son and a faithful vassal of the church, nor presume to invade a kingdom which was now part of the patrimony of St. Peter. "But," said Philip, "I have already expended enormous sums of money on this expedition, which I undertook at the pontiff's express commands, *and for the remission of my sins.*" The nuncio repeated his inhibition and withdrew. The French king, however, who was already on the road, continued his march to the coast. It appears, indeed, that Philip, who inveighed publicly against the selfish and treacherous policy of the pope, would not have been prevented from attempting the invasion by the dread of the thunders of the church, which again rumbled over his head.[2] But other circumstances

---

[1] *Matt. Parr.; Matthew Westminster, or Florilegus; W. Hemming; Chron. Mailros.; Annal. Waver.; Chron. T. Wykes.*
[2] Philip had been excommunicated, and his kingdom had been laid under an interdict, a few years before, by the reigning pope, Innocent III.

of a more worldly nature interfered: Ferrand, the new Earl of Flanders, demanded that certain towns which had lately been annexed to the French crown should be restored to him. Philip refused; and now, when he proposed to his great vassals that they should continue the enterprise against England, the Earl of Flanders, the most powerful of them all, said that his conscience would not permit him to follow his lord in such an unjust attempt; and so saying, he suddenly withdrew with all his forces. Philip, vowing he would make Flanders a mere province of France, marched after him, and, taking several of the earl's best towns on his way, sat down with his army before the strong city of Ghent. Fortunately for both parties, Ferrand had already a secret understanding with John, and now he applied to that king for help. John's fleet lay ready in the harbour of Portsmouth. Seven hundred knights, with a large force of infantry, embarked in 500 vessels, under the command of William, Earl of Holland, and William Longspear, Earl of Salisbury, one of the sons of "Fair Rosamond," and immediately made sail for the coast of Flanders. They found the French fleet at anchor at Damme, which was at that time the port of Bruges; it was three times more numerous than the English fleet; but most of the sailors and land-troops embarked with them were on shore plundering the neighbouring country, and committing all sorts of ravages in a district which, through the blessings of peace and commerce, had made a wonderfully rapid progress in civilization and the arts that adorn life. This was the first fleet that the French kings of the Capetian line had ever put to sea; and it was an unfortunate beginning for the French—their navy was annihilated. Philip thus lost the means of supporting his army in Flanders, or of transporting it to the English coast: half famished and overcome with vexation, he hurried across his own frontiers, leaving Earl Ferrand to recover with ease all that he had lost.

This first great naval victory transported the English people with joy; but with joy was mingled a malicious confidence and presumption in the heart of John, who now betrayed a determination to break the best part of his recent oaths. Being determined to carry the war into France, he summoned his vassals to meet him at Portsmouth. The barons went armed and appointed, as if ready to sail; but, when ordered to embark, they resolutely refused unless the king recalled the exiles, as he had promised to do. After some tergiversation John granted a reluctant consent, and Archbishop Langton, the Bishops of London, Ely, Hereford, Lincoln, and Bath, the monks of Canterbury, all, with their companions and numerous dependents, returned.

John and the archbishop met and kissed each other at Winchester; and there, in the porch of the cathedral church, Langton gave full absolution to the king, who again swore to govern justly, and maintain his fealty to the pope. It was, however, clear to all men that Langton placed no confidence in the king; and that the king, who considered him as the chief cause of all his troubles, regarded Langton with all the deadly hatred of which his dark character was capable. John now set sail with a few ships, but his barons were in no hurry to follow him, being far more eager to secure their own liberties than to recover the king's dominions on the Continent. They said that the time of their feudal service was expired, and they withdrew to a great council at St. Alban's, where Fitz-Peter, one of the king's justiciaries, presided, and where they published resolves, in the form of royal proclamations, ordering the observance of old laws, and denouncing the punishment of death against the sheriff's foresters, or other officers of the king who should exceed their proper and legal authority.

John got as far as the island of Jersey, when, finding that none followed him, he turned back with vows of vengeance. He landed, and marched with a band of mercenaries to the north, where the barons were most contumacious. Burning and destroying, he advanced as far as Northampton. Here Langton overtook him. "These barbarous measures," said the prelate, "are in violation of your oaths; your vassals must stand to the judgment of their peers, and not be wantonly harassed by arms." "Mind you your church," roared the furious king, "and leave me to govern the state." He continued his march to Nottingham, where Langton, who was not a man to be intimidated, again presented himself, and threatened to excommunicate all the ministers and officers that followed him in his lawless course. John then gave way, and, to save appearances, summoned the barons to meet him or his justices. Langton hastened to London, and there, at a second meeting of the barons, he read the liberal charter which Henry I. had granted on his accession; and, after inducing them to embrace its provisions, he made them swear to be true to each other, and to conquer or to die in support of their liberties. This was on the 25th of August. On the 29th of September a new legate from the pope, Cardinal Nicholas, arrived in England to settle the indemnity due to the exiles, and to take off the interdict. John renewed his oath of fealty to Innocent, knelt in homage before the legate, paid 15,000 marks, and promised 40,000 more to the bishops. The interdict was removed; and from this moment the court of Rome changed sides, and, abandoning the cause of liberty and the barons, stood for the king. This abandonment, however, did not discourage the nobles, nor did it even detach Archbishop Langton from the cause for which they had confederated.

A.D. 1214. A formidable league was now formed against the French king, and John was enabled to join it with some vigour. Ferrand, Earl of Flanders, Reynaud, Earl of Boulogne, and Otho, the new Emperor of Germany, nephew to John, determined to invade France and divide that kingdom among them, giving the English king all the country beyond the Loire for his share. Ferrand was to have Paris with all the Isle of France, Reynaud the country of Vermandois, and the emperor all the rest. John sent some English forces under the command of his half-brother, the Earl of Salisbury, to Valenciennes, where the confederates established their head-quarters, and then sailed himself to the coast of Poitou, where several of his former vassals joined him, and enabled him to advance to Angers. This diversion was well planned—it obliged Philip to divide his forces; and while he himself marched towards the frontiers of Flanders, he sent his son Louis into Brittany, whither the English king now advanced. John was kept in check, or lost his opportunity through cowardice and indolence, while his allies were thoroughly defeated at the battle of Bouvines—one of the most memorable battles of the middle ages, in which the emperor was completely ruined, and the Earl of Flanders, the Earl of Boulogne, and the Earl of Salisbury were taken prisoners, with an immense number of inferior lords and knights. Salisbury, the gallant Longsword, was captured by the Bishop of Beauvais, the very individual whom King Richard had loaded with chains, and upon whose coat of mail that king had been so facetious. This prelate, however, had become more prudent or more circumspect —he no longer wielded the sword, but fought with a heavy club, thus knocking people on the head without shedding blood, which was contrary to the canons of the church. He was not the only prelate in this fierce *mêlée*. Philip was chiefly indebted for his success to Guérin, Bishop-elect of Senlis, who also had some scruples of conscience, for he would not use a sword, but marshalled the French host, and directed the slaughter with a wand. This battle was fought on the 27th of July, near an obscure village called Bouvines, between Lisle and Tournay. On the 19th of October following, John begged a truce, and obtained one for five years, on condition of abandoning all the towns and castles he had taken on the Continent. He arrived in England on the 20th of October, and as if he would take vengeance on his English subjects for the reverses and shame he had suffered, he again let loose his foreign mercenaries on the land, and began to violate all his most solemn promises. Fitz-Peter, his justiciary, the only one of his ministers that could moderate his fury, had now been dead some months. John, who feared him, rejoiced at his death. "It is well," cried he, laughing as they told him the news; "in hell he may again shake hands with Hubert, our late primate, for surely he will find him there. By God's teeth, now for the first time I am king and lord of England."[1] But there were men at work resolute and skilful. Immediately after his arrival, the barons met to talk of the league they had formed with Langton. "The time," they said, "is favourable; the feast of St. Edmund approaches; amidst the multitudes that resort to his shrine we may assemble without suspicion." On the 20th of November, the saint's day, they met in crowds at St. Edmundsbury, where they finally determined to demand their rights, in a body, in the royal court at the festival of Christmas. The spirit of freedom was awakened, not soon to sleep again: they advanced one by one, according to seniority, to the high altar, and, laying their hands on it, they solemnly swore, that if the king refused the rights they claimed, they would withdraw their fealty and make war upon him, till, by a charter under his own seal, he should confirm their just petitions. They then parted, to meet again at the feast of the Nativity. When that solemn but festive season arrived, John found himself at Worcester, and almost alone; for none of his great vassals came as usual to congratulate him, and the countenances of his own attendants seemed gloomy and unquiet. He suddenly departed, and riding to London, there shut himself up in the strong house of the Knights Templars. The barons followed close on the coward's steps, and on the feast of the Epiphany (at every move they chose some day consecrated by religion) they presented themselves in such force that he was obliged to admit them to an audience. At first he attempted to browbeat the nobles. One bishop and two barons were recreants, and consented to recede from their claims, and never trouble him again, but all the rest were firm to their purpose. John turned pale, and trembled. He then changed his tone, and cajoled instead of threatening. "Your petition," he said, "contains matter weighty and arduous. You must grant me time till Easter, that, with due deliberation, I may be able to do justice to myself and satisfy the dignity of my crown." Many of the barons, knowing the use he would make of it, would not have granted this delay, but the majority consented, on condition that Cardinal Langton, the Bishop of Ely, and William, Earl of Pembroke, should be the king's sureties that he would give them the satisfaction

---

[1] *Matt. Paris.*

they demanded on the appointed day. The confederated nobles then retired to their homes. They were no sooner gone than John adopted measures which he fondly hoped would frustrate all their plans, and bring them bound hand and feet within the verge of his revenge. He began by courting the church, and formally renounced the important prerogative that had been hitherto so zealously contended for by himself and his great ancestors, touching the election of bishops and abbots. Having thus, as he thought, bound the clergy to his service, he turned his attention to the body of the people, whose progress had been slow, but pretty steady, and whose importance was now immense. He ordered his sheriffs to assemble all the free men of their several counties, and tender to them a new oath of allegiance. His next step was to send an agent to Rome, to appeal to the pope against what he termed the treasonable violence of his vassals. The barons, too, despatched an envoy to the Eternal City; but it was soon made more than ever evident that Innocent would support the king through right and wrong. He wrote a startling letter to Cardinal Langton; but that extraordinary priest was deaf to the voice of his spiritual chief where the interests of his country were concerned. To make himself still surer, John took the cross on the 2d of February, solemnly swearing that he would lead an army to the Holy Land. This taking of the cross, by which the debtor was exempted from the pursuit of his creditor—by which the persons, goods, and estates of the crusaders were placed under the immediate protection of the church till their return from Palestine —seemed to John the best of all defences.

On the appointed day in Easter week, the barons met at Stamford with great military pomp, being followed by 2000 knights, and a host of retainers. The king was at Oxford. The barons marched to Brackley, within a few miles of that city, where they were met by a deputation from the sovereign, composed of Cardinal Langton, the Earl of Pembroke, and the Earl of Warenne. The confederates delivered the schedule containing the chief articles of their petition. "These are our claims," they said, "and, if they are not instantly granted, our arms shall do us justice." When the deputies returned, and Langton expounded the contents of the parchment he held in his hand, John exclaimed, in a fury, "And why do they not demand my crown also? By God's teeth, I will not grant them liberties which will make me a slave." He then made some evasive offers, which the barons understood, and rejected. Pandulph, who was with the king, now contended that the cardinal-primate ought to excommunicate the confederates; but Langton said he knew the pope's real intentions had not been signified, and that unless the king dismissed the foreign mercenaries, whom he had brought into the kingdom for its ruin, he would presently excommunicate them.

The barons now proclaimed themselves "the army of God and of holy church," and unanimously elected Robert Fitz-Walter to be their general. They then marched against the castle of Northampton, but they had no battering engines; the walls were lofty and strong; the garrison, composed of foreigners, stood out for the king; and their first warlike attempt proved a failure. After fifteen days they gave up the siege, and marched to Bedford with anxious minds. On whichever side the free burghers of England threw their substantial weight, that party must prevail, and, as yet, no declaration had been made in favour of the confederates. But now anxiety vanished—the people of Bedford threw open their gates; and soon after messengers arrived from the capital with secret advice that the principal citizens of London were devoted to their cause, and would receive them with joy. Losing no time, they marched to Ware, and, not stopping to rest for the night, pursued their course to London, which they reached in the morning. It was the 24th of May, and a Sunday: the gates were open—the people hearing mass in their churches—when the army of God entered the city in excellent order and profound silence. On the following day, the barons issued proclamations requiring all such earls, barons, and knights, as had hitherto remained neutral, to join them against the perjured John, unless they wished to be treated as enemies of their country. In all parts of the kingdom the lords and knights quitted their castles to join the national standard at London. It is needless, say the old chroniclers, to enumerate the barons who composed the army of God and of holy church: they were the whole nobility of England. The heart of John again turned to water: he saw himself almost entirely deserted, only seven knights remaining near his person. Recovering, however, from his first stupefaction, he resorted to his old arts: he assumed a cheerful countenance; said what his lieges had done was well done; and from Odiham, in Hampshire, where he was staying, he despatched the Earl of Pembroke to London, to assure the barons that, for the good of peace, and the exaltation of his reign, he was ready freely to grant all the rights and liberties; and only wished them to name a day and place of meeting. "Let the day," replied the barons, "be the 15th of June—the place, Runnymede."[1]

On the morning of the appointed day, the king moving from Windsor Castle, and the barons

---

[1] *Matt. Par.*

from the town of Staines, the parties met on the green meadow, close by the Thames, which the barons had named. With John came eight bishops, Pandulph, Almeric, the master of the English Templars, the Earl of Pembroke, and thirteen other gentlemen; but the majority of this party, though they attended him as friends and advisers, were known to be in their hearts favourable to the cause of the barons. On the other side stood Fitz-Walter and the whole nobility of England. With scarcely an attempt to modify any of its clauses, and with a facility that might justly have raised suspicion, the king signed the scroll presented to him. This was Magna Charta—the GREAT CHARTER—a most noble commencement and foundation for the future liberties of England.[1] As the profound duplicity and immorality of John were well known, the barons exacted securities. They required that he should disband and send out of the kingdom all his foreign officers, with their families and followers; that for the two ensuing months the barons should keep possession of the city, and Langton of the Tower of London; and that they should be allowed to choose twenty-five members from their own body to be guardians or conservators of the liberties of the kingdom, with power, in case of any breach of the charter—such breach not being redressed immediately—to make war on the king; to distrain and distress him by seizing his castles, lands, possessions, and in any other manner they could, till the grievance should be redressed; always, however, saving harmless the person of the said lord the king, the person of the queen, and the persons of their royal children.

As soon as the great assembly dispersed, and John found himself in Windsor Castle safe from the observing eyes of his subjects, he called a few foreign adventurers around him, and gave vent to rage and curses against the charter. According to the chroniclers his behaviour was that of a frantic madman; for, besides swearing, he gnashed his teeth, rolled his eyes, and gnawed sticks and straws. The creatures who would be ruined and expelled by the charter, roused him by appealing to his passion of revenge, and he forthwith despatched two of them to the Continent to procure him the means of undoing all that he had been obliged to do. One of these adventurers went to Flanders, Poictou, Aquitaine, and Gascony, to hire other adventurers to come to England and fight against the barons; the other went to Rome, to implore the aid of Innocent. John then sent messengers to such governors of his castles as were foreigners or men devoted to him, commanding them silently, and without exciting notice, to lay in provisions, and put themselves in a state of defence. He caused the alarm himself, by instantly evading some of the clauses of the charter. On their departure from Runnymede, the barons, in the joy of their hearts, appointed a great tournament to be held at Stamford on the 2d of July. John, during their absence, formed a plot to surprise London, where the main strength of the party lay; but, being warned in time, the nobles put off the celebration of the tournament to a more distant day, and named a place for it nearer to London.

The king now withdrew to Winchester, where, alarmed at the whole course of his conduct, a deputation waited on him on the 27th of June. He laughed at their suspicions—swore, with his usual volubility, that they were unfounded, and that he was ready to do all those things to which he was pledged. He issued a few writs required of him, and then withdrew still further to the Isle of Wight, where he would mix with no society save that of the fishermen of the place and the mariners of the neighbouring ports, whom he tried to captivate by adopting their manners. Here he remained about three weeks (not months, as stated by Matthew Paris); for it appears from public instruments still extant, that he was at Oxford on the 21st of July, where he appointed a conference which he did not attend, posting away to Dover, where he staid during the whole of September, anxiously awaiting the arrival of his mercenary recruits from the Continent. When the barons learned that troops of Brabanters and others were stealing into the land in small parties, they despatched William D'Albiney, at the head of a chosen band, to take possession of the royal castle of Rochester. D'Albiney had scarcely entered the castle, which he found almost destitute of stores and engines of defence, when John found himself sufficiently strong to venture from Dover. The un-English despot, followed by Poitevins, Gascons, Flemings, Brabanters, and others—the outcasts and freebooters of Europe—laid siege to Rochester Castle at the beginning of October. The barons, knowing the insufficient means of defence within the castle, marched from London to its relief, but they were obliged to retreat before the superior force of the foreigners, who, day after day, were joined by fresh adventurers

---

[1] Many parts of the Great Charter were pointed against the abuses of the power of the king as lord paramount, and have lost their importance since the downfall of the system of feuds, which it was their purpose to mitigate. But it contains a few maxims of just government, applicable to all places and times, of which it is hardly possible to overrate the importance of the first promulgation by the supreme authority of a powerful and renowned nation. Some clauses, though limited in words by feudal relations, yet covered general principles of equity which were not slowly unfolded by the example of the charter, and by their obvious application to the safety and well-being of the whole community."—*Mackintosh.*

from the other side of the Channel. Fortunately for England, one Hugh de Boves and a vast horde of marauders perished in a tempest on their way from Calais to Dover. John bewailed this loss like a maniac, but he pressed the siege of Rochester Castle, and still prevented the barons from relieving it. After a gallant resistance of eight weeks, when the outer walls were thrown down, an angle of the keep shattered, and the last mouthful of provisions consumed, D'Albiney surrendered. John ordered him to be hanged, with his whole garrison; but Savaric de Mauleon, the leader of one of the foreign bands, opposed this barbarous mandate, because he feared the English might retaliate on his own followers, if any should fall into their hands. The tyrant was, therefore, contented to butcher the inferior prisoners, while all the knights were sent to the castles of Corfe and Nottingham.

The loss of Rochester Castle was a serious blow to the cause of the barons, who were soon after excommunicated by the pope; for the king's application to Rome had met with full success, notwithstanding a counter-appeal made by the English nation. Innocent declared that the barons were worse than Saracens for molesting a vassal of the Holy See—a religious king who had taken the cross. Thus emboldened, John marched from Kent to St. Alban's, accompanied by a most mixed and savage host. It was thought at one time he would turn upon London, but the attitude of the capital struck him with terror; and, leaving a strong division to manœuvre round it, and devastate the south-eastern counties, he moved towards Nottingham, marking his progress with flames and blood.

Alexander, the young King of Scotland, had entered into an alliance with the English barons, and, having crossed the border, was investing the castle of Norham. The whole northern country, moreover, was especially obnoxious to John, and thither he determined to carry his vengeance. A few days after the feast of Christmas, when the ground was covered with deep snow, he marched from Nottingham into Yorkshire, still burning and slaying, and becoming more savage the farther he advanced and the less he was opposed. Every hamlet, every house on the road, felt the fury of his execrable host— he himself giving the example, and setting fire with his own hands in the morning to the house in which he had rested the preceding night. His foreign soldiery put his native subjects to the torture to make them confess where they had concealed their money. All the castles and towns they could take were given to the flames; and the people of Yorkshire and Northumberland were reminded of the expedition of William the Conqueror. The Scottish king retired before a superior force, and John, vowing he would "unkennel the young fox," followed him as far as Edinburgh. Here, meeting with opposition, he paused, and then, never having any valour but when unopposed, he turned back to England, burning Haddington, Dunbar, and Berwick on his way. Near the borders, Morpeth, Mitford, Alnwick, Wark, and Roxburgh had been consumed already.

In the meantime the division left in the south committed equal atrocities, and, wherever the castle of a noble was taken, it was given, with the adjoining estate, to some hungry adventurer.

On the 16th of December, another sentence of excommunication was promulgated by the abbot of Abingdon and two other ecclesiastics; in this bull, Robert Fitz-Walter, the general of the confederacy, and all the principal barons, were mentioned by name; and the city of London was laid under an interdict. This measure excited some fear and wavering in the country, but the citizens of London had the boldness to despise it. According to Matthew Paris, they asserted that the pontiff had no right to interfere in worldly concerns; and, spite of the interdict, they kept open their churches, rang their bells, and celebrated their Christmas with unusual festivity.

But the barons, who were confined in London by the force that continually increased around them—who saw their property the prey to new invaders, and who knew the full extent of the danger to which the nation was exposed (the effect of the excommunication on the villeins in the country not being the least of these)—were sorely disquieted, and knew not what measures to adopt. Many meetings were held, and a variety of plans debated; but at last they unanimously resolved, in a moment of desperation, upon the very equivocal and perilous expedient of calling in foreign aid. They sent to offer the crown to Philip's eldest son, Prince Louis, who was connected with the reigning family by his marriage with Blanche of Castile, John's own niece; believing that, should he land amongst them, the mercenaries now with John, who were chiefly subjects of France, would join his standard, or at least refuse to bear arms against him. Philip and Louis eagerly grasped at this offer, but the wary old king moderated the impatience of his son, and would not permit him to venture into England until twenty-four hostages, sons of the noblest of the English, were sent into France. Then a fleet, with a small army, was sent up the Thames. It arrived at London at the end of February, and the commander assured the barons that Louis himself would be there with a proper force by the feast of Easter. Innocent, in the meanwhile, was not inactive in John's, or rather in his own cause; he despatched a new legate to England; and Gualo, on his journey, reached France in time to witness, and to endeavour to prevent, the preparations making for invasion. He boldly asked both king and prince how they dared attack the patrimony of the church, and threatened them with instant excommunication. To the astonishment of the churchman, Louis advanced a claim to the English throne through right of his wife, and departed for Calais, where his army was collecting. At the appointed time he set sail from Calais with a numerous and well-appointed army, and embarked on board 680 vessels. His passage was stormy. The mariners of the Cinque ports, who adhered to the English king, cut off and took some of his ships, but on the 30th of May he landed safely at Sandwich. John, who had come round to Dover with a numerous army, fled before the French landed, and, burning and ravaging the country, he went to Guildford, then to Winchester, and then to Bristol, where Gualo, the pope's legate, soon joined him. Leaving Dover Castle in his rear, Louis besieged and took the castle of Rochester. He then marched to the capital, where, on the 2d of June, A.D. 1216,

he was joyfully received by the barons and citizens, who conducted him, with a magnificent procession, to St. Paul's. After he had offered up his prayers, the nobles and citizens did homage and swore fealty to him. And then he, with his hand on the gospels, also swore to restore to all orders their good laws, and to each individual the estates and property of which he had been robbed. Soon after Louis published a manifesto, addressed to the King of Scotland and all the nobles not present in London. An immense effect was presently seen: nearly every one of the few nobles who had followed John now left him and repaired to London; all the men of the north, from Lincolnshire to the Borders, rose up in arms against him; the Scottish king made ready to march to the south; and, at first in small troops and then in masses, all the foreign mercenaries, with the exception of those of Gascony and Poictou, deserted the standard of the tyrant, and either returned to their homes or took service under Louis and the barons, who were now enabled to retake many of their castles. Gualo, the legate, did all he could to keep up the drooping, abject spirit of John; but at the very moment of crisis, on the 16th of July, the pope himself, the mighty Innocent, died, and left the church to be wholly occupied for some time by the election of a new pontiff.

Louis marched to Dover and laid siege to the castle, which was most bravely defended for the king by Hubert de Burgh; and at the same time some of the barons attacked Windsor Castle, which was equally well defended. When the siege of Dover Castle had lasted several weeks, Louis found himself obliged to convert it into a blockade. Withdrawing his army beyond reach of the arrows of the garrison, he swore that he

DOVER CASTLE.¹— From a view by Turner, R.A.

¹ Dugdale, in his *Monasticon*, quotes a record in old French, in which we are informed, that when Arviragus reigned in Britain he refused to be subject to Rome, and withheld the tribute, making the castle of Dover strong with ditch and wall against the Romans, if they should come. A ditch and mound of irregular form, a parallelogram with rounded corners, are still visible; and their antiquity is attested by the presence of Roman work within the ditch. An octangular building, still upwards of 90 ft. in height, the walls being 10 ft. thick, is considered to be the remains of a Roman pharos. It is believed that fortifications were erected on the site of Dover Castle, and that these were maintained and repaired during the Heptarchy; but there is no distinct account of the castle till the reign of Edward the Confessor, when Earl Godwin made some additions to it. The works were strengthened by William the Conqueror, and Dover Castle was then called the lock and key of the kingdom—*clavis et repagulum regni*. Henry II. in 1153, being the year before he ascended the throne, built a new keep in the castle similar to that at Rochester, and inclosed it with a new wall. The several succeeding kings from time to time continued to improve and make additions to the fortifications here, in particular Edward IV., who expended £10,000 in repairing and fortifying the several works. Henry VIII. and Queen Elizabeth both made extensive repairs, and Charles I. laid out a great deal of money on the state apartments, to prepare them for the reception of Henrietta Maria on her first arrival in this country. A bastion of earth was erected on the height at the north-west extremity of the castle, by direction of William, Duke of Cumberland, in 1745, and he likewise added to the barracks. The north turret of the keep of Dover Castle is 465·8 ft. above low-water mark, and 91·0 ft. above the ground on which it stands. The area within the fortifications comprises 35 acres.—Hasted's *History of Kent*.

would reduce the place by famine, and then hang all its defenders. The barons raised the siege of Windsor Castle entirely in order to repel John, who, after running from place to place, had at last made his appearance near them, and was pillaging the estates of some of those nobles. At their approach he fell back, and eluding their pursuit by skill, or, more probably, by hard running, he reached the town of Stamford. The barons wheeled round and joined Louis at Dover, where much valuable time was lost in inactivity, for that prince would neither assault the castle nor move from it. Other circumstances at the same time caused discontent; Louis treated the English with disrespect, and began to make grants of estates and titles in England to his French followers. Several barons and knights withdrew from Dover, and though few would trust John, all began to doubt whether they had not committed a fatal mistake in calling in the aid of a foreign prince. As these doubts prevailed more and more, and as the gloom thickened round the camp at Dover, where Louis had now lost nearly three months, the cause of John brightened in proportion. Soon after eluding the pursuit of the barons, he had made himself master of Lincoln, where he established his head-quarters for some time, making, however, predatory incursions on all sides. Associations were formed in his favour in several of the maritime counties, and the English cruisers frequently captured the supplies from the Continent destined for Louis.

At the beginning of October, marching through Peterborough, John entered the district of Croyland, and plundered and burned the farm-houses belonging to that celebrated abbey; he then proceeded to the town of Lynn, where he had a depôt of provisions and other stores. Here, turning his face again towards the north, he marched to Wisbeach, and from Wisbeach he proceeded to a place called the Cross Keys, on the southern side of the Wash. It is not clear why he took that dangerous route, but he resolved to cross the Wash by the sands. At low water this estuary is passable, but it is subject to sudden rises of the tide. John and his army had nearly reached the opposite shore, called the Fossdike, when the returning tide began to roar. Pressing forward in haste and terror, they escaped; but, on looking back, John beheld the carriages and sumpter-horses, which carried his money, overtaken by the waters; the surge broke furiously over them, and they presently disappeared—carriages, horses, treasures, and men, being swallowed up in a whirlpool, caused by the impetuous ascent of the tide and the descending current of the river Welland. In a mournful silence, only broken by curses and useless complaints, John travelled on to the Cistercian abbey of Swineshead, where he rested for the night. Here he ate gluttonously of some peaches or pears, and drank new cider immoderately. The popular story of his being poisoned by a monk may be true or false; but it is told in two ways, and was never told at all by any writer living at the time or within half a century of it; and the excess already mentioned, acting upon an irritated mind and fevered body, seems to be cause enough for what followed. He passed the night sleepless, restless, and in horror. At an early hour on the following morning, the 15th of October, he mounted his horse to pursue his march, but he was soon compelled, by a burning fever and acute pain, to dismount. His attendants then brought up a horse-litter, in which they laid him, and so conveyed him to the castle of Sleaford. Here he rested for the night, which brought him no repose, but an increase of his disorder. The next day they carried him with great difficulty to the castle of Newark, on the

REMAINS OF THE CASTLE OF NEWARK-ON-TRENT.[1]—From a view by Bartlett.

Trent, and there he sent for a confessor, and laid himself down to die. The abbot of Croxton, a

[1] The castle stood near the bank of the river Trent, which washed the western wall; and its remains exhibit vestiges of different periods, from that of the Normans to the time of Charles I. King John died here on October 18, 1216.

religious house in the neighbourhood, who was equally skilled in medicine and divinity, attended him in his last hours, and witnessed his anguish and tardy repentance. He named his eldest son, Henry, his successor, and dictated a letter to the recently elected pope, Honorius III., imploring the protection of the church for his young and helpless children. He made all the knights who were with him swear fealty to Henry, and he sent orders to the sheriffs of counties and the governors of castles to be faithful to the prince. Messengers arrived from some of the barons, who were disgusted with Louis, and proposed returning to their allegiance. This gleam of hope came too late—the "tyrant fever" had destroyed the tyrant. The abbot of Croxton asked him where he would have his body buried. John groaned, "I commit my soul to God, and my body to St. Wulstan!" and soon after he expired, on the 18th of October, in the forty-ninth year of his age, and the seventeenth of his wretched reign. They carried his body to Worcester, and interred it in the cathedral church there, of which St. Wulstan was the patron saint.[1]

In this way the dying malediction of the heart-broken Henry II. upon his rebellious children had not fallen in vain. Richard, after all his military glory, perished before a paltry fortress; John died a disgraced and baffled fugitive, in the midst of subjects who triumphed over his death as a happy national deliverance. It is but one of the many lessons which history delivers to crowned heads upon the guilt and the consequences of filial disobedience.

CHAPTER IX.—SCOTTISH ANNALS, &c.

A.D. 1057—1214.

Review of Scottish history during this period—Dominions of Malcolm Canmore—He invades England—His treaty with William the Conqueror—Nature of his homage to the English crown—War between Malcolm Canmore and William Rufus—Character of Malcolm's reign—Reigns of Donald Bane, Duncan, and Edgar—Reign of Alexander I.—His contests with the church—His character—Reign of David—His connection with Henry I.—His war in support of the claims of Matilda—He is defeated at the battle of the Standard—His useful reign—His death and character—He is succeeded by Malcolm IV.—Malcolm's unsatisfactory interviews with the King of England—His wars—His death in battle—Succeeded by his brother William—William invades England—He is taken prisoner at Alnwick—His liberation—His contest with the pope about the election of a bishop—Success of his resistance—He is released from the conditions of his ransom by Richard I.—His treaty with John—He is succeeded by Alexander II.—Summary of Irish affairs.

URING the whole of the period through which we have now passed, the three states of Albin, Pictland, and Strathclyde, which had formerly divided the northern part of the island, were consolidated into the single kingdom of Scotland, of which, however, the southern limits varied considerably at different times, for the proper Scotland lay all beyond the Forth and the Clyde, and the territory to the south of these rivers was not accounted as strictly forming part either of Scotland or England, till some ages after the Norman conquest. At the time of that event the Scottish king was Malcolm III., surnamed Canmore, or Great Head, whose reign commenced in 1057.[2] His dominions undoubtedly included the ancient kingdom of Strathclyde, or the district now forming the south-western part of Scotland, which had been conquered by Kenneth III. in the latter part of the preceding century;[3] and the district of Cumbria, lying on the same side of the island, but within what is now called England, was also at this time an appanage of the Scottish crown. With regard to the south-eastern portion of modern Scotland, or the district then known by the name of Lodonia or Lothian (now confined to a part of it), the state of the case is not so clear. The people appear to have been chiefly or exclusively Angles, mixed in later times with Danes, and the territory undoubtedly at one period formed part of the Anglo-Saxon kingdom of Northumbria. From the defeat, however, of the Northumbrian king, Egfrid, by the Picts, in 685,[4] it may be considered as having been withdrawn from the actual dominion of its former masters, although, perhaps, their claim to its sovereignty was never abandoned, and it may have been for short periods wholly or partially re-subjected by the English.

The south-western angle of Scotland, formerly called Galloway, and now forming the counties

[1] *Matt. Par.; Matt. West.* [2] See vol. i. p. 146.
[3] See vol. i. p. 144.

[4] See vol. i. p. 142.

of Wigton and Kirkcudbright, received various bodies of colonists from Ireland in the course of the ninth, tenth, and eleventh centuries, and these, mixed with the original population, were afterwards designated the "wild Scots of Galloway."

Malcolm had passed about fifteen years at the court of the Confessor before he became king, and in his long exile he must have formed various English connections, as well as become habituated to the manners of the sister country. He may, therefore, be supposed to have, from the first, kept up a more intimate intercourse with England than had been customary with his predecessors.

The principal events that make up the subsequent history of the reign of Malcolm, arose out of his connection with the unfortunate Edgar Atheling. Edgar fled to Scotland,[1] according to the most probable account, with his mother and his two sisters, in the beginning of 1068, and, soon after, Malcolm espoused Edgar's elder sister, Margaret. From some cause, which is not distinctly explained, Malcolm did not arrive with his forces in time to support the insurrection of the people of Northumbria,[2] in conjunction with the Danes and the friends of Edgar, in the following year; and it was not till after the complete suppression of that attempt, and the whole of the east coast, from the Humber to the Tyne, had been made a desert by the remorseless vengeance of the Norman, that the Scottish king, in 1070, entered England, through Cumberland, and spread nearly as great devastation in the western parts of York and Durham as William had done in the east. He commanded his soldiers to spare only the young men and women, and they were driven into Scotland to be made slaves.

It was not till 1072 that William found leisure to chastise Malcolm for this inroad. He then advanced into Scotland and wasted the country as far as the Tay, though the inhabitants, after the plan which they had been accustomed to pursue in such cases from the days of Galgacus, and which they continued to follow occasionally to a much later age, destroyed or removed everything of value as the invader advanced, so that, as the Saxon chronicler expresses it, " he nothing found of that which to him the better was." In the end, however, Malcolm came to him at Abernethy,[3] when, according to the *Saxon Chronicle*, a peace was arranged between the two kings, on Malcolm agreeing to give hostages, and to do homage to William as his liege lord. William then returned home with his army.

This transaction makes a principal figure in the controversy which was formerly carried on with so much unnecessary heat, and which still continues to divide historical inquirers respecting the alleged dependence, in ancient times, of the kingdom of Scotland upon the English crown. The position taken by the asserters of this dependence appears to be that, from a date long before the Norman conquest of England, the Anglo-Saxon kings of that country had, in some way or other, obtained possession of the sovereignty of the whole island, and the Kings of Scotland, as well as the Princes of Wales, had become their acknowledged vassals. We may say, without hesitation, that this notion is directly opposed to the whole course of the history of the two countries. The only subjection or homage which either the Scottish kings rendered, or the English crown claimed from them, before the Norman conquest, appears to have been, not for the kingdom of Scotland, but for territories annexed to that kingdom, or otherwise held by them, situated, or conceived to be situated, in England. Such was the lordship of Cumbria, or Cumbraland, after the donation of it by the English king, Edmund, to Malcolm I., in 946. Lothian, or a part of it,[4] may be considered to have been similarly circumstanced after the agreement between Kenneth IV. and Edgar in 971. There is reason to believe, also, that the Scottish kings were anciently possessed of other lands clearly within the realm of England, besides the county of Cumberland. For these possessions, of course, they did homage to the English king, and acknowledged him as their liege lord, exactly in the same manner as the Norman Kings of England acknowledged themselves the vassals of the crown of France for their possessions on the Continent.

When Malcolm III., however, on the seizure of the English crown by the Duke of Normandy, espoused the cause of Edgar Atheling, he necessarily, at the same time, refused to do homage for his English lands to the Norman invader, whom, by that very proceeding, he declared that he did not acknowledge as the rightful King of England. William, on the other hand, took

---

[1] See vol. i. p. 186.   [2] See vol. i p. 187
[3] This seems to be really the place meant by the "Abernithi" of Ingulphus, the "Abernithici" of Florence of Worcester, the "Abernitici" of R. de Diceto, and the "Abrenitici" of Walsingham; although Lord Hailes, Pinkerton, and other writers, have contended that it was more probably some place on the river Nith. Mr. Allen conceives that no doubt can exist as to its being Abernethy on the Tay.—*Vindication of the Ancient Independence of Scotland*, &c.

[4] Lord Hailes has endeavoured to show that the district anciently called Lothian, and perhaps considered as part of England, by no means included the whole of the south-east of Scotland, but only the counties of Berwick and East Lothian, and the part of Mid Lothian lying to the east of Edinburgh. And he adds, "only a small part of that territory could be considered as feudally dependent on England. Great part of those territories was the patrimony of St. Cuthbert."—*Remarks on the Hist. of Scotland* (Edin. 1772), chap. ii.

measures to maintain his authority, and to compel the obedience of his rebellious vassal, and these objects he completely attained by the submission of Malcolm at Abernethy. The latter now consented to make that acknowledgment of William's title, and of his own vassalage for the lordship of Cumberland and his other English possessions, which he had hitherto refused; he gave hostages to the English king, as the Saxon chronicler expresses it, and became his man.

After this Malcolm appears to have remained quiet for some years. He did not, however, finally abandon the cause of his brother-in-law, the Atheling; and in 1079, choosing his opportunity when the English king was engaged in war with his son Robert on the Continent, he again took up arms and made another destructive inroad into Northumberland. The following year after the reconcilement of William and his son, the latter was sent at the head of an army against Scotland; but he soon returned without effecting anything. It was immediately after this expedition that the fortress bearing the name of the Castellum Novum, on the Tyne, which

CASTLE OF NEWCASTLE-ON-TYNE.1—Scott's Border Antiquities.

gave origin to the town of Newcastle, was erected as a protection against the invasions of the Scots. When Rufus succeeded to the English throne, the two countries appear to have been at peace. But in the summer of 1091, we find Malcolm again invading Northumberland. Rufus immediately made preparations to attack Scotland both by sea and land; and, although his ships were destroyed in a storm, he advanced to the north with his army before the close of the year. We have already related[1] the course and issue of this new war. After being suspended for a short time by a treaty made, according to the Saxon Chronicle, "at Lothian in England," whither Malcolm came "out of Scotland," and awaited the approach of the enemy, it was renewed by the refusal of the Scottish king to do the English king right—that is, to afford him satisfaction about the matter in dispute between them, anywhere except at the usual place—namely, on the frontiers, and in presence of the chief men of both kingdoms. William required that Malcolm should make his appearance before the English barons alone, assembled at Gloucester, and submit the case to their judgment. "It is obvious on feudal principles," as Mr. Allen observes, "that if Malcolm had done homage for Scotland to the King of England, the Scotch nobles must have been rere-vassals of the latter, and could not have sat in court with the tenants in chief of the English crown." Yet it is evident that the nobility of both kingdoms had been wont on former occasions to meet and form one court for adjudication on such demands as that now made by the English king. The hostilities that followed, however, were fatal to Malcolm. He was slain in a sudden attack made upon him while besieging the castle of Alnwick, on the 13th of November, 1093.

The reign of Malcolm was one of the most memorable and important in the early history of Scotland. It was in his time, and in consequence, in great part, of his personal fortunes, that the first foundations of that intimate connection were laid which afterwards enabled the country to draw so largely upon the superior civilization of England, and in that way eventually revolutionized the whole of its social condition. From the time of Malcolm Canmore, Scotland ceased to be a Celtic kingdom. He himself spoke the language of his forefathers as well as Saxon; but it may be doubted if any of his children understood Gaelic, any more than their English mother. All his six sons, as well as his two daughters, received English names, apparently after their mother's relations. His marriage with the sister of Edgar

[1] The ancient name of Newcastle is derived from Pons Ælii, the second station from the eastern extremity of the Roman wall. Previous to the Conquest the town was called Monkchester, from the number of monastic institutions it contained. The town derived its present name from a fortress—built by Robert, eldest son of William the Conqueror, A.D. 1079 to 1082, on his return from an expedition into Scotland—to which, in contradistinction to some more ancient erection, the name of the New Castle was given. The remains consist of the massive keep, and a gate tower called the Black Gate. The keep is one of the finest examples of Norman military architecture in this country. It contains a lofty and spacious state apartment on the first story, and a dungeon and a remarkably fine chapel in the basement. [2] See vol. i. p. 213.

Atheling exercised a powerful influence both over the personal conduct of Malcolm and over public affairs. There is still extant a Latin *Life of Queen Margaret*, by her confessor Turgot, which is on various accounts one of the most interesting records of those times. Margaret was very learned and eloquent, as well as pious, and she exercised her gifts not only in the instruction of her husband, but also in controversy with the Scottish clergy, whose various errors of doctrine and discipline she took great pains to reform. Her affections, however, were not all set upon the beauty of spiritual things. She encouraged merchants, we are told by Turgot, to come from various parts of the world, with many precious commodities which had never before been seen in that country, among which are especially mentioned vestments ornamented with various colours, which, when the people bought, adds the chronicler, and were induced by the persuasions of the queen to put on, they might almost be believed to have become new beings, so fine did they appear. She was also, to adopt the summary of the monk's account given by Lord Hailes, "magnificent in her own attire; she increased the number of attendants on the person of the king, augmented the parade of his public appearances, and caused him to be served at table in gold and silver plate. At least (says the honest historian) the dishes and vessels were gilt or silvered over."

Malcolm is traditionally said to have, with the advice of his nobility, made various important innovations in the constitution of the kingdom, or the administration of public affairs. He appears to have restored the rule of law and order, which had been banished from the country by the civil wars that had preceded his accession; and it is probable that in the measures he adopted to accomplish this end, he imitated, as far as he could, the forms and usages of England. There is neither proof nor probability, however, for the statement which has been often repeated, that he introduced feudalism in a systematic form into Scotland. That state of things appears rather to have grown up gradually under the influence of various causes, and its complete establishment must be referred to a period considerably later than the reign of this king. The modern titles of Earl and Baron, however, are traced nearly to his time, and seem then, or very soon after, to have begun to supplant the older Celtic Marmor and Saxon Thane. Surnames also began to be used in this or the next reign. But on the whole, it was probably not so much by any new laws which were enacted by Malcolm Canmore (the collection in Latin which has been attributed to him is admitted to be spurious), or by any new institutions which he established, that Scotland was in a manner transformed into a new country in his days, as by his English education and marriage, the English manners which were thus introduced at his court, and the numbers of English of all ranks whom the political events of the time drove to take refuge in the northern kingdom. Much of the change, therefore, was really the effect of the Norman conquest of England, which in nearly the same degree that it made Saxon England Norman, made Celtic Scotland Saxon.

The disastrous close of the reign of Malcolm, whose own death was followed in a few days by that of his excellent queen—worn out, it is said, by her vigils and fastings, and other pious exercises—afforded an opportunity to his brother Donald Bane (or the Fair) to seize the throne. Malcolm's eldest son, Edward, had fallen with his father at Alnwick; his second, Ethelred, was a churchman; but he left four other legitimate sons, although they were all as yet under age. Donald is said to have remained till now in the Western Islands, where he had taken refuge, on the death of his father Duncan, more than fifty years before.[1] He now invaded Scotland with a fleet fitted out in the Western Islands, and, with the aid of the faction which had all along been opposed to the English innovations of Malcolm, carried everything before him. The children of the late king were hastily conveyed to England by their uncle Edgar Atheling; and Donald, as soon as he mounted the throne, expelled all the foreigners that had taken refuge at his brother's court.

He had reigned only a few months, however, when another claimant of the crown appeared in the person of Duncan, according to the common account, an illegitimate son of Malcolm Canmore. He had been sent, it seems, by his father as a hostage to England; and by now offering to swear fealty to Rufus, he obtained his permission to raise a force for the invasion of Scotland. He succeeded in driving Donald from the throne and mounting it himself in May, 1094.

But after a reign of only about a year and a half, Duncan was, at the instigation of Donald Bane, assassinated by Malpedir, Earl of Mearns, and Donald again became king about the end of the year 1095. After his restoration, he proceeded in his former course of policy, by favour

---

[1] It must be confessed that the great length of the interval— fifty-four years—between the dates assigned to the death of Duncan and that of Malcolm, throws some suspicion upon the common statement that the one was the son of the other. All that we know of the age of Malcolm is, that he was married about 1069 or 1070; that he reigned thirty-six or thirty-seven years, and that at his death, he left several children under age. As he fell in battle, however, it seems improbable that he was very old when he died. Pinkerton (who, by the by, places his accession—on the authority of the *Chronicle of Melrose*—in 1056, not in 1057) strongly insists that he must have been, not the son, but the grandson of Duncan.—*Inquiry*, II. 203, 204.

ing the Celtic, and depressing the Saxon population. Affairs proceeded in this train for about two years; but at length, in 1097, Edgar Atheling raised an army, with the approbation of the English king, and marching with it into Scotland, after an obstinate contest, overcame Donald, in the beginning of the following year, and obtained the crown for his nephew Edgar, the son of Malcolm Canmore. "Edgar, like Duncan," observes Mr. Allen, "appears to have held his kingdom in fealty to William. These two cases, and the extorted submission of William the Lion, during his captivity (to be presently mentioned), are the only instances I have found since the Conquest of any King of Scotland rendering fealty to England for his crown. Both occurrences took place after a disputed succession in Scotland, terminated by the arms and assistance of the English. Duncan was speedily punished for his sacrifice of the honour and dignity of the sceptre he unworthily held. Edgar appears to have repented of his weakness, and to have retracted before his death the disgraceful submission he had made in order to obtain his crown. One of his coins is said to bear the impress of 'Eadgarus Scottorum Basileus,' a title which, like Imperator, implied that the holder acknowledged no superior upon earth."[1]

On his second deposition, Donald Bane was deprived of the power of giving further disturbance, by being detained in prison, and having his eyes put out. Edgar retained the throne till his death, on the 8th of January, 1107; and during his reign the country appears to have enjoyed both internal tranquillity and freedom from foreign war. The accession of Henry I. to the throne of England, which took place in 1100, and his marriage the same year with Edgar's sister Maud, had the effect of maintaining peace between the two countries for a long course of years from this date. This favourable tendency of circumstances was not opposed by the disposition of Edgar, whom a contemporary chronicler describes as "a sweet-tempered, amiable man, in all things resembling Edward the Confessor; mild in his administration, equitable, and beneficent."[2]

Edgar, dying without issue, was succeeded by his next brother, Alexander I. Alexander strengthened his connection with the English king by a marriage with one of Henry's numerous illegitimate daughters, the Lady Sibilla, or, as she is called by other authorities, Elizabeth, whose mother was a sister of Walleran, Earl of Mellent. A dismemberment, however, of the Scottish kingdom, as it had existed for some reigns preceding, now took place, by the separation of Cumberland, which Edgar on his death-bed had bequeathed to his younger brother David. Alexander at first disputed the validity of this bequest; but the English barons taking the part of David, he found himself obliged to submit. By this arrangement, the King of Scotland would for the present (putting aside the doubtful case of Lothian) cease to be an English baron; and accordingly it appears that Alexander never attended at the English court. Nearly the whole history of his reign that has been preserved, is made up of a long contest in which he was engaged with the English archbishops on the subject of their assumed authority over the Scottish church.

Alexander did not long survive the settlement of this affair. He had about two years before lost his queen, who had brought him no offspring; and his own death took place on the 27th of April, 1124. The quality for which this king is most celebrated by the old historians is his personal valour, of which various remarkable instances are related, although some contests with revolted portions of his own subjects, of which there are obscure notices, seem to have been the only opportunities he had of displaying military talent. But he sufficiently proved his intrepidity and firmness of character, in the manner in which he defended and maintained the independence of his kingdom, in the only point in which it was attacked in his time. In the stand which he made here, he appears to have had with him the great body of the national clergy, and they and he were always on the best terms.

David, Earl of Cumberland, the youngest of the sons of Malcolm Canmore, now became king. Having lived from his childhood in England, his manners, says Malmesbury, were polished from the rust of Scottish barbarity. He had also, before he came to the throne, married an English wife, Matilda, or Maud, the daughter (and eventually heiress) of Waltheof, Earl of Nor-

---

[1] "The Scoto-Saxon period, which began (A.D. 1097) one and thirty years after the Saxon period of the English annals had closed, will be found to contain historical topics of great importance. The Gaelic Scots predominated in the former period; the Saxon-English will be seen to give the law in this. We shall perceive a memorable revolution take place, concerning which the North-British annals have hitherto been altogether silent: we shall soon perceive a new people come in upon the old, a new dynasty ascend the throne, a new jurisprudence gradually prevail; new ecclesiastical establishments settled, and new manners overspread the land. . . . In this period we shall see an Anglo-Saxon, Anglo-Norman, and Anglo-Belgic colonization begin in the country beyond the Forth, and a Scoto-Saxon dynasty commence. In our course we shall perceive the prevalence of the Celtic customs insensibly superseded by the introduction of new manners, and the influence of a Celtic government gradually reduced, by the establishment of an Anglo-Norman jurisprudence, and by the complete reform of a Celtic church."—Chalmers' *Caledonia*, vol. i. pp. 495-497. The "reform" of the Celtic church was unquestionably for the worse.

[2] *Aldred. Rival.*

thumberland, and the widow of Simon de St. Liz, Earl of Northampton. The King of Scotland was now again an English baron, by his tenure of the earldom of Cumberland; and accordingly, when Henry I., in 1127, called together the prelates and nobles of the realm, to swear that they would after his decease support the right of his daughter Matilda to the inheritance of the English crown, David was one of those that attended, and was the first who took the oath. In observance of this engagement, the Scottish king, on the usurpation of Stephen, led an army into England, and compelled the northern barons to swear fealty to Matilda. "What the King of Scots," said Stephen, when this news was brought to him, "has gained by stealth, I will manfully recover." He immediately collected a powerful force, and advanced at its head against David. They met at Newcastle; but no engagement took place: a compromise was effected (February, 1136), and David consented to withdraw his troops, on Stephen engaging to confer on his eldest son, Henry, the earldom of Huntingdon, with the towns of Carlisle and Doncaster, and promising to take into consideration his claims, in right of his mother, to the earldom of Northumberland. Earl Henry did homage to Stephen for the new English honour he was thus to receive; but David himself still refused to do so, although he appears to have retained the earldom of Cumberland in his own hands.

The war was, however, renewed before the end of the same year by David, on the pretence that Stephen delayed to put his son in possession of the county of Northumberland, but, in reality, in consequence of a confederacy into which he had entered with the Earl of Gloucester and the other partizans of the Empress Matilda, who were now making preparations for a grand effort to drive her rival from the throne. With the same impetuosity he had shown on the former occasion, David was again first in the field. A truce, negotiated by Archbishop Thurstan of York, gained a short space for Stephen; but in 1137, David entered Northumberland, and ravaged that unfortunate district for some time, without mercy and without check. In the beginning of the following year, however, he deemed it advisable to fall back upon Roxburgh at the approach of Stephen, who followed him across the Tweed, and made requital by wasting the Scottish border for part of the injury his own subjects had sustained. But the English king was soon recalled by other enemies to the south, and then David (in March, 1138) re-entered Northumberland, sending forward at the same time William, a son of the late King Duncan, into the west, where he and his wild Galwegians (on the 9th of June) gave a signal discomfiture to a party of English at Clitheroe. Meanwhile, Norham Castle, erected in the preceding reign by Bishop Flambard, on the south bank of the Tweed, to guard the main access from Scotland, surrendered to the Scottish king after a short siege; and from this point he marched forward, through Northumberland and Durham, to Northallerton, in Yorkshire, without opposition. Here, however, his barbarous host was met by an English force, collected chiefly by the efforts of the aged Archbishop of York. At the great battle of the Standard, fought on the 22d of August,[1] the Scots sustained a complete defeat. The victors, however, were not in a condition to pursue their advantage. King David retired to Carlisle, and soon after laid siege to the castle of Werk, which having reduced, he razed it to the ground, and then, to adopt the expression of. Lord Hailes, "returned into Scotland more like a conqueror, than like one whose army had been routed." The next year a treaty of peace was concluded between the two kings at Durham, by which David obtained the earldom of Northumberland, the ostensible object of the war, for his son, who enjoyed it till his death, and left it to his descendants.

David, however, was never cordially attached to the interests of Stephen. When, a few years after this, the cause of Matilda for a short time gained the ascendant, he repaired to the court of his niece, and endeavoured to persuade her to follow a course of moderation and policy, at which her imperious temper spurned. He was shut up with her in Winchester Castle, when she was besieged there by Stephen, in August and September, 1141,[2] and escaped thence along with her. It is said that he was indebted for his concealment afterwards, and his conveyance home to his own kingdom, to the exertions of a young man, named David Oliphant, to whom he had been godfather, and who chanced to be serving in the army of Stephen.

From this period the reign of David is scarcely marked by any events, if we except the disturbances occasioned by some piratical descents made upon the Scottish coasts by an adventurer of obscure birth, named Wimund, who gave himself out for a son of the Earl of Moray, but was at last, after giving considerable trouble, taken and deprived of his eyes, in 1151. In his latter years, however, David, relieved from foreign wars, applied himself assiduously to the internal improvement of his country, by the encouragement of agriculture, commerce, and manufactures, the establishment of towns, the erection of churches, monasteries, and other pub-

[1] See vol. i. p. 228. [2] See vol. i. p. 243.

lic buildings, and the reform of the law and its administration. Many of the statutes enacted by him are still preserved.

When the son of the Empress Matilda, afterwards Henry II., came over from the Continent, in 1149, to assert in person his claim to the English crown, he was met by the Scottish king at Carlisle,[1] and after receiving from him the honour of knighthood, bound himself, when he should become King of England, to make over to David the town of Newcastle, and the whole territory between the Tweed and the Tyne. David and his son Henry immediately invaded England, and advanced as far as Lancaster; but on the approach of Stephen, the Scottish army retired without risking a battle.

David did not live to witness the issue of the contest between Stephen and Henry. His death was probably hastened by that of his son Henry, which took place on the 12th of June, 1152, to the great grief of his countrymen, whom his amiable character had filled with hopes of a continuation of the same prosperity and happiness under his rule which they enjoyed under that of his father. Soon after this stroke, David fixed his residence at Carlisle; and there he expired on the morning of the 24th of May, 1153, having been found dead in bed, with his hands joined together over his breast in the posture of devotional supplication. Both the virtues and the capacity of this king have been extolled in the highest terms by the monkish chroniclers; but he seems, on the whole, to have deserved the praises bestowed upon him. It is true that, among the acts for which he is most eulogized, his donations to the church, and his founding of numerous religious houses, stand conspicuous—in allusion to which, his descendant, James I., is said to have feelingly complained of him as having been "a sore saint for the crown." But we may reasonably doubt whether it would have been for the advantage of the public interests that the funds thus expended should have remained in the possession of the crown; and it may also be questioned whether anything more effective could have been done to promote the civilization of a country just emerging from barbarism, as Scotland was at this period, than the planting over all parts of it these establishments, which were not only seminaries of piety and letters, but examples of ornamental architecture, and even central fountain-heads for diffusing knowledge, and the means of cultivating the civil and useful arts.[2]

The late Earl Henry's eldest son, though as yet only in his twelfth year, succeeded his grandfather, under the name of Malcolm IV. The notices we have of the events of his reign in the contemporary chroniclers, are scarcely sufficient to furnish a continuous or intelligible narrative; and in the lack of recorded facts, the writers of later date appear to have filled up the story by drawing on their invention with even more than their usual liberality. With a king of such tender age, the government must have been for some years in the hands of a regency; but there is no

[1] See vol. i. p. 246.

[2] In the time of David I. of Scotland, the church of that country still retained much scriptural purity, and was little subjected to Rome. The tone of the church's piety may be conjectured from what is recorded of the aged monarch's dying days, when it was the Psalms of David, not prayers to the saints, that occupied his thoughts. Then, too, it was that the influence of the Christian faith was most evident in fostering peaceful industry, in which respect we perceive its influence decline with its growing superstitions and subserviency to Rome. One is amazed to find so many clear proofs of there being a numerous, industrious, and apparently well-fed population in the south of Scotland in David's days, consisting largely, we may presume, of Anglo-Saxon immigrants driven by the Norman conquest from the northern parts of England. The influence of the numerous religious houses situated on the Tweed and its tributaries, was no doubt at that time beneficial, though in a far less degree than that of a purely Christian population would have been, such as that which produced such an outburst of peaceful industry, as once agricultural, manufacturing, and commercial, in the valley of the Rhone about this very period. But one would greatly err in supposing that the monks of those days, like the Trappists of later times, promoted agriculture by their own personal labours. Much rather were they like country gentlemen living in clubs, on very good terms with their numerous tenantry, and with neighbours who like themselves lived together in convents, and as nuns were the joint proprietors of pleasant estates. The laborious but often prejudiced George Chalmers, speaks thus of Roxburghshire in David I.'s time:—

"The kings, as we learn from the chartularies, were the greatest farmers of those times. David I. was not only the greatest husbandman himself, but the moving cause of husbandry in others. Early in the twelfth century, he founded the monasteries of Kelso, Melrose, and Jedburgh, and the monks were most extensive farmers. The kings had many manors and granges, with milns, malt-kilns, breweries, cattle, and studs in every shire. The followers of David who had supported his pretensions even during the reign of his brother Alexander, all followed his example and the fashion of the age as husbandmen. . . . But it was the several monks of the religious houses who were the greatest, perhaps the most intelligent cultivators of those times. Before the middle of the twelfth century, those monasteries possessed vast estates in all that constitutes opulence during rude times: in lands, in villeins, in cattle, and sheep, and in every article which can be produced by a well-managed husbandry. The same monks had other possessions in those times of great value. They had also, in various other districts of this shire, lands and tenements, which, as they were rented to cottagers, brought them considerable revenues."

Among the services rendered by their tenants, carriages formed an important item. Thus the husbandmen were bound to carry peats, salt, and coals to the monastery, and to take corn and wool to market. In Sprouston parish, where the monks had an estate, every husbandman was obliged to send a cart in summer weekly to Berwick, carrying corn thither, and returning with salt or coals. Their tenants must have been numerous. At Faudon, in Bolden parish, they had twenty-one cottages which paid £10 of rent yearly: at Bolden itself they had thirty-six cottages. On the whole, the abbot had under him at Bolden about seventy families. As in the charters we find proofs not only of draining and manuring land, but of *weeding* corn on the abbot's grange, the agriculture of that age could not have been contemptible; and in all its phases we recognize the superior industry and skill of the Saxon population.

account of any such arrangement. This was the first example of the Scottish throne having been occupied by a boy, and it may be regarded as having for the first time established the principle of hereditary succession as the rule of the monarchy in all circumstances. As might have been expected, however, the sceptre was not allowed to pass into the hands of so mere a pageant of a king without dispute. A few months only after Malcolm's accession, the public tranquillity was disturbed by what appears to have been more properly an invasion than an insurrection, being an attack made with the avowed object of effecting the conquest of the kingdom, by Somerled, the Thane of Argyle, whose daughter had married the adventurer Wimund. The provinces, it may be observed, of Argyle, Moray, Ross, and Galloway, seem still to have remained so many principalities, usually, indeed, acknowledging a sort of feudal dependence upon the Scottish crown, but scarcely considered as forming parts of the kingdom of Scotland, any more than the vassal dukedoms and earldoms of the crown of France were held to be integral parts of that kingdom. They had each its own chief, and in all respects its own government, with which that of the supreme sovereign rarely, if ever, interfered. In the present case the Thane of Argyle made war upon his sovereign just as any independent potentate might have made war upon another. All that we know of the events of the war is, that it lasted for some years; and then, in 1157, the King of Scotland appears to have made peace with the Thane of Argyle, just as he might have done with any other sovereign as independent as himself. To this date, also, is assigned Malcolm's first transaction with the English king. At an interview held at Chester he was induced not only to give up his claim to the territory on the north of the Tyne, promised to his father David, but also to abandon Cumberland, and whatever other lands and honours he possessed in England, with the exception only of the earldom of Huntingdon, which Henry either confirmed to him, or conferred upon him, taking it from his youngest brother David, to whom it appears to have been left by the late king. Malcolm at the same time is stated to have done homage to Henry in the same manner as his grandfather had to Henry's grandfather—that is to say, with the reservation of all his dignities. The accounts given of the whole of this affair by the old chroniclers are confused and obscure; but it is asserted by Fordun that Henry succeeded in effecting the agreement by bribing the advisers of the Scottish king, and taking advantage of his youth and inexperience; and that it produced a deep and settled hatred against Malcolm among all classes of his own subjects. Nor does his facility appear to have gained for him much gratitude or consideration from Henry. He repaired the following year to Carlisle to obtain the honour of knighthood from the English king; but this interview ended in a quarrel, and Malcolm returned home in disgust, and without his knighthood. When Henry, however, set forth on his expedition for the recovery of Toulouse, in 1159, Malcolm went with him to France, and was knighted by him there. But he had followed Henry's banner on this occasion in opposition to the judgment of the Scottish nobility, and after a few months a solemn deputation was sent to him to urge his immediate return to his dominions. The people of Scotland, the deputies were commanded to tell him, would not have Henry to rule over them. Malcolm felt it necessary to obey this call; but the faction opposed to the connection with England was not, it appears, to be satisfied with having succeeded in merely bringing him home. While he was holding a great council at Perth, Ferquhard, Earl of Strathearn, and five other noblemen, made an attempt to seize his person, and openly assaulted a tower in which he was lodged. The movement threatened to lead to a general insurrection, when an accommodation was brought about by the intervention of the clergy. Immediately after this, Malcolm applied himself to the reduction of those districts of his kingdom which, inhabited for the most part by races of foreign extraction, had never yet been completely brought under subjection to the general government, and in which revolts or disturbances were constantly breaking out. He found occupation for his restless nobility by leading them first against the wild Irish of Galloway, and then against the people of Moray, who seem to have been principally of Danish lineage. In his two first expeditions against Galloway he was repulsed; but in a third attempt he compelled Fergus, the lord of the country, to sue for peace, and to make complete submission. In regard to the province of Moray (at that time certainly not confined to the modern county of the same name, but comprehending apparently the whole or the greater part of what is now called Inverness), where rebellions had been incessant, Malcolm is asserted to have adopted the strong measure of removing the old inhabitants altogether to other parts of the kingdom, and replacing them with new colonies. The subjugation of Galloway and Moray was followed, in 1164, by another contest with Somerled, who had again risen in arms, and landed at Renfrew on the Clyde with a numerous force, which he had collected both from his own territories and from Ireland. The Thane of Argyle probably sympathized with the Lords of Galloway and Moray, or regarded their fate as of evil omen to himself. The issue of his present attempt, however, was eminently disastrous; his army was scattered with great slaughter in its first encounter with the king's forces, and both himself and his son were left among the slain.

It thus appears that Malcolm IV. was at least as successful as any of his predecessors in the maintenance of his proper authority as sovereign of Scotland, and that he probably extended the royal sway of the sceptre which they had left him in the country beyond the Tweed. His relinquishment, however, of the possessions which had been held by his grandfather in the south, and the partiality he evinced for a connection with England, seem to have been in the highest degree distasteful to the generality of his subjects. At the head of the party which this feeling raised against him, was his next brother, William, for whom his grandfather is said to have intended the earldom of Northumberland, and who accordingly considered himself to be deprived of his inheritance by the agreement with Henry which Malcolm had made in the commencement of his reign. Meanwhile, Malcolm is recorded to have, on the 1st of July, 1163, at Woodstock, renewed his homage to Henry, and also to have taken an oath of fealty to his infant son as heir apparent, and the relations between the two kings appear to have become more intimate than ever. The next notice that we have of the course of events in Scotland represents Malcolm as deprived of the government, and his brother William at the head of affairs as regent. Even the fact of this revolution, however, is involved in considerable doubt, and various accounts are given of the causes that led to it. It is certain that he died at Jedburgh, on the 9th of December, 1165, on which his brother William was raised to the throne.

Notwithstanding the part he had hitherto taken, William appears to have begun his reign by courting the alliance of the English king. He passed over to the Continent to Henry, while he was employed in reducing the revolted Bretons in 1166, and, as already mentioned, was with him while he kept court in the castle on Mount St. Michael in the close of that year. The *Chronicle of Melrose* (which is written throughout in an English spirit) says that William followed Henry to France "to do the business of his lord." It is probable that he expected to succeed by this conduct in his favourite object of recovering possession of Northumberland. Henry seems to have kept up his hopes by fair promises for some years: when his eldest son Henry was solemnly crowned at London, on the 14th of June, 1170, both William and his younger brother David, were present at the ceremony, and both did homage to the heir apparent, along with the other English barons; but in 1173, when the quarrel broke out between the English king and his son, William, tired of fruitless solicitation, changed his course, and, joining in confederacy with the "junior king," from whom he obtained a grant of the earldom of Northumberland for himself, and of that of Cambridge for his brother, he raised an army, and entered England as an enemy. But after merely ravaging part of the northern counties, he consented to a truce, which was eventually prolonged to the end of Lent in the following year. In 1174, however, he again invaded Northumberland. As before, his troops spread devastation wherever they appeared; but their destructive course was soon stopped. William, as has been already related, was on the 12th of July suddenly fallen upon at Alnwick by a party of Yorkshire barons, headed by Ranulf de Glanville, and made prisoner, with all his attendants. The Scottish king and his sixty knights, however, were not taken captive without resistance. As soon as William perceived who the enemy were, which was not till they were close upon him, for at first he had taken them for a returning party of his own stragglers, he cried out, "Now it will be seen who are true knights," and instantly advanced to the charge. But the numbers of the English (there were 400 horsemen with Glanville) made this gallantry wholly unavailing. The king was quickly overpowered and unhorsed, and was carried that same night to Newcastle, his attendants voluntarily sharing the fate of their sovereign. He was at first confined in the castle of Richmond, in Yorkshire; but after a few weeks Henry carried him across the seas to Falaise, in Normandy. In this strong fortress he remained shut up till the conclusion of the treaty of Falaise, in December following, by which William, with the consent of his barons and clergy, became the liegeman of Henry for Scotland and all his other territories. He was then liberated and allowed to return home, on delivering up to the English king the castles of Edinburgh, Stirling, Roxburgh, Berwick, and Jedburgh, and giving his brother David and many of his chief nobility as hostages for his adherence to the treaty.

The next event requiring to be noticed in the reign of William, is a remarkable contest in which he was engaged with the court of Rome. It began in 1178, when, on the death of Richard, Bishop of St. Andrews, the chapter elected as his successor John Scot, an Englishman of distinguished learning. The nomination of a bishop by the chapter, without the royal consent, was a stretch of ecclesiastical authority which had never been quietly submitted to, either in England or Scotland, although any actual conflict between the claims of the spiritual and the temporal powers had usually been avoided by the king and the chapter uniting in the election of the same person. But in the present case William had a particular motive for making a stand against the clerical encroachment, having destined the see for Hugh, his chaplain. "By the arm of St. James," he passionately exclaimed, when he heard of the election made by the chapter, "while I live John Scot shall never be Bishop of St. Andrews." He immediately seized the revenues of the see, and disregarding the appeal of John to Rome, made Hugh be consecrated, and put him in possession. When the pope, Alexander III., cancelled this appointment, and John was the following year consecrated in obedience to the Papal mandate, William instantly banished him from the kingdom. The pope, on this, resorted to the strongest measures: he laid the diocese of St. Andrews under an interdict; he commanded the Scottish clergy within eight days to install John; soon after he ordered them to excommunicate Hugh; and, finally, he granted legatine powers over Scotland to the Archbishop of York, and authorized that prelate, and the Bishop of Durham, to excommunicate the King of Scotland, and to lay the whole kingdom under an interdict, if the king did not forthwith put John in peaceable possession of the see. Still William was inflexible on the main point. He offered to make John chancellor, and to give him any other bishopric which should become vacant; but this was the only concession he would make. When the Archbishop of York and the Bishop of Durham called upon the clergy of the diocese of St. Andrews to yield obedience to John under pain of suspension, he banished all who complied with that summons. At last the two prelates went to the full extent of their tremendous powers, and actually pronounced sentence of excommunication against William, and laid the kingdom of Scotland under an interdict. But at this point the death of Alexander (in August, 1181) prevented further consequences. William lost no time in making application to the new pope, Lucius III., who, with the customary disregard of each sovereign pontiff for the decrees of his predecessor, consented to reverse the sentence of excommunication, and to recal the interdict. The affair was ended by the pope himself nominating Hugh to the bishopric of St. Andrews, and John to that of Dunkeld, and so, to use the words of Lord Hailes, "making *that* his *deed* which was the king's *will*." Lord Hailes observes that William, in the obstinate stand he made on this occasion against Pope Alexander, "seems to have been proud of opposing to the uttermost that pontiff, before whom his conqueror, Henry, had bowed."

Notwithstanding the success which is attributed to the measures taken by the preceding king, for reducing to a real obedience the various provinces that had before only acknowledged, at the utmost, a qualified dependence upon the Scottish crown, we find insurrections in these districts still disturbing the present reign.

In 1186, William, on the proposal of the English king, married Ermengarde, the daughter of Richard, Viscount Beaumont, and the descendant of an illegitimate daughter of Henry I., on which, as part of the dower of his *cousin*, Henry restored the castle of Edinburgh. Two years afterwards he also offered to give up the castles of Roxburgh and Berwick, if William would pay the tenths of his kingdom for the Holy War; but the Scottish barons and clergy made answer, "That *they* would not, although *both* kings should have sworn to levy them."

The accession of Richard I. to the English throne was followed, in a few months, by the release of William from the obligations which Henry, in the words of the charter of acquittance (dated December 5, 1189), "had extorted from him by new instruments, in consequence of his captivity," with the proviso only, that he should in future perform whatever homage had of right been performed, or had been of right due, by his brother Malcolm. There seems to be no pretence for denying that this was a full renunciation, by Richard, at least, of whatever new rights of sovereignty over Scotland had been created by the treaty of Falaise. For this acquittance, and the restitution of the castles of Roxburgh and Berwick, William agreed to pay 10,000 marks sterling.

William lived many years after this, but scarcely any events of importance mark the remainder of his reign. Some disturbances in Caithness, in 1196 and the following year, compelled him to march an army into that province, where he seized Harold, the Earl of Orkney and Caithness, who was at the head of the insurrection, and detained him in captivity until his son Torfin surrendered himself as a hostage. This was, perhaps, the earliest actual assertion by any Scottish king of his authority in that remote district; the earls of which, if they acknowledged any limitation of their independence, had probably been wont to consider themselves subject rather to the Danish than to the Scottish crown.

After the accession of John to the throne of England, William did homage to him (November 22, 1200) at Lincoln, "saving his own rights." A few years afterwards a misunderstanding arose between the two kings respecting a fort which John attempted to erect at Tweedmouth, and which William repeatedly demolished as soon as it was built. A war at last threatened to arise out of this quarrel; and, in 1209, the English king advanced to Norham, and the Scottish to Berwick, each at the head of an army. But no encounter took place; a treaty of peace was concluded by the intervention of the barons of both nations, by which William became bound to pay to John 15,000 marks, as a compensation, it is supposed, for his demolition of the fort, which John, on his part, is said to have undertaken not to rebuild. William also delivered his two daughters to John, that they might be provided by him with suitable matches.

William died, after a long illness, at Stirling, on the 4th of December, 1214, in the seventy-second year of his age, and forty-ninth of his reign. He was surnamed *The Lion*, on account, says Boyce, of his singular justice—which seems a strange reason. It is more probable that he took this title from the lion rampant, the coat armorial of the Scottish kings, which he appears to have been the first to introduce. The statutes attributed to him consist of thirty-nine chapters; but a few of them are believed to be interpolations of a later period. He left many natural children; but, besides his two daughters mentioned above, only one son by his wife Ermengarde de Beaumont, a youth in his seventeenth year, who succeeded his father, and was crowned at Scone on the 10th of December, 1214, by the name of Alexander II. The part taken by the new King of Scots, in conjunction with the English barons in their contest with John, has been related above.

We have now merely to add a notice of the few leading events, of subsequent date to Henry's expedition, which occur in the history of Ireland before it becomes mixed in one stream with that of England. The appearances of entire submission which had been exhibited during Henry's stay in the island were not long preserved after he left its shores. Before the close of the year 1172, the people had risen against the English domination in various districts; and, for the next three years, De Lacy, Strongbow, and their associates were kept in constant activity by the active or passive resistance of one part of the country or another. In 1175, Henry, in the hope that it might have some effect in subduing this rebellious temper, produced, for the first time, the bull which he had procured from Pope Adrian twenty-four years before, along with a brief confirming it, which he had received in the interval from Alexander III. William Fitz-Aldelm, and Nicholas, prior of Wallingford, were sent over to Ireland with the two instruments; and they were publicly read in a synod of bishops which these commissioners summoned on their arrival. In this same year, also, a formal treaty was concluded between Henry and Roderick O'Connor, by which the former granted to the latter, who was styled his liegeman, that so long as he continued faithfully to serve him, he should be king of the country under him, and enjoy his hereditary territories in peace, on payment of the annual tribute of a merchantable hide for every tenth head of cattle killed in Ireland. For some years after this, one chief governor rapidly succeeded another, as each either incurred the displeasure of the king by the untoward events of his administration, or, as it happened in some cases, awakened his jealousy by seeming to have become too popular or too powerful. But Henry never himself returned to Ireland. At length, in 1185, he determined to place at the head of the government his youngest son, John, then only in his nineteenth year; the lordship of Ireland, it is said, being the portion of his dominions which he had always intended that John should inherit. But this experiment succeeded worse than any other he had tried. The same evil dispositions which were afterwards more conspicuously displayed on the throne, showed themselves in John's conduct almost from the first day he began to exercise his delegated authority; by his insulting behaviour he converted into enemies those of the Irish chieftains who had hitherto been the most attached friends of the English interest; and he met with nothing but loss and disgrace in every military encounter with the natives. He was hastily recalled by Henry, after having been only a few months in the country. The government was then put into the hands of John de Courcy, who had some years before penetrated into Ulster, and established the English power for the first time in that province. De Courcy remained governor to the end of the reign of Henry; and from this date the history of Ireland may be considered as merged in the history of England.

CHAPTER X.—HISTORY OF RELIGION.

A.D. 1066—1216.

State of the English church at the Conquest—William founds Battle Abbey—His plans to depress the Anglo-Saxon clergy—Lanfranc raised to the primacy—Lanfranc's church reforms—Imperious demands of the pope on William—A uniform church-service introduced into England—Anselm succeeds Lanfranc as primate—Quarrels between Anselm and William Rufus—Anselm carries his appeal to Rome—Decision about ecclesiastical investitures—Anselm recalled to England at the accession of Henry I.—Anselm and Henry disagree about ecclesiastical investitures—Laws enforcing clerical celibacy—Death and character of Anselm—Question of ecclesiastical investiture revived in the reign of Henry II.—Thomas à Becket—His career till he becomes primate—His contest with Henry II. about the rights of the church—The Constitutions of Clarendon—They are opposed by Becket—Effects of his martyrdom in establishing his cause—Foreigners arrive in England—They are punished as heretics—History of the English church during the reigns of Richard I. and John—The controversy about ecclesiastical investiture still predominant—New monastic orders introduced into England—Prevalence of pilgrimages at this period—Soldier-monks—The Hospitallers and Templars.

HE first act by which the Conqueror expressed the joy of his heart for the victory of Hastings, was in accordance with the spirit in which he had professed to conduct his enterprise from its commencement, and betrayed none of that jealousy of the church which he showed at a later period. Up to this time the countenance of the pope and the church had been one of his main stays, and he had still to look to that quarter for much important aid in establishing his power. In these circumstances, and in the hour of triumph, when he gave orders for building the abbey of Battle, he was naturally liberal to profusion, both in the privileges which he granted to the new establishment and the revenues with which he proposed to endow it.

Although many of the higher churchmen had, during a great part of the reign of the Confessor, been in the Norman interest, and continued among the firmest friends of William after his seizure of the throne, the great body of the clergy were strongly attached to the national cause. Some of them had even taken arms and fought on the side of Harold at Hastings; and, in the course of the protracted contest which followed, before the country was finally subjugated, the English, in their resistance to the foreigners, had been on several occasions animated and led on by their priests. Hence it soon became a leading principle in the policy of William to depress the ecclesiastical power; while on the other hand the church, thus selected as a chief object of attack, rose on that account in the affections of the country, and grew every day to be more and more regarded as the strength and best representative of the patriotic cause.

Among the higher ecclesiastics who stood by what was considered as the English faction, the most conspicuous had all along been the Primate Stigand. He had refused, as we have already related, to put the crown on the head of the Conqueror, who was thereupon obliged to apply to Aldred of York to perform that office. Stigand, besides, lay under the displeasure of the court of Rome on other grounds. William, therefore, when he judged that the proper time had come, found no difficulty in effecting the removal of the obnoxious prelate: he was deposed by the Papal legates at a council held at Winchester in the early part of the year 1070. The person appointed by the king, with the consent of the barons, to be his successor, was the celebrated Lanfranc. Lanfranc had been a professor of laws in his native city of Pavia; but he had afterwards removed to Normandy, and opened a school at Avranches. Here he acquired great celebrity, and his seminary became the source from which the surrounding country was gradually provided with a lettered clergy. Of such importance were his services thought to be, that having, on the advance of old age, given up his public employment and retired to the monastery of Bec, he was after a few years induced, much against his own wish, to resume his occupation of schoolmaster or lecturer, and he continued to perform its duties with undiminished reputation till he was past the age of eighty, when William made him abbot of his new monastery of St. Stephen at Caen. He had nearly reached his ninetieth year when he was invited to the archbishopric of Canterbury.

Having once assumed his high office, which he did after much reluctance, Lanfranc showed himself determined to neglect neither its duties nor its rights. The first thing to which he applied himself was to recover for his church of Canterbury the numerous ancient possessions of which it had been deprived in the confusions, or by the arbitrary proceedings of the last few years. In pursuing this object, obliged as he was to contend with haughty barons, whom their liege lord could scarcely control, his intrepidity and perseverance enabled him to succeed in many instances. Even the powerful Odo, uterine brother to the king, was thus compelled to restore twenty-five manors which had formerly belonged to the see of Canterbury. The wealth thus recovered for the church was applied by Lanfranc to the promotion of its interests. He rebuilt the cathedral of Canterbury with Norman stone, repaired the sacred edifices, and erected churches and monastic establishments where they were considered most necessary. He also caused the bishops to remove their seats from the villages, in which many of them resided, to the larger towns: he is said to have introduced certain reforms into the monastic institutions, and he established schools in various parts of the kingdom. Lanfranc at the same time cordially co-operated with William in that particular point of ecclesiastical reformation which the latter no doubt had most at heart—the general substitution of a foreign for a native clergy. Very good reasons were easily found for the displacement of many of the English priests, on the ground both of ignorance and immorality; and, on the whole, it is probable that the result of their ejection was the settlement in the country of a more instructed body of pastors than it had previously possessed.

We must suppose that, whatever may have been the motives of another kind that principally actuated William, this was the end which Lanfranc kept in view, and by which he justified to himself the measures of severity in which he took part. His own elevation, indeed, had been one of the commencing moves of the royal scheme of reform; for it was at the council at which Stigand was deposed, held by the Papal legates in 1070, that the removal of the native clergy and the introduction of foreigners were begun. For some years after this, the course which had been thus entered upon was vigorously pursued, till the conversion of the spiritual estate to a community of interests and feeling with the civil government was pretty completely effected. In proof of this, we find that at the death of the Conqueror, only one English prelate—Wulstan, Bishop of Winchester—had been allowed to retain his bishopric. In many instances the crime of being an Englishman, or inability to speak the Norman tongue, was reckoned sufficient for clerical deposition in the absence of more substantial charges. Even the saints of the Saxon calendar shared in the fate of their worshippers. Their sanctity was denied, and their worship ridiculed. Of the unfortunate clergy, some endeavoured to make terms with a power they had no means of resisting, by consenting to descend to a humbler station in the church; others fled to Scotland. Their necessities, or the hope of vengeance, drove many to the forests, where they joined the bands of outlaws, and sanctioned with the rites of religion the wild struggle of independence which was there long maintained by the sparks of the popular spirit that were last in being trodden out, and also the deeds of rapine and cruelty with which it was doubtless plentifully deformed.

It appears that in most instances the higher church benefices were filled by William with men of learning and virtue; but it was impossible for him, whatever his wishes may have been, to prevent the intrusion of many unworthy persons into the inferior appointments. He had hired adventurers to his standard by promises of ecclesiastical as well as political preferment. The powerful barons, whose swords had hewn out his way to the throne, and now maintained him upon it, had kinsmen and retainers of the clerical order, whose demands could not be refused; and thus, though vacancies were rapidly made, they were still insufficient for a throng of greedy expectants, the gratification of whose demands, on the one hand, only deepened the miseries of the land, and the hatred of the unhappy people.

But while William was thus exercising his privileges of a victor in the church as well as the state, he was surprised by finding himself threatened with vassalage in turn. The subtle and imperious Hildebrand, now pope, by the title of Gregory VII., declaring that kings and princes were but the vassals of St. Peter and his successors, summoned William to do homage for the possession of England. The answer of the proud Norman was brief and decisive. The tax of Peter's pence, discontinued of late years in England, and now required by the pope, he declared that he would regularly pay; but the homage he peremptorily refused, alleging that it had never been promised by himself, nor rendered by any of his predecessors. With this answer to his demand, Gregory was obliged to remain satisfied for the present: he probably, indeed, expected no other, and only announced his claims with a view to their enforcement in more favourable circumstances, and that no future English king might be able to profess astonishment at their being advanced, seeing that they had first been pressed upon the Conqueror. William, in the meantime, taking advantage of the contest which arose between the pope and the emperor, and of his own remoteness from Rome, which enabled him to act with the more independence, commenced a vigorous warfare against the Papal encroachments. He ordered, first, that no pontiff should be acknowledged in his dominions without his previous sanction, and that Papal letters, before they were published, should be submitted to his inspection; secondly, that no decision, either of national or provincial synods, should be carried into execution without his permission; and thirdly, that the clerical courts should neither implead nor excommunicate any tenant holding of the crown *in capite*, until the offence had been certified to himself.[1]

During the latter period of William's reign an event occurred, arising out of the disorders of the Conquest, but from which an important benefit resulted to religion. No uniformity was observed in the public worship—the prayers, and their mode of recital, frequently depending upon the caprices of the officiating priest. In order to enforce a favourite liturgy among the Saxon monks of Glastonbury, Thurstan, their Norman abbot, entered the church with a band of archers and spearmen. The monks withstood even this armed demonstration; a desperate conflict commenced round the altar, and behind the great crucifix, which was soon stuck thick with arrows, while benches, candlesticks, and crosses were wielded in their defence by the brethren, several of whom were slain. This incident suggested the necessity of a form established by authority; and Oswald, Bishop of Salisbury, composed a church-service that became universal throughout the realm.[2]

Lanfranc did not long survive the accession of Rufus, for whom he materially assisted in securing the throne, and whose chief counsellor he continued to be while he lived. The archbishop, it is recorded, did not fail to press upon the new king the fulfilment of the oaths he had taken to observe the laws; but Rufus, now that he had obtained his end, was little inclined to give heed to these exhortations. The primate, however, maintained a considerable ascendancy over the irregular spirit of the king, by which his excesses were frequently restrained; and, with longer time, Lanfranc might perhaps have been also enabled to develope some of those better qualities, the elements of which Rufus undoubtedly possessed. But the archbishop, being nearly 100 years old, died in 1089, about two years after the commencement of the reign.[3]

Lanfranc was succeeded in his office of the king's chief adviser by the notorious Ralph Flambard. One of the chief sources to which the new minister looked for the supply of the royal coffers, was the plunder of the church. At his instigation, Rufus took to himself the revenues of all vacant bishoprics and abbacies, and in many cases kept the most important offices in the church unfilled for years, drawing the profits all the while into his own exchequer. In these cases the ecclesiastical estates were farmed out to those who offered the highest terms for the uncertain tenure, and who, of course, employed, without scruple, all the means at their command to repay themselves, and to make the most of their temporary occupation. The tenants under this system were ground to the earth by the most merciless exactions; and when, at last, an occupant was appointed to the benefice, he was usually required to pay a heavy premium for his promotion, which, again, he could only raise by a continuation of the same methods which had already produced so much suffering, and gone so far to exhaust the resources of the benefice.

This oppressive course of the king had continued for about four years, when, in 1093, he was seized with a dangerous sickness, and, under the agonies of terror and remorse, he became anxious to repair the wrongs he had done the church. Since the death of Lanfranc he had kept the see of Canterbury vacant, swearing that it should have no archbishop but himself; but now, impetuous in repentance as in guilt, he insisted that Anselm, the successor of Lanfranc in the abbacy of Bec, and whom that prelate had before his death expressed his wish to have also for his successor in the primacy, should forthwith be appointed archbishop. Anselm happening to be at the time in England, he was hurried to the bed-side of the king. A crozier was presented to him, but he refused to touch it, till the royal attendants unclenched his fingers, and forced the sacred staff into his struggling hand, when all with one accord burst forth into a *Te Deum* for the primate whom Heaven had sent them, while the helpless monk in vain protested against the whole proceeding. Anselm, upon accepting the primacy, stipulated for the restoration of all the church lands belonging to his see, and the implicit obedience of the king to his advice in all matters of religion; and to these demands William evasively replied that the archbishop's reasonable expectations would be fulfilled. But the penitence of the king vanished with his fit of illness, and he rose from his sick-bed with fresh vigour to resume the plunder of the church. His first quarrel with the primate was on the subject of the price to be paid by the latter for his promotion. As Rufus had not been accustomed to confer the higher benefices without a valuable consideration, Anselm was willing to comply with the usage; but, pleading his previous poverty, and the impoverished condition of the see, he offered only the sum of £500. Rufus eyed the money with disdain, and refused it, on which the primate bestowed it upon the poor. Afterwards he was given to understand that £1000 would be a more welcome offering, but he

[1] *Eadmer*, p. 6.   [2] *W. Malmes.; Chron. Sax.; Knyghton*.
[3] *Orderic.* pp. 241-245; *W. Malmes.* 117.

declared that he was unable to raise such a sum from his exhausted revenues.[1] When this answer was reported to the king, it filled him with fury. "As I hated him yesterday," he exclaimed, "so I hate him more to-day; and tell him that I shall hate him more bitterly the longer I live. I shall never acknowledge him for my archbishop."[2] A ground of open quarrel was soon found. About seven months after his forced acceptance of the see, the primate proposed, after the custom of his predecessors, to proceed to Rome to receive the pall from the hands of the sovereign pontiff; but there were at present two rival popes, between whom Rufus had not yet made his election. When Anselm, therefore, presented himself to request permission to set out on his journey, Rufus asked him, in real or affected surprise, to what pope he meant to go? Anselm at once answered that he should go to Urban II. Indignant at this arbitrary decision, the king instantly exclaimed, "As well tear the crown from my head as dispossess me of a right which is the peculiar prerogative of the English kings!" The archbishop, nevertheless, did not hesitate to announce that he intended to proceed on his journey, even without the leave of the king. In these circumstances a council of the nobility and prelates was forthwith assembled at Rockingham to decide upon the case. The bishops acknowledged the illegality of the primate's conduct; but when the king demanded his deposition, they declared that this could only be effected by the authority of the pope. They agreed, however, to unite in endeavouring to persuade him to retract his decision in favour of Urban, and to forego his journey, but Anselm would make no such concessions. The affair was thus fast advancing to a crisis, when the difficulty was solved by Rufus finding it expedient to acknowledge the claims of Urban, and by the pope, on the other hand, by way of returning the favour, dispensing with the personal attendance of Anselm, and transmitting the pall to England.

As Rufus, however, still persisted in keeping many of the chief offices of the church vacant, while Anselm felt it his duty to urge that proper persons should be appointed to the abbacies and other preferments, which the king thus retained in his own hands, the quarrel between them was not long in breaking out again with all its former violence. "Are not the abbeys mine?" exclaimed the Red King, when the archbishop pressed his unwelcome solicitations; "do what you please with the farms of your archbishopric, but leave me the same liberty with my abbeys!" Anselm eventually determined to go to Rome and lay the matter before the pope, deterred neither by the steady refusal of Rufus to grant him permission to leave the kingdom, nor by the confiscation and banishment which he was assured would follow his unauthorized departure. He set out on his journey in the spring of 1098, on foot, as a humble pilgrim, with a staff and wallet; and in this guise he reached Dover, where he underwent the indignity of a strict search from the king's officers, that he might carry no money out of England. He arrived, however, in safety at Rome, where he was greeted by the pope with the most distinguished welcome. Urban, addressing him in a long speech before his whole court, called him the pope of another world, while all the English in the city were commanded to kiss his toe.[3] The pontiff soon after sent a letter to Rufus, requiring the restitution of Anselm's property, which had been confiscated at his departure; but when the king understood that the bearer was a servant of the archbishop, he swore that he would tear out his eyes unless he instantly quitted the kingdom.

Before, however, it was known what reception the pope's application had met with, an ecclesiastical council, which was held at Rome in the close of this year, and at which Anselm was present, declared that the King of England deserved excommunication for his treatment of that prelate; but, at Anselm's request, made upon his knees, the pope refrained from actually pronouncing the sentence for the present. But this council is especially memorable, in the history of the church, for the decision to which it came upon the great question of investiture, which had now become the main point in the contest between the pretensions of the spiritual and of the temporal power in every part of Christendom. The matter in dispute was, simply, whether ecclesiastical persons, on being inducted into bishoprics and abbeys, should be permitted to receive the ring and crozier (by which the temporalities of the benefice were understood to be conveyed) from the hands of the prince. It is evident, however, that this ceremony involved the whole question of whether, in every country, the clergy should be under the dominion of the king or of the pope. Its observance, accordingly, had been for a long time as strongly protested against by the court of Rome, as it had been usually insisted upon by every temporal sovereign. The present council denounced excommunication both against all laymen who should presume to grant investiture of any ecclesiastical benefice, and against every priest who should accept of such investiture. It was alleged, with a daring freedom of language,

---

[1] Rufus exacted the same sum from his favourite Flambard, on presenting him with the bishopric of Durham. It is likely, however, that this able financier found no great difficulty in raising the money.   [2] *Eadmer*, pp. 21-25.

[3] *William of Malmesbury*, p. 127.

to be too horrible for hands that created the Creator himself—a power not granted even to the angels—and that offered him to the Father as a sacrifice for the world's redemption, to be placed in fealty between the hands of one who might be stained and polluted with every excess.[1]

Soon after this arrived the answer of Rufus to the pope's letter. "I am astonished," he wrote, "how it could enter your mind to intercede for the restoration of Anselm. If you ask wherefore, this is the cause:—when he wished to go away, he was plainly warned that the whole revenues of his see would be confiscated at his departure. Since, therefore, he would needs go, I have done what I threatened, and I think I have done right." Anselm was not recalled so long as Rufus lived.

When Henry Beauclerk succeeded, his defective title required the sanction of the church, and he, therefore, politically recalled Anselm from banishment at the commencement of his reign. He also promised neither to farm nor to sell the ecclesiastical benefices, as his brother had done, and to restore to the church all its former immunities; and he threw into prison the obnoxious Flambard, the agent of the late oppressions. After these concessions it was easy for the king to procure his marriage with Matilda, even though she was supposed to have taken the veil.

It was not long, however, before the quarrel respecting investiture was renewed by the demand of Henry that Anselm should do homage for his bishopric. To this demand the latter returned a decided negative. In consequence the vexatious subject was again referred to Rome, and, as might have been expected, the decision pronounced by Paschal II., who was now pope, was in favour of the church. Henry, notwithstanding, still commanded Anselm either to do homage or leave the kingdom; but the archbishop would do neither. He declared that he would abide in his province, and he defied any one to injure him there. A second deputation was thereupon sent to Rome, to intimate, in the name of the king and nobles, that unless the right of investiture was conceded they would banish Anselm, dissolve their connection with the Papal see, and withhold the usual payments.

Thus pressed, if we may believe the account given by Anselm's biographer, Eadmer, the court of Rome had recourse to a very strange and clumsy stratagem. Three bishops had brought the message of the king, and two monks had also arrived to plead the cause of the archbishop. To the bishops, it is affirmed, the pope verbally conceded the right of investiture as claimed by the king, but excused himself from committing the permission to writing, lest other sovereigns should demand the same privileges and despise his authority; while, by the monks, he sent letters to Anselm, exhorting him to resist all royal investitures and hold out to the uttermost. The deputies of both parties returned to London, and, at a great council held there (A.D. 1102), after the bishops had rehearsed their verbal commission the monks produced their letters. The pope afterwards declared the statement of the bishops to be false, and even excommunicated them as liars; but still Henry stood out. At length it was arranged that the archbishop should himself repair to Rome, to obtain a positive decision; and he set out on his journey, accordingly, on the 29th of April, 1103.

Some years of further negotiation followed, during which Anselm remained abroad. At last a compromise was effected by the pope consenting that, provided the king would abstain from insisting upon the investiture with ring and crozier, the bishops and abbots should do homage, in the same manner with the lay tenants in chief of the crown, for the temporalities of their sees. On the tedious controversy being thus brought to a close, Anselm returned to England in August, 1106.

Two years after this act of pacification, a council was held at London to enforce the obligation of clerical celibacy—a rule which both Anselm and his predecessor, Lanfranc, had always shown great zeal in promoting, although the subject had been partially lost sight of during the late controversies. Ten canons were now passed on this head, more rigid than any that had been hitherto promulgated. All married priests, of whatever degree, were commanded instantly to put away their wives, not to suffer them to live on any lands belonging to the church, and never to see them or converse with them except in urgent cases, and in the presence of witnesses. As a punishment for their crime in marrying, they were to abstain from saying mass for a certain period, and to undergo several penances. Those who refused to banish their wives were to be deposed and excommunicated, their goods were to be confiscated, and their wives, as adulteresses, to be made slaves to the bishop of the diocese.[2]

Anselm ended his troubled career in 1109, in the seventy-sixth year of his age and sixteenth of his primacy. His writings, which still remain, prove that he possessed a large share both of literary knowledge and metaphysical acuteness; and it deserves to be remembered, as one of his chief merits, that he zealously followed up, and even extended the plans of his predecessor Lan-

---

[1] The proceedings of this council are very minutely related by Eadmer, the companion of Anselm in his flight and banishment.

[2] Spelman's *Concilia*, i. p. 29.

franc, for the establishment of schools and the diffusion of learning in the country of his adoption. Whatever may be thought, also, of the course which he took in defence of what he conceived to be the rights of his station and of his order, or of some of his measures for the reform of the church over which he presided, it is evident that the contest he so perseveringly waged was for no merely personal or selfish objects. To his honour it is recorded that the English loved him as if he had been one of themselves.[1] After his death Henry was in no haste to fill the see of Canterbury, and he kept it vacant for the space of five years.

The ecclesiastical history of the remainder of the reign of Henry offers no events that require to be related. The conduct of the leading clergy, in the contention between Stephen and Matilda, has been detailed at sufficient length in a preceding chapter. The defective nature of Stephen's title afforded a favourable opportunity, which the ecclesiastical interest did not neglect, of extorting from the crown an acknowledgment of its haughtiest and heretofore most strenuously-disputed pretensions. Exemption from the royal investiture, and the right of carrying ecclesiastical causes by appeal to Rome, were conceded by Stephen, or usurped in spite of him, by a church that was daily improving in the art of profiting by every political emergency. It is not till the reign of Henry II., however, that the contest re-assumes much interest or distinctness, and to that period we will now therefore at once proceed.

The principal figure here is Becket. The legend of the origin of this celebrated personage is sufficiently romantic. Gilbert Beck or Becket, a Saxon yeoman, followed to the Crusades the pennon of his Norman lord, but being taken prisoner by an emir of the Saracens, he was thrown into a dungeon. The daughter of the infidel prince saw and loved the humble captive, and by her aid he effected his escape and reached his native country. Pining at his absence, the maiden afterwards conceived the wild idea of following his steps, though she knew no more of his language than his name, and that of the city in which he dwelt. She hastened to a seaport, and making her wishes known by repeating the word "London," she obtained a passage in a ship bound for England. Having reached the English capital, she went from street to street calling upon "Gilbert," until the invocation met the ear of the lost object of her affection. Having abjured her native faith, and been baptized, the foreign maiden became the wife of Becket, now a citizen of London. From this union was born Thomas, the future Archbishop of Canterbury, a man whose remarkable life was destined to be a fit sequel to this singular history.[2]

His education, his introduction at court by the patronage of Archbishop Theobald, the rapid progress which he made in the royal favour, his elevation to the chancellorship, and his subsequent appointment to the primacy, with the extra-

CONSECRATION OF BECKET AS ARCHBISHOP.—From Royal MS. 2. B. 7.

ordinary transformation which his mode of life and his whole character underwent upon the last-mentioned event, have been already related. There can be little doubt as to what Henry's design was in thus placing at the head of the church the man who had hitherto been the most compliant, as well as the most active and dexterous of his ministers in civil affairs. When the intention of making him primate was first intimated to Becket, he frankly declared to his friends that, in accepting the new dignity, he was aware that he must forfeit the favour either of God or the king. He expressed the same sentiment to Henry himself, but in such an equivocal manner that his remark seemed rather intended for a jest. Laughing, and holding up a corner of his gay robe, he cried, "A fine saint you are choosing for such a holy office." Many persons professed to be not a little shocked as well as astonished; but perhaps the indignant feelings of the Norman part of the community were as much excited by Becket's Saxon lineage

---

[1] Eadmer, *Hist. Nov.* 112.

[2] Brompton, in *X Scriptores*. The story is told by this author at great length and with considerable pathos.

as by the daring profanation at which they affected to be scandalized. Unclerical as the archbishop's former life had been, and notwithstanding his obnoxious promotion, the bishops, as well as the clergy generally, were at first delighted with such a primate, and the Saxon population, while they were charmed with his affability and humbleness of demeanour, had their exultation and affection heightened in regarding him as belonging to their own race.

The circumstances which led to the first breach between the king and the archbishop have already been stated. The whole course, indeed, of the contest between Henry and Becket is so interwoven with the general history of the kingdom, that a sketch of it, from its commencement to its close, has been necessarily given in relating the civil transactions of the period, and we have only now to fill up certain parts of that outline by a few additional details in regard to points belonging more especially to the subject of the present chapter.

The various matters in dispute between the two parties, it will be remembered, were all submitted to the great council of prelates and barons which met at Clarendon in January, 1164. A short review of what took place upon that occasion, and of the history of the decrees, or "Constitutions," as they were called, passed by the council, will best explain the conflicting claims of the king, on the one hand, and the archbishop on the other, and the relative positions in which the church and the state were left by the issue of the controversy.

The particular question which originated what eventually became a general contest about their respective rights between the crown and the spiritual estate, appears to have been—whether the clergy, when accused of crimes, should be tried and punished by the ecclesiastical or the civil courts. Filled, as many of the lower offices in the church were, with persons of little education, and whose emoluments were not such as to raise them above the habits and temptations of the lowest poverty, it is no wonder that, in an age of such general rudeness and disorder, some of the most serious offences, including even acts of violence and blood, should occasionally be committed by churchmen. It was alleged, however, with apparent reason, that the temptations to the commission of crime, in the case of a priest, were greatly augmented by the peculiar sort of trial and punishment to which it subjected him. During the Saxon times the clergy and laity were alike amenable to the courts of common law; but the Conqueror withdrew the bishops from the civil tribunals, and, in imitation of the order of things already existing in all the other countries of Christendom, placed them at the head of other courts of their own. The extent of the ecclesiastical jurisdiction thus established had, from the first, been a subject of uncertainty and dispute, but latterly the church courts had asserted the right of alone taking cognizance of all offences whatever committed by the clergy. One strong ground on which this claim was objected to by the civil authorities, was the inadequacy of the punishments which the ecclesiastical judges were considered to have the power of inflicting; for they were held to be restricted by the canons from pronouncing sentence of death, and, in consequence, for the most heinous offence committed by a priest, the heaviest retribution was stripes and degradation from his sacred office. It was also alleged that a natural partiality for their order induced those who presided in the church courts to treat the offenders that were brought before them with dangerous lenity, and sometimes, perhaps, made them shut their eyes altogether to the proofs of a churchman's guilt.

The Constitutions of Clarendon, as finally digested, were sixteen in number. They were presented for the acceptance of the council by the king, as a restoration or recognition of the ancient customs of the realm, or, as it was more specifically declared in the preamble, of the usages, liberties, and dignities which had prevailed and been maintained in the days of his grandfather and the other kings his predecessors. It must be admitted that this title was not a correct description as applied to all the articles. The instrument comprehended, as has been already observed, the entire scheme of reformation by which Henry proposed to bring the church under subjection to the civil authorities; and, however necessary certain of the clauses might be for this end, or however just and proper, they were undoubtedly innovations upon the laws and practice that had subsisted ever since the Conquest. The substance of the principal enactments was—that all cases, whether civil or criminal, in which a clergyman was concerned, should be tried and determined in the king's court; that appeals should lie from the archbishop to the king; and that no cause should be carried further than the archbishop's court (in other words, to Rome) without the king's consent; that no archbishop, bishop, or dignified clergyman, should depart from the kingdom without the king's leave; that no tenant in chief of the crown, and no officer of the royal household or demesne, should be excommunicated, or his lands put under an interdict, until application had been made to the king or the grand justiciary; that churches in the king's gift should not be filled without his consent; that when an archbishopric, bishopric, abbacy, or priory became vacant, it should remain in the custody of the king, who should receive all its

RELICS ASSOCIATED WITH THOMAS À BECKET.

(1) Ivory grace cup of Thomas à Becket; in the possession of P. H. Howard, Esq., of Corby.

(2) Mitre of Thomas à Becket; preserved in the Abbey of Sens, Normandy.

(3) Mitre of Thomas à Becket; belonged to the late Cardinal Manning.

(4, 5, 6, 7.) Leaden Tokens. (8) Leaden Ampula. Bought by pilgrims at Canterbury, and worn to show that they had visited the shrine of Thomas à Becket.

rents and revenues; that the election of a new incumbent should be made upon the king's writ, in the royal chapel, and with the assent of the king; and that the person elected should do homage and fealty to the king before being consecrated.

To these propositions Becket, at an interview with the king some time before the meeting of the council, had, although with much reluctance, promised that he would give his assent; and all the other bishops had also expressed their readiness to acquiesce in them. But now the archbishop, on being formally asked by the king to fulfil his promise, to the surprise of all present, peremptorily refused to give any other answer than that he would render obedience to the said ancient customs of the realm, saving the rights of his order. Terrified at the rage into which the king broke out at this unexpected opposition, Becket's brethren vehemently implored him to yield. Meanwhile the door of the antechamber being thrown open, discovered a band of knights standing clad in armour, and with their swords drawn. In these alarming circumstances Becket's firmness was at last shaken; and he promised that, if the meeting should be adjourned for the purpose of having the enactments digested into a regular form, he would then do what was required of him. But when he retired into solitude he was confounded at the thought of his weakness. Filled with remorse, he resolved even yet to draw back, to whatever of reproach or danger he might, by so doing, expose himself. When, therefore, the meeting re-assembled on the following day, and copies of the Constitutions were produced, he peremptorily refused his signature. Neither entreaties nor threats could now move him. Retiring from the council, he wrote to the pope an account of all that had taken place, soliciting absolution for the momentary lapse of which he had been guilty; and, as a penance for the same crime, he condemned himself to an abstinence of forty days from the service of the altar.[1]

The Constitutions of Clarendon, however, as assented to by the barons and the other prelates, became for the present the law of the land, notwithstanding the dissent and opposition of the archbishop.

It is only necessary to add here, that Henry, on his reconciliation with the pope, in 1172, only obtained absolution on solemnly promising to abolish all laws and customs hostile to the clergy that might have been introduced in his kingdom since the beginning of his reign—to re-instate the church of Canterbury in all the possessions it had held a year previous to Becket's departure; and to make restitution to all the friends of the late primate who had been deprived of their property. To these, it is said, were added some other engagements which were not committed to writing; and one version of the oath taken by Henry makes him acknowledge the kingdom of England to be held by him in feudal subjection to the pope. This article, however, has generally been held to be a forgery; and while on the one hand the evidence of its authenticity is very weak, its inherent improbability on the other is certainly strong.

Notwithstanding Henry's promise to abolish the customs that infringed upon the rights of the clergy, the Constitutions of Clarendon remained unrepealed for some years after this time. But if they were still nominally law, they were little better than a dead letter. All effective opposition to the cause of which Becket had been the great champion, was for the present put down by his martyrdom, and the wonders that were believed to have followed it. After the interment of the body, crowds of the afflicted repaired to the spot, where the lame recovered the action of their limbs, the blind received sight, and the sick were healed.[2] Every day added to the number of the pilgrims and the miracles, and consequently to the spread and fervour of the delusion. The enthusiasm became general, and messenger after messenger was despatched to Rome with fresh tidings of prodigies, and supplications that Becket might be made a tutelary saint for the blessing and protection of England. This favour was at last granted by the pope; and the 29th of December, the day on which the saint was assassinated, was assigned to him in the calendar.[3]

It was not, however, till the year 1176 that, at a great council held at Northampton, the repeal, or rather the modification, of the Constitutions of Clarendon was formally effected. It was there agreed, though not without much opposition from many of the barons—first, that the clergy should not be brought to trial before the temporal courts on any charges except for offences against the forest laws; and, secondly, that no bishopric or abbey should be kept in the king's hands longer than a year, except in circumstances which might make it impossible to have the vacancy filled up in that time. In this state the law continued the remainder of the period now under review.

Before dismissing this reign, an event remains to be mentioned, which, although otherwise insignificant, is memorable as the first instance on record of any opposition being made to the common faith, and as such may be regarded as the earliest harbinger of the Reformation in England. About the beginning of the year 1166, a synod was held at Oxford, in the presence of the king, for the arraignment of certain foreigners accused

[1] Gervase.   [2] Gervase; Matt. Par.   [3] Baron. Annal. 1173.

of heresy. It appears that five years before, several Germans, to the number of thirty men and women, had arrived in England, and began to disseminate their religious opinions; but as they had hitherto only converted one woman of low rank, and as their demeanour had been peaceful, they had been allowed to live unmolested. Attention, however, was at last called to the circumstance that their principles differed from the established creed, on which they were thrown into prison, and now brought for trial before the king. To the question of what was their belief, Gerard their leader answered that they were Christians, and venerated the doctrines of the apostles. But it is alleged that, when they were examined upon particulars, they spoke impiously of the eucharist, baptism, and marriage, and when urged with texts of Scripture, refused all discussion, declaring that they believed as they were taught, and would not dispute about their faith. When they were exhorted to recant, they received the admonition with scorn; and when threatened with punishment, they answered with a smile, "Blessed are they who suffer for righteousness' sake, for theirs is the kingdom of heaven." As heresy was new in England, the judges were at a loss how to act; but canons had already been enacted by the council of Tours against the Albigenses, and sentence was pronounced in conformity with these. The accused were condemned to be branded in the forehead with a hot iron, and to be publicly whipped and expelled out of Oxford, while the king's subjects were forbidden by proclamation to shelter or relieve them. The enthusiasts went to their punishment in triumph, singing, "Blessed are ye when men shall hate you and persecute you." Their garments were cut off by the waist, their brows were seared, and their backs torn with scourges; and thus bleeding, and almost naked, in the depth of winter, they wandered about unsheltered among the fields, until they died. Such is the obscure account delivered by the contemporary writers, in whose eyes dissent in belief from the church of Rome was an incomprehensible anomaly. It is probable that these strangers, from the notions ascribed to them on the institution of marriage and the sacraments, were Cathari, or Albigenses.

The history of ecclesiastical affairs in England during the reign of Richard I. is almost a blank; every feeling was absorbed in the great subject of the Crusades; and the clergy, who had already gained all for which they had contended at home, found ample scope for their belligerent propensities in the fields of Palestine, to which many of 'hem repaired in warlike array, notwithstanding the canons that had been enacted against their bearing arms. During this reign, the power of the popedom, which had been exerted in favour of Richard in the negotiations for his release, was also directed effectually against him when he showed symptoms of opposition to Rome. Hubert, the primate, jealous of the monks of Canterbury, and desirous to abridge their privileges, had determined to raise up against them a rival body, in the form of an establishment of canons regular, for whom he proceeded to erect a splendid edifice at Lambeth, with the approbation of Richard. But the monks of Canterbury, alarmed for their rights, and suspecting that the gainful relics of Becket would be transferred to the new house, fiercely opposed the project, and appealed to the pope, Innocent III., who warmly espoused their cause, and directed a bull to the archbishop, in 1198, commanding him in a very imperious style to desist immediately from his proceedings. He afterwards addressed another bull to Richard, whom he threatened for his contumacy in abetting the archbishop; warning him that if he persevered, he should soon find in his punishment how hard it was to kick against the pricks. By a subsequent mandate, also addressed to the king, Innocent declared that he would not endure the least contempt of himself or of God, whose place he held upon earth. The lion-hearted king and the rebellious archbishop were equally dismayed at these menaces, and the obnoxious building was destroyed.[1]

The history of the church in the reign of King John is principally a continuation of the same great contest respecting the appointment to the higher ecclesiastical offices between the clergy or the pope, on the one side, and the crown on the other, which had been carried on throughout the greater part of the preceding century. In the earliest ages of the Christian church, the election of bishops was by the voice of the clergy and the people of the diocese. After the establishment, however, of the feudal system in the different kingdoms of Europe, and the annexation to bishoprics of high political power and large landed possessions, the king naturally claimed the right of being at least a party in the nomination to an office which gave to its possessor so much weight in the state. The claim to a veto upon the election was as naturally extended to that of an absolute right of appointment, as soon as the crown found that it could not otherwise secure the office for its own nominee. Accordingly, this was substantially the position which the crown at last assumed, although the form in which it asserted its claim varied with circumstances. When it found itself obliged, for instance, to relinquish the absolute nomination of the bishop, it stood out for the right of granting or refusing to the individual elected that inves-

[1] *Gervase*, 1616-1624.

titure, without which he certainly could not draw the revenues of the see, even if he could exercise any of the spiritual powers of his office. The course taken by the church, on the other hand, equally varied in conformity to the course of events. In the first place, at a very early period, the interference of the laity was first reduced to a mere form, and then got rid of altogether. Subsequently the claim of the general body of the clergy of the diocese to a voice in the election was disputed, and the right of voting was asserted to reside solely in the chapter. As the chapter in many cases consisted of the monks of some religious house to which the cathedrals were held to belong, the natural enmity between the regular and the secular clergy here interfered materially to inflame the quarrel. This was the case, for instance, at Canterbury, where the chapter consisted of the monks of the great monastery of St. Augustine, who thus claimed the sole right of electing the Primate of all England. The regular clergy (that is, those living under monastic rule) were always, it may be observed, regarded by the court of Rome as the main support of its authority, and it usually took their side against the secular (so called, as living at large in the world). What the popes therefore endeavoured to effect in regard to the nomination of bishops, was to retain that power either in their own hands or in those of the chapters. Against the claim of the king to present in the first instance they constantly protested. In many cases, however, the chapters submitted to present the person named to them by the king. Even here, however, the question of investiture created a serious difficulty to be got over after the nomination had been settled. But the particular point upon which the dispute between John and Innocent III. hinged, was the power claimed by the Papal court of appointing to a bishopric vacated by the irregularity of the election, or by the unfitness of the person elected, the right being also assumed by it of deciding upon the irregularity or unfitness. It was upon the plea of such irregularity that the pope nominated Langton to the archbishopric of Canterbury.

Little or no change took place in the internal constitution of the English church in consequence of the Norman conquest; and its establishment remained through the whole of the period now under review nearly the same as it was before that event. The principal alteration was that made by the creation of two new sees—of Ely, in 1109, and of Carlisle, in 1133, in addition to the fifteen (including the two archbishoprics) that had existed in the Saxon times, being the same that still exist, with the exception of Oxford, Peterborough, Gloucester, Chester, and Ripon.

Before the Conquest the only order of monks known in England was that of the Benedictines,

BENEDICTINE MONK.[1]—From Dugdale.

or observers of the rule of St. Benedict, instituted in the early part of the sixth century, which some conceive to have been brought over by Augustine, but which was most probably unknown in the country till a considerably later period, and certainly was first generally established by St. Dunstan in the tenth century. Nor perhaps was the rule of St. Benedict ever strictly observed by the English monks till after the Conquest. In the course of the twelfth century two new orders were introduced—the Cistercians, or Bernardines, in 1128, and the Carthusians, in 1180. Both these, indeed, may be considered as branches of the Benedictines, only distinguished by subjection to a discipline of still greater severity. The order of the Carthusians especially (founded at Chartreux, in France, by St. Bruno in 1080, whence their establishments in England were corruptly called Charterhouses) was the strictest of all the monastic orders, the members never being allowed to taste flesh, and being restricted on one day of every week to bread,

CARTHUSIAN MONK.[2] From Dugdale.

water, and salt. The Carthusians never became numerous in England. The order of the Cistercians (instituted at Cisteux—in Latin, Cistertium—in Burgundy, in 1098, and afterwards greatly patronized by the celebrated St. Bernard) was chiefly distinguished by having its houses situated for the most part at a distance from all other habitations. There were a considerable number of them both in England and in Scotland.[3]

---

[1] The habit of the Benedictine monks was a black loose gown of stuff reaching to the heels, a cowl or hood of the same, and a scapulary. Under these was worn a habit of white flannel, and boots on the legs. From the outer habit, the Benedictines were commonly called Black Monks.

[2] The habit of the Carthusian monk was white, with an external coat of black stuff plaited.

[3] Among the many illustrations of mediæval manners which we owe to the Camden and similar societies, few are more in-

The most common form, however, which enthusiastic devotion assumed in the eleventh and twelfth centuries, was that of going on pilgrimage to some spot supposed to be of peculiar sanctity, either within the kingdom or abroad. After the martyrdom and canonization of Becket, his shrine at Canterbury became, and for ages continued to be the favourite resort of the pious, when they did not extend their penitential journey beyond the limits of their own country. Abroad, Rome, Loretto, but especially Jerusalem, Mount Sinai, and the other parts of the Holy Land, now attracted crowds of palmers,' "beyond the example of former times," to use the words of Gibbon, "and the roads were covered with multitudes of either sex, and of every rank, who professed their contempt of life, so soon as they should have kissed the tomb of their Redeemer. Princes and prelates abandoned the care of their dominions; and the members of these pious caravans were a prelude to the armies which marched in the ensuing age under the banner of the cross." Out of this practice of pilgrimage grew the Crusades, in which the spirit of devotion formed a strange alliance with the military spirit, each communicating something of its peculiar colour and character to the other. Four of these extraordinary expeditions belong to the present period, of which the first (the consequence of which was the establishment of the kingdom of Jerusalem) set out in 1097, the second in 1147, the third (that in which Cœur de Lion took so distinguished a part) in 1189, and the fourth (which resulted in the conquest of Constantinople from the Greeks) in 1203. The Crusades, however, though professedly religious enterprises, produced less effect upon the religion of the age in which they were undertaken than upon most of the other great constituents of its social condition. Among the phenomena that sprung out of the Crusades, none presented a more expressive type of their character than the religious orders of knighthood. The two earliest and most distinguished of these—the Knights Hospitallers of St. John, and the Knights Templars—both acquired establishments and extensive possessions in this country

soon after their institution; the principal seat of the former having been established at St. John's Hospital in Clerkenwell, London; that of the latter at the Temple (to which they had removed from a previous residence in Holborn), many years before the close of the twelfth century. As these two orders of military monks were so closely connected with the religious and civil history of the period, and were so influential, both as priests and soldiers, they require a fuller notice than we have given to the other monastic institutions. They had their origin in the oppression and cruelties with which the Christian pilgrims were visited in their journeys to the holy sepulchre. They first appeared in the form of Hospitallers, in the eleventh century, when they built an hospital dedicated to St. John within the walls of Jerusalem, for the reception and entertainment of pilgrims, and the relief of those who had been plundered in the journey, or were too poor to pay the exorbitant taxes levied by the infidels upon those who visited the sacred places. At first, they were but a community of monks, who followed the rule of St. Benedict, and devoted themselves to the humble duties of tending the sick and relieving the needy; but as their reputation increased, large donations of lands were bestowed upon the order, and gallant knights and men of high rank joined it, in the hope of thereby expiating their sins or escaping from the cares of the world. This wealth cherished ambition; these new recruits imparted a warlike spirit to the community; and during the Crusades, we find them risen into a great military power, at the head of which was a grand-master, exercising all the functions of a sovereign independent prince. Such an institution was particularly congenial to the warlike and devout spirit of the English; and, therefore, so early as A.D. 1100—only eight years after it was established at Jerusalem—a small body of these Hospital monks arrived in England, and during the same year, their house in London was erected. The branch thus planted in an English soil was quickly and abundantly fruitful; their commanderies, by which name their establishments were distinguished, were rich and nume-

---

teresting than the chronicle kept by the monk Jocelin, of St. Edmund's, in the twelfth century: *Chronica Jocelini de Brakelonda de rebus gestis Samsonis Abbatis Monasterii Sancti Edmundi*. In it the conventual fraternity present a very different aspect from that attributed to the monastic institutions of the middle ages by authors who think they cannot sufficiently exalt their merits. As landlords, they were so harsh as even to tear the doors from the cottages of their tenants in payment of arrears of rent. But Mr. Carlyle, in his *Past and Present*, has pronounced an opinion on Jocelin's work, part of which we may append:—" Jocelin, we see, is not without secularity. Our Dominus Abbas was intent enough on the Divine offices; but then—his account books? One of the things that strike us most, throughout, in Jocelin's *Chronicle*, and indeed in Eadmer's *Anselm*, and other old monastic books, written evidently by pious men, is this,

that there is almost no mention whatever of personal religion in them; that the whole gist of their thinking and speculation seems to be ' the privileges of our order,' ' strict exaction of our dues,' ' God's honour' (meaning the honour of our saints), and so forth."—See *Past and Present*, by Thomas Carlyle, p. 80.

[1] Pilgrims to foreign parts were properly called *palmers*, from the branches of the palm-tree, the emblem of victory, which they used to bear in their hands. In token of having crossed the seas, or of their intention of doing so, they were wont to put cockle or scallop shells in their hats—according to Ophelia's song in *Hamlet:*—

"How should I your true love know
From another one?
By his cockle hat and staff,
And by his sandal shoon."

rous; and so influential was the order throughout the country, that their superior ranked as the first of the English barons, and had, as such, a seat among the lords in parliament. This consequence they retained in England until the period of the Reformation, when their houses and endowments were swept away in the general confiscation. It is only necessary to add, that the Knights Hospitallers appear under different and successive names in history, according to the changes with which the order was visited. During the period of the Crusades, they were Hospitallers, from the Hospital they occupied; and Knights of St. John, from the name of the patron saint to whom the building was dedicated. Afterwards, on the expulsion of the Christians from the Holy Land, they were called Knights of Rhodes, in consequence of that island being assigned to them for their residence. The third change in their title occurred when, in consequence of the capture of Rhodes by the Turks, A.D. 1522, and their transference to the island of Malta, which was conferred upon their order by the Emperor Charles V., they adopted the name, which since that period they have retained, of "Knights of Malta."

A still more powerful and distinguished institution of soldier-monks, was that of the Templars, which originated A.D. 1118. At first they consisted of nine pious and valiant knights, who resolved, while their brethren of the Hospital devoted themselves to the care of the sick and the poor, to guard the highways that led to the holy sepulchre, and protect the pilgrims on their journey. They therefore selected for their patroness, the Virgin, whom they entitled "our dear Lady Mary," the "sweet mother of God;" and having adopted for their rule the canons of St. Augustine, they bound themselves by the three monastic vows of chastity, poverty, and obedience, to which, however, they added a fourth, of fighting incessantly in the defence of pilgrims and the Holy Land, against the heathen. Baldwin II., King of Jerusalem, assigned them a part of his palace for their abode; and as this building stood close by the church and convent of the Temple, the abbot and canons gave them a street leading to it from the palace, for the keeping of their stores and equipments; and from this circumstance, they obtained the names of "Brethren of the Temple of Solomon at Jerusalem," "Soldiers of the Temple," and "Templars."

During the first nine years of the existence of this order, its vow of poverty was strictly observed: the subsistence, and even the raiment of these gallant high-born soldiers were the alms which they received from the faithful; and even their first grand-master, Hugh de Payens, and his companion, Godfrey of St. Omer, had only one war-steed between them. This fact was carefully commemorated by the seal of the institution, which represented two Templar knights riding upon one horse; and it was hoped, that having this emblem constantly before their eyes, the brethren would be reminded of their original poverty, and the duty of Christian humility. And that such was at first the effect, may be learned from a letter of St. Bernard, the legislator of the order, seventeen years after it was instituted, and when it had acquired wealth and consideration. Speaking of the knights of the Temple, he says, "They go and come at a sign from their master; they wear the clothing which he gives them, and ask neither food nor clothing from any one else. . . . They never sit idle, or go about gaping after news. When they are resting from warfare against the infidels—a thing which rarely occurs—not to eat the bread of idleness, they employ themselves in repairing their clothes and arms, or do something which the command of the master or the common need enjoins. There is with them no respect of persons; the best, not the noblest, are the most highly regarded; they endeavour to anticipate one another in respect, and to lighten each other's burdens. No unseemly word or light mocking—no murmur or immoderate laughter—is let to pass unreproved, if any one should allow himself to indulge in such. They avoid games of chess and tables; they are adverse to the chase, and equally so to hawking, in which others so much delight. They hate all jugglers and mountebanks, all wanton songs and plays, as vanities and follies of this world. They cut their hair, in obedience to these words of the apostle, 'It is not seemly in a man to have long hair;' no one ever sees them dressed out; they are seldom ever washed; they are mostly to be seen with disordered hair, and covered with dust, brown from their corslets and the heat of the sun." After describing their fearless courage in battle, the illustrious abbot of Clairvaux adds, "Thus they are in union strange, at the same time gentler than lambs and grimmer than lions, so that one may doubt whether to call them monks or knights. But both names suit them, for theirs is the mildness of the monk and the valour of the knight. What remains to be said, but that this is the Lord's doing, and it is wonderful in our eyes? Such are they whom God has chosen out of the bravest in Israel, that, watchful and true, they may guard the holy sepulchre, armed with swords, and well-skilled in war."

A community so distinguished for valour, piety, and self-denial, and so powerful an instrument for the recovery of Palestine, and its maintenance against the infidels, was so completely accordant with the spirit and wants of the age, that the Templars rose into high favour both with the ecclesiastical and secular powers. They were soon enabled to doff the piebald and threadbare raiment of charity, in consequence of a decent uniform being appointed for them by Pope Honorius, which consisted of a white mantle, to distinguish them from the Hospitallers, who wore a black one. Afterwards, they were commissioned by Pope Eugenius III. to wear a red cross on the breast, as a sign of their constant exposure to martyrdom, and this likewise to distinguish them from their brethren of the Hospital, whose cross was white. They either received or adopted also their far-famed banner, called in old French, *Bauseant*, in consequence of the black and white stripes of which it was composed, this name being generally applied to a horse of these colours; and *Bauseant* became also the war-cry of the Templars, and a word of terror wherever it was heard. The banner itself bore the red cross of the order painted upon it, and the humble self-denying text of Scripture, "*Non nobis, Domine, non nobis, sed nomini tuo, da gloriam*"—("Not unto us, O Lord, not unto us, but unto thy name give the glory"). These distinctions, however, were but preludes to more substantial benefits, which flowed into the order in the form of rich high-titled neophytes, large territorial endowments, and powerful houses, called preceptories, which rose in every country in Christendom, so that the Templars were soon more distinguished than the earlier community of Hospitallers, of whom they were at first the humble imitators. And such was the confidence reposed in the integrity and strength of the order, that by the beginning of the thirteenth century, it had become the custom of sovereigns in troublous times to deposit their treasures in Temple houses, as places of assured security.

The connection of the Templars with England was profitable in the highest degree to their community, and this, from an early period, as may be seen from the account taken of their possessions in the country by royal authority, A.D. 1185.[1] During this year, also, they removed from their residence of the Old Temple on the south side of Holborn, to their new house at the western extremity of Fleet Street, the site of which is still called the Temple. At his departure from the Holy Land, Richard Cœur de Lion sought and obtained permission from the grandmaster to wear the habit of a Templar, that none might detect him in the dress of his avowed enemies; while John, his brother, attached himself to them as his best protection against the barons; bestowed upon them Lundy Island, at the mouth of the Bristol Channel, in addition to their other English possessions; and intrusted the sum of 20,000 marks to their keeping. In the succeeding reign, when Henry III. (A.D. 1252) complained of the arrogance of the Templars and Hospitallers, and threatened to resume the enormous possessions that had been inconsiderately bestowed upon them, he was answered by the prior of the former community in these authoritative words:—"What sayest thou, O king? Far be it that thy mouth should utter so disagreeable and silly a word. So long as thou dost exercise justice thou shalt reign; but if thou infringe it, thou wilt cease to be a king!" This significant language quickly reduced Henry to submission.

The dress by which the Templars were distinguished, was, with the exception of colour, the same as that of the Hospitallers, and was supplied, along with arms and equipments, from the common fund of the order. It consisted of a long white tunic, resembling in form that of the priests, and for head covering had a cap or hood attached to it; and both on front and back of the tunic, was a red cross of four arms, the lower one being the largest, so that it resembled the cross on which the Saviour suffered. Beneath this mantle, was a linen shirt, bound with a girdle. The arms of the Templar, besides the usual suit of plate and mail, consisted of a shield, sword, lance, and mace; and owing to the heat of the Syrian climate, and the necessity of employing himself in constant military service, these arms, offensive and defensive, were of a lighter description than those commonly used by secular warriors. When the Templar died, he was placed in a coffin in the habit of his order, and with his legs crossed; and it is in this costume and attitude that his effigy was represented upon his tomb. Such were the distinctive cha-

KNIGHT HOSPITALLER.—From Dugdale.

KNIGHTS TEMPLARS.
1 Jean de Dreux, Ch. | 2. Geoffrey of Magnaville, of St. Yved, Braine. | Temple Ch., London.

[1] Inquisitio, in Dugdale's *Monasticon*, vol. vi. part ii. p. 153, &c.

racteristics and costume of a community already doomed to ruin. Their crimes and arrogance were hated, their wealth and possessions were coveted; and though powerful, they were unable to make head against the hostility which they had so recklessly provoked. As a political community, they were obnoxious to kings and statesmen; while as an ecclesiastical body, they were condemned by popes and councils: and thus the twofold character in which their strength had originated, also insured their downfall. The history of their suppression belongs to the succeeding period.

CHAPTER XI.—HISTORY OF SOCIETY.

A.D. 1066—1216.

Causes of delay in progress at this period—Commencement of learning under the Norman conquest—Colleges and schools of this period—Institution of chivalry—Training for knighthood—Education of pages and squires—Ceremonial in the investment of knighthood—Growth of English cities—Extent and grandeur of London—Mercantile progress—Jewish money-lenders—Flemish manufacturers—Agricultural population—Classes into which they were divided—Architecture of the period—Abbeys and churches—Saxon and Norman styles of architecture—Architecture of houses—Castles of the nobility—Modes of life among the nobles—Their names, titles, and armorial distinctions—Their retinues and style of travelling—Dress and ornaments of the nobles—Female dress and ornaments—Domestic life of the upper classes—Their hours of meals—Their diet—Sports and pastimes of the nobility—Gambling—Minstrels, jugglers, stage-players, &c.—Hunting and hawking—Horse-racing—Sports and amusements of the common people—Bowling, kayle-pins, the sword-dance, &c.—Water-tournaments—Rustic imitations of chivalrous sports—Depression of the national spirit at this period.

HE conquest of England by the Normans was an event scarcely to be deplored. The Saxon occupation of the country had now lasted 600 years; but the rate of national progress had been so slow, and at the time of the Conquest itself appeared to be so decisively arrested, that any impulse, however rude and severe, would have been preferable to such a stagnation. For this want of improvement, also, such causes were in operation as to make any other kind of remedy hopeless. At their arrival in England, the Saxons were a very different kind of people from their predecessors the Romans, in everything but valour and the love of conquest; and after their coming, 350 years of wars with the Britons, and afterwards of contention among themselves, had elapsed. This was anything but favourable to the improvement of barbarian invaders, more especially as almost every trace of Roman civilization had been swept away in the conflict, so that scarcely a lesson was left them to learn, or model to copy. And even when England was transformed from a Roman province into a Saxon kingdom, new wars ensued during nearly the whole of the remaining 250 years, in which the English had to maintain their ground, and struggle for very existence against an enemy more destructive and barbarous than themselves. Where was then the time or the opportunity for improvement, especially when the work had to begin from the foundation? Even the labours of Alfred scarcely endured a single life-time, having been arrested by a new series of Danish invasions, in which the land was all but peopled anew with the most desperate of pirates and homicides. It was no wonder, therefore, if after the 600 years of interval, the Anglo-Saxons were so little superior to their ancestors who had arrived with Hengist and Horsa. They were still "toto orbe divisos"—as yet England formed scarcely a member in the great political family of nations; and upon the Continent her voice was unheard. But what made the case more hopeless still, was the degradation of the English aristocracy, who were sunk beneath the level of the people whom they were designed to elevate. Debased by profligacy, and immersed in gluttony, debauchery, and ignorance, the English thanes were at one time ready to sell the land and its inhabitants to Danish rovers, and at another to yield them up to the Norman conquerors. It is melancholy to think that Harold was the last of the Saxons, and that the fate of such a kingdom should have depended upon one man. But notwithstanding the gallant resistance of the people at Hastings, and the means still in reserve for twenty such conflicts, no sooner does Harold pass away, than the nobles despair and yield. It was full time that such leaders at least should be supplanted by a race of men, of whom any adventurous knight who could muster three or four score lances around his pennon might hope to win for himself a countship or even a kingdom, and establish a permanent dynasty; or who, even as a solitary wanderer and exile, was certain to become a chief in the territory that gave him a home. As might be expected, however, the first progress of the Normans after their conquest of England was slow, and from the same causes which had retarded that of the Saxons. Although superior to the conquered in refinement, they were still rude and illiterate; and as they were the smaller party, the utmost of their efforts for a long time were tasked, first to win, and afterwards to retain their ascendancy. The arts of war, therefore, rather than those of peace, occupied their immediate attention; and the march of civilization, instead of being accelerated, was in the first instance rather retarded by the change. But the shock was soon surmounted, and a foundation laid for future improvement during the course of the present period. William the Conqueror himself was a lover and patron of learning; Henry Beauclerk, his son, was distinguished for his scholarship; and Henry II. was not only accomplished in the learning of the period, but his sons also were distinguished for their literary acquirements. It is likewise to be noted, that although one of the earliest oppressions of the Conquest was the deposition of the English ecclesiastical diguitaries, yet their loss was little to be regretted on the score of learning, while their places were filled by foreign prelates of a much superior description. Of these, Lanfranc and Anselm were subtle metaphysicians and theologians; while Geoffrey, who established a school at Dunstable, and Godfrey, prior of St. Swithin's, were excellent Latin poets. Abbeys were also founded and libraries established for the promotion of literature and the extension of education; while schools in connection with cathedrals and monasteries were multiplied over the kingdom. It was chiefly, however, the clergy who availed themselves of these opportunities, for as yet, even of the Norman nobility, there were few who could either read or write. But, indeed, the education delivered at these seminaries was scarcely attractive enough for the stirring spirits of the young men of the day, being chiefly of a theological and scholastic character, mixed up, as might be supposed, with a full amount of the mere pedantry and show of scholarship. Such we learn from the description of Fitz-Stephen. "On holidays," he thus writes, "it is usual for these schools to hold public meetings in the churches, in which the scholars engage in demonstrative or logical disputations; some using enthymemes, and others perfect syllogisms; some aiming at nothing but to gain the victory, and make an ostentatious display of their acuteness, while others have the investigation of truth in view. Artful sophists on these occasions acquire great applause, some by a prodigious inundation and flow of words, others by their specious but fallacious arguments. After the disputations, other scholars deliver rhetorical declamations, in which they observe all the rules of art, and neglect no topic of persuasion. Even the younger boys in the different schools contend against each other in verse about the principles of grammar, and the preterites and supines of verbs." Thus early had that course of education been in full vigour in England which continued for centuries, and as long as the Aristotelian system prevailed. But the seminary which was finally to surpass and eclipse all these institutions is thus described by Peter of Blois, a lively writer who flourished in the reign of Henry II.:—" In the year 1109, Joffrid, abbot of Croyland, sent to his manor of Cottenham, near Cambridge, Master Gislebert [Gilbert], his fellow-monk, and professor of theology, with three other monks who had followed him into England, who, being very well instructed in philosophical theorems, and other primitive sciences, went every day to Cambridge, and, having hired a certain public barn, taught the sciences openly, and in a little time collected a great concourse of scholars; for, in the very second year after their arrival, the number of their scholars from the town and country increased so much, that there was no house, barn, nor church, capable of containing them. For this reason they separated into different parts of the town, and imitating the plan of the Studium of Orleans, brother Odo, who was eminent as a grammarian and satirical poet, read grammar according to the doctrine of Priscian, and of his commentator Remegius, to the boys and younger students that were assigned to him, early in the morning. At one o'clock, brother Terricus, a most acute sophist, read the logic of Aristotle according to the introductions and commentaries of Porphyry and Averroes, to those who were further advanced. At three, brother William read lectures on Tully's rhetoric and Quintilian's *Institutions*. But Master Gislebert, being ignorant of the English, but very expert in the Latin and French languages, preached in the several churches to the people on Sundays and holidays. From this little fountain which hath swelled into a great river, we now behold the city of God made glad, and all England rendered fruitful by many teachers and doctors issuing from Cambridge, after the likeness of the holy paradise." It will be noticed here, that in such a concourse of learned men from different countries, Latin was the conventional language, which was spoken with the ease and fluency of a living tongue. But to preach in it before illiterate rustic audiences, as Master Gilbert appears to have done!—The people, however, were probably charmed with the sound, and only the more convinced by how little they could comprehend. Such phenomena are not rare in preaching. In this way, Giraldus Cambrensis roused the people of Wales to arms, while preaching a crusade in 1166 for the recovery of the holy sepulchre. He harangued them in Latin, of which they did not understand a word; but they wept, and hurried forward in crowds to enrol themselves for the war in Palestine.

As chivalry constituted the main principle of Norman life at this period, its usages require our chief attention in a sketch of the social and domestic habits of this era. Having its origin in the forests of Germany, and being common to all the Teutonic tribes, the institution of chivalry was first imported into England by the followers of Hengist and Horsa, but in a form as rude and simple as the arms they wore, or the manners by which they were distinguished. How little, indeed, of the pomp and circumstance of chivalry could be manifested by those whose chief offensive weapons were an axe, a spear, and a long crooked seax or sword, while their only defensive armour was a leathern helmet and light wooden target! The arrival of the Normans with their more complete panoply of chain and scale armour, their higher imaginativeness, and greater love of splendour and display, completely changed the scene. They had engrafted upon the original chivalry of the naked North, the arts and refinements of the South, with which they very speedily superseded the rude knighthood of the Anglo-Saxons. The education of a noble youth of England, therefore, at this period—and every Norman family was accounted noble—had a reference to the military training by which he was to maintain the ascendancy of his countrymen, the deeds he was to achieve, and the spurs he was expected to win. For this purpose, he was placed as a page in the household of some knight or noble of approved military reputation, under whose instructions he learned, during this first step of his noviciate, those exercises by which he was improved in strength, dexterity, and hardihood, as well as in knightly courtesy and gracefulness of demeanour, while his lessons combined sport and amusement with proficiency. One of these was fighting at the *pel*, which was the stump of a tree about the height of a man, and marked all over with the different parts of the human body. This he was vigorously to attack both with edge and point, until he could hit each part at pleasure, covering himself all the while with his shield to prevent reprisal. Besides this training for a hand-to-hand combat on foot, he was taught a knight's chief duty on horseback by tilting at the *quintain*. This was a pole set upright in the earth, with a shield fastened to it with thongs of leather, which he was expected to detach from the pole with the point of his lance in full career, at the risk of being swept from the saddle if he failed. In these fierce ridings, the loss of his seat, or even of a stirrup, was to be eschewed as an inglorious failure. We find in one of the illuminated MSS. that this unshapely pole was at length elevated into the figure of a wooden Saracen, revolving upon a spindle, and armed with sword and shield. Here was an enemy sufficient to kindle the knightly and crusading zeal of the young tyro, as well as to task his utmost skill; for his object was to strike it full in the breast or face while he firmly maintained his seat, in which case his opponent, if made of flesh and blood, would have been a dead man. But if he struck aslant, or swerved from the centre, the Paynim wheeled rapidly round, and struck the assailant a degrading blow on the back with his wooden scimetar.

With these, and such exercises as these, amidst hot competition and merriment, the young pages of a noble household exercised themselves in the mimicry of war, by which they trained themselves to its stern realities. From the station of page the young aspirant attained to that of squire, in which he was not only to continue his military exercises, but join in the real business of war, by following his master to the field. During his intervals of leisure, he perfected himself in the arts of riding and tilting, and partook of the manly sports of hunting and hawking. The whole period of education for knighthood usually lasted seven or eight years—and from the demand it occasioned we may easily conceive how strongly a nobleman of high military repute must have fortified himself with future adherents, as well as how the friendships formed among the young pupils themselves, afterwards grew into political unions and coalitions. When the squire, after his long probation, was to obtain the coveted honour of knighthood, the investment was performed with such a combination of military and religious ceremonial as sufficed to mark it out as one of the very noblest of all earthly distinctions. Nights of prayer and watching in the chapel, and partaking of the eucharist, were to prepare him for the solemnity, as if the office for which he was in preparation was heaven-born and holy. To this was also attached in most cases the watching of his armour, which was hung over the altar. In this way, religion endeavoured to soften and ennoble by consecration an office so prone to violence and bloodshed. After these religious duties were fulfilled, and when the important day had arrived, the church was decked with the utmost splendour; a crowd was assembled, and after a solemn service in full choir, the priest at the altar administered the oaths of chivalry to the kneeling aspirant, and blessed his sword, which was thenceforth set apart to deeds of noble and generous emprise. These oaths were, that he would be loyal and obedient to his sovereign, a defender of the doctrines and immunities of the church, the champion of the ladies, and the especial protector of the orphan and the widow. His spurs were then buckled on by the lordly spectators present, or by the high-born ladies, whose honoured servant he was thenceforth to be considered. In like manner he was arrayed in his richest suit of armour; and when all was ready, the sovereign or the noble by whom the honour was to be conferred advanced and gave the accolade, exclaiming in a loud voice, "In the name of God, St. Michael, and St. George, I dub thee knight; be brave, hardy, and loyal." This accolade consisted of either one or three gentle strokes with the hand upon the cheek, or the flat of a sword upon the shoulder, indicating the last blows which the young knight was to receive without resentment or requital. Such were the principal ceremonies used on this important occasion, varying in splendour according to convenience and the rank of the recipient, but in every case made an imposing spectacle. There were times, however, when all this preparation and pomp were abridged; as in the case of active service, and especially upon a field of battle, after a signal victory had been won, when the young squire who had performed some remarkable deed of bravery, was thought worthy at once of the highest honours of chivalry. In this case, he was dubbed by the commander in the midst of blood and carcasses, and with shorn and hasty ceremonial. But a knighthood conferred in such circumstances was of higher account than when it was bestowed amidst the peaceful pomp of the chapel and with "unhacked rapier," as it was the attestation of a valour already tried and proved; and as such, the recipient was a knight banneret, and entitled to take precedence of his companions. With what fidelity the oaths of chivalry were kept, or with what indifference they were broken, the history of every country has sufficiently recorded. With regard to the tilts, tournaments, and magnificent pageantries to which the institution gave rise, these, although now in full force in Italy, France, and Germany, were not as yet fully naturalized in England, from the fear that they might become hotbeds of combinations and conspiracies. It is only when the kingly authority was more firmly established, and the influence of the aristocracy suppressed, that they will fall under our notice among the sports and festivals of England.

While learning and war—the church and the army—were thus provided for, we now turn our eyes to the general condition of society both in town and country. Already, not only "the sweet security of streets" was felt doubly needful in the new state of things, but also that spirit of centralization had vigorously commenced, which gives birth to national industry, wealth, and civilization. Thus, Bristol, Exeter, Winchester, Gloucester, and Chester, were already populous towns, to which may be added Dunwich, Lynn, Lincoln, and Norwich; and all of them were distinguished either for home or foreign trade, especially the latter, which was carried on with Ireland and the Continent. In like manner, the towns along the coast of England in general, which afterwards rose into opulence, were coming into note through their shipping and commercial enterprise. But even already the court and the Thames had imparted to London that pre-eminence which it still so immeasurably holds over every other English city; and the Latin style of Fitz-Stephen scarcely furnishes him with words of sufficient bulk and weight to describe its magnificence. It contained FORTY THOUSAND inhabitants! In the city and suburbs were 126 parochial churches and thirteen large conventual ones, while Ludgate was the extreme west end of the city. The inhabitants, too, were reckoned something better than mere ordinary citizens, and were called barons—just as the citizens of Rome in ancient times became the patricians of the overgrown Republic. Its traffic was carried on with every country, but chiefly with Germany; and the provisions that were garnered within its granaries, were the chief resource of the surrounding districts during the occasional visits of famine. A trade so brisk and so extensive, he adds, was also properly systematized, so that not only the merchants of every commodity, but the workmen of every craft had their respective places assigned to them. London also was curiously bounded, according to the ideas of the nineteenth century. The city was girdled with a great and high wall, having seven gates which were made double; and on the north and south it had towers and turrets at intervals; but on the south side, the wall was worn out and washed away by the ebb and flow of the Thames.[1] Such was the fate of the riverside fortifications in the time of Fitz-Stephen, and about the same period the stone bridge of London arose in their place, thus connecting both sides of the Thames, which had formerly been wedged asunder. Ludgate, as we have already mentioned, was the west end of London: the space between it and Westminster was a tract of fields and gardens. Smithfield, as yet a suburban locality, was then, as till lately, a cattle market, in which horses, cows, hogs, and other animals were sold. Moorfields was a large lake, formed by the confluence of several streams that turned mills. That great artery of London now called the City

[1] For a more particular account of London wall, the reader is referred to the engraving and note in vol. i. p. 41.

Road, with its countless ramifications of streets, consisted at that time of pasturage and corn-fields; while beyond that rural territory now known as Islington and Pentonville, a large tract of forest extended, stored with wild boars and other game, where the citizens enjoyed the recreation of hunting. Thus much for London, which even at that period was the marvel of foreigners on account of its greatness and its wealth. Well might the German barons who accompanied Richard I. exclaim, when they saw the magnificence of his reception within its walls: "O king! if our emperor had suspected this, you would not have been let off so lightly!"

While adverting to the mercantile character of the English towns, it is necessary to allude to those persons by whom the infant commerce and manufactures of the nation were at this period chiefly promoted. And first among the men of business, we may mention the Jews, who even at this early period had perceived the facilities which England possessed for gainful traffic, and who flocked thither in great numbers. True to their national character, and the doom imposed upon them of having no abiding home or resting-place, they neither dealt in land nor bulky articles of merchandise, neither built, created, nor manufactured; on the contrary, they dealt in money, the light symbol and representative of these substantialities; and that they might be enabled to gird up their loins and flee at a moment's warning, without the risk and labour of carrying gold and silver along with them, they symbolized the symbol itself, by the use of bills of exchange and letters of credit, so that they could carry their whole fortune away in the shape of a few scraps of paper or parchment. The towns were the natural abodes of such men, and especially the capital, where they pursued the vocation of money-lenders, and drove a thriving trade, on account of the prodigality of the Norman nobles. The law, too, was greatly in their favour, for while every Christian was prohibited from exacting any interest whatever upon a loan, the Jews were untouched by the statute, and might lay on their percentages to whatever amount they pleased. But although they were thus the brokers of the court, and money-lenders of royalty itself, their very profits made their situation more precarious than that of a farmer of taxes in the French revolution, or a Turkish pasha under the old régime; for like leeches they were compelled to disgorge as often as their tyrants were pleased to turn upon them; and in this way, the English kings were able to draw into the royal treasury the money of the people, without the odium of collecting it. The histories of Richard I. and John show how well these sovereigns understood such a simple and direct mode of finance. But this was not the worst which these outcasts of the world were compelled to endure; and the record of their sufferings during the crusading frenzy forms one of the most melancholy as well as atrocious episodes in the ancient chronicles of England.

It was fortunate that another class of people were already settled in the country, from whom its mercantile interests were to derive more substantial benefits than could ever be obtained from Jewish usurers. These were Flemish emigrants, who, in consequence of the bursting of their dikes, had been deprived of the territory which they had won from the sea, and were therefore obliged to seek a more permanent home. They first came to England in the time of the Conqueror, and as they were brave as well as industrious men, they were located on the frontier of Wales, where they formed a sort of steady break-water against the stormy invasions of the Welsh. This colony was soon increased by fresh arrivals; and Henry II., perceiving the benefits to be derived from such a people, not only enlarged their territory, but endowed them with many political privileges. England had hitherto not been a manufacturing country, but the arrival of these Flemings introduced the preparation and weaving of wool, so that, in process of time, not only the home market was abundantly supplied with woollen cloth, but a large surplus made for foreign exportation. Unlike the Jews, too, these Flemings, while they formed a gallant border defence against the Welsh, and diffused industrial arts and habits among the English, were not only Christians, but kinsmen of the Anglo-Saxon race, and distinguished for that probity in their commercial dealings which afterwards became the characteristic of the English merchants at large. From England, these Flemings gradually introduced themselves into Scotland, where David I. protected them, and allowed them to be governed by their own laws and usages, so that Flemish corporations were to be found in the chief towns of Fife, Angus, Aberdeen, and Inverness, and in Edinburgh, Peebles, Lanark, Dumbarton, Glasgow, Ayr, and Perth. In this way, not only the Scottish manufactures originated, but the trade of Scotland with Flanders, which continued for centuries, and was of great utility to both countries. How steadfast and true these wool-combers and weavers were to their plighted word when the barons and belted knights of the north stood aloof, or forswore themselves and became traitors, was afterwards manifested in an incident which the whole annals of chivalry cannot surpass. When Berwick was taken by storm in 1297, by Edward I., a building called the Red Hall was occupied by a company of thirty Flemish merchants, whose tenure of occupation was to defend it against the English to the last. They were summoned to surrender; but, true to their engagement, they continued their hopeless resistance for a whole day, until the building was set on fire, when they perished to a man in the flames.

We now pass from the towns to the rural districts, and from the nobles and citizens to the peasantry of England. In the *Doomsday Book* we find, that besides the land which was private property or common right, there was "terra regis," or land belonging to the crown, either by royal inheritance or forfeiture. Land itself was chiefly measured among the Saxons by the hide, and among the Normans by the caracute; but whether these measures were the same, or how many acres were comprised in each, it is now difficult to determine. As the expansion of the feudal system after the Norman conquest necessarily multiplied the tenures on which land was held, we now find the peasantry divided into *liberi homines*, or free men; *sochemanni*, or socmen; *bordarii*, or boors; *servi*, probably personal attendants; and *homines*, or men whose service, whatever it was, belonged to the feudal superior. All these seem to have more or less enjoyed a certain amount of personal property or freedom, although of what kind, and to what amount, we are unable to ascertain. Still, however, wherever bondage had existed in the Saxon times, it was either left undisturbed, or altered for the worse, through the right of the conquerors to do what they pleased with their own; and this must have chiefly fallen upon the *villeins*, who still composed the greater part of the English population. It was not, therefore, without cause that the cry was so popular and so frequent for the restoration of the laws of Edward the Confessor. Eadmer, the historian, informs us, that these serfs were so oppressed with exactions in the form of taxes, as sometimes to offer their ploughs to the king, having nothing more to bestow. As for the progress of agriculture, it must have been very slow in England during the whole of this period, on account of the internal wars and commotions that continued almost without a pause from the arrival of William the Conqueror to the death of King John.

The taste of the Normans for magnificent buildings was well attested by the churches, palaces, and castles which they erected in every land where they obtained the predominance; and after the conquest of so rich a country as England, these architectural predilections had scope for full exercise. Accordingly, while the greater part of the principal cathedrals and abbeys of the kingdom owed their origin to this period, a style of architecture was introduced superior to any that had yet been attempted in England. This, indeed, was to be expected where Norman prelates bore rule, and where the resources of the nation were at their command, for the realization of their utmost wishes. Such exertions gave full scope to the swelling ambition and superabundant activity both of bishop and noble, while they were enduring monuments of the power and talent of the founders. We almost lose sight, indeed, of the national oppression under which these glorious buildings arose, in the contrast which such achievements present to the doings of the thanes and bishops of the Anglo-Saxon period. But while monasteries and cathedrals were thus so largely multiplied, castles sprang up in still greater profusion. This was a natural consequence of the tenure by which the conquerors held possession; and during the reign of Stephen the necessity had so greatly increased, that 1115 castles were spread over the land. The style in which these edifices were erected, whether ecclesiastical, castellated, or domestic, was that prevalent at the time in Normandy; but it cannot in strictness be said to have been introduced into England at the Conquest, for Edward the Confessor, who had been brought up in the Norman court, had surrounded himself with Normans, and employed Norman architects on his buildings. It is expressly stated that he built the abbey church of Westminster in a "new style of architecture,"[1] and that many other churches were imitated from it. This must undoubtedly refer to the introduction of the Norman as a great improvement on the Saxon style; and the Conquest, which followed so closely on the death of this king, would extend and confirm the change. These buildings were no doubt considered magnificent in comparison with those which preceded them; but these also in their turn were soon deemed too small, and were swept away with as ruthless a hand as were those of their Saxon predecessors. Even the abbey of Westminster, built by the Confessor, suffered the same fate as the rest, no part, except possibly the crypt, being now in existence.

The Norman style continued in use for about 130 years—that is, until the time of Richard I., about the end of whose reign it passed into the early English style. It may be conveniently divided into three periods—the Early, from the Conquest to 1100; the Middle or enriched, from 1100 to about 1180; and the Transition, from about this time to the end of the century. These dates cannot be absolutely fixed, but are an approximation sufficiently near for general purposes. The Norman style is thus distinguished from the Saxon: in the Saxon the towers were lofty in proportion to their width, and were without buttresses or staircases; their masonry was peculiar,

[1] *Quam ipse novo compositionis genere construxerat.—Matt. Paris.*

and their windows, when of more than one light, were divided by a rude baluster, supporting a long impost through the thickness of the wall. In the Norman the towers were lower in proportion—were strengthened with buttresses, and had in general staircases, either in projecting turrets or within the thickness of the wall; their masonry had not the peculiar framework or quoins, and their windows were divided by small shafts instead of balusters. The mouldings, too, in the Saxon are few and simple, while in the Norman they are so numerous and ornamental, as to form an important characteristic of the style.

On the first view of a Norman building we are struck with its solid and massive, though somewhat flat appearance, while the absence of a spire, its comparatively low tower, round-headed windows and doors, almost flat buttresses, ornamented string courses, and the use of the zigzag and other mouldings in the most profuse manner, serve at once to distinguish it from any of the later styles. In the interior we find the same character: massive piers, round-headed windows, and a low vaulted or flat ceiling, impart an air of gloomy magnificence, which we never find in the buildings of a later period. This is particularly the case in the early structures; for the Normans, not being good builders, were obliged to compensate for want of skill by piling together immense masses of materials; but even then, instances are recorded of their edifices falling as soon as erected.

The general plan of small churches in this style is that of a parallelogram, consisting of a nave and chancel, with the tower either at the west end or at the junction of the two. In large churches the plan is generally cruciform, the tower being placed at the intersection of the cross, and sometimes the west end is flanked by two towers. The east end frequently terminated in a circular projection or *apse*, and in large conventual buildings or cathedrals there are frequently several of these both at the east end and on the transepts, where they served as chapels. Its vertical arrangements consisted of three tiers or stages, divided by mouldings or string courses, the lower of which was occupied by a semicircular arch resting on piers, separating the nave and choir from the aisles; the second contained the triforium (which in some instances was only a passage in the wall), the front of which opened into the body of the church by an arch, divided by a shaft into two lights, as at Norwich and Winchester Cathedrals, or subdivided into smaller arches, as at Malmesbury. This tier is by some early writers called also the *blind*-story, to distinguish it from the next or *clear*-story, in which are the windows above the aisles. In this upper story, also, there is a passage in the wall.

VOL. I.

When the building was vaulted or intended to be vaulted, a small shaft was carried up from the piers, and from this sprung the ribs and arches

PART OF THE SOUTH TRANSEPT AND NAVE, Peterborough Cathedral.

of the vaulting. In the early Norman buildings, however, the architects did not venture to throw vaults over the large spaces, but contented themselves with covering these with a flat boarded ceiling (as at Peterborough), and vaulting the aisles. The earliest vaults are what are called barrel vaults, that is merely a semi-cylinder reaching from side to side, as in the chapel of the Tower of London. Afterwards plain arches were thrown from pier to pier, and the space between was vaulted with diagonal groins without ribs, as in the crypt at Canterbury. These were at a still later period strengthened by vaulting ribs, which in later times were ornamented with the zigzag and other mouldings.

The piers which support the arches, are in the earlier examples strikingly solid and massive, being merely plain square or circular masses of masonry, sometimes having capitals and bases, and sometimes merely an impost to relieve the outline. The square piers were frequently recessed at the angles, and in some cases had half pillars attached to their sides; and the circular ones in some instances had the plain surface relieved by lines cut in a lozenge or spiral form, as at Durham and Norwich Cathedrals. As the style advanced, these solid piers were reduced to more moderate proportions of round or octagonal pillars, and in the time of the transition were frequently very tall and slender.

47–48

The capitals of these piers and pillars are among the most important features of this style. The upper member or *abacus* is in general square, and its profile is also square, having its lower edge sloped or *chamfered* off. It was sometimes cut up into smaller mouldings, but its general form remains; and it continues to the end of the style to be one of the most important characteristics. One of the earliest forms of the capital, and which with various modifications is found in all periods of the style, is what is called the *cushion capital*. It is frequently divided into two or many parts, and is also sometimes enriched with sculpture of foliage and figures; but under all these modifications it may still be taken as the primary form of the Norman capital. Throughout the whole of the Saxon and Norman period, there is an evident imitation of the classical styles, and of these the Corinthian seems to have made the greatest impression upon the minds of the workmen. We find in the Saxon capital the rudest possible imitation of the Corinthian volute, and it forms also one of the most striking marks of the early Norman. The volutes at the angles are distinct, and in place of the cauliculi, a plain block is left, as may be seen in the example from the chapel in the Tower of London, and this form, with some modifications, was in use in early Norman work, and is also very valuable in distinguishing this style. This imitation of the Corinthian capital continued throughout the style, but it was carried to the greatest perfection in the transition period, during the reigns of Henry II. and Richard I.,—a period at which Norman sculpture attained its greatest excellence, as the examples from Oakham Castle and Canterbury Cathedral will evince, in which the volutes, the cauliculi, and the foliage, are all evidently imitated. It may be also noticed, that in these examples the abacus is no longer square, but has its angles cut off; and in some instances it is circular, thus showing the transition to the circular form of the style that next came into use.

CUSHION CAPITAL.

CAPITAL—Chapel in Tower of London.

TRANSITION NORMAN CAPITAL, hall of Oakham Castle.

TRANSITION NORMAN CAPITAL, Canterbury Cathedral.

The arches were almost universally round-headed, until the period of the transition, when the pointed form was used along with or frequently instead of it. The pointed arch must not be taken as a *certain* criterion of transition date, as we have examples of it combined with solid early Norman piers, as at Malmesbury Abbey; but these examples are rare, and the mixture of the two forms may generally be taken as evidence of transition. The windows were universally round-headed, until the transition period. In the early examples they are quite plain, but they had afterwards frequently small shafts in the jambs, as at Steetley, or were enriched with the zigzag, as at St. Cross. Sometimes they were divided into two lights by a small shaft, and these again were frequently included under a large arch.

NORMAN WINDOW, Steetley, Derbyshire.

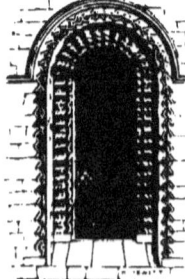

NORMAN WINDOW, St. Cross, Hampshire.

The doorways were the features on which the Norman architects lavished their decorations in greatest profusion; and though perfectly plain doors are to be found in this style, they were more frequently overlaid with ornament—and it is to

NORMAN DOORWAY, Earls-Barton, Northamptonshire.

this circumstance that they owe their preservation. In many instances, where every other part

CHEVRON MOULDING.

of the church has been rebuilt, the doorway has been preserved. Throughout the genuine Norman, the doorways were round-headed, but became pointed in the transition period. The door itself is often square-headed, and the space called the *tympanum*, between that and the arch, is frequently filled with sculpture, representing the three persons of the Trinity, saints, or allegorical devices, as at Barfreston, Ely, Rochester, Malmesbury, &c. The doorways were sometimes six or eight times recessed, and had as many shafts in the jambs; the capitals, imposts, jambs, and arches being elaborately carved with the mouldings peculiar to the style. The most prevalent of these is the zigzag or chevron. It is used in all parts of Norman buildings where ornament could be introduced, and at all periods of the style. It is the most easily executed of all decorations, and is therefore employed by various savage nations, for the ornaments of their weapons and canoes. We find it likewise in debased Roman work; but the most ancient example known is one on the Nineveh sculptures, brought home by Mr. Layard, where it occurs round the head of a window, as in Norman times, but in this instance it consists of only a single line. The other mouldings used are so numerous, that only a few of the most common can be enumerated. These are the lozenge, the billet, both round and square, the saw-tooth, the cable, the nail-head, the chain, the beak-head, the pellet,

the embattled, &c. Those of the early period, besides the zigzags, consist chiefly of lozenges, the billet, and such others as are shallow and easy of

LOZENGE MOULDING.

execution. For the ornamentation of flat spaces, a kind of shallow work cut on the surface in

BILLET MOULDING.

various patterns, as lozenges, scalework, &c., was much used. This was called *diaper work*, and was employed for the same purpose both in the

NAIL-HEAD MOULDING.

thirteenth and fourteenth centuries.[1] Small arcades, either simple or interlacing, were also used for the purpose of decoration, particularly on fronts and towers, as at Norwich.

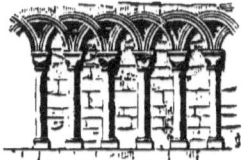

INTERLACING ARCADE, Norwich Cathedral.

The characters here given refer chiefly to the style in its purity; but soon after the middle of the twelfth century, towards the end of the reign of Henry II., a change came over it, by the introduction of the pointed arch. This seems to have been caused by the necessity of vaulting over spaces of unequal sides. It is evident, that though the semicircular arch might suit for the longer space, it would not for the shorter one, and therefore the use of the pointed arch was needed; and this once introduced, its convenience and applicability became so evident, that the use of the semicircular arch in the beginning of the next century, was entirely superseded by the

---

[1] See cut, St. Edmundsbury gateway, vol. i. p. 247.

pointed one. During this period, it was used not only for convenience but decoration, as may be seen at Oxford Cathedral, and in the remains of the Norman portion of Croyland Abbey, where

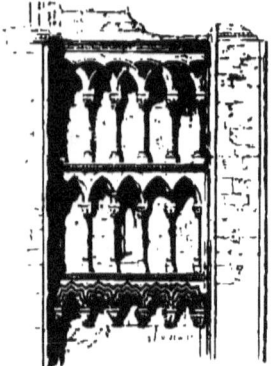

TRANSITION INTERLACING AND POINTED ARCADES.—Part of the west front, Croyland Abbey.

in both cases the round-headed and pointed arcades are used alternately, for the purpose of ornament. The Temple Church, London, and Oxford Cathedral, may be mentioned as good specimens of this period of transition, but by far the most valuable is Canterbury Cathedral. The rebuilding of this church was completed in 1110, and it was dedicated in 1130; but in 1172 it was almost entirely destroyed by fire, and the monks employed a Frenchman, named William of Sens, to rebuild it. He had nearly completed the choir in 1179, when having been injured by a fall, he resigned the work into the hands of another master, called William the Englishman, who continued the work, and completed what is called "Becket's Crown" in 1184. The whole of these proceedings are minutely recorded by Gervase, a monk of the place, who witnessed them, and his narrative is particularly valuable for distinguishing between early and late Norman work. If we examine the remaining portions of the old building, we shall find that they agree exactly in character with the early Norman work at Lincoln and elsewhere, while the portions built between 1172 and 1184 have the pointed arch, and the other features of the transition period.[1]

Of the *domestic buildings* of this period, as

[1] Professor Willis' *Architectural History of Canterbury Cathedral*. [The crypt—see cut, vol. i. p. 280—belongs to the former church; and the capital—figured on p. 370, vol. i.—to the latter.]

contradistinguished from the castellated, we have a few existing remains, which, though imperfect, can still enable us to trace their original arrangement. The usual ground plan of the house seems to have been a parallelogram, comprising merely a large room or hall, which occupied the entire height of the building, and two rooms at the end of the hall, the lower being the cellar, and the upper the *solar* or sleeping-room, which served also for a sitting-room, and was in fact the only private room in the house. To these a kitchen and other outhouses were attached; and in large houses there was a chapel. The king's houses at the time seem to have had no other accommodation. The hall served for the common living room of the master and his dependants. At one end the floor was raised a little higher than the rest, and on this raised part, which was called the *dais*, was placed crossways the principal table of the hall, and in the body were the tables for the servants and inferior guests. The floor of the hall served also for their sleeping place, the solar being reserved for the master and his family. The hall, as at Oakham Castle, was frequently divided into three parts by rows of pillars and arches, like the nave and aisles of a church; between these pillars curtains were hung, and by this means the aisles were separated from the body of the hall, and the sleeping apartments rendered more private. We find by Saxon MSS., particularly that of Cædmon, that this arrangement prevailed also

NORMAN DWELLING.—The Jews' House, Lincoln.

in Saxon times, and frequent allusions to it are to be found in the ancient poems and romances.

The hall was usually on the ground floor, but sometimes it was on the first floor; and, in this case, the lower story was vaulted, and the communication with the upper story was by an external staircase. A house of this kind is shown in the Bayeux Tapestry. The Jews' House, Lincoln, also a well-known example, has the principal room on the upper story, in which is the fireplace. The house is small, and appears to have had only two rooms; but this cannot now be ascertained, the original divisions of the interior being destroyed. This arrangement of having a large common hall was in use in the time of the Saxons, from whom the name is derived, and it was continued with little modification throughout the middle ages. The hall is sometimes called the *domus*, or house; and in the north of England we find the term *house-place* applied to the common sitting room in ordinary dwelling-houses, which have usually a *house-place* (or sometimes only *house*), *parlour*, and *kitchen*, thus showing that the same idea of the uses and arrangements of the rooms has been continued to our own time, and in all descriptions of dwellings. It is probable that the hall was warmed by a fire in the middle of the floor, with an opening or *louvre* in the roof over it, to allow the escape of smoke; but we have many fire-places and chimneys of this period still remaining, as at the Jews' House, Lincoln; a house at Christ

NORMAN FIRE-PLACE, Hedingham Castle, Essex.

Church, Hants; Conisbrough Castle; Rochester Castle; Hedingham Castle, &c.

We have but few materials for judging how the houses were furnished, our chief authorities being the illuminated MSS. of the time. It seems certain that in large houses tapestry was used to cover the walls, but this must refer to the "solar" only. The hall had probably only tables, benches, and seats. The bed must have been in the *solar*, or *private*. These, in the illuminations, have more the appearance of modern couches than beds; they are without hangings or testers, but they have pillows and bed-clothes. In some of the Saxon MSS. the beds have four posts, with head and foot boards, and are very similar to our modern French beds. The pillows are ornamented with various patterns, probably in embroidery. We also find stools, seats, and arm-chairs, of various designs, in common use, both in this century and the

one preceding it. All these appear to have been well executed, and some of them are enriched with ornamental carvings and mouldings. Many are evidently executed in the turning-lathe. The doors, shutters for the windows, chests, &c., exhibit in their hinges, bolts, and locks, specimens of ornamental ironwork; and their curtains are held up by rods and rings, as in modern houses. The lesser houses, the dwellings of the common people, both in town and country, seem to have been built of wood and plaster, and thatched with reeds and straw, but of these there are of course no examples remaining.

As might be expected, the strongholds of the Normans were of a more stately and imposing character than the straggling low-roofed granges in which the Saxon thanes had hitherto dwelt in safety; but still, they were built with a reference more to the means of resistance than those of elegance or comfort. The first defence of a castle was

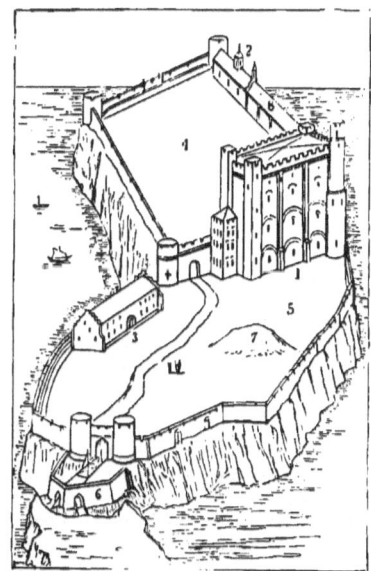

NORMAN CASTLE.—From a drawing in Grose's Military Antiquities.—1, The Donjon-keep. 2, Chapel. 3, Stables. 4, Inner Ballium. 5, Outer Ballium. 6, Barbican. 7, Mount, supposed to be the court-hill or tribunal, and also the place where justice was executed. 8, Soldiers' Lodgings.

the moat or ditch, that sometimes comprised several acres; and behind it was the outer wall, generally of great height and thickness, strengthened with towers at regular distances, and pierced with loop-holes through which missiles could be discharged at the assailants. Within these defences were three divisions, consisting of the outer ballium or lower court, the inner ballium or upper court, and the keep; while the main entrance through the outer wall was protected by the barbican, with its narrow archway, and strong gates and portcullis. It was no wonder that with such a net-work of walls, division of courts, and multiplied means for the defenders both of safety and annoyance, the dislodgment of an obnoxious magnate should have been so hard a task even when the royal banner marched against him. While so much was done for security and resistance, nothing was left for domestic comfort but the keep, which formed the residence of the

NORMAN KEEP, Hedingham Castle, Essex.

baron and his family. This was the innermost of all the buildings, to which the defenders retreated only in the last extremity, and was so strongly constructed, that in the ruins of castles it generally survives as a recording monument of departed greatness. A domicile erected on such a principle must, according to our modern ideas, have been sufficiently comfortless, where every window was a shot-hole, and every apartment a battery, and where light could not be admitted without also inviting an enemy. But such as it was, it was the constant home of lordly knights and high-born dames; and, therefore, their taste and ingenuity as well as their resources were employed to make the most of it.

But if the homes of the period still continued to be uncomfortable, all this mattered little with a people who cared not for domestic life, and whose happiness was to be found in action and open display. A large hall in which a crowd could be banquetted, rich armour, splendid dress, and a numerous retinue, constituted the chief insignia of distinction as well as source of happiness for a people who would have found an indoor life a very weariness. In these, therefore, the noble and wealthy of England were not want-

ing. And in the first place, who was that happy individual who paraded himself before the admiring crowd with such pomp and glitter? Had he been Tom, or Dick, or Harry, he would have been nothing, as these simple epithets might have belonged to any one; and he chose an addition to his one name, that the world might perceive he was somewhat. It was usually from the district in which he was born, or the estate which his ancestors had inherited, and hence the foreign places that were so often incorporated in the designations of our old English nobility. He thus showed that he had come from somewhere, and been the son of somebody, even before he fought his way to wealth and distinction at Hastings. If he held a place at court, this circumstance was equally good; and by using its title in addition to his Christian name, all the world could know that he was stabler or door-keeper to the sovereign, and therefore not a person to be overlooked. In this way, the *dapifers* were the chief nobles, and afterwards the Kings of Scotland. Or, if he had the good chance to be the son of an illustrious personage, even though it should be illegitimately, he added his father's name to his own, with the prefix of Fitz, and thus shone by the reflected light of his princely parentage. This distinction of a twofold appellation was so important, that when Henry I., by his right of royal wardship, resolved to bestow the hand of a rich and noble heiress upon his illegitimate son Robert, the lady flatly refused the match. "My father, and my grandfather," said the pouting beauty, "had each two names, and foul shame it were in me to marry a man who has only one." The king soon removed her scruples by giving his son the surname of Fitz-Roy, and the fortunate bridegroom was afterwards that illustrious Earl of Gloucester who so gallantly upheld the cause of Matilda in the reign of Stephen. Another mode of being known and distinguished was by the insignia of heraldry. As the different parts of defensive armour continued to increase until the wearer was completely covered from head to heel, it was generally impossible to recognize him in the confusion of conflict; and as no one cares to do brave deeds anonymously, the difficulty was removed by the adoption of some cognizance from which the champion could be recognized both by friend and enemy. In this case, some trivial ornament at first was thought enough; and thus the illustrious descendants of that count who wore a sprig of broom in his helmet, were afterwards famed throughout Europe for centuries under the name of Plantagenet. Sometimes the cognizance was a favourite war cry by which a leader animated his followers, or summoned them to the rescue. Sometimes it was an animal or other figure painted upon the shield.

which, like a sign-board, announced the resident of the iron mass behind it. In this way, quartered shields and embroidered surcoats, and crests and mottoes, grew into notice, and expanded into the complicated science of heraldry. Besides these different modes, the nobility of the period sought distinction in the throng of their followers; and these trains, especially in a long journey, were generally composed of strange materials. As inns were out of the question at this time throughout England, all the necessaries for an encampment or a bivouac had to be carried along with them; and thus waggons of provisions, ale, dress, and furniture accompanied the march. As feuds were frequent, and robber-barons to be found in every county, this singular retinue was defended in front, flank, and rear, by knights, squires, and spearmen, who were ready for the worst, though each mile should bring them a fresh encounter. And, finally, as such a kind of travelling was rather dull without the resources of amusement, jesters, dancers, mimics, and dicers, and sometimes still more questionable characters, formed part of the procession. All this upon a large scale was exhibited in the royal progresses of Henry II., as we learn from the letters of Peter of Blois; and we can easily conjecture how in such cases royalty was imitated by nobility.

But it was in dress that the Norman aristocracy of England chiefly showed their rank, wealth, and taste; and in this they resembled their ancestors the Danes, whose love of gay clothing and rich ornaments was almost equal to their craving for bloodshed and plunder. A liking of this nature could not well exist without capricious mutations, and therefore the changes in fashion from the time of William the Conqueror to that of Henry III. were so many that it becomes difficult as well as tiresome to follow them. At one time the hair of the men was shorn closely behind, and the upper lip shaved; at another, the hair was worn of such effeminate length that the church took the alarm; and while the practice was denounced by edicts, the long flowing locks of the male part of a congregation were often menaced by shears and razor, which the preachers plucked from their sleeves, when they arrived at the practical application of their sermons. Nay, on one occasion of this kind, when long beards were the order of the day, the Bishop of Sees, after declaiming against them before Henry I. and his courtiers, descended at the end of the discourse, and with his scissors cropped off the beards both of king and congregation. After such clerical rebukes, it is no wonder if, at the close of this period, we sometimes find the pictures of men without beard or mustachio—more especially as the monks were the limners. Even when the hair was not sufficiently long for the exquisite taste of the wearer, he sometimes enriched it with false locks, and thus flaunted a streamer that equalled the gayest. But what

SHIELD BEARING BADGE, HELMET, SWORD, AND BANNER.—From a MS. in the Bibliothèque de Mans.

country or generation has been free of such head-fopperies, from the ancient Egyptian periwig in the glass case of the British Museum, to the

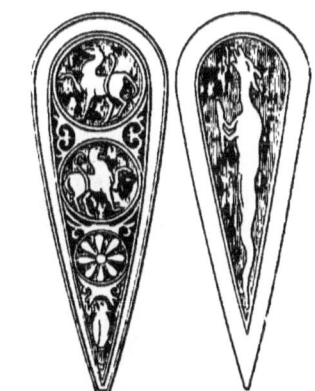

SHIELDS BEARING BADGES.—1. From a MS. Bible in the Bibliothèque Imperiale, Brussels, Depôt des Cordeliers. 2. From a Psalter in the same collection.

pigtail that was not unfamiliar in the days of our grandfathers? As for the general articles of dress at this period, they consisted of a hood, or a cap, shaped liked a Scottish bonnet, a cloak, a tunic, a pair of long tight hose, leg bandages, and shoes or short boots. All this, however, was but the ground-work, which fashion overlaid or transmuted at pleasure. In this way, cloaks became long or short; the sleeves of the tunic were sometimes so lengthened that the hand was overlapped and concealed; while the boots and shoes, instead of being adapted to the shape of the foot, and the convenience of walking or riding, were curled up at the points like rams' horns, and sometimes were fastened to the knee with a gold chain. To such extravagance was this fashion, which seems to have been an European one, afterwards carried in Germany, that the Austrian men-at-arms were unable to charge the Swiss at the battle of Sempach, until they had hewn off their boot points, which were so plentiful, the ballad informs us, that they would have filled a waggon. The costliness of the stuff of which these different articles of dress were made, and the richness with which they were befurred and embroidered, was a matter of great import; and William Rufus on one occasion threw away a new pair of hose, because they cost only three shillings, declaring that a king should wear nothing so cheap. He seems to have been of a different opinion from King Stephen, that "worthy peer," who thought his hose too dear at half-a-crown. Towards the close of this period the bonnet was sometimes discarded, that the hair might be more fully seen and admired; and in this case the exquisites of the time of King John wreathed their long locks into ringlets with curling-tongs, and bound them with gay ribbons. At other times, a streamer was attached to the hood, of such preposterous length that it nearly reached the middle of the leg. And yet, these were the men who could endure the heat of a Syrian campaign under a heavy load of armour, and fight gallantly from morning to night upon a fair field!

In all these fopperies, the male sex appear to have so completely anticipated the ladies, that little change can be found to have taken place in female costume and ornament. The gown and kerchief were still the principal articles of outer clothing, while the hair, which was worn long, was at one time plaited, and at another inclosed in a silken case, or bound with a ribbon. The under garment or tunic, where the front was given to view, was laced up, while its sleeves were so long that they were sometimes knotted up to prevent them from trailing on the ground—and the same was the case with the kerchiefs or veils, which would otherwise have dragged behind like a train. But these exaggerations were abandoned during the reign of Henry II., when a better taste discarded the long knotted sleeves and skirts for a more succinct and graceful costume. In this case, the gown was gathered closely to the waist with a girdle, and the veil demurely fastened beneath the chin, so that the whole head was covered. Sometimes the younger ladies wore their hair short and

GENTLEMEN OF THE TIME OF JOHN.—From an enamelled cup, presented by King John to the town of Lynn.

SLEEVE OF TWELFTH CENTURY, AND FEMALE WITH LONG KNOTTED SLEEVES.—From a Psalter in Douce's Collection.

curled, while the elder ones appear with a hood, furnished with a long streamer behind, like that of the gentlemen. The female ornaments of gold and articles of jewellery may be presumed to have been nearly or altogether the same as in the former period, as rings, chains, and brooches are adapted to every taste, and not liable to the mutations of more flexible or transitory articles.

In turning to the domestic style of life which now prevailed in England, we find that, with all the additional splendour which was introduced, little improvement was as yet made in the substantial comforts of a home. The floor was still carpeted, or rather littered, with rushes, however lordly might be the hall; and as these rushes appear to have been seldom renewed, they must have been plentiful receptacles both of damp and dust. On this account Fitz-Stephen quotes it as an instance of the princely magnificence of Thomas à Becket when chancellor, that he caused the floor of his dining-room to be covered every morning with clean straw or hay in winter, and green branches of trees in summer. The historian, however, adds a startling fact which we could not otherwise have surmised, and it is—that all this was for the comfort of those guests who were obliged at dinner to sit upon the floor, from no room being found for them at table! The general regulations in the daily routine of a household may be learned from the following rhyme of the period, which had probably all the authority of a well-established proverb:—

"Lever a cinque, diner a neuf,
Souper a cinque, coucher a neuf,
Fait vivre d'ans nonante et neuf."

To rise at five, to dine at nine,
To sup at five, to bed at nine,
Makes a man live to ninety and nine.

Here we have a four hours' morning fast before the first meal, followed by eight hours of endurance before the second and last succeeded. This,

and only two meals a-day, was perhaps the most marked change effected by the Conquest, when the four, and sometimes five heavy Saxon meals *per diem* of the preceding period are taken into account. Another striking change was in the new nomenclature imposed upon the articles of

LADIES OF THE TIME OF JOHN.—From an enamelled cup, presented by King John to the town of Lynn.

diet. While feeding and rearing, the animals suited to the table retained their Saxon names, but as soon as they were killed they became, to all intents, Norman. Thus a cow became beef, a calf veal, a sheep mutton, a sow pork, a deer venison, and a fowl a pullet. Amidst these transitions it is somewhat significant that bacon remained unaltered. We formerly noticed the large droves of swine that constituted the principal live stock of the Anglo-Saxon farmers. Their conquerors were probably too proud, as well as too dainty, to meddle with such fare, and had therefore left it untouched, as only fitted for the vanquished.

Of the style of cookery during the Norman period we only know that rich spices were in plentiful use, and that the Normans themselves were not only moderate, but also dainty eaters —epicures in the best sense of the term, in contrast to the Saxons, who, we must confess, were sheer gluttons in comparison. We learn the names of several choice dishes in Blount's *Ancient Tenures*, such as *diligrout, karumpie, maupigirnum*, but of what they consisted, or how they were prepared, we are left wholly in the dark. At solemn feasts the boar's head—that long after continued to be the chief ornament of the baronial hall and Christmas festival—was already a dainty dish, and as such was brought in at the coronation of Prince Henry, eldest son and junior king of Henry II., amidst a loud blare of trumpets. The peacock, in like manner, was such a cherished ornament of the table that either already, or soon after, kings, knights, and nobles were wont to swear solemnly over it before they ate it, when

LONG TRESSES AND FEMALE COSTUME.—From sculptures on the Port de Macons, Rouen Cathedral.

they pledged themselves to some great chivalrous enterprise. The crane was a bird for the common meals of nobles and princes. The finest wheat was made into simnel and wastel cakes, and spice-bread (*panis piperatus*), and used at the tables of the rich, in addition to common loaves; and the chief drinks, as before, were spiced wines, morat, pigment, and hippocras, for the wealthy, and ale and cider for the middle classes. But that much coarseness and discomfort still predominated at the board both of castle and palace—and that, too, at the period of Henry II.—may be learned from the following copious description, given by Peter of Blois, who doubtless had endured his full share of the annoyances he describes:—"I often wonder how any one who has been used to the service of scholarship and the camps of learning, can endure the annoyances of a court life. Among courtiers there is no order, no plan, no moderation, either in food, in horse-exercise, or in watchings. A priest or a soldier attached to the court has bread put before him which is not kneaded, not leavened, made of the dregs of beer; bread like lead, full of bran and unbaked; wine spoiled, either by being sour or mouldy—thick, greasy, rancid, tasting of pitch, and vapid. I have sometimes seen wine so full of dregs put before noblemen, that they were compelled rather to filter than drink it, with their eyes shut and their teeth closed, with loathing and retching. The beer at court is horrid to taste and filthy to look at. On account of the great demand, meat, whether sweet or not, is sold alike: the fish is four days old, yet its stinking does not lessen its price. The servants care nothing whatever whether the unlucky guests are sick or dead, provided there are fuller dishes sent up to their masters' tables. Indeed, the tables are filled (sometimes) with carrion, and the guests' stomachs thus become the tombs for those who die in the course of nature. Indeed, many more deaths would ensue from this putrid food, were it not that the famishing greediness of the stomach (which, like a whirlpool, will suck in anything) by the help of powerful exercise, gets rid of everything. But if the courtiers cannot have exercise (which is the case if the court stays for a time in town), some of them always stay behind at the point of death."

Such was the sorry kind of life enjoyed or endured by the paladins of Henry II. Well might they be trained and hardened for the worst that soon after was to be encountered in the crusade of Richard I. Indeed, after such an account, we may almost question if the story, which the minstrels of the day recorded, of Richard himself having eaten a Saracen boy, cooked into the likeness of pork, was wholly fabulous.

Of the sports and pastimes of England during this period, the authors and illuminated MSS. of the day are so full, that in most cases a brief notice is all we can afford. In regard to the sedentary amusements, dicing, as might be expected among such a military people as the Normans and Saxons, was keenly practised during the intervals of peace as a substitute for the excitement of conflict. It was at a game of dice, as we have seen, that the young sons of William the Conqueror were employed at the town of L'Aigle, when the dangerous quarrel broke out among them. Ten different games of dice were practised at the period; and so prevalent had these become that Richard I. of England, and his royal brother of France, were obliged, while on their way to Palestine, to enact the most stringent laws against them. By these it was decreed that only the two kings might play, and such of their retainers as they were pleased to command to that effect, and in their own presence; but in this case no noble, knight, or priest, was to lose more than 20s. in one day and night, under a penalty of four times that amount. In the same manner the servants of archbishops, bishops, earls, and barons, might play at the command of their masters; but if any menials presumed to partake of such indulgences without leave, they were to be whipped naked round the camp on three successive days. The same was to be the punishment of every soldier under the rank of priest or knight, while every sailor so offending was to be ducked three times in the sea. As it was known, however, that these rules were likely to be often infringed, in spite of the terrors of flogging and ducking, the offender was allowed to escape the punishment on payment of a fine towards the redemption of the holy sepulchre. The evil, however, went on in spite of the denunciations of the church, and even the halls of monasteries were pervaded with the rattle of the dice-box, while estates were lost and won, and hot blood and quarrels excited by the practice. This profusion with which property was staked was the natural consequence of the facility with which it had been acquired, and the Norman conquerors of England only acted as robbers or pirates are wont to do after every fortunate windfall.

But gambling, however attractive, was not sufficient for the castle of the Norman noble, where himself and his numerous throng of retainers lived in garrison, surrounded by dangerous rivals and an unsettled people; and other indoor sports were gladly welcomed to enliven the dulness of the passing day. For this purpose, there was the Norman troubadour and the Saxon gleeman, who led a homeless but merry life, wandering from hamlet to hamlet, and from tower to tower, singing to harp or rote the achievements of Rollo and Charlemagne, or the wild romances of the early Heptarchy. Next to these, were companies of strolling dramatists, who acted what the others sang; and as their plays were sufficiently coarse, both in language and incident, being adapted to the taste of their auditories, they were condemned by the church, while every priest was forbid to attend or countenance them. Then, there were buffoons, jesters, and mimics—men whose business it was to create the luxury of a laugh, and drive a trade in jokes; and posture-masters, tumblers, and dancers, who astonished the onlookers by their feats of agility. And though last not least, there was the juggler,

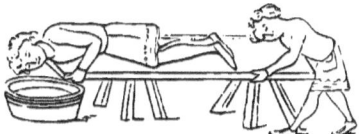

BOB-APPLE.—MS. Royal Library, 2. R. VII.

JUGGLER AND MUSICIAN.—Cotton MS. Tib. C. 6.

who generally headed the party, and whose feats in the art of sleight-of-hand imparted to the full what the poet calls "the pleasure of being cheated." Besides these feats of conjuration, he often exhibited that play of balls and knives which is still of common practice at every village fair, and which never ceases to startle the wondering or sympathizing spectators. These strange bands, who appear from the writers of the period to have been very numerous, were in all likelihood chiefly composed of Saxons dispossessed by the Conquest—men who had no alternative between such a precarious life, and that of outlaws in the greenwood—and who afterwards pursued from habit and inclination an employment they had adopted from necessity. In this way they recovered from their proud masters a small pittance of their own original inheritance, or amused their sorrowing countrymen amidst the severe inflictions of the Norman ascendancy. We find that not only men, women, and children were employed in these feats of dexterity and strength, but also bears, horses, and monkeys, who were taught to dance, fetch, and carry, and imitate the actions of human beings. Among the in-door amusements of the common people of this time, the game of *bob-apple* seems to have been a favourite. The tempting fruit was to be caught with the mouth as it floated in a large tub of water, while the diver was to attempt it poised upon his two hands, and leaning in ticklish balance over the flood below. To add also to his chance of a good ducking, the end of the platform on which he rested might be tilted up, by which his equipoise, however exact, was easily destroyed. Another mode of this game was to suspend the apple from the ceiling by a string, and attempt to secure it with the teeth only; and in this case, the abortive mumblings of the players afforded full scope for jeers and merriment.

Such, as we learn from paintings and chronicles, were the chief sedentary amusements of England during the period. In passing to the active sports, the first place must be given to hunting, as it formed not only so important a part in the history of the country, but was so fruitful a source of its misery. Mention has already been made of the depopulation of the New Forest, which the Conqueror appropriated to himself, and converted into a royal hunting ground. The great feudal Norman barons, among whom the land was subdivided, and who ruled over their own territory with regal authority, were not slow to imitate the example of the sovereign; and thus they inclosed large portions of their baronies for the preservation of game, having first destroyed the cottages, and driven out the occupants. In this way, new forests upon a limited scale were multiplied over the whole of England, and guarded with such jealous care by their proprietors, that to hunt the king's deer was visited with the penalties of high treason, while a trespass upon the inclosures of a noble was frequently expiated with loss of life or mutilation of limb. When the hunt was up, the same reckless disregard of common justice and humanity prevailed: the lordly train drove headlong through pasture-land and corn-field, indifferent to the desolation they occasioned or the families they ruined; while the wretched peasantry, instead of being permitted to bemoan themselves in their hovels, were obliged to wait at the door with food and refreshments for those who were thus trampling down their harvests. This furious love of hunting, too, was not confined to the nobler animals of game—to wild boars and stags—but descended even to rabbits; and in one of the illuminated MSS. of the period, we have a king and his attendants employed at full gallop in a rabbit-hunt. As many of the Anglo-Norman ladies partook of the military character, and had shared in the dangers of their lords, they were not to be excluded from a pleasure so suited to their dispositions; and therefore they too pursued the deer with hound and horn, and brought down the quarry with their arrows. Next to hunting, was the sport of hawking, which, as we have seen, had been in full favour in England prior to the Conquest. To the Norman nobles, however, it does not seem to have been sufficiently accompanied with stir, danger, and excitement, and therefore they left it as an effeminate amusement to women and priests. Horse-racing, which was practised upon a small scale in England, in the days of Bede and his contemporaries, does not as yet seem to have made great progress: indeed, during the whole period of chivalry, when mail-clad men were almost exclusively the riders, strength rather than speed was chiefly valued in a horse. We learn, however, from Fitz-Stephen, the biographer of Thomas à Becket, that horse-racing was occasionally practised with war-horses and hackneys in Smithfield.

While the active sports of the nobility of England were those of conquerors and tyrants, those of the common people were both few and cheerless. Hunting and hawking were out of the question, on account of the exclusive jealousy with which these amusements were guarded; and beyond a little poaching on their own grounds with clap-net and crossbow, with small birds for their game, they appear to have had nothing better—except, indeed, when they repaired to Sherwood, and enlisted among the bold outlaws of Robin Hood. We find, however, from the MSS. of the period, that several of those games, which are now the favourites of the commons of England, were in equal practice among the peasantry in the days of the earliest Plantagenets, and had perhaps been imported by their ancestors from the shores of the Baltic. The chief of these was bowling. Another, commonly called the game of kayle-pins, consisted in striking down small conical pieces of wood with the throw of a cudgel—a sport almost the same as that of nine-pins, now so common among children and schoolboys, and which is still kept up at country fairs, where the top of each pin supports a prize to reward the successful thrower. Cudgel-playing, and the fence of sword and buckler, are frequent in the pictorial delineations of this era, and were in great favour among the English commons, as they have always been among every martial people, in spite of the dangers with which they are attended. A more sportive form of these warlike amusements was the sword-dance, which was performed to the sound of music. In a picture of this kind, two dancers are manœuvring against each other with large swords and bucklers, while every movement is directed by a bag-piper's melody, so that the combatants know when to strike and ward in perfect safety. Amidst

SWORD-DANCE AND PIPER.—From Strutt.

these rougher sports, wrestling was certain not to be neglected; and one warlike form which it assumed, was the tilting of men horsed upon the backs or shoulders of their companions, where each grappled with his antagonist, and endeavoured to throw him to the ground. Foot-racing and the game of foot-ball, spear-throwing, and archery are also included among the sports of the period; while cock-fighting, bull-baiting, and bear-baiting—these chief amusements of a later day—appear to have been already commenced in England among the larger towns. Fitz-Stephen also describes a game in vogue among the London citizens which may be called the water-tournament, or rowing (not riding) at the ring,

WATER-TOURNAMENT.—MS. Royal Library, 2. B. VII.

which was performed in the following fashion:—A mast was set up in the midst of the river Thames, to which a shield was nailed; a boat was rowed at full speed against it, and a man standing in warlike attitude at the stern, with his lance or pole couched, took aim at the shield as he flew past it. But woe to the luckless wight who could not retain a firm footing, while his weapon closed or was shivered in the encounter! in this case, he was thrown backward like an unhorsed knight, and laid sprawling in the depths of the river, amidst a peal of universal merriment. But as drowning in addition to discomfiture would have been too much, boats were always in readiness to fish up the unsuccessful, so that nothing worse occurred than a sound ducking. The same drolling imitation of the sports of chivalry was practised on land. A pole of sufficient height was planted in the ground, at the top of which a transverse beam, having at one end a bag of sand and at the other

ANCIENT QUINTAIN, at Offham, Kent.

a board, revolved as easily as a weathercock to the touch. This board constituted the mark at which the peasantry, mounted on their clumsy untrained horses, rode with staves couched in full career; but no sooner was the board struck than the sand-bag revolved like the fist of a giant, and unseated the unlucky tilter by a blow between the shoulders, unless he eluded it by dexterous ducking or sharp spurring. By these two sports of land and water, the citizens and peasantry of England might furtively caricature the solemn military games of their Norman oppressors, and enjoy the merriment and stir of a tournament, without the bloodshed and broken bones with which it was usually accompanied.

Such is a brief sketch of the sports and amusements of the people of England during this period of transition. We know well that many others must have existed among them, in consequence of the exclusively Saxon character with which the sports of after periods were strikingly pervaded, when happier times than the present recalled them into active exercise. But from the Conquest to the death of John, the unfortunate natives were compelled to feel that they were a conquered people; and holding their very lives, as they did, at the pleasure of the victors, the spirit of nationality was almost crushed out of them, so that they were in no mood to play and be merry. But even at the close of this period, political causes were in operation through which they were to recover their rights, and become the free and independent people they had once been. Hereafter, therefore, we shall be enabled to recognize a more distinct, as well as more happy national physiognomy in the character and condition—the avocations and amusements—of the commons of "merry England."

BOOK IV.
PERIOD FROM THE ACCESSION OF HENRY III. TO THE END OF THE REIGN OF RICHARD II.—183 YEARS.
FROM A.D. 1216–1399.

CONTEMPORARY PRINCES.

England.
1216 HENRY III.
1272 EDWARD I.
1307 EDWARD II.
1327 EDWARD III.
1377 RICHARD II.

Scotland.
1249 ALEXANDER III.
1286 MARGARET.
1292 JOHN BALIOL.
1296 INTERREGNUM.
1306 ROBERT I.
1329 DAVID II.
1371 ROBERT II.
1390 ROBERT III.

France.
1223 LOUIS VIII.
1226 LOUIS IX.
1270 PHILIP III.
1285 PHILIP IV.

1314 LOUIS X.
1316 PHILIP V.
1322 CHARLES IV.
1328 PHILIP VI.
1350 JOHN.
1364 CHARLES V.
1380 CHARLES VI.

Castile and Leon.
1230 FERDINAND III.
1252 ALPHONSO X.
1284 SANCHO IV.
1295 FERDINAND IV.
1312 ALPHONSO XI.
1350 PEDRO.
1366 HENRY II.
1367 PEDRO (restored).
1369 HENRY II. (restored).
1379 JOHN I.
1390 HENRY III. and CATHERINE OF LANCASTER.

Germany.
1212 FREDERIC II.
1251 CONRAD IV.
1254 INTERREGNUM.
1273 RODOLPH.
1292 ADOLPHUS.
1298 ALBERT I.
1308 HENRY VII.
1314 LOUIS V.
1347 CHARLES IV.
1378 WENCESLAUS.

Popes.
1216 HONORIUS III.
1227 GREGORY IX.
1241 CELESTINE IV.
1243 INNOCENT IV.
1254 ALEXANDER IV.
1261 URBAN IV.
1265 CLEMENT IV.
1271 GREGORY X.
1276 INNOCENT V.

1276 ADRIAN V.
1276 JOHN XXI.
1277 NICHOLAS III.
1281 MARTIN IV.
1285 HONORIUS IV.
1287 NICHOLAS IV.
1294 CELESTINE V.
1294 BONIFACE VIII.
1303 BENEDICT XI.
1305 CLEMENT V.
1316 JOHN XXII.
1334 BENEDICT XII.
1342 CLEMENT VI.
1352 INNOCENT VI.
1362 URBAN V.
1370 GREGORY XI.
1378 URBAN VI. and CLEMENT VII.
1389 BONIFACE IX. and CLEMENT VII.
1394 BONIFACE IX. and BENEDICT XIII.

CHAPTER I.—CIVIL AND MILITARY HISTORY.

HENRY III., SURNAMED OF WINCHESTER.—ACCESSION A.D. 1216—DEATH A.D. 1272.

Henry III. succeeds his father John—The Earl of Pembroke appointed Protector—The Dauphin attempts to obtain the crown of England—His various encounters—His defeat at Lincoln—Defeat of a French fleet off Dover—The Dauphin compelled to abandon England—Reforms made in the laws—Earl of Pembroke dies—Quarrels among his successors in the regency—War proclaimed against France—Its inglorious termination—Hubert de Burgh, the chief minister, cruelly treated—Peter des Roches, his successful rival, banished—Henry III. marries Eleanor—Influx of foreigners into England—Unpopularity of Henry—He makes war on France—He is defeated—Applies to parliament for aid, and is refused—His iniquitous shifts to raise money—His solemn promises and oaths to parliament—His wasteful attempts to obtain Sicily for one of his sons—He is dismayed by an armed meeting of his parliament—The Earl of Leicester heads their opposition—Meeting of the "Mad Parliament" at Oxford—Its character and proceedings—The barons divided among themselves—Henry III. prepares to oppose them—A civil war commences—Leicester defeats Henry near Lewes—Prince Edward escapes from captivity—Edward raises an army—He defeats and slays Leicester at the battle of Evesham—Henry III. restored to the throne—Prince Edward departs to the Holy Land—Death of Henry III.

S soon as they had buried John at Worcester, the Earl of Pembroke, the marshal of England, marched with the royal army and Prince Henry, the deceased king's eldest son, to the city of Gloucester. On the day after their arrival, being the feast of St. Simon and St. Jude, Oct. 28th, 1216, Henry was crowned in the church of St. Peter, belonging to the abbey of Gloucester, by Gualo, the pope's legate, whose services in supporting the royal cause were of great value and efficacy. The ceremony was precipitated; no English bishops were present, except those of Winchester, Bath, and Worcester; no lay nobles, save the Earls of Chester, Pembroke, and Ferrers, and four barons. The scanty retinue was completed by a few abbots and priors. The prince took the usual oaths "upon the gospels and relics of saints." The crown had been lost, with the rest of the regalia, in the Wash, and, instead of it, Gualo put a plain ring of gold on his head. Henry was only ten years old when he went through these solemnities, without understanding them. It required no great force or persuasion to induce him to consent to do homage to the pope for England and Ireland, and to swear to pay the 1000 marks a-year which his father had promised. The clergy of Westminster and Canterbury, who considered their rights invaded by this hurried and informal coronation, appealed to Rome for redress; Gualo excommunicated the appellants, who, however, persevered; and this matter occasioned considerable trouble, which did not end till the ceremony was repeated in a more regular manner.

A great council was held at Bristol on the 11th of November following; and there the Earl of Pembroke was chosen Protector, with the title of *Rector Regis et Regni*. His pure character and many eminent qualities—his temper, prudence, and conciliating manners—his experience in public affairs, and his military skill—all seemed to point him out as the most eligible person; but some jealousies arose on the part of the great Earl of Chester, and Pembroke did not assume the style of "Rector" till the end of the month of November. At the same great council of Bristol, Magna Charta was carefully, and on the whole skilfully revised, with the view of satisfying the demands of the barons who adhered to Louis, without sacrificing the royal prerogative. These measures, however, were not considered conclusive, for Pembroke prudently left several clauses open for future discussion, when all the barons of the kingdom should be reconciled, and should meet again in one council. As yet the greater number of the nobles were on the side of Louis, who not only held London and the rich provinces of the south, but was powerful both in the north and the west, where the King of Scotland and the Princes of Wales supported his cause.[2]

HENRY III.1—From his tomb in Westminster Abbey.

When Lo is learned the death of John, he fancied that all opposition would presently cease. To take advantage of the consternation which he fancied must prevail amorg the royal party, he again pressed the siege of Dover Castle with great vigour, and, finding himself still incapable of taking it by force, he skilfully worked upon the fears and misgivings of the garrison, representing to them that they were fighting for a king who no longer existed, and whose death freed them from the obligation of their oaths of fealty. He tempted the governor, the brave Hubert de Burgh, with the most magnificent offers; and, when these failed, he threatened to put Hubert's brother to death. But threats were as ineffectual as promises; and, finding he was losing precious time, the French prince finally raised the siege, and returned to London, where the Tower, which had hitherto held out, was given up to him on the 6th of November. From London Louis marched to Hertford, and laid siege to the castle there, which he took on the 6th of December. He then attacked the castle of Berkhampstead, which he reduced on the 20th of the same month. Both these castles made a stout resistance, costing him many men; and the taking of that of Berkhampstead was a loss rather than a gain, for it led to a quarrel with Robert Fitz-Walter, to whom he refused the custody of the castle. But his mistrust of the English was made every day more evident. From Berkhampstead Louis marched to St. Alban's, where he threatened to burn the vast abbey to the ground if the abbot did not come forth and do him homage as legitimate King of England; but the abbot, it is said, escaped on paying a fine of eighty marks of silver. For a long period the carnage of war had been brought to a pause, by unanimous consent, on the seasons of our Saviour's birth and suffer-

---

[1] The tomb of Henry III. is on the north side of the shrine of the Confessor, and has been richly ornamented with inlaid work. On the top lies the effigy of the king. On the head is a crown of very simple and elegant form. His hands have supported the sceptre and orb, which have been removed. Over the left shoulder is thrown the royal mantle, fastened on the right by a fermail or clasp. Beneath is the tunic. The legs are boots, on which are represented, as embroidered in fret work, golden lions passant gardant; the same ornament decorates a square and a lozenge-shaped pillow which are placed under the head. The style in which this image is executed is of the finest cast; it is very probably Italian workmanship. The folds of the drapery are beautifully disposed, and the head has much of the simple majesty of the antique or Greek school. Sandford gives this inscription as remaining, in uncial characters, round the tomb of Henry III.:—

ICI: GIST: HENRI: LADIS: REY: DE: ENGLITERRE: SEYGNVR: DE IRLAVNDE: DVC DE AQVITAYNE: LE: FILZ: LE: ROY: IOHAN: IADIS: REY: DE: ENGLETERRE: A: KE: DEV: FACE: MERCY: AMEN.

[2] *Rymer; Carte; M. Paris.*

ing. Christmas was now at hand, and a truce was agreed upon which was to last till a fortnight

HERTFORD CASTLE.¹—From an old view in the British Museum.

after the Epiphany. At the expiration of this truce Pembroke willingly agreed to another, which did not expire till some days after the festival of Easter. Each party hoped to gain by this long armistice, and both were extremely active during its continuance. Louis, in Lent, went over to France to procure supplies of men and money; and Pembroke recruited in England, and drew off many of the nobles, during the absence of the French prince. Louis left the government in the hands of Enguerrand de Coucy, a nobleman of great quality, but of very little discretion, under whose misrule the French became more arrogant than ever, and the English barons were made to feel that, by securing the throne to a foreign prince, they should impose upon themselves foreign nobles for masters. At the same time the clergy, in obedience to the orders of Gualo the legate, read the sentence of excommunication in the churches every Sunday and holiday against the partizans of Louis. Hubert de Burgh, as constable of Dover Castle and warden of the Cinque ports, was in constant communication with the best mariners in England, and he kept them true to young Henry. Philip d'Albiney put himself at the head of a popular party in Sussex, where one William de Collingham collected a thousand gallant archers—rough English yeomen, who would allow of no truce with the French, and cared not for the armistice concluded by the Earl of Pembroke. On his way to the coast, Louis came into collision with these

sturdy patriots, who treated him very roughly, and would have made him a prisoner, but for the opportune arrival of the French fleet, in which he and his attendants embarked in great disorder. On his return from France with reinforcements, the mariners of the Cinque ports cut off several of his ships at sea, and took them by boarding. On this Louis landed at Sandwich, and burned that town to the ground in spite. He then, after making another unsuccessful attempt on Dover Castle, marched to London, where everything was falling into confusion.

On the expiration of the truce, the Earl of Pembroke recommenced hostilities by laying siege to the castle of Mountsorrel, in Leicestershire. Louis sent the Count of Perche with 600 knights and 20,000 armed men to relieve it. On their march, this mixed army of English, French, Flemings, and all kinds of mercenaries, committed great havoc, plundering the peaceful inhabitants, and wantonly burning the churches and monasteries. They succeeded, however, in their first object, Pembroke's forces raising the siege, and retiring before superior numbers. Flushed with this success, the Count of Perche marched away to Lincoln; the town received him, but the castle resisted; and when he laid siege to it, he was foiled by a woman—Nichola, the widow of Gerard de Camville, who held the custody of Lincoln Castle by hereditary right, and made a brave defence. While the confederates were wholly occupied with this siege, Pembroke suddenly collected a force of 400 knights, 250 cross-bowmen, many yeomen on horseback, and a considerable body of foot, and appeared before Lincoln in admirable order. The count for a time would not believe that the English would venture to attack him within a walled town; and though his superiority in cavalry would have given him an advantage in the open country, he rejected the advice of some English barons who were with him, and would not march out of the town. He continued to batter the castle until he found himself engaged in a fatal street contest. To animate Pembroke's force, Gualo now excommunicated Prince Louis by name, and pronounced the curse of the church against all his adherents, dispensing, at the same time, full absolution, and promises of eternal life, to the other party. The regent took advantage, in the most skilful manner, of the count's blunder: he threw all his crossbows into the castle by means of a postern.

---

¹ The remains of Hertford Castle consist of little more than an embattled wall and a mound, probably the base of the keep. An edifice of brick was built on the site of the castle, probably late in the time of James I., or in that of Charles I., or perhaps then re-edified, as some parts of it appear of earlier date.

A.D. 1216—1272.]   HENRY III.   385

These yeomen made great havoc on the besiegers by shooting from the castle walls; and seizing a favourable opportunity, they made a sortie, drove the enemy from the inside of the northern gate of the city, and enabled Pembroke to enter with all his host. The French cavalry could not act in the narrow streets and lanes: they were wounded and dismounted, and at last were obliged to surrender in a mass. The victory was complete: as usual, the foot-soldiers were slaughtered, but the "better sort" were allowed quarter: only one knight fell, and that was the commander, the Count of Perche, who threw away his life in mere pride and petulance, swearing that he would not surrender to any English traitor. This battle, facetiously called by the English "the Fair of Lincoln," was fought on Saturday, the 20th of May, 1217.

Its effect was to keep Louis cooped up within the walls of London, where plots and disturbances soon forced him to propose terms of accommodation. In the middle of June a conference was held at a place between Brentford and Hounslow, but it led to nothing.

Philip of France had been so scared by the threats of Rome, that he durst not send reinforcements in his own name; but he urged that he could not prevent Blanche of Castile, the wife of his son Louis, from aiding her own husband in his extremity; and under this cover another fleet and army was prepared for England. It was not till the 23d of August that this fleet could sail from Calais: it consisted of eighty great ships, and many smaller vessels, having on board 300 choice knights, and a large body of infantry. On the next day, the great festival of St. Bar-

SHIP OF THE TIME.¹—War Galley with iron prow or beak.—Camb. Matt. Paris.

tholomew, as they were attempting to make the estuary of the Thames, in order to sail up the

SEA FIGHT.²—Matt. Paris, Bennett Coll. C. V. XVI

river to London, they were met by the hero of Dover Castle, the gallant De Burgh. Hubert had only forty vessels great and small, but he gained the weather-gage, and by tilting at the French with the iron beaks of his galleys, sunk several of the transports with all on board. He after-

---

¹ Vessels of this kind seem to have been constructed in imitation of the war-galley of the Greeks and Romans, being fitted with a formidable beak of iron for the purpose of running into and splitting the vessels opposed to them. In this example the steersman bears a horn or speaking-trumpet. Besides the rowers the galley is manned by soldiers wielding crossbows, spears, axe, and sling. A banner is borne in front; the quarrels of the crossbowmen fly ahead.

² This illumination (Matt. Paris, Bennett Coll. C. V. XVI.) seems literally to illustrate a passage in De Burgh's defeat of the French ships off Dover, even to the decapitation of Eustace le Moine, or the monk, who had left his monastery in Flanders for the life of a sea-rover; and having given offence to the English, as well as being considered unworthy of knightly quarter, his head was struck off on the deck of the captured vessel. Here the vessels, for the purpose of a close hand-to-hand engagement, are grappled by a hook and chain. The combatants are armed with swords and pole-axes, and the broad Danish axe. In the assailing vessel a warrior plies a sling, and another, in a studded jerkin, discharges from a crossbow bottles of quicklime to blind the opponents. The different kinds of head-gear are worthy of notice.

VOL. I.   49—50

wards grappled with the enemy, fastening his ships to theirs by means of hooks and chains, and in the end he took or destroyed the whole fleet, with the exception of fifteen vessels. This decisive naval victory gave the death-blow to the project of Louis. That prince, however, acted generously and nobly in the midst of his difficulties: he would not abandon his friends, but said, when pressed, that he was ready to agree to any terms not inconsistent with his honour, or the safety of his English adherents. The prudent regent was glad enough to promise good terms to these barons, who, whatever might be their after errors, had been among the foremost champions of English liberty, and had assisted in obtaining the Great Charter, which he himself loved as much as any of them. There were also many other nobles, on the same side, equally averse to proceeding to extremities against countrymen, former friends, and relations. The final terms were easily settled in a conference held on the 11th of September, on an islet of the Thames near Kingston. It was agreed that the English barons who had continued to adhere to Louis, besides having their estates restored to them, should enjoy the customs and liberties of the kingdom, and all improvements thereof, equally with others. The privileges of London, as of all other cities and boroughs, were to be confirmed, and the prisoners on both sides taken since Louis' first landing, were to be released without ransom, unless where previous arrangements had been made between parties. Louis was to give up all the castles he possessed, and to write to Alexander, King of Scotland, and Llewellyn, Prince of Wales, to induce them to restore all the fortresses and places they had taken, if they would be included in the treaty. He also acquitted the English nobles of their oaths and obligations to him, and promised never to enter again into any confederacy with them to Henry's prejudice; and the barons made a like engagement on their own behalf. The French prince and his adherents swore to observe these articles, and to stand to the judgment of the church, upon which they were all absolved by the legate.[1] Louis was so poor, that he was obliged to borrow money from the citizens of London to defray the expenses of his journey home. On the 14th of September, a safe conduct was granted to him: he was honourably escorted to the sea-side by the Earl of Pembroke, and he sailed for France with his foreign associates. On the 2d of October, a few refractory barons, the only remnant of a great party, went to court, and were exceedingly well received there. On the fourth day of the same month, a new charter for the city of London was promulgated; and a few days later, the regent, for the general good of the nation, concluded with Haquin or Haco, King of Norway, a treaty of free commerce between the two countries. At the same time, this excellent regent's prudence and equity did more than a written treaty in reconciling conflicting parties at home. He was accessible and courteous to all, taking especial care that no man should be oppressed for his past politics. His authority, however, did not extend to the church, and Gualo severely chastised many of the English abbots and monks who had ventured to disregard his excommunications.

In all these transactions no mention had been made of Eleanor, the Maid of Brittany, who still occupied her dungeon or her cell at Bristol, nor was her name ever breathed during the civil wars which followed—a proof how little female right was then regarded; for, by the rules of succession as now recognized, she was the undoubted heiress to the throne. Henry began his reign in leading-strings, and owing to his weak and defective character, he never freed himself from such absolute guidance, but passed his whole life in a state of tutelage and dependence —being now governed by one powerful noble, or by one foreign favourite, and now by another. Isabella, the selfish queen-mother, abandoned her child in the midst of his troubles, and hurried back to Guienne in search of a new husband. It conveys a strange notion of the delicacy of those times, to find that the Count of la Marche, from whom John had stolen her, consented to take her back, and remarried her with great pomp. Every day the peace of the country was made more secure—"the evil will borne to King John seeming to die with him, and to be buried in the same grave."[2] But the determination to preserve the liberties which had been wrung from him was alive and active, and a second confirmation of Magna Charta was granted by the young king. Besides that the benefits of the charter were now extended to Ireland, several alterations were made in the deed, and a clause was added, ordering the demolition of every castle built or rebuilt since the beginning of the war between John and the barons. Other clauses were withdrawn, to form a separate charter, called the Charter of Forests. By this instrument, which materially contributed to the comfort and prosperity of the nation, all the forests which had been inclosed since the reign of Henry II., were thrown open; offences in the forests were declared to be no longer capital; and men convicted of the once heinous crime of killing the king's venison, were made punishable only by fine or imprisonment.

---

[1] Rymer.   [2] Speed Chron.

Meanwhile the spirit of insubordination which had arisen out of the civil war was gradually coerced or soothed by the valour and wisdom of the Earl of Pembroke, who was singularly averse to the cruelties and blood-shedding which had formerly disgraced all similar pacifications. But the excellent protector did not long enjoy the happy fruit of his labours: he died in the year 1219, about the middle of May, and was buried in the church of the Knights Templars at London, where his tomb or statue is still to be seen, with an inscription which scarcely exaggerates his virtues as a warrior and statesman. His authority in the state was now shared between Hubert de Burgh, the justiciary, the gallant defender of Dover Castle, and Peter des Roches (a Poictevin by birth), Bishop of Winchester. These ministers were jealous of each other: De Burgh was the more popular with the nation; but Des Roches, who had the custody of the royal person, possessed the greater influence at court, and among the many foreigners who, like himself, had obtained settlements and honours in the land. Dissensions soon broke out; but dangerous consequences were prevented by the skill of Pandulph, who had resumed the legateship on the departure of Gualo. On the 17th of May, 1220, young Henry was crowned again by Langton, Archbishop of Canterbury, whom the pope had permitted to return to the kingdom. In the following year, Joanna, the eldest sister of Henry, was married at York, to Alexander, the King of Scotland; and nearly at the same time, one of the Scottish princesses who had been delivered to John, and who had ever since remained in England, was married to Hubert de Burgh, the justiciary. Pandulph then returned to Rome, having previously demanded, in the name of the pope, that no individual should hold more than two of the royal castles. On his departure, however, little respect was paid to the orders from Rome. Many of the barons chiefly foreigners imported by John—refused to deliver up the fortresses which they pretended to hold in trust till the young king should be of age. While De Burgh insisted on their surrender, his rival Des Roches favoured the recusant chiefs. Plots and conspiracies followed; but in 1223, the justiciary, with the assent of the pope and the great council of the nation, declared Henry of age; and in the course of the following year he succeeded in getting possession of most of the disputed castles, taking some of them by siege and assault. Des Roches then gave up the struggle, under pretence of making a pilgrimage to Jerusalem, and many of the foreign adventurers followed him out of England. Though not a cruel man, Hubert de Burgh was far more severe than the Earl of Pembroke; for at the taking of Bedford Castle he hanged eighty of the foreign garrison, knights and others, who had been in the habit of committing frightful excesses in the country.

WILLIAM MARESCHAL [the elder], EARL OF PEMBROKE.[1]—From his effigy in the Temple Ch., London

A.D. 1225. In the following year (1225), one of the main springs of the English constitution, which checks the abuse of power, by the mode of allotting money, began its salutary movements. Louis, the French prince, who had now succeeded his father Philip on the French throne, unmindful of his promises, overran some parts of Guienne and Poictou, and took the important maritime town of Rochelle. The young king summoned a *parliament* (for that name was now coming into use) to meet at Westminster; and there Hubert de Burgh, having opened the proceedings by an explanatory speech, asked for money to enable the king to recover his own. At first the assembly refused to make any grant, but it was finally agreed that a fifteenth of all moveable property should be given, on the express condition, however, that the king should ratify the two charters. Henry, accordingly, gave a third ratification of Magna Charta, together with a ratification of the Charter of Forests, and sent fresh orders to some of his officers, who had hitherto treated them with little respect, to enforce all their provisions.[2] In the month of April, Richard, Earl of Cornwall, the king's brother, was sent to Guienne, under the guidance of the Earl of Salisbury, with an English army. But the French king had taken the cross against the Albigenses, an unfortunate people in the south of France, who were called heretics, and treated more cruelly than Saracens. A Papal legate interfered, threatened the English with excommunication if they raised obstacles to Louis in his holy war, and, at last, made both parties agree to a truce for one year.

---

[1] " He died in 1219 at his manor of Caversham, near Reading, in Berkshire. . . . Matthew Paris assigns to him the following epitaph, which styles him a Saturn, as a severe castigator of the Irish; an Apollo, as the glory and honour of England; a Mercury, as a diplomatist in Normandy; and a Mars, as a warlike and invincible knight against the French:—

Sum quem Saturnum sibi sensit Hybernia, Solem
Anglia, Mercurium Normannia, Gallia Martem.

The costume of this figure very well accords with the period of William Mareschal the elder's decease. He wears a hauberk of chain mail, long surcoat, and on his shield is a lion rampant.'
—Stothard's *Monumental Effigies of Great Britain.*

[2] *Matt. Par.; Brady.*

Before the term expired, the French king died at Paris, after a brief reign of three years, and was succeeded by his son Louis IX., who was only in his twelfth year. A stormy minority ensued; and Henry, who was now twenty years of age, might have taken advantage of it, had his character and his own circumstances been somewhat different from what they were. But the English king had little more real manhood than the child on the French throne; his barons were by no means anxious for the foreign war, and the armistice was subsequently renewed year after year, the English never recovering Rochelle, and the French making no further progress of importance. In the meantime, though he ruled with a firm hand, Hubert de Burgh was not always able to cause the government to be respected, and to maintain the tranquillity of the country.

A.D. 1229. It was at length, however, resolved to carry war into France. Henry was twenty-two years old, Louis only fifteen; but Blanche, the mother of the latter prince, and regent of the kingdom, had composed all dissensions, and put the kingdom into a posture of defence. When Henry went to Portsmouth, he found that the shipping provided was not sufficient to carry over his army, and after a violent altercation with Hubert de Burgh, who was accused of being the cause of this deficiency, the expedition was given up till the following year. At length the English king, elated by the promises and invitations of the barons of Guienne, Poictou, and even many nobles of Normandy, set sail for the Continent, and landed at St. Malo, in Brittany, where he was joined by a host of Bretons. He advanced to Nantes, where, like his father before him, he wasted his time and his means in feasts and pageantries, leaving the malcontents in Normandy and Poictou to curse their folly in committing their fortunes in the cause of so unwarlike a prince. In the meantime young Louis, accompanied by his mother, who shared all the hardships of a campaign, took several towns belonging to Henry. In the beginning of October the English king returned home, covered with disgrace; and his ally, the Duke of Brittany, was obliged to appear at the foot of the throne of Louis with a rope round his neck.[1] De Burgh had accompanied his master on this expedition; and, in spite of his known honour, bravery, and ability, the king, and some favourites with whom he had surrounded himself, attempted to throw all the blame of the miserable failure upon Hubert. The people, however, took a different view of the case, and set Henry down as a trifler and a coward. When he applied to parliament for a further grant of money, and complained of the poverty to which his French expedition had reduced him, they refused the aid, and told him that, through his thoughtlessness and extravagance, his barons were as poor as himself.

A.D. 1232. Hubert had now been eight years at the head of affairs. He enjoyed the good opinion of the people, whom he had never wantonly oppressed; but many of the nobles envied him his power, and hated him for his zeal in resuming the castles and other possessions of the crown. But for his tried fidelity, and his courage in the worst of times, that crown in all probability would never have been worn by the helpless Henry. But the proverbial ingratitude of princes was fostered in the present case by other circumstances, the most cogent of all being, that the minister was rich and the king wofully in want of money. On a sudden, Hubert saw his old rival Peter des Roches, the Poictevin Bishop of Winchester, reappear at court, and he must have felt from that moment that his ruin was concerted. In fact, very soon after, Henry threw off his faithful guardian and able minister, and left him to the persecutions of his enemies. The frivolous charges brought against Hubert almost lead to a conviction that he was guilty of no breach of trust or abuse of authority—of no real public crime whatever. Among other things, he was accused of winning the affections of the king by means of magic and enchantment.[2] The fallen minister took refuge in Merton Abbey. His flight gave unwonted courage to the king, who vapoured and stormed, and then commanded the mayor of London to force the asylum, and seize Hubert dead or alive. The mayor, who seems a strange officer to employ on such an occasion, set forth with a multitude of armed men; but the king being reminded by the Archbishop of Dublin of the illegality and sacrilegiousness of such a procedure, despatched messengers in a great hurry and re-called the mayor. In the end, the Archbishop of Dublin, the only one among the great men who did not forsake Hubert, obtained for him a delay of four months, that he might prepare for his defence, and for the interval, the king gave him a safe conduct. Relying on these letters-patent, De Burgh departed to visit his wife, the Scottish princess, at St. Edmundsbury; but he had scarcely begun his journey when the king, notwithstanding his plighted faith, listened to his enemies, and sent a knight —one Sir Godfrey de Crancumb—with 300 armed men, to surprise and seize him. Hubert was in bed at the little town of Brentwood, in Essex,

---

[1] Daru, Hist. de Bret.   [2] Matt. Par.

when this troop fell upon him. He contrived to escape, naked as he was, to a parish church, where, with a crucifix in one hand, and the host in the other, he stood firmly near the altar, hoping that his attitude and the sanctity of the place would procure him respect. His furious enemies, however, were not deterred by any considerations, and, bursting into the church with drawn swords, they dragged him forth, and sent for a smith to make shackles for him. The poor artizan, struck with the sad state of the great man, and moved with generous feelings, said he would rather die the worst of deaths than forge fetters for the brave defender of Dover Castle and the conqueror of the French at sea. But Sir Godfrey and his "black band" were not to be moved by any appeal: they placed the earl on horseback, naked as he was, and, tying his feet under the girths, so conveyed him to the Tower of London. As soon as this violation of sanctuary was known, an outcry was raised by the bishops; and the king was in consequence obliged to order those who had seized him to carry the prisoner back to the parish church; but at the same time he commanded the sheriff of Essex, on pain of death, to prevent the earl's escape, and to compel him to an unconditional surrender. The sheriff dug a deep trench round the sanctuary—erected palisades—and effectually prevented all ingress or egress. Thus cut off from every communication—unprovided with fuel and proper clothing (the winter was setting in)—and at last left without provisions, Hubert de Burgh came forth, on the fortieth day of his beleaguerment, and surrendered to the "black band," who again carried him to the Tower of London. A few days after, Henry ordered him to be enlarged, and to appear before the court of his peers; but it is said that this decent measure was not adopted until Hubert surrendered all his ready money, which he had placed for safety in the hands of the Knights Templars. When Hubert appeared in court in the midst of his enemies, he declined pleading: some were urgent for a sentence of death, but the king proposed an award which was finally adopted by all parties. Hubert forfeited to the crown all such lands as had been granted him in the time of King John, or been obtained by him, by purchase or otherwise, under Henry. He retained for himself and his heirs the property he had inherited from his family, together with some estates he held in fief of mesne lords. Thus clipped and shorn, the brave Hubert was committed to the castle of Devizes, there to abide, in "free prison," under the custody of four knights appointed by four great earls. Within these walls, which had been built by the famous Roger, Bishop of Sarum, whose adventures in some respects resembled his own, Hubert remained for nearly a year, when he was induced to adopt a desperate mode of escape, by learning that the custody of the castle had just been given to a dependent of his bitter enemy the Poictevin Bishop of Winchester. In a dark night he climbed over the battlements, and dropped from the high wall into the moat, which was probably in part filled with water. From the moat he made his way to a country church; but there he was presently surrounded by an armed band, led on by the sheriff. Circumstances, however, were materially altered: several of the barons who had before been intent on the destruction of the minister were now at open war with the king, and anxious to secure the co-operation of so able a man as De Burgh. A strong body of horse came down, released him from the hands of his captors, and carried him off into Wales, where the insurgent nobles were then assembled. Some eighteen months later, when peace was restored, Hubert received back his estates and honours: he was even re-admitted into the king's council; but he had the wisdom never again to aspire to the dangerous post of chief minister. At a subsequent period the king again fell upon him, but, it appears, merely to enrich himself at his expense, for the quarrel was made up on Hubert's presenting Henry with four castles.[1]

The Poictevin bishop, who succeeded to power on the first displacement and captivity of Hubert, soon rendered himself extremely odious to all classes of the nation. He encouraged the king's growing antipathy to the English barons, and to Magna Charta; he taught him to rely on the friendship and fidelity of foreign adventurers rather than on the inconstant affection of his own subjects; and he crowded the court, the offices of government, the royal fortresses, with hosts of hungry Poictevins, Gascons, and other Frenchmen, who ruled and wasted at their pleasure. The business of politics was as yet in its infancy: the nature of an opposition, constitutional and legal in all its operations, was as yet a discovery to be made; nor could men in their times and circumstances be expected to understand such things. The barons withdrew from parliament, where they were surrounded by armed foreigners, and took up arms themselves. When again summoned, they answered, that unless the king dismissed his Poictevins and other foreigners, they would drive both them and him out of the kingdom. Peter des Roches averted his ruin for the present by sowing dissensions among the English nobles. Several battles or skirmishes, which defy anything like a clear narration, were fought in the heart of England and on the Welsh borders. Richard,

---

[1] *Matt. Par.; M. West.; Wykes; Chron. Dunst.; Holinshed.*

Earl of Pembroke, the son of the virtuous protector, to whom King Henry was so deeply indebted, was treacherously and most barbarously murdered; and, following up his temporary success, the Poictevin bishop confiscated the estates of several of the English nobles without any legal trial, and bestowed them on adventurers from his own land. Edmund, the new Archbishop of Canterbury, who had succeeded Langton, took up the national cause, and threatened the king with excommunication if he did not instantly dismiss Des Roches and his associates. Henry trembled and complied: the foreigners were banished, and the archbishop for a short time governed the land with great prudence, and according to the charters. But Henry's dislike both of his native nobles and of the charters increased with his years, and his foreign favourites resumed their ascendancy.

A.D. 1236. Henry now married Eleanor, daughter of the Count of Provence, who came to England with a numerous retinue, and was soon followed by fresh swarms of foreigners. The Bishop of Valence, the queen's maternal uncle, was made chief minister. Boniface, another uncle, was promoted to the see of Canterbury; and Peter, a third uncle, was invested with the earldom of Richmond, and received the profitable wardship of the Earl Warenne. The queen invited over damsels from Provence, and the king married them to the young nobles of England of whom he had the wardship. This was bad enough, but it was not all: the queen-mother, Isabella, whom the nation detested, had now four sons by the Count of la Marche, and she sent them over all four—Guy, William, Geoffrey, and Aymer—to be provided for in England. The king heaped honours and riches upon these half-brothers, who were soon followed by new herds of adventurers from Guienne. Henry had resumed, with the pope's permission, nearly all the grants of estates he had made to his native subjects; but even the resources thus obtained were soon exhausted, and he found himself without money and without credit. When he asked aids from the parliament, the parliament told him that he must dismiss the foreigners who devoured the substance of the land, and they several times voted him small supplies, on the express condition that he should so do, and also redress other grievances; but he forgot his promises as soon as he got the money. The barons then bound him by oath; and Henry took the oaths, broke them, and acted just as before.[1]

A.D. 1242. Isabella, the queen-mother, added alike to the odium in which she was held by the English, and to the embarrassments and unpopularity of her son, by hurrying him into a war with France. Louis was now in the prime of manhood, and immeasurably superior in all eminent qualities to his rival. He was loved and respected by his subjects; whereas Henry was despised by his. When the English parliament was called upon for a supply of men and money, they resolutely refused both, telling the king that he ought to observe the truce which had been continually renewed with France, and never broken (so at least they asserted) by Louis. By means not recorded, Henry contrived to fill thirty hogsheads with silver, and, sailing from Portsmouth with his queen, his brother Richard, and 300 knights, he made for the river Garonne. Soon after his landing he was joined by nearly 20,000 men, some his own acknowledged vassals, some the followers of nobles who had once been the vassals of his predecessors, and who were now anxious, not to re-establish the supremacy of the English king in the South, but to render themselves independent of the crown of France by his means or at his expense.[2] Louis met Henry with a superior force on the banks of the river Charente, in Saintonge, and defeated him in a pitched battle near the castle of Taillebourg. The English king retreated down the river to the town of Saintes, where he was beaten in a second battle, which was fought on the very next day. His mother's husband, the Count of la Marche, who had led him into this disastrous campaign, then abandoned him, and made his own terms with the French king. Henry fled from Saintes right across Saintonge, to Blaye, leaving his military chest, the sacred vessels and the ornaments of his moveable chapel-royal, in the hands of the enemy. A terrible dysentery which broke out in his army, some scruples of conscience, and the singular moderation of his own views, prevented Louis from following up his successes, and induced him to agree to a truce for five years.

A.D. 1244. When Henry met his parliament this year, he found it more refractory than it had ever been. In reply to his demands for money, they taxed him with extravagance—with his frequent breaches of the Great Charter—they told him, in short, that they would no longer trust him, and that they must have in their own hands the appointment of the chief justiciary, the chancellor, and other great officers. The king would consent to nothing more than another ratification of Magna Charta, and therefore the parliament would only vote him twenty shillings on each knight's fee for the marriage of his eldest daughter to the Scottish king. After this he looked to a meeting of parliament as a meeting of his personal enemies, and to avoid it

---

[1] *Matt. Par.; Chron. Dunst.; Ann. Waverl.*   [2] *Meuray.*

he raised money by stretching his prerogative in respect to fines, benevolences, purveyances, and the other undefinable branches of the ancient revenue. He also tormented and ransacked the Jews, acting with regard to that unhappy people like a very robber; and he begged, besides, from town to town, from castle to castle, until he obtained the reputation of being the sturdiest beggar in all England. But all this would not suffice, and, in the year 1248, he was again obliged to meet his barons in parliament. They now told him that he ought to blush to ask aid from his people whom he professed to hate, and whom he shunned for the society of aliens; they reproached him with disparaging the nobles of England by forcing them into mean marriages with foreigners. They enlarged upon the abuse of the right of purveyance, telling him that the victuals and wine consumed by himself and his un-English household—that the very clothes on their backs were all taken by force and violence from the English people, who never received any compensation; that foreign merchants, knowing the dangers to which their goods were exposed, shunned the ports of England as if they were in possession of pirates; that the poor fishermen of the coast, finding they could not escape his hungry purveyors and courtiers, were frequently obliged to carry their fish to the other side of the Channel; and they added other accusations still more minute and humiliating.[1] In reply to the remonstrance of his barons, Henry gave nothing but fair promises which could no longer deceive, and he got nothing save the cutting reproof to which he had been obliged to listen.

The king now racked his imagination in devising pretexts on which to obtain what he wanted. At one time he said he was resolved to re-conquer all the continental dominions of the crown; but, unfortunately, all men knew that Louis had departed for the East, and that Henry, who had not shone in the field, had contracted the most solemn obligations not to make war upon him during his crusade. He next took the cross himself, pretending to be anxious to sail for Palestine forthwith; but here again it was well known he had no such intention, and only wanted money to pay his debts and satisfy his foreign favourites. At a moment of urgent necessity he was advised to sell all his plate and jewels. "Who will buy them?" said he. His advisers answered, "The citizens of London, of course." He rejoined bitterly, "By my troth, if the treasures of Augustus were put up to sale, the citizens would be the purchasers! These clowns, who assume the style of barons, abound in all things, while we are wanting in common necessaries."[2] It is said

that the king was thenceforth more inimical and rapacious towards the Londoners than he had been before. To annoy them and touch them in a sensitive part, he established a new fair at Westminster, to last fifteen days, during which all trading was prohibited in London. He went to keep his Christmas in the city, and let loose his purveyors among the inhabitants; he made them offer New-year's gifts; and shortly after, in spite of remonstrances, he compelled them to pay him the sum of £2000 by the most open violation of law and right.

In A.D. 1253, Henry was again obliged to meet his parliament, and this he did, averring to all men that he only wanted a proper Christian aid that he might go and recover the tomb of Christ. If he thought that this old pretence would gain unlimited confidence, he was deceived. The barons, who had been duped so often, treated his application with coldness and contempt; but they at last held out the hope of a liberal grant on condition of his consenting to a fresh and most solemn confirmation of their liberties. On the third day of May the king went to Westminster Hall, where the barons, prelates, and abbots were assembled. The bishops and abbots were apparelled in their canonical robes, and every one of them held a burning taper in his hand. A taper was offered to the king, but he refused it, saying he was no priest. Then the Archbishop of Canterbury stood up before the people and denounced sentence of excommunication against all those who should, either directly or indirectly, infringe the charters of the kingdom. Every striking, every terrific part of this ceremony was performed: the prelates and abbots dashed their tapers to the ground, and as the lights went out in smoke, they exclaimed—"May the soul of every one who incurs this sentence so stink and be extinguished in hell!" The king subjoined, on his own behalf—"So help me God! I will keep these charters inviolate, as I am a man, as I am a Christian, as I am a knight, and as I am a king crowned and anointed!" His outward behaviour during this awful performance was exemplary; he held his hand on his heart, and made his countenance express a devout acquiescence; but the ceremony was scarcely over when, following the impulse given him by his foreign favourites, he returned to his old courses, and thus utterly up-rooted whatever confidence the nation yet had in him.[3]

With the money he thus obtained he went to Guienne, where Alphonso, the King of Castile, had set up a claim to the earldom, and induced many of the fickle nobles to revolt against the English crown. This expedition was less dis-

---

[1] Matt. Par.; Matt. West.; Chron. Dunst.   [2] Matt. Par.   [3] Matt. Par.; Matt. West.; W. Hemingford.

honourable than the former ones; indeed it was successful on the whole, and led to a friendly alliance between England and Castile—Prince Edward marrying Eleanor, the daughter of Alphonso. But Henry concealed these arrangements for some time, in order to obtain a fresh grant from his parliament, under colour of carrying on the war. He returned penniless; for the partial re-establishment of his authority in the south of France seems never to have benefited his exchequer. The expedients to which he had recourse in England, rendered him more and more odious and contemptible. When his fortunes were at this low ebb, he blindly embarked in a project which immensely increased his embarrassments. This project was no other than to raise one of his sons to the throne of the Two Sicilies. On the death of Frederick II., who died excommunicated, Pope Innocent offered the crown to Henry for his second son, Prince Edmund; and the beggared and incapable king joyfully closed with the proposal, agreeing to march presently with a powerful army into the south of Italy, accepting an advance of money from the pope to enable him to commence the enterprise, and proposing also to raise what more it might be necessary to borrow on the pope's security. Had the energy and the means of the English king at all corresponded with the activity and cunning policy of the Roman priest, who only sought to make the Sicilies a fief of the Holy See, there is little doubt that the prince might have obtained a dependent and precarious throne; but Henry was placed in circumstances in which he could do little, and, wavering and timid, he did nothing at all, except giving his son the empty title of "King of Sicily." The pope ordered the English clergy to lend money for the expedition, and even to pawn the property of their church to obtain it.[1] The clergy of England were not very obedient; but whatever sums were raised were dissipated by the king or the Roman legate, and, in the end, the pope brought a claim of debt against Henry to the amount of more than £100,000, which, it was alleged, had been borrowed on the Continent, chiefly from the rich merchants of Venice and Florence. Henry, it appears, had never been consulted about the borrowing or spending of this money; but the pope was an imperative accountant—a creditor that could enforce payment by excommunication, interdict, and dethronement; and Henry was obliged to promise that he would pay, and to rack his weak wits in devising the means. Backed by the pope, he levied enormous contributions on the churches of England and Ireland. The native clergy were already disaffected, but these proceedings made them as openly hostile to the king as were the lay barons. The wholesale spoliation of the church had also the effect of lessening the clergy's reverence for the pope, and of shaking that power which had already attained its highest pitch, and which was thenceforward gradually to decline. When called upon to lay up some of the pope's bills, the Bishop of Worcester told Rustan, the legate, that he would rather die than comply; and the Bishop of London said that the pope and king were, indeed, more powerful than he, but if they took his mitre from his head, he would clap on a warrior's helmet. The legate moderated his demands and withdrew, fully convinced that a storm was approaching, and that the Sicilian speculation had completed the ruin of the bankrupt king.[2] As long as his brother Richard, the great Earl of Cornwall, remained in England, and in possession of the treasures he had hoarded, there was a powerful check upon insurrection; for though the earl's abilities in public affairs seem hardly to have been equal to his wealth, still the influence he possessed in the nation was most extensive. He had repeatedly opposed the illegal courses of the king, and had even been out in arms with the barons more than once; but he was averse to extreme measures, and, from his position, not likely to permit any invasion of the just prerogative of the crown. The Germans were setting up their empire for sale, and Richard's vanity and ambition induced him to become a purchaser. Having spent immense sums, he was elected, in the beginning of 1256, as "King of the Romans," which was considered the sure step to the dignity of emperor. But there was a schism among the electors, part of whom, a few weeks later, gave their suffrages to Alphonso, King of Castile. Richard, however, went over to the Continent, was crowned at Aix-la-Chapelle, and left the crown of England to be dragged through the mire.

A.D. 1258. A scarcity of provisions disposed the people to desperate measures. On the 2d of May, Henry called a parliament at Westminster. The barons, who had formed a new confederacy, went to the hall in complete armour. As the king entered, there was a rattling of swords: his eye glanced timidly along the mailed ranks; and he said, with a faltering voice, "What means this? Am I a prisoner?" "Not so," replied Roger Bigod; "but your foreign fa-

---

[1] "No country was so intolerably treated by this pope (Gregory IX.) and his successors as England throughout the ignominious reign of Henry III. Her church seemed to have been so richly endowed only as the free pasture of Italian priests, who were placed by the mandatory letters of Gregory IX. and Innocent IV. in all the best benefices. If we may trust a solemn remonstrance in the name of the whole nation, they drew from England in the middle of the thirteenth century, 60,000 or 70,000 marks, a sum far exceeding the royal revenue."—*Hallam.*

[2] *Matt. Par.*

vourites and your own extravagance have involved this realm in great wretchedness: wherefore we demand that the powers of government be intrusted and made over to a committee of bishops and barons, that the same may root up abuses and enact good laws." One of the king's foreign half-brothers vapoured and talked loudly, but as for himself, he could do nothing else than give an unconditional assent to the demands of the barons, who thereupon promised that, if he proved sincere, they would help him to pay his debts, and prosecute the claims of his son in Italy. The parliament then dissolved, appointing an early day to meet again at Oxford, where the committee of government should be appointed, and the affairs of the state finally adjusted.[1]

The present leader of the barons, and in all respects the most remarkable man among them, was the Earl of Leicester. It is evident that the monkish chroniclers were incapable of understanding or properly appreciating the extraordinary character of this foreign champion for English liberties; and those writers have scarcely left materials to enable us to form an accurate judgment. Simon de Montfort was the youngest son of the Count de Montfort in France, who had gained an unhappy celebrity in the barbarous crusades against the Albigenses. In right of his mother, Amicia, he had succeeded to the earldom of Leicester; but he appears to have been little known in England until the year 1238, when he came over from his native country, and married Eleanor, the Countess-dowager of Pembroke, a sister of King Henry. This match was carried by the royal favour and authority; for Richard, Earl of Cornwall, the king's brother, and many of the English barons, tried to prevent it, on the ground that it was not fitting a princess should be married to a *foreign* subject. But the earl had no sooner secured his marriage, and made himself known in the country, than he set himself forward as the decided opponent of foreign encroachment and foreign favourites of all kinds; and such was his ability, that he caused people to overlook the anomaly of his position, and to forget that he himself was a foreigner. He not only captivated the good-will of the English nobles, but endeared himself in an extraordinary degree to the English people, whose worth and importance in the state he certainly seems to have been one of the first to discover and count upon. His devotional feelings (which, upon no ground that we can discover, have been regarded as hypocritical) gained him the favour of the clergy: his literary acquirements, so unusual in those times, increased his influence and reputation. There seems to be no good reason for refusing him the merits of a skilful politician; and he was a master of the art of war as it was then understood and practised.

The favour of the king was soon turned into a hatred as bitter as Henry's supine and not cruel nature was capable of: it seemed monstrous that a foreigner should be, not a courtier, but the popular idol, and Leicester was banished the court. He was afterwards intrusted with the government of Guienne, where, if he did not achieve the impossibility of giving entire satisfaction to the turbulent and intriguing nobles, he did good service to the king, his master, and acquitted himself with ability and honour. Henry, however, was weak enough to listen to the complaints of some of his Southern vassals, who did not relish the firm rule of the earl. Leicester was hastily re-called, and his master called him traitor to his face. Thus insulted by a man he despised, the earl gave the lie to his sovereign, and told him that, but for his kingly rank, he would make him repent the wrong he had done him.[2] This happened in 1252. Leicester withdrew for a season into France, but Henry was soon reconciled, in appearance, and the earl returned to England, where his popularity increased in proportion to the growing weakness and misgovernment of the king. He was one of the armed barons that met in Westminster Hall, and now he was ready to follow up those demonstrations at Oxford.

On the 11th of June the parliament, which the royalists called the "Mad Parliament," met at Oxford. Having no reliance on the king, who had so often broken both promise and oath, the great barons summoned all who owed them military service to attend in arms on the occasion. Thus secured from the attack of the foreigners in the king's pay, they proceeded to their object with great vigour and determination. The committee of government was appointed without a

SIMON DE MONTFORT, EARL OF LEICESTER.
From a window in Chartres Cathedral.

---

[1] *Matthew of Paris; Chron. T. Wykes.; Rymer.*   [2] *Matthew of Paris.*

murmur on the part of the timid Henry: it consisted of twenty-four members, twelve of whom were chosen by the barons and twelve by the king. The king's choice fell upon his nephew Henry, the son of Richard, the titular King of the Romans; upon Guy and William, his own half-brothers; the Bishops of London and Winchester; the Earls of Warwick and Warenne; the abbots of Westminster and St. Martin's, London; on John Mansel, a friar; and Peter of Savoy, a relation of the queen's. The members appointed by the barons were the Bishop of Worcester; the Earls Simon of Leicester, Richard of Gloucester, Humphrey of Hereford, Roger of Norfolk, earl-marshal; the Lords Roger Mortimer, John Fitz-Geoffrey, Hugh Bigod, Richard de Grey, William Bardolf, Peter de Montfort, and Hugh Despencer. The Earl of Leicester was at the head of this supreme council, to the maintenance of whose ordinances the king, and afterwards his son Edward, took a solemn oath. The parliament then proceeded to enact that four knights should be chosen by the votes of the freeholders in each county, to lay before the parliament all breaches of law and justice that might occur; that a new sheriff should be annually chosen by the freeholders in each county; and that three sessions of parliament should be held regularly every year; the first, eight days after Michaelmas; the second, the morrow after Candlemas Day; and the third, on the first day of June.

The benefits derived from the acts of this parliament were prospective rather than immediate, for the first consequences were seven or eight years of anarchy and confusion, the fruits of insincerity and discontent on the part of the court, and of ambition and intrigue on the part of the great barons. Prince Edward, the heir to the throne, the Earl of Warenne, and others, took the oaths to the statutes or provisions of Oxford with unconcealed reluctance and ill-humour. Though their leaders were liberally included among the twenty-four guardians of the kingdom, the foreign faction was excessively dissatisfied with the recent changes, and said openly, and wherever they went, that the acts of Oxford ought to be set aside as illegal and degrading to the king's majesty. Irritated by their opposition and their secret intrigues, Leicester and his party scared the four half-brothers of the king and a herd of their relations and retainers out of the kingdom. The departure of these foreigners increased the popularity of the barons with the English people; but they were seduced by the temptations of ambition and an easy triumph over all opposition; they filled up the posts vacated in the committee of government with their own adherents, leaving scarcely a member in it to represent the king; and they finally lodged the whole authority of government in the hands of their council of state, and a standing committee of twelve persons. This great power was abused, as all unlimited power, whether held by a king, or an oligarchy, or a democracy, ever will be, and the barons soon disagreed among themselves.[1]

A.D. 1259. About six months after the meeting at Oxford, Richard, King of the Romans, having spent all his money among the Germans, was anxious to return to England that he might get more. At St. Omer he was met by a messenger from Leicester, who told him that he must not set foot in the kingdom unless he swore beforehand to observe the provisions of Oxford. Richard finally gave an ungracious assent: he took the oath, joined his brother, and immediately commenced organizing an opposition to the committee of government.[2] Soon after his arrival it was seen that the barons disagreed more than ever. The Earl of Gloucester started up as a rival to Leicester, and a violent quarrel—the first of many—broke out between these two powerful lords. Then there was presented a petition from the knights of shires or counties, complaining that the barons had held possession of the sovereign authority for eighteen months, and had done no good in the way of reform. A few improvements, chiefly regarding the administration of justice, were then enacted; but their slender amount did not satisfy the nation, and most of the barons were more anxious for the prolongation of their own powers and profits than for anything else. By degrees two factions were formed in the committee: when that of Gloucester obtained the ascendancy, Leicester withdrew into France. Then Gloucester would have reconciled himself with the king, but as soon as Prince Edward saw this, he declared for Leicester, who returned. The manœuvres and intrigues of party now become almost as unintelligible as they are uninteresting—reconciliations and breaches between the Leicester and Gloucester factions, and then between the barons generally and the court—a changing and a changing again of sides and principles, perplex and disgrace a scene where nothing seems fixed except Leicester's dislike and distrust of the king, and a general but somewhat vague affection among the barons of both parties for the provisions of Magna Charta.

A.D. 1261. Henry, who had long rejoiced at the division among the barons, now thought the moment was come for escaping from their authority. He had a Papal dispensation in his pocket for the oaths he had taken at Oxford, and this set his conscience quite at ease.

---

[1] Rymer; Annal. Burt.; Matt. West.   [2] Rymer.

On the 2d of February he ventured to tell the committee of government that, seeing the abuse they had made of their authority, he should henceforward govern without them. He then hastened to the Tower, which had recently been repaired and strengthened, and seized all the money in the mint. From behind those strong walls he ordered that the gates of London should be closed, and that all the citizens should swear fresh fealty to him. The barons called out their vassals and marched upon the capital. Prince Edward was amusing himself in France at a tournament, and it was agreed by both parties to await his arrival. He came in haste, and, instead of joining his father in the Tower, joined the barons. In spite of this junction—or perhaps we ought rather to say, in consequence of it—many of the nobles went over and joined the king, who published the pope's bull of dispensation, together with a manifesto in which he set forth that he had reigned forty-five years in peace and according to justice, never committing such deeds of wrong and violence as the barons had recently committed. For a time he met with success, and Leicester returned once more to France, vowing that he would never trust the faith of a perjured king.[1]

A.D. 1263. Another change and shifting of parts now took place in this troubled drama: the Earl of Gloucester was dead, and his son, a very young man, instead of being the rival, became for a while the bosom friend of Leicester. Prince Edward, on the other hand, veered round to the court, and had made himself unpopular by calling in a foreign guard. In the month of March young Gloucester called his retainers and confederates together at Oxford, and the Earl of Leicester returned to England in the month of April, and put himself at their head. The great earl at once raised the banner of war; and after taking several royal castles and towns, marched rapidly upon London, where the mayor and the common people declared for him. The king was safe in the Tower; Prince Edward fled to Windsor Castle; and the queen, his mother, attempted to escape by water in the same direction; but, when she approached London bridge, a cry ran among the populace, who hated her, of "Drown the witch!" and filth and stones were thrown at the barge. The mayor took pity on her, and carried her for safety to St. Paul's.[2]

The King of the Romans contrived to effect a hollow reconciliation between the barons and his unwarlike brother, who yielded everything, only reserving to himself the usual resource of breaking his compact as soon as circumstances should seem favourable. It is true his subjects had repeatedly exacted too much, but it is equally certain that he never made the smallest concession to them in good faith, and with a determination to respect it. Foreigners were once more banished the kingdom, and the custody of the royal castles was again intrusted to Leicester and his associates. This was done, and peace and amity were sworn in July; but by the month of October the king was in arms against the barons, and nearly succeeded in taking Leicester prisoner. This new crisis was mainly attributable to a condition exacted by that great earl, that the authority of the committee of government should not only last for the lifetime of the king, but be prolonged during the reign of his successor. Up to this point Prince Edward had pretended a great respect for his oath, professing to doubt whether an absolution from Rome could excuse perjury, and he had frequently protested that, having sworn to the provisions of Oxford, he would religiously keep that vow; but this last measure removed all his scruples, and denouncing the barons as rebels, traitors, and usurpers, he openly declared against them and all their statutes.

A.D. 1264. To stop the horrors of a civil war, some of the bishops induced both parties to refer their differences to the arbitration of the French king. The conscientious and justice-loving Louis IX. pronounced his award in the beginning of February. He insisted on the observance of the Great Charter; but otherwise his decision was in favour of the king, as he set aside the provisions of Oxford, ordered that the royal castles should be restored, and that the sovereign should have full power of choosing his own ministers and officers, whether from among foreigners or natives. The barons, who were better acquainted than Louis with the character of their king, well knew that if the securities they had exacted (with too grasping a hand, perhaps) were all given up, the provisions of the national charters would be despised, as they were previously to the parliament of Oxford; and they therefore resolved not to be bound by the award, which, they insisted, had been obtained through the unfair influence of the wife of Louis, who was sister-in-law to King Henry. The civil war was therefore renewed with more fury than ever. The strength of the royalists lay in the counties of the north and the extreme west; that of the barons in the midland counties, the south-east, the Cinque ports, and, above all, in the city of London and its neighbourhood. At the tolling of the great bell of St. Paul's the citizens of London assembled as an armed host, animated by one daring spirit. In the midst of this excitement they fell upon the unfortunate Jews, and, after plundering them, massacred

---
[1] *Matt. West.; Wykes.; Carte.*
[2] *Wykes.; West.; Trivet.; Chron. Dunst.*

above 500—men, women, and children—in cold blood. In other parts of the kingdom the royalists robbed and murdered the Jews under pretext of their being friends to the barons; and the barons' party did the like, alleging that they were allied with the king, and that they kept Greek fire hid in their houses in order to destroy the friends of liberty.[1]

The opening of the campaign was in favour of the royalists; but their fortunes changed when they advanced to the southern coast and endeavoured to win over the powerful Cinque ports. Leicester, who had remained quietly in London organizing his forces, at length marched from the capital with the resolution of fighting a decisive battle. He found the king at Lewes, in Sussex —a bad position, in a hollow—which Henry, relying on his superiority of numbers, did not quit on the earl's approach. Leicester encamped on the downs about two miles from Lewes. On the following morning, the 14th of May, leaving a strong reserve on the downs, he descended into the hollow. The two armies soon joined battle. On the king's side were the great houses of Bigod and Bohun, all the foreigners in the kingdom, the Percys with their warlike borderers, and from beyond the Borders, John Comyn, John Baliol, and Robert Bruce—names that were soon to appear in a very different drama. On the earl's side were Gloucester, Derby, Warenne, the Despensers, Robert de Roos, William Marmion, Richard Grey, John Fitz-John, Nicholas Seagrave, Godfrey de Lucy, John de Vesey, and others of noble lineage and great estates. Prince Edward, who was destined to acquire the rudiments of war in the slaughter of his own subjects, began the battle by falling desperately upon a body of Londoners, who had gladly followed Leicester to the field. This burgher militia could not stand against the trained cavalry of the prince, who chased and slew them by heaps. Eager to take a bloody vengeance for the insults the Londoners had offered his mother, Edward spurred forward, regardless of the manœuvres of the other divisions of the royalist army. He was as yet a young soldier, and the experienced and skilful leader of the barons made him pay dearly for his mistake. Leicester made a concentrated attack on the king, beat him most completely, and took him prisoner, with his brother the King of the Romans, John Comyn, and Robert Bruce, before the prince returned from his headlong pursuit. When Edward arrived at the field of battle, he saw it covered with the slain of his own party, and learned that his father, with many nobles besides those just mentioned, were in Leicester's hands, and shut up in the priory of Lewes. Before he could recover himself he was

LEWES PRIORY, as it appeared in 1773.[2]—Grose's Antiquities.

charged by a body of horse, and made prisoner. The Earl Warenne, with the king's half-brothers, who were again in England, fled to Pevensey, whence they escaped to the Continent.[3] The victory of the barons does not seem to have been disgraced by cruelty, but it is said to have cost

---

[1] *Wykes.; West.; Dunst.*

[2] "The great Cluniac priory at Southover, commenced in 1072 and completed in 1078, owes its origin to the piety or superstition of William, the first Earl de Warren, and his lady Gundreda, fifth daughter of William the Conqueror. . . . Its walls embraced an area of 32 acres, 2 roods, and 11 perches; and from the only description of it that remains—in the letter of Portuarus (published in Brown Willis' *History of Mitred Abbeys*, vol. ii. p. 26), addressed to his employer in the work of its destruction—it is evident that the building was not less remarkable for its magnificence than for its extent. The length of the church was 150 ft., having an altitude of 63 ft.; its circumference 1558 ft. It was supported by thirty-two pillars, standing equally from the walls, eight of which were very lofty, being not less than 42 ft. high, 13 ft. thick, and 45 ft. in circumference; the remaining twenty-four were 10 ft. thick, 25 ft. in circumference, and 28 ft. in height. The belfry was placed over the centre of the church at an elevation of 105 ft., and was supported by eight lofty pillars above mentioned. The roof over the high altar was 93 ft. high. The steeple stood at the front of the church, and was 90 ft. high; its walls were 10 ft. thick. On the right of the high altar was a vault, supported by four pillars, and from this recess there branched out five chapels, which were bounded by a wall 70 yards in length. A higher vault, supported by four massy pillars, 14 ft. in diameter and 45 ft. in circumference, was probably on the left side of the high altar, and correspondent with the one just mentioned, from which branched out other chapels or cells of the monks. The chapter house and the church were by far the most splendid portions of this stately pile. In the former were interred the remains of the founder of the monastery and of his countess, several of his successors in the barony, and some distinguished nobles, more or less connected with the establishment. The latter was richly adorned by the painter and the sculptor; and was distinguished by the magnificence of the funeral monuments by which it appears to have been crowded."—*Sussex Gurland, by James Taylor.*

[3] *Matt. Par.; Wykes; West.; Chron. Dunst.*

the lives of more than 5000 Englishmen, who fell on the field. On the following morning a treaty, or the "*Mise* of Lewes," as it was called, was concluded. It was agreed that Edward and his cousin Henry, the son of the King of the Romans, should remain as hostages for their fathers, and that the whole quarrel should be again submitted to a peaceful arbitration. But Leicester, who had now the right of the strongest, kept both the king and his brother prisoners as well as their sons, and, feeling his own greatness, began to be less tractable. Although the pope excommunicated him and his party, the people regarded the sentence with indifference; and many of the native clergy, who had long been disgusted both with pope and king, praised him in their sermons as the reformer of abuses—the protector of the oppressed—the father of the poor —the saviour of his country—the avenger of the church. Thus supported, and indeed carried forward by a boundless popularity, he soon forced all such barons as held out for the king to surrender their castles, and submit to the judgment of their peers. These men were condemned merely to short periods of exile in Ireland; not one suffered death, or chains, or forfeiture. Every act of government was still performed in the name of the king, whose captivity was made so light as to be scarcely apparent, and who was treated with every outward demonstration of respect. The queen had retired to the Continent before the battle of Lewes, and having busied herself in collecting a host of foreign mercenaries, she now lay at Damme, in Flanders, almost ready to cross over and renew the civil war. The steps taken by Leicester show at once his entire confidence in the good-will of the nation and his personal bravery and activity. He summoned the whole force of the country—from castles and towns, cities and boroughs—to meet in arms on Barham Downs, and having encamped them there, he threw himself among the mariners of England, and, taking the command of a fleet. cruised between the English and Flemish coasts to meet the invaders at sea. But the queen's fleet never ventured out of port, her land forces disbanded, and that enterprise fell to the ground.

The ruin of Leicester was effected by very different means. Confident in his talents and popularity, he ventured to display too marked a superiority above his fellows in the same cause; this excited hostile feelings in several of the barons, whose jealousies and pretensions were skilfully worked upon by Prince Edward, who had by this time been removed from Dover Castle, into which he had been thrown after the battle of Lewes, and placed, with his father, in the enjoyment of considerable personal liberty by the order of a parliament which Leicester had summoned expressly to consider his case, in the beginning of the present year (1265);[1] and which is memorable in the history of the constitution as the first in which we have certain evidence of the appearance of representatives from the cities and boroughs.[2] The Earl of Derby opened a correspondence with the prince, and the Earl of Gloucester set himself up as a rival to Montfort, and then, by means of his brother, Thomas de Clare, who had been placed about the prince's person, concerted a plan for releasing Edward. This plan was successful; and on Thursday in Whitsunweek the prince escaped on a fleet horse

---

[1] "The year 1265 was one of the most memorable in the annals of England. The barons, indignant at an award which imposed obedience on all English subjects, without affording them safety, again turned their arms against the recreant king. Two of the unhappy and inglorious victories of civil war were achieved by the vigorous genius of Prince Edward; while, on the other hand, Simon de Montfort, at the very moment of his fall, set the example of an extensive reformation in the frame of parliament, which, though his authority was not acknowledged by the punctilious adherents to the letter and forms of law, was afterwards legally adopted by Edward, and rendered the parliament of that year the model of the British parliament, and in a considerable degree affected the constitution of all other representative assemblies. It may, indeed, be considered as the practical discovery of popular representation. The particulars of the war are faintly discerned at the distance of six or seven centuries. The reformation of parliament, which first afforded proof from experience, that liberty, order, greatness, power, and wealth, are capable of being blended together in a degree of harmony which the wisest men had not before believed to be possible, will be held in everlasting remembrance."—Sir James Mackintosh, *Hist. of Eng.*, vol. i. p. 286.

[2] Of the cities and towns of England, M. Guizot remarks:— "Previous to the Norman Conquest, many were rich, populous, important; their inhabitants were seen taking part in national events; the citizens of Canterbury appeared, under Ethelred II., in the county court, and those of London concurred in the election of several kings. Nevertheless it is almost certain that the towns never sent deputies to the Saxon Witenagemot; their rights were confined within the circuit of their walls, and when they mingled in public affairs, it was in a casual and irregular way, without having a place assigned to them in the government by any institution—any permanent custom.

"After the Conquest, the decline of the towns was great; commerce, the source of their wealth, suffered most of all by the disorder and oppression that followed; York fell in a short time from 1607 houses to 967; Oxford from 720 to 243; Chester from 487 to 282; Derby from 243 to 140, &c. In losing their importance they lost also their rights; and the lord, whether the king or some other, within whose domain they were situate, disposed almost at his absolute will of the property and fortunes of their inhabitants.

"Dating from the reign of Henry I. they gradually recovered; from that prince the city of London received its first charter, and some articles prove that it had not lost all its ancient liberties. Under Henry II.—a prince who applied himself to the establishment of order—the towns advanced more rapidly; in several the inhabitants acquired from their lord the ownership of the ground on which they stood, and redeemed the individual tributes he arbitrarily imposed on them by a fixed impost, and by holding their town in *fee-farm*, a kind of tenure analogous to that of *socage*. They then formed themselves into a corporation, sometimes received a charter, and thus entered into possession of the municipal government. Grants of charters became frequent, dating from the reign of King John."—*Essais sur l'Histoire de France.*

which had been conveyed to him, and joined the Earl of Gloucester at Ludlow, where the royal banner was raised. The prince was made to swear that he would respect the charters, govern according to law, and expel foreigners; and it was upon these express conditions that Gloucester surrendered to him the command of the troops. This earl was a vain, weak young man, but his jealous fury against Leicester could not blind him to the obvious fact that but few of the nobility would make any sacrifices for the royal cause unless their attachment to constitutional liberty were gratified by such pledges.

About the same time Earl Warenne, who had escaped from the battle of Lewes, landed in South Wales with 120 knights and a troop of archers; and other royalist chiefs rose in different parts of the country, according to a plan which seems to have been suggested by the military sagacity of Prince Edward. The Earl of Leicester, keeping good hold of the king, remained at Hereford, while his eldest son, Simon de Montfort, with a part of his army, was in Sussex. The object of the prince was to prevent the junction of these separated forces, and to keep the earl on the right bank of the Severn. Edward destroyed all the bridges and boats on that river and secured the fords; but, after some skilful manœuvres, the earl crossed the Severn and encamped near Worcester, where he expected his son would join him. But Simon's conduct in war was not equal to his father's, for he allowed himself to be surprised by night near Kenilworth, where Edward took his horses and treasure, and most of his knights, and forced him to take refuge, almost naked, in the castle there, the principal residence of the De Montfort family. The earl, still hoping to meet his son's forces, advanced to Evesham, on the river Avon. On the morning of the 4th of August, as he looked towards the hills in the direction of Kenilworth, he saw his own standards advancing. His joy, however, was but momentary; for he discovered, when too late to retreat, that they were his son's banners in the hands of his enemies, and, nearly at the same time, he saw the heads of columns showing themselves on either flank and in his rear. These well-conceived combined movements had been executed with unusual precision—the earl was surrounded —every road was blocked up. As he observed the skilful way in which the hostile forces were disposed, he uttered the complaint so often used by old generals—"They have learned from me the art of war;" and then, it is said, he added, "The Lord have mercy on our souls, for I see our bodies are Prince Edward's." He did not, however, neglect the duties of the commander, but marshalled his men in the best manner. He then spent a short time in prayer and took the sacrament, as was his wont, before going into battle. Having failed in an attempt to force the road to Kenilworth, he formed in a solid circle on the summit of a hill, and several times repulsed the charges of his foes, who gradually closed round him, attacking at all points. The king being in the earl's camp when the royalists appeared, was encased in armour which concealed his features, and was put upon a war-horse. In one of the charges the imbecile old man was dismounted, and in danger of being slain, but he cried out, "Hold your hand, I am Harry of Winchester," and the prince, who happened to be near, ran to his rescue and carried him out of the mêlée. Leicester's horse was killed under him, but the earl rose unhurt from his fall, and fought bravely on foot. A body of Welsh were broken and fled, and the number of his enemies still seemed to increase on all sides. He then asked the royalists if they gave quarter? and was told that there was no quarter for traitors. His

KENILWORTH CASTLE.[1]—From a drawing by J Wykeham Archer.

gallant son Henry was killed before his eyes, the bravest and best of his friends fell in heaps

[1] The manor of Kenilworth was an ancient demesne of the crown: its castle was demolished in the war of Edmund Ironside and Canute the Dane, early in the eleventh century. Godfrey de Clinton, in the reign of Henry III., built here a strong castle, and

around him, and at last the great earl himself died with his sword in his hand.[1]

The hatred of the royalists was too much inflamed to admit of the humanities and usages of chivalry. No prisoners were taken; the slaughter, usually confined to the "meaner sort," who could not pay ransom, was extended to the noblest and wealthiest, and all the barons and knights of Leicester's party, to the number of 180, were despatched.[2] After the battle the corpse of Leicester was brutally mangled, and treated with every kind of indignity; but by the people his memory was affectionately cherished, and long after he was spoken of among them under the title of "Sir Simon the Righteous."

After the decisive victory of Evesham, the king, resuming the sceptre, went to Warwick, where he was joined by his brother, the King of the Romans, who, with many other prisoners taken by Leicester at Lewes, now first recovered his liberty. Early in the next month, on the "feast of the Translation of St. Edward," a parliament assembled at Winchester. Here it was seen that, even in the moment of success, the king could not venture to revoke any part of the Great Charter. His victory had been achieved by the arms of English barons, who, generally speaking, had concurred in the former measures against his faithless government, and whose opposition to the Earl of Leicester's too great power had in no sense weakened their love of constitutional safeguards, or their hatred of an absolute king. Led away, however, by personal animosities, the parliament of Winchester passed some severe sentences against the family and partizans of the late earl, and deprived the citizens of London of their charter.

A desperate resistance was thus provoked, and successive insurrections broke out in different parts of the kingdom. Simon de Montfort and his associates maintained themselves for a long time in the isles of Ely and Axholm; the Cinque ports refused to submit; the castle of Kenilworth defied several royal armies; and Adam Gourdon, a most warlike baron, maintained himself in the forests of Hampshire. Prince Edward's valour and ability had full occupation for nearly two years, and at last it was found necessary to relax the severity of government, and grant easier terms to the vanquished, in order to obtain the restoration of internal tranquillity. With this view a committee was appointed of twelve bishops and barons, and their award, called the "Dictum de Kenilworth," was confirmed by the

---

founded a monastery at the distance of about a quarter of a mile from it. The tower called Cæsar's is of the Norman period; the massive walls are in some parts 10 ft. in thickness. Large additions made by John of Gaunt are distinguished by the title of Lancaster buildings. Subsequent additions, called Leicester buildings, comprise the remains of a noble banqueting hall, called the White Hall, 86 ft. long by 45 ft. wide; and the Gate-house. These are all shown in the accompanying view, together with one of the towers belonging to the mural boundary, called Lunn Tower.

[1] *Contin. Matt. Par.; M. West.; Chron. Mailros.; Chron. Dunst.* "Though Simon de Montfort was slain—his lifeless remains outraged—his acts branded as those of an usurper—and his name, held in abhorrence by the powerful, was distinguished only by the blessings of the poor and the praise of the learned—yet, in spite of authority and prejudice, his bold and fortunate innovation survived.

"When the barons originally took up arms against John, they exercised the indisputable right of resistance to oppression. They gave a wholesome warning to sovereigns, and breathed into the hearts of nations a high sense of their rights. But in this first stage they knew not how to improve their victory; they took no securities, and made no lasting provision for the time to come. Both parties might have won successive victory with no other fruit than alternate tyranny.

"In the second stage of the contest the national leaders obtained, in the Great Charter, a solemn recognition of the rights of mankind; and some provisions which, by reserving to a national assembly the power over many taxes, laid the foundation of a permanent and effective control over the crown. Still the means of redressing grievances chiefly lay in an appeal to arms —a coarse and perilous expedient, which, however justifiable by an extreme necessity, is always of uncertain issue, and of which the frequent repetition is incompatible with the peace and order of human society. Such were the plans of government in the Great Charter, the provisions of Oxford, and the *mise* or agreement of Lewes.

"The third epoch is distinguished by the establishment of a permanent assembly, which was on ordinary occasions capable of checking the prerogative by a quiet and constant action, yet strong enough to oppose it more decisively if no other means of preventing tyranny should be left. Hence the unspeakable importance of the new constitution given to parliament by Simon de Montfort. Hence also arose the necessity under which the succeeding king, with all his policy and energy, found himself of adopting this precedent for his own purpose. It would have been vain to have legally strengthened parliament against the crown, unless it had been actually strengthened by widening its foundations, by rendering it a bond of union between orders of men jealous of each other, and by multiplying its points of contact with the people—the sole allies from whom succour could be hoped. The introduction of knights, citizens, and burgesses into the legislature, by its continuance in circumstances so apparently inauspicious, showed how exactly it suited the necessities and demands of society at that moment. No sooner had events thrown forward the measure, than its fitness to the state of the community became apparent. It is often thus that in the clamours of men for a succession of objects, society, by a sort of elective attraction, seems to select from among them what has an affinity with itself, and what easily combines with it in its state at the time. The enlargement of the basis of the legislature thus stood the test which discriminates visionary prospects from necessary repair and prudent reformation. It would be nowise inconsistent with this view of the subject, if we were to suppose that De Montfort, by this novelty, paid court to the lower orders to gain allies against the nobility—the surmise of one ancient chronicler, eagerly adopted by several modern historians. That he might entertain such a project as a temporary expedient is by no means improbable. To ascribe to him a more extensive foresight would be unreasonable in times better than his. On the supposition could be substantiated, it would only prove more clearly that his ambition was guided by sagacity—that he saw the part of society that was growing in strength, and with which a provident government ought to seek an alliance—that, amidst the noise and confusion of popular complaint, he had learned the art of deciphering its often wayward language, and of discriminating the clamour of a moment from demands rooted in the nature and circumstances of society."
—*Mackintosh.*

[2] Some ten or a dozen knights who were found breathing after the carnage were permitted to live, or, at least, to have that chance of living which their wounds allowed.

king and parliament. The Earl of Gloucester, whose personal quarrel with Leicester had been the chief cause of the overthrow of the baronial oligarchy and the restoration of Henry, quarrelled with the king and once more took up arms, alleging that even the "Dictum de Kenilworth" was too harsh, and that the court was seeking to infringe the provisions of Oxford, and breaking the promises given on the field of Evesham. The dissatisfied Londoners made common cause with him, and received him within their walls; but losing heart at the approach of the king's army, Gloucester opened negotiations, and submitted on condition of receiving a full pardon for himself. At the same time the Londoners compounded for a fine of 25,000 marks. The pope most laudably laboured to diffuse the spirit of mercy and moderation; and the gallantry and generosity shown by Prince Edward on one occasion did more in subduing opposition than a hundred executions on the scaffold could have done. In a battle, fought in a wood near Alton, the prince engaged Adam Gourdon hand to hand, and vanquished that redoubtable knight in fair single combat. When Adam was brought to the ground, instead of despatching him, he generously gave him his life. On that very night he introduced him to the queen at Guildford, procured him his pardon, received him into his own especial favour, and was from that time forward most faithfully served by Sir Adam.[1]

On the 18th of November, two A.D. 1267.[2] years and three months after the battle of Evesham, the king, in parliament at Marlborough, adopted some of the most valuable of the provisions of the Earl of Leicester, and enacted other good laws.[3] Thus all resistance was disarmed, and the patriots or the outlaws in the Isle of Ely, who were the last to submit, threw down their arms and accepted the conditions of the "Dictum of Kenilworth." As soon as the country was thoroughly tranquillized, Prince Edward and his cousin Henry took the cross, in which they were followed by nearly 150 English lords and knights. Having taken many precautionary measures in case his father should die during his absence, and having most wisely obtained the grant of a new charter, with the restoration of their liberties, to the citizens of London, and a free pardon to a few nobles who still lay under the king's ban, Edward departed with his wife, Eleanor, his cousin Henry, and his knights, in the month of July, 1270. Many of the choicest chivalry of England left their bones to bleach on the Syrian shore; but the fate of Henry d'Almaine, as they called the son of the King of the Romans, was more tragical, as well as much more unusual. He was assassinated in a church at Viterbo, in Italy, by his two cousins, Simon and Guy de Montfort, who, with their mother, the Countess of Leicester, King Henry's own sister, had been driven out of England, and who consi-

---

[1] *Contin. Matt. Par.*

[2] "It is curious that in the most disturbed period of this turbulent reign, when ignorance seemed to be thickening and the human intellect to decline, there was written and given to the world the best treatise upon law of which England could boast till the publication of Blackstone's *Commentaries* in the middle of the eighteenth century.* It would have been very gratifying to me if this work could have been ascribed with certainty to any of the chancellors whose lives have been noticed. The author, usually styled Henry de Bracton, has gone by the names of Brycton, Britton, Briton, Breton, and Brets; and some have doubted whether all these names are not imaginary. From the elegance of his style, and the familiar knowledge he displays of the Roman law, I cannot doubt that he was an ecclesiastic who had addicted himself to the study of jurisprudence, and as he was likely to gain advancement from his extraordinary proficiency, he may have been one of those whom I have commemorated, although I must confess he rather speaks the language likely to come from a disappointed practitioner than of a chancellor who had been himself in the habit of making judges. For comprehensiveness, for lucid arrangement, for logical precision, this author was unrivalled during many ages. Littleton's work on *Tenures*, which illustrated the reign of Edward IV., approaches Bracton; but how barbarous in comparison are the *Commentaries* of Lord Coke, and the law treatises of Hale and Hawkins!"—Campbell's *Lives of the Chancellors.*

[3] "I cannot conclude the present chapter without observing one most prominent and characteristic distinction between the constitution of England and that of every other country in Europe; I mean its refusal of civil privileges to the lower nobility,

* "This book must have been ritten between the years 1262 and 1267, for it cites a case decided in the 47th of Henry III., and takes no notice whatever of t e statute of Marlridge, which passed in the 52d of Henry III."

or those whom we denominate the gentry. In France, in Spain, in Germany, wherever, in short, we look, the appellations of nobleman and gentleman are synonymous. Those entitled to bear them by descent, by tenure of land, by office, or royal creation, have formed a class distinguished by privileges inherent in their blood from ordinary freemen. Marriage with noble families, or the purchase of military fiefs, or the participation of many civil offices were, more or less, interdicted to the commons of France and the Empire. Of these restrictions, nothing, or next to nothing, was ever known in England. The law has never taken notice of gentlemen. From the reign of Henry III. at least, the legal equality of all ranks below the peerage was, to every essential purpose, as complete as at present. Compare two writers nearly contemporary—Bracton with Beaumanoir—and mark how the customs of England are distinguishable in this respect. The Frenchman ranges the people under three divisions—the noble, the free, and the servile; our countryman has no generic class but freedom and villenage. No restraint seems ever to have lain upon marriage; nor have the children even of a peer been ever deemed to lose any privilege by his marriage with a commoner. The purchase of lands held by knight service was always open to all freemen. A few privileges indeed were confined to those who had received knighthood. But upon the whole there was a virtual equality of rights among all the commoners of England. What is most particular is, that the peerage itself imparts no privilege except to its actual possessor. . . . There is no part, perhaps, of our constitution so admirable as this equality of civil rights; this *isonomia* which the philosophers of ancient Greece only hoped to find in democratical government. From the beginning our law has been no respecter of persons. . . . It is, I am firmly persuaded, to this peculiarly democratical character of the English monarchy, that we are indebted for its long permanence, its regular improvement, and its present vigour."—Hallam's *State of Europe during the Middle Ages*, vol. ii, pp. 476-478.

dered the King of the Romans as the bitterest enemy of their house. That vain old man, the King of the Romans, was rejoicing in the possession or display of a young German bride, and was still flattering himself with the hopes of the imperial crown, when the melancholy catastrophe of his son reminded him of the vanity of human wishes. He did not long survive the shock; he died in the month of December, 1271; and in the following winter his brother, the King of England, followed him to the grave, expiring at Westminster, after a long illness and great demonstrations of piety, on the feast of St. Edmund, the 16th of November, 1272. Henry had lived sixty-eight years, and had been fifty-six years a king—at least in name.

CHAPTER II.—CIVIL AND MILITARY HISTORY.—A.D. 1272—1290.

EDWARD I., SURNAMED LONGSHANKS.—ACCESSION, A.D. 1272—DEATH, A.D. 1307

Prince Edward proclaimed king during his absence—His romantic exploits in Syria—Attempt to assassinate him—His return homeward—His tournament with the Count of Chalons—His coronation feast in London—The Jews in England robbed and cruelly persecuted—Edward's expedients to raise money—His design to reduce Britain into one kingdom—State of Wales at his accession—He invades Wales—The Welsh submit—Their subsequent rebellion—Edward again invades Wales—Llewellyn the Welsh prince slain—His brother David executed—Wales reduced to an English province—Affairs of Scotland—Reign of Alexander II. of Scotland—His contentions with the pope—His alliance with England—Feud of the Scottish families of Bisset and Athole—Assassination of the Earl of Athole—Appeal of Bisset from Alexander II. to the King of England as lord paramount—Consequences of this appeal—Death and character of Alexander II.—Succeeded by Alexander III.—Contentions of the Scottish nobles during his minority—Interferences of the King of England with the Scottish government—Revolutions they occasioned—Scotland invaded by the Norwegians—Their fleet shattered by a storm—They are defeated at Largs—Intercourse between Alexander III. and the King of England—Mortality in Alexander's family—His own sudden death at Burntisland—His daughter Margaret proclaimed Queen—Feuds and compacts of the Scottish nobility under her minority—Edward I. contracts his son to Margaret—She dies on her passage from Norway to Scotland.

FROM the abbey church of Westminster the barons, who had attended his father's funeral, went to the new temple and proclaimed the absent Edward by the style of "King of England, Lord of Ireland, and Duke of Aquitaine." This was on Sunday, the 20th of November, four days after the demise of Henry. A new great seal was made; Walter de Merton was appointed chancellor; Walter Gifford, Archbishop of York, the Earl of Cornwall, a surviving son of Richard, assumed conjointly the office of guardians or regents of the kingdom; and such wise measures were taken that the public peace was in no way disturbed; and the accession of Edward, though he was far away, and exposed to the chances of

GREAT SEAL OF EDWARD I.[1]

war and shipwreck, was more tranquil than that of any preceding king since the Conquest.

When Edward departed on the crusade he

[1] This seal measures 4 inches in diameter.

51—52

for Syria or Palestine, had turned aside to attack the Mussulman King or Bey of Tunis. The Kings of Sicily had some old claims to tribute from this African state, and the Italian crown, after hovering over the heads of so many princes, had at last settled on that of Charles of Anjou, who, with the assistance of the pope, won it from Manfred, the illegitimate Swabian, at the battle of the Grandella, fought near Benevento, in the year 1266. This Charles was the ferocious, unworthy brother of the amiable Louis IX.; and it is generally supposed that, for his own selfish ambition and interests, he craftily induced the French king to turn his arms against Tunis; though it is also probable that the exaggerated accounts of the wealth of that city acted as a strong temptation with the crusaders in general. Louis landed on the African shore in the midst of summer, and took the camp and town of Carthage; but the excessive heat of the climate, the want of provisions, and even of wholesome water, and the pestilential miasmata from bogs and swamps, soon caused dreadful maladies among his host. The king himself was attacked by a fatal dysentery, and he laid himself down to die among the ruins and fragments of ancient Carthage.

When Prince Edward arrived, he found that Louis was dead, and that more than half of his army had perished by disease. The survivors had, however, made advantageous terms with the Bey of Tunis, and showed little inclination to leave that country and encounter fresh dangers in Palestine. The English then re-crossed the Mediterranean to Sicily (a short voyage of 150 miles); but Edward would not renounce his project, or return home. He passed the winter at Trapani, vowing that, though all his soldiers should desert him, he would go to Acre attended only by Fowen, his groom. Early in the following spring he set sail from Sicily, and he landed at Acre,[1] which was now almost the only residue of the crusaders' conquests in the East, with a force which did not exceed 1000 men. But the fame of Richard was still bright on those shores; and, while the Mahometans trembled, the Christians gathered round the standard of the successor of Lion-heart, to whom Edward was scarcely inferior in physical strength and courage, while he was his superior in coolness and policy. Bondocar, the Sultan of Babylon, who had prepared to take Acre by assault, immediately retreated from its vicinity, and, crossing the desert, went into Egypt. Edward advanced, and obtained temporary possession of Nazareth, which was taken by storm. The prince, and many of the English with him, were soon after attacked with sickness, and returned to Acre, where they lingered some fifteen months, doing little or nothing; for the first enthusiasm among the Latin Christians had subsided upon seeing that Edward had scarcely any money, and received no reinforcements. The English chivalry distinguished itself by many feats of arms, and revived the glory of the national name; but, after all, the only other solid advantages gained were the capture of two castles and the surprise and partial plunder of a caravan. The Mahometans were not strong enough to attack Acre, which, chiefly by Edward's means, was so fortified as to be enabled to defy them for twenty years longer, when the Mamelukes of Egypt took it and drove the crusaders and their descendants from every part of the Holy Land. Edward on his side was always too weak to attempt any extensive operations. His presence, however, both annoyed and distressed the Turks, and an attempt was made to get rid of him by assassination. The Emir of Jaffa, under pretence of embracing the Christian religion, opened a correspondence with the English prince, and gradually gained his confidence. The emir sent letters and presents, till his messengers were allowed to pass and repass without examination or suspicion. On the Friday of Whitsunweek, about the hour of vespers, as Edward was reclining on a couch, with nothing on him but a loose robe, the emir's messenger made his usual salam at the door of his apartment: he was admitted; and as he knelt and presented a letter with one hand, he drew a con-

---

[1] 'Akka, under the name of St. Jean d'Acre, played an eminent part in the Crusades, especially when, after being taken in 1187, by Saladin, it fell into the hands of the Christians four years later. The latter kept possession for 100 years of this strong key to the land. In the beginning of this period, Jerusalem declined a little from its high station, and 'Akka increased in greatness and power, to a degree no other city in Palestine ever attained. Then the haven of 'Akka was crowded with ships from all the commercial nations in Europe. The pilgrim hordes first stopped ashore on its pier. Mighty kings and princes gathered their treasures within its walls, and adorned the fair city with splendid churches and palaces. Others again, such as Richard Cœur de Lion of England, Philip Augustus of France, and St. Louis, fortified it with almost impregnable walls and ramparts. During that period the Templars, the Hospitallers, the German Brethren of the Cross, and Knights of St. Lazarus, ruled in 'Akka with a high hand. In 1263, indeed, it was attacked, and even besieged till 1272, by Boudocar, King of Egypt; but Henri de Lusignan, King of Jerusalem, managed to make peace with him, and persuaded him to retire. But the year 1291 put an end for ever to 'Akka's power. After a bloody combat, the city fell into the hands of El-Ashraf, chief of the Saracens. The whole Christian population was barbarously massacred, excepting a few who escaped to the ships. The city was set on fire, and with it fell the sway of the Christians in Palestine. Dapper, in his description of its destruction, quotes the remark of a writer, who says—"All the elements seem to have united their powers to annihilate this city; the very soil was stained with the blood of its inhabitants; the waters swallowed them up like a river; the flames in a very short time reduced those splendid buildings to ashes, and the inhabitants were suffocated by the clouds of vapour and smoke which rose from the conflagration."—Van de Velde's *Syria and Palestine*, vol. i. p. 273.

cealed dagger with the other, and aimed a blow at the prince's heart. Edward, though wounded, caught the murderer in his iron grasp, threw him to the ground, and despatched him with his own weapon. The prince's wound was not deep, but the dagger had been smeared with poison: when he learned this fact, he made his will, and gave himself up as lost. The English soldiers would have taken a horrid vengeance upon the poor Turks in their power, but he restrained their fury, and made them reflect on what might befall the helpless Christian pilgrims then at Jerusalem. Fortunately there was at Acre an English surgeon with skill and nerve enough to pare away the sides of the wound; and the grand-master of the Templars sent some precious drugs to stop the progress of the venom. The piety, the affectionate attentions of his loving wife, Eleanor, may have contributed very effectually to his cure, but there is no good ground for believing that she sucked the poison from her husband's wound.[1]

Henry had already implored his son to return to England, and now Edward gladly listened to proposals of peace made by the sultan, who was so much engaged with other wars in the interior as to have little time to spare for the prosecution of hostilities on the coast. A truce was therefore concluded for ten years, and then Edward sailed again for Sicily. Theobald, Archdeacon of Liege, who had accompanied the prince to Palestine, had been recalled some months before from Acre to fill the vacant chair of St. Peter. At Trapani, Edward received an earnest invitation from this old companion and steadfast friend, now Gregory X., to

EFFIGY OF ELEANOR, Queen of Edward I.[2] From her tomb in Westminster Abbey.

visit him at Rome. The prince crossed the Faro of Messina to travel by land through the Italian peninsula. At a mountain village in Calabria he met messengers, by whom he was informed, for the first time, of the death of his father. By the month of February, 1273, he was at Rome; but his friend, the pope, being absent, he stayed only two days in the Eternal City, and then turned aside to Civita Vecchia, where the pope received him with honour and affection. Edward demanded justice on the assassins of Henry d'Almaine; but Simon de Montfort, one of them, had gone to account for his crimes before a higher tribunal; and as Guy de Montfort had absconded, the King of England was obliged to be satisfied with a very imperfect vengeance. Leaving the pontiff, he continued his journey through Italy, and was received in triumph at every town. The admiring Milanese presented him with some fine horses and purple mantles. His exploits in Palestine, limited as they had been, had gained him the reputation of being the Champion of the Cross; the dangerous wound he had received (if he had died of it he would have been enrolled among saints and martyrs) created an additional sympathy in his favour; and, as if people knew he would be the last king to embark in the Crusades, he was hailed with extraordinary enthusiasm. On crossing the Alps, Edward was met by a deputation from England. He travelled on to Paris, where he was courteously received by his cousin, Philip le Hardi, and did homage to that king for the lands which he held in France.

Notwithstanding the tranquil state of the

---

[1] *Hemingford; Chron. Pepini in Muratori; Matt. West.; Wykes.* The story of Eleanor's sucking the wound is not mentioned by any chronicler living near the time. It seems to be of Spanish origin, and to have been first mentioned a century or two after the time.

[2] Edward caused a monument to be erected to Eleanor's memory near that of his father in the Confessor's Chapel, on which is placed her recumbent image of copper, gilt; and round the verge of the tomb the following inscription in uncial letters:—
ICY GYST ALIANOR IADIS REYNE DE ANOLETERRE FEMME AL RE EDEWERD FIZ LE RE OVNTIF DEL ALME DE LI DEV PVR SA PITE EYT MERCI. AMEN.

The effigy of Queen Eleanor, like that of Henry III., is remark-able for the beauty of its execution. The form of the crown and the style of the drapery are so similar to that of the monument of Henry III., that it may be strongly conjectured that both effigies were executed by the same hand under the direction of Edward I. The features of the queen are remarkably regular, and have an air of commanding beauty. " The statue of Eleanor," says Walpole, "is said to have been modelled from her person after death, and probably by an Italian sculptor, from which all the others were copied (the figures on the crosses erected at the places where her body rested on the way to Westminster); and it has been asserted that it was considered as the worthy prototype of the numerous images of the Virgin Mary for a century afterwards."

country, and the loyal disposition of his subjects, it must excite some surprise to see, that after so long an absence, Edward had no anxiety to reach England.[1] Instead of crossing the Channel, he turned back from Paris, where he had stayed a fortnight, and went to Guienne. The motives generally assigned for his protracted stay on the Continent are, his wish to await the decisions of a general council of the church, which the pope had summoned to meet at Lyons, and the distracted state of Guienne, or Aquitaine, which province seems never to have been tranquil for a year at a time. But it is pretty evident that the English king entertained suspicions of Philip, a far less conscientious sovereign than his father, Louis IX., who had been severely blamed by the French for not taking advantage of the weakness of Henry III. to drive the English out of all their continental possessions. The dark shadows of some deep and disgraceful intrigues are visible; and it seems to us, that when the pope warned Edward against the swords of the assassins, he did not apprehend danger from the ruined and fugitive Guy de Montfort, so much as from more prosperous and more powerful agents. In the month of May, 1274, while the English king was in Guienne, he received a challenge, couched in all the nice terms and circumlocutions of chivalry, from the Count of Chalons, to meet him lance to lance in a tournament. This fashion was then at its height, and knights and nobles of high renown, and princes royal, were accustomed to defy each other in the name of God, of the blessed Virgin Mary, and of their respective saints and mistresses, and to invite one another, out of love and reverence, to joustings and tiltings, which often terminated in blood and death or fractured limbs. Edward considered himself bound in honour as a true knight to accept the count's challenge, and on the appointed day he entered the lists, as stalwart and fearless a combatant as ever sat in saddle. He was attended by 1000 champions; but the Count of Chalons rode to the spot with nearly 2000. Whispers of bad faith on the part of the count had already been heard, and the sight of this unfair advantage probably confirmed the worst suspicions of the English. The image of war was converted into its stern reality—a sanguinary battle ensued, in which the foot-soldiers took part as well as the knights. The English cross-bowmen drove the French infantry from the field, and then mixing with the English horse, who were far outnumbered by their opponents, they overthrew many of the count's knights by stabbing their horses or cutting their saddle-girths—two operations against all rule, and deemed infamous in the code of chivalry. The count himself, a man renowned for his physical strength, after charging Edward several times with his lance, rode in, and grasping the king round the neck, endeavoured to unseat him. Edward sat like a rock, and gave the proper touch with the spur—his war-horse sprang forward, the count was pulled out of his saddle, and hurled to the ground with a dreadful shock. He was remounted by some of his knights; but, sorely bruised and stupefied by his fall, he cried out for quarter. Edward was so enraged that he kept hammering on the iron armour of his suppliant foe for some time, and at last rejected his sword, and made him surrender to a common foot-soldier—an extremity of disgrace which a true knight would have avoided at the cost of life. The English had the best of the affray, taking many knights, who were obliged to ransom their persons, their arms, and their horses (where any were left alive), and *slaying* many of the French footmen—"because they were but rascals,' and no great account was made of them."[3]

A.D. 1274. Edward now turned his thoughts towards England, and sent orders to prepare for his coronation. If these orders were obeyed, the coronation feast must have been a sublime specimen of a well-loaded table; for 380 head of cattle, 430 sheep, 450 pigs, 18 wild boars, 278 flitches of bacon, and 19,660 capons and fowls, were ordered by the king for this solemn occasion.[4] As he travelled through France, Edward stopped at the pleasant town of

---

[1] He had written letters expressing some fear of the Londoners, and had several times commanded the "mayor, sheriffs, and commons" most carefully to keep the peace of the city. The measures adopted in consequence were more vigorous than legal. All persons suspected of having been partizans of the Earl of Leicester were hunted down in every ward, and, without form of trial or examination, thrown into prison till Edward's return.

It was a tranquillity, however, which seems to have encouraged the licentiousness of the barons. Speaking of Boston, in Lincolnshire, Camden says:—"This town was miserably ruined in Edward I.'s reign; for in that degenerate age and universal corruption of manners through the kingdom, certain warriors, whilst a tournament was proclaiming at the fair time, coming hither under the disguise of monks and canons, set the town on fire in many places, broke in upon the merchants with sudden violence, and carried away great quantities of goods, but burned more; insomuch that our historians write (as the ancients did of Corinth when it was demolished, that veins of gold and silver mixed together in one common current. Their ringleader, Robert Chamberlain, after he had confessed the fact and expressed his detestation of the crime, was hanged; but he could not by any means be brought to discover his accomplices."

[2] Rascal here means simply plebeian of the lowest class, the meaning attached to the term by Sir Thomas Smith, who, in his classification of English society, defines yeoman as "among the husbandmen, labourers, lowest and rascal sort of the people, such as be exempted out of the number of the rascalitie," &c. Thus, too, Pope—

"My blood
Has crept through veins of rascals since the flood."
(See *Imperial Dictionary*.)

[3] *Hem.ing.*; *West.*; *Trivet.*; *Holinshed.*   [4] *Rymer.*

Montreuil, to settle some differences which had long existed between the English and Flemings, and which had seriously committed the commercial interests of both countries. On the 2d of August, 1274, after an absence of more than four years, he landed at Dover, and on the 19th of the same month, "after the feast of the Assumption," he was crowned, together with his high-minded wife, in Westminster Abbey. The nation was proud of the valour and fame of their king, who was now in the prime of mature manhood, being in his thirty-sixth year; and the king had good reason to be proud of the affection, loyalty, and prosperity of the nation.

The government, however, was poor and embarrassed; and, in spite of all pretexts, this circumstance seems to have been the real whetstone of the animosity which Edward showed immediately after his accession to one class of his subjects—the unhappy Jews. The rest of the nation were now tolerably well protected from arbitrary spoliation by the Great Charter and the power of parliaments; but the miserable Israelites, considered unworthy of a participation in the laws and rights of a Christian people, were left naked to oppression, no hand or tongue being raised in their defence, and the mass of the people rejoicing in their ruin. As a zealous crusader, Edward detested all unbelievers, and his religious antipathies went hand-in-hand with his rapacity, and probably justified its excesses in his own eyes. The coin had been clipped and adulterated for many years, and the king chose to consider the Jews as the sole or chief authors of this crime.[1] To bring a Jew before a Christian tribunal was almost the same thing as to sign his death-warrant. Two hundred and eighty of both sexes were hanged in London alone, and many victims also suffered in every other town where they resided. As it was so common, clipped money might be found upon every person in the kingdom; but once discovered in the possession of an Israelite, it was taken as an irrefragable proof of guilt. The houses and the whole property of every Jew that suffered went to the crown, which thus had an interest in multiplying the number of convictions. Even before these judicial proceedings, the king prohibited the Jews from taking interest for money lent, from building synagogues, and buying lands or any free tenements. He put a capitation or poll-tax upon them, similar to the kharatch which the grand-seignior exacted from his Christian subjects: he set a distinctive and odious badge upon their dress, that they might be known from all others—another Turkish custom, which in its time has been the cause of infinite suffering.

Thirteen years later, when Edward was engaged in expensive foreign wars, and the parliament, in ill humour thereat, stinted his supplies, he ordered the seizure of every Jew in England; and on an appointed day, men, women, and children—every living creature in whose veins the ancient blood of the tribes was known or supposed to flow—were brutally arrested and cast into loathsome dungeons. There seems to have been no parity of justice on this occasion, and the Jews purchased their enlargement by a direct payment of the sum of £12,000 to the king. Edward might have continued to make good use of them from time to time in this manner, as most of his predecessors had done; but his fanaticism overcame his avidity for money, or, probably, he wanted a large sum at once, for he was now in the midst of his scheme for the subjugation of Scotland, and had just married two of his daughters. It was in the year 1290, soon after the sitting of a parliament at Westminster, that his proclamation went forth commanding all the Jews, under the penalty of death, to quit the kingdom for ever, within the space of two months. Their total number was considerable, for, though long robbed and persecuted in England, they had, notwithstanding, increased and multiplied, and their condition in the other countries of Christendom being still worse than here, the stream of emigration had set pretty constantly from the opposite side of the Channel. Sixteen thousand five hundred and eleven individuals received the king's pass, with the gracious permission to carry with them as much of their ready money as would pay the immediate expenses of their voyage. Houses, lands, merchandise, treasures, debts owing to them, with their bonds, their tallies and obligations, were all seized by the king. The mariners of London, and the inhabitants of the Cinque ports generally, who were as bigoted as the king, and thought it no sin to be as rapacious towards the accursed Jews, robbed many of them of the small pittance left them, and drowned not a few during their passage. Some few mariners were convicted and suffered capital punishment; for the king, to use the keen sarcasm of Hume, was determined to be the sole plunderer in his dominions.

Contemporaneously with these shameful proceedings against the Jews, Edward enacted many just and wise laws for his Christian subjects.[2]

---

[1] A few Christians were afterwards punished for the same offence.

[2] At the parliament which met in May, 1275, under the presidence of the Lord-chancellor Burnel, who had early distinguished himself not only in the civil and canon law, but in the common law of England, was passed THE STATUTE OF WESTMINSTER THE FIRST, deserving, says Lord Campbell, the name of a *code*, rather than an *act of Parliament*. "From this chiefly Edward I. has obtained the name of the 'English Justinian,' absurdly enough, as the Roman emperor merely caused a compilation to be made of existing laws; whereas the object now

The nature of his reforms shows the extent of the evil that had existed. In 1299 all the judges of the land were indicted for bribery, and only two of the number were acquitted; the chief justice of the court of king's bench was convicted of instigating his servants to commit murder, and of protecting them against the law after the offence; the chief baron of the exchequer was imprisoned and heavily fined, and so was Sir Ralph de Hengham, the grand justiciary. But perhaps, in some of these cases, we shall not greatly err if we deduct from the delinquency of the accused, and allow something for the arbitrary will of the accuser. It is known that the king was in great want of money, when, as the consequence of their condemnation, he exacted about 80,000 marks from the judges. In recovering, or attempting to recover, such parts of the royal domain as had been encroached upon, and in examining the titles by which some of the great barons held their estates, he roused a spirit which might have proved fatal to him had he not prudently stopped in time. When his commissioners asked Earl Warenne to show his titles, the earl drew his sword and said, "By this instrument do I hold my lands, and by the same I intend to defend them! Our ancestors, coming into this realm with William the Bastard, acquired their possessions by their good swords." Such title-deeds were not to be disputed; but there were other cases where men wore less powerful swords, and where written deeds and grants from the crown had been lost or destroyed during the convulsions of the country; and Edward seized some manors and estates, and made their owners redeem them by large sums of money. There was much bad faith in these proceedings, but, as the king chose his victims with much prudence, no insurrection was excited.

We must now retrace our steps, to take a regular view of this king's great operations in war. Edward was, to the full, as ambitious and fond of conquest as any prince of the Norman or Plantagenet line; but, instead of expending his power in foreign wars, he husbanded it for the grand plan of reducing the whole of the island of Great Britain under his immediate and undivided sway. He employed the claim of feudal superiority—a right most difficult to define, even if its existence had been admitted—with final success against Wales; and though, with regard to Scotland, i eventually failed, the ruin of his scheme there did not happen until after his death, and he felt, for a time, the proud certainty of having defeated every opponent. If the acknowledgment of the paramount authority of the English kings, extracted from unsuccessful princes, justified a forcible seizure of territory against the wishes of the people, Edward may be acknowledged to have had that right over Wales. Setting aside the somewhat doubtful vassalage of the Welsh principalities to our Saxon kings, on which the Norman conquerors impudently founded a pretension, as being the lawful heirs to those kings, we have repeated instances of a seeming submission, when the princes purchased peace by engaging to pay certain tributes, and to recognize the suzerainty of the English throne. When a weak state stood in this relation with a strong one, the feudal supremacy implied an almost unlimited right of interference and control; but when the relation existed between two states of equal power, it meant little or nothing beyond a mere ceremony. Thus the Kings of England, as vassals to the sovereigns of France for their territories on the Continent, had, for a long time, defied the authority of their liege lords, after making them tremble in Paris, their own capital. Those other nominal vassals, the great Dukes of Burgundy, although they had no separate sovereignty like the Normans and Plantagenets, repeatedly followed the same course. The forfeiture pronounced against John was generally considered as an unjustifiable stretch of the rights of supremacy, but it was well timed; it was directed against one who had made himself universally odious, and whose continental subjects, for the most part, at this crisis, preferred a union with

---

was to correct abuses, to supply defects, and to remodel the administration. Edward deserves infinite praise for the sanction he gave to the undertaking; and, from the observations he had made in France, Sicily, and the East, he may, like Napoleon, have been personally useful in the consultations for the formation of the new code; but the execution must have been left to others, and the chief merit of it may safely be ascribed to Lord-chancellor Burnel, who brought it forward in parliament.

"The statute is methodically divided into fifty-one chapters. Without exempting churchmen from civil jurisdiction, it protects church property from the spoliation of the king and nobles, to which it had been exposed. It provides for freedom of popular elections, then a matter of much moment, as sheriffs, coroners, and conservators of the peace were still chosen by the freeholders in the county court, and attempts had been made unduly to influence the election of knights of the shire almost from the time when the order was instituted. It contains a strong declaration to enforce the enactments of MAGNA CHARTA against

excessive fines, which might operate as perpetual imprisonment. It enumerates and corrects the great abuse of tenures, particularly with regard to the marriage of wards. It regulates the levying of tolls, which were imposed in an arbitrary manner, not only by the barons, but by cities and boroughs. It corrects and restrains the powers of the king's escheator and other officers under the crown. It amends the criminal law, putting the crime of rape on the footing to which it has been lately restored, as a most grievous but not a capital offence. It embraces the subject of "procedure" both in civil and criminal matters, introducing many regulations with a view to render it cheaper, more simple, and more expeditious.

"Having gone so far, we are astonished that it did not go farther. It does not abolish trial by battle in civil suits, only releasing the demandant's champion from the oath (which was always false), that he had seen seisin given of the land, or that his father, when dying, had exhorted him to defend the title to it."—Lord Campbell's *Lives of the Chancellors*, p. 164.

France to their old connection with England. The nature of Edward's right is scarcely deserving of a further examination: had no such claims existed he would have invented others; for he was determined on the conquest of the country, and internal dissensions and other circumstances favoured the enterprise. The expediency of the measure, and the advantages that have resulted from it, ought not to make us indifferent to the fate of a brave people who were fighting for their independence. The Anglo-Normans, who had been gradually encroaching on the territory for 200 years, accuse the poor Welsh of cruelty and perfidy, forgetting that they were themselves the aggressors, and had been guilty of treachery the most manifold, and of cruelties the most atrocious. Since the beginning of the reign of Henry II., civilization had advanced in the rich champaign of England, and had, from the circumstances in which the country was placed, retrograded in Wales; but there are Welsh writers of the time who trace in that land the most interesting picture of an hospitable and generous race of men, full of the elements of poetry, and passionately fond of their wild native music. Though chiefly a pastoral people, they were not rude or clownish. "All the Welsh," says Giraldus Cambrensis, "without any exception, from the highest to the lowest, are ready and free in speech, and have great confidence in replying, even to princes and magnates." The mass of the nation, however, notwithstanding this partial refinement, was poor and but rudely clad, as compared with their English contemporaries. Seldom has even a race of mountaineers made a longer or more gallant stand for liberty. When the sword of slaughter had passed over them to smite no more—when better times and better feelings came—though, as less numerous and far more exposed, they had been less fortunate than the Scots, their valour entitled them to the same admiration and sympathy; and perhaps the high national character of the United Kingdom of Great Britain may be in part owing to the fact, that no one portion of it fell an easy or degraded conquest to the other.

At the time of Edward's aggression, the principality of North Wales was still almost untouched by English arms; but the conquerors had established themselves in Monmouthshire, and held a somewhat uncertain and frequently disturbed possession of a good part of South Wales. This occupation had been effected very gradually by the great barons, who had made incursions at their own expense and with their own retainers. These lords were rewarded with the lands they gained from the Welsh. As they advanced they raised chains of fortifications, building their castles sufficiently near to communicate with and support each other. Thus, in Monmouthshire a regular chain of fortresses was occupied on the banks of the Monnow, the Wye, and the Severn. A second line stretched diagonally from Grosmont on the Monnow to the banks of the Rumney. In addition to these strong fortresses, many smaller castles were constructed for the purpose of keeping the natives in awe. The more advanced posts were often re-taken; and the day when one of these castles was destroyed was held by the Welsh—who foresaw the consequences of this gradual advance—as a day of universal joy, on which the father, who had just lost his only son, ought to forget his misfortune. But still the chains were drawn more and more closely around them by the persevering invaders; and, since the conquest of Ireland, extraordinary pains had been taken to secure the whole of the line through South Wales to Milford Haven, the usual place of embarkation for the sister island. In the wilderness of the Tivy, and in many of the more inaccessible moors, marshes, and mountains, the English were still defied. But the jealousies of the petty princes, and the rancorous feuds of the clans, defeated all their greater projects; and, at the critical moment which was to seal the fate of the whole country, Rees-ap-Meredith, the Prince of South Wales, was induced to join Edward and fight against Llewellyn, the ruler of the northern principality and the representative of a rival family. Llewellyn, moreover, was opposed by his own brother, David, who also rallied, with his vassals, round the standard of the English king.

In the wars between Henry III. and the barons, the Prince of North Wales had taken part with the latter, and had shown himself the steady friend of De Montfort. A body of northern Welsh had fought for that great earl against Edward at the battle of Evesham; and when De Montfort was dead, and his family ruined and scattered, Llewellyn still retained his old affection for the house, and agreed upon a marriage with Elinor de Montfort, daughter to the deceased earl. As that young lady was on her voyage from France to Wales, with Emeric, her youngest brother, she was taken by four ships of Bristol, and was sent to King Edward's court, where both brother and sister were detained as prisoners. Angry feelings had existed before, but this seizure of his bride transported Llewellyn with wrath, and bitterly complaining of the wrong and insult which had been done to him in a time of peace, he prepared for war. According to some accounts, he began hostilities by falling upon the English on his borders, killing the people and burning their towns; but this is not quite certain, and, at all events, Edward had long been employed in making preparations for conquest, and, what was equally notorious, and still more irritating to the unfortunate prince, he had been intriguing with Llewellyn's subjects and corrupting the Welsh chiefs with bribes and promises.

In A.D. 1277, after the feast of Easter, Edward departed from Westminster, and with a mighty force, which increased as he advanced, marched towards Chester. At Midsummer he crossed the Dee, and, keeping between the mountains and the sea, took the two castles of Flint and Rhuddlan. Cautious in the extreme, he made no further progress until he had repaired these fortresses and strengthened their defences. At the same time his fleet, which was skilfully managed by the mariners of the Cinque ports, co-operated along the devoted coast, blockading every port, and cutting off the supplies which Llewellyn had counted upon receiving from the Isle of Anglesey. On the land side every outlet was strongly guarded, and the Welsh prince, driven to the mountains, was soon in want of provisions. Edward avoided a battle with desperate men, and, girding in the barren mountains, waited the effects of a surer and more dreadful destroyer than the sword. When winter made its approach the condition of Llewellyn was horrible, and it finally obliged him to throw himself on the generosity of his enemy. On the 10th of November Edward dictated his harsh terms at Rhuddlan Castle. The English king afterwards remitted a tremendous fine, which so poor a country could never have paid; but he showed no great alacrity in making these concessions, and he let nearly a year elapse before he performed his promise of releasing Llewellyn's bride.

Such treaties as that imposed on this occasion upon the Welsh are never kept, and all Edward's art could not reconcile either the prince or people to the sense of degradation. He gratified Llewellyn's brother, David, who had fought for him, by marrying him to the daughter of an English earl, and making him an English baron; but, when David stood among his native mountains, he forgot these honours; he cursed his own folly, which had brought ruin upon his country, and had excluded him from the hope of succeeding, either in his own person or in that of his children, to the principality.¹ The English conquerors

were not sufficiently refined to exercise their power with moderation, and they derided the national usages, and insulted the prejudices of a susceptible and brave people. The invasion of their own demesnes, and the cutting down of the wood on the lands reserved to them by treaty, exasperated both Llewellyn and David; but it is perfectly clear that had these princes been converted into subservient vassals, or won by the kindest treatment to be solicitous for the preservation of the peace, they would still have been forced into war by the unanimous feeling of the Welsh people. On the night of Palm Sunday, March the 22d, of the year 1282, David surprised and took the strong castle of Hawardine, belonging to Roger Clifford, the justiciary, "a right worthy

HAWARDINE CASTLE, Flintshire.²—From Wood's Welsh Notes.

and famous knight," according to the English; a cruel tyrant, according to the Welsh. Several men who made resistance were killed, but the lord, who was caught in his bed, was only wounded, and then carried off as a prisoner. A general insurrection ensued: the Welsh rushed in arms from their mountains, and Llewellyn, joining his brother, laid siege to the castles of

---

² "It is probable that the site of Hawardine Castle was a Saxon stronghold; it is written Haordine in *Doomsday Book*. On the invasion of William, it was found in the possession of the gallant Edwin, and probably was one of the places of his residence. The remains are a fine circular tower or keep on the summit of a mount. This alone is pretty entire. On the removal of an accumulation of rubbish, in one place was discovered a long flight of steps, at the bottom of which was a door, and formerly a draw-bridge, which crossed a deep long chasm nicely faced with freestone, to another door leading to two or three small rooms, probably places of confinement. The several parts of this fortress seem to have been built at different times. It is surrounded by deep fosses. The castle was dismantled in 1645 by order of parliament.

---

¹ Llewellyn, it appears, had no children.

Flint and Rhuddlan. These strong places held out, but many of the new castles were taken and destroyed, and the English intruders were in some places driven across the marches. When the news was carried to Edward he affected surprise; but it has been suspected that he was not displeased with the opportunity, afforded by what had taken place, of making his conquest final and absolute. He was in want of money, and had no time to assemble a parliament; he therefore had recourse to the very unconstitutional means of a forced loan. He then sent out commissioners to raise an army, and despatched such troops as he had in readiness to the relief of Flint and Rhuddlan. He soon followed in person; and having assembled nearly all his military tenants and 1000 pioneers, he advanced into North Wales, leaving his fleet to act upon the coast and reduce the Isle of Anglesey. His pioneers cut down woods, and opened roads into the very fastnesses of Snowdon, whither the natives were again forced to retire. Some intrenched positions were carried, but not without a great loss; and in one affair, which appears to have been a regular battle, Edward was completely checked, if not defeated. But the means at his disposal made the struggle too unequal; reinforcements continually crossed the Dee, or came up from the coast, and he procured the services of foreign mercenaries, who were particularly well suited for mountain warfare. These were bands of Basques from the Pyrenees, whose method of

FLINT CASTLE.¹—From Roscoe's Wanderings in North Wales.

fighting, and whose general habits and manners differed little from those of the Welsh people, whom they were employed to hunt down like blood-hounds. These foreign hordes acted where the regular troops of the English king could not; accustomed in their own country to mountains far more rugged, they penetrated into every part of Snowdon, and the last bulwark of Welsh independence was forced. Edward, chiefly by means of his fleet, occupied Anglesey; but, in passing from that island to the main, a detachment of his forces sustained a severe loss. Between the sword and the waves there perished thirteen knights, seventeen esquires, and several hundred foot-soldiers. This reverse at the Menai Strait happened on St. Leonard's Day, the 6th of November. In another battle, Edward himself was worsted, being obliged to flee for protection to one of his castles, leaving the Lords Audley and Clifford dead on the field. Llewellyn was elated by these successes, and he fondly hoped that the severity of winter would force the English to retire; but Edward had collected a strong force in Pembrokeshire and Caermarthen, and he now sent it orders to advance through South Wales, and attack his enemy in the rear. Leaving his brother David to carry on the war in North Wales, his own principality, Llewellyn boldly turned his steps to the south to meet the new invaders. He had reached Bualth, in the valley of the Wye, when the English, under the savage Earl of Mortimer, appeared suddenly on the opposite side of the river. A Welsh force was on the neighbouring heights; but the prince had been left with only a few followers. The English crossed the river and surprised him before he had time to put on his armour; he was murdered, rather than slain in battle. They cut off his head and sent it to Edward, who forwarded it to London, there to be placed on the Tower.

The struggle for independence did not, however, end with this unfortunate prince. In spite of the submission of most of the Welsh chiefs, his brother David still kept his sword in his hand, and for six months he wandered a free man over his native wilds. At last he was betrayed by some unpatriotic Welshmen, and with his wife and children carried in chains to the castle of Rhuddlan. In the month of September following, an English parliament, assembled by

¹ Flint Castle was most probably founded by Edward I., although it has been said to have originated as early as the time of Henry II. Its ruins crest the summit of a freestone rock on the north side of the town, to which the castle was formerly attached by a bridge, which led to the barbican tower. It was dismantled in 1647 by order of the parliament.

Edward at Shrewsbury, pronounced the doom, not of the last champion of Welsh independence (for Madoc and others soon followed), but of the last sovereign prince of one of the most ancient ruling families of Europe. He was sentenced—1st. To be dragged by a horse to the place of execution, because he was a traitor to the king, who had made him a knight. 2dly. To be hanged, because he had murdered the knights in Hawardine Castle. 3dly. To have his bowels burned, because he had done the deed on Palm Sunday, the season of Christ's passion. 4thly. To be quartered, and have his limbs hung up in different places, because he had conspired the death of his lord the king in various parts. The sentence was executed to the letter, and it remained for many ages a revolting precedent in cases of high treason.[2]

Edward had far more patience and prudence than was common to the conquerors of his time; and he devised wise means for retaining peaceful possession of what he had gained by force. He did not move from Wales until more than a year after the death of Llewellyn, and he spent the greater part of that time in dividing the country into shires and hundreds, after the manner of England, and restoring order and tranquillity. Immediately after the affair of Bualth, he published a proclamation, offering peace to all the inhabitants, giving them, at the same time, assurances that they should continue to enjoy all their lands, liberties, and properties as they had done before. Some of the ancient usages of the country were respected, but, generally speaking, the laws of England were introduced and enforced. He gave charters with great privileges to various trading companies in Rhuddlan, Caernarvon, Aberystwith, and other towns, with the view of encouraging trade and tempting the Welsh from their mountains, and their wild, free way of living, to a more social and submissive state. When his wife Eleanor bore him a son in the castle of Caernarvon, he adroitly availed himself of that circumstance, by presenting the infant Edward to the people as their countryman, and telling them that he, who was born among them, should be their prince. The Welsh chiefs expected that this "Prince of Wales" would have the separate government of their country; for Alphonso, an elder brother of the infant Edward, was then alive, and the acknowledged heir to the English crown. For some time they indulged in this dream of a restored independence, and professed, and probably felt, a great attachment to the young Edward; but Prince Alphonso died; the illusion was also dissipated by other circumstances, and, in the sequel, the Welsh-born prince came to be regarded by his countrymen with very different feelings from either pride or affection.

CAERNARVON CASTLE.[1]—J. S. Prout, from his sketch on the spot.

After the subjugation of Wales, Edward's ambition rested for about four years—three of which he passed almost wholly on the Continent, where he was honourably engaged as umpire to settle a fresh dispute which had arisen between the Kings of France, Arragon, and the house of Anjou, respecting the island of Sicily. His ability and conduct in this matter gained him a great increase of reputation among foreign princes;[3] but the affairs of his own kingdom fell into disorder; the English people complained that he neglected their interests to take charge of what did not concern them; and the parliament at last refused him a supply which he had asked. The king then returned in haste, and, almost immediately after, he involved himself in the affairs of Scotland, which, with a few short intervals, entirely occupied him all the rest of his reign.

---

[1] This magnificent castle was built by Edward I. The space included within its walls and courts is an area of one mile in circumference. The exterior is complete in most of its parts, but the halls and chambers, which united a degree of palatial arrangement with the defences of an important stronghold, have fallen into decay. The castle stands at the west end of the town, and on the north and west its massive walls overhang the sea.
[2] *Hemingford; Chronicle of Dunstable Priory; Rymer; Carte.*
[3] *Rymer; Mezeray, Hist. Franc.; Giannone, Storia del Regno di Napoli.*

Before proceeding, however, to this part of the story of the English king, it will be most convenient to resume our Scottish narrative from the point to which we brought it down in the last Book.[1]

The reign of Alexander II., who succeeded to the throne in 1214, will not detain us long. After the death of John, the King of Scots continued to co-operate with Prince Louis of France and the confederated English barons; and he himself, his whole army, and kingdom were, in consequence, excommunicated by the legate Gualo; but the sentence seems to have been very little minded either by the people or their clergy. It was not even published by the latter till almost a twelvemonth had passed. In the meantime Louis made peace with Henry, without giving himself any concern about his ally. On this, Alexander, who was on his march into England, returned home. He soon after, however, effected his reconciliation both with the pope and the new King of England. On the 1st of December, 1217, he received absolution from the delegates of Gualo at Tweedmouth; and at the same time he surrendered to Henry the town of Carlisle, of which, although not of the castle, he had made himself master, and did homage for the earldom of Huntingdon and his other honours and possessions in England. On the 25th of June, 1221, Alexander married the Princess Joan, Henry III.'s eldest sister. A long period of uninterrupted peace and amity between the two countries was the consequence of these arrangements.

Notwithstanding the alliance that connected Alexander and Henry, and the friendship and frequent intercourse in which they lived—for the King of Scots made repeated visits to the English court—no final settlement of their claims upon each other had yet taken place. It was not till September, 1237, that at a conference, held at York, it was agreed that Alexander, who, among other things, laid claim, by right of inheritance, to the counties of Northumberland, Cumberland, and Westmoreland, should receive lands in the two former of the yearly value of £200 in full satisfaction of all his demands. The following year (4th March, 1238) Queen Joan died at Canterbury. She had left no issue, and within little more than a year (15th May, 1239) Alexander married again: his new queen was Mary, daughter of Ingelram de Couci, a great lord of Picardy. The chief bond that had attached the two kings was thus snapped; and Mary de Couci, whose family had been distinguished for its opposition to the English interests, is, besides, supposed to have exercised an unfavourable influence over the mind of her husband.

---

[1] See vol. I. p. 349.

It was some years, however, before the old friendship that had subsisted between him and Henry wholly gave way. Even in 1242 we find Henry, when about to set out on his expedition to France, confiding to Alexander the care of the northern Borders. But in this same year an event occurred which is especially memorable for the consequences attributed to it. An old feud had existed between the Bissets, a powerful family in the north of Scotland, and the house of Athole. At a tournament held at Haddington, Patrick, Earl of Athole, a youth distinguished for his knightly accomplishments, chanced to overthrow Walter Bisset. Within a day or two after, the Earl of Athole was found murdered in the house where he lodged, which was also set on fire. Suspicion immediately fell upon the Bissets: the nobility, headed by the Earl of March, immediately raised an armed force, and demanded the life both of Walter and of his uncle William Bisset, the chief of the family. It appears pretty certain that the latter at least was innocent of any participation in the murder: he urged, what seems to have been the fact, that he was not within fifty miles of Haddington when it was committed: he offered to maintain his innocence by the wager of battle; and, still further to clear himself, he had sentence of excommunication against the murderers published both in his own chapel and in all the churches of the kingdom. It seems to have been against him, nevertheless, that the rage both of the connections of Athole and of the people generally was chiefly turned. The savage notions of the period could not view what had taken place in any other light than as a ground for hunting to death the whole kindred of the supposed criminal; and the head of his family, as higher game, was naturally, in the spirit of this mode of considering the matter, pursued even with more eagerness than himself. The king, however, seems to have felt the injustice of the popular clamour: he interposed for Bisset's protection; and even the queen, according to Fordun, offered to make oath that he had no part in devising the crime; that is to say, she was so convinced of his innocence that she was willing to come forward as one of his compurgators, if the case should be submitted to that mode of trial. The opposite party, however, seem to have declined submitting the question to decision either by compurgation or by combat: they insisted that it should be brought before a jury; so that this affair is remarkable, in addition to its other points of interest, as a memorial of all the three great forms of judicial procedure in criminal cases which were then in use. Bisset refused the trial by jury, "on account of the malevolence of the people, and the implacable resentment of his enemies." At last, by the exertions of the king, it was agreed that he should be allowed to escape with his life on condition of forfeiting his estates and leaving the country. But he was still, notwithstanding, in the greatest danger from the secret determination of his enemies to have his blood; and it was only by remaining in concealment under the royal protection for about three months that he was at last enabled to make his escape to England. Whatever may have been his injuries, he now certainly showed little nobleness of character. Stung, possibly, with an indignant sense of the injustice he had experienced, he sought to avenge himself on his enemies at the expense not only of his country, but of its king, to whose zealous and energetic interposition in his favour he owed his life. It is said that he made his appeal to the King of England against the judgment that had been passed on him, on the plea that "Alexander, being the vassal of Henry, had no right to inflict such punishment on his nobles without the permission of his liege lord;" and that, at the same time, he further endeavoured to excite Henry against the Scottish king by describing the latter as devoted to the interests of France, and quoting instances in which, as he affirmed, English traitors who had escaped from prison were received and harboured at the northern court.[1]

These insidious representations may not improbably have had some part, along with other causes, in fomenting the hostile disposition which Henry not long after openly showed. At length, having fully arranged his plans, he proclaimed war against Alexander in 1244, and assembling a numerous army at Newcastle, prepared to invade Scotland. Some troops which had been sent to the assistance of Alexander by his brother-in-law, John de Couci, had been intercepted by Henry, who had also organized a confederacy of Irish chiefs to aid him in his enterprise, by making a descent upon the Scottish coast; but the country, nevertheless, prepared to make a vigorous resistance. The sword, however, was not drawn, after all; a negotiation took place between the two kings, and a peace was concluded at Newcastle (13th August), by which Alexander agreed always to bear good faith and love to his dear and liege lord, Henry, King of England, and never to enter into alliance with the enemies of Henry or of his heirs, unless they should unjustly aggrieve him.[2]

After this the Scottish king was engaged in war with his unruly vassal, Angus, Lord of Argyle, when he was taken ill, and died in the island of Kerarry, near the Sound of Mull, on the 8th of July, 1249, in the fifty-first year of his age, and thirty-fifth of his reign. Alexander,

like most of the other Scottish kings of those times, stood up throughout his reign for the independence of the national church. Although a favourer of the clergy, he does not appear to have gone into any extravagant expenditure for the aggrandizement of their order. He founded, indeed, no fewer than eight monasteries for the Dominicans or Black Friars; and Boece supposes that his partiality to these mendicants may have been occasioned by his having seen their founder, St. Dominic, in France, about the year 1217. "The sight of a living saint," observes Lord Hailes, "may have made an impression on his young mind; but perhaps he considered the mendicant friars as the cheapest ecclesiastics: his revenues could not supply the costly institution of Cistercians and canons regular, in which his great-grandfather, David I., took delight."

Alexander was succeeded on the throne by his only son, Alexander III., who was born at Roxburgh on the 4th of September, 1241, and was now consequently only in his ninth year. There was reason to apprehend that the King of England might endeavour to take advantage of this occasion to renew his attempt against the independence of the kingdom; and, therefore, by the patriotic advice of William Comyn, Earl of Monteith, no time was lost in proceeding to the coronation of the young king. The ceremony took place at Scone on the 13th of July, the Bishop of St. Andrews knighting the king as well as placing the crown on his head.

It would serve no useful end to load our pages with any detail of the intricate, and in great part, very imperfectly intelligible struggles of adverse factions that make up the history of the kingdom during this as during every other minority in those times. It is sufficient to state that at the head of one of the two great contending parties, was the powerful family of the Comyns, of which name it is said there were at this time in Scotland no fewer than thirty-two knights, several of whom were barons; the Baliols, among others, were adherents of this party. Among their most distinguished opponents were the Earl of March and Dunbar, the Earl of Strathern, the Earl of Carrick, the Bruces, the steward of Scotland, and Alan Durward, who held the office of great justiciary, and was also one of the most distinguished soldiers of the age. But many of the nobility were constantly changing sides, according to the course and apparent chances of the

---

[2] Nisi nos injuste gravent. Dr. Lingard describes this treaty as "an arrangement by which, though he eluded the express recognition of feudal dependence, he (Alexander) seems to have conceded to Henry the substance of his demand." In fact "the express recognition of feudal dependence" was not at all eluded by Alexander; it was made in the most distinct terms, but it was not made for the kingdom of Scotland, and therefore it was Henry, not Alexander, who conceded the point in dispute.

[1] Hailes, Ann. of Scot. 1. 188-190; Tytler, Hist. of Scot. 1. 4-6.

contest. The King of England also soon found a fair pretence for interfering in Scottish affairs, by giving his daughter Margaret in marriage to Alexander, according to an agreement which had been entered into soon after the births of the prince and the princess. Although neither party was yet quite eleven years old, the nuptials were celebrated at York with great magnificence on the 26th of December, 1251.

On this occasion Alexander, according to custom, did homage to Henry for his English possessions; but when the latter demanded homage also for the kingdom of Scotland, the young Scottish sovereign said "that he had been invited to York to marry the princess of England, not to treat of affairs of state; and that he could not take a step so important without the knowledge and approbation of his parliament." It was agreed, however, that Henry, in consideration apparently of his natural interest in the welfare of his son-in-law, should send a person in whom he placed confidence to Scotland, who might act in concert with the Scottish guardians of the young king. He sent, accordingly, Geoffrey of Langley, keeper of the royal forests, a man who had already acquired the worst reputation in England by the severity with which he exercised the powers of his odious office; but the Scottish barons, finding his insolence intolerable, soon compelled him to leave the country.

In 1255, we find the English king despatching a new mission to Scotland under pretence of inquiring into certain grievances complained of by the queen his daughter. At this time Robert de Ros and John de Baliol, two noblemen of the Comyn party, appear to have been at the head of the government under the name of regents. Queen Margaret complained that she was confined in the castle of Edinburgh—a sad and solitary place—without verdure, and, by reason of its vicinity to the sea, unwholesome; that she was not permitted to make excursions through the kingdom, nor to choose her female attendants; and that, although both she and her husband had by this time completed their fourteenth year, they were still excluded from each other's society. By a scheme concerted between Henry and the party opposed to the Comyns, the Earl of March, Durward, and other leaders of that party soon after this contrived to surprise the castle of Edinburgh, and to get possession of the king and queen. They were immediately conveyed to the north of England, where Henry was with an army; and at last, in a meeting of the two kings at Roxburgh (20th September, 1255), a new plan of government was settled, to subsist for seven years, that is, till Alexander should have attained the age of twenty-one, by which all the Comyns were deprived of office, and the

Earls of Fife, Dunbar, Strathern, and Carrick, Alexander the steward of Scotland, Robert de Bruce, Alan Durward, and other principal persons of the same faction, were appointed regents of the kingdom and guardians of the king and queen.

The settlement appears to have been maintained for about two years; but in 1257, a counter revolution was effected through the junction with the Comyns of Mary de Couci, Alexander's mother who had married John de Brienne, son of the titular King of Jerusalem, and had lately returne l from abroad, animated with all her old hereditary hatred of the English influence, and strengthened by her new alliance and by the favour and countenance of the pope. The lately expelled faction now suddenly rose in arms, seized the king and queen at Kinross, and so completely carried everything before them, that the principal adherents of the English interests found it necessary to save themselves by flight. There can be no doubt that, with whatever justice or by whatever means, the Comyns contrived to make theirs appear to be the patriotic cause, and to gain, at least for the moment, the popular voice. They probably made use of the old cry of independence, and worked upon the sensitive national jealousy of England with good effect. Even the king, now that he was in their hands, was of course compelled to act along with them, and submit to be their instrument. They put him at the head of their forces, and marched towards the English border, where it would appear that the adherents of the late government had rallied and collected their strength. No contest of arms, however, took place; the dispute was eventually settled by negotiation; and it was agreed that while the chief power should remain in the hands of the Comyns and the queen-dowager, to six regents of this party should be added four of the members of the late government. Mary de Couci and her husband were placed at the head of this new regency.

The coalition thus formed seems to have substantially subsisted till the king came of age, and took the management of affairs into his own hands, although, shortly after the new government was established, the Comyns lost their great leader, Walter, Earl of Monteith, poisoned, as was suspected, by his countess. In 1260, on the Queen of Scots becoming pregnant, she and her husband were permitted to go to her father in London, Henry engaging that neither the king nor his attendants should be required to treat of state affairs during their visit, and also making oath that he would not detain either the queen or her child, if her delivery should take place in England. In February, 1261, the Queen of Scots was delivered at Windsor of a daughter, who was named Margaret.

The year 1263 is the most memorable in the reign of Alexander. The Earl of Ross and other northern chiefs had, at the instigation of the Scottish king, invaded the Hebrides or Western Islands, which were under the dominion of Norway, and had signalized their descent, according to the Norwegian chroniclers, by the most frightful excesses of savage warfare. Haco, the Norwegian king, immediately prepared for vengeance. Having collected a great fleet, he sailed from Herlover in the beginning of July. The Orkney Islands, which, although formerly belonging to Norway, had been lately compelled to acknowledge the sovereignty of Scotland, were his first destination. Anchoring in the bay of Ronaldsvoe (now Ronaldshay), the formidable armament remained there for some weeks, during which the inhabitants, both of the islands and of the opposite mainland, were compelled to supply it with provisions and to pay tribute. It is recorded in the Norse chronicle of the expedition, that while the fleet lay at Ronaldsvoe "a great darkness drew over the sun, so that only a little ring was bright round his orb;" and it is found that the remarkable phenomenon of an annular eclipse must have been seen at Ronaldsvoe this year on the 5th of August. Such confirmations seem to revivify the long-buried past, and make its history read like a narrative of events of our own day. Haco now sailed for the south, and being joined as he proceeded by his allies, Magnus, the Lord of Man, and various Hebridean chiefs, he found himself at the head of above 100 sail, most of them vessels of considerable size. Dividing his force, he sent one powerful squadron to ravage the Mull of Cantyre; another, to make a descent on the Isle of Bute. The latter soon compelled the Scottish garrison of the castle of Rothesay, in that island, to surrender. In the meantime, Haco himself entered the Frith of Clyde, and anchored between the mainland and the Isle of Arran. Additional accessions had by this time increased his fleet to 160 sail. The Scottish government now attempted to avert the danger by negotiation: the abandonment of all claim to the Hebrides was offered by Alexander; but to these terms Haco would not listen. Some time, however, was thus gained, which was in various ways advantageous to the Scots and detrimental to their invaders. It allowed the former to improve their preparations for defence; it embarrassed the latter by a growing difficulty in obtaining provisions, and it exposed their fleet, upon a strange coast, to the hazards of the stormy season of the year that was fast approaching. Many of the inhabitants of the neighbouring country meanwhile had retreated for safety to the islets in Loch Lomond. There, however, they were soon attacked by a division of the invading force under the command of the King of Man, who, first sailing to the head of Loch Long, and plundering the shores as they passed, then dragged their boats across the neck of land that divides the two lakes. A devastating expedition into Stirlingshire followed. But now the heavens began to fight against them. One gale destroyed ten of their ships that lay in Loch Long; and soon after, on Monday, the 1st of October, a tempest of tremendous violence from the south-west attacked the main squadron lying under the command of Haco in the Clyde, and tearing nearly every ship from its moorings, after casting several of them on shore, drove the rest, mostly dismasted or otherwise disabled, up the Channel. The Scottish forces collected in the neighbourhood immediately fell upon the crews of the vessels that were stranded; but the Norwegians defended themselves with great valour; and assistance having been sent to them by Haco, when the wind was somewhat abated, they succeeded in driving off their assailants. As soon as daylight appeared, Haco, who had collected his shattered ships off the village of Largs, landed at the head of a strong force for the protection of two transports that had been among the vessels cast ashore the preceding afternoon, and which the Scots had attempted to plunder during the night. This movement may be said to have commenced what is called the battle of Largs. The Scottish army, led by Alexander, and the steward of Scotland, now came down from the surrounding high grounds. The handful of Norwegians, drawn up in three divisions, one of which occupied a small hill, while the other two were stationed on the shore, were greatly outnumbered by this force; and Haco, who as the engagement was about to commence, was, although with much difficulty, prevailed upon by his officers to row back to the ships for further aid. But he had scarcely got on board when another furious storm came on, and rendered the landing of more men for the present impossible. In the meantime the Scots had attacked the most advanced body of the Norwegians, who were soon obliged to flee in confusion. The rout immediately became general; numbers of the Norwegians threw themselves into their boats and attempted to regain their ships; the rest were driven along the shore amid showers of arrows from their pursuing enemy. Still they repeatedly rallied, and, turning round upon their pursuers, made an obstinate stand at every point where the ground favoured them. In this way, although still galled by the Scots hovering on their rear, they seem to have at length converted their flight into a slow and comparatively orderly retreat. Towards night a reinforcement from the ships having, notwithstanding the storm, which still continued effected a landing by extraordinary efforts, the foreigners, if we may trust to their own account, even made a general attack upon the Scottish army, and, after a short resistance, succeeded in driving it back. They then re-embarked in their boats and regained their ships. But on the water the elements had been doing their destructive work even with more effect than human rage on land. Haco's magnificent navy was now reduced to a few shattered vessels. The Norwegian king sailed away to the island of Arran, and from thence through a course of stormy weather to Orkney, which he did not reach till the 29th of October. He proceeded no farther on his homeward voyage. An illness seized upon him, under which he lingered for some weeks, and at last expired on the 15th of December.[1]

The battle of Largs is the great event of the reign of Alexander. The victory was among the most important the Scots ever won. It was their last conflict with the pirate kings. After negotiations which lasted for nearly three years, a peace was concluded with Norway, by which both the Hebrides and the Isle of Man, and all other islands in the western and southern seas, of which that power might have hitherto held or claimed the dominion, were made over in full sovereignty to Scotland. The Western Islands were never afterwards withdrawn from the Scottish rule.

There is little more to relate under the reign of Alexander. He was present with his queen, and many of his nobility, at the coronation of Edward I., in 1274, and on that occasion did homage, according to custom, for his English possessions. In 1278 he performed this ceremony a second time, declaring, according to the record preserved in the Close Rolls, that he became the liege man of his lord, King Edward of England, against all people. This was substantially the same acknowledgment that Alexander II. had made to Henry III. in 1244. It was no admission of Edward's claim of feudal superiority over Scotland, as is conclusively proved, if there could be any doubt on the subject, by the sequel of the record, which expressly states that Edward "received it, saving his right and claim to homage for the kingdom of Scotland, when it shall please him to bring it forward."

The government of Alexander, after he took the management of affairs into his own hands, made him universally beloved by his people; and peace and plenty blessed the land in his time. But clouds and storms were soon to succeed this sunshine.

Alexander had lost his queen, Margaret of England, in 1275; but, besides the daughter already mentioned, she had left him a son, named Alexander, born at Jedburgh on the 21st of January, 1264: David, a younger son, had died in his boyhood. In 1281 the Princess Margaret was married to Eric, King of Norway, and the following year the Prince of Scotland, now a youth of eighteen, was united to Margaret, daughter of Guy, Earl of Flanders. At this time the king himself, as yet only in his forty-first year, might reasonably have counted on a much longer reign; the alliances which he had formed for his children promised to enable him to transmit his sceptre to a line of descendants; and the people seemed entitled to look forward to the continuance of the present peace and prosperity of the country for many years. By a singular succession of calamities all these fair hopes were, one after the other, rapidly extinguished. First, in the latter part of the year 1283 died the Queen of Norway, leaving only an infant daughter. The death of Queen Margaret was followed by that of her brother, the Prince of Scotland, on the 28th of January, 1284. No time was lost by Alexander in taking the measures for the settlement of the succession which these events rendered necessary. On the 5th of February the parliament was assembled at Scone, when the estates of the kingdom solemnly bound themselves, failing Alexander and any children he might yet have, to acknowledge for their sovereign the Norwegian princess—"the Maiden of Norway," as she is called by the old writers. The following year (15th April, 1285), Alexander married Joleta, the young and beautiful daughter of the Count de Dreux. But within a year after his marriage, on the 16th of March, 1286, as Alexander was riding in a dark night between Kinghorn and Burntisland, his horse stumbled with him over a high cliff, at a place now known by the name of Kingswood End, when he was killed on the spot.

The loss of this excellent king would, in any circumstances, have been a heavy calamity to his country, but the blow could not have been received at a more unfortunate moment than the present.[2] A long minority was now the least evil the kingdom had to dread, and that evil was certain if a worse should not take its place. The

---

[1] See *The Norwegian Account of Haco's Expedition against Scotland*, in Islandic and English, with notes; by the Rev. James Johnstone, A.M., 12mo, 1782; and "Observations on the Norwegian Expedition against Scotland, in the year 1263, and on some previous events which gave occasion to that War," by John Dillon, Esq., in *Transactions of the Society of the Antiquaries of Scotland*, vol. ii. 4to. Edin. 1822, pp. 350-407.

[2] "But with the demise of Alexander III. without issue commenced warfare and anarchy which lasted, with little interruption, during 300 years. In that odious period of wretchedness we hear the monks incessantly cry out *Diram guerram!* Oppressive war! It became the very object of these hostilities, not to improve but to waste, not to save but to destroy. Agriculture was ruined; and the very necessaries of life were lost, when the principal lords had scarcely a bed to lie on."—Chalmers' *Caledonia*, vol. ii. p. 142.

life of an infant, in a foreign country, alone stood between the nation and all the sure confusion and miseries of a disputed succession. The first proceeding of the estates was to appoint a regency, at a meeting held at Scone, on the 11th of April. But scarcely, it would appear, had the throne of Queen Margaret been thus set up, when it began to be undermined by plots and secret treason. The rule of a female sovereign was new to the country; the attempt to transmit the crown to a daughter had already failed in England, even when made in the most favourable circumstances by Henry I.

The main strength of Margaret's cause lay in there being no other certain heir to the throne if she was set aside. The choice was between her and a disputed succession. Had it not been for this, it is more than probable that the settlement in her favour would have been wholly disregarded after Alexander's death. The next heir, if a male of mature age, and a native of the country, would at once have been preferred to the foreign female infant. Even as matters stood there was, it would seem, one party which had already formed the design of displacing Queen Margaret in favour of its own chief. Robert de Brus or Bruce, Lord of Annandale and Cleveland, was the son of Isabella, one of the three daughters of David, Earl of Huntingdon, the brother of William the Lion. He and a number of his adherents, including some of the principal of the Scottish nobility, held a meeting on the 20th of September, 1286, at Turnberry Castle, in Ayrshire, the seat of Bruce's son, Robert Bruce, called Earl of Carrick in right of his wife, and there entered into an agreement, by which they bound themselves to adhere to one another on all occasions, and against all persons, saving their allegiance to the King of England, and to him who should gain the kingdom of Scotland as the rightful heir of the late king.[1] The intention of the parties to this bond would appear to have been to obtain the crown for Bruce, by the aid of the King of England, whom, with that view, they were prepared to acknowledge as lord paramount of Scotland. Edward, however, had, for the present, another scheme of his own, with which this of theirs could not be suffered to interfere.

Two of the chief members of the regency, the Earl of Buchan and the Earl of Fife, died towards the close of the year 1288 (the Earl of Fife was murdered); and from this time violent divisions arose in the government, and all things began to tend to confusion and anarchy. One account is that the estates of Scotland now made a formal application to the English king for his advice and mediation towards composing the troubles of the kingdom. But this statement does not rest upon any certain authority. In the end of the year 1289, however, Eric, King of Norway, opened a negotiation with Edward on the affairs of his infant daughter and her kingdom; and at Edward's request the Scottish regency sent three of its members to take part in a solemn deliberation which was appointed to be held at Salisbury. It was here agreed that the young queen should be immediately conveyed either to her own dominions or to England, Edward engaging in the latter case to deliver her, on demand, to the Scottish nation, provided that good order should be previously established in Scotland, so that she might reside there with safety to her person. No mention was made in this convention of an English match for Margaret, but it appears that Edward had already obtained a dispensation from Rome for her marriage to her cousin, his eldest son. A report to that effect was very soon after spread in Scotland; whereupon the estates immediately assembled at Bridgeham, a village on the Tweed, and from thence addressed a letter to the English king, expressing, in warm terms, their gratification at the rumour that had reached them, and beseeching him to inform them if it was true. "If it is," they concluded, "we on our part heartily consent to the alliance, not doubting that you will agree to such reasonable conditions as we shall propose to your council." They wrote at the same time to the King of Norway, pressing him to send his daughter instantly to England.

Some months after this (on the 18th of July, 1290), a treaty was concluded at the same place, by which everything in regard to the proposed marriage was finally arranged. Many stipulations were made for securing the integrity and independence of the Scottish kingdom; and all points, both of substance and of form, relating to that matter, were regulated with elaborate scrupulosity. But the event of a few weeks rendered all the painstaking and onthtaking of no effect. The Maiden of Norway having at length set sail for Britain, fell sick on her passage, and landing on one of the Orkney Islands, died there about the end of September: she was in her eighth year.

---
[1] Tytler, *Hist. of Scot.*, i. 65.

SOME WORKS PUBLISHED BY

BLACKIE & SON, Limited,

LONDON, GLASGOW, EDINBURGH, AND DUBLIN.

A LIBRARY IN ITSELF.

THE POPULAR ENCYCLOPEDIA.
NEW ISSUE, REVISED.

A GENERAL DICTIONARY OF ARTS, SCIENCES, LITERATURE, BIOGRAPHY, AND HISTORY.

EDITED BY

CHARLES ANNANDALE, M.A., LL.D.,
Editor of Ogilvie's "Imperial Dictionary of the English Language."

Profusely Illustrated with Engravings.

To be completed in Fourteen handsome Volumes, super-royal 8vo, bound in rich cloth, red edges, at 12s. each.

The POPULAR ENCYCLOPEDIA is a perfect library in itself, superseding, practically, the necessity of having recourse to a large number of books on different topics, and furnishing, at moderate cost, a complete body of information on all subjects.

In its survey of human knowledge it will compare in point of fulness of detail with the best works of its size, while in its clear concise style, and in its avoidance of technicalities, the needs of the general reader have been constantly consulted.

It is a Universal Gazetteer.
It is a Universal History.
It is a Biographical Dictionary.
It is a Commercial Dictionary.
It is a Dictionary of Political Theories and Facts.
It is a Dictionary of the Sciences.

It is a Dictionary of Philosophy.
It is a Dictionary of Theology.
It is a Dictionary of the Fine Arts.
It is a Dictionary of the Practical Arts and Handicrafts.
It is a Dictionary of General Information.

This work has been aptly called a Conversations-Lexicon, since in it a man has the clue to all topics of interest and conversation in all professions, trades, and walks of life, and is enabled by it to equip himself to play a many-sided and intelligent part in the world.

It is A BOOK FOR THE HOUSEHOLD, being of value and interest to all its members, old and young alike. It is in itself a liberal education, and, indeed, the best POPULAR EDUCATOR, and it will be found of the highest service to the younger members of families in the prosecution of their studies, and especially in the preparation of their written exercises.

It abounds with pictorial illustrations, many printed in colours, which extend to above 200 pages of Engravings, including over 2000 separate figures. In addition, there is a series of coloured Maps, forming a valuable accompaniment to the geographical and historical articles.

NEW EDITION—REVISED AND GREATLY AUGMENTED.

BLACKIE'S
COMPREHENSIVE HISTORY OF ENGLAND.
CIVIL AND MILITARY, RELIGIOUS, INTELLECTUAL, AND SOCIAL.
FROM THE EARLIEST PERIOD TO THE PRESENT TIME.

ILLUSTRATED BY ABOVE ELEVEN HUNDRED ENGRAVINGS IN THE TEXT, AND SIXTY-FIVE FINELY ENGRAVED PLATES.

BESIDES THE NUMEROUS ILLUSTRATIONS PRINTED IN THE TEXT, EACH PART WILL CONTAIN TWO OR THREE SEPARATE PAGE ENGRAVINGS, ILLUSTRATING IMPORTANT HISTORICAL EVENTS, PORTRAITS OF SOVEREIGNS, &c.

The work will be completed in 26 parts, 2s. each; or 8 divisional-volumes, super-royal 8vo, handsomely bound in cloth, price 8s. 6d. each.

There is no man imbued with even the smallest spark of patriotism who does not desire to know the story of his country, and the career of those remarkable men who, in bygone years, helped to mould the people into a nation, and to build up those two most marvellous fabrics of modern times, The British Empire and The British Constitution. The tale is a wondrous one; fascinating as a romance; full of chivalrous exploits, and of high and lofty example for every condition of life.

THE COMPREHENSIVE HISTORY OF ENGLAND in telling this story will command the appreciative interest of the general reader, and become not only a useful book of reference but an entertaining and instructive work for the family.

A COMPLETE HISTORY OF THE ENGLISH PEOPLE.—Not only political, naval, and military, but also civil, religious, industrial, agricultural, and mercantile, presenting picturesque descriptions of the aspects of the various classes of society in successive periods; concise accounts of the progress of commerce, industries, and manufactures; and of the results arising from inventions and discoveries; sketches of the advance of literature and the fine arts; and the spread of general enlightenment.

ELEVEN HUNDRED ENGRAVINGS.—The Eleven Hundred Engravings, printed in the text, have been carefully prepared, with a view to the real elucidation of the History. They comprise Illustrations of the Dwellings, the Shipping, the Armour, Dress, Manners and Customs, and Utensils of our Ancestors at various periods; Views of Historical Sites, Buildings, and Monuments; Maps and Plans of Battles, Battlefields, Forts, Towns, &c.; Portraits and Statues of Illustrious Persons.

NEW AND REVISED EDITION.

The Casquet of Literature:

A SELECTION IN PROSE AND POETRY from the works of the best Authors. Edited, with Biographical and Literary Notes, by CHARLES GIBBON, Author of "Robin Gray", and revised by Miss MARY CHRISTIE. To be published in 6 volumes, bound in cloth, gilt elegant, with olivine edges, price 7s. 6d. per volume; also in 18 parts, price 2s. each.

The CASQUET OF LITERATURE will contain more than 1000 characteristic Selections from the writings of the most popular authors, accompanied by about 400 Biographical and Literary Notes. The stress of modern life leaves scanty leisure for recreation, yet in the evenings when the fireside is the only comfortable place, one needs something to refresh the jaded spirits, and obliterate for the time the worries of the day. For these purposes, what better than a good, breezy, entertaining book? Practically a guide to the best English literature, illustrated by a series of exquisite drawings.

600 of the greatest writers in the English tongue will be represented, including Tennyson, Browning, George Eliot, Addison, R. Louis Stevenson, S. R. Crockett, Ruskin, Andrew Lang, Douglas Jerrold, Mark Twain, J. M. Barrie, Anthony Hope. In fact, a book in which the reader is provided with the best work of poets, novelists, essayists, humorists, story-tellers, and artists. Material for desultory reading—the most delightful of all—of a lifetime. A casquet of inexhaustible treasure, inasmuch as beautiful thoughts and exquisite, like diamonds, never lose their brilliance or charm.

Blackie & Son's Publications. 3

DESCRIPTIVE ATLAS OF THE WORLD
AND GENERAL GEOGRAPHY.

COMPRISING

ABOVE ONE HUNDRED CAREFULLY EXECUTED MAPS; A DETAILED DESCRIPTION OF THE WORLD, PROFUSELY ILLUSTRATED; AND A COPIOUS INDEX OF PLACES.

PREPARED UNDER THE SUPERVISION OF

W. G. BLACKIE, Ph.D., LL.D.,
Fellow of the Royal Geographical Societies, London and Edinburgh.

To be completed in 12 divisions at 5s. each, forming a handsome volume, 16 inches × 12 inches.

The ATLAS will consist of sixty-four sheets of Maps, comprising seventy-five numbered maps and above thirty inset maps, making in all above ONE HUNDRED MAPS beautifully printed in colours, prepared from the most recent and most authoritative materials available.

While the older countries of the world will all be fully shown, special prominence will be given to Great Britain and its world-wide possessions, and also to the regions recently opened up by the enterprise of adventurous travellers.

Two of the maps are worthy of special notice. The Commercial Chart of the World, showing existing and available fields of commerce; and The British Empire at one view, showing all the possessions at home and abroad, drawn to one scale, and thereby enabling their relative size to be clearly appreciated.

The GENERAL GEOGRAPHY which accompanies the maps forms a very important section of the work. It supplies information geographical, historical, statistical, commercial, and descriptive, of the countries and regions of the world, and has been prepared from recent and authoritative sources. Its pages are enriched by a series of Pictorial Illustrations, consisting of striking views of natural scenery, remarkable edifices, town and river scenes, and picturesque groups of natives, and of animal life.

As a useful adjunct both to the Maps and the General Geography there will be given a Pronouncing Vocabulary of Geographical Names. In addition to this, an Extensive Index of Places will form a very useful section of the work.

To be completed in 14 parts, super-royal 8vo, at 2s. each; or in 4 divisions, stiff paper cover, at 7s. each, forming one handsome volume; or in 4 divisions, cloth, at 9s. each.

The Household Physician:

A FAMILY GUIDE TO THE PRESERVATION OF HEALTH AND TO THE DOMESTIC TREATMENT OF AILMENTS AND DISEASE. By J. M'GREGOR-ROBERTSON, M.B., C.M. (Hon.). With an Introduction by Professor M'KENDRICK, M.D., LL.D., F.R.S., Glasgow University. Illustrated by about 400 figures in the text, and a series of 19 Engraved Plates, many of them printed in colours.

This work is written in the simplest possible language, and includes full information on the conditions of health, and on the ordinary means, as regards food, clothing, exercise, &c., by which health may be maintained in the infant as well as in the full-grown person.

The book treats of the human body in health, and the various changes produced by disease. On Hygiene, or the conditions of health as regards food, drink, clothing, exercise, &c., and the rules to be observed for the promotion of health, both of individuals and communities. An explanation of the nature and mode of action of drugs and other remedial agents. On methods of dealing with Accidents and Emergencies, and on various ailments requiring surgical treatment. Also a chapter on Sick-nursing, and an Appendix containing recipes for Invalid Cookery and medical Prescriptions.

In 15 parts, super-royal 8vo, 2s. each; or 4 vols., cloth elegant, burnished edges, 9s. 6d. each.

NEW EDITION, Continued to 1890.

Gladstone and His Contemporaries:

Sixty Years of Social and Political Progress. By THOMAS ARCHER, F.R.H.S., Author of "Pictures and Royal Portraits," &c. Illustrated by a series of 34 authentic and beautifully executed Portraits.

"*This work is not so much a biography of Mr. Gladstone as a political History of England during his lifetime. It is a book which has evidently been compiled with no ordinary pains and care, and with a praiseworthy desire to be impartial.*"—Daily News.

"*It is probably true that the biographical form of history is the best in dealing with times within the memory of men yet living. The life of a man, prominent in affairs during a particular period, may be taken as a central point round which matters of more general history group themselves.*"—Standard.

THE HENRY IRVING SHAKESPEARE.—SUBSCRIPTION EDITION.

The Works of Shakespeare.

EDITED BY

HENRY IRVING AND FRANK A. MARSHALL.

With a General Introduction and Life of Shakespeare by Professor EDWARD DOWDEN, and nearly six hundred illustrations from designs by GORDON BROWNE and other Artists. To be completed in 25 parts, super-royal 8vo, 3s. each; or 8 volumes, cloth elegant, 10s. 6d. each, with gilt edges, 11s. 6d. each.

The universal popularity of the works of our GREAT DRAMATIST has induced the publishers to issue a sumptuous edition, of such comprehensive excellence that it is fitted at once to meet the requirements of the general reader, the lover of fine books, and the student of Shakespeare. This important edition in many respects has never been surpassed.

** Every subscriber for this edition of Shakespeare's Works will be presented, on the completion of his copy of the book, with an impression of the admirable PORTRAIT OF HENRY IRVING AS HAMLET, from the painting by EDWIN LONG, R.A., executed in Photogravure in the most finished manner by Boussod Valadon et Cie. (Goupil), of Paris. The size of the engraved surface is 19½ × 13½ inches, and with margin suitable for framing 27 × 20 inches.

"*On the care with which the text itself of the plays has been prepared we have nothing but praise to bestow. . . . The general result of this care and labour is, however, so good that we must congratulate all concerned in it; and in particular we must congratulate the publishers of the work on one especial feature which could hardly fail to ensure its success as a popular edition—it is profusely illustrated by Mr. Gordon Browne, whose charming designs, executed in facsimile, give it an artistic value superior, in our judgment, to any illustrated edition of Shakespeare with which we are acquainted.*"—The Athenæum.

"*This handsomely printed edition aims at being popular and practical. Add to these advantages Mr. Gordon Browne's illustrations, and enough has been said to recommend an edition which will win public recognition by its unique and serviceable qualities.*"—The Spectator.

In 17 parts, extra demy 8vo, at 2s. each; or 5 volumes, cloth elegant, gilt edges, at 8s. 6d. each.

NEW PICTORIAL EDITION.

The Works of Robert Burns,

With a series of Authentic Pictorial Illustrations, Marginal Glossary, numerous Notes, and Appendixes. Also the life of Burns by J. G. LOCKHART, and Essays on the Genius, Character, and Writings of Burns, by THOMAS CARLYLE and PROFESSOR WILSON. Edited by CHARLES ANNANDALE, M.A., LL.D., editor of the "Imperial Dictionary", &c.

In this edition of Burns his writings are presented in two sections, the one containing the poetry, the other the prose. Marginal explanations of Scottish words accompany each piece that requires such aid, enabling anyone at a glance to apprehend the meaning of even the most difficult passages.

The Pictorial Illustrations, which consist of Fifty-six beautiful Landscapes and Portraits, engraved on steel in the most finished manner, form a very distinctive feature of this edition. The Landscapes embrace the principal scenes identified with the Life and Writings of the Poet, and are from pictures painted by D. O. HILL, R.S.A.

Altogether in no other edition is so much light thrown from all points of view upon Burns the poet and Burns the man, and it may therefore be said to be complete in the best sense of the word.

In 18 parts, super-royal 4to, at 2s. each; in 6 divisions at 6s. each; and also in 2 volumes, large 4to, elegantly bound in cloth, gilt edges, price 24s. each.

The Natural History of Animals

(CLASS MAMMALIA—ANIMALS WHICH SUCKLE THEIR YOUNG), In Word and Picture. By CARL VOGT, Professor of Natural History, Geneva, and FRIEDRICH SPECHT, Stuttgart. Translated and Edited by GEO. G. CHISHOLM, M.A., B.Sc. Illustrated by above 300 fine Engravings on wood.

This account of the animals comprised in the class Mammalia has a decidedly popular character—not through lack of scientific value, but because the author presents the facts in an attractive form, and studies to smooth the path of those who can give only their leisure hours to learning the results of scientific research. The author's style is above all things clear, simple, and direct, and where occasion offers, lively and animated.

The artist has portrayed in the most spirited manner the animals as they appear in the varied circumstances of real life, in quest of their prey, caressing their young ones, or sporting with their fellows. The engravings have been executed in the most careful and finished manner, under Mr. Specht's own direction.

In 19 parts, 2s. each; or 6 divisional-volumes, super-royal 8vo, cloth elegant, 8s. 6d. each.

A History of the Scottish People

From the Earliest to the Latest Times. By Rev. THOMAS THOMSON and CHARLES ANNANDALE, M.A., LL.D. With 40 Original Designs by W. H. MARGETSON, ALFRED PEARSE, WALTER PAGET, GORDON BROWNE, and other eminent artists.

It is a full and detailed History of Scotland from the Earliest Times to the Latest.
It is a History of the Scottish People, their manners, customs, and modes of living at the various successive periods.
It is a History of Religion and Ecclesiastical Affairs in Scotland.
It is a History of Scotland's progress in Commerce, Industry, Arts, Science, and Literature.

In 14 parts, 2s. each; or 4 vols., super-royal 8vo, cloth elegant, 8s. 6d. each.

The Cabinet of Irish Literature.

A Selection from the Works of the Chief Poets, Orators, and Prose Writers of Ireland. Edited, with biographical sketches and literary notices, by CHARLES A. READ, F.R.H.S., author of "Tales and Stories of Irish Life," "Stories from the Ancient Classics," &c. Illustrated by a series of 32 admirable Portraits in mesochrome, specially prepared for this work.

The Publishers aim in this Work to supply a standard work in which the genius, the fire, the pathos, the humour, and the eloquence of Irish Literature are adequately represented. The specimens selected, which are arranged chronologically from the earliest to the present time, will both present a historical view of Irish Literature, and enable the reader to judge of the individual style and particular merit of each author, while to those not critically disposed the infinite variety presented in this convenient collective form will afford both instruction and amusement.

In 12 parts, demy 8vo, 2s. each; and 4 half-vols., cloth elegant, 7s. 6d. each; or gilt edges, at 8s. 6d. each.

The Poets and Poetry of Scotland:

FROM THE EARLIEST TO THE PRESENT TIME. Comprising Characteristic Selections from the works of the more Noteworthy Scottish Poets, with Biographical and Critical Notices. By JAMES GRANT WILSON. Illustrated by Portraits.

In the preparation of this Work the first object has been to present, not a collection of the ballads or songs, or the writings of the poets of any particular district of the country, but a comprehensive view of the poetry of Scotland in all its forms from the earliest to the present time. Besides original contributions and poems by living authors, the Work will contain poems, hitherto unpublished, by ROBERT BURNS, WILLIAM TENNANT, Mrs. GRANT of Laggan, JAMES HYSLOP, HENRY SCOTT RIDDELL, JOHN LEYDEN, WILLIAM MILLER, and others.
The Illustrations will consist of Twenty-four life-like Portraits, engraved on steel in the most finished manner.

In 15 parts, 2s. each; or two handsome vols., super-royal 8vo, cloth, 36s.

The Works of the Ettrick Shepherd,

IN POETRY AND PROSE. Centenary Edition. With a Biographical Memoir by the Rev. THOMAS THOMSON. Illustrated by Forty-four fine Engravings on steel, from Original Drawings by D. O. Hill, R.S.A., K. Halsewelle, A.R.S.A., W. Small, and J. Lawson.

Hogg's Works comprise *Tales in Prose*, illustrative of Border history and superstitions. They comprise likewise Poems of great imaginative power and descriptive beauty; Ballads full of humour and touches of tender pathos; and Songs which, besides being universally popular when first made public, are still cherished as among the finest productions of our native lyric muse.

"*Certainly we may now recognise him as the only one of Burns' followers who deserves to be named in the same breath.*"—Press.

To be completed in four half-volumes, super-royal 8vo, at 12s. 6d. each; or in twelve parts at 3s. 6d. each.

The Steam Engine:

A TREATISE ON STEAM ENGINES AND BOILERS. Comprising the Principles and Practice of the Combustion of Fuel, the Economical Generation of Steam, the Construction of Steam Boilers; and the Principles, Construction, and Performance of Steam Engines—Stationary, Portable, Locomotive, and Marine, exemplified in Engines and Boilers of Recent Date. By DANIEL KINNEAR CLARK, M.Inst.C.E., M.I.M.E.; Author of "Railway Machinery"; "A Manual of Rules, Tables, and Data for Mechanical Engineers"; &c. &c. Illustrated by above 1300 Figures in the Text, and a Series of Folding Plates drawn to Scale.

This work provides a comprehensive, accurate, and clearly written text-book, fully abreast of all the recent developments in the principles and practice of the Steam Engine.

Written in full view of the great advances of modern times, it expounds the principles and describes the practice exemplified in the construction and use of Steam Engines and Boilers, in all their varieties.

In 20 parts, 2s. each; or 5 divisions, royal 4to, 8s. each; or one vol., cloth, gilt edges, 42s.

Suggestions in Design;

A comprehensive series of Original Sketches in various Styles of Ornament, arranged for application in the Decorative and Constructive Arts, comprising 102 plates, containing more than 1100 distinct and separate "suggestions", by JOHN LEIGHTON, F.S.A. To which is added descriptive and historical letterpress, with above 200 explanatory engravings, by JAMES KELLAWAY COLLING, F.R.I.B.A.

These suggestions are throughout *original*, designed in the spirit, and with the proper art feeling of the various styles to which they severally belong, and are the accumulated result of long and arduous studies, extending over many years of investigation and thought.

This work will be found to be eminently suited to the wants of nearly every one who has occasion for decoration in whatever form;—to the worker in stone, wood, metal, ivory, glass, and leather—to the house-painter, decorator, &c. &c.

In 20 parts, super-royal quarto, 2s. each; or 8 divisions, 5s. each.

The Carpenter and Joiner's Assistant.

By JAMES NEWLANDS, late Borough Engineer of Liverpool. *New and Improved Edition.* Being a Comprehensive Treatise on the selection, preparation, and strength of Materials, and the mechanical principles of Framing, with their applications in Carpentry, Joinery, and Hand Railing; also, a complete treatise on Lines; and an Illustrated Glossary of Terms used in Architecture and Building. Illustrated by above One Hundred Engraved Plates, containing above Nine Hundred Figures; and above Seven Hundred Geometric, Constructive, and Descriptive Figures interspersed throughout the text.

"*We know of no treatise on Carpentry and Joinery which at all approaches this in merit. . . . We strongly urge our practical mechanics to obtain and study it.*"—Mechanic's Magazine.

In 24 parts, demy 4to, at 2s. each; or in 6 volumes, artistically bound in cloth extra, with olivine edges, at 10s. each.

The Works of Shakspeare,

Revised from the best Authorities; with a Memoir and Essay on his Genius by BRYAN W. PROCTER (Barry Cornwall), Annotations and Introductory Remarks on the Plays by Distinguished Writers, and numerous Illustrative Engravings from Designs by KENNY MEADOWS and T. H. NICHOLSON.

The most distinctive, as well as the most attractive feature of this edition of the Works of Shakspeare consists in the pictorial illustrations with which it is so copiously enriched. These are upwards of 750 in number, and bring most vividly before the reader the scenes and incidents occurring in the different plays.

By far the greater number are by the well-known artist KENNY MEADOWS, and so important are these illustrations that the edition of which they form a part has been appropriately named the *Kenny Meadows Shakspeare*.

Each play is accompanied by an original introduction, and explanatory notes from the pens of various writers distinguished for their critical acumen and their wide knowledge and high appreciation of Shakspeare's writings. Altogether this work will be found not unworthy of him who "was not of an age, but for all time".

Blackie & Son's Publications. 7

In 12 parts, small 4to size, price 2s. each; or 4 volumes, cloth elegant, gilt edges, 9s. each.

Our Sovereign Lady Queen Victoria:

HER LIFE AND JUBILEE. By THOMAS ARCHER, F.R.H.S., Author of "Pictures and Royal Portraits"; "Fifty Years of Social and Political Progress"; &c. Illustrated by a series of 28 highly-finished Etchings.

It is believed that for the multitudes of men and women who regard the Queen with a sentiment that may be spoken of as that of personal regard and affection, no more fitting memorial can be provided than a complete and worthy Life of our Sovereign Lady—a "Life" such as that which is here announced. The narrative presents a biographical rather than a historical record: a record, faithful, interesting, and well illustrated, of the Royal Family and of the Queen as Sovereign Lady rather than as Sovereign Ruler.

The ILLUSTRATIONS consist of a series of twenty-eight highly-finished etchings, including portraits of Her Majesty, the late Prince Consort, and all the members of their Family; also scenes and events in which the Queen has personally taken part.

In 23 parts at 2s. 6d. each; also 2 vols., cloth extra, gilt edges, price 35s. each.

Pictures and Royal Portraits,

ILLUSTRATIVE OF ENGLISH AND SCOTTISH HISTORY, from the Introduction of Christianity to the Present Time. This Work will comprise a Series of 69 Magnificent Plates engraved on steel in the most finished manner, with descriptive Historical Sketches, by THOMAS ARCHER. Printed on fine medium quarto paper, forming 2 elegant volumes, cloth extra, gilt edges, with richly ornamented boards.

"Pictures and Royal Portraits" will present a series of line engravings of historical designs, beautifully executed in steel, and produced in a new and attractive style, which imparts to them the appearance of highly-finished drawings in sepia. The series will include faithful reproductions of important paintings by some of the most eminent historical painters of the present century.

To be completed in 15 parts, folio (size 16¼ × 11¼ inches), price 5s. each.

The Practical Decorator and Ornamentist.

For the use of ARCHITECTS, PAINTERS, DECORATORS, and DESIGNERS. Containing one hundred Plates in colours and gold. With Descriptive Notices, and an Introductory Essay on Artistic and Practical Decoration. By GEORGE ASHDOWN AUDSLEY, LL.D., F.R.I.B.A., and MAURICE ASHDOWN AUDSLEY, Architect.

The highly practical and useful character of this important Work will at once commend it to those interested in decorative art, to whom it is more immediately addressed.

It will be found useful to the Modeller, the Plasterer, the Stone Carver, the Wood Carver, the Fret Cutter, the Inlayer, the Cabinetmaker, the Potter, the Engraver, the Lithographer, the House Painter, the Architect, the Interior Decorator, and, indeed, to every workman who has anything to do with ornament and design. To the student in drawing and ornamental design it presents a wide field of suggestive study.

Fourth Edition. Large 8vo (1000 pp.), cloth, 16s., or half-morocco, 20s.

A Manual of Rules, Tables, and Data

FOR MECHANICAL ENGINEERS, based on the most recent investigations. By DANIEL KINNEAR CLARK, author of "Railway Machinery", &c. &c. Illustrated with numerous Diagrams.

This book comprises the leading rules and data, with numerous tables, of constant use in calculations and estimates relating to Practical Mechanics;—presented in a reliable, clear, and handy form, with an extent of range and completeness of detail that has not been attempted hitherto. This (the fourth) edition has been carefully revised, and in its preparation advantage has been taken of many suggestions made by those using the former editions.

"*Mr. Clark writes with great clearness, and he has a great power of condensing and summarising facts, and he has thus been enabled to embody in his volume a collection of data relating to mechanical engineering, such as has certainly never before been brought together. We regard the book as one which no mechanical engineer in regular practice can afford to be without.*"—Engineering

To be completed in 21 parts, super-royal 8vo, 2s. each; or in 6 volumes, cloth extra, 9s. 6d. each.

NEW ISSUE.

The Imperial Bible-Dictionary,

HISTORICAL, BIOGRAPHICAL, GEOGRAPHICAL, AND DOCTRINAL. Edited by Rev. PATRICK FAIRBAIRN, D.D., author of "Typology of Scripture"; &c. With Introductions by the Right Rev. J. C. RYLE, D.D., Lord Bishop of Liverpool, and Rev. C. H. WALLER, M.A. Illustrated by about seven hundred Engravings.

This Edition will be augmented by an interesting discussion on the subject of INSPIRATION, by the Rev. C. H. WALLER, Principal of the London College of Divinity. To this is prefixed a luminous introduction on the same subject by the Right Rev. JOHN CHARLES RYLE, Lord Bishop of Liverpool.

The Work takes up in alphabetical order all the subjects which enter into the contents of the Bible, while the several books of which the Bible is composed in every case receive careful and attentive consideration. In the treatment of the different topics, full advantage is taken of the materials which modern criticism and research have accumulated.

The Pictorial Illustrations include representations of the plants and animals mentioned in Scripture, notable scenes and places, manners of social life, and the manifold productions of human skill. In addition to these illustrations, a Series of Views engraved on steel in the most finished manner, accompany the work.

New Issue, to be completed in 6 half-volumes, imperial 8vo, cloth extra, 9s. 6d. each.

The Whole Works of John Bunyan,

Accurately reprinted from the Author's own editions. Collated and edited, with an introduction to each treatise, numerous illustrative and explanatory notes, and a memoir of Bunyan, by GEORGE OFFOR. Illustrated by engravings on steel and on wood.

Among the Illustrative Engravings will be found the Portrait of Bunyan after Sadler; and a careful copy of the interesting Portrait by R. White, now in the British Museum; Views of Bedford, and Prison on Bedford Bridge; of Bunyan's Cottage, the Market-house and Church, Elstow; and of Bunyan's Tomb in Bunhill Fields. Also, a Series of beautiful Illustrations of *The Pilgrim* from Stothard's elegant designs; with Facsimiles of Bunyan's Writing, and of the earliest wood-cut illustrations of *The Pilgrim*, and to the *Life of Badman*.

All the excellencies of this much admired and highly valued edition of Bunyan's Whole Works (of which over twenty thousand copies have been sold) are retained, the work being simply reprinted with occasional improvements in typography.

Eleven vols., post 8vo, cloth, red edges, 3s. 6d. each; or in handsome case, £2, 1s.

Commentary on the New Testament,

Explanatory and Practical. With *Questions* for Bible-classes and Sunday-schools. By ALBERT BARNES. Edited by the Rev. ROBERT FREW, D.D. With numerous additional Notes, and an extensive series of beautiful Engravings and Maps, not in any other edition.

Shortly before his decease the Author completed a revision of his Notes on the New Testament, to the end of the Acts of the Apostles, the only section of the New Testament respecting the exposition and illustration of which modern research had accumulated new and important materials.

In making this new issue the first three volumes have been re-set so as to embody the author's latest corrections and additions, and they are now presented for the first time to readers in this country. This issue will consequently be the most complete and perfect of any published in Great Britain.

In royal 4to, cloth, gilt edges, 30s.

Family Worship:

A Series of Devotional Services for every Morning and Evening throughout the Year, adapted to the purposes of Domestic Worship; Prayers for Particular Occasions, and Prayers suitable for Children, &c. By above TWO HUNDRED EVANGELICAL MINISTERS. Illustrated by Twenty-six fine Engravings on steel. New and Improved Edition.

The work comprises 732 Services, adapted to be used in the family, being a service for *every* MORNING *and* EVENING throughout the year, with Special Services for the Morning and Evening of New-year's Day. Each Service is composed of Praise, Prayer, and Scriptural Exposition. Thus it points out a suitable psalm or hymn to be sung; next it refers to a portion of Scripture to be read from the Bible itself, and adds some brief explanatory and practical remarks; and the whole closes with a plain and earnest Prayer.

LONDON: BLACKIE & SON, LIMITED; GLASGOW AND EDINBURGH.

www.ingramcontent.com/pod-product-compliance
Lightning Source LLC
Chambersburg PA
CBHW031957300426
44117CB00008B/794